Empire & Revolution

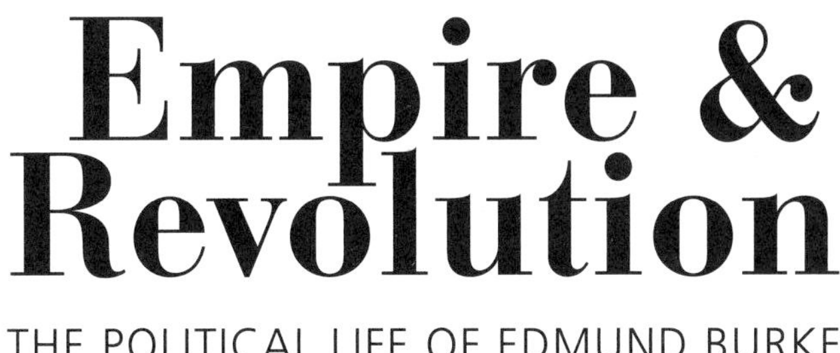

Empire & Revolution

THE POLITICAL LIFE OF EDMUND BURKE

Richard Bourke

PRINCETON UNIVERSITY PRESS
PRINCETON AND OXFORD

Published by Princeton University Press, 41 William Street, Princeton, New Jersey 08540
In the United Kingdom: Princeton University Press, 6 Oxford Street, Woodstock, Oxfordshire OX20 1TW

press.princeton.edu

Jacket image: Detail of *Portrait of Edmund Burke*, from the studio of Sir Joshua Reynolds, circa 1769. Image © National Portrait Gallery, London.

ISBN 978-0-691-14511-2

Empire and revolution : the political life of Edmund Burke / Richard Bourke.
pages cm
Includes index.
ISBN 978-0-691-14511-2 (hardcover : alk. paper) 1. Burke, Edmund, 1729–1797. 2. Statesmen—Great Britain—Biography. 3. Great Britain—Politics and government—18th century. 4. Political scientists—Great Britain—Biography. I. Title.
DA506.B9B66 2015
328.41'092—dc23
[B]
2014031021

British Library Cataloging-in-Publication Data is available
This book has been composed in Garamond Premier Pro

Printed on acid-free paper. ∞

Printed in the United States of America

3 5 7 9 10 8 6 4 2

Contents

Illustrations

Maps

Figures

Acknowledgements

This book has taken a long time to complete. I have consequently acquired a great many debts in the process of writing and researching it. It is a pleasure finally to record these. I owe particular thanks to colleagues in the history of political thought and political theory, above all to David Armitage, the late John Burrow, Alan Cromartie, Hannah Dawson, John Dunn, Raymond Geuss, Angus Gowland, Knud Haakonssen, Ross Harrison, Jeremy Jennings, Gareth Stedman Jones, Avi Lifschitz, Karuna Mantena, Sankar Muthu, Niall O'Flaherty, Philip Pettit, Nicholas Phillipson, Jennifer Pitts, J.G.A. Pocock, John Robertson, Fred Rosen, Silvia Sebastiani, Quentin Skinner, Michael Sonenscher, Tim Stanton, Sylvana Tomaselli, Richard Tuck, Georgios Varouxakis, Richard Whatmore, Donald Winch and David Wootton. The death of Istvan Hont during the final stages of my research has meant that I am unable to thank him in person for the benefit I received from his extraordinary knowledge of political ideas in the eighteenth century.

I have also benefited from conversations over the years with a number of Burke scholars, especially with David Bromwich, Seamus Deane, David Dwan, Iain Hampsher-Monk, Ian Harris, Paul Langford, F. P. Lock, Eamon O'Flaherty and Chris Reid. P. J. Marshall, who brings over fifty years' experience to the study of Burke, was particularly helpful in reading and commenting on large sections of a draft of the manuscript. I am also grateful to him for making available to me the materials for his edition of volume IV of the *Writings and Speeches of Edmund Burke*.

I would like to thank a number of colleagues whose specialist knowledge guided me. For help with France, I would like to thank Alex Fairfax-Cholmeley, Malcolm Crook, Ultán Gillen, Colin Jones, Munro Price and Michael Sonenscher; with Ireland, John Bergin, Paul Bew, Marielouise Coolahan, Ultán Gillen and Ian McBride; with the common law, Michael Lobban and Wilfred Prest; with eighteenth-century theology, Anthony Milton, Niall O'Flaherty and Isabel Rivers; with India, P. J. Marshall; with Britain, Joanna Innes and Steve Pincus; with America, Stephen Conway, who generously read my chapters on the colonies; with Locke, Hannah Dawson; with Hume, James Harris and Paul Sagar; with Tocqueville, Hugh Brogan; with the theory of language, Avi Lifschitz; with Montaigne, Felicity Green; and with Dutch painting, David Solkin and Joanna Woodall. I am grateful to the anonymous readers who reviewed the typescript for Princeton University Press for their scrutiny and advice. I have also greatly appreciated support from John Barrell, Cornelia Cook, Paul Hamilton, Eckhart Hellmuth, Christian Meier, Emer Nolan, Daniel Pick, David Simpson and Maurice Walsh.

The research for this book was made easier by the generous support of the John Carter Brown Library at Brown University (2004), the Clark Memorial Library at UCLA (2009), the Beinecke Library at Yale (2010) and the Huntington Library in San Marino (2011). The archivists at the Sheffield Archives, at the National Library of Ireland, and above all at the Northamptonshire Record Office, were indispensable. I am indebted to the AHRC for a term's funded research leave in 2004, and to the Alexander von Humboldt Stiftung for a Fellowship that I held in the History Faculty at the University of Munich in 2006–7. I would also like to express my thanks to the School of History at Queen Mary University of London for its constructive collegiality and forward-looking policy on research leave.

Princeton University Press has been exceptionally supportive at all stages. I am grateful to Ian Malcolm, then at Princeton, for commissioning the work. Al Bertrand, the publishing director, has been a sustaining presence. My editor, Ben Tate, has been a model of patience and encouragement. James Pullen, at the Wylie Agency, and before him Theo Collier, delivered indispensable advice. My copy-editor, Frances Brown, indexer Tom Broughton-Willett, and production editor Debbie Tegarden, have been meticulous throughout. The final preparation of the manuscript was undertaken in the conducive environment of the Wissenschaftskolleg zu Berlin. My thanks are due to the library staff for enabling me to make final checks.

Without Beatrice Collier, to whom my debts are incalculable, the book could not have been written.

Abbreviations

AAC Asian and African Collections (formerly Oriental and India Office Collections), British Library, London.

Add. MSS. Additional Manuscripts, British Library, London.

Archives parlementaires *Archives parlementaires de 1787 à 1860, première série (1787–1799)*, ed. M. J. Mavidal (Paris: 1875–).

Bodl. MSS. Bodleian Library Manuscripts, Oxford.

Cavendish Debates of the House of Commons *Sir Henry Cavendish's Debates of the House of Commons during the Thirteenth Parliament of Great Britain*, ed. John Wright (London: 1841–3), 2 vols.

Cavendish Diary Parliamentary Diary of Sir Henry Cavendish, 1768–1774, Egerton Manuscripts, British Library, London.

Cavendish Debates 1774 *Debates of the House of Commons in the Year 1774 on the Bill for Making more Effectual Provision for the Government of the Province of Quebec*, ed. John Wright (London: 1839).

Chatham Correspondence *Correspondence of William Pitt, Earl of Chatham*, ed. W. S. Taylor and J. H. Pringle (London: 1838–40), 4 vols.

CJ *Journals of the House of Commons.*

Corr. *The Correspondence of Edmund Burke*, ed. Thomas W. Copeland et al. (Chicago, IL: University of Chicago Press, 1958–78), 10 vols.

Correspondence (1844) *Correspondence of the Right Honourable Edmund Burke, between the Year 1744 and the Period of his Decease, in 1797*, ed. Charles William, Earl Fitzwilliam, and Lieutenant-General Sir Richard Bourke (London: 1844, 4 vols.

EB Edmund Burke.

Eg. MSS. Egerton Manuscripts, British Library.

Grafton, *Autobiography* *Autobiography and Political Correspondence of Augustus Henry, Third Duke of Grafton*, ed. William R. Anson (London: 1898).

Grenville Papers *The Grenville Papers: Being the Correspondence of Richard Grenville, Earl Temple, K.G., and the Right Honourable George Grenville, their Friends and Contemporaries*, ed. W. J. Smith (London: 1852–3), 4 vols.

Hoffman, *Burke* Ross J. S. Hoffman, *Edmund Burke, New York Agent, with his Letters and Intimate Correspondence with Charles O'Hara, 1761–1776* (Philadelphia, PA: The American Philosophical Society, 1956).

IOR India Office Records, Asia and Africa Collections, British Library, London.

LJ Journals of the House of Lords.

NLI MSS. National Library of Ireland Manuscripts

Northamptonshire MSS. Fitzwilliam Manuscripts at the Northamptonshire Record Office.

OSB Osborn Files, Beinecke Library, Yale University.

Parliamentary History *The Parliamentary History of England from the Norman Conquest in 1066 to the Year 1803*, ed. William Cobbett (London: 1806–20), 36 vols.

***Parliamentary Register* (Almon)** *The Parliamentary Register; or, History of the Proceedings and Debates of the House of Commons*, ed. John Almon (London: 1775–80), 17 vols.

***Parliamentary Register* (Debrett)** *The Parliamentary Register; or, History of the Proceedings and Debates of the House of Commons*, ed. J. Debrett (London: 1780–96), 45 vols.

PDNA *Proceedings and Debates of the British Parliaments Respecting North America, 1754–1783*, ed. R. C. Simmons and P.D.G. Thomas (Milwood, NY: Kraus International Publications, 1982–), 6 vols. to date.

***Reflections*, ed. Clark** Edmund Burke, *Reflections on the Revolution in France*, ed. J.C.D. Clark (Stanford, CA: Stanford University Press, 2001).

Rockingham Memoirs *Memoirs of the Marquis of Rockingham and His Contemporaries, with Original Letters and Documents Now First Published by George Thomas, Earl of Albemarle* (London: 1852), 2 vols.

Ryder Diary *Parliamentary Diaries of Nathaniel Ryder, 1764–1767*, ed. P.D.G. Thomas in *Camden Miscellany XXIII* (Fourth Series, vol. VII, Royal Historical Society, 1969).

TNA The National Archives, Kew, London.

Unpublished Letters, I, II and III F. P. Lock, "Unpublished Burke Letters (I), 1783–96," *English Historical Review*, 112:445 (February 1997), pp. 119–41; idem, "Unpublished Burke Letters (II), 1765–97," *English Historical Review*, 114:457 (June 1999), pp. 636–57; idem, "Unpublished Burke Letters (III), 1763–96," *English Historical Review*, 118:478 (September 2003), pp. 940–82.

W & S *The Writings and Speeches of Edmund Burke*, ed. Paul Langford et al. (Oxford: Oxford University Press, 1970–), 8 vols. to date.

Walpole, *Last Journals* *The Last Journals of Horace Walpole during the Reign of George III, from 1771–1783*, ed. A. Francis Steuart (London: J. Lane, 1910), 2 vols.

Walpole, *Memoirs* Horace Walpole, *Memoirs of the Reign of King George III*, ed. Derek Jarrett (New Haven, CT: Yale University Press, 2000), 3 vols.

***Works* (1808–13)** *The Works of the Right Honourable Edmund Burke* (London: 1808–13), 12 vols.

WWM BkP Wentworth Woodhouse Muniments, Sheffield Archives, Edmund Burke Papers.

Chronology

1730	Edmund is born in Dublin on 12 January to Richard and Mary (née Nagle) Burke.
1732	George Berkeley publishes *Alciphron.*
	Voltaire publishes his *Letters Concerning the English Nation* (the French version appeared a year later).
1736	Joseph Butler publishes *The Analogy of Religion.*
1737–41	Burke lives with his mother's Nagle relations in the Blackwater Valley of Co. Cork.
1741	Burke enrols as a boarder at Ballitore School in Co. Kildare on 26 May under the headmastership of the Quaker Abraham Shackleton.
1741–42	David Hume publishes *Essays, Moral and Political.*
1742	Robert Walpole resigns his seals of office on 11 February.
1744	Burke matriculates into Trinity College Dublin on 14 April and spends the next four years studying the curriculum.
1748	Burke is involved in editing and contributing to the periodical publication *The Reformer* between 28 January and 21 April.
	Charles-Louis de Secondat, Baron de Montesquieu publishes *The Spirit of the Laws* anonymously.
1750	Burke arrives in London to study for the bar at Middle Temple.
1752	Hume publishes his *Political Discourses.*
	Burke is introduced to his future publisher, Robert Dodsley.
1752–57	Burke composes assorted character sketches and essays on political and religious themes.
1754	David Mallet posthumously publishes *The Works of the Late Right Honourable Henry St. John, Lord Viscount Bolingbroke* in five volumes.
	John Leland publishes the first edition of his *View of the Principal Deistical Writers,* subsequently expanded.
1754–62	Hume publishes his *History of England* in six volumes.
1755	Jean-Jacques Rousseau publishes his *Discourse on the Origins of Inequality* in May.
1756	Burke publishes *A Vindication of Natural Society* anonymously on 18 May.
1756–63	The Seven Years' War draws Britain into campaigns in Europe, North America, Central America, Africa, India and the Philippines.

1757	Burke marries Jane Nugent on 12 March.
	The anonymously published *Account of the European Settlements in America* compiled by William Burke appears on 1 April with Edmund's contributions.
	Burke publishes his *Philosophical Enquiry into the Origin of our Ideas of the Sublime and Beautiful* anonymously on 21 April.
	The Pitt-Newcastle ministry assumes office in June.
	Burke begins work on *An Essay towards an Abridgement of English History*.
	Robert Clive secures a victory for the British East India Company over the Nawab of Bengal at the Battle of Plassey on 23 June.
	The Catholic Association is established in Dublin to campaign for relief from the popery laws.
c. 1757	Burke writes his fragmentary *Essay towards an History of the Laws of England*.
1758	Burke's son Richard is born on 9 February.
	William Blackstone publishes *A Discourse on the Study of the Law*.
	Emer de Vattel publishes *The Law of Nations*.
1758–65	Burke takes charge of editing and compiling *The Annual Register*.
1759	Burke accepts the position of secretary to William Gerard Hamilton.
	Adam Smith publishes *The Theory of Moral Sentiments*.
1760	George III accedes to the throne of Great Britain and Ireland on 25 October.
	The Catholic Committee is formed by Thomas Wyse, John Curry and Charles O'Conor to continue the work of the Catholic Association.
1761	Burke visits Dublin from late August as secretary to William Gerard Hamilton under the Lord Lieutenancy of Lord Halifax. Burke remains in Ireland until the following spring.
	Rousseau's *Nouvelle Héloïse* is published in Amsterdam.
1761–64	The Whiteboy disturbances persist in Munster.
1762	Rousseau publishes the *Social Contract* and *Émile*.
1762–65	Burke drafts his *Tracts relating to Popery Laws*.
1763–64	Burke accompanies Hamilton on official business to Ireland again.
1764	Burke drafts *An Address and Petition of the Irish Catholics* for the Catholic Committee.

1765	George Grenville's Stamp Act passes on 22 March.
	Burke becomes Secretary to the Marquess of Rockingham in July. The first Rockingham administration is formed that same month.
	The East India Company secures a right to the revenues (*Diwani*) of Bengal under the Treaty of Allahabad on 16 August.
1765–69	Blackstone publishes his *Commentaries on the Laws of England* in four volumes.
1766	Burke enters parliament as a member for Wendover in January.
	The Declaratory Act is passed along with the repeal of the Stamp Act on 18 March.
	The execution takes place of prominent Whiteboys during the spring.
	The Rockingham administration falls on 23 July. A new government is formed with William Pitt the Elder, now Lord Chatham.
	Burke publishes his *Short Account of a Late Short Administration* on 4 August as a vindication of the Rockingham government.
	William Beckford moves for a parliamentary inquiry into the East India Company on 9 December.
1767	The Townshend Revenue Act imposing new duties on the colonies passes into law on 29 June.
	Adam Ferguson publishes *An Essay on the History of Civil Society*.
1768	John Wilkes returns from exile and wins a seat in parliament as a member for Middlesex in February.
	Sir George Savile seeks leave to introduce a *Nullum Tempus* Bill on 17 February.
	The imprisonment of Wilkes leads to the St. George's Fields Massacre on 10 May.
	Burke takes out a mortgage on the Beaconsfield estate in Buckinghamshire in the spring.
	Chatham resigns from the government in October.
	The fourth edition of Thomas Pownall's *Administration of the Colonies* is published.
1768–70	The ministry is headed by the Duke of Grafton from 14 October.
1769	Burke publishes his *Observations on a Late State of the Nation* on 8 February.
	Wilkes is expelled from parliament in February.
1770	The Boston Massacre occurs on 5 March.
	Burke publishes his *Thoughts on the Cause of the Present Discontents* on 23 April.

1770–82	The government of Lord North is first established on 28 January, lasting for twelve years.
1772	A petition is presented to parliament in opposition to the clerical obligation to subscribe to the articles of the Church of England on 6 February.
	Harry Verelst publishes his *View of the Rise, Progress and Present State of the English Government in Bengal.*
	A Toleration Bill is introduced before the House of Commons in April.
	Alexander Dow publishes the third volume of his *History of Hindustan* (the first two volumes appeared in 1768) to which he prefixed "A Dissertation on the Origin and Nature of Despotism in Hindostan."
1773	The Tea Act passes into law on 10 May.
	The Regulating Act, designed for the better management of the affairs of the East India Company, becomes law on 21 June.
	The Boston Tea Party takes place on 16 December.
1774	The Boston Port Act is given the royal assent as the first of the Intolerable Acts on 31 March.
	Burke's *Speech on American Taxation* is delivered on 19 April.
	The Quebec Act becomes law on 22 June.
	Burke is elected MP for Bristol on 3 November.
1775	Massachusetts is declared to be in a state of rebellion on 9 February.
	The New England Restraining Act limiting colonial trade and fisheries is passed on 30 March.
	Restraints are imposed on colonial trade more generally in April.
	Conflicts at Lexington and Concord in North America trigger the start of the war between Britain and the colonies on 19 April.
	Burke's *Speech on Conciliation with the Colonies* is delivered on 22 March.
	Josiah Tucker responds to Burke in *A Letter to Edmund Burke, Esq.*
	The British parliament passes the Prohibitory Act blockading American ports on 22 December.
1776	Thomas Paine's *Common Sense* is published anonymously in Philadelphia on 9 January.
	The Continental Congress passes the Declaration of Independence on 4 July.
	Smith publishes *The Wealth of Nations.*
	Richard Price attacks the Declaratory Act in his *Observations on the Nature of Civil Liberty.*

1777	Burke's *Letter to the Sheriffs of Bristol*, written on 3 April, is published on 5 May.
	General Burgoyne is forced to surrender at Saratoga on 17 October.
	William Robertson publishes his *History of America* in three volumes.
1778	The Irish Volunteers are formed.
	Burke publishes *Two Letters on Irish Trade* on 12 May.
	A measure granting civil relief to Roman Catholics passes the Irish parliament on 6 August.
	Price challenges Burke's principles in connection with America in the Introduction to his *Two Tracts on Civil Liberty*.
1779	William and Edmund Burke publish *The Policy of Making Conquests for the Mahometans* in early summer.
	Christopher Wyvill is appointed secretary of the Yorkshire Association with a view to furthering the cause of political reform in Britain.
1780	Burke's *Speech on Economical Reform* is delivered on 11 February.
	Burke drafts his "Sketch for a Negro Code" after 9 April.
	Burke opposes shorter parliaments on 8 May.
	The Gordon Riots in London occur between 2 and 7 June.
	Burke loses his seat at Bristol on 9 September. He is nonetheless returned for Malton on Rockingham's interest.
1781	Burke intervenes in the Commons on the St. Eustatius affair on 3 May, 14 May, 30 November and 4 December.
	British forces under Lord Cornwallis surrender to the Americans at Yorktown on 19 October.
1782	The *First Report* of the Select Committee into the affairs of Bengal is published on 5 February.
	The British government authorises peace negotiations with America on 5 March.
	Legislative independence is granted to Ireland on 17 May.
	The second Rockingham administration lasts from March to July, when Rockingham dies. Burke was appointed paymaster of the forces for the duration.
	Further relief is granted to Irish Catholics from the popery laws on 27 July. Rousseau's *Confessions* is published posthumously.
1782–83	The Shelburne ministry is created in July and lasts until April the following year.
1783	The Fox–North coalition assumes office on 2 April under the leadership of the Duke of Portland. Burke is reappointed paymaster of the forces.

	The *Ninth Report* of the Select Committee into Indian affairs is published on 25 June.
	The Treaty of Paris ending hostilities with America is signed on 3 September.
	The *Eleventh Report* of the Select Committee into Indian affairs is published on 18 November.
	Burke delivers his *Speech on Fox's India Bill* on 1 December.
	George III dismisses the Fox–North coalition on 17 December. William Pitt the Younger is invited to form a new government.
1784	Pitt triumphs in the general election between 30 March and 10 May at the expense of "Fox's Martyrs."
	Burke publishes *A Representation to His Majesty* in protest against George III's support for Pitt on 14 June.
	Burke intervenes on parliamentary reform on 16 June.
1785	Burke debates Pitt's Irish commercial propositions on 21 February, 22 February and 19 May.
	Burke delivers a major *Speech on the Nawab of Arcot's Debts* on 28 February.
	Burke intervenes again on the issue of parliamentary reform on 18 April.
	Burke gives notice of a motion to be introduced against Warren Hastings on 20 June.
1786	Burke publishes the Articles of Charge against Hastings between 4 April and 5 May.
1787	Burke intervenes into the debates on the French commercial treaty on 29 January, 2 February, 5 February and 21 February.
	The first Assembly of Notables meets at Versailles on 22 February and is dissolved on 25 May.
	The House of Commons votes that Hastings should face trial on 10 May.
	Burke presents the Articles of Impeachment against Hastings between 14 and 28 May.
1788	The impeachment trial against Hastings opens with Burke's four-day speech between 15 and 19 February.
	Burke debates the abolition of the slave trade on 9 May and 2 June.
	Burke's earliest interventions into the Regency controversy are made on 8, 10, 18, 19 and 22 December.
	The second Assembly of Notables is convened between 5 October and 12 December.

1789 Emmanuel Joseph Sieyès publishes *What Is the Third Estate?* in January.

Burke intervenes into the debates on the Regency crisis on 6, 13, 19, 26 and 27 January and 2, 5, 6, 7, 9, 10 and 11 February.

Burke delivers his speech on the Presents Charge in the Hastings trial on 21 April and 7 May.

The Estates General meets at Versailles for the first time since 1614 on 5 May.

Burke speaks in the Commons against the slave trade on 12 and 21 May.

The Bastille is stormed in Paris on 14 July.

The National Assembly votes to adopt the Declaration of the Rights of Man and the Citizen on 26 August.

The King and Queen of France are harassed by a mob during the March on Versailles of 5–6 October.

The property of the French Church is nationalised on 2 November.

Price delivers *A Discourse on the Love of Our Country* on 4 November at the Meeting House in the Old Jewry, London.

The National Assembly issues *assignats* as a paper currency in December.

1790 Burke speaks in the Commons against the slave trade on 25 January.

Burke takes his first public stand on the French Revolution during his speech on the army estimates of 9 February.

The Civil Constitution of the Clergy initiates the formal subordination of the French Church to the government on 12 July.

Burke publishes *Reflections on the Revolution in France* on 1 November.

Burke delivers his speech recommending the continuation of the Hastings impeachment in the new parliament on 23 December.

1791 Burke completes his *Letter to a Member of the National Assembly* on 19 January and then sends it on the 28th. It is published on 27 April.

Burke agrees to limit the Hastings trial to the examination of specific charges in a speech on 14 February.

Paine publishes his *Rights of Man* on 16 March.

Burke splits with Charles James Fox on 6 May during an emotional debate on the Quebec Bill.

Louis XVI and Marie Antoinette are returned to Paris on 25 June after their attempt to flee to Varennes.

Burke publishes his *Appeal from the New to the Old Whigs* on 3 August.

In the Declaration of Pillnitz of 27 August Frederick William III of Prussia and Leopold II of Austria proclaim their support for Louis XVI.

The French Constitution is adopted and the National Constituent Assembly dissolved on 30 September.

The French Legislative Assembly meets on 1 October.

The Society of United Irishmen is formed on 14 October.

Burke writes and circulates his *Thoughts on French Affairs* in December.

Burke draws a dagger in the Commons during debate on the Aliens Bill on 28 December.

1792 Burke's *Letter to Sir Hercules Langrishe* is published in Dublin on 18 February.

Paine publishes part II of his *Rights of Man* in February.

Burke advocates enfranchisement of Catholics in his *Letter to Richard Burke* in late February.

France declares war against Austria on 20 April.

The Brunswick Manifesto of 25 July threatens French civilians with retribution in the event of the royal family being harmed.

The French monarchy is overthrown after the storming of the Tuileries on 10 August.

The September Massacres take place between 2 and 6 September.

The National Convention meets on 21 September. The following day the French Republic is declared.

1793 Louis XVI is guillotined on 21 January.

France declares war on Britain on 1 February.

Burke writes his *Observations on the Conduct of the Minority* in the spring urging the Duke of Portland to distance himself from Fox.

The Committee of Public Safety is created on 6 April.

A Relief Bill enfranchising Irish Catholics becomes law on 9 April.

Terror is declared the order of the day by the National Convention on 5 September.

The General Maximum is passed by the Convention Assembly on 29 September.

Burke starts his *Remarks on the Policy of the Allies* in October.

1794	The opposition Whigs split on 17 January as Portland resolves publicly to support the war against France.
	Burke's *Report* on the use of evidence and procedure in the Hastings trial is published on 20 April.
	Burke's nine-day speech in reply to Hastings's defence in the impeachment trial begins on 28 May.
	Burke retires from parliament on 21 June.
	Burke's son dies on 2 August.
1795	Earl Fitzwilliam arrives in Ireland as Lord Lieutenant on 4 January.
	Burke argues for Catholic emancipation in his *Letter to William Smith* of 29 January.
	Burke writes his second *Letter to Sir Hercules Langrishe* on 26 May.
	Burke starts work on his *Fourth Letter on a Regicide Peace* in October.
	The Directory is established in France on 2 November.
	Burke completes part of what would become *Thoughts and Details on Scarcity* in November.
1796	Burke's *Letter to a Noble Lord* is published on 24 February.
	Burke publishes the first and second letters on the prospect of peace with France as *Two Letters on a Regicide Peace* on 20 October.
	Membership of the Catholic Defenders increases as sectarian tensions in Ireland rise.
	A French fleet attempts to land at Bantry Bay on the southwest coast of Ireland in December.
1797	Burke continues to work on the *Third Letter on a Regicide Peace* but leaves it unfinished at his death.
	Burke dies at Beaconsfield on 9 July.

Empire & Revolution

Figure 1. *The House of Commons* by Karl Anton Hickel (National Portrait Gallery)

INTRODUCTION

1 Empire and Revolution

This is a book about the vicissitudes of empire and revolution as confronted by one of the leading political intellects of the eighteenth century. The confrontation was complicated in a number of distinct ways. In the first place the term "revolution" had a range of meanings. At its simplest it could denominate a change in the system of government. Yet it could also cover resistance to an established political order leading to the creation of a new regime. Finally it could refer to the subversion of government along with the various liberties it was supposed to protect. Over the course of his life, Edmund Burke defended revolution in the first two senses although he ardently set himself against the third. But while he supported the rights of legitimate rebellion, he also consistently upheld the authority of empire. However, the picture here was again a complex one. Burke cherished the rights of British imperial sovereignty, yet he vehemently opposed the standing policies of the Empire. Underlying this apparent ambivalence was a commitment to the rights of conquest accompanied by a repudiation of the "spirit of conquest." This referred to the attitude of usurpation that Burke believed had characterised European governments in the gothic past. Although governments of the kind had their origins in expropriation, they had gradually accommodated the "spirit of liberty." Nonetheless, modern liberty for Burke was a precarious achievement. It was capable of relapsing into the spirit of domination, not least in its interactions with the extra-European world. Burke's achievement was to analyse the conditions of freedom in minute practical and constitutional detail. His analysis drew on a historical vision of the character of modern politics. This book tries to capture the subtlety of that vision as it was expressed over the course of a parliamentary career. It aims to achieve this by reconstructing Burke's political thought in relation to the major developments of the age. This requires a full examination of current affairs as well as careful attention to intellectual context.

2 Oratory, Philosophy, History

In his own day, Burke was recognised as one of the pre-eminent political orators of the century. His career in the House of Commons was largely spent in opposition, which meant that his efforts were mostly dedicated to criticising policy. Criticism implied that a preferable course of action should be adopted. Burke was thus fundamentally a political advocate whose ultimate objective was persuasion. In that role, he was conscious of having a series of illustrious predecessors: in their different ways, Lord Somers, Lord Halifax and Robert Walpole had all shone in parliament.[1] Burke also faced impressive opposition at various stages: the Earl of Chatham, Charles Townshend, Henry Dundas and Pitt the Younger, to name just four. One-time allies who became his enemies, like Charles James Fox and Richard Sheridan, were equally outstanding public performers. Historians still study these figures today, but only Burke is widely read. His speeches were always topical in nature. His writings were similarly focused on immediate events. However, the appeal of his work derives from the sheer force of his eloquence rooted in the cogency of the positions he advocated.[2] Contemporaries were evidently enthralled by his rhetoric; posterity has likewise been captivated by his published work. It is important to understand what this implies. It does not merely show that his "language" is seductive. It points to the fact that his arguments are peculiarly powerful.

William Wordsworth, who heard Burke speak in the Commons in the early 1790s, described his audience in *The Prelude* as "Rapt" with attention.[3] The original vivacity of Burke's speeches has now been lost to history. What remains is the dexterity of his prose. William Hazlitt took his literary skill to be "his chief excellence."[4] This was of course intended as a denigration of his politics. Nonetheless, Hazlitt captured the extent to which his writing is imbued with urgency. He conveyed Burke's determination to impress on the minds of others the importance and vitality of his ideas. This made him, Hazlitt thought, the "most poetical" of prose writers, though in the end he strove to overpower rather than to please.[5] It would be possible to enumerate the figurative methods Burke employed to achieve his characteristic effects. However this can hardly act as a substitute for a direct encounter with his writing. Rhetoric works by moving a particular audience on a particular occasion. Practical criticism can describe its features but not explain why it succeeds. As Adam Smith

[1] See, however, Hume's strictures on modern eloquence: David Hume, "Of Eloquence" (1742) in idem, *Essays Moral, Political, and Literary*, ed. Eugene F. Miller (Indianapolis, IN: Liberty Fund, 1985, 1987).

[2] Paddy Bullard, *Edmund Burke and the Art of Rhetoric* (Cambridge: Cambridge University Press, 2011).

[3] William Wordsworth, *The Fourteen-Book Prelude*, ed. J. B. Owen (Ithaca, NY: Cornell University Press, 1985), bk. VII, line 517. The passage was heavily revised in the 1820s.

[4] William Hazlitt, "Character of Mr. Burke" (5 October 1817) in *The Complete Works of William Hazlitt* (London: J. M. Dent and Sons, 1930–34), 21 vols., VII, p. 229.

[5] Ibid. On Hazlitt's view of Burke, see David Bromwich, *Hazlitt: The Mind of a Critic* (Oxford: Oxford University Press, 1983), pp. 288–300.

observed, the technical rules of writing can never account for the power of language.[6] Rhetoric moves the passions by the force of argument; in politics, by the force of its moral claims.[7] Part of Burke's appeal can be found in the effectiveness of his reasoning. He achieved this by blending mastery of detail with a philosophical analysis of political relations. To this he added a remarkable gift of imagination that was capable of commanding the sympathy of his listeners and readers. The historian can recover the practicalities and the principles on which that imagination was brought to bear. Without these, moral language is evocative but empty—more appropriate to a conjurer than a public orator.

The attributes of the ideal orator had been a subject of inquiry since the elements of rhetoric came under systematic scrutiny in the city-states of the ancient world. Eighteenth-century politicians were familiar with the results: the textbooks of Aristotle and Quintilian were staple components of their education; the speeches of Demosthenes and Cicero were a constant resource.[8] In his *Institutio oratoria*, in addition to elocution and the figures of speech, Quintilian had emphasised philosophical wisdom as an essential characteristic of oratory.[9] Philosophy here meant moral philosophy, since the statesman or prosecutor, involved in counsel or litigation, stood in need of a proper conception of prevailing norms—like justice, equity or liberality. Burke excelled as a master of expressive flair but he was most conspicuous for his dexterity in moral argument. Having said this, he was concerned not with debating the foundations of the private virtues, but with the "morality" of public affairs. This was above all a matter for practical judgment, or prudence. The politician had to assess the probable course of events. "History," Burke wrote, "is a preceptor of prudence."[10] The statesman was a "philosopher in action."[11] This meant that he dealt in principles that were historically embedded. The justification of a course of action, which implied a judgment about the future, involved an account of how the present had been conditioned by the past.[12] Political science was essentially a historical form of inquiry, anticipating outcomes by interpreting the past.[13]

[6] Adam Smith, *Lectures on Rhetoric and Belles Lettres*, ed. J. C. Bryce (Indianapolis, IN: Liberty Fund, 1985), p. 40.

[7] See Quentin Skinner, "Retrospect: Studying Rhetoric and Conceptual Change" in idem, *Visions of Politics I: Regarding Method* (Cambridge: Cambridge University Press, 2002).

[8] Christopher Reid, *Imprison'd Wranglers: The Rhetorical Tradition of the House of Commons, 1760–1800* (Oxford: Oxford University Press, 2012).

[9] Quintilian, *Institutio oratoria*, I, Proemium, drawing on Cicero, *De inventione*, I, iii, 4 and *De oratore*, III, 56–81.

[10] EB to Dr. William Markham, post 9 November 1771, *Corr.*, II, p. 282.

[11] EB, *Thoughts on the Cause of the Present Discontents* (1770), *W & S*, II, p. 317.

[12] For Burke's historical consciousness see Friedrich Meinecke, *Die Entstehung des Historismus* (Munich: Oldenbourg, 1936), 2 vols., II, pp. 288–304; John C. Weston Jr., "Edmund Burke's View of History," *Review of Politics*, 23:2 (April 1961), pp. 203–29, and, most recently, Sora Sato, "Edmund Burke's Ideas on Historical Change," *History of European Ideas*, 40:5 (September 2014), pp. 675–92.

[13] For the fate of historical political science in Britain after Burke see John Burrow, Stefan Collini and Donald Winch, *That Noble Science of Politics: A Study in Nineteenth-Century Intellectual History* (Cambridge: Cambridge University Press, 1983).

"Burke was, indeed, a great man," Coleridge contended: "No one ever read history so philosophically as he seems to have done."[14] The historical idiom that interested Burke was "philosophical" history, first popularised by Montesquieu, Voltaire and Hume. History could be philosophical in two distinct senses: first, insofar as it rose above religious and political partisanship; and second, to the extent that it generalised about human affairs. Generalisation involved exploring how values were shaped by changes in society and government. The philosophies of the enlightenment provided versatile equipment for embarking upon this kind of exploration. By the middle of the 1750s, having moved to London to train for the Irish bar, Burke began to devote his attention to various aspects of the science of politics that had become controversial topics in the European enlightenment: the theory of the passions, the history of government, the role of providence in society. At the same time he began to immerse himself in contemporary affairs both as a journalist and as a man of business. In 1765 he became connected to the Whig magnate the Marquess of Rockingham, and within six months he had secured a seat in the House of Commons. He soon established himself as a formidable debater and publicist. His commitment to a career in public life was now settled. This did not entail sacrificing his ambitions as a man of letters, but it did mean that his intellectual and literary pursuits would be shaped by his involvement in practical affairs. As a member of parliament, Burke was exposed to the issues that dominated the age. His agenda was determined not by his intellectual enthusiasms but by the shifting fortune of events. Nonetheless, his response was informed by an education in the science of politics indebted to the insights of philosophical history.

Burke concerned himself with most of the issues that passed before the House of Commons during his tenure as a member of parliament. However, standing back from the plethora of topics that required the attention of government and opposition over the course of those thirty years, five main issues commanded his attention: the British constitution and parliamentary reform; the crisis in the American colonies between 1766 and 1783; the East India Company's management of Bengal and Madras from the attempts at reform under the Chatham administration down to the impeachment of Warren Hastings; Irish trade and government at various points over the same period; and the impact of the French Revolution on European affairs. These were decisive topics in politics at the time: the loss of empire in the west, the corruption of empire in the east, and a shift in the understanding of popular political rights. Burke applied his considerable powers of analysis to interpreting their significance, providing an angle from which to understand the course of modern history. An historical vantage can never provide the substance of historical truth, but it can certainly help us appreciate the stakes involved in past events. It can also generate new hypotheses for historical inquiry, potentially even the elements of a philosophy of history—a necessary prerequisite for any credible theory of politics. This book

[14] Samuel Taylor Coleridge, *Table Talk*, ed. Carl Woodring (Princeton, NJ: Princeton University Press, 1990), 2 vols., II, p. 213 (8 April 1833).

is concerned with Burke's vision of history and politics as these were worked out in response to the prevailing issues of the day. The Introduction first sets out the shape of that response, and then indicates its longer-term importance. I begin in the next section by sketching the main stages and preoccupations of Burke's career, and then conclude with a final section on his fundamental principles as these were worked out in relation to his view of European history.

3 Britain, America, India, Ireland, France

The affairs of Britain formed the central strand linking the various preoccupations that dominated Burke's imagination at different stages of his career. The country claimed to be governed by "revolution principles." These encompassed the Bill of Rights and the Act of Settlement as well as the precepts established by the Glorious Revolution. They also included provision for the toleration of dissent. The settlement that brought the conflicts of the seventeenth century to a close involved the constitutional regulation of both church and state.[15] After George III ascended to the throne in 1760, he was quick to recall the character of the bond between the two. In his Speech from the Throne, delivered on 18 November, he announced his determination to "adhere to and strengthen this excellent constitution in Church and State." This included maintaining "inviolable" toleration.[16] The expectation was that this "church-state" would protect political and religious liberties. This was achieved by fixing relations between crown and parliament whilst enabling the established Church to make room for nonconformity. However, the arrangements that were implemented in the late seventeenth century were adopted in the context of a developing polity. There was no guarantee that relations would not descend again into strife. The balance of the constitution and the status of the Church might need revision in order to secure them against degeneration. Throughout Burke's period on the public stage both topics were canvassed in society and debated among his peers. Above all, from the late 1770s onwards, partly under the influence of political arguments stimulated by America, challenges to the tenure and composition of the Commons began to receive attention in parliament and the press. During the same period, the entitlements of religious dissenters were contested on all sides.

Beginning with the "Cavalier" parliament in 1661, nonconformity was defined and variously restricted by a series of acts that were carried over the succeeding decades. The education, worship and political entitlements of dissenters were variously curtailed. The Toleration Act of 1689 offered some degree of relief. The Act granted freedom of worship under specified conditions to Christians who dissented from the thirty-nine articles of the Church of England. By the late 1760s, so-called

[15] J.C.D. Clark, *English Society, 1688–1832: Ideology, Social Structure and Political Practice during the Ancien Regime* (Cambridge: Cambridge University Press, 1985, 2000).

[16] *Parliamentary History*, XV, col. 982.

latitudinarian elements within the Anglican clergy were themselves seeking exemption from the articles of the Church, especially those relating to the doctrine of the trinity. As he made plain in 1772, Burke opposed relaxing discipline within the Church but promoted measures for removing disabilities that persecuted dissenters.[17] Magistracy ought never to interfere with matters between the deity and conscience.[18] However, as attacks on Anglicanism by rational dissenters like Joseph Priestley seemed to gather momentum, Burke came to believe that nonconformity would have to be monitored in case its exponents sought to undermine the security of the Church.[19] Moreover, heterodoxy would have to be restrained if it employed ecclesiastical means to provoke sedition, as Burke believed had taken place in the 1640s. Should the conditions of the mid-seventeenth century revive, dissent could no longer be regarded as a conscientious vocation and would instead have to be considered as a form of faction, and therefore as a potential vehicle for subversion.[20] Beginning in the late 1780s, Burke started to suspect this design on the part of prominent nonconformists. His suspicions intensified around 1790 in the context of the British reception of the French Revolution. Religion, he feared, was now being used as an instrument of power. Under these circumstances, the rights of conscience became a poor disguise for secular ambition. On top of that, the claim to a natural right to power was a problematic notion. While religious rights, like property rights, were "natural" to man, political rights were prescriptive rather than universal entitlements.

Burke insisted on the necessity of a political division of labour in any complex social structure. A successful distribution of the functions of government would preserve freedom and promote the happiness of citizens. However, equal participation in the organs of power directly militated against this principle. The equal exercise of the levers of government, as opposed to an equality of liberty under government, was incompatible with the practicalities of civil organisation. As Burke saw it, adherence to this brand of equal political rights, commonly designated the "rights of man," would be destructive of every conceivable mode of political subordination, and therefore of the distinction between society and government.[21] He followed the promotion of the idea of "equal rights" among critics of the constitution in the 1770s and 1780s. Increasingly after 1779, a variety of projects for political reform were conceptualised in these terms: shorter parliaments, the elimination of rotten boroughs and an increase in county representation were promoted under the banner of the rights of man. Burke opposed this general approach armed with a programme of reform that emphasised the desirability of popular liberty under the constitution.

[17] EB, Speech on Clerical Subscription, 6 February 1772, *W & S*, II, pp. 361–62.

[18] Northamptonshire MS. A. XXVII.103a (i).

[19] On rational dissent in the period, see Knud Haakonssen ed., *Enlightenment and Religion: Rational Dissent in Eighteenth-Century Britain* (Cambridge: Cambridge University Press, 1996).

[20] Northamptonshire MS. A. XXVII.100 (ii). Cf. Northamptonshire MS. A. XXVII.99 (ii): "N.B. Factions [&] Clubbs the instruments of . . . Revolution."

[21] EB, Speech on the State of the Representation of the Commons (16 May 1784), *Works* (1808–13), X, *passim*.

According to Burke, the best way of guaranteeing the liberty of the people was by instituting a system of government disposed to secure their rights and interests. In the case of Britain, this would involve revising arrangements as they existed rather than reconfiguring the whole polity *de novo*. In any given society, there would naturally be preferable ways of organising public power, but there was no universal template for the creation of political justice. The goal of government was to promote the general welfare while ensuring the protection of private rights. That involved enabling social and economic improvement as well as providing for the security of justice. In European societies in general, these aims could best be guaranteed by dividing the exercise of supreme power and ensuring that representation was effective. However, as Montesquieu emphasised in *The Spirit of the Laws*, the powers of government could be variously distributed among different bodies. Similarly, representation was disparately conceived as being served by impersonation, delegation or election. In their different ways, France, Spain, the Holy Roman Empire, the Dutch Republic and the Polish commonwealth sought to combine these assorted elements. Yet Burke thought it was in Britain that the powers of government were most effectively regulated while electoral representation was constitutionally guaranteed. By these means, a method had been found for combining political stability with popular representation. This combination, in turn, offered the best security to the strict administration of justice.

This whole edifice hinged on maintaining the integrity of the constitution. To achieve that, its component parts would have to be preserved in their due relations. From the middle of the 1760s, Burke took the proper functioning of the system to be under attack. The lodgement of overseas dominion in the hands of executive authority exacerbated an existing tendency. The growth of the influence of the crown meant that the democratic branch of government was effectively being perverted. Parliament had become an arena for acclaiming court power. By 1770, Burke was espousing the utility of "party" on behalf of his Rockinghamite friends in parliament as the best means of counteracting the prevailing means of corruption.[22] In pursuing "economical reform" in the early 1780s, he sought to rebalance the disordered equipoise of the constitution by reducing the overblown power of the monarch.[23] But by the end of the decade his priorities had shifted. It was now sham popularity that threatened to overturn the system of administration. Burke's worries had first been formed in the face of assorted campaigns for parliamentary reform, but they were intensified during the regency crisis and then with the Revolution in France. While his colleagues thought that Britain was immune to the French "malady," Burke was confident that there existed a general threat.[24] In pursuit of this conviction he abandoned his alliance with dissent and separated from the leadership of his party. It

[22] Classically in EB, *Thoughts on the Cause of the Present Discontents* (1770), *W & S*, II, *passim*.

[23] Most fully in EB, *Speech on Economical Reform*, 11 February 1780, *W & S*, III, *passim*.

[24] For the phrase, see EB, Debate on the Re-Commitment of the Quebec Government Bill, 6 May 1791, *Parliamentary History*, XXIX, col. 372.

would be years before he could reconcile with the Portland Whigs; his friendship with Charles James Fox would never recover.

A distinguishing feature of British politics in the late eighteenth century was the fact that the domestic constitution had to bear the strains of empire. Burke entered public life in the aftermath of the Seven Years' War. Looking back on that epic contest over ten years after its conclusion, it appeared to have been a moment of singular promise: "We had humbled every power which we dreaded," Burke recollected. This cleared the way for the establishment of "a New kind of Empire upon Earth."[25] There would be freedom in the colonies and justice in South Asia under the superintendence of liberal and enlightened power. Authority would be variously but prudently deployed among a diversity of peoples with multifarious beliefs. The British constitution was the source of this achievement, forming "the spirit and the power which conducted us to this greatness."[26] Yet soon this hopeful prospect was suffused with gloom. When Burke took his seat in the Commons in January 1766, the conflict with the American colonies was already underway. The debts incurred by Britain as a consequence of the war encouraged the government to raise new revenues across the Atlantic. Provincial protest and then resistance immediately ensued, initiating a challenge to the authority of the Empire. Domestic finance, overseas settlement and the balance of power were mutually implicated in the struggle for pre-eminence among the dominant powers. As Burke saw it, a series of ministries in effect modified the imperial constitution in order to prevail in the competition among European states. Innovation unsettled the system of governance. The practicalities of exercising the sovereignty of the crown-in-parliament over provincial assemblies in the new world threatened the British Empire with civil war.

On 22 December 1775, the government of Lord North passed the Prohibitory Act, blockading the conduct of American trade.[27] Burke saw this as an act of war directed against the colonies, bestowing a right of rebellion on the basis of self-defence.[28] This amounted to a justification of revolution on Burke's part. However, he was advocating revolution as an instrument of restoration, not insurgency in the name of innovation. Innovation, he believed, should be contrasted with reform just as improvement should be opposed to wanton destruction. Nothing had occurred by 1776 to suggest to Burke that this was an "Age of Revolutions."[29] Developments in America in the 1770s bore no relation to events in France in the 1790s. During both periods, Burke defended the right of a people to take up arms against tyranny: he adopted this position in 1788 in relation to the revolt of Benares in northern India seven years earlier, and he reiterated his commitment in the context of Irish

[25] EB, Notes for Second Conciliation Speech, ante 16 November 1775, WWM BkP 6:202.

[26] Ibid.

[27] 16 Geo. III, c. 5.

[28] EB, Notes on American Prohibitory Bill, WWM BkP 6:119.

[29] For early use of this now prevalent historiographical category see, for example, R. R. Palmer, *The Age of Democratic Revolution: A Political History of Europe and America, 1760–1800* (Princeton, NJ: Princeton University Press, 1959–64), 2 vols.

resistance in the years before the rebellion of 1798.[30] But while Burke never questioned the legitimacy of insurrection against despotism, he was clear about the obligation on the part of revolutionaries to re-establish government for the protection of property.

Even in the midst of the American Revolution, Burke rallied to the defence of British imperial sovereignty. As the war dragged on, he began to advocate the establishment of a federal compact between metropole and colonies as a means of accommodating the existence of "two legislatures" within a single imperial frame.[31] By 10 April 1778, he had accepted the need for a repeal of the Declaratory Act, and come to recognise the reality of American independence. Yet he still envisaged a role for the British Empire to the last: the Navigation Act, in some form, might be revived; George III might play a part in any new American arrangement.[32] Burke justified the authority of civilised empire at every stage of his career: British control of America was optimal for both parties; the separation of Ireland was anathema in any imaginable future; the conquest of Bengal was a legitimate act of war. Like most of his contemporaries, Burke had no clear conception of a world without empires. The globe was in effect populated by competing imperial powers: the French, the British, the Spanish, the Ottoman, the Mughal and the Maratha were just a few examples. Militant opposition to empire would entail dismantling each of these structures by means of a war intended to bring an end to the spirit of usurpation. As Burke saw it, when the French embarked on such a programme in 1792, in spite of their professed humanitarian intentions they unleashed the most belligerently imperial project that the world had seen since the early days of the Roman republic. Up until the founding of the first coalition against France, Burke's goal had been to regulate European competition by an effective balance of power. This, he thought, would enable Britain to employ its influence abroad in support of civil liberty and commerce. While the British appeared to Burke to be well placed to pursue that objective, the goal might still be thwarted by opposition forces at home. The fate of America illustrated the vulnerability of civilised empire to a resurgence of bygone attitudes of coercion and domination.

Soon after the fall of the first Rockingham administration in the summer of 1766, the new government under Lord Chatham turned its attention to India as a potential source of supply for the ailing British exchequer. With the repeal of the Stamp Act, signalling the collapse of Grenville's programme of taxation in the colonies, the prospect of new funds arising from the conquest of Bengal proved attractive as the new ministry assumed power. This inaugurated a conflict between the East India Company and the British government that was temporarily resolved in 1773 with the passage of Lord North's Regulating Act. The constitution of the Company was

[30] On the Benares episode see Northamptonshire MS. A. XXIX.36. For the rights of Irish Catholic insurgency see EB to Unknown, February 1797, *Corr.*, IX, p. 259.

[31] EB, *Letter to the Sheriffs of Bristol* (3 April 1777), *W & S*, III, p. 321.

[32] EB, Hints of a Treaty with America, March 1782, WWM BkP 27:219.

reconfigured, and a portion of its wealth was requisitioned by Westminster. Burke judged the interference to be an unwarranted act of power that compromised the liberty of a corporate institution. Reform was merely a pretext for the invasion of chartered privileges that were not merited by any proven act of delinquency in South Asia. Burke continued to doubt the intentions of the government of Lord North down to the collapse of his administration in 1782. Yet, during the same period, his sense of the culpability of the Company gradually deepened. He began to reimmerse himself in Indian affairs when the plight of the Raja of Tanjore was brought to his attention in 1778. The Raja was a victim of the territorial ambitions of the Nawab of Arcot in the Carnatic. Since the Nawab's exploits were being supported by British troops and, more insidiously, by loans issued by East India Company officials based in Madras, the southern British settlement on the Coromandel Coast was enabling expansion by a petty potentate. In fact, more than enabled, the Nawab was being encouraged so that the British could recoup their debts.[33]

By 1781, when Burke joined the Select Committee established to investigate the affairs of the subcontinent, India had acquired a profound significance in his mind. The work of the Committee focused his attention on Bengal, leading him to examine the constitution of the Company together with its foreign relations and tax collecting responsibilities. This resulted in a penetrating analysis of British power as it was channelled through the activities of a trading corporation. Mismanagement in the south had been indirectly orchestrated, but in the north the means of abuse were both extensive and direct. As Burke saw it, the Company had become a meticulously predatory bureaucracy bent on systematic exploitation.[34] Its objective was neither good government nor commercial advantage but a monstrous amalgamation of the two: a corporate monopoly devoted to its own political profit. Both commercial incentives and public duty were completely disregarded as rapacity and oppression were pursued. By the time that the Committee's eleven Reports had been compiled, Burke's mastery of Indian affairs was unrivalled in the House of Commons. His commitment to reform was also unsurpassed. Yet with the failure of Fox's India Bill in 1783, he was forced to seek redress through the impeachment of Warren Hastings. By the time that the prosecution of the Governor General became possible, Burke regarded all other issues in public life at the time as genuinely trivial by comparison.[35] He would devote much of the remainder of his career in parliament to representing India's interests before the imperial "senate." "I considered this Indian Affair to be what it had been, the object of far the greatest and longest labour of a very laborious life," he exclaimed to Dundas in 1792.[36] His involvement ultimately terminated with the acquittal of Hastings in 1794. By then his knowledge of the subcontinent was

[33] EB, *Speech on the Nabob of Arcot's Debts* (28 February 1785), *W & S*, V, *passim*.

[34] EB, *Ninth Report of the Select Committee* (25 June 1783), ibid., p. 201; EB, Speech in Reply, 28 May 1794, *W & S*, VII, p. 277.

[35] EB, Debate in the Commons on the Address of Thanks, 25 January 1785, *Parliamentary History*, XXIV, col. 1400.

[36] EB to Henry Dundas, 8 October 1792, *Corr.*, VII, p. 247.

prodigious indeed, though he distilled this into two fundamental maxims.[37] He contended, first, that despite the successive waves of Islamic conquest in the region culminating in the establishment of the Mughal dynasty in the sixteenth century, India had never been subject to a truly despotic power until the accession of the British to imperial dominion between 1757 and 1765. Second, he insisted that, whatever might be the facts concerning the history of Asian government, the exercise of authority over any population was bound by universally applicable minimal standards of conduct.

Accordingly, Burke's indictment of Warren Hastings and the Company over which he presided was guided by his interpretation of the law of nature and nations. He followed the claims of Locke against Grotius and Pufendorf: no power on earth could claim for itself the right to enslave a people. In fact, any population that was subject to such treatment was not only entitled but obliged to offer resistance against its oppressor. Burke would later come to examine the duty of resistance in relation to Ireland. While the law of nature and the practice of civilised nations were invoked by him as providing criteria by which misrule in India could be judged, he considered that the conduct of colonial administration in Ireland could be evaluated in terms of the standards set by the British constitution. The Glorious Revolution had issued in a settlement that affected the three kingdoms. The norms of administrative and constitutional propriety established in England and Scotland ought therefore in principle to be capable of extension to Ireland. However, the events of 1688–91 in the neighbouring island left a legacy there that was very different from that left on the British mainland. In the United Kingdom after 1707, the enduring spirit of party was contained and then pacified.[38] But in the sister kingdom the factious animosities of the seventeenth century found expression in a more ruthlessly proscriptive constitution that managed to sustain rather than defuse prevailing antipathies. Taken as a whole, the situation in Ireland raised three controversies at once. First, there was the question of the status of the Irish polity in relation to Britain that had rankled since the passage of the Declaratory Act in 1720.[39] Second, there was the related issue of the injustice of Irish trade restrictions. Finally, there was the searing dispute over the toleration of Roman Catholicism. The first two items concerned the legal and political relationship between the two islands, while the third involved the domestic organisation of the Irish state.

Burke addressed these related but distinguishable topics at three main points in his career: first, between the late 1750s and mid 1760s; second, during the fallout from the American Revolution in Ireland; and third, in the context of the influence of the French Revolution on Europe. During the earliest phase, before embarking on a parliamentary career, he considered the plight of Ireland under two headings:

[37] On Burke's own estimation of his grasp of the subcontinent see EB, Speech in Reply, 5 June 1794, *W & S*, VII, p. 401.

[38] J. H. Plumb, *The Growth of Political Stability in England, 1675–1725* (London: Macmillan, 1967); Steve Pincus, *1688: The First Modern Revolution* (New Haven, CT: Yale University Press, 2009).

[39] 6 Geo. I, c. 5.

on the one hand, in connection with his researches into English history, he investigated the origins of Ireland's dependence upon England; on the other, he explored the nature and significance of the popery laws imposed as restrictions on the civil and constitutional rights of Catholics in the aftermath of the Williamite victory in Ireland. Both these issues came together in the 1770s and 1780s, along with the resurgence of grievances about limitations on Irish trade. Over the course of the hostilities between Britain and the American colonies, the Irish sought liberalisation of restraints on their import and export trades. The complaint against the impact of the Navigation laws and related acts on Irish commerce inevitably reanimated controversy about Britain's legislative authority over Ireland. In addition, the need to win the support of the mass of the Irish population for the ongoing war effort gave rise to a determination on the part of the Westminster parliament to ease the civil and religious disabilities on Irish dissent, Catholic and Presbyterian alike. Burke advocated the extension of freedom of trade, and passionately espoused the cause of toleration. He was more sceptical about the grant of legislative independence that was conferred in 1782. The positions he carved out during the American crisis laid the foundation for his campaigns in the cause of Ireland in the aftermath of the French Revolution.

As the 1790s progressed, Burke steadily championed the extension of political rights to Catholics in addition to the civil liberties they had secured. The best hope that the disenfranchised had of receiving a liberal grant of privileges would in his opinion be at the behest of the imperial power at Westminster. Consequently, neither increasing measures of independence nor the triumph of complete separation would properly serve the interest of either community in Ireland. His view was that a parliamentary union was conceivable, but it would be a drastic resort that might well incite more strife than it would resolve. The brightest future lay in reducing the power of the "Junto," the presiding executive officers based at Dublin Castle, who were bent on maintaining what Burke saw as their venal grip on power by perpetuating their image as an indispensable link connecting the two kingdoms.[40] In the absence of achieving any meaningful reduction in the sway of "Ascendancy" rule, Burke came to see the Irish establishment as having inadvertently ensured that discontent would escalate into violent opposition. The principle of Ascendancy was publicised as guaranteeing Protestant security whereas in fact it was a means of sustaining a degrading and exclusive regime. In response, under the influence of French Revolutionary ideas, Catholics were liable to embrace the doctrine of the rights of man as a means of ventilating their legitimate complaints. In effect, in Burke's mind, they would be channelling their resentments into a political movement driven to dismantle the ramparts of civil society. In his final months, as disgruntled Catholics were being Jacobinised by the proselytism of the United Irishmen, it seemed to Burke that any hope of genuine reform had been thwarted by the forces of destruction.

[40] EB to William Windham, 30 March 1797, *Corr.*, IX, p. 301.

The prospect of destruction dominated the horizon throughout the 1790s. Foxite Whiggism was predisposed to interpret the Revolution in France as a popular rebellion against despotic power. Burke was certain that developments after the meeting of the assembly of notables in February 1787 exhibited nothing remotely of the kind. By the autumn of 1789, the character of events was already becoming clear. The French monarchy was not being challenged in the name of popular grievances. The *cahiers de doléances* undoubtedly recorded expressions of discontent, but none of these pointed to the need for a dissolution of the regime. Instead, the monarchy was being assailed by a fortuitous conspiracy of forces. Burke did not assume that this involved a deliberate confederacy of saboteurs.[41] Diverse actors inadvertently collaborated to subvert the existing state. Central to the process were disaffected nobles bent on advancing themselves at the expense of Louis XVI. The Revolution began as an opportunistic aristocratic revolt not a spontaneous rebellion of the people. With the collapse of the Estates General and the creation of the National Assembly in the summer of 1789, all constitutional restraints had been effectively destroyed: on Burke's reckoning, there was only a popular chamber confronting a king reduced to a cypher. He believed that a frivolous spirit of experimentation had come to dominate public deliberation: property, wisdom and experience barely played a role in legislation. Unpopular taxes were branded as feudal impositions. The Comte de Mirabeau attacked the property of the wealthiest landowning classes.[42] Talleyrand called into question the legitimacy of ecclesiastical possessions.[43] Thouret queried the rights of corporate ownership.[44] Burke was astounded by such threats to the very basis of civil society.[45] He thought that the sanctity of property required security at all levels. To cancel the titles of particular bodies or discrete individuals in support of a system of discrimination against nobility was a violation of the most rudimentary principles of justice.

By 1791, Burke was writing of the "fury" that attached individuals to their goods.[46] Being stripped of them by acts of power offended against basic instincts and inviolable rights. For this reason, the idea of prescription arose naturally in the human mind. Property rights had their origin in self-defence and were consolidated by usage. Both the right of possessors and sympathy with possession were "executive powers under the legislation of nature, enforcing its first law."[47] The depth of

[41] Though, as Burke saw it, the subversion of religion had involved deliberate conspiracy, already in evidence by 1773: see EB to the Abbé Augustin Barruel, 1 May 1797, *Corr.*, X, p. 38: "I have known myself personally five of your principal Conspirators."

[42] *Archives parlementaires*, IX, p. 195 (26 September 1789): "Frappez, immolez sans pitié ces tristes victimes, précipitiez-les dans l'abîme."

[43] Ibid., pp. 398ff. (10 October 1789).

[44] Ibid., pp. 485–87 (23 October 1789).

[45] EB to Earl Fitzwilliam, 12 November 1789, *Corr.*, VI, pp. 36–37.

[46] EB to Claude-François de Rivarol, 1 June 1791, ibid., p. 266.

[47] Ibid. Burke is implicitly referencing John Locke, *Two Treatises of Government*, ed. Peter Laslett (Cambridge: Cambridge University Press, 1960, 1990), bk. II, ch. 2, §§ 7, 13. The "first law" of nature prescribes "Peace and the *Preservation of Mankind*."

Burke's animosity against the French Revolution stemmed from two sources: first its violation of the laws of nature in the form of an assault on the rights to property; and second its hostility to the institutions of religion insofar as these inculcated fundamental duties. On his assessment, the dual attack on property and religion was facilitated by the collapse of domestic security, beginning with a mutiny in the armed forces in Paris and followed by the creation of the National Guard in July 1789. At that point, it seemed the main danger that the Revolution posed to Britain was in terms of the encouragement it gave through the medium of propaganda to sedition abroad. However the magnitude of the threat increased drastically over the next two years as the Legislative Assembly moved to extend the remit of the Revolution by military means. Looking back from the middle of the 1790s, Burke claimed that two principal characters had driven events thus far: on the one hand there were the men of letters, often committed to irreligion, and usually dedicated to grandiose revolutionary schemes; and on the other hand there were the politicians determined to salvage the dignity of France by employing the democratic "republic" as an instrument of empire.[48] Burke now claimed that, against all odds, Jacobinism had become a formidable opponent determined to prosecute ceaseless war against the recognised norms of civil society. As Pitt's ministry endeavoured to come to terms with the Directory in 1796, Burke preached relentless belligerence against what he regarded as an implacable foe. A war of annihilation had to succeed or everything would be lost.

Burke dealt with many of the issues that featured prominently in his career simultaneously. In the mid 1760s, when he was first exposed to the American crisis, he was obliged to adopt a position on the East India Company. In the same period he had to publicise perceived threats to the constitution and formulate the Rockinghams' view of party. Later on, as he came to terms with the gravity of the situation in India, he was still immersed in the intricacies of the American dispute. At the same time he was refining his ideas about representation in connection with both the colonies and Great Britain. In the 1790s, as he was fending off proposals for parliamentary reform, he was pressing for the repeal of anti-popery legislation in Ireland, doggedly pursuing the impeachment of Hastings, and challenging government policy on France. To present this jumble of issues in strict chronological sequence, with one topic intruding fast upon another, risks losing the thread of Burke's arguments about each of his major concerns. In the main body of this work, I have therefore separated his principal preoccupations, dividing America and India into stand-alone chapters. Britain and France are likewise given distinct treatment, while Ireland, which forms a crucial but less extensive portion of the Burke corpus, is examined in chapters dedicated to either British or French affairs, depending on which bears more heavily on the course of Irish events. By separating Burke's preoccupations in this way, it becomes possible to probe his most important positions in a sustained and integrated fashion.

At the same time, I have preserved, as seems appropriate, the broad chronological sweep of Burke's career. As events proceeded, Burke's response could not stand

[48] EB, *Second Letter on a Regicide Peace* (1796), *W & S*, IX, pp. 278–79.

still. It is necessary to chart how he adapted to developments. This process of change is plotted across the five main sections of this book. They deal, first, with his life in Ireland in the 1730s and 1740s, covering his immediate milieu and his years at school and university; second, with his arrival in London in 1750 and his life down to 1765, focusing on his legal training and intellectual development; thirdly, with his first nine years in parliament as tensions with the American colonists grew, covering his views on Ireland, Bengal and the colonies, and including his analysis of the growth of the power of the crown; fourthly, I treat Burke's succeeding eleven years in parliament in which he reassessed the scale of the Indian problem, appraised the impact of the war with the colonies on domestic politics, campaigned for the rights of Catholics by challenging the popery laws, and interrogated the relationship between members of parliament and their constituents; and, finally, in the last section, the book covers Burke's response to the French Revolution and his prosecution of the Hastings trial, while also presenting his responses to British political affairs and his reaction to Ireland's progress towards escalating conflict. Burke's career can be characterised in terms of abiding concerns, but it also displayed complicated patterns of development largely governed by the impact of events on established principles.

Besides its broadly chronological approach, the book identifies two overarching themes in terms of which Burke's development can be viewed. These were the spirit of conquest on the one hand, and the spirit of liberty on the other. Together they helped define his attitude to empire and revolution. Burke's idea of the spirit of conquest was a product of a vision of Europe that saw its various states as having emerged from the tyranny of feudal government. This, he thought, had meant progress towards a system of impartial justice and an escape from the extremes of baronial domination. These relics of the past had been replaced by the spirit of liberty which largely comprised the equitable application of law and mechanisms for securing political accountability. As Burke recognised, even the kings of eighteenth-century France supported an independent judiciary; even Frederick the Great was under pressure from the force of public opinion. From this vantage, the situation in Britain was happier still since the rights of the common citizen were in the hands of juries and opinion could make itself felt by means of elective representation. Burke's attachment to freedom was further refined by trying to understand it in a world-historical context: North America, having been peopled from Europe, extended the taste for liberty; many Asian governments were moderated rather than pure despotisms. For instance, in India under the Mughals public administration respected laws, protected property and deferred to manners. It was in the exercise of overseas European dominion that the spirit of conquest was most obviously revived, both in relations between the governments of the old world and the new and in the pursuit of commercial monopoly on the Indian subcontinent. Then, towards the end of his career, as Burke sought to curtail the effects of unmitigated despotism in the form of the East India Company, an unprecedented engine of oppression rose to power at the heart of Europe under the banner of the rights of man. As Burke saw it, the spirit of conquest had been rekindled in the mocking guise of freedom.

4 The Spirit of Conquest and the Spirit of Liberty

Burke's legacy to history has been a complicated affair. At different points during the course of the nineteenth century he enjoyed iconic status among each of the main British parties—Whigs, Liberals and Tories alike. He was also variously appropriated in Europe and America.[49] Two strands of interpretation have dominated his reception. On the one hand there has been a "liberal" rendition, largely based on his Irish, Indian and American writings, but including elements of his rejection of the powers of the crown under George III.[50] On the other hand there has been a "conservative" depiction, based partly on his assumed debt to medieval natural law, but mostly inspired by assorted statements denouncing the French Revolution.[51] Attempts to reconcile this dichotomy have led to the suggestion that there were in fact two Burkes, an early advocate of popular rights and a later apostate from progressive principles. This was originally a Foxite charge, forged in the heat of political dispute, but it has enjoyed considerable subsequent success as a scholarly hypothesis. This usually takes the form of questioning Burke's "consistency" and calling into question the "unity" of his thought. This is not the place to explore the coherence of these objections.[52] Nonetheless, it can at least be said that it is not obvious how practical judgments might be logically inconsistent in the way that the deductions of formal reasoning can be.

Contemporaries who accused Burke of blatant inconsistency were really charging him with a kind of infidelity: since he differed from former friends with whom he had agreed, the idea went, he must have betrayed a commitment which at one time

[49] The history of Burke's reception has yet to be written. Friedrich Gentz, Thomas Babington Macaulay, Alexis de Tocqueville, John Morley, William Ewart Gladstone, Matthew Arnold, William Edward Hartpole Lecky, Carl Menger, Andrew Bonar Law, John MacCunn, William Graham, Woodrow Wilson, Russell Kirk, Peter J. Stanlis and Friedrich Hayek have variously, and incongruously, championed his doctrines. The British context is currently being traced by Emily Jones, the German by Jonathan Green. The American reception has recently been treated by Seamus Deane, "Burke in the USA" in David Dwan and Christopher J. Insole eds., *The Cambridge Companion to Edmund Burke* (Cambridge: Cambridge University Press, 2012), and Drew Maciag, *Edmund Burke in America: The Contested Career of the Father of Modern Conservatism* (Ithaca, NY: Cornell University Press, 2013).

[50] The classic study in this idiom is John Morley, *Edmund Burke: A Historical Study* (London: 1867), but see more recently Conor Cruise O'Brien, *The Great Melody: A Thematic Biography of Edmund Burke* (London: Sinclair-Stevenson, 1992), drawing on Isaac Kramnick, *The Rage of Edmund Burke: Portrait of an Ambivalent Conservative* (New York: Basic Books, 1977).

[51] Russell Kirk, *The Conservative Mind: From Burke to Santayana* (Chicago, IL: Henry Regnery Co., 1953); Corey Robin, *The Reactionary Mind: Conservatism from Edmund Burke to Sarah Palin* (Oxford: Oxford University Press, 2011); Jesse Norman, *Edmund Burke: Philosopher, Politician, Prophet* (London: HarperCollins, 2013).

[52] On the issue of consistency in past thinkers, compare Peter Laslett, "Introduction" to John Locke, *Two Treatises of Government* (Cambridge: Cambridge University Press, 1960, 1990), pp. 82–83 and Quentin Skinner, "Meaning and Understanding in the History of Ideas," *History and Theory*, 8 (1969), pp. 3–53.

he had shared. However, Burke never obviously abandoned previously declared principles. What occurred instead was a disagreement about their application. This arose above all in response to the American and French Revolutions. For some of Burke's critics, like Richard Price and Joseph Priestley, both events were indicative of millenarian promise: since each appeared to look forward to impending spiritual deliverance, they were identified as somehow serving the same cause. For Burke, however, the Revolutions were radically different. The Americans began by appealing to older imperial arrangements before being forced into a posture of militant self-defence. The French, on the other hand, aimed at the destruction of a regime. In pursuing this they undermined both property and prescription. One might of course question Burke's judgment in arriving at this conclusion, but that does not establish inconsistency on his part.[53] The problem with the attempt to charge Burke with apostasy is that it is not in the end really about Burke at all, but about the historical significance of the French Revolution. A number of powerful historiographical traditions point to the events of 1789 as the gateway to modern progress. Thus Burke, as a prominent critic of the Revolution, is either associated with an ideology of reaction or accused of having abandoned the liberal values of his youth for the conservative principles of his old age.

Liberalism in this formulation is understood in terms of a commitment to natural rights, and conservatism in terms of a dedication to preserving the authority of the state. It is clear that by defending both these principles together Burke was opposed to the exclusive endorsement of them separately. As such, his writings cannot usefully be interpreted through the prism of party-political doctrines that lacked any purchase in his own time: neither "liberalism" nor "conservatism" can adequately capture Burke. At the end of his life, faced with the imminent prospect of insurrection in Ireland, he described the obligation to preserve the state as a cardinal responsibility: "The first duty of a State is to provide for its own conservation." Nonetheless, once secured, it was the overriding task of public authority to protect the rights of the people.[54] Burke articulated both perspectives in an early indictment of persecution: "Every body is satisfied," he argued, "that a conservation and secure enjoyment of our natural rights is the great and ultimate purpose of civil society."[55] In the 1790s, he identified three immediate threats to this "great . . . purpose": "Ascendancy," "Indianism" and "Jacobinism."[56] Each of these terms encapsulated a distinct mode of misgovernment rooted in the spirit of conquest. To Burke they stood for forces of

[53] Here I agree with David Bromwich, *The Intellectual Biography of Edmund Burke: From the Sublime and Beautiful to American Independence* (Cambridge, MA: Harvard University Press, 2014), p. 26: "There have been periods when the word *principle* seemed close to cant, but principle is the word that comes to mind when one thinks of Burke." On the other hand, it is of course true that principles are modified by circumstance. On this conundrum, see Ian Crowe, "Introduction: Principles and Circumstances" in idem ed., *Edmund Burke: His Life and Legacy* (Dublin: Four Courts Press, 1997).

[54] EB to the Rev. Thomas Hussey, post 9 December 1796, *Corr.*, IX, pp. 168–69.

[55] EB, *Tracts relating to Popery Laws* (1761–65), *W & S*, IX, p. 463.

[56] EB to Sir Hercules Langrishe, 26 May 1795, *Corr.*, X, p. 32.

reaction that posed a danger to the survival of the modern spirit of liberty. In 1758, David Hume contended that Britain could rival "the freest and most illustrious commonwealths of antiquity."[57] Burke was even more firmly committed to the British ideal of freedom. A properly historical examination of his politics must recover what he meant by the spirit of liberty and how he understood it to be imperilled by the spirit of conquest. However, the process of recovery is inhibited by what amounts to a dogmatic assumption that British freedom in the eighteenth century was a residue of the old regime while the French Revolution paved the way to a benign future. At the very least, this verdict is based on a radically simplified version of the past.

To make sense of Burke's rhetoric we need to understand his thought. The force of the one directly depends on the content of the other. Furthermore, to grasp the substance of Burke's ideas it is necessary to restore his arguments to two distinct though related contexts simultaneously: first, to the microscopic context of quotidian politics and, second, to the intellectual context of eighteenth-century political thought. Burke's political context is particularly rich and intricate. He supported government in the period 1765–6 during the first Rockingham administration. Then, between March and July 1782, he occupied the office of paymaster of the forces under the second Rockingham ministry. He accepted the position again in 1783 under the short-lived Fox–North coalition. For the rest of his time in parliament he had to conspire in opposition. Therefore, for the most part, reconstructing Burke's politics involves placing his arguments within the context of the policies he was rejecting. This requires a full description of the fortunes of eighteenth-century governments under the reign of George III. It demands attention to the pace and content of affairs on the basis of surviving memoirs, press reports and correspondence. Machiavelli, Grotius, Hobbes and Locke were clearly immersed in the trials of public life. Cicero even conducted his own political career. Yet Burke was obliged to respond more directly to the pressure of events, and his political context is accordingly more dense.

Precisely because of his commitment to the role of statesman, Burke's intellectual context is peculiarly difficult to decipher. He was not a systematic philosopher, but an engaged polemicist. As a result, he had no occasion to reveal the "foundations" of his thought. Nonetheless, by comparison with other orators and men of business in parliament, he was fluent in the intellectual traditions of the past. He wrestled with the legacy of Aristotle, Cicero, Suárez, Grotius, Coke, Hobbes, Pufendorf, Locke, Hutcheson, Berkeley, Montesquieu and Bolingbroke. He also evaluated the significance of Vattel, Rousseau, Hume and Smith. These figures are usually understood as "influences" on Burke. They would be better seen as thinkers whom he used. Unsurprisingly he used them in very different ways. He commonly resorted to the canons of jurisprudence to establish the agreed wisdom of the ages. It was in this fashion that he employed Philo, Justinian and Vattel. He also criticised moralists who embodied the antithesis of his own views: Mandeville, Bolingbroke and

[57] David Hume, "Of the Coalition of Parties" (1758) in idem, *Essays Moral, Political, and Literary*, ed. Eugene F. Miller (Indianapolis, IN: Liberty Fund, 1985, 1987), p. 495.

Rousseau were alike treated in this way. Beyond this, ascertaining an overarching Burkean philosophy has proved elusive. He admired the common law and respected the law of nations yet he considered both subordinate to the precepts of the law of nature. His responses to individual thinkers tended to be mixed. He was appalled by Hobbes's theory of law yet he adopted his conception of corporations. He accepted Locke's political premises but rejected his conclusions. He was captivated by Hume's ideas while being opposed to his religious scepticism. He misread Smith on morals, deferred to him on political economy, and helped educate him on the character of East India Company power.

As a result of his angular relationships with specific lawyers, philosophers and publicists, Burke is often aligned more generally with particular "schools" of thought. The idea of a school usually implies avowed discipleship, and this scarcely captures Burke's connection to his predecessors. He certainly tackled particular traditions, but he owed no allegiance to a consistent line of thought. He had no interest in presenting himself as heir to an intellectual inheritance: in the end his aim was to advocate a specific course of action at a particular point in time. None of this is to say that he lacked philosophical orientation: he was undoubtedly guided by intellectual commitments. His commitments on this score have been diversely interpreted, variously leading to his depiction as a natural lawyer, a proto-utilitarian and a proponent of historicism.[58] While these alternatives are usually presented as exclusive categories, in fact there is no necessary incompatibility between them. Natural law since Grotius sought to reconcile right with utility; Montesquieu aimed to study both through the history of morals, laws and government. For this reason, Montesquieu played a pivotal role in eighteenth-century political thought.[59] He was also an enduring presence in the mind of Edmund Burke. He enjoyed this privileged position for a number of reasons. First, Burke was attracted by Montesquieu's insistence that historical laws were ultimately answerable to a moral law. He was also impressed by his determination to relate both human and natural laws to *mores*, habitudes and customs. Next, he appreciated Montesquieu's inclination to elucidate historical laws by means of a comparative method. He was also persuaded by Montesquieu's ambition to pursue comparative study from a world-historical perspective, encompassing ancient and modern Europe along with Asian culture. Burke was further seduced by the clarity with which *The Spirit of the Laws* interpreted European history in terms of the processes of conquest and pacification. Finally, Burke was inevitably captivated by Montesquieu's claim that liberty was the basic principle underpinning the British system of government.

[58] See, respectively, Peter J. Stanlis, *Edmund Burke and the Natural Law* (1958) (New Brunswick, NJ: Transaction Press, 2003, 2009); Leslie Stephen, *English Thought in the Eighteenth Century* (London: 1876, 1881), 2 vols., II, pp. 225–26; Friedrich Meinecke, *Cosmopolitanism and the Nation State* (1907), trans. Robert B. Kimber (Princeton, NJ: Princeton University Press, 1970), p. 101.

[59] Sylvana Tomaselli, "The Spirit of Nations" in Mark Goldie and Robert Wokler eds., *The Cambridge History of Eighteenth-Century Political Thought* (Cambridge: Cambridge University Press, 2006).

Of course, none of this implies that Burke's politics strove to embody a specifically Montesquieuian doctrine. Nonetheless, *The Spirit of the Laws* offers a useful point of departure for beginning to understand Burke's conception of the spirit of liberty, and consequently the spirit of conquest over which he hoped it would prevail. For Montesquieu, this triumph had assumed its purest form in Britain in the aftermath of the Glorious Revolution. However, its very success left it exposed to unforeseen corruption. In *The Spirit of the Laws*, having reflected at length on his experiences during his visit to Britain between 1729 and 1731, Montesquieu devoted two chapters to the "constitution of England." The first, Chapter 6 of Book XI, was concerned with the form of the administration; and the second, Chapter 27 of Book XIX, was taken up with the *mores* and manners of the nation.[60] Montesquieu's treatment attracted extensive commentary from Hume to De Lolme and Madison.[61] In the same spirit, throughout his life, Burke credited what he saw as the commanding genius of the French baron.[62] Much like Hume, admiration did not make Burke an obedient disciple so much as an appreciative but critical reader of Montesquieu's work. In an early fragmentary study, the *Abridgement of English History*, Burke assessed the plausibility of the account presented in *The Spirit of the Laws* of the origins of "English" freedom; around thirty years later, in the *Reflections on the Revolution in France*, Burke returned to evaluate Montesquieu's take on the prospects for British stability.[63] During this period, and through the years that followed, it is clear that the British chapters of *The Spirit of the Laws* helped stimulate Burke's thought about national politics.[64] At the same time, the work as a whole was an inspiration for thinking more generally about constitutions.

According to Burke, the overriding achievement of modern European history was the liberation of jurisprudence from the hands of power.[65] Montesquieu had shown how the impartial administration of law had grown up with the establishment of an

[60] On the early composition of these chapters, see Paul A. Rahe, *Montesquieu and the Logic of Liberty: War, Religion . . . and the Foundations of the Modern Republic* (New Haven, CT: Yale University Press, 2009), pp. 40–42.

[61] F.T.H. Fletcher, *Montesquieu and English Politics* (London: Edward Arnold, 1939); David Lieberman, "The Mixed Constitution and the Common Law" in Goldie and Wokler eds., *Cambridge History of Eighteenth-Century Political Thought*; Ursula Haskins Gonthier, *Montesquieu and England* (London: Pickering, 2010); James Madison, "Federalist No. 47" in *The Federalist*, ed. George W. Carey and James McClellan (Indianapolis, IN: Liberty Fund, 2001), pp. 250–52.

[62] C. P. Courtney, *Montesquieu and Burke* (Oxford: Basil Blackwell, 1963); Seamus Deane, "Montesquieu and Burke" in idem, *Foreign Affections: Essays on Edmund Burke* (Cork: Field Day, 2005).

[63] EB, *An Essay towards an Abridgement of English History* (1757–c. 1763), *W & S*, I, p. 430. EB, *Reflections*, ed. Clark, p. 359 [275].

[64] See, for example, the record of Fox's intervention on 6 May 1791, *Parliamentary History*, XXIX, col. 391: "Mr. Fox alluded to what Mr. Burke had quoted from Montesquieu, and declared he agreed with Montesquieu in his observations on the British constitution."

[65] EB, *An Essay towards an History of the Laws of England* (c. 1757), *W & S*, I, p. 322. Cf. the Duke of Richmond opening his motion on the independence of the judiciary on 3 June 1783, *Parliamentary History*, XXIII, col. 963, with a citation from Montesquieu's *The Spirit of the Laws* on the essence of liberty as residing in the separation of judicial from legislative and executive power.

independent judiciary. The purity of justice was the clearest sign of an escape from the arbitrary whims of rulers. It marked the passage from feudal barbarism to the political culture of civilised Europe. Equity, Burke wrote, was ultimately "victorious over tyranny."[66] *The Spirit of the Laws* had encouraged its readers to think about this accomplishment in relation to the governments of the east as well as in connection with the republics of the ancient world. Burke was deeply critical of Montesquieu's claims about Asian politics, but he followed him in extolling post-feudal Europe as at least rivalling the constitutional triumphs of Greece and Rome. As he observed in the *Reflections*, the various member states of the modern European continent could be positively distinguished "from those states which flourished in the most brilliant periods of the antique world."[67]

Burke's understanding of the cast of European politics was based on an appreciation of the constitutional arrangements that facilitated the establishment of modern freedom. For Montesquieu, liberty in contemporary monarchies like Britain and France, unlike the freedom of antiquated Mediterranean city-states, was not a function of the direct exercise of popular power. Instead, it was a product of the feeling of security (*sûreté*) that came with the absence of fear.[68] Ancient liberty, by comparison, was both more precarious and more constrained. To begin with, it limited private interests in order to foster public virtue. By restricting private or "particular" desires, citizens' passions were focused exclusively on the common weal.[69] For this reason, the Greco-Roman republics were not "free by nature," Montesquieu thought: their liberty was preserved by the artifice of self-restraint.[70] Consequently, democratic republics in particular were exposed to corruption from two directions. They were compromised either by the introduction of luxury into society or by the excessive demand for equality on the part of ordinary members of the polity. In the former case, citizens would abandon their commitment to the cause of the commonwealth as they pursued the satisfactions of consumption instead; in the latter, respect for magistracy would decline as the people came to see themselves as equally competent to administer all offices of state. Given these vulnerabilities, Montesquieu concluded that freedom was better preserved by constitutional regulation on the model of modern monarchies than by promoting patriotic morals as required by the old republics. Where power was controlled by a system of checks and balances, abuses would be contained and the fear of arbitrary authority would give way to public confidence.[71]

[66] Ibid.

[67] EB, *Reflections*, ed. Clark, p. 239 [113].

[68] Charles-Louis de Secondat, Baron de Montesquieu, *De l'esprit des lois* (1748) in *Œuvres complètes*, ed. Roger Caillois (Paris: Gallimard, 1951), 2 vols., II, pt. II, bk. XI, ch. 6. Cf. ibid., pt. II, bk. XI, ch. 2: "on a confondu le pouvoir du peuple avec la liberté du peuple." Cf. EB, Debate in the Commons on the Bill for the Relief of Protestant Dissenters, 23 February 1773, *Parliamentary History*, XVII, cols. 778–79: "Montesquieu places liberty in an exemption from fear."

[69] Montesquieu, *De l'esprit des lois,* ed. Caillois, pt. I, bk. V, ch. 2: "passions particulières."

[70] Ibid., pt. II, bk. XI, ch. 4, and pt. I, bk. IV, ch. 5: "la vertu politique est un renoncement à soi-même."

[71] Ibid., pt. II, bk. XI, ch. 4.

Burke thought of the spirit of conquest as existing along a spectrum: at one extreme it found expression in unadulterated warfare while at the other it shaded into less violent if still absolute power. In international terms commerce was the opposite of conquest while domestically its antithesis was constitutional government. Montesquieu, for Burke, was the master theorist of the mechanisms by which constitutional government was regulated. Both of them saw regulation as a function of the separation of powers. Separation did not imply partitioning the branches of government so much as preserving their capacity for independent action. Thus, in the British case, the House of Lords enjoyed judicial privileges as well as playing a part in legislation. However, the crucial point was that in this instance, as equally in France, judicial decisions affecting the rights of the individual could never be controlled by executive power in the hands of the king. According to Burke, this arrangement provided for equality before the law. It was the precondition of justice in modern politics. As Montesquieu saw it, the separation of powers was most commonly organised in one of two ways. The first method took the form of a regime of "moderate" liberty and was exemplified by contemporary France. In this case, power was limited by separating judicial administration from legislative and executive authority combined. Montesquieu took the second method to have been perfected by the British. Theirs was a regime of "extreme" freedom under which power was restrained by keeping all three components of government distinct.[72] The administration of justice was left to juries and the hierarchy of courts, while legislation and execution were divided between parliament and the crown. Each power checked the other without paralysing the whole. The system of government successfully coordinated the countervailing decisions distributed among its independent branches.

Burke was a lifelong devotee of this "extreme political liberty."[73] Its extremity was a function of its apparent precariousness: where executive and legislative powers vied with one another, there was a constant possibility of constitutional implosion. Electoral representation lent both stability and fragility to this combination of forces. On the one hand it succeeded in moderating public opinion: the legislature was more enlightened than the general population. Therefore, unlike the assemblies of the ancient world, representative bodies facilitated deliberation.[74] However, representation also embroiled the nation in the tribulations of the constitution by promoting rival adherents of the two principal sources of power: on one side Tories traditionally rallied to the prerogatives of the crown, while on the other Whigs were disposed to support the privileges of parliament. For Burke and Montesquieu, unlike Hume, the two main parties exercised a positive influence on the whole: a sudden attempt by the executive on the rights of the legislature would cause the people to unite behind the privileges of parliament; a foreign threat to national security would

[72] Ibid., pt. II, bk. XI, ch. 6: "Dans la plupart des royaumes de l'Europe, le gouvernement est modéré, parce que le prince, qui a les deux premiers pouvoirs, laisse à ces sujets l'exercise du troisième."

[73] Ibid., pt. II, bk. XI, ch. 6. Cf. ibid., pt. III, bk. XIX, ch. 27, where Montesquieu refers to "États extrêmement libres."

[74] Ibid., pt. III, bk. XIX, ch. 27. Cf. ibid., pt. II, bk. XI, ch. 6.

encourage the population to rally in favour of the prerogatives of the king. As Burke himself argued a matter of months before his death, the British parties "by their collision and mutual resistance" had "preserved the variety of this Constitution in its unity."[75] Again, as both Burke and Montesquieu saw it, danger lay less in faction than in a protracted process of corruption: the state would perish when the influence of the crown finally overwhelmed the House of Commons. It was at that point that the legislature, in Montesquieu's phrase, would have become "plus corrompue que l'exécutrice."[76] In contrast to the disturbances of the 1640s, Britain in the eighteenth century was threatened less by the rise of factions that might culminate in civil war than by the gradual emergence of despotism through the elimination of effective parliamentary opposition. Burke's defence of party, and thus the original Rockinghamite platform, needs to be understood within this wider constitutional framework.

Burke believed that the process of corruption had been advanced under the venal ministries of George III. While this affected the integrity of the constitution at home its impact was most conspicuous in the wider Empire. Montesquieu had presented Britain as a haughty (*superbes*) commercial power immune to the temptations of territorial dominion.[77] The British were a jealous and monopolising people, prone to fret about the relative prosperity of their colonies. They nonetheless preserved their state free from the spirit of conquest.[78] However, from Burke's perspective, the situation changed dramatically in the aftermath of the Seven Years' War. First, the attitude of government towards the American provinces became more imperious. Next, the East India Company was permitted to operate as a ruthlessly oppressive power. In addition, an attitude of exclusive domination persisted in the administration of Ireland. Finally, in the 1790s, crisis loomed from another direction. Under the influence of the French Revolution, fawning populism threatened to undermine the division of social ranks, and with it the viability of constitutional government. As egalitarian rage was unleashed on the European continent, Jacobinism promised to complete the ruin of everything Burke held dear. He was utterly bereft of all complacent hope in progress. First the wars of religion had arrested the growth of enlightenment, and now the achievements of an age of liberty looked set to succumb to an era of darkness.

[75] EB, *Third Letter on a Regicide Peace* (1797), *W & S*, IX, p. 326. Cf. EB, Debate on the Bill to Prevent Traitorous Correspondence, 22 March 1793, *Morning Herald*, 23 March 1793: "Great rage and party animosity had subsisted between Whigs and Tories; yet he thought neither of them . . . were inimical to the Constitution. The Whig approved of the general form of the Constitution, but he leaned particularly to the democratic part of it. On the other hand, the Tory approved of the Constitution, and in doubtful cases he was inclined to support the prerogative of the Crown."

[76] Montesquieu, *De l'esprit des lois*, pt. II, bk. XI, ch. 6.

[77] Ibid., pt. III, bk. XIX, ch. 27.

[78] Ibid. Cf. Emer de Vattel, *The Law of Nations, or the Principles of the Law of Nature, Applied to the Conduct and Affairs of Nations and Sovereigns*, ed. Béla Kapossy and Richard Whatmore (Indianapolis, IN: Liberty Fund, 2008), p. 497: "England, whose opulence and formidable fleets have a powerful influence, without alarming any state on the score of its liberty, because that nation seems cured of the rage of conquest."

In 1792, two years before he finally retired from parliament, Burke called to mind the savagery of the spirit of conquest that accompanied the wars of religion in the seventeenth century. Ireland supplied a gruesome illustration of the phenomenon. Burke shuddered at the brutality of "confiscations" as well as the vindictiveness of "counter-confiscations."[79] Persecution and political upheaval had shaken governments and destabilised property. Prescription offered the only chance of enduring pacification; conscience presented the only means of imposing binding obligations. It astonished Burke that the French Revolution had dismissed these indispensable resources. Property as such had not been destroyed, but faith in property had been shattered. The integrity of "mine" and "thine" might never be the same again. Hostility to privilege in France had undermined all social distinctions. Prosperity, moral improvement and mutual trust had been immediate casualties of the mayhem. It was in this context that Burke observed towards the end of the *Reflections* how the "moderate" liberty of Montesquieu's France had proved more vulnerable than the extremity of British freedom to the ideal of primitive equality promoted by the Revolution.[80]

In Burke's mind, the idea of levelling all social ranks first posed a danger to Britain in the form of seductive propaganda.[81] However, through the 1790s, French ideology steadily proved its worth as a military force. It remained to be seen how the Revolution would fare under the impact of defeat. When Burke died in the summer of 1797, that was a complex judgment about the likely shape of the future. As it turned out, political attitudes were transformed in the course of the nineteenth century. The idea of government by estates was put on the defensive. Nonetheless, it can hardly be said that political values were completely overhauled, or that the institutions of the earlier period were comprehensively replaced. Revolutionary equality did not uproot the old European norms. Indeed, how many long-established conventions continue to define contemporary social and political experience remains an important question. The Revolution was a watershed, but it did not constitute a new epoch. Burke saw himself in his final years as an apologist for a disappearing world, yet his contribution was to help posterity see that no definitive breach in fact occurred.

[79] EB, *Letter to Richard Burke* (post 19 February 1792), *W & S*, IX, p. 657.

[80] EB, *Reflections*, ed. Clark, p. 359 [275].

[81] EB, *Substance of the Speech of the Right Honourable Edmund Burke in the Debate on the Army Estimates* (London: 1790), *passim*.

PART I

Reason and Prejudice

Early Formation, 1730–1750

OVERVIEW

This book is not a work of psychological biography. It does not seek to uncover the hidden motives that drove its protagonist.[1] It is not an exercise in personal biography either. It does not focus on the private life or pastimes of its subject.[2] Instead, its aim is to chart the progress of Burke's life in thought and politics. Nonetheless, his public actions and ideas did have a personal context. Burke was a lifelong devotee of religious tolerance. He came from a convert family, and was partly reared by Roman Catholic relations. He attended a Quaker school and a Church of Ireland university. This range of experience is not sufficient to account for his commitment to toleration. Even so, his mature principles are usefully seen against the background of his early years. Burke believed his family to have been expropriated in the seventeenth century during the reaction to the Irish rebellion of 1641. This gave him an acute awareness of the impact of confiscation on the attitudes of the Catholic gentry and nobility in Ireland. The Cromwellian settlement and the subsequent seizure of Catholic estates in the aftermath of the Glorious Revolution amounted to an experience of conquest on a major scale. A dramatic revolution in property had occurred, and only the passage of time could secure new titles by the operation of prescription.

[1] For the leading works in this genre, see Isaac Kramnick, *The Rage of Edmund Burke: Portrait of an Ambivalent Conservative* (New York: Basic Books, 1977); Conor Cruise O'Brien, *The Great Melody: A Thematic Biography of Edmund Burke* (London: Sinclair-Stevenson, 1992).

[2] The outstanding work of personal biography is F. P. Lock, *Edmund Burke: 1730–1797* (Oxford: Clarendon Press, 1998–2006), 2 vols.

Burke might have responded in a number of ways to this traumatic sequence of events. As it turned out, he rejected Jacobite revolution and Catholic retribution, arguing instead for the reform of the existing Hanoverian setup. So while Burke's background and experience do not predict his later beliefs, it is nonetheless right to recount the personal history in which those beliefs took shape.

I

—

THE BLACKWATER, BALLITORE, TRINITY AND *THE REFORMER*

1.1 Introduction

The first twenty years of Burke's life were spent in Ireland. His time was divided between Cork, Kildare and Dublin. These different locations corresponded to distinct cultural environments: his Catholic relations, his Quaker school and his Church of Ireland upbringing. In later life Burke would emphasise the hold of prejudice on the human mind. In his own case he was exposed to an array of incompatible prejudices. In a very real sense, the worlds of Roman Catholicism, dissent and established Protestantism were conspicuously divided from one another. It is interesting to ponder how Burke assimilated those divisions. As a youth he believed that custom could be educated by reason, enabling individuals to transcend their cultural confinement. It was only later, in the 1750s, that he came to contend that our rational faculties could productively be constrained by habit. This chapter presents the formation of Burke's early prejudices and charts his commitment to the idea that their cruder manifestations could be improved by a process of rational inquiry. By the late 1740s, while editing *The Reformer* after graduating from Trinity College Dublin, he was campaigning to accelerate that process by contributing to the refinement of national taste. He was committed to pursuing a career as a man of letters though obliged by parental pressure to train for the bar in London. It would take fifteen years before Burke's desire to succeed in the world of literature would be replaced by a resolution to take his chances in public life.

1.2 Family and Childhood in Historical Context

W.E.H. Lecky famously depicted Dublin in the middle of the eighteenth century as "the second city in the Empire."[1] Major public buildings and elegant private

[1] William Edward Hartpole Lecky, *A History of Ireland in the Eighteenth Century* (1892) (London: Longmans, Green and Co., 1913), 5 vols., I, p. 319.

residences were steadily constructed as the century progressed. A theatre on Smock Alley was founded in 1661; the Crow Street Theatre was established in 1758; a new music hall was based at Fishamble Street from 1741.[2] Dublin was the viceregal and administrative capital of the kingdom, boasting significant textile industries and a major port for trade. Having arrived in the city in June 1776, Arthur Young described it as exceeding his expectations: "the public buildings are magnificent, very many of the streets regularly laid out. . . . From everything I saw, I was struck with those appearances of wealth which the capital of a thriving community may be supposed to exhibit."[3] Much of what first caught Young's eye had been erected fifty years earlier. The number of inhabited houses had risen between 1711 and 1728 by more than 4,000; the development of Molesworth Fields accelerated after 1705, while Henrietta Street was laid out in the 1720s; Sackville Street and Gardiner's Mall were planned in the 1740s. Trinity College had been expanding from its Elizabethan quadrangle towards College Green since before the Williamite wars, and the Library, designed by Thomas Burgh, began construction in 1712. Early in 1729, the first stone of Parliament House was laid, and the building was complete within a decade.[4] Its Ionic columns faced onto a large equestrian statue of King William III, unveiled in 1701 on the eleventh anniversary of the Battle of the Boyne. A comparison of Thomas Phillips's 1685 *Map of the Bay and Harbour of Dublin* with Charles Brooking's 1728 *Map of the City and Suburbs of Dublin* illustrates the rate of suburban expansion.[5] During the first third of the eighteenth century, the city was predominantly Protestant in composition, with a total population of around 75,000, which rose in the middle decades to about 150,000.[6] However, by the 1760s the ratio between the denominations had reversed, with Roman Catholics now constituting the majority of residents.[7] By the time that Edmund Burke left Dublin for London in 1750, 80 per cent of the Protestant population were members of the established

[2]John Finegan, "Dublin's Lost Theatres," *Historical Record*, 47:1 (Spring 1994), pp. 95–99.

[3]Arthur Young, *A Tour in Ireland: With General Observation on the Present State of that Kingdom Made in the Years 1776, 1777 and 1778, and Brought down to the End of 1779* (Dublin: 1780), 2 vols., I, pp. 1–2.

[4]S. J. Connolly, *Divided Kingdom: Ireland, 1630–1800* (Oxford: Oxford University Press, 2008), p. 364.

[5]Samuel A. Ossory Fitzpatrick, *Dublin: A Historical and Topographical Account of the City* (London: Methuen and Co., 1907), ch. 5; Maurice Craig, *Dublin 1660–1868* (Dublin: Hodges, Figgis and Co., 1952), chs. 8–14; J. G. Simms, "Dublin in 1685," *Irish Historical Studies*, 14:55 (1965), pp. 212–26; Thomas Phillips, *Map of the Bay and Harbour of Dublin* (London: 1685); Charles Brooking, *Map of the City and Suburbs of Dublin* (London: 1728); Colm Lennon, *Dublin, 1610–1756: The Making of the Early Modern City* (Dublin: Royal Irish Academy, 2009).

[6]David Dickson, "The Demographic Implications of Dublin's Growth, 1650–1850" in Richard Lawton and Robert Lee eds., *Urban Population Development in Western Europe from the Late-Eighteenth Century to the Early-Twentieth Century* (Liverpool: Liverpool University Press, 1989). For comparisons with Edinburgh and Manchester, see R. B. McDowell, *Ireland in the Age of Imperialism and Revolution, 1760–1801* (Oxford: Oxford University Press, 1979, 1991), p. 20.

[7]Patrick Fagan, "The Population of Dublin in the Eighteenth Century with Particular Reference to the Proportions of Protestants and Catholics," *Eighteenth-Century Ireland*, 6 (1991), pp. 121–56, p. 143.

Church, although Presbyterians, Quakers, Baptists, Huguenots, Lutherans, Moravians and Methodists were also to be found among the denizens of the city.

Burke was born in Dublin on 12 January 1730.[8] He was baptised into the established Protestant Church of Ireland, probably in the Parish of St. Michan's. In 1733, if not before, he was living on the north side of the river Liffey, on Arran Quay, facing south and looking towards the medieval walls of the city. His father, Richard Burke, whose ancestors seem to have been originally based in Limerick, spent his youth in Co. Cork, and qualified as an attorney-at-law in the Court of Exchequer in Dublin.[9] In the surviving manuscript notes for a biography of Burke planned by the Irish historian William Monck Mason, a nephew of Burke's friend and correspondent John Monck Mason, we are told that the Burke family had held "considerable estates" around Limerick in the seventeenth century "which became forfeited during the rebellion of 1641."[10] Burke's great-grandfather, Mason went on, "possessing some property within Co. Cork retired thither, and subsequently settled near the village of Castletownroche."[11] Burke's mother, Mary Nagle, came from Ballyduff, near Castletownroche. She was descended from Richard Nagle, Attorney General under James II, although the family managed to escape the confiscation of their property under the Treaty that succeeded the war of 1689–91, and retained their lands into

[8] 1 January by the Julian calendar corresponds to 12 January by the Gregorian. A case can still be made for 1729 as the year of Burke's birth. The most likely date has been endlessly disputed: some biographers have identified 1728 as the relevant date, although most have alternated between 1729 and 1730. Many follow the registration information for Trinity College Dublin, available at TCD MSS. Mun/V/23/3, which records Burke's age as 15 ("agens 16") in April 1744. A birth date of 1729 is also implied by the memorial tablet in Beaconsfield Church, where Burke was buried, which gives his age as 68 in 1797. However, Burke's sister, Juliana, was baptised around January 1729, encouraging others to push the date of his birth one year forward, assuming she was baptised in the year of her birth. See National Archives of Ireland, "Register of the Parish of Castle Town Roche (1728)," M 5048. I have followed Lock, *Burke*, I, pp. 16–17, in giving Burke's birth date as 12 January 1730. However, a detailed case for the earlier date can be found at the Beinecke Library, "Collection of Letters and Notes Formed by Sir Richard Bourke in order to Establish Edmund Burke's Date of Birth" (1842–43), Osborn Manuscript File (OSB MS. File) 1578, and so the exact date must remain uncertain.

[9] The marriage licence bond between Richard Burke and his wife describes him as "Richard Bourke de Shanballyduff in Comit' Corc' gen' [of Shanballyduff in County Cork, gentleman]." The licence was destroyed with the records of the Four Courts in 1922, but is transcribed in Arthur P. I. Samuels, *The Life, Correspondence and Writings of the Rt. Hon. Edmund Burke LL.D., with the Minute Book of the Debating "Club" Founded by him in Trinity College Dublin* (Cambridge: Cambridge University Press, 1923), p. 2.

[10] William Monck Mason (1775–1859), "Manuscript Notes and Printed Excerpts Concerning the Lives and Works of Eminent Irish Men and Women," TCD MSS. 10531–2, fol. 32. Mason's main aim was to correct the errors in James Prior's 1824 biography of Burke. His uncle, John Monck Mason (1726–1809), was Burke's senior by three years at Trinity College. His correspondence with Burke between the 1760s and 1780s can be found in the Sheffield and Northamptonshire archives. Burke's Limerick ancestry is also proposed in Basil O'Connell, "Edmund Burke: Gaps in the Family Record," *Studies in Burke and His Time*, 10:3 (1968), pp. 946–48, p. 946.

[11] Mason, "Manuscript Notes," TCD MSS. 10531–2, fol. 32: "This property continued in the family upon the death of [Edmund's] elder brother Garret on 27 April 1765; it was sold . . . in 1792 or 1793, for somewhat less than £4,000."

the eighteenth century.[12] Ballyduff is located in the north-east of Co. Cork, in the Blackwater Valley, between Mallow and Fermoy. The area was then known as Nagle Country on account of the strength and extent of the Nagle families in the region, many of whom emerged comparatively unscathed by the forfeitures that succeeded the Williamite conquest of Ireland.[13] The father of Burke's mother, Garret Nagle, appears as a successful claimant in the lists of adjudications pertaining to the land settlement during the implementation of the Treaties of Limerick and Galway.[14] Nonetheless, viewed in longer-term perspective, it is notable that Catholic landed proprietorship had diminished in Cork to a mere 8 per cent in the 1690s, whereas it stood at around two-thirds in 1641, decreasing by a half by the end of the wars of the three kingdoms. The Catholic presence in the county was now concentrated around the Blackwater Valley, surrounded by Protestant settlers based in Mallow and Doneraile.[15] Sectarian tensions rose in the area in the 1720s, 1730s, 1760s and beyond, beginning with the execution of James Cotter, a leading Jacobite agitator from Carrigtwohill, for the "abduction" of a young woman, Elizabeth Squibb, commonly reckoned to have been a Quaker.[16]

In his *Ancient and Present State of the County and City of Cork*, Charles Smith reproduced an address presented to Queen Anne from the people of Cork in early 1713, congratulating her on her success in securing the Peace of Utrecht, but still lamenting the fact that the "unhappy and fatal divisions, which reigned and were fomented some years past, do yet continue in this kingdom."[17] Smith was recalling the party strife in Ireland surrounding Catholic and Tory hopes for a Jacobite succession. When the attempt led by Bolingbroke and the Duke of Ormonde to instal the Pretender failed, attention in Ireland focused on securing a Tory victory in the election of 1713. Cotter proceeded to raise a mob in Dublin on election day, marking himself out as a conspirator against the Revolution settlement. After being hanged for the rape of Squibb on 7 May 1720, he became the object of Catholic lament and adulation—a symbol of Jacobite allegiance, but also a focus for anti-Quaker senti-

[12]Joseph Napier, "Edmund Burke: A Lecture Delivered before the Church of Ireland Young Men's Christian Association, May 28th, 1862" in *Lectures, Essays and Letters* (Dublin: 1888), p. 111.

[13]Louis M. Cullen, "The Blackwater Catholics and County Cork Society and Politics in the Eighteenth Century" in Patrick O'Flanagan and Cornelius Buttimer eds., *Cork: History and Society* (Dublin: 1993), pp. 552–53.

[14]J. G. Simms, *The Williamite Confiscation in Ireland, 1690–1703* (London: Faber and Faber, 1956), p. 46.

[15]T. C. Barnard, "The Political, Material and Mental Culture of the Cork Settlers, c. 1650–1700" in Flanagan and Buttimer eds., *Cork*, p. 315, relying on research that now appears in David Dickson, *Old World Colony: Cork and South Munster, 1630–1830* (Cork: Cork University Press, 2005).

[16]Cullen, "The Blackwater Catholics," pp. 538–39. Squibb's Quaker allegiance is disputed in Neal Garnham, "The Trials of James Cotter and Henry, Baron Barry of Santry: Two Case Studies in the Administration of Criminal Justice in Early Eighteenth-Century Ireland," *Irish Historical Studies*, 31:123 (1999), pp. 238–42, p. 337.

[17]Charles Smith, *The Ancient and Present State of the County and City of Cork* (Dublin: 1750), 2 vols., II, p. 227.

ment in Cork. A Richard Burke based in Dublin, conceivably Burke's father, acted as a legal representative for Cotter.[18] However, whether the elder Burke played a role in the legal proceedings or not, there is no reason to believe that he identified with Cotter's politics. In fact, there are good grounds for supposing that he did not. He was, after all, as Edmund's intimate school friend Richard Shackleton was later to recall, a man of "punctual honesty" averse to matters of controversy.[19]

Richard Burke married Mary Nagle in the Diocese of Cloyne on 21 November 1724. It has often been assumed that, two years before the marriage, Burke's father had conformed to the established Church of Ireland for reasons of professional convenience—to be permitted to practise law under the constraints of the penal laws.[20] The evidence, however, continues to be disputed.[21] Nonetheless, the testimony of Richard Shackleton must carry considerable weight. In 1766, in response to an enquiry about Burke's character and formative education, Shackleton indicated that Richard Burke had raised his sons in the established Church in order to promote "his Children's Interest in the world" instead of troubling himself with "controverted points of Religion."[22] Acceptance of the new realities of Protestant Ireland was of course common, driven, as Burke himself put it, by the desire for family advancement and material prosperity.[23] Shackleton's formulation implies a pragmatic adaptation to church membership rather than a longstanding family commitment. It seems clear that the Burkes moved within a nexus of convert families in early to mid eighteenth-century Ireland, navigating a course between the Protestant establishment and surviving Catholic gentry and business interests.[24] Whether or not Burke's father entered the convert rolls on the grounds of expediency in 1722, it seems overwhelmingly probable that his ancestry was Catholic.

Presumably for this reason, Burke retained an interest in the rationality of conversion. Towards the end of his parliamentary career, as revolution raged in France and sectarian tension mounted in Ireland, he remarked: "Strange it is, but so it is,

[18] William Hogan and Líam Ó Buachalla eds., "The Letters and Papers of James Cotter Junior, 1689–1720," *Journal of the Cork Historical and Archaeological Society*, 68 (1963), pp. 66–95, p. 75n.

[19] [Richard Shackleton], "Biographical Sketch of Edmund Burke" [1766], OSB MS. File 2225.

[20] Basil O'Connell, "The Rt. Hon. Edmund Burke (1729–97): A Basis for a Pedigree," *Journal of the Cork Historical and Archaeological Society*, 60 (1955), pp. 69–74, p. 72; Conor Cruise O'Brien, *The Great Melody: A Thematic Biography of Edmund Burke* (London: Sinclair-Stevenson, 1992), pp. 3–4. Both base their findings on *The Convert Rolls*, ed. Eileen O'Byrne (Dublin: Irish Manuscripts Commission, 1981), p. 31. Burke's sister has also been identified as appearing on the *Convert Rolls*, p. 28—but the name in question is "Julian Burke." It is hard to see the connection with Edmund's sister.

[21] See, for example, Lock, *Burke*, I, p. 5.

[22] [Richard Shackleton], "Biographical Sketch of Edmund Burke" [1766], OSB MS. File 2225.

[23] EB to Richard Burke Jr., 20 March 1792, *Corr.*, VII, p. 101.

[24] Eamon O'Flaherty, "Burke and the Catholic Question," *Eighteenth-Century Ireland*, 12 (1997), pp. 7–27; idem, "Edmund Burke" in James McGuire and James Quinn eds., *Dictionary of Irish Biography* (Cambridge: Cambridge University Press, 2009), 9 vols.; Ian McBride, *Eighteenth-Century Ireland: The Isle of Slaves* (Dublin: Gill and Macmillan, 2009), pp. 325–26; idem, "Burke and Ireland" in David Dwan and Christopher J. Insole eds., *The Cambridge Companion to Edmund Burke* (Cambridge: Cambridge University Press, 2012).

that men driven by force from their habits in one mode of religion, have by contrary habits under the same force often settled in another."[25] The flight from religion inevitably produced a "dreadful void" in the mind of man unless compensated by the consolations of another mode of worship.[26] Even the transition to new beliefs could be disorientating, although prejudice facilitated an acceptance of what necessity had compelled. This testified to a human propensity to form habits, but it did not rule out the reasonableness of conversion. Individuals induced ("suborned") their "reason" to accept what their interest dictated, although the decision might for all that be perfectly rational. As far as Burke was concerned, a decision in favour of Protestantism evidently was. Nonetheless, socially and psychologically, this was a complex process: "Man and his conscience cannot always be at war. If the first races have not been able to make a pacification between the conscience and the convenience, their descendants come generally to submit to the violence of the Laws, without violence to their minds."[27] Converts were not just apostates from an abandoned faith; optimally, they were committed to an adopted form of worship.

At the beginning of the twentieth century William O'Brien surmised that Burke's ancestors, the "Bourkes", conformed to the Church of Ireland in the generation of his grandfather.[28] Be that as it may, the evidence certainly suggests that, at some point in the past, the Burke family converted. This is partly indicated by the pattern of interdenominational marriage, spanning at least two Burke generations, typical among convert families.[29] Marriage, as a general indicator of affiliation, might offer a clue to a tradition of political allegiance. Commonly, however, it does not. It is possible to identify patterns of convert behaviour and mutual support in eighteenth-century Ireland, but this did not entail a clearly delimited "convert interest." Moreover, however one might choose to fix Richard Burke's loyalties along the spectrum of possible allegiances in post-Williamite Ireland, it does not follow that Edmund's attitudes can be read off from his father's. The evidence points to a family ambition to succeed under the terms set by the Protestant regime in Ireland. "His father, Richard, was a protestant," Monck Mason asserted; Edmund, at any rate, certainly was.[30] Ultimately, this affiliation led him to reject the idea that a programme of conversion could resolve sectarian strife in Ireland. Denominational division was an insurmountable fact: "Two hundred years of history show it to be unalterable."[31] Politics would have to reconcile confessional diversity with the commitment to an established Church.

[25] EB, *Letter to Richard Burke* (post 19 February 1792), *W & S*, IX, p. 646.

[26] Ibid., p. 645.

[27] Ibid., p. 646.

[28] William O'Brien, *Edmund Burke as an Irishman* (Dublin: M. H. Gill and Son, 1924, 1926), p. 4.

[29] David Fleming, "Conversion, Mentality and Family" in Michael Brown, Charles Ivar McGrath and Thomas Power eds., *Converts and Conversion in Ireland, 1650–1850* (Dublin: Four Courts Press, 2004).

[30] Mason, "Manuscript Notes," TCD MSS. 10531–32, fol. 32.

[31] EB, *Letter to Richard Burke* (post 19 February 1792), *W & S*, IX, p. 651.

Burke's elder and younger brothers, Garret and Richard, remained unmarried, but his sister, Juliana, married Patrick William French, member of a prominent Catholic family from Galway.[32] Burke himself was to marry Jane Nugent, daughter of the Catholic physician Christopher Nugent, based in Bath, whose son is also known to have married a Nagle from Ballyduff.[33] It is notable that, in this vein, Burke remained on intimate terms throughout his life with Richard Hennessy, the Irish Catholic brandy merchant, whose family had intermarried for generations with the Nagles.[34] His "strong and affectionate memory" of Cork families like the Barretts and the Roches is similarly evident in much of his correspondence.[35] Writing about one of his relatives to the retired banker and politician Sir George Colebrooke, on 14 December 1794, Burke affirmed that he was "not deficient in natural affection to [his] kindred,"[36] although his Catholic and convert contacts extended far beyond kinship networks: Charles O'Hara, the Irish MP whose father had converted and subsequently married a Catholic, was an intimate correspondent down to 1776; Patrick Darcy, an Irish Jacobite who naturalised in France, was described by Burke as "an old" and "honoured" friend.[37] But of course none of this is indicative of crypto-Catholicism on Burke's part. Shackleton was explicit about the young Burkes having happily worshipped with "the other protestant boys" at school without ever showing "the least inclination to the Errors of the Church of Rome." As an adult, Shackleton went on, Burke was happy to expose the "Errors" of Catholicism, although he also thought that every church was fallible in its principles. Nonetheless, as Shackleton saw it, Burke took Anglicanism to contain "fewer" fallacies than the other branches of the Christian religion.[38]

Shackleton's sketch is a simple outline of the complex opinions that Burke would develop, but it is also resounding in its endorsement of his commitment to the Protestant faith. Shackleton surmised that his friend's reputation for secret partiality towards the Catholic religion had resulted from his marriage to a woman of the "Romish" persuasion who, like his parents, had originally come from Munster.[39] This suspicion extended to the wider network of his connections. Lord Charlemont recorded how the Duke of Newcastle sought to taint Burke at the start of his political

[32] Basil O'Connell, "The Rt. Hon. Edmund Burke (1729–97): A Basis for a Pedigree, Part II," *Journal of the Cork Historical and Archaeological Society*, 61 (1956), pp. 115–22, p. 119. Burke's mother, Mary Burke, gives a description of her visit to the Frenches in Loughrea, Galway, in *Correspondence* (1844), I, pp. 111–14.

[33] Basil O'Connell, "The Nagles of Ballygriffin," *Irish Genealogist*, 3:2 (1957), pp. 67–73.

[34] Cullen, "The Blackwater Catholics", pp. 537–38.

[35] See, for example, EB to Patrick Nagle, 21 October 1767, *Corr.*, I, pp. 328–29.

[36] EB to Sir George Colebrooke, 14 December 1794, *Corr.*, VIII, p. 99.

[37] Thomas Bartlett, "The O'Haras of Annaghmore c. 1600–c. 1800: Survival and Revival," *Irish Economic and Social History*, 9 (1982), pp. 34–52; S. J. Connolly, *Religion, Law, and Power: The Making of Protestant Ireland, 1660–1760* (Oxford: Oxford University Press, 1992), p. 141; EB to Count Patrick Darcy, 5 October 1775, *Corr.*, III, p. 228.

[38] [Richard Shackleton], "Biographical Sketch of Edmund Burke" [1766], OSB MS. File 2225.

[39] Ibid.

career in the eyes of his patron, the Marquis of Rockingham, by alleging that he was a man of "dangerous principles," having been reared "a Papist and a Jacobite."[40] Rockingham, we are told, soon dismissed the allegation, confirming his "entire confidence" in his secretary. The charge had been founded, Charlemont makes clear, "on Burke's Irish connections," which were often with individuals of the Catholic "persuasion," and on account of his involvement in unspecified "juvenile follies arising from those connections."[41] It is evident that Burke's background has long provided the opportunity to overinterpret the significance of his boyhood relationships. Charlemont himself was no exception to this tendency: having dubbed the imputation of Catholicism and Jacobitism to Burke as nothing less than a "calumny," he went on to describe his friend as afflicted with "an almost constitutional bent towards the Popish party."[42] However, this verdict was explicitly political in character, stemming from the experience of having battled against Burke over Catholic relief from the popery laws.

While there can be no doubt about Burke's extensive and intimate contact with the worlds of Irish Catholics and converts, it is less obvious what conclusions can be drawn from these connections. Some commentators have been tempted into unsupportable extremes, seeking to "explain" his literary output by way of reference to his Munster origins, or discovering a "layer" of "Irish" loyalism beneath his public pronouncements.[43] Psychobiographical accounts of the kind are prone to basic historical error. They assume, first, that it is possible to determine the character of belief solely by specifying its social context. Next, they suppose that a distinct and underlying set of attitudes can be surmised beneath the surface of expressed thought. On this basis, Conor Cruise O'Brien described what he termed Burke's "occasional appearances in the persona of an English whig" as amounting to "a flight from distressing and

[40] Historical Manuscripts Commission (HMC), *The Manuscripts and Correspondence of James, First Earl of Charlemont* (London: HMSO, 1891–94), 2 vols., I, p. 148.

[41] Ibid.

[42] Ibid., I, p. 149. Cf. ibid., II, p. 378.

[43] L. M. Cullen, "Burke, Ireland, and Revolution", *Eighteenth-Century Life*, 16 (1992), pp. 21–42, p. 24; Conor Cruise O'Brien, "Introduction" to Edmund Burke, *Reflections on the Revolution in France* (Harmondsworth: Pelican, 1968, 1986), pp. 30–38. O'Brien set the terms of debate for subsequent discussion of the Irish context of Burke's writing, which is given to suppose a native allegiance underlying publicly expressed doctrines. O'Brien derived his understanding of Burkean nativism from 'Ali Al 'Amin Mazrui, "Edmund Burke and Reflections on the Revolution in the Congo," *Comparative Studies in Society and History*, 5:2 (1963), pp. 121–33. On this debt, see Conor Cruise O'Brien, "Burke," New York University Archives (NYUA), Papers of the Albert Schweitzer Chair in the Humanities, Conor Cruise O'Brien Files, Box 5, Folder 8, pp. 7, 15–16. For the idea that a "substratum" of opinion underlies Burke's avowed positions, see also Katherine O'Donnell, " 'To Love the Little Platoon': Edmund Burke's Jacobite Heritage" in Seán Patrick Donlan ed., *Edmund Burke's Irish Identities* (Dublin: Irish Academic Press, 2006), p. 25. For the related notion that Burke can be read allegorically, see Luke Gibbons, *Burke and Ireland: Aesthetics, Politics and the Colonial Sublime* (Cambridge: Cambridge University Press, 2003), *passim*. For the contention that his dual heritage made him a "cultural cross-breed," see Michel Fuchs, *Edmund Burke, Ireland and the Fashioning of the Self* (Oxford: Voltaire Foundation, 1996), p. 311.

inconvenient reality into a decorous fantasy."[44] This kind of hypothesis is, of course, a recipe for substituting one's own ideas for those of one's subject of study.[45] Finally, as is particularly evident in the treatment of Burke, an approach based on psychology presumes that the relevant social context is altogether more transparent than it is. The convert nexus has often been conflated with a distinct convert "interest", binding strategic conformists to the goals of their Catholic brethren.[46] However, we lack good reasons to hypostatise the social world of the conforming gentry, merchant and professional classes into an ascertainable interest group bearing a determinate political complexion.

Convert lawyers, such as Richard Burke may have been, illustrate the cohesiveness of conformists. But they also show that conformity does not predict political principles. By 1689, four years after the accession of James II, the majority of Irish judges were recently appointed Catholics, although they lost their positions on account of the Jacobite defeat after 1690. While the civil articles of the Treaty of Limerick, published in 1691, entitled them to practise with such freedom as they had enjoyed under Charles II, pressure from expatriate Irish Protestants in London brought the introduction of a statute in 1692 requiring Catholic lawyers to profess their loyalty to the establishment by swearing a series of oaths to the religion of the new regime.[47] With this provision, imposed on the Irish legislature by Westminster, an era of penal legislation had effectively begun. In acts voted by the Irish parliament in 1698, 1704 and 1709, further restrictions on Catholic barristers and solicitors sparked a series of apparently strategic religious conversions. Hugh Boulter, Church of Ireland Archbishop of Armagh and Primate of All Ireland from 1724, infamously alluded in a letter to Lord Carteret to the "dangerous consequence" that could be expected to result from the increased number of "new converts practising."[48] Six months later, on 13 February 1727, he set out the wider context for his fears in a

[44] O'Brien, *The Great Melody*, p. 13. O'Brien's doubt about the "sincerity" of Burke's outward professions of belief is avowedly indebted to a suggestion made by Carl B. Cone, *Burke Newsletter*, 3 (1962), to which he refers in Conor Cruise O'Brien, "Burke," NYUA, Papers of the Albert Schweitzer Chair in the Humanities, Conor Cruise O'Brien Files, Box 5, Folder 8, p. 9. The germ of *The Great Melody* thesis, grounded on a Yeatsian hypothesis about the crux of Burke's thought, is contained in an essay from the 1960s: Conor Cruise O'Brien, "'Art is Man's Nature': Burke, Yeats and the Conservative Imagination," NYUA, Papers of the Albert Schweitzer Chair in the Humanities, Conor Cruise O'Brien Files, Box 7, Folder 8.

[45] For the perils of psychobiography, see Quentin Skinner, "Interpretation, Rationality and Truth" in idem, *Visions of Politics I: Regarding Method* (Cambridge: Cambridge University Press, 2002).

[46] See, for example, T. P. Power, "Conversions among the Legal Profession in Ireland in the Eighteenth Century" in Daire Hogan and W. N. Osborough eds., *Brehons, Serjeants and Attorneys: Studies in the Irish Legal Profession* (Dublin: Irish Academic Press, 1991), p. 153: "What emerged in the course of the century was a hybrid class of crypto-Catholics who had conformed in order to maintain or improve their landed status, career prospects, or political opportunities."

[47] Colum Kenny, "The Exclusion of Catholics from the Legal Profession in Ireland, 1537–1829," *Irish Historical Studies*, 25:100 (1987), pp. 337–57, pp. 350–52.

[48] Hugh Boulter, *Letters Written by His Excellency Hugh Boulter, D.D., Lord Primate of All Ireland, &c. to Several Ministers of State in England* (Oxford: 1769–70), 2 vols., I, p. 188.

letter to the Archbishop of Canterbury: "There are probably in this kingdom five papists at least to one Protestant."[49] Within another month he was appealing to the Duke of Newcastle that ground not be ceded to the burgeoning Catholic threat, in due course urging the Bishop of London to support a new bill that stipulated the need for a lapse of two years between conformity and the entitlement to practice: "as the law stands at present," Boulter complained, "a man may the day after his real or pretended conversion, be admitted a barrister, attorney, &c."[50] In 1733 an Irish statute based on a Westminster bill for regulating attorneys and solicitors provided that henceforth Protestant lawyers marrying Catholics would be disqualified from the profession. Burke's mother may have conformed to the Church of Ireland, but either way his father would have escaped this proscription since the act could not be retrospectively applied.[51]

There is a wealth of evidence suggesting that converts in eighteenth-century Ireland helped maintain the Catholic propertied interest under pressure from the popery laws, and that conformists were not absorbed into the Protestant Whig establishment.[52] Nonetheless, a balance of probabilities does not permit any absolute conclusions. For example, while Anthony Malone, the son of a Catholic convert—and the uncle of Burke's friend, the editor of Shakespeare, Edmond Malone—could be described in 1752 by George Stone, the Archbishop of Armagh, as "a name extremely unpleasing to the Protestant and whig interest in Ireland," the son of the convert John Fitzgibbon strenuously supported the ascendancy in the roles of Attorney General and Lord Chancellor.[53] Burke commented on both men in the early 1790s. Fitzgibbon's father was a relation of Burke, and a man of "firm and manly character," though Burke claimed that had he lived longer he would have been "astonished" by the zeal of his progeny.[54] Henry Grattan noted the "abhorrence" of the son for the

[49] Ibid., I, p. 210.

[50] Ibid., I, pp. 226, 229.

[51] On the religion of Burke's mother, see [Richard Shackleton], "Biographical Sketch of Edmund Burke" [1766], OSB MS. File 2225: "she was of a popish Family. I cannot say whether she legally conformed to the Church of England, but she practised the Duties of the Romish Religion, with a decent privacy."

[52] Thomas P. Power, "Converts" in T. P. Power and Kevin Whelan eds., *Endurance and Emergence: Catholics in Ireland in the Eighteenth Century* (Dublin: Irish Academic Press, 1990), refuting T. W. Moody and W. E. Vaughan, *A New History of Ireland IV: The Eighteenth Century, 1691–1800* (Oxford: Oxford University Press, 1986), p. 20.

[53] Power, "Conversions among the Legal Profession," pp. 171–73. Cf. David A. Fleming, "Conversion, Family and Mentality" in Michael Brown et al. eds., *Converts and Conversion*. For an account of both Fitzgibbons, *père* (1708–80) *et fils* (1749–1802), see Ann C. Kavanaugh, "John Fitzgibbon, Earl of Clare" in David Dickson, Dáire Keogh and Kevin Whelan eds., *The United Irishmen: Republicanism, Radicalism and Rebellion* (Dublin: Lilliput, 1993).

[54] EB to Richard Burke Jr., 20 March 1792, *Corr.*, VII, p. 101. Fitzgibbon senior acted as counsel to a Burke relation, James Nagle, during the Whiteboy disturbances of the 1760s: see EB to Patrick Nagle, 6 November 1766, *Corr.*, I, p. 276. For a less flattering portrait of Fitzgibbon Sr., see Kavanaugh, "John Fitzgibbon," pp. 116–18.

original religion of his father.[55] He was "hardly fit" for the office of lord chancellor, Burke contended, though his father might have plausibly filled the role.[56] Anthony Malone was the son of the erstwhile Catholic, Richard Malone.[57] Unlike the young Fitzgibbon, although Anthony Malone was passively inclined to accept the legitimacy of the existing establishment, Burke maintained that he still believed that it was based on proscription and discrimination.[58] There existed a pattern of convert experience in eighteenth-century Ireland, but nothing as determinate as a definite convert interest. Burke's experience exposed him to the plight of Catholics under the popery laws, and sensitised him to the consequences of what he saw as Protestant bigotry. Nonetheless, he was equally averse to the acquired habit of Catholic servility, and viewed both denominations as virtually condemned to prescribed roles. The result was unprepossessing, breeding pettiness on both sides: "The Protestants of Ireland are just like the Catholicks—the Cat looking out of the Window and the Cat looking in."[59] Despite this wariness, Burke's encounter with what he came to see as a dysfunctional society lent weight, and even passion, to his subsequent commitment to its reform. Even so, his exposure to sectarian antipathy did not predetermine the character of his response, nor dictate the precise shape of his ultimate policy preferences.

Nonetheless, passionate conviction was a marked feature of Burke's career, standardly represented as stemming from an undercurrent of "rage."[60] The object of this fury was the experience of injustice brought about by the subversion of a legitimate social order. However, it has always been difficult to see how an inchoate passion could be used to explain a complex political position, especially so fraught and contestable a position as one based on the idea of a "legitimate" order. In Burke's view, illegitimate subversion was commonly a product of the spirit of conquest, but the development of this view resulted in intricate forms of political argument that are not reducible to raw psychological states. They can of course be related to personal experience, but this relationship will not suffice to explain an entire worldview. The ascription of motives for the adoption of political principles can provide a context in which to interpret ideological commitment. We can invoke the likely incentives that helped inspire the commitment, but in themselves they cannot account for the accompanying system of thought.[61]

[55] Henry Grattan to EB, 25 March 1793, *Corr.*, VII, p. 364.

[56] EB to the Rev. Thomas Hussey, 17 March 1795, *Corr.*, VIII, p. 202. Burke was writing just after the failure of the Lord Lieutenancy of Earl Fitzwilliam.

[57] For Anthony Malone (1700–76), see McGuire and Quinn eds., *Dictionary of Irish Biography*.

[58] EB to Richard Burke Jr., 20 March 1792, *Corr.*, VII, p. 101.

[59] Ibid.

[60] See above all Isaac Kramnick, *The Rage of Edmund Burke: Portrait of an Ambivalent Conservative* (New York: Basic Books, 1977), *passim*, for the thesis that this "rage" was the product of latent aggression giving rise to "ambivalent radicalism."

[61] On the relationship between political principles and the motives that inspire their adoption, see Quentin Skinner, "Moral Principles and Social Change" in *Visions of Politics I*. Cf. Martin Hollis,

Burke's verdict on the turmoil of the 1640s and 1650s in Ireland provides an example of a personal investment in the outcome of that conflict, but it also illustrates the limitations involved in citing under-specified experiences as a key to the interpretation of political doctrine. In 1797, in the Preface to an edition of posthumous writings on French affairs, Burke's executor, French Laurence, saw fit to inform the public that his longstanding friend and confidant had possessed "the means of substantiating, that he was sprung from a family anciently ennobled in several of its branches, and possessing an ample estate, which his grandfather had actually enjoyed."[62] Whatever we might want to make of the claim that Burke's forebears were titled aristocrats, there remains the more plausible implication that his family had been victims of the seventeenth-century land confiscations in Ireland that attended the upheavals of the civil wars and their aftermath. It is impossible to confirm whether this had indeed been the fate suffered by Burke's ancestors, but Laurence is a dependable source for Burke's assumptions and beliefs, and the belief that his relatives had been dispossessed as a result of Cromwellian plantation is noteworthy. Under the Commonwealth, Catholic landownership was decimated as the estates of Irish royalists were transferred to veteran members of the New Model Army or to Scottish covenanter soldiers, or bought up by Protestant parliamentarians already resident in Ireland.[63] Burke's sense that his family had been plundered in the process is clearly significant; however it is hardly sufficient to predict comprehensively the perspective he adopted on the trials of seventeenth-century history and the impact that these had on his own age.

The Cromwellian enterprise found its justification in the Catholic rebellion of 1641, which had been accompanied by a massacre of Protestant settlers in Ulster.[64] Needless to state, this justification proved controversial, not least because the claims concerning the extent of wanton violence perpetrated against Ulster Protestants were highly contentious. But while the assumption that Protestant reprisals for 1641 represented an injustice does not entail any ambivalence about the revolution settlement of 1688–91, nor imply any reticence about the Anglican establishment of the eighteenth century, it does carry with it an implied censure for the zeal of Protestant and republican radicalism that threatened the security of property during the civil disturbances of the 1640s and 1650s. Robert Bisset, one of Burke's earliest biographers, clarified Laurence's claim that Burke's grandfather "actually enjoyed"

Models of Man: Philosophical Thoughts on Social Action (Cambridge: Cambridge University Press, 1977), pp. 132ff.

[62] French Laurence, "Preface" to *Two Letters on the Conduct of Our Domestick Parties with regard to French Politicks by the Late Right Hon. Edmund Burke* (London: 1797), p. xxiii.

[63] See John P. Prendergast, *The Cromwellian Settlement of Ireland* (1865) (London: Constable, 1996); Karl S. Bottigheimer, *English Money and Irish Land: The "Adventurers" in the Cromwellian Settlement of Ireland* (Oxford: Clarendon Press, 1971); Kevin McKenny, "The Seventeenth-Century Land Settlement in Ireland: Towards a Statistical Interpretation" in Jane Ohlmeyer ed., *Ireland from Independence to Occupation, 1641–1660* (Cambridge: Cambridge University Press, 1995).

[64] See below, this chapter, section 3, and chapter 4, section 7.

an estate before the Cromwellian conquest—it had been "confiscated," Bisset declared, presumably during the forfeitures that followed the success of Cromwell's campaign between 1649 and 1652.[65] In the nineteenth century, James Prior offered a corrective to the claims by Laurence and Bisset, based on the testimony of Richard Shackleton and his daughter, Mary Leadbeater, together with Burke's descendants, the Haviland-Burkes: it was Burke's great-grandfather, Prior assured his readers, who possessed an estate in Limerick, before this was "forfeited during one of those civil convulsions that have so often caused property to exchange possessors in that country."[66] From Limerick, the Burkes are alleged to have repaired to their remaining property in the Blackwater Valley, where presumably Edmund's father met his wife, Mary Nagle.

The full facts about Burke's genealogy are unlikely ever to be known, but his preparedness to present himself to a close associate like French Laurence as the descendent of dispossessed Irish ancestors gives edge to the declaration, formulated in the final year of his life, that his political mission had hitherto consisted in the project of defending property from the depredations of envy and avarice unleashed by the ordinances of "confiscating" tyrants.[67] Still, Burke's sense that he was the product of an ancestral experience of conquest that had been accompanied by the seizure of patrimonial estates does not in itself account for the character of his reaction to the spirit of conquest nor anticipate the doctrines he deployed to overcome its fury. Fighting broke out in Ireland in October 1641, and it was not brought to a conclusion until 1653. The massacre of Ulster Protestants that accompanied the outbreak of hostilities was commemorated in Ireland from early on during the Restoration, and continued after the Glorious Revolution through much of the eighteenth century. Sermons delivered annually on 23 October to mark the occasion were still intended to provoke outrage as late as the 1760s, reminding their audiences of the dissembling perfidiousness of the Catholic Irish.[68] Protestant sources estimated that the number of murdered settlers ran into the hundreds of thousands, as reported in John Temple's notorious *The Irish Rebellion*, which dwelled on the premeditated viciousness of the

[65] Robert Bisset, *The Life of Edmund Burke* (London: 1798). Cf. Peter Burke, *The Public and Domestic Life of the Right Hon. Edmund Burke* (London: 2nd ed., 1754), p. 2; Robert Murray, *Edmund Burke: A Biography* (Oxford: Oxford University Press, 1931), p. 3.

[66] James Prior, *Life of the Right Honourable Edmund Burke* (1824) (London: 5th ed., 1854). Prior had thanked Thomas Haviland Burke for information supplied about Burke in the advertisement to the second edition of the work (1826) and the Shackletons and Burke's niece, Mary Cecilia Haviland, in the advertisement to the fifth. In the second edition, Prior added the story of a former Mayor of Limerick and Burke relative (John Bourke) who had been imprisoned at the hands of Catholic confederates in 1646 on account of his support for the royalist cause. For a full treatment of this episode, see Thomas Macknight, *History of the Life and Times of Edmund Burke* (London: 1858–60), 3 vols., I, pp. 4–6.

[67] EB, *Letter to a Noble Lord* (1796) in *W&S, IX*, p. 167.

[68] T. C. Barnard, "The Uses of 23 October 1641 and Irish Protestant Celebrations," *English Historical Review*, 106:421 (1991), pp. 889–920.

assaults.[69] In due course Temple's opponents put the number of killings in the low thousands and traced the causes of the rebellion to Catholic frustration and alarm.[70]

In the fifth volume of the posthumous 1778 edition of his *History of England*, David Hume had added a note in which he represented attempts to deny the enormity of the 1641 massacres as exemplifying the dogmatism of party-minded commentators.[71] James Mackintosh relayed to Robert Bisset a conversation that he had in 1796 during which Burke made plain the personal offence he took at Hume's remark. At a meeting at David Garrick's that probably took place in the early 1760s, Burke had raised the matter with Hume, encouraging him to appreciate that these allegations had their origin in anti-Catholic bigotry, although Hume continued to be fixated with the barbaric cruelty that superstition seemed so effortlessly to excuse.[72] For Burke, the upheavals of the 1640s cast a shadow over seventeenth-century Irish history, from which the country had not fully recovered by the end of the eighteenth. His papers preserve the table of contents to "Eight Volumes of Manuscripts" concerned with Irish history, which evidently included numerous works devoted to the 1640s.[73] The Irish confederate wars forming the subject of these manuscripts, which set Catholics against Protestant settlers throughout the four provinces of Ireland, are most appropriately interpreted in the general context of the British constitutional crises of the mid to late seventeenth century, which should in turn be placed in the wider frame of confessional struggle across Europe in the same period.[74] Nonetheless, the fact remains that the persecuting zeal with which these wars were prosecuted ignited sectarian antagonisms that did not subside with the Restoration or during the aftermath of the Glorious Revolution. In fact, Protestant dread of Catholic insurgency outlasted the 1701 act of settlement and persisted into the life of the Hanoverian regime. For Burke, the 1640s had been a point of origin: the fallout from the collision perpetuated animosities originally stoked by the fear of persecution, giving rise in turn to a spirit of domination. Exposure to the fissures

[69] John Temple, *The Irish Rebellion, or an History of the Attempts of the Irish Papists to Extirpate the Protestants in the Kingdom of Ireland, together with the Barbarous Cruelties and Bloody Massacres which Ensued Thereupon* (London: 1646).

[70] See, for example, R. S., *A Collection of Some of the Murthers and Massacres Committed on the Irish in Ireland since the 23d of October 1641, with Some Observations and Falsifications on a Late Printed Abstract of Murthers Said to be Committed by the Irish* (London: 1662).

[71] David Hume, *The History of England, from the Invasion of Julius Caesar to the Revolution in 1688* (1754–62) (London: 1778), 8 vols., V, p. 505.

[72] Robert Bisset, *The Life of Edmund Burke* (London: 2nd ed., 1800), 2 vols., II, p. 426.

[73] WWM BkP 27:37. The following manuscripts are listed: *Heads of the Causes which Moved the Northern Irish to take Arms. 1641*; *Remonstrance of the Northern Catholicks Now in Arms*; Richard Bellings, *Fragmentum Historicum, or, the Second and Third Books of the War of Ireland, containing the Transactions in the Kingdom from 1642 to 1647*; *Apology of the Knights, Lords &c. of the English Pale for Taking Arms.*

[74] M. Perceval-Maxwell, *The Outbreak of the Irish Rebellion of 1641* (Dublin: Gill and Macmillan, 1994); Conrad Russell, *The Fall of the British Monarchies, 1637–1642* (Oxford: Clarendon Press, 1991); Jonathan Scott, *England's Troubles: Seventeenth-Century English Instability in European Context* (Cambridge: Cambridge University Press, 2000).

in the interdenominational politics of eighteenth-century Ireland preserved Burke from sectarian dogmatism but did not prescribe the terms in which he sought to resolve the ongoing confrontation.

Responding in 1771 to a surprise charge levelled by his son's godfather, William Markham, against himself, his brother Richard and his close friend William Burke for having unwittingly betrayed Jacobite sentiments in the course of private conversations, Burke was swift in defending the integrity of his conduct and principles. "People will say many things in Argument and when they are provoked by what they think extravagant Notions of their adversarys," Burke reasoned, but he was happy to base his convictions on the justice of "revolution principles" so long as these were adhered to in point of practice.[75] His ideas, he went on, had not been cobbled together out of assorted family pieties—"not patched out of party coloured Rags, picked from the filthy Dunghills of old women's superstitions, and children's Credulity"—but had rather been constructed out of systematic reflection on accumulated experience.[76] These were broadly speaking akin to Markham's brand of Whiggism, although the bishop could not now see this on account of the prejudices he had contracted, partly on the strength of misconstruing Burke's views on a subject which both men had debated "I dare say 20 times." The subject was none other than "the great Rebellion of 1641," responses to which Markham chose to construe as an index of patriotic loyalty.[77] Burke stood his ground: the rebellion had not lacked all provocation, nor taken the form of a general massacre. But, after the fact, it did convey the unpalatable truth that while passive obedience was an absurd doctrine, rebellion could not be justified a priori. This, in fact, was the lesson taught by the Glorious Revolution, and should be regarded as the cornerstone of Whiggism.[78] It moderated the hubris of aspiring liberty and restricted the presumptions of overweening authority.

The Cork Protestant Richard Cox began publishing his compendious account of the "Revolutions" of Ireland during his exile in Bristol after 1687.[79] When the second part of his *Hibernia Anglicana* appeared in 1690, it opened with a meditation on assorted "Controverted Points" in Irish history, focusing on the impact of 1641 and the shadow cast by the October massacre on relations between the denominations in Ireland.[80] Cox's overall question was how to arrest the recurrent pattern of Irish lawlessness and rebellion that continually upset the pacification of the natives in the wake of conquest. His approach to this question was to analyse the varieties of factionalism that had repeatedly beset the kingdom. Antipathy deriving from either

[75] EB to Dr. William Markham, post 9 November 1771, *Corr.*, II, p. 281.

[76] Ibid., p. 284.

[77] Ibid., p. 285.

[78] Ibid., p. 283.

[79] The phrase "Windings and Revolutions" is used to depict the progress of the civil dissensions in Ireland in the dedication "To the Reader" in *Hibernia Anglicana, or the History of Ireland from the Conquest thereof by the English to this Present Time* (London: 1689–90), Part II, n.p.

[80] Richard Cox, "An Apparatus, or Introductory Discourse" in ibid., n.p.

the diversity of customs or the clash of interests could ultimately be overcome, Cox contended, but differences between religious tenets seemed impossible to bridge: "there is no reconciliation to be made between God and Mammon," as he phrased his conclusion, where mammon represented the corruptions endemic to the Catholic faith.[81] The notion that Irish Catholics were implacable agents of rebellion was scarcely a plausible proposition for Burke, whose Nagle relatives held so constant a place in his affections: as he wrote to his uncle Patrick on 17 April 1759, "There are few persons in the world for whom I have so great a respect."[82] Thus, unsurprisingly, for Burke the lessons to be learned from the 1640s were utterly different from those adduced by Cox. Burke believed that religious zeal was too easily employed as a cover for political persecution. For Protestant ultras in the generations succeeding Cox, the Catholics of Ireland appeared to be in a condition of permanent revolt against the status quo, with the result that while they might be ultimately enlightened they should not in the short term be indulged. However, to Burke it seemed that Catholicism could induce pragmatic loyalty and so its adherents could be expected to respond to toleration. From this perspective, a scheme such as Cox's for reducing Ireland to civility by the eradication of popery seemed better calculated to perpetuate the Irish "Revolutions," or the cycle of insurgency and oppression.

Burke's intimacy with his Nagle relations first developed during the five years or so that he spent in the Blackwater Valley, beginning around 1737. Having received his earliest education from his mother and subsequently from assorted instructors, Burke was sent to reside with the Nagles in the country to preserve him from the dank conditions of Dublin city along the quays and help restore his frail constitution to health.[83] In Ballyduff, living with his uncle Patrick, he went to school in nearby Monanimy Castle, where he was first taught Latin by a Mr. O'Halloran, the village schoolmaster.[84] Kilcolman Castle, which had been occupied by Edmund Spenser during his period as secretary to Lord Grey from the 1580s, still stood on the opposite side of the river from Ballyduff. Burke was related to the poet on his mother's side, but his youthful admiration for his poetry was in due course matched by criticism of Spenser's support for the "genius and policy" of English government in Elizabethan Ireland.[85] Spenser's estate in Cork had been granted on forfeited lands for his services in securing a victory against the second Desmond rebellion, and its

[81] Richard Cox, "To the Reader" in ibid, Part I, n.p.

[82] EB to Patrick Nagle, 17 April 1759, *Corr.*, I, p. 125.

[83] For Burke's early schooling, see Mary Leadbeater, *The Annals of Ballitore* in *The Leadbeater Papers* (London: 1862), 2 vols., I, p. 46; Michael Kearney to Edmond Malone, 12 January 1799, Bodl. MS. Malone 39, f. 23. On conditions beside the Liffey, see Burke's reference in an early poem sent to Richard Shackleton on 9 June 1744 to "the foul river's Side" in *Corr.*, I, p. 13.

[84] Prior, *Life of Burke*, pp. 5–7.

[85] Spenser's son, Sylvanus, married Ellen Nagle, a great-aunt of Burke's mother: see EB to Richard Shackleton, c. 3 February 1746/7, *Corr.*, I, p. 80n. For Burke's early familiarity with Spenser's *Faerie Queene*, see EB to Richard Shackleton, ante 24 May 1744, ibid., p. 7; for criticism of Spenser's *View of the Present State of Ireland*, see EB, *Letter to Sir Hercules Langrishe* (1792) in *W & S*, IX, p. 615.

pastoral seclusion is celebrated in the famous scene depicted in *Colin Clouts Come Home Againe*, set in Spenser's castle under the western extremity of the Ballyhoura mountain range:

One day (quoth he) I sate (as was my Trade)
Under the foote of Mole, that Mountain hore
Keeping my Sheepe amongst the coolly Shade
Of the green Alders by the Mulla's Shore.

However, bucolic peace was easily shattered by political crisis. In the wake of the assault on Kilcolman Castle towards the culmination of Tyrone's rebellion, Spenser was forced to return to England with the manuscript of his *View of the Present State of Ireland*, advocating a drastic policy of conquest and subjugation.[86] Later, travelling through Munster in the 1740s, William Chetwood came to pay homage to the lyrical seductions of the poet but noted on his journey through Nagle country that the argument of the *View* met with pervasive disapproval.[87]

The name "Mulla" was intended by Spenser as a poetic term for the river Awbeg, a tributary of the Blackwater that makes an appearance in the invocation which opens a poem Burke sent to Shackleton on the "Christal flood" that passed through the valley beside Ballyduff: "O aid my voice that I may wake once more / The slumbering Echo on the Mulla's Shore."[88] The arresting beauty of the Munster countryside was to stay with Burke into his adulthood, but more particularly his personal and family attachments in the region continued to inspire gratitude. Writing to Patrick Nagle from London in October 1759, he commented that although he had now been absent from Cork for something in the region of eleven years "yet my remembrance of my friends there is as fresh as if it had been yesterday."[89] Some of Burke's relatives migrated around the Empire—moving to the War Office or into the militia, to the West Indies and into the East India Company—leaving him to worry about the depletion and impoverishment of the remainder of the "old stock."[90] Writing to his son Richard on 22 March 1792, he revealed how his early familial obligations left him "uneasy," conscious of the debts he owed to his uncle and immediate cousins—

[86] See Nicholas P. Canny, "Edmund Spenser and the Development of Anglo-Irish Identity," *Yearbook of English Studies*, 13 (1983), pp. 1–19; Ciaran Brady, "Spenser's Irish Crisis: Humanism and Experience in the 1590s," *Past and Present*, 111 (1986), pp. 17–49; Nicholas P. Canny, "Debate: Spenser's Irish Crisis: Humanism and Experience in the 1590s," *Past and Present*, 120 (1988), pp. 201–15; Brendan Bradshaw, "Sword, Word, and Strategy in the Reformation in Ireland," *Historical Journal*, 21 (1978), pp. 475–502.

[87] W. R. Chetwood, *A Tour through Ireland in Several Entertaining Letters* (Dublin: 1746), pp. 113–14.

[88] EB to Richard Shackleton, c. 3 February 1746/7, *Corr.*, I, pp. 79–80.

[89] EB to Patrick Nagle, 11 October 1759, ibid., p. 135.

[90] EB to Garrett Nagle, 27 December 1768, *Corr.*, II, p. 19n4; EB to Garrett Nagle, post 24 June 1779, *Corr.*, IV, p. 94; EB to Garrett Nagle, 2 August 1776, *Corr.*, III, pp. 284–85; EB to Colonel Isaac Barré, 16 July 1782, *Corr.*, V, p. 19n1. Reference to the "old stock" appears in EB to Garrett Nagle, 3 September 1777, *Corr.*, III, p. 371.

"all advanced in Life, and fallen, I believe, into Great Penury."[91] Burke was anxious to brief his son on the history of sectarian relations in which the Nagles had been submerged. Irish Catholics, Burke commented, were for the most part sunk in servility now that the old "Spirit of the Struggle" had been sapped under the weight of accumulated generations of religious prejudice, beginning with the reactions to "the pretended Massacre in 1641."[92] Burke generally counselled fortitude and perseverance in this context. In a letter sent to his cousin Garrett in September 1777, reviewing the diminished circumstances and the attrition of morale amongst the Nagles, he further advised his relatives to keep up their "old union and intercourse," to act in concert as "one family." "This," Burke added, "is the old burthen of my song."[93] The sentiment was developed into an operative principle throughout the vicissitudes of his adult life, but Burke first adopted it during the period of his early manhood.

1.3 School and University

On 26 May 1741 Burke was enrolled with his brothers as a boarder at the Quaker school run by Abraham Shackleton in Ballitore village in Co. Kildare. In her posthumously published *Annals of Ballitore*, Mary Leadbeater, the granddaughter of Abraham Shackleton, wrote of the village as "situated in a valley encompassed by gently rising hills, except where the river Griese takes its meandering course of about fourteen miles from its rising at Tubber."[94] The school stood on the road from Dublin to Cork, at the centre of a small "Colony of Quakers," surrounded by neatly presented orchards and gardens.[95] Abraham Shackleton had founded the school in 1726, attracting Quakers from the immediate vicinity and assorted students from overseas, but catering to a significant cohort of Irish Anglicans in the process, including, in the words of Leadbeater, "many persons of considerable note."[96] The future secretary of the United Irishman, James Napper Tandy, joined the school in 1749; Henry Grattan, the most outstanding Irish parliamentary patriot of his generation, had also been a pupil.[97] Students who were members of the established Church worshipped in the nearby town of Timolin, with an Episcopalian usher appointed to hear the established catechism in the school.[98] Nonetheless, fastidious attention to the Bible was encouraged by the headmaster, "a man of singular piety, Rectitude and

[91] EB to Richard Burke Jr., 20 March 1792, *Corr.*, VII, p. 106.

[92] Ibid., pp. 101–4.

[93] EB to Garrett Nagle, 3 September 1777, *Corr.*, III, pp. 371–72.

[94] Leadbeater, *Papers*, I, p. 15.

[95] W. R. Chetwood, *A Tour through Ireland*, p. 232.

[96] Mary Leadbeater ed., *Memoirs and Letters of Richard and Elizabeth Shackleton* (London: 1822), p. 3.

[97] E. J. McAuliffe, *An Irish Genealogical Source: The Roll of the Quaker School at Ballitore, Co. Kildare* (Dublin: Irish Academic Press, 1984).

[98] Michael Quane, "Ballitore School," *Journal of the Kildare Archaeological Society*, 14 (1966), pp. 174–209.

virtue," as Burke depicted him after his death in 1771.[99] In a co-authored poem on the subject of Ballitore, Burke paid tribute to his teacher as "the planter of the future age."[100] The compliment was regularly recited by Burke throughout his period as an undergraduate at Trinity as he passed on his respects to his old "Master," thanking him for the "favours" and "advantages" he had received.[101] By 1759, when he was making his way as a writer and journalist in London, Burke claimed that his education at Ballitore had in fact "made" him.[102] The feeling of obligation was lasting. With barely a month to live, anticipating the approach of his final "dissolution," Burke sent one of his last letters to Mary Leadbeater in Kildare, recollecting the "tender" sentiments still evoked by his teenage school days.[103]

By the time that Abraham Shackleton founded Ballitore, there already existed a number of Quaker schools throughout Ireland. George Fox, the founder of Quakerism in England, had recommended setting up schools as a means of propagating the faith in the 1660s, and between the late 1670s and early 1680s a number were founded in Ireland, first at Mountmellick and later in Dublin.[104] When the Shackletons arrived in the 1720s, the Quakers had been lobbying for relief from the civil and religious disabilities they had shared with other Protestant dissenters since the end of the seventeenth century.[105] Nonetheless, the aim of establishing complete liberty of conscience as originally envisaged by William Penn, comprising the freedom to worship as conscience dictated short of upsetting the requirements of civil government, was radically hampered by the designs of the clerical establishment which sought to maintain the Church's exclusive right to conduct marriages and regulate schools.[106] Members of the Society of Friends rejected the doctrine of predestination, and were committed to the notion that salvation was best secured by pursuing the "Light" within, although increasingly the community came to believe that its immediate access to Christ was assisted by the honesty and simplicity of its mode of living.[107] Mary Leadbeater recorded her father's early experience of being touched by "Divine love," and his consequent disposition to pour out his soul in emotion and

[99] EB to Richard Shackleton, ante 31 July 1771, *Corr.*, II, p. 226.

[100] EB and Richard Shackleton, "Panegyrick on Ballitore, MS in Verse" (1746), OSB MS. File 2234.

[101] EB to Richard Shackleton, post 14 April 1744, *Corr.*, I, p. 2; EB to Richard Shackleton, 29 June 1799, ibid., p. 24; EB to Richard Shackleton, 28 September 1752, ibid., p. 114.

[102] EB to Richard Shackleton, 10 August 1757, ibid., p. 124.

[103] EB to Mrs. William Leadbeater, 23 May 1797, *Corr.*, IX, p. 359.

[104] Michael Quane, "The Friends' Provincial School, Mountmellick," *Journal of the Royal Society of Antiquaries of Ireland*, 89:1 (1959), pp. 59–89; Michael Quane, "Quaker Schools in Dublin," *Journal of the Royal Society of Antiquaries of Ireland*, 94:1 (1964), pp. 47–68.

[105] John Bergin, "The Quaker Lobby and Its Influence on Irish Legislation, 1692–1705," *Eighteenth-Century Ireland*, 19 (2004), pp. 9–36.

[106] William Penn, *The Great Case of Liberty of Conscience* (1670) in *The Political Writings of William Penn*, ed. Andrew R. Murphy (Indianapolis, IN: Liberty Fund, 2002), p. 85: "By *Liberty of Conscience*, we understand not only a meer *Liberty of the Mind*, in believing this or that Principle of Doctrine, *but the Exercise of our selves in a visible Way of Worship, upon our believing it to be indispensably required.*"

[107] Richard S. Harrison, "'As a Garden Enclosed': The Emergence of Irish Quakers, 1692–1716" in Kevin Herlihy ed., *The Irish Dissenting Tradition, 1650–1750* (Dublin: Four Courts Press, 1995), p. 95.

prayer.[108] He understood religion to consist, as he himself wrote, in "an acquaintance with God in spirit."[109] He became, like Burke, a man of firm conviction; they were also both devoted to the Christian virtue of humility; but, unlike Burke, Shackleton shunned established religion and the machinations of Whig politics.[110] The Burkes, as Shackleton's wife was later to comment, "are quite different from us."[111] Nonetheless, it was through his school friend that Burke first encountered the pious rigours of the dissenting conscience. Whereas in England nonconformists made up 10 per cent of the population, Presbyterians in Ireland, especially in Ulster, rivalled the numbers in the established Church, with the result that hostility could more plausibly be expected from the ranks of dissent.[112]

By the early decades of the eighteenth century between 5,000 and 10,000 Friends resided in Ireland as loyal Protestants distinguished by their egalitarianism, their opposition to episcopacy, their reputation for integrity, their rudimentary attire, their impersonal mode of address, and of course their opposition to oaths and the payment of tithes.[113] Their convictions had cost them in terms of civil penalties, and so they carried an acute sense of a burden of past "sufferings."[114] Voltaire, in his *Lettres philosophiques*, had famously commended their plain frugality and sincerity whilst satirising their enthusiasm as "an epidemical distemper."[115] Nonetheless, in Voltaire's mind, a delusive faith in the inspired truths that Quakers assumed they had imbibed from the deity was no more destructive than the absurdities of the philosophy of Malebranche.[116] Friends were determined, but not militant; they supported dissent while diminishing sectarian animosity. As Voltaire saw it, nonconformity in Britain helped to restrain the pretensions of established authority, yet the divisions in its own ranks moderated the conflict between liberty and power.[117] Despite widespread interest in Voltaire's *Lettres* in eighteenth-century Ireland, the same balance of religious forces did not apply in the sister kingdom, where the Establishment confronted far more pervasive disaffection.[118] Whatever the levels of dissatisfaction,

[108] Leadbeater ed., *Memoirs of Richard and Elizabeth Shackleton*, pp. 5–6.

[109] University of California Santa Barbara Special Collections (UCSBSC), Ballitore Collection: Box 1, 1/3, Richard Shackleton to his Son, Dublin, 1 May 1776.

[110] Ibid., Ballitore Collection: Box 1, 1/3, Richard Shackleton to his Daughter, 30 July 1776.

[111] Elizabeth Shackleton to Richard Shackleton, 14 June 1776, OSB MS. 50, Box 4.

[112] S. J. Connolly, *Divided Kingdom: Ireland 1630–1800* (Oxford: Oxford University Press, 2008), p. 215.

[113] Phil Kilroy, *Protestant Dissent and Controversy in Ireland, 1660–1714* (Cork: Cork University Press, 1994), p. 84.

[114] Richard L. Greaves, *God's Other Children: Protestant Nonconformists and the Emergence of Denominational Churches in Ireland, 1660–1700* (Stanford, CA.: Stanford University Press, 1997), p. 359.

[115] Voltaire, *Letters Concerning the English Nation* (Dublin: 1733), p. 16; cf. Voltaire, *Lettres philosophiques* (1734) in *Mélanges*, ed. Jacques Van Den Heuvel (Paris: Gallimard, 1961), p. 8: "L'enthousiasme est une maladie."

[116] Voltaire, *Letters Concerning the English Nation*, p. 13.

[117] Ibid., p. 39.

[118] Josiah Martin, *A Letter from one of the People Called Quakers to Francis de Voltaire, Occasioned by his Remarks on that People, in his Letters Concerning the English Nation* (Dublin: 1749). See Graham

dissent among Quakers was determined yet constructive, focused on the tyranny of tithes, which were seen as amounting, in the words of one commentator, to an "antichristian Yoke of Oppression."[119]

Writing to Edward Newenham on 31 May 1778, Richard Shackleton gave vent to his longstanding objection to the obligation imposed on nonconformists to contribute to the revenues of the Church of Ireland through the payment of tithes. In enforcing this obligation, "the Magistrate" had intruded into "God's place"—assuming the right to "direct man's conscience in Matters of Religion, inflicting penalties and curtailing civil privileges if he will not believe and worship in a form and manner prescribed to him, as if it was in any person's power to shift his own opinions even at his own pleasure; and as if any offerings were acceptable to the Deity which did not proceed from a sincere and upright heart."[120] Exactly when Shackleton came to this view has to be a matter of speculation, but it is clear that he debated the content of his beliefs with Burke in the 1740s. Burke informed Shackleton in a letter sent from Arran Quay on 15 October 1744 how he felt that he could write to his friend with "greater freedom" on the subject of religion than anyone else, and by November he was imploring him to exercise the same liberty—setting out his own principles while criticising Burke's ideas: "You see that I tell you what I think amiss in yours."[121] Burke encountered a number of Huguenot students at Ballitore, whose families had settled at Portarlington in Co. Laois, and while at university he was capable of ridiculing their various migrations: "finding France to hot for 'em [they] retird [*sic*] to Holland, from thence to London, thence to Dublin, thence to Edenderry, thence to Ballitore thence to Portarlington—and where next."[122] But, despite appearances, he took persecution seriously, and sought earnestly to bridge the divergence in religious tenets between Shackleton and himself. As a teenager, Burke accepted the basic principle of toleration in accordance with which believers ought not be excluded from the means of achieving salvation on the basis of their disagreement with the dominant religion, although he remained troubled by the threat posed to the established Church by schism and sought the means to reconcile any divergence between doctrines.[123]

Burke would retain throughout his life a number of friends, many with Quaker backgrounds, whom he first met on account of his Ballitore connection—including Richard Brocklesby, his physician, and a pallbearer at his son's funeral; Michael Kearney, with whom he was still in contact in the early 1790s; Newcomen Herbert, whom he met through Shackleton and who became a member of the Debating Club

---

Gargett, "'Lettres philosophiques' in Eighteenth-Century Ireland," *Eighteenth-Century Ireland*, 14 (1999), pp. 77–98.

[119] Thomas Wight, *A History of the Rise and Progress of the People Called Quakers in Ireland from the year 1653 to 1700* (Dublin: 1751).

[120] Quoted in Quane, "Ballitore School," p. 192.

[121] EB to Richard Shackleton, 14 October 1744, *Corr.*, I, p. 33; EB to Richard Shackleton, 1 November 1744, ibid., p. 36.

[122] EB to Richard Shackleton, 11 June 1744, ibid., p. 17.

[123] EB to Richard Shackleton, 15 October 1744, ibid., p. 33.

at Trinity; Clement Zouch, who served him as a clerk during his political career; and Joseph Fenn Sleigh, who arrived at the school after Burke had left but with whom he later cultivated a lasting friendship. Burke's comrades were intelligent and motivated, and his own ability marked him out as a candidate for university, for which he was equipped with the requisite training. The effort evidently paid off: when Burke performed with distinction in an oral examination on Greek and Roman authors in the summer of 1746, one of his tutors at Trinity, the Reverend Dr. John Forster, "asked me from whose School I came . . . and I told him."[124] Lessons at Ballitore were for the most part in the classics—above all focusing on Greek and Latin verse—but also in history and mathematics. A surviving notebook of Abraham Shackleton's presenting an "Abridgement of English History, Done for the Use of Ballitore School" gives us a sense of the history curriculum in the school: covering the period from the Roman conquest of Britain to the England of the first two Georges, it includes the following commentary on 1641: "The Papists in Ireland thought this a favourable opportunity to throw off the English yoke by a general massacre of the Protestants; neither Age, Sex or condition received Pity . . . Friends murdered their intimates, Relations their Kinsmen, & Servants their Masters."[125] In general, teaching seems to have been rigorous, even exacting: a student once described the boys as being worked like "galley-slaves . . . book—book [—] book."[126] Despite this verdict, the school managed to inculcate in its more academic pupils a taste for polite learning. Burke and his friend Shackleton were above all seduced by the liberal pleasures of learning and letters: "The minds of both were strongly bent to literary acquirements; both were endowed with classical taste, solid judgment, and keen perception."[127] Leadbeater underlined the extent to which Abraham Shackleton had fostered this enthusiastic immersion, emphasising how "they climbed the heights of learning and picked the flowers of poetry together."[128] University, by comparison, would prove more arduous and routine.

Burke was admitted to Trinity College Dublin on 14 April 1744.[129] In that year, as usual, there were six days set aside in the Trinity calendar for the delivery of commemorative "public speeches" in the Hall: 20 January, marking the birthday of the Chancellor, then Frederick Prince of Wales; 30 January, commemorating the martyrdom of Charles I; 29 May, for the restoration of Charles II; 23 October, for the massacre of 1641; 30 October, to mark the birthday of George II; and 5 November, commemorating the Gunpowder treason.[130] Burke was registered as enjoying Pensioner ("Pens.") status, indicating that he was eligible to pay the standard fee.[131]

[124] EB to Richard Shackleton, 1 June 1746, ibid., p. 66.

[125] TCD MS. 3522.

[126] EB to Richard Shackleton, 1 June 1746, *Corr.*, I, p. 66.

[127] Leadbeater ed., *Memoirs of Richard and Elizabeth Shackleton*, p. 4.

[128] Leadbeater, *Leadbeater Papers*, I, p. 169.

[129] A brief sketch of Burke's academic career can be found in Thomas Hume to French Laurence, 27 April 1802, OSB MS. File 7762.

[130] TCD MSS. Mun/V/27/1/fol. 91r.

[131] "Catalogus omnium studentium in Collegium," TCD MSS. Mun/V/23/3.

"Fellow Commoners," by comparison, paid double the amount, while "Sizars," like Oliver Goldsmith, who was admitted in Burke's year, offered menial services in lieu of fees.[132] The majority of entrants at Trinity were Pensioners, with eleven Commoners and four Sizars being admitted out of total of seventy students in 1744.[133] The ages of the new entrants ranged from 14 to 19 years. Richard Malone, the son of Anthony Malone, registered in 1742; Burke's friend William Dennis registered in 1743. Apart from Burke, no other pupil from Ballitore School entered Trinity between 1742 and 1747.[134] The catalogue of students records Burke's father as "generosus" ("Gen."), a gentleman—a distinction to which his son was not indifferent.[135] When Richard Shackleton later described him as "an Attorney at Law of middling circumstances," Burke responded with conspicuous dismay.[136] His father, he insisted, was in fact "for many years not only in the first *Rank*, but the first man of his profession in point of practice and Credit."[137] Pedigree was an index of independent standing, and independence was fiercely coveted by Burke. When Shackleton's description found its way into the *London Evening Post* in 1770, Burke's irritation resurfaced, and he reasserted his sense of his dignity.[138] He was not in the control of any living person's "Patronage," and only took free favours from those on his "own Level."[139] Burke thought of himself as a rising talent in a world of hereditary privilege. Dependence on "the Great" would compromise his autonomy, which he would secure on the strength of effort and ability.

University did not prove the optimal nursery for his talents. Richard Shackleton would later attend lectures in Hebrew at the College, but in the meantime he sustained contact with his school friend at university, leaving a trail of correspondence by which we can follow their development. Looking back on the 1740s in 1766, Shackleton described the young Burke as having "an inquisitive & Speculative cast of mind." He went on: "He read much . . . & accumulated a Stock of learning of great Variety. His memory was extensive, his Judgement early-ripe."[140] Trinity, however, failed to cater to his intellect, offering a curriculum that seemed needlessly pedantic, lacking innovation and inspiration. The "course of Study", as Shackleton put it, "was not adapted to his taste."[141] While he graduated respectably, in the top half of his

[132] James Prior, *The Life of Goldsmith, M. B.: From a Variety of Original Sources* (London: 1837), 2 vols., I, p. 59.

[133] This information has been collated from "Catalogus omnium studentium in Collegium," TCD MSS. Mun/V/23/3.

[134] Ibid.

[135] Ibid.

[136] [Richard Shackleton], "Biographical Sketch of Edmund Burke" [1766], OSB MS. File 2225.

[137] EB to Richard Shackleton, 28 October 1766, *Corr.*, I, p. 274.

[138] *London Evening Post*, 14–17 April 1770.

[139] EB to Richard Shackleton, 19 April 1770, *Corr.*, II, p. 131.

[140] [Richard Shackleton], "Biographical Sketch of Edmund Burke" [1766], OSB MS. File 2225.

[141] Ibid.

class, his school friend Michael Kearney earned a fellowship for his achievements.[142] Writing to Edmond Malone in 1799, Kearney recalled how Burke had approached his studies in haphazard fashion, devouring the curriculum but usually after it had been examined.[143] A draft "Essay on Education" sketched by Richard Shackleton sets out what he took to be the shortcomings of the Trinity syllabus, indicating how Burke may have found it wanting. Scholarship in Ireland, compared with Glasgow or Leiden, was in Shackleton's eyes regimented and catechistic, confining literary study to glosses, commentary and grammar, and stifling the spirit of original inquiry.[144] The object of humanistic study was accordingly diminished—with Horace, for example, reduced to the persona of "a Country Schoolmaster," and Virgil to the level of a "farmer."[145] Montaigne, in Shackleton's opinion, offered a more promising approach: a pupil, as Montaigne had commented in his essay "Of the Institution and Education of Children," should not be soullessly memorising authors' precepts by rote—"It is requisite he indevor as much to feede him selfe with their conceits."[146] Education, Shackleton concluded, should not be "cramped" and mechanical, but should cultivate natural genius by the allurements of mimesis: "imitation," Shackleton noted, "is natural to man," and knowledge progressed by the aspiring seeking to emulate excellence.[147]

Burke had himself addressed the topic of the "Education of Boys" in a letter he wrote to Shackleton in July 1746, in which he dwells on the benefits to be derived from the study of "Humanity"—the "most essential . . . of all Sciences." Engagement with the ancient authors should be fostered with a view to distilling what their use of language substantively teaches instead of employing them as a vehicle for simple language acquisition.[148] In the pedagogy of the time, technical knowledge was privileged over the development of the higher faculties, disabling intellectual achievement. In Shackleton's estimate, genius would never flourish by encouraging memory at the expense of judgment, ensuring that Ireland compared to Switzerland or

[142] Lock, *Burke*, I, p. 41; EB to Richard Shackleton, 10 August 1757, *Corr.*, I, p. 124: "I hear with great Satisfaction . . . of Kearneys being chose a fellow in our College."

[143] Letters to Edmond Malone from Michael Kearney, 1797–1811, Letter of 12 January 1799, Bodl. MS. Malone 39, fol. 23.

[144] The University of Leiden was a popular resort for Irish and British (particularly Scottish) students at the time, noted for its religious toleration. See R.W.I. Smith ed., *Roll of the English-Speaking Students of Medicine at the University of Leyden* (London: 1932). See also Esther Mijers, "Irish Students in the Netherlands, 1650–1750," *Archivium Hibernicum*, 59 (2005), pp. 66–78, for a list of Irish students attending Leiden. For the intellectual culture of the university, see Esther Mijers, *"News from the Republic of Letters": Scottish Students Charles Mackie and the United Provinces, 1650–1750* (Leiden: Brill, 2012), part II.

[145] Richard Shackleton, "Essay on Education: Autograph MSS Draft" [n.d.], OSB MS. File 13408.

[146] Michel de Montaigne, *The Essayes or Morall, Politike and Millitarie Discourses of Lo: Michaell de Montaigne . . . The First Booke. First written by him in French. And now done into English by . . . Iohn Florio* (London: 1603), p. 71.

[147] Shackleton, "Essay on Education," OSB MS. File 13408. The rudiments of this pedagogical theory are to be found in Aristotle, *Poetics*, 1448b5–10, as Burke was aware: see EB, *A Philosophical Enquiry into the Origin of our Ideas of the Sublime and Beautiful* (1757, rev. ed. 1759), *W & S*, I, p. 225.

[148] EB to Richard Shackleton, 12 July 1746, *Corr.*, I, p. 69.

Scotland would produce few authors. "[W]e have so few men who make the least figure in the Learned world," Shackleton complained, resulting in general corruption and a pervasive "want of taste." As Ramus, Descartes and Locke could all testify, a university curriculum did not guarantee an education: the appropriate method of indoctrination was a prerequisite of success. The ancients had shown how learning could drive a man "into society"—rendering him of "use to the Commonwealth"—instead of fostering a culture of pedantic seclusion. University education in Ireland risked sharing the fate of the monasteries of Europe which, having been "Schools of Virtue and Learning became sinks of ignorance." With the petrification of knowledge, national prejudices would prosper, in turn fostering intellectual and religious bigotry. Letters bred taste, leading to enlightenment and toleration; pedantry corrupted manners, contracting the spirit of humanity.[149]

The course of study for undergraduates at Trinity College usually extended over a four-year period. The scientific component of the curriculum chiefly concentrated on logic, metaphysics, physics and astronomy: instruction in mathematics was pretty rudimentary, with Euclid only introduced in 1758, and algebra not studied until after 1808. In their first year, as junior freshmen, students were examined in Lucian, Sallust, Homer, Virgil, Theocritus, Ovid and Terence. Virgil and Homer were a staple in succeeding years. In addition, Juvenal, Epictetus, Justinian and Horace constituted the core curriculum for senior freshman. In the third year, junior sophisters studied Juvenal, Velleius, Cicero's *De officiis*, Xenophon's *Cyropaedia* and Livy. Senior sophisters, in their final year, covered Demosthenes, Aeschines, Sophocles, Suetonius, Tacitus, and Longinus on the sublime.[150] There were, in addition, prize compositions, the subjects for which in 1743 and 1746 were "Europa Libertas" and "On Peace and War" respectively.[151] On 4 July 1745, "Burk" was awarded a proemium for his Whitsuntide examinations.[152] The science course seemed to contemporaries to be more antiquated and arid. The first-year logic text was by the Dutch Ramist, Francis Burgersdijk, whose *Institutionum logicarum libri duo* had been composed back in the 1620s.[153] On 10 May 1744, Burke reported that he was due to begin work on the first nine chapters, complaining within a fortnight that the "hideous . . . Burgersdiscius" still lay on his bureau.[154]

[149] Shackleton, "Essay on Education," OSB MS. File 13408.

[150] TCD MSS. Mun/27/1/fols. 90, 99, 101. There is some brief advice about preparation for study at Trinity sent to Richard Shackleton in his capacity as schoolmaster for the sake of one of his school pupils from his own school friend, William Dennis, in an ALS to Richard Shackleton, April 1758, OSB MS. File 4326: "if he enters for the present class and intends to answer June examinations he must read Epictetus and the Second Six Books of Virgil with the first Book of Burgerdicius [*sic*]."

[151] "Subjects for the Bachelor Prize Exercises at Shrovetide," TCD MSS. Mun V/27/1/fol. 91r.

[152] TCD MSS. Mun/v/27/1/109v.

[153] Francis Burgersdijk, *Institutionum logicarum libri duo* (Leiden: 1626). Burgersdijk's works continued to appear on syllabuses at Oxford, Cambridge, Harvard and Yale down to the end of the eighteenth century.

[154] EB to Richard Shackleton, 10 May 1744, *Corr.*, I, p. 4; EB to Richard Shackleton, 24 May 1744, ibid., p. 7.

The staunch Whig Richard Baldwin occupied the position of Provost of Trinity throughout Burke's period in attendance at the university. Baldwin fled to England during the Jacobite takeover of the College in 1689, returning after the Battle of the Boyne to make good his ambition to impose sound Protestant principles on the institution. Little, however, occurred by way of academic innovation.[155] During a Provostship lasting from 1717 to 1758, not a single academic publication was authored by a Fellow of the College. The seventeenth-century syllabus was barely updated.[156] In addition to Burgersdijk, the 1618 *Logica* of Martinus Smiglecius appeared on the curriculum as a first-year text. However, post-Aristotelian philosophy was also represented: Jean le Clerc's *Logica, sive ars ratiocinandi* was studied alongside Burgersdijk and Smiglecius, and his *Physica* was studied in the second year under the heading of natural philosophy. Third-year students used Bernhard Varen's *Geographia generalis*, which covered the division between the earth and the heavens, the figure of the earth, its dimensions and magnitude, its motion and place in the "systemata mundi," its constitutive elements—its seas and rivers, woods and deserts—the determinants of the climate, and so on.[157] Varen, who attracted the attention of the Cambridge Platonists by employing Cartesian methods to supplant Scholastic orthodoxy, had twice been edited and emended by Isaac Newton. He represented a more innovative component of the science course at Trinity.

Varen's text also covered the wider universe, as did Edward Wells's *Young Gentleman's Astronomy*, which offered hypotheses explaining the motion, distribution and situation of the "Celestial Lights."[158] The study of the universe was evidently better calculated to fire Burke's imagination than the syllogistic reasoning of Francis Burgersdijk. Shackleton's interest in astronomy was signalled in a letter sent in the spring of 1744, which Burke noted in a reply he made in June.[159] Later that month, Burke himself offered a rhapsody on the "Beauty of the Heavens"—one deficient, as he conceded, in technical mastery, but nonetheless enthusiastic in the grandeur of its vision. The universe, Burke emphasised, should be appreciated for its beauty

[155] The contrast with the University of Edinburgh under the reforms initiated by William Carstares is telling: between 1703 and 1726, the curriculum and teaching practice at Edinburgh was entirely remodelled, first under Carstares and then under William Wishart, supported by the Earl of Ilay, later the Duke of Argyll. Leiden stood out as the model to be imitated. See Nicholas Phillipson, "The Making of an Enlightened University" in Michael Lynch et al eds., *The University of Edinburgh: An Illustrated History* (Edinburgh: Edinburgh University Press, 2003), pp. 60–63.

[156] John William Stubbs, *The History of the University of Dublin from its Foundation to the End of the Eighteenth Century* (Dublin: 1889), pp. 198–200; R. B. McDowell and D. A. Wells, *Trinity College Dublin, 1592–1952: An Academic History* (Cambridge: Cambridge University Press, 1982), pp. 37–46. There is a tendentious reconstruction of parts of the philosophical syllabus at Trinity in Francis P. Canavan, *The Political Reason of Edmund Burke* (Durham, NC: Duke University Press, 1960), Appendix A. The material is put to interpretative use in Burleigh T. Wilkins, *The Problem of Burke's Political Philosophy* (Oxford: Oxford University Press, 1967), pp. 33–34, 70.

[157] Bernhard Varen, *Geographia generalis* (Cambridge: 1681).

[158] Edward Wells, *Young Gentleman's Astronomy, Chronology and Dialling* (London: 1712).

[159] EB to Richard Shackleton, 11 June 1744, *Corr.*, I, p. 15n.

since it manifested "Variety and uniformity" together, corresponding to Francis Hutcheson's criterion for aesthetic decorum.[160] At this stage, Burke was approaching the subject armed with Virgil rather than Varen or Wells, citing the tribute paid in the second book of the *Georgics* to "the pathways of the stars and the heavens, the various lapses of the sun and the various labours of the moon."[161] But, as he warmed to his theme, Burke's treatment registered its indebtedness to a Christian sense of wonder:

> What grander Idea can the mind of man form to itself than a prodigious, glorious, and firy globe hanging in the midst of an infinite and boundless space surrounded with bodies of whom our earth is scarcely any thing in comparison . . . held tight to their respective orbits . . . by the force of the Creators Almighty arm.[162]

It was a sense of wonder that had been captured by Addison in *The Spectator* when he first published what he described as his "sublime" ode to celestial design in "The Spacious Firmament on High."[163] "Astronomy," he later argued, "is peculiarly adapted to remedy a little and narrow spirit."[164] The sheer magnitude of its objects and distances overwhelms the imagination, at once humbling and exhilarating the mind.

Burke would later develop these insights into the ideas of beauty and grandeur when he came to compose his *Philosophical Enquiry into the Origin of our Ideas of the Sublime and Beautiful* in the 1750s, but as an undergraduate his interests were changeable and diffuse. He worried in a letter to Shackleton of 15 October 1744 that he was "too giddy" when it came to discipline, leaving him with considerable intellectual range but little depth in any specific area of knowledge.[165] Two years later he again indicated how his interests were spread over diverse terrain: "I am deep in Metaphysics and poetry, I have read some history. I am endeavouring to get a little into the accounts of this our own poor Country."[166] The following spring he returned to his underlying regret. His studies usually began as "Sallies of passion" only to dissipate as his attention switched to a new enthusiasm. His procedure lacked method as he careered from a delight in natural philosophy to what he termed his "furor mathematicus" before being diverted into his "furor logicus," succeeded in turn by his "furor historicus," and developing, most recently, into a bout of "poetical madness."[167] Despite this apparently digressive approach to learning, Burke did roughly speaking progress through the undergraduate syllabus, supplementing it with reading

[160] EB to Richard Shackleton, c. 14 June 1744, ibid., p. 18. See below, chapter 3, *passim*.

[161] Virgil, *Georgics*, II, lines 477–78: "caelique vias et sidera monstrent, / defectus solis varios lunaque labores."

[162] EB to Richard Shackleton, c. 14 June 1744, *Corr.*, I, p. 18.

[163] Joseph Addison, *Spectator*, no. 465, 23 August 1712, reprinted in idem, *The Evidences of the Christian Religion* (London: 1730), pp. 238–39. Burke later pointed to the *Evidences* as a valued intellectual resource: see EB, "Christian Religion," WWM BkP 26:40–41.

[164] Addison, *Evidences*, p. 253.

[165] EB to Richard Shackleton, 25 October 1744, *Corr.*, I, p. 32.

[166] EB to Richard Shackleton, 21 July 1746, ibid., p. 68.

[167] EB to Richard Shackleton, 21 March 1746/7, ibid., p. 89.

of his own. Senior sophisters encountered metaphysics on the science curriculum in the form of Robert Baron's *Metaphysica generalis*, which offered a didactic exposition of the Aristotelian categories before treating the origin of evil together with an account of the sources of rationality and the nature of freedom of judgment (*arbitrium*).[168] But the final year also brought students into contact with ethics and jurisprudence. Burke left no record of his reading as a senior sophister; however, his letters down to 1747 show that he tended to reflect on the content of the undergraduate course, actively evaluating the variety of arguments he encountered.

Final-year moral philosophy was in the first instance based on the *Ethica, sive summa moralis disciplinae* of Eustachius a Sancto Paulo, which proceeded from the overriding telos of ethics, allegedly residing in the principle of "beatitude," through an analysis of the causes of human action, to a discussion of the passions of the soul.[169] A number of Robert Sanderson's *Praelectiones*, focusing in particular on his *De juramenti promissory obligatione* and *De obligatione conscientiae*, formed one of the main textbooks in jurisprudence and offered a casuistical treatment of topics ranging from passive obedience to the rights of conscience.[170] In addition to examining Sanderson, students were exposed to modern natural law theory through Samuel Pufendorf's *De officio hominis et civis juxta legem naturalem libri duo*.[171] Burke left no account of his youthful reaction to this crucial text in early modern philosophy, although he did hint at a general impatience with the "absurdities of Aristotle" in an early letter to Shackleton on the nature of human credulity.[172] Burke was above all keen to debate the topics he encountered, seeking to enliven intellectual effort with the thrill of open discussion. Where the opportunity for face to face conversation was wanting, he resorted to epistolary communication, apprising his friends of his responses to canonical and modern works—commending the "blameless" *De officiis* of Cicero, but preferring Sallust's history to Cicero's letters; sending his copy of Xenophon's *Cyropaedia* to Shackleton while mentioning an attempt to purchase an edition of Bayle's *Dictionary*; signalling his interest in Addison and Pope, and admiration for the work of Vincent Voiture.[173]

The counterpoint to Burke's commitment to sociable intellectual exchange in his early years was his persistent aversion to stoic teaching. Within a few months of arriving at university he was commenting ironically on the stoic doctrine of *apatheia*,

[168] Robert Baron, *Metaphysica generalis* (Leiden: 1657).

[169] Eustachius a Sancto Paulo, *Ethica, sive summa moralis disciplinae* (London: 1677).

[170] Robert Sanderson, *De juramenti promissory obligatione* (London: 1710); Robert Sanderson, *De obligatione conscientiae* (London: 1710).

[171] Samuel Pufendorf, *De officio hominis et civis juxta legem naturalem libri duo* (Lund: 1673).

[172] EB to Richard Shackleton, c. 5 March 1744/5, *Corr.*, I, p. 45.

[173] EB to Richard Shackleton, 5 December 1746, ibid., p. 74; EB to Richard Shackleton, 21 March 1746/7, ibid., p. 89; EB to Richard Shackleton and Richard Burke Sr., 29 November 1746, ibid., p. 72; EB to Richard Shackleton, 5 July 1744, ibid., p. 25; EB to Richard Shackleton, 10 July 1744, ibid., p. 29; EB to Richard Shackleton, 7 December 1745, ibid., p. 58; EB to Richard Shackleton, 16 January 1745/6, ibid., p. 60; EB to Richard Shackleton, 19 December 1746, ibid., p. 75.

particularly as exemplified by Epictetus.[174] In his *Discourses* and *Enchiridion*, Epictetus preached acceptance of the providential order of nature at the expense of native concern for one's own suffering or that of one's intimates. As he made plain in the *Discourses*, one ought not to pity the lamentations of a Priam or an Oedipus, weighed down by the burden of mere "external things" (*ta ektos*); instead, one should bear one's fortune with pride like Socrates, who submitted to his fate without complaint.[175] However, for Burke, self-command of the kind, exercised in the name of virtue, amounted not to a noble submission to the dictates of fortune, but to a denial of the spontaneous affections with which Providence had equipped human beings. Six months after his first reference to the stoics, writing to Shackleton when the river Liffey had just overflowed its banks and flooded his house on Arran Quay, Burke addressed himself to the topic of the sublime power of nature, wondering how to respond to its dreadful might—should one rage against the injustice of the Providential order of things, or submit with magnanimity even to the destruction of the world?[176] Burke returned to this theme in a letter of 28 December 1745, this time delivering a clear verdict in response to the philosophy of Seneca. The stoic philosophers, he commented, were but "Sorry Comforters," whose speculative injunctions habitually failed to take root in experience—the "tide of Passion is not to be stopp'd by such feeble dams" as theoretical precepts.[177] In the face of despondency, Burke counselled distraction rather than speculation, at one point advising Shackleton to adopt the remedy of Pascal by diverting the feeling of melancholy through constant occupation.[178]

1.4 The Club and *The Reformer*

In the eighth of his *Penseés* dedicated to the topic of "Divertissement," Pascal observed that "sans divertissement, il n'y a point de joie; avec divertissement, il n'y a point de tristesse."[179] As a result, Pascal concluded, solitude brings unhappiness, while bustle soothes. In flight from secluded reflection on the secular condition of man, human beings are driven to occupy themselves, and lose their melancholy thoughts in the enjoyment of the company of others.[180] In this spirit, Burke constantly sought to develop his ideas in conversation with others, preferring the cut and thrust of intellectual exchange to retirement into solitary contemplation. Together with friends, one could "mutually communicate" and thus navigate the difficulties and share the

[174] EB to Richard Shackleton, 24 May 1744, ibid., p. 8.

[175] Epictetus, *Discourses*, I, iv, 24–27.

[176] EB to Richard Shackleton, 25 January 1744/5, *Corr.*, I, p. 39.

[177] EB to Richard Shackleton, 28 December 1745, ibid., p. 59. For the notion that one can cure passions by precepts, see Seneca, *De ira*, III, lxi, 1.

[178] EB to Richard Shackleton, 16 January 1745/6, *Corr.*, I, p. 61.

[179] Blaise Pascal, *Penseés*, ed. Michel Le Guern (Paris: Gallimard, 1977), p. 122.

[180] EB to Christopher Nugent, September 1752, *Corr.*, I, p. 118.

pleasures of academic labour—"smoothing by that means the rugged path of knowledge, and deluding the tedious way by a friendly talk."[181] Much of Burke's self-image here was derived from Addison in *The Spectator*, to whom he twice refers in his early correspondence.[182] Just as Addison sought to relocate philosophy from "Closets and Libraries, Schools and Colleges" to "Clubs and Assemblies . . . Tea-Tables, and . . . Coffee-Houses," so Burke strove to convert learning into an extension of gregariousness.[183] Proselytism, Burke argued, is natural to man: no sooner have we stumbled upon a new discovery than we feel "uneasy to communicate the fruit of our labours to others."[184] Addison, once again in *The Spectator*, ascribed to this sociable instinct the desire among individuals to form themselves into "*Clubs*."[185] Accordingly, on 24 November 1744, we first find Burke plotting the establishment of a "Society" which would ultimately develop into a literary "Club," claiming William Dennis among its members.[186]

The club, or "Academy of Belles Lettres," was founded on 21 April 1747, the year after Burke took up residence in his college rooms, following his success in securing a scholarship. Meetings took place on George's Lane on a twice-weekly basis, falling on Tuesdays and Fridays and lasting from five in the afternoon till nine.[187] These sessions were intended to "improve" club members by exposing them to the refined and useful arts, and to the activities of conversation and debate. As the preamble to the laws of the club stated, "Each may become master of the Theory of Arts and science in his closet, but the practice & the benefit & the use of them can only be known and had in Society."[188] The original club members included Matthew Mohun, the first president, along with Andrew Buck, Joseph Hamilton, Abraham Ardesoif, Richard Shackleton and William Dennis. With the exception of Shackleton and Dennis, barely any record of the activities of these comrades survives. Dennis shared rooms with Burke, and played a prominent role in the club, although both men fell out of touch after their period at university. By the time that they caught up again in the 1750s, Burke was living in London and Dennis was in holy orders. In the club, Dennis was an eager participant, regularly contributing to its business and discussions, which included "speeching, reading, writing and arguing, in morality, History, Criticism, Politics, and all the useful branches of Philosophy."[189] Topics covered

[181] EB to Richard Shackleton, 24 November 1744, ibid., p. 37.

[182] EB to Richard Shackleton, 5 July 1744, ibid., p. 25; EB to Richard Shackleton, 16 January 1745/6, ibid., p. 60.

[183] Joseph Addison, *Spectator*, no. 10, 12 March 1711.

[184] EB to Richard Shackleton, c. 5 March 1744/5, *Corr.*, I, pp. 44–45.

[185] Addison, *Spectator*, no. 9, 10 March 1711.

[186] EB to Richard Shackleton, 24 November 1744, *Corr.*, I, pp. 3738; EB to Richard Shackleton, 4 July 1745, ibid., p. 50; EB and William Dennis to Richard Shackleton, 28 May 1747, ibid., pp. 90–91.

[187] This became South Great George's Street in the middle of the eighteenth century. See John Thomas Gilbert, *A History of the City of Dublin* (Dublin: 1861), 3 vols., III, ch. 3.

[188] "The Proceedings of the Club," TCD MSS. Mun/Soc/Hist/81, reprinted in Samuels, *Early Life*, pp. 226–95, p. 227.

[189] Ibid., p. 228.

extended from general themes, like "Luxury" and "Atheism," to reflection on historical characters and issues of contemporary political significance.

One of the goals of the club was to bring about a reformation of taste by refining the use of language, in the process educating manners and securing the role of religion in society. Burke had been applying himself to these subjects since his arrival at university, anxiously probing with Shackleton how the advancement of knowledge could improve the fortunes of religion. He was aware of the "Different Roads" towards Christian truth which both he and his friend earnestly pursued, and reflected on the "melancholy" fact that there existed "Diversities of Sects and opinions among us."[190] More than Shackleton, he lamented the reality of Church disunity, and was sceptical about the motives that lay behind much dissent. Too many sectaries in Ireland, it seemed, propagated schism on the basis of indifferent things (*adiaphora*) which had no implications for salvation: only divergence over essentials could justify dissent.[191] The only hope for enlightenment in the face of intemperate zeal was a commitment to humility and the practice of rational accounting. Burke fundamentally believed that he lived in "enlightened times," yet he wondered how intellectual progress and religious harmony could be maintained.[192] During his undergraduate days between 1744 and 1748, he contended that the process of enlightenment required that prejudice be supplanted by means of rational inquiry, although in the 1750s his position began to change. In hoping to bring Shackleton around to his own opinion, he implored him to cast off "Prejudice"—"the greatest obstacle we meet in search of truth."[193] Burke consistently reiterated this conviction in the 1740s, but after his move to London—above all, after his exposure to common law and his critical engagement with deism—his assessment of the role of prejudice in social life would change.

The impact of Berkeley's ideas is evident here. In *A Discourse Addressed to Magistrates and Men in Authority*, composed while Burke was still a child on Arran Quay, the Bishop of Cloyne expounded the wisdom of taking doctrines on trust in opposition to what he castigated as freethinking polemicists in Dublin inspired by the example of the Third Earl of Shaftesbury and Bernard Mandeville.[194] Freedom of thought was of course essential for facilitating the progress of knowledge, but such liberty had to be harnessed in support of church and state. "It is impossible . . . that the multitude should be philosophers," Berkeley wrote. Members of the manual and artisanal classes were expected to follow rules and accept conclusions, not inquire

[190] EB to Richard Shackleton, 15 October 1744, *Corr.*, I, pp. 32–33.

[191] EB to Richard Shackleton, 1 November 1744, ibid., p. 35.

[192] EB to Richard Shackleton, 21 March 1746/7, ibid., p. 89.

[193] EB to Richard Shackleton, c. 5 March 1744/5, ibid., p. 45.

[194] George Berkeley, *A Discourse Addressed to Magistrates and Men in Authority* (1736) in *The Works of George Berkeley*, ed. Alexander Campbell Fraser (Oxford: Oxford University Press, 1901), 4 vols., IV, p. 409. Berkeley was immediately responding to the recent establishment of the "Fraternity of Blasphemers," or Blasters Club, a society of deistical freethinkers.

into original causes or have recourse to the "deductions of science."[195] Society at large, therefore, depended on instruction by precept, which would then be "riveted by custom." This meant binding the public by means of prejudice: "Prejudices are notions or opinions which the mind entertains without knowing the grounds or reasons of them, and which are assented to without examination."[196] Individuals were motivated to pursue their interests and win respect, but these ambitions were in turn governed by "opinion." The formation of opinion, and the propagation of doctrines, was thus a central concern of the magistrate, who depended on the clergy to provide the requisite education. Correct principles had to be inculcated by authority and sustained by habit. Consequently, the "first notions which take possession of the minds of men, with regard to duties social, moral, and civil, may therefore justly be styled *prejudices*."[197] Burke became captivated by this argument after he had moved to London when he felt impelled to challenge the presumption of freethinkers in the mid 1750s. In the meantime, he was committed to the process of rational inquiry as a means of advancing the cause of objective truth.

In this spirit, in his correspondence with Shackleton in the 1740s, Burke insisted that there was no merit in idly following "Common opinion" in the face of plausible countervailing evidence: it was precisely by overturning cherished assumptions that barbarity, ignorance and superstition had been overcome. The desire for truth should be allowed to triumph over a stubborn opposition to enlightenment, yet to achieve this the reasoning faculty was forced to do battle with received wisdom.[198] A child "imbibes prejudice with its milk," thereby hoodwinking its powers of independent reasoning from the start.[199] However, if Burke wholeheartedly endorsed the procedures of rational inquiry in the 1740s, he was also committed to the refinement of the passions via the operation of religion and fine taste. Reason could correct error, but passion was required to motivate the soul. The education of the sentiments was therefore indispensable to the improvement of society and the cultivation of morals. Religion and the arts were the prime agents of this education, with Christianity standing as the most efficacious of religions. As Burke declared in an extempore explication of the Sermon on the Mount during a meeting of the club on 29 May 1749, the Christian religion marked an advance on heathen morality by educating the feelings of the heart.[200]

The relationship between religion, morality and taste was a central concern of Burke's between his graduation from Trinity in February 1748 and his departure for London in 1750. The principal surviving index of that preoccupation are the

[195] Ibid., pp. 487–88.

[196] Ibid., p. 486.

[197] Ibid.

[198] EB to Richard Shackleton, c. 5 March 1744/5, *Corr.*, I, p. 45; EB to Richard Shackleton, 15 [March] 1744/5, ibid., p. 48; EB to Richard Shackleton, 5 December 1746, ibid., p. 74.

[199] EB to Richard Shackleton, 19 March 1744/5, ibid., p. 50.

[200] "The Proceedings of the Club," TCD MSS. Mun/Soc/Hist/81, reprinted in Samuels, *Early Life*, p. 252.

writings that appeared in *The Reformer*, a weekly paper in which Burke was involved that ran to thirteen issues between 28 January and 21 April 1748. *The Reformer* was a collaborative miscellany comprising essays, poetry and assorted advertisements, to which Burke, Beaumont Brennan and Richard Shackleton variously contributed. Brennan was a budding comic playwright whom Burke first encountered around November 1746 and whose role in the production of *The Reformer* was later attested by contemporaries of Burke.[201] Dennis wrote to Shackleton in January 1748 soliciting his opinion of the first issue: "Who do you think the author?" he inquired.[202] A few weeks later Burke contacted Shackleton, complaining about his lack of leisure on account of his ongoing work on "the Reformer &c."[203] Burke's specific contributions to the publication cannot be established, although it is clear that he thought of it as a collaborative enterprise.[204] While the leading essays of each issue appear under various signatures, these evidently formed parts of a collective endeavour to purge Irish literary culture of ignorance and dullness. With this end in view, the first issue declared its mission to pit "*Spirit*" against depravity: depraved taste is deemed to have degraded manners and morality in Ireland, rendering her a latter-day Boeotia.

The echo of Pope's *Dunciad* was deliberate here, highlighting a concern that had preoccupied Burke for over two years.[205] On 5 December 1746 he proclaimed to Shackleton that Irish letters stood "on the verge of Darkness," about to realise the prophecy with which Pope closed the *Dunciad*—expecting the return of an "age of Lead" characterised by ignorance and barbarity.[206] The same diagnosis pervades the pages of *The Reformer*, which repeatedly charges native literary endeavour with the production of witless "Prodigies of Dulness."[207] In response, the aim of Burke and his associates was to expose contemporary literary folly, above all its manifestation in the theatre. The reformation of taste would in turn contribute to the improvement of morals and the cultivation of public spirit: "the Morals of a Nation have so great a Dependence on their Taste and Writings, that the fixing of the latter, seems the first and surest Method of establishing the former."[208] In a short pamphlet on the state of

[201] Lock, *Burke*, I, p. 56.

[202] Prior, *Life of Burke*, p. 21.

[203] EB to Richard Shackleton, 2 February 1747/8, *Corr.*, I, p. 101.

[204] EB to Richard Shackleton, May 1748, ibid., p. 102. Nonetheless, strangely enough, the work is usually treated as more or less Burke's own: see Samuels, *Early Life*, p. 160; T. O. McLoughlin, "The Context of Burke's 'The Reformer'," *Eighteenth-Century Ireland*, 2 (1987), pp. 37–55; idem, "Did Burke Write the *Reformer*?" *Notes and Queries*, 39:4 (December 1992), pp. 474–77.

[205] Alexander Pope, *The Dunciad*, book I, line 25, referring to Jonathan Swift's Ireland as "Bœotia." William Dunkins's *Boeotia! A Poem Humbly Addressed to His Excellency, Philip, Earl of Chesterfield* (Dublin: 1747) had recently appeared, although on its publication Burke wrote to Shackleton that it amounted to "the worst thing I ever saw of his" (21 March 1746/7, *Corr.*, I, p. 90). The designation of Ireland as Boeotia became commonplace: see Henry Grattan to Richard Burke Jr., 20 March 1793, *Corr.*, VII, p. 362: "I dont [*sic*] think England can call Ireland Boeotia nor yet a land of Slaves."

[206] EB to Richard Shackleton, 5 December 1746, *Corr.*, I, p. 74. Cf. Pope, *Dunciad*, book I, line 28.

[207] *Reformer*, no. 1., *W & S*, I, p. 67.

[208] Ibid., p. 66.

dramatic productions in Dublin the previous year, William Dennis had claimed that since the theatre represented "what is agreeable to society," it should be employed to promote what is beneficial to the public.[209] In broad outline, this perspective was shared by the collaborators on *The Reformer*: "PLAYS are the favourite Diversion of People of Fashion, and every one is sensible how much they influence their Taste and Manners."[210] From 1744, much of the calibre and character of productions for the stage in Dublin was determined by the actor-manager of the Theatre Royal in Smock Alley, Thomas Sheridan. By 1747, Sheridan was openly presenting himself as a "reformer of the stage," in response to which *The Reformer* was conceived as an instrument for publicising the alleged triviality of his endeavours.[211]

Sheridan's reforms were introduced in the wake of the Kelly riots in the Smock Alley theatre, beginning on 19 January 1747. The intimate and often inebriated atmosphere of the Theatre Royal had frequently resulted in scenes of minor uproar in previous years, but the stand-off between "gentlemen," "scholars" and "players" triggered by the lewd and outlandish behaviour of an audience member named Edmund Kelly gave rise to what Burke described to Shackleton as a singularly "grand Theatrical squabble . . . which divided the town into two parties as violent as whig and tory."[212] In the aftermath of the ensuing legal wrangle that occurred over a six-week period, Sheridan seized the opportunity to improve decorum in the theatre, setting an example that was later followed by Drury Lane.[213] For Burke and his allies, however, Sheridan's efforts represented trivial improvements that did little to raise the standard of public taste. The cosmetic nature of Sheridan's reforms were seemingly confirmed by his failure to stage Beaumont Brennan's *The Lawsuit*, spurring Burke, Brennan and colleagues into satirical opposition to the Dublin theatre establishment, beginning with Burke's first publication, a squib entitled *Punch's Petition to Mr. S[herida]n*, and continuing with Paul Hiffernan's serial, *The Tickler*, running alongside the issues of *The Reformer*.[214] The aim of each of these activities was, as William Dennis informed Shackleton, to establish "liberty on the stage, and taste among the people."[215]

The opposition to Smock Alley followed on the heels of a spirited defence of Sheridan's activities orchestrated by Charles Lucas in a series of anonymous pamphlets published in February and March 1747.[216] Lucas, descended from a Cromwellian officer who had settled in Co. Clare, had trained as an apothecary in Dublin

[209] William Dennis, *Brutus's Letter to the Town* (Dublin: 1747), p. 3.

[210] *Reformer*, no. 1, *W & S*, I, p. 67.

[211] Esther K. Sheldon, *Thomas Sheridan of Smock-Alley: Recording his Life as Actor and Theater Manager in both Dublin and London* (Princeton, NJ: Princeton University Press, 1967), pp. 81–95.

[212] EB to Richard Shackleton, 21 February 1747, *Corr.*, I, p. 82.

[213] Sheldon, *Thomas Sheridan*, p. 103.

[214] [EB], *Punch's Petition to Mr. S—n, to be admitted into the Theatre Royal* (Dublin: 1748), British Library, 1890.e.5(152).

[215] Prior, *Life of Goldsmith*, II, pp. 315–18.

[216] The context is treated in Ian Crowe, *Patriotism and Public Spirit: Edmund Burke and the Role of the Critic in Mid-Eighteenth-Century Britain* (Stanford, CA: Stanford University Press, 2012).

before entering public life as a representative of the Barber-Surgeons' Guild on the common council of Dublin Corporation in 1741.[217] Lucas's defence of Sheridan began with an attack on Kelly's credentials: as a Catholic from the western province of Connaught in Ireland, the "gentleman" instigator of the riots against Sheridan was pilloried for being an exemplar of native rebellion, and thus as an "Enemy of our happy Establishment." According to Lucas, the riots had been the work of "professed Papists" and "mercenary converts," ultimately threatening foreign invasion or an insurrection leading to massacre.[218] These portents of future catastrophe amounted to barely camouflaged references to both the ordeal of 1641 and the Jacobite rising of 1745. The prospect of such subversion prompted Lucas to pose the question: "shall we whose Ancestors came to subdue the Barbarity of the Natives of this Island . . . suffer their offspring to relapse . . . into the old hateful, exploded Slavery and Barbarism?"[219] In his third *Letter to the Free-Citizens of Dublin*, Lucas explained what he had meant to establish in his second: his invectives against native barbarism and popery had been intended not as a way of causing offence, but as a means of laying down some common principles. His argument was not with the tenets of the Catholic faith, but with submission to the temporal jurisdiction of the Pope.[220] Likewise, his quarrel with "*antient Irish Barbarism*" was to be taken not as an insult against any actually existing section of the Irish population, but as a rejection of a mode of life that he hoped had been eliminated through successive conquests over recent centuries, although the behaviour of Kelly suggested it was still alive in parts of Ireland.[221]

In the dedicatory epistle prefacing the second edition of Paul Hiffernan's *Tickler*, Lucas's "PATRIOTISM" was subject to derision.[222] In the middle of March 1747, in the fourth and fifth issues of his journal, Hiffernan proceeded to expose Lucas's campaign as the work of a levelling zealot who aspired, much like Cromwell, to enjoy the authority of a Caesar while rising on a tide of religious bigotry.[223] Reflecting ironically on Catholic loyalty in the wake of the '45 in Ireland, Hiffernan charged Lucas with sectarian opportunism: "Have not the villainous Papists, the pest of society . . . remain'd loyal in the late rebellion, for no other reason, but that you shou'd

[217] Seán Murphy, "Charles Lucas, Catholicism and Nationalism," *Eighteenth-Century Ireland*, 8 (1993), pp. 83–102; Jim Smyth, "Republicanism before the United Irishmen: The Case of Dr. Charles Lucas" in D. George Boyce, Robert Eccleshall and Vincent Geoghegan eds., *Political Discourse in Seventeenth- and Eighteenth-Century Ireland* (Basingstoke: Palgrave, 2001).

[218] [Charles Lucas], *A Letter to the Free-Citizens of Dublin* (Dublin: 1747), pp. 2, 5; [Charles Lucas], *A Second Letter to the Free-Citizens of Dublin* (Dublin: 1747), p. 10.

[219] [Lucas], *A Letter to the Free-Citizens*, p. 5.

[220] [Charles Lucas], *A Third Letter to the Free-Citizens of Dublin* (Dublin: 1747), pp. 18–19.

[221] Ibid., pp. 16–17.

[222] [Paul Hiffernan], *The Tickler: Nos. I, II, III, IV, V, VI, and VII* (Dublin: 1748), "To Ch–rl–s L–c–s, *Freeman*." On the wider "patriot" context, see Jacqueline Hill, *From Protestants to Unionists: Dublin Civic Politics and Irish Protestant Patriotism, 1660–1840* (Oxford: Oxford University Press, 1997), pp. 83–91.

[223] [Hiffernan], *Tickler*, pp. 22–25.

not have an opportunity to display your talents in suppressing them?"[224] Hiffernan had trained for the priesthood before moving to Montpellier to undertake the study of medicine.[225] At Montpellier he encountered Rousseau and took a BA in physic, before returning to Dublin around 1747 to embark on a literary career.[226] He helped arrange the publication of Burke's handbill, *Punch's Petition*, through Joseph Cotter, and maintained a dialogue with *The Reformer* in the pages of *The Tickler*, with *The Reformer* duly responding in its fifth issue. Virtually every one of the first eight issues of *The Reformer* carried an advertisement for Hiffernan's philosophical study, *Reflections on the Structure, and Passions of Man*, with additional notices appearing on 10 and 17 March assuring potential readers that the work would soon appear.[227] This endorsement of Hiffernan's work is intriguing, since the book contains an indictment of Protestant intolerance and the penal code.

The *Reflections* examines the operation of emulation as the "spring of all laudable actions" in society, threatened only by its degeneration into "Jealousy" and resentment—the "worst of Plagues the Breast of Man was e'er infected with," exposing social cohesion to the possibility of conflict.[228] Hiffernan goes on to observe that modern societies have been subject to a kind of "fury" unknown to the ancients, which takes its rise from disputatiousness in religion.[229] The pervasiveness of persecution in modern Europe could be traced to this source, including displays of bigotry in Ireland after 1745. At this point Hiffernan refers explicitly to Henry Brooke's *Farmer's Letters* which just three years earlier had railed against the kind of "Indolence" that prospers in an age of tranquillity. In the face of Irish complacency following the '45, Brooke called for a revival of the virtues of agrarian Rome as the surest means of securing colonial tenures and agricultural improvement against the prospect of native subversion. The enduring threat of popery called for vigilance: "History will ever remember . . . the horrid Massacre of Forty-One."[230] To Hiffernan this was tantamount to justifying a perpetuation of the penal laws, which encouraged younger siblings to plot against their elders, and sons likewise to "rise against their Fathers."[231] Ancient horror over filial and paternal conflict had been encapsulated

[224] Ibid., p. 25.

[225] For Irish Catholic students at Montpellier, see Hilde de Ridder-Symoens, *A History of the University in Europe II: Universities in Early Modern Europe, 1500–1800* (Cambridge: Cambridge University Press, 1996), p. 429.

[226] *The European Magazine*, 25 (February 1794), pp. 110ff.; *The European Magazine*, 26 (March 1794), pp. 179ff.; and R. R. Madden, *The History of Irish Periodical Literature, from the End of the Seventeenth to the Middle of the Nineteenth Century* (London: 1867), 2 vols., I, pp. 320–30.

[227] *Reformer*, no. 7, p. 4, and *Reformer*, no. 8., p. 4, Dublin City Library and Archive, Pearse Street. These advertisements are not carried in the reprint for *W & S*.

[228] Paul Hiffernan, *Reflections on the Structure, and Passions of Man. The Latter Reduc'd to One Common Principle* (Dublin: 1748), p. 89.

[229] Ibid., pp. 146–7.

[230] Henry Brooke, *The Farmer's Six Letters to the Protestants of Ireland* (Dublin: 1745, repr. 1746), pp. 6, 8, 9, 11.

[231] Hiffernan, *Reflections*, p. 152.

in the tragic myth of fratricidal antagonism concerning succession to the Theban throne between the sons of the accursed Oedipus, yet the constitution of modern Ireland on account of its penal regulations fostered this kind of divisiveness amongst the Catholic population, resulting in a "Nation where in almost every house such sons of OEDIPUS might be found."[232]

The closest that *The Reformer* came to espousing a repeal of penal legislation is contained in its bid to "establish a Spirit of Benevolence, good Sense and Religion in this City"—hardly, on the face of it, a determined call to action. Yet Burke's campaign against the popery laws was to become a persistent one from the 1760s to the 1790s.[233] If *The Reformer* circumnavigated the confessional divisions that polarised Irish society in the eighteenth century, the eleventh issue of *The Reformer* did nonetheless present "*Blind Zeal*," together with "*Infidelity*," as the enemies of true religion, which could alone infuse the moral life with the spirit of charity and lighten the weight of misfortune with the joy of hope.[234] For the most part, however, *The Reformer* aimed at the education of social morality via the cultivation of taste. Since the populace tended to emulate the gentry, while writers pandered to the fashions of the people, it was necessary to ennoble the manners of polite society by replacing the love of "*Lucre*" and the taste for "irrational Pleasures" with a more uplifting desire for glory.[235] To achieve this, men of learning and genius would have to be permitted to prosper in Ireland, thereby enabling reasoned attitudes to predominate over the sway of ingrained prejudice.[236] At the same time, men of fortune would have to be encouraged to promote the useful arts, and generally contribute to the public weal. In the absence of a reorientation of this kind, Ireland would continue to be "*the only Nation whose People entirely neglected their own Interest*."[237] If this amounted to something like the basic vision shared by the contributors to *The Reformer*, it was broadly indebted to the recommendations presented in Berkeley's *Querist*.

Berkeley had asked in the fifteenth *Querist* whether "a general good taste in a people would not greatly conduce to their thriving? And whether an uneducated gentry be not the greatest of national evils?"[238] These questions assumed that the amelioration of society depended on refining the existing division of ranks, but certainly not on subverting the social structure. In the period of Burke's youth, the main challenge in Ireland to the contemporary social order was launched by Charles Lucas during the paper war that accompanied his bid for election to the House of Commons when two seats became available in 1748–9 after the death of the sitting

[232] Ibid., pp. 155.

[233] *Reformer*, no. 2, 4 March 1748, *W & S*, I, p. 77.

[234] *Reformer*, no. 11, 7 April 1748, ibid., p. 116.

[235] *Reformer*, no. 1, 28 January 1748, ibid., p. 67; *Reformer*, no. 6, 3 March 1748, ibid., p. 93.

[236] *Reformer*, no. 1, 28 January 1748, ibid., p. 68; *Reformer* no. 2, 4 February 1748, ibid., p. 73.

[237] *Reformer*, no. 4, 18 February 1748, ibid., p. 83.

[238] George Berkeley, *The Querist* in *The Works of George Berkeley*, ed. Alexander Campbell Fraser (Oxford: Oxford University Press, 1901), 4 vols., IV, p. 423.

aldermen representing the city.[239] Lucas's campaign dominated political debate during Burke's final years in Dublin before his departure for Middle Temple.[240] A slew of publications accompanied the proceedings, a number of which were subsequently attributed to Burke.[241] It seems probable that, as his contemporary Michael Kearney later contended, Burke joined the ranks of campaigners against Lucas: certainly the politics of *The Reformer* diverged massively from the rhetoric of Lucas's *Censor*.[242] Years later, Burke identified Lucas as an upstart imposter, equating his patriotic posture with the kind of fanaticism that "banishes common Sense."[243] In 1749, it seems likely that Burke took issue with Lucas' demagogic pretensions. At the same time, assuming that Burke took an interest in the wider terms of the Lucas controversy, the encounter will have exposed him to the sectarian sub-structure of Irish politics.

In a series of twenty addresses to the freeholders of Dublin that appeared in 1749, Lucas subjected the constitutional organisation of the kingdom of Ireland to a variety of biting criticisms, in the process highlighting the troubled history of her relationship to England.[244] In the tenth *Address* in particular, Lucas resuscitated the argument of William Molyneux's 1698 *The Case of Ireland's Being Bound by Acts of Parliament in England, Stated,* in order to vindicate the kingdom's status as "a *free popular State,* or COMMON-WEALTH."[245] In supporting this claim, and in the process recasting his earlier indictment of native Irish slavery, Lucas presented the history of Irish rebellion as a reflex response to a catalogue of English oppressions, citing John Davies's famous 1612 tract, *A Discovery of the True Causes Why Ireland was never Entirely Subdued*, as a prime resource for his argument. Within months Richard Cox, a Cork MP for Clonakilty and grandson of the author of *Hibernia Anglicana*, was assailing Lucas's claims in a series of outraged pamphlets dwelling on the folly of his antagonists' position. Reanimating the old bitterness about 1641 that Burke would in due course set about rebuking, Cox accused his opponent of "sporting with the grievous Persecutions and *Massacres* of your *Ancestors*, justifying the infernal Barbarities of their Irish Enemies and Murderers."[246] Using Temple's *Irish*

239 See Seán Murphy, "Charles Lucas and the Dublin Election of 1748–9," *Parliamentary History*, 2 (1983), pp. 93–111; Seán Murphy, "The Corporation of Dublin, 166041760," *Dublin Historical Record*, 38:1 (December 1984), pp. 22–35.

240 R. B. McDowell, *Irish Public Opinion, 1750–1800* (London: Faber and Faber, 1944), pp. 11, 17.

241 Early biographers placed Burke in the anti-Lucas camp: see Bisset, *Burke* (1800), I, p. 28; Prior, *Life of Burke*, p. 31. Modern scholars have been divided on the issue: see Samuels, *Early Life*, pp. 180–202; Gaetano L. Vincitorio, "Edmund Burke and Charles Lucas," *Publications of the Modern Languages Association*, 68 (1953), pp. 1047–55; Seán Murphy, "Burke and Lucas: An Authorship Problem Re-examined," *Eighteenth-Century Ireland*, 1 (1986), pp. 143–56.

242 For consideration of Kearney's evidence, see Lock, *Burke*, I, pp. 60–61.

243 EB to Charles O'Hara, 3 July 1761, *Corr.*, I, p. 139.

244 These were all reprinted in *The Political Constitutions of Great-Britain and Ireland, Asserted and Vindicated* (London: 1751), 2 vols.

245 Ibid., I, p. 117.

246 [Richard Cox], *The Cork Surgeon's Antidote against the Apothecary's Poyson, for the Citizens of Dublin*, no. 6 (Dublin: 1749), p. 4.

Rebellion as a counterweight to Lucas's pleas, Cox revived the memory of Ireland's implacable Catholic rebels—rekindling the dialectic of fear and domination that, as Burke would come to argue from the 1760s on, afflicted Irish politics through the eighteenth century.[247] The antipathies generated by the upheavals of the seventeenth century persisted in Ireland through Burke's lifetime, whereas in Britain by the 1760s they appeared to have been more successfully integrated into the structure of political competition. This difference presented a contrast that Burke would soon observe at first hand.

[247] Ibid., p. 6. Cox's arguments were challenged in [Anon.], *A Letter to the Citizens of Dublin* (Dublin: 1749), often ascribed to Burke. There are, however, no compelling grounds for the attribution.

PART II

Antinomianism and Enlightenment

Intellectual Formation, 1750–1765

OVERVIEW

In the mid 1760s Burke definitively opted to embark on a political career. Before that time he hesitated between the world of letters and public affairs. Although he trained for the legal profession in the early 1750s, he soon registered his ambition to succeed in the field of writing. His literary exploits were conspicuously diverse, covering social commentary, philosophy and history. This resulted in a curious range of publications clustered around the middle of the decade: a satire on the political and religious ideas of Bolingbroke, the *Vindication of Natural Society*, in 1756; an anatomy of aesthetic sensibility, the *Philosophical Enquiry into the Origin of our Ideas of the Sublime and Beautiful*, in 1757; a jointly authored work on Europe's trans-Atlantic colonies, the *Account of the European Settlements in America*, in the same year; and an uncompleted narrative of the national past down to Magna Carta, the *Essay towards an Abridgement of English History*, that was initiated in 1757 but was still being revised in 1762. From 1758, Burke supplemented this activity by compiling *The Annual Register*, an overview of the year in politics and the arts. Then, in 1759, he accepted the post of assistant to William Gerard Hamilton. His literary output suffered under the pressures of the engagement and he decided to break with his patron at the start of 1765. When he accepted the role of secretary to the Marquis of Rockingham that same year, he resolved to channel his talents into the service of public business. Altogether, for fifteen years after his arrival in London, Burke's focus was fragmentary and indeterminate. Nonetheless, it was in this period that he laid down the foundations of his learning, evolved his characteristic intellectual positions, and immersed himself in enlightenment philosophical history.

Unlike Hume, Burke was not a precocious philosophical genius. Equally, he was not a diligent scholar like Immanuel Kant, who devoted a life to refining the underpinnings of his own thought. Instead, he was a man of brilliance whose gifts were realised in the cut and thrust of affairs. His literary skill was effortless, and his mental energy vast. That energy supplied him with an impressive stock of knowledge. But it was the application and adaptation of learning in the face of pressing events that stimulated Burke's peculiar genius as an analyst and commentator. He navigated a course through philosophy and history in his twenties and thirties and then allowed his knowledge to mature under the impact of great affairs of state. This process made him one of the outstanding political thinkers of the age, as well as one of its most powerful advocates. The sources of this achievement lay in the 1750s when he worked out the content of his basic ideas on a range of metaphysical and political themes: on the role of providence, the progress of society, the nature of the passions, the perils of reason, the operation of prejudice, the rights of conquest, and the politics of assimilation. Burke's deepest insights were a product of his career in parliament, yet many of the materials out of which he constructed them were gathered over the course of the previous decade. It was also at this time that he committed himself to fundamental positions that he would develop more fully as his public life progressed.

The character of Burke's thought has long been mischaracterised as conceived in opposition to the tendencies of the era. Three generations ago, Alfred Cobban depicted his values as in "revolt" against the eighteenth century insofar as he sought to privilege convention over contract and to subordinate the individual to the community.[1] The germ of this idea was contained in Novalis's remark over a century earlier that Burke's *Reflections* should be seen as a "revolutionary" book directed against the principles of the French Revolution.[2] This kind of response represented Burke as a "romantic" throwback, antipathetic to the prevalence of utilitarian values in society and to the impact of enlightenment on intellectual life.[3] This misconception was ironically a product of Burke's own rhetoric. Beginning in the 1790s, he vociferously denounced the "enlightened" ideals of the Revolution.[4] His intention was to ridicule the presumptuousness of natural reason and the pretensions of moral philosophies based on hostility to organised religion. In his own mind this amounted to a defence of true enlightenment founded on the goal of improved mental and moral attitudes under the influence of piety, prosperity and security. Subsequent historiography confused this picture by misconstruing Burke's antipathy to dogmatic irreligion as belated opposition to secular progress and material improvement. On

[1] Alfred Cobban, *Edmund Burke and the Revolt against the Eighteenth Century: A Study of the Political and Social Thinking of Burke, Wordsworth, Coleridge and Southey* (1929) (London: George Allen & Unwin, 1960).

[2] Novalis, *Blütenstaub* in *Werke,* ed. Gerhard Schulz (Munich: Beck, 1969), p. 349: "Es sind viele antirevolutionäre Bücher für die Revolution geschrieben worden. Burke hat aber ein revolutionäres Buch gegen die Revolution geschrieben."

[3] Richard Bourke, "Burke, Enlightenment and Romanticism" in David Dwan and Christopher J. Insole eds., *The Cambridge Companion to Edmund Burke* (Cambridge: Cambridge University Press, 2012).

[4] Richard Bourke, "Theory and Practice: The Revolution in Political Judgement" in Richard Bourke and Raymond Geuss eds., *Political Judgement* (Cambridge: Cambridge University Press, 2009).

that basis, enlightenment was represented as a naturalistic "project" devoted to the betterment of humanity.[5]

Notwithstanding these claims, Burke saw himself as promoting enlightened ideals from within a sceptical Anglican tradition.[6] His values were "latitudinarian" to the extent that they promoted toleration while seeking to preserve the established articles of the Church of England.[7] He had no absolute commitment to the verities of ecclesiastical doctrine. Instead, he was conscious of the precariousness of human judgment along with the need for a national consensus in matters of religion. What drove him to develop his views on theology and church government was his hostility to what he regarded as fanatical infidelity. In formulating his approach, he followed in the footsteps of earlier attempts to reconcile the worlds of faith and reason. It was commonly argued that the misalliance between the two was responsible for the excesses of the seventeenth-century wars of religion.[8] These conflicts had shattered political order, blighted learning and retarded prosperity. Burke saw this retreat into darkness as having had two principal causes: on one side, the attempt to reduce all moral reasoning to the inspired truths of religion characteristic of puritan "enthusiasm"; and on the other, the superstitious project to subordinate individual judgment to the decrees of papal authority. Burke followed Locke in attributing modern dogmatism to the twin misfortunes of superstition and enthusiasm. Both tendencies gave the human mind pretensions beyond its capacity. Burke went further: eighteenth-century irreligion replicated the same tendency. The deist project to realise the "freedom of philosophy" nurtured an uncritical belief in the oracles of reason. With this certainty came contempt for the utility of social habit, and disregard for the natural moral sentiments of mankind.

Burke believed that deism, like superstition and enthusiasm, fostered antinomian convictions. They each promoted a disregard for moral responsibility along with the values of society at large. In the 1640s this disregard corrupted the national sensibility and helped intensify the radicalism of the civil wars. For Burke it was

[5] For Jonathan Israel in *Radical Enlightenment: Philosophy and the Making of Modernity, 1650–1750* (Oxford: Oxford University Press, 2001), the "project" is best conceived as a form of "radical" enlightenment; for John Robertson in *The Case for the Enlightenment: Scotland and Naples, 1680–1760* (Cambridge: Cambridge University Press, 2005), human betterment from a properly enlightened perspective was focused on improvement in "this world, without regard for the existence or non-existence of the next" (p. 8).

[6] Iain Hampsher-Monk, "Burke and the Religious Sources of Sceptical Conservatism" in J. van der Zande and R. H. Popkin eds., *The Skeptical Tradition around 1800* (Dordrecht: Kluwer, 1998).

[7] J.C.D. Clark, "The Enlightenment, Religion and Edmund Burke," *Studies in Burke and His Time*, 21 (2007), pp. 9–38. For problems with "latitudinarianism" as a distinct position within the Restoration Church, see John Spurr, "'Latitudinarianism' and the Restoration Church," *Historical Journal*, 31:1 (1988), pp. 61–82; Dmitri Levitin, *Ancient Wisdom in the Age of Science: Histories of Philosophy in England, 1640–1700* (Cambridge: Cambridge University Press, forthcoming).

[8] This is discussed in J.G.A. Pocock, "Clergy and Commerce: The Conservative Enlightenment in England" in *L'Età dei lumi: studi storici sul Settecento europeo in onore di Franco Venturi*, ed. Raffaele Ajello et al. (Naples: Jovene Editore, 1985), pp. 528–29, 532; cf. idem, *Barbarism and Religion V: Religion: The First Triumph* (Cambridge: Cambridge University Press, 2010), p. 16.

in this context that the spirit of conquest was reborn after centuries of social and political improvement. He investigated this spirit from various angles in the 1750s as he contemplated the significance of the Seven Years' War. The war confirmed the moderating effects of the balance of power on European conflict. It prompted Burke to reflect on past examples of the passage from brute domination to subjection based on consent. In was in this spirit that he collaborated on the *Account of the European Settlements in America,* in which the severity of Spanish authority in the new world was analysed. During the same period he examined the progress of liberty in the *Abridgement of English History*, detailing the forms of assimilation that accompanied the subjugation successively imposed by the Romans, the Saxons and the Normans.

The chapters that follow in the second part of this book are largely concerned with Burke's various writings in the 1750s. While these do not form a convenient unity, they do register a preoccupation with overlapping themes. To begin with, Burke's admiration for the procedures of the common law encouraged his doubts about the effectiveness of natural reason. In this context he observed that, by comparison with pure reason, the kind of "artificial" reason employed in legal judgment built progressively on practical knowledge and experience. Like the civilised refinements of artificial society, it helped to promote the process of human improvement. Burke's early work continually returns to the conditions of improvement, leading him to explore the contribution made by the passions. In turn, his awareness of the motivating power of the passions made him conscious of the formation of "opinion" in society. Finally, Burke's sensitivity to the dependence of government upon opinion helped him understand the nature of the spirit of conquest and therefore grasp the relationship between pacification and assimilation.

II

NATURAL SOCIETY AND NATURAL RELIGION, 1750–1756

2.1 Introduction

Lady Montagu wrote to her friend Elizabeth Carter in 1759 about the merits of Burke's recent discussion of aesthetic experience in his *Philosophical Enquiry into the Origin of our Ideas of the Sublime and Beautiful.* Only "fools," she observed, "rush behind the altar at which wise men kneel and pay mysterious reverence."[1] The remark captures something of the attitude to mystery that Burke had arrived at by the middle of the 1750s. While the foolish might expect that they could penetrate metaphysical secrets, the wise were struck with awe in contemplating the operations of the universe. Burke settled on this perspective after an extensive study of theology. In the process he had grown sceptical about the powers of pure reason. This did not imply a rejection of the utility of rational inquiry. It meant instead that Burke accepted the limitations on human knowledge as had been emphasised in Locke's *Essay concerning Human Understanding.* Before developing his conception of the limits of natural reason, Burke had come to privilege the achievements of artificial reason. He acquired this preference during the course of his legal studies. The classic texts elucidating the wisdom of the common law had underlined the value of practical legal reasoning. From the vantage point of this tradition, lawyers did not proceed on the basis of abstract legal norms but rather argued "artificially" on the basis of experience. Legal judgment was improved through a process of empirical refinement by which the lawyer sought to ascertain the implications of precedent. The process was apt to generate suspicion of "natural" reason in favour of accumulated practical intelligence.

As this chapter shows, within five years of his arrival in London, Burke was extending his ideas about the limits of pure reason to contemporary debates about the mysteries of the creation and revelation. He first ventured along this path in a series

[1] *The Letters of Mrs. Elizabeth Montagu, with Some Letters of Her Correspondents* (London: 1809–13), 4 vols., IV, p. 211.

of essays that he wrote in the early 1750s on a clutch of intricately related themes: on the relationship between intellectual and ethical improvement, the foundation of morals and the truth of miracles. A number of fragmentary writings, including "Several Scattered Hints Concerning Philosophy and Learning" and "Religion of No Efficacy as a State Engine," present Burke's early attempts to grapple with the benighted legacies of cynicism and stoicism, the dangers of valorising speculation at the expense of established conventions, and the relationship between piety and the moral life. These efforts form the context for Burke's first major publication, *A Vindication of Natural Society*. The *Vindication* is less an exercise in political philosophy than a literary polemic concerned to expose the limits of deism. It is more interesting for the help it provides in recovering Burke's intellectual context than for the cogency of the analysis it supplies. Together with his early essays, it reveals the scale and depth of his suspicion of religious scepticism as publicised by men like John Toland, Anthony Collins, Matthew Tindal and Bolingbroke himself. It allows us to glimpse his early debts to Tillotson, Stillingfleet and Berkeley, as well as his enduring sympathy with the epistemologies of Locke and Butler. Burke emerges as a figure keen to credit natural sentiment and convinced of the ongoing bearing of divine providence on human life. The immortality of the soul and promise of an afterlife were essential to his conception of providential theodicy. In defending their credibility he betrays his commitment to rational analogy as a means of glimpsing the mysterious moral order of the world.

2.2 Custom and Common Law

Burke arrived in London around May 1750 to study for the bar at Middle Temple. Little evidence survives to record his experience of the transition, although a letter from a friend in Ireland does relay his first impressions: "Your account of London, I believe, is very just. All great cities from Rome down are the sinks of vice, and the graves of genius."[2] At last setting foot in the great metropolis, Burke must have been struck by the contrast it afforded with Dublin, in terms of both its relative debauchery and its outstanding cultural achievements. Burke's father had laid plans for his son's career at the Irish bar while Edmund was still a student at Trinity College: he

[2]Michael Smith to EB in Charles Henry Wilson, *The Beauties of the Late Right Hon. Edmund Burke . . . To Which is Prefixed, A Sketch of the Life* (London: 1798), 2 vols., I, p. xiii. The letter is printed as a response to one alleged to have been written by Burke. Both are reprinted in Robert Bisset, *The Life of Edmund Burke* (London: 2nd ed., 1800), 2 vols., I, pp. 201–18. Parts of the letter to Smith appear again in James Prior, *Memoir of the Life of Edmund Burke* (London: 2nd ed., 1826), 2 vols., I, pp. 36–40, but these passages are now assumed to have been sent to one Matthew Smith. The full letters to and from the same Matthew Smith are reprinted once more in Arthur P. I. Samuels, *The Life, Correspondence and Writings of the Rt. Hon. Edmund Burke LL.D., with the Minute Book of the Debating "Club" Founded by him in Trinity College Dublin* (Cambridge: Cambridge University Press, 1923), pp. 219–24. Burke's letter to Smith is presented as either a forgery, a part forgery or an editorial compilation in *Corr.*, I, Appendix, pp. 357–59.

had been entered at the Temple on 23 April 1747 with a view to taking up residence after the completion of his undergraduate studies.[3] Training to be a barrister was a bid for upward mobility—an advance on his father's status as an attorney. Given that neither Trinity College nor the King's Inns in Dublin offered legal tuition, enrolment at an English Inn, with a view to keeping eight terms in commons, had been a formal requirement for those wishing to practise as barristers in Ireland since the middle of the sixteenth century.[4] Originally, attendance at an Inn of Court in London was intended as a means of purging the profession of residual Gaelic customs derived from the old brehon laws.[5] By the beginning of the seventeenth century, the administration of statute and common law had become a prime instrument of colonial and imperial consolidation. In the penal era, the Catholic interest was also served by convert lawyers who received an education at the London Inns, although more usually the bar operated as a bastion of the Protestant establishment in Ireland.[6] At a total cost of around £1,500, the expense of qualification deterred more modest families. Admission had obvious advantages, including the right of those permitted to practise in the courts to style themselves "esquire."[7] In the event of being called to the bar, Burke could look forward to a professional life among the privileged ranks of the 200 barristers who operated in the Four Courts of Dublin; but, in the process, he would be abandoning his literary ambitions.

By the 1750s, more than one-third of the students enrolled at the Middle Temple came from Ireland, many of them moving in specifically Irish circles, and congregating at the Grecian coffee-house in Devereux Court off Fleet Street.[8] Some, like the Irish politician John Philpot Curran in the generation after Burke, fraternised on the margins of the fashionable literary world.[9] However, the details of Burke's own milieu have been more or less lost to history. In 1730, parliament decreed that appearance at commons for a minimum of twice each week for two weeks in every term

[3]Details of Burke's admission, including his bondsmen, are preserved at OSB MS. File 2229. Burke's father's psychological investment in his son's education is made evident in EB to Richard Burke (father), 11 March 1755, *Corr.*, I, p. 120.

[4]Colum Kenny, *King's Inns and the Kingdom of Ireland* (Dublin: Irish Academic Press, 1992).

[5]T. C. Barnard, "Lawyers and the Law in Later Seventeenth-Century Ireland," *Irish Historical Studies*, 28:111 (May 1993), pp. 256–82, p. 259.

[6]John Bergin, 'The Catholic Interest at the London Inns of Court, 1674–1800," *Eighteenth-Century Ireland*, 24 (2009), pp. 37–62. On Burke in connection with Irish convert lawyers, see Ian McBride, "Burke and Ireland" in David Dwan and Christopher J. Insole eds., *The Cambridge Companion to Edmund Burke* (Cambridge: Cambridge University Press, 2012), pp. 187ff.

[7]Toby Barnard, *A New Anatomy of Ireland: The Irish Protestants, 1649–1770* (New Haven, CT: Yale University Press, 2003), pp. 116–22. For Burke's own estimate of the cost of his education at the Middle Temple (at around £1,000), see Burke, *Corr.*, I, p. 274.

[8]Wilfrid Prest, "The Unreformed Middle Temple" in Richard Harvey ed., *History of the Middle Temple* (Oxford: Hart Publishing, 2011); Robert Murray, *Edmund Burke: A Biography* (Oxford: Oxford University Press, 1931), pp. 62–63.

[9]William Henry Curran, *The Life of the Right Honourable John Philpot Curran* (London: 1819), 2 vols., I, p. 75.

was a prerequisite for eligibility to be called to the bar.[10] Consequently, in the period outside term at least, students were free to reduce their costs by taking up residence in the country. Accordingly, Burke passed his time in Monmouth in the summer of 1751, and in Wiltshire the following year.[11] In the interval between the two he visited Surrey and Bristol.[12] Much of this time was spent in the company of perhaps his closest friend, William Burke, who enrolled at the Middle Temple in the same month as Edmund, and whose father had been on friendly terms with Burke's own.[13] William Burke had been educated at Westminster School before matriculating at Christ Church, Oxford, in 1747. He was ultimately called to the bar in November 1755, but in the interim he became an intimate friend and collaborator of Burke.[14] He was quick-witted and daring, ambitious yet distracted. In a character sketch that Burke drew of him during their early years together, he is presented as a figure more passionate than dependable—as a man of delicate taste, but lacking in diligence and judgment.[15] Nonetheless, he was a person to whom Burke could confide his aspirations and disappointments.

In a verse epistle sent to William in November 1750, Burke informed him of his tendency to neglect his legal studies while succumbing to the charms of poetic composition: "E'en I while arming for the wordy war / Neglect the spoils and trophies of the Bar."[16] Yet within a year, Burke wrote to Shackleton indicating that his work was proceeding satisfactorily—"my health is tolerable, thank God, my studies too."[17] Soon he was confirming his determination to make the most of his vocation. Over a year after the birth of Shackleton's first child, he used the occasion to reflect on his own achievements to date, dwelling in particular on his lack of poetic accomplishment: "I am no father nor ever was except of some metaphorical Children which were extremely shortlived and whilst they lived (as you know) too scandalous to be [owne]d." Admitting his past failures, he turned to his prospects for the future: "I hope my present [stu]dies may be attended [with more] Success, at least I have this comfort that tho a middling Poet cannot be endured there is some quarter for a mid-

[10] Prest, "The Unreformed Middle Temple."

[11] EB to Richard Shackleton, 31 August 1751, *Corr.*, I, p. 111; EB to Richard Shackleton, 28 September 1752, ibid., p. 112.

[12] Ibid., pp. 112–14.

[13] EB to Philip Francis, 9 June 1777, *Corr.*, III, p. 348, describes William Burke as "a friend, whom I have tenderly loved, highly valued, and continually lived with, in an union not to be expressed, quite since our boyish days."

[14] Joseph Welch ed., *Alumni Westmonasterienses* (London: 1852), p. 341; H.A.C. Sturgess ed., *Register of Admissions to the Honourable Society of the Middle Temple, from the Fifteenth Century to the Year 1944* (London: Butterworth and Co., 1949), 3 vols., I, p. 342; Dixon Wecter, *Edmund Burke and His Kinsmen* (Boulder, CO: University of Colorado Press, 1939), pp. 76–78.

[15] EB, "Phidippus" in *A Notebook of Edmund Burke, ed.* H.V.F. Somerset (Cambridge: Cambridge University Press, 1957), pp. 57–59.

[16] EB, "The Muse Divorced," *Corr.*, I, p. 105.

[17] EB to Richard Shackleton, 5 April 1751, ibid., p. 110.

dling Lawyer."[18] However, this newfound application never quite paid off. Burke was a voracious reader, but he could not enjoy his legal exercises—"I read as much as I can," he confided to Shackleton, "which is however very little."[19] The course of study proved difficult to master. After a year at the Temple, he was "just beginning to know something of what I am about, which till very lately I did not."[20] The problem was getting to know what it was he was supposed to know, since tuition was unstructured and haphazard.

Studious application notoriously eluded candidates for the bar in the eighteenth century, many of whom became sidetracked into dissolute entertainments, as illustrated by Henry Fielding in his comic drama, *The Temple Beau*.[21] The system of legal education that had prevailed in England down to the period of the civil wars began to disintegrate during the interregnum. In practice, after the Glorious Revolution, the Inns of Court played no significant role in training their students: formal lectures ceased before 1688, and aural exercises became something of a formality. Novices attended court, and participated in moots, but they largely relied on studying in private.[22] Occupying the four Inns of Court, located in the city's inner western suburbs, and populated by chapels, halls of residence and professional chambers, students could also benefit from collaborative study. But for the most part they resorted to uninspiring textbooks.[23] The expectation was that the sons of the nobility and gentry at the Inns not only would acquire sufficient legal learning "to serve their king and country," as Charles Worsley put it around 1730, but would also receive a liberal education in the process.[24] However, as Blackstone made clear in his *Discourse on the Study of the Law* of 1758, the expectation had been widely disappointed. Seduced by the "amusements" in the vicinity of Temple, and easily lost in the puzzles of English common law, "miscarriages" were a regular occurrence among aspirants to the bar. Not only was a methodical digest of the legal system badly needed, but a theoretical grasp of "first principles" was also necessary as a guide to practical conduct: "If practice be the whole he is taught, practice must also be the whole he will ever know," confining the budding legal intelligence to a menial maze of technical rules, unsuited to a cultivated gentleman.[25] In a review of Blackstone's *Discourse* in

[18] EB to Richard Shackleton, 31 August, ibid., p. 111.

[19] Ibid.

[20] Ibid.

[21] Henry Fielding, *The Temple Beau: A Comedy* (Dublin: 1730).

[22] David Lemmings, *Gentlemen and Barristers: The Inns of Court and the English Bar, 1680–1730* (Oxford: Clarendon Press, 1990), pp. 75–92.

[23] Wilfrid Prest, *William Blackstone: Law and Letters in the Eighteenth Century* (Oxford: Oxford University Press, 2008), pp. 63–68.

[24] Arthur Robert Ingpen ed., *Master Worsley's Book on the History and Constitution of the Honourable Society of the Middle Temple* (London: Chatto and Windus, 1919), pp. 117–18.

[25] William Blackstone, *An Analysis of the Laws of England, to which is Prefixed an Introductory Discourse on the Study of the Law* (Dublin: 1767), pp. l–liv. See also Paul Lucas, "Blackstone and the Reform of the Legal Profession," *English Historical Review*, 77:304 (July 1962), pp. 456–89; Michael Lobban, "Blackstone and the Science of Law," *Historical Journal*, 30:2 (June 1987), pp. 311–35; David Lieberman,

1759, *The Annual Register* noted its underlying ambition to be that of encouraging "persons of rank" back into the legal profession.[26]

Prior to the appearance of Blackstone's compendious *Commentaries on the Laws of England* in the mid to late 1760s, the standard study guides employed by students at the Inns of Court included Matthew Hale's overview of the legal system, *The Analysis of the Law*, and Henry Finch's *Nomotechnia*, which emphasised the prescriptive basis of the common law.[27] A standard place to start was also Thomas Wood's *An Institute of the Laws of England*, which provided an abstract of the law as it related to natural and civil "Persons," family and military matters, "Corporations," "Estates" and criminal law.[28] From such general surveys, students progressed to the first volume of Edward Coke's *Institutes*, the *Commentary upon Littleton*, and thence to the other *Institutes* and the *Reports*. Dudley Ryder left an account of his attempt to grapple with Coke's text in a diary entry for 18 February 1716: "Rose at 8. Read Coke all the morning. Was tired with one long case which I could not well comprehend. When that happens I am apt to think the law so difficult a study I shall never be able to do anything at it."[29] Between bouts of legal study, Ryder resorted to literature—reading "Boileau's reflections upon Longinus" and Madame Dacier on taste, annotating Cicero, perusing Tillotson and Chillingworth, and discussing the merits of Bishop Berkeley.[30] Burke's activities at Middle Temple seem to have closely resembled Ryder's, alternating between arduous attention to his textbooks and general reading in philosophy, theology and letters. However, in the end, his mind revolted from the narrow strictures of legal training. As Shackleton recalled, Burke "read the Law for a time with that intense Application which it necessarily requires, but he found that it would neither suit his habit of body or mind, to adopt that profession for a means of livelihood."[31]

Nonetheless, Burke retained from his study of the law a keen appreciation of legal reasoning as an antidote to the presumptuousness of purely "natural" reason.

"Blackstone's Science of Legislation," *Journal of British Studies*, 27:2 (April 1988), pp. 117–49. See further the review of Blackstone's *Discourse* in the *Monthly Review*, 19 (November 1758), pp. 486ff. Cf. Roger North's posthumously published *A Discourse on the Study of the Laws* (London: 1824), p. 1, and see also Lois Green Schwoerer, "Roger North and His Notes on Legal Education," *Huntington Library Quarterly*, 22:4 (August 1959), pp. 323–43.

[26] *The Annual Register for the Year 1758* (London: 1759), p. 452.

[27] Matthew Hale, *The Analysis of the Law: Being a Scheme or Abstract, of the Several Titles and Partitions of the Law of England, Digested into Method* (London: 1713); Henry Finch, *Nomotechnia; cestascavoir, Vn description del common leys dangleterre solonque les rules del arte Paralleles ove les prerogatives le Roy* (London: 1613). The *Nomotechnia* was translated as Henry Finch, *Law, or a Discourse Thereof, in Four Books* (London: 1661, 1759), and again, more professionally, as *A Description of the Common Laws of England* (London: 1759).

[28] Thomas Wood, *An Institute of the Laws of England, or the Laws of England in their Natural Order, according to Common Use* (London: 1720), 2 vols.

[29] William Matthews ed., *The Diary of Dudley Ryder, 1715–1716* (London: Methuen and Co., 1939), p. 184.

[30] Ibid., pp. 31, 65, 219.

[31] [Richard Shackleton], "Biographical Sketch of Edmund Burke" [1766], OSB MSS. File 2225.

In the spirit of Coke, Finch had depicted the common law as a species of "refined Reason" which, by a process of maturation, achieved the status of "Wisdom." In this he claimed to be following the argument of Plato's *Laws*, which assumed that the "common law of the city" (*tês poleôs koinon nomon*) reflected the reasoning faculty itself: "Common Law," as Finch put it, "is no other than Reason."[32] The question Finch next posed was what kind of reason this was, and his clear answer was that it could not be mere native reason, but should instead be understood as having grown "perfect" through cultivation. This characterisation is a conscious reference to Cicero's discussion of the rationality of law in his account of the origins of justice in *De legibus*. The Latin term "perfecta" is a variant reading of "confecta" as employed by Cicero in his depiction of legal reasoning as distinct from spontaneous ratiocination in being "confirmata et confecta" (fixed and developed) by the human mind.[33] In the first part of his *Institutes*, Coke presented a fuller description of developed "legall reason" as "an artificiall perfection of reason." No one is born a craftsman or "artificer" (artifex), Coke contended, and so the artificial excellence of legal intelligence could only be acquired by "long study, observation, and experience, and not of every mans [*sic*] natural reason."[34] Artificial reason, as Burke would learn to appreciate, was contextual, incremental, evolving and empirical.[35]

Coke's reason proceeded by "trial" and experience, but at the same time it strove for systematic comprehension.[36] In the Preface to the third part of his *Reports*, the mind of the judge is presumed to survey a vast "unitie." Just as in nature there exists a uniformity amidst teeming variety, so in law coherence can be discerned among myriad component parts. This overarching unity is seen as providential in nature: "Lex orta est cum mente divina" (law arose by divine intelligence), as Coke concluded.[37] However, the rationality of the law could not be ascertained by the isolated intellect alone. Insight required discipline in the form of application and

[32] Finch, *Description of the Common Laws of England*, p. 52, discussing Plato, *Laws*, 645a.

[33] Cicero, *De legibus*, I, vi, 18–19. "Perfecta" was last authoritatively given in J. Vahlen's Berlin edition of 1870.

[34] Edward Coke, *The First Part of the Institutes of the Laws of England. Or, A Commentary upon Littleton* (London: 1684), bk. II, ch. 6, sect. 138. On artificial reason, see J. U. Lewis, "Sir Edward Coke (1552–1633): His Theory of 'Artificial Reason' as a Context for Modern Basic Legal Theory," *Law Quarterly Review*, 84 (July 1968), pp. 330–42, and Charles Gray, "Reason, Authority and Imagination: The Jurisprudence of Sir Edward Coke" in Perez Zagorin ed., *Culture and Politics from Puritanism to the Enlightenment* (Berkeley, CA: University of California Press, 1980). For further analysis, see J. P. Sommerville, *Politics and Ideology in England, 1603–1640* (London: Longman, 1986); for the wider intellectual context, see Glenn Burgess, *The Politics of the Ancient Constitution: An Introduction to English Political Thought, 1603–1642* (London: Macmillan, 1992), ch. 2; for the political context, see Alan Cromartie, *The Constitutionalist Revolution: An Essay on the History of England, 1450–1642* (Cambridge: Cambridge University Press, 2006), ch. 7.

[35] On this, see J.G.A Pocock, "Burke and the Ancient Constitution: A Problem in the History of Ideas" (1960) in idem, *Politics, Language, and Time: Essays on Political Thought and History* (Chicago, IL: University of Chicago Press, 1971, 1989). Also, see below, chapter 13, section 3.

[36] Edward Coke, *The Twelfth Reports* in *The Reports of Sir Edward Coke*, ed. J. H. Thomas and J. F. Fraser (London: 1826), 7 vols., VI, p. 282.

[37] Coke, *Third Reports* in ibid., II, p. iv.

learning. The common law itself was a product of accumulated discipline, which entitled it to be considered "the perfection of reason": it had been "fined and refined" through a succession of ages at the hands of "an infinite number of grave and learned men."[38] While the individual mind was inevitably lacking, the accumulated deliberation of generations was wise. Since legal reasoning entailed constant exposure to this reality, it fostered diligence and humility in the process.

In the prefatory dedication to his *Report* on Irish cases, John Davies denominated the cumulative wisdom represented by the common law by the term "custome." National customs were seen as "full of Reason" to the extent that they catered to public utility as demonstrated by their continuation "time out of minde" and their ongoing acceptance and practicality. Unlike the Greeks and the Romans, the English had had no lawgiver; instead, their laws were connatural with the population and were reaffirmed experimentally on the basis of proven convenience. This argument implied that English legal custom constituted an uninterrupted tradition, and that therefore the Norman Conquest had involved a confirmation of the common law rather than the imposition of foreign customs: the forms of judicial proceeding may have changed, Davies accepts, but the traditional legal substance persisted.[39] In other words, although William the Conqueror had introduced the "marks" of conquest in support of his own dignity, he in fact subjected and conformed himself to the ancient constitution.[40] In the Preface to his third *Reports,* Coke had traced this claim to John Fortescue's *De laudibus legum Angliae*, dubbing the Norman Conquest a restoration rather than a revolution.[41] Coke combined this idea of the immemorial character of the common law with a radical commitment to its changelessness. While Burke would in due course distance himself from the extremity of this position, he adapted aspects of the thesis to suit his purposes.

First of all, later in his career, Burke insisted that the English constitution should be treated as if it were an entailed inheritance whose antiquity was an argument against wanton innovation. Next, he came to recognise that the loss of a national memory of conquest was an index of popular political consent. Finally, he grew committed to the notion that the rationality of a legal system transcended the abstract grasp of an individual's natural reason. Whereas the process of legal

[38] Coke, *First Institutes*, bk. II, ch. 6, sect. 138.

[39] John Davies, *Le Primer Report des Cases and Matters en ley Resolues and Adiudges en les Courts del Roy en Ireland* (Dublin: 1615), Preface, n.p.

[40] For this theme in the history of seventeenth-century political thought and historiography, see J.G.A. Pocock, *The Ancient Constitution and the Feudal Law: A Study of English Historical Thought in the Seventeenth Century* (Cambridge: Cambridge University Press, 1957, 1987); and J. P. Sommerville, "History and Theory: The Norman Conquest in Early Stuart Political Thought," *Political Studies*, 34 (1986), pp. 249–61. For a discussion of its legacy, see Quentin Skinner, "History and Ideology in the English Revolution" in idem, *Visions of Politics III: Hobbes and Civil Science* (Cambridge: Cambridge University Press, 2002), esp. pp. 262–63; and Harold J. Berman, "The Origins of Historical Jurisprudence: Coke, Selden, Hale," *Yale Law Journal*, 103 (May 1994), pp. 1651–1738, esp. pp. 1731–38.

[41] Coke, *Third Reports* in *Reports of Edward Coke*, II, pp. xxi–xxii.

argument implicitly acknowledged the surpassing complexity of the constitution, untutored reason was prone to self-inflation. The artificial intellectual capacity of the lawyer had to be cultivated, like prudence, as a learned craft. This capacity functioned in a context of respect for the medium in which it was put to work, and was therefore "presumptive" rather than presumptuous: practical intelligence of the kind trusted in the protocols of the field in which it operated rather than in the powers of the mind. Judicial judgment began by presuming the reasonableness of the law as a standard by which to assess particular cases. The lawyer did not evaluate individual actions in the light of an abstract norm of reason but instead specified their character by resort to analogy and comparison in order to subsume them under the provisions of the common law.

Matthew Hale had defended this species of "presumption" in favour of the rationality of the common law in his "Reflections" on Hobbes's *Dialogue between a Philosopher and a Student of the Common Laws of England*. The discovery of this rationality in the process of judicial decision-making depended less on a native facility for mathematical reasoning than on the acquired aptitude of "wise and knowing men."[42] The wisdom in question depended on the possession of a sufficiently wide "prospect" of the range of exigencies to which the law was intended to cater, together with an educated grasp of the collateral implications of each legal remedy. Since this process of consequential reasoning presupposed the rationality of the law, it appeared to Hale to be a "foolish and unreasonable thing for any to find fault w[i]th an Institution because he thinks he could have made a better."[43] It followed from this that, whereas speculative reason was prone to disregard the utility of established practices, trained intelligence was disposed to optimise the convenience of existing arrangements. Although Burke is unlikely to have encountered Hale's "Reflections" in manuscript, he knew his *History and Analysis of the Common Law* extremely well, and would have recognised its indebtedness to Coke's ideal of "artificial reason." As Burke developed these ideas, he began to conclude that natural reason, abstracted from the kind of practical context to which the educated intellect of the professional lawyer was committed, was liable to become intoxicated by its self-regarding subtlety. As he observed in a series of scattered "Political Observations" composed in the early 1750s, subtleties of the kind "are like Spirits drawn from Liquors": in being liberated from their sobering medium they "disorder the Brain."[44]

[42] Matthew Hale, "Reflections by the Lrd. Cheife Justice Hale on Mr. Hobbes His Dialogue of the Law" in William Holdsworth, *A History of English Law* (London: Methuen, 1956–72), 17 vols., V, pp. 504–5. For discussion, see D.E.C. Yale, "Hale and Hobbes on Law, Legislation and the Sovereign," *Cambridge Law Journal*, 3 (1972), pp. 121–56; Gerald J. Postema, *Bentham and the Common Law Tradition* (Oxford: Oxford University Press, 1986), pp. 61–80; and Alan Cromartie, *Sir Matthew Hale, 1609–1676* (Cambridge: Cambridge University Press, 1995), pp. 100–104.

[43] Hale, "Reflections," pp. 502–4.

[44] EB, "Some Political Scattered Observations" in *A Notebook of Edmund Burke: Poems, Characters, Essays and Other Sketches in the Hands of Edmund and William Burke*, ed. H.V.F. Somerset (Cambridge: Cambridge University Press, 1957), p. 101.

2.3 Philosophy and Learning

This exact reference to spirits drawn "from Liquors" disordering the brain occurs again in one of the most substantial essays to have been written by Burke before the appearance of his first significant publication, the *Vindication of Natural Society*, on 18 May 1756.[45] Along with his diffuse "Political Observations," this essay appears in a series of Notebooks containing youthful writings by Edmund and William Burke and bears the working title "Several Scattered Hints Concerning Philosophy and Learning."[46] The essay cannot be definitively dated, but it most likely belongs to the period around 1755. It brings together Burke's respect for artificial reason with his commitment to civilisation and his suspicion of dogmatism. Its main purpose is to justify a particular approach to enlightenment, vindicating the utility of knowledge as a means to virtue. The "End" of all knowledge, he wrote, should be "the bettering us in some manner."[47] Erudition for its own sake, on the other hand, defeats the purpose of intellectual inquiry: it becomes a badge of achievement or a route to "reputation," thereby undermining the vocation of philosophy proper. In catering to vanity, pure erudition betrays the mission of improvement and encourages what it ought really to correct. It increases self-regard, aggravates the passions, dogmatises opinion and reinforces vulgar prejudice. Erudition in itself, therefore, is an enemy of enlightenment unless it is employed practically in the service of society and religion. Knowledge involves the "Culture"—or cultivation—of the mind, but such refinement merely contributes to a display of ostentation unless it is harnessed to the advancement of piety and virtue.[48] The extremes of scepticism and rationalism were equally incompatible with enlightenment in Burke's view—the former since it delighted in inquiry for its own sake, never settling on fixed principles that might act as a guide to action; the latter since it was contemptuous of intellectual labour, thus combining actual ignorance with "intolerable pride."[49] Mental conceit, or the pride of reason, had long been a target for the enemies of deism. In his 1731 attack on Matthew Tindal, the nonjuring polemicist William Law alleged that the pretensions of reason often amounted to covert expressions of vanity.[50] Burke agreed that common sense in philosophy, like artificial reason in law, was habitually immune to its seductions.

[45] William B. Todd, *A Bibliography of Edmund Burke* (Godalming: St. Paul's Bibliographies, 1982), p. 26.

[46] EB, "Several Scattered Hints Concerning Philosophy and Learning Collected Here from My Papers" (c. 1755) in *Notebook*, p. 90. This printed work is one of a number of notebooks kept by William Burke and preserved among the Wentworth Woodhouse Muniments at the Sheffield Archives at WWM BkP 40–47. For discussion of the notebooks, see Richard Bourke, "Party, Parliament and Conquest in Newly Ascribed Burke Manuscripts," *Historical Journal*, 55:3 (September 2012), pp. 619–52.

[47] EB, "Philosophy and Learning," p. 85.

[48] Ibid., pp. 82–83.

[49] Ibid., p. 83.

[50] William Law, *The Case of Reason, or Natural Reason, Fairly and Fully Stated* (London: 1731).

In 1751 Jean-Jacques Rousseau had notoriously provoked the European defenders of the progress of modern knowledge by associating enlightenment with the decadence of morals.[51] "Philosophy and Learning" was likewise an attempt to reintegrate the arts and sciences with virtue, but without subjecting civilisation to thoroughgoing criticism.[52] In a review of Rousseau's *Letter to d'Alembert on the Theatre* that appeared in *The Annual Register* in 1760, the reviewer—probably Burke—refers to the *First Discourse* as a "satire upon learning" that gratuitously unsettles our dependable preconceptions.[53] Nonetheless, Burke's own analysis is not altogether lacking in critical import insofar as it focuses on the deleterious effects of unbridled pride on the mental attitudes of scholars and philosophers. As wide reading and extensive social intercourse appeared to Burke to be the most effective antidotes against pride, so narrow, mechanical learning was taken to be a means of reinforcing it. Menial education of the kind allegedly prevents an appreciation of the underlying principles of science, losing itself instead in the "littleness" of detail, contracting rather than liberalising intelligence. An open and liberal mind depended on a wide appreciation of the diversity of opinions and behaviour rather than a pinched or "confined" insistence on a limited array of "positive" tenets. This liberality is cultivated by exposure to "all the variety of Arts and Sciences, in the stories, opinions, Customs, manners, achievements of all ages and all nations." Such exposure fostered toleration and sociability, and generally enlightened attitudes without compromising values. As a result, it wore away the "little prejudices of little parties" that inflame animosity and generate conflict. A broad historical perspective on the multiplicity of beliefs humbles the pretensions of the community of the learned and defuses enlightened diffidence amongst them. Diffidence of the kind is not timidity, but caution: it promoted moral commitments that were neither vertiginously sceptical nor arrogantly presumptuous. It acted as a bulwark against mental *amour-propre*.[54]

Narrow scholarly application, then, encouraged dogmatism rooted in pride. What Burke cherished was the development of a "*versatile ingenium*" that could

[51] Jean-Jacques Rousseau, *Discourse on the Arts and Sciences (First Discourse) and Polemics*, ed. Roger D. Masters and Christopher Kelly (Hanover, NE: University Press of New England, 1992).

[52] Burke's complex relationship to Rousseau has been the subject of much unlikely speculation, including by C. E. Vaughan, *Studies in the History of Political Philosophy before and after Rousseau* (Manchester: Manchester University Press, 1925); Annie Marion Osborn, *Rousseau and Burke: A Study of the Idea of Liberty in Eighteenth-Century Political Thought* (Oxford: Oxford University Press, 1940); Alfred Cobban, *Rousseau and the Modern State* (London: George Allen & Unwin, 1954, 1964); David Cameron, *The Social Thought of Rousseau and Burke* (London: Weidenfeld and Nicolson, 1973); Mario Einaudi, "Burke on Rousseau," *Review of Politics*, 12:2 (April 1950), pp. 271–72. There is an important discussion in Ian Harris, "Religion and Social Order: The Case of Burke and Paine" in Michael Bentley ed., *Public and Private Doctrine: Essays in British History Presented to Maurice Cowling* (Cambridge: Cambridge University Press, 2002).

[53] *The Annual Register for the Year 1759* (London: 1760), p. 479. The review was addressed to the recent translation of Jean-Jacques Rousseau, *A Letter from M. Rousseau, of Geneva, to M. D'Alembert, of Paris, Concerning the Effects of Theatrical Entertainments on the Manners of Mankind* (London: 1759). On Burke's contributions to *The Annual Register*, see below, chapter 4, section 6.

[54] EB, "Philosophy and Learning," pp. 85–86.

range across various experiences and subject matter. Above all, he expected that the intellect would immerse itself in "business" instead of losing itself in the unworldliness of the *vita contemplativa:* "Man is made for Speculation and action; and when he pursues his nature he succeeds best in both."[55] However, this emphasis on the practicalities of *negotium* as a means of underwriting the usefulness of the arts and sciences was not intended to diminish the importance of the objects of taste in assisting in the improvement of society. The ornamental arts were not "practical" on the model of the applied sciences; their object was to polish our appreciation of the beautiful rather than to serve a more immediately utilitarian purpose. Nonetheless, they retained utility as an unintended by-product of their beauty to the extent that they improved our manners while they educated our taste. Aesthetic education implanted an "elegant disposition" in the process of refining sensibility: as Burke would later argue in his *Philosophical Enquiry into the Origin of our Ideas of the Sublime and Beautiful*, beauty supported virtue without being a source of moral worth.[56] The virtues, to be effective, had to be seductive. While moral precepts *in extremis* would have to be imposed upon the passions, they were best inculcated as "habits" which appealed to the imagination by virtue of their charm: "though rules, fear, interest, or other motives may induce us to virtue, it is the virtue of a bad soil, harsh and disagreeable."[57] But if the improvement of morals through the refinement of taste was preferable to normative coercion based on fear, it was also more effective than rational indoctrination.

Indoctrination by precept usually failed to impinge upon the motives to action, and so was received as an injunction but not heeded. Moreover, where moral injunctions were based exclusively on precepts of reason in this way, behaviour depended on a treacherous faculty for guidance. Burke believed that human error was most commonly an effect of the passions rather than a fault of reasoning, yet reason was often surreptitiously swayed by passion.[58] It habitually pretended to powers it did not possess, and was therefore prone to exult in its own capacity. In that sense it was perpetually in danger of being corrupted by the imagination whose "fancies" were easily mistaken for speculative truths. Imagination fed both superstition and enthusiasm, as illustrated by its role in Islamic and Methodist faith respectively. Methodism, for example, spuriously depended on the evidence of an inner "*light*" to gain purchase on the imagination where it could not convince the understanding.[59] Imagination was of course a staple feature of mental life and so ultimately integral to religion, but to avoid succumbing uncritically to the unaccountable claims of our fancy, the mind needed to learn to inhabit mystery and accept doubt.[60] For this,

[55] Ibid., p. 87.

[56] See below, chapter 3, section 5.

[57] EB, "Philosophy and Learning," pp. 87–88.

[58] Ibid., p. 88.

[59] Ibid., pp. 96–97. On the evangelical revival sparked by Methodism, see John Kent, *Wesley and the Wesleyans: Religion in Eighteenth-Century Britain* (Cambridge: Cambridge University Press, 2002).

[60] EB, "Philosophy and Learning," pp. 88–89, 92.

it was necessary to learn to live with uncertainty as compatible with firm conviction and steady resolution.[61] The maxim of unprejudiced inquiry—"Sapere aude"–enjoins boldness but not overconfidence in seeking out the reason of things, incrementally improving our understanding of effects without pretending to master the logic of final causes.[62] Straining after rational demonstration in the face of "dark and puzzling" appearances risked lapsing unawares into intellectual *hubris* with the result that pride induced the understanding to stray beyond its limits under the influence of an over-reaching imagination. At its most extreme, grandiosity of the kind was liable to grow destructive: in trusting excessively in its own presumed powers, reason grew contemptuous of established arrangements and conventions.[63]

As a result, it seemed wise to Burke to take our bearings from the existing state of things: "It is but reasonable that our general conduct should be a good deal modelled by the general Sense of the publick."[64] This meant that our beliefs and attitudes were best measured against common sense, which entailed crediting the reasonableness of customs. Burke's common law training is evident in this formulation, but his independence from many of its presuppositions is also apparent in what follows. While philosophical inquiry must begin with customs rather than ideals, custom should still be subject to rational criticism: "I would be its humble Servant but not its Slave."[65] Moreover, as Burke conceives it, custom is not limited to national traditions but has the character instead of *ius gentium*. "Custom," he wrote, "is to be regarded with great deference especially if it be an universal Custom." Universal custom, or the laws of peoples, arose by a process of experimental adaptation to suit convenience, and therefore possessed a "reasonableness" which abstract theory could never emulate. This did not disqualify the rational criticism of inherited practices, but it did mean that the reasoning faculty should remain appropriately phlegmatic in its approach when it strove to rationalise the utility of longstanding arrangements.[66] By comparison, "radical" or fundamental innovation implied contempt for the accumulated wisdom of experience, reducing properly rational inquiry into merely "splenetick" criticism.[67] Burke followed conventional wisdom in taking the doctrines of philosophical cynicism to have given expression to splenetic philosophy in its purest form, resulting in a pernicious assault on established institutions.[68]

[61] Ibid., p. 96.

[62] Ibid., pp. 92–95. On the application of this idea to the *Philosophical Enquiry*, see below, chapter 3, sections 3, 4 and 5. For the Newtonian sources of this commitment, see Henry Guerlac and M. C. Jacob, "Bentley, Newton, and Providence: The Boyle Lectures Once More," *Journal of the History of Ideas*, 30:3 (July–September 1969), pp. 307–18; P. M. Heimann, "Voluntarism and Immanence: Conceptions of Nature in Eighteenth-Century Thought," *Journal of the History of Ideas*, 39:2 (April–June 1978), pp. 271–83.

[63] EB, "Philosophy and Learning," p. 90.

[64] Ibid., p. 89.

[65] Ibid.

[66] See Burke's comment that reason functions best where it is "dephlegmatic" in ibid., p. 90.

[67] Ibid., pp. 90, 85.

[68] On this in connection with Burke's criticism of Rousseau, see below, chapter14, section 3.

There were two institutions in particular which Burke endeavoured to shield from this kind of remorseless attack in the 1750s—British constitutional liberty and the Anglican religion. The constitution had to be protected against the threat of corruption by the application of continuous critical vigilance; the Church of England had to be secured from deteriorating into dogmatism by maintaining a regime of toleration. Both edifices, in Burke's view, were endangered by the use of "pernicious" reason, or a cynical contempt for all established "forms and ceremonies."[69] Diogenes the Cynic appeared as the ideal-typical representative of pernicious criticism, disregarding the customs not just of the Greeks but of the wider world.[70] His philosophy was "shewy" yet had no "substance," Burke complained. As with the philosophy of the stoics, which he helped to inspire, Diogenes' combination of asceticism and cosmopolitanism set him at odds with the desires of human nature. His alleged indifference to his own burial as reported in Cicero's *Tusculan Disputations* is assumed to encapsulate his arrogance and scorn: " 'Without consciousness, what harm then could the mauling of wild beasts do me?' "[71] Burke responded with a defence of the practice of burial as exemplifying the wisdom of *ius gentium*: providence disposes us to provide for our own burial out of a concern for personal dignity, thus indirectly protecting society against infestation and disease that would inevitably accompany the spectacle of rotting flesh. At the same time, the ceremony nourishes "humanity" by catering to our sensitivities, throwing, as Burke put it, "a decent Veil" over our exposed condition. "What shall we say to that philosophy," he wondered rhetorically, "that would strip it naked?"[72]

From Burke's perspective, cynicism and stoicism were at war with human nature, trusting in austere reason at the expense of ordinary desires. A brief outline of the basic elements of stoic doctrine appeared in *The Gray's Inn Journal* in 1754. The journal was then edited by the Irish playwright Arthur Murphy, whom Burke had met through the Inns of Court in London about two years earlier. The article in question lays out the main ingredients of objections that Burke evidently would have accepted since they coincided with his own. Stoic philosophy, we are told, did not simply promote the "Suppression" of the passions but recommended that they be extirpated "totally from the human Heart." As a result of this drastic approach, feelings were made insensitive and attitudes rendered "callous," subverting the "Laws of Nature" which stoic reason was supposed to support.[73] This critique had been devel-

[69] EB, "Philosophy and Learning," p. 90.

[70] For the figure of Diogenes of Sinope in enlightenment thought, see Michael Sonenscher, *Sans-Culottes: An Eighteenth-Century Emblem in the French Revolution* (Princeton, NJ: Princeton University Press, 2008), esp. ch. 3.

[71] Cicero, *Tusculanae quaestiones*, I, 93.

[72] EB, "Philosophy and Learning," p. 91.

[73] *The Gray's Inn Journal*, 23 (2 March 1754), pp. 133–34. The article is anonymous and signed "N." The insensitivity of the stoic is implicit in David Hume, "The Stoic" (1742) in idem, *Essays Moral, Political, and Literary*, ed. Eugene F. Miller (Indianapolis, IN: Liberty Fund, 1985, 1987), and explicit, later on, in Elizabeth Carter, "Introduction" to *All the Works of Epictetus* (London: 1758). On Carter, see Christopher Brooke, *Philosophic Pride: Stoicism and Political Thought from Lipsius to Rousseau* (Princeton, NJ:

oped within Christian theology since the seventeenth century, attracting powerful proponents within the Anglican Communion. Méric Casaubon had argued in the Preface to his edition of the *Meditations* of Marcus Aurelius that of all the schools of the ancients it was the stoics who held opinions entirely "contrary to flesh and blood."[74] In this spirit, the Cambridge Platonist Henry More defended what he saw as the providential utility of the passions against ascetic ideals. Their adaptation to the purposes of the human frame was as evident as "the Structure of those Organs, which compose every animal body."[75] Robert South, a Church of England clergyman and Westminster schoolmate of John Locke, likewise chided the stoics for conflating sentiments with perturbations.[76] William Sherlock, a fellow Anglican with whom South would later become embroiled in controversy, similarly endorsed the spur that the passions provided to motivation.[77] Feelings, as George Stanhope put it in his edition of Epictetus, "are indeed the secret Springs that move and actuate us."[78] For his part, Burke believed that some modern adherents of sceptical rationalism had adopted the rigorous posture of the ancient stoic philosophers as a means of bolstering criticism of the institutions of religion and of indicting "artificial" society. In the *Vindication of Natural Society*, he ironically applied the deist critique of the "folly" of religion to the institutions of political society, "vindicating" natural appetites in the face of restraints imposed by government.[79] The aim was to condemn the pretensions of natural reason by exposing the absurdity of its conclusions. This was to be achieved by suggesting that the disaffected intellect could not convincingly dispense with the benefits of civilisation and religion. The outlines of this commitment to culture or "artifice" as providing the means of mental and moral improvement can be detected in "Philosophy and Learning."

Around the same period in which Burke was writing "Philosophy and Learning," he composed a fragment in which he presented one branch of our duties as active in nature, and based on the disposition to benevolence. This disposition expressed itself in the form of "Sympathy," which became a key concept in Burke's *Philosophical*

Princeton University Press, 2012), ch. 7. More generally, late seventeenth- and early eighteenth-century rebuttals of stoicism as a form of Spinozism, from Buddeus to Mosheim, tended to focus on the deism or atheism implicit in its physical theory. On this, see Christopher Brooke, "How the Stoics Became Atheists," *Historical Journal*, 49:2 (2006), pp. 387–402.

[74] Méric Casaubon, "A Discourse by Way of Preface" to *Marcus Aurelius Antoninus the Emperor, His Meditations* (London: 1673).

[75] Henry More, "Of the Passions in General, and of the Helps they Afford" in idem, *An Account of Virtue* (London: 1690), p. 34. Cf. James Lowde, *A Discourse Concerning the Nature of Man* (London: 1694), p. 24.

[76] Robert South, "Of the Creation of Man in the Image of God" in idem, *Sermons Preached upon Several Occasions* (London: 1737), 6 vols., I, p. 59.

[77] William Sherlock, "The Nature and Measure of Charity" in idem, *Sermons Preach'd upon Several Occasions* (London: 3rd ed., 1719), 2 vols., I, p. 215.

[78] George Stanhope, Preface to *Epictetus His Morals* (London: 1694).

[79] EB, *A Vindication of Natural Society: or, A View of the Miseries and Evils Arising to Mankind from Every Species of Artificial Society* (1756, 2nd ed. 1757), *W & S*, I, pp. 138–39.

Enquiry into the Original of Our Ideas of the Sublime and Beautiful.[80] Sympathetic feeling was quintessentially anti-stoic in nature.[81] For Anglican scholars like John Tillotson, this aptitude for fellow-feeling should be understood as a "natural affection" that was activated "precedent to all reason." The passion was particularly cultivated under the influence of the Christian faith, as evidenced by the ethic of charity towards enemies.[82] For Samuel Parker, charitable instincts were part of human design, leading him to the conclusion that cruelty and injustice were unnatural as well as unreasonable.[83] Richard Steele urged the same conclusion in the pages of *The Christian Hero*.[84] Human benevolence was in effect a "merciful" affection, as John Tottie put the case in a sermon delivered in 1750. It pointed to a principle of "Sympathy" or "Fellow-Feeling" activated by the distresses of human beings.[85] This principle was contrasted to the notion of moral "fitness" and the idea of the "beauty of virtue."[86] It was Anthony Ashley Cooper, the Third Earl of Shaftesbury, who was identified as conflating the beautiful and the moral. For Tottie, the appreciation of beauty only provided an "intellectual" motive to virtue, and was incapable of truly stirring the soul.[87] The Cambridge divine Thomas Rutherforth similarly upheld the pursuit of happiness against the pleas of "the disinterested Stoic."[88] Reason could only guide behaviour if it was supported by incentives that appealed to the expectations of human beings. It was Bishop Berkeley who had explained how Shaftesbury's aesthetic "sense" of morals could seem both unworldly and irreligious at the same time. The stoic disdain for passion associated virtue with disinterestedness, disconnecting moral action from the promise of reward. From this perspective, the ends of society could be achieved without the incentives of religion. As Berkeley saw it,

[80] EB, "Religion" in *Notebook*, p. 70.

[81] For discussion, see R. S. Crane, "Suggestions towards a Genealogy of the 'Man of Feeling'" in idem, *The Idea of the Humanities and Other Essays Critical and Historical* (Chicago, IL: University of Chicago Press, 1967), 2 vols., I. See also Norman Fiering, "Irresistible Compassion: An Aspect of Eighteenth-Century Sympathy and Humanitarianism," *Journal of the History of Ideas*, 37:2 (April–June 1976), pp. 195–218; *Jonathan Edwards' Moral thought and Its British Context* (Chapel Hill, NC: University of North Carolina Press, 1981).

[82] John Tillotson, Sermons 33 and 20 in *The Works of the Most Reverent Dr. John Tillotson* (London: 1728), 3 vols., I, pp. 298–99, 170. Cf. Hugo Grotius, *The Truth of the Christian Religion* (1627), ed. Maria Rosa Antognazza (Indianapolis, IN: Liberty Fund, 2012), pp. 116–19.

[83] Samuel Parker, *A Demonstration of the Divine Authority of the Law of Nature and of the Christian Religion* (London: 1681), p. 50.

[84] Richard Steele, *The Christian Hero* (London: 1790), pp. 80–81.

[85] John Tottie, *Sympathizing Affection: A Principle of Nature, Enforced by Reason and Religion* (London: 1751), pp. 2–4. Cf. David Fordyce, *The Elements of Moral Philosophy* (London: 1754), pp. 63–64.

[86] Tottie, *Sympathizing Affection*, pp. 22–23.

[87] Ibid.

[88] Thomas Rutherforth, *An Essay on the Nature and Obligations of Virtue* (Cambridge: 1744), p. 157. Rutherforth's argument was comprehensively directed against Shaftesbury, Francis Hutcheson, Samuel Clarke, John Balguy and William Wollaston (pp. 73, 118–52, 195).

Shaftesbury's ethical beauty entailed a renunciation of providence. If virtue had to be purified of the inducements of hope and fear, it had no use for the expectation of a future state.[89]

Berkeley developed his account of Shaftesbury in his dialogue *Alciphron*, a critical engagement with the pretensions of "free thought." Its titular character, representing an amalgam of freethinkers including Shaftesbury, described beauty as "natural" to man.[90] However, to Berkeley moral beauty was a "stoical enthusiasm" that sought to deprive the human species of its true religious nature.[91] For this reason, Shaftesburean stoicism seemed to share a common intellectual bent with scepticism and epicureanism. The strategy of *Alciphron* was to depict these diverse schools as facets of what Berkeley termed "minute" philosophy. He derived this category from Cicero's *De senectute*. At the close of that dialogue, the elder Cato dismissed the commonly perceived burdens of old age on the basis of his belief in the immortality of the soul, however much this might be disputed by "petty" (*minuti*) philosophers.[92] For Berkeley, petty—or "minute"—sceptics assailed faith, most usually in the name of reason.[93] Pretending to advance the cause of beneficent enlightenment, they in fact managed to bring about the reverse. As Euphranor, a character in the dialogue, put it: "If it were possible, they would extinguish the very light of nature, turn the world into a dungeon, and keep mankind for ever in chains and darkness."[94] Berkeley was averse not to the achievements of enlightenment, but to the resort to natural reason as a means of shattering faith. Minute philosophers, in nominally freeing the mind from the bonds of error, were happy to sacrifice utility to the overriding claims of truth. In the process they surrendered "useful truths" which were as probable as they were practically indispensable.[95]

As Burke saw it, natural reason claimed to lead back to natural desires. The fact was, however, that the "natural" appetites celebrated by modern sceptical philosophers were nothing more than philosophical projections. They followed from a pernicious attempt to barbarise and denature man. In their different ways, Thomas Hobbes, the Third Earl of Shaftesbury, Anthony Collins and Bernard Mandeville had variously contributed to this process. In their hands, the ancient schools of philosophy had been resuscitated and debauched in the service of a dogmatic assault upon religion. Modern scepticism had been directed towards the debilitation of

[89] George Berkeley, *Alciphron, or the Minute Philosopher in Seven Dialogues* (1732) in *The Works of George Berkeley*, ed. Alexander Campbell Fraser (Oxford: Oxford University Press, 1901), 4 vols., II, pp. 125–27.

[90] Ibid., p. 125.

[91] Ibid., p. 142.

[92] Cicero, *De senectute*, XXIII, 85.

[93] Cf. *The Tattler*, 18 February 1709: "I would fain ask a minute philosopher, what good he proposes to mankind by the publishing of his doctrines?"

[94] Berkeley, *Alciphron*, pp. 35–37. See also ibid., p. 227.

[95] Ibid., pp. 331, 335, 339.

knowledge, modern epicureanism towards the brutalisation of virtue, and modern stoicism towards purging ordinary human motivation. By "scepticism" Burke usually meant a brand of dogmatic rationalism that unsettled the grounds of belief by seeking to expose the claims of religion even though it entertained few doubts about its own pronouncements.[96] Anthony Collins's *Discourse of Freethinking* typified what Burke had in mind when criticising the notion that positive evidence could act as the sole criterion of assent.[97] This kind of approach gave rise, Burke thought, to the paradoxical result of calling moral certainties into doubt by a process of categorical assertion. This dogmatism of natural reason, in being turned against religion, was as commonly put in the service of epicureanism as it was employed to buttress stoicism.[98] In the 1770s Burke would call for a common front against epicureans. Like all freethinkers they were ultimately incapable of society because they exempted themselves from every bond of trust. Atheists, as he put it, were "dangerous animals," antinomian in theory and in practice.[99] For similar reasons Burke raised his voice against modern stoics in the 1750s.[100] Like epicureans they were determined to reverse the natural progress of civility by resort to the rudimentary instincts of savage nature. While Mandeville condoned the social utility of base appetites, Shaftesbury disregarded the civilized pleasures.[101] For Shaftesbury, the voice of reason was understood to accuse the passions, thereby commanding austerity and abstention. However, as Burke made plain in "Philosophy and Learning," this mode of thinking constituted a revolt against our condition as human beings. Luckily, true nature proved to be wiser than the imagined "nature" of natural reason: providence annexed pleasure to the satisfaction of needs, thus incentivising humans to better their condition, and in the process further the cultivation of virtue.[102]

[96] This was a primary basis of James Beattie's objection to modern scepticism in the postscript to his *An Essay on the Nature and Immutability of Truth in Opposition to Sophistry and Scepticism* (Edinburgh: 1771), pp. 543–44, which Burke admired. On the varieties of scepticism and freethought in the seventeenth and eighteenth centuries, see Richard H. Popkin and Arjo Vanderjagt eds., *Scepticism and Irreligion in the Seventeenth and Eighteenth Centuries* (Leiden: Brill, 1993); Peter N. Miller, "'Freethinking' and 'Freedom of Thought' in Eighteenth-Century Britain," *Historical Journal*, 36:3 (1993), pp. 599–617; Richard Popkin, *The History of Scepticism from Savonarola to Bayle* (Oxford: Oxford University Press, 2003).

[97] Anthony Collins, *A Discourse of Freethinking* (London: 1730), p. 3.

[98] On the revival of "epicurean" thought, see John Robertson, *The Case for the Enlightenment: Scotland and Naples, 1680–1760* (Cambridge: Cambridge University Press, 2007); see also Neven Leddy and Avi Lifschitz eds., *Epicurus in the Enlightenment* (Oxford: Voltaire Foundation, 2009).

[99] EB, Debate on Relief for Protestant Dissenters, 23 February 1773, *Parliamentary History*, XVII, col. 775n.

[100] EB to William Burgh, 9 February 1775, *Corr.*, III, p. 112.

[101] Burke's opposition to Mandeville later found expression in EB, Speech on Sixth Article: Presents, 21 April 1789, *W & S*, VII, p. 33. On Mandeville's moral and political thought, see E. J. Hundert, *The Enlightenment's Fable: Bernard Mandeville and the Discovery of Society* (Cambridge: Cambridge University Press, 2005).

[102] EB, "Philosophy and Learning," pp. 92, 96.

Burke's school friend Michael Kearney once remembered how his associate "always answered remarkably well in Locke."[103] In the *Essay Concerning Human Understanding*, Locke pointed to the infinite wisdom of the "Author of our being" in annexing to our ideas the "*perception of Delight*."[104] Human beings were invested with various capacities, including bodily movement and the ability to choose. Choice, however, had to be incentivised if the mind was to prefer one action to another. Without preferences, the human species would be reduced to fantastic idleness, and pass its time "in a lazy lethargic dream."[105] The impulse to pursue or avoid objects on the basis of pleasure and pain was therefore a providential inducement to human improvement. From this perspective, it was part of our nature to seek to acquire a culture, achieving progress by the acquisition of artificial means to develop from an originally savage state. As Burke saw it, artifice, in this sense, was part of nature: ceremony, government, luxury and elegance were essential to the progress of civilisation, whose development was integral to the providential scheme of nature.[106] Having accepted the benefits of artificial reason in the context of his legal studies and embraced the instinct for culture against the claims of modern sceptics, Burke brought together his overarching conclusions in the *Vindication of Natural Society* in the period after he had written "Philosophy and Learning." Instead of presenting the positive case for his argument, he justified the achievements of civilisation by satirically exposing attempts to undermine it as absurd. The satire, however, was subtle, and easily mistaken. As a result, the appearance of the *Vindication* was not an unambiguous success. To understand the ultimate import of the work, it has to be placed in the context of the theological controversies out of which it emerged.

2.4 Mystery, Association and Latitude

Looking back on his life from the vantage of 1757, Burke described his conduct over the previous years as "checquered with various designs."[107] By that stage he had married Jane Nugent, "daughter to a Popish Physician," and had begun to establish himself in the literary world of London.[108] However, earlier in the decade his career had

[103] Michael Kearney to Edmond Malone, 12 January 1799, "Letters to Edmond Malone from Michael Kearney, 1797–1811," Bodl. MS. 39, fol. 23.

[104] John Locke, *An Essay Concerning Human Understanding* (1689), ed. Peter H. Nidditch (Oxford: Oxford University Press, 1975, 1979), II, vii, § 3.

[105] Ibid.

[106] See EB, *An Appeal from the New to the Old Whigs, in Consequence of some Late Discussions in Parliament, relative to the Reflections on the Revolution in France* (London: 1791), p. 130; cf. EB, Speech in Reply, 12 June 1794, *W & S*, VII, p. 540.

[107] EB to Richard Shackleton, 10 August 1757, *Corr.*, I, p. 123. On this period in Burke's life, see Dixon Wecter, "The Missing Years in Burke's Biography," *Publication of the Modern Language Association*, 53:4 (December 1938), pp. 1102–25.

[108] William Dennis ALS to Richard Shackleton, July/August 1757, OSB MS. File 4324. Burke's marriage took place on 12 March 1757. See *Notes and Queries* (8 April 1882), pp. 274–75.

lacked direction. He had been dividing his time between London and the country, periodically visiting France; at the same time, he had been trying to advance his literary career while studying for the bar. Now he was considering emigrating to America, anxious for adventure as a means of improving his fortunes.[109] Over the last six years he had been struggling to commit himself to a definite objective—first exhausting himself with study, then craving poetic success; next seeking to diversify his talents as a writer, and finally aiming to deploy his literary skills in the field of politics. William Dennis indicated in a letter sent to Richard Shackleton in the summer of 1757 that Burke was making progress along this route: "He tells me poetry has utterly left him," Dennis reported, further noting that he seemed to be "writing pamphlets for the great ones" since he regularly visited Lord Egmont and was well acquainted with Granville.[110] After Burke's death, Michael Kearney confirmed this early connection to Granville: apparently the relationship was established soon after Burke's arrival in London.[111] Writing over forty years after the event, Kearney was presumably referring to the middle of the 1750s, when Burke, it seems, was considering a career as a man of business, involving himself in political affairs as a commentator and publicist while also hoping to realise his literary talents. This newfound sense of purpose had been preceded by uncertainty and doubt. In late 1750 or early 1751, Burke first encountered his future father-in-law, Christopher Nugent, a Roman Catholic from Ireland who had trained in France before settling to practise medicine in Bath. He resorted to Nugent for treatment when burdened by physical and mental stress. As Burke saw it, this recourse had "Restor'd his Life, and taught him how to Live."[112] In the same verse epistle, Burke dramatised his sense of irresolution by mocking his posture of drastic indecision through an invocation of the figure of the chronically distracted philosopher, unable to discover solitude in either the country or the city, as represented by Rabelais in his *Gargantua and Pantagruel*.[113]

The parable of the wavering philosopher aptly captured Burke's restlessness. He had started out in Dublin desiring literary success only to find himself in London on the path to a professional career during which he continued to aspire to the status of a writer, but without settling on the genre that would suit him best. In 1759, Dennis recalled the early dreams of the trio of aspiring authors—Burke, Beaumont Brennan and Richard Shackleton—who, along with himself, were originally thrown together by "the youthful vanity of writing."[114] Yet Burke was to discover that his

[109] EB to Richard Shackleton, 10 August 1757, *Corr.*, I, p. 123. According to Michael Kearney in a letter to Edmond Malone of 12 January 1799, "Letters to Edmond Malone from Michael Kearney, 1797–1811," Bodl. MS. Malone 39, fol. 24, Burke "had an offer of land in Carolina" from Granville.

[110] William Dennis ALS to Richard Shackleton, July/August 1757, OSB MS. File 4324.

[111] Michael Kearney to Edmond Malone, 12 January 1799, "Letters to Edmond Malone from Michael Kearney, 1797–1811," Bodl. MS. Malone 39, fol. 24.

[112] EB, "To Christopher Nugent" (Verse Epistle), September 1752, *Corr.*, I, p. 117.

[113] Ibid., pp. 115–16. The reference is to François Rabelais, *The Works of Francis Rabelais* (London: 1737), 5 vols., bk. III, ch. XIII, pp. 77–79.

[114] William Dennis ALS to Richard Shackleton, 6 October 1759, OSB MS. File 4327.

inchoate desires stood in need of a distinct objective. Part of his problem was finding a definite vehicle for his ambitions. As he later confided to Charles Butler, a campaigner for Catholic relief, "[a]fter the first years of youth are past, the mind requires more substantial food than mere reading; so that, to call forth literary application, it is necessary to superadd the stimulus of an ardent wish to attain a particular object."[115] In 1752, Arthur Murphy introduced Burke to his future publisher, Robert Dodsley.[116] Around the middle of the decade he began to make use of the connection, seeking out a more focused application for his talents. However, he still needed to reconcile his own designs with the priorities of his father. During a chance first encounter with the Armenian emigrant Joseph Emïn, in St James's Park around 1755, he openly presented himself as "a runaway son from a father."[117] In a letter of 11 March 1755, Burke was still having to justify his projects to his parent: "I have no Scheme or design, however reasonable it may seem to me that I would not gladly Sacrifice to your Quiet and submit to your Judgment."[118] Nonetheless, as he worked on the *Vindication of Natural Society*, an inkling of independence began to dawn, and with it coincided a drift towards political writing.

The *Vindication of Natural Society* combined Burke's various aspirations. These included his interests in politics, literature and theology. In a speech on Lord Barrington's motion for the expulsion of John Wilkes from parliament, which Burke delivered early in 1769, the orator recalled a snippet from early in his career: "a great portion of my time," he revealed to the House, "has been occupied in studying theoretical religion."[119] Evidence for this survives in a number of draft essays preserved in the notebooks of William Burke. Specifically, in "A Plan for Arguing," "Religion of No Efficacy as a State Engine" and a third piece on "Religion," Burke addressed himself to major issues in the philosophy of religion such as the rule of faith controversy and the nature of testimony, enthusiasm and providence. His preoccupation with these topics grew out of his immersion in the deist controversy, which gave rise to the idea of writing the *Vindication*. But, as a satirical imitation of Bolingbroke, the book at the same time illustrates Burke's desire for literary renown. Equally, as a critical assault on the idea of "natural society," the political orientation of the work can hardly be missed. It blended religious and political themes as part of an intricate indictment of freethinking rationalism and antinomian social criticism. Burke's target was a style of reasoning that he associated with irreligion which sceptically dismantled the foundations of all belief. Its influence would lead to the elimination of

[115] Charles Butler, *Reminiscences* (London: 1822–27), 2 vols., II, p. 102.

[116] Ralph Straus, *Robert Dodsley: Poet, Publisher and Playwright* (London: The Bodley Head, 1910), p. 254. On the Dodsley milieu in which Burke moved, see Ian Crowe, *Patriotism and Public Spirit: Edmund Burke and the Role of the Critic in Mid-Eighteenth-Century Britain* (Stanford, CA: Stanford University Press, 2012).

[117] Joseph Emïn, *Life and Adventures of Emin Joseph Emin, 1726–1809*, ed. Amy Apcar (Calcutta: Baptist Mission Press, 1918), pp. 49–53.

[118] EB to Richard Burke (father), 11 March 1755, *Corr.*, I, p. 119.

[119] EB, Speech on Wilkes's Expulsion, 3 February 1769, Cavendish Diary, Eg. MS. 216, fols. 232–33.

Christianity as well as to the destruction of society in general. Towards the end of his career, faced with the steady progress of Revolutionary ideology in Europe, Burke drew attention to "the horrible system of *Atheism*, which was now publicly *avowed* in France."[120] In the 1750s, Burke took the deistical denial of providence to be tantamount to eradicating religion altogether. He understood this denial to be a product of forms of scepticism that undermined all avenues to trust. It exploded social habitudes along with every tenet of faith. It was driven by a determination to annihilate mystery, and in the process it threatened to dissolve all confidence in society, and everything that supported benign credulity and civilisation.

Towards the end of the *Vindication*, the radical Baptist minister James Foster is cited as an exemplary exponent of the tenets of natural religion in opposition to the supposed mysteries of Christian revelation. In 1731, in *The Usefulness, Truth, and Excellency of the Christian Religion*, Foster had challenged the conclusions of Matthew Tindal's deist tract *Christianity as Old as the Creation*, but in the process defended the project of purging religion of superstitious doctrines and forms of worship.[121] Four years later, Foster summed up his position in a sermon "Of Mysteries" by declaring that "as we cannot in *reason*, we are not oblig'd by *revelation*, to carry our faith one jot beyond our understanding." By implication, matters of faith should be submitted before the tribunal of knowledge. As a result, Foster concluded, "Where the mystery *begins*, religion *ends*."[122] In the Introduction to his posthumously published *Letters or Essays Addressed to Alexander Pope*, Bolingbroke reminded his addressee of "a passage you quoted to me once . . . from a Sermon of FOSTER, and to this effect: 'Where mystery begins, religion ends.'" Foster's suggestion, Bolingbroke contends, betrays an admirable ambition to "purify Christianity from the leaven of artificial theology, which consists principally in making things that are very plain mysterious."[123] Burke was as sceptical about the assumption that Christianity could survive a full-blown assault on mystery as he was about the notion that social and political obligations could be comprehensively rationalised. In the *Vindication*, he sought to cast doubt upon the rational criticism of religion by ridiculing the application of comparable modes of argument to the history and legitimacy of political society.

The ostensibly serious claims of the *Vindication* are deliberately mocked by presenting them in the character of a Bolingbrokean social critic who promises to cleanse politics of every residue of mystery. As the pseudo-rationalist persona of the *Vindication* puts it: "A good Parson once said, that where Mystery begins, Religion ends. Cannot I say, as truly at least, of human Laws, that where Mystery begins, Jus-

[120] EB, Debate on Aliens Bill, 28 December 1792, *Diary*, 29 December 1792.

[121] James Foster, *The Usefulness, Truth, and Excellency of the Christian Religion* (London: 1731). For Foster's European influence, see Joris Van Eijnatten, *Liberty and Concord in the United Provinces: Religious Toleration and the Public in the Eighteenth-Century Netherlands* (Leiden: Brill, 2003), pp. 202–3.

[122] James Foster, *Sermons on the Following Subjects* (Dublin: 1735), p. 114.

[123] Henry St. John Bolingbroke, *The Works of the Late Right Honorable Henry St. John, Lord Viscount Bolingbroke* (London: 1754), 5 vols., III, p. 344.

tice ends?"[124] Of course, the aim of the *Vindication* was to undermine this proposition by satirising its implications as applied to practical affairs. At the same time, however, the intention was to challenge the suggestion that matters of faith could be reduced to truths of reason. This claim, famously advanced at the end of the seventeenth century by John Toland in *Christianity not Mysterious*, had preoccupied Burke through the early to mid 1750s. "Perhaps," he remarked in his essay on "Philosophy and Learning," "the bottom of most things is unintelligible; and our surest reasoning, when we come to a certain point, is involved not only in obscurity but contradiction."[125] This amounted to a reassertion of the priority of faith to reason in the face of persistent attempts, exemplified by Toland and his successors, to render every tenet of religious belief and worship consistent with rational explanation. "[W]e hold," as Toland put it, "that *Reason* is the Foundation of all Certitude."[126] From this perspective, all aspects of theology and all matters of scripture should be subject to rational accounting, and thus mystery would be discredited where it could not be explained.

Toland's radical intervention into the rule of faith controversy was explicitly designed to discredit two dominant approaches to characterising the relationship between mystery and understanding. In the first place, he wanted to show that there was nothing in the Gospel that could be said to be "contrary" to reason; and, in the second place, he wished to contend that none of the truths of scripture were "above" reason.[127] Toland was anxious to undermine the idea that "inspiration" rather than "reason" was essential to religious dogma. The notion of inspired truths had been widely credited in the writings of the early Protestant reformers, but it came to be associated with enthusiasm from the mid-seventeenth through to the mid-eighteenth century.[128] In opposition to enthusiastic conceptions of faith, a broad range of theologians after the English civil wars were anxious to rehabilitate reason as "an Instrument" of belief, even if it could not stand as a complete rule of faith.[129] Edward Stillingfleet was a prominent expositor of this view. In mounting his opposition to an inspired conception of doctrine as well as to the idea that faith could be above reason, Toland drew heavily upon socinian biblical criticism, presenting his project as a plain attempt to rationalise apparent mysteries in defence of a more intelligible

[124]EB, *Vindication*, p. 176.

[125]EB, "Philosophy and Learning," p. 93.

[126]John Toland, *Christianity not Mysterious: Or, A Treatise Shewing, that there is Nothing in the Gospel Contrary to Reason nor above It* (London: 1696), p. 6.

[127]Ibid. Burke later, in another context, adverted to the terms of this discussion. See EB, *Letter to Thomas Burgh* (1780), *W & S*, IX, p. 557: "as they say of faith, it is not contrary to reason, but above it."

[128]On the relationship between biblical interpretation, reason and inspiration in Luther and Calvin, see Alister McGrath, *Intellectual Origins of the Reformation* (Oxford: Blackwell, 1987). For the subsequent rationalisation of biblical criticism, see Gerard Reedy, *The Bible and Reason: Anglicans and Scripture in Late Seventeenth-Century England* (Philadelphia, PA: University of Pennsylvania Press, 1985).

[129]The position is attacked in Toland, *Christianity not Mysterious*, p. 5.

account of Christian revelation.[130] On the surface, therefore, he was launching an attack upon clerical attempts to mystify religion through the manipulation of opaque Scholastic jargon. But behind this exoteric justification of revealed religion as perfectly intelligible to the lay reason of even a "Brewer" or a "Baker," Toland's criticism periodically went further and challenged the foundations of faith altogether.[131] In this he claimed to be following in the footsteps of Lockean epistemology, depicting the acquisition of knowledge as "nothing else but *the Perception of the Agreement or Disagreement of our ideas*."[132] In fact, however, Toland's reduction of conviction to rational evidence represents a significant departure from the central message of Locke's *Essay*, and poses a problem for forms of belief that do not claim the status of knowledge.

In a sermon preached at the St. Laurence Jewry in London in April 1691, Stillingfleet argued that it was reasonable to credit mysteries that were not perfectly intelligible to us, and consequently that human beings were constantly required to repose their trust in matters that lay beyond their comprehension.[133] The criterion of reasonableness here was based upon the practical utility of belief, rather than the formal characteristics of propositions. In this, Stillingfleet's approach looked back to the pragmatism of "Great Tew Circle" Anglicans like Chillingworth and Hammond.[134] Its importance to Burke is implicit in the sham contempt for "consequences" paraded early on in the *Vindication*: the implication was that the possibility of acting on our beliefs counted for almost everything.[135] Crediting beliefs on the basis of their reasonableness, and appraising reasonableness in the light of the practical consequences of those beliefs, reconciled Burke, along with Chillingworth and Tillotson, to the

[130] On this, see Gerard Reedy, "Socinians, John Toland and the Anglican Rationalists," *Harvard Theological Review*, 70 (July–October 1977), pp. 285–304. On Toland within the wider context of freethinking polemic, see Justin Champion, *The Pillars of Priestcraft Shaken: The Church of England and its Enemies, 1660–1730* (Cambridge: Cambridge University Press, 1992). On socinianism in seventeenth-century England, see Sarah Mortimer, *Reason and Religion in the English Revolution: The Challenge of Socinianism* (Cambridge: Cambridge University Press, 2010).

[131] Toland, *Christianity not Mysterious*, p. xx. On Toland's esotericism, see Frederick C. Beiser, *The Sovereignty of Reason: The Defence of Rationality in the Early English Enlightenment* (Princeton, NJ: Princeton University Press, 1996), ch. 6.

[132] Toland, *Christianity not Mysterious*, p. 11.

[133] Edward Stillingfleet, "The Mysteries of the Christian Faith Asserted and Vindicated" in *The Works of Edward Stillingfleet* (London: 1709–10), 6 vols., III, pp. 346–62. For discussion, see Richard H. Popkin, "The Philosophy of Bishop Stillingfleet," *Journal of the History of Philosophy*, 9:3 (July 1971), pp. 303–19; Sarah Hutton, "Science, Philosophy and Atheism: Edward Stillingfleet's Defence of Religion" in Popkin and Vanderjagt eds., *Scepticism and Irreligion*.

[134] See Hugh Trevor-Roper, "The Great Tew Circle" in idem, *Catholics, Anglicans and Puritans* (London: Fontana, 1989), pp. 166–230.

[135] EB, *Vindication*, pp. 137, 139. Burke's debt here to the Anglican rationalist tradition is examined in Iain Hampsher-Monk, "Burke and the Religious Sources of Sceptical Conservatism" in J. van der Zande and R. H. Popkin eds., *The Skeptical Tradition around 1800* (Dordrecht: Kluwer, 1998).

existence of mysterious or "contrary" truths.[136] It was in this sense that Burke had espoused the unintelligibility of things at the conclusion of "Philosophy and Learning." This, however, was not seen as a disabling insight; it was an acknowledgement of the general "Contrariety in things" which could, despite the insurmountable mystery of existence, be credited "beyond any reasonable doubt."[137]

In *Christianity not Mysterious*, Toland explains our knowledge of the world in terms at once of "the means of information" and of the "grounds of perswasion." While the former, by which Toland meant the basic data we acquire about the world, depends on both experience and authority, the latter wins our assent by demonstration alone. We accept information about the world, such as the existence of a city named Carthage, on the basis of creditable authority. But the mind can only be convinced of definite truths to the extent that information acquires the status of certain knowledge.[138] In a *Letter* published in 1697 as a response to Toland's work, Peter Browne, the Church of Ireland Bishop of Cork and Ross and one time Provost of Trinity College Dublin, set out to show how the mind was persuaded not merely by evidence, but by the credit bestowed by authority as well. In other words, we do not simply receive information on the basis of authority, we also consent to truths on the very same terms: "*Authority*," Browne insisted, is also "a ground of Perswasion." As a result, we give our assent to innumerable propositions for which we have no certain evidence, and place our trust, even to the point of reverence, in ideas that we cannot comprehend.[139] The figure of Alciphron in Berkeley's dialogue of that name described his philosophical aim as being to "probe" prejudice and "extirpate" principles.[140] For all his doubts about the cogency of Browne's philosophical enterprise, Berkeley followed him in seeking to restore the dignity of prejudice. While Burke never became a disciple of the Bishop of Cloyne, he did accept the role of authority and custom in belief.

In his essay on "Philosophy and Learning," Burke signalled his commitment to the idea that trust and opinion represented an acceptable basis for claims about the world, even if these did not achieve the status of absolute certainty. In this, he was

[136] On John Tillotson in relation to Chillingworth and sceptical rationalism more generally, see Harry G. Van Leeuwen, *The Problem of Certainty in English Thought, 1630–1690* (The Hague: Martinus Nijhoff, 1963); Gerard Reedy, "Interpreting Tillotson," *Harvard Theological Review*, 86:1 (January 1993), pp. 81–103; Isabel Rivers, *Reason, Grace, and Sentiment: A Study of the Language of Religion and Ethics in England, 1660–1780* (Cambridge: Cambridge University Press, 1991), 2 vols., I, ch. 2; Patrick Müller, *Latitudinarianism and Didacticism in Eighteenth-Century Literature: Moral Theology in Fielding, Sterne and Goldsmith* (Frankfurt: Peter Lang, 2009), pp. 48–49.

[137] EB, "Philosophy and Learning," pp. 92–93.

[138] Toland, *Christianity not Mysterious*, pp. 14–22.

[139] Peter Browne, *A Letter in Answer to a Book Entitled Christianity not Mysterious, as Also to all Those who Set Up for Reason and Evidence in Opposition to Revelation and Mysteries* (Dublin: 1697), pp. 27–29. For discussion of the Irish context, see David Berman, "Enlightenment and Counter-Enlightenment in Irish Philosophy," *Archiv für Geschichte der Philosophie*, 64:2 (1982), pp. 148–65; idem, "Irish Philosophy and Ideology," *The Crane Bag*, 9:2 (1985), pp. 158–59.

[140] Berkeley, *Alciphron*, p. 40.

happy to present himself as a devotee of "academic" scepticism as defended by Cicero in the second book of his *Academica*. There we are told that even the truths of physical nature are ultimately shrouded in darkness, although the quest itself sustains and humanises both "spirit and intellect" (*animorum ingeniorumque*).[141] In citing this passage in both the essay on "Philosophy and Learning" and the Preface to the second edition of the *Philosophical Enquiry*, Burke was acknowledging the mind's dependence on verisimilitude rather than truth for the opinions that guide behaviour in the world.[142] This was of course a kind of scepticism, but it considered itself immune to the dogmatic rationalism of religious sceptics like Toland and Collins. The contention that natural or experimental philosophy falls short of a "science" capable of revealing the "inmost constitution of things" had been acknowledged by Locke insofar as he concluded that the physical laws of nature could only be ascertained by means of "analogy" on the basis of probability.[143] So while Locke's "way of ideas" had been appropriated by heterodox freethinkers like Toland, his epistemological scepticism was also deployed in polemics against deism by Tory divines like Peter Browne and Anglican Whigs like Joseph Butler.[144]

Locke's *Essay* cast a shadow over three generations of thought because it articulated the enduring preoccupations of the age, offering innovative if often controversial responses to basic questions about reason, faith and knowledge. The *Essay* argued for properly delimiting the provinces of reason and faith so that errors based on the inappropriate subordination of the one to the other could be dependably avoided. Crediting beliefs overtly contradicted by reason gave encouragement to "natural Superstition." It privileged credulity over rational inquiry.[145] Accordingly, Locke concluded that Tertullian's infamous pronouncement—"*Credo, quia impossibile est: I believe, because it is impossible*"—"might, in a good Man, pass for a Sally of Zeal; but would prove a very ill Rule for Men to chuse their Opinions, or Religion by."[146] A related and equally problematic folly sprang from the disposition to submit to personal revelation irrespective of what reason commanded. Locke dubbed im-

[141] Cicero, *Academica*, II, 122–28.

[142] EB, "Philosophy and Learning", pp. 92–93; Edmund Burke, *A Philosophical Enquiry into the Origin of our Ideas of the Sublime and Beautiful* (1757, rev. ed. 1759) in *The Writings and Speeches of Edmund Burke I: The Early Years,* ed. T. O. McLoughlin and James T. Boulton (Oxford: Oxford University Press, 1997), p. 191. In both places Burke cites Cicero, *Academica*, II, 127.

[143] John Locke, *Essay*, bk. IV, ch. iii, §§ 23–27.

[144] On the wide impact of Lockean epistemology on early eighteenth-century thought in Britain and Ireland, see John W. Yolton, *Locke and the Way of Ideas* (Bristol: Thoemmes Press, 1993). On Locke's own conception of the relationship between faith and knowledge, see Richard Aschcraft, "Faith and Knowledge in Locke's Philosophy" in John W. Yolton ed., *John Locke: Problems and Perspectives, a Collection of New Essays* (Cambridge: Cambridge University Press, 1969); David C. Snyder, "Faith and Reason in Locke's *Essay*," *Journal of the History of Ideas*, 47:2 (April–June 1986), pp. 197–213; Nicholas Jolley, "Locke on Faith and Reason" in Lex Newman ed., *The Cambridge Companion to Locke's "Essay Concerning Human Understanding"* (Cambridge: Cambridge University Press, 2007).

[145] Locke, *Essay*, bk. IV, ch. xviii, § 11.

[146] Ibid.

mediate revelation of the kind "enthusiasm." This involved the conviction of being "under the peculiar guidance of Heaven," born of a conceited confidence in the dictates of "a warmed and over-weening Brain."[147] Locke saw that the extremes of superstition and enthusiasm posed obvious problems for society insofar as they spread erroneous precepts as well as antinomian commitments and beliefs. Where the dictates of blind faith prescribed norms of behaviour, they might condone the most obnoxious forms of conduct. Roman Catholic claims that Christ's commission had been delegated to an infallible papacy ascribed moral truth to the whims of arbitrary authority. Submission to such authority bred superstition together with a disregard for an objective framework of justice. Equally, Protestant endorsements of religious "inspiration" encouraged belief in the idea of an elect order of citizen-saints. Enthusiasm of the kind gave rise to its own antinomian assumption that moral behaviour was finally subject to inspired religious truth. Establishing the proper bounds of knowledge and assent promised to furnish criteria by which these claims could be regulated. For Locke, this meant distinguishing the bases of certainty and probability, and uncovering the most common forms of error.

The association of ideas was one conspicuous source of error. Burke indicated his debt to the author of the *Essay* when he noted the same process in his *Abridgement of English History*: in the face of mystery the mind was disposed to blend "imagination and reason together, to unite ideas the most inconsistent."[148] Locke thought that preferences among human beings were often a product of association rather than deliberate discrimination. This meant that behaviour was largely determined by custom, which might well be benign, but might equally be mistaken.[149] A false conjunction of ideas could be perpetuated as custom, which rational argument could only with difficulty dislodge. This illustrated the power of prejudice over the human mind. Readers of Locke interpreted its efficacy diversely. The *Essay* argued that prejudice operated in the absence of positive proof. Locke recognised that this condition applied to most of the human species, who lacked the leisure and opportunity to accumulate the relevant evidence: "in this State are the greatest part of Mankind, who are given up to Labour, and enslaved to the Necessity of their mean Condition."[150] Under these circumstances, authority was needed for indoctrination, the results of which were transmitted by tradition. Prejudice was a function of the intellectual division of labour. While trust was therefore a necessary social solvent, it was also a means of perpetuating misguided assumptions.[151] Later, in a set of notes on the disparity between different liturgical practices, Burke applied the thought to

[147] Ibid., bk. IV, ch. xix, §§ 5–7.

[148] EB, *An Essay towards an Abridgement of English History* (1757–c. 1763), *W & S*, I, p. 353.

[149] Locke, *Essay*, bk. II, ch. xxiii, § 7.

[150] Ibid., bk. IV, ch. xx, § 2.

[151] On this, see John Dunn, "The Concept of 'Trust' in the Politics of John Locke" in Richard Rorty, J. B. Schneewind and Quentin Skinner eds., *Philosophy in History* (Cambridge: Cambridge University Press, 1984). For the wider philosophical context, see J. B. Schneewind, *The Invention of Autonomy: A History of Modern Moral Philosophy* (Cambridge: Cambridge University Press, 1998).

the choice of forms of worship: "the majority of men take their opinions of religion upon trust."[152] At the end of his life he generalised the argument still further: "The Mass of Mankind . . . are made to be led by others; habits and Customs are *their* support."[153] Among opposing congregations divided on aspects of religion, differences often came down to mere matters of opinion. Burke followed Locke in believing that disputes over religious tenets were best managed by the offices of humanity. In the absence of proof, where attitudes were formed by submission based on acts of trust, comity among believers was an obligation of charity.[154] Burke publicised his commitment to tolerant Protestantism in the 1770s. As he then saw it, Christianity had first flourished under a reign of liberality. While the eastern and western Churches accommodated rival sects they prospered and became exalted and "illustrious." Yet when the "Romish church" abandoned its forbearance of other faiths, it threatened and persecuted, and "commotions ensued." As a consequence, "the kingdom of darkness was erected on the ruins of Christian charity."[155]

In consistently espousing the virtue of latitude, Burke maintained a distance from the ecclesiology of Bishop Berkeley. In *Alciphron*, Berkeley chided latitudinarian laxity with having opened the door to deism, which ultimately gave encouragement to atheism.[156] Yet for Burke, toleration among Christians was a mark of piety, although his attitude to infidels was another matter.[157] His hostility to atheists would reach a crescendo in the 1790s in connection with the French Revolution: "Atheism, he said, was the centre from which ran out all their mischiefs and villainies."[158] Yet even then he still believed, in irenic fashion, that Christian dissent should always to be accommodated.[159] In 1779 he made plain his sense that all branches of the Christian religion contributed to a common undertaking. Each sect might be prone to error, but they were all equally to be respected. The plurality of divisions should be regarded less as schemes of mutual contradiction than as discrete methods for pursuing a common hope.[160] Dissent ought not to be regarded as a schismatic predilection unless it could be shown that it was deliberately factional—a tendency that

[152] Northamptonshire MS. A. XXVII.49.

[153] "Christian Religion," WWM BkP 26:40–41.

[154] Locke, *Essay*, bk. IV, ch. xvi, § 4.

[155] EB, Debate on Relief for Protestant Dissenters, 23 February 1773, *Parliamentary History*, XVII, cols. 781–82.

[156] Berkeley, *Alciphron*, p. 45.

[157] Cf. John Locke, *A Letter Concerning Toleration* (1689) in *A Letter concerning Toleration and Other Writings, ed.* Mark Goldie (Indianapolis, IN: Liberty Fund, 2010), pp. 52–53: "Those are not at all to be tolerated who *deny the Being of a God*. Promises, Covenants, and Oaths, which are the Bonds of Humane Society, can have no hold upon an Atheist. The taking away of God, though but even in thought, dissolves all."

[158] EB, Debate on War with France, 12 February 1793, *Morning Chronicle*, 18 February 1793.

[159] The inspiration was Grotian, and ultimately Erasmian. See Hans Posthumus Meyjes, "Tolérance et Irénisme" in Christiane Berkvens-Stevenlinck et al. eds., *The Emergence of Tolerance in the Dutch Republic* (Leiden: Brill: 1997).

[160] EB to Dr. John Erskine, 12 June 1779, *Corr.*, IV, pp. 84–85.

Burke came to think characterised Unitarians like Price and Priestley, but which was scarcely the standard attitude of nonconformists. With the exception of sects that agitated for the destruction of an established church-state, heterodoxy should be indulged rather than proscribed.[161]

Burke would later reveal that in his youth he had applied himself to representative samples of theological writing from every division of the Christian faith. Nothing conclusive could be drawn from these abstract investigations, which ultimately only served to "confound and bewilder."[162] In the end, this perplexity led Burke to deepen his attachment to the Church of England, but it also solidified his commitment to the principle of toleration. While toleration thus seemed to him a basic ingredient of the Christian message, he thought the dogmatism of sceptical deists promoted persecution.[163] It was a common refrain among polemical deists that religion was a source of bigotry, leading inexorably to sectarian prejudice and strife. Burke accepted Berkeley's inversion of this formula: Christianity was a morally emollient system of belief. Religion was commonly a pretext of animosity, but never its fundamental cause. As Crito argued in Berkeley's *Alciphron*, the identification of blind fury with religious piety by sceptics was the product of a pernicious brand of fanaticism. Minute philosophers ascribed "darkness, ignorance, and rudeness" to the very thing that "enlightened and civilized and embellished their country."[164] True enlightenment was not a vehicle for dogmatic hostility to religion but a means of reconciling the use of reason with the persistence of mystery. Mystery could be credited in the absence of demonstration on the basis of reasonable faith. The idea of reasonable faith implied degrees of probability extending from moral certainty to extreme implausibility. For Burke, Christian revelation, while not a mathematical certainty, nonetheless commanded our assent. Although the content of scripture was often miraculous in nature, its credibility could not reasonably be doubted.

2.5 Enthusiasm, Analogy and Particular Providence

Burke went so far as to assert that certain tenets of revelation were so credible as to leave less doubt than apodictic reasoning: "The highest Degree of testimony," he wrote, "leaves less doubt than Demonstration."[165] This argument appears in Burke's

[161] For Burke's "latitudinarian" commitments, see Frederick Dreyer, "Burke's Religion," *Studies in Burke and His Time*, 17 (1976), pp. 199–212; Clark, "The Enlightenment, Religion and Edmund Burke."

[162] EB, Speech on Gordon Riots, 20 June 1780, *W & S*, III, p. 606. Cf. the report in the *General Evening Post*, 21 June 1780, reproduced in the *Whitehall Evening Post*, 20–22 June 1780.

[163] On the range of attitudes to toleration in the period, see R. L. Emerson, "Latitudinarianism and the English Deists" in J. A. Leo Lemay ed., *Deism, Masonry and the Enlightenment: Essays Honouring Alfred Owen Aldridge* (Newark, NJ: Associated University Press, 1987); Richard Ashcraft, "Latitudinarianism and Toleration: Historical Myth versus Political History" in Richard Ashcraft et al. eds., *Philosophy, Science and Religion in England, 1640–1700* (Cambridge: Cambridge University Press, 1992).

[164] Berkeley, *Alciphron*, pp. 210–15, 227.

[165] EB, "Religion" in *Notebook*, p. 74.

fragment on "Religion," written at some point in the middle of the 1750s. The essay sketches a range of opinions on issues in morals and theology before concluding with an outline sketch of the credibility of miracles. The will of God is dimly displayed by the constitution of nature. Human beings thus stand to benefit from any additional illumination. It was reasonable to expect that the divinity would be willing to share further knowledge of "his Nature or his Will."[166] Scripture was a supplementary means of revealing the law of nature. It recorded the will of God, authenticated by "acts of Power."[167] These acts, in the form of miracles, were an instrument of persuasion, immediately witnessed and handed down by testimony to the faithful.[168] Human testimony left no doubt when it was "very strong."[169] As Burke stated in a fragment on the forms of argument, the credibility of an event could be judged in terms of conformity to experience, its probability with respect to time and place, and the credit of the individual reporting it.[170] On this basis, it could no more be doubted that the city of Rome existed than that "the Square of the Hypotenuse is equal to the Square of the two sides."[171] But if the Bible was a genuine record of the moral providence of God, it was nonetheless studded with inexplicable mysteries. For Spinoza, this was hardly surprising in a document designed to edify by stirring the imagination.[172] "Consequently," Spinoza wrote, "those who look in the books of the prophets for wisdom and a knowledge of natural and spiritual things are completely on the wrong track."[173] In a related vein, Toland held out the prospect of rationalising revealed mystery. For Burke, however, religion required more than natural reason: its appeal in addition lay, first, in the powerful feelings it evoked; and, second, in the fact that biblical mysteries were no more perplexing than the truths of nature. The first position pitted Burke against divines like Samuel Clarke who strove to rationalise Christianity in response to the deist challenge. The second attracted

[166] Ibid.

[167] Ibid.

[168] Some of the context for the debate about the credibility of miracles is provided by R. M. Burns, *The Great Debate on Miracles: From Joseph Glanvill to David Hume* (Lewisburg, PA: Bucknell University Press, 1981). Catholicism, by comparison, offered mediate revelation in the form of accumulated traditions. On the proneness of tradition to error, see Locke, *Essay*, bk. IV, ch. xvi, § 10: "*in traditional Truths, each remove weakens the force of the proof*... the more hands the Tradition has successively passed through, the less strength and evidence does it receive from them." For the distinction between Protestantism and Catholicism in these terms, see EB on the 1779 Dissenters Bill at WWM BkP 8:45: while for Catholics the rule of faith is "the Tradition of the Catholic Church and the scripture only as it is part of that Tradition," a Protestant "holds the Scripture of the old and New Testament as his sole rule of faith."

[169] EB, "Religion" in *Notebook*, p. 74.

[170] EB, "Plan for Arguing" in ibid., p, 45.

[171] EB, "Religion" in ibid, p. 74.

[172] Susan James, *Spinoza on Philosophy, Religion, and Politics* (Oxford: Oxford University Press, 2012), p. 49.

[173] Baruch Spinoza, *Theological-Political Treatise*, ed. Jonathan Israel (Cambridge: Cambridge University Press, 2007), p. 27.

him to the writings of Joseph Butler, whose *Analogy of Religion* he championed as a great philosophical resource.[174]

Clarke's first Boyle lecture, delivered in 1704 on the being and attributes of God, had presented such a consummate defence of natural religion that many contemporaries felt that he had disposed of the need for revelation.[175] He had thus sacrificed, it seemed, a major weapon in the armoury of Christian apologetics. Burke clearly believed that passion was one of religion's greatest aids. In another of his experimental essays from the mid 1750s, "Religion of No Efficacy Considered as a State Engine," he argued that the idea of instrumentalising religion could only end up weakening its force. Faith was an inducement to virtue, and virtue an asset to the commonwealth. Nonetheless, the attempt to justify belief on the basis of its public utility would rob it of its essential credibility: "as we confine the Ends of Religion to this world, we naturally annihilate its Operation, which must wholly depend upon the Consideration of another."[176] Endeavouring to co-opt religion in the service of reason of state, deists came to regard it as nothing better than superstition. At that point, Burke commented, they tended to cast it "to the Vulgar," losing all means of restraint in their own lives.[177] However, religion was better cherished as an emotionally compulsive attachment. The inspirational force of belief was widely affirmed by devotional poetry, as critics from Nicolas Boileau to John Dennis had testified, and as Edward Young had more recently dramatised.[178] Feelings of the kind were nothing if not "sublime."[179] Enthusiastic passions were only delusive, it followed, if their promptings were confused with the voice of reason. Burke accepted Locke's indictment of the sectarian enthusiasts of the civil war. Indeed, he would adopt the

[174] In a conversation recorded in 1797, Burke praised the intellectual achievement of Butler's *Analogy*. See WWM BkP 26:40–41, reprinted in facsimile in *Burke Newsletter*, 8 (1967), pp. 703–10, p. 704. James Prior, *Life of the Right Honourable Edmund Burke* (1824) (London: 5th ed., 1854), p. 128, records how Burke recommended Butler to his then client, James Barry, as the most compelling response to the challenge of deism. See also Sir Thomas Somerville, *My Own Life and Times, 1741–1814* (Edinburgh: 1861), p. 222: "Burke spoke with high admiration of Butler's *Analogy*, as containing the most satisfactory answer to the objections of philosophical sceptics." There are brief discussions of Burke's debt to Butler in Victor Hamm, "Burke and Metaphysics" in A. C. Pegis ed., *Essays in Modern Scholasticism* (Westminster, MD: Newman, 1944), and Francis Canavan, *Edmund Burke: Prescription and Providence* (Durham, NC: Carolina Academic Press, 1987), p. 9.

[175] Samuel Clarke, *A Demonstration of the Being and Attributes of God in answer to Mr Hobbes, Spinoza and their Followers, wherein the Notion of Liberty is Stated* (London: 1705).

[176] EB, "Religion of No Efficacy Considered as a State Engine," *Notebook*, pp. 67–68.

[177] Ibid., p. 68.

[178] For Boileau and Dennis, see Richard Bourke, "Pity and Fear: Providential Sociability in Burke's *Philosophical Enquiry*" in Michael Funk Deckard and Koen Vermeir eds., *The Science of Sensibility: Reading Edmund Burke's Philosophical Enquiry* (Heidelberg: Springer-Verlag GmbH, 2010). See also Edward Young, *Night Thoughts*, ed. Stephen Cornford (Cambridge: Cambridge University Press, 1989), V, line 176: "By Night an Atheist half-believes a God." For the theological context, see Isabel St. John Bliss, "Young's *Night Thoughts* in Relation to Contemporary Christian Apologetics," *Publication of the Modern Language Association*, 49:1 (March 1934), pp. 37–70.

[179] See below, chapter 3, section 4.

criticism himself in attacks on Richard Price from the 1770s.[180] Nonetheless, he also argued that "God has been pleased to give Mankind Enthusiasm to supply the want of Reason."[181]

Burke found the passion for religion displayed in Addison's *Spectator*, and retained the memory of the experience down to the year of his death.[182] Dictating some views on Christianity to Frances Crewe in 1797, he observed that the mind is made to "dissect and destroy all *Natural* enthusiasm." Left only to its devices, "we are all *cold* Beings!"[183] This was a perspective that he had already adopted by the middle of the 1750s.[184] Enthusiasm could make us feel the greatness of the almighty. If powerful emotions of the kind were confused with rational insight, the effects could be beguiling in the extreme. However, if guided and restrained by the conclusions of the rational faculty, the experience could be salutary: "It is true indeed that enthusiasm often misleads us. So does reason too. Such is the Condition of our Nature . . . But we act most when we act with all the Powers of our Soul; when we use Enthusiasm to elevate and expand our Reasoning; and our Reasoning to check the Roving of our Enthusiasm."[185] This tribute to flights of passion was also an endorsement of rational religion: it was anything but a reversion to antinomian enthusiasm.[186] But this commitment required an account of the role of reason in the realm of faith. Reason was fallible, but resourceful. It could help us if applied judiciously to experience. Mental discipline and industry could thus provide us with probable knowledge. Burke shared with Locke a sense of the solidity of empirical knowledge and an awareness of its drastic limitations. Beyond the restricted confines of the experimental knowledge of nature, Locke seemed to be saying, lay a "vast whole Extent" of mystery.[187] For Burke, the deists had been foolish enough to confuse the span of reason with the actual measure of things. On that basis they presumed to dismiss the mysteries of revealed religion. However, scriptural mysteries were in fact only to be expected, on the analogy of the experience of nature.[188] Therefore, alongside enthusiastic passion, the Bible was a second plank supporting belief in religion despite the miraculous nature of the dramatic events it depicts. For Burke, it was Bishop Butler who had shown most powerfully how assent to revelation was reasonable. Christ's message

[180] See below, chapter 9, section 6; chapter 13, section 6.

[181] EB, "Religion of No Efficacy Considered as a State Engine," *Notebook*, p. 68.

[182] See EB, "Christian Religion," WWM BkP 26:40–41.

[183] Ibid.

[184] Ross Carroll, "Revisiting Burke's Critique of Enthusiasm," *History of Political Thought*, 35:2 (Spring 2014), pp. 317–44.

[185] EB, "Religion of No Efficacy Considered as a State Engine," *Notebook*, pp. 68–69.

[186] For earlier theories of antinomian enthusiasm, see Michael Heyd, *"Be Sober and Reasonable": The Critique of Enthusiasm in the Seventeenth and Early Eighteenth Centuries* (Leiden: Brill, 1995), ch. 3.

[187] Locke, *Essay*, bk. IV, ch. iii, § 23.

[188] For this idiom in the eighteenth century, see Earl R. Wasserman, "Nature Moralized: The Divine Analogy in the Eighteenth Century," *English Literary History*, 20:1 (March 1953), pp. 39–76.

could be known as a "moral certainty" as befitted "Beings of limited Capacities."[189] Nature could not be grasped in the form of clear and distinct ideas: its laws could only be recognised as probable beyond doubt.[190] On the analogy of experimental reasoning about nature, the truths of revealed religion were surrounded by mystery, but they were nonetheless probable in themselves.

Locke had drawn attention to the utility of analogy in his discussion of degrees of ascent in the *Essay*. The probable organisation of those aspects of God's creation that were not immediately accessible to experience could be conjectured on the basis of our actual knowledge of nature. Cautious and responsible conjecture of the kind, which Locke dubbed "wary Reasoning from Analogy," commonly led to the discovery of important truths "which would otherwise lie concealed."[191] Butler traced the appeal to analogical reasoning to the Alexandrian theologian Origen.[192] Its usage seemed to license what was required to strengthen faith—namely, the establishment of likely hypotheses on the basis of known facts. This would enable us to reason "from that Part of the Divine Government over intelligent Creatures which comes under our view, to that larger and more general Government over them, which is beyond it."[193] Analogy provided for a process of reasonable extrapolation that might be more or less compelling as the degree of probability allowed. On this basis, Butler proceeded to recover the reasonableness of the Christian worldview, including the doctrine of a future state, a view of life in this world as a state of probation for the next, and belief in the apportionment of reward and punishment on the basis of moral desert.

This was an epic achievement in Burke's view because it justified the idea of God's moral government of the world in the face of sceptical assaults by deists like Bolingbroke. It was this aspect of Bolingbroke's philosophy that goaded Warburton into attack, and inspired him to recover the ideas of Alexander Pope from the distorting representation imposed by his one-time collaborator.[194] Bolingbroke encourages us to believe, Warburton wrote, "that an intelligent law made the world; and governs it

[189] Joseph Butler, *The Analogy of Religion, Natural and Revealed, to the Constitution and Course of Nature* (London: 1736), p. iii.

[190] Aaron Garrett, "Reasoning about Morals from Butler to Hume" in Ruth Savage ed., *Philosophy and Religion in Enlightenment Britain* (Oxford: Oxford University Press, 2012).

[191] Locke, *Essay*, bk. IV, ch. xvi, § 12.

[192] Butler, *Analogy*, p. iv. Its currency in the Schools and applicability in modern philosophy had been debated by Peter Browne, Archbishop King and George Berkeley. See, e.g., Berkeley, *Alciphron*, pp. 184–87. Precedents are discussed in Ernest Campbell Mossner, *Bishop Butler and the Age of Reason* (New York: Macmillan, 1936), pp. 80–82.

[193] Butler, *Analogy*, p. v.

[194] Pope's *Essay on Man* had originally been dedicated to Bolingbroke. For Pope's orthodoxy, and allegations of deism since Jean-Pierre de Crousaz, see Douglas Atkins, "Pope and Deism: A New Analysis," *Huntington Library Quarterly*, 35:3 (May 1972), pp. 257–78. For Pope's and Bolingbroke's political connections, see Howard Erskine-Hill, "Alexander Pope: The Political Poet and His Time," *Eighteenth-Century Studies*, 15:2 (Winter 1981–82), pp. 123–48; Isaac Kramnick, *Bolingbroke and His Circle: The Politics of Nostalgia in the Age of Walpole* (Ithaca, NY: Cornell University Press, 1968, 1982), ch. 8.

by his physical and general Laws; not by moral or particular."[195] Apparently Bolingbroke recognised the existence of divine laws, but not the "particular" providence involved in God's government of human conduct. Burke is sure to have closely followed this discussion.[196] The issues raised were fundamental to his own commitment to a theodicy that provided for a moral view of the universe. In the *Reflections on the Revolution in France*, he recalled the efforts of the French *philosophes* to dismantle every support that sustained the Christian vision of divine justice as he addressed the moral vacuity of military oaths in the new republic. He stated ironically: "I hope that handy abridgements of the excellent sermons of Voltaire, d'Alembert, Diderot, and Helvétius on the Immortality of the Soul, on a particular superintending Providence, and on a Future State of Rewards and Punishments, are sent down to the soldiers along with their civic oaths."[197] The systematic destruction of these components of the Christian faith had undermined the moral resources buttressing civilisation.

Two years after Burke's death, on 3 May 1799, Michael Kearney wrote to Edmond Malone about their friend's interests in theology, singling out his "fondness for those writers that deduce the attributes of a supreme being from the works of nature."[198] Burke's enthusiasm induced him to lend Kearney copies of physico-theological works by William Derham, John Ray and Bernard Nieuwentyt. Each of these authors had set out to display the wisdom of the creator as manifested in the works of the creation.[199] No "sparrow falls to the Ground without a purpose," Burke later asserted.[200] The underlying idea had played an important role in Grotian natural law theory: "the Will of God," Grotius wrote, "is revealed, not only through oracles and supernatural portents, but above all in the very design of the Creator;

[195] William Warburton, *A View of Lord Bolingbroke's Philosophy, in Four Letters to a Friend* (London: 1954–55), p. 70.

[196] *The Annual Register* provides some index of his preoccupations later in the 1750s, down at least to 1766. Aspects can be ascertained from: "Character of Voltaire by King of Prussia" in *The Annual Register for the Year 1758*, pp. 237–39; "Translation of a Letter from the late President Montesquieu, to Another of the View of Lord Bolingbroke's Philosophy" in *The Annual Register for 1760* (London: 1761), p. 189; "Physical Evil the Cause of Moral Good," extracted from the *Idler* in ibid., pp. 187–88; "A Short View of the Character and Writings of M. de Voltaire" in *The Annual Register for 1762* (London: 1763), pp. 48–50; "Review" of Warburton on the *Doctrine of Grace* in ibid., pp. 239–46; William Warburton's refutation of Voltaire in the *Divine Legation of Moses Demonstrated* (London: 1737–41), reprinted in *The Annual Register for the Year 1765* (London: 1766), pp. 207–15; "Advantages of the Social Principle over A Great Understanding towards Promoting the Happiness of Individuals," from John Gregory's *Comparative View of the Faculties of Man* (London: 1765) in ibid., pp. 227–33.

[197] EB, *Reflections*, ed. Clark, p. 383 [309].

[198] Michael Kearney to Edmond Malone, 3 May 1799, "Letters to Edmond Malone from Michael Kearney, 1797–1811," Bodl. MS. 39, fols. 29–30.

[199] William Derham, "A Demonstration of the Being and Attributes of God from the Works of Creation" in *A Defence of Natural and Revealed Religion Being an Abridgement of the Sermons Preached at the Lecture Founded by Robert Boyle* (London: 1737), 2 vols.; William Derham, *Physico-Theology: Or, A Demonstration of the Being and Attributes of God from His Works of Creation* (London: 1715); John Ray, *The Wisdom of God Manifested in the Works of the Creation* (London: 1709).

[200] EB to Unknown, 1795, *Corr.*, VIII, p. 364.

for it is from this last source that the law of nature is derived."[201] For Nieuwentyt in particular, who published his work in low Dutch so as to reach a national audience that had been treated to atheistic proselytism, the aim of the Christian philosopher was not merely to demonstrate the veracity of general providence, but to argue for the truth of "particular" providence as well: namely, to show that the "Eternal Being" was not only wise and powerful, but "Merciful" in addition.[202] God had not abandoned his creation to its own fortune, but continued to provide comfort for human aspirations and a framework of justification for morals. This benefaction depended on two articles of faith: the immortality of the soul and the doctrine of rewards and punishments. "Hope and fear are the Springs of everything in us," Burke wrote in his fragmentary essay on "Religion."[203] "To take away Providence," he went on, "would therefore be to take away Religion."[204] What he meant was that religion depended on particular providence, not the general idea of a wise and powerful creator. "Man has Ideas of Immortality, and wishes for it," Burke insisted.[205] He later noted that the assumption of immortality was "ancient, universal, and in a manner inherent in our nature."[206] Butler justified this idea as a probabilistic certainty based on analogical reasoning, dedicating the first two chapters of the *Analogy of Religion* to vindicating the reign of providence based on the promise of a future life and the prospect of rewards and punishments. Burke jotted the substance of his conclusions in an early fragment: "Man is sensible he has duties; that the Performance of these Duties must be agreeable to God; that being agreeable to God is the way to be happy."[207]

In Cicero's *De natura deorum* it is argued that the belief in providence is a precondition for piety (*pietas*), reverence (*sanctitas*) and religion (*religio*). Without these, moreover, "all trust [*fides*] and society [*societas*]" among human beings must be destroyed.[208] Atheism, from this perspective, was incompatible with social order. Burke claimed that the belief in immortality tended to "perfect" our nature: without it we were liable to sink to "the level of Inferiour Natures."[209] In the 1770s he would claim that even natural religion, founded either on reason or on instinct, was sufficient to sustain relations of trust between human beings, but only if it was based on ideas of immortality and an afterlife.[210] The Christian message had added meaning to these primitive intuitions by revealing a more refined relationship between

[201] Hugo Grotius, *Commentary on the Law of Prize and Booty* (c. 1604), ed. Martine Julia van Ittersum (Indianapolis, IN: Liberty Fund, 2006), p. 20.

[202] Bernard Nieuwentyt, *The Religious Philosopher: Or, The Right Use of Contemplating the Works of the Creator* (London: 3rd ed., 1724), p. v. This was a translation of *Regt Gebruik der Werelt Beschouwingen* (Amsterdam: 1715), dedicated to Lord Parker by J. Chamberlayne.

[203] EB, "Religion" in *Notebook*, p. 70.

[204] Ibid., p. 71,

[205] Ibid.

[206] EB, *An Essay towards an Abridgement of English History* (1757–c. 1763), *W & S*, I, p. 352.

[207] EB, "Religion" in *Notebook*, p. 71.

[208] Cicero, *De natura deorum*, I, 2.

[209] EB, "Religion" in *Notebook*, p. 72.

[210] EB to Dr. John Erskine, 12 June 1779, *Corr.*, IV, p. 85.

God and man. But why then had the Christian message not been revealed to all mankind at the beginning of the creation? This question had been provocatively posed by Matthew Tindal in 1730 as a means of challenging the need for revelation altogether.[211] Edmund Law, Cambridge philosopher and later Bishop of Carlisle, addressed the question in 1745 by reasoning probabilistically about God's distribution of benefits. "One who believed any thing of a God and his Providence," Law argued, "would naturally suppose that if a Revelation were to be made at all, it would be made according to the same method which is observed in the Government of the natural moral world."[212] The thesis drew on the powers of analogical argument to explicate the nature of the divine dispensation.[213] Christianity had been propagated in a "gradual, progressive and partial" manner as befitted the different stages of development among mankind.[214] This distribution of wisdom accorded with the ways of providence as evident more generally in life. Man was a morally progressive creature, requiring such ethical insights as would befit his stage of advancement. Christian truths were revealed to more developed understandings, as one would expect from the hand of a God who distributed just deserts.[215]

The reward of merit operated within a cosmic scheme of justice, but not within the scope of each individual life. As conflict between Britain and Revolutionary France began to intensify at the end of 1792, Burke returned to the themes of his early intellectual life. He reminded the Commons of the singular benefits derived from a programme of morality "founded upon the belief in the existence of God, and the comforts which individuals felt in leaving this world, in the hope of enjoying happiness in the next."[216] Burke's point was not merely that moral obligation required the sanction of an omnipotent deity. He was also keen to remind his auditors that the feeling of secular injustice was best compensated by the expectation of future happiness. This was a vital consideration for any advanced commercial society since the feeling of injustice might easily find expression under conditions of material inequality based on private property.[217] It was not always easy to explain to a man who stood in need of a dinner that "superfluities" were rightfully possessed over

[211] Matthew Tindal, *Christianity as Old as the Creation; or, the Gospel a Republication of the Religion of Nature* (London: 1730).

[212] Edmund Law, *Considerations on the State of the World, with regard to the Theory of Religion* (Cambridge: 1745).

[213] Law justified his case with reference to theological predecessors, specifically John Denne, *Sermon Preached for the Propagation of the Gospel in Foreign Parts* (London: 1730); John Conybeare, *The Defence of Revealed Religion* (London: 1732); Simon Browne, *Defence of the Religion of Nature, and the Christian Revelation* (London: 1732); and Butler's *Analogy*. See Law, *Considerations*, p. 9n.

[214] Ibid., p. 33.

[215] Ibid., pp. 10–11.

[216] EB, Speech on Aliens Bill, 28 December 1792, *Parliamentary History*, XXX, col. 187.

[217] For the persistence of opposition to the justice of the partition of property, see Michael Sonenscher, "Property, Community, and Citizenship" in Mark Goldie and Robert Wokler eds., *The Cambridge History of Eighteenth-Century Political Thought* (Cambridge: Cambridge University Press, 2006).

the claims of necessity.[218] Burke had underlined this point towards the end of the *Reflections*. A regime of property depended on the prior institution of civil obedience so that the acquisition of goods might be secure. Civil life implied respect for wealth which one did not oneself possess. Improvement was fuelled by a willingness to labour for what one hoped to obtain. Since it was commonly believed that the fruits of industry were not meritoriously allocated, the disproportionate division of secular wealth was made bearable by the idea of the "proportions of eternal justice." Particular providence was a guarantee of moral obligation, but it also facilitated social order through the consolations of a final reckoning. Whoever deprives a people of recompense of this kind, Burke thought, "deadens their industry, and strikes at the root of all acquisition as of all conservation." To pursue such a course by undermining the bases of Christian hope was to act the part of a "cruel oppressor, the merciless enemy of the poor and wretched."[219]

2.6 *A Vindication of Natural Society*

This argument was implicit in the *Vindication of Natural Society*, although the message is easily lost in the layers of parody. In an article for the *Monthly Visitor* published in 1797, it was asserted that the *Vindication* "has ever been considered as a master-stroke of deception."[220] The truth, however, is somewhat more complicated. In a review of the work that appeared within a month of its publication, the author was revealed to be "an ingenious young gentleman, a student in the *Temple*," but at the same time a general confusion about his intentions was reported.[221] The review then proceeded to summarise and refute the conclusions of the argument, depriving it altogether of its ironic purpose. The second edition of the work implicitly acknowledged that the irony of the original had been elusive, and thus that the satire was easily mistaken for genuine advocacy. The *Vindication* takes the form of a letter addressed to an unidentified figure, "Lord ****," posthumously published from the papers of a "Noble Writer." A mock Advertisement declares the letter to have been composed around 1748, and expects its author, the "Noble Writer," to be identified with Bolingbroke. The ensuing text is an elaborate imitation of Bolingbroke's prose with a view to parodying the evasiveness and pomposity of his style together with the superficiality presumed to be typical of his claims. However, the parody risks losing its edge by the sheer quality of the imitation, arguably undermining the critical import of the satire.[222]

[218] EB, Debate on Address of Thanks, 14 December 1792, *Parliamentary History*, XXX, col. 71.

[219] EB, *Reflections*, ed. Clarke, p. 411 [351].

[220] Anon., "Memoirs of the Right Honourable Edmund Burke," *Monthly Visitor* (October 1797), p. 317.

[221] *Critical Review* (June 1756), p. 420. Cf. *Gentleman's Magazine* (May 1756) for a similar result.

[222] Burke's irony has continued to be missed in twentieth-century interpretations of the *Vindication*. See, for example, Murray N. Rothbard, "A Note on Burke's *Vindication of Natural Society*," *Journal of the*

Burke's intentions can nonetheless be reconstructed from their context. The Preface to the second edition briefly adumbrates the general purpose: the aim of the work is to expose a particular mode of argumentation. Burke has the pseudo-philosophical style of Bolingbroke's posthumously published works in mind here, above all his late attacks on established religion and theology. His method is to expose Bolingbroke's posture of disabused reasonableness while casting doubt on his conclusions by a *reductio ad absurdum*. There are two objectives here which, in being pursued together, have blurred the exact import of Burke's message. The first objective was to demonstrate the disingenuousness of Bolingbroke's position, and the second was to explode his substantive points. Burke strove to mimic Bolingbroke's *faux* concessions to religious orthodoxy with a view to revealing his stance as an utter pretence. He was in little doubt that Bolingbroke's goal was to undermine religion, and that his avowed solicitousness for piety was mere bluff. For example, parodying the voice of Bolingbroke early on in the *Vindication*, the Noble Writer declares that, in ridiculing establishments, he does not in the least intend "to object to the Piety, Truth and Perfection of our most excellent Church."[223] However, obviously his "free inquiry" was designed to achieve exactly that.

At the same time, in addition to exposing Bolingbroke's specious show of candour, Burke endeavoured to shake up his intellectual method so as to reveal his putative insights as trivial flights of fancy. However, he did not pursue either of these aims by satirising Bolingbroke's treatment of those subjects through which he had caused most scandal: he did not explicitly tackle the topics of theology or religion but instead parodied Bolingbroke's procedure by applying it to political theory. The idea, therefore, was to show that the sceptical means employed by Bolingbroke to undermine religion could equally be deployed for the "Subversion of Government."[224] The assumption was that Bolingbroke himself would not accept the practical consequences of this mode of argument when applied to the subject of politics, and so the limits of corrosive reasoning would readily be made apparent.[225] Throughout the *Vindication*, the Noble Writer is presented as cherishing the truth over the consequences of its application: the idea that the destruction of long-held popular prejudices might be attended with "the most dangerous consequences" is ridiculed

---

History of Ideas, 19:1 (January 1958), pp. 114–18. For criticism of Rothbard, see John C. Weston Jr., "The Ironic Purpose of Burke's *Vindication* Vindicated," *Journal of the History of Ideas*, 19:3 (June 1958), pp. 435–41. Burke's irony is also noted throughout Frank Nowell Pegano, "Burke's Early Political Theory: *A Vindication of Natural Society*" (PhD thesis, Boston College, 1981), but without any historical sense of the object of Burke's satire. For a summary of the argument, see Frank N. Pegano, "Burke's View of the Evils of Political Theory: Or, *A Vindication of Natural Society*," *Polity*, 17:3 (Spring 1985), pp. 446–62. A more fully historical account of Burke's target is supplied by J. Boyd Cressman, "Burke's Satire on Bolingbroke in *A Vindication of Natural Society*" (PhD thesis, University of Michigan, 1956).

[223] EB, *Vindication*, p. 140.

[224] Ibid., p. 134.

[225] On this, see Iain Hampsher-Monk, "Rousseau, Burke's *Vindication of Natural Society*, and Revolutionary Ideology," *European Journal of Political Theory*, 9:3 (2010), pp. 245–66.

as an "Absurd and blasphemous Notion."[226] The aim of Burke's satire is to subvert this complacent assumption by delivering a vision of society that is a product of free inquiry, yet the consequences of which even Bolingbroke could not accept.

Two posthumous editions of Bolingbroke's works appeared under the editorship of David Mallet in 1754, one of them collecting all the writings he had produced and the other specifically presenting his "philosophical works."[227] It was the philosophical writings that attracted public attention, outraging orthodox sentiment by their irreverence and provocation. They were also widely seen as being disingenuous in the extreme: throughout, Bolingbroke protested his harmless intentions while cumulatively exploding the utility of organised religion. In the Introduction to his *Letters Addressed to Pope*, he claimed to be trying to restore the "honour of Christianity" by seeking the truth in his private capacity as a scholar.[228] However, to many the declaration seemed a charade: his intentions appeared impious and his objectives ultimately subversive. He "Blames the Free-thinkers for taking unbecoming Liberties," observed John Leland, "Yet writes himself without any regard to the rules of decency."[229] There were limits, Bolingbroke pretended, to freedom of wit and the spirit of ridicule; but in reality he strove to undermine the tenets of Christian faith.

According to Bolingbroke, the limits prescribed to a philosopher's freedom of inquiry were self-imposed, in accordance with the dictates of personal prudence, while those imposed on a church divine were a function of institutional bias. The implication was that the natural reason of philosophy served the truth while the clerical wisdom of the Church was skewed by institutional obligations. In a *Letter Occasioned by One of Archbishop Tillotson's Sermons*, Bolingbroke sought to denigrate the philosophical acumen of the clergy by insisting that they were encumbered by the requirements of their "theological system."[230] The philosopher, by comparison, was free to respond to the promptings of truth. For instance, while Bolingbroke had, as he tells us, at one time been disposed to assume that the beliefs of primitive man were monotheistic, on reflection he was at liberty to accept that the "first men" were most likely polytheists. Tillotson, on the other hand, was a slave to his presuppositions, and these derived from the demands imposed by his institutional commitments.[231] "Tillotson," as Bolingbroke put it, "was led by his prejudices"—guided by presumption steeped in "theological ostentation."[232] Burke would turn the tables on

[226] EB, *Vindication*, p. 139.

[227] Bolingbroke, *Works*, 15 vols.; Henry St. John Bolingbroke, *The Philosophical Works of the Right Honorable Henry St. John, Lord Viscount Bolingbroke* (London: 1754), 5 vols. Both editions carried the offending philosophical essays.

[228] Bolingbroke, *Works*, III, p. 334.

[229] John Leland, *A View of the Principal Deistical Writers that Have Appeared in England in the Last and Present Century* (London: 1755), 2 vols., II, p. 136.

[230] Bolingbroke, *Works*, III, p. 257. Bolingbroke is discussing the sermons collected in John Tillotson, *Sermons sur diverses matières importantes,* ed. J. Barbeyrac (Amsterdam: 1718), 2 vols. The sermons had been recommended to Barbeyrac by Locke.

[231] Bolingbroke, *Works*, III, p. 259.

[232] Ibid., pp. 266, 268.

Bolingbroke's critique, appealing to prejudice and presumption as a means of refuting dogmatic assertions.[233]

Again in the Introduction to the *Essays* addressed to Pope, Bolingbroke stridently contrasted the intellectual virtue of rational inquiry with the metaphysical delusions of Church dogma, declaring that he was a latecomer to the path of enlightened reason: originally, he had deferred to theological learning with an attitude of naïve "presumption," only to end up crediting his own faculties when he began to doubt unexamined assumptions that stood on authority alone: "I respect no authority enough to subscribe on faith to it."[234] Faced with clerical imposture, as he saw it, Bolingbroke began to construct a "first philosophy" on the secure basis of empirical inquiry, building on "particular experiments and observations" in opposition to the speculation of "hypothetical reasoning." In this he believed he was following the example of Locke, liberated from the kind of axiomatic reasoning that he associated with Leibnitz, and even Bacon.[235] By this he meant that he confined his inquiries within the "bounds of human knowledge," basing understanding on ideas either mediately or immediately derived from the observation of nature.[236]

To observe the natural world, of course, was to study the divinity as reflected in its works, but it was not to speculate about its nature, its attributes or its providence.[237] Such speculation, Bolingbroke made clear, went beyond the limits of legitimate rational inquiry since human understanding was incapable of comprehending the mind of God. However, if reason according to Bolingbroke could not penetrate metaphysical mysteries, it could expose the inconsistencies that pervaded superstition. Nonetheless, the process of exposure brought with it civic obligations. Bolingbroke insisted that the application of naked reason to the vulgar delusions of superstition carried with it a burden of public responsibility, without which the pursuit of enlightenment would foment dissidence and faction.[238] He accepted that devotion to the truth risked promoting heterodoxy, which in practice could be subversive of the established order in politics and religion. Given the potential for heterodox opinion to be politicised and organised into party-minded cabals, freedom of speech ought to be tailored to fit specific circumstances. It was salutary for Bolingbroke that Plato, Cicero, Varro and Erasmus all conceded the necessity of adapting one's message to match one's audience since the common run of humanity could not absorb the truths of reason without threatening the principles of social order.[239] There existed a middle way between shattering the foundations of society and government by exposing the religious sensibility to ridicule and the observance of blind obedience to established dogma.

[233] On this, see Hampsher-Monk, "Burke and the Religious Sources of Sceptical Conservatism."

[234] Bolingbroke, *Works*, III, pp. 320–22.

[235] Ibid, pp. 326–29.

[236] Ibid., p. 327.

[237] Ibid., p. 330.

[238] Ibid.

[239] Ibid., p. 331.

This *via media* depended, in the end, on a division of intellectual labour between the multitude who conformed their opinions to ancestral beliefs and leisured gentlemen engaged in the business of dispassionate inquiry without causing any disturbance to the public peace. Shaftesbury had memorably addressed the subversive danger posed by the criticism of religion at the start of the century: freedom of wit, he commented, is not to be "grossly us'd in publick Company." Instead, intellectual liberty should be reserved for the confines of the "*Club*"—that is, "amongst Gentlemen and Friends, who know one another perfectly well."[240] For Bolingbroke this meant that the truth should be sought "quietly" as well as "freely."[241] However, the suspicion was that this profession of discretion was a ruse on Bolingbroke's part, since at the same time he was explicit in wanting to pit the authority of lay inquiry against what he took to be the dogmatism of the clergy. The Church, in Bolingbroke's opinion, was incapable of enlightenment, having persisted in preaching pedantry and ignorance to the public, even after the "resurrection" of letters at the Renaissance.[242] There was, in effect, no possibility of "composition" with the clerical establishment.[243] The best one could expect was a decline in their credibility as priestly hegemony over men's minds was steadily replaced by the authority of enlightened gentlemen. Contention in human affairs had been a clerical fabrication, and thus philosophy promised an end to artificial party divisions: faction would be abolished along with theological controversy.[244]

Burke's idea for the *Vindication* was in all probability sparked by Bolingbroke's tentative application of the idea that theological artifice deranges the natural aptitudes of the mind to the process by which human nature is corrupted in civil society.[245] In the Introduction to his *Letters* to Pope, Bolingbroke contended that the operation of sectional interests on the passions of men in society generated prejudices that destroyed the impartiality of government. Prejudice was supported by intellectual imposture exemplified by clerical learning, which imported forms of "bias" developed in an era of ignorance into an "enlightened" age. For Bolingbroke, given this process of degeneration to which establishments were prone, truth would have to be continually restored by the light of nature, which Burke interpreted to mean that staple beliefs would be undermined by aggravated critical inquiry. The "most civilized nations," Bolingbroke argued, "are often guilty of injustice and cruelty." This

[240] Anthony Ashley Cooper, Third Earl of Shaftesbury, "Sensus Communis: An Essay on the Freedom of Wit and Humour" in idem, *Characteristicks of Men, Manners, Opinions Times* (1711) (Indianapolis, IN: Liberty Fund, 2001), p. 48.

[241] Bolingbroke, *Works*, III, p. 333.

[242] Ibid., pp. 341–42.

[243] Ibid., p. 343.

[244] Ibid., p. 335,

[245] For the idea that Rousseau's *Second Discourse* was a target of Burke's in the *Vindication*, see Richard Sewell. "Rousseau's *Second Discourse* in England from 1755 to 1762," *Philological Quarterly*, 17 (April 1938), pp. 97–114; F. P. Lock, *Edmund Burke*, I, p. 87; Ian Harris, *Burke: Pre-Revolutionary Writings* (Cambridge: Cambridge University Press, 1993), p. 6. For criticism, see Iain Hampsher-Monk, "Rousseau, Burke's *Vindication of Natural Society*, and Revolutionary Ideology."

failure of civility resulted, he thought, from the corruption of human beings as they are drawn out of their natural, "primitive" state under the influence of "artificial" interests and opinions. The accompanying decline of society can only be arrested at the behest of natural reason, which, as Bolingbroke saw it, should be employed to challenge the assumptions of traditional "custom." Custom, after all, was "a second and false nature," that ultimately bred divisiveness and faction.[246]

Burke's *Vindication* clears the ground for the development of an alternative theory of faction, beginning with a direct assault on the defence of natural society as outlined in the Introduction to Bolingbroke's *Letters* to Pope. For Bolingbroke, natural society was founded on the common interests of human beings, yet these were factionalised under the influence of false philosophical doctrines pedalled by the institutional or "artificial" reason of a designing clergy.[247] Faced with this fraudulent artifice, Bolingbroke commended the ambition of Montaigne to "naturalise" the inventions of the philosophy of the schools, citing his resolution to the effect that "je naturaliserois l'art": "If I was a philosopher, says Montaigne, I would naturalise art, instead of artilising nature."[248] The *Vindication of Natural Society* involves a wholesale application of this programme of "naturalisation" to the history of the institutions of government with a view to exposing Bolingbroke's naïveté. The goal, Burke implies, of bringing party to an end by purging vested interests in the name of a single, rationally shared objective will eventuate in the reverse of what is intended. Since uniformity of opinion would have to be despotically imposed, it would arouse the spirit of sedition against the tyranny of the common good.[249]

The *Vindication* opens by informing its readers that it will consider the destruction wrought by civil society by recounting the history of politics in both its external and internal relations. Beginning with the external activities of the state, the Noble Writer narrates the course of both civilised and barbarian histories as an unbroken sequence of war and devastation. Mimicking the display of learning which typically characterised Bolingbroke's writings, we are taken on a whirlwind tour of the Egyptian, Babylonian, Assyrian, Median and Persian monarchies, followed by snippets of Greek, Macedonian, Roman, Goth, Vandal and modern European affairs, to illustrate the claim that the record of history reveals nothing but a litany of crimes: conquest, subjugation, devastation and extirpation, without advantage either to the victors or to the vanquished, allegedly characterise the course of societies in their mutual relations. "I charge the whole of these effects on political society," the Noble Writer declares, aping the kind of indiscriminate condemnation found in Boling-

[246] Bolingbroke, *Works*, III, p. 315.

[247] Ibid., p, 319.

[248] Ibid., p. 315, translating the line from Montaigne's "Upon Some Verses of Virgil": "Si j'estois du mestier, je naturaliserois l'art autant comme ils artialisent la nature." See Michel de Montaigne, *Les essais de Michel de Montaigne,* ed. Pierre Villey and V.-L. Saulnier (Paris: Presses Universitaires de France, 1965), p. 874. I am grateful to Felicity Green for this reference.

[249] This subject is treated in Harvey C. Mansfield, *Statesmanship and Party Government: A Study of Burke and Bolingbroke* (Chicago, IL: University of Chicago Press, 1965), pp. 238–39.

broke.[250] A charge of irreligion at the same time lurks in Burke's presentation: the interminable round of bloodshed is used by the Noble Writer to exemplify "how severe a Scourge Providence intends for the human Race."[251] The implication is that the methods employed by Bolingbroke to destroy the idea of a beneficent deity can just as easily be used to obliterate the distinction between justice and exploitation, thereby reducing the history of government to a history of oppression. By these means, civilisation becomes indistinguishable from the barbarous past, and all history is collapsed into a procession of undifferentiated abuses.

Having reduced the history of society to an uninterrupted train of belligerence, the Noble Writer proceeds to offer some general reflections in which he explains the scale of human destruction in terms of the advent of political society. We are told that while a certain "haughtiness" and "fierceness" in human nature disposes the species to mutual confrontation and conflict, nonetheless it is the artifice of civil society itself that accounts for the frequency and cruelty of these contentions.[252] The reasons for this are seemingly twofold. First, the emergence of political society, in expanding the scale of organisation, is charged with increasing the means of destruction. But second, the birth of civil society apparently transforms the human passions in the process of instituting relations of "*subordination*." As the Noble Writer describes it, politics institutionalises a vicious dialectic between "Tyranny" and "Slavery," as a consequence of which fury and vengeance are unleashed through the experience of subjection to the caprice of rulers. Arcane reason of state on one side and popular malice on the other are taken to define the relationship between the government and the governed.[253]

Every system of government is presented in the *Vindication* as giving rise to despotism, resulting in disorder: "Take them in what Form you please, they are in effect but a Despotism," we are told.[254] This leads the Noble Writer to the deliberately outrageous conclusion that civil society as such is the source of political corruption. To lend plausibility to this claim, the reader is taken through the three principal forms of government so that the inadequacies of each can be paraded in turn. Monarchy, for example, is simply labelled by the term "despotism," while aristocracy is held to "differ but in Name."[255] In this vein, democracy is said to possess the same "Spirit" as "absolute Monarchy," as illustrated by the history of the ancient republics. Athens, for example, appears as a persecuting regime, averse to the triumph of merit and given to destabilising dissensions.[256] Beyond this, particular censure is reserved for mixed systems of government which are taken to combine the humours of each of the pure constitutional forms in a mixture leading to perpetual internecine struggle:

[250] EB, *Vindication*, pp. 151.
[251] Ibid., p. 143.
[252] Ibid., p. 152.
[253] Ibid., pp. 153–54.
[254] Ibid., p. 182.
[255] Ibid., p. 158.
[256] Ibid., pp. 161–65.

"such a Government must be liable to frequent Cabals, Tumults, and Revolutions, from its very Constitution."[257] The underlying cause of these collisions is the spirit of "Party," which drives the opposing interests of the polity into conflict. From this perspective, mixed regimes destroy the possibility of rational administration by fomenting angry factional divisions.[258]

Burke was perfectly aware that in the mid 1730s Bolingbroke had associated the "artifice" of party with the "darkness" of the age of superstition. The spirit of faction in English politics had subsided since the seventeenth century, Bolingbroke contended; and an end to national divisions could at least be contemplated. "Shall we suffer this light to be turned again into party-darkness?" he asked rhetorically.[259] Later on in *A Dissertation upon Parties*, Bolingbroke traces the origins of party in general to the diversity of opinions regarding politics and religion, identifying "sound philosophy" based on natural reason as the only hope for correcting aberrations of the kind.[260] To sharpen his point, he refers his reader to the philosophical preamble to the stoic proofs for the existence of God as articulated by Lucilius in book II of Cicero's *De natura deorum*. "Time destroys the contrivances of opinion," Lucilius remarked, "yet it confirms the judgments of nature."[261] In his *Dissertation*, Bolingbroke applied this appeal to natural reason to the subject of politics rather than religion, treating the defence of the prerogative rights of monarchy under Charles I as an example of vacuous opinion which sober judgment could not support: "when the same opinions revived at the Restoration," Bolingbroke asserted, they failed to take root and were soon "exploded."[262]

Bolingbroke's idea that false political opinions resulted from the misapplication of the laws of nature to specific cases under the influence of human passion was most fully elaborated in his *Fragments or Minutes of Essays* that appeared in the final volume of his *Works* of 1754. It followed from this analysis that party strife was a product of the insufficiency of reason. On this conception, civil society was corrupted under the influence of passion and prejudice. It was not, however, intrinsically iniquitous, as the *Vindication* suggested in its parodic version of Bolingbrokean theory. In Burke's satire, man in the state of nature is as yet unaffected by pride. It was the emergence of enlightenment with the birth of civilisation that gave rise at once to corruption and extravagance. Burke's Noble Writer encapsulated this position with a couplet from the third book of Pope's *Essay on Man*, a moral epistle on the "Nature and State of MAN" addressed to Bolingbroke: "Pride then was not; nor

[257] Ibid., p. 169.

[258] Ibid., p. 170.

[259] Henry St. John Bolingbroke, *A Dissertation upon Parties* (1735) in *Bolingbroke: Political Writings*, ed. David Armitage (Cambridge: Cambridge University Press, 1997), p. 4.

[260] Ibid., p. 30.

[261] Cicero, *De natura deorum*, II, ii, 5. In Bolingbroke, *Dissertation*, p. 30, this intervention in the dialogue is mistakenly ascribed to Balbus, and is paraphrased as follows: "Groundless opinions are destroyed, but rational judgments, or the judgments of nature, are confirmed by time."

[262] Bolingbroke, *Dissertation*, pp. 31–32.

arts, that Pride to aid; / Man walk'd with beast, joint tenant of the shade."[263] Bolingbroke's aim was to indict artificial society without crediting the idea of a natural state of man prior to the establishment of society. For Burke, however, this indictment undermined the conditions of religious piety, and with it the foundations of morality and civilisation. Bolingbroke contended that the "foundations of civil or political societies were laid in nature, though they are the creatures of art."[264] Art had vitiated the potentiality of nature.

Part of Bolingbroke's intention had been to criticise the idea of a state of natural liberty as presented in the work of Hobbes and Locke. There had never existed, he proposed, a purely natural condition that preceded the existence of political society: before civil society, communities subsisted within the society of the family, most usually under the supervision of paternal government. Pierre Bayle had been wrong, Bolingbroke protested, to associate barbarian existence with a condition of absolute licence. Following Sallust's depiction of the Getulians and Libyans as flourishing independently of "customs, laws, or the authority of rulers," Bayle had associated these "rude and uncivilized tribes" with pre-social life.[265] However, Bolingbroke objected, men "were never out of societies; for if they were divided into families before they were assembled into nations, they were in society from their original."[266] Nonetheless, if society and authority were natural to the human condition, they were prone to abuse in the hands of a creature as imperfect as man. As a consequence of the perennial human inability to apply the laws of nature with impartial rigour in civil society, the injustice and inhumanity evident in "civilised and enlightened" Europe often exceeded that apparent among "the Iroquois, Brasilians, or the wildest inhabitants of African deserts."[267] This was intended as a rebuke to the kind of enlightenment complacency that associated the progress of society with moral improvement. The implication was that culture or human "artifice" had not contributed to the betterment of civil society. If the natural state of man was not a pre-social condition, as Hobbes had suggested, neither was it a state of original depravity which had been corrected by improvements in mental and moral life.

As Burke saw, Bolingbroke's vision of the progress of man in society hinged on a set of claims about corruption bred by artifice. Bolingbroke's peculiar scorn was reserved for the history of religious culture. This was made apparent in the second of his *Letters to Pope*, "Some Reflections on the Folly and Presumption of Philosophers." Here Bolingbroke argued that the progress of religious wisdom had not

[263] Alexander Pope, *An Essay on Man* (1733–34) in *The Poems of Alexander Pope*, ed. John Butt (London: Routledge, 1963, 2005), "To the Reader," p. 501, and book III, lines 151–52. The lines are cited in Burke, *Vindication*, p. 181, as: "Then was not Pride, nor Arts that Pride to aid, / Man walk'd with Beast, Joint-tenant of the Shade."

[264] Henry St. John Bolingbroke, *Fragments or Minutes of Essays* in *Works*, V, p. 105.

[265] Ibid., p. 111. Bolingbroke is responding to an argument in the *Pensées diverses sur la comète* drawing on Sallust, *Jugurtha*, XVIII.

[266] Bolingbroke, *Fragments* in *Works*, V, p. 110.

[267] Ibid., p. 152.

been a history of enlightenment but a story of artificial imposture. Clerical abuse had successfully hoodwinked natural reason. As a result, Bolingbroke concluded, our most cherished religious notions are artful fabrications invented by a designing priestly caste. In presenting his case, Bolingbroke challenged what he took to be the prevalent Christian conception of the rise and progress of philosophy. Following the spurious claims of Josephus and Eusebius, scholars like Brochart, Huet and Stillingfleet had accepted the idea of the transmission of the arts and sciences, above all the acquisitions of religious truth, from east to west—bequeathed by the Egyptians to the Greeks.[268] In place of this trajectory, Bolingbroke presented the story of human awakening as the triumph of error and deception. His narrative was organised into two stages, beginning with error and ending in deception. The earliest societies, unable to intuit a final cause for the phenomena of nature, had explained events in terms of multiple efficient causes, which were worshipped as deities in themselves. The earliest religions were therefore polytheistic in character: the idea of a single godhead had not been a gift to the children of Adam. Monotheism, in other words, had been a late acquisition.[269] Its discovery had been an achievement of a philosophical elite. Yet this truth of first philosophy had not been imparted to the masses. Instead, they had been duped by a class of philosopher-legislators: "Religion, in the hands of these philosophical legislators, who succeeded to the authority of fathers of families, was a proper expedient to enforce obedience to political regimen."[270]

Since it was apparent that the earliest monotheists imposed doctrines on the people which they knew to be false, by manipulating spurious claims to privileged revelation, it seemed to Bolingbroke that they must have been eager to impose one particular artefact: the doctrine of rewards and punishments based on the immortality of the soul. The deception became all the easier with the emergence of church government, founded on the creation of a priestly order which wielded influence on the basis of power and wealth.[271] This was clearly a swipe at the Christian churches, the Anglican establishment in particular. They were captivated by error, and disposed to deceive their flock. Their methods were of ancient provenance, as Bolingbroke demonstrated in his account of the pagan religion among the Greeks. The character of the deity could only be discovered in his works: "Beyond this veil the eye of human reason can discover nothing."[272] However, the generality of mankind, as illustrated by the heroes of Homer's *Iliad*, were inclined to confuse the divinity with a multitude of polytheistic forces. At the other extreme, philosophers were prone to believe that they could penetrate God's essence, and decipher not only his physical effects but his moral nature as well.[273] The idea of God's particular providence, in other words, was a spurious theological interpolation generated by the presumption of

[268] Bolingbroke, *Works*, IV, pp. 12–13.
[269] Ibid., pp. 16–19.
[270] Ibid., p. 26.
[271] Ibid., p. 41.
[272] Ibid., p. 47.
[273] Ibid., p. 48.

philosopher-priests and perpetuated by modern Christian divines. The artifice of religion thus subverted natural reason with a superstitious belief in the moral economy of nature.[274]

During a debate on the Quebec Bill on 6 May 1791, Burke dedicated a "rapturous apostrophe" to the power of the deity whose ways were not accessible to "weak, incapable mortals."[275] All we had to guide us was the authority of experience. Nonetheless, this pointed to the probability of existence in the hereafter and the prospect of reward for industry and virtue. Without this foundation in hope, morality lacked dignity, reducing human motives to appetites and instincts. Burke opened the *Vindication* with the depiction of such a world. "The original Children of the Earth lived with their Brethren of the other Kinds in much Equality," he wrote.[276] Without a providential God, Burke was suggesting, humans would be vitiated and bestialised. In *Alciphron*, Berkeley had highlighted the position of moral sceptics as an inversion of true philosophical principles which "endeavour to raise and refine human-kind, and remove it as far as possible from the brute."[277] Freethinkers, by comparison, sought to strip the mind of its ornaments in order to divest it of its accumulated prejudices, "reducing it to its original state of nature."[278] As Burke saw it, it was the denial of particular providence that secured this result. The *Vindication* reported that the proponents of natural society doubted whether "the Creator did ever really intend Man for a State of Happiness."[279] All that was experienced was a succession of evils, without any justification or expectation of relief. The stoic doctrine of endurance could only offer sorry comfort. All artifice designed to alleviate this natural condition was doomed to add new misery to anguish. On this analysis of the possibilities for human improvement, habit offered no prospect for cultivating virtue: it only introduced "new Mischiefs", or aggravated old.[280] Education promised degradation instead of the means of moral advance.

In presenting this critical account of the achievements of artifice, the *Vindication* presented a mock challenge to Butler's moral thought. The real aim of the work, of course, was to endorse the claims of Butler by exposing the vacuity of Bolingbrokean argument. In the fifth chapter of the *Analogy*, devoted to the subject of moral improvement, Butler highlights the efficacy of moral habit as a vehicle for ethical education. Nature dictates, Butler observed, that habits are formed by continuous

[274] It was this argument in particular that drew criticism from Charles Bulkley, *Notes on the Philosophical Writings of Lord Bolingbroke* (London: 1755), p. 52. This work, like much else connected with the deist controversy, is listed in the sale catalogue of Burke's library. A version of this was published as *Catalogue of the Library of the Late Right Hon. Edmund Burke* (London: 1833).

[275] EB, Debate on the Quebec Bill, 6 May 1791, *Parliamentary History*, XXIX, col. 388.

[276] EB, *Vindication*, p. 138.

[277] Berkeley, *Alciphron*, p. 56.

[278] Ibid., p. 57

[279] EB, *Vindication*, p. 137.

[280] Ibid.

exercise.[281] Humans are so constituted, in other words, as to acquire culture, facilitating perception by the association of ideas and the readiness to act by repeated use.[282] This aptitude enables us to refine our nature for the benefit of civilised existence. Acclimatisation to luxury illustrates this capacity: ornaments gradually become requirements. By the same process, sensibilities can be cultivated and manners refined. The *Vindication* offered a sham critique of this process. Every day, we are told, the mind discovers "some craving want in the Body, which really wants but little."[283] This principle is then generalised into a feature of social life: we constantly invent "some new artificial Rule to guide that Nature which if left to itself were the best and surest Guide."[284] Butler's point, and Burke's too, was that artificial improvements were part of our nature, enabled by the disposition to form habits.

In the *Vindication* we are reminded of Bolingbroke's target in reprimanding artifice: theologians had contrived "imaginary Beings prescribing imaginary Laws" and then raised "imaginary Terrors to support a Belief in the Beings."[285] The idea of an imaginary being employed to inculcate imaginary terrors seemed to Burke no better than a presumptuous platitude of the kind popularised by generations of deist speculation. It was informed by a faith in natural reason that disregarded the "Power of Habits" as an instrument of moral progress.[286] Burke satirised the position in the *Vindication*, but in the aftermath of the French Revolution it was subject to a frontal attack that would dominate the final portion of his career. In 1794, after Burke had retired from parliament, his literary executor, French Laurence, planned an account of his career for *The Annual Register*. The *Vindication*, Laurence claimed, was intended to "startle" the disciples of Bolingbroke, "but the successors of the same school in France have gone the whole length of the principle in a desperate experiment on a great kingdom."[287] The moral and religious scepticism that Burke had challenged in the 1750s, it was being suggested, underlay the revolutionary spirit of the 1790s.

[281] Butler, *Analogy*, pp. 84–85. On nature in Butler, see Allan Millar, "Butler on God and Human Nature" in Christopher Cunliffe ed., *Joseph Butler's Moral and Religious Thought: Tercentenary Essays* (Oxford: Oxford University Press, 1992).

[282] Butler, *Analogy*, p. 82.

[283] EB, *Vindication*, pp. 137–38. For this theme in eighteenth-century political thought, see Istvan Hont, "The Early Enlightenment Debate on Commerce and Luxury" in Goldie and Wokler eds., *Eighteenth-Century Political Thought*.

[284] EB, *Vindication*, pp. 137–38.

[285] Ibid., p. 138.

[286] The phrase is from Butler, *Analogy*, p. 81.

[287] French Laurence, "Political Life of Edmund Burke: Annotated Proofs of a Contribution to the *Annual Register*" (c. 1794), OSB MS. File 8753.

III

THE *PHILOSOPHICAL ENQUIRY*: SCIENCE OF THE PASSIONS, 1757

3.1 Introduction

As Burke was writing *A Vindication of Natural Society* he had already substantially completed his *Philosophical Enquiry into the Origin of our Ideas of the Sublime and Beautiful*. Nonetheless, he revised his text and delayed its publication until after the *Vindication* had appeared. The *Philosophical Enquiry* has long enjoyed a privileged position in the Burke corpus, not least as a result of its early positive reception in Germany. In truth, however, the work is something of an oddity among Burke's writings. Its approach is explicitly philosophical in nature, and its subject matter comprises the causes of aesthetic pleasure. Burke never returned in a systematic way to the theme of the book again. Having said this, looked at less literally, the implications of Burke's study branch into a wider field, encompassing the social utility of the passions. From this perspective, the *Philosophical Enquiry* is an important document in Burke's development. As we shall see, it takes up the thread of preoccupations that absorbed him throughout his twenties. It begins with an exploration of the classical theory of mixed emotions, focusing on Aristotle's signature categories of pity and terror. It proceeds to elucidate the affective psychology of manners, probing the feeling of exhilaration unleashed by pride and the instinct for subordination based on fear. Challenging the deist assumptions of a number of predecessors, Burke argues for the dependence of moral taste on duty. In the process, he articulates the reliance of ethics on religion, and traces the origins and development of superstition. At the same time he investigates the association of ideas, the power of language and the standard of taste. The work also recapitulates Burke's antipathy to stoicism, along with his response to the leading moralists of the age, above all the writings of Hutcheson, Mandeville and Berkeley, as well as Dubos, Condillac, Hume and Smith. Although the *Enquiry* is not a comprehensive treatise in moral philosophy, it does provide us with access to Burke's theory of human nature as it sets about accounting for uniform features of the mind.

3.2 Wonder, Pleasure and Pity

Burke's *Philosophical Enquiry* was first published by Robert Dodsley on 21 April 1757. The following August he sent Shackleton a copy of the work, apologising for his "neglect" in not having been in touch sooner. The manuscript of the book, he informed his friend, "lay by me for a good while" before he finally decided that his effort should be "ventured" out.[1] Burke was more explicit about its composition in the Preface: "it is four years now since this enquiry was finished," he declared, indicating a completion date of 1753.[2] But his interest in the subject goes back still farther. In 1789, he informed Edmond Malone that the subject of his study had long been "rolling in his thoughts" since he began to address such topics during his college days.[3] This claim is easily ratified by reference to his correspondence: in a letter written to Shackleton during his Trinity years, Burke can be found analysing the character of mixed emotions, a subject that would draw his attention in the *Philosophical Enquiry*.[4] In a more elevated vein, he registered in an earlier letter the pleasure he took in witnessing "great tho' terrible Scenes" of nature which fill the mind "with grand ideas" and turn the soul "in upon herself." Burke was meditating on the psychological impact of natural disasters in the wake of his recent experience of the river Liffey having burst its banks. Events of the kind, he observed, impressed upon the human mind the potency of nature while still encouraging in us a belief in our own greatness: "I consider'd how little man is yet in his own mind how great!"[5] These stray ruminations would be developed into Burke's theory of "ambition" in the *Enquiry*, which he presented as part of a general account of human motivation.

The *Philosophical Enquiry* was an avowed work of criticism, but as such it contained the elements of a theory of the passions, at the same time examining the effects of emotion on social and religious life. For that reason, although the work is plainly not an exercise in theology or social theory, it contains the elements of an anthropology relevant to politics, morals and religion. Burke's title deliberately pointed to Francis Hutcheson's *Inquiry into the Original of Our Ideas of Beauty and Virtue* of 1725, although his purpose was to dissent from the conclusions of Hutcheson's work. In February 1747 Burke had composed a verse epistle "To Dr H[utcheso]N," evidently admiring the facility with which his addressee had anatomised the "structure of the passions," and traced them to their underlying causes.[6] But William Dennis was quick to notice Burke's divergence from his predecessor in

[1] EB to Richard Shackleton, 10 August 1757, *Corr.*, I, p. 123.

[2] EB, *A Philosophical Enquiry into the Origin of our Ideas of the Sublime and Beautiful* (1757, rev. ed. 1759). *W&S*, p. 188.

[3] James Prior, *Life of Edmond Malone, Editor of Shakespeare* (London: 1860), p. 154.

[4] EB to Richard Shackleton, c. 3 February 1746/7, *Corr.*, I, pp. 78–79.

[5] EB to Richard Shackleton, 25 January 1744/5, ibid., pp. 39.

[6] EB, "TO DR H--N," *W & S*, I, p. 31.

giving an account of both inquiries to Shackleton in March 1758. Dennis revealed that he was on his third reading of the *Philosophical Enquiry* since its appearance a year earlier, and considered it a "masterly performance." Its main thrust differed markedly from Hutcheson's conclusions, he went on: where Hutcheson's work corrupted the understanding of morals, Burke had evidently enlarged our sense of the operation of taste.[7]

Dennis ascribed the corrupting influence of Hutcheson's treatise to its having "indirectly" sapped religion by "representing virtue independent of it." Burke's *Enquiry* made no such attempt to reduce moral duty to the vagaries of taste, as Dennis saw it: instead, it established principles for judging the pleasures of the imagination by tracing the correspondence between our passions and the objects which arouse them. Therefore, while Burke set out to provide a science of taste, he kept the basis of aesthetic judgment distinct from the foundation of morals—an outcome poorly designed, perhaps, to please the modern "Crowd," as Dennis phrased it, but nonetheless one that would appeal to men of discernment.[8] What Dennis admired in the *Enquiry* was its lack of philosophical presumptuousness, and in this he was following the lead of Burke's own presentation of his intentions. The Preface to the first edition of the work claimed to be proposing its arguments as "probable conjectures, not as things certain and indisputable."[9] It was an exercise in Lockean empiricism, sceptical about metaphysical certainty, but nonetheless inclined to explain the effects of stimuli on the imagination in terms of providentially orchestrated "laws of nature" whose character could be observed, even if their rationale could not be decoded.[10] Burke was in search of the laws of criticism, but this required an account of human nature that could explain our motivations and reactions. In the process, he provided an account of sociability and a theory of subordination to authority, together with an analysis of the sentiments that supported religion. For this reason, it seems best to view Burke's work as built upon an anthropology which contained the rudiments of a theory of society and religion.

Burke begins the *Enquiry* by arguing that the instinct for novelty is a primordial characteristic of the human mind. "The first and simplest emotion which we discover in the human mind, is Curiosity," he declares.[11] The idea that curiosity, or the appetite for knowledge, is among the most basic of the emotions already had a long philosophical history. In *Les passions de l'âme,* Descartes presented curiosity as a feeling of wonder or "admiration," a sudden sensation of surprise in the soul triggered by an encounter with rare or extraordinary objects. In the face of something new, he claimed, we feel inspired to investigate further purely on account of the novelty of the object: what is out of the ordinary train of experience and expectation naturally

[7] OSB MSS. File 4325: "ALS to Richard Shackleton," March 1758.

[8] Ibid.

[9] EB, *Philosophical Enquiry*, p. 189.

[10] Ibid., p. 188.

[11] EB, *Philosophical Enquiry*, p. 210.

appears striking to us, and fills the mind with admiring curiosity.[12] This passion of wonder (*admiratio*) was understood by Descartes to be the "first" of all the emotions because, although the passion itself was useful insofar as it furthered human goals, it motivated action without regard to utility.[13] An object of curiosity might turn out to be beneficial, but as soon as its usefulness was ascertained the appetite for knowledge would have been gratified. Wonder was therefore antecedent to calculations of advantage.[14]

Charles Lebrun's 1698 *Conférence tenue en l'Academie Royale de Peinture et Sculpture* followed Descartes in adding admiration to the scholastic list of concupiscible passions.[15] He further observed that, unlike the other passions, this feeling caused no physical change in either the heart or the blood for the reason that it was indifferent to the calibre of its objects, which might equally turn out to be grand or mean. In the face of grandeur, admiration was joined to esteem, producing the feeling of veneration; in the face of meanness, it was joined to contempt, giving rise to disdain.[16] Lebrun's overall purpose was to illustrate how the passions could be represented by the plastic arts. Since he regarded admiration as the most tranquil of the emotions, the body should be represented as motionless under its influence, with even the face exhibiting scant muscular change on account of the experience. Thus wonder was best captured by a statuesque blank look.[17]

Burke's familiarity with Lebrun's *Conférence* is evident from his own account of the physical effects of the emotions. His depiction of the symptoms of love, for example, is almost identical to Lebrun's.[18] More generally, his absorption by the promise held out by "new," post-Cartesian philosophy to yield up the secret mechanics of

[12] René Descartes, *Les passions de l'âme* (Paris: 1649), p. 95. For discussion, see Amélie Oksenberg Rorty, "From Passions to Emotions and Sentiments," *Philosophy*, 57:220 (April 1982), pp. 159–72; Susan James, *Passion and Action: The Emotions in Seventeenth-Century Philosophy* (Oxford: Oxford University Press, 1997), ch. 5; Susan James "The Passions and the Good Life" in Donald Rutherford ed., *The Cambridge Companion to Early Modern Philosophy* (Cambridge: Cambridge University Press, 2006).

[13] For an account of the history of scientific and philosophical wonder, see Lorraine Daston and Katherine Park, *Wonders and the Order of Nature, 1150–1750* (New York: Zone Books, 1998). See also Caroline Walker Bynum, "Wonder," *American Historical Review*, 102:1 (February 1997), pp. 1–26; Michael Funk Deckard and Péter Losonczi eds., *Philosophy Begins in Wonder: An Introduction to Early Modern Philosophy, Theology, and Science* (Eugene, OR: Pickwick Publications, 2010). For the teleology of the passions in Descartes's thought, see Alison Simmons, "Sensible Ends: Latent Teleology in Descartes' Account of Sensation," *Journal of the History of Philosophy*, 39 (2001), pp. 49–75.

[14] Descartes, *Les passions de l'âme*, pp. 82–83.

[15] Charles Lebrun, *Conférence tenue en l'Academie Royale de Peinture et Sculpture* (Amsterdam: 1698), pp. 8–9. Cf. Nicolas Malebranche, *The Search after Truth* (1674–75), ed. Thomas M. Lennon (Cambridge: Cambridge University Press, 1997), p. 385, for a discussion of "wonder" in a neo-Cartesian vein.

[16] Lebrun, *Conférence,* p. 11.

[17] Ibid., pp. 10–11.

[18] EB, *Philosophical Enquiry*, p. 299. Cf. Lebrun, *Conférence*, pp. 19–20. Lebrun's work was widely known in the English translation of John Williams, which appeared as Charles Lebrun, *A Method to Learn to Design the Passions* (London: 1734). It was cited, for example, in William Hogarth, *The Analysis of Beauty* (1753), ed. Joseph Burke (Oxford: Oxford University Press, 1955) p. 138, although Burke seems not to have known Hogarth's work before preparing the second edition of his *Philosophical En-*

human nature is evident throughout the *Enquiry*. This involved extending the remit of the experimental method pioneered by Newton and Locke, whilst nonetheless practising the kind of rigorous analysis associated with the legacy of Descartes. Accordingly, Burke's debt to the science of morals and criticism as developed by Addison and Hutcheson is conspicuous in the *Enquiry*. Nonetheless, it is equally clear that he was keen to advance his own particular argument. James Prior claimed in his *Life* of Burke that the young pretender to literary fame had been at work on a "refutation" of the writings of Berkeley and Hume in the early 1750s.[19] Whatever we make of this specific claim, the *Enquiry* certainly drew upon the work of predecessors while also staking out its own territory. The work begins, as Lebrun began his, with an account of the primordial thirst for knowledge. However for Burke, unlike Lebrun, curiosity is an uneasy, restless passion; moreover, strictly speaking, it is not insatiable. Our interest in our environment is exhausted by familiarity: the mind grows sluggish with the advent of routine and would be reduced to weariness were it not motivated by further incentives. These incentives take many forms, as various as there are different kinds of pleasure and pain. Burke is interested in the derivation of these incentives from two particular sources: first, from the stimulus provided by assorted "powers" of nature, and second from the disposition of the "passions."[20]

What intrigues Burke in the *Enquiry* is the uniformity with which particular powers of nature stimulate specific dispositions in human beings. The objective of the work is to identify the final and efficient causes of these uniform responses, and so to contribute to an important branch of "anthropology," or the science of man. The specific branch of anthropology to which Burke addresses himself is "aesthetic" psychology, or the science of criticism, devoted to anatomising how the imagination is stimulated as against studying how the understanding and the senses operate.[21]

---

quiry. On Burke's debt to Lebrun, see Barbara C. Oliver, "Edmund Burke's 'Enquiry' and the Baroque Theory of the Passions'," *Studies in Burke and His Time*, 12:1 (Fall 1970), pp. 1661–76.

[19] James Prior, *Life of the Right Honourable Edmund Burke* (London: 5th ed., 1854), p. 38.

[20] EB, *Philosophical Enquiry*, p. 210.

[21] See Joseph Addison, *Spectator*, no. 411, 21 June 1712: "The Pleasures of the Imagination, taken in their full extent, are not so gross, as those of Sense, nor so refined as those of the Understanding." Cf. Francis Hutcheson, *An Essay on the Nature and Conduct of the Passions and Affections, with Illustrations on the Moral Sense* (1728), ed. Aaron Garrett (Indianapolis, IN: Liberty Fund, 2002), p. 17: 'the *Pleasant Perceptions* arising from *regular, harmonious, uniform* Objects; as also from *Grandeur* and *Novelty*. These we may call, after Mr. ADDISON, the Pleasures of the *Imagination*." On Hutcheson's debt to Addison, see Clarence DeWitt Thorpe, "Addison and Hutcheson on the Imagination," *English Literary History*, 2:3 (November 1935), pp. 215–34. For Addison's long-term impact, see Mark Akenside, *The Pleasures of the Imagination* (London: 1744), "Design," p. 3: "There are certain powers in human nature which seem to hold a middle place between the organs of bodily sense and the faculties of moral perception: They have been call'd by a general name, THE POWERS OF IMAGINATION. Like the external senses, they relate to matter and motion; and at the same time, give the mind ideas analogous to those of moral approbation and dislike." Cf. Dugald Stewart, *Philosophical Essays* (Edinburgh: 1810), 209n: "What Mr Addison has called *Pleasures of Imagination*, might be denominated, more correctly, the pleasures we receive from the objects of *Taste*; a power of the mind which is equally conversant with the pleasures arising from sensible things, and with such as result from the creations of genius." The term "aesthetics"

According to the *Enquiry*, aesthetic psychology is based on general psychology, and so, in the process of analysing aesthetic responses, Burke presents us with an account of the psychological reactions that support society, religion and politics in general. At the same time, he outlines his conception of the role of psychology in ethics, and of the relationship between the passions and providential design. Therefore, from this short tract on our ideas of the sublime and beautiful, we get a sketch of Burke's approach to how the principles of psychology are connected to morality and theodicy. These ramifying implications account for the difficulty commentators have experienced in categorising the work in terms of a definite overarching concern.[22]

Burke's initial move in developing his new approach to the psychology of the imagination is to revise Locke's theory of the interdependence of pleasure and pain as laid out in the *Essay Concerning Human Understanding*. In book II, chapter vii of the *Essay*, Locke elucidates the role of pleasure and pain in motivating human action and understanding. All kinds of satisfaction and delight, and likewise all forms of unease and torment, are annexed to each of our ideas and so govern our thoughts and sensations, according to Locke. Without the wise addition of these positive and negative feelings to our ideas, human life would be reduced to a "lazy lethargic Dream," incapable of settling on a specific course of action or reflection in preference to another, and so unable to employ our faculties as the "Author of our being" intended.[23] But Locke further conjectured that the "Sovereign Disposer," while providing for the efficient preservation of human existence through the appropriate exercise of the functions of the body and its parts, subjected each individual life to an interminable quest for satisfaction in order that we might seek our fullest enjoyment in our maker "*for evermore*."[24] Burke conceded these general arguments, but he went on to challenge Locke's analysis of the relationship between pleasure and pain.

Locke declared himself satisfied with his account of the divine rationale underpinning the response to pleasure and pain; however, he doubted that he had clari-

---

is a subsequent coinage of Alexander Baumgarten's, though what he meant by this term had already been covered in a non-technical idiom by Addison's "Pleasures of the Imagination." See Paul Guyer, "The Origins of Modern Aesthetics, 1711–1735" in idem, *Values of Beauty: Historical Essays in Aesthetics* (Cambridge: Cambridge University Press, 2005).

[22] Thus commonly Burke's politics are collapsed into his criticism, or his criticism no less straightforwardly into theology. The latter interpretation is pursued by F. P. Lock, *Edmund Burke* (Oxford: Oxford University Press, 1998), 2 vols., I, p. 98. For previous comment on the relationship between aesthetics and politics in Burke, see Neal Wood, "The Aesthetic Dimension of Burke's Political Thought," *Journal of British Studies*, 4 (1964), pp. 41–64; Christopher Reid, *Edmund Burke and the Practice of Political Writing* (Dublin: Gill and Macmillan, 1985), ch. 3; Frans De Bruyn, "Edmund Burke's Natural Aristocrat: The 'Man of Taste' as a Political Ideal," *Eighteenth-Century Life*, 11 (1987), pp. 41–60; David Bromwich, "The Sublime before Aesthetics and Politics," *Raritan*, 16 (1997), pp. 30–51. For recent attempts to place the *Enquiry*, see Michael Funk Deckard and Koen Vermeir eds., *The Science of Sensibility: Reading Edmund Burke's Philosophical Enquiry* (Heidelberg: Springer-Verlag GmbH, 2010).

[23] John Locke, *An Essay Concerning Human Understanding* (1689), ed. Peter H. Nidditch (Oxford: Oxford University Press, 1975, 1979), II, vii, § 3.

[24] Ibid., II, vii, §§ 5, 6.

fied the nature of the stimulus itself.[25] Burke agreed with Locke's assessment of what he had achieved in the *Essay*, but he also wanted to pinpoint its deficiencies. That objective had already been pursued by Lord Kames in his *Essays on the Principles of Morality and Religion*. The Lockean notion that human actions are solely motivated by the search for pleasure and the avoidance of pain was challenged in Kames's critical essay on the aesthetic theory of Jean-Baptiste Dubos, "Our Attachment to Objects of Distress." The sociable nature of human beings had been so designed, according to Kames, that we feel affection for objects that arouse unpleasant emotions such as grief, thus demonstrating that self-love is offset by sympathetic instincts.[26] Burke was similarly alert to the existence of sentiments that appeared to undermine attempts to reduce motivation to selfish principles, but he developed his own particular critique of the legacy of Locke. In a footnote to the first edition of the *Enquiry* he observed that "Mr. Locke thinks that the removal or lèssening of a pain is considered and operates as a pleasure, and the loss or diminishing of pleasure as a pain." "It is this opinion," he added, "which we consider here."[27] Burke accepted Locke's contention that pain and pleasure were irreducible ideas, "incapable of definition," as he put it.[28] However, he objected to the claim that pain resulted from the depletion of pleasure, or pleasure from the alleviation of pain. It is on the basis of this fundamental objection that Burke develops his own theory and stakes his claim to originality in the field.

"I can never persuade myself," Burke began by observing, "that pleasure and pain are mere relations, which can only exist as they are contrasted."[29] What Burke was challenging was the notion that ease and discomfort, satisfaction and distress, were entirely relative to one another, existing along a spectrum such that the diminution of the one entailed an increase in the experience of the other. On the contrary, both of these states represented self-contained ideas, discretely circumscribed rather than dependent on one another. Between the two extremes of pain and pleasure lay the neutral state of "tranquillity," and both the depletion of enjoyment and the removal of discontent involved progress towards this distinct condition of "indifference" rather than a passage from one of the extremes into its opposite. It was by restoring the ideas of pleasure and pain to their integrity in this way that Burke was able to develop a more nuanced account of the manifold variety of each. More particularly, it enabled him to discover much of that variety in the subtly diverse conditions

[25] Ibid., II, vii, § 6.

[26] Henry Home, Lord Kames, *Essays on the Principles of Morality and Natural Religion* (1751), ed. Catherine Moran (Indianapolis, IN: Liberty Fund, 2005), pp. 14–16. Kames's criticism of Dubos was presumably directed at the recent translation of Jean-Baptiste Dubos, *Réflexions critique sur la poésie et sur la peinture* (1719) as *Critical Reflections on Poetry, Painting and Music, with an Inquiry into the Rise of the Theatrical Entertainments of the Ancients*, trans. Thomas Nugent (London: 1748), 3 vols.

[27] EB, *Philosophical Enquiry*, p. 212n. These lines are a virtual quotation from Locke, *Essay*, II, xx, § 16.

[28] EB, *Philosophical Enquiry*, p. 211. Cf. Locke, *Essay*, II, xx, § 1.

[29] EB, *Philosophical Enquiry*, p. 212.

through which experience passed in the process of changing from a definite state of pleasure or pain towards the neutral state of indifference.

In this Burke exhibited a distinct preference for the classical analysis of pleasure over Locke's less differentiated theory. Naturally there existed a multitude of competing classical perspectives on the canonical theme of pleasure.[30] Burke drew specifically on a tradition of argument inaugurated by Plato in his *Philebus*, and subsequently developed in Aristotle's *Rhetoric*. In his *Enquiry into the Original of Moral Virtue*, which Burke may well have read as he worked on his *Philosophical Enquiry*, Archibald Campbell had been emphatic in insisting that "*Pleasure is Something else than the removal of Pain*," footnoting the *Philebus* as his source for the insight.[31] In the *Philebus*, Socrates had argued against the idea that a stream of sensations must always be experienced as an increase or diminution of enjoyment. There is a third, neutral condition between pleasantness and unpleasantness, pointing to the conclusion that freedom from pain is not equivalent to feeling pleasure. Relief may simply restore us to the indifferent position from which we started.[32] In addition, the physiology of enjoyment is inescapably affected by the mental states of memory and desire such that, for example, the pleasure that accompanies the gratification of appetite is increased by the anticipation of satisfaction. So it goes for the experience of the emotions in general, Socrates concludes: the laughter provoked by ridicule in comedy is tinged with pain, just as the spectacle of tragedy induces sorrow mixed with joy.[33]

The same applies to anger, fear, longing, lamentation, love and jealousy: each of these mixed emotions has a bittersweet effect. Socrates cites the example of Achilles' description of his tormented wrath as "far sweeter" than flowing honey after learning of the death of Patroclus in book XVIII of the *Iliad*.[34] The pain of anger thrills in expectation of revenge. In the *Enquiry*, Burke points to the relief experienced just after an escape from imminent danger as blending the emotions in a similarly complex way, giving rise to a "sort of mixt passion of terror and surprize." *The Iliad*, once again, provides Burke with an example:

> As when a wretch, who conscious of his crime,
> Pursued for murder from his native clime,

[30] On this broad subject, see J.C.B. Gosling and C.C.W. Taylor, *The Greeks on Pleasure* (Oxford: Oxford University Press, 1982); C.C.W. Taylor, *Pleasure, Mind and Soul: Selected Papers in Ancient Philosophy* (Oxford: Oxford University Press, 2008).

[31] Archibald Campbell, *An Enquiry into the Original of Moral Virtue* (1727) (London: 1733), p. 266. For an account of Campbell's ideas and career, see Anne Skoczylas, "Archibald Campbell's *Enquiry into the Original of Moral Virtue*, Presbyterian Orthodoxy, and the Scottish Enlightenment," *Scottish Historical Review*, 87:293 (April 2008), pp. 68–100.

[32] Plato, *Philebus*, 43c1–d9.

[33] Ibid., 48a1–9, 50b1–5. For discussion, see Dorothea Frede, "Disintegration and Restoration: Pleasure and Pain in Plato's *Philebus*" in Richard Kraut ed., *The Cambridge Companion to Plato* (Cambridge: Cambridge University Press, 1992).

[34] *Philebus*, 47e8–9, citing Homer, *Iliad*, XVIII, lines 108–9.

Just gains some frontier, breathless, pale, amaz'd;
All gaze, all wonder.[35]

It is these mixed states that absorb most of Burke's attention in the *Enquiry*, above all the mixed sentiment that characterises exposure to the sublime. Ambivalent feelings of the kind are brought about by memory and desire operating on the immediate data of perception: a recent release from danger anticipates complete security, the disappearance of pleasure is consoled by its recollection. Even the restoration of tranquillity is tinged by its preceding state.[36]

Burke dedicates section V of part I of the *Enquiry* to the feelings that attend the termination of joy to illuminate his case more clearly. The cessation of pleasure can affect the mind in one of three ways, he argues. Either it simply comes to an appropriate end, restoring us to tranquillity; or it is suddenly interrupted, inducing disappointment; or the former enjoyment is utterly lost, resulting in grief. But even grief, the most extreme of these conditions, is distinct from positive pain. We indulge the experience, and even savour it, because the negative sensation is suffused with the memory of satisfaction. Distress is unpleasant without mitigation, whereas melancholy reflection kindles "pleasing woe."[37] Aristotle, in his *Art of Rhetoric*, had already subjected ambivalent sentiments of the kind to intense scrutiny, at one point following Plato in citing Achilles' mournful wrath as a kind of bitterness alleviated by the sweet anticipation of revenge.[38] But the two passions that most concern Burke, and to which Aristotle devoted a substantial amount of attention, are pity and fear.[39]

Pity and fear represented for Burke two specific but highly significant ways in which the feelings of pleasure and pain operated in the human mind. They were significant because they resulted from two fundamental instincts that drove the affections, those of "*self-preservation*" and "*society*" respectively.[40] These jointly motivating passions were famously anatomised by Grotius in the Prolegomena to the first edition of *The Rights of War and Peace* in terms of a drive to self-interested utility

[35] EB, *Philosophical Enquiry*, p. 213, citing Pope's translation of Homer, *Iliad*, XIV, lines 590–3.

[36] EB, *Philosophical Enquiry*, pp. 212–13.

[37] Ibid., pp. 215–16. Burke takes the quotation from Pope's translation of Homer, *Odyssey*, IV, line 127, where Menelaus is lamenting the loss of his companions in the Trojan War.

[38] Aristotle, *Rhetoric*, 1370b9–10.

[39] Cf. EB, *Hints for an Essay on the Drama* (c. 1761), *W & S*, I, p. 558: "Tragedy turned . . . on melancholy and affecting subjects . . . its passions, therefore, [are] admiration, pity and fear." In the *Annual Register for the Year 1758* (London: 1759), p. 278, Burke prefaced an account of the Black Hole of Calcutta by J. Z. Holwell with remarks on these Aristotelian passions: "Perhaps the human mind can have no entertainment at once more congenial and more useful to it, than . . . stories of extraordinary distresses, and wonderful deliverances. In the former part our humanity is cultivated; in the latter it is inspired [with] a spirited hope and trust in Providence . . . They have the effect which Aristotle attributes to good tragedy, in correcting the passions of terror and pity."

[40] EB, *Philosophical Enquiry*, p. 216. "[S]elf-preservation in individuals is the first Law of Nature," Burke later wrote. See the notes for EB, Speech on the Unitarian Petition, 11 May 1792, Northamptonshire MS. A. XXVI. 96.

on the one hand and an appetite for society on the other.[41] Burke's view of human nature as expressed in the *Philosophical Enquiry* evidently conformed to the basic outlines of Grotius' scheme. Within this framework, he argued that fear was ultimately motivated by a concern with our own self-preservation while pity inclined us towards society with others. By the time that Burke came to write the *Enquiry*, these two passions had absorbed the attention of innumerable modern natural lawyers and moralists from Hobbes to Mandeville and Rousseau. The positive content of these emotions, as well as their presumed social implications, had been a subject of recurrent controversy. The assessment of these implications was of course dependent on the interpretation of their content. But their content, in turn, was dependent on the context in which they were expressed: context affected the gradations of intensity with which they were felt, as did their relation to other neighbouring sentiments. But of principal importance among these diverse possible relations was their intricate connection to one another.

One of Burke's achievements in the *Enquiry* was to redefine the nature of the relationship between pity and fear. Hobbes had argued in *Leviathan* that "*Grief*, for the Calamity of another, is Pitty," but he went on to trace the form of pity under investigation to a self-regarding fear for one's own welfare. The seemingly sociable impulse of compassion, in other words, is based on the apprehension that "the like calamity" might befall oneself.[42] "Thus Fear and Compassion," as Bishop Butler later summarised Hobbes's account, "are the same Idea."[43] One implication of this argument is that the reality of self-love underlies the appearance of sociability. This equation was established by recasting the relationship between pity and fear as developed by Aristotle in his *Rhetoric*. In that work, fear was explicitly defined as a species of apprehension that would provoke fellow-feeling if an anticipated mishap were actually to afflict another person.[44] Later in the *Rhetoric*, Aristotle presented his case more emphatically still by claiming that whatever occasion men might have "to fear for themselves" would arouse their pity should others be afflicted.[45] In other words, pity (*eleos*) is fear (*phobos*) for the welfare of our fellows. However, since pity in that case amounted, as Hobbes put it in his vivid rendition of Aristotle's text, to

[41] Hugo Grotius, "Prolegomena" (1625), *The Rights of War and Peace*, ed. Richard Tuck (Indianapolis, IN: Liberty Fund, 2005), III, p. 1747. Interpretations of Grotius' analysis have varied widely. On the meaning of the social instinct in his writings, see Richard Tuck, "Grotius and Selden" in J. H. Burns and Mark Goldie eds., *The Cambridge History of Political Thought 1450–1700* (Cambridge: Cambridge University Press, 1991), pp. 499–529; Annabel Brett, "Natural Right and Civil Community: The Civil Philosophy of Hugo Grotius," *Historical Journal*, 45.1 (2002), pp. 31–51. Christopher Brooke, *Philosophic Pride: Stoicism and Political Thought from Lipsius to Rousseau* (Princeton, NJ: Princeton University Press, 2012), ch. 2.

[42] Thomas Hobbes, *Leviathan*, ed. Noel Malcolm (Oxford: Oxford University Press, 2012), 3 vols., II, pt. I, ch. 6, p. 90.

[43] Joseph Butler, *Fifteen Sermons Preached at the Rolls Chapel* (London: 1726), p. 81n. Butler was commenting on Thomas Hobbes, *Elements of Law, Natural and Politic*, ed. Ferdinand Tönnies (London: Frank Cass & Co., 1969), pt. I, ch. ix, § 10, p. 40.

[44] Aristotle, *Ars rhetorica*, 1382b12.

[45] Ibid., 1386a14.

a "perturbation of the mind, arising from the apprehension of hurts, or trouble to another," the question remained of what could move us to compassion under these unenticing conditions.[46] Given that anxious concern for another provoked discomfort, it was necessary to ask how imaginative identification of the sort resulted in sympathy rather than aversion.

Hume took up this question at various stages in his career, beginning with the *Treatise of Human Nature*. In the midst of an account of mixed passions in the *Treatise*, Hume acknowledged that, since pity is a form of "uneasiness" arising from "the misery of others," it might be expected to repulse rather than awaken fellow-feeling. Pity, however, is activated by sympathy, which Hume construes as a benevolent affection that induces a feeling of pleasure. Under the influence of benevolence, pity can, when it is sufficiently powerfully stimulated, subordinate the specifically uncomfortable element to an overall positive experience.[47] In this way, both the Hobbesian and the Mandevillian attempts to reduce apparently other-regarding passions to forms of self-love were refuted by appeal to the common experience of humanity and goodwill.[48] As Hume put the case later, in his *Enquiry Concerning the Principles of Morals*, "natural philanthropy" operated in the human breast alongside partiality, envy and malice, and its operation added to the fund of human happiness.[49] But while Burke was equally committed to the existence of a philanthropic principle in human nature, he resisted the idea that the incentive to identification was wholly based on the idea of positive pleasure.

Burke came to address the issue in section XIV of part I of the *Enquiry*. In the immediately preceding section, he had indicated how he reckoned that the puzzle of painful sympathy was equivalent to the familiar conundrum of why "objects which in reality would shock, are in tragical, and such like representations, the source of a very high species of pleasure."[50] Now we are told that a proper examination of this enduring mystery requires an explanation of "how we are affected by the feelings of our fellow creatures in circumstances of real distress."[51] A credible account of this process would involve anatomising the precise experience of pity and fear, thereby clarifying the source of either sentiment in the instincts for society and self-preservation respectively. If pity for the distress of others involves a process of substitution whereby we place ourselves imaginatively in their place, the act of identification involves contracting the unpleasant feeling of discomfort that accompanies

[46] Aristotle, *A Briefe of the Art of Rhetorique, Containing in Substance all that Aristotle hath written in his Three Bookes of that Subject, Except Onely What is not Applicable to the English Tongue*, trans. Thomas Hobbes (London: 1637), p. 93.

[47] David Hume, *Treatise of Human Nature* (1739–40), ed. David Fate Norton and Mary J. Norton (Oxford: Oxford University Press, 2000), pp. 245–50.

[48] Ibid., p. 239. On the dynamics of sympathy and interpersonal comparison in Hume, see Annette Baier, *A Progress of Sentiments: Reflections on Hume's Treatise* (Cambridge, MA: Harvard University Press, 1991), pp. 147–51.

[49] David Hume, *An Enquiry Concerning the Principles of Morals* (1751), ed. Tom L. Beauchamp (Oxford: Oxford University Press, 1998), p. 114.

[50] EB, *Philosophical Enquiry*, p. 221.

[51] Ibid., p. 221.

alarm. Notwithstanding this incremental increase in unwanted trouble, we do not "shun" upsetting images of the kind. On the contrary, people are commonly drawn to harrowing spectacles of suffering, the more so if the scenes in question are known actually to have occurred. We admire the incessant triumphs of Scipio Africanus, but we are drawn in awe to the death of the stoic Cato the Younger.[52]

What attracts us is the admixture of pity and fear, Burke makes clear. He then glosses the fear in question as a feeling of "terror" sparked by witnessing another person's miserable fate. Moreover, the kind of terror Burke has in mind produces "delight" rather than second-hand agony.[53] It is this assertion that has the best claim to being an original insight in the *Enquiry*, and for this reason the argument of the book is organised around it.[54] The most tantalising formulation of Burke's case is contained in his statement that "terror is a passion which produces delight when it does not press too close, and pity is a passion accompanied with pleasure, because it arises from love and social affection."[55] Burke implicitly presents a typology of fear in the *Enquiry*, indicating how it modulates according to circumstance to produce terror, dread, astonishment and awe. However, he also argues that even the more unsettling instances of the passion—fear, terror and dread—are capable of causing exhilaration in spectators under the appropriate conditions. At the same time, he locates sympathy among the family of sociable instincts that encompass attachment, affection, friendship and sexual love. For Burke, there is no mystery about the attraction to these kinds of relationship since they afford a positive pleasure in themselves. However, delight in danger, in the threat of harm and destruction, is less easily explained. Yet its explanation yields insights into the life of the imagination and consequently into the passions that animate religion, society and politics.

Burke dedicates an early section of the *Enquiry* to explicating the difference between pleasure and delight. While the diminution of pain may not be equivalent to a positive pleasure, it can have a character that is "far from distressing" and may even be positively "agreeable." Burke elects to denominate this pleasing release from distress or danger by the term "*Delight*" in order to distinguish it from simple pleasure and unadulterated pain.[56] According to this scheme, the human frame is constituted so as to experience certain forms of privation as enjoyable, and even thrilling. These typically involve the feeling of apprehension—a sense of threat that stops short of overwhelming alarm. The passion of fear is ultimately triggered by the instinct for self-preservation and as a result unleashes the most powerful of the emotions. We are horrified by the prospect of pain and death—indeed, what is finally distress-

[52]Ibid., p. 222. Cf. Hume, *Treatise*, p. 387 and Hume, *Enquiry*, p. 179, for the comparative attractions of the "amiable" Caesar and the "awful" Cato as drawn by Cicero.

[53]EB, *Philosophical Enquiry*, p. 222.

[54]Herbert A. Wichelns, "Burke's 'Essay on the Sublime and Beautiful' " (PhD thesis, Cornell University, 1922), pp. lxviii–lxix, notes the centrality of delight to Burke's argument, but takes his treatment to be derived from Dubos and Hume.

[55]EB, *Philosophical Enquiry*, p. 222.

[56]Ibid., pp. 213–14.

ing about the range of possible torments is that they are emissaries of the supreme "king of terrors." When distress and danger press too close we are pained and panic-stricken, and clearly beyond enjoyment, "but at certain distances, and with certain modifications, they may be, and they are delightful, as we every day experience."[57]

In Burke's eyes this principle accounts at once for certain pleasures of the imagination and for specific forms of social behaviour. It explains the thrill that accompanies exposure to the sublime, and goes some way towards accounting for the positive effects of tragedy. The spectacle of harm or danger, where it does not bear down on the spectator as an existential threat, can elicit delight in the midst of unease—sometimes evoking amazement, always awakening concern. We have established that the attempt to analyse "mixed" emotions of this type extends back to the treatment of the passions in Plato and Aristotle, but the impulse to explore these ambivalent states received a new lease of life around the beginning of the eighteenth century with the emergence of a project to apply the new science of the passions to aesthetic sensibility or "the pleasures of the imagination." Addison, for example, had observed in *The Spectator* that where a deformity in nature appears on a scale of sublime greatness, "there will be a Mixture of Delight in the very Disgust it gives us."[58] Burke's aim in the *Enquiry* was not only to identify a new category of feeling under the term delight, and to illustrate how its pleasant effects could be combined with negative sentiments, but to show how the resulting complex of emotions contributed to the appreciation of diverse aesthetic objects as well as to the support of social attitudes and tastes.

The result was a revision of what Burke considered to be the obnoxious legacy of Mandeville to social thought. In his *Essay on Charity and Charity-Schools*, Mandeville had conceded that the objects that arouse compassion, much like those that inspire fear, are capable of so completely disturbing the imagination as to occasion "great Pain and Anxiety."[59] In addition to having these disquieting effects, Mandeville presented commiseration as a counterfeited virtue, pretending to be motivated by disinterested charity whilst in reality being a product of raw passion. Pity was a primitive, instinctive response to misfortune automatically triggered by scenes of suffering near at hand. It was an immediate, sensory, reactive impulse: "when the Object does not strike, the Body does not feel it."[60] On the basis of this analysis, Mandeville hoped to show that in acting out of pity we were covertly serving ourselves. That claim represented a modification of the thesis advanced by Pierre

[57] Ibid., p. 217.

[58] Addison, *Spectator*, no. 412, 23 June 1712.

[59] Bernard Mandeville, *An Essay on Charity and Charity-Schools* (1723) in *The Fable of the Bees: Or, Private Vices, Public Benefits*, ed. F. B. Kaye (Indianapolis, IN: Liberty Fund, 1988), p. 255. For the comparison of pity with fear, see ibid., pp. 257, 258.

[60] Ibid., p. 257. On this aspect of Mandeville's thought, together with his debt to and departure from Dutch republican thought and French Jansenism alike, see E. J. Hundert, *The Enlightenment's Fable: Bernard Mandeville and the Discovery of Society* (Cambridge: Cambridge University Press, 1994), ch. 1. See also E. J. Hundert, "Bernard Mandeville and the Enlightenment's Maxims of Modernity," *Journal of the History of Ideas*, 56:4 (October 1995), pp. 577–93.

Nicole in his *Essais de morale* to the effect that charity was a form of "self-regard" (*amour-propre*).[61] Mandeville's position was closer to an observation of Thomas Browne's: "by compassion we make others misery our own, and so by relieving them, we relieve ourselves also."[62] Burke's aim was to explain this process while maintaining a critical distance from Mandevillian scepticism.

In following Browne, Mandeville was contending that the very process of acting out of pity conveniently "eases us."[63] Tokens of compassion, like rescuing the vulnerable and engaging in bouts of alms-giving, offset the discomfort caused by the actual experience of identifying with suffering. However, it remained unclear why human beings should be drawn into such costly fellow-feeling in the first place. Mandeville had a theory about how acts of counterfeit charity could purge the aggravation caused by pity, but not about why the spectator was drawn to commiserate as such. Burke believed that his analysis offered a solution to this conundrum. At the same time, he thought it helped to explain one of the foundations of social cohesion. Since a spectacle of suffering could be dreadful without overwhelming the spectator with terror, it was capable of arousing delight rather than pain, enabling us to sympathise with the afflicted. The mind was able to extend sympathy to objects of pity as well as to expressions of happiness—it could take delight in scenes of destruction and also take pleasure in those that aroused joy.[64] In the process of identifying with adversity in particular, the feeling of delight offered a definite incentive to pity misfortune. Sympathetic attachment, as Burke saw it, is strengthened "by the bond of a proportionable delight; and there most where our sympathy is most wanted, in the distress of others."[65]

Delight thus offers an incentive to affectionate identification with affliction, lending support to social solidarity in general. Burke speculated about the instrumentality or "final cause" underlying this arrangement. Since "our Creator" ordained that "we should be united by the bond of sympathy," that bond was purposefully strengthened where it appeared to be most needed—namely, in circumstances where we encounter other humans in distress.[66] Burke's innovation here was to claim that a mental state derived from the instinct for self-preservation fortified the impulse to society. His aim in this was to reconcile the appetite for self-love with the ob-

[61] Pierre Nicole, *Essais de morale* (Paris: 1672), 4 vols., II, p. 220. On Nicole and his wider milieu, see Lionel Rothkrug, *Opposition to Louis XIV: The Political and Social Origins of the French Enlightenment* (Princeton, NJ: Princeton University Press, 1965); Nannerl Keohane, *Philosophy and the State in France: The Renaissance to the Enlightenment* (Princeton, NJ: Princeton University Press, 1980), pp. 283–311; Dale Van Kley, "Pierre Nicole, Jansenism and the Morality of Enlightened Self-Interest" in Alan C. Kors and Paul Korshin eds., *Anticipations of the Enlightenment* (Philadelphia, PA: University of Pennsylvania Press, 1987).

[62] Thomas Browne, *Religio Medici* (London: 4th ed., 1656), pp. 129–30. Cf. François de la Rochefoucauld, "La pitié" in *Maximes*, ed. Jean Lafond (Paris: Gallimard, 1976), maxime 264.

[63] Mandeville, *Essay on Charity*, p. 258.

[64] EB, *Philosophical Enquiry*, p. 221.

[65] Ibid., p. 222.

[66] Ibid., p. 222.

servable characteristics of sociability. But in addition to facilitating a novel account of pity, Burke's category of "delight" was intended to make sense of a wider set of psychological responses. It provided the key to his account of the sublime in the *Enquiry*, and, as Lessing, Nicolai and Mendelssohn in due course noted, it offered an original explanation of how tragedy brought enjoyment.[67] But it was also designed to clarify the nature of political deference, and to illuminate crucial aspects of religious experience. The social and religious implications of delight inspired by fear will be addressed in the third section of this chapter. But first we need to examine Burke's understanding of beauty, and the sympathetic sensibility on which its appreciation is based.

3.3 Beauty, Sympathy and Utility

The purpose of the first part of the *Enquiry* is to trace the passions that give rise to the feelings of the sublime and beautiful to their sources in two fundamental human instincts—those, as has already been shown, of self-preservation and society. As a result of this approach, Burke was obliged to present his underlying theory of sociability, and in the process laid the groundwork for an account of the role of sentiment in politics and religion. In parts II and III of the *Enquiry*, Burke turns his attention to identifying the sorts of impressions that induce the feelings of beauty and sublimity. In part III he begins negatively by first indicating the kinds of qualities that are mistakenly assumed to cause the feeling of beauty before settling on those ideas that do evoke the beautiful. The procedure in part II is more straightforward, systematically presenting those ideas—obscurity, power, privation, vastness, infinity, magnificence and so on—that cause the feeling of the sublime. In both cases, the catalogue of qualities that are taken to arouse beautiful or sublime sentiments is preceded by a short account of the nature of the passion itself, describing the range of its intensity and isolating its precise content. Here Burke builds on the analysis in part I, drawing on the anatomy of the emotions he developed there. Accordingly, sublime objects are identified as those which induce feelings associated with pain and danger, sensitivity

[67] See Jochen Schulte-Sasse, *Lessing, Mendelssohn, Nicolai: Briefwechsel über das Trauerspiel* (Munich: Winkler, 1972). See also Moses Mendelssohn, *Rezensionsartikel in Bibliothek der schönen Wissenschaften und der freyen Künste* (1756–59) in *Gesammelte Schriften: Jubiläumsausgabe IV*, ed. Eva J. Engel (Stuttgart: Friedrich Frommann Verlag, 1977), pp. 216–36, p. 235. Cf. Mendelssohn to Lessing, 2 April 1758, in Moses Mendelssohn, *Briefwechsel I* in *Gesammelte Schriften: Jubiläumsausgabe XI*, ed. Bruno Straus (Stuttgart: Friedrich Frommann Verlag, 1974), p. 185. See also Gotthold Ephraim Lessing, *Bemerkungen über Burkes Philosophische Untersuchungen über den Ursprung unserer Begriffe vom Erhabenen und Schönen* (175859) in idem, *Gesammelte Werke*, ed. Paul Rilla (Berlin and Weimar: Aufbau-Verlag, 1968), 10 vols., VII, pp. 273–74. For the impact of Burke on Lessing, see William Guild Howard, 'Burke among the Forerunners of Lessing,' *Publication of the Modern Language Association*, 22:4 (1907), pp. 608–32. For the wider, central European reception of the *Enquiry*, see Tomas Hlobil, "The Reception of Burke's *Enquiry* in the German-Language Area in the Second Half of the Eighteenth Century (A Regional Aspect)," *Estetika*, 44:1–4 (2007), pp. 125–50.

to which derives from an ineradicable instinct for survival; while beautiful objects are identified as those that induce feelings associated with amity and love to which we are prone on account of our sociable nature.[68]

According to Burke, the sociable nature of human beings is rooted in the disposition to "sympathy."[69] We have already examined the ways in which sympathy can be aroused by objects of pity, but for Burke it can equally be sparked by the prospect of pleasure. Sympathy therefore covers an extensive range of affections, as diverse as the variety of forms of interaction. Conspicuous amongst this variety, besides sympathy with distress, is the passion of "love," which Burke proceeds to analyse into two distinct categories involving sexual desire on the one hand and social affection on the other. These categories, however, overlap: in human beings, sexual desire has an obvious social dimension. Nonetheless, Burke is clear that "lust," or the passion for "generation," must be distinguished from the instinct for "*general society*." Pure lust is both spontaneous and undiscriminating, whereas sexual desire in humans is affected by particular qualities that prompt us to decide between available options. These qualities range from physical appeal to attributes of character, just as with forms of attraction driven exclusively by social appetite. The social appetite *per se* is a "general" affection for the species capable of being extended to the natural habitat at large. This general impulse embraces all socially estimable characteristics, but it also encompasses a sense of fellowship with animals and the inanimate world.[70] The utility of sympathy in the moral world is obvious: fellow-feeling motivates the command of conscience. However, the reason why we are attracted to natural objects is a mystery. Burke speculates that this arrangement probably serves some "great end," even though its purpose cannot be discerned. While providence in this case can be assumed to be at work, it cannot be definitively explained: "his wisdom is not our wisdom, nor our ways his ways."[71]

When Shaftesbury set about rationalising his philosophical enthusiasm for beauty in the character of Theocles as presented in his rhapsodic dialogue *The Moralists*, he did so by delivering a rapturous hymn to nature. Beauty was discovered in the pastoral bounty of "fruitful and exuberant Nature" conceptualised on a cosmic scale: pastures, oceans, deserts, mountains, grottos and caverns elicited admiration alongside stars and planets in a tribute to universal concord. But the object of admiration was the divine intelligence that composed the elements of nature into a complex order: sympathy with the natural world derived from the utility of design.[72] Accord-

[68] Hugh Blair soon took issue with Burke's categories. See Hugh Blair, *Lectures on Rhetoric and Belles Lettres* (Dublin: 1783), 3 vols., I, p. 66: "He seems to stretch his theory too far, when he represents the Sublime as consisting wholly in modes of danger, or of pain."

[69] EB, *Philosophical Enquiry*, pp. 220–21.

[70] Ibid., pp. 217–19.

[71] Ibid., p. 220, echoing Isaiah 55:8.

[72] Anthony Ashley Cooper, Third Earl of Shaftesbury, "The Moralists, A Philosophical Rhapsody" in idem, *Characteristicks of Men, Manners, Opinions Times* (1711) (Indianapolis, IN: Liberty Fund, 2001), 3 vols., II, pp. 193–225.

ingly, in a fragment on "The Beautiful" (*to kalon*), Shaftesbury described the "love of cosmetic and natural beauty" as a desire for "symmetrical and orderly arrangement which is born of the need for harmony within."[73] The inner desire for harmony is gratified by the appearance of decorous order in the universe. Shaftesburean love of beauty was thus modelled on a combination of stoic sympathy (*sympatheia*) and Platonic utility (*chrêsimotês*) such that fellowship with rational creatures culminates in admiration for universal design.

Francis Hutcheson similarly linked the appreciation of beauty to an apprehension of the intelligence of the deity. As he put it in his *Essay on the Nature and Conduct of the Passions*, "Grandeur, Beauty, Order, Harmony, wherever they occur, raise an Opinion of a MIND, of *Design*, and *Wisdom*."[74] However, Burke's sympathy with beauty is an immediate feeling of tenderness that does not regard the functionality of the objects it esteems. It shares with the Shaftesburean and Hutchesonian social instinct a disregard of personal advantage: it does not pursue the "possession" of the object of its affection, thus distinguishing it from sexual desire.[75] However, unlike the taste for the beautiful in Shaftesbury, it is not activated by an appreciation of the fittingness of design. Shaftesbury's debt to Plato's *Hippias Major* is conspicuous in his thinking. The beautiful, as Socrates pointed out to Hippias in that dialogue, is "whatever is useful" (*ho an chrêsimon*).[76] However, Burke is at pains to insist that beauty is indifferent to "convenience." Functionality is discerned by reason and appeals to the understanding, whereas beauty directly arouses the passion of love, as indicated by the automatic feeling of affection induced by qualities like smoothness, delicacy and grace.[77]

According to Burke, the mistaken notion that the feeling of beauty is caused by an appreciation of utility is responsible for the assumption that figures please on account of their proportionality.[78] Both these ideas, he recognised, "arose from the

[73] Anthony Ashley Cooper, Third Earl of Shaftesbury, "The Beautiful" in *The Life, Unpublished Letters, and Philosophical Regiment of Anthony, Earl of Shaftesbury* (1900), ed. Benjamin Rand (Bristol: Thoemmes Press, 1995), p. 247.

[74] Hutcheson, *Essay on the Nature and Conduct of the Passions*, p. 116.

[75] EB, *Philosophical Enquiry*, p. 255. Hutcheson's isolation of the sense of beauty from the feeling of advantage likewise distinguished imaginative pleasure from the sentiment of possession or "Ideas of Property." See Hutcheson, *Essay on the Nature and Conduct of the Passions*, pp. 114–15.

[76] Plato, *Hippias Major*, 295c3. Cf. Xenophon, *Memorabilia*, III, viii. There is some discussion of the Platonic theory of beauty in relation to utility in Monroe C. Beardsley, *Aesthetics from Classical Greece to the Present* (Tuscaloosa, AL: University of Alabama Press, 1966), pp. 42–43; R. G. Collingwood, "Plato's Philosophy of Art," *Mind*, 34:134 (1925), pp. 154–72.

[77] EB, *Philosophical Enquiry*, pp. 255–56, 273–78.

[78] Ibid., p. 266. The association of beauty with proportionality was standard among Classical and Renaissance theories of art and architecture. See, for example, Vitruvius, *Ten Books on Architecture*, ed. Ingrid D. Rowland (Cambridge: Cambridge University Press, 1999). The argument circulated widely in the eighteenth century. See, for example, George Berkeley, *Alciphron; Or, the Minute Philosopher* (1732) in *The Works of George Berkeley*, ed. Alexander Campbell Fraser (Oxford: Oxford University Press, 1901), 4 vols., II, p. 138.

Platonic theory of fitness and aptitude," as elucidated in the *Hippias Major*.[79] The merits of that theory were widely debated in the first quarter of the eighteenth century, as indicated by the appearance of a French translation together with a commentary on the dialogue by de Maucroix that was appended to the second edition of Jean-Pierre de Crousaz's *Traité du beau*.[80] Burke claimed that, if it were true that proportionality gratified our sense of beauty, its appeal would have to derive from one of three sources: either it was based on the mechanical attraction of definite mathematical ratios; or it could be ascribed to the seeming appositeness of customary proportions; or, finally, it resulted from the fitness of given dimensions to an ascertainable purpose.[81] But empirical investigation showed each of these hypotheses to be false, not least the underlying assumption responsible for the rest—namely, the idea that the appearance of beauty was a product of the perception of convenience. Burke conceded that utility was pleasing to the intellect, but it did not affect the mind with a "sense of its loveliness."[82] We are disposed to admire intricacy in design, both in artefacts and in natural creation; but these please us by eliciting the "acquiescence of the understanding" rather than by arousing the passions of the imagination.[83] Burke contended that, wherever providence seeks to guide human behaviour, our responses are designed to react without the mediation of the will.[84] So it was with the response to the beautiful: beauty captivates the soul by automatically alluring our imagination without the intervention of the reasoning faculty.[85]

The sentiment of beauty is thus an immediate feeling of "love" or fellowship with objects in the natural and moral worlds. Addison had argued that beauty impacts directly on the mind, spreading satisfaction throughout the soul, diffusing a sense of "Cheerfulness" and "Joy." The appreciation of physical beauty acts as a temptation to "multiply," whereas the visual appeal of nature endears God's workmanship to us: "it is impossible for us to behold his works with coldness and indifference, and to survey so many Beauties without a secret Satisfaction and Complacency."[86] Addison accepted Locke's case for secondary qualities as set out in book II, chapter VIII of the *Essay Concerning Human Understanding*, leading him to the conclusion that the ornamentation of nature was largely a matter of perception.[87] As a result, Addison concluded, "our Souls are at present delightfully lost and bewildered

[79] Ibid., p. 263.

[80] Jean-Pierre de Crousaz, *Traité du beau* (1715, 2nd ed. 1724) (Paris: Fayard, 1985), pp. 441–89.

[81] EB, *Philosophical Enquiry*, pp. 255–68.

[82] Ibid., p. 261.

[83] Ibid., p. 269.

[84] Ibid., p. 268.

[85] Ibid., p. 269.

[86] Addison, *Spectator*, no. 413, 24 June 1712. Cf. James Arbuckle, "Hibernicus's Letter, No. 5, Saturday 1 May 1725" in *A Collection of Letters and Essays on Several Subjects Lately Publish'd in the Dublin Journal* (London: 1729), 2 vols, I, p. 40. On Arbuckle's relations with Hutcheson and the Molesworth Circle, see W. R. Scott, "James Arbuckle and his Relation to the Molesworth–Shaftesbury School," *Mind*, 8:30 (April 1899), pp. 194–215.

[87] Locke, *Essay*, II, viii, §§ 13–14.

in a pleasing Delusion."[88] But the delusion was nothing other than the experience of beauty, which draws us into a feeling of contentment with the world. But, for Burke, Addison's "complacency" was really a feeling of attraction, prompting the claim that beauty was a "social quality": exposure to it inspires us "with sentiments of tenderness and affection."[89] Equally, these warm feelings of pleasure are evoked by exposure to particular company. The sentiment of "complacence" lies dormant when we confront the abstract idea of a general society of our fellows, but in the face of "*particular society*"—"Good company, lively conversations, and the endearments of friendship"—sociability is aroused from a gregarious instinct to a positive pleasure.[90]

Burke's observation about the pleasures of "particular" society was directed against the tenets of stoic philanthropy. The revival of stoic ideas concerning the natural sociability of man was associated with both Shaftesbury and Hutcheson.[91] Hutcheson's resuscitation of Zeno's ideal, as reported in Cicero's *De finibus*, of a life lived "according to nature" (*secundum naturam vivere*) was intended as an assault on Epicurean and Augustinian accounts of moral motivation that sought to reduce human psychology to the depraved appetite of self-love.[92] In Hutcheson's Christianised rendition of the stoic doctrine, the virtuous life entailed conducting oneself "according to what we may see from the Constitution of our Nature, we were intended for by our Creator."[93] This design was evident in the human capacity for disinterested action expressed in both the "Esteem" of virtuous behaviour and "Love" of benevolent motives.[94] The natural sense of mankind was drawn alike to what was decent (*decorum*) and honourable (*honestum*) by a "general kinship" and "universal affection."[95] In explicit contradiction of the principles advanced by "civilian" lawyers

[88] Addison, *Spectator*, no. 413, 24 June 1712.

[89] EB, *Philosophical Enquiry*, p. 219.

[90] EB, *Philosophical Enquiry*, p. 220. On the sentiment of "complacence," cf. Francis Hutcheson, "Reflections on the Common Systems of Morality" (1725), which originally appeared as a letter to *The London Journal* under the pseudonym of Philanthropos, in idem, *Two Texts on Human Nature*, ed. Thomas Mautner (Cambridge: Cambridge University Press, 1993), p. 100.

[91] For the important divergences between these two figures, however, see Stephen Darwall, *The British Moralists and the Internal "Ought" 1640–1740* (Cambridge: Cambridge University Press, 1995), ch. 8.

[92] Cicero, *De finibus*, IV, vi, 14. Cf. Diogenes Laertius, *Vitae philosophorum*, VII, iv. The phrase is cited in Hutcheson, *Essay on the Nature and Conduct of the Passions*, Preface, p. 8. On Hutchesonian moral philosophy as a critical response to the Augustinian precepts of "Reformed dogmatism," see James Moore, "The Two Systems of Francis Hutcheson: On the Origins of the Scottish Enlightenment" in M. A. Stewart ed., *Studies in the Philosophy of the Scottish Enlightenment* (Oxford: Oxford University Press, 1990). For his association of "self-love (*philautia*)" as the principal spring to action with Epicureanism, see Francis Hutcheson, "On the Natural Sociability of Mankind: Inaugural Lecture" (1730) in idem, *Logic, Metaphysics, and the Natural Sociability of Mankind*, ed. James Moore and Michael Silverthorne (Indianapolis, IN: Liberty Fund, 2006), p. 202.

[93] Hutcheson, *Essay on the Nature and Conduct of the Passions*, Preface, p. 8.

[94] Francis Hutcheson, *An Inquiry into the Original of Our Ideas of Beauty and Virtue* (1725), ed. Wolfgang Leidhold (Indianapolis, IN: Liberty Fund, 2004), pp. 102–3.

[95] Hutcheson, "On the Natural Sociability of Mankind," p. 206. On the nature of "moral sense" in Hutcheson, see D. D. Raphael, *The Moral Sense* (Oxford: Oxford University Press, 1947); William

like Pufendorf, Hutcheson insisted that human beings were sociable not merely in the "secondary" sense of being forced to congregate on account of native indigence and weakness, but in the "primary" sense of being drawn to fellowship "without regard to its advantage or pleasure."[96] This same disinterestedness was evident in our sympathy with beauty: "there must be a Sense of Beauty," as Hutcheson put it in the *Inquiry*, antecedent to the prospect of utility or "Advantage."[97] While we naturally admire the utility of nature, our admiration is independent of any hope of advantage.

Nonetheless, admiration for beautiful and benevolent actions increases in proportion to the extent to which they serve the utility of others. As Hutcheson saw it, the moral sense is particularly drawn to those actions which have "the most universal unlimited Tendency to the greatest and most extensive Happiness of all the rational Agents, to whom our Influence can reach."[98] This meant, in Burkean parlance, that devotion to "general society" was more agreeable to moral taste than our commitment to "particular society" in the form of family and friends. Burke would have recognised this claim as an expression of the stoic commitment to the doctrine of rational kinship. "We are by nature fitted [*apti*]," as Cato put it in book III of Cicero's *De finibus*, "to associations [*coetus*], assemblies [*concilia*] and cities [*civitates*]." All particular associations, however, must yield to the most complete, cosmopolitan association—the community of all rational creatures—which is preferable to every partisan attachment.[99] In one of the essays which he prefaced to his 1727 translation of Richard Cumberland's *De legibus naturae*, John Maxwell sought to capture the basic point of the stoic argument by ascribing to the ancient moralists the view

---

Frankena, "Hutcheson's Moral Sense Theory," *Journal of the History of Ideas*, 16:3 (June 1955), pp. 356–75; D. F. Norton, *David Hume: Common-Sense Moralist, Sceptical Metaphysician*, (Princeton, NJ: Princeton University Press, 1982), ch. 2. For the contrast with Hume, see James Moore, "Utility and Humanity: The Quest for the *Honestum* in Cicero, Hutcheson, and Hume," *Utilitas*, 14:3 (2002), pp. 365–86.

[96] Hutcheson, "On the Natural Sociability of Mankind," p. 205. For Hutcheson's relation to Pufendorf, see Knud Haakonssen, *Natural Law and Moral Philosophy from Grotius to the Scottish Enlightenment* (Cambridge: Cambridge University Press, 1996), ch. 2.

[97] Hutcheson, *Inquiry into the Original of our Ideas of Beauty and Virtue*, p. 26. On this theme in eighteenth-century criticism, see Paul Guyer, "Beauty and Utility in Eighteenth-Century Aesthetics" in idem, *Values of Beauty*.

[98] Hutcheson, *Inquiry into the Original of Our Ideas of Beauty and Virtue*, p. 126.

[99] Cicero, *De finibus*, III, xix, 63–64. Cf. Hierocles as preserved in Stobaeus, 4.671,7–673,11, reproduced in *The Hellenistic Philosophers*, ed. A. A. Long and D. N. Sedley (Cambridge: Cambridge University Press, 1997), 2 vols., 57G: "although the greater distance in blood will remove some affection, we must try hard to assimilate them." On the theme of "social" *oikeiôsis* in stoic ethics, see briefly Ernst Oberfohren, *Die Idee der Universalökonomie in der Französischen Wirtschaftswissenschaftlichen Literatur bis auf Turgot* (Jena: Gustave Fischer, 1905), pp. 3ff., and more fully in Julia Annas, *The Morality of Happiness* (Oxford: Oxford University Press, 1993), pp. 262–76, 303–11; Gisela Striker, "The Role of *Oikeiôsis* in Stoic Ethics" in idem, *Essays on Hellenistic Epistemology and Ethics* (Cambridge: Cambridge University Press, 1996); Tad Brennan, *The Stoic Life: Emotions, Duties, and Fate* (Oxford: Oxford University Press, 2005), p. 211; A. A. Long, *From Epicurus to Epictetus: Studies in Hellenistic and Roman Philosophy* (Oxford: Oxford University Press, 2006), ch. 16.

that "the whole is of greater regard than a part, and a City than a Citizen," while ultimately each individual was a "Citizen of the World."[100] Although Hutcheson argued in the same cosmopolitan vein that universal benevolence was more "amiable" than personal affection, Burke was clear that immediate ties were more endearing than general human fellowship.[101] For Burke, in other words, sympathy was partial by its nature.

Two years after the first appearance of Burke's *Enquiry*, Adam Smith emphasised in his *Theory of Moral Sentiments* that although sympathy is commonly taken to be coextensive in meaning with pity, it should properly be understood to denote "our fellow-feeling with any passion whatever."[102] This signalled a departure from the system of Mandeville, but also from the modification of Mandeville's conception of fellow-feeling as formulated by Rousseau in his second *Discourse*. Sympathy was not a refinement of self-love, as Mandeville had argued, or a form of natural compassion, as Rousseau artfully construed the Mandevillian position.[103] Smith underlined the deficiency evident in previous accounts: "Our sympathy with sorrow, though not more real, has been more taken notice of than our sympathy with joy."[104] Smith's admiration for Burke's *Enquiry* was related by Dugald Stewart to James Prior in the period between the appearance of the first and second editions of Prior's memoir of

[100] John Maxwell, "Concerning the Imperfectness of the Heathen Morality" in Richard Cumberland, *A Treatise of the Laws of Nature* (1672), trans. John Maxwell (1727), ed. Jon Parkin (Indianapolis, IN: Liberty Fund, 2005), p. 71. Much of Maxwell's material was borrowed from Richard Brocklesby's *An Explication of the Gospel—Theism and the Divinity of the Christian Religion* (London: 1706). On this, see Jon Parkin, "Forward" to Cumberland, *Treatise of the Laws of Nature*, p. xix, n. 20.

[101] Hutcheson, *Inquiry into the Original of Our Ideas of Beauty and Virtue*, p. 125; EB, *Philosophical Enquiry*, p. 220.

[102] Adam Smith, *The Theory of Moral Sentiments*, ed. D. D. Raphael and A. L. Macfie (Indianapolis, IN: Liberty Fund, 1982), p. 10. On sympathy as an enabling condition of moral evaluation in Smith, see T. D. Campbell, *Adam Smith's Science of Morals* (London: George Allen & Unwin, 1971); on the preconditions of human sympathy, see Eugene Heath, "The Commerce of Sympathy: Adam Smith on the Emergence of Morals," *Journal of the History of Philosophy*, 3:3 (1994), pp. 447–66. On the relationship between sympathy and self-interest in Smith, see Nicholas Phillipson, "Adam Smith as Civic Moralist" in Istvan Hont and Michael Ignatieff eds., *Wealth and Virtue: The Shaping of Political Economy in the Scottish Enlightenment* (Cambridge: Cambridge University Press, 1983), pp. 182–91; Donald Winch, *Riches and Poverty: An Intellectual History of Political Economy in Britain, 1750–1834* (Cambridge: Cambridge University Press, 1996), pp. 103–9.

[103] See Jean-Jacques Rousseau, *Discours sur l'origine et les fondements de l'inégalité parmis les hommes* (1755) in *Œuvres complètes III: Du contrat social, écrits politiques*, ed. Robert Derathé et al., p. 154, for the view that Mandeville's account of pity represented a departure from his usual "froid et subtil" style. For Smith's view of Rousseau as having blended the ideas of Mandeville with the principles of Plato, see his "Letter to the *Edinburgh Review*" (1755–56) in Adam Smith, *Essays on Philosophical Subjects*, ed. W.L.D. Wightman (Indianapolis, IN: Liberty Fund, 1982), p. 251.

[104] Smith, *Theory of Moral Sentiments*, p. 43. Cf. John Clarke, *The Foundation of Morality in Theory and Practice* (York: 1726), esp. pp. 51–53, for the idea that benevolence is founded on self-satisfaction. On Clarke as an important precursor for Smith and Hume, see Luigi Turco, "Sympathy and Moral Sense, 1725–1740," *British Journal for the History of Philosophy*, 7:1 (1999), pp. 79–101.

Burke's life, though it is not clear when Smith originally read the work.[105] It is clear, however, that Burke alighted on what he saw as the overlap in both their accounts of sympathy after the appearance of Smith's *Theory of Moral Sentiments* in 1759.

Burke received a copy of Smith's *Theory* from Hume in April 1759, finally writing to the author on 10 September to register his appreciation of the work.[106] He was "convinced," he told Smith, of the "solidity and Truth" of the overall argument, apparently interpreting Smith's "natural" account of the passions as facilitating both an illustration of the wisdom of providence and a criticism of the perfectionism of stoic self-denial. Burke focused on three aspects of the work in particular. First, he noted that Smith had succeeded in basing his science of morals on the broad foundations of "Human Nature." He then went on to remark how this attention to observed behaviour, along with fidelity to the actual operations of the mind, was an essential qualification in a true "Philosopher," as well as in "a good Christian." Finally, he contrasted this willingness to factor the full range of human passions into a system of morals with the more "contracted" approach of the ancients, above all the "magnificent delusion" of stoic ethics.[107] In Burke's view, Smith had produced a realistic account of the psychological sources of moral motivation that exhibited the providence of intelligent design. He further reckoned that sympathy held this edifice together. In a brief and schematic review of *The Theory of Moral Sentiments* for *The Annual Register*, Burke interpreted Smith as combining an analysis of moral duties with an account of "moral sensations."[108] Smith seemed to have succeeded, in other words, in pursuing the "natural" method of experimental observation without reducing moral sentiment to self-interest or self-regard.[109] Since sympathy coexisted with the selfish passions as a principle of human nature that interested us in the fortunes of others, it seemed to Burke to enable the transition from moral "sensations" to the judgment of "duties."

[105] Prior, *Life of Burke*, p. 38n. The footnote recording Smith's admiration for the *Enquiry* was first added to the second edition of Prior's biography, which bore the title of *Memoir of the Life and Character of the Right Hon. Edmund Burke, with Specimens of his Poetry and Letters, and an Estimate of his Genius and Talents, Compared with those of his Great Contemporaries* (London: 1826), 2 vols.

[106] David Hume to Adam Smith, 12 April 1759, *The Letters of David Hume*, ed. J.Y.T. Greig (Oxford: Oxford University Press, 1932), 2 vols., I, p. 303.

[107] EB, *Corr.*, I, pp. 129–30. For a divergent modern interpretation, see D. D. Raphael, *Adam Smith* (Oxford: Oxford University Press, 1985), p. 73, where the category of "sympathy" in Smith is traced to the stoic idea of cosmic *sympatheia*.

[108] *The Annual Register for the Year 1759* (London: 1760), p. 485. Burke evidently cooled to what he later came to see as Smith's infidelity. See the report of his response to Smith's account of Hume's death in James Boswell, *Boswell in Extremes, 1776–1778*, ed. C. M. Weis and F. A. Pottle (New York: McGraw Hill, 1970), p. 270, discussed in Nicholas Phillipson, *Adam Smith: An Enlightened Life* (London: Allen Lane, 2010), p. 247.

[109] For a reconstruction of the wider context of debate about self-interest that informs Smith's moral theory, see Pierre Force, *Self-Interest before Adam Smith: A Genealogy of Economic Science* (Cambridge: Cambridge University Press, 2003).

Smith's account of sympathy was clearly indebted to Hume's.[110] In the process of explaining the natural esteem felt for the rich and powerful in his *Treatise of Human Nature*, Hume observed how sympathy involved us in the affairs of others, forcing us to "partake" in their satisfactions as well as sufferings.[111] Broadly speaking, the power of sympathy could be observed acting through "the whole animal creation," automatically exciting "pity and terror" in human beings.[112] However, besides feeling pity and fear at the plight of others, we also imaginatively participate in their joy. In the *Enquiry Concerning the Principles of Morals*, Hume highlighted the articulation of this insight in Horace: "The human countenance, says HORACE, borrows smiles and tears from the human countenance."[113] The reference here is to Horace's *Ars poetica*, where the poet draws on the Aristotelian concept of sympathy (*sympatheia*) to explain aesthetic response in terms of a basic instinct for emulation or mimesis: "ut ridentibus arrident, ita flentibus adsunt / humani vultus" [as human faces smile upon those smiling, they weep in response to weeping].[114] Hume described this capacity for sympathy as a "contagion," passed on from agent to spectator by infectious pleasure.[115] On the basis of this seductive process of mutual imitation, we identify with the pleasing prospect of general social utility extending beyond any selfish concern with our own exclusive welfare. Furthermore, according to Hume, sympathy with either the pleasing aspect or the utility of objects accounts for the experience of beauty.

Hume proposed that the appearance of utility accounts for the greater part of beauty: "How considerable a part this is of beauty will easily appear upon

[110]For their exchange on the subject after the publication of the *Theory of Moral Sentiments*, see David Raynor, "Hume's Abstract of Adam Smith's *Theory of Moral Sentiments*," *Journal of the History of Philosophy*, 22:1 (1984), pp. 51–79. For Hume's debts to his predecessors, and to Hutcheson in particular, see Carolyn W. Korsmeyer, "Hume and the Foundations of Taste," *Journal of Aesthetics and Art Criticism*, 35:2 (1976), pp. 201–15. For a broader historical sketch, see Dabney Townsend, "From Shaftesbury to Kant: The Development of the Concept of Aesthetic Experience," *Journal of the History of Ideas*, 48:2 (1987), pp. 287–305.

[111]Hume, *Treatise*, p. 231.

[112]Ibid., pp. 234, 368.

[113]Hume, *Enquiry*, p. 109.

[114]Horace, *Ars poetica*, lines 101–2. Hume's citation employs Richard Bentley's "adflent" instead of "adsunt." Horace's debt to Aristotle is examined in C. O. Brink, *Horace on Poetry I: Prolegomena to the Literary Epistles* (Cambridge: Cambridge University Press, 1963), pp. 98–99. The term *sympatheia* appears in Aristotle, *Problemata*, 886a25–887b6. In *Ars rhetorica*, 1408a5, the idea of fellow-feeling is signalled by the verb *synomoiopatheô*.

[115]Hume, *Enquiry*, p. 131. For differences in Hume's treatment of sympathy in the *Enquiry* by comparison with the *Treatise*, see Norman Kemp-Smith, *The Philosophy of David Hume: A Critical Study of its Origins and Central Doctrines* (London: Macmillan, 1941, 1966), p. 151; Nicholas Capaldi, *David Hume: The Newtonian Philosopher* (Boston, MA: Twayne, 1975), pp. 180–87; Terence Penelhum, *David Hume: An Introduction to His Philosophical System* (West Lafayette, IN: Purdue University Press, 1992), p. 155. For continuities in the argument, see John B. Stewart, *The Moral and Political Philosophy of David Hume* (New York: Columbia University Press, 1963), p. 329; Kate Abramson, "Sympathy and the Project of Hume's Second *Enquiry*," *Archiv für Geschichte der Philosophie*, 83:1 (2001), pp. 45–80; Rico Vitz, "Sympathy and Benevolence in Hume's Moral Psychology," *Journal of the History of Philosophy*, 42:3 (2004), pp. 261–75.

reflection."[116] The feeling of beauty substantially derives from our sympathy with the pleasure which a proprietor takes in the "fitness" of their possession.[117] In both the *Treatise* and the second *Enquiry*, Hume illustrates his point with reference to Quintilian.[118] In book VIII of the *Institutio oratoria*, in the process of considering the appropriate use of ornament (*ornatus*) in rhetoric, Quintilian observes how the refinements of beauty are capable of inspiring an audience with passionate emotion. In arriving at this conclusion, he tells us, he followed the suggestions of both Aristotle and Cicero for whom ornament evokes admiration, and thereby awakens sympathy.[119] However, beautiful refinement has to be to the purpose, since beauty pleases above all by its appositeness. Quintilian makes his point by invoking the conventions of Roman pastoral: landscapes charm insofar as they appear to service the needs of social life.[120] Thus, planting vines in a symmetrical fashion is agreeable to the eye, not least because the arrangement benefits the nourishment of the crop. "True beauty," Quintilian concluded, "is never separable from utility."

Notwithstanding Burke's insistence that the beautiful bore no relation to purpose in Hume's and Quintilian's sense, Smith claimed in the *Theory of Moral Sentiments* that the identification of utility as a principal source of beauty had been noted by virtually every commentator on the subject. But he further reckoned that even Hume, although an "ingenious" writer on this topic, had failed to separate the pleasure conferred by the purpose of an artefact from its facility or fitness in promoting that end. What in fact attracts us to utility, in Smith's opinion, is less the enjoyment of the benefit administered by an artefact than the aptness of the instrument in furthering some end: we are capable of admiring the propriety of a given contrivance over and above the advantage it is designed to procure.[121] This admiration for the beauty of contraptions is diffused through every avenue of life, attracting us to the conveniences that accompany wealth and luxury, and at the same time naturally driving us to abandon stoic apathy in favour of the imagined charms of intricacy and refinement, spurring us in the process to industry and ambition.[122] But if beauty fosters ambition, Smith also noted that it can inspire enthusiasm for improving the variety of institutions that secure the public welfare, and on the same basis it recommends the appearance of virtue to our taste.[123] A virtuous character pleases by the appo-

[116] Hume, *Treatise*, p. 368.

[117] Ibid., pp. 368–69.

[118] Ibid., p. 369n; Hume, *Enquiry*, p. 109n.

[119] Quintilian, *Institutio oratoria*, VIII, iii, 5–7. See Aristotle, *Ars rhetorica*, 1404b11. Quintilian cites a fragmentary passage in a letter from Cicero to Brutus that has not otherwise survived: "nam eloquentiam quae admirationem non habet non iudicio." The identification of eloquence with the ability to inspire admiration can likewise be found in Cicero, *De oratore*, III, xiv, 52–53. For discussion, see G. L. Hendrickson, "Cicero's Correspondence with Brutus and Calvus on Oratorical Style," *American Journal of Philology*, 47:3 (1926), pp. 234–58.

[120] See Virgil, *Georgics*, II, lines 1–70, on the adornment of nature with abundance through labour; cf. Horace, *Odes*, II, xv, lines 1–8, where cultivation is seen to have occurred at the expense of rustic charm.

[121] Smith, *Theory of Moral Sentiments*, pp. 179–80.

[122] Ibid., pp. 181–83.

[123] Ibid., p. 187.

siteness of their behaviour just as a system of government can be appreciated for its beauty. But, once again, what delights us is less the utility secured by the action than the "propriety" with which a given end is pursued.[124]

Burke's argument in the *Enquiry* similarly concluded that virtuous behaviour endeared itself to spectators on the basis of its beauty, yet he conceived of the beauty of virtue as appealing less in terms of its propriety than on account of the spontaneous feeling of sympathy it engendered. Even so, this was to concede that the appeal of moral qualities to taste promoted virtue. To illustrate his point, Burke compared the aesthetic attributes of the exemplary characters of Caesar and Cato as drawn by Sallust, exactly as Hume had done in both the *Treatise* and the second *Enquiry*.[125] However, whilst acknowledging that the attributes of beauty could appropriately be applied to virtue, Burke went on to underline the danger involved in confounding the two. In urging caution in this way, he was not only distancing himself from Epicurean naturalism, but also signalling his divergence from Shaftesbury and Hutcheson. Attempts to reduce moral qualities to the attributes of beauty had "given rise to an infinite deal of whimsical theory," he contended, just as efforts to explain the sentiment of beauty in terms of utility had distorted the true character of aesthetic appeal. Moral philosophy was ultimately concerned to establish the "science of our duties" on the basis of how reason restrained our sentiments in compliance with ascertainable norms.[126] In the end, although our sentiments might naturally be disposed to favour virtue, the passions had to be judged by the tribunal of conscience, and ethics established on a more secure foundation than could be afforded by mere taste. Taste provided vital support in sustaining religion, politics and morals, but it did not supply criteria of judgment adequate to the defence of piety or justice.

3.4 Sublimity, Reverence and Fear

Burke was careful in the *Enquiry* to distinguish beautiful from sublime characters. We "love" Caesar as depicted by Sallust, he declared: we feel "familiar" with him, and are happy to follow his lead. What draws us is the beauty or "loveliness" of his persona, which embodied the "softer" virtues of "kindness" and "liberality."[127] Caesar's virtues, as Hume had argued, are "amiable" rather than "awful."[128] Cato, on the other hand, as Burke portrayed him, was a beacon of the "strong virtues." His qualities were sublime rather than companionable and indulgent, presenting us with "much

[124] Ibid., p. 189.

[125] EB, *Philosophical Enquiry*, p. 271. Cf. Hume, *Treatise*, p. 387; Hume, *Enquiry*, p. 179. See also Richard Steele, *The Christian Hero: An Argument Proving that no Principles but those of Religion are Sufficient to Make a Great Man* (London: 1701), pp. 5–10, for an early eighteenth-century recapitulation of Sallust's comparison. For Sallust's juxtaposition, see *Bellum catilinae*, LIV, vi.

[126] EB, *Philosophical Enquiry*, p. 272.

[127] Ibid., p. 271.

[128] Hume, *Treatise*, p. 387; Hume, *Enquiry*, p. 179. Cf. EB, *Philosophical Enquiry*, p. 271, where the term "amiable" is twice used to capture the humane or sympathetic virtues.

to admire, much to reverence, and perhaps something to fear; we respect him, but we respect him at a distance."[129] In his account of "Qualities Immediately Agreeable to Ourselves" in the second *Enquiry*, Hume had identified such awe-inspiring magnanimity with the "GREATNESS of MIND" and "Dignity of Character" that Longinus had likened to the experience of the sublime.[130] Hume followed Boileau in associating such venerable self-command with the conduct of Medea in Corneille's *Médée*.[131] Conspicuously, he did not mention Boileau's adoption of Longinus' celebration of the *fiat lux* as exemplifying the quintessence of the sublime, despite the fact that debate about the character of that pronouncement had done so much to involve the sublime in intellectual controversy from the late seventeenth century onwards.[132] However, as early as 1744, Burke had identified the spectacle of the creation as encapsulating sublimity at its utmost: "Sun, earth, moon[,] Stars[,] be ye made, and they were made! The word of the Creator sufficient to create universe from Nothing."[133] Awesome command was magnificent and inspired reverence automatically.

Longinus' point had been that the simple utterance, as reported in *Genesis*, "God said: 'Let there be Light,' and there was Light; 'Let there be Earth,' and there was Earth," perfectly captured the idea of omnipotence. Such an image of power, he believed, exalted the human mind.[134] Sublimity of style evoked dignity of soul, which is excited by the spectacle of overwhelming greatness: humans naturally respect the image of surpassing grandeur, which prompts them to contemplate their own exultant nature.[135] In the *Philosophical Enquiry*, Burke denominated this disposition to glory by the term "ambition," describing it as a "satisfaction" arising from the contemplation of excelling our fellows. Such pride, he went on, produces "a sort of swelling and triumph that is extremely grateful to the human mind." Moreover, this feeling of distinction operates with singular force when the mind is confronted with an astounding spectacle, since consciousness feels ennobled by the dignity of the objects which it contemplates. "Hence proceeds," Burke concluded, "what Longinus has observed of that glorying and inward sense of greatness, that always fills the reader of such passages in poets and orators as are sublime."[136]

[129] EB, *Philosophical Enquiry*, p. 271.

[130] Hume, *Enquiry*, p. 132.

[131] Hume, *Enquiry*, p. 133. Hume was following Boileau in depicting Medea's assertion of personal fortitude in the phrase "Moy, Moy, dis-je, & c'est assez" (Pierre Corneille, *Médée*, act I, scene v) as exhibiting the sublime in style and conception. See Nicolas Boileau-Despréaux, "Réflexion x ou refutation d'une dissertation de Monsieur Leclerc contre Longin'" (1710) in *Œuvres* (Amsterdam: 1714), 2 vols., II, Réflexion x.

[132] On this, see Richard Bourke, "Pity and Fear: Providential Sociability in Burke's *Philosophical Enquiry*" in Michael Funk Deckard and Koen Vermeir eds., *The Science of Sensibility: Reading Edmund Burke's Philosophical Enquiry* (Heidelberg: Springer-Verlag GmbH, 2010).

[133] EB Burke to Richard Shackleton, c. 14 June 1744, *Corr.*, I, p. 18.

[134] The citation appears in Longinus, *On the Sublime*, IX, 9–10.

[135] Ibid., VII, 2–3; XXXV–XXXVI.

[136] EB, *Philosophical Enquiry*, pp. 225–26.

Burke contrasted the passion of ambition with "imitation" insofar as the latter prompts us to emulate rather than surpass our peers. Emulation is a potent instrument of education and socialisation—"This forms our manners, our opinions, our lives"—and leads us by the pleasures of sympathy rather than the precepts of reason.[137] Burke elucidates his argument by way of reference to Aristotle's concept of mimesis as developed in the *Poetics*.[138] We take pleasure in the products of artful imitation, Aristotle proposed, but we equally enjoy the activity of imitation itself: mimesis is an instinct in evidence from childhood, and mankind is the most mimetic (*mimêtikôtaton*) of the animals.[139] For Burke, imitation confines our aspirations to socially approved norms, since in emulating each other we approximate one another's desires. It is, as Burke put it, "a form of mutual compliance which all men yield to each other," thereby conforming us to a standard without any feeling of constraint.[140] It binds us to one another through an exchange of reciprocal pleasure. With ambition, however, we strive beyond our fellows, and are imaginatively seduced into transcending our own abilities. The admiration of the sublime takes us beyond ourselves, inducing a feeling of pride as the soul expands to embrace objects at the limit of its comprehension, or to exercise self-control beyond the natural human capacity. As Addison had argued, providence has so arranged things that the mind is naturally astonished by an impression of limitlessness, fostering devotion at the intimation of boundless power.[141] In this vein, Burke construed ambition to be driven by the emulation of something more than human, reminding us of a greatness beyond ourselves.

Awareness of surpassing greatness ennobles the mind, but it also confirms our relative vulnerability. At the very moment that the idea of greatness swells our pride, the feeling of sublimity awakens the instinct of self-preservation since the prospect of vulnerability induces the passion of fear. Yet, as Burke had already explained in part I of the *Enquiry*, the objects of fear, when experienced at a sufficiently safe distance, can excite delight.[142] The passions belonging to self-preservation turn on pain and danger, and consequently inspire dread. But, when the prospect of pain or danger is sensed without the agent being overwhelmed by a situation of real threat, the accompanying emotion of terror confers what Burke terms "delight," since under these secure circumstances the perception of remote distress is experienced as a release from discomfort, and therefore as a diminution of pain. Burke summarises his case with the pronouncement, "Whatever excites this delight, I call *sublime*."[143] In elucidating this insight, he further pointed out that although the diminution of pain is not a pleasure, it can produce the thrill of relief shadowed by the horror of an escape from danger. Properly understood, therefore, the feeling of the sublime

[137] Ibid., p. 224.

[138] Ibid., p. 225.

[139] Aristotle, *Poetics*, 1448b5–10. Cf. *Ars rhetorica*, 1371a21–1371b25. On this, see EB, *Hints for an Essay on the Drama* (c. 1761), *W & S*, I, p. 555: "we are imitative animals."

[140] EB, *Philosophical Enquiry*, p. 224.

[141] Addison, *Spectator*, no. 413, 24 June 1712.

[142] EB, *Philosophical Enquiry*, p. 226.

[143] Ibid.

has three component parts. First, it delights the mind with the prospect of a distant and therefore manageable threat; second, it fills the soul with pride in the contemplation of grandeur; and finally, it induces reverence before an image of magnificence. As a result of this complex combination of responses, the overwhelming passion of fear is modified into a form of delightful terror that modulates between astonishment and respect.

In the conclusion to part I of the *Enquiry*, Burke commented that men commonly act appropriately "from their feelings," while subsequently poorly reasoning about what their sentiments enjoin.[144] Ultimately, Burke reserved a role for reason in evaluating the justice of moral sentiment. However, in our everyday moral conduct, we happily rely on our passions, which deliver impulses in advance of being processed by the reasoning faculty. Astonishment and horror are clear examples: they hurry the mind onwards "by an irresistible force," anticipating rather than resulting from calculation, proceeding from instinctive responses that have yet to be rationalised. The same can be said of the more moderate effects of the sublime such as induce the states of "admiration, reverence and respect."[145] While these sentiments are crucial for the maintenance of society and religion, they are founded on self-preservation, not sociability. Each of them, moreover, shares a common source. "Terror," Burke proposes, is the overarching passion, either openly or latently animating the mind with a range of affections extending from horror to devotion. Burke took the variety of responses induced by terror to be evident from linguistic usage, since many languages employ a single term to depict diverse reactions. Thus "wonder" and "fear" are both signalled by the single Greek noun *thambos*; "terror" as well as "respect" by the word *deinos*; to "revere" and to "fear" by the verb *aideô*. The same can be said of single terms in the Latin and French languages, which invoke a multiplicity of senses by using a single word—as with *vereor*, *stupeo*, *attonitus* and *étonnement*.[146]

Burke illustrates the way in which these distinct yet related passions are evoked instinctively, without the intervention of rational speculation, by itemising their causes in part II of the *Enquiry*. Obscurity, power, privation, vastness, infinity, magnitude and the like, all bring about the feeling of the sublime. They have this effect on account of the fear they provoke. This response is most conspicuous in the case of obscurity and power. "To make any thing very terrible, obscurity seems in general to be necessary," Burke observed.[147] Obscurity shrouds in mystery and augments the authority of what is feared. However, authority is ultimately founded on the perception of power, subjection to which induces submission based on either terror or respect. The effects of power and obscurity are apparent in life as well as in literature. Milton intensifies terror by shrouding its objects in obscurity; Job evokes transcendent power by underlining the timidity it provokes.[148] The experience of the sublime,

[144] Ibid., p. 228.
[145] Ibid., p. 230.
[146] Ibid., p. 231.
[147] Ibid.
[148] Ibid., pp. 231–32, 238.

in proceeding from fear at the point where it is being modified into a manageable passion, proves to be fundamental to Burke's treatment of both religious awe and social deference. Both devotion to the divinity and submission to our superiors are generated by apprehension induced by relative positions of power. "I know of nothing sublime," Burke commented, "which is not some modification of power."[149]

In a long section on the subject of "Power" added to the second edition of the *Enquiry* in 1759, Burke elaborated on the psychology of radical subordination. Fear in the end is based on vulnerability in the face of death, and what horrifies us about power is its capacity to realise this ultimate terror. At its most extreme, in the face of omnipotence, "we shrink into the minuteness of our own nature, and are, in a manner, annihilated before him."[150] In his review of the first edition of the *Enquiry*, Goldsmith had objected to the suggestion that the sublime is excited more by "terror" than it is by admiration and love. "It is certain," he argued, "we can have the most sublime ideas of the Deity, without imagining him a God of terror."[151] Burke's extended meditation on power in the second edition of the *Enquiry* directly addresses this concern.[152] It is indeed right that the Christian conception of God "humanised" our idea of the divinity, Burke conceded. Both philosophy and revelation make available to us a "complex idea" of the deity as a blend of power, wisdom, justice and goodness.[153] But this refined and abstract notion derived from theological speculation is distinct at once from primitive and pagan conceptions of the godhead. What fires the imagination, as opposed to the understanding, is the image of divinity as an overwhelming power. In our conception of the deity we are apt to confuse the effect of our ideas with their cause. We are capable of ascending to a higher "intellectual" grasp of God's attributes, but we are nonetheless condemned by our limited faculties to make that progress to a purer understanding via more basic "sensible images."[154] These images appeal to the imagination, simplifying complex attributes into a more rudimentary perception in which the impression of surpassing power predominates.

Burke's argument here amounts to the claim that the natural disposition to religion is founded on superstition. Revelation and speculation are both capable of improving this basic inclination into a more refined form of piety and devotion. Nonetheless, these supplements have been grafted onto a primordial exposure to dread. Ritual, solemnity and ceremonial pomp register the enduring impact of a fundamental impulse to placate the passion of fear. Neither the most basic nor the most developed forms of worship can altogether dispense with some acknowledgement

[149] Ibid., p. 236.

[150] Ibid., p. 239.

[151] [Oliver Goldsmith], Review of the *Philosophical Enquiry*, *Monthly Review*, 16 (May 1757), pp. 473–80, p. 475.

[152] On the religious significance of these passages, see F. P. Lock, "Burke and Religion" in Ian Crowe ed., *An Imaginative Whig: Reassessing the Life and Thought of Edmund Burke* (Columbia, MO: University of Missouri Press, 2005).

[153] EB, *Philosophical Enquiry*, p. 239.

[154] Ibid.

of the underlying terror that ignites religious sentiment, nor consequently with ritual displays of reverential awe. "Almost all the heathen temples were dark," Burke remarked in this context.[155] The atmosphere of gloom was itself a tribute to the sublime object of devotion. Druidic practices and American savages alike exhibited a penchant for supplication; even Christian ceremony recognised the requirements of the imagination. It followed that while superstition could be reduced, it could never be completely eradicated. Burke contended that it is "our ignorance of things that causes all our admiration, and chiefly excites our passions."[156] Enlightenment was capable of improving this condition, but science could never penetrate to the inner secrets of nature, and thus superstition could never be totally abolished. Burke arrived at this conclusion in a spirit of Lockean resignation in a passage on the inscrutability of causation with which he opened part IV of the *Enquiry*: "The great chain of causes, which linking one to another even to the throne of God himself, can never be unravelled by any industry of ours. When we go but one step beyond the immediately sensible qualities of things, we go out of our depth."[157]

Burke's claim that religious feeling proceeds from ignorance and superstition is distinct from the sceptical argument that fear is the cause of belief. He cited the notorious line from the Silver poet Statius, to present the view from which he wanted to dissent: "primus in orbe deos fecit timor" (fear first created gods in the world).[158] While Burke accepted that fear stands at the origin of religious sentiment, he insisted that it is not the source of religious belief. The idea of God precedes the dread of him, although fear will inevitably follow from the concept of omnipotence. "It is on this principle," he commented, "that true religion has, and must have, so large a mixture of salutary fear; and that false religions have generally nothing else but fear to support them."[159] In this context, he noted that throughout the annals of pagan literature the idea of divinity is inseparable from a sacred feeling of obeisance. Even Lucretius, "a poet not to be suspected of giving way to superstitious terrors," confessed to a feeling of sublime horror in the face of the spectacle opened up by the Epicurean philosophy of nature.[160] Platonism first introduced, and Christianity properly established, the passion of love as defining our relationship to our maker. But the love in question at the same time has an element of veneration since overwhelming superiority instils an attitude of abasement. Indeed, the fact that a regime of dedicated contemplation is a prerequisite for the achievement of a state of adoration clearly indicates that the passion of terror precedes the habit of devotion.[161]

After paying considerable attention to the passion of fear in the *Ars rhetorica*, Aristotle was equally clear that what panicked the mind was the prospect of destruction or great pain. In social life, the intention accompanied by the capacity to do harm is

[155] Ibid., p. 231.
[156] Ibid., p. 233.
[157] Ibid., p. 283.
[158] Ibid., p. 241, citing Statius, *Thebaid*, III, line 661.
[159] EB, *Philosophical Enquiry*, p. 241.
[160] Ibid., p. 240.
[161] Ibid., p. 241.

a source of anxiety, and consequently the "signs" of malevolent purpose are primed to induce fear. Thus enmity and anger armed with power can inspire dread, just as outraged virtue, or injustice, is equally likely to do. Indeed, any experience of being at the mercy of another is a potential occasion for alarm, not least because most people are disposed to commit injustice "whenever they can."[162] It follows from this that social power is liable to induce submission as a consequence of natural timidity. Montesquieu commented in the *Spirit of the Laws* that man in the state of nature above all feels his weakness. His "timidity," as a result, "would be extreme," as is evidenced by the condition of the savages of North America: "everything makes them tremble, everything makes them flee."[163] The exploitation of such sentiments under a despotic government requires that the faults of the ruler be kept from view: "He is hidden," Montesquieu wrote, "and one remains in ignorance of his condition."[164]

In the same vein, Burke argued in the *Enquiry* that, because despotism depends on arousing fear, the chief power will be sequestered as much as possible "from the public eye."[165] However, it followed from Burke's analysis that a depleted level of power, especially under conditions of reduced ill will on the part of whoever is in authority, diminished the intensity of the terror it could provoke, so that the symbols of power displayed before the public in a civilised regime could foster subjection based on reverence rather than unadulterated dread. Submission could be elicited on the basis of sublime delight without needing to evoke excessive fear. This insight would prove important to Burke's understanding of political psychology. It appeared to show that awe and veneration can sustain authority in politics in the absence of unmitigated servility. It also implied that admiration flourishes in a context of deference where power commands respect without the threat of immediate danger. This implication argued against natural histories of government that traced the origins of subjection solely to gratitude for protection from fear.[166] As Burke saw it, not only did the fear of authority continue to exact obedience but, further, the feeling of submission could be agreeable to the mind as terror relaxed into the sentiment of respect.

Burke drew on medical science to argue that mind and body were fitted to one another to produce this result. He noted that, when it comes to pain, the body reacts as a warning to the mind; but in the case of danger, the mind is activated to stimulate the body, contracting or tensing the nerves and thereby exercising the organs.[167] The analysis here agreed with the argument developed by Lévesque de Pouilly, who claimed that providence had wisely ordained that labour and discomfort could be agreeable since stimulation excited the body from languor and aroused the mind

[162] Aristotle, *Ars rhetorica*, 1382a25–1382b20.

[163] Charles-Louis de Secondat, Baron de Montesquieu, *De l'esprit des lois* (1748) in *Œuvres complètes*, ed. Roger Caillois (Paris: Gallimard, 1951), 2 vols., I, pt. I, bk. I, ch. 2.

[164] Ibid., pt. I, ch. 14, p. 59.

[165] EB, *Philosophical Enquiry*, p. 231.

[166] See, for example, Polybius, *Historiae*, VI, vi.

[167] Ibid., pp. 284–88.

from melancholy.[168] Burke's point was that our aesthetic responses are uniformly caused by identifiable stimuli, or by qualities we learn to associate with particular events and circumstances. Accordingly, in social life, we automatically react to the beauty and elegance of manners as well as to the imposing spectacle of power. Without the fortuitous tendency to delight in the feeling of awe, subordination could only be secured on the basis of naked force, and rebellion only subdued by overwhelming terror. Under this arrangement of things, all politics would be founded on the spirit of conquest, and all conquest on the perpetuation of violence and fear.

3.5 Language and Taste

The fifth and final part of the *Philosophical Enquiry* was devoted to the subject of "Words." A key component of Burke's purpose in analysing this subject was to examine the peculiar power of language to persuade. By comparison with painting, poetry and rhetoric were deficient as means of description, yet they were unsurpassed as vehicles for compelling an audience.[169] Burke's claim was directed against the view developed by Dubos to the effect that painting surpassed poetry in its impact on the soul.[170] Following Horace, Dubos had argued that the empire of sight was dominant over the human mind, providing the imagination with a singular source of pleasure.[171] The imagination is stirred less vividly by aural impressions than by visual images, Horace claimed in the *Ars poetica*.[172] Dubos set about illustrating his point with the depiction of Cupid in one of Horace's *Odes* as "whetting his fiery darts on stone imbrued with blood."[173] The image is forceful, Dubos notes, because it strikes our visual sense, but it does so by means of "artificial signs."[174] That is, the

[168] Louis-Jean Lévesque de Pouilly, *Theorie des sentimens agréables: où après avoir indiqué les règles, que la nature suit dans la distribution du plaisir, on établit les principes de la théologie naturelle et ceux de la philosophie morale* (Paris: 1748), p. viii. Cf. Dubos, *Critical Reflections on Poetry, Painting and Music*, I, p. 5; David Hume, "Of Tragedy" (1757) in *Essays Moral, Political, and Literary* (Indianapolis, IN: Liberty Fund, 1985, 1987), p. 217.

[169] Ibid., pp. 316–17.

[170] Debate on this subject became widespread in the eighteenth century. James Harris, *Three Treatises: The First Concerning Arts; the Second Concerning Music, Painting and Poetry; the Third Concerning Happiness* (London: 1744), p. 94, placed poetry above the other "mimetic" arts. Burke's copy of Harris's *Treatises* is located at the Clark Library, UCLA. For discussion, see Richard Bourke, "Aesthetics and Politics in Edmund Burke," *UCLA Centre for Seventeenth- and Eighteenth-Century Studies and William Andrews Clark Memorial Library: The Centre and Clark Library Newsletter*, 50 (Fall 2009), pp. 7–9.

[171] Dubos, *Critical Reflections on Poetry, Painting and Music*, I, ch. 40.

[172] Horace, *Ars poetica*, lines 179–82. Horace's point was in fact that visual stimulus, like the sight of Medea murdering her children, might be excessive. On the reception of this passage, see H. C. Nutting, "Horace, *Ars Poetica* 179ff.," *Classical Philology*, 16:4 (October 1921), pp. 384–86.

[173] Horace, *Odes*, II, viii, lines 14–15: "et Cupido, / semper ardentis acuens sagittas / cote cruenta."

[174] Dubos, *Critical Reflections on Poetry, Painting and Music*, I, p. 321. On the artifice, and arbitrariness, of the sign in the eighteenth century, see Avi Lifschitz, "The Arbitrariness of the Linguistic Sign: Variations on an Enlightenment Theme," *Journal of the History of Ideas*, 73:4 (2012), pp. 537–57.

description excites ideas, conjuring an image in the mind, yet it does so through the artifice of language, leaving us at a distance from immediate impressions. Burke's aim in the final section of the *Enquiry* was to contest this verdict. Later, in the 1770s, he would write that "poetry will always rank first among human compositions."[175] This was partly because of its philosophical aptitude for contributing to the study of human nature. But it was also because of the forcefulness of its impact upon the mind. To illustrate this last point in the *Philosophical Enquiry*, Burke built his case in part around two literary images of the sublime, one from the King James Bible and one from Milton's *Paradise Lost*.

Burke's biblical example concerns a recurrent Old Testament phrase. The best way of depicting an angel in painting, Burke claims, is to "draw a beautiful young man winged." There are very few ways of effectively "enlivening" such an image. Prose and poetry, however, are different, as a common portrayal of angels illustrates: the addition of a single word can transform the force of representation, for example in the image of "the angel of the Lord."[176] The qualification made the subject at once awesome and grand. Burke's second example is taken from Milton's description of the fallen angels in the second book of *Paradise Lost*:

> Through many a dark and dreary vale
> They pass'd, and many a region dolorous
> O'er many a frozen, many a fiery Alp;
> Rocks, caves, lakes, fens, bogs, dens and shades of death,
> A universe of death.[177]

This picture works by heightening the experience of the sublime: successive regions of death are at last revealed as instances of a whole "universe of death." The depiction is "great and amazing," but also "beyond conception."[178] We cannot literally picture such a staggeringly bold image, calling into question whether it is truly an "image" at all. Thus for Burke, poetry is not properly a mimetic form of art.[179] It functions by evocation rather than description. It uses "tokens" to gain purchase on the minds of other people. It lays hold of the imagination rather than the understanding by manipulating common "modes of speech." It innovates, in other words, by using figures of speech. The rhetorical adaptation of language is peculiarly adept at evoking passion, thereby appealing to the enduring sentiments in man. At the start of the eighteenth century, John Dennis had described this effect as "Poetical Enthusiasm."[180] Burke followed him in admiring its ability to move the soul. For Dennis, this form of transport had been identified by Longinus as a "fullness of Joy mingled with Astonishment," giving rise on the part of the spectator to a feeling of

[175] EB to William Richardson, 18 June 1777, *Corr.*, III, p. 354.
[176] EB, *Philosophical Enquiry*, p. 318.
[177] Milton, *Paradise Lost*, II, lines 18–22, misquoted at EB, *Philosophical Enquiry*, p. 318.
[178] Ibid., p. 319.
[179] Ibid., p. 317.
[180] John Dennis, *The Advancement and Reformation of Poetry* (London: 1701), p. 29.

"noble Pride."[181] This kind of sublimity was inspired by religious sentiment above all else.[182] The salutary effects of enthusiastic expression in religious poetry demonstrated, in turn, the dependence of devotion on passion as well as reason. Dennis's analysis was ultimately a plea for revealed religion, which could inspire by its resort to religious language. According to this account, Socrates' contempt for revelation gave rise to a damaging cleavage between sentiment and rationality.[183] Modern deism repeated the same separation of religion from the inspirational support of revelation.[184] It was on the basis of a commitment to the same idea that Burke had been keen to resuscitate the virtue of enthusiasm: "God has been pleased to give Mankind an Enthusiasm to supply the want of Reason."[185]

There is a difference, Burke suggested, "between a clear expression, and a strong expression."[186] Clarity of expression had been prized in modern philosophy since the advent of Cartesian "distinct" ideas. However, force of expression carried benefits of its own. These had been amply demonstrated by Robert Lowth in his Oxford lectures on the poetry of the Hebrews, which had been published in 1753. Here Lowth pointed to religious experience as constituting the origin of poetry. Both shared a will to express the more violent passions, which were conveyed by ardent and vehement forms of speech.[187] Such language worked by arousing sympathy in its auditors rather than by visual depiction. In this role, rhetorical speech was exceptionally winning: "We yield to sympathy, what we refuse to description."[188] This testified to the power of language to move the emotions by fellow-feeling. The sentiment of a writer or speaker, Smith observed in his *Lectures* on rhetoric, is successfully communicated "by *sympathy*."[189] The point had been made in the previous century in Bernard Lamy's *Rhetorique*: language was a means of effecting mutual "sympathie."[190] Lamy illustrated his argument by recourse to the *Ars poetica*. As noted earlier in this chapter, Horace observed in a famous passage how human beings are moved to smile by smiling faces just as they are grieved by others' weeping. Poetry achieved this outcome by mixing formal beauty with charm: "Non satis est pulchra esse poemata; dulcia sunto."[191] Burke cited this line in his *Reflections on the Revolution in France*,

[181] Ibid., p. 47.

[182] John Dennis, *The Grounds of Criticism in Poetry* (London: 1704), p. 81: "Longinus did not fully know that the sublime was derived from religion, though he instinctively knew it."

[183] Dennis, *Advancement and Reformation of Poetry*, pp. 100–102.

[184] Ibid., pp. 158–78.

[185] EB, "Religion of no Efficacy Considered as a State Engine" in *A Notebook of Edmund Burke*, ed. H.V.F. Somerset (Cambridge: Cambridge University Press, 1957), p. 68.

[186] EB, *Philosophical Enquiry*, p. 319.

[187] Robert Lowth, *De sacra poesi Hebraeorum* (Oxford: 1753), p. 16.

[188] EB, *Philosophical Enquiry*, p. 319.

[189] Adam Smith, *Lectures on Rhetoric and Belles Lettres* (Indianapolis, IN: Liberty Fund, 1985), p. 25. The lecture was delivered on 29 November 1762.

[190] Bernard Lamy, *La rhetorique ou l'art de parler* (Amsterdam: 4th ed., 1699), pp. 111–12.

[191] Horace, *Ars poetica*, line 99. Freely translating, this gives: "It is not enough for poetry to be beautiful; it must also inspire."

employing it to emphasise the fact that in order to inspire love an object must be experienced as "lovely."[192] In the *Philosophical Enquiry*, he tried to show how this sympathy was triggered by the rhetorical properties of language.

In the Introduction to his *Treatise Concerning the Principles of Human Knowledge*, Berkeley had contended that it was not solely the function of language to communicate ideas by means of words: "There are other ends, as the raising of some passion, the exciting to or deterring from an action, the putting the mind in some particular disposition."[193] This was not achieved, Berkeley went on to argue, by conjuring ideas in the mind: language did not represent in this way, as Burke later asserted.[194] It stirred the passions, as Berkeley put it, "without any ideas coming between."[195] Signs, as the character of Euphranor put it in *Alciphron*, can raise emotions, and thereby produce "dispositions or habits of mind."[196] Condillac later observed how this effect was originally achieved by gesture, modulation and intonation of the voice—by the language of "action."[197] He cited Warburton on the declamation of the prophets to show how communication originally required vivid denotation.[198] Emphatic signification, first achieved by gesture, was later achieved by figurative speech.[199] Burke adopted this perspective in the *Enquiry*: "Now, as there is a moving tone of voice, an impassioned countenance, an agitated gesture, which affect independently of the things about which they are exerted, so there are words, and certain dispositions of words, which being peculiarly devoted to passionate subjects . . . touch and move us more than those which far more clearly and distinctly express the subject matter."[200]

In absorbing the arguments of Condillac, Burke was also making use of Berkeley's criticisms of Locke. Locke had argued that words excite "*Ideas*" in the mind, yet for Berkeley a term might have a powerful effect without conjuring any idea in

[192] EB, *Reflections*, ed.. Clark, p. 241 [115–16]. For discussion, see Bourke, "Pity and Fear," pp. 152–55.

[193] George Berkeley, *A Treatise Concerning the Principles of Human Knowledge* (1710) in *Works*, I, p. 251.

[194] For the likely impact of Berkeley's theory on Burke, see Dixon Wecter, "Burke's Theory Concerning Words, Images, and Emotion," *Publication of the Modern Languages Association*, 55:1 (March 1940), pp. 167–81.

[195] Berkeley, *Treatise*, p. 252.

[196] Berkeley, *Alciphron*, p. 344. For comment, see David Berman, "Cognitive Theology and Emotive Mysteries in Berkeley's 'Alciphron'," *Proceedings of the Royal Irish Academy*, 18C (1981), pp. 219–29; Kenneth P. Winkler, "Berkeley and the Doctrine of Signs" in idem ed., *The Cambridge Companion to Berkeley* (Cambridge: Cambridge University Press, 2005).

[197] Etienne Bonnot de Condillac, *Essay on the Origin of Human Knowledge* (1746), ed. Hans Aarsleff (Cambridge: Cambridge University Press, 2001), pp. 115–18. For discussion, see Avi Lifschitz, *Language and Enlightenment: The Berlin Debates of the Eighteenth Century* (Oxford: Oxford University Press, 2012), pp. 27–28.

[198] William Warburton, *The Divine Legation of Moses Demonstrated* (London: 1737–38), 2 vols., II, p. 86.

[199] Condillac, *Origin of Human Knowledge*, pp. 183–84.

[200] EB, *Philosophical Enquiry*, p. 319.

particular.[201] The promise of a "good thing" is sure to thrill an auditor, and the threat of imminent "danger" to inspire fear, yet in each case nothing specific is conceived in the mind of the auditor. "Even proper names themselves," Berkeley concluded, "do not seem always spoken with a design to bring into our view the ideas."[202] In such cases, meaning was a function of association made durable by custom: thus, the name "Aristotle" could be used to impress an argument with authority irrespective of the content and relations of propositions. To those in the habit of crediting Aristotelian ideas, the customary associations of the proper name should inspire reverence and thereby illicit assent.[203] As with Berkeley, the final part of Burke's *Philosophical Enquiry* began with Locke. Most conspicuously, it reproduces a variant of Locke's division of language into words depicting "simple" ideas, "mixed modes" and "substances."[204] Burke renders these as "*simple abstract* words," like "red," "blue" or "square"; "*compounded abstract* words," like "virtue," "honour" or "magistrate"; and "*aggregate* words," like "man" and "horse."[205] Mixed modes—Burke's compound abstract words—pose peculiar problems for Locke. These generally refer to moral qualities or social practices and relations, like "*Honour, Faith, Grace, Religion, Church*," and their signification, Locke observes, is often doubtful.[206] Indeterminate signification results from the process of association, as a result of which the interpretation of values can become unhinged form their foundation in the laws of nature as prescribed by God.[207] Burke noted how Locke himself observed of mixed modes that children learn their names "before they have their *ideas*."[208] Yet while for Locke this highlighted the dangers of the moral confusion wrought by language, for Burke it showed the associative power of speech.

According to Burke, a word like "honour" receives its meaning by repeated use on appropriate occasions. Locke also saw that this is how a child learns to use moral vocabulary. Yet the associations of the word can readily become detached from the occasions in which it was originally used. As a result, Burke notes, "when words commonly sacred to great occasions are used, we are affected by them even without the occasions."[209] In the *Essay*, Locke focused on the diversity of moral behaviours potentially generated by this indeterminacy of meaning. By comparison, in the *Enquiry*, Burke concentrated his attention on the power of language that this

[201] John Locke, *Essay Concerning Human Understanding*, ed. Peter H. Nidditch (Oxford: Oxford University Press, 1975), III, ii, § 8.

[202] Berkeley, *Treatise*, p. 252.

[203] Ibid., pp. 252–53.

[204] Locke, *Essay*, III, iv–v.

[205] EB, *Philosophical Enquiry*, p. 309.

[206] Locke, *Essay*, III, ix, § 9. On this, see James Tully, *A Discourse on Property: John Locke and His Adversaries* (Cambridge: Cambridge University Press, 1980, 1982), p. 8; Hannah Dawson, *Locke, Language and Early-Modern Philosophy* (Cambridge: Cambridge University Press, 2007, 2011), pp. 222–29; Steven Forde, "Mixed Modes," *Review of Politics*, 73 (2011), pp. 581–608.

[207] EB, *Philosophical Enquiry*, pp. 310–11; Locke, *Essay*, III, ix, § 9.

[208] Ibid., III, v, § 14.

[209] EB, *Philosophical Enquiry*, p. 311.

highlighted. This does not imply that he did not appreciate Locke's worries: he knew that Locke's unease was a concern about morals at one remove. An associative creature whose moral ideas were driven by fashion might never conform their actions to properly ethical norms.[210] Burke shared this alarm but pointed to a method for overcoming the difficulty. Armed, as he thought, with a solution to scepticism about moral norms, he was happy to draw out the value of custom and association, as illustrated by his thoughts about the rhetorical uses of language. In surviving draft notes for the *Reflections on the Revolution in France*, he berated the reductiveness of rationalist theories of morals as exemplified by dominant strains of Revolutionary ideology: "It reduces," he wrote, "all our ideas to a few simple principles inadequate [to] the various relations of a complicated nature & therefore destroys the dignity [of human values]." However, in reality, he went on, all "our moral ideas are mixed modes."[211] They are fabricated in the midst of the contingencies of social life: "custom multiplies, refines & distinguishes them."[212] Yet beneath the operation of custom and the process of association there were standards of judgment to which contingent evaluations are obliged to submit.

Sympathetic critics of Locke's moral thought in the first half of the eighteenth century were similarly happy to adapt his theory of association to the demands of developing a robust ethical philosophy. John Gay's "Preliminary Dissertation" prefacing the third edition of Edmund Law's translation of William King's *Essay on the Origin of Evil* provides one influential example. Moral values, Gay observed, were commonly sustained in the form of "Habits" founded on "the *Association* of Ideas."[213] However, while it was true that this attachment to habitual norms based on the association of ideas enabled human beings to pursue virtue without reflection, the power of association also had its dangers: it might prompt us to transfer our partiality to virtue to "improper Objects, and such as are of a quite different Nature from those to which our Reason had at first directed them."[214] It was therefore necessary to resort to criteria by which habits might be judged. A "moral sense" of the kind that had been advocated by Shaftesbury and Hutcheson could not perform this task in Gay's opinion. Such a sense could be nothing other than "innate" ideas of moral behaviour. Since "occult" ideas of the kind were nowhere to be observed, our moral sensibility in being expressed as an automatic reflex could be ascribed to nothing more solid than habits or instincts. However, acting on habit supplied no means of

[210] This problem in Locke was commonly identified as his actual conclusion. On this, see Daniel Carey, *Locke, Shaftesbury and Hutcheson: Contesting Diversity in the Enlightenment and Beyond* (Cambridge: Cambridge University Press, 2006); for an analysis of the problem, see Dawson, *Locke*, ch. 9.

[211] Northamptonshire MS. A. XXVII.75.

[212] Ibid.

[213] John Gay, "Preliminary Dissertation Concerning the Fundamental Principles of Virtue or Morality" in William King, *An Essay on the Origin of Evil*, trans. Edmund Law (Cambridge: 3rd ed., 1739), p. xxxi.

[214] Ibid., p. liii.

adjudicating between rival impulses.[215] There was no such thing, in other words, as a true moral sensibility or ethical "taste." The pursuit of virtue required standards by which behaviour could be judged. The character of Euphranor in Berkeley's *Alciphron* similarly exposed the doctrine of moral taste as espoused by Shaftesbury: "Should it not therefore seem a very uncertain guide in morals, for a man to follow his passion or inward feeling; and would not this rule infallibly lead different men different ways, according to the prevalency of this or that appetite or passion?"[216]

A fundamental objective of Burke in the *Philosophical Enquiry* was similarly to challenge the idea that discrimination simply varied as "this or that appetite" happened to predominate.[217] Human beings were not reducible to pleasure seeking animals whose values were formed and reformed by processes of association.[218] While association was a powerful mental aptitude, "it would be absurd . . . to say that all things affect us by association only."[219] Burke accepted with Locke that "when we go one step beyond the immediate sensible qualities of things, we go out of our depth."[220] The final causes of things were inaccessible to the human mind.[221] Nonetheless, the efficient causes of human passions could be systematically accounted for, establishing uniformity in human responses to stimuli. This was an encouraging result for Burke, since it pointed to a common sensibility in the species. If this did not exist, he solemnly noted, the "ordinary correspondence of life" could not be maintained.[222] But there was more to human sensibility than automatic reactions. Taste was not reducible to a "species of instinct" which, as Hutcheson taught, responded to moral worth in the same way that it approved of beauty.[223] In a substantial introductory essay that Burke added in 1759 to the second edition of the *Philosophical Enquiry*, he set about showing how aesthetic judgment involved evaluating the data of experience rather than merely amounting to an instinctive sensory response.

There was a resurgence of interest in the question of taste from the middle of the 1750s in Europe. In 1752, in the second volume of the *Encyclopédie*, Diderot had contributed an article on the "Beautiful," which included an extensive account of

[215] Ibid., pp. xxx–xxxi.

[216] Berkeley, *Alciphron*, p. 129.

[217] Paddy Bullard, *Edmund Burke and the Art of Rhetoric* (Cambridge: Cambridge University Press, 2011), p. 91.

[218] On this, see French Laurence, "Political Life of Edmund Burke: Annotated Proofs of a Contribution to the *Annual Register*" (c. 1794), OSB MS. File 8753: "the principles of [Burke's] treatise [on the sublime and beautiful] are in direct opposition to those of lord Bolingbroke and the new . . . schools of France. . . . For while they derive all the duties of man to his kind from the single motive of self-interest, he considered sympathy as a primary passion, and the principal link in the great chain of society."

[219] EB, *Philosophical Enquiry*, p. 284. Cf. EB, *Letter to a Noble Lord* (1796), *W & S*, IX, p. 171: "under the direction of reason, instinct is always in the right."

[220] EB, *Philosophical Enquiry*, p. 283.

[221] On this, see Steffen Ducheyne, "'Communicating a Sort of Philosophical Solidity to Taste': Newtonian Elements in Burke's Methodology in the *Philosophical Enquiry*" in Vermier and Deckard eds., *Science of Sensibility*, pp. 62–64.

[222] EB, *Philosophical Enquiry*, p. 196.

[223] Ibid., p. 208.

Hutcheson and his disciples.[224] Four years later, in the fifth volume, Montesquieu's posthumous essay on "Gout" appeared, together with contributions by Voltaire and D'Alembert.[225] A translation of excerpts from Montesquieu's essay was published in *The Annual Register* three years later.[226] In 1757, Hume included an essay on "The Standard of Taste" as the final element in his *Four Dissertations*.[227] Hume's essay in particular was a *tour de force*. It set about showing how the sceptical doctrine of the relativity of taste could be challenged by analysing the common-sense assumption that aesthetic preferences could be discriminated by a "true" standard of taste. A standard of taste was "a rule, by which the various sentiments of men may be reconciled."[228] Hume was clear that this could not be based on any objectively available criteria. Nonetheless, this did not render taste a function of the idiosyncratic preferences of individuals. It was a common assumption of social life that these preferences could be rated. Moreover, Hume believed that he could show that the idea of adjudicating between the range of tastes could in fact be justified. He built his case on what he took to be two facts. First, notwithstanding the apparent diversity of taste, it was observable that there was considerable uniformity in the aesthetic perceptions of mankind. Just as with secondary qualities there are shared perceptions of colour without the objective existence of attributes like "blue" and "green," so there is a common response to beauty even though this is based on nothing more robust than subjective sentiment. "Some particular forms or qualities," Hume concluded, "from the original structure of the internal fabric, are calculated to please."[229] However, this did not reduce the standard of beauty to habitual reactions to objects of mental pleasure. This brought Hume to his second point. Aesthetic excellence was not determined by the average response. Instead, preferences could be discriminated in terms of better and worse, pointing to a standard that could decide between alternatives. This process of discrimination depended on expert critics in a position to establish norms of beauty.[230]

[224] Despite this, Diderot's relationship to Burke is usually viewed exclusively in terms of the former's debt to the latter: see Gita May, "Diderot and Burke: A Study in Aesthetic Affinity," *Publications of the Modern Language Association*, 75:5 (December 1960), pp. 527–39.

[225] For the circumstances surrounding Montesquieu's contribution, see Downing A. Thomas, "Negotiating Taste in Montesquieu," *Eighteenth-Century Studies*, 39:1 (Autumn 2005), pp. 71–90. For the contributions by Voltaire and D'Alembert, see idem, "Taste, Commonality and Musical Imagination in the Encyclopédie" in Daniel Brewer and Julie Chandler Hayes eds., *Using the Encyclopédie: Ways of Knowing, Ways of Reading* (Oxford: Voltaire Foundation, 2002).

[226] *The Annual Register for the Year 1758* (London: 1759), pp. 311–19.

[227] For a comparison between Burke's argument and Hume's, see Dario Perinetti, "Between Knowledge and Sentiment: Burke and Hume on Taste" in Vermier and Deckard eds., *Science of Sensibility*.

[228] David Hume, "Of the Standard of Taste" (1757) in idem, *Essays Moral, Political, and Literary*, ed. Eugene F. Miller (Indianapolis, IN: Liberty Fund, 1985, 1987), p. 229.

[229] Ibid., p. 233. Cf. David Hume, "The Sceptic" (1742) in idem, *Essays*, pp. 163–64.

[230] Peter Kivy, "Hume's Standard: Breaking the Circle," *British Journal of Aesthetics*, 7:1 (1967), pp. 57–66; Korsmeyer, "Hume and the Foundations of Taste"; Noël Carroll, "Hume's Standard of Taste," *Journal of Aesthetics and Art Criticism*, 43:2 (Winter 1984), pp. 181–94; Roger A. Shiner, "Hume and the Causal Theory of Taste," *Journal of Aesthetics and Art Criticism*, 54:3 (Summer 1996), pp. 237–49.

Much of Hume's essay was given over to analysing the characteristics that made an expert critic. These were essentially five in number.[231] They comprised a keen sensibility, or "delicacy" of taste; good sense in appreciating the relations between parts of a work; freedom from prejudice, involving openness to the intentions of the work without the intrusion of personal interest; a degree of practice in employing the discriminating faculties; and accumulated exposure to the activity of comparison. These attributes of the fine critic could be compressed into two characteristics: the possession of a fine sensibility, and an aptitude for judgment.[232] Burke invokes these same criteria in his "Introduction on Taste." The imagination, Burke believed, is uniformly affected by invariable laws, giving rise to definite "principles of Taste."[233] These principles enabled the critic to circumvent the sceptical notion that the diversity of aesthetic responses rendered the judgment of taste "vain" and "frivolous."[234] While Burke's argument concurred with the Humean assumption that there was conformity among ideas of beauty, it also agreed that it was possible to evaluate these ideas. The sentiment of approbation in the judgment of taste was based on two capacities: sensibility on the one hand, and judgment on the other. Both of these were susceptible to degrees of discrimination. Sensibility might be delicate, and judgment cultivated. The pleasures of the imagination were largely based on the faculty of "wit."[235] Burke takes his conception of this mental power from Locke. While the analytical faculties separated and distinguished, wit—or "fancy"—establishes comparisons. The mind was pleased by resemblances, exemplified by metaphors and allusions, giving rise to instantaneous exhilaration.[236] The question for Burke's "Introduction" was how these resemblances could be adjudicated—how the pleasures of wit could be rated by an agreed standard.

Burke's answer lay in the degree to which taste could be refined. Human beings relished the same mental pleasures, but they did not always do so with the same facility: there were differences in sensitivity and differences in mental effort.[237] These differences could be ranked so as to provide for degrees of elegance, yielding a standard for discrimination.[238] At the same time, the ability to arrive at this standard could be progressively improved with practice by repeated exposure to comparative

[231] The fullest account is in Peter Jones, *Hume's Sentiments: Their Ciceronian and French Contexts* (Edinburgh: Edinburgh University Press, 1982), pp. 93–106.

[232] These traits were later singled out for attention in Blair, *Lectures on Rhetoric*, I, p. 23. See also Henry Home, Lord Kames, *Elements of Criticism* (1762), ed. Peter Jones (Indianapolis, IN: Liberty Fund, 2005), 2 vols., II, p. 727.

[233] EB, *Philosophical Enquiry*, pp. 197–98.

[234] Ibid., p. 198.

[235] For wit and imagination in literary history, see M. H. Abrams, *The Mirror and the Lamp: Romantic Theory and the Critical Tradition* (Oxford: Oxford University Press, 1953, 1971); James Engell, *The Creative Imagination: Enlightenment to Romanticism* (Cambridge, MA: Harvard University Press, 1981).

[236] Locke, *Essay*, II, xi, § 2.

[237] EB, *Philosophical Enquiry*, p. 206: "the degree in which these principles prevail in the several individuals of mankind, is altogether as different as the principles themselves are similar."

[238] Ibid., p. 205.

exercises. By this process, different qualities, forms and manners were juxtaposed and evaluated. Over time, if circumstances permitted, aesthetic judgment could become steadily more discriminating. The human sense of decorum was therefore capable of improvement. As a consequence, the assessment of beauty as well as the judgment of morals could in principle be educated. "Indeed," Burke claimed, "it is for the most part in our skill in manners, and in the observances of time and place, and of decency in general . . . that what is called Taste . . . consists; and which is in reality no other than a more refined judgement."[239] For Hume, the process of refinement had served to distinguish ancient and modern morals, with modern "decency" and "humanity" challenging the preference.[240] Similarly on Burke's account, systems of morals, like the science of criticism, might in principle be gradually perfected.[241] Yet while the improvement of manners was forwarded by refinements in humanity, the evaluation of behaviour had to extend beyond the moral imagination to encompass the realm of our duties.[242] Providence placed human beings in a position to perform their obligations by providing them with an aptitude for sympathy and taste. Yet, in the end, a benevolent disposition of mind was a duty to God.[243] The *Philosophical Enquiry* sought to illustrate the wisdom of providence in providing for dependable means of discrimination. Nonetheless, it was not the intention of the work to resolve our duties into the empire of taste. As Shaftesbury had shown, the philosophy of beauty might be co-opted into the armoury of deism, yet for Burke the sense of decorum was merely a branch of the science of duty. Manners assisted morals, but they did not determine their content.

[239] Ibid., p. 206.

[240] Hume, "Standard of Taste," p. 246.

[241] EB, *Philosophical Enquiry*, p. 208.

[242] For the phrase "moral imagination," see EB, *Reflections*, ed. Clark, p. 239 [114]. For a discussion of the phrase in Burke, see Russell Kirk, "The Moral Imagination," *Literature and Belief*, 1 (1981), pp. 37–49; David Bromwich, "Moral Imagination," *Raritan*, 27:4 (Spring 2008), pp. 4–33.

[243] EB, "Religion" in *Notebook*, p. 70.

IV

CONQUEST AND ASSIMILATION, 1757–1765

4.1 Introduction

Between 1757 and 1765 Burke shifted his attention from literary pursuits to the demands of public business. In 1759, he accepted the patronage of William Gerard Hamilton and soon found his energies swamped by the demands of his employer. His aim had been to cultivate his reputation in the republic of letters while simultaneously deepening his investment in politics. Initially Burke's prospects of achieving this aim looked promising: he collaborated on *An Account of the European Settlements in America* while writing essays on the state of current affairs. He also undertook to write an *Abridgement of English History*. By the time that the work was due, he had also agreed to edit and compile *The Annual Register*. However, before long, Hamilton's claims on his time began to crowd out research and writing. He visited Ireland on official business in the early 1760s, and it was in this period that he began to compose his work on the Irish popery laws. But his ambitions as an author continued to be frustrated, and by 1765 he had abandoned the manuscript in draft. From that date onwards, Burke's writings were connected exclusively to parliamentary or party business. His great polemical works, which appeared later in his career, were all constructed as responses to immediate events. Consequently, they were not directly products of study and meditation. Nonetheless, his deepest concerns were related to the intellectual projects that he nurtured in the 1750s. These projects included his early historical writing.

Burke's early histories seem a world away from the metaphysical concerns exhibited in the *Vindication* and the *Philosophical Enquiry*. The limits of natural reason and the science of the passions were hardly the most appropriate subjects for historical narrative. Nonetheless, themes that were central to Burke's philosophical writings reemerge in both the *Account* and the *Abridgement*, not least his persistent fascination with the spiritual habits of mankind. The role of religion in general, and of Christianity in particular, surfaces in Burke's history of England and his account of the new world. The chastening effect of the idea of an afterlife on human morals is noted in connection with both the Britons and the American savages. The ethical psychology presented in the *Philosophical Enquiry* similarly reappears in the analysis of consent that underpins Burke's treatment of the Saxon system of government as well as the subjection of the Incas to the Spanish. This particular topic proved to be pivotal to the major preoccupation that dominates Burke's historical works around 1757: namely, the theme of conquest along with the prospects of assimilation and pacification.

It is fair to assume that Burke's interest in both the justification of conquest and the practicalities of achieving civil peace was rooted in his awareness of his family's misfortune arising out of the Cromwellian conquest of Ireland. The land seizures after 1649, together with the subsequent expropriation that accompanied the Glorious Revolution, was by any reckoning a major event in British and Irish history. In any case, Burke's consciousness of these episodes never moved him to vengeance. He believed that conquest was an act of war that was best followed by assimilation: insurgency against settlers, which would entail counterconfiscation, seemed abhorrent and counterproductive at the same time. It was in this context that Burke first developed his ideas about subordination and consent. Modern ideology tends to view these states as antithetical bases for subjection, yet for Burke they blended into one another along a graduated spectrum. Nonetheless, he was sure that only consent could offer a legitimate basis for government. The *Account*'s depiction of what was in effect the mockery of acquiescence that obtained under the Spanish Empire in America was intended as an endorsement of forms of subjection based on compliance. Compliance, however, was seen by Burke as an intricately contextual value: the conformity of soldiers under their commanders, for example, was distinct from civil acquiescence. Burke's history of England rejected the prevalent idea that the value of consent celebrated in eighteenth-century Britain was part of a lineage extending into the Saxon past. In reality, British history had been a process of contingent improvement, not a teleological progression. In Ireland the contingencies were differently arranged, and improvement was consequently curtailed: under the penal statutes imposed on the Roman Catholic population, the spirit of conquest prevailed over toleration and consent.

Burke's transition from history and philosophy to politics was neither immediate nor categorical. As he was working on his histories of England and America he also undertook his earliest forays into political essay writing. His activities in the early to mid 1750s are difficult to reconstruct: his correspondence is incredibly sparse, and further evidence is hard to collect. Nonetheless, the survival of a series of manuscript essays on matters of current political concern—on political parties, on shorter parliaments, on the militia, and on the dependency of Ireland—open a window onto one aspect of Burke's early development. Already, it seems, he had a deep concern with the constitutional organisation of the British polity. Along with his narrative histories, these writings show him to be immersed in the works of Hume and Montesquieu. In some sense Burke was their student, though certainly not their disciple. Along with both these precursor philosophical historians, Burke was enamoured of the spirit of modern liberty as exemplified by the British constitution. He was also preoccupied with the forces that might unsettle its balance and thereby tip the system into anarchy or conquest. Burke's analysis proved to be different from the claims of his predecessors. Indeed, his positions largely demonstrate an attitude of independence that was to survive into his period as a Rockingham MP.

4.2 The Spirit of Conquest: *An Account of the European Settlements in America*

On 5 January 1757, Burke acknowledged receipt of fifty guineas from his publisher in payment for the copyright for *An Account of the European Settlements in America.*[1] The work was then published in London in two volumes at the start of April, three weeks before the *Philosophical Enquiry* appeared.[2] Burke never fully admitted authorship of the work. Reading the book in November 1789, James Boswell claimed that it was "everywhere obvious" that Burke had contributed a great deal to its composition.[3] Yet apparently Burke insisted that he "did not write it; I do not deny that a friend did, and I revised it."[4] That friend was William Burke, who seems to have been working on the text in the summer of 1756 when both he and Burke spent some months in the town of Monmouth near the Welsh border. In discussing Burke's early writings in a sketch of the statesman's life that was to appear in *The Annual Register* in 1794, French Laurence, although a very close collaborator at the time, did not mention the work alongside the *Vindication* and the *Enquiry.*[5] In a draft for what was intended as an authoritative biography of Burke, William Monck Mason, on the other hand, did: "[Richard] Shackleton always said it was solely [Burke's]."[6] Such a definitive verdict seems unlikely. The *Account* went through multiple editions in the eighteenth and nineteenth centuries, the last in Burke's lifetime appearing in 1777, yet he never so much as alluded to the work. This, perhaps, is unsurprising since much of it is derived from the travel literature of the period. More telling is the fact that philosophical reflection on the variable state of human manners recurs throughout the *Account*, strongly indicative of the hand of Burke, and scarcely char-

[1] Add. MS. 20723, fol. 35.

[2] William B. Todd, *A Bibliography of Edmund Burke* (Godalming: St. Paul's Bibliographies, 1982), p. 29.

[3] James Boswell to William Johnson Temple, 28 November 1789, *Letters of James Boswell Addressed to the Rev. W. J. Temple* (London: 1857), p. 318.

[4] Ibid.

[5] French Laurence, "Political Life of Edmund Burke: Annotated Proofs of a Contribution to the *Annual Register*" (c. 1794), OSB MS. File 8753.

[6] William Monck Mason (1775–1859), "Manuscript Notes and Printed Excerpts Concerning the Lives and Works of Eminent Irish Men and Women," TCD MSS. 10531–2, fol. 35. Mason also reports that Lord Macartney ascribed it to Richard Burke Sr. and William Burke.

acteristic of anything we know that William wrote.[7] The *Account* is very much a compilation, interspersed with analysis and reflection. It seems probable that Burke's avowed "revision" of the work took the form of supplementary passages of philosophical history added to the main body of narrative.

When Charles O'Hara wrote to Burke in 1762 about the inhabitants of the island of Inishmurray off the coast of Sligo, he knew that he would be charmed by the chaste simplicity of their existence.[8] He recognised Burke's fascination with the range of human customs, as would become evident in his writings through the rest of his career. More immediately, the diversity of national manners was a prominent theme in *The Annual Register*. Under Burke's editorship, it featured Antoine-Yves Goguet on the Spartans, Pierre de Charlevoix on the Native Americans, Anquetil-Duperron on Zoroastrianism, and the Abbé de Saint-Pierre on the varieties of culture.[9] Burke would later put Charlevoix's *Histoire et description de la Nouvelle France* to use in his speeches on the American war.[10] The work of Cadwallader Colden and Joseph-François Lafitau would feature in the same context.[11] By the middle of the 1750s, Burke was enthralled by the writings of philosophical historians.[12] It was then that he first read the histories of Voltaire and Hume.[13] He would later pay fulsome tribute to the writings of William Robertson.[14] Reading Robertson's multi-volume

[7] F. P. Lock, *Edmund Burke: 1730–1797* (Oxford: Clarendon Press, 1998–2006), 2 vols., I, pp. 125–27. For a characteristic production of William Burke, see his *Remarks on Letter Address'd to Two Great Men* (London: 1760).

[8] Charles O'Hara to EB, 10 August 1762, *Corr.*, I, p. 146. Burke hoped that O'Hara would manage to secure the island for himself. See EB to Charles O'Hara, ante 23 August 1762, ibid., p. 147: "I wish you may get it with all my heart: for I know that you will be no Cortez, Pizarro, Cromwell or Boyle."

[9] See, respectively, "Characters" in *The Annual Register for the Year 1760* (London: 1761), pp. 1–9; "Characters" in *The Annual Register for the Year 1761* (London: 1762), pp. 10–12; "Antiquities" in *The Annual Register for the Year 1762* (London: 1763), pp. 103–12; "Literary and Miscellaneous Articles" in ibid., pp. 153–60. See also an account of the Jesuits in Paraguay in "Literary and Miscellaneous Essays" in *The Annual Register for the Year 1758* (London: 1759), pp. 362–67; "Account of the Laplanders" by M. de Juterbog from the *Journal oeconomique* in "Characters" in *The Annual Register for the Year 1759* (London: 1760), pp. 328–41; an "Account of the Origin of Chivalry" by Voltaire in "Antiquities" in *The Annual Register for the Year 1760*, pp. 176–78; Swift on Manners in "Literary and Miscellaneous Articles" in *The Annual Register for the Year 1762*, pp. 166–69; and the "Rise of Chivalry" extracted from Richard Hurd's *Letters on Chivalry and Romance* in "Antiquities" in ibid., pp. 134–38.

[10] WWM BkP 27:244, reproduced in *W & S*, III, p. 366, referring to Pierre François Xavier de Charlevoix, *Histoire et description de la Nouvelle France* (Paris: 1744), 3 vols.

[11] Cadwallader Colden, *History of the Five Indian Nations of Canada* (New York: 1727); Joseph-François Lafitau, *Mœurs des sauvages américains, comparées aux mœurs des premiers temps* (Paris: 1724).

[12] For an account of the European genre, see Karen O'Brien, *Narratives of Enlightenment: Cosmopolitan History from Voltaire to Gibbon* (Cambridge: Cambridge University Press, 1997, 2005).

[13] His response to both was sceptical. For Hume, see below, section 3 in this chapter. For Voltaire, see EB, "Voltaire" in *A Notebook of Edmund Burke, ed.* H.V.F. Somerset (Cambridge: Cambridge University Press, 1957).

[14] Burke's tribute came in 1777. In the meantime, William Robertson, *History of Scotland during the Reigns of Queen Mary and of King James VI* (London: 1759) was reviewed in *The Annual Register for the Year 1759*, pp. 489–94; and William Robertson, *History of the Reign of the Emperor Charles V* (London: 1769) was reviewed in *The Annual Register for the Year 1769* (London: 1770), pp. 254–72.

History of America in 1777, he claimed that he derived the greatest pleasure from "the discussion on the Manners and character of the Inhabitants of that new World."[15] Historical study, in examining human nature in all its aspects, contributed to the elimination of aggravating prejudice. This was a peculiar achievement of eighteenth-century letters since, unlike the historical insights of all other periods, the present age was in a position to inspect every stage of human development: "there is no state or Gradation of barbarism, and no mode of refinement which we have not at the same instant under our View."[16] The impartial reconstruction of the customs of Europe and China, of Persia and Abyssinia, and of North America and New Zealand, had all been profitably undertaken. Burke was clearly captivated by the results. It seems highly likely that this preoccupation with human nature under varying conditions explains his willingness to contribute to the *Account*.

By the time that the *Account* appeared in print, Britain had been at war with France for almost a year. On 28 June 1756, the island of Minorca had been captured by the French in the opening naval contest of the Seven Years' War. Two years earlier, disagreements over control of the confluence of the forks of the Ohio brought French settlers in New France into conflict with British colonists on the eastern seaboard of North America, erupting into violence in May 1754.[17] Months later, the British government under Newcastle sent General Braddock to lead an expedition to bolster the position of the colonists. A struggle between the European powers thus began across the Atlantic, spearheaded by provincial militants with the backing of metropolitan governments. War was officially declared in Europe on 18 May 1756. Maritime strength, terrestrial security and financial stability were now being staked in a major competition among the dominant powers of Europe.[18] The diplomatic revolution in the wake of the War of the Austrian Succession meant that Britain was allied to Prussia against France, Austria and Russia.[19] By the spring of 1757, when the Burkes' *Account* appeared, Britain had been struggling to get the better of the French: defeats at Oswego and Fort William Henry added to the embarrassment of Minorca.[20] As a result, as the Preface to the first edition of the *Account* pointed out, the affairs of America were suddenly of major interest to the public.[21]

[15] EB to Dr. William Robertson, 9 June 1777, *Corr.*, III, p. 350.

[16] Ibid., p. 351.

[17] For these events, see Marc Egnal, *A Mighty Empire: The Origins of the American Revolution* (Ithaca, NY: Cornell University Press, 1988), chs. 2–6.

[18] Daniel A. Baugh, "Great Britain's 'Blue-Water' Policy, 1789–1815," *International History Review*, 10 (1988), pp. 35–58. For the domestic financial infrastructure, see John Brewer, *The Sinews of Power: War Money and the English State, 1688–1783* (New York: Alfred A. Knopf, 1989).

[19] Brendan Simms, *Three Victories and a Defeat: The Rise and Fall of the First British Empire* (London: Allen Lane, 2007), pp. 408–11.

[20] Fred Anderson, *Crucible of War: The Seven Years' War and the Fate of Empire in British North America, 1754–1766* (New York: Vintage, 2000), pts. II and III.

[21] [Edmund and William Burke], *An Account of the European Settlements in America. In Six Parts.* (1757) (London: 6th ed., 1777), 2 vols., I, Preface, n.p. The Preface remained unchanged from the first edition.

After setbacks in America, combined with the loss of Minorca, the patriot opposition in parliament was roused to consternation. An invasion scare in the summer of 1756 added to the pressure on the Newcastle administration. The Dutch, now required for assistance, promptly declared their neutrality. Hessian and Hanoverian troops were deployed for national defence in preference to widespread calls for the embodiment of a militia. On top of the spate of American and domestic crises, the situation on the continent began to look grim. Britain's ally, Frederick the Great, originally engaged for the defence of Hanover, launched an attack on Saxony in August 1756 in anticipation of an Austrian campaign for the recovery of Silesia. Britain, bound in league with her, would be drawn into the affairs of Europe.[22] William Pitt was swept into office as Secretary of State for the Southern Department, promising to save the honour of the nation.[23] The Great Commoner now lent his support to a policy of continental warfare as a means of guaranteeing the security of the colonies.[24] It was reckoned that the plight of Europe would determine the fate of the settlements in the new world. The "balance of continents" was now an issue for domestic reason of state.[25] One speaker in the House of Commons declared that "we have our eye upon America, when we fix it upon any spot of the globe, where the power of France is to be curbed or her injustice chastised."[26] The French would therefore have to be challenged on the European mainland. And yet it was clear that their objective was to expand across the Atlantic, and so the aim of the British had to be to inhibit their attempts at colonial aggrandisement. "The French, Sir, consider power as their ultimatum," the speaker continued. Yet they knew that the source of power lay in national wealth, and that the source of "English riches" lay in its commerce with the new world.[27] The war in Europe would be fought over the political economy of empire.

The *Account* aimed to add to the knowledge that was required for judging the condition of trade and politics in America. "The war we now carry on principally regards our colonies," it was asserted. This proved at least that the British had "come at last to know their value."[28] However, it seemed to the authors of the *Account* that grasping their true significance was no mean feat since until now reports of the new world had been drafted "to gratify the low prejudices of parties."[29] There were two

[22] Franz A. J. Szabo, *The Seven Years' War in Europe, 1756–1763* (Edinburgh: Longman, 2008), ch. 1.

[23] Horace Walpole, *Memoirs of the Reign of King George II*, ed. John Brooke (New Haven, CT: Yale University Press, 1985), 3 vols., III, p. 1.

[24] Brendan Simms, "Pitt and Hanover" in Brendan Simms and Torsten Riotte eds., *The Hanoverian Dimension in British History, 1714–1837* (Cambridge: Cambridge University Press, 2007). For the wider context, see Daniel A. Baugh, "Withdrawing from Europe: Anglo-French Maritime Geopolitics, 1750–1800," *International History Review*, 20 (1998), pp. 1–32.

[25] The phrase occurs as a chapter heading in Walter L. Dorn, *Competition for Empire, 1740–1763* (New York: Harper and Brothers, 1940).

[26] *Parliamentary History*, XV, col. 788.

[27] Ibid., col. 787.

[28] [Burkes], *Account*, II, p. 48.

[29] Ibid., I, Preface, n.p.

reasons for this. First, given the state of disunity among British settlements, rival colonies promoted antithetical views. However, second, the politics of the new world stirred the interests of contending empires, each with distinct investments in the representation of their provinces. Therefore, a philosophical history of Europe's settlements in America would strive to rise above conflicting provincial and imperial passions. Politics would be viewed from a cosmopolitan perspective, and with that detachment would come a wider field of inquiry. The narrative of events would be supplemented with philosophical speculation, and human nature would be explored in the context of shifts in society and government.

The historical part of the *Account* was intended to frame the analysis of commerce. The principal events examined included the discovery of America and the conquest of the Mexican and Peruvian civilisations that thrived in the midst of a savage continent. In addition, the manners of the Native Americans would form a key part of the inquiry, and the politics and habits of the British colonists would be studied. When and where each plantation was established would be recounted. However, the ultimate goal was clear: "My principal objective, in treating of the settlements, was, to draw every thing towards their trade, which is the point that concerns us most materially."[30] At the end of his career, looking back on his years of application before entering parliament, Burke referred to his early immersion in political economy. This was before the subject engrossed "the thoughts of speculative men in other parts of Europe."[31] The *Account*, after all, predated Quesnay's *Tableau économique*.[32] Burke was familiar with the *Journal oeconomique* by the end of the 1750s.[33] As he noted in his *Letter to a Noble Lord* in 1796, systematic investigation of trade began in England in the seventeenth century, yet it was still in its infancy in the middle of the 1750s.[34] Josiah Tucker's first pamphlet on commerce appeared in 1749; Hume's essays on trade and money appeared in 1752.[35] The *Account* was building on aspects of the earliest literature on political economy, focusing on the traffic of six European empires.[36] The Burkes analysed the history of each of these settlements in turn: the Spanish, the Portuguese, the French, the Dutch, the Danish and, finally, the British.

[30] Ibid. For discussion of the work from this perspective, see Richard Whatmore, "Burke on Political Economy" in David Dwan and Christopher J. Insole *eds., The Cambridge Companion to Edmund Burke* (Cambridge: Cambridge University Press, 2012).

[31] EB, *Letter to a Noble Lord* (1796), *W & S*, IX, p. 159.

[32] François Quesnay, *Tableau économique* (Paris: 1758).

[33] *The Annual Register* began including excerpts from the journal in 1759.

[34] EB, *Letter to a Noble Lord* (1796), *W & S*, IX, pp. 159–60.

[35] Josiah Tucker, *A Brief Essay on the Advantages and Disadvantages, which Respectively Attend France and Great Britain* (London: 1749); David Hume, *Political Discourses* (Edinburgh: 1752).

[36] For the earlier literature, see Istvan Hont, "Free Trade and the Economic Limits to National Politics: Neo-Machiavellian Political Economy Reconsidered" in idem, *Jealousy of Trade: International Competition and the Nation-State in Historical Perspective* (Cambridge, MA: Harvard University Press, 2005); David Armitage, *The Ideological Origins of the British Empire* (Cambridge: Cambridge University Press, 2000), ch. 6.

The *Account* is neatly divided into six parts. The first two are concerned with the conquest of the new world and the customs of the Native Americans respectively, and the final four with the various settlements of the European powers. The conquest itself is introduced by an overview of Europe, which forms the background to the eruption of the old world into the new. This is structured in terms of a vision of the progress of Protestant enlightenment: between the fifteenth and early seventeenth centuries, the monarchies of Europe were politically consolidated; gunpowder was discovered and movable type invented; ancient learning was revived, and the Reformation initiated. Literature began to soften manners, and states began to perfect the art of policy. Politeness and the sense of honour entered the culture of courts. Barbarism was steadily consigned to the past. Scholastic philosophy was superseded by rigorous enquiry, and empirical study reached beyond the purely "sensible horizon." The system of the heavens was plotted for the first time.[37] In the context of these general improvements in society, knowledge and politics, Columbus emerged as an enterprising Genoese projector bent upon discovering a western passage to the East Indies.[38] Having combatted the prejudices of his opponents, determined to "enlighten ignorance" and vanquish "obstinate incredulity," he set sail with the support of Ferdinand and Isabella of Spain on 3 August 1492.[39] Thirty-three days later, he landed with his crew on the Bahamas—"and here it was, that the two worlds, if I may use the expression, were first introduced to one another."[40] The event would transform the fortunes of both regions of the globe.

In the Preface to the *Account*, the Burkes underlined their debt to "the judicious collection called Harris's Voyages."[41] This referred to James Harris's *Navigantium atque Iterantium*, a two-volume collection of voyages actually compiled by John Campbell.[42] In his Dedication to the work, Campbell indicated his purpose to be that of "setting the History and Advantages of Commerce in a true Light."[43] His aim was to argue that commerce was the principal source of national wealth since it operated as a stimulus to industry.[44] In offering a route to plenty, it was also a means of securing power: "The Power attained either by Policy, or Arms, is but of short

[37] [Burkes], *Account*, I, pp. 3–5. For the history of variants on this "enlightened narrative" in Europe, see J.G.A. Pocock, *Barbarism and Religion II: Narratives of Civil Government* (Cambridge: Cambridge University Press, 1999). Relatedly, see also J.G.A. Pocock, *Barbarism and Religion IV: Barbarians, Savages and Empires* (Cambridge: Cambridge University Press, 2005).

[38] The main accounts on which eighteenth-century chroniclers of the journeys of Columbus drew included those of Antonio de Herrera y Tordesillas and Peter Martyr. For versions of the story closer in time to the *Account*, many of whose details overlap with those of the Burkes, see [Anon.], *The History of the Voyages of Christopher Columbus, in order to Discover America and the West-Indies* (London: 1747).

[39] [Burkes], *Account*, I, pp. 8–9.

[40] Ibid., p. 10.

[41] Ibid., Preface, n.p.

[42] Lock, *Burke*, I, p. 128.

[43] [John Campbell], *Navigantium atque Iterantium; Or, a Compleat Collection of Voyages and Travels* (London: 1744–48), 2 vols., I, Dedication, n.p.

[44] Ibid.

continuance, in comparison of what is acquired by Trade."[45] However, large commercial enterprise involved copious hazards and only remote benefits. As the Burkes noted, the conquest of the new world was incentivised by more immediate gain: "A remote prospect of commerce and the improvement of manufactures, by extending colonies, would never have answered the purpose."[46] What animated adventurers was the "insatiable thirst for gold."[47] The same point was later reiterated in Adam Smith's *Wealth of Nations*: the enterprises of Europeans following on from Columbus were motivated by the search for precious metals. "It was the sacred thirst for gold," Smith recapitulated, "that carried Oieda, Nicuessa, and Vasco Nugnes de Balboa, to the isthmus of Darien, that carried Cortez to Mexico, and Almagro and Pizzarro to Chilli and Peru."[48] The unintended benefit of the colonial system was an important observation in the *Account*: "Even amongst ourselves, the most trading and reasoning people in Europe, right notions in these matters began late . . . Our colonies were settled without any view of those great advantages which we draw from them."[49]

The slow development of the science of political economy proved fortuitous. During the renaissance, the "speculative knowledge of trade" was in a rudimentary condition.[50] The avid pursuit of baubles drove the ambition of states and explorers. More realistic designs would have moderated policy, leading to the gradual development of trans-Atlantic commerce. A more languid process would most likely have resulted in a more equal contest between conquerors and conquered since the Native Americans would have become habituated to European manners and the use of arms. However, then "it would have been next to impossible to have made those extensive settlements in the new world."[51] The rational benefits of colonial industry were an unexpected by-product of the irrational ambition which flooded the Americas with newcomers. Religious persecution had also stimulated emigration, but likewise this can hardly be claimed as a sane basis for colonial policy. This brings the Burkes to the fundamental question behind the *Account*: how ought colonial enterprise to be conducted, given the curious history of its beginnings? The starkest piece of advise on offer was to avoid the approach adopted by Spain. After first supporting the exploits of a philosopher-adventurer like Columbus, the Spanish court reverted to discouraging enterprise. With such treatment the "spirit of invention" expires.[52] By comparison, Colbert offered encouragement to experiment and invention, laying a foundation for industry and effort.[53] "By these means," the *Account* professed,

[45] Ibid., Introduction, p. vii.

[46] [Burkes], *Account*, I, p. 48.

[47] Ibid., p. 47.

[48] Adam Smith, *An Inquiry into the Nature and Causes of the Wealth of Nations*, ed. R. H. Campbell and A. S. Skinner (Indianapolis, IN: Liberty Fund, 1976), 2 vols., II, p. 562.

[49] [Burkes], *Account*, I, p. 48.

[50] Ibid.

[51] Ibid., p. 49.

[52] Ibid., p. 63.

[53] For Colbert's role in helping to foster balance-of-trade arguments in England, see Laurence Bradford Packard, "International Rivalry and Free Trade Origins, 1660–1678," *Quarterly Journal of Econom-*

"France advanced during the reign of Lewis the fourteenth, and under this minister, more than it had done in many reigns before."[54]

If Spain was at best inconstant in the encouragement it lent to discoverers, its policy was still more flawed regarding the governors it instituted. These were imbued with a spirit of exploitation, leading to the ill treatment of those whom they had subjugated. The extermination of millions, as reported by Las Casas, might, the Burkes accepted, have been an exaggerated account, yet there was no doubting the severity which conquering magistrates employed.[55] The suggestion was that Spanish *imperium* had been secured with insufficient humanity. Yet this did not imply a blanket opposition to "empire." The theme of conquest would play a significant role in Burke's subsequent career and so its examination in the *Account* has a wider relevance for his thought. He would later accept the conquest of both Ireland and India as having been legitimately secured by the rights of war. However, he was also clear that the duties of government succeeded any contest of arms. This contention formed part of a worldview that recognised the overthrow of peoples as an invariable feature of human history. Moreover, it was a feature that was probably impossible to eliminate. Behind the story of the English annexation of Ireland lay a prior history of belligerence, barbarism and servitude. Subjection was a necessary part of the process of civilisation. Similarly, behind the European conquest of Asia lay a longer history of invasion and takeover. What troubled Burke about India was not the change of regime but the inadequacy of the replacement that occurred. Successful conquest was a political process that Burke was in principle happy to approve. He associated success with pacification, followed by the progressive establishment of civilisation. Examples of such a process of benign subordination played a conspicuous role in the history recounted by the *Account*. Prior to European settlement, there had been two cases of conquest: first, the foundation of Mexico; and second, the creation of Peru.

The Burkes were conscious of both processes as examples of pre-European conquest. The empire of Montezuma, they stated explicitly, was "founded on conquest." The death of the Aztec ruler was conjured in melancholy tones, yet nonetheless it was recognised that, while he was a prince of "capacity" and "courage," he remained "artful, hypocritical and cruel." His crown had been elective, conferred in view of his considerable merits, though his primary achievement had been to extend his Mexican dominion.[56] Like Pompey, his resourcefulness had been better adapted to securing power than to holding it under conditions of duress.[57] The ruler of the Incas, Manco Cápac, was likewise a figure of genius, skilled in the acquisition of power,

---

ics, 37:3 (May 1923), pp. 412–35. For conspicuous examples of the Colbertian policy of investment in domestic industry, see Abbott Payson Ushe, "Colbert and Governmental Control of Industry in Seventeenth Century France," *Review of Economics and Statistics*, 16:11 (November 1934), pp. 237–40.

[54] [Burkes], *Account*, I, p. 65.

[55] Ibid., pp. 126–29. The reference is to Bartolomé de las Casas, *Brevísima Relación de la Destrucción de las Indias* (Seville: 1552). The demographics were in fact far more disturbing than they imagined. See J. H. Elliott, *Spain and its World, 1500–1700* (New Haven, CT: Yale University Press, 1989), p. 10.

[56] [Burkes], *Account*, I, p. 71.

[57] Ibid., p. 93.

but in addition adaptable under adversity. By exploiting the natural superstition of his people, "he brought a large territory under his jurisdiction."[58] The rule of the Incas was despotic, but "filial" rather than "slavish."[59] The contrast here was intended to distinguish Asia from Peru, where subjection was based on affection rather than the sword. It was the process of civilising subjection that impressed the Burkes. Cápac had "united and civilized the dispersed and barbarous people; he bent them to laws and arts; he softened them by the institutions of a benevolent religion."[60] This passage had many parallels in Roman conquest literature and was duplicated in European histories that followed a similar pattern.[61] The results were also the same: "there was no part of America in which agriculture and the arts were so much and so well cultivated."[62] Conquest could be legitimised in terms of its outcomes and by means of prescription, even if the original subjugation had no justification.

According to Montesquieu, the only possible justification for conquering a people had to be based on the threat they posed to peace: "Du droit de la guerre dérive celui de conquête."[63] In a philosophical interlude early in the *Account*, the Burkes—most probably Edmund—provided an overview of the pretexts commonly used to vindicate subjection. The first was derived from the idea of natural slavery prevalent among the Greeks and accepted by Aristotle in his *Politics*.[64] It was a notion that would play a prominent role in rationalising the acquisition of Spanish America.[65] According to the Burkes it was a doctrine, given that it was baseless, that could hardly hope to exonerate the conduct of the Spaniards. The Burkes were thinking in particular of the conquest of Hispaniola, notable for the extremity of its violence. But the point applied to two further means of pretending to authority adopted by Europeans in their transactions with the new world. Both these popular pretexts were condemned as spurious: the first was the papal claim to territorial jurisdiction based on the spiritual authority of the office of bishop, and the second was the concept of the dominion of grace which gained a foothold among the English during the

[58] Ibid., p. 133.

[59] Ibid., p. 134.

[60] Ibid.

[61] See, for example, Tacitus, *Agricola*, 21. As a source for Burke in this idiom, see John Davies, *Discoverie of the True Cause why Ireland was never Entirely Subdued nor Brought under Obedience of the Crowne of England, untill the Beginning of His Majesties Happie Raigne* (London, 1612). For discussion, see Richard Bourke, "Edmund Burke and the Politics of Conquest," *Modern Intellectual History*, 4:3 (November 2007), pp. 403–32. See also below, chapter 9, section 5 and chapter 14, section 6.

[62] [Burkes], *Account*, I, p. 134. For the theme of civilising agriculture versus nomadic barbarism in early modern European political thought, see Richard Tuck, *The Rights of War and Peace: Political Thought and International Order from Grotius to Kant* (Oxford: Oxford University Press, 1999, 2002).

[63] Charles-Louis de Secondat, Baron de Montesquieu, *De l'esprit des lois* (1748) in *Œuvres complètes*, ed. Roger Caillois (Paris: Gallimard, 1951), 2 vols., II, pt. II, bk. X, ch. 3.

[64] [Burkes], *Account*, I, pp. 31–32.

[65] Anthony Pagden, *The Fall of Natural Man: The American Indian and the Origins of Comparative Ethology* (Cambridge: Cambridge University Press, 1982), ch. 3.

period of the civil wars.[66] Both claims were ultimately antinomian in character: spiritual authority was used to abrogate moral standards. But while the actions of Europeans in vanquishing the Indians enjoyed little justification, the perpetrators had no sense of the impropriety involved. Therefore the conduct of the victors had to be explained in terms of their commitment to the ideological justice of their cause. Ideas, however, could have no force unless they enjoyed some plausible support. In this case, ideological conviction was supplemented by a characteristic of human nature.

The Burkes described this characteristic as a species of credulity. While human beings were morally equal they were not practically upon the same level. Superior skill and aptitude was esteemed as "fitness" to rule. This perception of distinction was easily translated into a "right": by a habitual tendency of the human mind, a fact was converted into a norm.[67] An ability to govern became a title to rule. This operation of prejudice was Janus-faced in its consequences. On the one hand it enabled necessary subordination, on the other it facilitated political domination. In the former capacity it could expedite the passage to legitimate subjection on the back of violent oppression. As the *Account* saw it, deference could "palliate the guilt and horror of a conquest."[68] The point was not to celebrate a supine disposition but to show that, without a rudimentary aptitude for concession, rapprochement between liberty and authority could not occur. Without this means of accommodation, servitude could never develop into legitimate submission. Yet, equally, by an abuse of acquiescence the most frightful tyranny could be instituted. The subjugation of Mexico exemplified such exploitation. Burke recalled its severity at the end of his career, comparing the French nobility under the Revolutionary regime to Spain's hapless Aztec victims: "They were found in such a situation as the Mexicans were, when they were attacked by the dogs, the cavalry, the iron, and the gunpowder of a handful of bearded men, whom they did not know to exist in nature."[69]

Similarly, the Incas of Peru were poignant victims of oppression. At the hands of greedy magistrates and overbearing priests, they were economically exploited and held in social contempt: "Complaints are answered with new indignities, and with blows, which it is a crime to return."[70] An annual festival in the city of Lima reenacted their former freedom, ventilating the depression of a people bowed down in bondage.[71] The reenactment inspired the Indians with overwhelming rage as they juxtaposed their remembered freedom with their current degradation. Subordination, by implication, was not based on consent: conquest never yielded to civilised government and consequently never generated liberal submission. In the language

[66] [Burkes], *Account*, I, p. 31.

[67] Ibid., p. 32.

[68] Ibid.

[69] EB, *Letter to a Noble Lord* (1796), *W & S*, IX, pp. 174–75.

[70] Ibid., p. 257.

[71] Ibid., pp. 258–59, based on Amédée-François Frézier, *Relation du voyage de la mer du Sud, aux côtes du Chili, du Pérou et de Brésil, fait pendant les années 1712, 1713, et 1714* (Paris: 1715), p. 249. The Burkes refer to Frézier in the *Account*, I, p. 251.

of Montesquieu, the Spanish never looked to the preservation of their colonies which they chose instead to regard as expendable objects of their will. "The purpose of conquest is preservation [conservation]," the *Spirit of the Laws* commented; "servitude" can never be its end.[72] The Spanish, in the eyes of the Burkes, confused dominion with servility, basing their administration on the prerogatives of power rather than the duties of government.

The Spanish Empire forms a central plank of the *Account of the European Settlements* because its methods offered a model of how not to construct a government. Spain was ultimately animated by the spirit of conquest rather than the pacific arts of reciprocity and commerce. "Jealousy is the glaring character of the court of Spain," the *Account* declared.[73] Its operation affected the conduct of domestic trade by strangling ambition and innovation. Its enormous accretions of gold failed to extend the national wealth; prosperity was sacrificed to excessive security: "No country in Europe receives such vast treasures as Spain. In no country in Europe is seen so little money."[74] It was closer to Montesquieu's fictional Persia than it was to his putative France. Its chief characteristics were a by-word for exploitative dominion: "In government tyranny; in religion bigotry; in trade monopoly."[75] Its colonies were afflicted by the same temperament, leading to yet more terrible results. Spanish governors were driven by avidity and envy, ravenously preying on their people. These in turn were maintained in a state of permanent fear: the creoles were loathed by the Spanish while despising the blacks in turn. The native population grew progressively disconsolate—"humble, dejected, timorous, and docile," longing for a government of their own kind.[76] The Europeans had exported a system of divide and rule.[77] Altogether, Spain was manifestly a declining power: Cromwell had displayed poor judgment in collaborating with the French, "then rising into a dangerous grandeur," as the Spanish, with whom he battled, were independently exhausted.[78]

If the law of nations were properly respected across the globe, Montesquieu claimed, then it would make sense to speak of the benefits that could accrue to vanquished peoples. However, the Spanish pursued dominion with lethal results. "What good could the Spanish not have done the Mexicans?" Montesquieu asked. Yet a trail of disaster followed in their wake.[79] The Burkes were equally blunt: the Spanish refused all means of retaining their conquests except what amounted to "extirpating the people."[80] However, this was an indictment not of the project of empire, but of the systematic abuse of imperial power. Legitimate conquest, colonial

[72] Montesquieu, *De l'esprit des lois*, pt. II, bk. X, ch. 3.
[73] [Burkes], *Account*, I, p. 234.
[74] Ibid., p. 296.
[75] Ibid., pp. 296–67.
[76] Ibid., pp. 238–43.
[77] Ibid., p. 258.
[78] Ibid., II, pp. 63–64.
[79] Montesquieu, *De l'esprit des lois*, pt. II, bk. X, ch. 4.
[80] [Burkes], *Account*, I, p. 296.

settlement and cultural improvement should be extolled. Towards the end of the second volume of the *Account*, the authors list a succession of munificent conquerors—Christopher Columbus, Philippe de Longvilliers de Poincy, Pedro de la Gasca, Lord Baltimore and William Penn—who had "brought into the pale of civility and religion" a variety of "rude and uncultivated parts of the globe."[81] In due course, their deeds would be mixed with fable to become the founding myths of nations. Their achievements could be equated with Osiris, Bacchus and Orpheus—agents of cultivation and progenitors of civilisation.[82] There was no shame in such endeavour but only in its miscarriage, as illustrated by the willing acquiescence of Indians in the settlements instituted by the Jesuits, where subjection was united with "contentment and satisfaction."[83]

The Burkes' idea that subjection can be traced to an instinct for subordination is based on the analysis of Native American savages, largely indebted to the observations of Lafitau. The aborigines of the continent appeared remarkably similar in their customs and stood as an image of the antiquity of all nations.[84] They were superstitious rather than religious in a cultivated way, and consequently had "scarce any temples."[85] Crucially, they credited the immortality of the soul, as illustrated by their meticulousness in caring for the dead. The *Account* points to the "festival of souls" as a means of illustrating this devotion. The information is derived from chapter 7 of the second volume of Lafitau's *Mœurs de sauvages américains*. The festival was conducted among the seven nations of the Iroquois confederacy living around the Saint Lawrence River valley. The ceremony involved disinterring and mourning the bodies of the dead. While this entailed the most horrendous displays of bodily mortality, it also demonstrated the "tendre piété" of the Indians.[86] According to Lafitau, this behaviour went to discount the arguments of atheists against the universality of religious sentiment. For the Burkes it showed how religion smoothed "our rugged nature into humanity."[87] Even so, cruelty was rife among these savage populations, indicating the advantages of the Christian religion, particularly as it taught "compassion to our enemies."[88]

Admitting the mixture of brutality and amity among the Indians, on the whole they appeared "hardy, poor, [and] squalid," while always remaining devoted to liberty.[89] They were not easily roused to anger, but when sufficiently provoked they were given to boundless fury.[90] Their predominant occupation was war, and glory

[81] Ibid., II, pp. 221–22.

[82] Ibid., p. 222.

[83] Ibid., pp. 285–86. Cf. the rebellious dissatisfaction of the Chileans in ibid., pp. 272–73.

[84] Ibid., pp. 167–68.

[85] Ibid., p. 173.

[86] Lafitau, *Mœurs de sauvages américains*, p. 448.

[87] [Burkes], *Account*, I, p. 186.

[88] Ibid., pp. 199–200.

[89] Ibid., pp. 168–69.

[90] Ibid., pp. 171–73.

was the supreme object of their affections.[91] Equally, they were strongly averse to dependence, or obedience to command, although they were susceptible to persuasion by those whom they admired. Here the habit of conceding to authority was apparent even among the most wilfully free-spirited. Their chiefs were revered as fathers, acting by persuasion rather than coercion. Their great councils were populated by those who enjoyed "consideration."[92] Even so, despite the signs of deference based on admiration, there existed no system of criminal jurisdiction: "the crime is either revenged or compromised by the parties concerned."[93] Their rudeness and simplicity meant a lack of jurisprudence. It was indicative of a fundamental absence of civility. This condition made European observers "sensible of the value of commerce, the arts of a civilized life, and the lights of literature."[94] This of course was more than "some" philosophers were ready to admit. Rousseau was the most obvious candidate for this censure. The arts and sciences as well as cultivation and commerce meant progress from a rudimentary equality of conditions. Civilisation drew "the sting of our natural vices, and softened the ferocity of the human race."[95]

Conspicuous in the *Account* is its admiration for the French. The Portuguese, the Dutch and the Danes receive comparatively terse treatment. France takes centre stage because of the buoyancy of its trade, thanks to the cumulative impact of intelligent commercial policy. This began with Richelieu and was perfected by Colbert; it was centred on "what serves most effectually to support commerce, colonies and establishments abroad."[96] The volume of sugar, indigo and coffee exports from their West Indian settlements was an indication of economic strength: "We have the greatest reason to be jealous of France in that part of the world."[97] Indeed, in general, though the French had been regularly subjected to patriotic derision in Britain, in truth their commercial success should be an object of emulation. The attention they bestow upon the trade of their colonies ought to act as a spur to British industry—it ought "to rouse us out of that languor into which we seem to have fallen."[98] The current conflict with France was part of a longstanding contest, stretching back for a century and more. The struggle was for "superiority in arms, in politics, in learning, and in commerce."[99] Victory could not be had by assailing commerce in time of war. The only solution was for a polity to outpace its rivals by exceeding it in competitive edge: "While the spirit of trade subsists, trade itself can never be destroyed."[100]

[91] Ibid., pp. 188–90.
[92] Ibid., pp. 176–78.
[93] Ibid., pp. 180–82.
[94] Ibid., p. 200.
[95] Ibid.
[96] Ibid., II, pp. 4–5.
[97] Ibid., pp. 22–23.
[98] Ibid., p. 48.
[99] Ibid., p. 49.
[100] Ibid., p. 17.

The conspicuous admiration of *Colbertisme* in the *Account* most likely explains Burke's refusal to acknowledge his involvement in the work: "that great, wise, and honest minister Colbert, one of the ablest that ever served any prince."[101] Exclusive monopolies are criticised within national jurisdictions, but intelligent regulation is commended.[102] The spirit of commerce is approved as an engine of widening sociability, yet the advantage of a favourable balance of trade is also applauded.[103] As regards the West Indies, the exorbitant duty on sugar together with the burden of maintaining an establishment is contrasted with the more conducive policy of the French.[104] More generally, a liberalisation of trade within the Empire is encouraged, and the "round-about" trade, including its impact on Ireland, is criticised.[105] At the same time, a trade surplus against competitor-empires was to remain the goal of commercial policy. The basic premise of the *Account* is that the application of executive planning to commercial regulation, as perfected across the Channel, could be married to the spirit of political liberty in the British colonies. It was possible, in other words, to learn from the French, without imposing their institutions in America as a blueprint for the political economy of empire.

British plantations were a product of the love of liberty rather than a result of ministerial planning, and their administration had to respect the terms of their original foundation. The attachment to freedom had both a religious and a political aspect. It was dissent from the national Church that drove many colonists to emigrate, imbuing them with an enthusiasm for liberty. This had its advantages for the mother country by opening up a vent for "fiery, restless tempers."[106] Paradoxically, devotees of liberty who had fled as refugees often scourged religious dissenters in their turn. Having been molested on account of their conscientious commitments their zeal primed them to vex their brethren in America. Harassment had disposed them to retaliation: "They judge of the hatred of the adverse side by their own."[107] The cycle of dissent and persecution in the colonies led the Burkes to espouse the virtue of toleration: "In all persuasions the bigots are the persecutors; the men of cool and reasonable piety are favourers of toleration."[108] It was a sentiment to which Burke would remain committed for the rest of his career. Unity of faith was preferable to a multiplicity of beliefs, yet with the advent of diversity charity should be practised.[109]

[101] Ibid., p. 4.

[102] Ibid., pp. 3, 8, 47, 60; ibid., pp. 182–23.

[103] Ibid., I, pp. 47, 112.

[104] Ibid., pp. 110–16.

[105] Ibid., p. 115. This would later preoccupy Burke during his first spell in parliament. See EB to Charles O'Hara, 1 March 1766, *Corr.*, I, p. 240, and below, chapter 5, section 2; chapter 6, section 5; and chapter 8, section 3.

[106] [Burkes], *Account*, II, p. 106.

[107] Ibid., pp. 152–53.

[108] Ibid., p. 153.

[109] Ibid., p. 199.

Political liberty among the British in the new world was no less conspicuous than the taste for religious freedom. This was particularly apparent in the colonies of North America. In New England above all, while there existed holders of considerable estates who let their lands to farmers, the majority of the colonists were independent yeomen whose properties were partitioned by "gavelkind" among the children of the family. This had the result that the settlers were generally of moderate means, and possessed of "a very free, bold, and republican spirit."[110] Given this temper among the North Americans, royal government was best adapted as a means of administration. This combined an assembly of elected representatives with a governor and council appointed by the crown. Proprietary colonies were similarly constituted. Yet under charter governments, such as were settled on New England, Connecticut and Rhode Island, power was vested "more dangerously" in the body of the people: "It is to all purposes a mere democracy."[111] Executive officers were elected rather than appointed, rendering these settlements less tractable to the metropolis. In Massachusetts the governor lacked an establishment of his own, rendering him dependent on local representatives, and thus a tool of popular forces in the province.[112] Republican sentiment in the colonies made settlers nervous about executive privilege. They zealously guarded the right to consent. Imperial imposition was liable to be construed as a reversion to the prerogatives of Stuart power. Under these circumstances, government risked appearing as an instrument of subjugation and a tool of persecution. In the 1760s and 1770s, Burke set about recovering for a metropolitan audience the likely consequences of that appearance. London would be faced with the stark alternative of conquest or conciliation.

4.3 *An Abridgement of English History*: The Romans to Christianity

With the *Account* and the *Philosophical Enquiry* published, Burke was hoping to set out for America in August 1757.[113] However, the plan was impeded by the onset of the war.[114] At the same time, he was contracted by Dodsley to write a history of England that was ultimately published posthumously as *An Essay towards an Abridgement of the English History*.[115] On 25 February 1757, he agreed to compose a single-volume narrative that would extend "from the time of Julius Caesar to the end of

[110] Ibid., p. 167. Much in the Burkes' account of New England is dependent on William Douglass, *A Summary, Historical and Political, of the First Planting, Progressive Improvements, and Present State of the British Settlements in North America* (Boston: 1749), 2 vols.

[111] [Burkes], *Account*, II, p. 300.

[112] Ibid., p. 302.

[113] EB to Richard Shackleton, 10 August 1757, *Corr.*, I, p. 123.

[114] The idea of emigrating still appealed to Burke four years later: see EB to Charles O'Hara, 10 July 1761, ibid., p. 141.

[115] Six sheets of the work were printed in 1760. This text survives at the Bodleian Library in Oxford. A revised manuscript was published in 1812. See Todd, *Bibliography*, pp. 42–43.

the reign of Queen Ann [*sic*]."[116] It was expected that Burke would submit his work by the end of 1758. The idea was that a concise overview could survey material that had hitherto appeared in multi-volume histories. The work was still being revised by Burke in 1763.[117] Although rumours of its imminent publication were circulating the previous year, Burke never completed the project.[118] What survives is therefore a fragment of the intended whole, although it nonetheless amounts to a substantial body of writing covering the period from the Roman invasion to Magna Carta.[119] The *Abridgement* is divided into three books, covering Roman, Saxon and Norman Britain respectively. Its principal theme is the conquest and coalition of peoples in connection with the progress of freedom.

Burke opens with a synoptic overview of the protracted contest between civility and barbarism in Europe, a staple theme in enlightenment historiography more generally, and a subject of fascination to the ancient historians, evident as early as Thucydides.[120] Burke's story begins as a struggle between the north and south of the continent. The great landmass extending westwards from the extremities of Tartary to the ocean had long been the haunt of plundering shepherding warriors, familiar since Herodotus as uncouth Scythians.[121] Tribal societies of the kind dominated the north of the continent, waging perpetual war upon one another. Various nations triumphed, but the mode of life stood still, until at last they encountered the military force of the Romans. The Roman Republic was a product of southern European settlement. Nomadism had been extinguished by the peninsular geography of Greece and Italy which sheltered communities who could embark on a settled life of cultivation. The mechanical and learned arts ultimately followed. Military discipline accompanied the acquisitions of civility. Accordingly, the settlements of the south, as Burke observed, "came greatly to excel the northern nations in every respect."[122] The conquest of Britain was a product of conflict between the ferocity of the Gauls and the civility of the south spearheaded by Rome. Caesar prosecuted a strategic rather than an "absolute" conquest of the island.[123] His aim was to neutralise potential support for the Gauls rather than extend Roman dominion beyond the mainland. He

[116] Isaac Reed, "Notes on an Abridged History of England Undertaken by Edmund Burke," Boswell Papers, Yale University Library, MS. C. 2349, cited in T. O. McLoughlin, "Edmund Burke's 'Abridgment of English History'," *Eighteenth-Century Ireland*, 5 (1990), pp. 45–59.

[117] EB to William Gerard Hamilton, March 1763, *Corr.*, I, pp. 164–65.

[118] Thomas Gray to Horace Walpole, 28 February 1762, *The Yale Edition of the Correspondence of Horace Walpole*, ed. W. S. Lewis (New Haven, CT: Yale University Press, 1937–83), 48 vols., XIV, p. 122.

[119] The fullest treatment of Burke's sources (ancient and medieval) appears in Sora Sato, "Edmund Burke's Ideas on History" (PhD thesis, University of Edinburgh, 2013), pp. 24–32.

[120] Pocock, *Barbarians, Savages and Empires*, pp. 2–6; Nicholas Phillipson, "Providence and Progress: An Introduction to the Historical Thought of William Robertson" in Stewart J. Brown ed., *William Robertson and the Expansion of Empire* (Cambridge: Cambridge University Press, 1997, 2008); Thucydides, *History of the Peloponnesian War*, I, iiff.

[121] Herodotus, *History*, IV, iff.

[122] EB, *An Essay towards an Abridgement of English History* (1757–c. 1763), *W & S*, I, pp. 338–39.

[123] Ibid., p. 344.

achieved his purpose in the course of two expeditions into the south of England and withdrew to the continent before turning on Rome.[124]

A more durable reduction of Britain began under the principate, at first apathetically, under Tiberius and Caligula, but more determinedly under Vespasian.[125] Substantial tracts of territory, extending north into Caledonia, were properly brought under the yoke with the expedition of Agricola, recorded by Tacitus, his son-in-law. Beginning in 77 AD, Agricola's campaigns were manifested by humanity, his administration by moderation: "the island, when he had reduced it, was treated with great lenity . . . he pitied the condition and respected the prejudices of the conquered."[126] His aim was to secure a "perfect" conquest, which meant winning over the vanquished to acquiesce in Roman authority. This meant supplementing the art of military command with an aptitude for civilian rule. In pursuit of this, Agricola proceeded with equanimity and forbearance. War, Cicero argued in *De officiis*, should only be undertaken for the sake of peace.[127] Under various incarnations, this became a staple Roman norm. Peace, for Agricola, entailed equitable administration: "He knew . . . that the conquest is neither permanent nor honourable, which is only an introduction to tyranny."[128]

Burke charted the imperial administration of the Romans as part of the context for the subjugation of the British under Vespasian. He distinguished the status of allies, municipalities, provinces and colonies, and traced the administration of subject territories from the Republic to the Empire, recounting the passage from the authority of praetors in the earlier period to the era of the procurators. Throughout he noted the operation of a close-knit *esprit de corps* serving the interest of imperial security. Later, in his Indian writings, he would identify this as a negative characteristic of British government in Asia.[129] It could function positively, he seemed to think, under propitious circumstances. Otherwise it could be employed as an instrument of repression: it was "a firm and useful bond of concord in a virtuous administration; a dangerous and oppressive combination in a bad one."[130] Burke identified a sequence of policies animating the progress of Roman arms. In the early days of the Republic, war was a means of survival, and its conduct was therefore focused on the destruction of the enemy. However, with greatness came stability, and with stability civil policy. Thus, even while prosecuting war, the Romans of the Empire "looked towards an accommodation."[131] The law of nations was elaborated in accordance with this disposition—"common rules" were established, and moderation was identified with sound reason of state. Burke equated this improvement with modern policy:

[124] Ibid., pp. 342–45.
[125] Ibid., pp. 359–65.
[126] Ibid., pp. 366–67.
[127] Cicero, *De officiis*, I, xxiii.
[128] EB, *An Essay towards an Abridgement of English History* (1757–c. 1763), *W & S*, I, p. 367.
[129] EB, Speech on the Opening of Impeachment, 15 February 1788, *W & S*, VI, pp. 285–86.
[130] EB, *An Essay towards an Abridgement of English History* (1757–c. 1763), *W & S*, I, p. 371.
[131] Ibid., pp. 368–69.

the politics of imperial Rome were "more like those of the present powers of Europe, where kingdoms seek rather to spread their influence, than to extend their dominion; to awe and weaken, rather than to destroy."[132]

This comparison, however, had its limitations. Ancient governments, like that of the Romans, continued to exhibit "something of the spirit of conquest."[133] Yet this "spirit," it appeared to commentators, could manifest itself along a spectrum extending from the unrestrained impulse to usurp to milder forms of coercive pacification. While Burke could chide the policy of conquest among the Romans it was generally said that their approach was relatively civilised in character. The strategy of extending the privileges of citizenship to those who supported Roman arms was frequently observed in the ancient literature on both the Republic and the Empire. In the *Annals*, Tacitus had extolled the wisdom of "mixing" the conquered with their conquerors; Livy had commended extending the rights of freedom to the vanquished.[134] Grotius singled out the wisdom of these procedures in his *Rights of War and Peace*, championing the "prudent Moderation of the old *Romans*."[135] Above all he meant the Romans of the early commonwealth, who had incorporated the Sabines, the Latins and the Italians. Burke noted that the provinces of the Empire were less fortunate. Imperial Rome was civilised, he accepted, but still severe. He would acknowledge the benefits bestowed upon the Britons yet criticise the relatively wilful management of the Roman provinces when viewed from the angle of more liberal regimes. The revenues that Rome imposed on subject allies were harsh, often obliging them to have recourse to extortionate loans to keep up their payments.[136] For this reason, ancient moderation compared unfavourably with the temperate government of modern colonies: the Roman system of provincial taxation seemed "rather calculated for the utter impoverishment of nations, in whom a long subjection had not worn away the remembrance of enmity, than for the support of a just commonwealth."[137]

For Burke, the remembrance of enmity indicated an absence of rapprochement. With successful subjugation, hostility subsided as the benefits of government were disseminated. A "perfect" conquest entailed a full pacific accommodation, meaning an end to any residual belligerent attitude on either side. As we have seen, the persistence of animosity survived the conquest of Peru. As Burke vividly realised from comparative knowledge of Britain and Ireland, ongoing antipathy similarly characterised colonial relations in the sister kingdom. This represented a failure of political "coalescence." Whatever the relative deficiencies of Roman imperial government when placed in world-historical perspective, the goal of reconciliation was lauded

[132] Ibid., p. 369.

[133] Ibid., p. 376.

[134] Tacitus, *Annals*, XI, xxiv, 7; Livy, *Ab urbe condita*, VIII, xiii, 16.

[135] Hugo Grotius, *The Rights of War and Peace*, ed. Richard Tuck (Indianapolis, IN: Liberty Fund, 2005), 3 vols., III, p. 1500.

[136] EB, *An Essay towards an Abridgement of English History* (1757–c. 1763), *W & S*, I, p. 375.

[137] Ibid., p. 376.

among ancient commentators as an essential feature of the *pax romana*. For Seneca the triumph of the Empire could be explained in terms of the "commingling" (*permiscere*) of victor and vanquished.[138] Agricola exemplified the spirit of compliance by which populations coexisting in the context of Roman conquests were encouraged to "coalesce and settle." In general terms, over time, "the several parts blended and softened into one another."[139] These "parts" included both colonial settlers and provincial subjects. With barbarous subjects such as the Britons had originally been, coalescence required an initial process of refinement. This is what Agricola had delivered: "In short he subdued the Britains by civilizing them; and made them exchange a savage liberty for a polite and easy subjection."[140]

Conquest was an "unhappy" but sometimes "necessary" undertaking.[141] It was necessary when nations posed a threat to peace. According to the annals of classical and modern historiography, barbarians and savages were peculiarly disposed to militancy, and thus existed in a state of enmity with civilised powers. The Britons, like the Gauls, exhibited these characteristics. They were products of the waves of northern European migration, which followed the pattern of the earliest peoples who spread across the earth. The cause of this dispersal was twofold: the mode of subsistence and the habit of war. Migration had occurred not under pressure of population growth, but on account of the tendency among hunters and pastoralists to wander. This was exacerbated by the scattering effects of constant conflict, underlining for Burke the aggressive and combative nature of migrant nations.[142] Accordingly, as with the Gauls, the Britons were "like all barbarians, fierce, treacherous and cruel."[143] This depiction of pastoral societies was indebted to Herodotus, Caesar and Tacitus, whose accounts of warlike shepherds became a *topos* in later literature. Much of it seemed to have been confirmed by accounts of hunter societies in North America, particularly in the writings of Lafitau and Charlevoix. What followed from this analysis was a faith in the benefits of civilisation.

Despite their rude condition, elements of improvement could be detected among the Britons. This was evident from their government and institutions of religion. The first provided a system of justice, the second a fear of the hereafter. Both phenomena were cultivated under the supervision of druids. Their "cardinal doctrine," Caesar wrote, was the immortality or transmigration of souls.[144] Burke elaborated on the earlier description: "The Druids were eminent above all the philosophick lawgivers of antiquity for their care in impressing the doctrine of the soul's immortality on

[138] Seneca, *De ira*, II, xxxiv.

[139] EB, *An Essay towards an Abridgement of English History* (1757–c. 1763), *W & S*, I, p. 373.

[140] Ibid., p. 368.

[141] Ibid.

[142] Ibid., pp. 346–47.

[143] Ibid., p. 348.

[144] Caesar, *De bello Gallico*, VI, 14.

the minds of their people, as an operative and leading principle."[145] He compared their rites and attitudes favourably with other heathens, and presented the duties of their office along with the content of their worship.[146] His sympathetic account contrasts with the portrait supplied by Hume, for whom the authority of the druids rested on "the terrors of their superstition."[147] Hume's *History of England* had started to appear in 1754, with the final instalment being published in 1761. Burke had to face the challenge of writing in its shadow. Tobias Smollett's *Complete History of England*, produced in little more than fourteen months, was a comparatively hurried and conventional affair.[148] It was Hume's work that had to be reckoned with, and Burke did so by absorbing its insights while criticising some of its conclusions. Hume would remain a counterpoint throughout Burke's literary and political career. He admired Hume's philosophical detachment and systematic view of politics, yet he regarded his religious scepticism as corrosive and prone to bigotry. Hume's disdain for superstition was a case in point. For Burke, primitive beliefs provided a basis for subsequent enlightenment. Religion was the germ of improvement, not of mental and moral corruption: "The first openings of civility have been everywhere made by religion."[149]

The improvement of British manners before the coming of the Romans had progressed furthest in the south, where settlements had been established. To the north, assorted tribes lived by war and pasturage. While the druids supplied religion, medicine and education, they also administered justice: "they seem to have had the sole execution and interpretation of whatever laws subsisted among this people."[150] Laws were of course few, as government was minimal. Liberty therefore met with few restraints. Society more nearly approximated the original equality of mankind. Civilisation entailed a departure from these primitive conditions, bringing peace and luxury with increased social stratification. The achievement of Agricola was to draw the Britons along that path. As Tacitus recounted: an "uncouth" (*rudes*) and "scattered" (*dispersi*) population was brought into subjection by the allurements of "cultivation" (*humanitas*) deployed by their conquerors.[151] Burke followed this lead: Agricola had reduced the Britons by civilising them. The policy thus pursued was exemplary—offering a "perfect model" for binding "a rude and free people."[152] Hume had come to the same conclusion: Agricola accustomed the Britons to the "conveniences

[145] EB, *An Essay towards an Abridgement of English History* (1757–c. 1763), *W & S*, I, p. 352.

[146] Ibid., pp. 354–58.

[147] David Hume, *The History of England* (Indianapolis, IN: Liberty Fund, 1983), 6 vols., I, p. 6.

[148] Tobias Smollett, *A Complete History of England* (London: 1757–58), 4 vols. A fifth volume, continuing the *History*, appeared in 1765. On the speed of composition, see Tobias Smollett to William Huggins, 13 April 1756, *The Letters of Tobias Smollett*, ed. Lewis M. Knapp (Oxford: Oxford University Press, 1970), p. 55.

[149] EB, *An Essay towards an Abridgement of English History* (1757–c. 1763), *W & S*, I, p. 349.

[150] Ibid.

[151] Tacitus, *Agricola*, 21.

[152] EB, *An Essay towards an Abridgement of English History* (1757–c. 1763), *W & S*, I, p. 368.

of life" and employed every available method "to render those chains, which he had forged, both easy and agreeable to them."[153]

According to Burke, the Roman Empire underwent three great changes in its history. The first was the removal under Antoninus of all distinctions between municipality, colony and province. This led to the amalgamation of peoples of the Empire into a single category of citizenship: "every mark of conquest was finally effaced."[154] The second was the division of the eastern from the western Empire under Diocletian around 293 AD, and the third was the conversion of Constantine to Christianity in 312 AD. In Britain, the influence of Roman civility steadily declined, but the Christian faith would later penetrate the south of the country during the aftermath of the Saxon invasions. These began with the intrusion of Hengist under the rule of Vortigern in the fourth century. Before long, waves of militant Saxons broke in upon the British, whom they effectively, Burke concluded, destroyed. With the Britons there perished the remnants of Roman learning until the rebirth of letters together with the Christian religion under the reign of Ethelbert, the king of Kent, around 600 AD. The Anglo-Saxons were converted with incredible rapidity, beginning with the king, followed by the nobles and then the people.[155] The monastery was the principal institution of the Saxons' religion, and the primary means of improving the manners of the population. Originally, they were "such as might be expected" of a rude people—"fierce, and of a gross simplicity."[156] Without arts, trade or manufactures, war was their only occupation and hunting their only pleasure.[157] The transition to Christianity was gentle rather than abrupt. Popular superstitions were reconciled to the new faith.[158] Conversion was also aided by assorted benefactions: the clergy manumitted baptised slaves; the donations of the wealthy were funnelled through the monks. The religious life was frugal and characterised by devotion, and monasteries provided both places of refuge and sites of burial. Seclusion placed a bar between barbarous existence and spiritual life. Gleams of early enlightenment soon began to dawn.[159]

Burke monitored the state of learning by surveying the works of Bede. The saint's achievements were curtailed by the decline of Roman science, which had been corrupted since the period in which the Empire had flourished.[160] Nonetheless, the search for knowledge brought mental improvement in its train: "These speculations,

[153] Hume, *History*, I, p. 10.

[154] EB, *An Essay towards an Abridgement of English History* (1757–c. 1763), *W & S*, I, p. 380.

[155] Ibid., pp. 390–91.

[156] Ibid., p. 392.

[157] Ibid., p. 393.

[158] Ibid., p. 395.

[159] Ibid., pp. 396–400.

[160] Burke seems to have had in mind his reliance on Epicurean physics in his cosmological thesis *De rerum natura*, modelled on Isidore of Seville. For discussion of some of Bede's sources, see M.L.W. Laistner, "Bede as a Classical and a Patristic Scholar," *Transactions of the Royal Historical Society*, 16 (1933), pp. 69–94.

however erroneous, were still useful; for though men err in assigning the causes of natural operations, the works of Nature are by this means brought under consideration; which cannot be done without enlarging the mind. The science may be false and frivolous, the improvement will be real."[161] The spread of knowledge and the improvement of manners had been mutually reinforcing. Learning disseminated reflection; teaching corrected morals. The Christian message ameliorated social intercourse: "The manners of the Saxons underwent a notable alteration by this change in their religion; their ferocity was much abated, they became more mild and sociable, and their laws began to partake of the softness of their manners, everywhere recommending mercy and a tenderness for Christian blood."[162] Scruples came to predominate, and brutality declined. Hume drew more or less the opposite conclusion: Christianity in Britain had been corrupted from the start, imparting credulity and superstition to its practitioners. More specifically, as Hume saw it, monastic life suppressed the active virtues; belief in miracles tampered with the progress of learning; reverence for the clergy encouraged servility among the people; and morals were perverted by the availability of absolution.[163]

While Burke took codes of conduct to have improved among the Saxons, politics remained mired in confusion. This was largely a result of the failure to settle the means of succession, which meant that a sequence of rulers had tottered on their thrones.[164] To remedy these disorders, King Alfred reformed the laws and institutions of government. During a period of tranquillity after subduing rampaging Danes, he settled the affairs of state. First of all he effectively garrisoned the kingdom: a militia was established, and the navy was improved. He then provided for the incorporation of the Saxons and the Danes by subjecting both communities to a uniform system of laws. In the aftermath of perpetual ravages by invaders, the country had been reduced to a state of indigence and incivility. In response to this King Alfred endeavoured to pacify the country by providing for the efficient administration of justice. Towards this end, shires, hundreds and tithings were established. Burke originally attributed their institution to Alfred, though he later added a note suggesting that their introduction was gradual and therefore not the result of "any single design."[165] Similarly juries, usually ascribed to the initiative of Alfred, in fact never did "prevail amongst the Saxons," though even Hume attributed their origin to this period.[166] According to Burke, Alfred was responsible for collecting a body of

[161] EB, *An Essay towards an Abridgement of English History* (1757–c. 1763), *W & S*, I, p. 402.

[162] Ibid., p. 404.

[163] Hume, *History of England*, I, p. 51.

[164] EB, *An Essay towards an Abridgement of English History* (1757–c. 1763), *W & S*, I, p. 406.

[165] Ibid., p. 411n. Contra, for example, Thomas Carte, *A General History of England* (London: 1747–50), 2 vols., I, p. 309.

[166] EB, *An Essay towards an Abridgement of English History* (1757–c. 1763), *W & S*, I, p. 411; Hume, *History*, I, p. 77.

laws, and generally improved the state of learning. He may have even established the University of Oxford.[167]

It has already been observed that Burke had a dual purpose in the *Abridgement.* His first concern was to elucidate the dynamics of conquest, and his second was to chart the progress of liberty. Both goals were intended to serve a further end: to dismantle the mythology of the ancient constitution. To begin with, the business of conquest presented a complicated picture. The Romans, the Saxons, the Danes and the Normans had all set about subjecting a vanquished people to government, but they achieved their purpose with varying results. The Romans brought civility, but their Empire did not last, giving way to ruination and decline: deserted villas, depopulation, diminished towns and the depletion of trade.[168] Desolation and plunder had succeeded a period of improvement before the economy and society began to recover in the seventh century.[169] By comparison with the Romans, the Danes were merely marauders, never establishing a distinct polity of their own, although they did acquire kingship under a "truly great" prince, King Canute.[170] Canute represented a continuation of the Saxon regime: he chose to rule by "the inclination of his subjects" rather than by "right of conquest."[171] He revived older Saxon statutes, and governed with moderation. Nonetheless, what interested Burke was the fact that the Saxons were easy prey to the Normans. This touched on the inherent deficiencies of Saxon government, leading Burke to present a sketch of the basic principles of their administration along with an analysis of their customs and social structure. This enabled him to highlight the development of their system of government in opposition to the image of a static "constitution." It also helped him to portray the essential crudeness of their scheme of liberty against previous celebrants of Gothic freedom. Finally, it permitted him to distinguish the Norman polity from its predecessors, once more emphasising discontinuities in the trajectory of English history, undermining the illusion of a seamless passage of freedom from the Germanic arrangements described by Tacitus to the triumph of parliament in the seventeenth century. Burke never completed the later instalments of his history, although its challenge to national pieties is evident in what remains. He weaves a narrative that emphasises circumstantial development and shows how a system of primitive liberty managed contingently to improve.

[167] EB, *An Essay towards an Abridgement of English History* (1757–c. 1763), *W & S*, I, p. 412, based on John Spelman, *The Life of Alfred the Great* (London: 1709), p. 144.

[168] For a retrospective overview extracted from the works of Bede, see Joel T. Rosenthal, "Bede's Ecclesiastical History and the Material Culture of Anglo-Saxon Life," *Journal of British Studies*, 19:1 (Autumn 1979), pp. 1–17.

[169] M. M. Postan, *The Medieval Economy and Society: An Economic History of Britain in the Middle Ages* (Harmondsworth: Penguin, 1975), p. 16.

[170] EB, *An Essay towards an Abridgement of English History* (1757–c. 1763), *W & S*, I, p. 419. Cf. EB, *An Essay towards an History of the Laws of England* (c. 1757), *W & S*, I, p. 328.

[171] EB, *An Essay towards an Abridgement of English History* (1757–c. 1763), *W & S*, I, p. 419.

4.4 *An Abridgement of English History*: The Anglo-Saxons and the Norman Conquest

In capturing the primitivism of Saxon institutions as well as their evolution, followed by the rupture introduced by the Normans, Burke's *Abridgement* displayed its debt to Hume's *History of England*. In both works, English history resembled more a process of contingent development than a story of the perseverance of primordial liberty. This represented a challenge to Bolingbrokean shibboleths, as well as to the main import of Paul de Rapin de Thoyras's influential *L'Histoire d'Angleterre*. Rapin, whose multi-volume history first appeared at The Hague between 1724 and 1725, was a Huguenot émigré who had been wounded assisting Williamite forces at the Siege of Limerick in 1690 before settling in Holland.[172] His work was immediately translated by Nicolas Tindal, the nephew of Matthew Tindal, with the last of fifteen volumes appearing in 1731.[173] In the second volume of Tindal's version of the *History*, Rapin's lengthy "Dissertation on the Government of the Anglo-Saxons" appears, containing an account of the laws, manners and constitution of the Heptarchy. Here, pristine Saxon liberties, preceding the establishment of monarchy, are explored in detail.[174] The wisdom of Rapin is repeatedly invoked throughout Bolingbroke's *Remarks on the History of England*.[175] He is further cited as an authority in the *Dissertation upon Parties*, where Bolingbroke presents, in Letter XII, a sketch of the trajectory of English freedom. The Britons, Bolingbroke argued, were "freemen."[176] He follows Sidney in dismissing accounts of aboriginal monarchy as "senseless."[177] The Britons, the Saxons and the Normans alike maintained the indelible marks of native freedom: "as far as we can look back, a lawless power, a government by will, never prevailed in Britain."[178] In this spirit, the Saxon Witenagemot is equated with the "high court of Parliament," and the Normans are presumed to have reverted to the original laws of the vanquished: an indomitable spirit of liberty persistently reigned.[179]

[172] Rapin died in 1725: his history was then continued by other hands down to 1745.

[173] Tindal later produced continuations down to 1745. On Rapin, see Hugh Trevor-Roper, "A Huguenot Historian: Paul Rapin" in Irene Scouloudi ed., *Huguenots in Britain and their French Background, 1550–1800* (Basingstoke: Macmillan, 1987); M. G. Sullivan, "Rapin, Hume and the Identity of the Historian in Eighteenth-Century England," *History of European Ideas*, 28 (2002), pp. 145–62.

[174] Paul de Rapin-Thoyras, *The History of England, as well Ecclesiastical as Civil* (London: 1725–31), 15 vols., II, pp. 137ff.

[175] Henry St. John Bolingbroke, *Remarks on the History of England* (1728–30) (London: 1743), pp. 76, 99, 105, 145, 149, 162, 206.

[176] Henry St. John Bolingbroke, *A Dissertation upon Parties* (1733–34) in *Political Writings*, ed. David Armitage (Cambridge: Cambridge University Press, 1997), p. 113.

[177] Algernon Sidney, *Discourses Concerning Government* (1698), ed. Thomas G. West (Indianapolis, IN: Liberty Fund, 1990), p. 512.

[178] Bolingbroke, *Dissertation upon Parties*, p. 114.

[179] Ibid., p. 115. Cf. Bolingbroke, *Remarks*, Letter IV.

Burke, like Hume before him, set about exposing these assumptions. Hume's scepticism about the enduring features of an "ancient constitution" began in the 1750s after an earlier admiration for Rapin.[180] As he progressed in writing the *History*, his doubts increased.[181] Hume followed Tacitus' *Germania* in depicting the northern nations, of whom the Saxons were an offshoot, as the bearers of "a fierce and bold liberty." According to Tacitus, the "German" tribes in general chose their kings (*reges*) on the basis of distinction (*nobilitas*) and their generals on the basis of merit (*virtute*). Government, however, was by consultation, and the authority of rulers was limited to persuasion.[182] In building upon Tacitus, Hume did not construe these arrangements as a model of pristine virtue. *Optimates*, or magnates, dominated the Saxon assemblies. By the time that the Norman conquerors arrived on the scene, government "was become extremely aristocratical."[183] This, in itself, was not an original statement. James Tyrrell had argued explicitly that "the Government of the Ancient *English Saxons* was rather Aristocratical than Monarchical."[184] However, Hume's purpose was to illustrate the shortcomings of the form of government. In claiming that the regime was neither a monarchy nor a popular state, part of his aim was to undermine the prejudices of Whigs and Tories who repaired to the Saxon original to find the constitution in embryo. But he was also keen to outline the inherent deficiencies of the Saxon regime. Burke followed this sceptical line, and indeed pushed it still further, rejecting "visionary" attempts to "settle the ancient Constitution in the most remote times exactly in the same form, in which we enjoy it at this day."[185]

The monuments of British antiquity not only pointed to essential discontinuities separating Saxon Britain from subsequent developments, they also demonstrated the "rudeness" of these primitive conditions. Burke stressed this fact to confute the "panegyrical declamations" which men like Bolingbroke had bestowed upon the ancient constitution.[186] It was perfectly clear that Saxon liberty was an entirely crude affair. It was a product of both ignorance and unpromising conditions. Together these ensured that freedom was arbitrary and despotic: it promoted licence among the powerful and unequal justice among the rest. Moreover, the forms of authority and social relations were military in character. The combination of these features limited agri-

[180] Duncan Forbes, *Hume's Philosophical Politics* (Cambridge: Cambridge University Press, 1975, 1985), p. 261. See also Nicholas Phillipson, *David Hume: The Philosopher as Historian* (London: Penguin, 2011), chs. 5–7; R. J. Smith, *The Gothic Bequest: Medieval Institutions in British Thought, 1688–1863* (Cambridge: Cambridge University Press, 1987, 2002), pp. 74–83.

[181] David Hume to James Oswald, *The Letters of David Hume*, ed. J.Y.T. Greig (Oxford: Oxford University Press, 1932, 1969), 2 vols., I, p. 179.

[182] Tacitus, *Germania*, VII, XI.

[183] Hume, *History*, I, pp. 160–65.

[184] James Tyrrell, *The General History of England as well Ecclesiastical as Civil* (London: 1696–1704), 3 vols., I, p. xxxix.

[185] EB, *An Essay towards an Abridgement of English History* (1757–c. 1763), *W & S*, I, p. 443.

[186] Ibid., p. 444.

cultural improvement as well as suppressing commerce and individual industry.[187] Civil authority was weak, while personal authority was strong. The office of rule was barely distinguishable from the person of the ruler, and the idea of political representation was non-existent.[188] Since authority was exercised by means of personal qualities, subordination lacked formality and stability. Hume had described the "ancient Germans" as "little removed from the original state of nature."[189] By this he meant that society was on a permanently military footing, with bands of soldiers acclaiming the martial virtues of their leaders. Burke followed suit: archaic conditions under the Saxons and the Germans were governed by the relationship between chiefs (or lords) and *comites* (or vassals).[190] The *comites* were bound together by ties of fraternity while allying themselves deferentially with the great.[191] Society and authority were based on military service, with soldier confederates devoting themselves to distinguished leaders in the field. This system was supported by "two principles in our nature": ambition on the one hand, and admiration on the other.[192] Within these passions lurked the germ of human subordination. Civilisation could only regularise and mollify subjection. Allegiance was distinguished from conquest by the presence of consent. This began as "voluntary inequality and dependence."[193] It developed into a relationship of emulation and friendship. Warburton had examined this species of personal allegiance in his treatment of the relationship between Nisus and Euryalus in book IX of Virgil's *Aeneid*.[194] Similarly, Burke argued, the cultivation of loyalty on the basis of admiration lies at the origin of the relationship between "Knights and their Esquires in this country."[195] The improvement of Europe was a product of the regulation of inequality and the removal of arbitrary dependence.[196] Subordination remained a constant, although its terms and conditions varied widely.

[187] Ibid., p. 429.

[188] William Lambard, *Archeion: Or, A Commentary upon the High Court of Justice in England* (London: 1635), pp. 241–44, had claimed that the system of representation could be traced to Saxon England.

[189] Hume, *History*, I, p. 174.

[190] EB, *An Essay towards an Abridgement of English History* (1757–c. 1763), *W & S*, I, pp. 429 and 431, follows Tacitus, *Germania*, XIII, and Caesar, *De bello Gallico*, VI, 15, in denominating German "comites," or martial fellows, as "ambacti."

[191] EB, *An Essay towards an Abridgement of English History* (1757–c. 1763), *W & S*, I, p. 432. Charles-Louis de Secondat, Baron de Montesquieu, *De l'esprit des lois* (1748) in *Œuvres complètes*, ed. Roger Caillois (Paris: Gallimard, 1951), 2 vols., II, pt. VI, bk. XXX, ch. 3, describes them as "compagnons."

[192] EB, *An Essay towards an Abridgement of English History* (1757–c. 1763), *W & S*, I, p. 431.

[193] Ibid.

[194] William Warburton, *The Divine Legation of Moses Demonstrated* (London: 1737–41), 2 vols., bk. II, sect. IV.

[195] "Literary and Miscellaneous Essays" in *The Annual Register for the Year 1763* (London: 1764), p. 178. This is the germ, celebrated in EB, *Reflections*, ed. Clark, p. 238 [113], of "that generous loyalty to rank and sex, that proud submission, that dignified obedience, that subordination of the heart, which kept alive, even in servitude itself, the spirit of an exalted freedom."

[196] See the extract from Voltaire's *Essai sur les mœurs* in *The Annual Register for the Year 1764* (London: 1765), pp. 167–68, on the "necessary inequality between conditions."

It is clear that Burke admired the process by which subjection was ameliorated rather than the crude original out of which it grew. Montesquieu, he recalled, extolled the "fine system" of the Germans. Towards the conclusion of his famous analysis of "the English constitution" in book XI of the *Spirit of the Laws*, he claimed that the British took "their idea of political government" from the mode of subordination originally hatched in the German forests.[197] Yet for Burke the primitive model "was far from being a fine one," and it contained no more than "the faint and incorrect outlines of our Constitution."[198] While Saxon government was premised on the consent of the governed, power was nonetheless exercised by arbitrary means. The modern constitution retained a component of popularity, but it had gradually eliminated the element of caprice. By implication, inequity and wilfulness pervaded the original frame. These traits inevitably followed from the division of ranks. To begin with, society was originally divided into freemen and slaves—those who conducted warfare, and those who tilled the ground. Among the freemen were included both thanes and freeholders. Thanes supported their family and dignity by means of their estates, whose demesne lands were cultivated by slaves. A number of stations intervened between the thanes and their slaves, comprising varying degrees of dependency and freedom, corresponding in turn to distinct modes of property, and providing access to different levels of juridical protection.[199] The highest court, the Witenagemot, was dominated by great men, while the many were commonly present to acclaim but not deliberate.[200] Burke's overall message thus became clear: "To the reign of Henry II. the citizens and burgesses were little removed from absolute slaves."[201] Most aggravatingly, taxation was arbitrary, and justice uneven.

In addition to its constitutionally unprepossessing characteristics, the Saxon regime was also weak and disunited. As a result, it was easy prey to a conqueror like William of Normandy: "one battle gave England to the Normans, which had cost the Romans, the Saxons and the Danes, so much time and blood to acquire."[202] Burke traces the vulnerability of the Saxons to the shortcomings of their polity. To begin with, the Danes had not yet fully incorporated with the English.[203] Next, the great men of the nation were divided and disheartened.[204] This pointed to a fundamental problem with the nobility, as well as to the insecurity of the monarchy in general. As a consequence of the operation of gavelkind, by which estates were gradually diminished over generations, the main body of the gentry were depleted in resources while great wealth was concentrated among the more powerful thanes. The nobility were therefore too great "to obey" yet too few "to protect," leaving the country exposed

[197] Montesquieu, *De l'esprit des lois*, pt. II, bk. XI, ch. 6.
[198] EB, *An Essay towards an Abridgement of English History* (1757–c. 1763), *W & S*, I, p. 430.
[199] Ibid., pp. 432–38.
[200] Ibid., pp. 440–41.
[201] Ibid., p. 441.
[202] Ibid., p. 426. Cf. Hume, *History*, I, p. 187.
[203] EB, *An Essay towards an Abridgement of English History* (1757–c. 1763), *W & S*, I, p. 428.
[204] Ibid., p. 428.

to infiltration.[205] The absence of obedience was caused by the uncertainty of succession which affected the Saxon, and then the Norman crown. The rules of tanistry governed accession to the throne, which meant that election and heredity were blended in an unstable mix.[206] As a result, the government of the territory lacked force while the community lacked cohesion. The Normans could therefore overmaster the country and remodel its constitution at their pleasure.

Nonetheless, William proceeded to manage his acquisition with moderation.[207] He erected garrisons across the country, and defeated even the resurgent English interest. Forfeited lands were distributed among his followers on feudal tenures, although the majority were confirmed in their holdings with a view to uniting "the two nations under the wings of a common parental care."[208] According to Hume's calculations, William created 700 chief tenants on feudal terms, while a further 60,000 knights in fee service were subordinated to them.[209] In one sense the Norman invasion represented a new order of things: "novum seclorum nascitur ordo," as Spelman put it.[210] Burke concurred: the "English laws, manners, and maxims were suddenly changed."[211] Nonetheless, at the same time, feudal tenures perpetuated already existing difficulties: the people were oppressively subjected to magnates, while the tenure of the king remained insecure. Down to Henry II, the succession of the crown continued to be disputed, while the power of the barons was extended.[212] Burke's narrative covers the period down to the introduction of Magna Carta, which he saw as one of the earliest attempts to remedy feudal abuses. In this, he was following in the footsteps of previous commentators who had criticised the injustices of the feudal order. He began, like most earlier historians, by observing that German

[205] Ibid., p. 427.

[206] Ibid., pp. 433–35.

[207] The notion that William "acquired" rather than "conquered" can be found in Henry Spelman, *Glossarium archaiologicum* (London: 1687), p. 145. Cf. John Skene, *De verborum significatione* (Edinburgh: 1681), under "Conquestus."

[208] EB, *An Essay towards an Abridgement of English History* (1757–c. 1763), *W & S*, I, pp. 459, 464. On this, see the review of George Lyttleton, *The History of the Life of King Henry the Second, and the Age in which he Lived* (London: 1767), 3 vols., in *The Annual Register for the Year 1767* (London: 1768), p. 265: "In this period we see the conquest of one mighty nation by another; the union and incorporation of both nations; the manner how by slow degrees they were melted into one."

[209] Hume, *History*, I, p. 204. Cf. EB, *An Essay towards an Abridgement of English History* (1757–c. 1763), *W & S*, I, pp. 464–65. This contrasts with Robert Brady's claims in his *Complete History of England from the First Entrance of the Romans unto the end of the Reign of Henry III* (London: 1685), pp. 192–93, that William the Conqueror completely extirpated the existing English nobility.

[210] Henry Spelman, "Of Parliaments" in idem, *Reliquae Spelmannianae: The Posthumous Works of Sir Henry Spelman* (London: 1723).

[211] EB, *An Essay towards an Abridgement of English History* (1757–c. 1763), *W & S*, I, p. 453. Cf. Jean Louis De Lolme, *The Constitution of England; Or, An Account of the English Government* (1771, 1778), ed. David Lieberman (Indianapolis, IN: Liberty Fund, 2007), p. 27: "the establishment of the feudal system in England, was an immediate and sudden consequence of the conquest which introduced it."

[212] EB, *An Essay towards an Abridgement of English History* (1757–c. 1763), *W & S*, I, pp. 464–65, 493.

nations were Scythian in origin. Subsistence was dominated by pasturage and hunting. Early agriculture was conducted on the basis of an annual division of territory.[213] It was the process of conquest, triggered by the decline of Rome, that established more durable estates. Territory was appropriated by conquerors as a means of managing and subordinating the vanquished. Before long, the control of these territories became hereditary.[214] Burke distinguished this arrangement from specifically feudal property: first, Saxon estates were not hereditable "fiefs," insofar as they did not descend intact to their heirs; and second, they were not burdened with services and dues.[215]

Like Saxon territories, feudal lands were a product of relations of conquest. Yet while the Saxons comprised a confederacy of independent soldiers, the Norman Conquest established more regular civil subjection. This was also founded on military discipline, but it tended to bind retainers more closely to their chiefs, and vassals more rigorously to their lords. Hume's *History* had offered an indictment of its provisions, drawing explicitly on Montesquieu and Robertson.[216] Under the conquering chiefs of the Germans, property became steadily more secure, with possessions becoming more durable despite the dependence of barons on the king and of vassals on their barons.[217] Even so, social and political relations continued to be oppressive. The monarch governed the country with the consent and advice of his magnates, yet the dependents of the barons were exposed to arbitrary authority. At the same time, commercial and mercantile wealth remained modest and static, while the serfs and the lesser vassals were excluded from public life and exposed to the impositions of their superiors.[218] The Commons, correspondingly, had no political existence, and so "the people" had no stake in public tribunals.[219] Magna Carta succeeded in correcting the extremity of authority, balancing established prerogatives with new privileges. "The object of Magna Charta," Burke wrote, was "the correction of the

[213] Ibid., p. 450.

[214] Ibid., p. 451.

[215] Ibid., p. 452. The point at which hereditary fiefs with feudal dues were introduced into England had, as Burke knew, been widely debated in the seventeenth century. See John Selden, *Titles of Honour* (London: 1614), pp. 300–302; Matthew Hale, *The History of the Common Law of England* (London: 1713), pp. 107, 223–25; Henry de Bracton, *On the Laws and Customs of England* (Cambridge, MA: Harvard University Press, 1968–77), 4 vols., II, pp. 37–38. On the transition from allods to fiefs, see Montesquieu, *De l'esprit des lois*, pt. VI, bk. XXXI, ch. 8.

[216] Hume, *History*, I, p. 455n. Cf. Montesquieu, *De l'esprit des lois*, pt. VI, bk. XXX, chs. 1–25, and William Robertson, *History of Scotland during the Reign of Queen Mary and of King James VI* (London: 1759), 2 vols., I, pp. 12–19. See also Henry Home, Lord Kames, *Essays upon Several Subjects Concerning British Antiquities* (Edinburgh: 1747); John Dalrymple, *An Essay towards a General History of Feudal Property in Britain* (London: 1757). For comment on Robertson's thesis, see *The Annual Register for the Year 1759*, p. 490: "his account of the ancient feudal constitution is one of the best specimens of his mastery."

[217] Hume, *History*, I, pp. 457–58. Cf. Montesquieu, *De l'esprit des lois*, pt. VI, bk. XXX, ch. 16, based on Jacques Cujas, *De feudis libri quinque* (Cologne: 1593): "at first the lords could take fiefs away at will . . . later they secured them for a year, and afterward gave them for life."

[218] Hume, *History*, I, pp. 462–63.

[219] Ibid., pp. 468–71.

feudal policy."[220] This did not transform either the balance of property or the system of government, but merely diminished the "overgrown branches" of feudal dues and services.[221] In this way the reform began of what Burke condemned as "the worst imaginable" form of government—a "feudal aristocracy."[222] As the privileges of the barons were secured, so the rudimentary liberties of the people were confirmed. The foundations of civilised freedom were laid even though "the thing itself was not yet fully formed."[223]

Hume had clearly indicated that the consummation of English liberty was neither the inevitable fulfilment of primitive custom nor even a discovery of native genius. Magna Carta was the fruit of French resistance, for example.[224] Burke's endorsement of this scepticism about the ancient constitution is particularly evident in a fragment that survives from the late 1750s, the *Essay towards an History of the Laws of England*. The *Essay* barely extends from the Saxon Conquest to the Norman. Nonetheless, its principal purpose is clear. Accounts of the common law as well as the history of English government, from the writings of Matthew Hale to the polemics of Bolingbroke, seemed to Burke to be united in their incoherent commitment to two contradictory ideas: first, a belief in the "eternity" of English legal provisions, and second a faith in their perpetual "improvement."[225] According to Burke, this curious amalgamation of incompatible ideas was a product of overwhelming national vanity, disposed to treat the customs and laws of the polity as both distinguished by their wisdom and hallowed by their antiquity.[226] This perspective was further exacerbated by divisive party views determined to trace the original form of the constitution either to a condition of primordial monarchical purity or to pristine republican institutions.[227] Both conceptions rely on unlikely accounts of British antiquity, and then collapse the progress of institutions into their original simplicity. The various modifications of legal practices brought about by changes in manners, commerce and religion are thus obscured or even denied.[228]

As far as Burke was concerned, the monuments of British antiquity overwhelmingly indicated the "rudeness" of the institutions first introduced by the Saxons.[229] Their original simplicity was naturally modified over time: they were altered by

[220] EB, *An Essay towards an Abridgement of English History* (1757–c. 1763), *W & S*, I, p. 544.

[221] Ibid., p. 456. Cf. John Millar, *An Historical View of the English Government* (Indianapolis, IN: Liberty Fund, 2006), p. 237: the Charter "produced a reciprocal diminution of . . . power [between king and nobles]. But though the freedom of the common people was not intended in those charters, it was eventually secured to them."

[222] EB, *An Essay towards an Abridgement of English History* (1757–c. 1763), *W & S*, I, p. 457.

[223] Ibid., p. 551.

[224] Hume, *History*, I, pp. 470–71.

[225] EB, *An Essay towards an History of the Laws of England* (c. 1757), *W & S*, I, p. 324.

[226] Ibid., p. 323.

[227] Ibid., pp. 324–25.

[228] Ibid., p. 325.

[229] He explicitly takes issue with one of Bolingbroke's sources: Nathaniel Bacon, *Historical and Political Discourse of the Laws and Government of England* (London: 1647–51).

contingencies, and fed by various influences, including an assortment of foreign customs and elements of the civil law. Nonetheless, it was the Norman Conquest that revolutionised English legal provisions: "At this time the English jurisprudence, which hitherto had continued a poor stream . . . was all at once . . . replenished with a vast body of foreign learning."[230] However, this did not ensure that the constitution was improved. Norman laws and feudal tenures were not "adopted" but rather "imposed." They introduced new rigours into the government of England, yet they were not enforced by impartial administration. The history of the emergence of a national constitution was a story of contingent improvisation and adaptation. This outlook is developed in a review of the first volume of Hume's *History* published in *The Annual Register* for 1761, most probably written by Burke: it is curious to observe, the author proposes, "from what a strange chaos of liberty and tyranny, of anarchy and order, the constitution, we are now blessed with, has at length arisen."[231] Burke's *Abridgment* arrived at a similar conclusion. British institutions were neither a reflection of Saxon liberty nor the culmination of the Norman constitution. Instead, British history was a product of conquest and pacification, giving rise to a protracted struggle between liberty and authority. The establishment of modern freedom with the Glorious Revolution had at no point been a predetermined outcome. Instead, British developments had given rise to an evolving dynamic in which privilege and prerogative were variously contested. The British constitution of the eighteenth century was likewise a product of the convergence of contingencies, which for that reason might easily be undone.

4.5 The Science of Constitutional Freedom

It is clear that the concerns expressed in the *Abridgement of English History* carried over into Burke's analysis of contemporary politics. In the year in which he first undertook to deliver a single-volume account of the national past, he was also at work on a number of political essays which sought to examine the contemporary dynamics underpinning the constitution. Four essays from 1757 have survived: "Hints of Ireland," "Considerations on a Militia," "On Parties" and "National Character and Parliament."[232] It makes sense to discuss these essays in reverse order, since the last invokes a context relevant to the others. "National Character and Parliament" addresses the issue of shorter parliaments, a controversial issue since the passage of the Septennial Act in May 1716. Burke consciously raised the issue with reference to the Seven Years' War on the grounds that the mood created by that "unsuccessful" con-

[230] EB, *An Essay towards an History of the Laws of England* (c. 1757), *W & S*, I, p. 331.

[231] *The Annual Register for the Year 1761*, p. 301.

[232] These have all been reprinted in Richard Bourke, "Party, Parliament and Conquest in Newly Ascribed Burke Manuscripts," *Historical Journal*, 55:3 (September 2012), pp. 619–52.

test might be favourable to a consideration of constitutional reform.[233] Reform of the kind is dependent on a comprehensive political theory, Burke seemed to imply. Such a theory involved an analysis of the principles of a polity in connection with its social structure and political organisation. In the British case this required an appreciation of national "character" together with an understanding of the channels through which it moved. This entailed examining the "genius" of the people in relation to the form of government through which it found expression. British politics were animated by the "Spirit" of freedom, yet at the same time they were conducted by the combination of powers that constituted the complex machinery of government. Burke likened the national genius to the character of the Romans in contrast to the modern French and the ancient Athenians and Thebans. Under an "Absolute" regime, such as that which prevailed in France, government was reducible to administration.[234] However in Britain, much like Rome, the spirit of the people was decisive since the polity was founded on the principle of freedom. Yet freedom, as opposed to licence, presupposed constitutional government.

Burke's point arose out of the development of an argument in Hume. In his 1741 essay, "That Politics May Be Reduced to a Science," Hume claimed that "absolute governments must very much depend on the administration."[235] It was far different in the case of a mixed monarchy like the British where decision-making was determined by countervailing forces. In this instance, government was a function of the form of government, not the passions of individual leaders. The same principle applied to the Roman constitution under which everything depended on general "Causes," as Burke phrased it, rather than simply on the humours of individual men. This formulation was intended as a criticism of Sallust, in particular his reduction of the fate of the Roman commonwealth to a struggle between *virtus* and *fortuna*. In his study of the Jugurthine war, the Roman historian had presented individual moral agency as the best means of regulating the world of chance.[236] It was a theme that governed the opening sections of his account of the Catilinarian conspiracy: during the period in which the *mores* of the republic were failing, avarice, luxury and ambition had vitiated moral excellence, enabling fortune to overmaster terrestrial affairs.[237] Machiavelli would later demonstrate that while an explanatory framework of the kind might usefully illuminate the dynamics of principalities, it could not properly account for the fate of constitutional government. The fate of republics, based on relations between organised yet opposing forces, was not reducible to the dispositions of individual rulers. Montesquieu revived this perspective in his *Grandeur des Romains et leur décadence*: Rome rose to greatness not by fortune, but by "un certain

[233] EB, "National Character and Parliament" in Bourke, "Party, Parliament and Conquest," p. 641.

[234] Ibid., p. 640.

[235] David Hume, "That Politics May Be Reduced to a Science" (1741) in idem, *Essays Moral, Political, and Literary*, ed. Eugene F. Miller (Indianapolis, IN: Liberty Fund, 1985, 1987), p. 15.

[236] Sallust, *Bellum Jugurthinum*, I, 2–5.

[237] Sallust, *Bellum Catilinae*, I, 3–7; X, 2–5.

plan."[238] Burke supported this conclusion in "National Character and Parliament": Sallust, he noted, had improperly ascribed the fortunes of the Republic "to the Virtues & Capacity of particular men."[239] The polity of Athens, as a pure democracy, was as variable as its generals; the strength of Thebes had wholly depended on the aptitudes of Epaminondas. However the Romans, like the Britons, had a durable character deriving from their "haughtiness."[240] This spirit was sustained by an enduring "Scheme" or design, containing the secret of their political success. This was nothing less than a general plan of liberty embodied in a system of constitutional restraints.[241]

Because constitutional government was a system of checks and balances, it was prone to disturbance and corruption over time. The role of parliament was pivotal in maintaining a regular composition of forces since it was there that the competing elements of the republic collided. Liberty might be threatened by the growing power of the Commons or by the expanding influence of the crown: the former could best be curtailed by the patronage of the monarch, the latter by the potency of parliament. It had commonly been claimed that shorter parliaments added to the weight of the popular element in the constitution. Burke's goal in "National Character and Parliament" was to show how this could only serve to compromise legislative independence. The replacement of the 1694 Triennial Act with a scheme for extending the tenure of parliament to seven years had been introduced to stabilise Whig government in domestic and foreign affairs, but had long been challenged as a scheme for extending the power of parliamentary faction.[242] In his *Dissertation upon Parties*, Bolingbroke had argued in this vein that "domestic tranquillity may be . . . better secured under triennial, nay, annual Parliaments, than under Parliaments of longer continuance."[243] Enthusiasm for triennial elections was revived in 1755 in the pages of Richard Beckford's *The Monitor*.[244] As Burke saw it, however, a more extended tenure bestowed on parliament the character of a "Senate" in which members naturally combined to thwart the ambitions of the prince. The collision served to pro-

[238] Charles-Louis de Secondat, Baron de Montesquieu, *Considérations sur les causes de la grandeur des Romains et de leur décadence* (1734) in *Œuvres complètes*, ed. Roger Caillois (Paris: Gallimard, 1951), 2 vols., II, p. 173.

[239] EB, "National Character and Parliament" in Bourke, "Party, Parliament and Conquest," p. 641.

[240] Cf. Montesquieu, *De l'esprit des lois*, pt. III, bk. XIX, ch. 27: "les nations libres sont superbes."

[241] EB, "National Character and Parliament" in Bourke, "Party, Parliament and Conquest," p. 641.

[242] A positive case for the Septennial Bill was mounted by [Daniel Defoe], *The Alteration in the Triennial Act Considered* (London: 1716). The contrary case was effectively put by, inter alia, [Archibald Hutcheson], *A Speech Made in the House of Commons April the 24th, 1716, against the Bill for the Repeal of the Triennial Act* (London: 1722). For the general context, see Owen C. Lease, "The Septennial Act of 1716," *Journal of Modern History*, 22:1 (March 1950), pp. 42–47.

[243] Bolingbroke, *Dissertation upon Parties*, p. 106.

[244] *The Monitor*, 23 August 1755; 21 August 1756. Richard Beckford was the younger brother of William, a Pittite who rose to prominence in the City of London. For the general aims of this publication, see Marie Peters, "The 'Monitor' on the Constitution, 1755–1765: New Light on the Ideological Origins of English Radicalism," *English Historical Review*, 86:341 (October 1971), pp. 706–27.

mote the welfare of the commonwealth: "the People cannot suffer a great deal whilst there is a Contest between the different Parts of the Constitution."[245]

The effectiveness of this contest depended on securing the independent power of Whig grandees. After the loss of Minorca, the old corps of Whigs was subjected to "patriot" disdain at the hands of the Pittite publicist and divine, John "Estimate" Brown. Burke knew Brown's work through his earlier attack on the deist assumptions of Shaftesbury's *Characteristicks*.[246] Six years later, in his *Estimate of the Manners and Principles of the Times*, Brown returned to his concern with irreligion with an attack on the infidelity of Bolingbroke, but he also turned his fire against the "parties" of Great Britain.[247] Reviewing the book in 1759, *The Annual Register* described it as a satire on the times for which the nation at large had been prepared on account of "our ill success in the war."[248] The *Estimate* amounted to a Sallustian indictment of the degenerate morals of the age, culminating in a condemnation of the "*vain, luxurious*, and *selfish* EFFEMINACY" of national manners.[249] These features had weakened the bonds of union that feed the power of the state. Their divisive impact had been intensified by the conduct of political factions. Montesquieu had spoken of rival parties ("divisions") at Rome as permanent and necessary components of a free commonwealth.[250] Brown claimed in response that factions might be either "*salutary*" or "*dangerous*" depending upon their "*foundation*."[251] Burke examined the same terrain in his essay "On Parties," but came to a diametrically opposite conclusion.

Brown had situated his analysis in the context of the rise of parliament to power and dignity during the aftermath of the Glorious Revolution. Before long, he claimed, parliament was corrupted by means of "influence" exercised through the executive gift of places and pensions.[252] At the same time, representatives were bought off by private interests in town and country alike, completing the "great Chain" of partisan politics extending from the borough to the court.[253] Power was engrossed by a

[245] EB, "National Character and Parliament" in Bourke, "Party, Parliament and Conquest," p. 642. Cf. EB, Debate on Wilkes's Re-election, 17 February 1769, *Cavendish Debates of the House of Commons*, I, p. 231: "the alteration from a triennial to a septennial parliament was, I think, an improvement of the constitution." For subsequent discussion of shorter parliaments, see below, chapter 8, section 5.

[246] John Brown, *Essays on the Characteristics of the Earl of Shaftesbury* (1751), ed. D. D. Eddy (Hildesheim and New York: Georg Olms Verlag, 1969). Brown had been influenced by the "utilitarian" doctrines of Edmund Law, which he used to critique the moral thought of Wollaston and Clarke as well as the "moral sense" ideas of Shaftesbury and Hutcheson. See ibid., pp. 114–15, 132–35, 136n.

[247] On Bolingbroke, see John Brown, *An Estimate of the Manners and Principles of the Times* (London: 2nd ed., 1757), p. 56. Hume is similarly pilloried for irreligion in ibid., p. 83.

[248] *The Annual Register for the Year 1758*, p. 444. Extracts from John Brown's *Thoughts on Civil Liberty, Licentiousness, and Faction* (London: 1765) were included in "Essays" in *The Annual Register for the Year 1765* (London: 1766), pp. 222–26. Burke returned to the subject of Brown in EB, *First Letter on a Regicide Peace* (1796), *W & S*, IX, p. 192.

[249] Brown, *Estimate*, p. 29.

[250] Montesquieu, *Considérations sur les causes de la grandeur des Romains*, p. 119

[251] Brown, *Estimate*, p. 106.

[252] Ibid., p. 109.

[253] Ibid., p. 111.

factious nobility incapable of serving the general welfare. What was needed in response, Brown concluded, was "SOME GREAT MINISTER" capable of restoring public virtue.[254] Pitt was the obvious candidate for the task. Since the accession of the Duke of Newcastle to the position of first minister in the spring of 1754, national counsels had been divided into opposing camps. Henry Fox, a follower of the Duke of Cumberland, opted to maintain his support for the endangered Newcastle ministry. Pitt, however, was drawn into a more precarious course—setting up in opposition to the new government, winning favour with potentially influential Tories, and laying claim to various tenets of patriot rhetoric. Integrity, economy and efficiency became his watchwords.[255] As the Newcastle ministry buckled in the early stages of the war, Pitt's posture paid off: by the autumn of 1756 the government had fallen, propelling Pitt into a shortlived partnership with the Duke of Devonshire. This new ministry fell as early as April 1757, yet Pitt was back in office with the Duke of Newcastle by June, demonstrating the potency of popularity as well as the ongoing strength of the old corps of Whigs in the Commons. Brown's pamphlet was a paean to the patriot leader. Burke's essay "On Parties," however, was a meditation on the threat of demagogic politics at a time when Whig aristocracy was under assault from popular rhetoric.

Burke framed his discussion in the context of the decline of party in general and the rise of mere faction in its stead.[256] In the aftermath of 1745, Jacobitism became a spent force in national politics, depriving the Tory party of much of its rationale: "The Jacobite interest was what really kept Life in both Partys, they gave a real Design to what was only Speculation in the tories, & the whigs had thereby a real ground to oppose them."[257] In the place of genuine parties, factions had emerged, serving to divide the spoils of office in the absence of any sustaining constitutional principle. Parties, Burke went on, were necessary elements in any mixed or republi-

[254] Ibid., p. 221.

[255] Lucy Sutherland, "The City of London and the Devonshire-Pitt Administration, 1756–1756," *Proceedings of the British Academy*, 46 (1960), pp. 147–73; Paul Langford, "William Pitt and Public Opinion, 1757," *English Historical Review*, 88 (1973), pp. 54–79; Marie Peters, *Pitt and Popularity: The Patriot Minister and London Opinion during the Seven Years' War* (Oxford: Oxford University Press, 1980); Linda Colley, *In Defiance of Oligarchy: The Tory Party, 1714–1760* (Cambridge: Cambridge University Press, 1982), pp. 276–82; J.C.D. Clark, *The Dynamics of Change: The Crisis of the 1750s and English Party Systems* (Cambridge: Cambridge University Press, 1982, 2002).

[256] For the context for this discussion, see David Thomson, "The Conception of Political Party in England in the Period 1740 to 1783: An Essay in Constitutional Thought; Being an Examination of the Evolution and Acceptance of the Idea of Party, from Bolingbroke to Burke" (PhD thesis, University of Cambridge, 1938); Richard Pares, *King George III and the Politicians* (Oxford: Oxford University Press, 1953, 1988), ch. 3; Archibald S. Foord, *His Majesty's Opposition, 1714–1830* (Oxford: Oxford University Press, 1964), pts. IV–VI; John Brewer, *Party Ideology and Popular Politics at the Accession of George III* (Cambridge: Cambridge University Press, 1976, 1981), pp. 39–136; J.C.D. Clark, "The Decline of Party, 1740–1760," *English Historical Review*, 93:368 (July 1978), pp. 499–527; B. W. Hill, *British Parliamentary Parties, 1742–1832: From the Fall of Walpole to the First Reform Act* (London: George Allen & Unwin, 1985), chs. 4–6.

[257] EB, "On Parties" in Bourke, "Party, Parliament and Conquest," p. 644.

can system of government, animated by opposing principles. For Bolingbroke, such divisions had been little better than artificial fabrications deployed by partial interests in the state to engross power in the hands of prevailing Whiggism.[258] Only a patriot king, he later argued, could hope to recover a nation from the ensuing moral and political degeneration.[259] He would achieve this goal by governing on a patriot platform in the absence of political parties: "party is a political evil, and faction is the worst of all parties."[260] For Burke, on the other hand, party was a means of principled association. He contrasted this with medieval and ancient factions—with the Greens and the Blues during the death throes of the Roman Empire, or the partisans of Marius and Sulla or Caesar and Pompey during the decline of the Republic.[261] The same spectacle was on show in the contemporary Dutch Republic in which Orangists and Republicans vied to establish a pure regime, albeit on opposite principles.[262] This was entirely different from principled opposition. In this case, antagonists supported rival powers in the interest of a shared regime: "to form a Party there must be an object[,] the Real Aggrandisement of some of the Powers which form the Political Constitution of every state."[263] Burke was thus advocating the formation of parties on the basis of definite "principles" in order to serve the goal of moderation in mixed regimes.[264]

Hume had identified the existence of "Parties from *principle*" as a distinguishing feature of modern times.[265] In addition to the differences founded on their distinct interests, the parties of Great Britain opposed one another on the basis of divergent principles of the kind, and for that reason threatened the constitution with subversion.[266] After he had completed the Stuart volumes of his *History*, with Newcastle and Pitt conspiring to sustain effective government, Hume returned to the subject of party in 1758. Parties of principle that diverged to the point justifying "opposition by arms" had long subsided in Britain, giving way to a general desire to abolish such distinctions in favour of a coalition between hitherto divergent positions.[267] However, as Burke saw it, a bland assimilation of principles posed problems too. Organised antipathy might endanger a polity, but it also preserved the "vigour" of a constitution.[268] In its absence a properly republican regime would imperceptibly

[258] Bolingbroke, *Dissertation upon Parties*, pp. 29, 37, 39–40.

[259] Henry St. John Bolingbroke, *The Idea of a Patriot King* (1741–49) in *Political Writings*, ed. Armitage, p. 249.

[260] Ibid., p. 257.

[261] EB, "On Parties" in Bourke, "Party, Parliament and Conquest," p. 645.

[262] Ibid.

[263] Ibid.

[264] Cf. the claim that parties have always existed and always will in EB to Richard Shackleton, 25 May 1779, *Corr.*, IV, pp. 79–80. For discussion, see Harvey C. Mansfield, *Statesmanship and Party Government: A Study of Burke and Bolingbroke* (Chicago, IL: University of Chicago Press, 1965), pp. 15–16.

[265] David Hume, "Of Parties in General" (1741) in idem, *Essays Moral, Political, and Literary*, p. 60.

[266] David Hume, "Of the Parties of Great Britain" (1741) in ibid., p. 65.

[267] David Hume, "Of the Coalition of Parties" (1759) in ibid., pp. 493–94.

[268] EB, "On Parties" in Bourke, "Party, Parliament and Conquest," p. 646.

degenerate into an unmixed state, which is precisely what had been occurring in recent British history: "We are very obviously grown in effect whatever Appearances may be, into a perfect Democracy."[269] Ministers now rose in parliament on the basis of popular power, never solely on the basis of royal favour. After the accession of George III three years later, Burke began to revise his analysis of 1757. Yet in both cases his alarm was indicative of acute sensitivity about mixed regimes as harbouring within themselves the means of their destruction. Principled opposition offered the best security, he thought, against both monarchical ambition and the demagoguery of popular leaders.[270]

It was in this spirit that Burke opposed, in March 1757, the campaign to revive the militia. The image of a national defence force manned by men drawn from the plough and the loom and officered by responsible men of property in the counties had an established appeal among Tory and Country publicists since the accession of William III.[271] After the introduction of a new Militia Bill by the Townshend brothers in December 1755, Pitt was swift to lend his full support.[272] Initially blocked by opposition in the Lords, a Militia Act was passed in 1757.[273] Many years later, Burke recalled the protests that accompanied its establishment.[274] His essay opposing its introduction was written between the second and third readings of the Bill in support of the critical stance originally propounded by Granville and Hardwicke.[275] Although Burke would revise his view after the deployment of the standing forces of the kingdom against the American colonists in the 1770s, in 1757 he pointed out that "all fears for our Liberty from our Army . . . are in a manner vanished."[276] The alarms of the seventeenth century had been allayed by the reconciliation of defence with the spirit of the constitution: parliament granted supply while the crown directed the armed forces, mirroring the "mutual & necessary Dependence" of the powers of the state.[277] In the *Abridgement*, Burke traced the origin of the institution

[269] Ibid.

[270] Cf. Newcastle's account of Cumberland's view of 25 November 1764 to the effect that "Opposition" was beneath the old corps Whigs, even though the "Young Men" should be free to pursue this: Add. MS. 32964, fol. 109. See also Lord Hardwicke's reticence about long-term opposition: George Harris, *Life of Lord Chancellor Hardwicke, with Selections from his Correspondence, Diaries, Speeches and Judgements* (London: 1847), 3 vols., III, p. 351.

[271] Lois C. Schwoerer, *No Standing Armies! The Antimilitary Ideology in Seventeenth-Century England* (Baltimore, MD: Johns Hopkins University Press, 1974). See, more generally, Isaac Kramnick, *Bolingbroke and His Circle: The Politics of Nostalgia in the Age of Walpole* (Ithaca, NY: Cornell University Press, 1992).

[272] Paul Langford, *A Polite Commercial People: England, 1727–1783* (Oxford: Oxford University Press, 1989, 1992), p. 230.

[273] J. R. Western, *The English Militia in the Eighteenth Century: The Story of a Political Issue* (Baltimore, MD: Johns Hopkins University Press, 1974).

[274] EB to John Coxe Hippisley, 3 October 1793, *Corr.*, VII, p. 442.

[275] See Bourke, "Party, Parliament and Conquest," p. 636.

[276] EB, "Considerations on a Militia" in ibid., p. 648. For his later perspective, see EB, *Letter to the Sheriffs of Bristol* (3 April 1777), *W & S*, III, p 329,

[277] EB, "Considerations on a Militia" in Bourke, "Party, Parliament and Conquest," p. 648.

to the reign of Henry II: "he armed the whole body of the people" against the insolence of the barons.[278] Yet Burke came to believe that such armament was counterproductive in the modern age. As late as 1752, Hume had continued to lament the absence of a militia as a means of curtailing incipient threats to liberty.[279] Burke, however, preferred the security offered by purely legal restraints. Forty years later he still doubted the utility of the militia: "I do not like in time of War any permanent body of regular Troops in so considerable a number as perhaps to equal the whole of our other Force."[280]

In his "Idea of a Perfect Commonwealth" of 1752, Hume extolled the Swedish combination of a militia with a standing army.[281] Such commentary, Burke noted in 1757, failed to regard the diminutive proportions of the militia in that country as well as the incomparable character of the Swedish constitution. In Britain the proposed size of the militia threatened the predominance of the regular forces, whereas elsewhere citizen armies were kept in "intire Subordination."[282] Burke conceded that a militia had been proposed "by some good men," but more usually it was a component of a disgruntled Tory agenda that began with their opposition to the Revolution settlement and was perpetuated by their hostility to the Whig conception of the balance of power.[283] For the latter, continental alliances needed to be maintained, and a standing force was necessary to service that arrangement.[284] Yet Burke's hostility was focused more clearly on the domestic threat posed by a militia than on the extent to which it would compromise national defence. It was common to think of the people in arms as offering security to constitutional liberty. Yet this perception was based on a fundamental misconception of modern politics. Under primitive regimes appropriate to a pastoral existence, or feudal societies tied almost exclusively to agricultural produce, the resort to arms might serve as an effective means of protecting privileges. Yet with the passage from rudeness to refinement came the transition to constitutional freedom under which liberties were supported by a regulated system of government: "Our liberty is defended by the force of civil institutions," Burke wrote—not by resort to military means.[285]

Before the commercial age, populations were relatively impoverished and dispersed across great stretches of territory. They were consequently disinclined to conspire against authority, and disabled from engaging in subversive cabals. The situation was very different in urban environments. As a consequence, the ancient

[278] EB, *An Essay towards an Abridgement of English History* (1757–c. 1763), *W & S*, I, p. 517.

[279] David Hume, "Of the Protestant Succession" (1752) in idem, *Essays*, p. 509. For discussion, see John Robertson, *The Scottish Enlightenment and the Militia Issue* (Edinburgh: John Donald, 1985), ch. 3.

[280] EB to French Laurence, 18 November 1796, *Corr.*, IX, p. 118.

[281] David Hume, "Idea of a Perfect Commonwealth" (1752) in idem, *Essays*, p. 647n. The comment was removed from collections of Hume's *Essays* after 1768.

[282] EB, "Considerations on a Militia" in Bourke, "Party, Parliament and Conquest," p. 650.

[283] Ibid., p. 649.

[284] Ibid., p. 650.

[285] Ibid., p. 651.

republics disarmed the mass of their citizens except when they assembled for external war.[286] The disorders that overwhelmed medieval and renaissance cities illustrated the peril of populations under arms. Ancient Constantinople and medieval Paris were continually mutinous, while Ghent from the thirteenth century was "furious & ungovernable."[287] Demagogues could prey on ready ears. This problem, Burke went on, was multiplied in modern polities, where trade had formed each country into a grand metropolis. In 1790, with the spectacle of the French Revolution before him, Burke observed how the urban centres of commercial monarchies and republics exacerbated the threat of modern insurgency. Country life was continually "dissolving into individuality" as gentlemen, peasants and yeomen went about their isolated tasks: "combination and arrangement" was foreign to them.[288] The situation was far different in modern Paris: "The habits of burghers, their occupations, their diversion, their business, their idleness, continually bring them into mutual contact."[289] They were constantly exposed to the electric speed of communication, and immediately prone to respond to incitement and alarm. To empower this mass with weaponry was a recipe for tumult. Defections in the royal army in 1789 as well as the insurgent mood in the National Guard under Lafayette's command convinced Burke that his precautionary stance had been perfectly well grounded.[290]

With an upsurge in food riots across Britain in 1757, Burke's disdain for popular armament carried an immediate charge.[291] Modern cities provided the means of unleashing disturbances, while levelling rhetoric could supply the requisite justification for mobilising crowds. As Burke would later emphasise in 1795, dearth might become a weapon at the disposal of demagogues.[292] Despite the fact that current shortages could be explained in terms of the poor harvest, it was not hard to imagine how economic hardship might be construed in political terms: "how easy would it be," Burke speculated, "to give the people[']s fluctuating Minds some dangerous turn, to confound natural with political Evils to animate them with hopes of Gain and Plunder."[293] Scarcity provided conditions for opportunistic attacks on property.

[286] Ibid.

[287] Ibid., p. 652.

[288] EB, *Reflections*, ed. Clark, p. 363 [281–82].

[289] Ibid., p. 364 [283].

[290] See below, chapter 11, section 5.

[291] John Stevenson, *Popular Disturbances in England, 1700–1870* (London: Longman, 1979), p. 91; Nicholas Rogers, *Crowds, Culture and Politics in Georgian Britain* (Oxford: Oxford University Press, 1998), pp. 58–75. On the phenomenon more generally, see R. B. Rose, "Eighteenth-Century Price Riots and Public Policy in England," *International Review of Social History*, 6:2 (1961), pp. 277–92; E. P. Thompson, *The Making of the English Working Class* (Harmondsworth: Penguin, 1963), ch. 3; George Rudé, *The Crowd in History, 1730–1848: A Study of Popular Disturbances in France and England* (New York: John Wiley and Sons, 1964); E. P. Thompson, "The Moral Economy of the English Crowd in the Eighteenth Century," *Past and Present*, 50:1 (February 1971), pp. 76–136; Dale Edward Williams, "Morals, Markets and the English Crowd in 1766," *Past and Present*, 104:1 (August 1984), pp. 56–73.

[292] See below, chapter 16, section 5.

[293] EB, "Considerations on a Militia" in Bourke, "Party, Parliament and Conquest," p. 652.

The availability of arms could convert a mass of protesters into a phalanx of insurgents. Property might be pillaged, and prescription undermined. Already by the end of the 1750s Burke was analysing the supports sustaining civil society, and was conscious of how their security might be undermined.

4.6 *The Annual Register*

Burke's attention in 1757 was also drawn to Ireland. In "Hints of Ireland" he sketched the constitutional status of the kingdom by examining the history of its relations to the British monarchy. It was a subject that he explored more fully in his *Abridgement of English History*. Both these accounts together represent Burke's earliest treatment of a subject to which he would be obliged to return at various stages of his career. What distinguished him as a commentator on Irish affairs was his willingness to examine the constitutional subordination of the kingdom in conjunction with an account of the position of Roman Catholics. He would turn to the issue of religious toleration in Ireland after a period spent in Dublin in the early 1760s. But in the meantime his attention was absorbed by the progress of the war in Europe and the colonies. This was largely determined by his involvement in editing the *Annual Register*. The main aim of that periodical was to provide an overview of the year's developments in an accessible and synoptic form. Burke was engaged by Dodsley to undertake the work in April 1758.[294] His primary responsibility in compiling the *Register* extended down to 1765; a looser connection with the journal continued into the 1790s.[295] When Burke became more heavily involved in public life, a friend of his, Thomas English, took primary charge of the publication, although he was assisted by other associates of Burke. For the period between 1758 and 1765, Burke devised the "historical article" for each year, providing an account of the main occurrences over the previous twelve months.[296] He also selected documents and took charge of the reviews. Some of these were presumably written by himself, although attempts to ascribe definite authorship have shown this to be impossible to confirm.[297]

The period from 1759 proved to be one of considerable frustration for Burke. On the positive side, he had become settled in his private life. He married on 12 March

[294] Ralph Straus, *Robert Dodsley: Poet, Publisher and Playwright* (London: Bodley Head, 1910), pp. 257–58.

[295] Bertram D. Sarason, "Edmund Burke and the Two *Annual Registers*," *Publications of the Modern Language Association*, 68 (1953), pp. 496–508; T. O. McLoughlin, *Edmund Burke and the First Ten Years of the "Annual Register," 1758–1767* (Salisbury: University of Rhodesia Press, 1975).

[296] John C. Weston Jr., "Burke's Authorship of the 'Historical Articles' in Dodsley's *Annual Register*," *Papers of the Bibliographical Society of America*, 51 (1957), pp. 244–49.

[297] Thomas W. Copeland, *Edmund Burke: Six Essays* (London: Jonathan Cape, 1950), chs. 3 and 4; James E. Tierney, "Edmund Burke, John Hawkesbury, the *Annual Register*, and the *Gentleman's Magazine*," *Huntington Library Quarterly*, 42 (1978), pp. 7–72; Lock, *Burke*, I, pp. 165ff.

1757, soon moving to Battersea just outside London.[298] His first son, Richard, was born on 9 February 1758. Christopher, a second son who died in childhood, arrived ten months later. The Burkes now moved to Marylebone, closer to central London. In the years that followed, Burke cultivated a number of close friendships. By 1759 he had got to know David Hume pretty well. Oliver Goldsmith and Arthur Murphy were close acquaintances. Joshua Reynolds, David Garrick, Elizabeth Montagu and Samuel Johnson became steadfast friends.[299] The Literary Club, located above the Turk's Head on Gerrard Street in Soho, provided a venue for sociability from 1764. Nonetheless, Burke looked back on these years as a lost opportunity in his intellectual and literary trajectory. His sole achievement was his work on *The Annual Register*: the *Abridgement* lay unfinished and his work on Ireland bore little fruit. Most of his energy was exhausted by his engagement to a new patron, William Gerard Hamilton.

Hamilton had entered parliament as a follower of Henry Fox in 1754. Within two years he joined Lord Halifax at the Board of Trade, accompanying him to Ireland as Chief Secretary in 1761.[300] Having failed in the autumn of 1759 to secure the position of consul at Madrid, Burke accepted the role of secretary to Hamilton.[301] By now the fortunes of the British in the Seven Years' War had begun to recover. The conflict stretched over an extensive theatre of operations, virtually spanning the globe; it affected Europe, North America, Central America, West Africa, South Asia and the Philippines. Serious contests occupied the British and the French across America, encompassing Canada, Pennsylvania and the Caribbean islands. Battles were similarly conducted over the fate of Silesia and for the control of the Carnatic in South Asia. Over the same period, Prussia and Sweden launched counter-attacks in Pomeranian territory. On 1 August 1759, the allies prevailed over the forces of Louis XV at Minden in Westphalia. Burke noted the desultory performance of the commander-in-chief of the British forces, yet there was no denying the improved position of the allies.[302] Wolfe's victory at Quebec on 13 September 1759 was a further major boon. Two naval victories similarly disabled the French, first in the Mediterranean and then in Quiberon Bay. The Prussians, on the other hand, were sorely pressed: Frederick suffered a bruising defeat at the Battle of Kunersdorf; the following summer the Austrians routed his army at Landshut. Nonetheless, when parliament met in the wake of British victories by sea and land, Pitt was openly ebullient about the prospects for the future. Lord Villiers moved an address extolling the "glories" of the previous months.[303]

[298] *Notes and Queries*, 5 (8 April 1882), pp. 274–75.

[299] Donald C. Bryant, *Edmund Burke and His Literary Friends* (St. Louis, MO: Washington University Studies, 1939).

[300] Thomas W. Copeland, "Burke's First Patron," *History Today*, 2 (1952), pp. 394–99.

[301] On the Madrid posting, see EB to Mrs. Elizabeth Montagu, 24 September 1759, *Corr.*, I, pp. 131–34.

[302] EB to Robert Dodsley, c. 6 September 1759, ibid., pp. 127–28.

[303] *Parliamentary History*, XV, col. 953.

That same year, Burke composed the first of his accounts of the progress of the war: *The Annual Register* for 1758, written in 1759, opened by tracing the origins of the current struggle for power in Europe. It was, Burke wrote, "an almost general and very important war," and for that reason merited a narrative of its beginnings and subsequent course.[304] He recollected the desperate situation a year into the war. With repeated setbacks abroad and the changes of ministry at home, "we almost despaired of our military virtue; public spirit appeared extinguished, and the rage of faction burned with the utmost violence."[305] The nation was divided into the supporters of Leicester House, the followers of Newcastle and the partisans of Pitt. At its most extreme, these divisions took the form of a polar opposition between the devotees of "influence" and the champions of "popularity": the former camp endorsed the executive management of parliament, registered their concern for the balance of power in Europe, and publicised their commitment to the war on the continent; their rivals espoused the cause of independence in public life, advertised the need for popular backing for the ministry, and advocated the primacy of the navy and the militia.[306]

The extremity of these polarities threatened the country with ruin: "it was high time our domestic factions should be composed at last."[307] The reasonableness of a medium course between a naval and a continental war urged itself upon dispassionate observers. With the establishment of a coalition between the contending parties, Britain was in a position to apply itself to victory and reverse the humiliation of 1756–7: "There reigned in both houses [of parliament] the most perfect and unprecedented union."[308] Power and patriotism were now combined, liberty and order reconciled. The fruits of cooperation began to appear with the successes at Minden and Quebec, yet still there was no end to hostilities in sight. After the opening flurry of excitement, the various powers in the struggle had grown steadily more cautious. Parity among the contenders had gradually become apparent, though none of them was prepared to withdraw and accept even minor losses. Victory would now be a matter of marginal skill together with the command over resources.[309] It seemed to Burke by the end of 1759 that Britain might have the edge in the competition. The management of finance supplied a clear advantage: while France was virtually bankrupt, British credit continued to appear buoyant. The government had succeeded in borrowing 6 million pounds at favourable interest with repayments to be covered by a tax on malt. Only the failure of Britain's allies could now compromise this lead.[310]

Burke was thinking of the plight of Frederick the Great. By 1760, his forces were under considerable strain from the Russians and facing further pressure from

[304] "The History of the Present War" in *The Annual Register for the Year 1758*, p. 2.
[305] Ibid., p. 10.
[306] Ibid., pp. 10–13.
[307] Ibid., p. 13.
[308] "The History of the Present War" in *The Annual Register for the Year 1759*, p. 7.
[309] Ibid., pp. 1–2.
[310] Ibid., p. 56.

the combined strength of France's allies. British support for Prussia in the form of subsidies for its troops would be subject to renewed scrutiny by opponents of continental warfare. Even Newcastle recognised that the Prussian leader had become a liability.[311] The problem was compounded by the accession of George III on 25 October 1760. The new king and his favourite, the Earl of Bute, favoured the pursuit of a naval campaign against France, redirecting attention from the operations in Europe. That November, Israel Mauduit revived the fortunes of the old "blue-water" strategy with an attack on Britain's embroilment in the German war.[312] The new king, in his speech from the throne, made clear his scepticism about the virtue of further entanglements across the Channel.[313] By March 1761, Holderness had been replaced by Bute as Northern Secretary. A reorientation of policy was underway, and hopes for a resolution began to increase. "The stocks rise," Burke wrote in the summer of 1761: a cessation of operations was expected soon.[314] In the midst of these developments, what staggered Burke was how indecisive the military contest was proving to be. Despite a string of defeats, Frederick the Great was still secure in his dominions: he had not been "despoiled of a single town."[315] The most notable feature of the current epic struggle between the great powers was that individual victories were incapable of deciding the war. The Duke of Brunswick's success in driving the enemy form the Rhine left the European balance where it stood; Broglie failed to enter Hanover after his victory at Bergen; the French could still advance their cause after the rout at Minden.[316] The clash was at an impasse, yet despite the apparent stalemate contention persisted.

Even so, the terms on which peace might be secured continued to be debated. William Burke contributed to the stream of polemic. In his *Remarks on the Letter Address'd to Two Great Men*, he accepted that Britain's overall aim should be "to possess a just Weight, and Consideration in *Europe*; and that the power of the nation should be rather respectable than terrible."[317] The question was how that "Weight" could be achieved, above all in terms of the balance of colonial empires. Specifically, Britain had to decide on whether Canada should be retained, in which case the sugar island of Guadeloupe would be given up to the French.[318] William was keen to insist upon the folly of this proposal: "I shall not hesitate to say, that an Island Colony, is always more advantageous than a Continental one, for the Mother Country."[319] The

[311] Philip C. Yorke, *The Life and Correspondence of Philip Yorke, Earl of Hardwicke, Lord High Chancellor of Great Britain* (Cambridge: Cambridge University Press, 1913), 3 vols., III, p. 313.

[312] Israel Mauduit, *Considerations of the Present German War* (London: 1760).

[313] *Parliamentary History*, XV, cols. 981ff.

[314] EB to Charles O'Hara, 3 July 1761, *Corr.*, I, p. 138.

[315] "The History of the Present War," in *The Annual Register for the Year 1760*, p. 1.

[316] Ibid., p. 2.

[317] [William Burke], *Remarks on the Letter Address'd to Two Great Men, in a Letter to the Author of that Piece* (London: 3rd rev. ed., 1760), p. 17.

[318] This had been proposed in December 1759 in [Anon.], *A Letter Address'd to Two Great Men, on the Prospect of Peace* (London: 1769), to which William Burke was responding.

[319] [William Burke], *Remarks*, p. 46.

northern colonies were keen on the retention of Canada for the purposes of their own security, yet the commercial interest of Britain appeared to William to lie in the south.[320] Trade with the Caribbean was based on "natural" reciprocity, whereas the produce of New England overlapped with that of the metropole.[321] Moreover, the northern colonies would be ultimately tempted by independence: "they must live wholly on their own Labour, and in process of Time will know little, enquire little, and care little about the Mother Country."[322]

For the moment, peace negotiations could make no headway, and the blockage in accepting a resolution to the war continued. A general lesson could be drawn from this experience, Burke thought. The balance of power was successfully maintaining the liberty of Europe, but it could not compel the protagonists to agree a peace. The extent of the war was fantastic, with the result that a conclusion became all the more elusive. A loss in one portion of the sprawling theatre might be compensated by a gain in another. The intrigues in every court ensured the dispute would be protracted as rival powers pushed for any marginal advantage. Equality of power enjoined treating with the enemy; pride propelled the opponents to maintain their disagreements: "the spirit of intrigue, which is the political distemper of the time, that anxious foresight which forms the character of all the present courts," was inhibiting the adoption of moderate counsel.[323] The following year Burke returned to the same theme. Terms for peace had been proposed at the end of 1759, but the war still spluttered on in 1761. The sublime battles that dominated the early stages of the conflict—those "vast events that astonish the mind"—had been succeeded by smaller skirmishes and the machinations of cabinets. The antagonists faced one another in a position of parity, but they would not conclude a treaty on that basis: they wanted instead to compel their enemies to accept a deal, to drive them to the table as a matter of "*necessity*." This, in effect, was a policy of conquest in lieu of accepting the need for rapprochement on equal terms. It was, Burke noted, a widely popular posture, yet at the same time it was practically forlorn: "In fact, it is to the last degree difficult to reduce any of the great powers of Europe to this disgraceful necessity."[324]

George III was now arguing for a separate peace with France, abandoning the Prussians to their fate. Pitt nonetheless insisted on maintaining the current

[320] For the wider context, see W. L. Grant, "Canada versus Guadeloupe: An Episode of the Seven Years' War," *American Historical Review*, 17 (1911–12), pp. 735–43; Peter N. Miller, *Defining the Common Good: Empire, Religion and Philosophy in Eighteenth-Century Britain* (Cambridge: Cambridge University Press, 1994), pp. 172–74.

[321] [William Burke], *Remarks*, p. 49. Cf. [William Burke], *An Examination of the Commercial Principles of the Late Negotiation between Great Britain and France in 1761* (London: 2nd ed., 1761), pp. 24–25, where he advances the same argument, this time in opposition to Benjamin Franklin, *The Interest of Great Britain, with Regard to her Colonies* (London: 1760). Burke briefly alludes to William Burke's position in EB to Charles O'Hara, ante 23 August 1762, *Corr.*, I, p. 148.

[322] [William Burke], *Remarks*, p. 50.

[323] "The History of the Present War," in *The Annual Register for the Year 1760*, p. 3.

[324] "The History of the Present War" in *The Annual Register for the Year 1761*, p. 2.

"system."[325] The fortunes of Frederick the Great then shifted dramatically: Peter III succeeded Elizabeth of Russia and recalled his troops from the heart of Prussia, thus enabling Frederick to concentrate his forces against the Austrians. While Prussia prospered, Britain was newly assailed: Spain joined the war with France in January 1762, with Portugal being recruited as a British ally. Pitt had been keen to launch a pre-emptive strike against the Bourbon alliance and resigned when Bute and Newcastle refused to support his schemes. According to Burke, the cabinet regarded Pitt as dangerous and extreme: "They thought his principles too violent and they did not perfectly like his person."[326] Moves towards a settlement got under way after his withdrawal. On 28 July 1762, the Duke of Bedford was sent to Paris to negotiate a peace. He was, as Charles O'Hara commented to Burke, "the properest man in England to bring the French to speak with precision." Nonetheless, Burke's friend worried about the outcome of the talks, arguing that Spain and Portugal would have to be included in any settlement.[327] Burke himself aired his displeasure later that autumn: "I own I think it hard to form an idea of a shameful peace, if this is not the most shameful that ever was made."[328]

When parliament opened on 25 November 1762, Burke expected the sparring over foreign policy to be conducted with singular "acrimony." Pitt was set to attack the peace as "*felonious*" and "inglorious."[329] Newcastle had been replaced by Bute in May 1762, and so the Duke looked set to oppose the new first minister. As it turned out, the king's speech opening the new session proved bland and uneventful.[330] Newcastle adapted poorly to his new role in opposition. It was the end of an era in British public life. The Pelhams had formed an interest in parliament and the nation, exemplified by Newcastle's politicking and largesse. He formed an edifice of power that would prove difficult to shake. Under George II, Burke observed, Newcastle directed government almost without the king's "control."[331] At first, with the inauguration of the new regime, the influence of Newcastle appeared as solid as ever. However, he lacked a key ingredient of preponderating power—"the r[oyal] confidence," upon which the effective management of parliament still depended.[332] With the favourite now installed in the senior counsels of the nation, Newcastle's days were numbered. A group of supporters followed him out of government, creating space for the inclusion "of those called Tories, or country gentlemen."[333] Exploded party

[325] Richard Middleton, *The Bells of Victory: The Pitt-Newcastle Ministry and the Conduct of the Seven Years' War, 1757–1762* (Cambridge: Cambridge University Press, 1985, 2002), p. 170.

[326] "The History of the Present War" in *The Annual Register for the Year 1762*, p. 46.

[327] Charles O'Hara to EB, 10 August 1762, *Corr.*, I, p. 145.

[328] EB to Charles O'Hara, 30 October 1762, ibid, p. 152.

[329] EB to Charles O'Hara, 23 November 1762, ibid., p. 155,

[330] EB to Charles O'Hara, 25 November 1762, ibid., p. 156.

[331] "The History of the Present War" in *The Annual Register for the Year 1762*, p. 46.

[332] Ibid.

[333] Ibid., p. 47.

distinctions now reappeared on the scene, distracting both the nation and the Commons. Under these circumstances, further prosecution of the war became difficult. The connection between the old corps and the monied interest made peace a priority because the ministry feared for its ability to sustain financial credit. Burke concluded: "These causes co-operated to render the intentions of the British ministry towards peace altogether cordial and sincere."[334] Since his accession to the throne, George III informed parliament, he had been focused on bringing about an honourable peace. Now "an immense territory" had been added to the Empire, and "a solid foundation for the increase of trade and commerce" had been laid."[335] It was time to reach an agreement with the French.

Burke was doubtful about what had been achieved. He was scathing about Lord Egmont's support for the crown in the House of Lords: "The general drift of his discourse was to shew we are a reduced, beggard, depopulated, undone Nation, who are notwithstanding very Victorious[,] glorious &c. &c in the stile which you will find the bon ton among us at present."[336] The galleries were cleared for the discussion of the peace preliminaries, preventing Burke from actually attending the debates.[337] He was nonetheless determined to keep himself informed. The position of the government dismayed him: it was, after all, "a bad peace."[338] Too much had been conceded from a position of strength. Over the course of the war, British forces had seized Canada, Guadeloupe, Martinique, Dominica, Tobago, St. Vincent, Grenada, Pondicherry, Senegal, Manilla, Havana and Belle Île. French control of the St. Lawrence had come to an end. Yet now it was proposed that Martinique and Guadeloupe should returned to the enemy, while French fishing rights off the Newfoundland coast were to be restored. Despite his opposition to the concessions, Newcastle's performance in the Lords appeared "ridiculous." Equally disappointing, Pitt delivered an apology for his own behaviour instead of tackling the substance of the peace preliminaries.[339] In general, opposition was "warm" but "ineffective."[340] For the government, Lord Halifax performed "above par." Only Lord Mansfield, "with his usual dexterity," impressed.[341] The Treaty of Paris was finally signed on 10 February 1763. Within two months George Grenville would replace Lord Bute as First Lord of the Treasury. Britain had emerged victorious after years of arduous struggle, yet many regarded the peace as a respite instead of a settlement. Vergennes already looked

[334] Ibid.

[335] *Parliamentary History*, XV, col. 1234.

[336] EB to Charles O'Hara, 25 November 1762, *Corr.*, I, p. 158.

[337] EB to Charles O'Hara, 9 December 1762, ibid., p. 158.

[338] EB to Charles O'Hara, 12 December 1762, ibid., p. 160.

[339] Ibid.

[340] "The History of Europe" in *The Annual Register for the Year 1763*, p. 33. Cf. "The History of Europe" in *The Annual Register for the Year 1764*, p. 18: on the "peace, to which so trifling an opposition had been made in parliament."

[341] EB to Charles O'Hara, 12 December 1762, *Corr.*, I, p. 160.

forward to a renewal of hostilities.[342] The sheer extent of British territory, and the complexity of its commerce, promised fresh challenges in the immediate term.[343]

Attacks by a confederacy of American Indian tribes led by Pontiac, the Ottawa chief, against British settlers around the Great Lakes showed that the frontiers of the Empire posed a problem for the metropole. Forts across North American territory would have to be defended. Expectations of costs were liable to induce alarm as the nation sought to manage its extravagant debt. Nonetheless, public attention for the most part reverted to the domestic scene: "dissentions" at home "supplied the place" of foreign entanglements.[344] Party now seemed to Burke a positive aspect of the constitution: given the healthy state of the British constitution, "jars" were likely to do "very little mischief." In fact they represented a positive development, ensuring that national character would not stagnate: "There are times, when the spirit of liberty, must owe something to the spirit of faction."[345] Burke's personal situation was less promising, however. His lack of literary achievement had begun to irritate and depress him. In 1763, he was awarded £300 on the Irish establishment, but the security failed to bring him psychological relief. Up until now, while he delivered on his obligation to Dodsley regarding *The Annual Register*, his time and efforts had been monopolised by his patron. Though he thought of himself as engaged to Hamilton as a sort of "companion" in the MP's studies, his energy and attention had been engrossed.[346] He was therefore unable to make any headway with his career as an author, not having published a new work since 1757. He began to panic. His resentment rose. He started to regard Hamilton's demands as an imposition, indeed as a presumptuous interference with his freedom.

Burke needed the intervals between public business for his own projects—"to study and consult proper books."[347] The summers were likely to offer the most fertile period for research. However, the opportunity was consistently denied him. By July 1764, his strained relationship with Hamilton was reaching breaking point. At that time, Burke's brother was heading off to accept a posting in the Caribbean, while Hamilton himself was dismissed as Chief Secretary to the Lord Lieutenant.[348] Burke began to cast about for vacancies abroad.[349] With Hamilton back in London still holding a seat in the House of Commons, he seems to have sought to bind Burke to permanent secretarial service. This smacked of "settled servitude" to Burke, who

[342] Simms, *Three Victories*, p. 502.

[343] *The Annual Register for the Year 1763*, "Preface." Burke seems to have completed most the work on this year's *Register* by February 1764. See EB to James Dodsley, 19 February 1764, *Corr.*, I, pp. 174–75. The work appeared on 17 May 1764.

[344] *The Annual Register for the Year 1764*, "Preface."

[345] Ibid.

[346] EB to William Gerard Hamilton, March 1763, *Corr.*, I, pp. 164–65.

[347] Ibid., p. 165.

[348] EB to Richard Shackleton, 17 July 1764, ibid., pp. 175–76.

[349] EB to William Young, 31 December 1764, ibid., pp. 176–77.

duly bridled.[350] Angry recrimination on both sides followed.[351] The relationship was irreparably at an end. By July 1765, both William and Edmund Burke had been recommended to the Marquess of Rockingham. A new ministry, headed by Rockingham, was in the process of formation. By 11 July Burke was installed as private secretary to the Marquess.[352] His career was about to take a turn for the better. He would manage to reconcile immersion in routine politics with his ambitions as literary figure. Soon he would also reveal his genius as a public orator: the following January he secured a seat in House of Commons.

4.7 The Irish Popery Laws

The Earl of Halifax was appointed Lord Lieutenant of Ireland on 20 March 1761. He arrived in Dublin on 6 October for the opening of parliament on College Green two weeks later.[353] His main agent in the Irish legislature would be Hamilton as Chief Secretary. Burke set off in the summer to prepare the way for his superiors. Before long he established contact with his friends and intimates. Beaumont Brennan, who had gone to London, was now dead; however, Burke was soon in touch with Richard Shackleton and William Dennis.[354] He had reconciled with his father the previous year, although Burke senior died three months after his son took up residence in Dublin Castle.[355] While this was Burke's first visit to Ireland since 1750, the country's problems had not been absent from his thoughts in the interim. Its current predicament, he thought, was a legacy of its past. Historical analysis drew him back towards the advent of the Norman Lordship. It was necessary to have some sense of the original state of the country to understand the impact of the conquest and its aftermath. This, however, was to enter into uncertain territory. "The people of Ireland lay claim to a very extravagant antiquity," Burke remarked in the *Abridgement*. Yet he believed that the resulting "tales" frequently bordered on "absurdity."[356]

[350] EB to William Gerard Hamilton, ante 12 February 1765, ibid., p. 180.

[351] EB to William Gerard Hamilton, ante 12 February 1765, ibid., pp. 182–87; EB to William Gerard Hamilton, 10 April 1765, ibid., pp. 188–89; Hamilton's Notes on EB's conduct, ibid., pp. 189–91; EB to Henry Flood, 18 May 1765, ibid., pp. 192–95; EB to John Monck Mason, post 29 May 1765, ibid., pp. 195–98; EB to John Hely Hutchinson, May 1765, ibid., p. 198–201.

[352] EB to Charles O'Hara, 11 July 1765, ibid., p. 211.

[353] See "Dunk, George Montagu" in the *Dictionary of Irish Biography, from the Earliest Times to the Year 2002*, ed. James Maguire and James Quinn (Cambridge: Cambridge University Press, 2009), 9 vols.

[354] EB to Richard Shackleton, 25 August 1761, *Corr.*, I, pp. 142–43.

[355] EB to Agmondesham Vesey, 10 September 1760, ibid., pp. 136–37. The way for a meeting was still being prepared the following year: see EB to Charles O'Hara, 3 July 1761, ibid., p. 139.

[356] EB, *An Essay towards an Abridgement of English History* (1757–c. 1763), *W & S*, I, pp. 509–10. Burke's scepticism was presumably directed against Roderick O'Flaherty, *Ogygia, seu, rerum Hibernicarum chronologia* (London: 1685). He subsequently developed a sympathetic interest in the study of Irish antiquities as it revived in Ireland around this time. See Clare O'Halloran, *Golden Ages and Barbarous Nations: Antiquarian Debate and Cultural Political in Ireland, c. 1750–1800* (Cork: Field Day, 2005). Some of Burke's interest can be traced through his relationship with Charles Vallencey: see

By the time the Normans arrived, the natives still retained the primitive manners of "the original Celtae," despite their conversion to the Christian religion.[357] This meant that, like the Saxons, they retained the customs of gavelkind and tanistry. The latter was attended "with very great and pernicious inconveniences," most particularly disputes over succession.[358] On the other hand, the offices of judge and other professions were kept within specific hereditary orders. "Scythian" attitudes still prevailed; defence was preserved by a militia; and there was only the sparsest scattering of towns. Above all, the people were "addicted" to pasturage instead of practising agriculture.[359]

The beginning of the end for the "mere" Irish came with the intrusion of the Normans between 1169 and 1172.[360] Landing at Waterford on 11 October 1171, Henry II accepted pledges of fealty from the Irish kings, and proceeded to incorporate the Lordship of Ireland within the Angevin Empire. According to Burke, he left the Irish chiefs "everything but the honour of their independency."[361] Feudal tenures were accordingly introduced into the country, though these were confined within the territories that supported a Norman allegiance. Burke gestured at the story down to 1603: it would prove "long" before the English were able to "subdue the island," yet "the continual efforts of the Irish, for more than four hundred years, proved insufficient to dislodge" their opponents.[362] Final subjection came at the start of the Jacobean reign, celebrated in John Davies's tract on the defeat of "the Irishry," though "perfect" conquest in the form of comprehensive pacification eluded British policy down to the eighteenth century.[363] Part of this failure stemmed from the aborted project of assimilation, beginning with the antipathies between feudal settlers and native barbarians, and continuing with the animosity between colonial Protestants and Roman Catholics. It also derived from controversy about the terms of Irish subjection, based on the disputed terms of loyalty to Henry II.

Walter D. Love, "Edmund Burke, Charles Vallencey and the Sebright Manuscripts," *Hermathena*, 95 (1961), pp. 21–35; Monica Nevin, "General Charles Vallancey, 1725–1812," *Journal of the Royal Society of Antiquaries*, 123 (1993), pp. 19–58. Burke also corresponded with Sylvester O'Halloran, whose contributions to the subject started to appear in the 1770s. For Burke's relationships with Irish antiquaries more generally, see Walter D. Love, "Edmund Burke and an Irish Historiographical Controversy," *History and Theory*, 2:2 (1962), pp. 180–98. His "Countenance" and "Encouragement" are acknowledged in Charles O'Conor, *Dissertations on the History of Ireland, to which is Subjoined a Dissertation on the Irish Colonies Established in Britain* (Dublin: 2nd ed., 1766), p. xv.

357 EB, *An Essay towards an Abridgement of English History* (1757–c. 1763), *W & S*, I, p. 509.

358 Ibid. p. 511.

359 Ibid., p. 512.

360 Mere was the standard term for pure. See Joep Leerssen, *Mere Irish and Fíor-Ghael: Studies in the Idea of Irish Nationality, its Development and Literary Expression prior to the Nineteenth Century* (Cork: Field Day, 1996).

361 EB, *An Essay towards an Abridgement of English History* (1757–c. 1763), *W & S*, I, p. 513.

362 Ibid., p. 514.

363 On John Davies, *Discoverie of the True Cause why Ireland was never Entirely Subdued nor Brought under Obedience of the Crowne of England, untill the Beginning of His Majesties Happie Raigne* (London: 1612), see below, chapter 9, section 5 and chapter 14, section 6.

Burke's fragmentary essay from 1757, "Hints of Ireland," was intended to address disagreement about the relations between the two kingdoms. Ireland had been invaded by Henry II, but it had not been subject to violent subjugation according to Burke. Edward Coke had argued that Ireland "originally came to the kings of England by conquest."[364] Subsequent commentators were determined to clarify what this meant. William Molyneux was prominent amongst them. In 1698, in the context of mounting controversy over restrictions on Irish trade, Molyneux rejected claims that the parliament in Dublin was subject to the legislative authority of Westminster.[365] He noted, citing Spelman, that while Henry II was certainly a "conqueror," his title was based on acquisition by peaceful annexation.[366] The crucial point was that Ireland was governed by consent, which for Molyneux carried the corollary that the parliament of England had no jurisdiction over the sister kingdom.[367] Burke added to this discussion in "Hints of Ireland" by clarifying the nature of the "Homage" paid by the Irish. First this was a personal relationship between lord and vassal, and did not automatically transfer to later generations. Second it implied reciprocity on both sides rather than "absolute" power on the part of Henry II. Finally, and most importantly, it was not possible to offer homage to a corporate person, and so fealty to the English parliament could never have been part of the original bargain. Ireland, in short, was not held by the English by "right of Conquest": government was instead established on the basis of mutual "compact." Therefore, "neither expressly nor tacitly" could the Irish "have been supposed to give the *People* of England, any power over their Lives, Liberties, or Estates."[368]

Conclusions of this kind were commonly used to bolster "patriot" politics in Ireland.[369] Burke, however, had little enthusiasm for the cause. As he prepared to move his family to Dublin to serve under Hamilton, Charles Lucas had returned to Ireland to launch a campaign for shorter parliaments. "I own I am somewhat out of humour with patriotism," Burke admitted to Charles O'Hara when reflecting on Lucas's campaign.[370] O'Hara was a descendant of a prominent Gaelic family

[364] Edward Coke, "Calvin's Case, or the Case of the Postnati" in *The Seventh Part of the Reports* (London: 1608) in *The Selected Writings of Sir Edward Coke*, ed. Steve Sheppard (Indianapolis, IN: Liberty Fund), 3 vols., I, p. 218.

[365] Patrick Kelly, "William Molyneux and the Spirit of Liberty in Eighteenth-Century Ireland," *Eighteenth-Century Ireland*, 3 (1988), pp. 133–48. See also Jacqueline Hill, "Ireland without Union: Molyneux and His Legacy" in John Robertson ed., *A Union for Empire: Political Thought and the Union of 1707* (Cambridge: Cambridge University Press, 1995).

[366] William Molyneux, *The Case of Ireland's Being Bound by Acts of Parliament in England, Stated* (Dublin: 1798), pp. 12–13. For his account of the relevant events Molyneux substantially followed Giraldus Cambrensis, *Expugnatio Hibernica* (1189), ed. A. B. Scott and F. X. Martin (Dublin: Royal Irish Academy, 1978).

[367] Molyneux, *The Case*, p. 17. The debate is alluded to in the review of Ferdinando Warner, *The History of Ireland* (London: 1763) in *The Annual Register for the Year 1763*, pp. 257–64, most likely by Burke.

[368] EB, "Hints of Ireland" (1757) in Bourke, "Party, Parliament and Conquest," p. 643.

[369] On the career of patriot politics in Dublin, see Jacqueline Hill, *From Patriots to Unionists: Dublin Civil Politics and Irish Protestant Patriotism, 1660–1840* (Oxford: Oxford University Press, 1997).

[370] EB to Charles O'Hara, 3 July 1761, *Corr.*, I, p. 139.

which had been reconciled to the Protestant establishment without severing its ties to the Catholic majority. His mother was a Catholic, and his male ancestors were converts.[371] His correspondence with Burke exhibits a rare openness and intimacy. Both were committed to the cause of Catholic relief under the Hanoverians. They also shared an allegiance to Whig principles in politics, which included disdain for the kind of "fanatical spirit" that Burke detected in Lucas.[372] However, opposition to patriot posturing did not imply passive obedience to reigning power. A proposal in 1762 to have the number of troops on the Irish establishment increased met with acquiescence on the part of the Irish government. Burke found this supine acceptance at once docile and aggressive: fawning towards authority, imperious towards the Catholic Irish. He reported that assurances had been given by the Protestant establishment to the effect that the measure was agreeable to "the whole People of Ireland."[373] Burke's reference to the entirety of the population was ironic. As he was acutely aware, the phrase usually elided Catholic residents in the country: only Anglicans properly constituted the "people" of Ireland.[374] Burke claimed to be perplexed by the attitudes of the prevailing minority: "For my part this same people of Ireland, their notions and their inclinations have always been a riddle to me."[375] They abhorred a civil while they coveted a military establishment, Burke observed. They were, he implied, a garrison settlement: jealous of their liberty in relation to the metropole yet anxious to preserve their privileges over the majority population.

Their paradoxical position was explicable in terms of their character: "The Truth is this military servitude is what they have grown up under; and like all licentious, and wild, but corrupt people, they love a Jobb better than a Salary."[376] This was Burke's earliest reference to the jobbish character of the administration in Ireland. Corruption was a function of its garrison mentality. Members of government clung to power by pleading their loyalty to the Protestant cause and their indispensable role in securing the connection between the two kingdoms. Success in that venture depended on advertising threats to existing constitutional arrangements. Towards that end, fears of a reprise of 1641 were encouraged. Popularity could be won amongst the Protestant electorate by fostering sectarian prejudice, associating Catholicism with bloody rebellion. As a result, both the constituencies and sections of the administration were disposed towards intolerance. "I hate to think of Ireland," Burke confided to O'Hara, "though my thoughts involuntarily take that turn, and whenever

[371] See above, chapter 1, section 2.

[372] EB to Charles O'Hara, 3 July 1761, *Corr.*, I, p. 139.

[373] EB to Charles O'Hara, 30 December 1762, ibid., p. 161.

[374] The phrase had been resonant since [Jonathan Swift], *A Letter to the Whole People of Ireland* (Dublin: 1724), addressed in practice to full Protestant members of the civil community. On this, see S. J. Connolly, *Divided Kingdom: Ireland, 1660–1800* (Oxford: Oxford University Press, 2008), pp. 226–27.

[375] EB to Charles O'Hara, 30 December 1762, *Corr.*, I, p. 161.

[376] Ibid.

they do meet only with objects of grief and indignation."[377] The grief was caused by the continuation of the popery laws in Ireland, the indignation by the attitude of the Protestant minority. Burke's consternation rose during his stay at Dublin Castle in 1761, and persisted through the lord lieutenancy of Halifax. The chief cause was the treatment meted out to the perpetrators of agrarian disorders that began in Munster around 1761.[378] In Burke's view, landlords and local magistrates were equally culpable in their behaviour. Their persecuting conduct was reminiscent of the severity of unfeeling conquerors—Cortez, Pizzarro and Cromwell were Burke's examples.[379]

Agrarian outrages were being deliberately misrepresented as a form of incipient rebellion. Burke returned to this theme in 1763. As alarm about rural atrocities rose, which Burke attributed to the social grievances of agrarian levellers, he wrote to his lawyer complaining about opportunistic Protestant bigotry: "they are reviving Rebellion stories."[380] These "stories" referred to feats of massacre expected of Irish Catholics since the circulation of narrative accounts of the horrors of 1641. John Temple's *Irish Rebellion*, in publicising appalling tales of the unanticipated ferocity of Catholic rage, gave currency to forebodings of native insurgency that would inevitably take revenge upon Protestant estates.[381] Attempts to counteract the impact of Temple's history had been under way among pro-Catholic publicists since 1740.[382] John Curry, whose grandfather had fallen as a Catholic cavalry officer at the Battle of Aughrim in 1691, systematically applied himself to challenging sectarian assumptions about 1641 in the aftermath of the Jacobite rising of 1745. This resulted in his 1747 *Account of the Irish Rebellion*, whose arguments were reformatted in 1758.[383] In the 1760s, Curry became a correspondent of Burke, whom he expected to help revise the "myth" of 1641.[384] By then, together with Thomas Wyse and Charles O'Conor, he had formed the Catholic Committee to campaign for the repeal of the popery laws.[385] Wyse was a Waterford Catholic whose son converted in 1763; O'Conor was a scholar and activist whose family estates had been confiscated

[377] Ibid., p. 162.

[378] See below, chapter 5, section 3.

[379] EB to Charles O'Hara, ante 23 August 1762, *Corr.*, I, p. 147.

[380] EB to John Ridge, 23 April 1763, ibid., p. 169.

[381] John Temple, *Irish Rebellion; or an History of the Beginning and First Progresse of the Generall Rebellion Raised within the Kingdom of Ireland upon the . . . 23 Oct. 1641* (London: 1646).

[382] [Anon.], *Some Considerations of the Laws which Incapacitate the Roman Catholicks of Ireland* (Dublin: 1740), p. 26, emphasises the de facto loyalty of the Catholics of Ireland.

[383] [John Curry], *A Brief Account from Authentic Protestant Writers of the Causes, Motives and Mischiefs of the Irish Rebellion of . . . 1641* (London: 1747). The material was reworked for [John Curry], *Historical Memoirs of the Irish Rebellion, in the Year 1641* (London: 1758). In due course Curry wrote the *Historical and Critical Review of the Civil Wars in Ireland* (London: 1775) in order to refute the claims of Thomas Leland, *History of Ireland, from the Invasion of Henry II* (London: 1773), 3 vols.

[384] John Curry to EB, 24 February 1764, WWM BkP 1:31; John Curry to EB, 8 June 1765, WWM BkP 1:49. For Burke's relations with Curry and Charles O'Conor at this time, see John C. Weston, "Edmund Burke's Irish History: A Hypothesis," *Publications of the Modern Language Association*, 77:4 (September 1962), pp. 397–403.

[385] Thomas Wyse, *Historical Sketch of the Late Catholic Association* (London: 1829), 2 vols.

in 1691.[386] Their campaign with Curry aimed at the assimilation of the Catholic population on the basis of loyalty to the idea of revolution principles. Refutation of the false allegations surrounding 1641 was a component of the project to vindicate Catholic allegiance in the context of the Protestant succession.

In the first of his Stuart volumes, which appeared in 1754, Hume had revived the spectre of 1641 in a rendition of the rebellion based largely on Temple and his disciples. "Without provocation, without opposition," he claimed, "the astonished English, living in profound peace, and full security, were massacred by their nearest neighbours, with whom they had long upheld a continued intercourse of kindness and good offices."[387] These claims seemed like a serious provocation to Burke, who regarded the partiality of the "philosophical" historian of Britain as a product of general prejudice against religion. Burke later claimed that he had studied these events "with more Care than is common," leading him to the conclusion that the rising had been provoked.[388] O'Conor was likewise dismayed by the presumptuousness of Hume.[389] After all, the depiction in the *History* of the turmoil surrounding 1641 took the form of an indictment of "superstition." "Amidst these enormities," Hume wrote, "the sacred name of Religion resounded on every side."[390] There was a vicious circularity, Burke came to believe, between the misrepresentation of events in 1641, the portrayal of ongoing Catholic discontent as malevolent subversion, and the maintenance of penal statutes for the purpose of persecuting popery. Any attempt to alleviate the laws against Catholics heightened sensitivities and stirred sectarian responses. A proposal to raise five regiments of Catholic soldiers in Ireland for service in the final stages of the Seven Years' War, reported in *The Annual Register* for 1762, was typical of the alarmist reaction prompted by schemes for relief.[391] The plan was swiftly abandoned, but not without the incitement of religious hostility. Two years before his death, Burke recalled the ensuing events: "This gave rise to a

[386] Francis Plowden, *An Historical Review of the State of Ireland* (London: 1803), 2 vols., I, pp. 320–22; Olga Tsapina, "'With Every Wish to Reconcile': *The Memoir of the Life and Writings of Charles O'Conor of Belanagare* (1796) and Religious Enlightenment in Ireland," *Eighteenth-Century Studies*, 45:3 (Spring 2012), pp. 409–22.

[387] Hume, *History*, V, p. 342.

[388] EB to Dr. William Markham, post 9 November 1771, *Corr.*, II, p. 285.

[389] Charles O'Conor to John Curry, 12 June 1762, *The Letters of Charles O'Conor of Belanagare*, ed. Catherine Coogan Ward and Robert E. Ward (Ann Arbor, MI: Irish-American Cultural Institute, 1980), 2 vols., I, p. 134. See also [Charles O'Conor], "A Letter to David Hume, Esq. on Some Misrepresentations in His History of Great Britain," *Gentleman's Magazine* (April–May 1763), pp. 55–64, 65–78. There is an account of the letter in Robert E. Ward, "A Letter from Ireland: A Little-Known Attack on David Hume's *History of England*," *Eighteenth-Century Ireland*, 2 (1987), pp. 196–97. For O'Conor's involvement in the controversy over 1641 in general, see Walter D. Love, "Charles O'Conor of Belanagare and Thomas Leland's 'Philosophical' *History of Ireland*," *Irish Historical Studies*, 13:49 (March 1962), pp. 1–25. See also Joseph Liechty, "Testing the Depth of Catholic/Protestant Conflict: The Case of Thomas Leland's *History of Ireland*, 1773," *Archivium Hibernicum*, 42 (1987), pp. 13–28.

[390] Hume, *History*, V, p. 343

[391] "The Chronicle" in *The Annual Register for the Year 1762*, p. 76.

Scene of murderous persecution, which continued with more or less violence during the Government of two or three Lord Lieutenants."[392] The malicious prosecution of suspected agrarian agitators or "Whiteboys" (*Buachaillí Bána*) was viewed by Burke as at least partly fostered by this context.[393] However, the problem derived not from active prejudice in government circles, but from "the evil spirit of the Country Gentlemen."[394] This was exacerbated, Burke conceded, by the prostrate attitude of Catholic victims, inured to passivity as a consequence of their depressed status. Nonetheless, the principal cause of animosity was popular prejudice in the countryside rather than residual bigotry among government officials, although jobbish power was prepared to capitalise on the illiberality of the constituencies.

This was the context in which Burke first began to campaign against the impact of the popery laws in Ireland. The Glorious Revolution of 1688 was not secured in Ireland until 1691, when the civil and military articles of the Treaty of Limerick were signed.[395] The military articles provided for the disbandment of Jacobite forces, granting safe passage to the bulk of the army to serve on the continent of Europe. The civil articles dealt with the religious and property rights of the defeated, at first guaranteeing the retention of estates to former rebels on condition of swearing allegiance to the new regime. Forfeiture of property belonging to non-juring Jacobites followed. In the wake of the Cromwellian and Restoration settlements, the Catholic share of profitable land was reduced to 22 per cent. By 1703 it had diminished further by another 8 per cent.[396] Before that date the Irish parliament, first convened under the new dynasty in 1692, had begun to introduce legislation that would supplement the terms of the settlement. This resulted in the passage of a series of "penal" statutes designed to remove any residual "papist" threat to the new regime by curbing the civil, religious and political rights of Catholics.[397] While the regulations did not amount to criminal statutes, they carried serious civil penalties. To the average reader they appeared as "a species of jargon," according to Burke.[398] They read more like a digest of legal chicanery than a system of hostile oppression. Perhaps for that reason, Burke observed, many of the relevant Bills met scarcely any opposition.[399] When one

[392] EB to Earl Fitzwilliam, 10 February 1795, *Corr.*, VIII, p. 147.

[393] On Whiteboyism, see below chapter 5, section 3.

[394] EB to Earl Fitzwilliam, 10 February 1795, *Corr.*, VIII, p. 147.

[395] In fact, the sense of insecurity among the victors persisted down to the end of the Nine Years' War, and beyond. See Ian McBride, *Eighteenth-Century Ireland: The Isle of Slaves* (Dublin: Gill and Macmillan, 2009), pp. 180–93.

[396] J. G. Simms, *The Williamite Confiscation in Ireland, 1690–1703* (London: Faber and Faber, 1956), p. 160.

[397] It has commonly been observed that these were not "penal" insofar as they were not criminally punitive. See S. J. Connolly, *Religion, Law, and Power: The Making of Protestant Ireland, 1660–1760* (Oxford: Oxford University Press, 1992), p. 3. For Burke, however, the laws imposed amounted to a "system of penalty and incapacity" and were thus, literally, "penal laws": see EB, *Tracts Relating to Popery Laws* (1761–65), *W & S*, IX, p. 453.

[398] Ibid., p. 481.

[399] Ibid.

complex set of proposals was debated before the Irish Commons in February 1704, only spokesmen for the Catholic community gave critical responses.[400] In general, the provisions passed into law "with the highest . . . applauses."[401] The penal "code" was a diverse and complex set of instruments, introduced for various purposes over a period of more than thirty years.[402] Nonetheless, taken together, the regulations amounted to a system of proscription whose presentation under the guise of legal technicalities discouraged feelings of sympathy for its victims.[403]

To begin with, in 1695, measures were introduced disarming the Catholic population. In the same year they were prevented from being educated in universities in Europe in order to obstruct communications between subversives and the continent.[404] Two years later, Catholic bishops were required to leave the country.[405] Again in 1797 it was enacted that the estates of Protestant heiresses married to Catholics would descend to their nearest Protestant relatives. Equally, a Protestant male proprietor marrying a Roman Catholic would incur the restrictions imposed on the delinquent faith. A major act of 1704 prevented Catholics inheriting estates from Protestants, as well as from acquiring land by purchase. Catholic leases were henceforth limited to thirty-one years. In addition, existing Catholic property was to be exempt from primogeniture, which meant that estates would effectively be "gavelled" and thus progressively reduced as property passed down the generations.[406] Nonetheless, a son who conformed to the established Church could inherit the property entire. In 1709, attempts to evade these restrictions were subject to forfeiture, with the property passing to individuals who "discovered" the misdemeanour. In addition, after 1691, members of parliament and officeholders were required to repudiate Catholic teaching, the doctrine of transubstantiation in particular.[407] Then, in 1728, Catholics were formally excluded from the electoral franchise.[408]

[400] J. G. Simms, "The Making of a Penal Law (2 Ann., c. 6)," *Irish Historical Studies*, 12:46 (October 1960), pp. 105–18, at p. 116.

[401] EB, *Tracts Relating to Popery Laws* (1761–65), *W & S*, IX, p. 481.

[402] For an overview of the popery laws see: Maureen Wall, *The Penal Laws, 1691–1760* (Dundalk: Dundalgan Press, 1967); Thomas Bartlett, *The Rise and Fall of the Irish Nation: The Catholic Question, 1790–1830* (Dublin: Macmillan, 1992), ch. 2; Connolly, *Religion, Law, and Power*, ch. 7; McBride, *Eighteenth-Century Ireland*, pp. 195–202; James Kelly, "The Historiography of the Penal Laws," *Eighteenth-Century Ireland: Special Issue on New Perspectives on the Penal Laws*, 1 (2011), pp. 27–52.

[403] EB, *Tracts Relating to Popery Laws* (1761–65), *W & S*, IX, p. 481.

[404] "Securing the Protestant Interest: The Origins and Purpose of the Penal Laws of 1695," *Irish Historical Studies*, 30:117 (May 1996), pp. 25–46.

[405] The Banishment Act (9 Will. III, c. 1) was "An Act for banishing all Papists exercising any Ecclesiastical Jurisdiction, and all Regulars of the Popish Clergy out of this Kingdom."

[406] The Popery Act (2 Ann., c. 6), an "Act to prevent the further growth of popery," was further amended in 1709.

[407] Matthew O'Conor, *The History of the Irish Catholics from the Settlement in 1691* (Dublin: 1813), p. 115.

[408] The Disenfranchising Act (1 Geo. II, c. 9) was "An Act for further Regulating the Election of Members of Parliament, and Preventing the Irregular Proceedings of Sheriffs and other Officers in Electing and Returning such Members."

According to Charles O'Hara, the government of Ireland in the middle of the eighteenth century had fallen to the "descendants of adventurers" and consequently exhibited a "spirit of domination."[409] For Burke the administration's advocates in the 1750s and 1760s were perpetuating a system of "abject servitude."[410] Between the Treaty of Limerick and the Treaty of Utrecht, there was patent alarm among Protestant settlers that the impulse to rebel would be renewed among Roman Catholics. Yet to many in the 1750s it seemed obvious that the wars of religion were definitively over, and that the Jacobite peril had been finally laid to rest. Certainly Catholicism persisted in Ireland, but "popery" in the sense of a threat to the civil establishment was dead.[411] In the Advertisement prefacing his 1755 pamphlet on *The Case of the Roman-Catholics of Ireland*, Charles O'Conor made plain his contention that "*Popery* is not so dangerous to the *Protestant* Interest *here* as it was *then* imagined."[412] As he had argued two years earlier, the Catholic faith was perfectly compatible with a free constitution.[413] Burke also adopted this position around 1760.[414] After the establishment of the Catholic Committee on Essex Street in Dublin on 2 April 1760, Wyse, O'Conor and Curry approached Burke to draft an address proclaiming the loyalty of the Catholics of Ireland to George III. This resulted in the completion in 1764 of an *Address and Petition of the Irish Catholics*, disclaiming all seditious intent on the part of their co-religionists.[415] In support of this claim, Burke pointed to "our dutiful, peaceable submissive behaviour for more than four-score years."[416] This was a plea to have Irish Catholics judged by their "own actions" in their "own times" rather than under the influence of "controversial writers" whose purpose was to tarnish the current generation by exaggerating the history of rebellion among their forebears.[417] There was, Burke commented elsewhere, an "interior History of Ireland" that was based on proper evidence drawing on credible records. The conclusions to which it pointed called Temple and Clarendon into doubt.[418]

409 NLI, O'Hara Papers, Notes on the History of Sligo, MS. 20, 397.

410 EB, *Address and Petition of the Irish Catholics* (1764), *W & S*, IX, p. 460.

411 The distinction was emphasised earlier, in Edward King, *The Case of Toleration Consider'd with Respect to Religion and Civil Government* (Dublin: 1725). For discussion, see Ian McBride, "Catholic Politics in the Penal Era: Father Sylvester Lloyd and the Devlin Address of 1727" in Bergin et al. eds., *New Perspectives on the Penal Laws*, pp. 115–48.

412 [Charles O'Conor], *The Case of the Roman-Catholics of Ireland* (Cork: 1755), p. iv. For the context, see Robert Coogan Ward and Catherine Coogan Ward, "The Catholic Pamphlet of Charles O'Conor (1710–1791)," *Studies: An Irish Quarterly Review*, 68:272 (Winter 1979), pp. 259–64.

413 [Charles O'Conor], *Seasonable Thoughts Relating to our Civil and Ecclesiastical Constitution* (Dublin: 1753), p. 12.

414 This is confirmed in EB, *Letter to Sir Hercules Langrishe* (1792), *W & S*, IX, p. 635.

415 EB, *Address and Petition of the Irish Catholics* (1764), ibid., p. 430. For the dating, see John Curry to EB, 18 August 1778, *Correspondence* (1844), II, pp. 237–38.

416 EB, *Address and Petition of the Irish Catholics* (1764), *W & S*, IX, p. 432.

417 Ibid.

418 EB, *Tracts relating to Popery Laws* (176165), ibid., p. 479. Burke had in mind Edward Hyde, Earl of Clarendon, *True Narrative of the Rebellion and Civil Wars of England* (Oxford: 1702–3), 3 vols.

Above all, the 1764 *Address* was designed to highlight the deleterious effects of the 1704 Popery Act together with its supplementary provisions introduced in 1709.[419] Burke understood these measures to be an affront to the purpose of society insofar as they impeded opportunities for improvement by enshrining insecurity of property and the division of estates among the remnants of the Catholic gentry.[420] By empowering discoverers to challenge ownership, and enabling sons to dispossess their fathers, they also compromised trust in both society and the family.[421] In the early 1760s, as Burke pondered the dysfunctional character of Irish political society, he also set about drafting a detailed analysis of penal legislation, later collected as a series of *Tracts relating to Popery Laws*. Without examining the original circumstances under which the various pieces of legislation had been introduced, he nonetheless claimed that the overall "intention of the Legislature" was apparent from the evident tendency of the measures.[422] Despite the dissimulating manner in which their significance was presented, Burke had no doubt that the provisions constituted a system of persecution.[423] He discussed the regulations under six main headings: rules governing the tenure of property; restrictions regarding the acquisition of land; limitations on education; prohibitions on bearing arms; laws governing marriage; and restraints upon the practice of religion.[424] He then concentrated on three particularly heinous results: the reduction in the "substance" of the Catholic population; the disincentive to industry caused by insecurity of property; and the corruption of relations within the family. The first was largely achieved by the gavelling clause in the 1704 Popery Act: under this provision, the landed property of Catholics would in due course "be wholly dissipated."[425] The second iniquitous consequence was likewise a product of this Act given that industry and labour depended on stable acquisition.[426] Burke then turned his attention to his third concern, the "extraordinary Effects" which rules governing the transmission and descent of estates would have on "interior natural relations in all popish families."[427]

One of the most shameful results of the penal laws derived from the rules governing conversion. If the son of a popish proprietor should conform to the established faith, the father would be rendered a mere tenant of his progeny. All children, including the female offspring, might acquire the same dominion.[428] Husbands and wives could equally deprive one another of their "natural" roles upon conversion

[419] For discussions of these penal statutes in particular see W. N. Osborough, "'Catholics, Land and the Popery Acts of Anne" in T. P. Power and Kevin Whelan eds., *Endurance and Emergence: Catholics in Ireland in the Eighteenth Century* (Dublin: Irish Academic Press, 1990).

[420] EB, *Address and Petition of the Irish Catholics* (1764), *W & S*, IX, p. 430.

[421] Ibid., pp. 430–31.

[422] EB, *Tracts relating to Popery Laws* (1761–65), ibid., p. 434.

[423] Ibid., p. 549.

[424] Ibid., p. 436.

[425] Ibid., p. 437.

[426] Ibid., pp. 476–77.

[427] Ibid, p. 437.

[428] Ibid., p. 438.

to the Church of Ireland.[429] Burke described the penal system in general terms—as it affected conscience, property and the family—as a "singular" programme of disqualification.[430] It was certainly different, and in many ways worse, than any comparable scheme in Europe with which he was familiar. One distinguishing feature was the magnitude of its application. Louis XIV's Revocation of the Edict of Nantes in 1685 was officially presented as affecting a mere fraction of the French population. Despite this misrepresentation, the number of its victims amounted, in absolute terms, to only half of those affected in Ireland. In relative terms this constituted a twentieth of those implicated in the penal code.[431] The volume of Irish casualties was sufficient to make up "a great people," rendering the popery laws an exceptional affront to public morality.[432] Given the sheer extent of their object, the popery laws could be regarded as directed against virtually a whole nation: "A Law against the majority of the people, is in substance a Law against the people itself."[433] For Burke this amounted to an infraction against the principles of natural law.[434] He explicated the oppressiveness of the arrangement in terms of two fundamental principles: the rules of justice, which ought to be the object of any system of law; and the common good, which was the rationale for the establishment of any civil community.

Burke referred to these two principles under the terms "equity" and "utility." The first was the more complex norm since it comprehended the idea of justice, although Burke dealt with it in only the most cursory fashion. The goal of justice was to render each their own (*suum cuique tribuere*) without prejudice.[435] Its chief characteristic was therefore to proceed impartially, treating like objects indiscriminately. This was "the great rule of equality," based on our common nature as creatures of the deity.[436] Equality of the kind, Burke concluded with Philo of Alexandria, was the "mother of justice" (ἔστι γὰρ ἰσότης . . . μήτηρ δικαιοσύνης).[437] This was not intended to provide for equality indifferently. Things might be distributed unequally in accordance with differential merit. Nonetheless, crucially, the same rules ought to be applied without exception in like cases.[438] The popery laws clearly vitiated this principle of

[429] Ibid., pp. 440–41.

[430] Ibid., p. 452.

[431] Ibid., p. 460.

[432] Ibid., p. 453.

[433] Ibid., p. 454.

[434] On Burke and natural law, see below chapter 8, section 6; chapter 12, section 3; chapter 12, section 6.

[435] The principle derives from Justinian, *Institutiones*, I, i, 1–3: *iuris praecepta sunt haec: honeste vivere, alterum non laedere, suum cuique tribuere.*

[436] EB, *Tracts relating to Popery Laws* (1761–65), *W & S*, IX, p. 456.

[437] Philo, *De specialibus legibus* in *The Works of Philo*, ed. F. H. Colson and G. H. Whitaker (Cambridge, MA: Harvard University Press, 1929–53), 10 vols., VIII, bk. IV, xlii, 231, cited in EB, *Tracts relating to Popery Laws* (1761–65), *W & S*, IX, p. 456. For Philo's debt to an eclectic tradition of natural law thinking including Cicero and extending back to Antiochus of Ascalon, see Richard A. Horsley, "The Law of Nature in Philo and Cicero," *Harvard Theological Review*, 71:1/2 (January–April 1978), pp. 35–59.

[438] On justice and equality see below chapter 13, section 4. Cf. Philo, *De specialibus legibus*, bk. IV, xii, 71: "the good judge must draw a veil over the disputants."

jurisprudence by distributing benefits differentially on the arbitrary basis of religion. This, in fact, was not justice, but persecution. The same point applied to Burke's second principle, that of utility. By this he meant specifically "public" utility, or the common good, in terms of which alone political society could be justified. Burke vindicated this claim on the basis of consensus among legal authorities and as a conclusion of rational inquiry. He cited his authorities not on account of their membership of a specific "school," but as a sample of diverse opinion through the ages. Cicero, Paulus and Suárez, though widely different in their approach, agreed that public utility was a principle of generality: it ought to comprehend the community as a whole rather than some inappropriately privileged portion.[439]

In addition to establishing an authoritative consensus, Burke built his case on rational argument. Towards this end he outlined his view of the legitimacy of law. Just laws could not be based on arbitrary will but had to derive from the sovereignty of the people: "in all forms of government the people is the true legislator."[440] That sovereignty was expressed indirectly by reposing trust in government, or directly by empowering the people as a whole. Either way, it was the duty of government to exercise judgment in favour of the supreme rights of the population. Yet these rights were not invented by the people themselves: they derived, as Burke put it, from "a superior Law."[441] His argument here was explicitly directed against Hobbes: men did not have a right to make what laws they pleased.[442] The constitutions of commonwealths, he argued with Cicero, were not in a position to supply an objective measure of value.[443] Burke would later condemn the idea of relative justice as enshrining a form of "geographical" morality, rendering duty dependent on the whims of time and place.[444] The law did not oblige merely on account of its institution but on the basis of its moral force to bind. Given the principle of public utility, it ought in general terms to unite its citizens in support of the common allegiance they owed as members of the state. This mutual allegiance stood as a surpassing obligation that defined the parameters of their political lives. Against this, the popery laws were premised on the existence of a partial religious fellowship that trumped the commitment to common citizenship. On this assumption, German Protestants were

[439] Burke makes his point with citations from Cicero, *De officiis*, III, vi; *The Digest of Justinian*, ed. Theodor Mommsen and Paul Krueger (Philadelphia, PA: University of Pennsylvania Press, 1985), bk. I, i, 11 (from Julius Paulus); Francisco Suárez, *Tractatus de legibus, ac Deo legislatore* (Naples: 1872), I, vii.

[440] EB, *Tracts relating to Popery Laws* (1761–65), *W & S*, IX, p. 454.

[441] Ibid., p. 455. Burke's position is widely indebted to natural law arguments but in its denial of the right to enslave oneself is substantially based on Locke. See below chapter 12, section 6. For the underlying assumptions in Locke see Timothy Stanton, "Authority and Freedom in the Interpretation of Locke's Political Theory," *Political Theory*, 39 (2011), pp. 5–30.

[442] EB, *Tracts relating to Popery Laws* (1761–65), *W & S*, IX, p. 455.

[443] The argument is based on Cicero, *De legibus*, I, xv.

[444] EB, Speech on the Opening of Impeachment (16 February 1788), *W & S*, VI, p. 346.

closer associates of Irish Anglicans than their fellow Catholics, corrupting domestic patriotism by means of "foreign affections."[445]

Burke would later challenge what he took to be this spurious brand of cosmopolitan benevolence in the context of the French Revolution.[446] He was in fact generally sceptical about declarations of charity whose effects entailed nothing but injury to its putative beneficiaries. The proselytism of those who sought to impose conformity in Ireland was invariably based on this posture of goodwill. The misery that resulted from self-declared humanity was justified in terms of its benefit to remote posterity.[447] The remainder of the *Tracts* offered a blistering indictment of the logic underlying the doctrine of coercive benevolence. Burke followed Bayle and Locke in claiming that attempts to enforce conviction could never lead to genuine conversion.[448] It was "one thing to persuade, another to command," as Locke put it.[449] This commitment brought Burke to reflect on the prospects for enlightenment in the context of a diversity of faiths. Moral improvement was a concrete achievement that resulted from the free exercise of human faculties under conditions of prosperity and peace. Speculative improvement was a more doubtful acquisition since the criteria that claimed to establish the superiority of beliefs were themselves controversial. In any case it seemed clear to Burke that neither moral nor speculative enlightenment could be coercively imposed. Beliefs and attitudes were not adopted as matters of convenience, above all in connection with "final things" or eternal happiness.[450]

Improvement could only proceed on the basis of consensus. For this reason, toleration was a basic constituent of enlightenment.[451] The necessary connection between enlightenment and toleration meant that moral and religious improvement were matters for persuasion.[452] People could only be enlightened on the basis of consent, which was generated by a mixture of rational agreement and customary attachment. As Burke had come to realise by the middle of the 1750s, opinions were sustained by a blend of conviction and veneration. Veneration need not

[445] Ibid., p. 461. On this theme in Burke, see Seamus Deane, *Foreign Affections: Essays on Edmund Burke* (Cork: Field Day, 2005).

[446] See below chapter 14, section 3.

[447] EB, *Tracts relating to Popery Laws* (1761–65), *W & S*, IX, p. 463.

[448] Pierre Bayle, *A Philosophical Commentary on these Words of the Gospel, Luke 14: 23, "Compel them to Come in, that My House May be Full* (Indianapolis, IN: Liberty Fund: 2005), p. 54; John Locke, *A Letter Concerning Toleration* (1689) in *A Letter Concerning Toleration and Other Writings*, ed. Mark Goldie (Indianapolis, IN: Liberty Fund, 2010), pp. 31–32. For discussion of the principles involved, see John Dunn, "The Claim to Freedom of Conscience: Freedom of Speech, Freedom of Thought, Freedom of Worship?" in idem, *The History of Political Theory and Other Essays* (Cambridge: Cambridge University Press, 1996); Timothy Stanton, "Natural Law, Nonconformity, and Toleration: Two Stages on Locke's Way," *Proceedings of the British Academy*, 186 (2013), pp. 50–85.

[449] Locke, *Letter Concerning Toleration*, p. 14.

[450] EB, *Tracts relating to Popery Laws* (1761–65), *W & S*, IX p. 464.

[451] Ibid., p. 465.

[452] Ibid., p. 466.

amount to blind attachment or superstition. It arose out of an "implicit admiration" for long-held beliefs that had the practicality of usage in their favour.[453] The "stable prejudice of time" disposed the mind to maintain its assent in support of habitual assumptions.[454] As Locke had argued in his *Essay Concerning Human Understanding*, when it came to the operation of conviction, the authority of custom did most of the work for most individuals.[455] Certainly, Burke concluded, public authority could not supply the place of voluntary agreement: "The coercive authority of the State is limited to what is necessary for its existence."[456] Force was never sufficient to convince the human mind. For this reason, influence rather than power was the principal means of reforming opinion. But even then, presumption was always "on the side of possession."[457] Only encouragement, armed with favours and the prospect of benefits, could hope to shape the world of human judgment and allegiance.

[453] Ibid.

[454] Ibid., p. 467.

[455] John Locke, *An Essay Concerning Human Understanding* (1689), ed. Peter H. Nidditch (Oxford: Oxford University Press, 1975, 1979), IV, xx, § 2. For discussion see above chapter 2, section 4.

[456] EB, *Tracts relating to Popery Laws* (1761–65), *W & S*, IX, p. 467.

[457] Ibid., p. 466.

PART III

Party, Sovereignty and Empire, 1765–1774

OVERVIEW

Oliver Goldsmith wrote of Burke in 1774 that he gave up to party "what was meant for mankind."[1] There is a poignancy to this portrait, which takes Burke to have bartered his talents for the petty spoils of politics. Yet Goldsmith's point was not that Burke was, in the old sense, a creature of party, sacrificing his ideals to the demands of power. On the contrary, he presented his friend as a man of public principle, and thus a misfit: "for a patriot, too cool; for a drudge, disobedient; / And too fond of the *right*, to pursue the *expedient*."[2] Despite this first-hand testimony, there is a school of eighteenth-century scholarship that finds its claims implausible.[3] Professions of principle in parliament, Lewis Namier believed, were displays of ambition cloaked in a show of morals.[4] Succeeding historians of ministerial conduct under George III were inclined to add to this assumption the belief that since Burke played the role of counsellor among Whig grandees he must have been their minion.[5] All the evidence, however, points another way. Although Burke abided by the codes of eighteenth-century politeness, he prized his self-sufficiency and intellectual independence. Nonetheless, Burke's life underwent an enduring change after 1765 when he entered public life on a more committed and permanent basis. His literary aspirations would

[1] Oliver Goldsmith, "Retaliation: A Poem" in *The Complete Poetical Works of Oliver Goldsmith* (London: Henry Frowde, 1906), p. 88, line 32.

[2] Ibid., lines 39–40.

[3] On this tendency among generations of eighteenth-century British high-political historians, see Conor Cruise O'Brien, *The Great Melody: A Thematic Biography of Edmund Burke* (London: Sinclair-Stevenson, 1992), pp. xli–lix, who dubs all offenders, somewhat loosely, "Namierite."

[4] Lewis Namier, *England in the Age of the American Revolution* (London: Macmillan, 1930, 1970), pp. 40–41.

[5] Richard Pares, *King George III and the Politicians* (Oxford: Oxford University Press, 1953, 1988), p. 13; John Brooke, *The Chatham Administration, 1766–1768* (London: Macmillan, 1956), p. 309.

in a basic sense continue, but these were now channelled into a career in the House of Commons. From this point forward, his writings and speeches were occasioned by the course of practical affairs. Moreover, for the most part he was obliged to act with a body of collaborators.

The Rockingham Whigs with whom Burke would associate sought to distinguish themselves among assorted parliamentary groupings as a party committed to politics based on principle. Twenty-first-century readers are disposed to treat this stance with suspicion since it seems that political conduct cannot be dissociated from the pursuit of "interests." Given this reality, a profession of principle is liable to appear a dubious posture. Yet there are two points to be made about this: first, even a posture limits the options that can be taken in pursuing interests; and second, adherence to principle among the Rockinghams meant promoting particular interests.[6] Burke took the lead in thinking about how their programme should be presented, which in practice meant developing a distinct political theory. In this he drew on his experience of historical and philosophical research to carve out a position on domestic and imperial affairs. Leading parliamentarians of the eighteenth century like Chatham and Fox were classically trained and humanistically educated men. Burke, however, was steeped in the enlightenment science of politics. Accordingly, he brought a deeply historical mind and a generalising intelligence to bear on the major issues of the day. In reconstructing the singular contribution made by Burke, commentators have struggled to keep these aptitudes in play. Political historians obliged to deal with his interventions have tended to downplay his intellectual bent, while historians of ideas and political theorists have tended to treat him as an academic philosopher.[7] More recent intellectual historians have restored a fuller context to Burke's ideas, elucidating his sources with greater care and precision, yet this work has largely been limited to articles and chapters.[8] In general these have emphasised Burke's connection to other thinkers rather than the pragmatic demands of eighteenth-century

[6]On the first point, see Quentin Skinner, "Moral Principles and Social Change" in *Visions of Politics I: Regarding Method* (Cambridge: Cambridge University Press, 2002).

[7]In the former category, see Frank O'Gorman, *Edmund Burke: His Political Philosophy* (Bloomington, IN: Indiana University Press, 1973); Paul Langford, "Edmund Burke" in *Oxford Dictionary of National Biography* (Oxford: Oxford University Press, 2004), 60 vols. In the latter, see John McGunn, *The Political Philosophy of Edmund Burke* (London: Edward Arnold, 1913); Peter J. Stanlis, *Edmund Burke and the Natural Law* (1958) (New Brunswick, NJ: Transactions Press, 2003, 2009); and Charles Parkin, *The Moral Basis of Burke's Political Thought* (Cambridge: Cambridge University Press, 1956).

[8]See, for example, J.G.A Pocock, "Burke and the Ancient Constitution: A Problem in the History of Ideas" (1960) in idem, *Politics Language and Time: Essays on Political Thought and History* (Chicago, IL: University of Chicago Press, 1971, 1989); Frederick Dreyer, *Burke's Politics: A Study in Whig Orthodoxy* (Waterloo, Ont.: Wilfrid Laurier University Press, 1979); Iain Hampsher-Monk, *A History of Political Thought: Major Thinkers from Hobbes to Marx* (Oxford: Blackwells, 1992, 2001), ch. 6; Donald Winch, *Riches and Poverty: An Intellectual History of Political Economy in Britain, 1750–1834* (Cambridge: Cambridge University Press, 1996), pt. II; David Armitage, "Edmund Burke and Reason of State," *Journal of the History of Ideas*, 61:4 (October 2000), pp. 617–34; Jennifer Pitts, *A Turn to Empire: The Rise of Imperial Liberalism in Britain and France* (Princeton, NJ: Princeton University Press, 2005), ch. 3.

policy. For this reason, a comprehensive study relating Burke's politics to his principles has not been previously undertaken.

Burke's early years in parliament were awash with dramatic events. To begin with there was a sequence of short-lived administrations under the Marquess of Rockingham, the Earl of Chatham and the Duke of Grafton, followed by the more durable tenure of Frederick, Lord North, beginning in late January 1770. Under each of these ministries there was a need for informed discussion in the House of Commons across a bewildering array of topics: the fate of political party under George III between 1765 and 1774; the limits of toleration in the early to mid 1770s; the Stamp Act crisis in 1765; agrarian protest in Ireland in 1766; the Bengal revenues in 1767; the Townshend duties in the same year; new legislation relating to landed property beginning in 1768; the expulsion of Wilkes in 1769; the Boston Massacre in 1770; the doctrines of the Anglican Church in 1772; the regulation of the East India Company in 1773; and the impact of the Tea Act throughout 1774. All of these items needed urgent attention in fast succession. Each episode forms a part of one of the three larger narratives that make up the chapters in the third part of this book. The first covers the trajectory of British affairs over the course of four successive ministries. The second examines the progress of the contest with America between the Declaratory Act and the closure of the Boston Port. And the third explores the government's handling of the East India Company down to the passage of Lord North's Regulating Act. Irish developments are examined separately but included in the British chapter since they form a part of a wider debate about religious toleration. In contesting policy in connection with each of these controversial matters, Burke was obliged to act with his fellow Rockinghamites in parliament. Even so, it was in these years that he acquired his reputation for a highly individual approach that combined erudition with philosophical abstraction. Yet despite this singularity of style, Burke shared with his colleagues a dedication to the politics of principle, although their position has to be distinguished from airy moralism.

For Burke and his Rockingham friends alike, a principled stand in parliament did not imply transcending interests or withstanding the temptations of public office. The Rockinghams were keen to embrace the burdens of power and happy to manage parliament with the aid of the king's "influence." They were neither patriot purists subservient to the people, nor a country opposition appalled by the power of the crown. Equally, they were determined to avoid becoming tools of George III. Indeed, "principle" for them implied avoiding these extremes and thus maintaining their independence from slavish populism and court flattery. However, although the Rockinghams regarded themselves as a party of government, they were sure that the nature of monarchical influence had changed under George III. As Burke emphasised in 1770 in his first major piece of political writing, the *Thoughts on the Cause of the Present Discontents*, the new king seemed anxious to govern through favourites and dependants rather than in alliance with Whig gentlemen and grandees. His view of party was adapted to address this situation. As we have seen, as early as 1757 Burke had set about justifying opposing parties under the constitution. Their job was to restore the balance among the powers of government in the interest of either parliament or the king. From Burke's perspective, ever since the reduction of the prerogatives of the crown in the aftermath of 1688, the king was expected to govern by placing his influence at the disposal of the administration. Ministers, he thought, should be drawn from men of property and ability—members who had independent standing as well as popular support, and who were therefore in a position to command a following in parliament. In the aftermath of the Seven Years' War, with an increase in the national debt together with enlarged military and naval establishments, the king was in a position to put his patronage to corrupt use by excluding men of natural means and acquired aptitudes from office. For Burke and his colleagues after 1765, the tribulations of government down through the 1770s had been caused by this insidious form of constitutional corruption.

The consequences of this corruption seemed obvious to Burke: the calibre of government had declined, the constituencies were increasingly estranged from parliament, and the executive began to encroach upon the privileges of the people. These tendencies were evident in a number of developments, including a rise in the intensity and frequency of unrest, legislation directed against the prescriptive title to property, and a growing disregard for the rights of parliament. Domestic upheavals spilled over into the management of the Empire. The response to the mood of protest spreading through America was a particularly serious symptom of executive presumptuousness. The invasion of chartered privileges enjoyed by the East India Company was another flagrant example of the abuse of ministerial power. Throughout this period, Burke opposed the view that faction was the cause of public turmoil as well as deformations in the system of government. On the contrary, party was the cure for a range of domestic problems and by extension for emerging crises in the Empire. As Burke understood the matter, the demise of genuine parties under George III had encouraged the extension of ministerial power and distorted the prevailing conception of the rights of sovereignty. Burke complained that the supremacy of the crown-in-parliament was being confused with the omnipotence of executive authority. To the extent that this confusion was being implemented in practice, it was eroding the corporate rights of the East India Company and deepening the estrangement between the American colonies and the mother country. Burke's aim was to restore the branches of the constitution to their proper function as a means of saving the government of the Empire from the spirit of conquest.

V

PARTY, POPULARITY AND DISSENT

BRITAIN AND IRELAND, 1765–1774

Figure 2. Lord Bute upsets the balance of the constitution by improper use of prerogative powers. Anon., *The Constitution* (1770), BM 4430 (British Library), in Nicholas K. Robinson, *Edmund Burke: A Life in Caricature* (Yale: 1996), p. 22.

5.1 Introduction

Developments in Britain and Ireland during his early years in parliament proved formative politically and intellectually for Burke. Popular protest and government repression were conspicuous features of the period. In Ireland in 1766 agrarian agitation met with a dramatic judicial response. The execution of suspects provoked outrage in Burke, leading him to reflect on underlying sectarian tensions together with their constitutional implications. The popular prejudices supporting the popery laws were exploited rather than moderated by a corrupt establishment. To Burke, the contrast with the ethos of British politics was stark. On the mainland, the rage of faction formed by divided opinions on church and state had long subsided. The combination of an established Church with the toleration of dissent was broadly accepted. At the same time, a mixed system of government comprising parliament and monarchy was widely supported. Nonetheless, while civil and ecclesiastical relations were broadly harmonious, surreptitious developments counselled against complacency.

Throughout the course of Burke's first years in the Commons, the main threat to domestic consensus seemed unlikely to come from the growth of religious conflict. In 1772, he opposed the idea of relieving the Anglican clergy of the duty of subscribing to the tenets of the established Church on the grounds that the security of religion required a community of belief based on agreed doctrines and a uniform liturgy. Yet he insisted that this should be accompanied by generous toleration. For Burke, only the extremes of irreligion and politically seditious beliefs ought to impose limits on the virtue of charity towards religious difference. Before the late 1780s, he entertained no serious fear of either of these prospects and was consequently happy to extend the bounds of toleration. However, the organisation of politics presented a less assuring picture. While superficially the system of government was healthy, agreement about how to sustain it was eroding. Specifically, the power of the crown under George III along with the disposition of ministries were undermining the constitution. The exclusion of Wilkes from parliament in 1769 betrayed government contempt for liberty and a disregard for popular sentiment. Ministerial support for a *Nullum Tempus* Bill, seeking to promote the claims of the crown against the prescriptive right to property, offered another indication of the creeping power of the court. In addition, the official reaction to riots revealed a punitive attitude to public disquiet and a failure to diagnose the reasons for the ferment. In response, Burke provided his party with a probing analysis of the causes for the growing alienation of the public from the administration.

From the moment that the Rockinghams assumed office in 1765, they set about deliberately cultivating out-of-doors opinion. While Pitt might pose as a patriot who in fact curried the crown's favour, the Rockinghams would stand their ground as at once popular and independent. That meant disdaining the allurements of the people and the court—collaborating with the public without becoming sycophants, cooperating with the monarchy without becoming its dependents. In this they thought they were continuing the legacy of the Whigs, acting as intermediaries between the populace and the king. Yet George III denied them the role after 1762, governing instead though undistinguished favourites operating without an independent following in parliament or significant support in the country at large. Under these circumstances, government became increasingly remote from the population, reducing politics to a standoff between ministry and mob. Burke's theory of party was intended as a set of remedial propositions in terms of which the "system" of George III could be opposed. The Rockinghams would be justified in resisting a corrupt court in the interest of a sustainable constitutional balance. Popularity, deliberation and executive authority would be restored to government, securing liberty against decline into incipient tyranny.

5.2 The Rockingham Connection

By February 1765, Burke's relationship with William Gerard Hamilton had come to an acrimonious conclusion. At the end of the previous year, he was applying for the position of London agent for the conquered islands of Grenada, the Grenadines, Dominica, St. Vincent and Tobago. The application came to nothing, but it indicated Burke's desire for a fresh beginning. As he sought a new position, George Grenville was still heading the administration of the country. On the eve of the 1765 session, Burke felt that the political scene was in a state of stagnation: "though Parliament is on the point of meeting, one sees none of that eagerness and movement, which usually precedes a Session in which much has been expected."[1] When parliament opened after the recess on 10 January 1765, George III looked forward to the marriage of his youngest sister to the prince of Denmark, the continuation of peace with France and Spain, the prudent management of public finances, and the reduction of the national debt.[2] However, by the spring of 1765, the ministry was in serious trouble as the king's relations with Grenville deteriorated beyond repair. At that point, Burke was still lamenting the effects of his connection with Hamilton. In May he was writing of his former patron's intention of reducing him to a kind of domestic slavery. His bitterness was still raw: "Six of the best years of my Life he took from every pursuit of Literary reputation or of improvement of my fortune."[3] Burke felt that he was losing ground to ambitious contemporaries: there had never before been a more favourable period for those interested in a political career, yet the opportunities seemed on the verge of passing by. Even Burke's friends were growing anxious that he should secure a position that would enable him to display his abilities and talents.[4]

[1] EB to [William] Young, 31 December 1765, *Corr.*, I, pp. 176–77.
[2] Walpole, *Memoirs*, II, pp. 76–77; *Parliamentary History*, XVI, cols. 1–2.
[3] EB to John Hely Hutchinson, [May 1765], *Corr.*, I, p. 200.
[4] John Monck Mason, 28 June 1765, WWM BkP 1:53.

Charles Townshend looked likely to come to the rescue. On 8 June, he was appointed paymaster general in Grenville's ministry, and in the preceding months he had been developing a friendship with Burke.[5] At the time, the government found itself in a highly unstable position. Its handling of the Regency Bill alienated George III, who was already anxious to rid himself of his First Lord of the Treasury.[6] The dismissal of Grenville was finalised on 10 July 1765. On the tenth of that month, the first Rockingham ministry was formally inaugurated, with Charles Watson-Wentworth, the second Marquess of Rockingham, installed at the head of a new administration. Burke was offered the post of private secretary to Rockingham, consolidating a relationship that would prove pivotal to his career. "I have got an employment of a kind humble enough," Burke informed O'Hara.[7] He nonetheless hoped to make something of the position, even though the appointment was neither an official one nor directly remunerated. As Burke was appointed Secretary to the First Lord of the Treasury, William Burke became Under-Secretary of State to Henry Seymour Conway. They had both benefited from a recent connection with Lord John Cavendish and William Fitzherbert.[8] A "little gleam of prosperity," Burke wrote to David Garrick, had suddenly brightened his prospects.[9] To begin with, Burke hoped to continue his association with Townshend even as he committed himself to Rockingham. "This may prove a nice card to play," commented O'Hara.[10] Before long, however, Burke was exclusively focused on the Rockingham connection, which would dominate his activities down to 1782.

Rockingham was an improbable choice to head the Treasury. Poor health and inexperience, he confided at the time, made him an unlikely leader of the ministry.[11] Walpole was astonished at the result: "I never heard a more wild proposal, nor one more fraught with greater improbability of success."[12] As late as 30 June 1765, the future of the minority was still in doubt. At a meeting at Newcastle's Claremont residence in Surrey, the Old Whigs were divided on whether to form an administration without the participation of Pitt.[13] Among many who would join the Rockingham administration, support from Pitt was a prerequisite of success.[14] For his part,

[5] EB to John Monck Mason, post 29 May 1765, *Corr.*, I, p. 197; Henry Flood to EB, 30 June 1765, WWM BkP 1:47; Charles Townshend to EB, 23 June 1765, WWM BkP 1:52.

[6] Paul Langford, *The First Rockingham Administration, 1765–1766* (Oxford: Oxford University Press, 1973), pp. 7–8.

[7] EB to Charles O'Hara, 11 July 1765, *Corr.*, I, p. 211.

[8] EB and William Burke to Charles O'Hara, 4 July 1765, ibid., p. 207. William ascribed the break to the intercession of O'Hara. See also EB to Charles O'Hara, 9 July 1765, ibid., p. 210.

[9] EB to David Garrick, 16 July 1765, ibid., p. 211.

[10] Charles O'Hara to EB, 11 July 1765, in Hoffman, *Burke*, p. 231.

[11] Ross J. S. Hoffman, *The Marquis: A Study of Lord Rockingham, 1730–1782* (New York: Fordham University Press, 1973), pp. 78–79. For Rockingham's subsequent view that "it was with the greatest reluctance I cam into Office in the year 1765," see EB, "Thoughts" (July 1779), *W & S*, III, p. 450.

[12] Walpole, *Memoirs*, II, p. 163. Cf. *Grenville Papers*, III, p. 208.

[13] *Rockingham Memoirs*, I, pp. 218–20; Walpole, *Memoirs*, II, p, 162.

[14] Sir George Colebrooke to the Duke of Newcastle, 4 July 1765, Add. MS. 32967, fol. 226; Henry Flood to Edmund Burke, 27 July 1765, WWM BkP 1:55.

the Great Commoner had not only declined to form a new administration, he was also refusing to cooperate with Newcastle and his associates. The "leading men" in the opposition, as Burke informed Charles Townshend, were affronted not only by Pitt's withholding his confidence from them, but by his failure to demonstrate his respect for them as well.[15] By 4 July 1765, Burke was reporting the ongoing confusion surrounding negotiations, although Pitt's position remained firm, while "the Whigs are resolved to try whether they cannot make up an administration by themselves."[16] On 9 July the "immense stir" was continuing. In the midst of ongoing uncertainty, it was clear that Townshend would refuse to accept a major role in the government. Nonetheless, the principal positions were soon decided: William Dowdeswell was destined to be Chancellor of the Exchequer, while Conway and the Duke of Grafton were being named as Secretaries of State.[17] At this late hour Burke's future was still not settled. As negotiations proceeded he fell foul of the Duke of Newcastle's machinations, who was insinuating to Rockingham that his choice for Secretary had been reared a Jacobite.[18] But the controversy soon blew over, and once Burke was installed in his new position he applied himself with an ardour that would become notorious.

The new government was formed by the intercession of the Duke of Cumberland, but it was studded with inexperienced members and had insufficient depth of support in the House of Commons. Charles Townshend retained his position in the paymaster's office; Charles Yorke accepted the job of Attorney General; Lord Winchelsea became Lord President, and the Duke of Newcastle Lord Privy Seal. Lord Northington was made Lord Chancellor and Lord Egmont First Lord of the Admiralty, maintaining the positions they had held under Grenville.[19] News of a violent reaction to colonial policy in America arrived in waves through autumn and winter. Even so, the attention of the new ministry was focused on foreign policy as it sought to develop an Anglo-Prussian alliance that would withstand any unity of purpose between Austria and the Bourbon powers.[20] In addition, the government endeavoured to define itself by its opposition to the Cider Excise and the issuing of General Warrants. In this they were staking a claim to the legacy of Pitt, hoping to establish their reputation as a patriot administration. As the ministry bedded down, Burke immersed himself in the details of daily business, preserving his independence and garnering respect. His friend Agmondesham Vesey was pleased to hear that his new connection was proving so beneficial.[21] Before long, his energy

[15] EB to Charles Townshend, 25 June 1765, *Corr.*, I, p. 205.

[16] EB to William Burke, 4 July 1765, ibid., p. 206.

[17] EB to Charles O'Hara, 9 July 1765, ibid., p. 210.

[18] Duke of Newcastle to the Duchess of Newcastle, 31 October 1765, Add. MS. 33078, fol. 35; Francis Hardy, *Memoirs of the Political and Private Life of James Caulfield, Earl of Charlemont* (London: 1812), 2 vols., II, pp. 281–82; EB to David Garrick, 16 July 1765, *Corr.*, I, p. 211.

[19] Langford, *First Rockingham Administration*, pp. 24–39.

[20] Ibid., pp. 84–85.

[21] Agmondesham Vesey to EB, 27 July 1765, WWM BkP 1:57.

and application became vital to the administration.[22] Already in November 1765 Burke was preparing to enter parliament, anxious to make a figure and eagerly anticipating this "considerable Step in the World" in a letter to Sir George Macartney in December.[23] On 24 December he informed O'Hara: "yesterday I was elected for Wendover, got very drunk, and this day have an heavy cold."[24] Burke acquired his seat through the patronage of Lord Verney, who first offered it to William Burke, who passed it on to Edmund. It would prove the major breakthrough of his career, providing him with a field in which to exercise his talents. The transition from literary apprentice to public orator was nearly complete.

At the end of 1765, Burke still betrayed an interest in the affairs of "the Literary world," updating Macartney on a recent response of Robert Lowth to William Warburton.[25] His preoccupation with the controversies of the mid 1750s still lingered. Nonetheless, in early January 1766 Thomas Leland indicated how Burke was moving on: "Your head is filled with questions, divisions and majorities;—Canada Bills, Jetees, Manilla ransoms, and stamp-duties. My thoughts are employed on Lowth and Warburton."[26] The transition was not as extreme as might be supposed. Burke's eloquence would be put in the service of parliamentary persuasion, and his intellect employed in devising political argument. His intelligence had been formed by combining historical study with philosophical reflection. Over the course of a parliamentary career that would last nearly thirty years, Burke would continue to add to this fund of knowledge, though he would also draw on his accumulated stores. Despite the obtrusive interference of Hamilton, he had familiarised himself with competing strains of enlightenment thought, especially in Britain, to which he brought an enduring set of firmly held convictions. Taking his seat in January 1766, he unleashed these powers of analysis on the contemporary political scene, rigorously developing insights through powerfully compelling argument, immediately cutting a figure in House of Commons debates. Burke presented what amounted to "a new political philosophy," as one admirer commented, one that was securely grounded in practical affairs.[27]

As Burke prepared to take his seat, the American crisis had just emerged as the dominant issue before parliament. Grenville's Stamp Act had passed on 22 March 1765, driven by the need for revenue and pleaded with a disregard for conse-

[22]Joseph Yorke to Lord Hardwicke, 15 April 1766, Add. MS. 35368, fol. 40; Earl of Buckinghamshire to George Grenville, 11 June 1766, Add. MS. 22358, fol. 35.

[23]Charles O'Hara to EB, 22 November 1768, *Corr.*, I, pp. 218–19; EB to Sir George Macartney, post 23 December 1765, ibid., p. 222. On "making a figure" in the House, see Christopher Reid, *Imprison'd Wranglers: The Rhetorical Culture of the House of Commons, 1760–1800* (Oxford: Oxford University Press, 2012), pt. III.

[24]EB to Charles O'Hara, 24 September 1765, *Corr.*, I, p. 223.

[25]EB to Sir George Macartney, post 23 December 1765, ibid., pp. 222–23. Burke is referring to [Robert Lowth], *A Letter to the Right Reverend Author of the "Divine Legation of Moses Demonstrated"* (London: 1765).

[26]Thomas Leland to EB, 9 January 1766, WWM BkP 1:77.

[27]James Marriott to EB, 8 February 1766, WWM BkP 1:83.

quences.[28] As the colonists rose in protest, the fundamentals of government were made matters of contention. The reciprocal obligations of obedience and protection became objects of aggravated dispute. "Little did he weigh the danger of a contest between the mother country and such distant, extensive, and now powerful subjects," Horace Walpole later commented of Grenville.[29] After news of the disturbances in America had reached Britain, the King's Speech on 17 December 1765 acknowledged that the matter required the attention of parliament. Grenville did his utmost to stymie the government's prospects, but to no avail: "hitherto the unstable administration stands firm," Burke wrote to John Ridge the day after his election, ". . . never did an adversary shew more fury and impotence together than G. Grenville."[30] Grenville opposed ministerial measures at every turn in late December. The American business was then deferred till the new session in January. As Burke waited to enter the Commons after the Christmas recess, William Markham expressed the hope that he would "appear at once in some important question."[31] He was not disappointed. Within days of parliament meeting on Tuesday 14 January, after weeks of intense debate about the handling of the crisis, Burke intervened in the debate on the American colonies. David Garrick, who was present for the proceedings, extolled Burke's "Virgin Eloquence."[32] Performing in parliament was commonly experienced as a terrifying event, with fewer than half the members in the middle of the eighteenth century actually contributing to debate.[33] In the cramped rectangular space of St. Stephen's Chapel where the Commons met, Burke had thrown himself into the major controversy of the early reign of George III. It would absorb much of his attention down to 1783.[34]

The attempt to manage the American crisis prompted the government to review the Navigation Acts in general. Burke threw himself into the enterprise with zeal: "Ned is so taken up that he has scarce time to eat, drink, or sleep," Burke's wife informed his sister just after her marriage to Patrick French.[35] In early March, Burke described to O'Hara the Rockinghams' plans for "a compleat revision of all the Commercial Laws, which regard our own or foreign Plantations."[36] The overlapping and competing interests of West Indian, West African and North American trade

[28] This was Rockingham's verdict by October 1765: see the Marquess of Rockingham to Viscount Irwin, 25 October 1765, Historical Manuscripts Commission, *Report of Manuscripts in Various Collections: The Manuscripts of the Hon. Frederick Lindley Wood, M. L. S. Clements, Esq., Philip Unwin, Esq.* (London: 1913), VIII, p. 183.

[29] Walpole, *Memoirs*, II, p. 93.

[30] EB to John Ridge, 24 December 1765, *Corr.*, I, p. 225.

[31] Dr. William Markham, 29 December 1765, ibid., p. 226.

[32] David Garrick to EB, 18 January 1766, ibid., p. 233.

[33] P.D.G. Thomas, *The House of Commons in the Eighteenth Century* (Oxford: Oxford University Press, 1971), p. 229.

[34] See chapters 6 and 9 below.

[35] Jane Burke and EB to Juliana French, 6 February 1765, *Corr.*, I, p. 236.

[36] EB to Charles O'Hara, 1 March 1766, ibid., p. 239.

had been anxiously lobbying the government since the advent of the new ministry.[37] The determination of the Newcastle Whigs to secure themselves against the fate that befell the party in 1762 encouraged them to foster a popular base as a form of insurance against the wilfulness of an unsympathetic monarch. Encouraged by a rising generation of "Young Whigs," the Rockinghams courted support from dominant commercial interests as an index of popularity out of doors.[38] In early March, Burke reported to O'Hara that negotiations were underway to reconcile the ambitions of West Indian and North American traders. Their agreement would free up the ministry to bring forward a "regular and digested scheme."[39] Burke relished helping to devise its contents—"it is a Business I like"—and wondered how Ireland might be made to benefit by a transformation of the laws of trade.[40] On 7 March, a motion to repeal the Cider Act carried successfully.[41] However Burke's main effort in the spring of 1766 was concentrated on reorganising the Empire. Disturbances in the American colonies pointed to a crisis in imperial subjection. The traditional means of enforcing provincial subordination included revenue extraction and commercial regulation. Since the parliamentary imposition of taxation in America had sparked resistance, the Rockinghams set about regenerating American allegiance.

This was to be achieved not merely by repealing the Stamp Act, but also by revising the terms of trade throughout the Empire. Burke played a major role in reconceptualising the current system. Rockingham, O'Hara hinted, was much indebted to Burke's formulation of policy. "The undertaking is great," he assured his friend, and it owed much to Burke's enterprise as well as his intellect.[42] The ambition of Burke's plans has rarely been noted, largely on account of the extraordinary condescension with which the Rockingham administration has been treated by historians.[43] Part of his aim was to include Ireland in the new system of imperial trade, though his colleagues were largely focused on the American islands and continent.[44] "The revision to be made of the Trade laws was not proposed to be total; but only so far as they regarded America," Burke updated O'Hara.[45] Nonetheless, Burke searched

[37] Lillian M. Penson, "The London West India Interest in the Eighteenth Century," *English Historical Review*, 36 (1921), pp. 373–92; George L. Beer, *British Colonial Policy, 1754–1765* (New York: Macmillan, 1907).

[38] On "Little" or young Whigs, see the Duke of Newcastle to the Marquess of Rockingham, 19 June 1765, Add. MS. 32967, fol. 69. For discussion, see Lucy Sutherland, "Edmund Burke and the First Rockingham Administration," *English Historical Review*, 47:185 (January 1932), pp. 46–72.

[39] EB to Charles O'Hara, 1 March 1765, *Corr.*, I, p. 240.

[40] Ibid.

[41] Burke spoke for 30 minutes on the subject: EB to Charles O'Hara, 11 March 1766, ibid., p. 244.

[42] Charles O'Hara to EB, 15 April 1766, in Hoffman, *Burke*, p. 344.

[43] Langford, *First Rockingham Administration, passim*: the ministry is generally presented as naïve and unrealistic, largely in reaction against the judgments of the Whig historians. Thomas Babington Macaulay, *Essay on the Earl of Chatham* (London: 1887), is singled out for criticism at p. 42. The pitfalls of anti-Whiggism, apparent in Langford, are well diagnosed in Herbert Butterfield, *George III and the Historians* (London: Collins, 1957).

[44] EB to Charles O'Hara, 1 March 1766, *Corr.*, I, p. 240.

[45] EB to Charles O'Hara, 27 March 1766, ibid., p. 246.

for Irish regulations that might be revised under an American Act. O'Hara was to inform him of articles for inclusion, considering sugar, woollen fabrics and cottons at various stages. "I have considered all the proposals you have made concerning Trade," Burke duly reported, but he regarded "every one of them" as impracticable.

The fact was that any liberalisation of commerce of the kind that Burke sought inevitably encountered the political reality of opposing interests. At every turn a freer trade was opposed by "some predominant prejudice."[46] Pitt would later reveal his hostility to Burke's ideas.[47] Only time and the work of persuasion could prevail upon adverse reasoning.[48] The British fear was that Irish products would compete with metropolitan manufactures: "you must remember," Burke admonished O'Hara, "Cotton is the Basis of one of the most extensive and most favourite manufactures of England, that of Manchester."[49] Having begun to draft his plans with an eye to including Ireland, Burke finally came to realise that the Irish commercial relations constituted a "System" in itself. Scrutiny and reform would have to wait for another season.[50] As early as 1749, Josiah Tucker had complained of the competitive animosity that encouraged Britain to cramp the commerce and manufactures of Ireland: "If *Ireland* gets rich, what is the Consequence? *England* will be rich too."[51] Tucker's plans, however, formed part of a bid for an incorporating union. In the meantime, policy in Britain was driven by rivalry, and Irish liberty fell prey to metropolitan anxiety. Back in 1748, Montesquieu had described the British as supremely (*souverainement*) jealous in commercial affairs, more put out by the prosperity of rivals than pleased with the progress of its own good fortune.[52] Burke encountered the same attitude in 1766.

The Rockinghams nonetheless proceeded with their plans to establish free ports in the Caribbean. By early May 1766 an agreement was struck that a port was to be opened to Spanish trade in Jamaica, and another for the commerce of the North American colonies in Dominica.[53] Originally, Pitt had strenuously opposed himself to the measure, forcing Burke to travel to Hayes to win him over to the government side.[54] However, by now, Pitt had begun to conspire to weaken the standing of the ministry: "the truth is, he determined to be out of humour," since he wished

[46] Ibid.

[47] The Earl of Chatham to the Duke of Grafton, Grafton, *Autobiography*, p. 108.

[48] Burke later recollected his bruising attempt to enlarge Irish trade. See EB, *Letter to Thomas Burgh* (1780), *W & S*, IX p. 561: "I found that the house, surrendering itself to the guidance . . . of the accidents of court favour, had become the sport of the passions of men, at once rash and pusillanimous."

[49] EB to Charles O'Hara, 27 March 1766, *Corr.*, I, p. 247.

[50] Ibid.

[51] Josiah Tucker, *A Brief Essay on the Advantages and Disadvantages which Respectively Attend France and Great Britain with Regard to Trade* (London: 1749), p. 28.

[52] Charles-Louis de Secondat, Baron de Montesquieu, *De l'esprit des lois* (1748) in *Œuvres complètes*, ed. Roger Caillois (Paris: Gallimard, 1951), 2 vols., II, pt. III, bk. XIX, ch. 27.

[53] This passed as 6 Geo. III, c. 49.

[54] As late as 11 May 1766 Pit was describing the provision for a free port in Dominica to Thomas Nuthall as an "unsolid idea." See *Chatham Correspondence*, II, p. 421.

to expose any weakness in the administration.[55] In early April, Burke was feeling confident about the standing of the government in the House of Commons. As they closed their examination of witnesses in favour of opening Dominica as a free port and prepared to draft resolutions as the basis for a new trade act, opposition to the ministry seemed to have expired. This stirred in Burke a feeling of optimism: "So much popularity never was possessed by any set of people who possessed great offices."[56] Nonetheless, Rockingham was clearly exposed on two fronts: first, he still depended on collaboration from Pitt; failing that he would have to placate the ambitions of the king's friends, still associated with the shadowy figure of Lord Bute.[57] Since neither Newcastle nor Rockingham would unite with disciples of Bute, their party had to rely on at least tacit support from Pitt. This support was now slowly withdrawn, causing upset to the passage of commercial legislation. Equally, the king's friends set about qualifying the terms of the new provisions. In cabinet, they frittered the new measures down to a minimum, mutilating the architecture of Rockingham's grand design. Even this, Burke conceded, was better than nothing.[58] But then Pitt changed tack, withdrawing his opposition to the new dispensation. Accordingly, with the requisite votes available in the Commons and the Lords, on 6 June 1766 the Rockingham's commercial policy received the royal assent. The trade of the American colonies was permitted to expand, while West Indian commerce was opened to the Spanish Empire.[59]

The Rockinghams had challenged the basis of Grenville's legislation. In the process, they had undermined the rationale of fundamental aspects of the Navigation Acts while securing colonial submission to the metropole. O'Hara was alive to the intended scale of the new provisions, and Burke admitted that the aim was to reconfigure the trade of the Empire, in effect abolishing a system of commercial restraint insofar as this could be harmonised with mercantile prejudice.[60] Any substantial revision to the political economy of the Empire implied a recalibration of political relations with the colonies. O'Hara could only surmise what Burke and his friends were up to, but nonetheless appreciated the essence of the proposed scheme. A liberalisation of trade was to take place in conjunction with the repeal of the Stamp Act. It was a gesture of munificence that served the interest of the metropole while winning over the provinces by a display of generosity. Since the benefactor was the British legislature, magnanimity on the part of parliament would confirm its authority. A gesture in favour of liberty was at the same time an act of "dominion." The

[55] EB to Charles O'Hara, 23 April 1766, *Corr.*, I, pp. 251–52.

[56] EB to Charles O'Hara, 8 April 1766, ibid., p. 248.

[57] Specifically, Grafton and Conway pressed for some kind of union with Pitt, while Northington and Egmont sought cooperation with the Bute faction.

[58] EB to Charles O'Hara, 23 April 1766, ibid., p. 251.

[59] F. Armytage, *The Free Ports System in the British West Indies* (London: Longmans, Green and Co., 1953).

[60] Charles O'Hara to EB, 15 April 1766, in Hoffman, *Burke*, p. 344; EB to Charles O'Hara, 23 April 1766, *Corr.*, I, p. 252.

regeneration of American commerce would "derive its existence wholly from the British legislature," instilling loyalty in the process of confirming subordination.[61] As it turned out, the full range of the Rockinghams' plans did not make it onto the statute book, yet the overarching plan was to promote serious reform. After the fall of the administration on 23 July 1766, having lasted just a year and twenty days, Burke would defend its work in a brief celebratory pamphlet. Trade, he wrote, had been "set free"; the commerce of the colonies had been extended without detriment to the mother country; West Indian and continental interests had been coordinated; and imperial supremacy had been reconciled with colonial subordination.[62]

Although Pitt ultimately relinquished his opposition to the Dominican free port, he maintained his campaign against the ministry from April through to July. Rockingham's government, Burke later remarked, had been removed "upon a Plan settled by the Earl of *Chatham*."[63] On the eve of the formation of the Rockingham administration, Burke had entertained the idea of "taking in Lord Bute."[64] At the very least, the new ministry should avoid instigating a quarrel with the king's friends, and ought to aim to establish a broad-based administration, including a proportion of Tories and men of business. This was a plea for cooperating with the followers of George III, though it was not a plan that the Whig grandees were to find either credible or bearable. After the fall of the ministry, Burke affirmed on their behalf: "With the Earl of Bute they had no personal connection; no Correspondence of Councils. They neither courted him nor persecuted him."[65] The result was that they had been opposed in office by a conspiracy of placemen and pensioners, obliging them to appeal to "the Confidence of the Nation."[66] The nation included the public and opinion in the Commons. To encourage the former, the Rockinghams had organised support from commercial interests; to ensure the latter, they hoped to sustain cooperation with William Pitt.[67] However, the Rockinghams' problem was that their refusal to combine with the king's men was not compensated for by effective collaboration with Pitt.[68] In Burke's judgment, their dependence on the Great Commoner had itself proved an obvious source of weakness. When in April 1766 Pitt began to draw away from them, they lost a material "prop" on which they leaned.[69] Pitt challenged them publicly during the militia debate on 14 April 1766. The followers of Bedford and Grenville then attacked Dowdeswell's budget plans. At this time, Pitt was signalling his preparedness to form a government, but on terms

[61] Charles O'Hara to EB, 15 April 1766, in Hoffman, *Burke*, p. 345.

[62] EB, *Short Account of a Late Short Administration* (1766), *W & S*, II, p. 55.

[63] Ibid., p. 54.

[64] EB and William Burke to Charles O'Hara, 4 July 1765, *Corr.*, I, p. 208.

[65] EB, *Short Account of a Late Short Administration* (1766), *W & S*, II, p. 56.

[66] Ibid.

[67] Ibid., p. 55, on being the first administration to hold free public consultations.

[68] Frank O'Gorman, *The Rise of Party in England: The Rockingham Whigs, 1760–1782* (London: George Allen & Unwin, 1975), p. 158.

[69] EB to Charles O'Hara, 21 April 1766, *Corr.*, I, p. 250.

that included the exclusion of Newcastle and Rockingham. When the bid failed, the Duke of Grafton set about resigning from the ministry.[70] The foundations of the government were shaken, and the end was drawing near. "Mr. Pitt," as Walpole commented, "was grown impatient for power."[71] David Hume expressed the general sense of the terms on which he expected his ambitions to be fulfilled: he wished to model an administration "as he pleases."[72] Burke took this to be symptomatic of an underlying syndrome. Pitt aimed to destroy party in the garb of patriotism. He wanted to monopolise government by winning the backing of the court after securing his own base by popular appeal. Accordingly, on 24 April 1766, he made what Burke described as a "fine flaming patriotick Speech, chiefly against any sort of connections." Burke was clear about what Pitt's position entailed: it meant destroying all connections except connection with himself.[73]

5.3 The Whiteboy Disturbances

Although Burke largely failed to incorporate revision of the Irish trade laws into the reformation of American commercial regulations, he did at least manage to introduce an Irish Soap Bill before the Commons.[74] The aim was to permit the importation of soap manufactured in Ireland into West Indian plantations. Burke kept O'Hara informed of the progress of the Bill between March and April 1766.[75] However, at this time he was equally preoccupied with the revival of sectarian strife in Ireland.[76] The origins of the conflict lay in rural discontent, the first instance of regional agrarian rebellion since the activities of the Houghers in the early eighteenth century.[77] The agitation of the 1760s, orchestrated by an oath-bound society of "Levellers" or "Whiteboys," soon impacted on relations between Roman Catholics and the Protestant establishment.[78] Typically, protestors engaged in the kind of disorder that

[70] Grafton, *Autobiography*, p. 71.

[71] Walpole, *Memoirs*, III, p. 37.

[72] David Hume to Lord Hertford, 8 May 1766, *The Letters of David Hume*, ed. J.Y.T. Greig (Oxford: Oxford University Press, 1932), 2 vols., II, p. 43.

[73] EB to Charles O'Hara, 24 April 1766, *Corr.*, I, p. 252.

[74] *CJ*, XXX, p. 825.

[75] EB to Charles O'Hara, 29 March 1766, *Corr.*, I, p. 247; EB to Charles O'Hara, 8 April 1766, ibid., p. 249.

[76] L. M. Cullen, "Burke, Ireland, and Revolution," *Eighteenth-Century Life*, 16 (1992), pp. 21–42.

[77] W.E.H. Lecky, *History of Ireland in the Eighteenth Century* (London: Longmans, Green and Co., 1913), 4 vols., I, pp. 136–37; J. S. Donnelly, "Irish Agrarian Rebellion: The Whiteboys of 1769–1776," *Proceedings of the Royal Irish Academy*, 83C (1983), pp. 293–331. The passivity of Ireland over recent generations was emphasised in Anon., *An Inquiry into the Causes of the Outrages Committed by the Levellers, or White-Boys, in the Province of Munster* (np: 1762), included as an appendix to [John Curry], *A Candid Enquiry into the Causes and Motives of the Late Riots in the Province of Munster in Ireland* (London: 1767), pp. 25ff.

[78] Ian McBride, *Eighteenth-Century Ireland: Isle of Slaves* (Dublin: Gill and Macmillan, 2009), pp. 312–19.

Burke, at least, would expect of "an oppressed or a licentious people."[79] This included the maiming of cattle, the levelling of ditches, breaching perimeter walls and launching arson attacks on barns. For one contemporary pamphleteer, such conduct betrayed the true rights of the people by resort to popular violence in defiance of legal redress.[80] In due course, the situation gave rise to inter-denominational hostility on account of the judicial response to the campaign in Munster. What dismayed Burke was the deliberate attempt to implicate Roman Catholics in general in the petty criminal activities of the more depraved rural classes.

In fact, according to the findings of John Aston, the chief justice of the common pleas appointed with Anthony Malone to head a commission of inquiry into the outrages, Catholics and Protestants were involved "promiscuously" in the violence.[81] The disturbances, nonetheless, revived religious bigotry in Munster, which was exploited as a means of withholding concessions from Catholics during the parliamentary session of 1761–2, when Burke was present in Dublin as secretary to Hamilton.[82] Years later, Burke recalled the succeeding period as having unleashed "insane prejudice and furious temper" among "the lower part of the prevailing faction."[83] The lesser Protestant gentry had fanned the flames of hatred by alleging a general conspiracy against the Hanoverian settlement. The suggestion was that agrarian violence had been encouraged among the lower Catholic orders, with the implication that the real initiative lay with the more reputable members of the community. As Burke later recalled: "All classes in the obnoxious description, who could not be suspected of the lower crime of riot, might be involved in the odium, in the suspicion, and sometimes in the punishment, of a higher and more criminal species of offence."[84] In other words, they could be charged with treasonous subversion against the current regime.

The Whiteboy protests began in the south of Ireland in the autumn of 1761, quickly spreading through Tipperary, Limerick, Waterford and Cork.[85] Although the activities of the Whiteboys were largely aimed at redressing agrarian grievances,

[79] EB, *Letter to Sir Hercules Langrishe* (1792), *W & S*, IX, p. 602.

[80] Anon., *The True Friends of Liberty: To the White-Boys of the South, the Oak-Boys of the North, and the Liberty-Boys of Dublin* (Dublin: 1763), p. 15.

[81] Aston's report can be found among Burke's papers, and is reprinted in *Correspondence* (1844), I, pp. 38–41.

[82] The episode is discussed in Louis M. Cullen, "The Blackwater Catholics and County Cork Society and Politics in the Eighteenth Century" in Patrick O'Flanagan and Cornelius Buttimer eds., *Cork: History and Society* (Dublin: 1993), pp. 565–71.

[83] EB to Richard Burke Jr., 20 March 1792, *Corr.*, VII, p. 101. Cf. EB, *Letter to William Smith* (29 January 1795), *W & S*, IX, p. 664.

[84] EB, *Letter to Sir Hercules Langrishe* (1792), ibid., p. 602. Cf. EB, *Letter to Lord Kenmare* (21 February 1782), ibid., pp. 569–70, on the "inhuman proceedings" of the period.

[85] WWM BkP 8:1; W. P. Burke, *The History of Clonmel* (Waterford: N. Harvey and Co., 1907), pp. 361–405; Maureen Wall, "The Whiteboys" in T. D. Williams ed., *Secret Societies in Ireland* (Dublin: Macmillan, 1973); James S. Donnelly, "The Whiteboy Movement 1761–1765," *Irish Historical Studies*, 21:81 (March 1978), pp. 20–54; Vincent Morley, "George III, Queen Sadhbh and the Historians," *Eighteenth-Century Ireland*, 17 (2002), pp. 112–20.

their supporters were soon construed as abetting Jacobite insurrection.[86] A criminal campaign was "metamorphosed" into a "conspiracy against the state."[87] Five hundred conspirators were imprisoned over a period of four years, and leading culprits were condemned to be executed. Burke found the reaction excessive in its severity. The idea that a fully fledged rebellion had been orchestrated by George III's Roman Catholic subjects in Ireland in league with the monarchy of France was so implausible as to be preposterous.[88] "The *affected* fears of a few leading, designing, but nominal protestants," argued John Curry, "have produced *real* terrors in all the sincere, and well meaning professors of the established religion."[89] Already in August 1762, as legal proceedings against the accused were passing through the courts, Burke wrote to Charles O'Hara of the "Horrors" of the Munster circuit.[90] Among those affected was Burke's relation, Garret Nagle, arrested on suspicion of lending assistance to the Whiteboys. Official conduct had been nothing less than "criminal" in Burke's opinion.[91] The establishment had colluded in popular prejudice, seeking to implicate respectable Catholic subjects in disturbances that had been perpetrated by the disgruntled rural poor.

The judicial response to the Munster disturbances was brought to a climax in 1766.[92] In the spring of that year a series of executions were carried out on the basis of suspect evidence. These included the hanging of James Farrell, James Buxton and Father Nicholas Sheehy, a parish priest from Clogheen in Tipperary.[93] Curry presented the Sheehy case as the Irish equivalent of the Calas affair in France, whose persecution had inspired Voltaire to write his *Traité sur le tolérance*.[94] Petitions and speeches by Sheehy and his co-defendants are to be found among Burke's papers.[95] In his final declaration, Buxton protested that he had "never heard . . . of a Rebel-

[86] Ironically, as Burke himself noted, the origin of the association with Jacobitism could be traced to William Fant, a mentally unstable Protestant attorney who first inspired the Whiteboys. See WWM BkP 8:1.

[87] EB, *Letter to Sir Hercules Langrishe* (1792), *W & S*, IX, p. 602.

[88] WWM BkP 8:1. At the start of the disturbances at the end of the Seven Years' War, the unlikelihood of the allegation was systematically laid out in a series of queries collected as Anon., *An Alarm to the Unprejudiced and Well-Minded Protestants of Ireland, or Seasonable Queries upon the Rise, Danger, and Tendency, of the White-Boys* (Cork: 1762).

[89] [Curry], *A Candid Enquiry*, p. 23.

[90] EB to Charles O'Hara, ante 23 August 1762, *Corr.*, I, p. 147.

[91] WWM BkP 8:1.

[92] R. R. Madden, *The Literary Life and Correspondence of the Countess of Blessington* (London: 2nd ed., 1855), 2 vols., I, pp. 484ff.

[93] A cousin of Burke's had married a sister of Sheehy's around 1755. See Cullen, "The Blackwater Catholics," p. 573.

[94] [Curry], *A Candid Enquiry*, Preface. Burke referred to the Calas affair after in debate on the Protestant riots against Catholic toleration in Scotland in 1779: see WWM BkP 8:51. On Sheehy, see Thomas P. Power, "Father Nicholas Sheehy, c. 1728–1766" in Gerard Moran ed., *Radical Irish Priests, 1660–1970* (Dublin: Columba Press, 1998).

[95] WWM BkP 8:2, 3, 4, 8, 9. Printed versions of the materials appear as an appendix in [Curry], *A Candid Enquiry*, pp. 49ff.

lion intended in this Kingdom," nor equally of any "Massacre" either planned or imagined.[96] He also revealed that he had been encouraged to give evidence against another Burke relation, James Nagle.[97] O'Hara had been updating Burke on the fate of Sheehy since February. On 20 March he wrote that evidence of an insurrection was still expected.[98] Burke was growing exasperated by his willingness to credit such spurious charges. "I find you go on in Ireland plotting; alarming; informing; seizing; and imprisoning as usual."[99] The Irish government appeared to ignore, or even collude in, the proceedings: "I see, that weak unsystematick Government will be more odious, as well as more contemptible, than wicked Government."[100] The contrast with Britain was stark, where liberality prevailed among men of the rarest ability. "Are you not ashamed," Burke asked O'Hara? As a result of fabricated fears in Munster, rumours of unlikely assassinations, massacres and rebellions in Ireland were rife at Westminster, each new wave as implausible as the last.[101] Yet, as persecution spread through the south of Ireland, toleration governed Rockinghamite policy in regard to French Catholics in Quebec.[102] Burke grew incensed and argued for intervention, while O'Hara insisted that interference would only inflame the situation.[103]

After the fall of Rockingham and the instalment of Pitt following his elevation as the Earl of Chatham to the House of Lords, the outgoing Whigs expected to keep a foothold in the administration by maintaining the allegiance of those who continued to hold their offices in the new regime.[104] Burke preferred to go out with Rockingham, although he registered some interest in acquiring a position under the incoming ministry. He would, Grafton believed, represent a considerable gain as "the readiest man upon all points perhaps in the whole House."[105] Rapprochement between Chatham and the Newcastle Whigs proved untenable, and when Rockingham and his friends went into opposition on 25 November 1766 Burke eagerly followed them into the ranks of the minority.[106] Before Burke definitively committed

[96] WWM BkP 8:9a. Patrick Nagle raised the case with Burke in November 1766. Burke was far from sure that his life was not "in the greatest danger." See EB to Patrick Nagle, 6 November 1766, *Corr.*, I, p. 276. James Nagle conformed to the established Church on 22 December 1766.

[97] WWM BkP 8:8.

[98] Charles O'Hara, 20 March 1766, in Hoffman, *Burke*, p. 340.

[99] EB to Charles O'Hara, 8 April 1766, *Corr.*, I, p. 249.

[100] EB to Charles O'Hara, 21 April 1766, ibid., p. 250.

[101] EB to Charles O'Hara, 24 May 1766, ibid., p. 255.

[102] The policy, however, was hampered by Northington: see R. A. Humphreys and S. M. Scott, "Lord Northington and the Laws of Canada," *Canadian Historical Review*, 14 (1933), pp. 54–62; Philip Lawson, *The Imperial Challenge: Quebec and Britain in the Age of the American Revolution* (Montreal and Kingston: McGill-Queen's University Press, 1994), ch. 4.

[103] Charles O'Hara to EB, 15 April 1766, in Hoffman, *Burke*, p. 346. Cf. Charles O'Hara to EB, 5 December 1767, *Corr.*, I, p. 338.

[104] Langford, *First Rockingham Administration*, p. 261.

[105] The Duke of Grafton to the Earl of Chatham, 17 October 1766, *Chatham Correspondence*, III, pp. 110–11.

[106] On the events that precipitated the move of the Rockinghamites into opposition, see John Brooke, *The Chatham Administration, 1766–1768* (London: Macmillan, 1956), pp. 46–62.

to the fate of the Rockinghamites, he spent some weeks in Ireland managing his personal affairs.[107] He had not visited since 1764, and he used his time to assess the state of politics in the country. A quarter of a century later, looking back on this period in Ireland, he noted the improvement since the 1740s and 1750s. Among the ministerial class in Dublin, the prejudices of the previous generation had been sloughed off, although these were still kept up among the squirearchy throughout the country. By August 1766, even the "shameful rage in Munster" had been virtually exhausted.[108] But what continued to haunt Burke was the fact that, under conditions where Roman Catholics were excluded from the franchise, persecution could pay dividends among rulers devoid of principle without the population affected being able to represent its case.

As Burke put it in his *Letter to Sir Hercules Langrishe* of 1792, the manufacture of treasonous plots among the Catholic population could be made to answer to the purposes of Protestant electioneering. In turn, those condemned simply had "no hold" on their putative representatives since these were drawn exclusively from an adverse denomination.[109] While religious bigotry was effectively on the decline in Ireland, it could be reignited through the kind of chicanery that flourished under a corrupted constitution. Instead of purging the constitution of the means by which prejudice was perpetuated, Burke believed that the crown was determined to increase its sway over Irish affairs. Nonetheless, he viewed the campaign for a Septennial Act, intended to strengthen the Irish parliament against the executive, as a distraction from more pressing concerns.[110] Since the Glorious Revolution, Irish parliaments were only dissolved upon the death of the reigning monarch, giving rise to the patriot goal of limiting their duration. But when that objective was embodied in an Octennial Bill, which received the royal assent in February 1768, Burke was unimpressed.[111] Shorter parliaments, in his view, were poorly equipped to limit the ambitions of the crown.[112] In any case, the Octennial Act was intended to ease the passage of a military augmentation Bill in Ireland, which Burke was virtually alone in opposing in the Commons.[113] Augmenting the Irish forces in peacetime served

[107] Mary Burke to Ellen Hennessy, 25 October 1766, *Correspondence* (1844), I, p. 112; EB to Charles O'Hara, 19 August 1766, *Corr.*, I, pp. 264–65; EB to the Marquess of Rockingham, 21 August 1766, ibid., pp. 266–67; EB to Richard Shackleton, [August 1766], ibid., pp. 267–8.

[108] EB to Richard Burke Jr., 20 March 1792, *Corr.*, VII, p. 102; cf. EB to Charles O'Hara, 27 November 1767, *Corr.*, I, p. 337.

[109] EB, *Letter to Sir Hercules Langrishe* (1792), *W & S*, IX, p. 603.

[110] EB to Charles O'Hara, 24 May 1766, *Corr.*, I, p, 255.

[111] EB to Charles O'Hara, 20 February 1768, ibid., p. 342.

[112] Burke had addressed the general theme in EB, "[National Character and Parliament]," reprinted in Richard Bourke, 'Party, Parliament and Conquest in Newly Ascribed Burke Manuscripts," *Historical Journal*, 55:3 (September 2012), pp. 619–52.

[113] Thomas Bartlett, "The Augmentation of the Army in Ireland, 1767–1769," *English Historical Review*, 96:380 (July 1981), pp. 540–59. For the role of the Octennial Bill in smoothing the passage of the Augmentation Bill, see the "The History of Europe," in *The Annual Register for the Year 1768* (London: 1769), p. 83.

no practical purpose; its sole contribution would be to inflate the military charge on the Irish establishment. As Burke saw it, the debts and expenses of Ireland were a cost to the Empire, and therefore to Britain.[114] What he found particularly irksome was the British ministerial invocation of the Whiteboy disturbances as a pretext for raising troop levels across the Irish Sea.[115] The ministry ought to address the ways in which agrarian violence could be exploited for sectarian purposes instead of using popular discontent to augment the forces of the crown.

Burke's dedication to what seemed to him the tolerant liberality of Whigs like Rockingham acquired a boost from his exposure to prejudice in Ireland in the mid 1760s.[116] The comparison between the two kingdoms was based not on an assessment of personalities, but on an understanding of the constitutional arrangements under which political characters were formed. The country was rotten and required urgent attention.[117] Sectarianism in Ireland had led to the construction of a divisive constitution, and the constitution now perpetuated the prejudicial attitudes that had been formed in the bitter struggles of the seventeenth century. By comparison, the rage of party in Great Britain had steadily subsided through an alliance between Whig families and the Hanoverian crown. With that alliance under threat since the accession of George III, it became necessary to campaign for the independence of parliament. It was this goal which the Rockinghams made their own after the summer of 1766. From that point forward, they would refuse to accept office except on terms of independence. For that they would have to remain intact as a collaborating corps. As Rockingham later argued in justifying his conduct in the 1760s, his role in politics was to keep together "a set of valuable men" ready to enter government as a counterweight to corruption.[118] Circumstances shook the Rockinghams from the habits of court Whiggism, while their commitment to business distinguished their conduct from earlier country oppositions.[119] They were committed to decisive administration, but for this they would have to free themselves from the divisiveness of the court.

[114]WWM BkP 27:94. Cf. EB, Speech on Prorogation of Irish Parliament, 3 May 1770, *W & S*, IX, p. 485.

[115]EB to Charles O'Hara, 20 February 1768, *Corr.*, I, p. 343.

[116]See his comment in EB, Letter to Thomas Burgh (1782), *W & S*, IX, p. 551, on the "known liberal principles in government, in commerce, in religion" of the Rockinghams in connection with Ireland.

[117]Burke expressed this view on 25 November 1767 in responding to the government's plans to augment the army establishment in Ireland. See EB to Charles O'Hara, 27 November 1767, *Corr.*, I, p. 337.

[118]The position was formulated by Burke: see EB, "Thoughts" (July 1779), *W & S*, III, p. 450.

[119]As a result of their refusal to act the part of king's men, the Rockinghams have often been identified as a country party. See C. Collyer, "The Rockingham Connection and Country Opinion in the Early Years of George III," *Proceedings of the Leeds Philosophical Society*, 8 (1952–55), pp. 251–75; Langford, *First Rockingham Administration*, p. 284; O'Gorman, *Rise of Party*, p. 228; Warren M. Elofson, "The Rockingham Whigs and the Country Tradition," *Parliamentary History*, 8 (1989), pp. 90–115. On the other hand, for the persistence of court Whiggism in Burke's thinking, see Reed Browning, "The Origins of Burke's Ideas Revisited," *Eighteenth-Century Studies*, 18 (1984), pp. 57–71.

5.4 Property and Popularity: *Nullum Tempus* and Wilkes

By the end of 1766, Burke had absorbed the implications of the Rockinghams' year in office. George III was not to be trusted as an honest broker among the Whigs; the king's friends threatened to unbalance Britain's mixed system of government; and Chatham stood exposed as a courtier who postured as a patriot. The situation forced the remaining Rockingham loyalists into opposition. Yet many of the Marquess's erstwhile followers retained their positions under Chatham, and were headed for years of service under the government of Lord North. This greatly reduced the strength of the minority. At the same time, opposition Whiggism was irredeemably fractured, with the Grenvilles and the Bedfords alienated from the residual Rockinghamites. Opposition might be respectable, Burke noted in December, but under current circumstances it was ineffective as an immediate route to power.[120] The following July, with Chatham incapacitated due to illness, Grafton and Conway approached Rockingham to induce him to accept office, but the negotiations misfired, and the prospect of ongoing exclusion from office stretched into the distance. Even so, Burke's reputation as a speaker continued to grow. "Mr. Bourke has made himself very considerable," Lord George Sackville wrote to General Irwin in the spring of 1767. His performances were "ingenious," both opening and in reply.[121] As much as Burke relished the practicalities of administration, it was as an opposition debater that he refined his rhetorical skills. Sixteen years would pass before Burke's friends were again in office. As early as December 1766, Burke had accepted that the view of a return to government was "dim and remote," but this position perfectly suited his disposition.[122]

As Burke saw the matter, the goal of the Rockinghams was to build a party of principle. For this they would have to develop a reputation for devotion to the public by cultivating opinion out of doors whilst winning credit for their consistency within the Houses of Parliament.[123] This would involve conducting themselves as partisans, concerting to bolster their strength against the predominance of the crown. The crown prospered in the absence of Whig unity by successfully enlisting court friends. The "power of the Crown arises out of the weakness of Administration," Dowdeswell pleaded in a memorandum in July 1767.[124] Strong government

[120] EB to Charles O'Hara, 23 December 1766, *Corr.*, I, p. 284.

[121] Historical Manuscripts Commission, *Report on the Manuscripts of Mrs. Stopford-Sackville* (London: 1904), p. 120.

[122] EB to Charles O'Hara, 23 December 1766, *Corr.*, I, p. 285.

[123] On the need for enduring popular support, see EB to the Marquess of Rockingham, 21 August 1766, ibid., p. 267. For principled consistency as the key to this, see the Marquess of Rockingham to the Duke of Newcastle, 16 March 1767, Add. MS. 32980, fols. 296–97.

[124] William Dowdeswell, "Thoughts on the Present State of Public Affairs" in Gaetano L. Vincitorio ed., *Crisis in the "Great Republic": Essays Presented to Ross J. S. Hoffman* (New York: Fordham University Press, 1969), pp. 1–13.

would require a unity of purpose for which the Rockingham party stood but which other connections failed to support.[125] Burke was therefore happy to play a long game, avoiding political dependence and campaigning on the basis of conviction. The appeal to party against the executive implied a principled alliance: "there are no contradictions to reconcile; no cross points of honour or interest to adjust; all is clear and open; and the wear and tear of mind, which is saved by keeping aloof from crooked politics, is a consideration absolutely inestimable."[126] It was in this spirit that Burke applauded Rockingham's refusal of office in July 1767. By then, the "Bute influence" had lost all its terrors for Chatham and his associates, but for Rockingham and Burke it remained a threat to the constitution: "L[or]d Bute is seldom a day out of town," Burke advised his patron on 1 August 1767.[127] Under the circumstances, the Rockinghams were right to reject all inducements to power.[128] Their goal should be to enter an administration from a position of strength, based on independence from the corruptions of influence. This meant assuming office in collaboration with other parties, inhabiting government as a "Corps" that would draw all connections into a focus. From that position the Rockinghams could unite the Whig interest against court faction.[129] They would thus play an essential constitutional role in reducing the power of the executive by diminishing the presence of the king's friends, exemplified by the privileges accorded the associates of Lord Bute.[130]

The Rockingham connection was now confirmed as the focus of Burke's activities. As he wrote to the Duke of Newcastle in the autumn of 1767: "I have, from inclination and principle, a strong attachment to that System of which your Grace forms so eminent a part."[131] Having resolved to oppose the ministry, there was little chance of rapid change, but the compensation was that the Rockinghams' consciences were clean.[132] This posture suited Burke above all others. Honesty, it seemed, was the only available policy.[133] In December 1767 he communicated to O'Hara his commitment to acting with consistency in the Commons. He had entered parliament not for preferment, but as a "refuge."[134] Maintaining his relative independence in politics offered security against the dependence that he had

[125] See the Marquess of Rockingham to the Duke of Newcastle, Add. MS. 32975, fol. 307.

[126] EB to Charles O'Hara, 23 December 1766, *Corr.*, I, p. 285.

[127] EB to the Marquess of Rockingham, 1 August 1767, ibid., p. 316. On the persistence of the fear of Bute among the Rockinghamites, see O'Gorman, *Rise of Party*, p. 182. For Rockingham's own alarm, see the Marquess of Rockingham to the Earl of Hardwicke, 2 July 1767, *Rockingham Memoirs*, II, p. 53.

[128] EB to John Hely Hutchinson, 3 August 1767, *Corr.*, I, p. 319.

[129] O'Gorman, *Rise of Party*, p. 209. Rockingham was determined to play a hegemonic role. On this, see John Brewer, *Popular Ideology and Popular Politics at the Accession of George III* (Cambridge: Cambridge University Press, 1976), pp. 91–92.

[130] EB to the Marquess of Rockingham, 1 August 1767, *Corr.*, I. p. 317. In fact the evidence suggests that Bute withdrew from politics at this time.

[131] EB to the Duke of Newcastle, 30 August 1767, ibid., p. 325.

[132] EB to James Barry, 24 August 1767, ibid., p. 323.

[133] This was the theme of EB, Letter to the *Public Advertiser (c. 1768), W & S*, II, pp. 74–75.

[134] EB to Charles O'Hara, 11 December 1767, ibid., p. 340.

experienced as a client of Hamilton. Acting in party facilitated independent judgment, whereas solitary action entailed exposure to coercive individuals, which might force one into dependence on the crown. Becoming an MP was a manifest liberation for Burke; distinguishing himself in debate gave solidity to that freedom. Reflecting on his position of relative autonomy within a party, he recalled the oppression of Hamilton as an attempt to ruin him when he "first began to meddle in Business."[135] The Rockinghamites for Burke meant constitutional salvation as well as personal release from bondage. They offered a means of promoting talent under the protection of property. By comparison, as Burke noted in his Speech on the Address of 24 November 1767, the new government, now effectively under the Duke of Grafton, enabled the crown to divide and rule by acting against the unity of party: "Is it not notorious that they only subsist by creating divisions among others? Their plan is to separate party from party? Friend from friend?"[136] The current ministry, Burke commented the following year, comprised a set of men who had "separately betrayed every friend and renounced every principle in order to acquire their present situation."[137] This was a price that the Rockinghams would not pay.

Rockinghamite cohesion was sustained by the commitment of its members to the claims of the people against the crown. In practice, this meant serving the cause of property under the constitution. An opportunity to rally supporters around that issue emerged in 1768. The previous year Sir James Lowther, a relation of Bute's, issued a claim against lands in Cumberland including Inglewood Forest and the Socage of Carlisle in the possession of the Bentinck family since 1705, and currently occupied by the Rockinghamite peer, the third Duke of Portland.[138] Since Inglewood Forest was inhabited by up to 400 freehold tenants, Lowther's control of the territory would confer upon him the ability to influence voters against Portland's candidate in the forthcoming election of 1768.[139] Because William III's grant of the Cumberland estates omitted to specify all lands occupied by Portland, Lowther, acting through his lawyer William Blackstone, was in a position to issue a claim against the landlord on the grounds that *nullum tempus occurrit regi*: irrespective of the practical use of the lands between 1705 and 1767, no amount of time could run against the rights of the crown. Ministerial support for Lowther raised alarm among sections of the landed interest in parliament since the *nullum tempus* provision under which the claim against Portland was pleaded amounted to a declaration against the principle of prescription.[140] Accordingly, on 17 February 1768, Sir George Savile

[135] Ibid.

[136] EB, Speech on Address, 24 November 1767, *W & S*, II, p. 73.

[137] EB, "Tandem" to the *Public Advertiser*, 4 August 1768, *W & S*, II, p. 91.

[138] O'Gorman, *Rise of Party*, pp. 215–16.

[139] On the estimated number of voters, see the Duke of Portland to Charles Yorke, 17 February 1768, Add. MS. 35638, fol. 228.

[140] On this, see Paul Lucas, "On Edmund Burke's Doctrine of Prescription; Or, an Appeal from the New to the Old Lawyers," *Historical Journal*, 11:1 (1968), pp. 35–63, esp. at p. 55. As Burke saw it, the

brought in a *Nullum Tempus* Bill in defence of prescriptive right. The Bill sought to render void any claim by the crown on property held in possession for over sixty years.[141] "It was a most honourable day for us," the Marquess of Rockingham remarked afterwards.[142] The motion was lost by a margin of only twenty votes, encouraging Savile to resurrect the topic in the next session.[143] The Bill successfully passed the following year, placing prescription upon the statute book.[144] It was a measure, Burke later commented, in which he had "a very full share" in bringing to fruition.[145]

The debate over *nullum tempus* enabled Burke to challenge a principle that he held to be "fundamentally contrary to natural Equity."[146] The aim of the Bill, he argued, was to reduce "to one equitable & uniform standard" the rights of the crown and the subject in litigation over property.[147] This was essential, he went on, for the stability of possessions, the security of liberty, and the British constitution. He also tried to show through precedents drawn from Gaius and Justinian that faith was the foundation of property, and prescription the basis of faith.[148] This represented Burke's first public display of his commitment to large territorial possessions, secured under prescriptive right, as offering the best guarantee for the safety of property in general, and thus the peace of society altogether. Hume had claimed that it was commonly imagined that a just distribution of property might be secured on the basis of the science of morals: on this assumption, the knowledge of virtue would reward the deserving according to the rules of merit. Yet the partiality of human judgment, by which one person's award of merit appeared to another to be ill deserved, rendered any such arrangement impracticable.[149] Alternatively, the rules of property might be based on the idea of equal allocation, exemplified by Spartan equality and Roman agrarian laws. However, as Hume further noted, a verdict of the kind would be pernicious in its practical effects: an inquisition was required to maintain it, and

---

resuscitation of *nullum tempus* potentially affected "perhaps half the Landed property of the Kingdom". See WWM BkP 11:1.

[141] R. M. Kerr, in a note to his edition of William Blackstone, *Commentaries on the Laws of England* (London: 1862), 2 vols., I, bk. 2, ch. 17, shows the gradual contraction of the span of immemorial usage, taking the Prescription Act of 1832 (2 & 3 Will. IV, c. 71) as his example.

[142] The Marquess of Rockingham to the Earle of Albemarle, 23 February 1768, *Rockingham Memoirs*, II, p. 73.

[143] Burke briefly intervened in the debate: *Cavendish Debates of the House of Commons*, I, p. 52. A record of the votes cast is located at WWM BkP 11:8.

[144] 9 Geo. III, c. 16.

[145] EB, *Letter to a Noble Lord* (1796), *W & S*, IX, p. 171.

[146] EB, "Mnemon" to the *Public Advertiser (4 March 1768)*, *W & S*, II, p. 80. Cf. *The Annual Register for the Year 1768*, pp. 78ff. for substantially the same argument. In due course, Granville Sharp would claim that this principle of equity could be inferred from common law: see Granville Sharp, *A Short Tract Concerning the Doctrine of Nullum Tempus Occurrit Regi* (London: 1779), p. 11.

[147] WWM BkP 11:16.

[148] WWM BkP 11:18.

[149] David Hume, *An Enquiry Concerning the Principles of Morals* (1751), ed. Tom Beauchamp (Oxford: Oxford University Press, 1998), p. 90.

a tyranny to enforce it.[150] Ultimately, the rights of property had to be adjudicated through the provisions of the civil laws. These, however, were best constructed in accordance with the sentiment of justice.[151] That sentiment was supported by mental dispositions that enabled humans to associate possession with the right to property.[152] The perception of justice involved extrapolating general rules in conformity with these habits of mind. The most obvious rule was that justice should be served by the stability of property over time: in the absence of consent to alienate possessions, external goods should be durably ascribed to their possessors. The requirement of stability militated against redistribution, converting the inequality of fortunes into a principle of justice.[153]

Hume went on to argue that the stable ownership of external goods was generally supported by five principles which the human mind was disposed to embrace. These were present possession, first occupation, prescription, accession and succession. However, the first and second of these were potentially in conflict with one another, as illustrated by the controversy over *nullum tempus*: an original occupier and a present possessor were commonly different people, requiring adjudication between competing claims. Hume resolved this conflict by resort to the principle of prescription: "Present possession . . . is not sufficient to counter-balance the relation of first possession, unless the former be long and uninterrupted."[154] The recourse to length of time as conferring legitimacy upon present possession was an explicit invocation of the principle of prescription as decisive in the determination of ownership. On the basis of these observations, Hume derived two "laws of nature": first, "*that upon the first formation of society, property always follows the present possession*"; and second, that afterwards "*it arises from first or from long possession*."[155] Since a dispute between an original and a present owner can only be resolved by length of possession, the passage of time, giving rise to prescription, acted as the primary criterion of proprietorship.[156]

[150] Ibid., p. 91. Cf. Henry Home, Lord Kames, *Historical Law-Tracts* (Edinburgh: 1758), 2 vols., I, pp. 125–26.

[151] For Hume this was an acquired sentiment rather than a primordial instinct. See James Moore, "Hume's Theory of Justice and Property," *Political Studies*, 24:2 (1976), pp. 103–19. On the foundations of artificial virtues of the kind in the human aptitude for rational reflection, see Stephen Buckle, *Natural Law and the Theory of Property: Grotius to Hume* (Oxford: Oxford University Press, 1991, 2002), p. 287.

[152] David Hume, *A Treatise of Human Nature* (1739), ed. David Fate Norton and Mary J. Norton (Oxford: Oxford University Press, 2000, 2008), p. 323n.

[153] Ibid., p. 330.

[154] Ibid., p. 326n.

[155] Ibid., p. 327n. Cf. Thomas Rutherforth, *Institutes of Natural Law, Being the Substance of a Course of Lectures on Grotius's De Jure Belli ac Pacis* (Cambridge: 2nd ed., 1779), p. 117, for whom the right of prescription is based on a presumption of dereliction in the previous possessor.

[156] The point resolves a key problem in Locke. See Alan Ryan, *Property and Political Theory* (Oxford: Basil Blackwell, 1984), p. 34.

In his contributions to the *nullum tempus* debate, Burke similarly presented prescription as the basis of stable possession. "He that establishes prescription establishes property," he argued.[157] The debt to Hume is clear: "Possession during a long tract of time conveys a title to any object."[158] To secure possession, Burke believed, was the grand objective of all law.[159] This was of course the achievement of civil society under sovereign authority, yet effective authority had to be underpinned by supporting popular opinion. Property, that is, was secured by political power on the basis of an opinion of its justice. Burke's most famous intervention into public debate, the *Reflections on the Revolution in France*, took its bearings from this fundamental commitment to the original right of property as based on the law of nature. When the issue came before parliament in 1771, Burke seized upon the opportunity to argue for the incorporation of prescriptive title into national legislation. This would provide a means of enshrining in statute law a principle derived at once from natural law and the law of nations.[160] The idea that prescriptive right had a basis in the law of nations had been proposed by Hugo Grotius in *The Rights of War and Peace*. Without some presumption that length of possession could confer title, "Disputes about Kingdoms, and their Boundaries, would never be at an End."[161] For Grotius the passage of time implied the consent of the previous owner, and so prescription was a form of tacit consent.[162] On this basis, in addition to having a basis in the law of nations, it also had a foundation in natural law.[163]

Equally for Burke, prescriptive claims might be codified in positive law, but originally they were based on natural law. "The principle of prescription," he claimed, was a fundamental precept of law: its positive recognition was based on the "Law of nature."[164] Natural law prescribed that use conferred a title to ownership. The

[157] WWM BkP 11:19.

[158] Hume, *Treatise*, p. 326. The Humean origins of Burke's ideas were generally, though imprecisely, canvassed in Friedrich Meinecke, *Die Entstehung des Historismus* (Munich and Berlin: Oldenbourg 1936), 2 vols., I, vi, 3. See also Mario Einaudi, "The British Background of Burke's Political Philosophy," *Political Science Quarterly*, 49 (1934), pp. 576–98; H. B. Acton, "Prejudice," *Revue internationale de philosophie*, 21 (1952), pp. 323–36.

[159] WWM BkP 11:16.

[160] EB, *Nullum Tempus* Amendment Bill, 20 February 1771, *Cavendish Debates of the House of Commons*, II, p. 318. Cf. EB, Speech on the Church *Nullum Tempus* Bill, 17 February 1772, *Parliamentary History*, XVII, col. 305.

[161] Hugo Grotius, *Rights of War and Peace*, ed. Richard Tuck (Indianapolis, IN: Liberty Fund, 2005), 3 vols., II, p. 484. Grotius is taking issue with the natural lawyer Gabriel Vásquez.

[162] Ibid., p. 491. Jean Barbeyrac modified this claim in his edition of Samuel Pufendorf, *De iure naturae et gentium libri octo* (Lund: 1672), bk. IV, ch. xii, § 8, n. 3.

[163] This is implied at Grotius, *Rights of War and Peace*, II, p. 496.

[164] WWM BkP 11:7. Cf. WWM BkP 1:16: "an act of Limitation is a Law not of choice & expedience, but of the strictest Duty. It is a Debt from Legislature to the people. It is the Law of Nature, not made, but only explained & inforced by positive statute." See also EB, *Nullum Tempus* Amendment Bill, 20 February 1771, *Cavendish Debates of the House of Commons*, II, p. 318: "I never felt so clear a conviction in my life, as that such a right of long possession is founded upon the immutable law of nature."

passage of time, which transformed use into custom, converted possession based on use into a right to property.[165] For Burke this right depended not on actual or implied consent, but on the simple fact of immemorial usage: a questionable title, over an expanse of time, gradually yielded to legitimate possession. Conquest, including the seizure of estates, over time gave rise to a rightful claim of dominion, although this claim carried with it an obligation to render justice. "Upon what other foundation," William Paley later wrote of prescription, "stands any man's right to his estate? The right of primogeniture, the succession of kindred, the descent of property, the inheritance of honours, the demand of tithes, tolls, rents, or services . . . upon what are they founded, in the apprehension at least of the multitude, but upon prescription?"[166] Already committed to this conception in the 1760s, Burke concluded that nothing could be more destructive to the institution of property than an arbitrary attempt on prescriptive title. The events of 1789 in France, beginning with the claim of the National Assembly on the corporate property of the Gallican Church, represented an assault on prescription of a kind that Burke had long feared, but on a scale that he could not have imagined in the Britain of the 1760s. In the face of such an assault, it was not merely privilege but justice itself that was threatened with extinction.

The defenders of *nullum tempus* argued that the rent which the resumption of old titles such as the crown's to Portland's Cumberland estates made a new stream of revenue available to the government.[167] From Burke's perspective, on the other hand, the permanent existence of a fixed civil list establishment at the disposal of the crown made this an unpersuasive plea. Besides, it was parliament, and not the king, that had a claim upon national revenues. Altogether, the principle of *nullum tempus* bore the obnoxious appearance of an invasive prerogative. Such excessive prerogative claims should be rejected by the friends of monarchy since they could only render royal authority offensive to the public mind.[168] Kings might have an interest in the servitude of their people, but never in imbuing them with hatred.[169] A prerogative claim to overrule prescription was a potential source of public terror that posed a threat to common equity. It could only be explained as a relic of barbarism. Political liberty,

[165] "Prescription" and "custom" gradually became interchangeable in eighteenth-century usage, but originally they were technically distinct. See William Blackstone, *Commentaries on the Laws of England* (London: 1765), 4 vols., II, pp. 263–64.

[166] William Paley, *The Principles of Moral and Political Philosophy* (1785) (Indianapolis, IN: Liberty Fund, 2002), p. 287. Cf. Dugald Steward, *The Philosophy of the Active and the Moral Powers of Man* in *The Collected Works of Dugald Stewart*, ed. William Hamilton (Edinburgh: 1854–60), 11 vols., VII, p. 271: "while a regard for legal property is thus secured, among men capable of reflection, by a sense of general utility, the same effect is accomplished, in the minds of the multitude, by habit and the association of ideas; in consequence of which all the inequalities of fortune are sanctioned by mere prescription; and long possession is conceived to found a right of property as complete as what, by the law of nature, an individual has in the fruits of his own industry."

[167] *The Annual Register for the Year 1768*, p. 81.

[168] WWM BkP 11:1.

[169] Ibid.

by comparison, was based on natural equality, on the basis of which individuals were entitled to litigate "aequo iure."[170] The crown should have no privileged claims in respect of private property. The plea of *nullum tempus* thus ran counter to the basic principles of civil equality in enlightened regimes. It also posed a particular danger to the British constitution: since, as the case of Inglewood Forest made clear, landed property brought with it leverage in elections, attempts to resume dormant titles in favour of the king promised to increase the political influence of the crown.[171] What Burke saw as the "natural connection" between landlord and voter would be severed in favour of corrupt ministerial influence.[172] Whereas landed grandees won the support of freehold tenants, the executive would govern the votes of electors on the basis of fear rather than gratitude. Consequently, "all the sacred Bands that hold the Nation together" would be "broken in a moment," and the constitutional balance based on the representation of the counties would be perilously undermined.[173]

Burke was again returned for Wendover on Verney's interest in the general election 1768. The previous year, he had taken a house on Charles Street off St. James's Square, within walking distance of parliament.[174] In the spring of 1768, he gathered all his resources to "cast a root in this Country": he purchased a 600 acre estate at Beaconsfield in Buckinghamshire, 24 miles from London.[175] The Gregories estate at Beaconsfield would offer Burke the chance to become "a farmer in good earnest."[176] It would also provide a welcome retreat and a family residence for the remainder of his career. Writing to Richard Shackleton to update him on his situation, Burke also mentioned the position of the party: they were still holding themselves aloof from the machinations of the court.[177] Their clout was considerably reduced since their period in office. Rockinghamite support in the House of Commons had diminished from 111 to 54 by 1768.[178] Against this background, the *Nullum Tempus* Bill offered a powerful means of rallying the landed interest. Major points of principle were an essential method of sustaining the viability of opposition to the crown. The fate of Wilkes soon offered another focal point.[179]

170 WWM BkP 11:7.

171 EB to the Marquess of Rockingham, 29 June 1769, *Corr.*, II, p. 38.

172 WWM BkP 11:1.

173 Ibid.

174 He moved to Fluyder Street in September 1769. He moved again for the 1772 session of parliament, returning to Charles Street in 1779, where he remained until about 1785. See F. P. Lock, *Edmund Burke, 1730–1797* (Oxford: Oxford University Press, 1998–2006), 2 vols., I, pp. 242, 286, 326, 440.

175 EB to Richard Shackleton, 1 May 1968, *Corr.*, I, p. 351. On the details of Burke's financial transactions regarding this purchase, see Dixon Wecter, *Edmund Burke and his Kinsmen: A Study of the Statesman's Financial Integrity and Private Relationships* (Boulder, CO: Library of the University of Colorado, 1939), pp. 27–28.

176 EB to Richard Shackleton, 1 May 1968, *Corr.*, I, p. 351.

177 Ibid.

178 O'Gorman, *Rise of Party*, p. 220.

179 On the symbolic status of Wilkes, see Brewer, *Party Ideology and Popular Politics*, ch. 9.

The opening session of 1769 was dominated by the consequences of Wilkes's election to parliament for Middlesex. Controversy over the wayward idol of "liberty" had been in abeyance for about four years. After being successfully prosecuted for obscene and seditious libel on 19 January 1764, Wilkes remained on the continent as an outlaw from justice, until his return to contest a seat in the 1768 election. In the interim he had canvassed the assistance of the Rockinghams, but it was the prospect of a seat in parliament that drew him back to Britain.[180] The election, which stretched through the spring from 16 March to 6 May, saw Wilkes successfully returned, a "triumphant tribune" as Walpole described him.[181] Yet the process was accompanied by riots and disorderly behaviour, culminating in the "Massacre" of over half a dozen protestors at St. George's Fields on 10 May 1768.[182] This "tragic scene" of "blood, horror, and confusion," as a deputy marshal at the King's Bench Prison overlooking the Fields presented it, was only the most extreme event in a sequence of turbulent days in London during which a mob besieged the Houses of Parliament and the coal-heavers rampaged in the streets.[183] Walpole marvelled at the series of outrages perpetrated "in a vast capital, free, ungoverned, unpoliced, and indifferent to everything but its pleasures and factions!"[184]

Three days after the St. George's Fields shootings, Burke descried the succession of "tumults upon tumults" in the House of Commons, and demanded that the underlying causes be examined.[185] When a Bill was introduced to empower the king to call out the militia in response to ongoing disturbances, Burke reiterated the point: "The cause is a general one, which has inflamed the people, from one end of the kingdom to the other."[186] The Rockinghams had long resolved to support "the Cause not the Person" of Wilkes: "he is not ours; and if he were, is little to be trusted."[187] As a result, Burke set about developing a general diagnosis that would contribute to an analysis of the British political scene. This would amount to a restatement of the essentials of Whig doctrine, elucidating the role of the people in parliamentary politics. The principles of publicity and popular representation were distinguishing features of public life in Britain, yet when liberty had to be asserted by means of

[180] Burke sets out his and the Marquess of Rockingham's attitude in EB to Richard Burke Sr., ante 14 January 1766, *Corr.*, I, p. 231.

[181] Walpole, *Memoirs*, IV, p. 7.

[182] George Rudé, *Wilkes and Liberty* (Oxford: Oxford University Press, 1962), ch. 3.

[183] William Prentice, *The Extraordinary Case of William Prentice, Late Deputy Marshall of the King's Bench Prison, with a Short but Precise Narrative of the Transactions in St. George's Fields* (London: 1768), p. 24. I am grateful to Joanna Innes for referring me to this pamphlet.

[184] Walpole, *Memoirs*, IV, p. 22.

[185] EB, Address on the King's Proclamation for Suppressing the Riots, 13 May 1768, *Cavendish Debates of the House of Commons*, I, p. 14. Cf. EB, Debate on Re-election of Wilkes, 7 April 1769, *Parliamentary History*, XVI, col. 583.

[186] EB, Speech on the Militia Bill, 16 May 1768, *Cavendish Debates of the House of Commons*, I, p. 22.

[187] EB to Charles O'Hara, 9 June 1769, *Corr.*, I, pp. 352–53. Cf. the Duke of Newcastle to the Duke of Portland, 11 April 1768, Add. MS. 32989, fols. 219–20.

insurgency the constitution risked being overturned.[188] Even so, while the violence of popular protest made the Rockinghams wary of Wilkes's cause, the assault of the ministry on freedom of the press and the right of election brought the opposition into alignment with the popular movement that Wilkes inspired.[189]

When parliament opened on 23 January 1769, Wilkes was still in prison, and facing a renewed charge of seditious libel. Joseph Martin, a new opposition MP, moved that Wilkes should be protected by parliamentary privilege, appealing to Whig principles "in support of liberty."[190] In the ensuing debate, Burke focused on the conflict between the laws of libel and the liberty of the press.[191] By its high-handed treatment of libellous criticism, government was offending against the spirit of the constitution. Over the next year, Burke would connect the conduct of the Grafton ministry to new tendencies in the management of public affairs that he traced back to the accession of George III. Popular sentiment, he suggested, was being gradually disregarded as the approach of the administration became steadily more draconian. On 9 February 1769, in response to an attack on the Rockinghams by the Grenvillite publicist William Knox, Burke illustrated the new spirit by way of reference to the Grenville ministry in *Observations on a Late State of the Nation*.[192] The suggestion was that the harsh measures adopted by the current administration were already in evidence in the early 1760s. Knox had offered a direct provocation by accounting for the malaise in Britain and the colonies in terms of the record of the Rockingham administration. Burke retorted with a description of the oppressive habits of Grenville's government, under which, it was alleged, the "inclinations of the people were little attended to."[193] Filling ninety-eight pages in demy quarto, the *Observations* was Burke's first substantial pamphlet publication, largely taken up with a general account of the prospects for British power in comparison with French. In the process, it pointed to the underlying causes of discontent.

In trying to establish continuity between the character of public business under Grenville and the recent disturbances under Grafton, Burke recalled the riot of the

[188] EB, Motion respecting St. George's Fields Riots, 23 November 1768, *Cavendish Debates of the House of Commons*, I, p. 70. Cf. the Duke of Newcastle to the Marquess of Rockingham, Add. MS. 32990, fol. 39: "we must be either governed by a mad, lawless Mob, or the peace be preserved only by military force."

[189] WWM BkP 12:9: "I see a manifest design to *destroy* the Liberty of the press on one side & to encourage the most flagitious License on the other to make the press an instrument against the Liberties of the subject & to destroy it as a support to them."

[190] *Cavendish Debates of the House of Commons*, I, p. 116.

[191] EB, Speech on Wilkes's Privilege, 23 January 1769, *W & S*, II, p. 101. Cf. EB, Proceedings against Wilkes for a Seditious Libel, 16 December 1768, *Cavendish Debates of the House of Commons*, I, p. 109; EB, Debate on Lord Barrington's Motion for the Expulsion of Wilkes, 3 February 1769, Cavendish Diary, Eg. MS. 217, fol. 231; EB, Debate on Motion for the Expulsion of Wilkes, 10 February 1769, *Cavendish Debates of the House of Commons*, I, p. 227.

[192] For the publication date, see William B. Todd, *A Bibliography of Edmund Burke* (Godalming: St. Paul's Bibliographies, 1982), p. 71.

[193] EB, *Observations on a Late State of the Nation* (1768), *W & S*, II, p. 184.

Spitalfields weavers in the spring of 1765.[194] The "licentiousness and tumults of the common people, and the contempt of government . . . had at no time risen to a greater or a more dangerous height," Burke remarked.[195] Grenville's supporters, like those of Bedford and Chatham, were disposed to attribute the spirit of protest to the workings of faction or the impact of luxury. In his *Thoughts on the Cause of the Present Discontents* of 1770, Burke ridiculed the idea that prosperity produced discord.[196] Conway had suggested in 1768 that luxury had combined with faction to instil rebelliousness.[197] The reality was, however, that the measures adopted to suppress the mob had been more severe than the violence of the crowd. This stemmed, Burke thought, from the weakness of government, connected to the decline of party. As a result, power was applied directly to a defenceless population, leading to a mood of disaffection: "a disposition to the use of forcible methods ran through the whole tenour of administration."[198] The previous year, Burke was already explaining these desperate procedures in terms of a theory of constitutional corruption. The fault lay, he thought, with those who had been complicit in the destruction of "every personal dignity."[199] Burke was complaining about the studied disregard of George III for the Newcastle–Rockingham connection, which Burke associated with the spirit of independent Whiggism.

Burke looked back to a time when, under the dominance of the Pelhams, Whig grandees collaborated with the gentlemen of the Commons to deliver good government under a cooperative monarch. There was no question of seeking to diminish the dignity of the crown: "The Crown of Great Britain cannot, in my opinion, be too magnificent," Burke asserted.[200] Burke's commitment to royalty did not begin with the regency crisis, nor suddenly emerge in response to the French Revolution. Monarchy was an integral part of the mixed system of government. Royalty, he declared, was "the oldest and one of the best parts of our constitution."[201] Nonetheless, it was essential that its power be restrained within due bounds. It was the job of the Lords and Commons to provide the necessary limit. In order for the check to function, administrations would have to be composed of men of independent standing in parliament and the country. Current arrangements undermined that requirement. By comparison, prior to the accession of George III, the king retained his dignity and ministries their own weight. The "upper ranks were kept in order by a sense of their own importance": public esteem, based on social standing, engendered an attitude

[194] For an account, see the *London Gazette*, 21 May 1765. The subject is touched on in Rudé, *Wilkes and Liberty*, pp. 12, 38.

[195] EB, *Observations on a Late State of the Nation* (1768), *W & S*, II, p. 185.

[196] EB, *Thoughts on the Cause of the Present Discontents* (1770), ibid., p. 254.

[197] *Cavendish Debates of the House of Commons*, I, p. 15.

[198] EB, *Observations on a Late State of the Nation* (1768), *W & S*, II, pp. 184–85.

[199] EB, Debate on King's Proclamation for Suppressing Riots, 13 May 1768, *Cavendish Debates of the House of Commons*, I, p. 14.

[200] EB, Debate on the King's Message respecting the Civil List Debt, 28 February 1769, ibid., p. 273.

[201] Ibid.

of responsibility.[202] At the same time, the gentry and nobility, acting through the two Houses, operated as a bulwark against the despotism of the crown. They stood as a kind of "isthmus between arbitrary power and anarchy," securing the constitution against democracy and tyranny. The British had achieved what Montesquieu desired: an institutionalised intermediary body of sufficient social and political authority to be able to curb the ambitions of an expansive executive power. This "middle class," as Burke described it, between the monarch and the people possessed the wherewithal to mediate between popular frenzy and monarchical oppression.[203] To achieve that end, while checking the crown, parliament had to act in alliance with the people: "we are not to set ourselves against the people," Burke insisted.[204] In the face of definite provocation by government, the populace would certainly "be roused at last," pitting parliament against the privileges of the people out of doors.[205]

By 15 December 1768, after the member for Middlesex had published a letter from Viscount Weymouth signalling the need for troops in advance of the St. George's Fields Massacre, which included a provocative preface accusing the minister of premeditation, Grafton had determined to expel Wilkes from the Commons. The matter came before parliament in the new year. For all his contempt for Wilkes, Burke was appalled.[206] After his initial expulsion, Wilkes repeatedly stood again, only to meet with ejection three more times. Ultimately, it was decided that he was incapable of assuming a seat in the Commons, and Henry Luttrell was substituted in his place.[207] The government was disqualifying a member of the House "contrary to the unanimous opinion of the whole country," Burke protested. The populace at large would "take fire," he predicted, as parliament and people grew mutually estranged.[208] Beginning with the appointment of Lord Bute to head a ministry in 1762, George III had treated parliament as an "appendage" of the crown. The populace had consequently been cut loose from its moorings as government became separated from independent men of rank. Only an aristocracy could bind the multitude: "This is it that sways."[209] The people were disposed to attach themselves to individual leaders rather than campaign on abstract principles alone. This explained

[202] EB, Debate on King's Proclamation for Suppressing Riots, 13 May 1768, ibid., p. 15.

[203] Ibid.

[204] EB, Debate on Wilkes's Petition for Redress of Grievances, 27 January 1769, Cavendish Diary, Eg. MS. 216, fol. 210.

[205] Ibid., fol. 211.

[206] EB, Debate on Barrington's Motion for the Expulsion of Wilkes, 3 February 1769, Cavendish Diary, Eg. MS. 217, fols. 231–32: "In 1763, you took away privilege, you now take away the capacity of sitting in parliament."

[207] P.D.G. Thomas, *John Wilkes: A Friend to Liberty* (Oxford: Oxford University Press, 1996), ch. 6; Arthur H. Cash, *John Wilkes: The Scandalous Father of Civil Liberty* (New Haven, CT: Yale University Press, 2006), chs. 9 and 10.

[208] EB, Debate on Wilkes's Re-election, 17 February 1769, *Cavendish Debates of the House of Commons*, I, p. 231.

[209] Ibid.

the attraction of the "crowd" to the pageant of Wilkes.[210] If men of substance were disabled from representing popular sentiment, the people would be seduced into extra-parliamentary agitation.

Throughout the spring of 1769, Burke supported the public demand for popular representation. "I am pleading the cause of the people," he declared in the middle of April.[211] In his Speech on the Address to parliament the following year, he connected the turmoil in Britain to the crisis in the colonies: "The same baneful influence under which this country is governed, is extended to our fellow sufferers in America."[212] He summed up the conduct of government over the course of the previous two years: "military executions" had been carried out and countenanced; the debts on the civil list had been employed to promote corruption; the spurious claims of prerogative had threatened the rights of property; and the House of Commons had pitted itself against the rights of the people by unilaterally "declaring" elected members to be ineligible.[213] Altogether, these developments had served to diminish the representative role of the Commons. "The Peers represent themselves, we represent the people," Burke reminded his colleagues early in 1769.[214] Despite this, the Commons had increasingly appeared as "an assembly of inquisitors" rather than "an assembly of gentlemen." As such, they did not "represent those who sent them hither."[215]

The construction of ministries without due regard to the popularity of their members was leading to a contest between the government and the "mob." "Who, Sir, are the representatives of this mob," Burke pleaded in debate on the civil debt?[216] The first duty of government was to provide for order and security, yet an enlightened system of rule should also cater to popular liberty. British arrangements achieved that goal by means of representation. "Let us not forget," Burke urged his colleagues in the chamber, "from what original we spring."[217] However, the popular origins of the lower House ought not to render it a channel for the resentments of the people. The direct expression of popular attitudes was not the task of constitutional poli-

[210] EB to Charles O'Hara, 11 April 1768, *Corr.*, I, p. 349.

[211] EB, Debate on Onslow's Motion for Declaring in Favour of Luttrell, 15 April 1769, *Cavendish Debates of the House of Commons*, I, p. 378.

[212] EB, Speech on Address, 9 January 1779, *Parliamentary History*, XVI, col. 722.

[213] Ibid. On attempts by the Commons to usurp the role of legislator, see WWM BkP 12:1, 3, 6, 9. Burke recurred to this theme during the regency crisis: see the *Morning Herald*, 23 December 1788. See also EB to the Earl of Charlemont, 9 May 1769, *Corr.*, II, p. 23, on the confusion between the judicial role of the Commons and the legislative authority of parliament. Cf. EB to Charles O'Hara, 31 May 1769, ibid., pp. 26–27 on "this New, usurped, and most dangerous power of the house of Commons, in electing their own Members."

[214] EB, Debate on Proceedings against Wilkes for Seditious Libel, 2 February 1769, Cavendish Diary, Eg. MS. 217, fol. 96.

[215] EB, Debate on Lord Barrington's Motion for the Expulsion of Wilkes, 3 February 1769, Cavendish Diary, Eg. MS. 217, fol. 233.

[216] EB, Debate on Motion for an Inquiry into the Civil Debt, 1 March 1769, *Cavendish Debates of the House of Commons*, I, p. 287.

[217] Ibid.

tics. As Burke would repeatedly insist through the 1780s and 1790s, proclaiming grievances in the absence of structured deliberation was a recipe for escalating violence.[218] The administrations of Grenville and Grafton had defied the desires of the people, diluting the substance of parliamentary representation. Public authority had inevitably collided with national sentiment. That was an argument not for reproducing popular judgment, but for the constitutional reconciliation of the rights of the people with the duties of government. It was the ambition of Burke's *Thoughts on the Cause of the Present Discontents* to show how that objective might be achieved.

5.5 *Thoughts on the Cause of the Present Discontents*

Burke embarked on what was to become the *Thoughts on the Cause of the Present Discontents* in the early summer of 1769.[219] At that time, the Rockinghams were conspiring with the Grenvillites to launch a petitioning campaign throughout the country in alliance with the followers of Wilkes and the Society of Gentlemen Supporters of the Bill of Rights.[220] About twenty counties and a clutch of boroughs were involved in the campaign, which was inaugurated at a dinner on 9 May 1769. Burke took part, along with other members of the opposition: "All the minority, (however composed) dines today at the Thatched House," Burke wrote to a friend in Dublin, the first Earl of Charlemont.[221] The campaign proved to be founded on an uneasy alliance. Rockingham was reluctant to lend his support to the measure, and many followers were squeamish about the association with Wilkes. The Society for a Bill of Rights led the way in the metropolis and some western shires, with the parliamentary opposition taking the initiative in the remaining counties: Rockingham in Yorkshire, Dowdeswell in Worcestershire, and Temple in Buckinghamshire. Success in the shires was mixed. "Our petition goes *slowly*," Dowdeswell informed Burke in the autumn of 1769.[222] Activity in London was altogether more enthusiastic, spurred on by John Horne at the head of the Bill of Rights Society, and supported by a number of reform-minded MPs: James Townshend, John Sawbridge and Joseph Mawbey prominent among them. To the chagrin of Burke and Rockingham, these men were determined, along with Alderman William Beckford, to connect the cause of Wilkes to demands for more regular parliaments, a reduction of the standing army, place and pension bills, and also a "more equal" representation. In the 1760s, the

[218] EB, Debate on the Conduct of the Government during Tumults, 8 March 1769, ibid., p. 308.

[219] For the process of composition, see Donald C. Bryant, "Burke's Present Discontents: The Rhetorical Genesis of a Party Testament," *Quarterly Journal of Speech*, 43 (1956), pp. 115–26.

[220] On the strategy of petitioning in the period in general, see Mark Knights, "Participation and Representation before Democracy: Petitions and Addresses in Premodern Britain" in Ian Shapiro et al., *Political Representation* (Cambridge: Cambridge University Press, 2009).

[221] EB to the Earl of Charlemont, 9 May 1769, *Corr.*, II, pp. 23–24.

[222] William Dowdeswell to EB, 5 September 1769, ibid., p. 70. For a report on progress, see also the Marquess of Rockingham to EB, 30 July 1769, ibid., p. 50.

main constituency for such a programme was to be found in the City of London together with the greater metropolitan area.[223] The Rockinghams were anxious to retain control of the agenda, yet they feared their parliamentary rivals would capitulate to unwelcome measures that threatened the viability of the constitution.[224]

Burke remained optimistic that the Rockinghams could maintain a leading role. This would be based on the authority of Whig grandees in the party. It was permissible to stir up popular support, Burke thought, if education came in tow. "There is a great Spirit all over the Northern part of the Kingdom," he wrote to O'Hara. If it was "improved, supported, and rightly directed," it could not fail to assist in building a popular following.[225] Burke believed that the people should be participants in any system of popular government. Their feelings were often signalled by extra-parliamentary agitation, yet legislative action had to be pursued by means of representation. Logically, representatives could not be vehicles for the medley of competing judgments to be found among the masses out of doors, yet they had to take account of dominant feelings in the nation: "it is our duty to indulge the people out of doors."[226] This obliged members of parliament to deliberate on their behalf, not to act as delegates under instruction. Burke's position was developed in opposition to rival claims. On 1 March 1769, Joseph Mawbey announced in the Commons that he was acting under instructions, provoking disapproval from among some members.[227] The Chathamite, Isaac Barré, defended Mawbey's stance, so long as instructions embodied "the true voice of the people" and were delivered "in the spirit of the constitution."[228] Jeremiah Dyson, an expert in the House on parliamentary procedure, demurred: "I conceive there is, and ever has been, the most essential difference between deputies appointed to act according to the orders of those who send them, and representatives of the people who are chosen to act and to judge for them."[229] Burke, of course, was to develop this view over the course of the 1770s. For the moment his response was laconic: the "doctrine of instructions," he asserted, was "unfounded in reason." If unopposed, it would "destroy the constitution."[230] Burke recognised that the organisation of popular sentiment was one of the overriding challenges facing the conduct of free government. The *Thoughts on the Cause of the Present Discontents* was an attempt to show how organisation might proceed.

[223] Lucy S. Sutherland, *The City of London and the Opposition to Government, 1768–1774* (London: Athlone Press, 1959), *passim*. See also Simon Macoby, *English Radicalism, 1762–1785* (London: George Allen & Unwin, 1955); John Brewer, "English Radicalism in the Age of George III" in J.G.A. Pocock ed., *Three British Revolutions: 1641, 1688 and 1776* (Princeton, NJ: Princeton University Press, 1980).

[224] The Marquess of Rockingham to EB, 17 July 1769, *Corr.*, II, p. 48.

[225] EB to Charles O'Hara, 28 August 1769, ibid., p. 57.

[226] EB, Debate on Motion for an Inquiry into Civil Debt, 1 March 1769, *Cavendish Debates of the House of Commons*, I, p. 287.

[227] *Cavendish Debates of the House of Commons*, I, p. 282.

[228] Ibid., p. 283.

[229] Ibid., p. 285.

[230] EB, Debate on Motion for an Inquiry into Civil Debt, 1 March 1769, *Cavendish Debates of the House of Commons*, I, p. 287.

On 29 June 1769, Rockingham wrote to Burke encouraging him to continue with his pamphlet.[231] At that point, Burke's work was at an early stage of development. Even so, the basic idea was clear: his aim was to anatomise the whole "system" since 1760.[232] A month later, Burke was toying with the idea of presenting his argument in the form of a letter to be addressed to a Whig stalwart whose principles were still intact.[233] The implication was that the Whig position was as relevant as it had been under the first two Georges. If anything it was more necessary than ever, above all since the position faced an existential threat. The threat came, Burke believed, from the misguided conception that George III had of the constitution. The roots of this misconception lay in an alleged project devised by courtiers among the reversionary interest under the Pelhams to concoct a species of patriot monarchy. Burke's claim was that George III's father, Prince Frederick, had transmitted these ideas to his son, who tried in turn to realise them at the expense of Newcastle and then of the Rockingham Whigs.[234] This had brought about "a great change" in British affairs.[235] The change may have been facilitated by the education of the prince in the idioms of patriot kingship as originally espoused by Bolingbroke, but it had been carried into effect by irresponsible courtiers—the "king's friends," as Burke depicted them in the *Present Discontents*. Their activities threatened the integrity of the constitution, and had already given rise to public disorder as a result. Burke's worry was that in exposing a system so dear to the king without being certain of widespread popular support, the Rockinghams would be rendered ineligible for office.[236] Nonetheless, Burke's allegations against the court had to be explicit since corruption had proceeded insensibly. Even fundamentalist republicans, he thought, failed to notice the subtle difference: like most critics of public institutions, they were wise about the deficiencies and corruptions of the past but had little purchase on the current deformation of the British government.[237]

Whigs were accustomed to defending the rights of parliament against the crown, and they continued in an apparently similar vein under George III. However, the

[231] The Marquess of Rockingham to EB, 29 June 1769, *Corr.*, II, p. 39.

[232] Ibid.

[233] EB to the Marquess of Rockingham, 30 July 1769, ibid., p. 52.

[234] EB, *Thoughts on the Cause of the Present Discontents* (1770), *W & S*, II, p. 260. Cf. EB to O'Hara, 30 September 1772, *Corr.*, II, pp. 336–37. The claim has long been challenged: see Namier, *England in the Age of the American Revolution*, pp. 83–93. The details of George III's original ambitions are analysed in *Letters from George III to Lord Burke, 1756–1766*, ed. Romney Sedgwick (London: Macmillan, 1939), Introduction. However, many of his conclusions are suggestively challenged in Richard Pares's review of Sedgwick's edition in the *English Historical Review*, 5:219 (July 1940), pp. 475–79. See also Richard Pares, *King George III and the Politicians (Oxford: Oxford University Press, 1953)*, p. 71 (incl. footnote 2) for a more ambiguous statement on this subject.

[235] EB, *Thoughts on the Cause of the Present Discontents* (1770), *W & S*, II, p. 256.

[236] EB to the Marquess of Rockingham, post 6 November 1769, *Corr.*, II, pp. 108–9. Cf. EB to the Marquess of Rockingham, 18 December 1769, ibid., p. 122

[237] EB, *Thoughts on the Cause of the Present Discontents* (1770), *W & S*, II, p. 257.

threat to parliament was to be found no longer in attempts to undermine its outward forms, but in the operation of a new species of "influence." Most Whigs who laid claim to the legacy of the Pelhams accepted the necessity of influence or "corruption" as an essential means of reconciling executive with legislative power.[238] To effect decisions, ministries had to carry votes in the House of Commons, for which they needed to incentivise potentially cooperative members.[239] Yet influence of this kind had always been employed for the support of ministers of state with a view to carrying public business in accordance with their designs.[240] The problem facing the constitution since the accession of George III was that influence was being developed in new ways. This represented a departure from previous procedure under the Hanoverians. Since the Glorious Revolution, the "power of the Crown, almost dead and rotten as Prerogative, has grown up anew, with much more strength, and far less odium, under the name of Influence."[241] Between Walpole and Newcastle, this system of management successfully reconciled order with liberty. After 1760, however, influence was put in the service of a system of court favouritism.[242] This was facilitated by the fall-out from the Seven Years' War: overseas conquest, an increase in the national debt, as well as enlarged military and naval establishments, added considerably to the opportunities for court patronage.[243] Yet the key thing was that patronage was extended by George III to advance the interest of the crown against the Commons.[244] The court, as Burke presented it, was separated from the ministry, creating what he termed a "*Double Cabinet*."[245] A court conspiracy, Burke suggested, had set about freeing the crown from control by what was perceived to be an oligarchy of Whig ministers. In theory, the king was to be made his own master.[246] In practice, Britain would be brought to resemble the monarchy of France.[247]

It had long been argued by critics of court Whiggism that the patronage of the crown had been monopolised by ministers under the first two Georges who had thereby created a government of the few. The clerical publicist John Douglas was a prominent example. In 1761, he welcomed the new reign as promising an end to faction based on court corruption. Executive influence, channelled through Whig

[238] For a classic formulation, see David Hume, "Of the Independency of Parliament" (1741) in idem, *Essays Moral, Political, and Literary*, ed. Eugene F. Miller (Indianapolis, IN: Liberty Fund, 1985, 1987), p. 45.

[239] See John B. Owen, "Political Patronage in Eighteenth-Century England" in Paul Fritz and David William eds., *The Triumph of Culture: Eighteenth-Century Perspectives* (Toronto: A. M. Hakkert, 1972).

[240] EB, *Thoughts on the Cause of the Present Discontents* (1770), *W & S*, II, p. 269.

[241] Ibid., p. 258.

[242] Ibid., p. 261: by this means, "a cabal of the closet and back-stairs was substituted in the place of a national administration."

[243] Ibid., p. 262.

[244] The abuse of the Commons, Burke argued, entailed the abuse of "the whole": Northamptonshire MS. A. I.39B, reproduced as EB, Speech on Parliamentary Incapacitation, 31 January 1770, *W & S*, II, p. 234.

[245] EB, *Thoughts on the Cause of the Present Discontents* (1770), *W & S*, II, pp. 260, 274.

[246] Ibid., p. 266.

[247] Ibid., p. 303.

managers, pretended to offer a corrective to "*Democratical* encroachments on prerogative," whereas in reality it merely extended aristocratic privilege.[248] From Burke's perspective, however, Douglas's preferred scheme depended on the most credulous expectations of virtuous conduct on the part of rulers. Government in the interest of the public good without the support of party required an effort of "supernatural virtue" among the ruling class. This, Burke believed, involved a system of perfection "far beyond the Visionary Republic of Plato."[249] Real politics, by comparison, stood in need of patronage. Influence in this sense, Burke accepted, offered reasonable means of managing the Commons since favour was dispensed to support the ministry of the day. When government was in the hands of men of "popular weight and character" they wielded influence in a way that benefited the Commons rather than constituting an accession to royal power.[250] Under these circumstances, despite the existence of "corruption" as a resource of the crown, its employment depended on the concurrence of Whig magnates along with their merchant and gentry supporters. Since these figures possessed independence, on the basis of either their public standing or their commitment to party friends, they were preserved from being co-opted as mere instruments of the court. In their hands, government was a tool of the people as much as it was a lever of the king. Wealth and nobility conspired to preserve the rights of the people by offsetting the private interests of the crown: men of "great natural interest or great acquired consideration" governed through the Commons with reference to the country rather than as functionaries of the court.[251]

It has long been recognised that the ambitions of George III did not involve attempts to subvert the constitution.[252] Yet in emphasising the continuity between personal monarchy under George III and the extensive powers of the crown under his predecessors, historians have often missed the basic point of the Rockinghams' case, which was that the conduct of the new king eroded the authority of party, thus eliminating the potency of the main intermediary power capable of intervening between the court and the population.[253] From Burke's perspective, this development wore the appearance of a revival of Bolingbroke's scheme for redeeming a corrupt nation by means of the virtue of a patriot king. In 1738, in order to lend authority to the ambitions of Leicester House, Bolingbroke championed the prospect of a patriot monarch: "To espouse no party, but to govern like the common father of

[248] John Douglas, *Seasonable Hints from an Honest Man on the Present Important Crisis of a New Regime and a New Parliament* (London: 1761), p. 37.

[249] EB, *Thoughts on the Cause of the Present Discontents* (1770), *W & S*, II, p. 265.

[250] Ibid., p. 259.

[251] Ibid. Cf. EB to Dr. William Markham, post 9 November 1771, *Corr.*, II, p. 270: "The Rank in Office is to be rated by the Rank which men hold in Parliament, and by that only."

[252] Lewis Namier, "Monarchy and the Party System" in idem, *Personalities and Powers* (London: Hamish Hamilton, 1955). In this spirit, Burke's *Present Discontents* has commonly been presented as "fictitious." See *Letters from George III to Lord Burke*, ed. Sedgwick, p. xviii. For a sceptical review of this conclusion, see Herbert Butterfield, *George III and the Historians* (London: Collins, 1957).

[253] EB, *Thoughts on the Cause of the Present Discontents* (1770), *W & S*, II, pp. 259–60.

his people, is so essential to the character of a Patriot King."[254] For a king to govern on patriot principles, liberated from party and, by implication, from the customary venality of Whig administrations, would require introducing virtue in the place of influence. In practical terms, this would have to begin by a purge of the court, an attack on the spirit of luxury, and a reduction of the power of parliament. Under the monarchy of George III, each of these objectives had been tangibly advanced. As a result, intermediary power within the state was being depleted. In 1790, Burke would refer to Bolingbroke as a "superficial" writer who nonetheless made one valuable observation.[255] This was that, while monarchy cannot plausibly be grafted onto republican government, republican forms can be used to temper established monarchy. As Burke saw it, despite this observation, Bolingbroke's recommendations would have destroyed the popular elements of the constitution capable of restraining the monarchy in Britain. The aim of the *Present Discontents* was to show how the means of resisting the crown had declined under George III. This had been initiated by a system of court favouritism inaugurated under Bute.[256] Rank and independent consideration lost their authority in the state; property and connection were disregarded; all initiative was drawn into the circle of the prince.[257]

Burke would later argue in this vein that the reduction of the intermediary orders of the state facilitated the institution of despotism. As he put it in the phraseology of Montesquieu, in France after 1790 the removal of all barriers against concentrated power would render even a newly constructed monarchy "the most completely arbitrary power that has ever appeared on earth."[258] The defence of the system of intermediary ranks was not, as is commonly assumed, a vindication of aristocratic government: "I am no friend to aristocracy, in the sense in which that word is usually understood." A purely aristocratic regime, Burke stated, would establish an "austere and insolent domination."[259] He would later claim that he was neither an antagonist nor an abject admirer of nobility: he held the order in "decent and cold respect," as befitted a core constituent of a mixed constitution which would be destroyed by the predominance of aristocratic power. At the same time, he was not an adherent of "the rich and powerful against the poor and the weak." Partiality to aristocracy in this sense was repugnant.[260] Yet he was not opposed to the accumulation of wealth in families since this was the only means of securing property in general. With this objective in view, in the *Present Discontents* Burke promoted an alliance between

[254] Henry St. John Viscount Bolingbroke, *Political Writings*, ed. David Armitage (Cambridge: Cambridge University Press, 1997), p. 257.

[255] EB, *Reflections*, ed. Clark, p. 293 [187].

[256] It began with the slaughter of the Pelhamite innocents: see EB, *Thoughts on the Cause of the Present Discontents* (1770), *W & S*, II, p. 264.

[257] Ibid., pp. 264, 268, 280.

[258] EB, *Reflections*, ed. Clark, p. 359 [275]. Cf. Montesquieu, *De l'esprit des lois*, pt. II, bk. XI, ch. 6.

[259] EB, *Thoughts on the Cause of the Present Discontents* (1770), *W & S*, II, p. 268. Cf. the misleading comments in Pares, *King George III and the Politicians*, p. 60.

[260] EB, Speech on Fox's Marriage Bill, 15 June 1781, *The Works of the Right Honourable Edmund Burke*, ed. French Laurence and Walker King (London: 1792–1827), 16 vols., V, pp. 414ff.

the peerage and the House of Commons as the best means of securing the liberty of the people. Such an alliance combined popularity and circumspection with a dependable means of stabilising the distribution of property. The peerage accorded weight and influence to the acreage of the country without erecting the nobility into a disconnected caste. After all, elevation to the Lords was dependent on popular favour insofar as membership of the upper chamber was a consequence of service in the lower House.[261] Burke's theory of party offered an account of how the coalition between Commons and Lords could most readily be cemented. Party preserved the peerage from co-optation by the court while ensuring its collaboration with the representative element in the constitution. The king, the Lords and the Commons, separately and conjointly, performed a representative function in the state. Individually, they stood for distinct interests, while together they represented the common good. "Government," Burke wrote, ". . . is an institution of Divine authority."[262] By this he meant that its obligation to the people was more than a merely secular duty. Its object, nonetheless, was the general welfare. Its origin, in this sense, lay in the people. Yet this origin characterised every form of government.[263] Popular government, however, ought to have a more particular connection with the people at large. Under the British constitution, this connection was supplied by the House of Commons, which was representative in a peculiar sense.

As Burke saw it, the lower House was originally intended as a check upon executive power. It restrained the standing organs of the state in conformity with its sense of prevailing popular demands. The Commons performed this function insofar as it bore "some stamp of the actual disposition of the people at large."[264] It deliberated on the basis of sympathy with national feeling. Direct election, however imperfect a method of selecting representatives, was the best means of securing the requisite correspondence.[265] The people might be misled in their judgments, but their sentiments were mostly sound: "Whenever the people have a feeling, they commonly are in the right."[266] It was the job of a representative assembly to ascertain that feeling. In the aftermath of the Wilkes crisis, parliament had steadily been discouraged from performing that role, since successive ministries had stigmatised the favour of the people.[267] Popular favour, of course, was a problematic principle: acclamation was an essential part of popular liberty, yet it was also the means of erecting democratic tyranny. Burke had addressed this issue at length in March 1769 as he moved

[261] EB, *Thoughts on the Cause of the Present Discontents* (1770), *W & S*, II, p. 268.

[262] Ibid., p. 292.

[263] Ibid.

[264] Ibid.

[265] WWM BkP 12:2: "If all representatives were to be trusted, one Election would serve for all. If all Electors were to be trusted & Elections had no inconveniences attached to them, it were no matter if there were Elections every month." Of course, neither condition obtained, so periodic elections offered the most practical remedy.

[266] EB, Debate on Civil List Debt, 2 March 1769, *Cavendish Debates of the House of Commons*, I, p. 306. Cf. EB, *Thoughts on the Cause of the Present Discontents* (1770), *W & S*, II, p. 255.

[267] Ibid., pp. 295–96.

for a committee of inquiry into the St. George's Fields Massacre. The duty of MPs, he remarked, was "to separate the feelings of the people from their judgement; to consider their interest with their real intentions."[268] Popular sentiment inevitably included an element of "popular dross" unleashed by the activities of "violent, factious men."[269] The House of Commons was at once a representative and a deliberative chamber, which had to echo the attitudes of the people without being bound by their proposals. The disorders attending the Wilkes affair pointed to both these requirements: mob sentiment could not reasonably be replicated by parliament, but neither could public outrage simply be ignored. The role of the Commons in giving vent to popular grievances ensured that the violence of British crowds was less desperate than their European equivalents.[270] This pointed to the achievement of moderate liberty, under which the rights of the people were reconciled with constitutional order.

Burke's conception of the popular provisions included in the British state led him to reflect on Rousseau's *Contrat social*. A "foreigner has said," he reminded the Commons, "that the people of England are free but once in seven years, and that then they made so bad an use of their freedom they deserve not to be free at all."[271] Burke recognised that members of parliament had recently supported oppressive ministries which pitted magistracy against the will of the people. But he also proceeded to observe how the constitution of the British government acted against the separation of administration from the public. Nonetheless, the Wilkes débâcle, in prompting government to resort to hostile measures against the population, threatened the consensual basis of government in Britain. The prospect of relying on the military as the standard means of riot control seemed to Burke an extreme example of the general tendency. It threatened to erect the organs of public order into an adverse corporation in the state. The whole drift of previous constitutional history had been

[268] EB, Debate on the Conduct of Government during Tumults, 8 March 1769, Cavendish Diary, Eg. MS. 219, fol. 6. Cf. WWM BkP 8:71, reproduced as EB, Speech on St. George's Fields Massacre, 8 March 1769, *W & S*, II, p. 225.

[269] Cavendish Diary, Eg. MS. 219, fol. 5.

[270] Ibid., fols. 17–18. Burke had the recent disturbances in Madrid in mind. These were discussed in "The History of Europe," in *The Annual Register for the Year 1766* (London: 1767), pp. 14ff. The episode was also discussed in Horace Walpole to Henry Seymour Conway, 6 and April 1766, *Yale Edition of the Correspondence of Horace Walpole* (New Haven, CT: Yale University Press, 1937–83), 48 vols., XXXIX, pp. 60–66.

[271] EB, Debate on the Conduct of Government during Tumults, 8 March 1769, Cavendish Diary, Eg. MS. 219, fols. 9–10. See Jean-Jacques Rousseau, *Contrat social* (1762) in Robert Derathé et al. eds., *Œuvres complètes* (Paris: Pléiade, 1964), III, p. 430: "Le peuple Anglois pense être libre; il se trompe fort, il ne l'est que Durant l'élection des membres du Parlement; sitôt qu'ils sont élus, il est esclave, il n'est rien. Dans les courts momens de sa liberté, l'usage qu'il en fait mérite bien qu'il la perde." Rousseau's recent widely publicised visit to Britain gave currency to discussion of his writings in the capital. Burke was well informed about Rousseau's dispute with Hume at this time. On their disagreements, see Paul H. Meyer, "The Manuscript of Hume's Account of His Dispute with Rousseau," *Comparative Literature*, 4:4 (Autumn 1952), pp. 341–50; Dena Goodman, "The Hume–Rousseau Affair: From Private Querelle to Public Process," *Eighteenth-Century Studies*, 25:2 (Winter 1991–92), pp. 171–201; John Hope Mason, "Rousseau in England," *Daedalus*, 137:2 (Spring 2008), pp. 96–101.

pulling the other way, from the establishment of a jury system to the reduction of the power of the clergy: "we have constantly entertained a jealousy of all bodies of men who have a separate interest, and separate feelings of their own, distinct from the mass, and body of the people."[272] The tenure of magistrates concerned with public order, particularly of constables and sheriffs, ensured conformity between the population and local administration. Britain was, "perhaps, the only country in the world in which there is a popular magistracy."[273] Originally, this was exemplified by the election of sheriffs: it was "ordained by statute," as Blackstone noted, "that the people should have election of sheriffs in every shire, where the shrievalty is not of inheritance." This exhibited, he went on, "a strong trace of the democratical part of our constitution," although subsequently their appointment was vested in the crown.[274] Nonetheless, even if the office was by royal appointment since Henry VI, its personnel were drawn from the common people for a particular term.[275] Like the constables, they shared the "common feelings" and "interests" of the people: "In both the superior and inferior judicatures, and in the executive part of our constitution, the law is executed by the people upon the people; and therefore furnishes a security for a fair, mild, equitable, and legal government."[276]

At the outset of the *Present Discontents*, Burke emphasised that he had no interest in the "abstract value" of popular rights.[277] What concerned him was the relationship between government and opinion. In a mixed regime, opinion was formed by the attitudes of the public at large, amongst whom officials were obliged to maintain their reputation. It was the job of parliament to overawe the ministries of the day, while at the same time revering the sentiments of the people.[278] These tasks could not be effectively performed by isolated members of both Houses. United strength was required to hold the executive to account as well as to recall representatives to their duty. Party was the means of providing that unity of purpose, directed towards securing the common good. The Grenvilles and the Bedfords undermined that goal by seeking office in the interest of particular advantage rather than to further the public weal.[279] Chatham, on the other hand, professed the cause of public virtue

[272] EB, Debate on the Conduct of Government during Tumults, 8 March 1769, Cavendish Diary, Eg. MS. 219, fol. 15.

[273] Ibid., fol. 16.

[274] Blackstone, *Commentaries* (1862 ed.), bk. 1, ch. 9. The relevant statute providing for election to the office of sheriff was 28 Edw. I, c. 8.

[275] For the organisation of local administration, see Bryan Keith-Lucas, *The Unreformed Local Government System* (London: Croom Helm, 1979); David Eastwood, *Government and Community in the English Provinces, 1700–1870* (London: Palgrave, 1997).

[276] EB, Debate on the Conduct of Government during Tumults, 8 March 1769, Cavendish Diary, Eg. MS. 219, fol. 16.

[277] EB, *Thoughts on the Cause of the Present Discontents* (1770), *W & S*, II, p. 252.

[278] Ibid., pp. 278–79.

[279] EB to the Marquess of Rockingham, 29 October 1769, *Corr.*, II, p. 101: "the Bedfords, and Grenvilles, and other knots, who are combined for no public purpose; but only as a means of furthering their joint strength, their private and individual advantage."

while attacking the only means of its realisation. Burke once referred to the "significant, pompous, creeping, explanatory, ambiguous" character of the "true Chathamic style."[280] Given its explicit assault on the court system, the *Present Discontents* was forced to underplay the extent of the Rockinghamite aversion to what they saw as the self-regarding isolation cultivated by the elder Pitt.[281] Pitt advocated the ideal of a patriot ministry, formed on the basis of "measures" rather than "men."[282] Such an arrangement had to rely on individual integrity rather than on the discipline that came from acting in corps.

Pitt's ideal looked back to John Brown's jeremiad from the 1750s, the *Estimate on the Manners and Principles of the Times*, which, Burke recalled, had affected a "terror of the growth of an aristocratic power, prejudicial to the rights of the Crown, and the balance of the constitution."[283] Brown had sought to revise Montesquieu's notion that parties ("*Divisions*") were necessary to the strength of a republican regime.[284] Where party furthered the ambitions of aristocratic interest, as it had done since the accession of William III, it disseminated a spirit of selfishness throughout the polity: "Thus the great Chain of political Self-Interest was at length formed; and extended from the *lowest Cobler* [*sic*] in a *Borough*, to the *King's first Minister*."[285] The achievement of the *Present Discontents* was to invert the charge of faction levelled against a system of principled connection between men of weight and talent in parliament. Sallust had pointed out that friendship among good men amounted to faction among the wicked: "haec inter bonos amicitia, inter malos factio est."[286] In Burke's scheme, party connection was described as a form of friendship while courtiers were branded a factious combination.[287] From this perspective, since Chatham was a creature of the closet *malgré lui*, he was a conduit for the promotion of faction in the state.

As the Rockinghams' saw it, the main obstacle to the formation of honest combination against court intrigue was the posture of other proprietary groups identi-

[280] EB to the Marquess of Rockingham, 9 July 1769, ibid., p. 43.

[281] EB to the Marquess of Rockingham, post 6 November 1769, ibid., p. 109: "The whole attack on Pitts [*sic*] Conduct must be omitted, or we shall draw the Cry of the world upon us." Cf. EB on the Chatham Ministry of 1767 in Speech on American Taxation, 19 April 1774, *W & S*, II, p. 450. See also the comments in WWM BkP 6:55 and WWM BkP 31:47. Portland found Burke's treatment of other opposition groups too severe: see the Duke of Portland to the Marquess of Rockingham, 3 December 1769, Rockingham, *Memoirs*, II, pp. 144–47.

[282] EB, *Thoughts on the Cause of the Present Discontents* (1770), *W & S*, II, p. 318. On Pitt's programme, see Brewer, *Party Ideology and Popular Politics*, ch. 6; Michael C. McGee, "'Not Men, but Measures': The Origins and Import of an Ideological Principle," *Quarterly Journal of Speech*, 64 (1978), pp. 141–54.

[283] EB, *Thoughts on the Cause of the Present Discontents* (1770), *W & S*, II, p. 267.

[284] Charles-Louis de Secondat, Baron de Montesquieu, *Considérations sur les causes de la grandeur des Romans et de leur décadence* (1734) in *Œuvres complètes,* ed. Roger Caillois (Paris: Gallimard, 1951), 2 vols., II, ch. 8. For further discussion see above chapter 4, section 5.

[285] John Brown, *An Estimate on the Manners and Principles of the Times* (Dublin: 1758), p. 71.

[286] Sallust, *Jugurthine War*, XXXI, 15.

[287] EB, *Thoughts on the Cause of the Present Discontents* (1770), *W & S*, II, p. 321. In its original classical context, friendship (*amicitia*) included the relationship between political patron and client. See Ronald Syme, *The Roman Revolution* (Oxford: Oxford University Press, 1939, 1960), p. 157.

fied with the Whig cause. Conway perfectly illustrated the problem: attracted to the Chathamite call to serve in the name of virtue, his angelic profession of conscience made him a tool of court designs. Walpole recalled how in 1768 Burke along with Lord John Cavendish had inveighed against the dissolution of connections, "which Conway took as leveled at him."[288] The issue flared up again in 1769 when Burke crossed swords with Conway on the issue of subserviency. Beckford, Rigby and Conway might seek to associate court service with an impartial commitment to public business, but to Burke their avowed "candour" was self-interest in disguise.[289] Party, Burke believed, reconciled collaboration with independence. It permitted dedication to a common cause without sacrificing self-respect and self-reliance: "When I find good men, I will cling to them, adhere to them, follow them in and out."[290] This was not a form of slavish deference, but the best means available of serving the public good. The grandees of the Rockingham party represented "the genuine voice, the unsuborned testimony . . . of their country."[291] The devotees of "conscience," like Conway and Pitt, were courtiers arrayed in patriot apparel.[292] There was a fundamental lesson to be drawn from this. Political virtue was not a function of individual intention but a result of constitutional arrangement. "It is not enough, in a situation of trust in the commonwealth, that a man means well to his country," Burke proclaimed.[293] Power must be organised so as to attract the honourable and discourage the mercenary: "The elevation of the one, and the depression of the other, are the first objects of all true policy."[294] Responsibility to parliament, rather than the lure of court favour, provided incentives for attracting the public-spirited into government. Party was the only means of supporting them against the crown, while at the same time disposing them to represent the people.

5.6 Liberality and Religious Dissent

1770 opened with a crisis for the Grafton ministry. The Lord Chancellor, the Earl of Camden, resigned on 17 January. Grafton followed suit on the 26th, discouraged by dwindling numbers in the House of Commons. Two days later, George III appointed Lord North as First Lord of the Treasury, just in time for a vote on the state of the nation. "Lord North had neither connections . . . nor popularity with the country,"

[288] Walpole, *Memoirs*, IV, p. 15.

[289] On this exchange, together with the developing connotations of "candour," see Christopher Reid, "Speaking Candidly: Rhetoric, Politics, and the Meanings of Candour in the Later Eighteenth Century," *British Journal for Eighteenth-Century Studies*, 28 (2005), pp. 67–82.

[290] EB, Debate on the King's Message respecting the Civil List Debt, 28 February 1769, Cavendish Diary, Eg. MS. 218, fol. 221.

[291] Ibid., fol. 222.

[292] EB, *Thoughts on the Cause of the Present Discontents* (1770), *W & S*, II, p. 319. The allegations against Conway were to persist down to 1782. See Charles James Fox on this theme in *Parliamentary History*, XXXII, cols. 169–70.

[293] EB, *Thoughts on the Cause of the Present Discontents* (1770), *W & S*, II, p. 315.

[294] Ibid., p. 278.

Walpole commented, yet he managed to stave off the victory of the opposition.[295] Over the next months, the mood of urgency declined as national turmoil abated. The strength of the opposition was steadily depleted, with Richmond announcing his reluctance even to travel into town.[296] By the time that Burke's *Present Discontents* appeared in print, the situation it was originally designed to influence had been reconfigured. Nonetheless, over the next few years, dismay among the Rockinghams about the presumption of the court increased their fears of a continuing constitutional imbalance. However, they failed to unite the opposition around a plan for its reduction. While they collaborated on a campaign to bring down the debt on the civil list, they failed to develop a shared perspective on how to improve the minority's fortunes. Chatham endorsed the idea of a more equal representation, while the Rockinghams rejected calls for more frequent parliaments and a place bill.[297] None of this gave hope for a common platform. The pressure of public opinion also began to ease: by the summer of 1770, the petitioning movement was exhausted. At the same time, talent started to drain from the opposition: Temple began to withdraw from public life and his brother, George Grenville, died on 13 November. By the end of the year, as Burke observed, Grenville's supporters were thought to be "upon the Wing, if not actually flown."[298] The Rockinghams would have to fall back on their own imperfect resources.

This predicament could offer Burke very little encouragement. He did not, he reported, have the "least glimmering of hope" that the party's endeavours would meet with success any time soon.[299] The Earl of Bute, he was aware, was a spent force, yet the system he introduced allegedly continued to prosper. Accordingly, in the autumn of 1772, Burke was still complaining about the machinations of the closet. The crown was charged with continuing to discount the claims of the Rockinghams, and with disregarding the "Natural powers and interests of the Country." Instead, it concentrated its resources on "private influence and Court Cabal."[300] Burke had long realised that the people were both a necessary and a potent weapon in politics; yet they were also a conspicuously wayward instrument. Public life ought to be conducted exclusively for their sake; however, they certainly posed a threat to its integrity. The people had to be wooed, but they ought to be cultivated appropriately. Unfortunately, they were often courted by undesirable suitors. Mixed government offered the only means of co-opting them beneficently. Under its auspices, aristocracy could be secured against the spirit of domination by being bound to the power of a representative assembly. At the same time, popularity could be liberalised by an

[295] Walpole, *Memoirs*, IV, p. 141.

[296] O'Gorman, *Rise of Party*, p. 272.

[297] The position was set out in EB, *Thoughts on the Cause of the Present Discontents* (1770), *W & S*, II, pp. 308ff.

[298] EB to the Marquess of Rockingham, 29 December 1770, *Corr.*, II, p. 175.

[299] Ibid., p. 176.

[300] EB to Charles O'Hara, 30 September 1772, ibid., p. 336.

alliance with grandees. A structural affinity between nobility and the people was necessary for the security of property as well as generosity in public counsels. Yet the coalition between the two orders was a precarious affair, threatened with dissolution from two opposing directions: the people might be seduced by either one of two rival supplicants. On the one hand, they might be adopted by demagogic leaders; on the other, they might be solicited by the crown.

Burke habitually cast Chatham, and by this stage Shelburne too, in the role of demagogue. At the end of 1770, he represented both as playing the same part. The elder Pitt, Burke wrote to Rockingham, was endeavouring to "discredit" the Marquess by captivating the affections of the people. At the same time, Shelburne was consorting with populist leaders in the City of London.[301] In less than a year, Burke would dismiss this cohort as comprising "treacherous patriots," professing public virtue while servicing themselves.[302] In Burke's eyes, demagoguery was a vehicle for personal ambition secured by exploiting immoderate popular passions. It was altogether distinct from serving the welfare of the people, for which it was sometimes necessary to promote their interest at the expense of their inclinations. It might be advisable, Burke proclaimed during the regency crisis, to oppose the wishes of the people "whenever they attempted to ruin themselves."[303] In reality this meant counselling against popular inducements wielded by unscrupulous politicians. Monarchical tyranny proceeded by equally meretricious means. The *Present Discontents* was a determined effort to anatomise its procedures under George III. If the crown were permitted to outflank every obstacle to its ambition, then Britain would fall prey to the fate of Sweden under Gustavus III. The 1772 *coup* by the king of Sweden against the reigning constitution was described in *The Annual Register* as "one of the most extraordinary revolutions, considered in all its parts, which we can meet with in ancient or modern history."[304] For Burke it signalled the worst fate that might await the British monarchy. As Montesquieu had predicted, Britain could expect a drift rather than a rush towards despotism.[305] Most alarmingly it was likely to proceed by garnering popular support.

Burke expressed his fears to O'Hara in 1772: "the Court may assume as uncontrolled a power in this country as the King of Sweden has done in his."[306] Modern historians have mostly seen this as extravagant gloom on Burke's part, yet it is possible to recover the rationale for dire foreboding of the kind. From Burke's vantage, the complacency of retrospect would surely appear naïve. Like many of his contemporaries, he saw the British regime as a fragile mechanism that was the

[301] EB to the Marquess of Rockingham, 29 December 1770, ibid., p. 175.

[302] EB to Charles O'Hara, post 14 July 1771, ibid., p. 222.

[303] EB, Speech on the King's Illness, 22 December 1788, *Parliamentary History*, XXVII, col. 819.

[304] "History of Europe," in *The Annual Register for the Year 1772* (London: 1773), p. 7.

[305] Charles-Louis de Secondat, Baron de Montesquieu, *De l'esprit des lois* (1748) in *Œuvres complètes*, ed. Roger Caillois (Paris: Gallimard, 1951), 2 vols., pt. II, bk. XI, ch. 6.

[306] EB to Charles O'Hara, 30 September 1772, *Corr.*, II, p. 336.

outcome of a series of historic struggles. "Our constitution," he wrote, "stands on a nice equipoise, with steep precipices, and deep waters upon all sides of it." Incremental change might trigger revolution: "In removing it from a dangerous leaning towards one side, there may be a risque of oversetting it on the other."[307] Prerogative had collided with freedom throughout the course of modern history, and there was little reason to expect the contest suddenly to relent. Power sought to secure itself against rival powers, leading to instability, and potentially to crisis. The crown could advance its position by abusing its influence, and in the process it might cut off all avenues to redress. The resistance of the Commons was the primary impediment to the crown, yet if its independence were compromised the liberty of the people would decline. In detaching members of the lower House from their aristocratic alliances, the main bulwark against the monarchical will was steadily corrupted. Tyranny could progress, greeted by popular applause. The court "system," Burke thought, "had favour in the Eyes of the vulgar."[308] Court and mob were steadily approximating one another: the venal instincts of the one could trade on the slavishness of the other. This vicious circularity was not easily overcome. An appeal to public opinion was one obvious reserve, although the populace seemed indifferent and stupefied.[309] Rousing them would have to avoid the demagogic rhetoric of men like Chatham. Party spirit was the best means of averting this recourse, since it was premised on collaboration between nobility and commons. Burke cast this collaboration in terms of Roman *amicitia*—as a pledge of reciprocal friendship between aspiring ability and settled greatness.[310] The free clientage between commoners and the propertied peerage was the only means of upsetting the servile patronage of the court. For Burke, Hamilton had exemplified the aristocratic abuse of a client relationship, yet Rockingham showed how a "little platoon" might harmonise deference with independence.[311] Party provided a method by which this kind of combination could offer resistance to incipient despotism on the political stage.

Every commercially complex society that had emerged against the backdrop of feudal Europe had to develop social and political relationships capable of reconciling widely different gradations of wealth and status. Above all, what Burke termed "rising merit" ought to be accommodated by hereditary privilege: the alternatives

[307] EB, *Thoughts on the Cause of the Present Discontents* (1770), *W & S*, II, p. 311.

[308] EB to Charles O'Hara, 30 September 1772, *Corr.*, II, p. 336.

[309] EB to William Dowdeswell, 27 October 1772, ibid., p. 352.

[310] EB, *Thoughts on the Cause of the Present Discontents* (1770), *W & S*, II, p. 316. See also EB, Speech on Resolution on Future of the Impeachment, 11 May 1790, *W & S*, VII, p. 93: "With regard to friendship, it was, Mr. Burke said, if any thing, superior even to love of one's country, as it was the source and spring, the animating soul, whence originated every other virtue." Cf. Cicero, *De amicitia*, 10. For discussion of the Roman context, see P. A. Brunt, "'Amicitia' in the Late Roman Republic," *Proceedings of the Cambridge Philological Society*, 11 (January 1965), pp. 1–20. On the general value in classical thought, see David Konstan, *Friendship in the Classical World* (Cambridge: Cambridge University Press, 1997).

[311] For this motif in connection with the *Reflections on the Revolution in France*, see chapter 13, section 4 below.

were either oppression or civil conflict. As a self-proclaimed "*Novus Homo*," Burke felt he had an insight into the larger structural arrangement.[312] Faced with a personal attack by William Bagot in the Commons on 2 April 1770, he defended himself against allegations of factiousness by appealing to his industry and virtue as a public servant.[313] As the fate of Charles I had shown, such service was disregarded at the peril of the constitution. The long parliament had begun by diminishing the role of the Lords and the crown, and ended by eliminating the influence of constituents.[314] With this lesson in mind, Burke insisted that new men should be permitted to rise "under the wings of establish'd Greatness."[315] This was the surest means of staving off resentment, which inclined the talented to resort to rebellion, and then placed the nobility in the hands of "Mechanicks." Aggravated talent would likewise appeal "ad populum."[316] Burke was conscious of the need for commoners to defer to grandees, yet he cherished his self-command, and prized exertion over privileged indolence.[317] In fact, throughout his political career, culminating in his *Letter to a Noble Lord* of 1796, he battled against the inertia which he associated with the condition of hereditary greatness. Party was the best means of spurring the nobility into action, since it placed them in a confederacy with proactive men of business. As regards the Rockinghams themselves, this meant that the call for initiative generally came form Burke, who was perpetually obliged to stir his friends into accepting the need for engagement. A party, Burke wrote to Rockingham, "will putrifye and dissipate, if not kept healthy and compact by continual agitation and enterprise."[318]

As the ferment associated with the Wilkes campaign diminished, mobilisation became increasingly difficult to achieve. "The Country is dead," as Burke put it to O'Hara in July 1771.[319] The feeling of stagnation persisted for the next few years,

[312] William Burke to William Dennis, 6 April 1770, *Corr.*, II, pp. 128–29.

[313] The assault began on 30 March 1770, during the third reading of Grenville's Controverted Elections Bill, as an attack on party as a means of wounding the constitution "through the sides of the ministry." See *Parliamentary History*, XVI, col. 919.

[314] Northamptonshire MS. A. I.39B, reproduced as EB, Speech on Parliamentary Incapacitation, 31 January 1770, *W & S*, II, p. 234.

[315] William Burke to William Dennis, 6 April 1770, *Corr.*, II, p. 128. Cf. EB, Speech on Grenville's Controverted Elections Bill, 30 March 1770, *Parliamentary History*, XVI, col. 921: Burke "compared the benefit derived to society from the unactuated load of landed abilities, which descended from generation to generation, in the useless members of the community, and that which derived from the acquirements, improvements, and activity of mental abilities, and shewed that either might be pernicious, and yet that both were a real benefit wherever and whenever they mixed, but always more so when acting in mutual aid of each other."

[316] William Burke to William Dennis, 6 April 1770, *Corr.*, II, p. 128.

[317] "Birth and fortune" would fail to win public support and admiration so long as they were accompanied by vice and inertia, Burke contended. See Northamptonshire MS. A. I.39A, reproduced as EB, Speech on Middlesex Election, 15 April 1769, *W & S*, II, p. 230.

[318] EB to the Marquess of Rockingham, 29 December 1770, *Corr.*, II, p. 175.

[319] EB to Charles O'Hara, post 14 July 1771, ibid., p. 222. Cf. EB to William Dowdeswell, 27 October 1772, ibid., p. 352: "the Nation quietly acquiesces in those measures which we agitate with so much eagerness."

until the American crisis became an overriding topic in the Commons. In the aftermath of the upheaval of the later 1760s, a sonorous calm had succeeded, Burke lamented to Shackleton.[320] The court continued to capitalise on the enthrallment of parliament. By 1773, Burke was remarking on servility as "shocking and unnatural," yet perplexingly still common in the world.[321] Along with the seizure of East Indian patronage, the ministry was still hankering after the destruction of Wilkes.[322] In this disconsolate mood, Burke defensively insisted on the propriety of his past conduct: he ought not to be surprised if rectitude had condemned his party to protracted labour in the wilderness. Yet the narrowing of prospects was dispiriting, not least since it reduced the opportunities for action: "Want of any pleasing hope, want of Object, want of pursuit, inaction without repose, has thrown me into such a troubled sort of sleep for a long time past."[323] The Rockinghams had sought to take a lead in the City of London while principally appealing to the "large-acred part of the Nation."[324] But three obstacles had been placed in their way: first, they had competitors for the leadership of the diverse interests of the City, many of whom could trump them in their popular appeal; second, the court was gradually reducing the independence of the Commons, rendering opposition ineffective; and finally, resistance to the crown was in the hands of the party's leaders, whose habits generally inclined them to somnolent inaction. Relentlessly, but usually thanklessly, Burke struggled between 1770 and 1774 to assail the government, supporting Grenville in his Controverted Elections Bill, defending the constitutional role of the jury, opposing the ministry over the land tax and the Falkland Islands, and objecting to attempts to regulate the corn trade and prevent the printing of parliamentary reports.[325]

In the face of this discouraging campaign, Burke repeatedly considered the merit of secession from parliament. Responding to one such proposal in November 1772, the Duke of Richmond admitted "how very desperate" the situation of the party was.[326] Without Burke's application, the whole edifice would fall to pieces. Richmond's letter prompted Burke to compose a lengthy and considered response. He

[320] EB to Richard Shackleton, ante 31 July 1771, ibid., p. 227.

[321] EB to Charles O'Hara, 20 August 1773, ibid., p. 452.

[322] EB to William Dowdeswell, 27 October 1772, ibid., 351.

[323] EB to Charles O'Hara, 20 August 1773, ibid., p. 451.

[324] EB to the Marquess of Rockingham, 29 December 1770, ibid., p. 175.

[325] EB, Speech on Grenville's Controverted Elections Bill, 30 March 1770, *Parliamentary History*, XVI, cols. 920–21; EB, Speech on Address, 13 November 1770, *W & S*, II, pp. 334ff.; EB, Speech on the Corn Trade, 16 November 1770, *Cavendish Debates of the House of Commons*, II, pp. 55–56; EB, Speech on the Land Tax, 12 December 1770, ibid., pp. 211–12; EB, Speech on Convention with Spain, 25 January 1771, *W & S*, II, pp. 339ff.; EB, Complaint against Printers, 8 February 1771, *Cavendish Debates of the House of Commons*, II, pp. 259–60; EB, Speech on Jury Bill, 7 March 1771, *W & S*, II, pp. 343ff.; EB, Proceedings against Printers, 12, 14 and 18 March 1771, *Cavendish Debates of the House of Commons*, II, pp. 384, 387–88, 391, 395–97, 413–15, 419; EB, Committee on the Corn Trade, 14 April 1772, *Parliamentary History*, XVII, col. 479; EB, Speech on Corn Bill, 30 April 1772, Cavendish Diary, Eg. MS. 241, fols. 61–66, 72–73, 75–77; Speech on Corn Trade, 17 and 26 March 1773, Cavendish Diary, Eg. MS. 245, fols. 21, 158–65, 170–71; EB, Speech on Grenville's Election Act, *W & S*, II, pp. 396ff.

[326] The Duke of Richmond to EB, 15 November 1772, *Corr.*, II, p. 371.

extoled the role of the peerage as perpetuating national culture, particularly its constitutional forms. Unlike the fleeting significance of lesser commoners like Burke, Richmond and his ilk carried with them a sense of permanency by virtue of their awareness of durable family greatness that accompanied the institution of entailed estates. By comparison, Burke famously remarked, ordinary citizens "are but annual plants" that perish with the season.[327] Burke's comments were meant as encouragement, not flattery.[328] The purpose of his letter was to counteract the kind of lethargy and dissipation of effort which the chiefs of the Rockingham party typically exhibited.[329] Richmond exemplified the problem: he ought to concentrate his energy on pressing issues of public concern, yet his efforts were diffused through a variety of pursuits.[330] The great should lead by example, braced by their consciousness of the watching public. It was their station that made them sensitive to the value of reputation. Yet their position also made them languid and unsystematic, leaving them poorly equipped for the business of opposition.[331] The intermediary ranks, Burke saw, were easily dissolved into their individual families, yet they needed to combine if their weight was to carry influence. As Burke perceived it, it was the duty of ability to lend its energy to aristocratic importance. This, he insisted, was not creeping adulation, as hypocritically alleged by ingratiating court favourites. Self-respect and independence were matchless values for Burke. "As to those that are called great, I never paid them any Court," he once wrote.[332] Unlike the French nobility, the British peerage dealt freely and openly with commoners.[333] Business brought both descriptions into frequent contact with one another, forcing nobles to be judged by men who were more or less their peers, and enabling ordinary gentlemen to support aristocracy in preference to fawning popularity.

"All good men are partial to nobility," Burke noted, quoting Cicero, in the *Reflections*.[334] The pro-aristocratic alliance between commoners and peerage was not a recipe for perfectly beneficent government, but it did insure the constitution against the domination of a haughty patrician caste, and protect the state from the extremes

[327] EB to the Duke of Richmond, post 15 November 1772, ibid., p. 377.

[328] This has commonly been misunderstood: see, for example, Pares, *King George III and the Politicians*, p. 13: "Edmund Burke, the theorist and the high priest of snobbery."

[329] Burke later commented on this to William Baker in a letter of 12 October 1777, *Corr.*, III, p. 388: "those whom you and I trust" habitually show "a want of stimulus to ambition."

[330] EB to the Duke of Richmond, post 15 November 1772, *Corr.*, II, p. 374.

[331] Ibid., p. 373.

[332] EB to Richard Shackleton, 22 April 1770, ibid., p. 131. This was a constant theme in Burke's pronouncements at this time. Cf. EB, Speech on the Address of Thanks, 13 November 1770, *Parliamentary History*, XVI, col. 1045: "neither fear nor dependency have altered my principles."

[333] EB to the Duke of Richmond, post 15 November 1772, *Corr.*, II, p. 375. Cf. Northamptonshire MS. A. I 39A, reproduced as EB, Speech on Middlesex Election, 15 April 1769, *W & S*, II, p. 230: an "English Gentleman," by comparison with a nobleman on the continent, "has no rank above his fellow Citizens . . . [except what] his Manners, his affability, his Knowledge, [and] his popular use of his fortune" can provide.

[334] EB, *Reflections*, ed. Clark, pp. 308–9 [205]: "*Omnes boni nobilitati semper favemus*, was the saying of a wise and good man." The quotation is from Cicero, *Pro Sestio*, IX, 21.

of pure democracy and monarchy. It also served to liberalise legislation and policy. The security of extensive property cherished long views, and facilitated a larger perspective.[335] "I Live and have Lived in Liberal and humanized company," Burke proclaimed to William Markham in 1771.[336] Rockingham, Portland, Richmond and Dartmouth were men of integrity, honour and patriotism, disposed at once to public and private virtue. Those who possessed these qualities stood as a barrier against innovation and bigotry. Security helped to fortify the mind against fanaticism, and the forms of persecution that usually followed in its wake. In the 1770s, sectarian partiality had an opportunity to express itself in connection with religion. The position of dissent, and the truth of the doctrines of the established Church, were potential subjects of generalised dispute.[337] As far as Burke was concerned, a national Church together with the Toleration Act protected the public from contention over the forms of religious worship. It was the job of religion to achieve the salvation of souls, yet any community of the faithful had to agree on core tenets of doctrine and on the mode of organisation of their church. Since it had proved impossible in modern Europe either to fabricate or to enforce uniformity of worship or belief, toleration appeared to be the only practical solution. In England, the Act of Toleration, which had received the royal assent on 24 May 1689, provided for freedom of worship among dissenters who had taken the oaths of allegiance and supremacy. At the same time, nonconformists were expected to reject the doctrine of transubstantiation and accept the truth of the trinity.[338] As Burke saw it, toleration extended the latitude of private judgment while maintaining the authority of the Church.

The meaning of this latitude became an issue in the 1770s, as a number of Anglicans came more openly to question the necessity of clerical subscription to the thirty-nine articles defining the doctrines of the Church of England.[339] This led to a petition being presented to the House on Commons on 6 February 1772 by Sir William Meredith.[340] The petition itself had been agreed at a meeting held at the Feathers Tavern on the Strand in London on 16 July 1771, inspired by the publi-

[335] EB to the Duke of Richmond, post 15 November 1772, *Corr.*, II, p. 377.

[336] EB to Dr. William Markham, post 9 November 1771, ibid., p. 262.

[337] For the intellectual context, see John Gascoigne, "Anglican Latitudinarianism, Rational Dissent and Political Radicalism in the Late Eighteenth Century" in Knud Haakonssen ed., *Enlightenment and Religion: Rational Dissent in Eighteenth-Century Britain* (Cambridge: Cambridge University Press, 1996, 2006).

[338] W. K. Jordan, *The Development of Religious Toleration in England* (Cambridge, MA: Harvard University Press, 1936–40), 4 vols.; Ursula Henriques, *Religious Toleration in England, 1787–1833* (London: Routledge and Kegan Paul, 1961), chs. 1 and 2; R. B. Barlow, *Citizenship and Conscience: A Study in the Theory and Practice of Religious Toleration in England during the Eighteenth Century* (Philadelphia, PA: University of Pennsylvania Press, 1962).

[339] For a discussion of this episode, see B. W. Young, *Religion and Enlightenment in Eighteenth-Century England* (Oxford: Oxford University Press, 1998), ch. 2. For aspects of the surrounding debate, see Charles F. Mullett, "Some Essays on Toleration in Late Eighteenth-Century England," *Church History*, 7:1 (March 1938), pp. 24–44.

[340] For the petition, see *Parliamentary Register* (Debrett), VI, pp. 168–71.

cation in May 1766 of Francis Blackburne's *Confessional*, a work that had challenged the reasonableness of subscription to doctrinal articles which were known to be diversely interpreted.[341] The business of generating support for the petition largely devolved to Theophilus Lindsey, a son-in-law of Blackburne who left the Church when the petition failed, prompting him to establish a Unitarian chapel on Essex Street in London.[342] The Feathers Tavern Petition attracted backing from Christopher Wyvill, John Cartwright and the Duke of Grafton, wining particular support from sections of opinion within Cambridge: John Jebb, Edmund Law and Richard Watson set about endorsing it.[343] Sir George Savile and Sir John Cavendish supported Meredith in favour of the petition, yet Burke pursued his own independent line. Requiring clerics to propagate the doctrines of the Church did not compromise freedom either of conscience or of worship; it merely defined the character of a national institution. For Meredith, on the other hand, the thirty-nine articles had their origins in an age of barbarism, and should be subject to revision at a time when "liberal and enlarged notions" prevailed.[344] Burke conceded that official doctrine might not represent the complete "truth," yet certain peace was more valuable than controverted truth.[345] The current, imperfect tenets that defined the English confession were products of human frailty, and so liable to be disputed; yet they currently won the support of the majority of its members. Renewed controversy would undermine the dominant consensus, and potentially revive the tumults of the seventeenth century. Burke accepted the idea of religious reform, but that would require generating consent for change. To reform a legal establishment widespread grievances would have to be in evidence. Either way, some confession was needed to sustain a community of belief, and this could only be provided by an agreed doctrinal core.

Burke was conscious at this time of the existence of what he termed "Lay bigotry and Anti-priestcraft," but he was nonetheless anxious to distinguish his case from

[341] During the debate in parliament on clerical subscription, one speaker (Thomas Fitzmaurice, Lord Shelburne's brother) referred to Blackburne's work as pivotal: *Parliamentary History*, XVII, col. 262. The Preface to the second edition referred the reader to the authority of Locke: see Francis Blackburne, *The Confessional; or, a Full and Free Inquiry into the Right, Utility, Edification and Success of Establishing Systematical Confessions of Faith and Doctrine in Protestant Churches* (London: 1767). For discussion, see Peter N. Miller, *Defining the Common Good: Empire, Religion and Philosophy in Eighteenth-Century Britain* (Cambridge: Cambridge University Press, 1994), pp. 309–13.

[342] Thomas Belsham, *Memoirs of the Late Reverend Theophilus Lindsey* (London: 1812), pp. 51–67; G. M. Ditchfield, "The Subscription Issue in British Parliamentary Politics, 1772–1779," *Parliamentary History*, 7:1 (1988), pp. 45–80.

[343] A list of 197 signatories is reproduced in *Monthly Repository*, 13 (1818), pp. 15–17. For the Cambridge connection, see John Gascoigne, "Anglican Latitudinarianism and Political Radicalism in the Late Eighteenth Century," *History*, 71:231 (February 1986), pp. 22–38; idem, *Cambridge in the Age of Enlightenment: Science, Politics and Religion from the Restoration to the French Revolution* (Cambridge: Cambridge University Press, 1988, 2002), pp. 194–98.

[344] *Parliamentary History*, XVII, col. 246. This was the Cavendish line too: see ibid., cols. 270–71.

[345] EB, Speech on Clerical Subscription, 6 February 1772, *Parliamentary History*, XVII, col. 282n. This portion of Burke's speech is reproduced from *Works of Edmund Burke*, V, pp. 323–26, based in turn on Northamptonshire MSS. A. XXXVI. 23, 26A, 26B, 26C, 26D.

the high Church arguments articulated by Sir Roger Newdigate who represented legislative change as constitutionally subversive.[346] On the contrary, Burke claimed, "Our ancestors were neither so bigoted nor so ill informed as to leave no door open for reformation."[347] Nonetheless, reform should not be secured at the risk of destroying the Church, and with it the constitution to which it was indissolubly bound. It was the plea of the supporters of the Feathers Tavern Petition that the law should bend to the conscience of the individual.[348] Religion, they believed, was a matter of private judgment based on an engagement with the truths of scripture. Burke accepted that belief was a matter of conscience, and that Christian conscience was guided by revelation. However, religion was a public as well as a private matter since worship was an organised activity. In fact, it could not plausibly be otherwise conceived: if worship were to be based on a naked encounter with the scriptures, belief would be condemned to the most hectic diversity so as to render religious practice incompatible with social discipline.[349] Burke followed Locke in describing a church as a "voluntary society."[350] For Burke, however, this conception was compatible with a church establishment: one might voluntarily associate with the Church of England, or conscientiously dissent from its provisions. In the latter case, one was free to join another recognised church of one's choosing. An establishment amounted to a tax paid for the support of those who performed the rituals and purveyed the tenets of a church. In the event of a set of clergymen disputing the precepts of the establishment, they were effectively declaring their separation from the Church. An establishment was not an instrument of persecution so long as conscientious dissent was tolerated. Freedom of conscience was not in conflict with clerical subscription.

Nonetheless, conscientious doubts among members of the clergy continued to assert themselves. Edward Evanson alerted the archbishop of Canterbury to his uncertainty about aspects of the Nicene and Athanasian creeds soon after his appointment as vicar of Tewkesbury in 1769. In the absence of a response, he adapted the liturgy to suit his personal preferences. This gesture was compounded by an Easter sermon he delivered on the resurrection in 1771, leading to the commencement of legal proceedings against the vicar.[351] The following year, Evanson published an anonymous pamphlet setting out his difficulties with the doctrine of the trinity, while broadly criticising the folly and superstition of prevailing orthodoxy in the

[346] EB, Speech on Church *Nullum Tempus* Bill, 17 February 1772, *W & S*, II, p. 367. For Newdigate, see *Parliamentary History*, XVII, cols. 251–66. His points were then adopted by Lord North: see ibid., cols. 272–74.

[347] EB, Speech on Clerical Subscription, 6 February 1772, *W & S*, II, p. 360.

[348] Some suspected the petitioners of wishing to destroy all church establishments and propagate socinian beliefs. See *Parliamentary History*, XVII, cols. 262, 264. Burke did not share this view in the 1770s.

[349] EB, Speech on Clerical Subscription, 6 February 1772, *W & S*, II, pp. 361–62.

[350] John Locke, *A Letter Concerning Toleration and Other Writings*, ed. Mark Goldie (Indianapolis, IN: Liberty Fund, 2010), p. 15.

[351] G. Rogers, "Some Account of the Life, Religious Opinions, and Writings, of Edward Evanson" in Edward Evanson, *Sermons* (Ipswich: 1807), 2 vols.; John Stephens, "The London Ministers and Subscription, 1772–1779," *Enlightenment and Dissent*, 1 (1982), pp. 43–71.

Church of England.[352] In 1775, his prosecution failed on a technicality, although he resigned his living voluntarily in 1778. When William Meredith moved on 5 May 1774 for a committee to reconsider the issue of clerical subscription, Burke drew attention to Evanson's case as effectively proving his point: "subscriptions are necessary," he bluntly asserted.[353] In 1779, when the Presbyterian MP Sir Henry Hoghton again moved for a committee on the subscription issue, Burke underlined the difference between a qualification to preach and the private rights of conscientious dissent.[354] Without the former, clergy would be allowed to alter the liturgy however they wished, or even preach one set of beliefs while publishing another. Should this be permitted, the kingdom would soon be filled "with schism and confusion."[355] Every opinion that was not directly destructive of religion ought to be tolerated, in Burke's view, but that principle should not be extended at the expense of the national Church.

Burke elaborated his position on 3 April 1772 in response to a Bill introduced by Hoghton for the relief of dissenting schoolmasters and ministers. Under the Toleration Act, dissenters were exempted from subscribing to the rituals, homilies and government of the Church of England. However, the confirmation of the duty on the part of the Anglican clergy to subscribe to the tenets of the established confession in the aftermath of the failure of the Feathers Tavern Petition questioned the validity of imposing any requirement for subscription on those dissenting from ceremonies and doctrines of the Church.[356] The existing exemption on the part of nonconformists from subscription to articles 34, 35, 36 and part of 20 in practice excluded them from the Anglican faith, Burke recognised, and so obliging them to pledge themselves to additional tenets of the Church was "absurd."[357] The dissenters did not wish to participate in the emoluments of the Anglican establishment, and consequently their bid to procure full liberty of conscience should be permitted. Although Burke's view prevailed in the House of Commons, the Bill met with stern resistance in the Lords. By comparison with the Feathers Tavern Petition, support for a Bill to relieve dissenters was extensive, yet still there were divisions within nonconformist ranks, largely over suspicions that complete exemption from doctrinal articles would promote heterodoxy outside the Church. Accordingly, when a renewed attempt was made to secure relief in 1773, efforts were made to render the

[352] Edward Evanson, *The Doctrines of a Trinity and the Incarnation of God Examined on the Principles of Reason and Common Sense* (London: 1772), pp. 10–11.

[353] EB, Speech on Clerical Subscription, 5 May 1774, *W & S*, II, p. 466.

[354] EB, Notes for Speech on Dissenters Bill, April 1779, *W & S*, III, p. 433.

[355] EB, Speech on Clerical Subscription, 5 May 1774, *W & S*, II, p. 467. Cf. Immanuel Kant, *Was ist Aufklärung?*, ed. Horst D. Brandt (Hamburg: Felix Meiner Verlag, 1999), pp. 23–24, where a clergyman is taken to be justified in preaching one doctrine yet publishing another.

[356] Anthony Lincoln, *Political and Social Ideas of English Dissent, 1763–1800* (New York: Octagon, 1971), ch. 2.

[357] EB, Speech on Toleration Bill, 3 April 1772, *W & S*, II, p. 369.

application more conciliatory.[358] Even so, the ongoing effort to increase toleration raised the alarm that a concerted assault on trinitarian orthodoxy was underway.[359] For one contributor to the debate on the second reading of the Toleration Bill on 17 March 1773, socinianism, deism and infidelity were conspicuously on the rise.[360]

For Burke, however, the nonconformist petitioners, and rational dissenters at large, were allies in the battle against religious scepticism. Diversity, it was true, need not be encouraged; yet, as a fact, it had to be tolerated. Nonetheless, Burke noted two exceptions to this charitable indulgence. Firstly, a magistrate was entitled to restrain religious freedom where dissension was propagated "to raise a faction in the state."[361] Secondly, given that infidelity represented an attack on organised society, atheism should never "be supported, never . . . tolerated."[362] Burke had recently returned from Paris, where he had been shocked by the widespread contempt for the basic tenets of religion.[363] It was also at this time that he commended the postscript to James Beattie's *Essay on Truth* as a "masterly" achievement.[364] Hume's *Treatise of Human Nature* was a principal target for Beattie, though he also had his doubts about Berkeley's *Treatise Concerning the Principles of Human Knowledge*.[365] What attracted Burke was Beattie's assault on "our modern Pyrrhonists" who were alleged to be inculcating bigotry while pretending to reduce its influence. "I see propagated principles," Burke declared, "which will not leave to religion even a toleration."[366] Scepticism, he was suggesting, was disposed to persecution. By scepticism, of course, Burke did not mean disbelief, but a conceited determination to undermine all reasonable opinions. An individual might doubt the veracity of Christian revelation, yet, so long as they maintained a "pious silence" in the face of uncertainty, they could not be deemed an enemy to religion and civil society.[367] Dogmatic atheism, however, was another matter: its modern exemplars had devoted themselves to brutalising human nature, to sapping the foundations of moral virtue, and to ridiculing the truths of scripture and the rule of providence.[368] Freethinkers, as Crito argued in Berkeley's

[358] Richard Price to the Earl of Shelburne, 23 February 1773, *The Correspondence of Richard Price*, ed. W. B. Peach and D. O. Thomas (Durham, NC: Duke University Press, 1983–94), 3 vols., I, p. 156.

[359] G. M. Ditchfield, "'How Narrow Will the Limits of this Toleration Appear?' Dissenting Petitions to Parliament, 1772–1773," *Parliamentary History*, 24:1 (February 2005), pp. 91–106.

[360] Clement Tudway, reported in the Cavendish Diary, Eg. MS. 243, fols. 345–46.

[361] EB, Speech on Toleration Bill, 17 March 1773, *W & S*, II, p. 385.

[362] Ibid., p. 388.

[363] A record of Burke's trip survives in a series of letters that can be found at *Corr.*, II, pp. 411–22. Burke's reaction to the prevailing systems of unbelief is recorded in James Prior, *Life of the Right Honourable Edmund Burke* (1824) (London: 5th ed., 1854), pp. 135–36.

[364] James Beattie, *London Diary, 1773*, ed. Ralph S. Walker (Aberdeen: Aberdeen University Press, 1946), pp. 33–38.

[365] James Beattie, *An Essay on the Nature and Immutability of Truth in Opposition to Sophistry and Scepticism* (Edinburgh: 1771), pp. 542–44.

[366] EB, Speech on Toleration Bill, 17 March 1773, *W & S*, II, p. 389.

[367] Ibid.

[368] EB, Speech on Toleration Bill, 17 March 1773, *Parliamentary History*, XVII, col. 782.

Alciphron, had destroyed the "hopes of men," degrading human nature to the level of animal life.[369] In the face of this ongoing onslaught, Burke believed, toleration was a means of uniting with fellow Christians to defeat an assault against piety and morals: "I would have Christians united; I would have them join in every attempt to crush the powers of darkness, and trample under foot the foe to God and man."[370]

Replying to a letter from William Burgh in 1775, Burke made plain what he understood to be the scope of toleration. Civil protection included complete immunity from interference with any form of worship, and accordingly Burke would afford toleration "to Jews[,] Mahometans and even Pagans."[371] With even fewer qualms he was happy to extend toleration to every branch of the Christian faith. At this time, Burgh was proposing to dedicate the second edition of his work refuting the Unitarian principles of Theophilus Lindsey to Burke.[372] In response, Burke found it necessary to insist that he could never view dissenters as mere schismatics, although in the 1790s he would conclude that this is exactly what Price and Priestley were.[373] For the moment, he regarded even heterodox dissent as expressing a commitment to "our common hope."[374] Another age, Burke predicted, would embrace this disposition to charity, and recognise its promotion as a sign of religious devotion. "I have no doubt," Burke wrote to an American correspondent, "that the spirit of intolerance will vanish Away by degrees, both on our side of the water and on yours."[375] In Grotian spirit, while Burke was happy to denounce the forms of persecution that had flourished in the era of Roman Catholic tyranny, he nonetheless appreciated the commonalities that existed across all strands of the Christian religion.[376] He could find nothing "capitally amiss" in any division of the reformed or unreformed churches except "their mutual hatred for one another."[377] Christian strength lay in a common commitment to combat religious indifference and thwart the rising presumption of "Epicurism."[378]

[369] George Berkeley, *Alciphron; or the Minute Philosopher* in *The Works of George Berkeley*, ed. Alexander Campbell Fraser (Oxford: Oxford University Press, 1901), 4 vols., II, p. 49.

[370] EB, Speech on Toleration Bill, 17 March 1773, *Parliamentary History*, XVII, col. 783.

[371] EB to William Burgh, 9 February 1775, *Corr.*, III, p. 112.

[372] The original work was William Burgh, *A Scriptural Confutation of the Arguments against the One Godhead by the Reverend Mr. Lindsey* (London: 1775).

[373] On this, see John Seed, "'A Set of Men Powerful Enough in Many Things': Rational Dissent and Political Opposition in England, 1770–1790" in Haakonssen ed., *Enlightenment and Religion*, p. 157.

[374] EB to William Burgh, 9 February 1775, *Corr.*, III, pp. 111–12.

[375] EB to John Cruger, 30 June 1772, *Corr.*, II, p. 310.

[376] Hugo Grotius, *The Truth of the Christian Religion* (1627), ed. Rosa Antognazza (Indianapolis, IN: Liberty Fund, 2012), p. 125: "the Difference of Opinions that is amongst Christians, cannot hinder their Agreement in the principal things." For discussion of Grotius' debts to an Erasmian tradition, and his impact on English latitudinarian theology, see Hugh Trevor Roper, "The Religious Origins of the Enlightenment" in idem, *The Crisis of the Seventeenth Century: Religion, the Reformation, and Social Change* (Indianapolis, IN: Liberty Fund, 1967).

[377] EB to William Burgh, 9 February 1775, *Corr.*, III, pp. 112.

[378] Ibid.

VI

COLLISION WITH THE COLONIES, 1765–1774

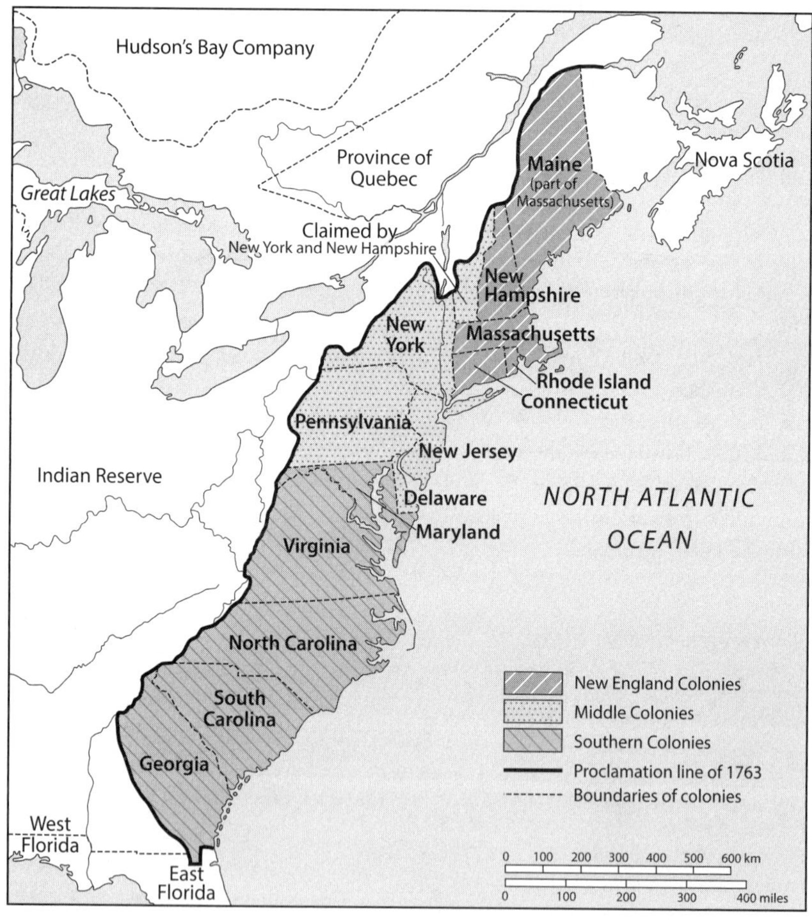

Map 1. Map of the American Colonies

6.1 Introduction

Burke's parliamentary career began with a major political crisis that would loom large in national debates for a further seventeen years. The rift with America represented the most dramatic controversy to emerge during the first half of the reign of George III. Colonial resistance mounted a challenge to the composite structure of the Empire and to the nature of metropolitan authority. This chapter charts Burke's response to the developing situation down to the eve of the outbreak of the war of independence. From the beginning he was wary about a contest over "rights," pitting the claims of the colonists against the government. Practical accommodation should be the goal of either side. By December 1765, Burke had decided that the repeal of George Grenville's Stamp Act offered the only means of reconciling both sides. This was of course to be accompanied by an assertion of imperial sovereignty designed to proclaim the juridical supremacy of the crown-in-parliament. The position was carefully crafted in opposition to Pitt and Grenville: the former was playing the patriot card in deferring to colonial sentiment, the latter pushing the executive line that the British were unaccountable. While imperial authority was necessarily supreme, Burke countered, it had to be responsive to colonial consent. Already by the autumn of 1766, Burke suspected that the Chathamites were changing course: suddenly they were pressing the claims of metropolitan power, having forgotten their devotion to the rights of the provinces. In accordance with this change, Rockinghamite policy was being overturned as early as 1767 by the advancement of Charles Townshend's scheme for imposing duties that would yield a revenue in the colonies. From that point on, conflict with America began to intensify, driving the government towards imperiousness rather than conciliation. The Boston Massacre, the Tea Act and the Intolerable Acts followed, driving relations with the colonies towards mounting hostility.

Burke's opposition to the policies of Chatham, Grafton and North occurred against the backdrop of a pledge to the value of consent. In the mid 1760s, the Rockinghams were hard at work aligning themselves with public opinion in an effort to make good the idea that they represented the people without appearing to be subordinate to the popular will. They understood themselves to be in tune with the sentiments of the public, particularly the attitudes of merchants and the city, while still maintaining a commitment to deliberation and judgment fostered by parliamentary procedure. Government failure to recognise the weight of colonial opinion appeared to Burke as a betrayal of these ideals. The failure was determined by the attitude of British power, which grew more oppressive as its dependence on the provinces became apparent. The colonies had progressed from being mere trading corporations to enjoying the status of substantial though subordinate commonwealths. From Burke's vantage, they had representative assemblies whose decrees should be respected even if their authority was accountable to Westminster. Yet instead of approaching them in the spirit of superintending benefaction, successive governments had treated them as mischievous delinquents. Ministries appeared determined to administer rather than guide them even as they lacked the instruments to succeed. Burke reckoned that colonial populations schooled in the principles of British liberty would not submit to have their revenues as well as their commerce controlled. More importantly, they had the means of resisting what they saw as arbitrary impositions, which meant that Britain was obliged to employ its authority rather than its force if it was to hope to steer its subjects in America towards compliance. Under successive Secretaries of State for the colonies—first under the Earl of Hillsborough between 1768 and 1772, and then under the Earl of Dartmouth down to 1774—the provinces dreaded coercion as imperial government feared rebellion. Driven by pride to assert its will as it felt its effectiveness recede, Burke warned that the seat of Empire was losing its credibility in a desperate bid to uphold its dignity. Westminster could only govern in accordance with opinion yet improvidence persistently drove it to attempt to rule by terror.

6.2 The Stamp Act Crisis

In his Speech on American Taxation of 19 April 1774, Burke admitted that the subject of the colonies moved him to "sadness."[1] He had watched the policy shifts of successive administrations compromise imperial authority and inflame colonial sentiment over a period of nine years. Throughout that time, he stated, he held fast to a single position, whose defence he put in the service of Rockinghamite policy on the colonies, and which he pointedly described as the "system of 1766"—referring to the year in which Lord Rockingham headed the treasury.[2] In pursuing this steady course, despite the jibes of court favourites, he had sacrificed preferment for the sake of public honour. Honour meant adhering to principles rather than seeking places, and Burke claimed that he had been devoted to the same principles regarding America since before he secured a seat in the House of Commons.[3] By implication, his core commitments were embodied in the provisions for colonial government adopted by the Rockinghams in 1766.

On 17 January 1766, a raft of petitions was presented to the House of Commons from merchants around Britain complaining about the decay of trade with the American colonies in the aftermath of the Stamp Act. This was part of a concerted campaign to consolidate support for the ministry in opposition to Grenville's measure. William Meredith approached Burke to present the Manchester petition. This gave rise to Burke's first trial in parliament. In a full House, the atmosphere was electric and intimidating. The opposition benches, where Burke stood, comprised four staggered rows, facing—across the floor of the House—the supporters of the government. The speaker occupied a platform situated in the middle, while galleries

[1] EB, *Speech on American Taxation* (19 April 1774), *W & S*, II, p. 462.
[2] Ibid.
[3] Ibid.

ran along either side of the chamber. "I felt like a man drunk," Burke admitted to Charles O'Hara.[4] He was writing in a state of excitement the day after his maiden speech, stealing a moment in the Commons before the lobby bell sounded. Meredith had unexpectedly passed the task to Burke, forcing him to react without due preparation.[5] Soon he was in debate with Lord Frederick Campbell, and then George Grenville. "I was now heated," Burke revealed; he was eager for more, but then George Savile broke his flow by catching the Speaker's eye. He was nonetheless relieved, having "plunged" straight in, thus overcoming the fear of his first performance. Immediately afterwards he felt "stouter," if a little "giddy," sensing a kind of "swimming" in his brain.[6] He was elated but still grounded by the momentousness of the occasion—the most significant, Pitt had argued, since the Glorious Revolution.[7]

Burke's first intervention into parliamentary debate occurred in the midst of a crisis of colonial confidence. The Stamp Act had passed on 22 March 1765, becoming effective the following November, but opposition to the measure had been mounting since it was first mooted in the spring of 1764.[8] This had originally occurred in the context of ministerial plans for regulating colonial trade, presented in a series of resolutions before the Commons in March 1764.[9] On taking office in the summer of 1763, in the aftermath of the Peace of Paris, Grenville was under considerable pressure to manage the spiralling costs of the national debt, and to raise funds for the maintenance of a standing army in America. Some of this was to be met by imposing duties on colonial imports—Madeira, wine, coffee, pimento, indigo, painted calicoes, linen and molasses.[10] This last regulation, which together with the rest would soon become known as the Sugar Act, amounted to an attempt to enforce the ineffective Molasses Act of 1733 by reducing the cost of the duty in order to ease its collection. It was intended, like the others, as a preferential tariff designed to benefit British trade, but had the additional purpose of relieving the exchequer.[11] Opposition in the colonies was immediate and vociferous, beginning in the assemblies and

[4] EB to Charles O'Hara, 18 January 1766, *Corr.*, I, p. 232.

[5] See the description in Christopher Reid, *Imprison'd Wranglers: The Rhetorical Culture of the House of Commons, 1760–1800* (Oxford: Oxford University Press, 2012), pp. 145–46.

[6] EB to Charles O'Hara, 18 January 1766, *Corr.*, I, p. 233.

[7] Pitt had made this claim on 14 January 1766. The fullest record of the debate appears in the *Parliamentary Register* (Almon), VII, pp. 61–77. For the comparison with 1688, see PDNA, II, p. 86. Cf. Walpole, *Memoirs*, III, p. 8.

[8] The act passed as 5 Geo. III, c. 12.

[9] *CJ*, XXIX, pp. 934–35. The provision of a stamp tax was first proposed by Grenville in the fifteenth and final of his resolutions on colonial trade to the Commons.

[10] The relevant figures are presented by Burke in "Supplies Granted by Parliament for the Service of the Year 1764" in *The Annual Register for the Year 1764* (London: 1765), pp. 164–65, and are presented verbatim in Adam Anderson, *An Historical and Chronological Deduction of the Origin of Commerce, from the Earliest Accounts to the Present Time* (London: 1764, 1790), 4 vols., IV, pp. 65–67.

[11] On new commercial regulation under the Grenville ministry, see O. M. Dickerson, *The Navigation Acts and the American Revolution* (Philadelphia, PA: University of Pennsylvania Press, 1951), ch. 7; J. J. McCusker and R. M. Menard, *The Economy of British America, 1607–1789* (Chapel Hill, NC: University of North Carolina Press, 1985), ch. 3.

among the merchant class, spreading through the population down to the justices of the peace. Enforcement by the navy was indiscriminate and heavy handed. Agents were dispatched to Westminster to complain.[12]

Discontent arising in the aftermath of the Sugar Act did not deter the government from contriving to extract more revenue. The national debt had risen over the course of the Seven Years' War to the staggering sum of £129,586,789, while the annual expense of maintaining troops in North America was estimated in the region of £250,000.[13] Yet in response to the ministerial plan to impose a duty to help meet these costs, representatives were sent to Britain to question the right of parliament to impose taxes on the colonies at all.[14] Taxation required concurrence through representation, it was protested.[15] The development of a position of principled opposition occurred against a backdrop of more tangible complaints. Armed sea cutters were being used off the coasts of Britain and Ireland to intercept smuggled cargoes, while naval officers in American waters were required to play the part of revenue inspectors. Merchant seamen were treated roughly and left with little by way of redress since only the Lords of the Admiralty and Treasury were available on appeal, thus depriving the accused of a trial by a jury of their peers. Perhaps more remarkably, it seemed that trade itself was being attacked by a new vigilance on the part of the navy to ensure compliance with commercial regulations that were usually ignored.[16] "Thus were our North American colonies put to the severest trial of their love and respect for the mother country," Burke commented in *The Annual Register* for 1765.[17]

[12] Edmund S. Morgan and Helen M. Morgan, *The Stamp Act Crisis: Prologue to Revolution* (1953) (New York: Macmillan, 1962), pp. 52–58.

[13] The figure for the national debt is for the year 1764. See *CJ*, XXIX, p. 760. Cf. the figures in Adam Smith, *An Inquiry into the Nature and Causes of the Wealth of Nations*, ed. R. H. Campbell and A. S. Skinner (Indianapolis, IN: Liberty Fund, 1981), 2 vols., I, p. 354. Ten thousand British troops were stationed on the American continent. For the cost, see *CJ*, XXIX, p. 681; for discussion, see John Shy, *Toward Lexington: The Role of the British Army in the Coming of the American Revolution* (Princeton, NJ: Princeton University Press, 1965).

[14] Burke took a particular interest in the government's negotiations with colony agents, later annotating and taking issue with Israel Mauduit's *Mr. Grenville' Offer to the Colony Assemblies to Raise the Supply Themselves* (London: 1775), which can be found at WWM BkP 6:147. Burke also drafted an unpublished response. For this, see WWM BkP 6:148–53.

[15] The case was famously put in James Otis, *Rights of the British Colonies Asserted and Proved* (Boston: 1764). Otis's statement to that effect before the Massachusetts House of Representatives was included as an appendix to the work. See ibid, pp. 70–80. The pamphlet was to serve as the basis for Jasper Mauduit's representations to parliament on behalf of Massachusetts Bay. See *The Gentleman's and London Magazine* (London: 1767), p. 149.

[16] For the context of commercial restrictions, and their origins in the Board of Trade, see Thomas W. Barrow, "Background to the Grenville Program, 1757–1764," *William and Mary Quarterly*, 22:1 (January 1965), pp. 93–104.

[17] "The History of Europe" in *The Annual Register for the Year 1765* (London: 1766), p. 23. This volume was first published on the unusually late date of 27 June 1766. For discussion of the tightening up of navigation restrictions after 1763, see Thomas C. Barrow, *Trade and Empire: The British Customs Service in Colonial America* (Cambridge, MA: Harvard University Press, 1967).

At this point, political passions in the colonies were raised to new heights against the anticipated designs of British power. Hitherto, resentment was confined to aggravated individuals, whereas now colonial discontent was increasingly concerted. Associations to boycott British imports were deliberately formed, while colonial assemblies instructed their agents to present their principled disapproval. The legitimacy of legislative acts would be put to the test, and the authority of parliament called into question. With the opening of parliament on 10 January 1765, parliamentary supremacy was proclaimed in the speech from the throne, helping to make an issue of what was ordinarily taken for granted.[18] Eleven days later, in connection with the Navy estimates, Charles Townshend felt compelled to reiterate the "*supremacy of this country* over the colonies," later eliciting an outraged response from Alderman William Beckford: "The colonies . . . are more free than Ireland," he declared.[19] In *The Annual Register* Burke presented an argument that he would often repeat: no one would ultimately benefit from contention over questions of right since political relations would be damaged no matter how the dispute was decided, and if it was not the disagreement would feed acrimony and suspicion.[20] When colonial petitions were presented on 15 February, parliament refused to have them read. Charles Yorke, the Attorney General, characterised colonial legislation as equivalent to the promulgation of mere "by-laws."[21] Among the colonists, remarks of this kind felt like an affront, and soon the Sons of Liberty were protesting in the streets of Boston, while the Stamp Act Congress registered a deepening sense of grievance.[22] The "Spirit of Democracy," General Gage reported, was animating sentiment against the mother country.[23]

Burke speculated that the upheaval over the Stamp Act might have been avoided if the measure had been introduced all of a sudden and without fanfare.[24] In that case, the opportunities for organisation would have been curtailed, and the population could have grown to accept what in practice might have been less oppressive than its dire anticipation made it appear. Instead, political activists, given time and opportunity to prepare, fomented disaffection among all ranks of the people.[25] The

[18] *CJ*, XXX, pp. 2–4.

[19] Townshend's remark is reported in the Parliamentary Diary of James Harris, reprinted in PDNA, II, p. 4. Beckford's riposte came on 23 January, and is contained in Walpole, *Memoirs*, II, p. 34, reprinted in PDNA, II, p. 8.

[20] "The History of Europe" in *The Annual Register for 1765*, p. 26.

[21] The statement appears in Parliamentary Diary of James Harris, reproduced in PDNA, II, p. 26.

[22] Morgan and Morgan, *The Stamp Act Crisis*, chs. 7 and 8.

[23] Thomas Gage to Henry Seymour Conway, 12 October 1768, *The Correspondence of General Thomas Gage with the Secretaries of State, 1763–1775*, ed. Clarence Edwin Carter (New Haven, CT: Yale University Press, 1933), 2 vols., I, p. 69.

[24] "The History of Europe" in *The Annual Register for 1765*, p. 49. The suggestion is again made in EB, *Observations on a Late State of the Nation* (1769), *W & S*, II, p. 188. For an analysis of the delay in introducing the Stamp Act, see Edmund S. Morgan, "The Postponement of the Stamp Act," *William and Mary Quarterly*, 7:3 (July 1950), pp. 353–92.

[25] "The History of Europe" in *The Annual Register for 1765*, pp. 49–50.

material they had to work with was of course easy to inflame, so anger spread like wildfire across vast tracts of colonial territory. Burke contended that news of the passage of the Stamp Act reached New England first, ensuring that opposition would rise to a height of fury, reviving the old spirit of republican independence.[26] All differences in public sentiment and religion were overcome, and with it the best assurance of submission to the British interest.[27] Unity even spread among the colonies themselves, above all between New England, New York, New Jersey, Philadelphia, Virginia, the Carolinas and Maryland.[28] Nonetheless, colonial protest met with little support in the House of Commons, although Isaac Barré made a stand in defence of the rights of Americans.[29]

In the midst of the first stirrings of unrest in anticipation of the Stamp Act, Burke recognised that the manner of defraying the expenses of the nation would determine the future of Britain and its Empire. He had explained in *The Annual Register* for 1764 that he expected the Peace of Paris to endure, despite the powerful alliance between France and Spain. He also admitted that it was difficult to predict who would make most of the terms of the peace. Everything would depend on fine judgments in political economy—on the flexibility and stability of the political systems of Europe, on the judicious management of the resources of each state, and on the skill of French and British ministers in capitalising on those resources.[30] Principal among these resources were industry and trade. In a review of Adam Anderson's 1764 *Historical Deduction of the Origin of Commerce*, *The Annual Register* underlined what was already obvious. Habits of trade were "influenced by the manners of mankind," while commerce was an integral part of national policy.[31] The prospects for trade were therefore pivotal to the power and prosperity of the state, but its regulation would depend on the manners and opinions of those affected.

Burke would later point to the War of the Austrian Succession and its aftermath as marking a crucial period in the development of British attitudes to the relation between trade and power.[32] The Treaty of Aix-la-Chapelle, signed in October 1748, brought less a settlement of the European struggle for empire than a respite in which plans were laid that would lead to its intensification. After the resumption of hostili-

[26] Ibid., p. 50. In fact the earliest stand was taken by Patrick Henry in the Virginia House of Burgesses on 29 May 1765, though it was on the suggestion of James Otis, based in Massachusetts Bay, that the Stamp Act Congress was convened the following October. Physical resistance began in Boston in August with the obstruction of tax collection and attacks upon property.

[27] Ibid.

[28] Ibid., p. 56.

[29] Barré's first recorded intervention on the American issue occurred on 21 January 1765 and is noted in the Parliamentary Diary of James Harris, reproduced in PDNA, II, p. 4. He made a more extensive and impassioned statement on 6 February 1765. See PDNA, II, p. 16.

[30] "The History of Europe" in *The Annual Register for 1764*, p. 10.

[31] "An Account of the Books Published in 1764," ibid., p. 250.

[32] Edmund Burke, Speech on the Opening of Impeachment, *W & S*, VI, p. 311. Burke was then focusing on developments in the east rather than the west.

ties in America in 1754, and then in Europe in 1756, British prospects in the Great War for Empire that ensued looked grim until the capture of Quebec in 1759.[33] By 1763, Britain was in a position to agree a peace on favourable terms, which in America involved securing extensive new tracts of territory delimited into three main areas from which the French and Spanish were at last excluded. These comprised the region of Canada, the territory between the Appalachians and the Mississippi, together with East and West Florida, all of them making, as Burke put it in 1764, Britain's "American empire complete."[34] In comparison with the coastal and West Indian colonies, these were undeveloped, sparsely populated areas.[35] They could not be made to yield immediate profit, and if they were ever to be rendered "beneficial in traffic" they would first have to be made absolutely secure.[36] Expanses of "savage" country evidently represented a mainly strategic gain to the British, but in the longer term, due to the varieties of soils and climates in the region, the new acquisitions would make an addition to agriculture and commerce. However, not every portion of these territories was to be subjected to British government. The American interior east of the Mississippi was to be retained as hunting ground for the native Indian population until such a time as they assimilated to British politics and culture through the processes of settlement and trade.[37]

In the meantime, in line with the Royal Proclamation of 1763, conflict between colonial settlers and the Indian population was to be avoided by the curtailment of private land purchases beyond the Appalachians and the presence of the British military to regulate the border. That regulation necessarily came at a cost, and in 1764 Burke was clear about who should meet it. "For the present," he wrote, the troops are "maintained by Great Britain." However, with the advent of a more "settled season" they would be paid—"as is reasonable"—by the colonies they were intended to protect.[38] It would later become clear that the terms of payment proposed by Westminster would unsettle political relations between the colonial and parliamentary components of Britain's composite monarchy.[39] By 1766, Burke was proposing to

[33] For the phrase "Great War for Empire," see Lawrence Henry Gipson, "The American Revolution as an Aftermath of the Great War for the Empire, 1754–1763," *Political Science Quarterly*, 65:1 (March 1950), pp. 86–104.

[34] "The History of Europe" in *The Annual Register for the Year 1763* (London: 1764), p. 18.

[35] William Burke underlined this point with reference to Canada in his *Examination of the Commercial Principles of the Late Negotiation Between Great Britain and France in 1761, in which the System of that Negotiation with Regard to our Colonies and Commerce is Considered* (London: 1762), pp. 80–81.

[36] "The History of Europe" in *The Annual Register for the Year 1763*, p. 18. This volume first appeared on 16 May 1764.

[37] Ibid., p. 32.

[38] Ibid., p. 21.

[39] On composite monarchy as an early modern political system, see H. G. Koenigsberger, "Monarchies and Parliaments in Early Modern Europe: *Dominium Regale* or *Dominium Politicum et Regale*," *Theory and Society*, 5:2 (March 1978), pp. 191–217; J. H. Elliott, "A Europe of Composite Monarchies," *Past & Present* (November 1992), pp. 48–71; Istvan Hont, *Jealousy of Trade: International Competition and the Nation-State in Historical Perspective* (Cambridge, MA: Harvard University Press, 2005), pp. 456–63. For application to the American context, see H. G. Koenigsberger, "Composite States,

resolve the antagonism by having the colonies contribute to the overall British welfare through the growing volume of trade rather than by taxing colonial commerce. Robert Walpole was taken to have established a clear policy precedent by rejecting American taxation in 1739.[40] It would be far better, Burke reported him as having commented, if commercial latitude was maximally extended to America, with the British exchequer benefiting indirectly from the boost to domestic productivity and exchange. "This," *The Annual Register* presented Walpole as having concluded, "is taxing them more agreeably both to their own constitution, and to ours."[41]

The extent of colonial resistance to the Stamp Act was evident in Whitehall by 5 October 1765.[42] The first Rockingham administration had replaced Grenville's ministry in July, and Burke was appointed private secretary to the First Lord of the Treasury at the same time. He was immediately set to work on government business.[43] By the time he was elected to the Commons in December, plans for amending the Stamp Act had been drafted by the administration. Rockingham had been collaborating with Barlow Trecothick, a London Alderman, to organise petitions to parliament setting out the detriment to British trade expected when the new act came into force.[44] Details of a campaign to mobilise British merchants survives in a document in Burke's hand from November.[45] The mobilisation was intended as a means of educating parliament before a policy was finally put before the Commons. By early December, Henry Seymour Conway, the Secretary of State for the Southern Department, had been informed that the Stamp Act had not been enforced in New York, and it did not look as though it was likely to be successful elsewhere in the colonies. If the inconvenience of its non-enforcement did not bring it into effect in the near future, only a substantial military force could ensure its implementation.[46]

Representative Institutions and the American Revolution," *Historical Research*, 62:148 (June 1989), pp. 135–53.

[40]The episode to which Burke is referring is discussed in Alvin Rabushka, *Taxation in Colonial America* (Princeton, NJ: Princeton University Press, 2008), p. 449.

[41]"The History of Europe" in *The Annual Register for the Year 1765* (London: 1766), p. 25. This is substantially the position later advocated in EB, *Speech on American Taxation* (19 April 1774), *W & S*, II, pp. 428–29. Cf. Walpole, *Memoirs*, II, p. 93: "It had been proposed to Sir Robert Walpole to raise the revenue by imposing taxes on America, but the minister, who could foresee beyond the benefit of the actual moment, declared it must be a bolder man than himself, who should venture on such an expedient."

[42]The news was relayed via Governor Francis Bernard's letter of 31 August to Lord Halifax. See Langford, *Rockingham Administration*, p, 80.

[43]A letter from Rockingham to Lord Shelburne from 11 July 1765 survives in Burke's hand. See *Corr.*, I, p. 211n.

[44]John L. Bullion, "British Ministers and American Resistance to the Stamp Act, October–December 1765," *William and Mary Quarterly*, 49:1 (January 1992), pp. 89–107.

[45]Northamptonshire MS. A. XXVII.81.

[46]Thomas Gage to Henry Seymour Conway, 4 November 1765, *Correspondence of Gage*, I, p. 71.

In the face of American recalcitrance, the Lord Chancellor reported to the king on 12 December that the cabinet were minded to yield in the face of rebellion.[47]

The question was how exactly they would yield. For his part, Burke had made up his mind by 31 December 1765: "my resolution is taken," he wrote to O'Hara.[48] Grenville had been looking increasingly shabby in Burke's eyes: "He shews I think no Talents of a Leader; he wanted the stage of administration to give him figure."[49] His incompetence was being particularly noted in connection with American affairs. Since parliament met on 17 December, he had been agitating for stern measures to be adopted against the colonists, displaying what Burke saw as his own weakness in the process.[50] Even so, preparations were required over the Christmas recess before the government could settle on a way forward. Burke conveyed to O'Hara that while he had settled on repeal, the ministry had yet to fix its plan "conclusively."[51] In the interval before the meeting of parliament in January, there were "wonderful materials of combustion at hand."[52] Parliament faced its gravest challenge since the accession of George III, and the government had to decide whether to modify the Stamp Act, to suspend it in order to buy time before settling on an approach, or to repeal it and thus be done with it for good.[53] Writing to Newcastle on 2 January 1766, Rockingham anticipated that "*Very Few*" would support a repeal.[54] His task would be to convert this number into a majority over the following months.

At a meeting of ministers on 27 December, Charles Yorke had proposed preceding any alteration in the Act with a declaratory resolution asserting the authority of parliament.[55] On 2 January, Rockingham commended the wisdom of such an assertion, which was to be modelled on the Irish Dependency Act of 1720, championed by Charles Yorke's father, Philip Yorke, later Earl of Hardwicke.[56] It was also clear

[47] Lord Northington to George III, 12 December 1765, *The Correspondence of King George the Third from 1760 to December 1783*, ed. Sir John Fortescue (London: Macmillan, 1927–28), 6 vols., I, p. 429.

[48] EB to Charles O'Hara, 31 December 1765, *Corr.*, I, p. 229.

[49] EB to Charles O'Hara, 24 December 1765, ibid., p. 224. Cf. EB to John Ridge, 24 December 1765, ibid., p. 225: "never did an adversary show more fury and impotence together than G. Grenville."

[50] Grenville had settled on his course of action before he knew the content of the King's Speech. See P.D.G. Thomas, *British Politics and the Stamp Act Crisis: The First Phase of the American Revolution, 1763–1767* (Oxford: Oxford University Press, 1975), p. 155.

[51] EB to Charles O'Hara, 31 December 1765, *Corr.*, I, p. 229.

[52] Ibid.

[53] See Langford, *First Rockingham Administration*, ch. 5.

[54] Add. MS. 32973, fol. 12. Burke later claimed that the ministry had settled on its programme before the meeting of parliament. See EB, *Speech on American Taxation* (19 April 1774), *W & S*, II, p. 439.

[55] Thomas, *British Politics and the Stamp Act Crisis*, pp. 162–3.

[56] *Statutes at Large from the First Year of the Reign of George the First to the Ninth Year of the Reign of George the Second* (London: 1786): 6 Geo. I, c. 5. For an account of the meeting, see Rockingham to Newcastle, Add. MS. 32973, fols. 11–13. For Philip Yorke's support of the Irish Dependency Act, see *The History and Proceedings of the House of Commons, 1714–1727* (London: 1742), VI, pp. 198–218.

that Rockingham had decided in favour of conciliation.[57] The viability of this course of action became clearer with Pitt's intervention into the parliamentary debate on 14 January 1766.[58] It was at this point that Pitt declared his support for repeal, dramatically increasing the likelihood that the government would have the numbers to carry the measure in the face of reluctance on the part of George III and the opposition of his friends in the House of Commons.[59] Burke recalled the occasion to O'Hara, parodying the appearance of Pitt in St. Stephen's Chapel as a lone eminence with obedient followers in tow: "Last Tuesday we drew up the Curtain, and discovered the Great Commoner, attended by his train, *solus*."[60] His performance, Burke later commented, was merely a bid for popularity that also served the purpose of antagonising his brother-in-law, Grenville.[61] His maxims were designed to appeal rather than to tackle outstanding problems, while his politics were made to serve his independent ascendancy at the expense of concerted action with his peers.[62]

Burke was scathing, summarising Pitt's speech as an attempt to decry the late ministry while keeping his distance from the new government—specifically by denying any right on the part of Britain to "impose an interior Tax on the Colonies."[63] "Taxation is no part of the governing or legislative power," Pitt had proclaimed.[64] The distinction between legislation and taxation, he was suggesting, was essential to the security of liberty: whereas the crown and peers participated with the lower House in making laws, taxation was a prerogative of the Commons alone. Pitt envisaged a similar relation between colonial assemblies and the sovereign parliament as obtained between the Commons and other components of the constitution. The concerted will of parliament was supreme in all matters of government, yet it could only determine taxation on the basis of popular consent: supply was a gift that only the representatives of property could grant, and this status was enjoyed by the popular branch in state and empire.[65] This was a striking doctrine, presented in critical circumstances, which implied that a resolution of the colonial crisis would clarify the

[57] Burke was to insist on this point in EB, *Speech on American Taxation* (19 April 1774), *W & S*, II, p. 441, when he dismissed the idea that the Rockinghams were driven to embrace repeal out of deference to Pitt. Thomas, *British Politics and the Stamp Act Crisis*, pp. 162–63.

[58] He expressed his determination to Thomas Nuthall from Bath on 9 January 1766 that he would deliver his "mind and heart" on the state of America when the session opened. See *Chatham Correspondence*, II, p. 362.

[59] William Pitt to Lady Chatham, 15 January 1766, ibid., pp. 363–70; Langford, *First Rockingham Administration*, pp. 142–43.

[60] EB to Charles O'Hara, 18 January 1766, *Corr.*, I, p. 231.

[61] WWM BkP 6:55.

[62] See the account of Chatham, EB, *Speech on American Taxation* (19 April 1774), *W & S*, II, pp. 450–51.

[63] EB to Charles O'Hara, 18 January 1766, *Corr.*, I, p. 232.

[64] PDNA, II, p. 85. The debate of 14 January 1766 can be found in *Parliamentary Register* (Almon), VII, pp. 61–77. The precise import of Pitt's speech is examined in Ian R. Christie, "William Pitt and American Taxation, 1766: A Problem of Parliamentary Reporting," *Studies in Burke and His Time*, 17 (1976), pp. 167–79.

[65] PDNA, II, p. 86.

constitutional configuration of the Empire. In challenging Pitt's claims, the Rockinghams would require a theory of empire of their own. According to one correspondent, Burke's speeches in early 1766 seemed "a kind of new political philosophy."[66] He was conceptualising the Empire at a moment of political reckoning, examining its relations with reference to current constitutional thinking in the light of the rapid growth in colonial prosperity and strength.

6.3 Agitation for Reform

The final adoption of an American policy among Rockingham's supporters was agreed at a series of meetings on 19, 21 and 24 January 1766. A Declaratory Act proclaiming the right of parliament to "bind the Colonies and *People of America* . . . in all Cases whatsoever" was to be promulgated, followed by a series of concessions on trade, concluding with the repeal of Grenville's Stamp Act.[67] The major divisions on repeal would come in late February and early March, but in the meantime the Rockinghams set about winning support for the measure. As their campaign got under way, there was a debate in the Commons on 27 January about whether to receive a petition from the North American Congress, assembled in what many regarded as "a dangerous federal union."[68] To the dismay of David Hume, Pitt argued in favour of receiving the petition, claiming that the "original compact" between parliament and colonies had been broken.[69] However such a claim, according to Fletcher Norton, amounted to sounding "the trumpet to rebellion," invoking the inflammatory language of seventeenth-century popular resistance by way of objecting to current government policy.[70] Both Dowdeswell and Conway judged Pitt's gesture out of order, and argued against having the petition read. Burke, however, took a different tack: he was in favour of accepting the petition, but drew the opposite conclusion from Pitt. The very act of petitioning, far from implying that the contract of government had been violated, was an implicit acknowledgement of the authority of Westminster over the colonies.[71]

It was this intervention in January 1766 that first brought Burke to the attention of Horace Walpole. As Walpole described him, this new member—"an Irishman, of a Roman Catholic family," the narrowness of whose fortune had kept him down—

[66] James Marriott to EB, 26 February 1766, *Correspondence* (1844), p. 103.

[67] Rockingham to Charles Yorke, 19 January 1766, Add. MS. 35430, fol. 32. For the Declaratory Act, see *Statutes at Large from the Twenty-Sixth Year of the Reign of King George the Second to the Sixth Year of the Reign of King George the Third* (London: 1786): 6 Geo. III, c. 12.

[68] Walpole, *Memoirs*, III, p. 13.

[69] David Hume to Lord Hertford, 27 February 1766, in J.Y.T. Greig ed., *The Letters of David Hume* (Oxford: Oxford University Press, 1932), 2 vols., II, pp. 18–19. For Pitt's remarks, see Walpole, *Memoirs*, III, p. 13.

[70] Ibid., p. 14.

[71] Ibid.

poured out fresh ideas with inexhaustible fertility, proving a scourge to Grenville as well as the darling of his party.[72] His knowledge and facility allegedly outshone Pitt's, though his approach seemed somewhat bookish by comparison. At the same time his vanity, Walpole complained, drove him to seek the applause of his peers. Altogether, Walpole thought that his talent as a speaker outdid his skills as a politician, since he failed to study the motives of men inferior in ability.[73] In any case his capabilities were on display in early February, beginning with his intervention into the debate on the declaratory resolution. This was the first of a series of resolutions on American affairs proposed to a committee of the whole House, sparking a significant debate with major contributions from across the House: from William Blackstone, Alexander Wedderburn, Isaac Barré, Hans Stanley, Richard Hussey and Charles Yorke, among others.[74] Four more resolutions were debated over the following weeks—condemning the insurrections in America; indicting the colonial assemblies for encouraging disorder; urging the punishment of those responsible for acts of violence; and recommending compensation for those affected by the disorders—but on 3 February Conway opened in favour of the first resolution, defending the right of parliament to bind the people of the colonies.[75] He never had been, he made clear, a supporter of the internal taxation of America, but he nonetheless defended the "legal right" of parliament to do so. Yet if Westminster had this undoubted right, Conway was sure that it ought not to be exercised in point of "policy and justice."[76] In theory the right of government was absolute and uncontrollable, but in practice its authority should be tempered by circumstance. Charles Yorke pointed in a similar vein to the need to separate the question of right from "the question of expediency."[77] It was this argument that Burke was to make his own: "Principles should be subordinate to government," as Walpole summarised his case.[78]

The surviving manuscript evidence shows that Burke's speech on American affairs on 3 February 1766 presented a general account of the constitution of the Empire. Central to that account was the juridical distinction between the supreme right of sovereignty and the circumstances that limited the practical application of that right.[79] It was an argument that Burke would reiterate in relation to the French Revolution and in connection with the rights of British power in South Asia. It was

[72] Ibid.

[73] Ibid., pp. 14–15.

[74] There is an account in Lawrence Henry Gipson, "The Great Debate in the Committee of the Whole House of Commons on the Stamp Act, 1766, as Reported by Nathaniel Ryder," *Pennsylvania Magazine of History and Biography*, 86:1 (January 1962), pp. 10–41.

[75] Walpole, *Memoirs*, III, p. 17.

[76] *Ryder Diary*, p. 261.

[77] Ibid., p. 263.

[78] Walpole, *Memoirs*, III, p. 18.

[79] For the context of Burke's arguments, see Richard Bourke, "Sovereignty, Opinion and Revolution in Edmund Burke," *History of European Ideas*, 25:3 (1999), pp. 99–120; H. T. Dickinson, "The Eighteenth-Century Debate on the Sovereignty of Parliament," *Transactions of the Royal Historical Society*, 5th Series, 26 (1976), pp. 189–210; idem, "Britain's Imperial Sovereignty: The Ideological Case against the

vital, he later claimed, to distinguish between the legally "unaccountable" nature of the supreme authority of a country, which was not in doubt, and the limitations that bound its actual usage.[80] An "Ideal," speculative right and its practical exertion should not be confounded, yet Grenville had unhelpfully blended them in his defence of his own failed policies.[81] Metaphysical precepts should not guide the practical business of government, Burke contended.[82] The question of right was in some sense perfectly clear. As Burke formulated this during debate over the Townshend duties, the right of "this Country" is "sacred," since without it "our Dominion cannot exist."[83] By the very nature of sovereignty, its supremacy could not be rendered subordinate. If the supremacy of parliament were made juridically dependent upon the colonies, America would occupy the seat of empire. But not only was the dependency of the colonies evident from "the usual course of the British constitution," it was also obvious from the original charters of the colonies.[84] Unlike Pitt, Burke was clear that this dependency had to imply a right of taxation vested in the British parliament: "I think we have the clearest right imaginable," Burke insisted, "not only to bind them Generally with every Law, but with every mode of Legislative Taxation."[85] Nonetheless, once the location of sovereignty had been decided, a long list of difficulties remained. Above all, the question remained of how the rights of sovereignty were to be exercised. Burke's answer involved him sketching his view of the constitution of the colonial Empire, and the means of attachment between the settlers and the mother country.

The resolution in favour of a declaratory provision was carried with the support of virtually all members of the Commons, with the exception of William Pitt and his followers, and received the royal assent on 18 March. The accompanying debate set out the variety of perceptions of how the government of the Empire should be organised, as well as the history on which these perceptions had been based. The crisis of 1765 was generally situated within the wider context of the reconfiguration of the British monarchy since 1640.[86] It was recognised all round that attempts at constitutional adjustment in the 1630s had given rise to civil war in the 1640s,

American Colonies" in idem ed., *Britain and the American Revolution* (London and New York: Longman, 1998).

80 EB, Speech on the Opening of Impeachment, *W & S*, VI, p. 351. Cf. EB, Speech on American Disturbances, 6 February 1775, *W & S*, III, p. 83: absolute sovereignty, Burke insisted, was distinct from unlimited government.

81 WWM BkP 6:129, reproduced in EB, Speech on Declaratory Resolution, 3 February 1766, *W & S*, II, p. 46.

82 WWM BkP, 6:127 in ibid., p. 49.

83 Northamptonshire MS. A. XXVII.55 and A. XXVII.59.

84 Ibid.

85 Ibid. Cf. *The Annual Register for 1765*, p. 37, on the "absurdity" of colonial assemblies "pretending to be exempt from the taxation of parliament, because authorized by charter to tax themselves."

86 This contextualisation was standard in the pamphlet literature as well. See William Knox, *The Claim of the Colonies to an Exemption from the Internal Taxes Imposed by Authority of Parliament, Examined* (London: 1765), p. 8.

and the worry was that mismanagement in the 1760s would lead to a conflagration within the Empire as a whole a century after the resolution of the crises of the three kingdoms of England, Scotland and Ireland. Hans Stanley, on 3 February, realised that a failure to resolve the current collision might terminate in the "miseries of civil war."[87] This was a realisation at which Burke had also arrived by the start of the parliamentary session. One of his earliest prepared statements involved defending the administration against Grenville's charge that the government had failed to respond to the American tumult. Burke was clear that the Rockingham ministry had originally expected the Stamp Act to implement itself. Faced with the closure of the courts and the ports, the Americans would be forced to accept the use of stamps to avoid the inconvenience of a halt to business and trade. Only after 1 November did it become clear that the colonists would risk hardship by deciding to resist. Burke's notes defending government action between July and December 1765 set out the impracticality of military enforcement in the short term, while assuming that such a course would never be desirable even if favourable conditions were to obtain. It would have taken, Burke estimated, up to 500 troops to quell the disturbances in New England, and these would have to have been transported across the continent from frontier territories. "Mountains, Desarts, Woods, Snows, and all the accumulated horrors of an American winter" forbade this course of action.[88] Even in the campaign season a military response represented the "inglorious" option of employing violence against "fellow citizens." It would also require reinforcements from across the Atlantic, which could only really set out in the spring. There was nothing therefore in need of an urgent decision before parliament met. "There is time enough," Burke concluded, "to open the Theatre of Civil war."[89]

Nobody, of course, wanted civil war. The question was how it could be dependably avoided. Rockingham's supporters appreciated that staving off civil implosion meant preserving the balance of the domestic constitution as well as maintaining order in the colonies. However, the domestic balance was now implicated in the wider imperial balance. British stability depended upon uniform authority being preserved among the components of a mixed system of government united under the sovereignty of parliament. Charles Yorke believed that, in the absence of cohesion based on subordination, the British Empire would fall victim to the disaggregation that afflicted both the Netherlands and Poland-Lithuania.[90] By contrast, Pitt's argument had been that the colonies could maintain a relationship with the crown that would bypass the legislative will of parliament. To many this seemed to reverse

[87] *Ryder Diary*, p. 262.

[88] Northamptonshire MS. A. XXVII.52, reproduced in EB, Speech on Stamp Act Disturbances, January–February 1766, *W & S*, II, p. 44. Burke reiterated the point in his *Observations on a Late State of the Nation* (1769), *W & S*, II, pp. 190–91.

[89] EB, Speech on Stamp Act Disturbances, January–February 1766, *W & S*, II, pp. 44–45.

[90] Grey Cooper's notes on the Declaratory debate of 3 February 1766, printed in H.W.V. Temperley, "Debates on the Declaratory Act and the Repeal of the Stamp Act, 1766," *American Historical Review*, 17:3 (April 1912), pp. 563–86, p. 566.

the drift of modern constitutional history whereby the crown had been made dependent on the British parliament. As the Rockinghams saw it, the Empire would have to adapt to this salutary arrangement or imperil the Revolution settlement. Yorke, for one, was explicit on the subject: the vital principle of the Empire was the sovereignty of Britain, and any exception to this arrangement would upset "the balance of the constitution" by exempting a dependent dominion from the authority of Westminster.[91] A pact between subject territories and the crown under which the former granted taxes directly to the latter would undo the bands that fastened the king to the Houses of Parliament and augment the monarchical element of the constitution. It was this same fear of an extension of the power of the court that decided the Rockingham party against ministerial attempts to reform the East India Company between 1767 and 1773.[92] Parliamentary supremacy, moreover, enjoyed constitutional precedents, the case of Ireland most conspicuous among them. The Irish parliament, like the American assemblies, had to be subordinate to British sovereignty and could not negotiate independently with the crown. If it did, the political settlement of the Glorious Revolution would be undone, and the Declaration of Right undermined.[93]

Yorke pointed out that Ireland would have been lost in the 1640s, and again in the 1690s, were it not for initiatives taken by the "legislative power of this country"—specifically meaning intervention by the Westminster parliament.[94] It was by an act of the British parliament that 12,000 troops had been placed on the Irish establishment after the Peace of Ryswick, and it was the British Commons that had condemned Molyneux's *Case of Ireland . . . Stated* on 27 June 1698.[95] Yorke thought it appropriate to raise the case of the neighbouring island since James II had by all accounts been anxious to secure its subjection exclusively to himself instead of to "the whole legislative authority of Parliament."[96] Current American claims risked fuelling a replay of Stuart ambition in accordance with which a colony, in William Blackstone's words, might become a "separate dominion under one head."[97] As everyone saw, this image of colonial legislatures granting supply to a monarchical head was supported by a theory of representation: it was as representative bodies that colonial assemblies pleaded their status as partners in the Empire. Hence Hans Stanley's argument for the subordination of America on the basis of its being represented virtually: he could see "no difference" between the virtual representation of

[91] *Ryder Diary*, p. 267.

[92] See below, chapter 7.

[93] Pitt put the contrary case in parliament on 4 March 1766 when he cited William Molyneux's adversaries, including William Atwood, to illustrate how even they conceded that "the right of taxing does not necessarily follow the right of governing." See *Ryder Diary*, p. 316.

[94] Ibid., p. 264.

[95] Ibid. For the vote on Molyneux's tract, see *CJ*, XXI, p. 331.

[96] *Ryder Diary*, p. 265. Yorke noted that he had sought John Selden's advice on the issue, only to be disappointed by the response. See ibid, and cf. Grey Cooper's notes in Temperley, "Debates on the Declaratory Act," p. 567.

[97] *Ryder Diary*, p. 264. Ibid., p. 268.

the disenfranchised in Britain and the virtual representation of North America.[98] Prior to their representation in the Commons, Durham and Chester had been liable to taxation: there was, as Blackstone argued, no essential connection between taxation and representation in the history of English constitutional procedure. In fact, although it was true that the Commons initiated grants of revenue, the Lords and the crown still participated in processing taxation legislation.[99] And even if taxation were inseparable from representation, the British parliament was accustomed to represent dependencies, as illustrated by the declaration of 1648 proclaiming the subjection of Guernsey, Jersey and Ireland.[100] The same principle applied to colonial America, as exemplified in the preamble to the Navigation Act of 1651. Only Calais, from without the realm, ever sent representatives to Westminster.[101]

It was with this image of the colonies as subordinate corporations in mind that Yorke likened them to Roman *coloniae*: "They went out upon charter, carrying with them the laws and enjoying the protection of the mother country."[102] The same idea was implicit in the opening clauses of the 1757 legal opinion delivered by Charles Pratt and Charles Yorke, then Attorney General and Solicitor General respectively, reiterating earlier claims to the effect that settlers from the British realm carried with them the provisions of the common law and statute.[103] On 3 February 1766, Yorke contrasted this with the tendency among Greek *apoikia* to assert their relative autonomy in relation to the metropolis. But such analogies, Burke soon argued, missed the point: "We cannot resort to the example of Roman or Greek colonies."[104] A decade later, Adam Smith was again anxious to discount the parallel between modern colonial expansion and either Greek or Roman settlements. Above all, Smith noted, the utility of British colonies bore no relation to their original purpose, which had been driven by the desire of lucre in the west on the back of the failure of a scheme for commerce in the east.[105] By comparison, Greek and Roman settlements arose "either from some irresistible necessity, or from clear and evident utility."[106] Equally, Burke observed, precedents in British law were inapplicable under the circumstances. When the colonies were first settled by charter in America, their populations were inconsiderable and their trade extremely modest. But they had since then grown to merit being regarded as commonwealths in their own right, and were hardly little more than corporations in point of politics, even if they remained such in point

[98] Ibid., p. 262.

[99] Ibid., p 268

[100] Ibid. For the relevant Act, see *CJ*, V, pp. 577–80.

[101] *Ryder Diary*, p. 268.

[102] Ibid., p. 265. Cf. Grey Cooper's notes in Temperley, "Debates on the Declaratory Act," p. 567.

[103] On the Pratt-Yorke (Camden-Yorke) opinion, see Sheila Lambert ed., *House of Commons Sessional Papers of the Eighteenth Century* (Wilmington, DE: Scholarly Resources, 1975), 147 vols., 26, Item 1. See also below, chapter 7.

[104] *Ryder Diary*, p. 273.

[105] Smith, *Wealth of Nations*, II, p. 564.

[106] Ibid., p. 558.

of law.[107] "The object is wholly new in the world," Burke asserted of the colonies in 1769.[108] Proposals therefore had to be drawn from circumstances as they now existed, rather than from precedents that did not fit the current case.

For all his commitment to the idea that the British parliament enjoyed absolute authority over legislation, including taxation, in relation to its overseas dominions, Burke recognised that there was something inadequate about treating the colonies as replicas of domestic corporations. "Is there a single trait of resemblance," he asked his colleagues on 3 February, "between those few Towns disseminated through a represented County, and a great growing people spread over a vast quarter of the Globe?"[109] It was preposterous, he was suggesting, to equate New England with an unrepresented borough in an English county. Other members of parliament had expressed the anxiety that admitting to a problem with imperial representation would fan the flames of popular discontent. The principles being adopted by the Americans, complained Alexander Wedderburn, had first been aired by Wat Tyler in the days of Richard II, and more recently by the enemies of Charles I.[110] Hans Stanley was still more outspoken in defence of current arrangements: the Americans suffered no hardship in being virtually represented, and to redress their grievance would invite reform of domestic representation. Yet to broaden the franchise at home would turn elections into popular tumults, Stanley feared.[111] Burke was equally sceptical about revising the domestic system, but he still thought it made no sense to view the colonies as adequately represented if the preferences of their assemblies were disregarded. Parliament was certainly the supreme representative organ of the Empire, but this did not discount accepting subordinate representation. The colonies had to be subordinate, but they also had to be free. As Burke described the dilemma: "There is not a more difficult subject for the understanding of men than to govern a Large Empire upon a plan of Liberty."[112]

This touched on what Hume saw as the paradox of republican empire. The conquests of a monarchy are uniformly subject to the regulations of the prince whereas the acquisitions of a free state are usually distinguished from the home territory "by restrictions on trade, and by taxes" imposed as tribute by the republic on its dominions.[113] However, it was mere dogmatism, Burke thought, to insist that *libertas* and *imperium* were on a collision course under the empire of a free people.[114] All

[107] Grey Cooper's notes in Temperley, "Debates on the Declaratory Act," p. 571.

[108] EB, *Observations on a Late State of the Nation* (1769), *W & S*, II, p. 194.

[109] WWM BkP, 6:127 reproduced in EB, Speech on Declaratory Resolution, 3 February 1766, *W & S*, II, p. 48.

[110] *Ryder Diary*, p. 272.

[111] Ibid., p. 262.

[112] WWM BkP, 6:126 reproduced in EB, Speech on Declaratory Resolution, 3 February 1766, *W & S*, II, p. 47.

[113] David Hume, "That Politics May Be Reduced to a Science" (1742) in idem, *Essays Moral, Political and Literary*, p. 19.

[114] For this theme in the history of political thought, see J.G.A. Pocock, *The Machiavellian Moment: Florentine Political Thought and the Atlantic Republican Tradition* (Princeton, NJ: Princeton University

governments were exposed to a contest between liberty and authority, yet the art of politics had to strive to reconcile them. In the case of America, since taxation was the most sensitive aspect of administering the colonies, the privilege of granting supply should sensibly be left to their assemblies. Given the complex and variegated situation of the peoples of America between the tropics and the North Pole, it seemed to Burke that were one to design constitutions at least for the coastal settlements, "it would be right totally to leave the affair of internal Taxation to themselves."[115] This compromise pointed to a model of colonial empire based on an idea of "superintendancy" that permitted local immunities.[116] Provincial supply was exactly such a species of immunity, and bestowing it upon the assemblies of North America would bind them to the mother country in a "reciprocation of benefits."[117] The settlers would benefit their sovereign and enjoy the dignity of benefaction in return. Admission to a dignified form of subordination of the kind had the happy consequence of reconciling the liberty of consent with the authority of revenue extraction. Since an incorporating union, by which American representatives would "coalesce into the Mass of the particular constitution of this Kingdom," was a circumstantial impossibility, there was no option but to bestow upon a freedom-loving people a token of their freedom.[118] This entailed acknowledging the representative status of their assemblies, albeit conceding their subjection to the superintending authority of Westminster.

When it came to America, Burke believed, there was no medium between conquest and consent. Consent could only be won through representative assemblies standing as an image of the parent institution. This meant conferring upon them the privilege of taxation without permitting them to undermine the supremacy of the centre. By means of their assemblies, the colonies had carried with them–"across the ocean into the woods and desarts of America"—a local exemplification of the British constitution.[119] Popular assemblies were revered as the household gods of the Englishman, ensuring the colonists' attachment to their dependency. That attachment required that the instinct for liberty should be satisfied even if the authority of the Empire implied subjection: "An Englishman must be subordinate to England, but he must be governed according to the opinion of a free land. Without subordination, it would not be one Empire. Without freedom, it would not be the British Empire."[120]

Burke intervened relatively late in the debate of 3 February, which lasted into the early hours of the morning. Over the next week, as his brother Richard confirmed,

---

Press, 1975, 2003); for its persistence in British imperial thought, see David Armitage, *The Ideological Origins of the British Empire* (Cambridge: Cambridge University Press, 2000).

[115]WWM BkP, 6:126 reproduced in EB, Speech on Declaratory Resolution, 3 February 1766, *W & S*, II, p. 47.

[116]WWM BkP, 6:129 in ibid.

[117]WWM BkP, 6:126 in ibid., p. 48.

[118]WWM BkP, 6:127 in ibid., p. 49.

[119]Ibid.

[120]*Ryder Diary* in ibid., p. 50.

he spoke on nearly every ministerial resolution, winning him applause as well as the compliments of Pitt.[121] On 5 February, the government's resolutions came under renewed scrutiny, with one being completely recast and Grenville adding two of his own; yet none of this brought the Commons to a division. Nonetheless, the opposition sensed that the ministry stood on precarious ground, prompting Grenville to press for an address calling for enforcement of the Stamp Act on 7 February. It was crucial for the government to defeat the motion, leading Burke to argue that its passage would prematurely silence legitimate complaints. The ongoing mayhem in North America was of course disturbing, but the grievances which had given rise to it nonetheless merited a hearing. Grenville's motion was ultimately beaten, but Burke's counterblast still has its interest. The complaints of the Americans deserved an inquiry, but so did the distresses of British merchants. The people were pleading at the doors of the Houses of Parliament, and it was the duty of the House of Commons to listen: "Nothing can hurt a popular assembly so much as the being unconnected with its constituents."[122] The Commons derived its rights by representation, and representation implied sympathy with the population represented.

The best chance of securing the repeal of the Stamp Act was by presenting its continuance as a national disaster afflicting British commerce and domestic manufacture. Rockinghamite strategy was intended to compel parliament to recognise this prospect, in the process packaging their policy as an expression of popular feeling. This was enabled by the extensive series of petitions presented to the Commons from trading and manufacturing towns around Britain. The petitions were intended as indices of discontent, although drafting them had been organised, at least indirectly, by the administration. They were, in truth, tokens of mercantile displeasure, mobilised and concerted with the blessing of the government. It is in this context that Burke's claim about the sympathetic connection between the "popular assembly" and its constituents has to be seen. A leading Glaswegian trader, Archibald Henderson, wrote to Burke on 9 February enclosing a memorial that set out the deleterious effects which merchants "far removed from the seat of deliberations" were experiencing on account of the North American situation. The debts due from Maryland and Virginia alone exceeded half a million sterling, yet without functioning courts in the colonies credit was at the mercy of personal trust.[123] Earlier, in January 1766, Burke referred to an imminent breakfast between himself and the Glasgow merchants, indicating that relations had been developing for some time.[124] In fact, the meeting was part of a larger scheme begun in November of the previous year to establish a

[121] Richard Burke Sr. to James Barry, 11 February 1766, *Corr.*, I, p. 237. For other contemporary accounts of Burke's performances on the American issue, see James Marriott to EB, 8 and 26 February 1766, *Correspondence* (1844), pp. 97–98, 102–3. Cf. James West to Newcastle, 21 February 1766, Add. MS. 32974, fol. 47. For Burke's own acknowledgement of words of encouragement from Pitt, see EB to Charles O'Hara, 1 March 1766, *Corr.*, I, p. 241.

[122] EB, Speech on Enforcement of Stamp Act, 7 February 1766, *W & S*, II, p. 52.

[123] *Correspondence* (1844), pp. 99–100.

[124] EB to the Marquess of Rockingham, *Corr.*, I, p. 235.

committee of London merchants that would correspond with the regions and coordinate the petitioning of the Commons.[125] The following July, days after the fall of the Rockingham administration, Burke boasted that the late ministry had been the first to propose and encourage "public Meetings, and free Consultations of Merchants from all Parts of the Kingdom."[126] Government, he was arguing, had consulted public opinion, and its policies had won out-of-doors support.

In reality, opinion at large meant mercantile opinion, and its free expression had been aided by political machinations. The great western trading interests to Africa, the West Indies and North America had been rising in political importance from the second third of the eighteenth century. During the depression after the Seven Years' War, and particularly during the non-importation agreements sparked by the Stamp Act crisis, British commercial interests trading in American waters rose to political prominence.[127] But their rise was partly abetted by Rockinghamite strategy itself, which aimed to use opposition to Grenville as a symbol of the *vox populi*. This goal was facilitated by the sudden harmony between West Indian and North American interests brought about by their common antagonism to commercial policy since 1764. It was also stoked by constant administrative attention from Burke. Never before, *The Annual Register* commented, was the public so deeply interested in the affairs of parliament.[128] This was partly a result of the constant stream of petitions, twenty-six in all, that arrived at Westminster from 17 January onwards—coming from Liverpool, Lancaster, Bristol, Hull, Glasgow, Birmingham, Leicester, Leeds, Manchester, Nottingham and Wolverhampton.[129] Presented successively over a fortnight, the petitions increased alarm about impending commercial ruin, spreading fear about a decline in manufacturing, as well as about rising indebtedness and unemployment.[130] Such was the impact of the petitions on the House of Commons that members of the opposition regarded them as products of "ministerial artifice."[131] In addition to Glasgow, Burke had been in contact with Birmingham and Lancaster, and most probably with other cities besides.[132] He was proving an effective and industrious man of business, mediating between the ministry and opinion outside parliament.

Since the government was effectively facilitating agitation, it was essential that popular protest remain under its control. Burke acknowledged that the alliance between Trecothick, Rockingham and the merchants of the regions had been the

[125] See Northamptonshire MS. A. XXVII.81. For discussion, see Bullion, "British Ministers and American Resistance," p. 104.

[126] EB, *Short Account of a Late Short Administration* (1766), *W & S*, II, P. 55.

[127] Lucy Sutherland, "Edmund Burke and the First Rockingham Ministry," *English Historical Review*, 47:185 (January 1932), pp. 46–72.

[128] "The History of Europe," in *The Annual Register for the Year 1766* (London: 1767), p. 35.

[129] Thomas, *British Politics and the Stamp Act Crisis*, p. 187.

[130] Walpole, *Memoirs*, III, p. 28

[131] "The History of Europe," in *The Annual Register for 1766*, p, 37.

[132] See the address of thanks from the merchants of Lancaster to Burke dated 12 June 1766 in *Correspondence* (1844), p. 104. For Birmingham, see Northamptonshire MS. A. XXV.79.

primary means of securing the success of the government's scheme. On the back of a circular letter dispatched to the outports and manufacturing towns on 6 December 1765, he noted in pencil how it was the merchants who had aided the ministry in quieting the Empire.[133] Since the resignation of Newcastle in 1762, young Whigs like Charles Townshend had been contriving to deepen the party's base in extra-parliamentary activity, and now the campaign for the Stamp Act's repeal was providing those in power with credible out-of-doors support.[134] The attitudes of a properly representative sample of the whole body of British merchants would always have "great weight" in the commercial deliberations of the Rockinghams, Burke later claimed.[135] In 1766, policy was indeed benefiting from what Hardwicke termed the "universal clamour" of the merchant and manufacturing classes, and Burke's assumption was that the agitation would remain responsive to the party's lead.[136] The performance of witnesses summoned to give evidence before the American committee between 11 and 18 February 1766 appeared to bear out that expectation.[137] Trecothick himself delivered his evidence on the first day of the proceedings, emphasising the distress under which domestic trade was labouring, supporting the ministry in what seemed a rehearsed plea for the wisdom of repeal.[138]

In response to Grenville's call for the enforcement of the Stamp Act on 7 February, Burke highlighted the existence of mercantile discontent. He reminded his audience how merchants and manufacturers believed that they had been brought to the "brink of ruin" by the previous government's measures. "Let us hear them," he urged the Commons.[139] In his *Observations on a Late State of the Nation*, Burke spoke with pride of the attention bestowed by the ministry on the trading interest through dinners held in December 1765 and January 1766 at the houses of Sir George Savile, Rockingham and Dowdeswell.[140] In August 1766, after the fall of the ministry, Hardwicke wrote to Rockingham about his alliance with the merchant class, commending his reliance on their support: "You are really beating the late Great Commoner at his own weapons."[141] During the same period, sensing that Chatham's new ministry was being built on shaky foundations, Burke urged his leader to consolidate his advantage. Popularity, he commented, "is current coin, or it is nothing."[142] As

[133] *Rockingham Memoirs*, I, p. 319.

[134] Sutherland, "Burke and the First Rockingham Ministry," p. 54. See also Lucy Sutherland "The City of London in Eighteenth-Century Politics" in Richard Pares and A.J.P. Taylor eds., *Essays Presented to Sir Lewis Namier* (London: Macmillan, 1956), p. 67.

[135] EB, *Observations on a Late State of the Nation* (1769), *W & S*, II, p. 191.

[136] *Rockingham Memoirs*, I, pp. 284–85. Cf. Walpole, *Memoirs*, III, p. 29: "in reality it was the clamour of trade, or the merchants and the manufacturing towns, that had borne down all opposition."

[137] Evidence that witnesses had been coached can be found in *Grenville Papers*, IV, p. 387.

[138] Add. MS. 33030, fols. 88–113. The suggestion that his evidence was rehearsed derives from a remark by Newcastle presented in Thomas, *British Politics and the Stamp Act Crisis*, p. 217.

[139] EB, Speech on Enforcement of Stamp Act, 7 February 1766, *W & S*, II, p. 52.

[140] EB, *Observations on a Late State of the Nation* (1769), *W & S*, II, p. 201.

[141] 24 August, *Rockingham Memoirs*, II, pp. 9–10.

[142] EB to Lord Rockingham, 21 August 1766, *Corr.*, I, p. 267.

Burke understood it, the aim of the Rockinghams should be both to cultivate and to give direction to popular opinion. Public support was politically essential, but it was fickle and easily exploited. It could never be ignored, but it had to be appropriately formed. Ultimately, in the 1790s, the Whigs would divide over the role of popularity in politics.[143] But, in orchestrating agitation for the repeal of the Stamp Act, the Rockinghams managed to link parliament to out-of-doors opinion in a way that Burke thought could act as a model for the conduct of national politics. At the same time, America showed how popular sentiment could be dangerously inflamed, and how government might struggle to remain in the ascendant. Constitutional politics had to serve the good of the people, and so the consent of the population was a precondition for its stable functioning. However, consent had to be carefully formed and courted; it had to be managed by a responsive and public-spirited leadership.

6.4 Sovereignty and Authority

Events over the period 1766–7 dramatised the difficulty of this undertaking. In debate on the repeal of the Stamp Act on 21 February 1766, Conway referred to the open "rebellion" of America.[144] The situation called to mind the upheaval of the seventeenth-century civil wars. There was, however, a key difference, as Pitt noted. In the 1640s, opposition to the monarchy divided the population, whereas now colonial sentiment was united: "There never was an instance where the whole country was united to a man in a revolt as in the case of America."[145] Pitt was adamant that this called for conciliation, but what if American resistance then persisted? In that case, the colonies would continue to be bound by the Navigation Acts, and should be maintained as a seller's market for British manufactures.[146] If the colonists then bridled at this subordination, Pitt concluded, "we shall act against them with the whole force of this country."[147] Paradoxically, although the colonies enjoyed an inalienable right to tax themselves in Pitt's mind, their preferences could nonetheless be fairly overridden by the "force" attached to British supremacy.[148] At a push, if they challenged the primacy of manufacturing in the mother country, even taxation could legitimately be imposed.[149]

[143] See below, chapters 11, 13, 14.

[144] *Ryder Diary*, p. 304.

[145] Ibid., p. 309.

[146] For the theory of colonial dependence into which this recommendation fits, see Klaus E. Korr, *British Colonial Theories, 1570–1850* (Chicago, IL: University of Chicago Press, 1944), pp. 9–10.

[147] *Ryder Diary*, p. 309.

[148] On the paradoxes of Pitt's American policy, see Marie Peters, "The Myth of William Pitt, Earl of Chatham, Great Imperialist, Part II: Chatham and Imperial Reorganisation, 1763–78," *Journal of Imperial and Commonwealth History*, 22:3 (1994), pp. 393–431.

[149] As reported by James West to Newcastle on 21 February 1766. See Add. MS. 32974, fol. 47.

During the debates of 4 March on the passage of the Declaratory Bill and the repeal of the Stamp Act, Pitt expressed his surprise at having been treated by his colleagues as "an overheated enthusiastic leveller," given his determination to preserve America in subjection.[150] He remarked on the fact that Ireland was subordinate, yet not taxed by the British parliament. The ensuing debate, Walpole recalled, "turned chiefly on the resemblance or non-resemblance of Ireland and America."[151] The essential thing for Pitt was to confer upon America exactly the same privileges that had been settled upon Ireland under William III. Nathaniel Ryder presents Richard Rigby and George Hay as having supported Pitt in his stand against the Declaratory Bill. Burke commended Rigby's defence of the privileges enjoyed by Ireland, but nonetheless spoke in favour "of the whole plan of conduct of the present Ministry," ultimately regarding the comparison between Ireland and the colonies as imperfect.[152] The important thing was to recognise that the absolute right of sovereignty did not license the practical use of every power which that right could claim. The colonies did not have absolute jurisdictional rights, as Pitt presumed, but they ought to enjoy practical immunity from parliamentary interference in the control of their own revenues.

The question before parliament was how to secure American consent while maintaining the authority of parliament. There were two aspects to the maintenance of authority in Burke's mind, one juridical and the other pragmatic. From a juridical point of view, finality in the determination of law was implicit in the idea of sovereignty, and the assertion of parliamentary supremacy catered to that requirement. At the same time, the very assertion of sovereignty, as embodied in the Declaratory Bill, served to buttress the exercise of authority. Dowdeswell made this point in the debate of 4 March: the aim of legislation was to curb American resistance, and the proclamation of parliament's right would itself bolster British authority.[153] It was a perspective which Burke wholeheartedly shared. As he was to argue three years later, without the assertion of a principle of supreme jurisdiction, British authority would "vanish into an empty name."[154] In addition, however, there was the pragmatic issue to be considered: a supreme right did not imply its unconditional exercise. From a practical point of view, the exercise of sovereignty depended upon consent. As Hume had observed, even the mamluks had been led by winning their compliance.[155] Under a regime of liberty, the requirements of compliance were closely guarded and adhered to, and the expectation that authority would respect consent was carefully nurtured. Yet if the need for consent placed practical limits on the capacity of

[150] Walpole, *Memoirs*, III, p. 52.

[151] Ibid.

[152] *Ryder Diary*, pp. 316–17; Walpole, *Memoirs*, III, p. 52; EB to Charles O'Hara, 4 March 1766, *Corr.*, I, p. 241.

[153] *Ryder Diary*, p. 317.

[154] EB, *Observation on a Late State of the Nation* (1769), *W & S*, II, p. 196.

[155] David Hume, "Of the First Principles of Government" (1742) in idem, *Essays Moral, Political and Literary*, pp. 32–33.

government, it could not rightfully contradict the claims of sovereignty. As Burke saw, supreme jurisdiction was compatible with a liberal use of power, but it was not legally accountable to the populace.

Pitt had consulted Camden and had been reading Locke in preparation for his opposition to the Rockinghams' Declaratory Bill.[156] He was, he confessed, a solitary figure, and had developed his ideas based on "the best light he could collect from old books and old doctrine."[157] Locke had contended that whereas a soldier might be commanded by his superior "to march up to the mouth of a Cannon," yet he could not be deprived of "one penny of his Money" without his consent.[158] This consent, Pitt thought, could be obtained by representation, and American representation was embodied in colonial assemblies.[159] Burke's counterclaim was that consent was a practical requirement of imperial politics, yet colonial privileges could not logically overrule the right of parliament.[160] Despite the familiarity of the topic, and the complexity of the theme, Burke was apparently alone on 4 March 1766 in managing to sustain the interest of the House in the technicalities of parliamentary sovereignty.[161] Pitt, in particular, was impressed, although Burke was by now acquiring a reputation for abstruseness—"Those who dont [*sic*] wish me well, say I am abstracted and subtile [*sic*]," as he informed O'Hara.[162] About a week later, John Ridge, full of admiration for Burke, adverted to his "refined and Metaphysical" style in debate.[163] By the end of the ministry it could be said of him that, although "descended form a Garret," he was something of a "metaphysician," indeed a "Man of Learning & imagination," even if these attributes gave his arguments an otherworldly quality.[164] His contribu-

[156] Two extracts from Locke's *Two Treatises of Government* on taxation (*Second Treatise*, ch. 11, §§ 138 and 142) can be found in Pitt's hand in the Chatham Papers, TNA, PRO 30/8/74, fol. 436. This is followed in the same manuscript by a resolution on the clergy's right to tax themselves arrived at by a conference of the two Houses of Parliament in 1671.

[157] *Ryder Diary*, p. 316.

[158] John Locke, *Two Treatises of Government*, ed. Peter Laslett (Cambridge: Cambridge University Press, 1960, 1990), bk. II, ch. 11, § 139. On the context for Locke on taxation, see John Dunn, "Consent in the Political Theory of John Locke," *Historical Journal*, 10:2 (1967), pp. 153–82, pp. 170–71.

[159] On 15 July 1768, in a letter to William Knox, Grenville invoked Locke in support of his own idea that while taxation by right required popular consent, consent need not be measured in terms of "distinct" representation. See Huntington Library, San Marino, Grenville Letter Book, ST. 7, V. 2.

[160] For a comparative discussion of Burke's and Pitt's views during the debates on the repeal of the Stamp Act and the passage of the Declaratory Bill, see Albert von Ruville, *William Pitt, Earl of Chatham, 1708–1778* (London: 1907), 3 vols., III, pp. 171–73.

[161] See D. H. Watson, "William Baker's Account of the Debate on the Repeal of the Stamp Act," *William and Mary Quarterly*, 26:2 (April 1969), pp. 259–65, p. 262.

[162] 1 March, *Corr.*, I, p. 241. See the diary comment by James Harris on Burke's performance on 21 February 1766 as "ingenious" but "saucy" in PDNA, II, p. 286.

[163] John Ridge to EB and William Burke, ante 8 March 1766, *Corr.*, I, p. 243. Cf. Charles O'Hara to EB, 20 February 1766 in Hoffman, *Burke*, p. 331: "Some people say you are too abstracted; others that you take in too great a compass for debate, that your turn is rather for writing, than speaking in public, all commend you."

[164] Letter to Grenville, 11 June 1766, Add. MS. 22358, fol. 35.

tions in parliament were indeed subtle and refined, yet they made sense within the context of eighteenth-century jurisprudence: imperial government was prudentially limited by past "*usage*" insofar as this shaped the content of consent, but sovereignty could not be restricted by a "*right*" superior to itself.[165]

The Declaratory Bill passed the Commons without a division on 4 March, with both it and the repeal of the Stamp Act becoming law on 18 March. Unrest, however, persisted in the colonies. Discontent continued in connection with the Currency Act of 1764, and also in relation to the Quartering Act of 1765.[166] In addition, after the change of ministry in July 1766, the need to relieve the British exchequer persisted. Chatham and Beckford pinned their hopes on new acquisitions in the East Indies, although the attention of government still focused on America as well.[167] Grafton and Shelburne were exploring how quit rents might "*incidentally*" offer a means of supply, while Townshend pursued a scheme to meet some of the cost of magistrates and governors in the colonies by raising a revenue from duties.[168] As Townshend indicated to the Commons on 26 January 1767 that he planned to do "something" to create a revenue in America, the dispute over the Quartering Act was reaching a crisis.[169] Chatham's cabinet had instructed Shelburne to write to the recalcitrant New York assembly demanding compliance with the terms of the Act, which obliged relevant colonies to provision British soldiers with barrack supplies. The burden of the Act fell disproportionately on New York, and in December its assembly informed the British ministry of its unanimous decision not to comply with Shelburne's injunction. "America affords a gloomy prospect," Chatham wrote to Shelburne in the new year. The province of New York appeared unaccountably distracted, "infatuated" with the spirit of rebellion.[170] A petition sent at this time by merchants in the colony objecting to trade restrictions previously imposed under the Grenville and Rockingham ministries seemed an index of further discordant

[165] See the report by the Rev. R. Palmer of the Commons debate of 21 February 1766 in Lionel Cust ed., *Records of the Cust Family, Series III: Sir John Cust, Third Baronet, P C., M.P. for Grantham 1742–1770, Speaker of the House of Commons 1761–1770* (London: Mitchell, Hughes and Clarke, 1927), p. 97.

[166] See Joseph Ernst, "The Currency Act Repeal Movement: A Study of Imperial Politics and Revolutionary Crisis, 1764–1767," *William and Mary Quarterly*, 25:2 (April 1968), pp. 177–211; Lawrence Henry Gipson, *The British Empire before the Coming of the American Revolution* (New York: Alfred Knopf, 1936–70), 15 vols., XI, pp. 45–54; Shy, *Toward Lexington*, ch. 6.

[167] For Chatham's hopes of securing significant returns from Bengal, see below chapter 7.

[168] The idea that quit rents could "incidentally" be used to generate funds was communicated by Shelburne to Chatham on 1 February 1767. See *Chatham Correspondence*, III, p. 185. The origins of Townshend's plans are discussed in Robert J. Chaffin, "The Townshend Acts of 1767," *William and Mary Quarterly*, 27:1 (January 1970), pp. 90–121. Cf. Robert J. Chaffin, "The Townshend Acts Crisis: 1767–1770" in Jack P. Greene and J. R. Pole eds., *The Blackwell Encyclopedia of the American Revolution* (Oxford: Blackwell, 1991).

[169] For Townshend's announcement, see the Roger Newdigate Diary, Newdigate Papers, Warwick County Public Record Office, cited in Chaffin, "The Townshend Acts Crisis: 1767–1770," p. 143 n. 9.

[170] 3 February 1767, *Chatham Correspondence*, III, pp. 188–89.

views.[171] The Declaratory Act, Shelburne suggested, had spread jealousy and alarm such that the slightest imposition was greeted with dismay.[172]

On 13 May 1767, Townshend laid before parliament his proposals for securing the submission of New York. A Restraining Act, preventing the assembly from exercising its legislative functions until it complied with the provisions of the Quartering Act, duly passed in the Commons in June, although by then New York had voted sufficient sums to meet its obligations. In advance of this outcome, Burke was deeply critical of the administration's plan, which proposed in effect to punish public opinion.[173] He interpreted the Restraining Bill as having been foisted by the ministry on Townshend—a "dwarf" of a measure, kitted out in the "Panoply of a Giant."[174] The entire Bill, Burke reckoned, was misconceived, resorting to legislation to enforce an executive order while still holding out the possibility that New York would not comply. Everything smacked of a "confusion of Ideas": judicature was confounded with parliament, law with policy, civil legislation with criminal regulation.[175] Parliament, in the process, would be brought into disrepute. In suspending the assembly, imperial government was unavoidably disabled at the same time, ironically highlighting the dependence of British administration on American cooperation: "how do you enforce your act? By suspending their Legislature—observe that during this suspense [*sic*] of their authority; you suspend your own."[176] The measure promised to inflate the importance of New York while simultaneously diminishing the effectiveness of London: "By calling in their assemblies to assist you, you confess a sort of dependence."[177] In addition, compulsion was being applied to a deliberative body, amounting, as Burke saw it, to an exercise in tyranny since British legislation was acting as an arm of the executive in restraining the liberty of a colonial organ of administration.[178] Finally, Burke found the Bill to be crudely punitive in nature. Given that the citizen body along with the delinquents would fall victim to a dissolution of the machinery of government, the measure was liable to affect the innocent as much as the guilty.[179] At the same time, with punishment being inflicted in defence

[171] The petition can be found at *CJ*, XXXI, pp. 158–60. Burke proposed that it be brought before the House of Commons on 16 February 1767 on the assumption that no action would follow: the petition, after all, was an attack in the previous administration. See *Ryder Diary*, p. 330.

[172] Shelburne to Chatham, 6 February 1767, *Chatham Correspondence*, III, p. 191.

[173] Northamptonshire MS. A. XXVII.82.

[174] EB, Speech on Suspension of New York Assembly, 13 May 1767, *W & S*, II, p. 58. More specifically, he appears to have thought that it was the brainchild of Chatham: see Walpole, *Memoirs*, III, p. 135. For Burke's scepticism about Chatham's posture as a leading "Friend of America" after November 1766, see WWM BkP 6:55: "a return to the principles of the Stamp Act was intended."

[175] Northamptonshire MS. A. XXVII.79.

[176] EB, Speech on Suspension of New York Assembly, 13 May 1767, *W & S*, II, p. 59.

[177] Ibid. See Walpole, *Memoirs*, III, p. 135.

[178] EB, Speech on Suspension of New York Assembly, 13 May 1767, *W & S*, II, p. 59: "the very Essence of Tyranny."

[179] Ibid.

of the military establishment, the army would become "odious" to the population of New York.[180]

Townshend opened the proceedings of the American committee at around 5 p.m. on Wednesday 13 May. It was just under a week since he had regaled the House of Commons with his famous "champagne speech," an extempore effusion of "bacchanalian enthusiasm," as Walpole recalled, that displayed the minister's wit, as well as the incongruities of his character.[181] By comparison, five days later, the vital business of the American committee demanded serious treatment, and Townshend delivered a comprehensive view of the situation. The hunger for liberty across the Atlantic should be seen in relative context, he suggested: there, as elsewhere, the taste for freedom meant independence from the yoke of superiors, not a general concern for the welfare of those exposed to arbitrary power, as the tenacious defence of slavery in the southern colonies attested.[182] Against the background of assertiveness in America, Townshend remarked that three issues demanded the attention of the House. First was the indemnity clause which the Massachusetts legislature had built into its Act for compensating the victims of the Boston riots of the previous year, although happily the Privy Council had the matter already in hand. Second, as already noted, was the restiveness arising out of the Quartering Act, affecting New York in particular. And last was the set of adverse resolutions promulgated by various provincial assemblies. In relation to all these matters, the government of America could be seen to depend on the goodwill of colonial legislatures, and Townshend accordingly indicated a desire that the "salaries of governors and judges in that part of the world be made independent of their assemblies."[183] Grenville, for his part, advanced the idea of an oath to "test" colonial allegiance. However Townshend's plan was to enforce subordination by using import duties as a source of revenue that could meet some of the cost of American administration.[184]

Burke responded to Townshend's proposals in a speech of 15 May, which ranged over the assorted American issues that had arisen the previous Wednesday. He expected colonial distress to increase on account of the array of divisive measures brought into play at once: "A standing army, Quarters enforced, Legislature suspended, Taxes laid on, Tests imposed."[185] This busy stream of policy would inevitably inflame opinion, and should be replaced by the operation of steady political management. Grenville's proposal for a test of allegiance seemed peculiarly

[180] Northamptonshire MS. A. XXVII.79.

[181] Walpole, *Memoirs*, III, pp. 130–31.

[182] Ibid., p. 134.

[183] Ibid., p. 133. The new taxes were not introduced until the following Friday: on the 13th he merely indicated his future plans. See P.D.G. Thomas, "Charles Townshend and American Taxation in 1767," *English Historical Review*, 83:326 (January 1768), pp. 33–51, p. 44.

[184] Walpole, *Memoirs*, III, p. 133. The idea may have gone back to 1753–54 during Townshend's time at the Board of Trade. See Sir Lewis Namier and John Brooke, *Charles Townshend* (London: Macmillan, 1964), pp. 147, 179. But cf. Thomas, "Townshend and American Taxation," p. 51.

[185] EB, Speech on Townshend Duties, 15 May 1767, *W & S*, II, p. 64.

misplaced. The 1673 Test Act had been designed to protect an established arrangement of church and state, not to found a new system of allegiance. Grenville's scheme, by comparison, would operate as a means of exclusion instead of acting to define the terms of inclusion. Loyalty could be clarified, but not imposed on a population: the attempt to enforce principles of membership would prove powerless against the reality of popular sentiment. This went to the fundamental problem of obedience, the elusive foundation of every political system. Populations might grow to consent to government, or simply be habituated to it, but they could never be reasoned into it for the convenience of their governors.[186] The attempt to test allegiance was really an index of desperation quite in line with the mood of the Chatham administration. The dynamics of government since Pitt came to power had been driven by a determination to subordinate the colonies, with ministers striving by "emulation" to limit their freedom of manoeuvre.[187] Burke thought that Townshend's duties were being recommended in this spirit.

Walpole argued that Chatham was anxious to appear in popular mantle, while beneath there lurked a commitment to British power and authority.[188] Burke was inclined to agree with this diagnosis. Later he remarked on Chatham's habit of regarding the "mob" as raw material to be manufactured at will.[189] Upon his elevation to the Lords, Burke expected Pitt to be "at least as despotic there as ever he was with us."[190] He found a clue to the future when Augustus Hervey moved the Address in November 1766, appearing to disown the repeal of the Stamp Act.[191] Burke assumed that Chatham himself was behind the change of attitude. In a note jotted on his own copy of the *Thoughts on the Cause of the Present Discontents*, he recalled that after his return from Ireland in the late summer of 1766 he sensed that a reversion to "the Principles of the Stamp Act" was in the offing.[192] Chatham had even gone so far as to intimate to Rockingham that he had come to think with George III that the Declaratory Act enjoined stern measures. While Burke accepted that it would have been improper to expose Chatham's posture as the leading "friend of America," it was not in fact necessary to unmask his punitive stance since Townshend was happy to embrace that role in the open.[193] His proposed duties were a belated sign of this, Burke claimed, since they attempted what should have been recognised to be impossible under the circumstances: colonial subservience in commercial policy as well as subjection to metropolitan taxation.[194]

[186] Ibid., p. 63.

[187] Ibid., p. 62.

[188] Walpole, *Memoirs*, III, p. 135.

[189] Notes from the Commonplace Book of Samuel Rogers, Add. Ms. 47590, fol. 26.

[190] EB to Charles O'Hara, post 11 November 1766, *Corr.*, I, p. 279.

[191] Ibid., pp. 279–80.

[192] WWM BkP 31.

[193] Ibid.

[194] EB, Speech on Townshend Duties, 15 May 1767, *W & S*, II, pp. 61–62.

6.5 Disquisition and Consent

This reaction indicates that Burke was opposed to the Townshend Acts from the start.[195] In his Speech on the Address delivered on 8 November 1768, he reminded the Commons that he had opposed the government measures in the spring of 1767. He now proclaimed that he expected to prove "a true prophet, that you will never see a single shilling from America."[196] Burke's reasoning was consistent with his original reaction to provincial resistance: the imposition of taxes for the purpose of revenue degraded the political dignity of the colonies by overriding their legislative function. As such, it offended the spirit of liberty in the new world, and undermined the bonds of affection that sustained the imperial relation. Townshend's duties, Burke admitted, were "well chosen." Import levies on wine, fruits, glass, lead, paints, paper and pasteboards were unlikely to affect British trade adversely: they enlarged foreign commerce, insofar as the trade was permitted at all, but without endangering domestic manufacture.[197] In fact, the idea of duties on wine and fruits was indebted to regulations originally planned by the Rockinghams.[198] Nonetheless, Burke was clear that the rationale for the taxes undermined their acceptability among the colonists. As he declared in May 1767: "It is impossible that the Same Country could be at once subservient to your Commerce and your Revenues."[199] The point was not that such dual subservience was impossible a priori, but that political communities circumstanced such as the North American colonies were would never submit to taxation for imperial supply when they were already bound in subjection by the terms of the Trade and Navigation Acts.

As Burke saw it, this was the thinking that underlay the reform of British commercial regulations by the Rockingham ministry in 1766. The original plan of action as laid out in a letter to Charles Yorke on 17 January 1766 had been to follow up the Declaratory resolution with "*Considerations on Trade*" before settling on a final determination of the Stamp Act.[200] Ascertaining the state of imperial commerce involved presenting to the Commons an extensive array of relevant opinion—"from the greatest Philosopher to a Shoe maker," as Burke recalled the process in

[195] *Pace* Paul Langford, "The Rockingham Whigs and America, 1767–1773" in Anne Whiteman et al. eds., *Statesmen, Scholars and Merchants: Essays in Eighteenth-Century History Presented to Dame Lucy Sutherland* (Oxford: Oxford University Press, 1973), p. 137.

[196] EB, Speech on Address, 8 November 1766, *W & S*, II, p. 96.

[197] Ibid. Townshend's duties were later modified to exclude wine and fruits from Spain and Portugal, and to include a new duty on tea from the east.

[198] See Dowdeswell's comment on Townshend's duties in Dowdeswell MSS., Dowdeswell to Rockingham, 14 August 1768, cited in Langford, "The Rockingham Whigs and America," p. 147: "Had [they] been proposed in our time I should have liked the thing well enough, but I would have advised sending it out under some other name, made commerce its first object, and the revenue a secondary object."

[199] EB, Speech on Townshend Duties, 15 May 1767, ibid., p. 62.

[200] The Marquess of Rockingham to Charles Yorke, Add. MS. 35430, fol. 32.

November 1768.[201] Thereafter, the Rockinghams embarked on a major study of the state of the Navigation Acts with a view to revising some of their key provisions. Burke in particular applied himself with diligence to the task. By the end of the parliamentary session, he was being described as more than merely Rockingham's "Right hand": he was in fact, it was claimed, "both his hands."[202] Nearly thirty years later, in his *Letter to a Noble Lord*, Burke wrote of the impact of his efforts at this time on his mental and physical constitution. All things being equal, a total revision of British commerce might then have been attempted. As it happened, with circumstances limiting opportunities, much was in any case achieved. "The first session I sat in Parliament," he commented, "I found it necessary to analyze the whole commercial, financial, constitutional and foreign interests of Great Britain and its Empire." His labours stretched him to breaking point: "I seemed to myself very near death," as he recalled.[203] Nonetheless, significant reform of imperial commerce was achieved.

The aim of the Rockinghams was to free up areas of colonial trade whose restriction had deleterious effects in both America and Britain. It was generally agreed, for instance, that particular elements of the commerce between Jamaica and Spanish America could be beneficially liberalised, providing an outlet for imperial manufactures and a source of bullion and raw materials. At the same time, the ministry broke new ground in backing North American schemes to open colonial trade with the Caribbean, although this directly threatened monopolies enjoyed by British West Indian planters.[204] As Burke waited for the Repeal of the Stamp Act to make its way through the Lords in March 1766, he wrote to O'Hara to inform him that the ministry was now preparing "for a complete revision of all the Commercial Laws, which regard our own or the foreign Plantations, from the act of Navigation downwards."[205] It was an avowedly ambitious scheme, and the North American and West Indian interests were already in negotiation over its contents. Burke hoped that Ireland might somehow be roped into the arrangement by being permitted to import sugars directly.[206] On 15 April Joseph Henderson revealed how since the beginning of the session he had been collaborating intensively with Rockingham, as Burke's assistant, to develop and bring the proposals to fruition.[207] However, Pitt proved a serious obstacle on the way to complete agreement. "His forte was his fancy, his feeble was

[201] EB, Speech on Address, 8 November 1768, *W & S*, II, p. 96. The reference to the philosopher and the shoe maker are to Benjamin Franklin and John Hose of Cheapside.

[202] Letter to Grenville, 11 June 1766, Add. MS. 22358, fol. 35.

[203] EB, *Letter to a Noble Lord* (1796), *W & S*, IX, p. 159.

[204] Langford, *First Rockingham Administration*, pp. 200–201. For the paramountcy of the West Indian interest in British colonial policy down to 1766, see G. L. Beer, *British Colonial Policy, 1754–1765* (New York: Macmillan, 1907), ch. 6; Richard Pares, *War and Trade in the West Indies, 1739–1763* (Oxford: Oxford University Press, 1936), ch. 9.

[205] EB to Charles O'Hara, 1 March 1766, *Corr.*, I, pp. 239–40.

[206] Ibid., p. 240. On 11 March he informed O'Hara that he had composed recommendations on the subject. See ibid., p. 244.

[207] Joseph Henderson to John Temple, *Collections of the Massachusetts Historical Society*, Sixth Series, IX (Boston: 1847), p. 72.

his ignorance," Burke once quipped to Grattan about Pitt.[208] Under pressure from Beckford and his own connections with West Indian planters, Chatham objected to the establishment of a free port in Dominica. On 8 April Burke wrote that the examination of witnesses on the issue of free ports had been completed, and that resolutions preparatory to a "New American Trade act" were being formulated.[209] However, by the 23rd he was lamenting the fact that the "Great Commoner sets his face against it."[210]

Burke was amazed by the peevishness of Pitt, perversely opposed to "so salutary and unexceptionable a measure."[211] In a better mood, he had been known to support an overhaul of the trade restrictions enshrined in Grenville's Sugar Act, which was the intention underlying the new regulations proposed by the Rockinghams. On 15 April O'Hara wrote to Burke about claims to the effect that the ministry were devoted solely to "undoing what their predecessors had done."[212] The rumour was not mistaken, Burke confirmed a week later: "We are, it is true, demolishing the whole Grenvillian Fabrick."[213] This was of course a considerable undertaking, with major commercial and political implications, not least since Grenville had presented his measures as a pillar of the Navigation Acts.[214] These measures were partly designed to give preferential treatment to the produce of the West Indian colonies by prohibitively taxing rival French commodities imported into the northern colonies.[215] These particular regulations were part of a still larger project to subordinate the trade of the colonies to the interest of the metropole while maintaining the Anglophone Atlantic community as "one Nation."[216] The guiding principle of this arrangement was the idea of a balance of trade to be maintained against Britain's European competitors. This would be achieved by confining the trade of the colonies to the mother country, and securing the navigation of commerce to British ships.[217] The Rockinghams, on the other hand, were determined to meet the complaints of the North American colonies against West Indian monopolies while also establishing free ports in the Caribbean. All this was envisaged as making a positive contribution to Britain's

[208] Notes from the Commonplace Book of Samuel Rogers, Add. MS. 47590, fol. 29.

[209] EB to Charles O'Hara, *Corr.*, I, p. 248.

[210] EB to Charles O'Hara, 23 April 1766, ibid., p. 251.

[211] Ibid.

[212] Hoffman, *Burke*, p. 344.

[213] EB to Charles O'Hara, 23 April 1766, *Corr.*, I, p. 252.

[214] It was a vision that Grenville was still defending in a letter of 27 June 1768 to William Knox. See Huntington Library, San Marino, Grenville Letter Book, ST. 7, V. 2.

[215] The rationale of the policy is outlined in the Grenvillite pamphlet by Thomas Whateley, *Consideration on the Trade and Finances of this Kingdom* (London: 1766), p. 70.

[216] Thomas Whateley, *The Regulations Lately Made concerning the Colonies, and the Taxes Imposed upon them, Considered* (London: 1765), p. 40. For Grenville's own ideas of subordination in terms of the Navigation Acts as embodying the "established principle & policy of every other European nation with respect to their Colonies," see his letter to William Knox of 27 June 1768 in Huntington Library, San Marino, Grenville Letter Book, ST. 7, V. 2.

[217] Whateley, *Regulations Lately Made* (1765), p. 88.

imperial trading balance, but it was still presented as a piece of judicious liberalisation which would bring to an end the "ruinous Impositions" of the 1764 Sugar Act.[218] Colonial commerce with foreign territories was opened, while rival trading interests in the Empire were reconciled.[219]

All this was achieved, Burke noted, while increasing British revenue derived from North America.[220] He was anxious to demonstrate that revenue was not simply a function of taxation, since it could be derived from an intelligent management of trade. Nonetheless, when it came to colonies established with a view to commerce, regulation should not be employed as an instrument of supply. In the wake of the Townshend duties, Burke commented that tax did not always entail revenue, since the exchequer might be full while the country lay "ruined."[221] Equally, revenue might be collected without resorting to direct taxation. "I am ag[ains]t every Tax which is not engrafted on some Benefit," Burke stated during the debate on suspension of the New York assembly.[222] As he clarified in his *Observations on a Late State of the Nation*, the commercial principles that the Rockinghams adopted in 1766 were an attempt to put these ideas into practice. In this context he presented the status of all twenty-six American provinces as specifically "commercial" in character, meaning that their position under the imperial constitution rendered them "an unfit object of taxation."[223] He was writing when resistance to Townshend's measures was under way, and he interpreted the Chancellor of the Exchequer's policy as a repetition of the mistakes already made by Grenville: the Chatham administration, he argued, had in effect chosen to return to policies "of the very same nature" as those already rejected in 1765, with the consequence that "America is in disorder again."[224] This blunder was a product of a misconception of the British Empire and a consequence of constricted ideas about how its trade could be made beneficial. Properly understood, colonial trade was not purely a form of commercial activity, but a "creature of law and institution."[225] While the Navigation Acts marked the beginning of this institutional arrangement, their nature and significance had not been grasped by Grenville or his disciples. A more searching account of the constitution of the Empire would reveal the character of British dominion and the interests of its subjects in its commerce.

In the *Observations*, Burke presented his own understanding of these matters in opposition to the arguments of William Knox. Knox had presented himself in *The Present State of the Nation* as advocating the implementation of the "old navigation

[218] The relevant Acts are embodied in 6 Geo. III, c. 52 and 6 Geo. III, c. 49. For the citation, see EB, *Short Account of a Late Short Administration (1766)*, *W & S*, II, p. 55.

[219] Ibid., pp. 55–56.

[220] Ibid., p. 55: "The Revenue was improved and settled upon a rational Foundation."

[221] Northamptonshire MS. A. XXVII.55.

[222] Northamptonshire MS. A. XXVII.79.

[223] EB, *Observations on a Late State of the Nation* (1769), *W & S*, II, p. 166.

[224] Ibid., p. 198.

[225] Ibid., p. 193.

laws," but it was unclear whether he was endorsing specifically the Navigation Act of 1660, precursor legislation in 1649 and 1651, or the multitude of amendments added since the seventeenth century.[226] Presumably, Burke reckoned, he would want to include the duties that made up part of Grenville's Sugar Act. These, however, seemed to Burke to have been a product of an excessive "rage for regulation."[227] In addition to particular restrictions designed to limit foreign imports and boost West Indian exports, Grenville's reforms embraced, as already noted, a new naval establishment intended to enforce stringent regulation by preventing the conduct of all contraband trade.[228] To the Rockinghams these seemed counterproductive provisions born of a misguided zeal to prevent European access to colonial markets while drastically confining North American trade. Consequently, in 1766, the ministry worked to replace this scheme of narrow regulation with a relaxation of restrictions on colonial commerce. A new arrangement was ultimately agreed between the North American and West Indian trading interests in the spring of 1766, finally becoming law on 6 June.[229] The new Act opened areas of French and Spanish trade to British colonial markets, while permitting the colonies to sell direct to European rivals.[230]

Burke presented these provisions in the *Observations* as a programme of commercial "enlargement."[231] The idea was to free up new areas of commerce, while still falling short of the establishment of a comprehensively free trade. As Burke presented it, it would involve a stimulus to growth in exchange and manufacture without threatening the advantages expected from a balance in favour of British trade. The new provisions included a reduction on the duty on foreign molasses into North America to 1*d*. per gallon, the same as the sum levied on West Indian molasses. Since the duty fell equally on the French and British product, it could not be presented as a preferential tariff designed to benefit imperial trade, and so had every appearance of being a duty imposed for the purpose of revenue.[232] Therefore, the "system of 1766," as Burke later dubbed it, had in fact included an element of taxation. Nonetheless, the Rockinghams insisted after the introduction of the Townshend duties that commerce, and not revenue, should be the "first object" of regulation, and Burke explained their priorities in terms of the historic constitution of the colonies.[233] The colonies were "evidently founded in subservience to the commerce of Great Britain,"

[226] On Knox, see Leland J. Bellot, *William Knox: The Life and Thought of an Eighteenth-Century Imperialist* (Austin, TX: University of Texas Press, 1977).

[227] EB, *Observations on a Late State of the Nation* (1769), *W & S*, II, pp. 182–82.

[228] Ibid., p. 186.

[229] Langford, *Rockingham Administration*, pp. 202–6.

[230] The details are set out in Frances Armytage, *The Free Port System in the British West Indies: A Study in Commercial Policy, 1766–1822* (London: Longmans, Green and Co., 1953), pp. 36–42.

[231] EB, *Observations on a Late State of the Nation* (1769), *W & S*, II, p. 200.

[232] This much, in fact, was admitted by Dowdeswell in a letter to Rockingham of 14 August 1768. See Clements Library, Michigan, Dowdeswell MSS., cited in Langford, "Rockingham Whigs and America," p. 147.

[233] Dowdeswell to Rockingham, 14 August 1768, ibid.

which could only be expected to relax its jealousy by degrees.[234] This subservience was based on a double monopoly over the colonies—first, of their imports, which were expected to be drawn from Great Britain and, second, of their exports, which were expected to be conducted via the metropole. The same conception dictated that they were to receive the manufactures of the mother country in exchange for their own "raw" products.[235] To subject colonies in this situation to additional methods of revenue extraction would thwart the original purpose of their foundation. The existing benefit to the seat of empire was considerable: America cultivated its lands, traded its produce and navigated its wares by means of British capital, directly contributing profit to metropolitan commerce and, indirectly, revenue to its treasury.[236] Hitherto, it had done so on the basis of an "artificial commerce," comprising restrictions imposed by the mother country. Such restraints depended on a "powerful authority" located at Westminster, the proliferation of whose provisions was inimical to the spirit of liberty in the colonies. Consequently, due respect had to be paid on the part of the imperial government to the "temper and disposition" of the provinces.[237] Minimally, this entailed the absence of direct taxation; optimally, it involved opening up their overly regulated trade.

The failure to observe these principles had unleashed a "dangerous spirit of disquisition" in America.[238] Burke was not enamoured of the results. News of the Boston riots reached London in July 1768, leaving Burke to remark that matters seemed "to grow serious" there.[239] The activities of James Otis in the spring of the same year had provoked his ire: Otis's fundamentalist opinions would "scatter firebrands, and death."[240] But this was no justification for the government's various actions in seeking to bring the colonies to book. "The affairs of America prosper ill in their hands," Burke commented to O'Hara.[241] After the establishment of a new board of commissioners and the passage of the Townshend Acts in the summer of 1767, the sense of colonial grievance started to mount. The Massachusetts Bay assembly began to remonstrate against the measures as early as December, and a circular letter laying out its main objections was dispatched to other colonies at the same time. The response of the imperial government was decisive and swift. On 22 April 1768 Lord Hillsborough, recently appointed Secretary of State to the newly created American department, ordered the Massachusetts resolutions to be rescinded, while other assemblies were to be prorogued if they attempted to condone the circular letter. The colonies, however, were defiant, many forming associations to prohibit the importation of

[234] EB, *Observations on a Late State of the Nation* (1769), *W & S*, II, p. 192. For the idea of commercial "jealousy," see Hont, *Jealousy of Trade*, Introduction.

[235] EB, *Observations on a Late State of the Nation* (1769), *W & S*, II, p. 192.

[236] Ibid., p. 193.

[237] Ibid., p. 194.

[238] Ibid., p. 188.

[239] EB to the Duke of Portland, 30 July 1768, *Corr.*, II, p. 11.

[240] EB, Speech on Address, 8 November 1768, *W & S*, II, p. 96.

[241] EB to Charles O'Hara, 1 September 1768, *Corr.*, II, p. 14.

British goods. Troops were sent to Boston in anticipation of resistance to authority, but their arrival in October became the occasion for further rebellion. "What, Sir, will become of this insolent town of Boston," Stanley wondered in seconding the Address on 8 November 1768. Should the troops be withdrawn, he predicted, "the riots will begin again."[242] Burke, however, was scathing in response. Hillsborough's orders had threatened a colonial assembly with "annihilation," prompting, when the assembly was dissolved, an illegal congregation to be formed in its place—a "Vermin" substitute, as Burke colourfully condemned the Boston Convention.[243] However, if the consequences of misgovernment in America were disturbing, the resolutions of the ministry were equally misplaced: "There is no such thing as governing the whole body of the people contrary to their inclinations."[244]

The ineliminable requirement of consent as a precondition for successful government was a constant refrain of Burke's utterances into the 1770s. He also recognised that consent was different from static acclamation: the terms of support for government were as variable as popular opinion, and opinion became more exacting in its expectations of the system of rule as the people grew to embrace the ideal of liberty. Burke could admire the persistent American commitment to the ideal of freedom, but he was perturbed by some of its acrimonious expressions. The colonists, he wrote in the *Observations*, were a "haughty and resentful people."[245] This was his view in February 1769, exactly a year after the publication of John Dickinson's *Letters from a Farmer in Pennsylvania,* which had denied the right of Britain to tax America and advocated the boycott of British goods.[246] On 1 November 1768 Knox had written of the "revolt of New England," responding to the aftermath of riots in Boston the previous June.[247] The establishment of the Massachusetts Convention in September, which counterposed the power of popular demonstration to the authority of the royal governor, represented an equally tangible threat. The people of New England were a "refractory" population, Newcastle concluded.[248] Ultimate rebellion was inevitable, George Savile thought.[249] Burke expressed his disdain for colonial methods in the *Observations*, condemning "the insolence of the mutinous spirits in America."[250] This was to acknowledge the "spirit of faction" highlighted in the King's Speech of the previous November.[251] In responding to Pownall's motion to repeal the Townshend measures in the spring of 1769, Burke pointed to the extent of the

[242] *Cavendish Debates of the House of Commons*, I, p. 35.

[243] EB, Speech on Address, 8 November 1768, *W & S*, II, p. 97.

[244] Ibid.

[245] EB, *Observations on a Late State of the Nation* (1769), *W & S*, II, p. 188.

[246] The idea of "withholding from Great-Britain all the advantages she has been used to receive from us" was canvassed in Letter III. See John Dickinson, *Letters to a Farmer in Pennsylvania: To the Inhabitants of the British Colonies* (1768) (London: 1774), p. 34.

[247] *Grenville Papers*, IV, pp. 394–95.

[248] Add. MS. 32990, fols. 340–41.

[249] *Rockingham Memoirs*, II, p. 76.

[250] EB, *Observations on a Late State of the Nation* (1769), *W & S*, II, p. 190.

[251] *Cavendish Debates of the House of Commons*, I, p. 31.

colonies' poor behaviour.[252] But he also saw that their antagonism fed on the perceived hostility of government. As Rockingham noted, mismanagement by the government had become a serious issue.[253] A vicious dialectic was in train.

As Burke saw it, this dialectic was based on heated imaginations giving rise to misconceptions on both sides. The Americans, for their part, believed that the government was determined to oppress them, while the British thought that the colonists were set upon rebellion.[254] "America is more wild and absurd than ever," Burke wrote in the aftermath of the disturbances of the summer of 1769.[255] Not only had acts of defiance in Virginia, Rhode Island, Massachusetts and Connecticut outraged government opinion, but members of the opposition were clearly also appalled.[256] Irritation on the ministry's part was all the more intensely felt since the cabinet had decided the previous May that Townshend's duties on glass, china, paper and paints should be repealed, with only the tax on tea being retained. In the new year, the Grafton administration fell apart, with the Chathamites, excepting Hawke, now departing from the ranks of government. The policy of partial repeal was confirmed by the new cabinet on 2 March 1770, and Lord North introduced a Bill to that purpose three days later in the Commons. Unlike the "anti-commercial" duties on British manufactures, there were no grounds for abandoning the tariff on East Indian tea, a luxury commodity whose cost had already been reduced by the removal of all duty on its export in 1767: in effect, North argued, taxation at 3*d*. in the pound should be seen as a veritable bounty by the Americans.[257] As he saw it, colonial assertiveness had resulted from vacillation in the imperial government, above all from the decision to repeal the Stamp Act in 1766.[258] Blame was being laid at the door of the opposition in parliament, with Rockinghamite policy being associated with the disturbances across the Atlantic.

6.6 The Tea Act

The Rockinghams' response came on 9 May 1770. It was on that day that Burke moved eight resolutions of censure against government, surveying the ineptitude of policy towards America under Chatham, Grafton, and now Lord North. The repeal of the Stamp Act, he suggested, had been an exercise in practical wisdom. It was thereafter that damaging vacillation had set in, as the administration departed from the "ground of peace" that the Rockinghams had established, and proceeded to

[252] EB, Speech on Townshend Duties, 19 April 1769, *W & S*, II, p. 231.

[253] Marquess of Rockingham to EB, 17 July 1769, *Corr.*, II, p. 47.

[254] EB, Speech on Townshend Duties, 19 April 1769, *W & S*, II, p. 231.

[255] EB to Marquess of Rockingham, 9 September 1769, *Corr.*, II, p. 77.

[256] Peter D. G. Thomas, *The Townshend Duties Crisis: The Second Phase of the American Revolution, 1767–1773* (Oxford: Oxford University Press, 1987), ch. 8.

[257] *Cavendish Debates of the House of Commons*, I, pp. 484–86.

[258] Ibid., p. 486.

overload the idea of parliamentary sovereignty with burdensome demonstrations of power.[259] The repeated aim of the government had been to salvage its authority, but it did so by a series of exercises in force. As a result, in seeking to recover its dignity, it attracted suspicion and scorn. Burke's comments at this point were being made in the aftermath of the Boston Massacre of 5 March 1770, when a small contingent of British soldiers had fired upon an angry crowd on King Street, killing five and injuring six others. On 1 May, Burke described the event as an "eruptive" symptom of an underlying distemper "which pervades the whole empire."[260] The previous week, on 26 April, Barlow Trecothick had moved for an account of the tragedy, prompting Burke to denounce government policy since the appointment of Lord Hillsborough. A plan to reform the constitution of Massachusetts Bay, originally put before the cabinet in February 1769, had appeared ham-fisted and provocative: "It has inflamed the people," Burke noted.[261] In a similar vein, the threat of trying Boston radicals for treason or misprision of treason, publicly wielded by Hillsborough in a letter to Barnard of 20 February 1769, was at once galling and half-hearted: "You showed your ill will to America, at the same time you dared not execute it."[262] A series of measures designed to impose order had compromised public authority and incited popular animosity. Burke's resolutions of 9 May were intended to itemise the accumulated incidents of misgovernment while pointing to an underlying pathology.

The pathology was rooted in a misconception of the nature of authority. Under pressure from popular protest in America, the British government had sought to enforce its will by resort to the crude deployment of executive power: by issuing commands, and then relying on its troops. Ultimately this would terminate in a policy of conquest that was bound to fail. On 26 April, pondering the implications of the massacre, Burke advocated an alternative course. The Americans could only be conquered by policy, never by the employment of naked force. Certainly this would require fixity of purpose embodied in resolute government. Part of Burke's point was that Britain's posture in America was one of merely blustering assertiveness: its stand was brutal, yet somehow compromised, continually wavering in its determination to prosecute its objectives. Power was made to appear terrifying and ineffective at the

[259] EB, Debate on Resolutions Relating to the Disorders in North America, 9 May 1770, *Parliamentary History*, XVI, col. 1003. The report is based on *Parliamentary Register* (Almon), VIII, pp. 339–43.

[260] EB, Motion for Address on Hillsborough's Circular, 1 May 1770, PDNA, III, p. 263. For parallels in the mistreatment of Ireland and the colonies at this time, see the transcription of a Burke speech in manuscript by French Laurence from 1770 at OSB MS. File 2237: "Their support must be purchased by the removal of every cause of discontent. This is the only magic, the only charm which can draw their affection, which can convert & unite the different members of the empire, & make it act, as if inspired by one soul."

[261] EB, Motion for Address on Disorders in America, 26 April 1770, ibid., p. 257. Burke is specifically complaining about a version of the plan issued by Governor Bernard and then publicised in the House of Commons.

[262] Ibid., p. 258. The suggestion was that alleged offenders might be charged under an Act of Henry VIII. For discussion, see Bernard Knollenberg, *Growth of the American Revolution: 1766–1775* (1975) (Indianapolis, IN: Liberty Fund, 2003), ch. 9.

same time. However, as Burke argued, exactly the reverse was what was required: government had to appear as a benefit to the people while commanding respect on account of its tenacity. America needed firm direction based on durable consent: "Conquer it by your strong government. Conquer it by your laws."[263] However, this did not mean managing the colonies by perpetual intervention. Parliament should superintend, but not administer. "Parliament can't govern the detail of America," as Burke put it.[264]

It was precisely government in detail that Britain had been pursuing, Burke believed. The results were not encouraging. Sections of the population in various northern colonies had revolted against both the civil and the military power. On 9 May Burke resolved to examine how imperial policy had misfired. Horace Walpole summed up his performance as a "fine oration tending to censure Lord Hillsborough and the administration for their absurd and contradictory orders to the governors of the colonies, to which variations he imputed the troubles existing there."[265] Burke was more modest in his recapitulation to Charles O'Hara: he had not, he informed him, lost any "Credit" in setting out his case.[266] In personal terms, the speech was in fact a triumph. Before Burke rose, as William Burke reported, "expectations were very great, the House very full." After he had finished, he stood higher in the estimation of the public than ever before.[267] His argument was based on a series of documents laid before the House, including the preamble to Townshend's Act of 29 June 1767, the King's Addresses to parliament of 10 March and 8 November 1768, copies of Hillsborough's letter of instructions to Governor Bernard of 22 April 1768 along with his circular letter to the colonies of 21 April 1768, copies of communications between the Massachusetts assembly and Governor Bernard, as well as subsequent documents of public significance that passed among the Americans and between them and the mother country. The idea was to build up a picture of the tendency of recent policy, beginning with the fall of the Rockinghams but concentrating on the period since Hillsborough had become responsible for the American department. It was essential that the Commons should see the thrust of recent initiatives and developments in a comprehensive, "universal light."[268] For the past three years, the Rockinghams had abstained from pressing their own measures or calling for inquiries into the situation in North America. The moment for a proper diagnosis had now arrived.

The avowed aim of Burke's intervention was to restore the credit of parliament that had been squandered in connection with the management of the colonies. Now that the ministry was also in conflict with the East India Company, the salvation of

[263] EB, Motion for Address on Disorders in America, 26 April 1770, PDNA, III, p. 258.

[264] Ibid., p. 259.

[265] Walpole, *Memoirs*, IV, p. 174.

[266] EB to Charles O'Hara, 21 May 1770, *Corr.*, II, p. 139.

[267] William Burke to Charles O'Hara, 15 June 1770, in Hoffman, *Burke*, p. 472. Despite this claim, the debate did not figure in contemporary discussions: see Thomas, *Townshend Duties*, p. 187n.

[268] EB, Motion for Resolutions with regard to America, 9 May 1770, PDNA, IV, p. 299.

the Empire was at stake—one part "tottering" and the other "tumbling" in the face of the administration's apparent contempt for the forms of freedom.[269] In both portions of Britain's overseas dominion, the executive was overextending its authority. However, the government of the western provinces, much like the eastern, would have to be administered by local institutions of rule. America could not be managed from a distance of 3,000 miles: ministry and parliament would have to trust in the devolved powers of the colonies, rather than cabinet second-guessing the determinations of popular assemblies stationed in the new world.[270] This was a point on which Burke dwelt in the notes for his speech of 9 May. The role and responsibilities of parliament in Britain and those of the apparatus of government in America had to be kept separate: the task of the British was to oversee by establishing general laws and conferring general powers, advertising its beneficence by the liberality of its grants; whereas government in America should manage the detail of administration, operating within the bounds set by the mother country. Restless attempts to break in upon the regular operation of colonial government wore the appearance of arbitrary conduct. Trust in the process of devolution, on the other hand, was a demonstration of imperial "Magnanimity."[271] "The trust is great," Burke conceded, "but it is a trust that is necessary until you are beaten out of it by every abuse."[272]

Having established broad principles of government, Burke proceeded to outline how these had been subverted. The idea was not to dwell upon individual instances of mismanagement, but to point to systematic failure, to "a whole Body and System of disorder."[273] At the root of individual acts of folly lay the misconceived principles of what Burke viewed as "a weak, violent, inconsistent, Senseless System of Government."[274] Much of the incendiary behaviour to which this connected series of acts of misgovernment had given rise across the Atlantic was blameable. So too were some of its supporting ideological doctrines—not least what Burke cautiously described as "perhaps" an "improper sense of liberty", meaning the appeal to popular entitlements at the expense of public order.[275] However, Burke's emphasis on 9 May was on the improvidence of government, condemned to repeat its errors on account of its defensive attachment to its own dignity. The concern with "dignity" had distorted judgment: it "fretted men exceedingly."[276] In its name, a succession of ministries destroyed the public tranquillity. The Rockinghams, by comparison, had pursued a course with prudence: it was certain that the repeal of offensive legislation

[269] Ibid., p. 300.

[270] Ibid.

[271] Northamptonshire MS. A. XXVII.67, reprinted in EB, Speech on American Resolutions, 9 May 1770, *W & S*, II, p. 325.

[272] EB, Motion for Resolutions with regard to America, 9 May 1770, PDNA, IV, p. 300.

[273] Northamptonshire MS. A. XXVII.67, reprinted in EB, Speech on American Resolutions, 9 May 1770, *W & S*, II, p. 326.

[274] Northamptonshire MS. A. XXVII.60.

[275] EB, Motion for Resolutions with regard to America, 9 May 1770, PDNA, IV, p. 300.

[276] Ibid., p. 301.

would quieten the colonies. There remained the remote possibility that such a concession would in future embolden the Americans to stake out their rights offensively. But whereas such a conceivable scenario might lie in "the Womb of time," it was the height of imprudence to gamble an existing peace out of concern for the diminution of dignity that it was felt had occurred in procuring it.[277] This, Burke thought, was improvidence, brought about by pride; and it was this syndrome that informed the pathological mismanagement of the colonies. A new "spirit" entered into the corridors of power from 1767, a determination to redeem a loss of face by high-handed acts of authority. Since this determination was motivated by underlying pride, it failed to arm itself with a sober sense of the probable consequences.

The first fruit of imperial pride was a resolution to "test" colonial loyalty. This mission was obviously misconceived from the start, not least since it was pursued through attempts to circumvent the provincial assemblies, which stood as the prime objects of colonial allegiance. The aim of circumvention, Burke emphasised, was explicit in the preamble to Townshend's Act, which advertised its intention to employ colonial revenue to defray the "Charge of the Administration of Justice, and the Support of Civil Government" in America.[278] It therefore ought to be seen for what it was—as "an act not of Revenue but of Policy."[279] As such, it amounted to a paradoxical attempt to find support for government "independent of the affection of the people."[280] Unsurprisingly, instead of winning support, it generated alarm.[281] When popular alarm challenged the imperial plan, the government made a show of determination by adopting a series of provisions that operated as tokens of executive vigour. However, the vigour was never properly calculated to succeed, and as it floundered the administration repented of its measures. "You ought to have looked into all the consequences of that Scheme," Burke chided the ministry.[282] Having threatened the dissolution of colonial assemblies that failed to comply, Westminster was bereft of means of realising its designs as soon as provincial legislatures were actually prorogued. Imperial magistracy had endeavoured to make a parade of its potency without in fact being able to deliver. Government fulminated, dispatched its troops, threatened prosecutions, and then withdrew. In response, the Americans launched associations and combinations designed to thwart metropolitan policy. "Every senseless[,] arbitrary enforcement brought a new insult on your authority on

[277] Northamptonshire MS. A. XXVII.67, reprinted in EB, Speech on American Resolutions, 9 May 1770, *W & S*, II, p. 326.

[278] 7 Geo. III, c. 46.

[279] Northamptonshire MS. A. XXVII.65.

[280] EB, Motion for Resolutions with regard to America, 9 May 1770, PDNA, IV, p. 301.

[281] Northamptonshire MS. A. XXVII.19: the dissolution of the assemblies sapped the "Life & Soul of the whole."

[282] Northamptonshire MS. A. XXVII.67, reprinted in EB, Speech on American Resolutions, 9 May 1770, *W & S*, II, p. 328.

their side," Burke concluded.[283] Altogether, popular fury was kindled and effective government disabled.

Authority had to stand on two foundations—first, upon its wisdom and, next, upon its power. Without these, its credit sunk, and trust was compromised. Where trust declined, the spirit of faction revived, giving rise to disputatious doctrines of government. Accordingly, after its suspension, the New York assembly proclaimed itself the source of its own powers, predicating its rights on "the law of nature."[284] Government threatened, menaced and violated the constitutions of North America, while the colonies protested and then subverted established norms in the language of natural right.[285] The confrontation was increasingly polarising, but it had begun with a simple mistake: instead of conceding from strength and then bolstering its authority, the government proclaimed its authority and then exposed its power: "They began first with Violence, with harshness and menace—and they ended with the most humiliating concessions."[286] The consequence was resoundingly negative in Burke's opinion: "The malignity of your will is abhorred, the debility of your government contemned [*sic*]."[287] Yet whatever Burke and his comrades might have thought, the resolutions were comfortably rejected. Moreover, despite the bleak diagnosis of Burke's speech, the situation in America began to look up for the ministry in the months after the opposition made its stand. To begin with, the non-importation agreement began to break down among New York's merchants, with the end of the embargo spreading to other colonies as the months progressed. Therefore, by 1771, Lord North was in a position to derive satisfaction from the restoration of trans-Atlantic commerce, and also from the legacy of recrimination among colonial agitators who had originally sought to implement the boycott. Policy planning in relation to the colonies now went into abeyance. Dartmouth succeeded Hillsborough on 14 August 1772 and, although friction between colonial merchants and customs officials persisted, there was a hiatus in parliamentary deliberation on America until the debate over a new Tea Bill in April 1773.

Burke commended the appointment of Dartmouth in a letter to James De Lancey six days after his appointment, the same day reporting the change to the Committee of Correspondence of the New York assembly.[288] It was De Lancey, a prominent political operator in New York politics while also being an associate of Rockingham, who had first recommended Burke as a potential agent for the province. On 27 December 1770, Burke was confirmed in the post, promising in the spring that he

[283] Northamptonshire MS. A. XXVII.10.

[284] EB, Motion for Resolutions with regard to America, 9 May 1770, PDNA, IV, p. 303.

[285] An early example can be found in Richard Bland, *An Inquiry into the Rights of the British Colonies* (Williamsburg: 1766), reprinted in the *Virginia Gazette* on 30 May 1766, and again in London in 1769.

[286] Northamptonshire MS. A. XXVII.66, reprinted in EB, Speech on American Resolutions, 9 May 1770, *W & S*, II, p. 330.

[287] *Parliamentary History*, XVI, col. 1005.

[288] EB to James De Lancey, 20 August 1772, *Corr.*, II, pp. 326–27.

would open his mind "fully and confidentially" to De Lancey. He had the advantage, he noted, of being close to the scene where colonial business was transacted, and of having a clear sense of the character of British affairs.[289] His letters to the Committee of Correspondence would be drier and more officious, outlining the state of play and keeping his judgments to a minimum, while generally aiming to serve the colony's interest.[290] This included presenting official policy as well as developments in government thinking about a variety of matters—from negotiations concerning the boundaries between New York, New Hampshire, New Jersey and Canada, to government Bills and political appointments.[291] His staple task was following instructions issued by the assembly in relation to its legislative Acts as these were scrutinised by the Board of Trade before confirmation by the Privy Council. Throughout, Burke accepted his status as an agent, not a representative, delegated to act in accordance with the assembly's determinations.[292] He also defended the role of agent as a servant of the province, not an arm of the imperial machine. "I have always been and shall ever be earnest to preserve the Constitutional dependence of the Colonies on the Crown, and Legislature of this Kingdom," he informed De Lancey on 4 December 1771.[293] This included opposing ministerial plans to alter the role of the New York agency by permitting the governor and council to participate in his election.[294]

A considerable proportion of Burke's correspondence with America between 1772 and 1773 was taken up with government policy in connection with the East India Company. On 31 December 1772, he reported to the New York Committee of Correspondence that the Company's trade was much larger than it had ever been before, although ministerial demands on its revenues were larger than any increase could bear.[295] The King's Speech of 26 November had held out the state of India as a principal concern of government, yet Burke doubted the ministry's resolution to tackle alleged abuses, presenting North as determined to extend the powers of the crown. This would be secured, Burke predicted, by monopolising the management of Asian money and affairs. The British public, envious on account of the increase in conspicuous wealth among Company "nabobs," was happy to teach the corporation a lesson.[296] As Burke underlined to John Cruger, the speaker of the New York assem-

289 EB to James De Lancey, 9 June 1771, ibid., p. 215.

290 EB to James De Lancey, 20 August 1772, ibid., pp. 328–29.

291 Much of the correspondence, reprinted in *Corr.*, is contained in Hoffman, *Burke*, pp. 194–272.

292 On this, see EB to James De Lancey, 20 August 1772, *Corr.*, II, p. 329.

293 Ibid., pp. 290–91.

294 Thus bringing New York into line with arrangements in the West Indian and southern colonies. See James J. Burns, *The Colonial Agents of New England* (Washington, DC: Catholic University of America Press, 1935); Edward P. Lilly, *The Colonial Agents of New York and New Jersey* (Washington, DC: Catholic University of America Press, 1936). Should the measure be approved, Burke notified the Committee of Correspondence, "your Agency should become in part at least an Appointment by Ministry," and Burke would resign his position under those conditions. See *Corr.*, II, p. 293.

295 EB to the Committee of Correspondence of the New York Assembly, 31 December 1772, *Corr.*, II, p. 397.

296 See below, chapter 7.

bly, this amounted to a contrivance by a self-aggrandising court to play upon a popular sense of resentment.[297] More immediately, however, the ministry had to restore the flagging fortunes of eastern trade. A boost might be supplied by dealing with "the supply of three years Sales of Tea" now stored in Company warehouses.[298] This had in part been accumulating as a result of the North American non-importation agreements, together with the ease with which the Dutch could smuggle tea into the colonies. The easiest solution to overcoming the confinement of the Company's trade was to lower the price of one of its staple exports. But if it could be agreed all round that the cost of tea might usefully be reduced, the government's method for achieving this proved fateful for North America.

The North ministry opted to maintain Townshend's duty on tea while removing the tax on its re-export from Britain. Under an Act of 1698, the East India Company had been granted the exclusive right to export merchandise from Asia.[299] Under a further Act of 1721, the direct import of East Indian wares into the colonies was prohibited, obliging all items of trade to pass through the British emporium.[300] Upon re-export, these were subject to duties. In 1773, North proposed to offer a drawback, or rebate, on the charge on tea. Since this would reduce its cost in North America, smuggled produce would not be able to undersell its British rival. On 26 April 1773, North defended the retention of the Townshend levy in the face of objections from Dowdeswell: "as long as the duty remains, the Americans will not take the tea."[301] Dowdeswell's prediction proved right. To influential opinion in America, the combination of a reduced price with the retention of the tax seemed a calculated attempt to confirm the parliamentary right to revenue by stealth. At the same time, under the provisions of the Tea Act, the East India Company acquired a monopoly on distribution in the colonies. Therefore, in addition to the offence caused by the politics of the measure among leaders of opinion, American merchants felt affronted by their exclusion from the trade. Smugglers were equally alarmed by the new arrangements as their business was put at a competitive disadvantage.[302] Accordingly, the mood in the colonial ports of New York, Philadelphia and Charleston was defiant, but it was in Boston that the will to resist was driven to open sabotage when on 6 December 1773 the East Indian cargo on board the *Dartmouth* was emptied into the harbour.

[297] EB to John Cruger, 16 April 1773, *Corr.*, II, p. 430.

[298] EB to the Committee of Correspondence of the New York Assembly, 31 December 1772, ibid., p. 397. Cf. EB, *Speech on American Taxation* (19 April 1774), *W & S*, II, p. 416.

[299] 9 and 10 Wm. III, c. 44.

[300] 7 Geo. I, c. 21.

[301] PDNA, III, p. 488.

[302] At a cost of 2*s*. per pound, the East India Company tea would out-perform its Dutch competitor. See P.D.G. Thomas, *Tea Party to Independence: The Third Phase of the American Revolution, 1773–1776* (Oxford: Oxford University Press, 1991), p. 11. For the causes of social and political ferment over the Tea Act, see Arthur M. Schlesinger, *The Colonial Merchants and the American Revolution* (New York: Columbia University Press, 1917); B. W. Labaree, *The Boston Tea Party* (New York: Oxford University Press, 1964); J. W. Tyler, *Smugglers and Patriots: Boston Merchants and the Advent of the American Revolution* (Boston, MA: Northeastern University Press, 1986).

"The conduct of the American's [*sic*] can not be justified," Rockingham declared to Burke on 30 January 1774.[303] However, his outrage was soon to be modified in light of the government's response. News of the disturbances in America reached India House on Threadneedle Street on 19 January 1774, although even before then Burke was wondering whether colonial affairs might be brought before parliament.[304] On 2 February, in the process of informing the New York assembly of the fate of a Boston petition before the Privy Council demanding the removal of Governor Hutchinson, Burke noted that the tea ships débâcle was under consideration: "As yet I do not find any measures have been taken in consequence, though I do not think the matter will be altogether kept out of Parliament."[305] A message from Burke the previous day to General Charles Lee struck a less guarded and more melancholy note. The continent of America held out "infinite Objects of Curiosity" to the inquiring mind, Burke commented. So much had been done there, and so much "undone" besides.[306] There remained, he continued, great opportunities for experiment in the colonies, where a lot might still be accomplished, or destroyed. The current state of distraction boded ill for the immediate future, and recalled the sequence of mistakes that had brought affairs to their current "confusion."[307] The Rockinghams were powerless to affect any positive change, so Burke was reluctant to speculate in any detail on the subject.[308] However, soon the ministry's actions would force his hand. Wedderburn, the Solicitor General, expatiated on the situation in Boston when defending Governor Hutchinson before the Privy Council on 29 January, inveighing against the assembly and town meetings of New England.[309] On the same day the cabinet met to consider its response to American resistance. By 19 February the ministry had decided that the Boston port should be closed, with a cabinet meeting of 28 February resolving that American papers should be laid before parliament on 7 March.[310]

A large tranche of documents was presented to parliament when an address was moved on 7 March by George Rice, envisaging a series of measures for securing the dependence of the colonies. Burke saw these as likely to be framed in the same spirit as the long and "doleful" sequence of political miscarriages to date, leaving American politics "expiring in convulsions."[311] He expressed alarm at the prospect of a punitive response, anticipating the redesign of colonial governments and the adoption of new principles of commercial regulation.[312] "I can never give my assent to proceeding to actual force against the Colonies," Rockingham had admitted to Burke on

[303] The Marquess of Rockingham to EB, 30 January 1774, *Corr.*, II, p. 516.

[304] See EB to the Committee of Correspondence of the New York Assembly, 5 January 1774, ibid., p. 503.

[305] Ibid., p. 522.

[306] Ibid., p. 517.

[307] Ibid., p. 518.

[308] Ibid.

[309] For Burke's reaction, see his letter to Rockingham, 2 February 1774, ibid., p. 524.

[310] Thomas, *Tea Party to Independence*, pp. 30–39.

[311] PDNA, IV, p. 42.

[312] *Parliamentary History*, XVII, col. 1161.

30 January.[313] Yet military enforcement is what Burke was now led to expect. "As soon, I say, as the civil government of those colonies shall depend for support on a military power, the former will be that moment at an end," he proclaimed.[314] What in fact confronted parliament on 14 March, however, was a Bill to close Boston harbour until the Tea Act was accepted and compensation duly paid to the East India Company, a proposal that took the Commons by surprise. A number of colonies had openly subscribed to "pernicious" political doctrines, North admitted, but it was in Boston that these ideas were put into effect, resulting in deliberate acts of violence.[315] Burke took his stand against North's recommendations on 25 March, as the Bill was set to pass its third reading. The measure was disproportionate, and bound to be ineffective, he wagered.[316] America could either be made subservient to each single British law, or "left to govern itself by its own internal policy."[317] Similarly, tax could be raised by either coercion or consent, yet the government had settled on a noxious mixture of the two. Resistance to the duty in America was universal, so punitive measures could only serve to increase the intensity of resistance against them.[318] While the colonies had clearly signalled their defiance, in truth they had not actually risen in "Rebellion," as Burke jotted in his notes made in advance of 25 March.[319] The leading agitators might reasonably be punished, but not Bostonians as a whole, particularly while other offending colonies were exempt from retribution: "the distemper is general, but the punishment local," Burke remarked. Yet, while only Boston was proscribed, other colonies were just as recalcitrant.[320] These would be provoked into greater truculence on account of the example to be made of Boston, placing the government in a state of enmity with its own provinces: "this is the day then that you wish to go to war with America," he observed.[321] The outlook was bleak, and the consequences potentially disastrous, with French power likely to be tempted to exploit Britain's vulnerability.

On 6 April 1774, Burke wrote to the New York Committee of Correspondence summarising the mood of the British parliament in the wake of North's prescriptions concerning Boston port. The Act had received royal assent on 31 March, and was due to come into effect on 1 June.[322] In the meantime, as Burke noted, there was a general feeling of suspicion directed against the colonies, "both within doors and without," exemplified by North's depiction of assorted American provinces as infused with an

[313] *Corr.*, II, p. 516.

[314] *Parliamentary History*, XVII, col. 1161.

[315] Speech of Lord North, 14 March 1774, PDNA, IV, p. 56.

[316] EB, Speech on Boston Port Bill, 25 March 1774, *W & S*, II, pp. 404–5.

[317] *London Evening Post*, 31 March 1774.

[318] EB, Speech on Boston Port Bill, 25 March 1774, *W & S*, II, pp. 404–5; cf. *London Evening Post*, 31 March 1774.

[319] WWM BkP 6:75.

[320] *London Evening Post*, 31 March 1774.

[321] Ibid.

[322] 14 Geo. III, c. 19.

"evil disposition" resulting in "dark designs" and "turbulent Conduct."[323] The ministry was putting pressure on the Commons to take sides, interpreting opposition as an index of disloyalty.[324] In his notes for his speech of 25 March, Burke commented that he had never seen a more belligerent mood on display in the House—"such songs of Triumph not only without Victory but without Battles."[325] Behaviour of the kind, he thought, was a lesson in how to lose an empire, whose precariousness was founded on a "premeditated ignorance of our true situation."[326] As he observed in his letter to the New York assembly, opinion in parliament was driven by the need to assert authority—inspired by the general sense that "*some Act* of Power was become necessary," however much it might expose the government's desperation.[327] Moderation was expiring on the other side of the Atlantic, and being openly disdained in the House of Commons. Rival accounts of the rights of authority and the rights of man confronted one another across a chasm of mutual misunderstanding, which only an improbable act of wisdom could hope to bridge.

[323] EB to the Committee of Correspondence of the New York Assembly, 6 April 1774, *Corr.*, II, p. 527.

[324] Cf. Burke's complaint on 25 March 1774 to the effect that Charles James Fox had been metaphorically "tarred and feathered" for his opposition to government policy on America in PDNA, IV, p. 123.

[325] WWM BkP 27:40.

[326] Ibid.

[327] EB to the Committee of Correspondence of the New York Assembly, 6 April 1774, *Corr.*, II, p. 528.

VII

A REVOLUTION IN IDEAS

THE INDIAN EMPIRE, 1766–1773

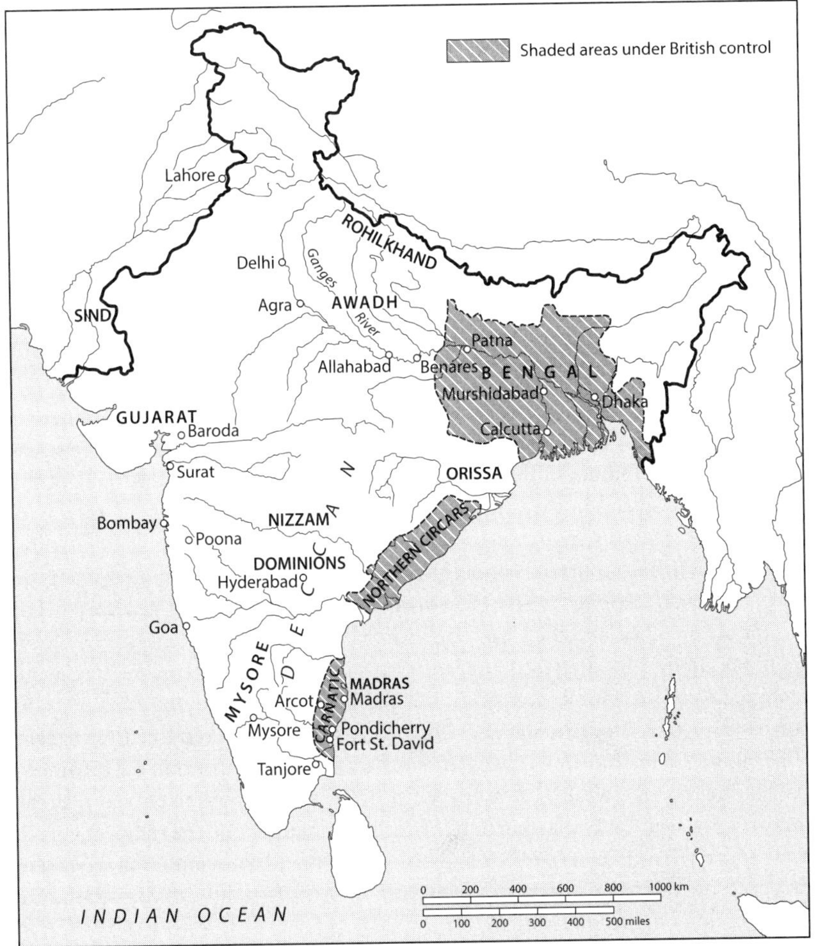

Map 2. Map of the Indian Subcontinent

7.1 Introduction

Burke's response to developments in India between the start of the Chatham ministry and the early years of the North administration occurred against the backdrop of his engagement with domestic events in conjunction with the American crisis. In each case, his thinking was framed by the context of British constitutional concerns, above all his alarm about the decline of party and the rise of an imperious style in court and ministerial circles. India posed a particular threat in the context of these preoccupations: the access to patronage that the conquest of Bengal might deliver into the hands of the British crown filled Burke with dismay. British military might had been demonstrated on the subcontinent in crucial battles fought in 1757 and 1764, resulting in the grant of administrative authority to the East India Company under the nominal sovereignty of Asian powers. The passage of the Company from trade to power politics was now more or less complete. With this new status came responsibility for Bengal's taxation revenues. The ultimate right to this resource, and thus the beneficiary of the expected funds, soon became a subject of controversy in British politics. An inquiry into the ownership of the proceeds was instituted in the early days of the Chatham administration. A division of the spoils was agreed between the Company and the ministry without the question of entitlement finally being settled. Nonetheless, parliament was now invested in the Company's affairs. State interference persisted over the following seven years, culminating in the passage in 1773 of Lord North's Act to regulate the constitution of the Company.

Developments in Asia created a licence to intervene. Financial and credit crises in 1772 followed by allegations of abuse against Company servants deepened suspicions about the conduct of the corporation. When news of the catastrophe of the Bengal famine spread in the early 1770s, outrage against the Company increased. Britain had created a virtual *imperium in imperio*, which the metropole found difficult to control. The Court of Proprietors, the Court of Directors and the servants on the ground were criticised for the growth of private trading monopolies, the corrupt receipt of "presents" and the expanding frontier of war. Burke believed that reform should begin by extending the Company's legal powers. The government, it seemed, preferred to tinker with its constitution while appropriating an increasing percentage of its profits. As with America, Lord North appeared determined to manage affairs minutely instead of devolving initiative to responsible agents in the provinces. As envy against the wealth of returning "nabobs" spread, Burke believed that the ministry was bent on employing public hostility to undermine the rights of corporate property. An alliance between mobbish instincts and court ambition seemed in prospect: the reckless management of expansion in the east threatened to erode the means of domestic accountability.

7.2 War, Trade and Revenue

In 1767 *The Annual Register*, by then under the editorship of Burke's admirer Thomas English, described the situation in Bengal as a political "labyrinth" from which the East India Company could not easily escape. The pursuit of trade seemed to entail deepening political involvement in Asian territories while regional politics drew the Company into war. Even in the wake of Britain's recent military successes, on account of which an advantageous peace was established over sizeable tracts of the Indian north-east, a threat to stability was still expected from the Marathas and the Afghans.[1] Yet the interplay between trade and war was nothing new: as one early nineteenth-century commentator noted, it was during the War of the Austrian Succession, at the latest, that both Britain and France became "military powers in India."[2] Since the 1740s, the British had been involved in open conflict with the French, which in turn dragged them into alliances with Indian rulers in the south-east, luring them into the affairs of both the Deccan and the Carnatic: while the French won support from the Nizam of Hyderabad, the British entered an alliance with the Nawab of Arcot.[3] By then, British trade was centred in Calcutta in south Bengal, in Madras on the Coromandel Coast and, on the western side of the peninsula, in Bombay. Robert Orme remarked in his 1763 *History of the Military Transactions of the British Nation in Indostan* that the East India Company's settlements, taken together, had been "continually engaged in war" since 1745.[4] It was at this time, as Adam Smith later commented, that "the spirit of war and conquest seems to have taken possession of their servants in India, and never since left them."[5] But it was in Bengal that the British were first established as a territorial power between the Battle of Plassey in 1757 and the Company's assumption of responsibility for provincial revenues in 1765. At the beginning of this process, Burke interpreted events on the subcontinent as amounting to a transfer into the hands of the British Empire of "a vast kingdom, yielding in its dimensions to few in Europe, but to none in the fertility of its soil, the number of its inhabitants, and the richness of its commerce."[6] Over the following years, the impact of eastern developments on British domestic politics would ramify in complicated ways. Above all, controversy

[1] "The History of Europe" in *The Annual Register for the Year 1766* (London: 1767), p. 28.

[2] David Macpherson, *The History of European Commerce with India* (London: 1812), p. 177.

[3] J. H. Parry, *Trade and Dominion: The European Overseas Empires in the Eighteenth Century* (London: Phoenix Press, 1971), ch. 9; Om Prakash, *European Commercial Enterprise in Pre-Colonial India* (Cambridge: Cambridge University Press, 1998), chs. 6 and 7.

[4] Robert Orme, *A History of the Military Transactions of the British Nation in Indostan, from the year 1745, to which is Prefixed a Dissertation on the Establishments Made by Mahomedan Conquerors in Indostan* (London: 1763–78), 2 vols., I, pp. 33–34.

[5] Adam Smith, *An Inquiry into the Nature and Causes of the Wealth of Nations*, ed. R. H. Campbell and A. S. Skinner (Indianapolis, IN: Liberty Fund, 1976), 2 vols., II, p. 749.

[6] "The History of the Present War" in *The Annual Register for the Year 1758* (London: 1759), p. 32.

would ensue about how the "richness" of Asian commerce could best facilitate the growth of British power and prosperity.

The bid for supremacy in the Seven Years' War formed the wider context for the struggle in South Asia.[7] "A war between maritime powers is felt in all parts of the world," Burke observed at the outset of the Franco-British contest. "Not content with inflaming America," he went on, "the dissensions of the French and English pursued the tracks of their commerce, and the Ganges felt the fatal effects of a quarrel on the Ohio."[8] Reviewing Orme's *History* in 1764, *The Annual Register* regarded the British as having advanced from being a "trading" to a "conquering" people in the east.[9] The Company, as Burke put it in the same issue of *The Annual Register*, had been elevated into an "arbiter of kingdoms."[10] Within a year, the implications of this transformation were being debated in the press. In *The Annual Register* for 1765 Burke observed that French treaties of conquest on the subcontinent were signed on behalf of the crown rather than the *Compagnie des Indes orientales*. This gave them a solidity which Britain's acquisitions might be deemed to lack. Also diverging from British procedure, the Dutch took direct charge of their conquests. The East India Company, by contrast, had hitherto tended to operate through Indian Viziers and Nawabs, establishing native rulers as "an empire in an empire," which in practice meant that the British had constructed an empire "against itself."[11] It was clear that if British power could be effectively organised in South Asia, the Company's provincial acquisitions "could not fail greatly to forward the payment of our national debts." The question was whether in exercising administrative functions directly over an Indian population, Company servants could be trusted to fulfil the role of governors with justice and responsibility. If British authority was deployed with equity and honour, then a "just claim to dominion" might be readily obtained. But it remained to be considered on what terms the "vast revenues" annexed to that dominion might be employed for the benefit of the British public.[12] During the negotiations preceding the Peace of Paris of 1763, the Bute ministry had informed the French that British territories in Asia were to be regarded as the "legal and exclusive property of a body corporate, belonging to the English nation," and in which, as a consequence, the government had no right to interfere.[13] By 1766, however, the

[7]Within that context, however, South Asian developments followed a logic of their own. See P. J. Marshall, "The British in Asia: Trade to Dominion, 1700–1765" in idem ed., *The Oxford History of the British Empire II: The Eighteenth Century* (Oxford: Oxford University Press, 1998), p. 501.

[8]"The History of the Present War" in *The Annual Register for the Year 1758*, p. 30.

[9]*The Annual Register for the Year 1764* (London: 1765), p. 256. The review, given its date, might well be by Burke.

[10]"The History of Europe" in *The Annual Register for the Year 1758*, p. 34.

[11]"The History of Europe" in *The Annual Register for the Year 1765* (London: 1766), p. 15.

[12]Ibid., p. 16.

[13]Macpherson, *History of European Commerce*, pp. 192–3n. This passage had been cited in *The Annual Register for the Year 1773* (London: 1774), p. 96, to demonstrate the "exclusive and undoubted right of the East-India Company to those territories it possessed, whether acquired by conquest or otherwise."

meaning of an "exclusive property" residing in the "nation" was being reexamined with a view to establishing its practical implications.

Between 1766 and 1773, Burke focused on the question of how the Company's corporate property might be harnessed to the British national welfare, but without destroying the balance of the constitution. In the first instance, the issue appeared to depend on how the Company's title to sovereignty on the subcontinent was construed. It was only later in his career that Burke came to question whether the justness of British dominion would be best preserved by vesting administrative discretion in the corporation alone. Thus, in a letter of 27 November 1766 to Charles O'Hara, he took it for granted that the East India Company was "a great resource," albeit one that would require skilled management to make it serve the "national advantage."[14] How the Company could best be organised to deliver that result was by now a question of recognised complexity. Burke's letter was sent at a time when East Indian affairs were being scrutinised by the Chatham ministry with a view to redefining their relationship to government. In general terms that scrutiny gave rise to a reconceptualization of parts of the Indian subcontinent in relation to Britain's overseas dominion. The Company could now be regarded as "part of the empire," *The Annual Register* commented when reflecting on Robert Clive's success in establishing British sovereignty in Bengal.[15] It was against this background that the Directors of the Company had been alerted on 28 August 1766 to the ministry's intention of establishing a parliamentary inquiry to examine its affairs.[16] By 29 October the supporters of the "Laurence" Sulivan faction within the Company were attempting to seize the initiative, calling for a General Court, scheduled for 14 November, to consider proposals for making use of the "Territorial Revenues acquired by the Company" in such a way that both private trade and the general public might enjoy "solid and lasting Advantages."[17] Chatham, however, had other plans. Like Burke, he saw the Company as a potential source of revenue for the British government, still overwhelmed by debts acquired during the course of the Seven Years' War. But rather than negotiate a mutually agreeable contribution, Chatham was determined to force the Company's hand.

At the point at which Burke was writing to O'Hara in late November 1766, the position of the Rockinghams in relation to the government had come to a head: "affairs are come to a Crisis," as Burke put it.[18] The previous July, when the king called upon Pitt to form a government during Rockingham's final period as First Lord of the Treasury, the expectation was that the incoming first minister would construct a

[14] EB to Charles O'Hara, 27 November 1766, *Corr.*, I, p. 281.

[15] "The History of Europe" in *The Annual Register for the Year 1766*, p. 30.

[16] Charles Lloyd to George Grenville, 30 August 1766, *Grenville Papers*, III, p. 312; Walpole, *Memoirs*, III, p. 80; Lucy S. Sutherland, *The East India Company in Eighteenth Century Politics* (Oxford: Oxford University Press, 1952), p. 157; John Brooke, *The Chatham Administration, 1766–1768* (London: Macmillan, 1956), p. 72.

[17] AAC, IOR, B/82: Court Book, April 1766–April 1767, fols. 240–41.

[18] EB to Charles O'Hara, 27 November 1766, *Corr.*, I, p. 280.

government on the basis of the outgoing administration.[19] When Pitt's brother-in-law, Lord Temple, resolved "to have nothing to do in the administration," Burke and his associates assumed that their role would be correspondingly enhanced: Temple's departure narrowed the "ground of disagreement" between Pitt and the Rockinghamites, increasing the possibility of cooperation between the two.[20] However, that sense of prospective harmony was not to endure, deteriorating from suspicion into antagonism and recrimination, rekindling anxieties about the role of Bute, and raising alarm among the Rockinghamites about the outlook for their party.[21]

This period of indeterminacy proved a time of reckoning for Burke himself. As Newcastle, Rockingham, Richmond, Winchelsea and Dowdeswell were swept from favour, Burke shared in the "ill humour" of the leaders of the Old Corps, smarting from their treatment at the hands of Pitt.[22] Conway was the principal link connecting the two ministries, retaining his position as Secretary of the Northern Department and continuing in his role as Leader of the Commons, with Shelburne taking over the Southern Department from the Duke of Richmond. Since Chatham opted for the office of Lord Privy Seal, the Duke of Grafton took up position as head of the Treasury, while Charles Townshend was "kicked up" to become Chancellor of the Exchequer and Charles Pratt, by now Lord Camden, replaced Northington as Lord Chancellor.[23] Nonetheless, in the face of this reallocation of the major offices of state, the remnants of the Rockinghams were advised to keep their places, and Burke pondered whether to attempt to join the administration himself. However, a definite opportunity did not arise and, on 29 July, he conveyed his disappointment to O'Hara, indicating that no offer had yet been made: "As to myself, I hear nothing," he confided.[24] This mood of uncertainty, tinged with a mixture of defensiveness and irritation, lasted through the summer. On 19 August Burke revealed again that he had "had no civility from any of the New People."[25] Six days later O'Hara responded, confessing his own surprise.[26]

Over the next six weeks the outlook began to brighten. By the opening of parliament on 11 November 1766, Burke was delighting in the feeling of being courted, even if no offers were tangibly forthcoming: Conway, on Burke's retelling, would only declare the ministry's "intentions and hopes" of offering him employment.[27] This was a friendly approach, but not a compelling one. In exchange for well-meaning promises, Burke was expected to lend his support to the decisions of the

[19] Charles Pratt to Thomas Walpole, 24 July 1766, Grafton, *Autobiography*, p. 94.

[20] EB to the Duke of Portland, 17 July 1766, *Corr.*, I, p. 260; EB to the Earl of Dartmouth, 18 July 1766, ibid., p. 261.

[21] Frank O'Gorman, *The Rise of Party in England: The Rockingham Whigs, 1760–1782* (London: George Allen & Unwin, 1975), p. 188.

[22] EB to Charles O'Hara, 29 July 1766, *Corr.*, I, p. 262.

[23] Ibid., p. 263

[24] Ibid., p. 264.

[25] Ibid.

[26] Charles O'Hara to EB, 25 August 1766, Hoffman, *Burke*, p. 358.

[27] EB to Charles O'Hara, post 11 November 1766, *Corr.*, I, p. 279.

government. Against the background of Pitt's apparent wariness of Burke, this was at least a vote of confidence in his abilities, but it was not enough to entice him into backing the administration.[28] The context of this refusal is provided by a letter dispatched by William Burke in London on 4 October to O'Hara in Sligo while Edmund was visiting his sister at Loughrea in Galway. As a result of recent developments, William explained, the Burkes' finances were in a state "to second our views of independency."[29] William anticipated that, as the political season approached, the government might seek an addition of strength by recruiting talent to the remaining executive posts. Edmund, he thought, might conceivably be a beneficiary of this last push. However, since his and William's fortunes had recently improved, they could now consult their political preferences rather than having to serve their immediate interests. The death of William's father, and of Edmund's brother, had brought them new resources. But in addition, William had recently been speculating in East India stock, aided by the generosity of Lord Verney, and assisted by a loan from Henry Fox.[30] As the fortunes of the Company seemed to rise, he expected to make an easy killing. "Wills [*sic*] news," Burke soon confirmed, "is indeed marvelous." He then observed: "This certainly leaves one with some freedom of Conduct."[31]

In a letter to O'Hara composed in the days following the opening of parliament, Burke clarified how he planned to use his freedom. Rockingham had instructed his followers to attend the Cockpit meeting of government supporters on 10 November. In addition, Burke was present at a private meeting of men of business convened by Conway on the eve of the Cockpit.[32] These gestures were intended to exhibit the Rockinghams' distance from Grenville's opposition without amounting to a "contract" to support the ministry.[33] Burke's doubts about the dependability of Chatham were deepening at this time, and he resolved to maintain his allegiance to Lord Rockingham come what may, even though his party's course would be determined by the conduct of Pitt. "I had begun with this party," Burke reflected, and although it was now caught between opposition and support for the administration, the "point

[28] Pitt's reluctance to co-opt Burke into government office is evident from his response to Grafton's recommendation of him on 17 October 1766. See *Chatham Correspondence*, III, pp. 110–11, for Grafton's comment, and Grafton, *Autobiography*, p. 108, for Pitt's response.

[29] Hoffman, *Burke*, p. 361.

[30] Lucy S. Sutherland and John A. Woods, "The East India Speculations of William Burke," *Proceedings of the Leeds Philosophical and Literary Society, Literary and Historical Section*, 11 (1966), pp. 183–216; Lucy S. Sutherland and J. Binney, "Henry Fox as Paymaster General of the Forces," *English Historical Review*, 70:275 (1955), pp. 229–57, esp. pp. 241–42.

[31] EB to Charles O'Hara, 21 October 1766, *Corr.*, I, p. 272. The Burkes were noted for their "common purse," as mentioned by Mrs. Vesey in a letter to Lady Montagu on 28 May 1777, reprinted in Reginald Blunt, *Mrs. Montagu, "Queen of the Blues": Her Letters and Friendships, 1762–1800* (London: Constable, 1923), 2 vols., II, p. 23. Nonetheless, Burke later distanced himself from William's Indian investments. See EB to Adrian Heinrich von Borcke, post 17 January 1774, *Corr.*, II, p. 513: "I have never had any concern in the Funds of the East India Company."

[32] EB to Charles O'Hara, post 11 November 1766, *Corr.*, I, p. 277.

[33] Ibid.

of honour" lay with those who were "out of power." Consequently, whether he accepted a position under Chatham or not, it would have to be understood that he would be "revocable" to his own party should they ever pitch a standard for outright opposition.[34]

The issue was then decided with the advent of the "Crisis" among Rockingham's supporters to which Burke referred in his letter of 27 November. Ten days previously, the Rockinghams had been crudely rebuked by the dismissal of Edgcumbe from his post as treasurer of the Household. The Duke of Portland, Lord Bessborough, Lord Scarborough and Lord Monson duly resigned, construing Pitt's move as an insult that could not be ignored. "All hopes of accommodation are over," as Portland put it.[35] The resignations of Charles Saunders, Admiral Keppel and William Meredith soon followed. It appeared to the Rockinghams that "L[or]d Chatham had resolved the ruin of the Party," Burke reported.[36] They were now set on a course of opposition to the Chatham ministry, with the management of India having emerged as the first item on the agenda of government business. Walpole speculated on the context for Pitt's design: "With indignation he beheld three Indian provinces, an empire themselves, in the hands of a company of merchants, who authorized by their charter to traffic on the coast, had usurped so mighty a portion of his dominions from the prince who permitted their commerce with their subjects."[37] The extensive wealth of the Company appeared to Pitt as a "gift from heaven" that promised to deliver the "*redemption* of the nation."[38] Chatham's idea was to launch an inquiry into the affairs of the East India Company as a prelude to imposing a financial settlement between it and the British state. Beyond that, as Grafton put it, "Lord Chatham never did open to us, what was his real and fixed plan."[39] That is, it was clear that Chatham sought to establish the rights of the British government to the revenues of the East India Company; however, it was not clear what arrangements he envisaged for the extraction of this wealth once the entitlement of the crown had been established.[40] Consequently, the logic of his position was not apparent to his supporters, with the result that opposition to his approach was readily developed within his own ministry.

Chatham's optimism about the prospect of deriving a significant income from the Company was in part a product of a general impression that the British acquisition of the territorial and customs revenues for the provinces of Bengal, Bihar and

[34] Ibid., p. 279. Cf. Walpole, *Memoirs*, III, p. 73: "Burke had said he would take nothing, but on proviso of resigning, if Lord Rockingham went into opposition."

[35] Portland to Newcastle, 21 November 1766, Newcastle Papers, Add. MS. 32978, fols. 11–13. For discussion and context, see John Brooke, *The Chatham Administration*, pp. 57–58.

[36] EB to Charles O'Hara, 29 November 1766, *Corr.*, I, pp. 282–83.

[37] Walpole, *Memoirs*, III, p. 79.

[38] The Earl of Chatham to the Duke of Grafton, 7 December 1766, Grafton, *Autobiography*, p. 110.

[39] Ibid.

[40] On Chatham's preoccupation with the legal entitlement of the Company to its territorial revenues, see Huw V. Bowen, "A Question of Sovereignty? The Bengal Land Revenue Issue, 1765–1767," *Journal of Imperial and Commonwealth History*, 16:2 (January 1988), pp. 155–76.

Orissa after her assumption of the *Diwani* in 1765 would entail a significant increase in the profitability of the eastern trade. "The great acquisitions of power, dominion, and riches, which have been made in the East Indies," declared *The Annual Register* in connection with these events, "are become objects of the highest importance and consideration."[41] A more specific expectation was articulated in a letter sent by Thomas Townshend to Chatham on 6 September 1766. "There is good reason to believe," Townshend began, that "the treaties concluded in Bengal by Lord Clive, will be productive of a clear yearly revenue of two millions sterling." Within a few years, he went on, such a sum would substantially redeem the nation's debt.[42] But Chatham had already been apprised of this possibility by Clive himself, who had informed him back in 1759 about his assessment of the opportunities for aggrandisement held out to British imperial ambition in the aftermath of the Battle of Plassey. "Now I leave you to judge," as he put it to the Secretary of State, "whether an income yearly of upwards of two millions sterling . . . be an object deserving the public attention."[43] Having defeated the forces of Siraj-ud-Daula, the Nawab of Bengal, at Plassey on 23 June 1757, it seemed clear to Clive that the Company could successfully pursue a policy of territorial expansion. At the same time, he anticipated that it would be possible to take "possession of these rich kingdoms," by which he meant securing a grant from the Mughal Emperor of the right to assume control over revenue collection.[44] But the question remained of how these new powers might in practice be administered: "so large a sovereignty may possibly be an object too extensive for a mercantile company," Clive mused, "and it is to be feared they are not of themselves able, without the nation's assistance, to maintain so wide a dominion."[45]

With the signing of the Treaty of Allahabad on 16 August 1765, which enshrined the terms of peace concluded between the British, the Mughal Emperor, Shah Allam II, the Wazir of Awadh, Shuja-ud-Daula and the new Nawab of Bengal, Najm-ud-Daula, the rights of *Diwani* did indeed fall to the East India Company.[46] This afforded "a degree of triumph," as *The Annual Register* phrased it, "unknown even

[41] *The Annual Register for 1766*, p. 20.

[42] *Chatham Correspondence*, III, p. 61. In a letter to George Grenville dated 30 September 1765, Clive estimated the revenues of the Company at 4 million: see Philip Lawson, "Parliament and the First East India Inquiry, 1767," *Parliamentary History*, 1 (1982), pp. 99–114, p. 100. This, he reckoned, would yield a surplus of 1½ million per annum: see P. J. Marshall, *Problems of Empire: Britain and India, 1757–1813* (London: George Allen & Unwin, 1968), p. 58. The figure of 2 million sterling was bandied about the pamphlet literature in the mid 1760s. See, for example, Anon., *A Letter to the Proprietors of East-India Stock* (London: 1766), p. 4; cf. *The Annual Register for 1766*, p. 29. The Company servant John Zephaniah Holwell went so far as to estimate the revenues of the Company at just under 14 million: see his *Interesting Historical Events, Relative to the Province of Bengal, and the Empire of Indostan* (London: 2nd ed., 1766–67), 3 vols., I, p. 204.

[43] Robert Clive to William Pitt, 7 January 1759, *Chatham Correspondence*, I, p. 390.

[44] Ibid.

[45] Ibid., pp. 389–90.

[46] Henry Dodwell, *Dupleix and Clive: The Beginning of Empire* (London: Frank Cass & Co., 1920, 1967), pp. 213–37.

to ancient Rome."[47] The Nawab's deputy would henceforth manage the provincial finances, while the actual collection of the revenues was to be conducted through a variety of intermediaries. Nonetheless, the process would be overseen by the Company's resident at the Nawab's *Durbar*, and the perceived need for British military paramountcy was addressed: troop numbers in Bengal rose from 3,000 in 1756 to 26,000 by 1766.[48] The Company thus governed a judicial and civil administration devolved upon indigenous office holders.[49] Overall, these developments promised relief to the British exchequer, but the terms on which the extraction of revenue was to be conducted remained controversial. Writing to Chatham on 9 September 1766, Thomas Townshend contended that the present constitution of the company was "very inadequate" to the demands of government over distant territories, implying that the relationship between the Company and its possessions needed urgent adjustment. That adjustment could best be effected by redefining the relationship between the Company and the state, Townshend thought.[50] However Charles Townshend, Thomas Townshend's cousin, was determined to negotiate a settlement with the Company's Directors that would preserve the current arrangements governing the status of the corporation.[51] What was required, he insisted to Chatham, was an "amicable" arrangement between the ministry and the Directors: the idea of transferring responsibility for the collection and remittance of Indian revenues from the Company to the government was fraught with "endless difficulties," and ought to be avoided at all costs.[52]

Pitt himself had long worried about the best means of dividing responsibility for the "vast" territories of the subcontinent over which the British had come to exercise control between 1757 and 1765.[53] From the combination of the old and new companies into the United Company of Merchants of England Trading to the East Indies in 1709 down to the conclusion of the Seven Years' War in 1763, relations between the corporation and the government had been harmonious, sustained by a common commitment to the terms of the Company's charter. But, as successive ministries turned to tackle the national debt after the Peace of Paris, Britain's relations with its Indian territories, much like its relationship to the North American colonies, were subject to new strains as the Treasury sought to alleviate the financial exigencies of the nation. Chatham's ally, the MP for the City of London Alderman

[47] *The Annual Register for 1766*, p. 22.

[48] Huw V. Bowen, *Revenue and Reform: The Indian Problem in British Politics, 1757–1773* (Cambridge: Cambridge University Press, 1991), p. 12.

[49] B. B. Misra, *The Judicial Administration of the East India Company in Bengal, 1765–1782* (New Delhi: Motilal Banarsidass, 1961), pp. 21–6.

[50] Thomas Townshend to the Earl of Chatham, 9 September 1766, *Chatham Correspondence*, III, p. 62.

[51] On Townshend's behaviour in relation to East India Company business in 1767, see Namier and Brooke, *Townshend*, pp. 155–72.

[52] Charles Townshend to the Earl of Chatham, 4 January 1767, *Chatham Correspondence*, III, p. 156.

[53] See his comments to Clive's agent, John Walsh, recorded in John Malcolm, *The Life of Robert, Lord Clive* (London: 1836) 3 vols., III, p. 189.

William Beckford, put the matter bluntly: "Unless you can procure a revenue of a million per annum without new taxations and oppressions on the people, there can be no salvation arise to Israel."[54] Suspicious of the East India Company's monopoly over Asian trade, and siding with Pitt against Conway and Charles Townshend over the terms on which the government ought to appropriate Company wealth, it was Beckford who proposed the motion to launch an inquiry into the state of India's affairs to a sparsely attended House of Commons on 25 November 1766.[55] "Men were amazed," Horace Walpole remarked, "to see a machine of such magnitude entrusted to so wild a charioteer."[56]

Burke shared with Chatham the general aim of ensuring that the Company would prove a benefit to the British nation, but he departed from him and Beckford in insisting that this depended on maintaining the integrity of the Company's corporate property. This did not rule out a revision of the terms of the Company's charter, nor intelligent reform of its constitution. Indeed, as we shall see, Burke conceded that the discretion lodged in the Company's administration of the subcontinent was in need of judicial regulation. Abuses, he came to recognise, had certainly occurred, and they needed to be corrected. Burke was clear, however, that these abuses did not extend to the fact of conquest itself, which had been a legitimate achievement of East India Company servants, secured by right of war. Subjugation was a brutal yet glorious fact. The question for policy was how to maintain this evident fact as a legitimate right. As Burke viewed the situation between Beckford's motion for an inquiry and the introduction of Lord North's Regulating Bill seven years later, the rights of conquest depended on the ongoing advantage which British dominion secured to the metropole and its Asian provinces alike. But such advantage could not plausibly be advanced by pursuing, as Chatham seemed intent upon doing, the conquest of the Company's acquisitions by government violation of chartered privileges. This approach, Burke would soon argue, threatened to destroy credit and unsettle the rights of property, which would then deprive Britain and India of any benefit whatever.[57] It could only be achieved, moreover, by extending the corruption of the British constitution—perverting, as Burke would maintain in 1772 and 1773, its balanced arrangement by the introduction of a purely demotic monarchy that risked declining headlong into tyranny. The parliamentary inquiry launched by Beckford in 1766 would soon appear as a key stage in this process of perversion.

[54] Chatham Papers, TNA, PRO 30/8/19, fol. 91, Beckford to Chatham, October 1766, cited in Lawson, "Parliament and the First East India Inquiry," p. 99.

[55] *CJ*, XXXI, p. 25.

[56] Walpole, *Memoirs*, III, p. 82.

[57] On the East India Company as a pillar of national credit, see P.G.M. Dickson, *The Financial Revolution in England: A Study in the Development of Public Credit, 1688–1756* (London: Macmillan, 1967); H. V. Bowen, *The Business of Empire: The East India Company and Imperial Britain, 1756–1833* (Cambridge: Cambridge University Press, 2006), ch. 2.

7.3 Rights of Conquest

Beckford's motion was introduced in the context of suspicion directed against the sudden prosperity associated with the eastern trade. The ostentatious opulence paraded by returning Company servants or "nabobs," setting themselves up in the country and targeting parliamentary boroughs for electoral gain, had been generating concern.[58] *The Annual Register* reported the common belief that "luxury, corruption, and the extreme avidity for making immense fortunes in a little time, had so totally infected the company's servants, that nothing less than a general reform . . . could preserve the settlement from certain and immediate destruction."[59] It has long been recognised that the popular reaction against an apparent invasion of British public life by Company servants had been based on exaggerated impressions held by contemporary observers. Most European traffickers toiled for a modest fortune, or died in the course of business in India itself.[60] Nonetheless, between 1760 and 1780, around 200 Company officials returned to Britain from trading factories stationed around Bengal, Madras and Bombay, with a conspicuous proportion of them having amassed considerable wealth—much of this through private trade, some from personal gifts.[61] A number of these nabobs controlled parliamentary seats, while others strove for peerages, or connections to be secured through marriage. In addition, at least seventy members of the House of Commons held shares in East India stock in 1764—a significant number, even if these members' diverse concerns cannot plausibly be taken to constitute a unified Indian "interest."[62] In the face of a growing suspicion of the rise in the nabobs' influence, publicists began to question the trustworthiness of servants on the subcontinent, especially after their elevation from merchants into rulers. After the Battle of Buxar, the Company had been transformed, as one commentator put it, "from a commercial, into a military corporation." In the process, he went on, erstwhile provincial merchants had been promoted into being governors of princes whom they subjected to "more absolute vassalage" than the meanest "feudatories" of the king of France.[63]

[58] See, for example, *Letters of Horace Walpole, Fourth Earl of Orford*, ed. P. Toynbee (Oxford: Clarendon Press, 1905), 16 vols., V, p. 29. For general account, see James M. Holzman, *The Nabobs in England, 1760–1785: A Study of the Returned Anglo-India* (New York: Columbia University Press, 1926); P. J. Marshall, *East Indian Fortunes: The British in Bengal in the Eighteenth Century* (Oxford: Oxford University Press, 1976).

[59] *The Annual Register for 1766*, p. 27.

[60] Holden Furber, *John Company at Work* (Cambridge, MA: Harvard University Press, 1948).

[61] Philip Lawson and Jim Phillips, "'Our Execrable Banditti': Perceptions of Nabobs in Mid-Eighteenth-Century Britain," *Albion*, 16:3 (Autumn 1984), pp. 225–41, p. 227.

[62] *Additional Grenville Papers, 1765–1767*, ed. J.R.G. Tomlinson (Manchester: Manchester University Press, 1962), pp. 96–9; Huw V. Bowen, "'Dipped in the Traffic': East India Stockholders in the House of Commons, 1768–1774," *Parliamentary History*, 5:1 (December 1986), pp. 39–53.

[63] Anon., *Reflections on the Present State of our East India Affairs, with Many Interesting Anecdotes never before Made Public* (London: 1764), pp. 20–21. For criticism of the presumptuousness of Com-

British commercial enterprise, it seemed, was yielding to the spirit of conquest.[64] Reflecting on the wider context of Chatham's ambition to establish the supremacy of the crown over the Company, Horace Walpole questioned whether it can ever have been the intention of the British state in granting a commercial monopoly to a trading corporation to establish dominion in far away places through the agency of "a set of private merchants."[65] Observers were left to wonder by what "treachery, fraud, violence and blood" such an extraordinary feat of aggrandisement had occurred, while politicians were obliged to decide on the administration of the conquests.[66] Chatham was evidently anxious to subordinate East India House to the House of Commons, but at a cost of invading the property of the Company. Walpole accordingly noted that most MPs who "had property in the East India Company, [and] most of those who had any other property . . . took the alarm."[67] The Rockinghams were to the fore in representing this concern, spontaneously coordinating around a common position: "You cannot think with what spirit and system our little Corps went," as Burke depicted the scene in the Commons after Beckford had put his motion.[68] As for himself: "I jumped up instantly on Beckfords [*sic*] making his motion and took my own Ground," Burke reported to O'Hara.[69] Although Burke does not mention the basis for his objection on 25 November, at least the quality of his intervention was relayed by Henry Flood to Lord Charlemont: "Our friend Burke rose first in opposition and acquitted himself very honourably."[70] At this stage, as he told O'Hara, Burke proceeded "very cautiously" lest he narrow his party's options in the future.[71] But at least his independence from the ministry was not in doubt: he had broken off all negotiations with "the powers that be" and was cherishing his freedom of action "in the fair open Sea."[72]

The House divided on Beckford's motion by 76 to 129 in favour of establishing a committee of inquiry, but not without members of the government itself amending his call for an examination into the conduct "of all or any persons concerned in the direction or administration of the said Company."[73] The ministry, in short, was divided against itself: never before had a government cut "a more shameful figure," Burke later complained.[74] With Conway and Townshend in the Commons

pany servants corrupted through opulence and power during this period, see also Anon., *Considerations on the Present State of the East-India Company's Affairs* (London: 1764), pp. 14–15.

[64] On this, see John Dunning, *A Letter to the Proprietors of East-India Stock, on the Subject of Lord Clive's Jaghire* (London: 1764), p. 7.

[65] Walpole, *Memoirs*, III, p. 79.

[66] Ibid.

[67] Ibid., p. 80.

[68] EB to Charles O'Hara, 29 November 1766, *Corr.*, I, p. 283.

[69] EB to Charles O'Hara, 27 November 1766, ibid., p. 281.

[70] As reported in *Chatham Correspondence*, III, p. 144n.

[71] EB to Charles O'Hara, 27 November 1766, *Corr.*, I, p. 281.

[72] EB to Charles O'Hara, 29 November 1766, ibid., p. 283.

[73] *CJ*, XXXI, p. 25.

[74] EB to Charles O'Hara, 27 November 1766, *Corr.*, I, p. 281.

plotting a course that diverged from Chatham, Grafton and Shelburne in the Lords, ministers in the lower House were "beat about like footballs."[75] In coming out against the government, the Rockinghams were joining forces with the Bedfords and the Grenvilles in challenging Beckford's plans; "but we did not go in their Train," Burke insisted. Instead, they took up a position of principle, disdaining "factious opposition."[76] The principle in question centred on the chartered rights of a trading corporation, whose property in its own business ought not to be violated on the whim of government. But the issues which that principle was designed to cover were not so easily addressed. The extent of the Company's possessions on the subcontinent were an evident fact, but did the fact of possession constitute a claim to absolute property, and did the rights of property carry with them both the obligations and the burdens of government?

These issues came into focus on Tuesday, 9 December when Beckford moved for the Company's papers to be laid before the House, hoping to have their various "charters, treaties, [and the] revenue in Bengal" brought under investigation.[77] In the process, Walpole observed, he "expatiated" on the "devastation" committed by Company servants in Bengal. It was not the established proprietors of East India stock who profited from this treatment, Beckford added, but adventurers, like William Burke, speculating on the rise in the Company's credit.[78] Peregrine Cust, the Speaker's brother, at first lent support to the government line. The private concerns of Leadenhall Street could not be separated from those of the public: it was not individual enterprise, but the British navy, that had sustained the Company's settlements against French interlopers and the Country powers. Nonetheless, in opposition to Beckford, Cust also dampened the expectation of national redemption from the revenues of Bengal: the forts and armaments of the Company were a permanent drain on her resources.[79] Others questioned whether Bengal was in fact a permanent acquisition, while the Rockinghams disputed the propriety of hauling Company Directors before the bar, accusing potential partners whom one ought to treat as equals. "We fought the best battle we could," was Burke's verdict. Holding out until midnight for a three-month adjournment, they were "as spirited as you could wish," he informed O'Hara. As for himself, he spoke twice, the first time "for upwards of an hour," being "well heard."[80] The Company was accused so that "their property might be confiscated," he is reported to have declared.[81] Next he rounded on Chatham, whom he depicted as presiding *in absentia* over the treasury bench like the awesome deity before the roll call of the angels in book V of Milton's *Paradise Lost*. The government, he went on, was making a dangerous attempt on the operation of

[75] Ibid.
[76] Ibid.
[77] Walpole, *Memoirs*, III, p. 88; *CJ*, XXXI, p. 42.
[78] Walpole, *Memoirs*, III, p. 88.
[79] Ibid.
[80] EB to Charles O'Hara, 23 December 1766, *Corr.*, I, p. 286.
[81] Walpole, *Memoirs*, III, p. 88.

free government without a tangible advantage in the offing.[82] High-handed authority, Burke asserted, was threatening to compromise the standing of the "National Credit" to which Pitt had owed his victories in the last war.[83]

Burke's performance on 9 December was among his most outstanding to date, exhibiting the weakness of the ministry by exposing the reticence of both Townshend and Conway. William Burke was effusive on the subject to O'Hara: "I believe no man ever got so much credit, by a single effort. The town rang with it, and have not yet done with it."[84] Nonetheless, an inquiry was overwhelmingly endorsed by the House of Commons, leaving the General Court to empower the Directors of the East India Company to seek an agreement on the best terms available. That search was repeatedly frustrated over the following months as Chatham failed to concert with either his Chancellor of the Exchequer or his Minister in the Commons. The basis of their disagreement lay in the question of whether the right of the Company to its territorial acquisitions on the subcontinent should be determined in advance of a practical agreement over the allocation of revenues. For Chatham, this prior determination was crucial, whereas for Townshend and Conway a settlement should take precedence over a statement of juridical entitlement. To Burke it appeared that "the great Guide," as he now began to style Chatham, was intent on "contesting the right of the E. I. company" in the teeth of practical politics and the judgment of his principal ministers in the Commons.[85] But if the position *de jure* of the Company was to be established in advance, it was debatable whether this was a decision for parliament or the courts. As Conway reported to Chatham on 24 January 1767, Grenville had raised this issue two days previously in the Commons.[86] It was a topic that was to resurface as a bone of contention over the following months.

Parliamentary controversy over the privileges and obligations of the East India Company was ultimately based on the contested events of South Asian history that occurred between 1757 and 1765. Having travelled north from Madras to repulse the aggression of Siraj-ud-Daula against the British settlement in Calcutta, Clive installed Mir Jafar as Nawab of Bengal, based at Murshidabad, in June 1757. Therewith, under the appearance of continuity, a series of "revolutions" in the government of Bengal began.[87] The primary commitment of the new establishment was to

[82] As reported in a letter from Matthew Fetherstonehaugh to Robert Clive, reprinted in Chatham, *Correspondence*, III, p. 145n.

[83] EB to Charles O'Hara, 23 December 1766, *Corr.*, I, p. 286.

[84] WB to Charles O'Hara, 27 December 1766, in Hoffman, *Burke*, pp. 381–2

[85] EB to Charles O'Hara, 15 January 1767, *Corr.*, I, p. 291.

[86] Henry Seymour Conway to the Earl of Chatham, 24 January 1767, *Chatham Correspondence*, III, p. 175; Conway is reported to have lent his support to Grenville's claim in a letter from Beckford to Chatham of 27 January 1767, ibid., p. 177.

[87] Burke counted "three capital revolutions" between 1757 and 1764 in *The Annual Register for the Year 1764*, p. 34. On the conservative character of the "revolution" of 1757, see P. J. Marshall, *Bengal: The British Bridgehead, Eastern India, 1740–1828* (Cambridge: Cambridge University Press, 1987, 1990), pp. 78–79. For the pattern of change in South Asia in the eighteenth century more generally, see P. J. Marshall ed., *The Eighteenth Century in Indian History: Evolution or Revolution?* (Oxford: Oxford University

ensure the progress of business as usual. As Luke Scrafton, then a Company representative at the Nawab's court, understood the situation, the British aimed to revert from their newfound political role to purely "commercial" activity, while the independence of the Nawab was to be guaranteed despite the military presence of the British.[88] But political relations were shaped by facts on the ground: the dominance of the Company had been demonstrated in arms, and the impulse to interfere in the politics of Bengal proved irresistible. Trade and war became interdependent; in fact they had never been cleanly separated in commercial colonies in Asia.[89] The need for resources encouraged the demand for territory, impacting on the political ambitions of the Company.[90] As Clive's successor as Governor of Bengal, Henry Vansittart, saw it, the need for funds bred the perception that "countries" would have to be "ceded."[91] In the end, Vansittart claimed, "other ideas than those of commerce" came to determine the purposes of the Company: "from a system of oeconomy and commerce, they entered upon a political and military system."[92] Accordingly, in finding Mir Jafar recalcitrant, Vansittart opted to instal a successor, Mir Kasim, as Nawab in October 1760. But the Calcutta Council under Vansittart was divided, and within a few years relations between the British and the Nawab had broken down again, largely over the rights of private traders in Bengal. Withdrawing into northern India in 1763, Mir Kasim joined forces with the Mughal Emperor and the Wazir of Awadh against the British, and met with defeat at the Battle of Buxar the following year.

Government ministers, above all the Nawab's deputy or *naib*, together with more junior administrative appointments in Bengal, were henceforth controlled by the British. Responsibility for defence likewise fell to the Company, which was duly elevated to the status of *Diwan*, or administrator, of the revenues of Bengal by direct grant from the Emperor. A succession of Nawabs continued in the increasingly cer-

Press, 2003). The vestigial survival of "corporate" practices and assumptions in the period after 1757–65 is examined in Philip J. Stern, "Conclusion" in *The Company-State: Corporate Sovereignty and the Early Modern Foundations of the British Empire in India* (Oxford: Oxford University Press, 2011).

[88] Luke Scrafton, *Observations on Mr. Vansittart's Narrative* (London: 1766), p. 2. Scrafton is responding to the argument set forth in Henry Vansittart, *A Narrative of the Transactions in Bengal from the Year 1760 to the Year 1764* (London: 1766), 3 vols.

[89] On the longstanding dependence of British trade on force, see P. J. Marshall, "British Expansion in India in the Eighteenth Century: A Historical Revision," *History*, 60 (1975), pp. 28–43, esp. pp. 31–32. Cf. the different emphasis in S. Arasaratnam, "Trade and Political Dominion in South India, 1750–1790: Changing British–Indian Relationships," *Modern Asian Studies*, 13:1 (1979), pp. 19–40.

[90] For the problems involved in extrapolating "policy" from this process, see Marshall, "British Expansion in India," pp. 28–43.

[91] *Fort William—India House Correspondence, III, 1760–1763*, ed. R. R. Sethi (New Delhi: National Archives of India, 1968), p. 290.

[92] Henry Vansittart, *A Letter to the Proprietors of East-India Stock* (London: 1767), p. 20. In asserting this, Vansittart is refuting the claims of Scrafton.

emonial role of *Nazim*, or governor, in subjection to the British.[93] "We must indeed become the Nabobs ourselves," as Clive put it.[94] Governor Pownall later underlined the extent of the change: the native government of Bengal had been "dissolved," he exclaimed—"the sovereignty annihilated."[95] Accession to the *Diwani* represented a significant increase in the territorial power of the East India Company, but the question remained as to whether this increase should be understood as an extension of the property rights of the trading corporation, or as an acquisition by conquest to the British state. On 16 April 1767, the Chairman of the East India Company put a series of propositions to Chatham with a view to securing an agreement concerning the revenues of Bengal, beginning with an account of the "State of the Facts" that would help determine the "matter of right between the Crown & the Company."[96] From the Company's perspective, its right to the revenues was a function of the "free and perpetual gift" (*altamga*) bestowed upon it of the "Civil Office" of *Diwan* held under the Emperor in exchange for a share of the relevant rents and taxes collected.[97] The Company's right to occupy that office was ultimately provided for under the terms of its 1698 Charter, which conferred upon it "an unlimited right to hold possessions of any sort of nature that might be granted or ceded to them by the Country Powers."[98] The implications of this entitlement in the aftermath of victory at Plassey were outlined in the Pratt-Yorke opinion of 24 December 1757, in which the Attorney General and Solicitor General clarified for the Privy Council the relative rights of dominion in India in response to a petition from the East India Company. This opinion specified that although all territories in possession of the Company were subject to parliamentary sovereignty since British subjects "carried with them your majesty's Laws wherever they form Colonies," districts acquired by treaty remained

[93] Dodwell, *Dupleix and Clive*, pp. 238–43; Abdul Majed Khan, *The Transition in Bengal, 1756–1775: A Study of Saiyid Muhammad Reza Khan* (Cambridge: Cambridge University Press, 1969), pp. 78–102.

[94] Percival Spear, *Master of Bengal: Clive and his India* (London: Thames and Hudson, 1975), p. 146.

[95] Thomas Pownall, *The Right, Interest, and Duty of the State, as Concerned in the Affairs of the East Indies* (London: 1773), pp. 39–40.

[96] "Papers Transmitted by the Chairman of the East India Company to the Earl of Chatham, 16th Apr. 1767," Chatham Papers, TNA, PRO 30/8/99, Part III, fols. 188–260.

[97] Rajat Kanta Ray, "Indian Society and the Establishment of British Supremacy, 1765–1818" in Marshall ed., *Oxford History of the British Empire II*, p. 511.

[98] "Papers Transmitted by the Chairman of the East India Company," Chatham Papers, TNA, PRO 30/8/99, Part II, fol. 9. For an account of the Company's successive charters around this time, see Arthur Berriedale Keith, *A Constitutional History of India, 1600–1935* (London: Methuen, 1936), pp. 9–20. The fullest discussion of the Pratt-Yorke opinion in the context of India is provided by Bowen, *Revenue and Reform*, pp. 53–54. There is some discussion of the opinion, particularly of its impact on the settlement of North America, in Thomas Perkins Abernethy, *Western Lands and the American Revolution* (New York: D. Appleton-Century Company, 1937), p. 21; and Jack M. Sosin, *Whitehall and the Wilderness: The Middle West in British Colonial Policy, 1760–1775* (Lincoln, NE: University of Nebraska Press, 1961), pp. 229–30.

the property of the Company while dominion acquired by conquest was vested in the crown.[99]

The application of this opinion to the situation of the Company after 1765 proved controversial, since although the *Diwani* had been granted by the Mughal, and had therefore not been acquired by right of conquest, the Emperor himself had been made a prisoner of the British with the assistance of the king's forces—making him, de facto, a conquest of the crown.[100] For opponents of the Company like Beckford and Chatham, this meant that the *Diwani* had itself been acquired by conquest, and was therefore at the disposal of the British sovereign. It followed that the distribution of its proceeds should be determined by a parliamentary inquiry. To Burke, this resolution was tantamount to a resort to "force," since he construed Chatham's eagerness to labour the question of jurisdiction as a means of rejecting all negotiation with the Company, imposing upon her by "Violence" instead.[101] On 20 February 1767, the question of whether territorial jurisdiction in Bengal should be regarded as Company property was keenly debated, with Burke siding with the opposition lawyers, Thurlow and Wedderburn, who questioned how far "it was legal for the House of Commons to interfere its authority in deciding [in] any way about the property of individuals," with ministerial supporters "adopting the contrary opinion"—namely, "that the conquests were made by the King, and not by the Company."[102] At a cabinet meeting on 3 March the issue was debated once more, but still without generating consensus.[103] When the India business next came before the House of Commons, "Grenville, Burke and Wedderburn treated Chatham and Beckford with scorn, and laboured to raise a spirit against the idea of force to be put on the Company."[104] The controversy, however, persisted. On 9 March the MP for Roxburghshire, Gilbert Elliot, trumpeted the public's right to the proceeds of conquest which, ipso facto, could not be viewed as "free grants following from the dictates of Eastern gratitude."[105]

In the end, as Burke predicted, the Chatham ministry opted to pursue a negotiated settlement. "In the Indian affair," as Burke put it to O'Hara on 17 March 1767, "he [Chatham] will I am satisfied get off his high ground, and take that method which reason ought at first to have directed, but which Necessity at length compels him to pursue, that of fair Treaty and Negotiation upon terms of mutual ad-

[99] "Papers Transmitted by the Chairman of the East India Company," Chatham Papers, TNA, PRO 30/8/99, Part II, fol. 9.

[100] Ibid., Part III, fols. 188–260.

[101] EB to Charles O'Hara, 7 and 14 March 1767, *Corr.*, I, pp. 297–300.

[102] Mr. Rouet to Baron Mure, 21 February 1767, *Selections from the Family Papers Preserved at Caldwell* (Glasgow: 1854), 3 vols., II, ii, pp. 107–8; cf. *Ryder Diary*, p. 332. Burke consistently maintained, well into the 1780s, that Britain's territorial acquisitions in the East Indies were not in any way annexed or united to the crown. See EB, *A Representation to His Majesty, Moved in the House of Commons . . . June 14, 1784* (London: 1784), p. 17.

[103] Walpole, *Memoirs*, III, p. 101.

[104] Ibid., p. 103.

[105] *Ryder Diary*, p. 335.

vantage."[106] Ten days later, the interrogation of witnesses before a Committee of the House of Commons began. By the middle of April, Thomas Rous, Deputy Chairman of the Company and a Director for more than twenty years, was confirming the lack of control exercised over Company servants from East India House—"Great Licentiousness," he stated, had characterised their proceedings on the subcontinent.[107] One conspicuous reason for this was presented by Warren Hastings on 31 March: since the Directors were regularly replaced at the discretion of the Court of Proprietors, and their orders might plausibly be overturned before they reached Bengal, servants grew used to regarding regulations as negotiable.[108] More fundamentally, but equally damaging, it was being contended, in the words of Henry Vansittart, that "a commercial Company and Military Company cannot long subsist at the same time for the Expence and Inconvenience on the one side must over balance the advantages on the other."[109] Nonetheless, in a letter sent to O'Hara at this time, Burke was sceptical about the achievements of the government concerning India: "All they do is run a blind muck at the Companys [*sic*] right to their acquisitions, without knowing the practicality or regarding the Justice of the measure."[110] Similar sentiments were articulated on 14 April when the Company's jurisdictional entitlements were again defended—this time by Charles Yorke, Attorney General under Rockingham, and co-signatory to the Pratt-Yorke opinion of a decade earlier.[111] Asserting the right of the corporation to their territorial possessions, he emphasised their status as a "grant" bestowed out of favour and not in fear.[112] Burke, it seems, accepted the implications of this conclusion: the acquisitions were by right the Company's own.

Yorke was opposed by Fletcher Norton, Attorney General under Grenville, who insisted that if the territories had not been acquired by right of conquest, they should be regarded as illicit plunder and returned to the "country powers."[113] However "nobody," Walpole recorded, "wished to see that."[114] Yet if opinion was united in wanting to derive some public benefit from the Company's successes, division persisted about the means of achieving this. Burke looked with "horror" upon the idea of subjecting the corporate rights of the Company to parliamentary restriction. No convincing attempt had been made to negotiate a beneficial outcome, and yet in practical terms it would prove impossible to proceed without the Company's agreement and cooperation. The spirit of the government's proceedings was

[106] EB to Charles O'Hara, 17 March 1767, *Corr.*, I, p. 300.

[107] "Substance of the Evidence taken before an Open Committee of the House of Commons on the State of Bengal &c. in 1767," BL Add. MS. 18469, fols. 66r–v.

[108] Ibid., fols. 20v–21r.

[109] Ibid., fol. 12v.

[110] EB to Charles O'Hara, 30 and 31 March 1767, *Corr.*, I, p. 303.

[111] *Ryder Diary*, p. 339.

[112] Ibid. Yorke was focusing in this instance on the grant of territories from the Nawab of Arcot.

[113] Ibid.

[114] Walpole, *Memoirs*, III, p. 119.

oppressive in the extreme, converting the House of Commons into a judicial tyranny: "We set ourselves up as Judges upon a point of Law, to decide between Subject and the Crown a matter of property of the greatest concern and magnitude without the least colour of right; at once Judge and party!"[115] But, as Burke spoke, negotiations between the government and the Company were happily proceeding under the direction of Lord Shelburne, reducing the significance of Beckford's inquiry, at least in the short term.[116] By 1 May one of the Directors, Sir George Colebrooke, felt ready to pronounce in parliament on the prospect of an "accommodation" on the Indian business.[117] "They have come to a temporary agreement with the E. India directors," Burke noted.[118] However, one day later the whole affair was thrown into disarray once more.

On 6 May the Court of Proprietors, in defiance of the Directors, voted to reject the terms being agreed with the government and resolved to raise the Company dividend to 12½ per cent. The result was consternation among government supporters at such a unilateral affront to the ministry's efforts at negotiation. Accordingly, the following day, the Company was obliged to lay papers before the House explaining its actions and, on 8 May, notice of a Bill to regulate the dividend on East India stock was introduced by Jeremiah Dyson.[119] Over the following month, the mood of outrage at the Proprietors' effrontery was further exploited by the ministry, sealing an agreement to the effect that, while the Company would be confirmed in its territorial possessions, it would also be forced to pay the government £400,000 per annum.[120] At the same time, a resolution was introduced to prevent the practice of vote splitting in sessions of the General Court while, as a concession, a reduction in the duty on tea was also proposed.[121] The plan to reduce the dividend from 12½ to 10 per cent thus remained the only outstanding matter of controversy. For opponents of the Bill, government regulation of dividend payments appeared arbitrary and whimsical, even if the timing of the Company's proposed increase could be deemed impertinent.[122] Far more impertinent, Burke thought, was the government's plan to subvert the laws of commerce and credit for reasons of punitive regulation. On 25 May, the House went into committee to consider the Bill, and counsel on behalf of the Proprietors presented evidence against a reduction. The following day, the debate lasted until one in the morning, with the government ultimately prevailing, although both Townshend and Conway voted with the minority.[123] The measure, Burke insisted to

[115] EB to Charles O'Hara, 30 and 31 March 1767, *Corr.*, I, p. 303.

[116] Sutherland, *East India Company Politics*, pp. 162–76. Beckford was later to complain, during a debate on 16 December 1768 on a petition to free East India trade, that he had not been "supported by the government" in 1767. See *Cavendish Debates of the House of Commons*, I, p. 105.

[117] *Ryder Diary*, p. 341.

[118] EB to Charles O'Hara, 5 May 1767, *Corr.*, I, p. 311.

[119] Walpole, *Memoirs*, III, pp. 129–30.

[120] The agreement was embodied in statute as 7 Geo. III, c. 57.

[121] Lawson, "East India Inquiry," p. 110.

[122] Ibid., p. 111.

[123] *Ryder Diary*, p. 350.

the House, amounted to a "Revolution" in the principles of free government.[124] If the debt obligations of the Company to the government were being met, any forcible extraction from the corporation was tantamount to "robbery."[125]

Burke's dramatic stance derived from his sense that Dyson's proposal constituted an arbitrary restraint upon commercial profit, and an attempt to regulate credit by means of public intervention. The idea that market confidence could be determined by public authority had been subjected to substantial criticism since the collapse of John Law's scheme for regulating the value of credit during his period as Controller General of Finances in France in the early eighteenth century.[126] Thirty years later, in the *Spirit of the Laws*, Montesquieu was still meditating on the causes behind Law's failure, associating his system with unmitigated despotism.[127] This association facilitated Burke's denunciation of the government's plan.[128] "I suppose there is nothing like this to be found in the Code of Laws in any Civilised Country upon Earth," he declared.[129] "Civilised" here entailed a commitment to civil liberty, which ultimately rested on the security of property: "I always took it to be an invariable rule and what distinguished Law and Freedom from Violence and Slavery . . . that the property vested in the Subject by a known Law" would be secure against invasion from "any power or authority whatsoever."[130] The only grounds on which an infringement of this principle could be defended would consist in a plea of overriding public interest.[131] It was indeed on the basis that an increase in the dividend would be detrimental to public credit that ministerial supporters argued in favour of its restriction. Moreover, it was commonly asserted on the government side that the motive behind the proposed increase was market manipulation in the interest of financial speculation. However, Burke protested, the notion that government counter-manipulation

[124] EB, Speech on East India Dividend Bill, 26 May 1767, *W & S*, II, p. 65.

[125] WWM BkP 9:30. Cf. WWM BkP 9:21, on the perception that property was being "endangered." Burke returned to this episode repeatedly in the years that followed, notably in EB, Speech on East India Restraining Bill, 18 December 1772, *W & S*, II, p. 378.

[126] On John Law, see EB, *Reflections*, ed. Clark, p. 408 [346]. For discussion of Law's schemes, see Michael Sonenscher, *Before the Deluge: Public Debt, Inequality, and the Intellectual Origins of the French Revolution* (Princeton, NJ: Princeton University Press, 2007), pp. 40–1, 108–20; Michael Sonenscher, *Sans-Culottes: An Eighteenth-Century Emblem in the French Revolution* (Princeton, NJ: Princeton University Press, 2008), pp. 260–72.

[127] Charles-Louis de Secondat, Baron de Montesquieu, *De l'esprit des lois* (1748) in *Œuvres complètes*, ed. Roger Caillois (Paris: Gallimard, 1951), 2 vols., II, pt. I, bk. ii, ch. 4; pt. IV, bk. xxii, ch. 10.

[128] Burke was later to reprobate Law as a "bubble projector" in the Debate on the Renewal of the East India Company's Charter, 21 March 1780, *Parliamentary Register* (Debrett), XXI, cols. 313–14.

[129] EB, Speech on East India Dividend Bill, 26 May 1767, *W & S*, II, p. 65. In the 1780s, Burke came to see that the rise in the price of Company stock, and consequently in the value of its dividend, had been artificially inflated by the use of public revenues for investment in trade. See EB, *Ninth Report of the Select Committee* (25 June 1783), *W & S*, V, pp. 223–28.

[130] EB, Speech on East India Dividend Bill, 26 May 1767, *W & S*, II, p. 65.

[131] Cf. EB, *Third Letter on a Regicide Peace* (1797), *W & S*, IX, pp. 346–7: "To force that market, or any market, is of all things the most dangerous. . . . The monied men have a right to look to advantage in the investment of their property. To advance their money, they risk it; and the risk is to be included in the price."

could put an end to stock-jobbing was itself fallacious.[132] At the same time, he went on, the idea that subverting the basic principles of commercial freedom over a paltry difference in the value of the dividend would serve the national welfare betrayed a poor grasp of the underlying public interest.[133]

Looking back on the events of 1767 in his *Observations on a Late State of the Nation*, Burke saw the restriction on the Company's dividend as having been carried by the king's friends operating without the full support of the cabinet. After all, Townshend, together with all former Chancellors of the Exchequer in the Commons, opposed the measure. So too did Conway. The Bill was therefore carried with a "high hand"—conducted by men like Jenkinson and Dyson, acting on the promise of "*some sort of secret support*."[134] Thus, like so much else during this period, Burke saw Indian legislation as a creation of the "double cabinet" with measures concocted by the court behind the backs of leading ministers in the Commons. This had the effect of converting legislative power into an arm of the executive. At the same time, in seeking to employ a parliamentary inquiry as a means of contesting the right of the East India Company to its possessions in Asia, it transformed the legislative chamber into a quasi-judicature, collapsing judicial into legislative power, which had already been reduced to a tool of the court: "The original plan seems to have been, to get the house of commons to compliment the crown with a sort of juridical declaration of a title to the company's acquisitions in India."[135] As a result of this arrangement, oppressive measures came naturally to the government, but in the process it threatened to overturn the principal advantage which East Indian trade could offer the British nation. Among the main benefits to be derived from a trading company, Burke thought, was the revenue collected from customs imposed on its commerce and the support which its enterprise lent to public credit. This last advantage depended on preserving the corporate integrity of the Company: as soon as the government trespassed on its freedom, the principle of the Company's right to its property was imperilled, and with that both confidence and credit were compromised. Since credit, in fact, was a function of confidence, it could not be coerced: "power and credit are things adverse, incompatible," Burke insisted.[136] Thirty years later, when the Revolutionary government of France issued paper *assignats*, hoping to establish credit on the basis of unaccountable authority, Burke's response was even more pointedly one of outrage.[137]

[132] EB, Speech on East India Dividend Bill, 26 May 1767, *W & S*, II, p. 67. It might, in fact, encourage it. On this, cf. [Anon.], *A Letter to a Minister, on the Subject of the East India Dividend* (London: 2nd ed., 1767), p. 7.

[133] EB, Speech on East India Dividend Bill, 26 May 1767, *W & S*, II, p. 66.

[134] EB, *Observations on a Late State of the Nation* (1769), ibid., p. 173.

[135] Ibid., p. 172.

[136] Ibid., p. 175.

[137] *Reflections*, pp. 403–4. On this theme in Burke, see J.G.A. Pocock, "The Political Economy of Burke's *Reflections on the Revolution in France*" in idem, *Virtue, Commerce, and History: Essays on Political Thought and History, Chiefly in the Eighteenth Century* (Cambridge: Cambridge University Press, 1985).

In 1768, *The Annual Register* recalled how the East India Company Proprietors moved for an increase in the dividend on the assumption that "great revenue and a flourishing trade" could not be reconciled with an artificially deflated dividend.[138] From their perspective, a low return on investment served only to depress the present value of stock, catering to the interest of prospective jobbers instead of current East India share holders: "the possessors of property were the only people who could not enjoy any of the advantages arising from it."[139] But whereas the Proprietors could only see the profitability of the Company, the Directors were preoccupied with its debts, and so less sanguine about the future price of stock. Burke's point in the late 1760s was that this divergence could not be reconciled by executive fiat, with the ministry imposing restrictions on the profits anticipated from the Company. This, he was certain, was tantamount to a subversion of the appropriate relationship between government and corporate enterprise on the scale of the East India Company. It was crucial that relations between the state and the corporation be conducted not in terms of a subordinating, contractual arrangement whereby protection was extended in return for absolute obedience, but rather as a relationship based on a process of negotiation where both parties met as "equal dealers, on the footing of mutual advantage."[140] The kingdom would in fact be "ruined" if parliament should ever resort to "governing by detail," doling out portions of property as the administration saw fit.[141] But other councils prevailed, and the Dividend Bill passed in the Commons by 151 to 84 votes, only to come up for renewal early in the new year.[142] The renewal duly passed on 25 January 1768: "We got rid of the E. I. question in our house," Burke informed O'Hara. "We battled it for about six hours," but the opposition found themselves in a sizeable minority.[143] It was then carried in the House of Lords on 4 February, with the Bedfords, having joined the ministry, voting against their government.[144]

Burke viewed ministerial interference in Asian affairs between 1766 and 1767 in the context of what he took to be a wider constitutional crisis. As we have seen, he construed this putative crisis to be the product of government expansion at the expense of aristocratic power, secured through the corruption of the legislature and exemplified by the Pittite doctrine of "measures, not men." The growth of eastern patronage was a related source of alarm—"the Company having more places to bestow than the First Lord of the Treasury," as Walpole later claimed. The consequence was clear in the minds of opposition politicians: "the exorbitant wealth of our empire"

[138] "The History of Europe" in *The Annual Register for the Year 1767* (London: 1768), p. 41.

[139] Ibid., p. 42.

[140] EB, *Observations on a Late State of the Nation* (1769), *W & S*, II, p. 172.

[141] WWM BkP 9:21.

[142] The Dividend Bill was ultimately enacted as 7 Geo. III, c. 49.

[143] EB to Charles O'Hara, c. 1 February 1768, *Corr.*, I, p. 342.

[144] *LJ*, XXXII, pp. 65, 67, 68–69. For an account, see Walpole, *Memoirs*, III, p. 203. The Bill was enacted as 8 Geo. III, c. 11. For a narrative of the political machinations of the time, see Brooke, *Chatham Administration*, pp. 336–7.

went "hand in hand with the advance of prerogative."[145] Attempts to reform the Company were, from this perspective, mere pretexts for the pursuit of ministerial aggrandisement. A surviving manuscript note from the period encapsulates Burke's thinking:

> what plans of improvement have been proposed[?]—what errors corrected[?]—what frauds & violence detected & punished[?]—Is any thing of these proposed[?]—Not a syllable[!]—your mixture of law & policy is no more than is convenient for you to take the E. I. companys [*sic*] money . . . you are apprehensive that their right & your conveniency will not coincide.[146]

Like most political developments from the mid 1760s, Burke interpreted ministerial policy as a symptom of the corruption of the frame of national government. In conducting East Indian business, precedents ought to have been drawn from the "unpolluted fountain of constitutional principles," whereas in fact they were drawn from "occasional practice" modified by the demands of perceived exigency.[147] This paved the way for a subversion of chartered privileges, and consequently posed a challenge to the security of property. Prior to government attempts to regulate the Company, there was not a single instance in living memory in which the House of Commons had endeavoured to arrogate to itself the right to determine the property of the subject. "Here we stand on the very edge of the Law," Burke declared, "contending at the last hour for the policy of charters, the practice of civilised nations and the honour of Parliament." Parliamentary intrusion into the rights of private justice represented a "dreadful crisis," an "agonizing extremity of the constitution." Only an appeal to "superior Ranks & Talents" held out the hope of defending the public interest. Accordingly, Burke called upon the representatives of property, standing and influence in the community to safeguard the welfare of the people.[148]

7.4 Company Discretion

The agreement of May 1767 obliging the Company to contribute half of its annual profit to the government was due to expire on 1 February 1769, and so negotiations to renew its terms began in August 1768. By October of that year, the Duke of Grafton had assumed the reigns of government, as Chatham continued to sink under the afflictions of protracted illness. The previous autumn, the Bedfords had separated themselves from the opposition to the ministry and gradually came over to the court: places were duly found for Gower, Sandwich, Rigby and the rest.[149] At the same time, responsibility for the Colonies was separated from the South-

[145] Walpole, *Memoirs*, IV, p. 88.
[146] WWM BkP 9:31.
[147] Ibid.
[148] Ibid.
[149] Brooke, *Chatham Administration*, ch. 8.

ern Department, with the result that the Earl of Hillsborough "kissed hands for the American department" in the new year.[150] Charles Townshend had died in September 1767, eliciting from William Burke the judgment that while he ought to have been "the leading Man and Minister in this vast Empire," he was in fact "incapable of Good"—too eager to show his parts, he could not settle on any principle.[151] He was replaced on 7 October by Lord North as Chancellor of the Exchequer, who was later appointed Minister in the Commons. North took over the post from Conway who resigned on 20 January 1768, with Weymouth taking charge of the Northern Department. A General Election followed between March and May, prompting the return of Wilkes to the British political scene. Burke retained his seat, and settled at Beaconsfield. On 19 July news of the first disturbances in Boston in response to the Townshend Duties reached London. Three months later, just a week after Chatham resigned, Shelburne stood down as Secretary of State, leaving Weymouth to transfer to the Southern Department, with Rochford replacing him in his old post. Meanwhile Thomas Bradshaw, Grafton's Secretary to the Treasury, arranged for the renewal of negotiations with the East India Company.

The Company and the ministry concluded their discussions in January 1769, with the administration having approached the business on the basis of the tendentious assertion that entitlement to the revenues and acquisitions on the subcontinent lay by right in the crown. The usual sum of £400,000 was to be paid to the government, although this time the agreement was to last for five years. The outstanding dispute over the dividend was also settled: while the Company would be permitted to increase its payments to 12½ per cent, it could only raise the rate by a single percentage point in a given year. The Company was never again allowed to increase its dividend at will.[152] It could, however, lower its payments to the public in circumstances where its was forced to reduce its dividend to the Proprietors. These proposals were put to the vote in a ballot held at East India House on Leadenhall Street on 9 February, winning the support of the General Court and the endorsement of the Court of Directors. This consensus was produced against a background of Company dissension, weakening, the Rockinghams thought, the bargaining strength of the corporation.[153] Nonetheless, even under these conditions, the Company agreed a set of proposals to be put in the form of a petition and submitted them to the House of Commons on 27 February. The "bad posture of Indian affairs" was now subjected to renewed attention, pitting MPs against the Company, Directors against their servants, and leading East Indian representatives against one another as Governor Johnstone blamed Robert Clive for the "misfortunes" in the east.[154]

When the proposals contained in the petition were debated in committee they were commended by Lord North as a bargain for the country which he hoped

[150] Walpole, *Memoirs*, III, p. 200.

[151] William Burke to EB, post 4 September 1767, *Corr.*, I, pp. 326–27.

[152] Sutherland, *East India Company Politics*, pp. 184–5.

[153] The Marquess of Rockingham to EB, 31 May 1769, *Corr.*, II, p. 28.

[154] Walpole, *Memoirs*, IV, pp. 71–72.

could be accepted by a process of "amicable agreement," notwithstanding "the clear right and claim of the Crown" to the Company's acquisitions.[155] Despite this last assertion, it was clear to all members present that the rival claims to dominion had never been finally settled. Burke was clear why this had been the case: it was plain, he argued, that the ministerial claim had no credible foundation, and that the government was driven to invoke its putative "right" as a means of subtly overawing the Company.[156] In the end, however, it was found that interfering with the dividend was a more effective method of intimidating the Directors into accepting the 1767 treaty.[157] Nonetheless, with the question of territorial right came that of political responsibility, a topic which carried with it a certain urgency in 1769. As a succession of speakers addressed the merits of the petition before parliament, the reality of war in southern India threw a shadow over the proceedings: "there is nothing but war from the Carnatic to the Decan," Isaac Barré remarked.[158] There was a general sense among opposition speakers that the ongoing appetite for conquest in Asia, which brought with it new opportunities along with extravagant expenses, imperilled the future of Britain's Empire in the east. The advent of war threatened at once the value of Company stock, the size of the dividend to the Proprietors, and the stability of public credit. These were misfortunes, Burke reflected, that could not be dissociated from the exercise of power and influence on the subcontinent, and so responsibility for them could not be avoided: "You are plunged into empire in the East," he informed the Commons, "you have formed a great body of power there; you must abide by the consequences."[159]

The question before the House was whether these consequences could be mitigated. "The orient sun never laid more glorious expectations before us," Burke declared.[160] But these hopes were parried by the prospect of political setbacks held out by the probability of conflict on the subcontinent: "That we shall not enjoy peace in that part of the world for ever is true, any more than in this."[161] This statement was a concession to Lord Clive's fear that India would continue to be a scene of militant strife threatening the viability of the Company. Instability in Asia, after all, offered new opportunities to France. "It is not possible for France to see these possessions in the hands of the English," George Colebrooke noted, "and not desire to

[155] *Cavendish Debates of the House of Commons*, I, p. 252. Cf. North's statement to the effect that "the Crown is fully entitled to assert the rights of the public" in the Commons debate on a petition for establishing an open trade in the east on Friday 16 December 1768, in ibid., p. 106.

[156] EB, Speech on East India Settlement, 27 February 1769, *W & S*, II, p. 221. For a subsequent restatement of the position, cf. EB, Speech on North's East India Resolution, 5 April 1773, *W & S*, II, pp. 390–91.

[157] EB, Speech on East India Settlement, *W & S*, II, pp. 221–22. Cf. the reference in EB, *Observations on a Late State of the Nation* (1769), *W & S*, II, p. 174, to "mock enquiries, and real rescinding bills."

[158] *Cavendish Debates of the House of Commons*, I, p. 257.

[159] EB, Speech on East India Settlement, 27 February 1769, *W & S*, II, p. 220.

[160] Ibid.

[161] Ibid.

wrest them from us."[162] The point was felt more keenly still by Clive: "France! She has lost all sight of America . . . [and] she will look for an equivalent . . . in the East Indies."[163] Burke, however, was sanguine about the outcome: "If we make war, shall we not conquer? If we conquer, shall we not keep?" France, currently "baffled," was not an imminent threat.[164] Yet Barré, Colebrooke, Vansittart, Clive, Grenville and Thomas Walpole were altogether less complacent. Since August 1767, the Company Presidency at Madras had been feeling the effects of being drawn into the First Anglo-Mysore War, as Haidar Ali, the Sultan of Mysore, conspired with the Nazim of Hyderabad to check the East India Company in the south-east. The British were allied with the ruler of the Carnatic, Muhammed Ali Khan Wallajah, commonly styled the Nawab of Arcot, which drew them further into the contests of the region. Vansittart believed the balance of forces inherently unpredictable, not least since he deemed the relationship with the Nawab fundamentally unstable—"he has broken treaties already; he will give the French assistance."[165] Meanwhile, the Nazim was anxious to inhibit British attempts to gain control of the Northern Circars, which eased the Company's passage between Madras and Bengal. For his part, Haidar Ali, "risen from being a common seapoy, to become master of a considerable part of the Malabar coast," was extending his base beyond Mysore on either side of the southern peninsula, affecting the British Presidencies of Madras and Bombay.[166]

By 1769, *The Annual Register* was describing the British conflict with Haidar Ali as having been "wantonly" embarked upon by the Company "to answer their own private purposes and emolument."[167] This view was shared by critics of the Company in the House of Commons. British servants in the Indies were, in Barré's words, forever "striking out new wars": "not content with the revenues which they already have, but thirsting for more—it is impossible but India must be a scene of confusion."[168] Thomas Walpole was likewise anxious about the activities of Company servants, whose excesses dictated that Britain's eastern venture would amount to little more than a "golden dream." The Directors were forever catching up with their officials, ultimately obliged to condone what they had not originally endorsed: "Whatever the gentlemen abroad think proper to enter into, the Company must ratify."[169] The spirit of conquest, in other words, was being driven by the avarice of servants on the ground, with the Directors forced to lend support to their initiatives after the fact.[170] Even the Council at Calcutta was forever belatedly adapting to

[162] *Cavendish Debates of the House of Commons*, I, p. 258.

[163] Ibid., p. 263.

[164] EB, Speech on East India Settlement, 27 February 1769, *W & S*, II, pp. 220–21.

[165] *Cavendish Debates of the House of Commons*, I, p. 259.

[166] "The History of Europe" *in The Annual Register for the Year 1768* (London: 1769), p. 66.

[167] "The History of Europe" in *The Annual Register for the Year 1769* (London: 1770), p. 48.

[168] *Cavendish Debates of the House of Commons*, I, p. 257.

[169] Ibid., p. 256. On the failure of instructions from the Direction in London to compel action in South Asia, see Marshall, *East Indian Fortunes*, p. 129.

[170] On this, see Robert Travers, *Ideology and Empire in Eighteenth-Century India* (Cambridge: Cambridge University Press, 2007), pp. 14–15. Cf. Bowen, *Revenue and Reform*, p. 68: "Thoughts of future

new developments in the field. As Harry Verelst, who succeeded Clive as Governor of Bengal in 1767, came to describe this dynamic process, Company servants "proceeded to dominion" without their masters having properly understood "the situation to which they had advanced."[171] But for Isaac Barré it was the Direction that ought to shoulder responsibility: their leadership was not adequate to the task of imperial governance. The administration of a dominion "containing sixteen millions of inhabitants, and producing a revenue from four to eight millions a year, could not be wisely and safely managed by twenty-four gentlemen in Leadenhall-street." Above all, the government of the East India Company was rendered incoherent by annual elections to the Court of Directors which had the effect of subjecting policy to the fortunes of Company faction.[172] For Vansittart this was an argument for following the example of the French, whose instructions to their servants were more practicable and precise: the Directors of the British East India Company "only give out a general principle, that we do not mean to extend our territories." But under conditions of regional conflict, this principle proved inoperable, forcing servants into conflict with the designs of East India House.[173]

Burke dissented from these strictures, disputing the proposals of Vansittart and Clive. "Do not take a plan from a French Company," he urged. Discretion among Company servants was structurally unavoidable: "You can tell them what wars are wanton, what necessary. Your past experience will tell you, that you must leave a great deal to the discretion of [the Company's] officers."[174] However, for Clive, discretion was an inherent problem which bred a process of unplanned expansion that would terminate in the loss of the territories in the east: "it is a miracle," he exclaimed, "we have preserved them so long."[175] Mindless expansionism, Colebrooke concurred, could only end in tears: "By extension of territory, the Roman empire was dissolved."[176] The best solution, in Clive's view, was to begin by extending the tenure

---

conquest found no place in the corporate Company mind." This of course depends on how one interprets this corporate "mind." For a typical statement of Company policy that captures the Directors' predicament, see the instructions dispatched from East India House to Fort William on 9 March 1763 in *Fort William–India House Correspondence, III: 1760–1763, ed.* R. R. Sethi (New Delhi: National Archives of India, 1968), p. 188: "for we are by no means desirous of making further Acquisitions or engaging our Forces in very distant projects, unless the most absolute necessity should require it."

[171] Harry Verelst, *A View of the Rise, Progress, and Present State of the English Government in Bengal, Including a Reply to the Misrepresentations of Mr. Bolts, and Other Writers* (London: 1772), p. 55.

[172] *Cavendish Debates of the House of Commons*, I, p. 257.

[173] Ibid., p. 259.

[174] EB, Speech on East India Settlement, 27 February 1769, *W & S*, II, p. 220. Burke later came to see Leadenhall Street as colluding in this discretion, to the disadvantage of the inhabitants of India. See EB to Lord Loughborough, c. 17 March 1796, *Corr.*, VIII, p. 428.

[175] *Cavendish Debates of the House of Commons*, I, p. 262.

[176] Ibid., p. 258. The process is described by J. D. Nichol, "The British in India, 1740–1763: A Study of Imperial Expansion into Bengal" (PhD thesis, University of Cambridge, 1976), pp., 4–5, 304, as "sub-imperialism." For Clive as an exemplar, see Bruce Lenman and Philip Lawson, "Robert Clive, the 'Black Jagir', and British Politics," *Historical Journal*, 26:4 (December 1983), pp. 801–29. For an attempt to connect this process to metropolitan party politics, see James M. Vaughn, "The Politics of Empire: Met-

of the Directors, without which they could not exercise the appropriate influence over their army or control their "civil agents." As a consequence of the distracted state and ineffective authority of the Direction, conquest was inadvertently foisted on the Company by the uncoordinated activities of local avidity and entrepreneurialism. The Proprietors were at loggerheads with the Directors, the Directors in conflict with the servants, and the servants defied by the military officers of the Company.[177] For Grenville, with whom Clive was closely allied at this time, this state of affairs called for parliamentary scrutiny of the Directors, whose tenure should be extended at the same time.[178] A version of this conclusion was pressed by Colebrooke as well: the British could not proclaim sovereignty over the North American colonies whilst remaining merely merchants in the east.[179] But all this must have appeared to Burke as a means of empowering the executive, encroaching upon the corporation as Grenville and Grafton had encroached on the colonies. The Direction was already supervised by the Proprietors, and this scrutiny would deliver the requisite remedies in the east: "Men continually watched by their constituents, it works them into vigour."[180]

Ten years later James Macpherson confidently convicted the East India Company of fundamental defects in the principles of its organisation, focusing on the incapacity of its Directors—their remoteness from the scene of action, their political ineptitude, and the "fugitive" nature of their authority. Vanity prompted them to inflate their political status, which in turn encouraged returning servants to seek a position on the Direction. The result was that the Company was administered by managers consumed by self-regard but devoid of a sense of responsibility. "Thus," he concluded, "the injustice and oppression committed by the servants of the Company in India, instead of being checked by the authority of the Directors, were too frequently encouraged by their approbation."[181] But where others in the late 1760s had raised doubts of a similar nature about the capacity of the Company to regulate its behaviour in Bengal and Madras, Burke saw in the assorted calls for the reform of East Indian affairs a pretext for court aggrandisement at the expense of the public welfare. As he reflected in his *Observations on a Late State of the Nation* around this time, zeal for reform was commonly staked on parliamentary claims to sovereign right, but such declarations of entitlement offered little guidance about the appropriate means to action.[182] A viable scheme of renovation, he observed, had to be conformable to the "true spirit of prior establishments." Such conformity would have to include securing the purpose to which an institution was supposed to answer.

ropolitan Socio-Political Development and the Imperial Transformation of the British East India Company, 1675–1775" (PhD thesis, University of Chicago, 2009).

[177] *Cavendish Debates of the House of Commons*, I, p. 262.

[178] Ibid., p. 267.

[179] Ibid., p. 258.

[180] EB, Speech on East India Settlement, 27 February 1769, *W & S*, II, p. 221.

[181] James Macpherson, *The History and Management of the East India Company from its Origin in 1600 to the Present Times* (London: 1779), p. 161.

[182] EB, *Observations on a Late State of the Nation* (1769), *W & S*, II, p. 175.

In the case of the East India Company, one of its principal uses derived from the support it lent to the stability of public credit. This function meant that government could not unilaterally command its obedience: on the contrary, the state was crucially dependent on the welfare of the Company which, given its position, "stood upon a principle of [its] own"—"distinct from, and in some respects contrary to, the relation between prince and subject." The obligations underwriting the relations between public authority and corporate property thus represented "a new species of contract superimposed upon the old contract of the state."[183] As Burke saw it, the task facing opposition politicians in the late 1760s was therefore one of enabling the Company to secure politically what the ministry sought to bypass: its rightful status as an independent force in negotiations with the government.

Three months after the renewal of the government's 1767 agreement with the East India Company passed in the House of Commons, Rockingham wrote to Burke outlining a proposal for increasing the political effectiveness of the Company.[184] The letter was sent three days after news had reached London of Haidar Ali's invasion of the Carnatic, reportedly coming within sight of the Company's settlement at Fort St. George, at once threatening British interests and causing the value of stock to plummet. Under these circumstances, the Company urgently needed to bolster its credit. Rockingham thought this could best be achieved by composing existing dissensions among the Directors. These divisions had deepened during the preparations for elections to the Court of Directors, extending over a six-month period from October through April 1769.[185] Throughout these months, "Laurence" Sulivan was waging a campaign against those currently in the ascendant in the Directors' Court, supported by the Johnstones and Vansittart, and aided in his ambitions by Lord Shelburne. Meanwhile Colebrooke, a new addition to the Court, was conspiring to dominate its proceedings, provoking intense suspicion among his colleagues—at one moment allying himself with the ministry, then opposing them in parliament in the debate over the Company's petition. At the same time Clive, recently returned from his Governorship of Bengal, was warily backing the Directors. Faced with these divisive struggles, Rockingham strove to secure reconciliation among the protagonists, thereby restoring to the Company a unity of purpose. This would boost its prospects in the context of the present "calamity," but it would also offer the Directors "*permanent* security" against interference from the government.[186]

The bid to effect some kind of coalition among leading figures in the Company soon ended in acrimony, and was overtaken in the wake of the disturbances in southern India by a Company scheme to restore confidence and impose order on the affairs of the subcontinent. This was to be achieved by dispatching a commission of Supervisors to monitor developments on the subcontinent first hand. This plan, as

[183] Ibid.

[184] The Marquess of Rockingham to EB, 31 May 1769, *Corr.*, II, pp. 27–28.

[185] Sutherland, *East India Company Politics*, pp. 182–3.

[186] The Marquess of Rockingham to EB, 31 May 1769, *Corr.*, II, p. 28.

Rockingham noted in a letter to Burke on 9 July 1769, produced its own additional conflicts among the players at East India House.[187] But to distrust among the Directors was added their suspicion of the ministry when the government resolved on what Burke described as its "extraordinary" insistence that its own nominee, the naval captain Sir John Lindsay, be included among the Supervisors to be sent to India.[188] Weymouth took the lead in this proposal, conspiring to have plenipotentiary powers conferred upon Lindsay, enabling him to treat directly with the country powers and bestowing upon him the authority to negotiate with the Nawab of Arcot. [189] Ultimately, Vansittart was appointed one of the three Supervisors, along with Luke Scrafton and Francis Forde, with Lindsay dispatched separately to assist them with their inquiries.[190] The *Aurora*, carrying the Supervisors, never reached its destination, while Lindsay's interference in the administration of East India affairs ended in failure. Grafton's ministry was now approaching its end, with Lord North succeeding him as First Lord of the Treasury in January 1770. The government promptly moved to mollify the ongoing antagonism among Company figures. This cleared the way for the Directors to address themselves to allegations of corruption in Asian affairs, which acquired renewed force after a radical deterioration in the state of Bengal along with the publication of critical accounts of the conduct of the Company under Clive.

7.5 Popular Prejudice and Court Design

Walpole recorded his reaction to conditions in Bengal in his *Memoirs* for 1771. "From the East Indies came bad news," he recalled: "a dreadful famine had depopulated Bengal and swept away multitudes."[191] The problem for the Company was that this development was imputed to the conduct of its own servants—accused, as Walpole went on, of "every species of tyranny and plunder."[192] The principal charges were those of exploitation motivated by the desire to secure gifts and other emoluments from the Country powers, and the illegitimate establishment of private trading monopolies. Walpole's *Last Journals* relates how controversy was particularly stirred by the publication in 1772 of William Bolts's *Considerations on Indian Affairs* and the third volume of Alexander Dow's *History of Hindustan*, both of which charged Clive in particular with misdemeanours in Bengal, exposing Company malpractices to general scrutiny.[193] Nonetheless, the Directors' own attempts to reform the affairs

[187] The Marquess of Rockingham to EB, 9 July 1769, ibid., pp. 48–49.

[188] EB to the Marquess of Rockingham, 13 August 1769, ibid., pp. 54–55.

[189] Bowen, *Revenue and Reform*, pp. 67, 78–79, 82.

[190] Sutherland, *East India Company Politics*, pp. 195–200.

[191] Walpole, *Memoirs*, IV, p. 242.

[192] Ibid.

[193] Walpole, *Last Journals*, I, p. 72. Extracts from Bolts were serialised in the *London Magazine* and the *London Evening Post*: see Bowen, *Revenue and Reform*, p. 95. In a letter to Bolts on 5 May 1786, *Corr.*, V,

of the Company between 1771 and 1772, both as a result of circumstantial pressure and in response to the rising tide of public criticism, largely ended in failure, with the major changes in the administration of the Indian presidencies between 1772 and 1774 being traceable to the efforts of Warren Hastings in Bengal and to the actions of the government in London. The efforts of Hastings were commended to Burke in the summer of 1772 by George Dempster, an independent-minded Rockinghamite active at India House, who noted the Governor's reputation for "good-sense and integrity."[194] At that time, Hastings was endeavouring to implement a series of judicial reforms while revising the system of revenue collection in Bengal.[195] Meanwhile, North's ministry was on the verge of preparing itself to intervene decisively into the management of Asian affairs. The government would soon be obliged, in Walpole's words, to "assist or correct" the Company.[196]

When the "great revolution" in the administration of the Company finally came in the form of North's Regulating Act of 1773, it had largely been provoked by the financial and credit crises of 1772.[197] But this overhaul was preceded by initiatives launched from within the Direction, sometimes loosely concerted with elements in the ministry, to place East Indian arrangements on a more acceptable footing. This began with attempts to reform the recruitment of troops to the Company's forces, which met with effective opposition when it reached the Commons in April 1771.[198] Next, on 30 March the following year, Laurence Sulivan introduced the East India Judicature Bill. The aim here was to bring about a significant reformation: to reconfigure the administration of justice in Bengal, to outlaw participation in trade on the part of the province's Governor and Council, and to increase the control of the Directors over their servants on the subcontinent.[199] However, this measure was scuppered by General Burgoyne's motion to set up a Select Committee to investigate prevalent abuses in the British administration of India. Following the demise of

p. 263, Burke described his book as being "the first that turned the national attention to the state of our affairs in the East Indies." For a more general look at accounts of India in the press in the early 1770s, see Jeremy Osborn, "India and the East India Company in the Public Sphere of Eighteenth-Century Britain" in Huw V. Bowen et al. eds., *The Worlds of the East India Company* (Woodbridge: Boydell, 2002).

194 George Dempster to EB, 4 August 1772, *Corr.*, II, p. 322.

195 For judicial reforms, see B. B. Misra, *The Central Administration of the East India Company, 1773–1834* (Manchester: Manchester University Press, 1959), pp. 229–32; G. R. Gleig ed., *Memoirs of the Life of the Right Honourable Warren Hastings* (London: 1841), 3 vols., I, pp. 263ff. On revenue reform, see Marshall, *Bengal*, pp. 116–24.

196 *The Yale Edition of Horace Walpole's Correspondence*, ed. W. S. Lewis (New Haven, CT: Yale University Press, 1937–83), 48 vols., XXIII, p. 441.

197 The phrase is from *The Annual Register for the Year 1772* (London: 1773), p. 101.

198 A brief outline of Burke's contribution to the debate can be found in the *General Evening Post*, 16 April 1771; a fuller yet very patchy account appears in the Cavendish Diary, Eg. MS. 229, fols. 19–27, 143–55. For the context of the Bill, see Arthur N. Gilbert, "Recruitment and Reform in the East India Company Army, 1760–1800," *Journal of British Studies*, 15:1 (Autumn 1975), pp. 89–111; Huw V. Bowen, "The East India Company and Military Recruitment in Britain, 1763–71," *Bulletin of the Institute of Historical Research*, 59:139 (1986), pp. 78–90.

199 *Parliamentary History*, XVII, cols. 327–8; Bowen, *Revenue and Reform*, pp. 93–101.

the Judicature Bill, there was an attempt to revise the Commission of Supervisors, with Burke approached in late July on Colebrooke's recommendation as the leading candidate for the position, although the precise number of potential appointees had yet to be established.[200] Dempster urged the role upon Burke as offering "a field for Genius[,] probity and Industry." "You will find that country in a singular and almost unprecedented state of Anarchy and Despotism," he warned. Nonetheless, this presented an opportunity for statecraft: "You will have a system of Government to contrive for it and[,] as the Artists say[,] upon a new principle."[201] The offer came to Burke while he was staying at Goodwood with the Duke of Richmond, but he promptly resolved to decline it, informing Colebrooke of his decision on 5 August.[202] Later on, Adam Smith, Adam Ferguson and James Steuart were likewise approached to serve, but none accepted.[203]

Within a month of Burke's decision the cataclysmic state of the Company's finances had become apparent to members of parliament: on 22 September 1772 the Directors informed the Court of Proprietors that a decision on the annual dividend would have to be deferred as they sought an emergency loan from the government to shore up their solvency. This declaration came in the wake of the credit crisis that broke the previous June with the fall of the Scottish banker Alexander Fordyce, spreading to the continent and triggering stagnation and a depression.[204] The situation engendered what Burke termed a "Labyrinth of difficulties" for both the government and the Company.[205] Anticipating how the business of the new parliament would pan out, he expected the Indian crisis to be "our sole employment."[206] The corporation at this point was "shaken to its foundations."[207] Accordingly, after the recess, North moved for the appointment of a Committee of Secrecy to investigate the current straits in which the Company found itself with a view to introducing legislation to ameliorate its predicament.[208] However, first, the government settled on a Bill to restrain temporarily the appointment of Supervisors to be dispatched to India. It was, Burke wrote to Portland, a "monstrous Bill," of a piece with the general attitude of the ministry.[209] Nearly two months earlier, Burke had recognised the "strange state of derangement" in which the Company found itself, afflicted by the

[200] EB to the Duke of Richmond, 4 August 1772, *Corr.*, II, pp. 31–20; Colebrooke, *Reminiscences*, I, p. 99. See also EB to Dowdeswell, 6–7 November 1772, *Corr.*, II, p. 365.

[201] George Dempster to EB, 4 August 1772, *Corr.*, II pp. 321–22.

[202] EB to the Duke of Richmond, 4 August 1772, ibid., p. 320; William Burke to Charles O'Hara, 31 July–1 August 1772, Hoffman, *Burke*, pp. 529–30; Charles O'Hara to EB, 11 September 1772, ibid., pp. 531–34.

[203] *Correspondence of Adam Smith*, ed. Ernest Campbell Mossner and Ian Simpson Ross (Indianapolis, IN: Liberty Fund), pp. 163–4.

[204] Sutherland, *East India Company Politics*, pp. 223–25.

[205] EB to the Marquess of Rockingham, 29 October 1772, *Corr.*, II, p. 354.

[206] Ibid.

[207] EB to John Stewart, 30 October 1772, ibid., p. 358.

[208] EB to the Duke of Richmond, 26 November 1772, ibid., pp. 388.

[209] EB to the Duke of Portland, 18 December 1772, ibid., p. 392.

"unmeaning hostility" of the government.[210] It was "unmeaning" because counterproductive: the ministry was perpetually harrying the corporation, but without a credible plan for resolving its problems. Burke by this time was prepared to concede—"perhaps erroneously"—that there had been "great mistakes and mismanagement" in the Company's conduct.[211] But he could not credit the resolution of the government.

Back in September, Burke had complained to O'Hara about the character of parliamentary proceedings in connection with India. Much alarm had been generated, but then the matter was neglected. "There is nothing deserving to be called Law in that Country," he reminded O'Hara, and yet the attempt to redress the deficiency in the form of the Judicature Bill was conspicuously allowed to lapse in the House of Commons.[212] Burke explained this malaise in terms of the wider constitutional predicament. As he had been at pains to emphasise since the fall of the Rockingham ministry, the court consistently bypassed "the Natural powers and interests of the Country" in favour of "private influence and . . . Cabal."[213] The aristocratic component of the constitution, in other words, was being marginalised by the executive's success in courting popular opinion. Rockingham confirmed Burke in his sense of the clear and mounting danger: "All thinking men must already acknowledge that the influence of the Crown and the means of corruption are become very dangerous to the Constitution and yet the enormous addition of power, which Government are aiming at, by subjecting the E[ast] India Company to their controul, does not strike and alarm so much as it ought."[214] Chatham in due course recognised the domestic threat posed by Asian patronage: "English kings would become moguls . . . we shall have conquered ourselves," he objected to Shelburne.[215] But Rockingham immediately linked the ambitions of the crown to attempts to pillory Company conduct in Bengal. As he observed to Burke, the principal actors with the ear of the closet were prone to "laugh in their sleeve" as popular indignation put the Company in the dock.[216] Burke himself repeated the same sentiment in November: "the designs of the Court coincide exactly with the phrensy of the people."[217] The Asian calamity had become an instrument of impending popular tyranny. How "nearly the Court and the Mob approach one another in their sentiments," as Burke exclaimed to O'Hara.[218]

[210] EB to John Stewart, 30 October 1772, ibid., p. 358.

[211] Ibid., pp. 358–9.

[212] EB to Charles O'Hara, 30 September 1772, ibid., p. 337. It passed its second reading on 4 May, but did not get past examination by Committee on 18 May: *CJ*, XXXIII, p. 736 and pp. 770–71.

[213] EB to Charles O'Hara, 30 September 1772, *Corr.*, II, p. 336.

[214] The Marquess of Rockingham to EB, 24–28 October 1772, ibid., p. 344. On this topic, see W. M. Elofson, "The Rockingham Whigs in Transition: The East India Company Issue, 1772–1773," *English Historical Review*, 104:413 (October 1989), pp. 947–74.

[215] The Earl of Chatham to the Earl of Shelburne, 17 July 1773, *Chatham Correspondence*, IV, p. 285.

[216] The Marquess of Rockingham to EB, 24–28 October 1772, *Corr.*, II, p. 345.

[217] EB to William Dowdeswell, 6–7 November 1772, ibid., p. 365.

[218] EB to Charles O'Hara, 30 September 1772, ibid., p. 336.

There exists a longstanding assumption that Burke's defence of the East India Company against attempts by the crown to intervene in its affairs from 1766 down to 1773 was guided by considerations of either personal or political advantage, steadily giving way to a deepening "humanitarian" concern from around 1775.[219] There are three problems with this presentation of the evidence. First, it assumes, without warrant, that Burke's alarm about what he saw as the court's campaign against the Company can be explained as personally and politically convenient, while his subsequent dismay at East India Company malpractice evidently transcended partisanship. Secondly, the idea of a conversion to a "humanitarian" position does not fit with Burke's avowed principles: his condemnation of abuses in the later 1770s and 1780s was conducted in terms of Christian commitment rather than a norm of secular "humanity."[220] As Burke put the point indignantly to Joshua Reynolds's niece, Mary Palmer, on 19 January 1786, Indian victims of British oppression commanded attention precisely because they could be regarded as "images of the great Pattern."[221] Just under a month earlier, William Burke confessed to Edmund's son that he could not fully fathom his father's depth of concern for "the black primates" of Hindustan.[222] By comparison, defending those who had suffered at the hands of Company rule, Burke was indeed appealing to a common principle of humanity. But, as he had been at pains to emphasise since his assault on the tenets of deism in the 1750s, it was the Christian deity, and not humanitarian sentiment, that underwrote our duty to our fellows.

Finally, Burke's aversion to Company reform before 1777 was not motivated by a desire for political or personal gain at the expense of a commitment to the obligations of imperial rule. Instead, he was opposed to what he saw as the hypocrisy of successive governments using an appeal to charity as a cover for the ambitions of the court. Despite the sound and fury trumpeted against the Company, credible schemes for reform were never developed. On the other hand, executive leverage over the Company and a share in its profits steadily increased. Burke was as committed to the duty that bound the government of India in the period 1766–73 as he was in the period 1777–85. However, complaints against the Company during the first phase of British ministerial intervention into its affairs appeared shrill, personalised and controversial. William Bolts's charges against Clive and the Company had "inflamed

[219] Sutherland, *East India Company Politics*, pp. 58, 367; Holden Furber, "Edmund Burke and India," *Bengal Past and Present: Journal of the Calcutta Historical Society*, 76 (1957), pp. 11–21, esp. p. 14; Cone, *Burke I*, p. 243. Lock, *Burke I*, pp. 237–38.

[220] On the theological roots of "humanitarianism," see Norman Fiering, "Irresistible Compassion: An Aspect of Eighteenth-Century Sympathy and Humanitarianism," *Journal of the History of Ideas*, 37:2 (April–June 1976), pp. 195–218. For the Christianised use of the Roman idea of *humanitas* in the eighteenth century, see Laurence Dickey, "Doux-Commerce and Humanitarian Values: Free Trade, Sociability and Universal Benevolence in Eighteenth-Century Thinking," *Grotiana*, 22/23 (2001–2), pp. 271–318.

[221] EB to Joshua Reynolds, 19 January 1786, *Corr.*, V, p. 255.

[222] Chatham Papers, TNA, PRO 30/8/118, fol. 123, cited in P. J. Marshall, "Introduction" to idem ed., *W & S*, V, p. 11.

the nation" by means of "what may at least be call'd a partial representation."[223] Even so, Burke did not deny the existence of malpractice. Instead, he pleaded for a credible method of redress.

Launching his motion for a Select Committee on East Indian affairs on 13 April 1772, General Burgoyne inveighed against "the most atrocious abuses that ever stained the name of civil government."[224] In the ensuing debate, Burke recognised that Company business in India had been administered by means of "discretionary power," and that discretion of the kind was always liable to abuse: "This has been the case," he affirmed, "with the East-India Company."[225] But had parliament or the Ministry ever truly sought reform? The King's Speech at the opening of the new session on 21 January 1772 had drawn attention to the "danger" that proceeded from the government of remote places, and yet Clive, two months later, could remind his audience in the Commons how nothing in reality had been done.[226] Government had refused to address how the Company's charter might be rendered fit for purpose. Indeed, from the start, their sole concern had been with "the immediate division of the loaves and fishes."[227] Burke had suspected as much since 1766 and, by the end of 1772, during the final day of debate on the Bill to restrain the Company's plan to send new Supervisors into the East, he charged the government with "improvidence" and parliament with "short-sightedness" in not forming a system of administration suitable to the constitution of a commercial monopoly.[228] "They pretended reformation, and they meant nothing but plunder," Burke exclaimed.[229]

In practice government countenanced mismanagement: "Session after session had passed away and they took no one step in the Business."[230] The directors had been left without the means of controlling their servants, the system of revenue collection had been instituted without any check upon its proceedings, and a tyrannical scheme of "double government" had been permitted to continue in the Carnatic, while Westminster pressed exclusively for the seizure of territorial revenue. As the ministry derided the authority of the Company, Burke fretted that the Ganges would pour forth "a new tide of corruption" as the control of East India offices fell to the crown. "I dread," Burke declared melodramatically, "the infection of that place . . . Was it not the sudden plunder of the East that gave the final blow to the

[223] EB, Debate on Judicature Bill, 30 March 1772, Cavendish Diary, Eg. MSS., 239, fol. 263.

[224] *Parliamentary History*, XVII, col. 454.

[225] *W & S*, II, p. 372, as reported in the *London Magazine*, and reprinted in *Parliamentary History*, XVII, cols. 461–63.

[226] 21 January 1772, *Parliamentary History*, col. 233.

[227] Ibid., 30 March 1772, col. 363.

[228] Ibid., 8 December 1772, col. 672.

[229] EB, Speech on East India Restraining Bill, 18 December 1772, *W & S*, II, p. 378. Cf. Burke on the Regulating Bill, WWM BkP 9:17: "The very grievances w[hich] first inflamed you to this disdain will be them that remain unredressed." This remained Burke's verdict until the end: it still constituted a core complaint in EB, *Ninth Report of the Select Committee* (25 June 1783), *W & S*, V, p. 221.

[230] EB, Speech on East India Restraining Bill, 18 December 1772, *W & S*, II, p. 380. Cf. Burke's intervention on the Regulating Bill, 10 June 1773, Cavendish Diary, Eg. MS., 250, fols. 215–16.

freedom of Rome?"[231] In the same idiom, Alexander Dalrymple had warned three years earlier that Roman liberty had fallen prey to "Asiatic conquests."[232] Yet Thomas Pownall drew the opposite conclusion: the conquest of the east brought an opportunity to extend the empire of liberty, as the Romans had done after their victories over Illyria and Macedonia. He cited Livy to make his point: Roman arms brought freedom to the enslaved, "non liberis seruitutem."[233] To achieve this, he argued, the government should act as what he termed a "state-holder," which meant retaining "executive power and command of the army" while presiding over the "establishment and execution of the civil officers." However it was precisely this prospect that Burke feared, and the new year made his nightmare a reality.

The opening session of 1773 was crowded with East India business. The third report of the Committee of Secrecy was published on 9 February, the previous two reports having appeared on 7 and 17 December. A series of Resolutions setting out the terms for a loan of £1,400,000 to the Company to help resolve its current financial difficulties were debated in March and laid before the House on 27 April.[234] Meanwhile, the revelations publicised by Burgoyne's Select Committee continued to cause a stir, leading to a debate on the Committee's reports on 10 May. Resolutions on these reports introduced ten days later produced ructions in the Commons, focusing attention on the culpability of Clive, and dividing the ministry and opposition alike. The loan to the Company was to be conditional upon the due regulation of the affairs of the Company, and so the ministry set about preparing a Bill for the reform of its administration. Resolutions to that effect were ready by 3 May. These were incorporated into the Regulating Bill, introduced at the end of the month, which finally became law on 21 June.[235] The Act provided for the extension of the tenure of Directors to four years; restrictions on voting qualifications among the Proprietors; the reform of the judicial system in Bengal, including the appointment by the crown of three judges and a Chief Justice to a Supreme Court; and the creation of a Governor General with authority over all three Indian presidencies, along with a council of four, all appointed by parliament in the first instance. These provisions were intended as an emergency remedy that would be revisited when the East

[231] 18 December 1772, *Parliamentary History*, cols. 672–3. On the theme of the threat posed by the east to western empires in the context of debates about the future of the East India Company, see P. J. Marshall, *The Making and Unmaking of Empires: Britain, India, and America, c. 1750–1783* (Oxford: Oxford University Press, 2005), p. 197; on the general concern with the comparative fortunes of Roman imperial history, see Anthony Pagden, *Lords of All the World: Ideologies of Empire in Spain, Britain and France, 1500–1800* (New Haven, CT: Yale University Press, 1997).

[232] Alexander Dalrymple, *Vox Populi, Vox Dei: Lord Weymouth's Appeal to a General Court of India Proprietors Considered* (London: 1769), p. 12. On Dalrymple and his connection to the Rockinghams, see Asma Ahmad, "The British Enlightenment and Ideas of Empire in India, 1756–1773" (PhD thesis, University of London, 2005), ch. 4.

[233] Thomas Pownall, *The Right, Interest, and Duty of the State, as Concerned in the Affairs of the East Indies* (London: 1773), p. 47, citing Livy, *Ab urbe condita*, XLV, 18, 1–3: "not servitude to the free."

[234] Subsequently embodied in the Loan Act of 13 Geo. III, c. 64.

[235] 13 Geo. III, c. 63.

India charter came up for renewal in seven years' time. "The session is ended," Burke wrote with resignation to the Committee of Correspondence of the New York General Assembly on 2 July: "The East India Companys [*sic*] Political and Financial Affairs are put into the hands of the Crown."[236]

The session was indeed over, but the legislation had yet to be given practical effect. Anticipating its implementation, Burke expected still more "infractions" of the Company's charter along with "further additions to the power of the Crown."[237] However, these would hardly remedy the disorders in East Indian politics, which could only be plausibly checked by the Court of Proprietors.[238] In the end, the "ragged scaffolding" of the ministry's new regulations would stand as "a monument to the folly of the Builders."[239] Burke itemised the grievances against Company misdemeanours as amounting to the corrupt receipt of gifts, the exploitation of private monopolies, abuses in the management of the revenue, and evidence of "Anarchy & Military Violence" in the provinces.[240] According to him, the government's position was that each of these malpractices could be attributed to the constitutional organisation of the Company and its inability to exercise power effectively.[241] Yet from the start Burke had disputed this diagnosis.[242] Abuses, however exaggerated, could not be denied; it was also true that they arose from discretionary authority.[243] But what this called for was an extension of the Company's lawful powers embodied in the clauses of a new charter. Burke had formulated this position most clearly back in 1772. In his Speech on the East India Select Committee of 13 April in that year, he complained that a system of arbitrary government had been foisted upon the Company by the failure of successive ministries to compose a "comprehensive and well-digested code of laws" by means of which the Directors could regulate their governors, who in turn could keep their servants in awe of their legitimate instructions: "Where no laws exist, men must be arbitrary; and very necessary acts of government will often be . . . represented by the interested and malevolent as instances of wanton oppression."[244] By reconstituting the legal framework for the manage-

[236] EB to the Committee of Correspondence for the New York Assembly, 2 July 1773, *Corr.*, II, p. 442.

[237] Ibid.

[238] EB, Speech on East India Regulating Bill, 10 June 1773, *W & S*, II, p. 395.

[239] WWM BkP 9:17.

[240] Ibid., 27.

[241] Ibid.

[242] See, for example, Burke's contribution to the debate on the Judicature Bill, 30 March 1772, Cavendish Diary, Eg. MS., 239, fol. 265: "I deny th[at] Now, Sir, with regard to the impossibility of Traders governing."

[243] As late as 1789 Burke would maintain that some of the abuses of 1772 had been exaggerated. See EB, Speech on Sixth Article: Presents, 21 April 1789, *W & S*, VII, p. 42.

[244] EB, Speech on East India Select Committee, 13 April 1772, *W & S*, II, p. 373.

ment of Company affairs, it would be possible to "cure its corruption [and] punish its delinquents," but without inflating the discretion of the crown.[245]

The alarming aggrandisement of the patronage of the court was being brought about in Burke's view by "a strange Revolution in our Ideas."[246] The spectacle of East Indian wealth had brought with it a derangement of social attitudes and national cohesion. The higher ranks of society had grown supine, while the vulgar were easily seduced.[247] Most disturbingly, all ranks were disposed to envy in the face of an influx of conspicuous luxury. The result was, as Burke saw it, that the nobility was inclined to regard the claims of the Company indignantly as an "exaltation of Plebeian insolence," while the lower and middling orders grew to resent nabob prosperity as the harbinger of a diminution in their relative standing.[248] This combination of attitudes had succeeded in corrupting national judgment as "Popular prejudice & Court design" corroborated one another.[249] As a consequence of this, legislation was bereft of deliberative wisdom and moderation, being reduced to executive decrees supported by corrupted popular sentiment. Seeking to characterise this arrangement in the debate on the Restraining Bill on 18 December 1772, Burke illustrated his point by resort to Aristotle, an author who, apparently, is "more spoken of than read."[250] It was equivalent, Burke claimed, to government by popular decrees (*psephismata*), which accelerated "the ruin of every state."[251] This was a form of polity, as Aristotle had argued in Book IV of the *Politics*, in which the multitude (*to plethos*) are supreme (*kurion*) and supersede the law by their *psephismata*.[252] Burke's point was subtle: a court governing without an independent aristocracy amounted to a popular tyranny. It marked the point at which monarchy and democracy blended into one another. This amalgamation was a recipe for imperial tyranny, which would compromise the legitimacy of British authority in the east.

From his earliest interventions into the debate on the legal status of the East India Company in the 1760s to his final, angry indictment of the conduct of Warren Hastings in the 1790s, Burke defended the legitimacy of the British conquest of Asian territories. He was, by extension, a defender of the rights of the British Empire in the east. Reflecting on the enormous acquisition of wealth that had attended that process, Burke conjectured that there was "something of a divine providence in it."[253] Intimations of providence, however, were not sufficient to justify the entitlement to

[245] EB, Speech on East India Restraining Bill, 7 December 1772, Cavendish Diary, Eg. MS., 242, fol. 100.

[246] WWM BkP 9:41.

[247] EB, Speech on North's East India Resolutions, 5 April 1773, *W & S*, II, p. 392.

[248] WWM BkP 9:40. Cf. EB to Charles O'Hara, 20 August 1773, *Corr.*, II, p. 452: the Commons "voted down the East India Company out of Envy."

[249] WWM BkP 9:40.

[250] *Parliamentary History*, XVII, col. 673.

[251] Ibid., where *psephismata* is mistranscribed as "*phephismata*."

[252] Aristotle, *Politics*, 1292a5–10.

[253] EB, Proceedings against Clive, 21 May 1773, Cavendish Diary, Eg. MS., 248, fol. 261.

rule. Nonetheless, Burke did vindicate the rightfulness of the acquisitions that had been made. Bengal had been secured by right of conquest, which in practice meant that British sovereignty had been established by right of war. From the perspective of civil government, such a right wore the appearance of a violent crime. But in the context of military engagement such apparent criminality was a necessary act of power. It therefore made no sense to question a title to rule by exposing the violence of its origins.[254] "I will venture to say", Burke contended in defence of Clive on 21 May 1773, that "no nation ever formed a tribunal to sit and inquire by what Crimes it was they acquired an augmentation of their empire."[255] A veil of silence should be drawn over the original assertion of might, with each bloody manifestation of force consigned to oblivion. Likewise, as Athenian and Roman precedent recommended, the perpetrators of violence should be pardoned by "acts of amnesty."[256] What counted was what could be expected from a new institution of power, and whether its acts were likely to be checked by just procedures. Yet there was no reason to believe that ministerial usurpation of Company prerogatives was a vehicle for increasing the accountability of British rule. As Burke argued in connection with North's Regulating Bill, only dire "necessity" or manifest "delinquency" could justify the violation of corporate prerogatives.[257] As things appeared in the summer of 1773, neither criterion could plausibly be invoked as a pretext for depriving the East India Company of its legitimately acquired dominion.

Responding to a letter from Adrian Heinrich von Borcke, the son of Frederick the Great's distinguished chancellor, inquiring about the prospects for East India stock in January 1774, Burke commented on the complexity of recent Asian affairs compared with the days in which the Company was confined to "moderate commerce."[258] Since then, domestic political contention had spilled over into the management of the Empire, which was in turn embroiled in the intricate politics of Europe and the subcontinent. This situation was burdened by the finances of the Company, which recently stood on "the precipice of general bankruptcy": ironically, a "monopoly of the most lucrative trades, and the possession of imperial revenues" had brought the government to the "verge of beggary and ruin."[259] Burke could see one advantage arising out of these difficulties. The sheer "Magnitude of this Object," the scale of responsibility resulting from newly acquired dominion over millions, meant that the issues that it threw up could no longer be hidden from view. Almost everything connected with the Company had become "very publick," and public-

[254] On this, see Paul Lucas, "On Edmund Burke's Doctrine of Prescription; Or, an Appeal from the New to the Old Lawyers," *Historical Journal*, 11:1 (1968), pp. 35–63. See also, crucially, EB, *Letter to Richard Burke* (February 1792), *W & S*, IX, pp. 653–57.

[255] EB, Proceedings against Clive, 21 May 1773, Cavendish Diary, Eg. MS., 248, fol. 254.

[256] Ibid., fols. 260–61. Cf. EB, Speech on East India Select Committee, 13 April 1772, *W & S*, II, pp. 373–74.

[257] WWM BkP 9:17.

[258] EB to Adrian Heinrich von Borcke, post 17 January 1774, *Corr.*, II, p. 513.

[259] EB, *Speech on American Taxation* (19 April 1774), *W & S*, II, p. 416.

ity would provoke debate about the fundamentals of imperial government.[260] Three years later, events in Madras would draw Burke into East India business once more, a subject that would then pursue him to the grave. His estimation of the gravity of Company delinquency would certainly change, but his assessment of the failures of North's Regulating Act would remain, together with his doubts about the government's determination to place the management of Asia on a viable constitutional footing.

[260] EB to Adrian Heinrich von Borcke, post 17 January 1774, *Corr.*, II, p. 513.

Figure 3. Burke at the start of the American War in the guise of Ulysses guides his companion (the artist, James Barry) to safety by calmly admonishing caution.
James Barry, *Ulysses and a Companion Fleeing from the Cave of Polyphemus* (1776), Crawford Art Gallery, Cork.

PART IV

Conquest, Conciliation and Representation, 1774–1785

OVERVIEW

Burke's character has been commonly presented as an amalgamation of passion and prudence. Reviewing Robert Southey's *Colloquies* on the progress of society in 1830, Thomas Babington Macaulay depicted the statesman as choosing his side "like a fanatic" while defending it "like a philosopher."[1] The eleven years covered by the fourth part of this book extend from the beginning of the fourteenth parliament into the first year of the sixteenth. They were dominated, in the first instance, by the government of Lord North, which lasted from January 1770 until March 1782. They were followed by a succession of short-lived administrations—the second Rockingham ministry for four months, Shelburne's for the following seven and the Fox–North Coalition for a further eight—before the accession of William Pitt the Younger in 1784. Burke occupied the position of paymaster of the forces under Rockingham and then again under North and Fox, his only experience of office before returning to opposition. His fortunes in this period were mixed: he rose to a position of authority during his years as MP for Bristol yet was subject to bouts of ridicule after the election of 1784. Still, throughout this time he was recognised as a thoroughly achieved orator, having spoken in well over 200 debates in his first nine years in the Commons. He had demonstrated a complete set of abilities: meticulous preparation, ready wit, tactical intelligence, artfulness, vehemence, and force of delivery.[2] Some of these attributes can be glimpsed in the speeches that Burke carefully

[1] Thomas Babington Macaulay, "Southey's Colloquies on Society" (1830) in idem, *Critical and Miscellaneous Essays* (Philadelphia, PA: 1843–44), 5 vols., I, p. 284.

[2] There is a neat description in Paul Langford, "Edmund Burke" in *Oxford Dictionary of National Biography* (Oxford: Oxford University Press, 2004), 60 vols. Fur a fuller exploration, see Paddy Bullard, *Edmund Burke and the Art of Rhetoric* (Cambridge: Cambridge University Press, 2011).

reworked for publication between 1774 and 1785, from his famous interventions on conciliation with America to his searing attack on the Nawab of Arcot's debts.[3] Fanaticism and philosophy were indeed recurrent traits. Yet Macaulay's representation might usefully be reversed: Burke adopted his positions with due deliberation before proceeding to defend them with fervent passion.

Burke sat as a member for Bristol for six years from 1774. In that time, his command of the political problems facing the British Empire deepened. Relations with the colonies continued to deteriorate, erupting into conflict in 1775. During the following years he strenuously opposed the conduct of the war, gradually reappraising how imperial relations could best be structured. When he lost his seat for Bristol in September 1780, victory against America looked forlorn, and within a year the siege of Yorktown sealed the fate of British forces. Nonetheless, even as late as the peace negotiations that ensued, Burke hoped that the former colonies would play some role within the Empire. However, it was immediately apparent that separation would be complete. By this stage, as he lamented the loss of empire in the west, Burke's involvement in the affairs of India became a major preoccupation. In 1773 he had supported reforming the Company by extending its legal powers. Within a decade he saw that it was government by the corporation that had failed. Westminster, he concluded, would have to intervene. This did not involve abandoning his commitment to chartered rights nor developing a new account of the conditions under which they should be forfeited. From the start Burke had accepted that national sovereignty should prevail over the entitlements of subordinate jurisdictions in the Empire. At the same time he believed that supreme authority should relinquish its powers in the interest of protecting the rights of corporate property. Yet he also thought that this arrangement ought to be overruled where a dependent administration like the East India Company had violated the fundamental rights of man.

Burke began to see the Company as radically delinquent after he immersed himself in the affairs of Madras from the late 1770s. By the early 1780s, on account of his role on the parliamentary Select Committee charged with investigating abuses on the subcontinent, his grasp of the systematic nature of the problem was at once detailed and profound. Burke recognised that loss of confidence in the prospects for colonial representation caused the breach that led to the conflict between Westminster and the American provinces. He now saw that the Indian provinces were bereft of representation of any kind. In grasping what Burke meant here, it is important to appreciate that "representation" had a range of meanings in eighteenth-century parlance, extending from the idea of being answerable to an electorate to the figure of an unelected recipient of popular trust. According to Burke, a regime that failed to represent in any sense was illegitimate: it disregarded the interests of the people whom it ruled. As the British experience of America had shown, representative government required popular conciliation. Since in the colonies electoral or "actual"

[3]On the rhetorical characteristics of the published writings, see Christopher Reid, *Edmund Burke and the Practice of Political Writing* (Dublin: Gill and Macmillan, 1985).

representation existed in the form of local assemblies, Burke proposed that conciliation ought to include investing provincial legislatures with credible fiscal powers. But he believed that even in the absence of elected deputies governments should be representative in a more general sense. They were entrusted with the duty of "virtual" representation, which meant sympathizing with the people whom they ruled. Later in his career, Burke struggled to coax parliament to sympathise with Indians and thought of mechanisms that might be devised for ensuring that it would. The East India Company, however, was another matter: its servants seemed to Burke to be systematically incapable of identifying with its subjects since their corporate interest forced them to pursue the Company's profit irrespective of the consequences for the local population. For this reason, the corporation was disposed to behave like a conqueror in Asia instead of striving to conciliate the manners and opinions of the people.

As Burke arrived at this conclusion in the early 1780s conditions in Ireland were steadily improving for Roman Catholics. This was partly a product of the mood of toleration that animated politics at Westminster. In the 1770s, the influence of this attitude began to be felt in Dublin: in 1778 and again 1782, relief was granted from the most aggravating of the popery laws. During the same period, a range of Irish trade restrictions were lifted under pressure from agitation orchestrated by the Volunteers. Introduced in the context of the American crisis, these religious and commercial reforms had not resulted from regular procedures that gave voice to either the Protestant or Catholic populations. As a result, in 1782, Protestant Ireland demanded legislative independence from Britain. With Catholics excluded from parliament and the vote, this left them without any electoral means of promoting their agenda. More importantly, as Burke would later argue, the Irish establishment was ill disposed to provide them with even virtual representation. This was largely a consequence of the residual spirit of conquest that guided the politics of the ascendancy in Ireland. The situation was likely to continue without remedy as long as Catholics were deprived of actual representation. Throughout the decade between 1774 and 1784, the strength of Burke's attachment to electoral politics was in evidence. He was forced to explain his commitment in the context of what he saw as a range of challenges to effective representation in Britain, beginning with arguments in favour of instructions for MPs and ending with claims to a natural right to representation in the people. Both proposals, Burke believed, would subvert the constitution. The British system of government certainly called for reform, but Burke was anxious that reform should not be a pretext for revolution.

VIII

REPRESENTATION AND REFORM

BRITAIN AND IRELAND, 1774–1784

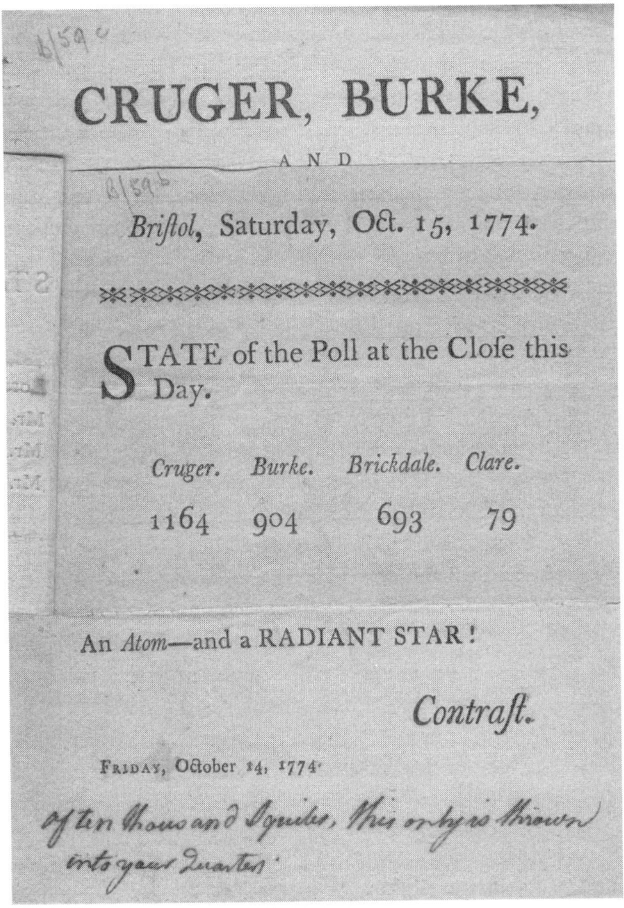

CRUGER, BURKE,

AND

Briſtol, Saturday, Oct. 15, 1774.

STATE of the Poll at the Cloſe this Day.

Cruger.	*Burke.*	*Brickdale.*	*Clare.*
1164	904	693	79

An *Atom*—and a RADIANT STAR!

Contraſt.

FRIDAY, October 14, 1774.

of ten thousand Squibs, this only is thrown into your Quarters.

Figure 4. Results of the Bristol Poll, 1774. Beinecke Library, Yale.

8.1 Introduction

In sitting as a member of parliament for a populous commercial city, Burke was forced to think seriously about his obligations as a representative. In doing so he could draw on his experience in the House of Commons as well as on his efforts in mobilizing opinion out of doors. Immediately following his election in 1774, the propriety of acting on instructions from constituents was raised on the hustings. Burke thought about the issue in broad constitutional terms: it touched on the relationship between the Commons and the constituencies as well as the role of election under a mixed system of government. By 1779, Burke's energies were more deeply absorbed in constitutional reform. The increase in the debt on the civil list as well as the patronage afforded by the American war were contributing to the growth of the power of the crown. In response, Burke emphasized the need for economy as a means of redress: the volume of pensions should be diminished, defunct places discontinued, and sinecures in the gift of the king brought to an end. However, before long, Burke's extra-parliamentary collaborators in the cause of "economical" reform were pushing for measures he believed would undermine the constitution. By 1780, conflict with the colonies was reaching the apogee of crisis, discontent in Ireland was contributing to popular militancy, and public protest was affecting confidence in the British system of government. Shorter parliaments were advocated along with manhood suffrage. The commitment to a more equal representation spread. Yet for Burke proposals of the kind were merely tokens of innovation often inspired by incoherent ideas about natural rights in politics.

Writing about the enlightenment in 1971, Franco Venturi contrasted the relationship between ideas and politics in England with philosophical activists seeking reform on the continent.[1] In the rest of Europe, *philosophes* were independently or "autonomously" organised and thereby freed from the institutional influence of religion. Partly as a consequence of this, in France in particular, political and theological criticism was directed against traditional arrangements in ecclesiology and government.[2] However in England, if not Scotland, the situation appeared to be different. On Venturi's understanding, based largely on the political sociology of Lewis Namier, government was structured around an oligarchy of interests without reference to ideas, doctrines or principles. Under these circumstances, a "parti des philosophes" had no coherent *raison d'être*. Accordingly, Venturi concluded, political reform played a comparatively negligible role in the national culture.[3] Yet in fact competing principles pervaded public discussion and reform was a permanent

[1]Franco Venturi, *Utopia and Reform in the Enlightenment* (Cambridge: Cambridge University Press, 1971), pp. 126ff.

[2]Derek Beales, *Enlightenment and Reform in Eighteenth-Century Europe* (London and New York: I. B. Tauris, 2005, 2011), pp. 60ff.

[3]Venturi, *Utopia and Reform*, pp. 132–34.

feature of political life in Britain. For Burke, a vital objective of criticism was ensuring that reform contributed to the progress of society rather than the disintegration of existing institutions that facilitated moral and political improvement. With the introduction of ideas of personal representation into debates about parliamentary reform from the late 1770s, Burke believed that British politics was toying with the means of its destruction. The appeal of individual representation derived from the idea of a natural right to self-government. Civil society, however, was founded on the surrender of that right, substituting trust in government for pre-political self-mastery.

As his intervention in 1781 into debate on the British treatment of St. Eustatius showed, Burke recognised that while government might have its origin in subjugation, the act of conquest should be aimed at conservation. For this reason, where one people was in a position to subject another to its authority the rights of war were immediately succeeded by the obligations of trust. Therefore, although political society was premised on the relinquishment of self-government, governors had a duty to represent the governed. Under the British constitution, elected members of parliament comprised that portion of the representative system that was peculiarly sensitive to the wishes of the people. Nonetheless, as Burke saw it, the House of Commons was not comprised of delegates from the constituencies. Instead, it was a deliberative forum that had to reconcile two duties: first, it was responsible for channeling popular sentiment; but second, it was also charged with serving the common good. Any political system should be judged on its ability to reconcile these potentially discordant purposes. Rulers were there to obey the inclinations of the ruled, but also to judge how their interests could best be advanced. This required them to moderate popular fury, which was usually aroused by a clash of opinion concerning religion or by resentment over the unequal distribution of wealth. In 1780 the Gordon riots displayed the consequences of blind rage as well as the role of representatives in curbing mob enthusiasm. During his tenure in Bristol, Burke similarly felt obliged to oppose patriotic fervor against the Americans as well as mercantile support for trade restrictions in the Empire.

Burke was particularly concerned about restrictions imposed on Irish trade. For example, in 1779, he supported commercial concessions on the export of Irish wool. In 1785, as Pitt moved to introduce a system of free trade in the form of a series of commercial propositions, Burke still favoured a plan of liberalization, though he demanded that this should cater to ongoing British fears. National sentiment could never be disregarded even if it required leadership and guidance. Religious prejudice presented the clearest example of the need for moderation. Imperial policy in India favoured a regime of toleration. The Irish parliament was encouraged in the same direction by Westminster. In 1778, the right to hold leases on property for 999 years was granted as a concession to Roman Catholics. Relief was then extended in 1782. From Burke's perspective, the political process had succeeded in correcting popular bigotry. Under the regime of anti-popery legislation in Ireland, the dictates of conscience were employed as a pretext for the exercise of communal power.

However, the use of authority to support prejudice in effect replicated popery, which the penal laws were at least nominally designed to eliminate. On the whole, Burke accepted that reforming government had to be answerable to the feelings of the people but he also believed it should protect them from the consequences of their folly.

8.2 Bristol

The parliamentary session of 1774 ended on 22 June. A dissolution, followed by an election, was generally expected. The fourteenth parliament beckoned, so Burke was forced to prepare for his return to the House of Commons. However, with Lord Verney's financial affairs in an increasingly precarious state, Burke would be obliged to relinquish his seat at Wendover. William Burke would likewise be forced to give up Great Bedwyn, and would in fact never sit in parliament again. Edmund was altogether more fortunate. On 28 June 1774, Thomas Wilson, an associate of Wilkes, wrote to Burke about the prospect of his representing "the second city in the kingdom," namely Bristol.[4] The sitting representatives, Viscount Clare and Matthew Brickdale, had fallen from grace due to their support for North's policy in the colonies.[5] For the previous two elections, a pact had awarded the Bristol seats to a Tory and a Whig candidate. As the crisis in America deepened, Henry Cruger, a well-connected American merchant living in the city, decided to oppose one of the sitting members.[6] The Boston Port Bill, which threatened to blockade New England trade, had passed into law on 31 March 1774. Burke's famous speech on American Taxation was delivered towards the end of the following month. As he spoke, the volume of the Bristol trade to New York, Philadelphia, the Carolinas and Virginia was in decline, and manufacturing output was being seriously affected.[7] If political relations failed to improve, imports were expected to fall by the end of the summer, depriving Bristol of access to tobacco, sugar, molasses, rum, coffee and hemp. The slave trade, conducted by British ships sailing from West Africa to the West Indies, also looked forward to disruption.[8] The state of Bristol qualified as a national affair. By 1770, the annual customs receipts for the city amounted to £200,000; the excise contributed half that amount again.[9] "A Contest in a place of that Magnitude is a

[4]Reverend Dr. Thomas Wilson to EB, 28 June 1774, *Correspondence* (1844), I, p. 465.

[5]Claude Nugent, *A Memoir of Robert, Earl Nugent* (London: 1898).

[6]A. Everett Peterson, "Henry Cruger" in the *Dictionary of American Biography* (New York: Scribner's, 1928–36), 20 vols.; Henry C. Van Schaack, *Henry Cruger: The Colleague of Edmund Burke in Parliament* (New York: 1859).

[7]John Latimer, *The Annals of Bristol in the Eighteenth Century* (London: 1893); Ernest Barker, *Burke and Bristol: A Study of the Relations between Burke and His Constituents during the Years 1774–1780* (Bristol: J. W. Arrowsmith: 1931).

[8]C. M. MacInnes, "Bristol and the Slave Trade" in Patrick McGrath ed., *Bristol in the Eighteenth Century* (Newton Abbot: David and Charles, 1972).

[9]Kenneth Morgan, *Bristol and the Atlantic Trade in the Eighteenth Century* (Cambridge: Cambridge University Press, 1993), p. 23.

serious Affair," Burke wrote to Wilson.[10] Victory was sure to enhance his standing in the party, as well as his authority in the House of Commons.

While Burke's Bristol backers were canvassing on his behalf, Wilkes supporters at Westminster were soliciting his candidacy. Westminster had three seats and about 9,000 electors–the City of London had 6,000, and Bristol about 5,000.[11] While Westminster's "popular party" was approaching Burke, Charles Stanhope, styled Lord Mahon, was also contesting a seat.[12] In the *Public Advertiser* on 15 September he set out his credentials: he would support "Revolution Principles"; oppose "influence" at elections; seek the repeal of the Quebec Act, which gave a boost to "Popery"; and renounce the Septennial Act so as to "strengthen and increase the due and necessary Relation between Representative and Constituent."[13] Writing to Rockingham, Burke snubbed the "illiberal Tone" of the Mahon manifesto as indicating the demotic appeal on which his candidacy was based.[14] Burke's own chances, he soon recognised, were not strong, but the opening at Bristol still remained. On 2 October, Rockingham assured Burke that his presence at parliament was "necessary," and offered him the security of one of his own seats.[15] By then, Richard Champion, a merchant with a growing interest in porcelain manufacture, had clarified the opportunity at Bristol. The gentlemen of the town might still support the incumbents, but the tradesmen and manufactures were openly discontented and could probably be brought to vote for Cruger and Burke. In addition, Champion wrote, the "graver Sort among the Dissenters would indisputably declare for you."[16]

On Tuesday 11 October 1774, Burke was elected for Malton. By that stage, Lord Clare had withdrawn his candidacy at Bristol, opening the way for Burke. Richard Champion duly nominated him on 8 October, a day after the poll was officially opened, while Burke was still up north. His brother Richard went south to take charge of the Bristol campaign, writing to Shackleton on the eleventh to inform him of Burke's Quaker support.[17] As Richard wrote, Burke was preparing to travel to the busy scene of the election. He breakfasted with Rockingham on his way south, reaching Bristol on the afternoon of Thursday 13 October.[18] Rockingham communicated his awareness of the "weight and importance" of Bristol in a letter sent to

[10] EB to Dr. Thomas Wilson, 1 July 1774, *Corr.*, III, p. 3.

[11] P. T. Underdown, "Henry Cruger and Edmund Burke: Colleagues and Rivals at the Bristol Election of 1774," *William and Mary Quarterly*, 15:1 (January 1958), pp. 14–34, p. 15.

[12] EB to the Marquess of Rockingham, 18 September 1774, *Corr.*, III, p. 29. Stanhope's association with the Chathamites particularly repelled Burke.

[13] *Public Advertiser*, 15 September 1774.

[14] EB to the Marquess of Rockingham, 18 September 1774, *Corr.*, III, p. 29.

[15] The Marquess of Rockingham to EB, 2 October 1774, ibid., p. 48. Rockingham controlled two seats at Malton in Yorkshire and one at Higham Ferrers in Northamptonshire. He alerted Burke to an opening at Malton three days later: see the Marquess of Rockingham to EB, 5 October 1774, ibid., p. 56.

[16] Richard Champion to EB, 1 October 1774, ibid., p. 47.

[17] Richard Burke Sr. to Richard Shackleton, 11 October 1774, ibid., p. 65.

[18] The Marquess of Rockingham to EB, 17 October 1774, ibid., p. 66.

Burke's wife on the twenty-sixth.[19] By the middle of the eighteenth century, there were 40,000 residents in the city, rising to 64,000 by 1801.[20] The town itself had retained its shape as a medieval walled city, although with its narrow streets intermixing workshops and housing, and peopled with merchants, manufactures, shipwrights and hauliers, it exuded the spirit of modern commercial bustle. Catherine Macaulay and Josiah Tucker were among its more prominent residents.[21] Burke's speech on his arrival in the city extolled its national importance as "a main pillar in the commercial interest of Great-Britain."[22] A handbill reported his intention to focus his efforts on the "Welfare of Commerce."[23] In this way, Burke avoided the "popular" causes which Cruger was making his own.[24] Instead, he sought to capitalize on fears about trade being heightened by the colonial dispute.[25] A "great crisis in our affairs" was fast approaching, he contended, whose origins lay in "our unhappy contest with America."[26] He looked down upon current events as from a great precipice. The spectacle beneath was discouraging, not least since the various plans for resolving the ongoing dispute failed to offer coherent remedial action. Burke invoked the Declaratory Act to signal his devotion to the metropolitan welfare, championing the "necessary constitutional superiority of Great-Britain."[27] In his usual manner, he defended imperial supremacy as compatible with American liberty.

The contest at Bristol lasted for twenty-three days, with the poll finally closing on 3 November. Cruger took first place in the election with over 3,500 votes. Burke led over Brickdale by 251 votes. He wrote to his sister with pride, breaking the fresh news: "The Election lasted a month . . . This is the second City in the Kingdom; and to be invited, and chosen for it without any request of mine, at no expence to myself . . . is an honour."[28] The following day, he issued a handbill thanking his electors, promising to promote "to the best of my judgment, the true interests of those from whom it is derived."[29] Brickdale planned to petition against the validity of the result, though ultimately his strategy would fail. Burke did not return to Beaconsfield until the evening of 18 November. In the intervening period, he was absorbed in post-election celebrations, before travelling first to Bath and then to Oxford, where

[19] The Marquess of Rockingham to Jane Burke, 17 October 1774, ibid., p. 68.

[20] Walter Minchinton, "The Port of Bristol in the Eighteenth Century" in McGrath ed., *Bristol in the Eighteenth Century*.

[21] Although Tucker had succeeded to the Deanship of Gloucester, he retained his rectory at Bristol. See G. E. Weare, *Edmund Burke's Connection with Bristol from 1774 to 1780* (Bristol: 1894), p. 9.

[22] EB, Speech on Arrival at Bristol, 13 October 1774, *W & S*, III, p. 59.

[23] EB, Appeal to Bristol Electors, 13 October 1774, ibid., p. 61.

[24] Cruger, having been a Tory, tacked towards the Wilkes faction in response to his dismay at American policy. See Underdown, "Henry Cruger and Edmund Burke," p. 17.

[25] He consciously adopted a platform. On this, see Henry Jephson, *The Platform: Its Rise and Progress* (London: 1892), 2 vols., I, pp. 70–72.

[26] EB, Speech on Arrival at Bristol, 13 October 1774, *W & S*, III, p. 58.

[27] Ibid., p. 59.

[28] EB to Juliana French, 2 November 1774, *Corr.*, III, pp. 73–74.

[29] EB, Thanks to the Bristol Voters, 3 November 1774, *W & S*, III, p. 62.

he would meet Jane. He was voted the freedom of Bristol on 12 November; in the run-up he feared that the "dinners would never end."[30] In the midst of this merriment, it was clear that Burke took his public duty seriously. His understanding of his responsibilities was presented as the poll was declared. Cruger, as the leading candidate, addressed the crowd from the hustings first. "It has long been my opinion that the electors have a right to instruct their members," he declared.[31] Burke used his own address to undermine this contention. Instructions to members of parliament had been issued in the seventeenth century; in the eighteenth they became a popular tool of the opposition. Prior to the 1760s, these were largely orchestrated. Thereafter, they acquired a momentum of their own, beginning with moves by Middlesex, Westminster and the City to instruct members of parliament to protest against the expulsion of Wilkes. In 1771, the idea of obliging representatives to commit themselves to pledges was adopted by the Society of Supporters of the Bill of Rights.[32] Three years later William Baker, by now a good friend of Burke, was pressed to bind himself by a "test" as a condition for holding his Westminster seat.[33] As he mounted the hustings in 1774, Burke was acutely aware of controversy surrounding instructions.

More remotely, the status of the representative had been keenly considered in English constitutional history since the seventeenth century. In the midst of the first Civil War, in the fourth part of his *Institutes*, Edward Coke observed that a member of parliament, even though he is chosen for a particular borough or county, "serveth for the whole Realm, for the end of his coming thither, as in the writ of his election appeareth, is generall"—namely, to help conduct the affairs of the kingdom as a whole.[34] Even so, Rapin de Thoyras, in his *Dissertation sur les whigs et les torys* of 1717, complained that English "Députez" were not instructed by their constituents, and if they were these representatives were not obliged to discuss their mandates.[35] Notwithstanding this complaint, by the 1760s Anthony Ellys, the bishop of St. David's, was contending in his posthumously published volumes on the *Liberty Spiritual and Temporal of the Subjects of England*, that what de Thoyras saw as a defect was a consummate advantage. One of the achievements of the British constitution, Ellys contended, was that deliberation was not in the hands of the population at large. "Gothic" constitutions, by comparison with ancient republics, "left only the choice

[30] EB to Jane Burke, 8 November 1774, *Corr.*, III, p. 74; EB to Sir Abraham Isaac Elton, c. 15 November 1774, ibid., p. 77.

[31] *Felix Farley's Bristol Journal*, 5 November 1774.

[32] The idea was first developed by Catherine Macaulay in her response to Burke's *Present Discontents*: see her *Observations on a Pamphlet Entitled, Thoughts on the Cause of the Present Discontents* (London: 1770), pp. 30–31.

[33] Lucy Sutherland, "Edmund Burke and the Relations between Members of Parliament and their Constituents," *Studies in Burke and His Time*, 10 (1968), pp. 105–21. Baker's response to the request that he be bound by a pledge is reproduced at pp. 120–21.

[34] Edward Coke, *The Fourth Part of the Institutes of the Laws of England, Concerning the Jurisdiction of the Courts* (London: 1644), p. 14.

[35] Paul Rapin de Thoyras, *Dissertation sur les whigs et les torys* (The Hague: 1717), p. 160.

of representatives to the people," at the same time investing these deputies, "when once chosen, with a discretionary power, to act as they saw fit, within the established bounds of the constitution."[36] Ellys cited Cicero's *Pro Flacco* to make his point: "all the republics of the Greeks are governed by the rashness of the assembly while sitting." The greatness of these city-states collapsed, Cicero went on, on account of the "immoderate liberty and licentiousness of the popular assemblies."[37] For Ellys, the gothic mode of deputing representatives facilitated the selection of competent administrators, guarding against the intemperance and imprudence of constituents. Since members of parliament were expected to deliberate for the common good, regional conflicts were avoided just as much as popular prejudices were amended. Binding instructions threatened to undermine both of these achievements.[38] Burke's familiarity with Ellys's arguments cannot be doubted: large portions of the fourth section of part two of his *Liberty Spiritual and Temporal*, dealing with the folly of electoral tests and pledges, were excerpted in 1766 in the review of Ellys's work published in *The Annual Register*.[39]

Before long, the subject surfaced in parliament itself. In a debate on the civil list debt on 1 March 1769, Alderman Beckford had declared that other members of parliament might think that instructions from voters were not to be respected by their representatives, yet he did regard them. "I think it is the law and custom of parliament," he proposed.[40] Sir Joseph Mawbey, who had begun as a supporter of the Rockinghams but increasingly came to align himself with the cause of Wilkes, was quick to agree: "I have had the honour to receive this very day a set of instructions from my constituents."[41] Mawbey's announcement met with derision, yet Barré sprung to his defence: "The notion of members receiving instructions from their constituents has been treated by a certain part of the House with great contempt. I do not rise for the sake of encouraging a factious disposition; but when instructions, proceeding from the true voice of the people come to us in the spirit of the constitution, they are not to be laughed at."[42] At this point Jeremiah Dyson, an expert on parliamentary procedure, delivered his verdict. Attempts to bind representatives by

[36] Anthony Ellys, *Tracts on the Liberty, Spiritual and Temporal, of the Subjects of England* (London: 1763–65), 2 vols., II, p. 122.

[37] Cicero, *Pro Flacco*, 16: "Graecorum autem totae res publicae sedentis contionis temeritate administrantur . . . libertate immoderata ac licentia contionum."

[38] Ellys, *Tracts*, II, pp. 118ff.

[39] "An Account of Books Published in 1765" in *The Annual Register for the Year 1765* (London: 1766), pp. 298–303.

[40] *Cavendish Debates of the House of Commons*, I, p. 280; cf. ibid., p. 285. On the subject in general, see Paul Kelly, "Constituents' Instructions to Members of Parliament in the Eighteenth Century" in Clyve Jones ed., *Party and Management in Parliament, 1660–1784* (Leicester: University of Leicester Press, 1984). See also C. S. Emden, *The People and the Constitution* (Oxford: Oxford University Press, 1956), pp. 22–25; B. Kemp, "Patriotism, Pledges and the People" in M. Gilbert ed., *A Century of Conflict, 1850–1950: Essays for A. J. P. Taylor* (London: Hamilton, 1966).

[41] *Cavendish Debates of the House of Commons*, I, p. 282.

[42] Ibid., p. 283.

issuing instructions had no authority under the constitution. Rigby returned to the issue on 2 March, reaffirming the substance of Dyson's remark.[43] The day before, Burke had already been forced to declare his hand: "As to the doctrine of instruction to representatives," he intervened, "it is unfounded in reason; if not put down, it will destroy the constitution."[44] In response to Cruger's pronouncements on 3 November 1774, Burke delivered a fuller exposition of his views. "I wish that topick had been passed by," Burke revealed, yet since it had been raised he felt compelled to make a response. Cruger might choose to declare at the conclusion of the poll in favour of the "coercive authority" of instructions, but Burke was bound to demur.[45]

In 1791, recounting his record as a public champion of liberty, Burke returned to his stance taken at Bristol in 1774. Writing in the face of deepening divisions within his party, he recalled with pride his steady refusal to court vacuous "popularity," instancing his renunciation of instructions in the midst of his post-electoral address: he was, he declared, "the first man who, on the hustings, at a popular election, rejected the authority of instructions from constituents."[46] Indeed, the subsequent discredit into which the doctrine of binding instructions had fallen might be attributed to the authority of Burke's determined intervention. Never before, he asserted, had the issue been treated in such a comprehensive fashion.[47] Facing his constituents, both those who had voted for him and those who had not, he affirmed it his duty to consider their interest rather than his own, and to nurture "the strictest union, the closest correspondence, and the most unreserved communication" with them.[48] But this was quite distinct from acting as a popular agent. This touched on the fundamental nature of popular representation, the complexity of which drew Burke's attention repeatedly through his career.

To begin with, representation had to be considered in three dimensions. First, any organized society was composed of diverse and potentially competing "wills," understood as individuals possessing their own "interests." It was the job of politics to render these interests mutually compatible, which meant establishing a representative interest. This common interest was represented by the state.[49] However,

[43] Ibid., p. 302.

[44] Ibid., pp. 287–88.

[45] EB, Speech at the Conclusion of the Poll, 3 November 1774, *W & S*, III, p. 68

[46] EB, *An Appeal from the New to the Old Whigs, in Consequence of Some Late Discussions in Parliament, relative to the Reflections on the Revolution in France* (London: 1791), pp. 32–33.

[47] Ibid.

[48] EB, Speech at the Conclusion of the Poll, 3 November 1774, *W & S*, III, p. 68.

[49] This perspective has been developed most fully by Thomas Hobbes. See Quentin Skinner, "The State" in Terence Ball et al. eds., *Political Innovation and Conceptual Change* (Cambridge: Cambridge University Press, 1989); idem, "Hobbes and the Purely Artificial Person of the State" in idem, *Visions of Politics III: Hobbes and Civil Science* (Cambridge: Cambridge University Press, 2002); David Runciman, "Hobbes's Theory of Representation: Anti-Democratic or Proto-Democratic" in Ian Shapiro et al. eds., *Political Representation* (Cambridge: Cambridge University Press, 2009). For Burke's debt to Hobbes's argument, see EB, *An Appeal from the New to the Old Whigs*, p. 69; see also chapter 14, section 5 below.

secondly, in constitutional terms, this representative interest was formed by collaboration between distinct forces operating through different branches of government.[50] In this sense, the different components of the constitution might themselves be seen as performing a representative function: the peers and the crown were "representative," and of course the House of Commons was too.[51] However, the Commons was representative in a more specific sense, and so the way in which it "presented" the community had to be analysed.[52] This was a third aspect of representation, relevant in particular to modern popular governments, and one that was absent from purely monarchical or aristocratic regimes. The king represented the crown, the Lords represented the peers, yet the Commons represented the non-ennobled "people." Since the people in this limited sense excluded both monarch and peers, the Commons did not represent the population as a whole: it stood for the commonalty. According to contemporary estimates, the Commons was elected by between 250,000 and 300,000 voters.[53] Burke was acutely aware that these constituted a diverse grouping, necessarily comprising distinct "descriptions." The diversity of the commonalty was complicated by the fact that it included what might be described as members of an aristocracy who were nonetheless not counted among the nobility.[54] The commonalty thus composed a variety of gradations, together with a number of determinate interests.[55] In the end, the preferences of the commons were as manifold as the number of members comprising it, yet in practical terms these could be grouped into particular, dominant interests: land, commerce, the army and the professions prominent among them.[56] The electoral process that populated the Commons allowed these interests to be represented.

[50] On various applications of this doctrine in eighteenth-century thought, see Bryan Garsten, "Representative Government and Popular Sovereignty" in Ian Shapiro et al. eds., *Political Representation* (Cambridge: Cambridge University Press, 2009).

[51] Burke made this point in EB, Debate on Proceedings against Wilkes for Seditious Libel, 2 February 1769, Cavendish Diary, Eg. MS. 217, fol. 96.

[52] This sense of representation dominates modern accounts. For discussion, see Bernard Manin, Adam Przeworski and Susan Stokes, "Introduction" to idem eds., *Democracy, Accountability and Representation* (Cambridge: Cambridge University Press, 1999); Mónica Brito Vieira and David Runciman, *Representation* (Cambridge: Polity, 2008).

[53] Arthur Young, *Political Essays Concerning the Present State of the British Empire* (London: 1772), p. 34; John Gray, *The Right of the British Legislature to Tax the American Colonies* (London: 1775), p. 28.

[54] The term "aristocracy" has this wider sense in EB, Speech on the Bill to Amend the Marriage Act, 15 June 1781, *The Works of the Right Honourable Edmund Burke*, ed. French Laurence and Walker King (London: 1792–1827), 16 vols., V, pp. 414–19. Cf. EB, *Appeal from the New to the Old Whigs*, pp. 139ff.

[55] Cf. John Shute Barrington, *The Revolution and Anti-Revolution Principles Stated and Compar'd* (London: 1714), pp. 49–50; William Meredith, *The Question Stated, Whether the Freeholders of Middlesex Lost their Right by Voting for Mr. Wilkes* (London: 1769), p. 14.

[56] Samuel H. Beer, "The Representation of Interests in British Government: Historical Background," *American Political Science Review*, 51:3 (September 1957), pp. 613–50.

This medley of interests shared an underlying concern: that of "property."[57] This basic interest was clearly a common concern since competing rights in finance, agriculture and trade were potentially sectional claims in respect of this shared concern. This in effect created the problem of representation. Competing claims to property had to be reconciled, and only a representative interest could serve that end. This interest had to be fabricated: it did not "naturally" emerge. If it did, there would be no need for politics or representation. Land and commerce held pride of place as principal interests in society, since the defence of these in practice served all other interests as well. In the Commons, commerce was more fully represented than land according to Burke. Of course the Lords, in representing what Burke termed national "dignities," served the interest of extensive property in land at the same time.[58] In 1770 Burke had observed that the lower House was not intended as "a representative of the landed property only, but of the commercial interest chiefly, as appeared from the establishment of the boroughs, essential parts of that representation, existing in times earlier than any annals or history can give testimony of."[59] Commerce was a key element of the national interest, yet the Commons represented local concerns at the same time. The volume of parliamentary legislation steadily increased through the eighteenth century. By the 1780s, there was an average of 120 items added to the statute book each year, and a proportion of these involved provisions for specific counties and towns: highway bills, improvement bills, workhouse bills, enclosure bills and harbour bills were introduced by particular members.[60] To this extent, MPs often acted as agents for local interests. Nonetheless, it was commonly assumed that their job was to represent the national interest over all: "Every member," Speaker Onslow claimed, "as soon as he is chosen, becomes a representative of the whole body of the Commons."[61]

Bristol was particularly active in canvassing its MPs, and Burke was himself prepared to act with partiality to the city. On 26 March 1777, he accepted David Garrick's advice to support a proposal to grant a license for a playhouse at Birmingham.[62] Yet after his Bristol friends became involved in opposing the measure, he voted against the license on 29 April.[63] William Burke wrote to Garrick explaining

[57] Paul Langford, "Property and 'Virtual Representation' in Eighteenth-Century England," *Historical Journal*, 31:1 (March 1988), pp. 83–115.

[58] EB, Speech in Reply, 5 June 1794, *W & S*, VII, p. 427.

[59] EB, Speech on Grenville's Controverted Elections Bill, 30 March 1770, *Parliamentary History*, XVI, cols. 920–21.

[60] Langford, "Property and 'Virtual Representation'," p. 84.

[61] John Hatsell, *Precedents and Proceedings in the House of Commons* (London: 1781), 4 vols., II, p. 55.

[62] David Garrick to EB, 29 April 1777, WWM BkP 1:955; EB, Speech on Birmingham Playhouse Bill, 26 March 1777, *W & S*, III, pp. 286–88.

[63] EB, Speech on Birmingham Playhouse Bill, 29 April 1777, ibid., pp. 336–38. The incident is covered in P. T. Underdown, "Religious Opposition to Licensing the Bristol and Birmingham Theatres," *University of Birmingham Historical Journal*, 6 (1958), pp. 149–60.

that Edmund had "yielded."[64] Burke wrote for himself on the subject that same day: "I have had such instructions, as in wisdom, and indeed in common Decency, I cannot wholly resist."[65] He could not, he felt, set his face against the wishes of his constituents "unless the Cause they espouse is indeed a bad one."[66] This final qualification was indicative of Burke's view. It was necessary to be sensitive to local opinion, and equally to the sentiments of the nation at large. Yet the highest role of a representative was to deliberate on the national interest, and for this they would have to subordinate particular interests to the common good, and interpret popular feeling in accordance with their own prudence. On this last topic Burke was both consistent and resoundingly clear. One should trust in the common people to the extent that one should trust in the schemes of princes: both were fickle, self-interested, and sometimes self-destructive.[67]

Writing to Rockingham at the beginning of 1777, Burke reminded his patron of the fitfulness of popular opinion: it was "full of Levity, and the very creature of Fortune."[68] In Britain it was necessary to regard the state of public sentiment, but one could only do so safely if one was prepared to educate it. The leadership among the Rockinghams, as he informed Charles James Fox later that same year, "do very much look to the people," but more than was wise for those "who do so little to guide and direct the public opinion."[69] This did not imply a disregard for the people: the best instincts and highest duties of the statesmen should be geared towards serving them.[70] The question was how, politically, this objective could best be secured. Mere popular declamation, such as was favoured by Lord Shelburne, was not to be trusted: at one point, Burke recalled, Shelburne remarked that the people "were never in the wrong," but before long he was lamenting their rejection of his candidates in the City of London.[71] It was right, Burke claimed in his *Letter to the Sheriffs of Bristol*, that politicians should "follow" rather than "force" the inclinations of the public. Their job was to gather the "general sense of the community."[72] This, however, could never mean reproducing constituents' judgments.[73] It meant deliberating on the basis of their ascertainable feelings. For this, he proposed in his 1774 Speech in Bristol, their "wishes ought to have great weight" with their member of parliament. In practice, this meant that their opinion should have his "high respect," and their business his "unremitting attention."[74]

[64] William Burke to David Garrick, 29 April 1777, *Corr.*, III, p. 336n.

[65] An example can be found in John Turton to EB, 26 February 1777, WWM BkP 1:936.

[66] EB to David Garrick, 29 April 1777, *Corr.*, III, p. 336.

[67] EB to John Bourke, 11 July 1776, ibid., p. 281.

[68] EB to the Marquess of Rockingham, 6 January 1777, ibid., p. 311.

[69] EB to Charles James Fox, 8 October 1777, ibid., p. 381.

[70] *Pace* Richard Pares, *King George III and the Politicians*, pp. 43–4.

[71] EB to John Bourke, 11 July 1776, *Corr.*, III, p. 281.

[72] EB, *Letter to the Sheriffs of Bristol*, 3 April 1777, *W & S*, III, p. 315.

[73] EB, *Observations on the Conduct of the Minority* (Spring 1793), *W & S*, VIII, p. 433.

[74] EB, Speech at the Conclusion of the Poll, , *W & S*, III, 3 November 1774, pp. 68–69.

Burke went on to flesh out his conception. His presentation of his thoughts on the duties of a representative received perhaps his fullest attention in his Speech at the conclusion of the 1774 poll.[75] Here he drew a distinction between will and deliberation. The public will was clearly superior to the will of the representative. This might be described as the people's "inclination." Yet public life was not simply an expression of popular preference; it offered a means of ascertaining the national interest. That interest should be made to accord with the mood of the nation, but it also had to be conducive to its long-term benefit. That was not a matter of spontaneous inclination: it had to be arrived at by a process of deliberation. Deliberation depended on "reason and judgement," which drew conclusions on the basis of discussion.[76] For Burke, it made no sense to entrust future welfare to transient feeling or popular prejudice. Attitudes had to be debated, reflected upon, evaluated. Mandates ensured that decisions preceded deliberation, inverting the only process by which a policy could be reasoned. Representation was a popular trust as well as "a trust from Providence."[77] The member of parliament was entrusted to debate on the basis of conscience, not reproduce the conclusions of authoritative mandates. It was the deliberative process that generated a representative interest. Before that there existed opposing preferences, which politics was supposed to reconcile.

Representation refined, assuaged and harmonised. Without it rival purposes jostled and conflicted. A process of mandating ambassadors to parliament entailed charging them with promoting an existing clash of interests without any room for reasoned compromise. This was to ignore the fact that "Parliament is a *deliberative* Assembly of *one* Nation, with *one* Interest, that of the whole."[78] Unity was required for decisions to be made, which could never result from a collision of wills vying in a hostile congress: "wide-spread interests must be considered; must be compared; must be reconciled if possible."[79] These interests were both local and sectional, derived from the complex political geography of the country as well as a variety of social sectors. By the mid 1770s, putative anomalies in the representation of the political geography of Britain was being widely debated. Burke was pleased to declare of the Commons in 1794 that "we . . . represent in a body by the Knights of shires, the landed interest . . . by Cities [we] represent the trading interest. By the Boroughs and sometimes by the Cottages it is our glory that we represent the people of England."[80] The landed interest, the trading interest and more generally "the people of England," could be analysed into large proprietors, gentry and tenant farmers,

[75]The best discussion remains James Conniff, "Burke, Bristol, and the Concept of Representation," *Western Political Quarterly*, 30:3 (September 1977), pp. 329–41. See also Melissa S. Williams, "Burkean 'Descriptions' and Political Representation: A Reappraisal," *Canadian Journal of Political Science*, 29:1 (March 1996), pp. 23–45.

[76]EB, Speech at the Conclusion of the Poll, , *W & S*, III, 3 November 1774, p. 69.

[77]Ibid.

[78]Ibid.

[79]Ibid., p. 70.

[80]EB, Speech in Reply, 5 June 1794, *W & S*, VII, p. 427.

comprising about fourteen per cent of the electorate; the manufacturers and merchants, who made up another significant sector; the retailors, amounting to a further fifth of the whole; craftsmen, constituting another third; and agricultural workers and unskilled craftsmen, who made up about twenty-eight per cent.[81] These voters selected members for borough and county seats. These seats were often distributed in proportion to population or the tax return, or some estimated amalgamation of both, although often an electoral district was demographically inconsequential, while great cities like Birmingham and Manchester had no representation at all.[82] Nonetheless, it was clear that a large multiplicity of preferences, based on an assortment of regions and orders, could be voiced in the House of Commons. A representative chamber had to draw this medley together on the basis of collaborative prudence. A system of mandates would contradict that outcome, and subvert the process that brought it about.

Burke's tenure at Bristol lasted until September 1780. During his six years as a representative for the city, he served its cause in parliament, at the treasury and the admiralty to the fullest extent compatible with his conscience and sense of his duty. Above all, he resisted attempts by London merchants to gain advantages over Bristol, and sought equal treatment of its port with other rivals in the kingdom.[83] Nonetheless, with the advent of war against the American colonies, opinion in Bristol substantially swung behind the government, and Burke was left defending positions against his own constituents. By 1777, his conduct was eliciting explicit criticism, not least for his failure during the secession of the Rockinghams to appear in parliament to oppose the American Treasons Act.[84] In his *Letter to the Sheriffs of Bristol* of 3 April 1777, he offered a robust defence of his conduct, and in the process presented an elevated conception of the office of the legislator. The sovereign lawmaker was not bound by the regulations of subordinate courts, but only by "the great principles of reason and equity, and the general sense of mankind."[85] Armed with these guiding norms, members of parliament should seek "to enlarge and enlighten law by the liberality of legislative reason."[86] This ambition ought particularly to be expressed in relation to the great issues of empire. Yet while Burke's passion and intelligence was drawn to consider these weighty subjects, he was expected, as a member for Bristol, to attend to "*the small Tithes*."[87] Burke used this phrase in a letter

[81] Frank O'Gorman, "The Unreformed Electorate of Hanoverian England: The Mid-Eighteenth Century to the Reform Act of 1832," *Social History*, 11:1 (January 1986), pp. 33–52.

[82] These apparent anomalies were intensively analysed in the 1790s, first in Thomas Oldfield's *History of the Boroughs* (London: 1792), 3 vols., and then in the *Report of the Society of the Friends of the People on the State of the Representation* (London: 1793). For discussion, see Frank O'Gorman, *Voters, Patrons, and Parties: The Unreformed Electoral System of Hanoverian England, 1734–1832* (Oxford: Oxford University Press, 1989), pp. 18–19.

[83] The best treatment is in P. T. Underdown, "Edmund Burke, the Commissary of His Bristol Constituents, 1774–1780," *English Historical Review*, 73:287 (April 1958), pp. 252–69.

[84] 17 Geo. III, c. 9.

[85] EB, *Letter to the Sheriffs of Bristol*, 3 April 1777, *W & S*, III, p. 295.

[86] Ibid.

[87] EB to Richard Champion, 26 June 1777, *Corr.*, III, p. 356.

to Richard Champion in 1777. Since February of that year, the soap-makers of the city had been urging him to oppose a Bill pending before parliament which they felt would have an adverse effect on business. On 2 June, the Bill passed, without any action on Burke's part. On the twenty-sixth of the month he apologized to Champion for his negligence, lamenting the fact that constituents judged their representative "solely by his merits as their special Agent."[88] He felt it was more strongly in the interest of electors that MPs should attend to the "Main lines" of their duty, which was to deliberate on major affairs of state.

Nonetheless, in applying himself to major issues of national policy, Burke antagonized the electorate by adopting a succession of unpopular stances. Early in September 1780, he determined to give up the opportunity to stand again for Bristol.[89] But then, on 6 September, a sudden change of fortune forced him reluctantly back into the race. He was sick with a heavy cold, and exhausted from stomping the pavements, yet he was still expected to glad-hand, canvass and cajole.[90] Three days later, he finally withdrew from the contest. He spoke for just five minutes outlining his resolution, but still, as Champion reported, there were "very few dry Eyes" in the audience.[91] The speech was carried by the *Whitehall Evening Post*, the *Morning Chronicle*, the *Morning Post* and the *Public Advertiser*. "The Representation of Bristol was an Object on many accounts dear to me," Burke declared.[92] Yet it was clear that he had lost the support of the voters. Only one Whig candidate could plausibly be returned in the general election, and the honour was unlikely to fall to Burke.[93] But even before he withdrew from the election, as he fought his last campaign, he knew he had estranged many erstwhile supporters. Entering the final struggle on 6 September, he set out a detailed defence of his conduct to date. Towards this end, he urged his audience at the Guildhall to regard "the *whole tenour*" of his conduct, above all his independence from the court: no one would serve the people, he remarked, "whilst there is a court to serve, but those who are of a nice and jealous honour."[94] He counted himself among those with the requisite independence of spirit, and proceeded to defend his record against charges of having neglected his constituents.

Burke only visited Bristol twice since his election in 1774. He vindicated this choice in terms of his assiduousness at Westminster. Yet even there he seems to have alienated the Bristol voters. His opposition to the slave trade was well known, and his opposition to commercial monopolies widely publicized. In general, he had

[88] Ibid.

[89] EB to the Marquess of Rockingham, 7 September 1780, ibid., p. 275.

[90] Ibid., p. 278.

[91] Richard Burke Sr. to the Marquess of Rockingham, 9 September 1780, ibid., p. 280; Richard Champion to the Marquess of Rockingham, 11 September 1780, ibid., pp. 280–81n.

[92] EB, Speech on the Hustings at Bristol, 9 September 1780, *W & S*, III, p. 666.

[93] Ian R. Christie, "Henry Cruger and the End of Edmund Burke's Connection with Bristol," *Transactions of the Bristol and Gloucestershire Archaeological Society*, 74 (1956), pp. 153–70.

[94] EB, Speech at Bristol Previous to the Election, 6 September 1780, *W & S*, III, p. 625.

acted according to his best judgment rather than the instructions of his constituents. As recently as 28 February 1780, he had voted in favour of Lord Beauchamp's Bill to relieve the plight of insolvent debtors in the face of calls from Bristol to oppose the measure.[95] He was not inclined to apologize for his behaviour. Even when he could not face former supporters with whom he had come to disagree, he would never sacrifice his own prudence to their sensitivities. The fate of America provided a potent example. After the British victory over the colonists in the battle of Long Island on 27 August 1776, the whole country was seduced by the rising "spirit of domination." At length, Bristol was converted to the cause: "We lost all measure between means and ends; and our headlong desires became our politics and our morals."[96] Burke took a stand against the mood of punitive militancy which had seized the dominant attitude of the public: "I conformed to the instructions of truth and nature, and maintained your interest, against your opinions, with a constancy that became me."[97] He saw himself as bound to look to the opinions of the electorate, but above all to opinions which regarded the future. "I was not to look to the flash of the day . . . you chose me . . . to be a pillar of the state, and not a weathercock on the top of the edifice, exalted for my levity and versatility."[98] A representative was a servant of the public interest, not the agent of incompatible popular whims.

It is impossible to appreciate Burke's understanding of his role without grasping both his reverence for the primacy of the people's will and his alarm at the possible folly of their judgment. "When they call for bread, I would not give them the Kingdom," he once announced during debate on the corn trade.[99] Over a year later he affirmed that it was the duty of the member of parliament "to look the p[eople] in the face whenever our instruction is greater than theirs . . . [and] make them trust it whether they will or not."[100] The distribution of property was a divisive subject of the greatest importance to a state which could not be safely left to the partiality of the populace. The same went for imperial policy, which had to be secure against popular pride. The civil war with the colonies illustrated the dangers. It had disposed the crowd to arrogance and peremptoriness: "They are naturally proud, tyrannical, and ignorant," Burke observed in this context–"bad scholars and worse masters," he concluded.[101] Yet at the same time he insisted that he would always follow their "humour." Private and party interests were "nothing in comparison."[102] It was the glory of the Commons, he underlined in the 1790s, to protect "the lower order of

[95] EB, Speech on Insolvent Debtors Bill, 28 February 1780, ibid., pp. 552–53. For the petition drawn up against the Bill, see EB to James Hill, 25 April 1789, *Corr.*, IV, pp. 231–32.

[96] EB, Speech at Bristol Previous to the Election, 6 September 1780, *W & S*, III, pp. 628–29.

[97] Ibid., p. 634.

[98] Ibid.

[99] EB, Debate on the Corn Trade, 13 April 1772, Cavendish Diary, Eg. MS. 240, fol. 206.

[100] EB, Debate on the Corn Trade, 26 March 1773, Cavendish Diary, Eg. MS. 245, fol. 166. For further discussion, see below, chapter 16, section 5.

[101] EB to the Duke of Portland, 3 September 1780, *Corr.*, IV, p. 274.

[102] Ibid.

the people."[103] Even if they were poor instructors, they were masters nonetheless, and representatives were ultimately commanded "to obey."[104] This obedience was not enforced by encouraging representatives to betray their principles. Instead, it was safeguarded by two less immediate methods. The first was clearly articulated by Anthony Ellys in emphasizing how the people were secured against misgovernment: "if they do not approve [their representative's] conduct . . . they may, after a short time, lay them aside, and send other persons more likely to serve them well."[105] Burke accepted the verdict of the people in the same terms. "I received your Trust in the face of day," he conceded on 9 September 1780, "and in the face of day, I accept your dismission."[106] The right of removing deputies was the most potent weapon wielded by a people as a consequence of their "actual" representation. Yet there was a second means of restraining the conduct of members of parliament: by raising their awareness of the duties of "virtual" representation. As Burke would argue in respect of Ireland in 1792, in some respects the latter was more effective than the former.[107]

The demerits of virtual representation had been widely publicized since the advent of the American crisis.[108] Burke himself explicitly rejected it as a sufficient index of consent for the purpose of conducting colonial government. Nonetheless, to be virtually represented offered great security to a people: it ensured "a communion of interests, and a sympathy in feelings and desires between those who act in the name of any description of people, and the people in whose name they act, though the trustees are not actually chosen by them."[109] It was perfectly possible that the processes of actual representation might distort the results achieved by virtual representation. In the end, it was the virtual correspondence or community of interest that was essential: election was just a means of securing that result. The "undone millions of India" could expect to be productively served in circumstances where their virtual representation was guaranteed.[110] Yet, as Burke underlined in his Speech on the Rohilla War Charge against Hastings in 1786, there was in fact no community of sentiment between Britain and the subcontinent.[111] It was the job of the Commons to represent British territories in South Asia.[112] As Burke emphasized at the opening of the Presents Charge during the Hastings impeachment, members of parliament were "representatives of the inhabitants of Bengal."[113] That meant

[103] EB, Speech in Reply, 5 June 1794, *W & S*, VII, p. 427.

[104] EB to Richard Champion, 26 June 1777, *Corr.*, III, p. 356.

[105] Ellys, *Tracts*, II, p. 122.

[106] EB, Speech on the Hustings at Bristol, 9 September 1780, *W & S*, III, p. 667.

[107] EB, *Letter to Sir Hercules Langrishe* (1792), *W & S*, IX, p. 629.

[108] John Phillip Reid, *The Concept of Representation in the Age of the American Revolution* (Chicago, IL: University of Chicago Press, 1989), pp. 53ff.

[109] EB, *Letter to Sir Hercules Langrishe* (1792), *W & S*, IX, p. 629.

[110] The phrase appears in EB, Speech on Debate on Address, 25 January 1785, *W & S*, IX, p. 585.

[111] EB, Speech on Rohilla War Charge, 1 June 1786, *W & S*, VI, p. 94.

[112] EB, Speech in Reply, 7 June 1794, *W & S*, VII, p. 458.

[113] "Minutes of Proceedings of the Trial of Warren Hastings," Tuesday 21 April 1788, Add. MS. 24229, fol. 7.

that they should serve their interests on the basis of sympathy, although in practice metropolitan affairs disregarded the plight of the provinces. A concordance of sentiments might occasionally be stimulated, but it was difficult to sustain. As Burke commented, once again in connection with Ireland, virtual representation "cannot have a long or sure existence, if it has not a substratum in the actual."[114] His career as a member for Bristol provided a vivid experience of how that substratum operated in practice. The vote, Burke saw, was ultimately the "Shield" of the subject, which protected against public oppression as well as private persecution.[115]

8.3 Trade and Tumult in Ireland

A major cause of the estrangement of Bristol voters from Burke's candidacy can be attributed to his position on Ireland after 1778 when he supported concessions to the mercantile interest of the country. As he put it himself, his stance brought on the suspicion that he had "acted rather as a native of Ireland, than as an English member of parliament." In response, in his Speech at Bristol Previous to the Election of 6 September 1780, he claimed that the limits of his "true country" were coterminous with the sphere of his duties.[116] By this he meant that his conduct should be answerable to a tribunal less partisan than merely local patriotism. Nonetheless, in spite of this avowedly cosmopolitan perspective, he proceeded to define his obligations in terms of the welfare of the British Empire, whose fortunes would determine the fate of England, Ireland and Bristol. "A new world of policy was opened," he observed, "to which it was necessary we should conform whether we would or not . . . my only thought was how to conform our situation in such a manner as to unite to this kingdom, in prosperity and in affection, whatever remained of the empire."[117] The progress of American arms over the course of the colonial crisis, particularly the French support that the colonists enjoyed from 1778, had undermined the security of the Empire.[118] In the face of these developments, British strength depended on the continuing allegiance of Ireland, which now hung on its prosperity and its constitutional status.

Irish sympathies were at first stirred by the contest with America, particularly among the patriot Whig interest.[119] There had been a substantial influx of settlers

[114] EB, *Letter to Sir Hercules Langrishe* (1792), *W & S*, IX, p. 629.

[115] EB, *Letter to Lord Kenmare* (21 February 1782), *W & S*, IX, p. 570.

[116] EB, Speech at Bristol Previous to the Election, 6 September 1780, *W & S*, III, p. 630. Cf. EB, Speech on Trade Concessions to Ireland, 6 December 1779, *W & S*, IX, p. 542, where he claimed to have acted "with the best dispositions for promoting the mutual interest of both kingdoms."

[117] EB, Speech at Bristol Previous to the Election, 6 September 1780, *W & S*, III, p. 630.

[118] Stephen Conway, *The British Isles and the War of American Independence* (Oxford: Oxford University Press, 2000, 2003), pp. 16–17.

[119] Vincent Morley, *Irish Opinion and the American Revolution, 1760–1783* (Cambridge: Cambridge University Press, 2002), p. 95.

into the colonies from Ireland since the early seventeenth century, giving rise to a diverse range of trans-Atlantic connections.[120] Emigration from Presbyterian Ulster had been rising over recent decades, with over 20,000 transporting themselves across the Atlantic between 1769 and 1774.[121] More importantly, while the colonists in the 1760s and 1770s looked to the history of Irish debates concerning the nature of the relationship between the two kingdoms, the Irish were now captivated by the revival of questions in the colonies about constitutional dependence in the Empire.[122] "If Ireland was to rebel and resist our laws, I would tax it," Richard Rigby declared in the British House of Commons as contention with the colonies was reaching the point of crisis.[123] The next day, he was forced to make a retraction under pressure from Irish opinion.[124] The following year, a chorus of support for the American cause rang through the Irish parliament.[125]

The din, however, was caused by opposition voices alone.[126] The Irish government itself accommodated imperial policy. Burke reminded Richmond in September 1775 that "Ireland is always a part of some importance in the general System."[127] Given the current distempers of the Empire, it could practically be said to hold the balance of power. However, instead of interposing its will to give heft to American resistance, it proved supine in the face metropolitan policy. Burke reiterated his disappointment throughout the following year.[128] But if Dublin Castle connived with Westminster, substantial sections of patriot opinion identified with the colonies, even if this declined as the 1770s progressed.[129] Charles O'Hara informed Burke from Dublin in the summer of 1775: "[H]ere we sympathize more or less with the

[120] R. B. McDowell, *Irish Public Opinion, 1750–1800* (London: Faber and Faber, 1944), pp. 40–42; Kerby A. Miller, *Emigrants and Exiles: Ireland and the Irish Exodus to North America* (Oxford: Oxford University Press, 1985), ch. 4.

[121] R. J. Dickson, *Ulster Emigration to Colonial America, 1718–1785* (London: Routledge, 1966), p. 60; David Dickson, *New Foundations: Ireland, 1660–1800* (Dublin: Irish Academic Press, 1987, 2012), p. 159.

[122] Charles McIlwain, *The American Revolution: A Constitutional Interpretation* (New York: Macmillan, 1924); Robert L. Schuyler, *Parliament and the British Empire* (New York: Columbia University Press, 1929); Patrick Kelly, "William Molyneux and the Spirit of Liberty in Eighteenth-Century Ireland," *Eighteenth-Century Ireland*, 3 (1988), pp. 133–48.

[123] 22 April 1774, *Parliamentary History*, XVII, col. 1287.

[124] As reported by Governor Johnstone, *Parliamentary History*, XVIII, col. 63.

[125] *A Narrative of the Proceedings and Debates of the Parliament of Ireland* (London: 1776). For the parliamentary response in general, see Maurice R. O'Connell, *Irish Politics and Social Conflict in the Age of the American Revolution* (Philadelphia, PA: University of Pennsylvania Press, 1965), pp. 26–27. Supporters included Lords Leinster, Charlemont, Irnham, Meath and Powerscourt, and George Ogle.

[126] Conway, *British Isles and the War of American Independence*, pp. 13–14.

[127] EB to the Duke of Richmond, 26 September 1775, *Corr.*, III, p. 218.

[128] EB to Charles O'Hara, 7 January 1776, ibid., pp. 244–45; EB to Lord Charlemont, 4 June 1776, ibid., p. 271.

[129] Vincent Morley, *Irish Opinion and the American Revolution, 1760–1783* (Cambridge: Cambridge University Press, 2002). Support declined in the face of worries about the state of Catholic opinion, particularly after the Bourbons entered the war against the colonies.

Americans; we are in water colours, what they are in fresco."[130] The Irish attorney, John Ridge, gave his impressions that autumn: "All Protestants as far as I can see, especially the Presbyterians . . . are . . . friends to the American cause."[131] It was opposition to slavish subordination to the seat of empire that united Protestant opinion with their brethren across the Atlantic.[132] Under British metropolitan regulations, imperial dependence had a commercial as well as a political dimension. As Ireland was drawn deeper into the contest with the colonies, both these issues generated increasing public controversy.

Commercial restraints operated as a longstanding grievance in Ireland. First, the cattle acts under Charles II banned the sale of Irish livestock in England, although the measure was repealed in 1776.[133] Later, concerted action by English merchants in the south-west of the country, above all at Exeter and Bristol, had led to a prohibition on the export of Irish woollen products in 1699.[134] Burke's hostility to the measure was still palpable nearly a century later: "the whole Woollen Manufacture of Ireland, the most extensive and profitable of any, and the natural staple of that Kingdom, has been in a manner so destroyed by restrictive laws of *ours*."[135] More generally, Irish trade was limited by the Navigation Acts and by the imposition of duties on a range of merchandise. Of course, the system of regulations included benefits for Irish commerce: linen products prospered in the absence of import duties, and Irish shipping was free to participate in the colonial trade.[136] Equally, the export of provisions to America steadily rose throughout the century.[137] However, colonial produce, notably sugar and tobacco, had to be imported via the "round-about" trade through Britain, and the tariff regime favoured British products at the expense of

[130] Charles O'Hara to EB, 5 June 1775, Hoffman, *Burke*, p. 585.

[131] John Ridge to EB, 25 September 1775, ibid., p. 600.

[132] Roman Catholics petitioned the government with its support: R. B. McDowell, *Ireland in the Age of Imperialism and Revolution, 1760–1801* (Oxford: Oxford University Press, 1979, 1991), pp. 241–42.

[133] John O'Donovan, *The Economic History of Livestock in Ireland* (Cork: Cork University Press, 1940).

[134] L. M. Cullen, *Anglo-Irish Trade, 1660–1800* (New York: Augustus M. Kelley, 1968), p. 5; H. F. Kearney, "The Political Background to English Mercantilism, 1695–1700," *Economic History Review*, 11:3 (April 1959), pp. 484–96. See also Istvan Hont, "Free Trade and the Economic Limits to National Politics: Neo-Machiavellian Political Economy Reconsidered" in idem, *Jealousy of Trade: International Competition and the Nation-State in Historical Perspective* (Cambridge, MA: Harvard University Press, 2010); Jim Smyth, "'Like Amphibious Animals': Irish Protestants, Ancient Britons, 1691–1707," *Historical Journal*, 36:4 (December 1993), pp. 785–97.

[135] EB, *Two Letters on the Trade of Ireland* (1778), *W & S*, IX, p. 516. Cf. John Hely Hutchinson, *The Commercial Restraints of Ireland Considered in a Series of Letters to a Noble Lord* (Dublin: 1779), pp. 155ff., on the origins of British attitudes in colonial policy. The importation of woollen yarn into Britain was permitted by legislation after 1753 (26 Geo. II, c. 11).

[136] Though duties were imposed on coloured, checked and printed linens in 1711 (10 Anne, c. 19).

[137] Thomas Truxes, *Irish-American Trade, 1660–1783* (Cambridge: Cambridge University Press, 1989); T. M. Devine, "The English Connection and Irish and Scottish Development in the Eighteenth Century" in T. M. Devine and David Dickson eds., *Ireland and Scotland, 1600–1850* (Edinburgh: John Donald, 1983).

Irish goods.[138] Restrictions continued to be imposed into the eighteenth century: for instance, the importation of hops was prohibited in 1710, and the exportation of glass in 1746.[139] On the other hand, the export of preserved beef, pork, butter and salted fish to the West Indies grew exponentially as the century progressed, and Irish linen benefited from bounties after 1743. Nonetheless, complaints about restrictions were pervasive after mid-century. As with the North American and West Indian colonies, Arthur Young commented, Irish trade had been governed by the spirit of monopoly, infused with the "maxims" of the counting house.[140]

Since his earliest days in parliament in 1766, Burke had been concerned to reduce the limitations on Irish trade.[141] In 1773, in a Letter to Sir Charles Bingham contesting plans to impose an absentee tax upon landlords resident more than six months out of Ireland, Burke addressed himself to these historic commercial disadvantages. He was aware that restraints had raised a storm of protest in the 1720s and 1740s.[142] The economic drain that was alleged to have followed absenteeism was another persistent complaint.[143] While Burke supported Irish arguments for liberalizing trade, he presented a tax on absenteeism as a retrograde step.[144] The British connection, he insisted, was vital to Irish prosperity. This was increased by what he termed the "free communication" of peoples between the two islands, enhanced by the existence of proprietors in both jurisdictions.[145] To penalize this arrangement by introducing residency requirements would damage the means of mutual support between the two kingdoms.[146] Mutual support could not mean equal power: for the several bodies that comprised the "complicated mass" constitutive of the British Empire to cohere with one another, supreme authority had to reside "somewhere"—and "that

[138] On "round-about" trade, see Adam Smith, *An Inquiry into the Nature and Causes of the Wealth of Nations*, ed. R. H. Campbell and A. S. Skinner (Indianapolis, IN: Liberty Fund, 1976), 2 vols., I, p. 491. For details of enumerated goods subject to this diversion, see R. C. Nash, "Irish Atlantic Trade in the Seventeenth and Eighteenth Centuries," *William and Mary Quarterly*, 42:3 (July 1985), pp. 329–56.

[139] L. M. Cullen, *An Economic History of Ireland since 1660* (London: B. T. Batsford, 1972, 1987), pp. 37–39, 75–76.

[140] Arthur Young, *A Tour in Ireland with General Observations on the Present State of that Kingdom* (London: 1780), 2 vols., I, pp. viii, ix.

[141] See above, chapter 5, section 2.

[142] On Jonathan Swift, Bishop Berkeley and others in this context, see James Kelly, "Jonathan Swift and the Irish Economy in the 1720s," *Eighteenth-Century Ireland* 6 (1991), pp. 7–36; Patrick Kelly, "Berkeley's Economic Writings" in Kenneth P. Winkler ed., *The Cambridge Companion to Berkeley* (Cambridge: Cambridge University Press, 2005); S. J. Connolly, *Divided Kingdom: Ireland, 1630–1800* (Oxford: Oxford University Press, 2008), pp. 345–46.

[143] Ibid., p. 347. See Thomas Prior, *A List of the Absentees of Ireland* (Dublin: 1729).

[144] See also EB to French Laurence, 16 March 1797, *Corr.*, IX, pp. 283–84, in response to the Whig opposition's resurrection of plans for an absentee tax, and EB to French Laurence, 1 June 1797, ibid., p. 365. Cf. Smith, *Wealth of Nations*, II, p. 895, who was sympathetic to the tax.

[145] EB, *Letter to Sir Charles Bingham* (30 October 1773), *W & S*, IX, p. 489.

[146] Cf. EB to Earl Fitzwilliam, 15 March 1797, *Corr.*, IX, p. 283, for Burke's response to Grattan's attempt to introduce a similar tax during the crises of the 1790s.

somewhere," Burke contended, "can only be in England."[147] The metropolis was charged with regulating the policy and administration of its subordinate provinces, including the laws of a dependent kingdom such as Ireland. This was achieved under the various modifications of Poynings' Law by providing the English Privy Council with a role in Irish government, an arrangement that Burke believed served to liberalize legislation.[148] Any challenge to this system of organisation would threaten the cohesion of the Empire. But while imperial sovereignty was necessarily final and supreme, its policies should foster security and liberty. As Burke saw it, commerce was the most obvious candidate for enjoying the privilege of freedom: "I do not mean to impeach the Right of the Parliament of Great Britain to make Laws for the Trade of Ireland. I only speak of what Laws it is right for Parliament to make."[149]

A threat to the customary supremacy of the British legislature was posed by a plan announced before both Houses of the Irish parliament on 25 November 1775 to dispatch 4,000 soldiers stationed in Ireland to America, replacing them with foreign Protestant troops.[150] Without any prior consultation with the House of Commons, it was proposed that the troops should be charged on the British establishment.[151] As Burke made plain in his notes for a speech on this subject in February 1776, this provision would undermine the authority of the "*presiding Legislature*."[152] The superior rights of the British parliament were fundamental to the constitution of the Empire established at the Glorious Revolution. It was then that the principles governing relations between the two islands "underwent an accurate Survey and obtained a *thorough repair*."[153] Fundamental to this reformation was the constitution of the military, designed in response to the misdemeanours of the late seventeenth-century monarchy. Positioned only twelve hours sail from the mainland, Ireland was close to the "bosom" of the Empire.[154] Since James II had provocatively introduced Irish regiments into England, a triple "jealousy" had governed parliament's policy towards Ireland. This comprised, first, alarm about the existence of standing armies in general; second, opposition to the introduction of foreign troops into Britain; and, third, a specific concern for the military situation in Ireland.[155] These fears

[147] EB, *Letter to Sir Charles Bingham* (30 October 1773), *W & S*, IX, p. 488.

[148] Ibid., p. 489.

[149] EB, *Two Letters on the Trade of Ireland* (1778), *W & S*, IX, p. 515.

[150] Burke had been hoping for a rather different result. As he wrote to the Duke of Richmond, 26 September 1775, *Corr.*, III, p. 218: "If they [the Irish parliament] should only add to this, a *suspension* of *extraordinary* grants of supplies for Troops employed *out* of the Kingdom, in Effect employed against their own clearest rights and privileges, they would preserve the whole Empire from a ruinous war." Troops were being moved from Ireland to the colonies in early 1775: see Charles O'Hara to EB, 25 January 1775, Hoffman, *Burke*, p. 576.

[151] Burke first raised objections in early December 1775: see EB, Bill to Prohibit American Trade, 1 December 1775, *London Evening Post*; PDNA, 2 December 1775, VI, p. 313.

[152] EB, Speech on Foreign Troops in Ireland, 18 February 1776, *W & S*, IX, p. 499.

[153] Ibid., p. 501.

[154] Ibid., p. 500.

[155] Ibid., p 501.

could only be allayed by requiring the consent of the Commons for the maintenance of a standing force, which in turn presupposed the control of the British legislature over the Irish parliament.[156] That meant that while the expense of Ireland's defence should be provided for out of Irish coffers, its character should be determined by the cast of British policy.[157] This was the hard and necessary reality governing imperial subordination. Yet, as Burke had argued in 1773, as long as this subordination of parts subsisted, it was vital that Irish property be represented in the British Commons.[158] This would serve to mitigate the application in practice of the rights which accompanied the superior jurisdiction of Westminster. Above all, it held out the possibility of reforming commercial monopolies.

Despite what seemed to Burke its obvious advantages, the existence of this mitigated exercise of authority had attracted criticism since the days of Molyneux and Swift.[159] It was regularly said, Burke was aware, "that Ireland, in many particulars, is not bound to consider itself as part of the British body" because "this country, in many instances, is mistaken enough to treat you as foreigners, and draws away your money by Absentees, without suffering you to enjoy your natural advantages in trade and commerce."[160] In response to what Burke viewed as these legitimate complaints, he set out his attitude to commercial regulation. "No man living," he proclaimed, "loves restrictive regulations of any kind less than myself; at best, nine times out of ten, they are little better than laborious and vexatious follies." Moreover, as was apparently the case with Ireland, such limitations operated as "oppressions" as well as "absurdities."[161] The American crisis intensified Irish feelings of resentment. "We know that *you*," the colonial Congress admitted, "are not without your grievances."[162] The British naval and military demand for Irish provisions in the midst of war preparations prompted the government to embargo Irish exports to the colonies by order in council on 3 February 1776.[163] Among Irish patriots, the move was reminiscent of the severe restrictions already introduced by Lord North against the rebellious colonies.

The previous year, North had implemented what seemed to his opponents a punitive policy of constraining traffic out of New England. Burke protested against

[156] The 1689 Bill of Rights outlawed the maintenance of a standing army in peacetime without the consent of parliament: 1 Will. & Mar., Sess. 2, c. 2.

[157] EB, Speech on Foreign Troops in Ireland, 18 February 1776, *W & S*, IX, p. 499n4.

[158] EB, *Letter to Sir Charles Bingham* (30 October 1773), ibid., p. 490.

[159] Robert Mahony, "Protestant Dependence and Consumption in Swift's Irish Writings" in S. J. Connolly ed., *Political Ideas in Eighteenth-Century Ireland* (Dublin: Four Courts Press, 2000); Patrick Kelly, "The Politics of Political Economy in Mid-Eighteenth-Century Ireland" in ibid.

[160] EB, *Letter to Sir Charles Bingham* (30 October 1773), *W & S*, IX, p. 494.

[161] Ibid.

[162] *An Address of the Twelve United Colonies of North America to the People of Ireland* (Philadelphia, PA: 1775), p. 11

[163] Theresa M. O'Connor, "The Embargo on the Export of Irish Provisions, 1776–1779," *Irish Historical Studies*, 2:5 (1940), pp. 3–11; Truxes, *Irish-American Trade, 1660–1783*, pp. 238–45; Conway, *British Isles and the War of American Independence*, pp. 61–62.

the measure in March 1775, presenting it as, in effect, an attempt to destroy overseas dominion by a foolhardy attempt to bolster British authority.[164] North's plan included proposals to prohibit the relevant colonies from fishing off the Newfoundland coast. However, the legislation was to be accompanied by measures to encourage Irish commerce.[165] As well as expanding the opportunities for fishing, bounties were to be granted on the importation of flax seed, and the export of raiment for troops was to be permitted.[166] Nonetheless, Burke objected to the spirit of these apparently generous provisions. While they had merit when viewed from a limited perspective, they had not arisen from any "liberal" opinion in favour of Ireland or been "based upon an enlarged and general idea." They were, instead, a side-product of ministerial despotism in the colonies, "giving Ireland spoils taken from America."[167] Burke proposed an amendment to consider the issue of trade more generally. This should include consideration of the importation of sugars into Ireland directly and a plan to lift restraints on the export of Irish woollens.[168] The amendment, however, was rejected. Charles O'Hara largely confirmed Burke's scepticism about North's intentions: "the present object seems to be merely with a view to keep Ireland in good humour, while America is in ferment."[169]

On 17 March 1778, the king's message respecting the alliance between the colonies and France was read before the Houses of Parliament.[170] The "civil war" with the colonies would now be complicated by a European war. In that context, the loyalty of Ireland became more urgent than ever before. The sister kingdom was now, as Burke bluntly stated, "the chief dependency of the British Crown."[171] Yet its commerce was forced to operate at a continuous disadvantage. The distress of the country, as *The Annual Register* claimed, had reached its present "alarming and deplorable state, under the unhappy consequences of the American war."[172] In this situation, Earl Nugent, formerly MP for Bristol as Lord Clare, moved for a committee to enquire into the state of the trade of Ireland on 2 April 1778.[173] Current arrangements, he announced, were impolitic and unjust, calling for a thorough revision of the system.[174] The opposition largely supported the government's proposals. For William

[164] EB, Speech on Restraining Bill, 6 March 1775, *W & S*, III, p. 98.

[165] For discussion of the benefits, see Sir Lucius O'Brien, *The Substance of Two Speeches in the House of Commons in Ireland on the Subject of Fisheries* (Dublin: 1776).

[166] These provisions passed as 15 Geo. III, c. 45.

[167] EB, Speech on Fishery Bill, 11 April 1775, *W & S*, IX, p. 496.

[168] EB to Charles O'Hara, 26 April 1775, *Corr.*, III, p. 152. Lifting the prohibition on the export of woolens was proposed by the Duke of Richmond's brother-in-law, Thomas Conolly, but supported by Burke. See *Parliamentary Register* (Almon), I, pp. 428–30.

[169] Charles O'Hara to EB, 3 May 1775, Hoffman, *Burke*, p. 580.

[170] *Parliamentary History*, XIX, cols. 912–13.

[171] EB, Speech on Irish Trade, 2 April 1778, *W & S*, IX, p. 504.

[172] "The History of Europe" in *The Annual Register for the Year 1778* (London: 1779), p. 172.

[173] *Parliamentary History*, XIX, cols. 1100–2.

[174] Ibid., col. 1102. Reform had broad-based government support: see McDowell, *Ireland in the Age of Imperialism*, pp. 250–51.

Baker, the current restrictions defeated their own purpose. William Meredith applied this insight to the state of woollen manufacture. Unable to export to England, the Irish exchanged their produce with France, enabling that country to rival Britain in the precise area which had provoked envy.[175] Over the following days, a succession of resolutions were passed in the House of Commons recommending in the face of objections from British merchants that Ireland should be permitted to extend its trade by exporting hitherto prohibited commodities and importing directly from the colonies. This raised fears that cheap labour and low taxes in Ireland would "ruin" manufacturing towns in England.[176] Not only were these apprehensions foundationless in Burke's opinion, current exigencies made them a relative luxury.[177] As Burke wrote to Samuel Span, a Master of the Merchants Hall in Bristol, it was necessary "to improve the portion of this Empire which is left to us to enable every part to contribute in some degree to the strength and welfare of the whole."[178] The benefits of liberalization lay far off. What made the gesture urgent was the need to satisfy Irish opinion in order to foster a sense of common interest. The measures on the table were of largely symbolic importance. They were, as Burke made plain in a letter to Champion, for the most part "frivolous," and had they been substantial Ireland lacked the capital to derive major benefits from the concessions. What moved the Commons was the determination not to be diverted by another rebellion, which a deterioration in relations with Ireland might effect.[179]

After Burke had transmitted the resolutions on Irish trade to the Society of Merchant Adventurers of Bristol, he received a reply from Span setting out the Society's objections, recommending a union between the two kingdoms as the best means of resolving disputes.[180] Burke published his response as *Two Letters on the Trade of Ireland*, a joint missive sent to Span as well as Hartford, Cowles and Co., iron merchants in Bristol who had similarly objected to Burke's stance. An incorporating union between both kingdoms was a "great question of state," Burke acknowledged, but it was one on which he would not pronounce before the occasion arose.[181] In the meantime, he would deal with the situation at hand. This centered on the attitude of the British government, which had been conducting imperial policy under the powerful delusion that affairs of state could be regulated according to the whims

[175] *The Annual Register for the Year 1778*, p. 173. For Baker's and Meredith's contributions to the debate, see *Parliamentary History*, XIX, cols. 1103–5.

[176] Ibid., col. 1111.

[177] EB, *Two Letters on the Trade of Ireland* (1778), *W & S*, IX, p. 510: "Ireland pays as many taxes, as those who are the best judges of her powers, are of opinion she can bear." Cf. EB, Speech on Irish Trade, 6 May 1778, *Parliamentary History*, XIX, col. 1121.

[178] EB to Samuel Span, 9 April 1778, *Corr.*, III, p. 426.

[179] EB to Richard Champion, 11 April 1778, ibid., p. 427. Cf. EB to Richard Champion, 14 April 1778, ibid., pp. 429–30.

[180] For the wider context for the proposal, see James Kelly, "The Origins of the Act of Union: An Examination of Unionist Opinion in Britain and Ireland, 1650–1800," *Irish Historical Studies*, 25:99 (May 1987), pp. 236–63.

[181] EB, *Two Letters on the Trade of Ireland* (1778), *W & S*, IX, p. 510.

of its rulers.[182] This proud and imperious disposition had engendered the schism with America. Now that the ministry was seeking to revise this approach in connection with Ireland, the narrow interests of municipal traders threatened to revive the spirit of jealousy, and thereby punish Ireland by strangling its commerce. Given the similarity of climate and the proximity between both kingdoms, it was inevitable that there would be overlap in produce and manufactures.[183] Competition, however, did not mean zero-sum rivalry: "The prosperity arising from an enlarged and liberal system improves all its objects: and the participation of a trade with flourishing Countries is much better than the monopoly of want and penury."[184]

The defence of imperial controls imposed on Irish traffic focused on the mother country's contribution to security. It was a strangely counterproductive argument from Burke's perspective: in effect, he pointed out, the role of the military included the enforcement of unpopular restraints on trade. An army kept up to "cramp" prosperity is an instrument of national servitude.[185] *Ceteris paribus*, freedom of trade was a fundamental human liberty. Opposition to it was based on the misguided apprehension that justice to others brought with it a disadvantage to ourselves.[186] This fear was inevitable yet contrary to natural right. "God has given the Earth to the Children of Man," Burke wrote.[187] Restriction of trade in the absence of overriding need was in effect a violation of the laws of nature. For that reason Burke associated oppressive regulation not only with injustice but also with impiety. The unbounded right to traffic was at once "more rational, more just, and more religious."[188] What the law of nature prescribed was also enjoined by revelation: "Man shall eat his Bread by his Labour."[189] Labour gave rise to property as an instrument of self-preservation. By the same natural right, the obligations of contract and freedom of exchange could not with justice be unilaterally cancelled. The unconstrained dynamics of production, consumption and demand could only reasonably be hampered on the basis of a plea of necessity. Necessity implied a right of self-defence in the face of hostile forces. It had no bearing on Britain's relations to Ireland since both kingdoms shared a common interest. That common interest was their mutual utility: "if Ireland is beneficial to you, it is so, not from the parts in which it is restrained, but from those in which

[182] Ibid., p. 508.

[183] Ibid., p. 509.

[184] EB to Samuel Span, 9 April 1778, *Corr.*, III, p. 426. Cf. James Caldwell, *An Enquiry how far the Restrictions Laid upon the Trade of Ireland are a Benefit or Disadvantage to the British Dominions in General* (London: 1779), p. 10.

[185] EB, *Two Letters on the Trade of Ireland* (1778), *W & S*, IX, p. 515.

[186] Ibid., p. 507. The view was soon encapsulated in [Anon.], *Impartial Thoughts on a Free Trade to the Kingdom of Ireland* (London: 1779).

[187] EB, *Two Letters on the Trade of Ireland* (1778), *W & S*, IX, p. 515, citing Psalms, 114:16.

[188] Ibid., p. 514. Cf. EB, *Thoughts and Details on Scarcity* (1795), ibid., p. 137: "the laws of commerce, which are the laws of nature, and consequently the laws of God." For the providential basis of commercial sociability, see Jacob Viner, *The Role of Providence in the Social Order: An Essay in Intellectual History* (Philadelphia: American Philosophical Society, 1972).

[189] EB, *Two Letters on the Trade of Ireland* (1778), *W & S*, IX , p. 515, citing *Genesis*, 3:19.

it is left free, though not unrivalled. The greater its freedom, the greater must be your advantage."[190] Commercial competition between political allies could only serve to advance the interest of both.

Burke pursued this argument with vigour on the second reading of the Bill to permit the importation of colonial goods into Ireland on 6 May 1778. He demonstrated how much of the alarm about Irish trade had been based on the most deluded fantasies about her position. These fears had longstanding roots in the "rich country-poor country" debate, extending back into the seventeenth century.[191] A common assumption was that the long-term advantages arising from Ireland's low-wage economy would in due course give her an edge in the competitive struggle for markets.[192] Burke estimated that Britain's opportunities for traffic and its accumulated wealth were greater than those of Ireland by a factor of forty. At the same time, proportionately compared, Irish taxes were four times as stringent as those in Britain. These factors combined made the apprehension that Irish trade would supplant its chief rival an extraordinarily misguided perception on the part of its main competitor.[193] The incidence of blind "terrors" was well illustrated by the response to proposals to legalise the exportation of sailcloth, cordage and iron from Ireland.[194] Heated petitions were soon launched against the measures.[195] However, it transpired that these commodities could already be freely imported.[196] The petitioners "had not felt from the reality, what they dreaded from the idea," Burke commented.[197] Behind this dread lay the spectre of losing market share, yet the worry was based on a basic misunderstanding. Parity of advantage between Britain and Ireland was as remote a possibility as it was a persistent concern: "The great disproportion of capital effectually destroys the possibility of an equality," Burke contended.[198] However much Irish

[190] Ibid., p. 517.

[191] On this, see Bernard Semmel, "The Hume-Tucker Debate and Pitt's Trade Proposals," *Economic Journal*, 75:300 (December 1965), pp. 759–70; Istvan Hont, "The 'Rich Country–Poor Country' Debate in Scottish Classical Political Economy" in Istvan Hont and Michael Ignatieff eds., *Wealth and Virtue: The Shaping of Political Economy in the Scottish Enlightenment* (Cambridge: Cambridge University Press, 1983); idem, "The 'Rich Country–Poor Country' Debate Revisited: The Irish Origins and French Reception of the Hume Paradox" in Margaret Schabas and Carl Wennerlind eds., *David Hume's Political Economy* (London: Routledge, 2007).

[192] This assumption, and its consequences, is discussed in Istvan Hont, "Free Trade and the Economic Limits to National Politics: Neo-Machiavellian Political Economy Reconsidered" in John Dunn ed., *The Economic Limits to Modern Politics* (Cambridge: Cambridge University Press, 1990); David Armitage, *The Ideological Origins of the British Empire* (Cambridge: Cambridge University Press, 2000), ch. 6.

[193] EB, Speech on Irish Trade, 6 May 1778, *W & S*, IX, p. 521.

[194] The phrase appears in EB, Speech on Irish Trade, 5 May 1778, ibid., p. 519. Cf. EB, Speech on Irish Trade, 4 May 1778, ibid., p. 518, on the "preposterous" tendency to alarm.

[195] *CJ*, XXXVI, p. 950. See EB, *Letter to Thomas Burgh* (1780), *W & S*, IX, p. 549: "petitions crowded in upon one another."

[196] Sailcloth was only subject to restrictions for as long as the Irish parliament granted bounties on its export, as per 23 Geo. II, c. 32. The importation of iron was permitted under 7 and 8 Will. III, c. 5.

[197] EB, Speech on Irish Trade, 6 May 1778, *W & S*, IX, p. 522.

[198] Ibid., p. 521.

trade should be permitted to prosper freely, it was never to be expected that it could overhaul the British. Ireland could be expected to progress under a liberal regime, but a disproportion between it and Britain would remain. Burke's argument followed the contention made famous by Hume: "the increase of riches and commerce in any one nation, instead of hurting, commonly promotes the riches and commerce of all its neighbours."[199] The causes of suspicion between commercial rivals lacked foundation. The advance of Irish trade would forever be offset by improvements in British manufacture. Both would continue to find appropriate outlets for their commodities. "The lowness of labour is a nugatory argument," Burke claimed: by the time that Irish manufacture could ever rival British products, the price of labour in both jurisdictions would be at par.[200]

The success of British mercantile interests in limiting the relaxation of Irish trade restrictions was causing consternation in Dublin by 1779. The opposition occurred in the midst of a rising force of volunteer soldiers that had been forming for the defence of the kingdom since 1778. Spain entered the American war a year after the French. With Irish troops already engaged across the Atlantic, the south of Ireland was perilously exposed. In response to the failure to fund a new militia Act in 1778, military associations formed on a voluntary basis offered security to home defence. On a smaller scale, local military bands had formed earlier in the decade, but in 1778 the formation of volunteer corps on a national scale gathered momentum.[201] Numbers rose from 15,000 in 1779 to over 40,000 by 1780.[202] Catholics, who under the penal laws were prohibited from bearing arms, were for the most part excluded from this popular show of strength. Soon the Volunteers were flexing their muscles. On 4 November 1779, a Dublin contingent massed in the city calling for free trade.[203] Earlier in the year, demands for the boycott of British goods had been raised, and a non-importation movement spread through the south of the country. In March 1779, Burke had protested that the administration, in the process of losing one portion of the Empire, "was now likely to drive another into rebellion."[204] Opinion in the Irish Commons rose against the government. Walter Hussey Burgh's amendment in the Dublin parliament in favour of free trade was unanimously passed, with North having to concede the export of wool and glass by December 1779.

Burke's response to the Volunteers mixed resignation with alarm. Since the legal provision of defence in Ireland had failed, the people were "in the right" to arm

[199] David Hume, "Of the Jealousy of Trade" in *Essays*, p. 328. For the explicit use of Hume to support the Irish case, see William Eden, *A Letter to the Earl of Carlisle on the Representations of Ireland respecting a Free Trade* (Dublin: 1779), pp. 27–28.

[200] EB, Speech on Irish Trade, 6 May 1778, *W & S*, IX, p. 522.

[201] McDowell, *Ireland in the Age of Imperialism*, pp. 255–6.

[202] Connolly, *Divided Kingdom*, p. 403.

[203] For the surrounding debates, see George O'Brien, "The Irish Free Trade Agitation of 1779," *English Historical Review*, 38 (October 1923), pp. 564–81 and 39 (January 1924), pp. 95–109.

[204] EB, Speech on Irish Trade and the State of Ireland, 12 March 1779, *W & S*, IX, p. 530.

themselves.[205] Their decision to do so, however, was hardly comforting. Burke was amazed that the British Commons practically ignored these citizen soldiers who constituted an "illegal military force."[206] At the end of the year, Burke viewed with scepticism Lord North's belated efforts to confer legitimacy upon the burgeoning military associations in Ireland by retrospectively legalising their existence.[207] He was dismayed by the potential for popular insurgency, noting darkly that the troops were electing their own officers.[208] He commended the refusal of the Lord Chancellor of Ireland to vote his approval of the Volunteers in the Lords.[209] But while widespread armament was a worrying development in Ireland, it was evidently a product of ministerial folly in Britain.[210] Spurned by the metropolis, the "sister" kingdom came to view itself "as free and independent." This trajectory was reminiscent of the response in the colonies, where resistance had steadily escalated in response to crude acts of power.[211] In receiving notice of the critical reaction of Irish parliamentarians to the Rockinghams' conduct in the face of North's trade concessions, Burke articulated his reaction to the Volunteers at length.[212] He conceded, with some irony, the passive part that he had played in contrast to the proactive posture of Irish Whigs—"at the head," he added provocatively, "of forty thousand men."[213] He also revealed his preferred approach, which was to get the principle of free trade accepted in the British parliament before gradually enlarging the extent of commercial concessions to Ireland.[214] By comparison, the extraction of national benefits by the threat of military force was illiberal and potentially subversive of the constitution.

Indeed, it was altogether subversive, if justifiable de jure. The Irish were in the early flush of victory, drawing confidence from their palpable military strength.[215] They would be well advised to reflect on where their conduct was likely to lead. A militia had been raised without commission. This could only be termed legitimate in terms of the rights of resistance. This army, Burke remarked, "did not so much contradict the spirit of the law, as supersede it." Since its justification was not based on constitutional procedure, it must derive from an authority "still higher."[216] This

[205] Ibid.

[206] Ibid., p. 531. For Burke's response to the Volunteers, see Conor Cruise O'Brien, *The Great Melody: A Thematic Biography of Edmund Burke* (London: Sinclair-Stevenson, 1992), pp. 178ff.

[207] EB, Speech on Trade Concession to Ireland, 6 December 1779, *W & S*, IX, p. 540. Cf. the more upbeat response of Fox in *Parliamentary History*, XX, cols. 1226ff.

[208] EB, Speech on Trade Concession to Ireland, 6 December 1779, *W & S*, IX, pp. 540–41.

[209] Ibid., p. 541. Burke had been in contact with the Lord Chancellor the previous spring: see EB to the Marquess of Rockingham, 30 April 1779, *Corr.*, III, p. 66.

[210] Burke was keen to occlude the weak position from which the British were forced to negotiate. See EB to the Marquess of Rockingham, 9 May 1779, *Corr.*, IV, pp. 70–71.

[211] EB, Speech on Trade Concession to Ireland, 6 December 1779, *W & S*, IX, pp. 538–40.

[212] The terms of his response are set out in Thomas Burgh to EB, 27 January 1780, *Corr.*, IV, pp. 201–2.

[213] EB, *Letter to Thomas Burgh* (1780), *W & S*, IX, p. 546.

[214] Ibid., p. 549.

[215] Ibid., pp. 546, 548.

[216] Ibid., p, 557.

was the authority of popular resistance, which could not be denied in the face of the need for national defence. As Burke would later insist in the 1790s, this was the final expedient of desperation. It was also a perilous method of redress. Soldiers could not offer a permanent political solution, "and would prove but a poor shelter for your liberty."[217] There was an inkling of a grim future in the posture of the Irish parliament which had placed its trust in the British ministry at the expense of the opposition, "composed of the far greater part of the independent property and independent rank of the country."[218] Having acted a great part by resort to unconstitutional means, Irish methods threatened to overthrow the balance of forces in the Empire: they had managed to coerce the crown and thus, indirectly, the British commons, bolstering the power of the king against the authority of parliament.[219] The following year Burke underlined the extent of his discomfort: "An independent army was established in Ireland,—this was a weighty consideration; and the more so, as the liberty of this country was involved in it."[220] As Burke explained the situation in Ireland in 1778 to his Bristol constituents in 1780, the whole country was "instantly in a flame." In arming to resist the threat from France, the Irish actually "cast off" the power of Britain. The country was then on the verge of "an abyss of blood and confusion." Ireland demanded freedom with arms in its hands, lacking any sanction from the law. Britain was simply incapable of restraining this move: not a single executive officer or judicial body in the sister kingdom would recognise the authority of the king's army in the country.[221]

The menace of the Volunteers persisted into 1782. In Armagh, on Friday 15 February, the first Dungannon Convention resolved under Lord Charlemont that Ireland should be granted legislative independence, that Poynings' Law regulating the transmission of Irish legislation should be amended, that Irish judges should be granted security of tenure, and that a limited mutiny Bill should be agreed.[222] "Volunteers from every quarter paid their tribute and applause," Francis Dobbs observed.[223] On 14 March, the Irish parliament adjourned for four weeks, and in the interlude the North administration fell. By the end of the month a government under Rockingham had succeeded, with Burke assuming the role of paymaster general. On 8 April, the day on which the members of the new ministry took their seats, the former Irish chief secretary, William Eden, moved for the repeal of the Declaratory Act

[217] Ibid., p. 548.

[218] Ibid., p. 547.

[219] Ibid., pp. 558–9.

[220] EB, Speech on Mutiny Bill, 20 February 1781, ibid., p. 564. Cf. Samuel Johnson's allegations of rebellion recorded in *Dr. Campbell's Diary of a Visit to England in 1775*, ed. J. L. Clifford (Cambridge: Cambridge University Press, 1947), pp. 94–95.

[221] EB, Speech at Bristol Previous to the Election, 6 September 1780, *W & S*, III, pp. 630–31.

[222] Edmund Curtis and R. B. McDowell eds., *Irish Historical Documents, 1172–1922* (London: Routledge, 1943), pp. 233–5. For a contemporary account, see Charles Henry Wilson, *A Compleat Collection of the Resolutions of the Volunteers, Grand Juries &c. of Ireland* (Dublin: 1782).

[223] Francis Dobbs, *A History of Irish Affairs* (Dublin: 1782), pp. 65–66.

establishing the legislative subordination of Ireland.[224] It was a proposal, Burke responded, of considerable magnitude that threatened to "tear asunder the connection between England and Ireland."[225] Within days, he was elaborating on his position to his old friend John Hely Hutchinson, a member of the Irish parliament and the provost of Trinity College: "The repeal desired could only serve to disgrace the British Legislature, without serving that of Ireland in any degree."[226] Burke had no desire to see the Irish legislative process separated from British parliamentary proceedings.[227] Some concession, nonetheless, was necessary from the ministry, since "no reluctant tie" could be "a Strong one."[228] Still, Burke expected the introduction of "some clear and solid settlement" establishing the respective rights of the kingdoms.[229] A mere act of repeal was an empty gesture lacking constitutional specificity. What was required was a compact regulating relations between the two countries.

On 16 April 1782, Henry Grattan proposed in the Irish Commons that the key elements of the Dungannon resolutions be recommended to the king.[230] Rockingham felt obliged to accede to the demand. In June, the British parliament repealed the Declaratory Act, and in July it agreed to modify the provisions of Poynings' Law. Burke was forced to accept the inevitable, recognising that Ireland "was to be placed on a footing of equality with Great Britain."[231] Yet even in this context he reminded his audience that there was no juridical limit to the discretion of British power. Coordinate status had been conceded to the kingdom of Ireland, although the fact remained it was still the "less powerful state."[232] The country might now be "*constitutionally*" independent, Burke later argued, but "*Politically* she never can be so."[233] Burke recounted this insight again in the final year of his life: "At Bottom Ireland has no other choice, I mean no other rational choice."[234] Already dissatisfied with Grattan's "Revolution," Henry Flood sought to secure the concession of independence by a further "renunciation" of British legislative authority in Ireland.[235] In

[224] *Parliamentary History*, XXII, cols. 1241–46.

[225] EB, Speech on Irish Crisis, 8 April 1782, *W & S*, IX, p. 581.

[226] EB to John Hely Hutchinson, post 9 April 1782, *Corr.*, IV, p. 440.

[227] Thomas H. D. Mahoney, *Edmund Burke and Ireland* (Cambridge, MA: Harvard University Press, 1960), pp. 132–33.

[228] EB to the Earl of Charlemont, 12 June 1782, *Corr.*, IV, p. 460.

[229] EB to John Hely Hutchinson, post 9 April 1782, ibid., p. 440. The view was shared among Rockinghamites in general: see P. J. Marshall, *Remaking the British Atlantic: The United States and the British Empire after American Independence* (Oxford: Oxford University Press, 2012), pp. 139–40.

[230] The published version of his speech appears in *The Speeches of the Right Hon. Henry Grattan*, ed. Daniel Owen Madden (Dublin: 1871), p. 70.

[231] EB, Speech on Irish Affairs, 17 May 1782, *W & S*, IX, p. 582. He nonetheless assured Thomas Lewis O'Beirne on 7 June 1782 that "I most Sincerely Sympathise in the Joy which you feel in Common with the Whole Kingdom" (*Corr.*, IV, p. 457).

[232] EB, Speech on Irish Commercial Propositions, 19 May 1785, *W & S*, IX, p. 591.

[233] EB to the Rev. Thomas Hussey, 18 May 1795, *Corr.*, VIII, p. 247.

[234] EB to Unknown, February 1797, *Corr.*, IX, p. 257.

[235] For the surrounding debate, see Stephen Small, *Political Thought in Ireland, 1776–1798* (Oxford: Oxford University Press, 2002), pp. 113–15.

the face of this attempt on the dignity of the British parliament, Burke emphasised the finality of the existing repeal "of all claim to the right of legislative or judicial power over Ireland, in every case whatsoever."[236] Yet he remained acutely aware of the realities of power underlying the new constitutional arrangement. "Ireland is an independent Kingdom to all intents and purposes," he acknowledged to Charlemont in the summer of 1783.[237] Nonetheless, circumstances pointed to the superior capacity of Britain, with which Ireland would at all times be wise to reckon.[238]

Burke's restiveness about two coordinate legislatures in the Empire stemmed from his awareness of the potential for mutual jealousy that this created.[239] "The old link is snapped asunder," he reminded the Lord Lieutenant, the Duke of Portland, in May 1782.[240] It remained to be seen how business would henceforth be transacted. Britain had already given a "dreadful" example of how the abuse of power could inflame relations between metropole and province. It was now incumbent on Ireland not to repeat the exercise by imposing itself high-handedly on Britain.[241] Even short-term moderation was no guarantee of success: the scope for future friction palpably remained. Fourteen years after the establishment of Grattan's parliament, Burke reiterated his original dissatisfaction: "I never liked, as is well known, that total independence of Ireland which, without, in my opinion, adding any security to its Liberty, took it out of the common constitutional protection of the Empire."[242] Legislative autonomy had been conceded to Ireland, yet there was little gain in terms of either administrative efficiency or constitutional freedom in the Empire. On the contrary, the management of Ireland was now in the hands of a restrictive clique.[243] Burke lamented that arrangement until the year of his death. Ireland prospered best in subordination to "*Imperial* politics," destined in that role to live and die with Britain.[244]

William Pitt was equally alarmed about the prospect of a contest between the two kingdoms. By 1784, demands for protective tariffs were already being raised in Dublin. Accordingly, Pitt began to search for means by which the two countries "may exercise the rights of legislation, without clashing with each other on the one

[236] EB, Speech on Affairs of Ireland, 20 December 1782, *W & S*, IX, p. 583.

[237] EB to the Earl of Charlemont, 5 August 1783, *Corr.*, V, p. 103.

[238] Irish Bills, in being presented to George III, would still be scrutinised by the British Privy Council and law officers. See J. C. Beckett, "Anglo-Irish Constitutional Relations in the Later Eighteenth Century" in idem, *Confrontations: Studies in Irish History* (London: Faber and Faber, 1972).

[239] See, in this connection, John Hely Hutchinson to EB, 6 April 1782, *Corr.*, IV, p. 436, who regarded the repeal of the Declaratory Act as a measure likely to be "productive of dissidence and discord between the two Kingdoms." His tone suggests that he expected Burke's agreement with his position. Cf. EB to French Laurence, 20 November 1796, *Corr.*, IX, p. 126.

[240] EB to the Duke of Portland, 25 May 1782, *Corr.*, IV, p. 455.

[241] Ibid.

[242] EB to Earl Fitzwilliam, 20 November 1796, *Corr.*, IX, p. 122. Burke went so far as to ascribe the measure to Lord North, clearly blaming its introduction on the conduct of the previous administration (ibid., p. 123).

[243] See EB to Sylvester Douglas, post 30 December 1793, *Corr.*, VII, p. 509.

[244] EB to Unknown, February 1797, *Corr.*, IX, p. 257.

hand, or on the other being encumbered by the necessity of actual and positive concert on every point of common concern."[245] This was to be achieved by introducing a commercial settlement that would revise the Navigation Acts, establish a free trade between both countries in their own products, and secure a form of reciprocity in commercial duties.[246] The details of the eleven commercial propositions resulting from this ambition were negotiated intensively between mid-December 1784 and early January 1785.[247] In February the chief secretary, Thomas Orde, put the scheme to the Irish parliament. It included a measure to appropriate any surplus from the revenue on the Irish hereditary fund for the support of the Empire.[248] The prospect of an imperial contribution provoked opposition in Ireland, while fears for domestic manufactures inspired protests in British towns. By the time the revised scheme, now expanded to twenty propositions, reached the Irish parliament in August 1785, opposition had become focused on the restraint on the Irish legislature implied by the requirement that British colonial regulations be replicated in Ireland. Pitt's plan, it was clear, was heading for defeat.

Burke intervened in the debate on the commercial propositions in February and again in May 1785. The opposition was still smarting after its defeat in the general election of 1784, exacerbated by Pitt's insistence on protracting the scrutiny of Fox's election for Westminster. Fox and North hoped to discomfit Pitt by harrying him on the Irish issue, with William Eden and Lord Sheffield supplying stores of ammunition.[249] In approaching the general issue of mobilising the party, Burke felt that Fox was proceeding without a coherent set of principles, seeking to wound the government come what may.[250] The rift between the two figures was already underway. Even so, Burke set his face against the administration along with his friends.[251] On 21 February 1785, he complained that the ministry's measures lacked genuine reciprocity, and expressed doubt about Ireland's capacity to contribute revenue to an imperial fund given the country's recent management of its expenditure.[252] On

[245] Lord Ashbourne, *Pitt: Some Chapters in His Life and Times* (London: 1898), pp. 85–86.

[246] Vincent T. Harlow, *The Founding of the Second British Empire, 1763–1793* (London: Longmans, 1952–64), 2 vols., I, pp. 558ff.; John Ehrman, *The Younger Pitt: The Years of Acclaim* (London: Constable, 1969, 1984), pp. 197–99. For the wider intellectual context, see James Livesey, "Free Trade and Empire in the Anglo-Irish Commercial Propositions of 1785," *Journal of British History*, 52:1 (January 1785), pp. 103–27.

[247] James Kelly, *Prelude to Union: Anglo-Irish Politics in the 1780s* (Cork: Cork University Press, 1992), p. 96.

[248] Ehrman, *Pitt: The Years of Acclaim*, p. 203.

[249] Paul Kelly, "British and Irish Politics in 1785," *English Historical Review*, 90:365 (July 1975), pp. 536–63.

[250] EB to William Windham, 14 October 1784, *Corr.*, V, p. 177.

[251] A pamphlet, [Anon.], *A Reply to the Treasury Pamphlet, Entitled "The Proposed System of Trade with Ireland Explained"* (London: 1785), is often ascribed to Burke on the authority of a contemporary opponent. It seems unlikely that Burke would issue an anonymous pamphlet on Irish commerce when he was speaking openly on the subject in the Commons at the time. See William B. Todd, *A Bibliography of Edmund Burke* (Godalming: St. Paul's Bibliographies, 1982), p. 272.

[252] EB, Speech on Irish Commercial Propositions, 21 February 1785, *W & S*, IX, pp. 586–87.

19 May, he reiterated his suspicions, but he also considered more deeply the relations between the two kingdoms, explaining where his loyalties would lie in a contest between the two powers.[253] A week earlier, Fox had presented his sense that Pitt's proposals compromised the legislative independence of Ireland.[254] In taking up the debate seven days later, Burke turned to consider what Ireland's legislative autonomy implied. Free trade was of course desirable, but it needed to be established at first in principle, and then introduced strategically, without prejudice to British interests. The current levels of British debt could not bear a reduction in manufacture which ill-judged reciprocity might entail.[255] The adversity of Britain would mean the ruin of its sister kingdom, which was still subordinate to the mother country in terms of authority and wealth. Juridical equality might be established between the two islands, but Britain's practical supremacy was in effect a "decree of nature." It was the British who ultimately bore the burden of Empire, wielding "the great trident that was to move the world."[256]

8.4 Persecution and Toleration: Catholic Relief and the Gordon Riots

The American crisis, in negatively impacting upon Irish commerce, also raised the wider issue of Catholic emancipation. Writing to Charles James Fox in 1777, Burke noted how the history of Ireland had failed to instruct British policy in America. "Surely the state of Ireland ought for ever to teach parties moderation in their victories," he mused. Legislation introduced in opposition to a people could only breed hostility to the laws, making those who have little to lose more or less "dangerous" to established power.[257] But if the lessons of Ireland were forgotten in drafting policy for the colonies, nonetheless the state of America encouraged generosity elsewhere. On 7 April 1778, in the midst of debating the liberalisation of commercial policy, Thomas Townshend broached the topic of the penal laws against Irish Catholics. He hoped, he said, that Ireland could be delivered from its prolonged bondage.[258] However, as Lord North pointed out, since the popery laws originated for the most part in the Irish parliament, it was in Dublin that redress would have to begin.[259] In the 1760s, Blackstone remarked that fears of the Stuart pretender had all but vanished in Britain, and that the power of the papacy in Europe had declined to feeble

[253] Ibid., p. 590. Cf. *Morning Post*, 20 May 1785, for further reporting on Burke's description of his divided allegiance.

[254] *Parliamentary History*, XXV, col. 610.

[255] EB, Speech on Irish Commercial Propositions, *W & S*, IX, p. 590

[256] Ibid., p. 591. The reference is to Poseidon in Greek myth who, armed with a trident, shakes the world.

[257] EB to Charles James Fox, 8 October 1777, *Corr.*, III, p. 387.

[258] *Parliamentary History*, XVII, col. 1111.

[259] Ibid., col. 1112.

dimensions.[260] Within twenty years Burke could declare that toleration was "a late ripe fruit in the best climes."[261] Roman Catholic worship had prospered in Holland even in the face of its official proscription, and more recently it was tolerated after the conquest of Silesia.[262] Even in Ireland, Burke noted at the start of 1780, men of "Liberal Spirits" were rising to prominence.[263] This was "an enlightened age," he proclaimed in the same year.[264] He was surveying the fate of the Christian denominations in Europe in general. Frederick the Great had initiated the construction of St. Hedwig's Catholic Cathedral in Protestant Berlin in 1747. Protestantism was progressively indulged under Maria Theresa in Austria, and Catholicism under Gustavus III of Sweden.[265] Yet in Ireland the status of Catholics remained unaltered for three quarters of a century. Catholics in Grenada were granted the vote in 1768; in 1774 toleration was extended to the province of Quebec.[266] In the same year, a test enabling them to pledge their loyalty to the established regime passed in the Irish parliament. Promoted by the Church of Ireland bishop of Derry, Frederick Hervey, and modelled on the Gallican articles of the French Church, the oath cleared the ground for consideration of a relaxation of the penal laws.

By the 1770s, the Catholic Committee had been campaigning for relief for over a decade; religious services were openly conducted throughout Ireland; and arguments for employing members of the majority faith in the British army were regularly canvassed. At the same time, a Bill to permit Catholics to invest money in mortgages on land had been introduced before the Irish parliament, as was a measure to grant them long leases on marshland.[267] But it was in 1778 that the first

260 William Blackstone, *Commentaries on the Laws of England* (London: 1765–69), 4 vols., IV, p. 57. The passage was transcribed by Burke and can be found at WWM BkP 27:205.

261 EB, Thoughts on Approaching Executions, 10 July 1780, *W & S*, III, p. 614.

262 Christine Kooi, "Popish Impudence: The Perseverance of the Roman Catholic Faithful in Calvinist Holland, 1572–1620," *Sixteenth Century Journal*, 26:1 (Spring 1995), pp. 75–85; Francis Kugler, *The Life of Frederick the Great, Comprehending a Complete History of the Silesian Campaigns* (New York: Perkins, 1902), ch. 17.

263 EB to Lord Kenmare, 22 January 1780, *Corr.*, X, p. 7.

264 EB, Speech at Bristol Previous to the Election, 6 September 1780, *W & S*, III, p. 651.

265 Burke made these observations two years after the passage of the relief Act: see ibid., pp. 651–52. A more sceptical view of Maria Theresa is provided by Derek Beales, *Joseph II: In the Shadow of Maria Theresa, 1741–1780* (Cambridge: Cambridge University Press, 1987), pp. 465–66. For Sweden, see H. A. Barton, "Gustavus III of Sweden and the Enlightenment," *Eighteenth-Century Studies*, 6:1 (1972–73), pp. 1–34.

266 The situation in Grenada proved to be a brief interlude. Toleration for Irish Catholics is discussed in the wider imperial context in Jacqueline Hill, "Religious Toleration and the Relaxation of the Penal Laws: An Imperial Perspective, 1763–1780," *Archivium Hibernicum*, 44 (1989), pp. 98–109. On Grenada, see John Garner, "The Enfranchisement of Roman Catholics in the Maritimes," *Canadian Historical Review*, 34:3 (1953), pp. 203–18.

267 W. J. Amherst, *The History of Catholic Emancipation and the Progress of the Catholic Church in the British Isles* (London: 1886), 2 vols., I, ch. 1; W.E.H. Lecky, *History of Ireland in the Eighteenth Century* (London: Longmans, Green and Co., 1913), 4 vols., II, pp. 180ff.; Eamon O'Flaherty, "Ecclesiastical Politics and the Dismantling of the Penal Laws in Ireland, 1774–1782," *Irish Historical Studies*, 26:101 (May 1988), pp. 22–50.

substantial attempt to reform the popery laws got under way with the passage of an Act proposed by the affluent Dublin MP Luke Gardiner, that permitted Catholics to hold leases for a term of 999 years and to bequeath their estates intact to a single heir.[268] The measure had been sponsored by the British government on the back of recent toleration granted to English Catholics.[269] Sir George Savile's Bill for repealing the Act against the growth of popery in England received the royal assent on 3 June.[270] This was followed by Richard Cavendish's motion to repeal the prohibition on Catholics purchasing forfeited estates, which passed, Burke noted, with "unanimity and satisfaction."[271] Burke later commented that the values underlying this legislation were shared by "all who are distinguished in this Kingdom, for learning, integrity, and abilities, and all parties and descriptions of men."[272] On 25 April, the speaker in the Irish Commons, Edmund Sexton Perry, confirmed to Burke that Gardiner's measure was intended to follow in the footsteps of Savile's Bill.[273] Burke himself elucidated British strategy in early June 1778: "Parliament wished to speak its sense, as clearly as it could do without using its authority, to Ireland."[274] Britain had set an example which it was hoped Ireland would emulate by introducing what Burke would later call "this first faint sketch of toleration."[275]

Earlier in his parliamentary career, in the middle of April 1771, during a debate on a Bill intended to regulate military recruitment into the East India Company, Burke had reflected on the situation of Roman Catholics in Ireland. The proposal to admit them into Company forces involved dangers arising from their peculiar position as a body of men trusted to wield arms without possessing the privileges of citizenship. It was "indecent," Burke complained, to entrust defence to individuals denied the benefits of "human society."[276] Government would be better employed blunting the edge of persecution by addressing the grievances manifested among

[268] 17 and 18 Geo. III, c. 4.

[269] Robert E. Burns, "The Catholic Relief Act in Ireland, 1778," *Church History*, 32:2 (June 1963), pp. 181–206; Robert Kent Donovan, "The Military Origins of the Roman Catholic Relief Programme of 1778," *Historical Journal*, 28:1 (March 1985), pp. 79–102; Thomas Bartlett, *The Fall and Rise of the Irish Nation: The Catholic Question, 1690–1830* (Dublin: Gill and Macmillan, 1992), pp. 82–92; Karen Stanbridge, *Toleration and State Institutions: British Policy towards Catholics in Eighteenth-Century Ireland and Quebec* (Oxford: Lexington Books, 2003), pp. 167–77.

[270] It was widely believed that Burke drafted Savile's Bill. See Paul Levack, "Edmund Burke, His Friends, and the Dawn of Irish Catholic Emancipation," *Catholic Historical Review*, 37:4 (January 1952), pp. 385–414. He certainly wrote the preamble: see EB, Preamble for Catholic Relief Bill, May 1778, *W & S*, III, pp. 384–85.

[271] EB to Edmund Sexton Perry, 19 May 1778, *Corr.*, III, p. 449.

[272] EB to Job Watts, 10 August 1780, *Corr.*, IV, p. 261.

[273] Edmund Sexton Perry to EB, 25 May 1778, *Corr.*, III, p. 450.

[274] EB to Unknown, c. 3 June 1778, ibid., p. 455. Burke had drafted the Petition of English Catholics seeking redress from penal legislation in 1778: see EB, Draft Address for the Catholics, April 1778, *W & S*, III, pp. 376–79.

[275] EB, Speech at Bristol Previous to the Election, 6 September 1780, ibid., p. 649.

[276] EB, East India Recruitment Bill, 12 April 1771, Cavendish Diary, Eg. MS. 229, fols. 24–25.

this "oppressed people."[277] Hitherto, policy had focused on gaining converts at the expense of seeking to promote their civil welfare. The aim of the penal laws, as one anonymous pamphleteer reminded his readership, was to prevent the further growth of popery. An interest in the laws and civil constitution of the kingdom, which would foster industry and help dispel the mists of ignorance, could best be promoted by security of property. At that point, the author concluded, conversions would proceed in tandem with enlightenment.[278] Burke, however, was sceptical about proactively seeking conformity, however much the unity of the Christian churches might be desirable. In a manuscript note on the attitude of Irish Protestants, he commented that Catholics "must either be their Converts or their Slaves."[279] This attitude contradicted sound reason of state, which always precluded resort to persecution: "no good Constitution of Governm[en]t can find it necessary for its security to form any part of its subjects to permanent slavery."[280]

The intensity of Burke's commitment to Catholic toleration is most palpable in his correspondence with Sexton Perry, conducted as Gardiner's Bill was making its passage through the Irish Commons. The supporters of the Bill confronted "Gigantick prejudice" as they sought to restore over one and a half million souls to the rights of civil society.[281] Catholics were "aliens in their own Country . . . outlaws without charge or process."[282] The magistrate, Burke insisted, should not be confused with a proselyte seeking to provide for apostles rather than citizens in a commonwealth. He recalled the case of India, where the British presided over extensive territories that were both pagan and Muslim in denomination. It would be absurd to seek to alter or annihilate these existing faiths. The country could not be converted, though it should be governed for its benefit, "and our own."[283] Burke regarded Gardiner's measure as limited, but necessary, in seeking to cater to a fundamental principle. Ireland exhibited the spectacle of an oppressed "Multitude," disabled in terms of its civil entitlements and persecuted in its choice of religious worship. The current measure focused on the most basic of disqualifications—the inability securely to hold and transmit property. As Burke put it to an unknown correspondent at the time, the Bill "affirmed that *property* was to be encouraged in

[277] *General Evening Post*, 16 April 1771.

[278] [Anon.], *An Enquiry into the Policy of the Penal Laws Affecting the Popish Inhabitants of Ireland* (London: 1775), pp. 87–89. The pamphlet was reviewed in the *Monthly Review*, 53 (July 1975), pp. 17–21.

[279] Northamptonshire MS. A. XXVII.2.

[280] Northamptonshire MS. A. XXVII.95.

[281] Burke estimated the Catholic population of Ireland at 1,600,500 (EB, Speech at Bristol Previous to the Election, 6 September 1780, *W & S*, III, p. 650). Modern assessments place the total population of the country at about 4 million, with Catholics comprising three quarters of the whole. See K. H. Connell, *The Population of Ireland, 1750–1845* (Oxford: Oxford University Press, 1950), pp. 4–5, 25. Burke estimated that, by comparison, there were 50,000 Catholics in England (EB, Speech at Bristol Previous to the Election, 6 September 1780, *W & S*, III, p. 650). That number has more recently been put at 60,000: T. G. Holt, "A Note on Some Eighteenth-Century Statistics," *Recusant History*, 10 (1969–70), pp. 3–11.

[282] EB to Edmund Sexton Perry, 16 June 1778, *Corr.*, III, p. 457.

[283] Ibid., p. 438.

the acquisition, and quieted in the holding."[284] In Britain there existed a consensus around this right, providing grounds on which Anglican and Presbyterian, as well as Whig and Tory, could happily rally: "it was the clear opinion of every body," Burke proclaimed, "that property ought to have the same security and freedom in every part of the British dominions."[285] After the Bill had passed the Irish Commons on 6 August 1778, Burke rejoiced at the thought that its beneficiaries would soon "have a Country."[286] With divisions of Volunteers massing across the country, its opponents were bound to vent their disappointment: "There will be much arming, much blustering, and many pretended fears and apprehensions on this occasion," Burke wrote to his Catholic cousin, Garret Nagle.[287] It was advisable under the circumstances to welcome victory with humility.

To Burke's mind, toleration was a crucial component of enlightenment.[288] In this he was following standard Protestant histories of the Reformation that associated reformed religion with deliverance from the persecution characteristic of the "dark ages" that succeeded the primitive church.[289] The demography of Ireland made the provision of toleration peculiarly urgent. "We think," Burke declared, "that in no case should the few become the victims of the many." In fact he went further: wherever a contest unfortunately presented itself, "the few ought to be offered up for the safety of the multitude."[290] In his *Tracts relating to the Popery Laws* of 1765, Burke had dwelt with singular horror on the idea of converted sons acceding to the property of their Catholic fathers. On 16 June 1778, when the future of Gardiner's Bill looked unpropitious, as an amendment providing for a conforming child to be granted maintenance instead of his parent's estate was being debated in the Irish House of Commons, Burke expatiated to Sexton Perry on the baseness of the measure. It appealed to an ostensible principle of religion as a means of deforming the moral relations of the family: "To corrupt family relations is to poison fountains; for the sources of the commonwealth are within the Households; and errors there are irretrievable."[291] After the passage of Gardiner's Bill, Burke had occasion in the autumn of 1780 to examine the attempt to secure it in the wider context of religious turmoil since the schism in the Catholic Church in the sixteenth century. The persistence of religious hostility in Ireland demonstrated that the Reformation was not yet complete there. The popery laws should be seen as a relic of persecution, not as a pillar of the Protestant faith. Burke further considered that the pursuit of persecu-

[284] EB to Unknown, c. 3 June 1778, ibid., p. 455.

[285] Ibid., pp. 455–56.

[286] EB to Edmund Sexton Perry, 12 August 1778, *Corr.*, IV, p. 14.

[287] EB to Garrett Nagle, 25 August 1778, ibid., p. 19.

[288] EB to Unknown, c. 3 June 1778, *Corr.*, III, p. 456.

[289] Gilbert Burnet, "Epistle Dedicatory" to *The History of the Reformation of the Church of England . . . The First Part* (London: 1715); Gilbert Burnet, Preface to Lucius Caecilius Firmianus Lactantius, *A Relation of the Death of the Primitive Persecutors* (Amsterdam: 1687), p. 27.

[290] Northamptonshire MS. A. XXVII.2.

[291] EB to Edmund Sexton Perry, 16 June 1778, *Corr.*, III, p. 457.

tion by open violence could be less damaging than its establishment by a process of codification. In particular, penal statutes that interfered with property and the family were "outrages on our nature." They corrupted at once the rights and feelings of humanity by an insidious policy of cruelty.[292]

Burke was fascinated all his life by the root causes of religious chauvinism. Its explanation lay in the dynamics of the Reformation itself. While attempts to purge Catholicism of superstition and tyranny represented one of the greatest "periods of human improvement," the effort soon ran into complications and reversals.[293] Secular interests were distinct from the higher purpose of salvation, yet the two were often combined in point of practice. Under the unreformed Church and during the wars of religion alike, the two became problematically entwined. Here Burke was implicitly rejecting the common deist charge that religion was the source of the civil strife of the seventeenth century. In fact, Burke thought, religious sentiment was then debased by the instinct for power: "the enthusiasm of religion threw a gloom over politics; and political interests poisoned and perverted the spirit of religion on all sides."[294] The intermingling of spiritual goals with secular ambition had been difficult to avoid given the circumstances of the Reformation, where peoples were pitted against their rulers and populations against magistrates. Conflict bred antagonism; the experience of adversity induced fear and retaliation. In Ireland in the aftermath of the Glorious Revolution these passions were particularly acute. The Protestant establishment resorted to tyrannical measures to secure itself—opposing to popery, as Burke sarcastically remarked, "another Popery," by which he meant a code of prejudice backed by power.[295]

Toleration would transform the civil welfare of Roman Catholics, but it would also alter relations between their Church and the state. This was more obviously to be expected in the aftermath of a new set of relief measures, introduced on 5 February 1782 by John Dillon on behalf of Gardiner. The successful passage of the 1782 Bills as amended in debate enabled Catholics to purchase and bequeath land on the same terms as Protestants. At the same time, the services and duties of the clergy were to be officially recognised.[296] This raised the sensitive issue of the regulation of the Catholic Church, hitherto exempted from civil control on account of its unofficial status. The issue of ecclesiastical appointments would have to be resolved, along with the education of priests. In the midst of a debate during the passage of Gardiner's new measures, Hely Hutchinson proposed that members of the Catholic

[292] EB, Speech at Bristol Previous to the Election, 6 September 1780, *W & S*, III, p. 640.

[293] Ibid., p. 639.

[294] Ibid.

[295] Ibid., p. 640.

[296] John Fitzgibbon forced Gardiner to group his proposals under four heads. See *The Parliamentary Register, or the History of the Proceedings and Debates of the House of Commons of Ireland* (Dublin: 1784), I, p. 241.

clergy might be trained along with Protestant undergraduates at Trinity.[297] Burke obviously supported the relaxation of penal statutes, but he had his doubts about prevailing suggestions for regulating the clergy. Viscount Kenmare, who by now played a prominent role in Catholic politics in Ireland, kept him abreast of the range of proposals being discussed.[298] "All parties look up to you, as the greatest Ornament of your Country and this Age," Kenmare informed him after the heads of the Bill had been sent to the Lord Lieutenant.[299] By then the proposals had stirred controversy within the Catholic hierarchy.[300] Burke set out his own objections in a lengthy letter to Kenmare.

In the letter he was critical of Hely Hutchinson's proposals. He explained himself directly after his letter had been circulated, admonishing his friend that he could hardly love his country "and hate and persecute four fifths of its Inhabitants."[301] The circumstances under which the Catholic clergy were currently educated only added to their legal degradation. The schooling of the laity ought to be addressed by the state, but so too should the training of religious orders. Burke estimated that there were 4,000 priests in Ireland, many of whom, in the absence of expectations of lucrative returns, were drawn from the lower ranks of the population.[302] There was no institutionalised arrangement for their domestic education. Many received what they could from abroad by investing their earnings from petty employment, only later to return in a state of abject poverty. Despised by their Protestant neighbours and disparaged by their more fortunate Catholic fellows, they contracted the habits and manners of the poor. The popery laws, Burke was suggesting, added debasement to oppression by inhibiting the means of acquiring an education with dignity that would enable the clergy to improve their "rational Nature." His conclusion was damning: "To render humanity fit to be insulted, it was fit that it should be degraded."[303] Current proposals intended to remedy this situation he believed would actually exacerbate the problem. Catholic training required the availability of necessary discipline, developed and refined in appropriate seminaries. It was not possible to inculcate correct clerical teaching under circumstances that militated against the values of the denomination. In relation to Roman Catholics in particular, priests could not be prepared for celibacy and the hearing of confession in an atmosphere, as at Trinity College, where such practices were held in contempt.[304]

[297] McDowell, *Ireland in the Age of Imperialism*, pp. 192–3; *Irish Parliamentary Register*, I, pp. 309–10.

[298] Viscount Kenmare to EB, 5 February 1782, *Corr.*, IV, pp. 400–402.

[299] Viscount Kenmare to EB, 14 March 1782, ibid., p. 422.

[300] O'Flaherty, "Ecclesiastical Politics," pp. 46–49.

[301] EB to John Hely Hutchinson, post 9 April 1782, *Corr.*, IV, p. 441.

[302] EB, Letter to Lord Kenmare, 21 February 1782, *W & S*, IX, p. 571. This was a common observation, though remuneration and social standing in fact varied. See Ian McBride, *Eighteenth-Century Ireland: Isle of Slaves* (Dublin: Macmillan, 2009), pp. 250–51.

[303] EB, Letter to Lord Kenmare, 21 February 1782, *W & S*, IX, p. 572.

[304] Ibid., p. 573.

Religion was perpetuated by indoctrination, and so clerical pedagogy had to be a concern of the state. To cultivate the piety of members of their flock, priests and ministers could only instruct by winning respect. The Catholic clergy gained credit by living apart from the community and employing a range of ceremonies and observances. By comparison, Anglican pastors, integrated into society, were esteemed for liberal learning, commanding admiration as a result.[305] In either case, ecclesiastics were charged with improving their congregations. To achieve this they needed to be equipped with the means of bringing it about. Since toleration provided recognition of the clergy, regulation became a matter for public policy. Under those circumstances, it was essential that the process of remedying old injustice should not become an occasion for devising new insults. Much of what was proposed was a product of ignorance, originally engendered by contempt. Burke likened existing schemes for rehabilitating the clergy to a plan "to feed a sick Gentû with Beef Broth, and to foment his Wounds with Brandy."[306] The feeling of supremacy was a poor nursery for considered reform. In some cases it was detrimental to remedial action altogether, giving rise instead to feelings of bigotry. A clause freeing Irish Presbyterians from the sacramental test had been added to the Catholic Relief Bill of 1778, though it was struck out by the English Privy Council.[307] Had the measure been successful it would have made dissenters in Ireland eligible for political office. Burke believed that the spectacle of toleration for Catholics made them eager to secure an increment of power for themselves: "Those who are long used to power over others, will consider a condition of equality as a State of Degradation."[308] The reaction in Scotland, however, was considerably more irate. When the idea of extending the relief Acts to the other side of the border began to be debated at the end of 1778, Scottish Protestants grew restive and alarmed. Lord Weymouth was forced in the new year to try to restore some calm.[309] James Boswell appealed to Burke to resist the idea of a Scottish Bill.[310]

Boswell's move was a poorly considered strategy. A response from Burke mixed ridicule with disapproval. Edinburgh and Glasgow had actively opposed the prospect of a Bill. Before long, eighty-five societies in the west of Scotland had banded together to halt its introduction north of the Tweed.[311] On 1 December 1778, the first meeting of the newly formed Society of Friends to the Protestant Interest, commonly referred to as the Protestant Association, had taken place. It selected a committee of correspondence within days. They petitioned Edinburgh Council in

[305] Ibid., p. 574.

[306] Ibid., pp. 572–73.

[307] Burke was closely involved with the British scrutiny of the Bill: see EB to Edmund Sexton Perry, 3 July 1778, *Corr.*, IV, p. 3.

[308] EB to Luke Gardiner, 24 August 1778, ibid., p. 17.

[309] *Caledonian Mercury*, 13 February 1779.

[310] James Boswell to EB, 22 February 1779, *Corr.*, IV, pp. 43–4.

[311] Colin Haydon, *Anti-Catholicism in Eighteenth-Century England, c. 1714–1789: A Political and Social Study* (Manchester: Manchester University Press, 1993), p. 207.

early January. Glasgow followed suit in the next weeks. By February 1779, 20,000 signatures had been collected against the measure.[312] Protest was soon accompanied by violence. On 6 February, Edinburgh Catholics were forced to flee from angry mobs; three days later, the disorder spread to Glasgow. During the course of the riots, the chapel, house and library of George Hay, the Catholic Bishop of Daulis, had been plundered by a furious crowd.[313] The shop of a small-time grocer, Daniel Macdonald, had been attacked, and the pottery works of Robert Bagnal were destroyed. "The American rebellion is more to my Taste than that which you are cooking in the North," Burke wrote to Boswell.[314] Equivocation in respect of the virtue of toleration appeared to Burke to be ethically confused. "I am apt to be as much puzzled by moral Mysteries as others are with religious," he quipped. Burke's friend in Edinburgh, the historian William Robertson, had ordered the university to be closed, causing obvious dissatisfaction in Burke: "Full as little do I understand why the University should share the Fate of the Masshouses."[315] Burke publicised his distress in the House of Commons in the middle of March. A "paroxysm of religious phrensy" had been unleashed over the border, he told his peers.[316] Boswell might indulge his fears of a return to the wars of religion, but for Burke the pettiest persecution had erupted in an enlightened age. Looking back in 1780, he presented Savile's relief Act as having set the tone for Europe. By granting a degree of toleration to Catholics, it secured the position of Protestants on the continent.[317] By comparison, bigoted insurgency in the great Scottish cities was retrograde and counterproductive.

Burke accepted that the Bill could not be forced upon North Britons in the face of such antagonistic passions. Nonetheless, it seemed obvious that Roman Catholics should be compensated for their losses. Accordingly, Burke drafted a petition and presented it on their behalf. In the process, he explained that zeal was a positive quality if accompanied by other virtues. Yet if it was suffered to gather momentum independent of approvable aims, it would turn out to be "the most mischievous thing in the world."[318] It was a lucky thing that 15 million subjects in South Asia were persecuted only by avarice and not by bigotry as well.[319] An anonymous pamphlet issued in Scotland in early 1779 had urged the Protestant faithful to sever ties

[312]Eugene Charlton Black, "The Tumultuous Petitioners: The Protestant Association in Scotland, 1778–1780," *Review of Politics*, 25:2 (April 1963), pp. 183–211; R. K. Donovan, *No Popery and Radicalism: Opposition to Roman Catholic Relief in Scotland, 1778–1782* (New York: Garland, 1987).

[313]Hay later came to London to secure compensation for Scottish Catholics. He wrote to Burke about his disappointed mission on 12 July 1779. See *Corr.*, IV, pp. 99–102.

[314]EB to James Boswell, 1 March 1779, ibid., p. 45.

[315]Ibid., p. 46. On this episode, see Alexander du Toit, "'A Species of False Religion': William Robertson, Catholic Relief and the Myth of Moderate Tolerance," *Innes Review*, 52 (Autumn 2001), pp. 167–88.

[316]EB, Speech on Scottish Riots, 15 March 1779, *W & S*, III, p. 425.

[317]EB, Speech at Bristol Previous to the Election, 6 September 1780, ibid., p. 652.

[318]EB, Speech on Scottish Catholic Petition, 18 March 1779, ibid., p. 429.

[319]Ibid., p. 430.

with Roman Catholics through employment, commerce or general society.[320] Burke misattributed the work to the secretary of the Protestant Association, which had in fact issued its own statement against the proposed relief.[321] However, this document was equally subject to criticism by Burke, who wrote to Ralph Bowie, one of its authors, on 31 March 1779. While Bowie and his colleagues had not called for actual boycotts, they had agitated against liberal relations with Roman Catholics. Even accepting that they were motivated by a commitment to religion, their discriminatory language—their "railing and invective"—inevitably fomented feelings of hatred in the people at large.[322]

Burke's suspicion of popular politics must be set in this context. Human beings were creatures of prejudice, in all senses of the term—animated by warmth or bitterness towards their fellows as perceptions and circumstances changed. It was the job of politics to represent their common interests, as much as possible in accordance with their humours and sentiments, but not to the extent of violating the principles of justice. Representatives should therefore serve by promoting moderation: "we ought to correct the Bigotry of the people."[323] Popular animosity placed obstacles in the way of this objective by pitting illiberal prejudice against the aspirations of decency. In the weeks following the Scottish riots, John Erskine, an evangelically minded minister at Greyfriars Church in Edinburgh, wrote to Burke to draw attention to their shared sentiments on America and to resist being dubbed a firebrand by Catholic victims of the recent disorders.[324] He was, he protested, a figure of moderation in the Scottish Church.[325] Having taken the trouble to read Erskine's publications on both the colonies and the idea of Catholic relief, Burke responded at length to his letter two months later. He was surprised to learn that Erskine sought to prove his "*Moderation*" by dispatching works expressive of disdain.[326] Along with William Porteous and John Macfarlan, ministers in Glasgow and Edinburgh respectively, Erskine had been keen to articulate his worries about the persistence of inimical practices in the

[320] [Anon.], *A Letter to All Opposers of the Repeal of the Penal Laws against Papists in Scotland* (Edinburgh: 1779). For Burke's reaction, see EB, Speech on Scottish Catholic Petition, *W & S*, III, p. 426.

[321] [Anon.], *A Short View of the Statutes at Present in Force in Scotland against Popery* (Edinburgh: 1779).

[322] EB to Patrick [*id est* Ralph] Bowie, 31 March 1779, *Corr.*, IV, pp. 55–56.

[323] EB, "Thoughts on Approaching Executions," 10 July 1780, *W & S*, III, p. 615. Cf. EB, Debate on the Bill for the Regulation of the Civil List Establishments, 15 February 1781, *Parliamentary History*, XXI, col. 1226: temperate government "administered justice and mercy, without being influenced by the petulance, or disturbed by the clamours of the subject."

[324] For Erskine, see Jonathan M. Yeager, *Enlightened Evangelicalism: The Life and Thought of John Erskine* (Oxford: Oxford University Press, 2011). Presbyterian ministers had been accused of fomenting bias in the pulpit and in pamphlets in the period prior to the Scottish disturbances in the *Memorial to the Public in Behalf of the Roman Catholics of Edinburgh and Glasgow* (London: 1779), pp. 10–11.

[325] Dr. John Erskine to EB, 24 April 1779, *Corr.*, IV, p. 63.

[326] EB to John Erskine, 12 June 1779, ibid., p. 85. Burke was taking issue with John Erskine, *Considerations on the Spirit of Popery* (Edinburgh: 1778).

Church of Rome.[327] As unenlightened votaries of their priests, the poor and illiterate papists who predominated in Scotland had an under-developed sense of charity towards other Christians.[328] For Burke, however, Erskine's pronouncements merely substituted personal animosity with a more learned antipathy to rival religious tenets. His sentiments would do little to mollify "the blind fury of the Multitude."[329]

Since civil society was an instrument of pacification, it made no sense to enable a system of representation to be employed as a means of subverting its justice. When an MP was elected into the House of Commons, he was commissioned to give voice to the feelings of the people in conformity with the good of the community. This could never include a licence to mistreat or oppress.[330] When Burke came to articulate this sentiment in defence of his conduct as an MP for Bristol on 6 September 1780, he referred once more to his experience in supporting Catholic relief in Scotland. Catholics, it was often said, were partisans of monarchy. Their disabilities, consequently, were sometimes defended in terms of Whiggish dogma. To Burke, however, it mattered little what shape the apology for discrimination took. What counted was that it amounted to a factious doctrine masquerading as a plea for liberty. Republics and monarchies might equally persecute, irrespective of the pieties of Whig ideology.[331] Liberty had to be supported by generosity, and it was potentially destroyed by pride. What particularly disturbed republican liberty was divisiveness terminating in faction. In the eighteenth-century British church-state, toleration was a bulwark against civil strife, yet its principles often conflicted with popular conceptions of freedom. The goal of popular freedom was commonly sustained by emulation, which instilled a jealous partisanship towards religious and political attachments. "This disposition is the true source of the passion, which many men in very humble life, have taken to the American war," Burke observed.[332] They were zealously solicitous for *their* colonies, *their* dependents. Pride was fed by the feeling of superiority that membership of the dominant group provided. The vaunted symbols of liberty were merely the marks of pre-eminence, which the lower ranks of society paraded before such objects of their prejudice as were unhappily dependent on their mercy. "The desire of having someone below them," Burke discerned, "descends to the very lowest of all."[333]

327 Dr. John Erskine to EB, 16 July 1779, *Corr.* IV, p. 103. His colleagues had published two sermons on the subject: William Porteous, *The Doctrine of Toleration, Applied to the Present Times* (Glasgow: 1778), John Macfarlan, *A Defence of the Clergy of the Church of Scotland in Opposition to the Repeal of Penal Laws against Roman Catholics* (Edinburgh: 1778).

328 Erskine, *Spirit of Popery*, pp. 2–4.

329 EB to Dr. John Erskine, 12 June 1779, *Corr.*, IV, p. 85.

330 EB, Speech at Bristol Previous to the Election, 6 September 1780, *W & S*, III, p. 660.

331 Ibid., p. 659.

332 Ibid. For discussion of the Gordon Riots in the context of the American war, see Nicholas Rogers, "The Gordon Riots and the Politics of War" in Ian Haywood and John Seed eds., *The Gordon Riots: Politics, Culture and Insurrection in Late Eighteenth-Century Britain* (Cambridge: Cambridge University Press, 2012); Brad A. Jones, " 'In Favour of Popery': Patriotism, Protestantism, and the Gordon Riots in the Revolutionary British Atlantic," *Journal of British Studies*, 52 (January 2013), pp. 79–102.

333 EB, Speech at Bristol Previous to the Election, 6 September 1780, *W & S*, III, p. 659.

Burke's hatred of demagoguery derived from his contention that its practitioners were prepared to manipulate these repellent attitudes. When writing about the Gordon Riots just months after the event, he focused his invective on "the wicked instigators" of the affair. Stealthily, behind the scenes, without ever having to face official retribution, they incited "the blind rage of the populace, with a continued blast of pestilential libels, which infected and poisoned the very air we breathe in."[334] On Friday 2 June 1780, in the aftermath of the Scottish reaction to prospective Catholic relief, Lord George Gordon petitioned parliament for the repeal of Savile's Act. Gordon had been active north of the border since the summer of 1779, getting elected president of the Protestant Association in England in November of that year.[335] On Monday 29 May 1780, he announced his plans for a monster petition at a meeting at the Coachmaker's Hall in London.[336] On the day that he presented the document to the Commons, a large crowd of about 60,000 marched on Westminster from St. George's Fields.[337] Assorted members of the Lords were assaulted en route to their chamber. Gordon harangued the crowd with reports of events in St. Stephen's Chapel, berating opponents of the petition for repeal—"particularly Mr. Burke, the member for Bristol."[338] After the protesters were dispersed by the House Guard, they descended on Lincoln's Inn and St. James's Square, targeting Catholic chapels for vandalism. Over the following days the scope of the attacks was widened, peaking on 7 and 8 June and leaving the "Metropolis in flames," before the military managed to restore order with considerable loss of life.[339]

Burke learned of an impending attempt on his own house on 5 June, after Savile's place had already been attacked. Soldiers were posted on the orders of the government to provide him with protection. The following day, having had his books and furniture removed, he moved his wife to General Burgoyne's for safety. On Wednesday 7 June, he mingled with the crowds, at one point being forced to draw his sword. "Some of them were malignant and fanatical," he reported to Shackleton, while others were simply "dissolute and unruly."[340] He was happy to debate the issues with them, but he would not be deviated from his course: "I was neither to

[334] Ibid., p. 654.

[335] Eugene Charlton Black, *The Association: British Extraparliamentary Organisation, 1769–1793* (Cambridge, MA: Harvard University Press, 1963), pp. 153–54.

[336] *London Magazine*, 69 (1780), pp. 282–83.

[337] Estimates vary between 40,000 and 60,000. See J. Paul de Castro, *The Gordon Riots* (Oxford: Oxford University Press, 1926); George Rudé, *Paris and London in the Eighteenth Century: Studies in Popular Protest* (London: Collins, 1970), p. 270; Christopher Hibbert, *King Mob: The Story of Lord George Gordon and the Riots of 1780* (1958) (Stroud: Sutton, 2004), pp. 34ff.

[338] "An Account of the Late Riots in the Cities of London and Westminster" in *The Annual Register for the Year 1780* (London: 1781), p. 258.

[339] Haydon, *Anti-Catholicism*, p. 241; George Rudé, "The Gordon Riots: A Study of the Rioters and their Victims," *Transactions of the Royal Historical Society*, 6 (1956), pp. 93–114.

[340] EB to Richard Shackleton, 13 June 1780, *Corr.*, IV, p. 246. On Burke's typology of the rioters, see Iain McCalman, "Mad Lord George and Madame La Motte: Riot and Sexuality in the Genesis of Burke's Reflections on the Revolution in France," *Journal of British Studies*, 35:3 (July 1996), pp. 343–67.

be forced nor intimidated from the straight line of what was right."[341] For all his first-hand exposure to the scale and ferocity of the riots, having spent at least four nights keeping watch over the London homes of friends, he was dismayed by the deployment of the military to maintain order. In the Commons debate on the disturbances on 6 June 1780, with troops occupying the streets around parliament, he likened the city of London to St. Petersburg and Berlin as the ministry installed the military "on the ruins of civil government."[342] *The Annual Register* remarked that the "invincible jealousy of military power," long characteristic of popular sentiment in Britain, was giving way to a toleration of garrisons and encampments.[343] Burke reserved his praise for the Catholic denizens of the city, estimated to number about 5,000 residents, who showed restraint in the face of persistent provocation.[344] As was made plain in the Commons resolutions against the Protestant Association, which he had helped to draft before they were moved on 20 June, the groundswell of bigotry would merely encourage the persecution of Protestants in Europe.[345] Despite the mood in the country, and even in parliament itself, Burke was keen to redouble attempts to extend religious indulgence further.[346] He would not be deflected by the "Cries of the people."[347]

Despite the determination in the Commons to face down the upheavals and resist the pressure for repealing Catholic relief, Savile himself introduced a Bill on 23 June 1780 to secure the Protestant religion from the suspected growth of popery. Burke made a stand against what he saw as this deluded apprehension. The proposed measures to restrain papists included interfering with the education of their children, in violation, Burke claimed, of the fundamental rights of parents. Thomas Aquinas could be quoted against such barbaric recommendations, illustrating how "the darkness of the 12th Century" might be summoned "against the light of the 18th."[348] Gloomy fears continued to be held of the Catholic population because of their habit of skulking underground in order to avoid giving offence. They should assert themselves through petitions, and pledge their allegiance openly. In due course, Burke believed, this would relieve them of the suspicion of adhering to "secret and concealed dogmas."[349] Yet for all his detestation of the attitudes of the rioters, Burke realised that their mindset was a product of circumstances. He

[341] EB to Richard Shackleton, 13 June 1780, *Corr.*, IV, p. 246.

[342] EB, Speech on Gordon Riots, 6 June 1780, *W & S*, III, p. 603.

[343] "The History of Europe" in *The Annual Register for 1781* (London: 1782), p. 138.

[344] EB, Speech at Bristol Previous to the Poll, 6 September 1780, *W & S*, III, p. 656. Rudé, "Gordon Riots," pp. 108–9, estimates the Catholic population at 14,000, about half of them immigrant Irish labour. This figure was revised upwards to 25,000 in Nicholas Rogers, *Crowds, Culture and Politics in Georgian Britain* (Oxford: Oxford University Press, 1998), p. 155.

[345] EB, Resolutions after the Gordon Riots, ante 18 June 1780, *W & S*, III, p. 604.

[346] Lord North to EB, 18 June 1780, *Corr.*, IV, pp. 250–51.

[347] WWM BkP 8:32.

[348] EB, Speech on the Bill to Secure Protestantism, *W & S*, III, pp. 609–10.

[349] EB to Lord Loughborough, 15 June 1780, *Corr.*, IV, p. 249.

emphasised this consideration when he came to address the mode of punishment that might appropriately be doled out to participants in the Gordon Riots.

By July 1780, sixty-two rioters had been condemned to death for their role in the violence, and twenty-five were actually executed.[350] Burke wrote to the Lord Chancellor, Edward Thurlow, with a set of proposals, pleading various issues in mitigation.[351] He set out a scheme for limited punishment in preference to the spectacle of mass hangings: six solemn executions should be carried out, all scheduled on a single day, to avoid diminishing respect for justice by unleashing an orgy of retribution. Punishment should humble rather than "irritate," and it should be concentrated on the most conspicuously guilty perpetrators.[352] Burke followed up his "Thoughts" with "Additional Reflections on the Executions," which he sent on 18 July to Lord Bathurst.[353] He noted that the "chief delinquents" had so far escaped.[354] The individuals who had selected particular properties for attack eluded capture; so too had the principal agitators who had assembled the mobs, along with those who directed operations. Bigoted preachers were never questioned, conspiring politicians barely accused. Those who had been fingered to bear the brunt of responsibility were "a poor thoughtless set of creatures" who had been fired by inexpensive rhetoric that would now cost them their lives.[355] This outcome prompted Burke to reflect on the underlying causes. It should be borne in mind, he suggested, "that the whole Nation has been for a long time guilty of their Crime."[356] Toleration, he contended, was a "new virtue" in Britain, just as it was an incipient novelty across Europe. It was being cultivated by the enlightened against a background of historic bias that had been publicised for generations in the pulpits and the press. Detestable crimes based on religious antipathy would have to be spectacularly, if precisely, punished. Nonetheless, it should be recollected that these misdeeds had been fomented by the national culture, and as such should also be viewed as the results of a collective crime.[357]

8.5 Economy and Innovation: Political Reform in Britain

When the Duke of Richmond rose on 2 June 1780 to present his promised motion on shorter parliaments, he was forced to lament "the riotous proceedings" currently in progress in Palace Yard.[358] The Gordon Rioters were baying in the vicinity as he spoke. On their way to the chamber, Lords Mansfield, Stormont, Hillsborough,

[350] Rudé, "Gordon Riots," p. 99.

[351] EB to Lord Thurlow, 10 July 1780, *Corr.*, IV, 254.

[352] EB, "Thoughts on Approaching Executions," 10 July 1780, *W & S*, III, p. 613.

[353] EB to Earl Bathurst, 18 July 1780, *Corr.*, IV, p. 256.

[354] EB, "Some Additional Reflections on the Executions," *W & S*, III, p. 616.

[355] Ibid.

[356] EB, "Thoughts on Approaching Executions," 10 July 1780, *W & S*, III, p. 614.

[357] Ibid., p. 615.

[358] *Parliamentary History*, XXI, col. 665.

Townshend, Bathurst, Sandwich and Northumberland had been threatened and manhandled.[359] It was an unpropitious scene for introducing a popular measure. In response to the mayhem out of doors, Richmond assured his peers that although he was commonly reckoned a friend of the people he was also a devotee of the rights and privileges of parliament. "He had been honoured with the name leveller, because he took delight in reformation."[360] But the designation, he insisted, was inappropriate. He was certainly an advocate of reform, yet his plan was not to "mix all distinctions of men indiscriminately, but to distinguish them clearly."[361] Richmond was a descendant of Charles II, and drew an income of £19,000 per annum by the time the first Rockingham administration formed.[362] Burke marked him out as a "considerable man" when he first heard him speak in 1766.[363] In due course he would come to play a leading role in defending the Rockingham line against the American war. But before long he would gravely disappoint Burke as a proponent of irresponsible forms of parliamentary reform. When Richmond addressed the Commons at the outset of the Gordon Riots, Burke had already developed his own proposals for reforming government. His object was to reduce the extensive powers of the crown. Richmond professed a desire to achieve the same objective, but to Burke his methods were certain to undermine his goals.

Agitation for reform in 1780 was occurring against a background of rising crisis. It was "one of the most critical periods in our annals," Burke commented in the 1790s.[364] French Laurence, Burke's literary executor, presented the following picture: "Towards the close of the year 1779 when the people began to grow tired of the American War & the parliament still continued to support it with unabated determination," the question of reform acquired immediate topicality.[365] General Burgoyne's losses at Saratoga in the autumn of 1777 had damaged British expectations of ready victory in the American war. The transformation of the struggle into a battle against the Bourbon powers had further damaged confidence in the resilience of the Empire. The trade dispute with Ireland and the rise of the Volunteers contributed to the growing sense of pressure and alarm. Part of Burke's case against the colonial war had been the tendency of the conflict to add to the power of the crown. The expansion of the naval and military establishments, along with the increase in revenue officers, had extended patronage through the kingdom. This contributed to a longstanding concern about the powers of the crown under the monarchy of George III. Ever since Lord North's attempts to regulate the revenue and govern-

[359] Thomas Holcroft, *A Plain and Succinct Narrative of the Late Riots and Disturbances in the Cities of London and Westminster* (London: 1780), pp. 16–17.

[360] *Parliamentary History*, XXI, col. 665.

[361] Ibid., col. 666.

[362] Alison Olson, *The Radical Duke: Career and Correspondence of Charles Lennox, Third Duke of Richmond* (Oxford: Oxford University Press, 1961).

[363] EB to Charles O'Hara, 11 March 1766, *Corr.*, I, p. 244.

[364] EB, *Letter to a Noble Lord* (1796), *W & S*, IX, p. 151.

[365] French Laurence, "Notes on Parliament" (c. 1794), OSB MS. File 8751.

ment of the East India Company, the Rockinghams had viewed the problem within an imperial frame.[366] The rising debts on the civil list had given them occasion to articulate their worries. In February and again in March 1769, Burke had drawn attention to the burden on the Commons. In April 1777 he returned to the familiar theme. It was right that under a mixed system of government the crown should be supported in the degree of splendour requisite to the dignity of the royal household.[367] There was, however, a line to be drawn between dignity and corruption. The civil list had been inaugurated with the Civil List Act of 1698, intended to divide the expenses of government without disturbing the balance of the constitution. As part of that division, parliament was to assume responsibility for the cost of the armed forces and servicing the public debt. At the same time, the crown was to be granted sufficient revenue to maintain the costs of government and assorted royal establishments.[368] These included the salaries of ministers, officers, ambassadors and consuls, as well as the "privy purse," royal palaces and parks. A decision to borrow against the fund was made under Queen Anne. Despite attempts to regulate the list in the early years of George III, expense exceeded income throughout the reign. In his *Thoughts on the Present Discontents*, Burke argued that unaccountable debt on the list could supply an inexhaustible fund for corruption.[369] By 1777, the repayment of borrowing against the list was £600,000 in arrears.[370]

The debts on the civil list were a potent symbol of "influence," which Burke described as a term of art for the practice of corruption.[371] Undue influence, he would later remark, "preyed on the very vitals" of the constitution.[372] Nonetheless, the Rockinghams remained committed to the tenets of court Whiggism. Their aim was to modify its perversion into what they saw as a new Toryism by distinguishing reasonable influence from its increasingly corrupt usage.[373] Out of fear of the expanding power of the court, crown contracts, offices, placemen and pensions came under scrutiny. In the later phase of Lord North's ministry, there were fifty government officers in parliament, twenty-five members occupying positions at court, sixty-five

[366] W. M. Elofson, *The Rockingham Connection and the Second Founding of the Whig Party* (Montreal and Kingston: McGill-Queen's University Press, 1996); W. M. Elofson, "The Rockingham Whigs in Transition: The East India Company Issue, 1772–1773," *English Historical Review*, 104:413 (1989), pp. 947–74.

[367] EB, Speech on Civil List Debts, 16 April 1777, *W & S*, III, p. 332.

[368] E. A. Reitan, "The Civil List in Eighteenth-Century British Politics: Parliamentary Supremacy versus the Independence of the Crown," *Historical Journal*, 9:3 (1966), pp. 318–37.

[369] EB, *Thoughts on the Cause of the Present Discontents* (1770), *W & S*, II, pp. 303ff.

[370] *CJ*, XXXII, p. 334.

[371] EB, Speech on the Civil List Debts, 18 April 1777, *W & S*, III, p. 334. Cf. WWM BkP 14:12.

[372] EB, Debate on the Regulation of the Civil Establishment, 15 February 1781, *Parliamentary History*, XXI, col. 1239.

[373] EB, Speech on Public Expenses, 15 December 1779, *W & S*, III, p. 472; EB, Letter for Lord Rockingham, January 1780, ibid., p. 480. On the addition of "Country" components to the Rockinghamite platform, see W. M. Elofson, "The Rockingham Whigs and the Country Tradition," *Parliamentary History*, 8 (1989), pp. 90–115.

naval and military officers, thirty sinecurists in various roles, eleven beneficiaries of government contracts, the same number holding secret service pensions, and twenty-four sitting for government seats.[374] In response, in the spring of 1778, a series of motions were put to parliament for dealing with placemen in the Commons.[375] By 1779, a month before Spain completed its preparations for entering the American war on the side of the French, Burke was addressing the pointlessness and extravagance of the contest. A committee under Frederick Montagu had taken evidence in May confirming the hostility of the Americans to the metropolitan government, the erection of military fortresses across every stretch of colonial territory, and the effectiveness of the enemy in withstanding conquest.[376] The British, therefore, had little positive to expect in future save a mortgage on their properties determined by the cost of the national debt.[377] Radical economies were consequently called for. Since these would generate debate on the distribution of public expenditure, they would raise the issue of the balance of forces between the executive and the legislature. As such, they would form a part of the wider discussion about the remit of political reform. This embraced the issue of more frequent parliaments, the question of the franchise and the character of representation. With the demise of the Wilkite movement by 1779, agitation for these objectives shifted to metropolitan activists and the Yorkshire Association established by Christopher Wyvill.[378] In Burke's mind, the task for the Rockinghams was to promote public economy in collaboration with extra-parliamentary forces whilst steering the appetite for reform away from constitutional innovation. "*To innovate is not to reform*," as Burke clarified in 1796.[379] Popular protest would have to be channelled into skilful renovation. Having berated the supine character of public opinion during the American crisis, the advent of a popular campaign held major attractions for the Rockinghams. Yet it also posed a challenge to their control of the agenda.

Christopher Wyvill had started his career as a rector in Essex, having graduated and been ordained at the University of Cambridge. After campaigning against clerical subscription in the early 1770s, Wyvill moved to Yorkshire to assume the life of a country gentleman, having inherited substantial estates in the north of the county.[380]

[374] Ian R. Christie, "Economical Reform and 'The Influence of the Crown'" in idem, *Myth and Reality*, pp. 300, 306.

[375] Frank O'Gorman, *The Rise of Party in England: The Rockingham Whigs, 1760–1782* (London: George Allen & Unwin, 1975), pp. 406–7.

[376] EB, Speech on Supply, 31 May 1779, *W & S*, III, p. 440.

[377] Ibid., p. 439.

[378] The Middlesex by-election of 1779 caused by the death of Sergeant Glynn revived metropolitan activity. See EB to the Marquess of Rockingham, 17 October 1779, *Corr.*, IV, p. 159.

[379] EB, *Letter to a Noble Lord* (1796), *W & S*, IX, p. 156. Cf. EB, *Letter to William Elliot* (26 May 1795), ibid., p. 40.

[380] Ian R. Christie, *Wilkes, Wyvill and Reform: The Parliamentary Reform Movement in British Politics, 1760–1785* (London: Macmillan: 1962), pp. 70–71; idem, "The Yorkshire Association, 1780–1784: A Study in the Political Organisation" in idem, *Myth and Reality in Late-Eighteenth-Century British Politics and Other Papers* (Berkeley and Los Angeles: University of California Press, 1970), pp. 263ff.

In November 1779, he undertook to establish a movement for reform, hoping to begin by petitioning the House of Commons for a committee on the state of the civil list. The expectation was that sinecures would be called into question, and that unnecessary or unmerited places and pensions would be rescinded. From his base in the North Riding, Wyvill called a county meeting as a prelude to founding a Yorkshire Association. This would establish a precedent for other counties to follow. The weight of opinion, it was hoped, would have an impact on the general election, due the following year, by helping to return members less susceptible to corruption. This would clear the ground for a more ambitious scheme of reform: "if once the fund of corruption was reduced, it would be an easy matter to carry the other regulations which are thought necessary to restore the freedom of Parliament."[381] These "other regulations" would prove diverse in nature, attracting varying degrees of public support. If indulged without deliberation they might compromise the constitution; if pursued without consultation they might break the unity of the movement. Soon, the Marquess of Rockingham would be warning that "the times, and the circumstances of the times, *are critical*."[382] Judicious management might restore the government of the country to health. A precipitous decision might sabotage the national consensus.

With this in mind, the Rockinghams were keen to confine the remit of the Association. In his correspondence with Stephen Croft, a leading gentleman in the city of York and a prominent member of the county Association, the Marquess was determined to avoid "speculative propositions," above all the proposals for shorter parliaments, the extension of the franchise and an increase in the country membership of the Commons.[383] This aim was most likely to succeed if opposition proposals for public economy prospered in the Commons. With that end in view, on 3 November 1779, Rockingham informed Burke that he was sharpening his "shears" as a prelude to urging retrenchment on the ministry. He now believed that the incompetence of the administration was generally felt, and that the time was ripe for launching an attack.[384] Burke spent the following weeks developing and refining a set of proposals, which were distributed among colleagues by 27 November.[385] On 7 December, the Duke of Richmond pressed for "the most rigid and exact oeconomy" in the Lords.[386] Rockingham lent support in demanding a "reformation of the constitution"—on the assumption that this would mean a "restoration."[387] Shelburne attacked the wasteful distribution of government contracts, and announced his intention to move for an

[381] Christopher Wyvill to William Anderson et alia, 29 November 1779, *Political Papers, Chiefly Respecting . . . a Reformation of the Parliament of Great Britain* (York: 1794–1802), 6 vols., III, p. 117.

[382] The Marquess of Rockingham to EB, 31 March 1780, *Corr.*, IV, p. 217,

[383] The Marquess of Rockingham to Stephen Croft, 12 December 1779, cited in O'Gorman, *Rise of Party*, p. 627n47.

[384] The Marquess of Rockingham to EB, 3 November 1779, *Corr.*, IV, p. 161.

[385] The Marquess of Rockingham to EB, 27 November 1779, ibid., p. 171.

[386] *Parliamentary History*, XX, col. 1257.

[387] Ibid., col. 1260.

inquiry into army extraordinaries.[388] On 14 December Burke informed Shelburne of his own intention to inaugurate reform, assuring him that his purpose coincided with the Earl's.[389] The following day he presented his plan to the House of Commons. The scheme was simple. He promised to introduce a measure after the Christmas recess that would reduce public expenditure by £200,000 and cut the number of members dependent on crown munificence by fifty.[390] Burke presented this as a programme of radical reform that would remedy the distemper of the constitution. By curtailing the means at the disposal of the executive branch of government, it would restore the legislature to its proper independence.

Burke announced his scheme in the context of international turmoil. St. Vincent and Grenada had been captured by the French the previous summer. Jamaica was felt to be in danger, and relations with Ireland had deteriorated dramatically.[391] But if change was imperative, the means of effecting it were sparse. The abolition of corruption would be opposed by vested interests in the Commons, leaving the opposition to depend on the dwindling numbers of independents. Corruption functioned by means of a vicious circularity in public proceedings. Influence bred prodigality, and prodigality spread corruption: "they become," Burke claimed, "reciprocally cause and effect."[392] The power of opinion out of doors was needed to assist in breaking the circle. For that reason, the Rockinghams took a close interest in the Yorkshire Association, and in the allied organisations that sprung up in emulation. Burke threw himself into a range of supporting activities. He advocated the creation of committees to concert the business of associations, and corresponded with numerous counties to promote the cause of reform.[393] A county meeting for Yorkshire was fixed for 30 December. Six hundred gentlemen and a group of peers descended upon the Assembly Rooms at York. Rockingham was delighted with the unanimity of opinion.[394] The Duke of Portland attended a similar event at Middlesex where a petition and resolutions were drafted. It went well—"very well"—Burke informed Rockingham.[395] He was keen to present his proposals to the Commons as a matter of priority to capitalise on the burgeoning support in the counties: "Our strength is without," he advised Portland.[396] By the middle of the month, Burke was ready with a draft of two new Bills. Within weeks he had composed a complete set of proposals. On 8 January 1780, Savile presented the 8,000 signatures collected at Yorkshire to the Commons. Three days later Burke outlined his plan for economical reform.[397] Be-

[388] Ibid., col. 1266.

[389] EB to the Earl of Shelburne, 14 December 1779, *Corr.*, IV, p. 174.

[390] EB, Speech on Public Expenses, 15 December 1779, *W & S*, III, p. 474.

[391] Ibid., p. 472.

[392] Ibid., p. 471.

[393] EB, Answers to Queries, post 16 December 1779, ibid., p. 478.

[394] The Marquess of Rockingham to EB, 6 January 1780, *Corr.*, IV, p. 183.

[395] EB to the Marquess of Rockingham, 7 January 1780, ibid., pp. 188–9. Rockingham passed on his approval in the Marquess to Rockingham to EB, 13 January 1789, ibid., p. 193.

[396] EB to the Duke of Portland, 16 January 1780, ibid., p. 196.

[397] A sketch of the plan survives in manuscript at WWM BkP 14:30–34.

tween February and June, when Burke's Establishment Bill was rejected, questions of administrative reform dominated the agenda.

Burke's *Speech on Economical Reform*, ultimately published on 6 March, presented an elaborate understanding of the British system of government along with an account of how it could be profitably overhauled.[398] The plan is rarely looked at on its own terms. Instead, it is usually judged beside competitor schemes that are associated, teleologically, with progress towards the future. In a letter to Christopher Wyvill in December 1780, John Jebb described economical reform as a raging tempest fit to do no better than drown a fly.[399] By this time, partly under the influence of Major John Cartwright, Jebb was openly proposing equal representation and the creation of universal manhood suffrage.[400] Back in 1777, Burke had politely distanced himself from what he saw as Cartwright's "speculative ideas for the improvement of the constitution."[401] In 1780 these ideas were being mobilised in a national movement, and Burke took their dissemination rather more seriously. From his perspective, the Rockinghams' plans for national renewal were bold and comprehensive without risking a descent into civil conflict. As he would later insist to the Duke of Bedford, they did not consist in paltry attempts at marginal repairs. He sought "radical, Systematick Oeconomy," he later declared.[402] He had "acted on state principles," he insisted in 1796: "I found a great distemper in the commonwealth; and according to the nature of the evil and of the object, I treated it."[403] Burke took the business of reform extremely seriously, partly because it probed the limits of government stability but also because it raised the issue of popular consent. Later, in his *Observations on the Conduct of the Minority* of 1793, he considered the conditions under which a "pretended Reform" would give way to a "real Revolution."[404] The distinction between the two was a matter for careful judgment since the government of the kingdom comprised interlocking elements contingently preserved in a delicate balance. A perilous shift in the prerogatives of one of these components could endanger the viability of the edifice as a whole.

Burke believed that the intricacy of the apparatus of British power was seldom properly appreciated. Not only were the branches of government "balanced as

[398] Todd, *Bibliography*, p. 101. A pirated edition of the speech appeared on 17 February. See ibid., p. 100. Leave to introduce the Bill was obtained on 11 February 1780: *CJ*, XXXVII, p. 884.

[399] John Jebb to Christopher Wyvill, 19 December 1780, Wyvill, *Papers*, IV, p. 500. For conflict between parliamentary and economic reformers at this time, see George Stead Veitch, *The Genesis of Parliamentary Reform* (1913) (London: Constable, 1965), pp. 75ff.

[400] John Jebb, *Address to the Freeholders of Middlesex* (London: 1779). For Jebb's trajectory, see Anthony Page, "'Liberty has an Asylum': John Jebb, British Radicalism and the American Revolution," *History*, 87:286 (2002), pp. 204–26.

[401] EB to Major John Cartwright, post 18 February 1777, *Corr.*, III, p. 329. Burke was responding the arguments contained in John Cartwright, *Take Your Choice!* (London: 1777).

[402] EB to Joseph Harford, 4 April 1780, *Corr.*, IV, p. 219.

[403] EB, *Letter to a Noble Lord* (1796), *W & S*, IX, p. 154.

[404] EB, *Observations on the Conduct of the Minority* (Spring 1793), *W & S*, VIII, p. 444.

opposing interests," they were also necessarily "connected as friends."[405] If the terms of this alliance were significantly compromised, the opposition of interests would descend into mutual hostility. "To act on the principles of the constitution . . . has been from the beginning the rule of my conduct," Burke declared in 1777.[406] The alternative of dissolving the fabric of government was a recipe for civil mayhem. The constitution should be renovated, not haphazardly destroyed. This had to be brought about by a return to first principles, based on the independence of parliament.[407] Yet renovation of the kind was fraught with difficulty. It was obliged to elude two powerful seductions at once: the blandishments of power and the sirens of popularity. Both of these were supported by potent rhetorical resources. Power was bolstered by the claims of ancestral authority, while popularity could invoke "the desires of the people."[408] Both forms of legitimation were Janus-faced, with a beneficial and a treacherous aspect. The appeal of age-old conventions was an instance of this double-sidedness. As Burke would argue at length in the *Reflections*, the authority of ancestral usage secured government against forms of innovation that threatened it with sudden disintegration. Yet it was clear to Burke that antiquity, while it naturally conferred authority, could only be justified in terms of public utility. Delinquency was an abuse no matter what its pedigree. It was this fact that Charles I had failed to recognise, Burke reflected: he "defended himself on the practice of the Stuart who went before him."[409] However, inveterate misconduct was all the worse for being archaic. The same applied to dysfunctional offices and jurisdictions. Feudal relics that were a drain upon public resources ought properly to be consigned to oblivion. When the rationale for "old establishments" disappeared, "it is absurd to preserve nothing but the burthen of them."[410]

The preservation of venerable institutions in the face of their impracticality seemed to Burke an unsustainable species of superstition. With this in mind, he proposed bringing an end to superannuated corporations, and radically reducing the royal household. Subordinate jurisdictions like Lancaster and Chester, sheltering a host of sinecures, should be eliminated; in the same spirit, the great wardrobe, the jewel office, and the treasurer of the chamber should be expunged. The proliferation of useless offices had been used to compensate pliable MPs, providing the crown with purchase on the will of parliament. This means of corruption had to be terminated. At the same time, public finance and the system of accounting should be subject to auditing. Waste and profusion should also be curtailed. Crown lands were to be sold off, and the surveyor-general abolished. The paymaster of the forces and the treasurer of the navy were to be rationalised. Pensions were to be limited to £60,000 a year. Defunct places, like the clerk of the pells, were to be discontinued. The Board

[405] Ibid., p. 441.
[406] EB, *Letter to the Sheriffs of Bristol* (3 April 1777), *W & S*, III, p. 328.
[407] EB, *Address to the Colonists* (January 1777), ibid., p. 284.
[408] EB, *Speech on Economical Reform* (11 February 1780), ibid., p. 490.
[409] Ibid., p. 491.
[410] Ibid., p. 510.

of Trade was to be dismantled, and the American Secretary annulled. These economies were to be introduced in accordance with seven principles of conduct directed towards the goal of extinguishing malign influence. "Influence," of course, was necessary in British politics. After all, the parts of the constitution were held together by "friendship."[411] But this was very different from a system of servility whereby the monarch bought off parliament by a proliferation of minor posts that remunerated at the expense of public virtue. This was the point at which influence descended into corruption. It enabled the king to ignore the claims of distinguished members of parliament in favour of habitual courtiers. This had been the theme of the *Present Discontents*, but it was also fundamental to the *Speech on Economical Reform*. "Kings," Burke observed, "are naturally lovers of low company."[412] He called to mind the dependence of the Roman emperors on flatterers. Monarchy, he was suggesting, benefited from intermediary powers. The chief person of the state needed to be bridled by dependent greatness rather than reverenced by servile minions. Influence, Burke was saying, could not safely be abandoned. His was no country programme opposed to active administration.[413] Executive power required ways and means, but it ought to be grounded on the authority of parliament. Unnecessary places and docile officers sabotaged that result.

Popularity was as big a pitfall as the claims of ancestral authority. On the one hand it was essential, on the other it was deceptive. One thing was certain: the powers of government were conferred to service the good of the people. As soon as it was suggested in the spring of 1780 that the civil list was the property of the king, Burke emphasised the popular origins of all power, monarchical and republican alike: "Wherever Government wa[s] property, subjection must be slavery." He likened the ministerial position to the claims of Jacobitism, above all the idea that the title to rule was *jure divino*, terminating in the doctrine that "the people were made for Kings, not Kings for the people."[414] In a mixed system of government with a representative component, the duty of public service was not only paramount, it was also enforced by the sacred trust that bound representatives to their constituents. Burke had rejected Hume's suggestion that civilised monarchy in France was as committed to the principles of justice as mixed government in Britain.[415] Under the unopposed rule of one, liberty was a "connivance" rather than a practical power in the people. "What is connivance but a state under which all slaves live?," Burke had asked when defending the right of toleration.[416] A right had to be distinguished from an indulgence that might be revoked. The anticipation of revocation was in fact a state of fear. "Montesquieu places liberty in an exemption from fear," Burke once reminded the

[411] Ibid., p. 528.

[412] Ibid., p. 532.

[413] See, for example, EB, *Thoughts on the Cause of the Present Discontents* (1770), *W & S*, II, p. 310.

[414] EB, Speech on the Civil Establishment Bill, 8 March 1780, *W & S*, III, p. 555.

[415] EB, *Letter to the Sheriffs of Bristol*, 3 April 1777, *W & S*, III p. 299, taking issue with David Hume, "Of Civil Liberty" in idem, *Essays and Treatises* (London: 1758), p. 60.

[416] EB, Speech on Toleration Bill, 17 March 1773, *W & S*, II, p. 383.

Commons.[417] Representation made the enjoyment of liberty a power in the hands of the people rather than lucky connivance on the part of authority. Optimally it aligned the Commons with opinion out of doors: "Let the commons in parliament assembled, be one and the same thing with the commons at large," Burke urged in his *Speech on Economical Reform*.[418] Yet the goal of popular sympathy became complicated over the months that followed. "The people are the masters," Burke affirmed to his colleagues. Members of parliament, on the other hand, were "expert artists."[419] As the Association movement developed between February and June, relations between master and artist came under increasing strain.

Burke's reforms were to be embodied in a number of Bills, the first—on the civil establishment—introduced on 23 February 1780.[420] North aimed to defeat the opposition by detailed debate on individual clauses. On 8 March, in a committee of the whole House, the provision to annul the American Secretary was defeated by seven votes. Yet five days later the Board of Trade was successfully abolished.[421] The good fortune of the Rockinghams did not last. On 20 March the attempt to retrench the royal household failed. Burke was distressed: "the whole Systematick part of the principle of the Bill, that which cost me far the most pains . . . is totally rejected."[422] On 6 April the critics of government prospered: Dunning's famous motion on the expansion of court power carried by just over fifteen votes. The principle of parliamentary scrutiny of public accounts was also established.[423] But thereafter the impetus for reform became unstuck. Burke's work was slowly dismantled in committee. The independents in the Commons began to take fright at assaults on prerogative. Then, on 8 May 1780, the divisions in the ranks of the opposition were publicly displayed as they divided over Sawbridge's motion for shortening the duration of parliaments.[424] Fox supported the motion, Burke was emphatically against. Richmond then proceeded to unveil his plan in the Lords, opting for annual parliaments and a universal franchise.[425] Gloom replaced the cheer of early spring among opposition groups. Shelburne withdrew from politics, accusing his colleagues of pusillanimity.[426] The Rockinghams were disgruntled, and increasingly divided. Relations with the Association movement grew suspicious and tense.[427]

[417] Ibid. as reported in *Parliamentary History*, XVII, cols. 778–79.

[418] EB, *Speech on Economical Reform*, 11 February 1780, *W & S*, III, p. 549.

[419] Ibid., p. 547.

[420] *Parliametnary History*, XXI, cols. 111ff.

[421] *Parliamentary History*, XXI, col. 278.

[422] EB to Unknown, post 20 March 1780, *Corr.*, IV, p. 214. See *Parliamentary History*, XXI, col. 309.

[423] *Parliamentary History*, XXI, cols. 340–74.

[424] Ibid., cols. 594–615.

[425] Ibid., cols. 686–88.

[426] Earl of Shelburne to Isaac Barré, December 1780, Lord Fitzmaurice, *Life of William, Earl of Shelburne* (London: 1875–76) 3 vols., III, pp. 106–7.

[427] This despite the fact that at least twelve of the twenty-seven county meetings were inspired by Rockinghamite connections, and that seven party members were active on the committees, some occupy-

The diversity of possible reforms was the midwife of division. Back in November 1779, Walker King had updated Burke on the reform enthusiasms of the Duke of Richmond. He had embraced the idea of annual parliaments, and hoped to extend the vote "to every Man of 21 years of age and upwards without exception."[428] He had also fallen under the influence of Burgh and Cartwright, and was committed to establishing some form of association. Cartwright had been pressing since 1776 for "a grand national association for the restoration of the constitution."[429] He was deliberately drawing on Burgh's proposal to supplement "[i]nstructing, petitioning, remonstrating and the like" with a popular movement, organised to demand a reconstituted parliament.[430] By early January 1780, Burke himself was lamenting the ineffectiveness of issuing petitions—"lately petitioning has fallen into discredit"—and banking instead on the authority of a popular movement at large.[431] Yet the example of people in protest in Ireland and America was disturbing rather than heartening. Between 11 and 20 March 1780, twelve counties and a handful of cities and boroughs sent deputies to Wyvill's conference in London to agree a plan of national association. Proposals were to be taken back by the delegates to the counties, returning to the Yorkshire committee on 25 March. Rockingham was dismayed by the proceedings that ensued. They were, as he informed Burke, "*strange*, *precipitate*, and . . . tending to nothing but the accumulation of *perplexities*."[432] He was already opposed to suggestions that tests might be imposed on MPs: "being elected a representative, if it implies a trust, is most highly honourable, but if it is to lock up your reasoning faculties . . . it would be a disgraceful bondage."[433] He was even more perturbed by the idea that "*the people*" were not represented.[434] The subject of rotten boroughs might usefully be addressed, and the duration of parliaments might conceivably be revised, but these were issues with complicatedly ramifying consequences, and needed to be treated with the utmost care.[435] Burke was even more alarmed by the drift of the popular tide. He wrote to Richmond after the vote on Sawbridge's Bill

---

ing more than one position. See N. C. Phillips, "Edmund Burke and the County Movement, 1779–1780," *English Historical Review*, 76:299 (April 1961), pp. 254–78.

[428] Walker King to EB, 5 November 1779, *Corr.*, IV, pp. 165–66.

[429] Cartwright, *Take Your Choice*, p. 89.

[430] James Burgh, *Political Disquisitions* (London: 1774), 3 vols., III, pp. 455–56. For discussion, see Herbert Butterfield, *George III, Lord North and the People, 1779–1780* (London: Bell, 1949), pp. 259–63; Carla H. Hay, "The Making of a Radical: The Case of James Burgh," *Journal of British Studies*, 18:2 (1979), pp. 90–117; Pasi Ihalainen, *Agents of the People: Democracy and Popular Sovereignty in British and Swedish Parliamentary and Public Debates, 1734–1800* (Leiden: Brill, 2010), pp. 249–50.

[431] EB to the Duke of Bolton, 2 January 1780, *Corr.*, IV, p. 179.

[432] The Marquess of Rockingham to EB, 31 March 1780, ibid., p. 216.

[433] The Marquess of Rockingham to Pemberton Milner, 28 February 1780, *Rockingham Memoirs*, II, p. 396. Wyvill had indicated his support for instructions by the end of January 1780: see Wyvill, *Papers*, I, pp. 67–68.

[434] The Marquess of Rockingham to Pemberton Milner, 28 February 1780, *Rockingham Memoirs*, II, p. 397.

[435] The Marquess of Rockingham to Henry Clerk Zouch, ibid., pp. 404–6.

for shorter parliaments proclaiming his timidity in the face of fundamental change to those parts of he constitution "under which I was born."[436]

In his *Speech on Economical Reform*, Burke had famously remarked that while he was devising his recommendations he had not followed the people but had rather "*met it on the way*."[437] Yet before long he would find that their paths were subtly diverging. It was of course difficult to access the sense of "the people," since it was almost impossible to identify its genuine voice amidst the multitude of agents who claimed to articulate its will. In the notes for his speech on the duration of parliaments delivered on 8 May 1780, Burke observed that in every district of the kingdom there was always "some leading man, some agitator, some wealthy merchant or considerable manufacturer, some active attorney, some popular preacher, some Money-Lender, &c., &c., who is followed by the whole Flock."[438] Behind official representatives lay layers of representation, each one providing opportunities for flattering, canvassing and cajoling the "desires" of the population. Fidelity to popular sentiment was no more assured in the county delegate than it was in a national deputy. It was certainly not more likely that they would serve the common interest. By the early summer of 1780 Burke was describing the Association movement as a "*faction*" whose prominent activists were often "despotic" in character.[439] Nonetheless, despite the elusive character of the people's voice, it was ultimately possible to ascertain the overwhelming sense of the nation. More than that, it was essential that politics should act at its behest. The best political system was the one that captured it with fidelity and justice. Even where the people were deceived in their choice of an object, it was proper that they be permitted to pursue their preference.

In a letter to Joseph Harford, who had moved the Bristol petition in favour of economical reform, Burke underscored the primacy of popular sentiment: "It would be a dreadful thing if there were any power in this Country of strength enough to oppose with effect the general wishes of the people."[440] In the end the population would have its way, whatever the consequences. Yet the next worst thing to impeding the popular will was permitting it to engineer the destruction of the common good. Popularity was therefore a potentially expensive political virtue. Burke worried about the cost in his own county of Buckinghamshire, where Lord Stanhope, whose credentials he would challenge in the *Reflections on the Revolution in France*, was pressing for major constitutional change, including triennial parliaments and the addition of one hundred new county members in the Commons.[441] Burke wrote to the chairman of the country meeting on 12 April 1780. The constitution, he admitted, was certainly flawed, but to repair its faults the whole edifice would have to be viewed together as a complicated array of prerogatives and forces. This was a com-

[436] EB to the Duke of Richmond, post 8 May 1780, *Corr.*, IV, p. 236.
[437] EB, *Speech on Economical Reform*, 11 February 1780, *W & S*, III, p. 493.
[438] EB, Speech on Duration of Parliaments, 8 May 1780, ibid., p. 593.
[439] EB to the Duke of Richmond, post 8 May 1780, *Corr.*, IV, p. 236.
[440] EB to Joseph Harford, 4 April 1780, ibid., p. 220.
[441] Butterfield, *George III, Lord North, and the People*, pp. 383–7.

plicated theoretical enterprise, requiring an extended process of deliberation. Would the addition of one hundred knights of the shires, or the proliferation of electoral competitions throughout the kingdom, improve the fate of liberty, or compromise its operation?[442] Burke returned to the subject of more frequent parliaments in the Commons on 8 May. Taking a stand against Sawbridge's motion, and thus against Fox and Cavendish too, Burke was eloquently committed to the electoral powers of the people but wary of the distempers that more frequent contests were likely to cause. "To govern according to the Sense and agreeably to the interests of the People is a great and glorious Object of Government," he recognised.[443] Yet while elections were indispensable to ascertaining the popular sense, they were also potential instruments of malign influence and corruption. Their cost acted against the honest canvassing of men of integrity; their frequency was an opportunity for the machinations of the court.[444] More frequent parliaments would not bypass the corruptions of the political process. Instead, they would exacerbate the deforming features of the existing system.

A year before his death, in the *Letter to a Noble Lord*, Burke returned to consider the upheavals of 1780. The popular passions of that year could be observed in three dimensions. First, there was the general feeling that reform was a national priority; second, there was the complex reality of relations between rulers and ruled; and third, there was the prospect of frenzy and fury on the part of the populace. All reform had to be based on the first of these considerations: politics dealt with grievances, and these proceeded from popular sentiment, which it was the job of representatives to remedy and redress. "It was my aim to give the People the substance of what I knew they desired," Burke argued in this connection.[445] However, as a representative, rather than a delegate, he was also determined to conform his actions to what seemed "right," whether the populace happened to desire it or not. The people, for their part, were then entitled to dismiss him. In the meantime, it was his duty to oppose measures that he was convinced would convulse the state. This raised the second aspect of popular passion, based on the balance of responsibility between government and governed. The relationship between constituent and representative was a quintessentially political one. The deputy was to act on the feelings of the principal, yet this might take a variety of forms. For instance, the representative might either inflame or flatter the voter. However, optimally, he would deliberate on the constituent's behalf. Where public servants combined the characteristics of sensitivity and integrity, the political division of labour could be expected to operate well. Yet when representatives acted as sycophants, or as vehicles for prejudice, the third dimension of popular politics lurched into view: moderation would be sacrificed to blind fury.

[442] EB to the Chairman of the Buckinghamshire Meeting, 12 April 1780, *Corr.*, IV, pp. 227–28.

[443] EB, Speech on the Duration of Parliaments, 8 May 1780, *W & S*, III, p. 590.

[444] Ibid., pp. 592–94.

[445] EB, *Letter to a Noble Lord* (1796), *W & S*, IX, p. 155. Cf. EB to the Chairman of the Buckinghamshire Meeting, 12 April 1780, *Corr.*, IV, p. 228.

Burke expected this development to take one of two forms: either it would stimulate religious antagonism or it would undermine the system of private property. He remembered 1780 as having engendered the means of upheaval.[446] The Association movement became an engine of potentially subversive activity. A national convention "nosed" parliament, sitting with pretensions to an authority over the established sovereignty. Many of its proposals "went in their certain, and, in my opinion, not very remote effect, home to the utter destruction of the Constitution of this kingdom."[447] Burke was now writing in the aftermath of the French Revolution. Had the proposals circulating in many of the Association committees been realised, then Britain, rather than France, might have had the privilege of performing "the death dance of Democratick Revolution."[448] On fuller consideration, Burke believed that Britain enjoyed one advantage securing it against all-out fervour: it lacked the doctrine of the rights of man.[449] Nonetheless, if proposals for annual parliaments and manhood suffrage had succeeded, the British mixed system of government would have been demolished, and some species of untrammelled democracy would have imperilled the society of ranks: "a gate would have been opened, through which all property might be sacked and ravaged."[450] As it happened, a programme of social resentment failed to materialise. Instead, the spirit of persecution seized large sections of the populace, demonstrating the potential intemperance of the crowd. The Gordon Riots stood as an enduring caution: "Such was the distemper of the publick mind," Burke recalled, "that there was no madman, in his maddest ideas, and maddest projects, who might not count upon numbers to support principles and execute his designs."[451]

8.6 Norms and Nature: From the Election to St. Eustatius

By the summer of 1780, with a dissolution of parliament in the offing, the programme of economical reform was fast expiring. In July, William Courtenay, the chairman of the Devonshire county committee, approached Burke to revive his Bill in the next session. Burke, however, did not expect to have the requisite support.[452] He reported the same reticence to Christopher Wyvill the following month: "it will not be possible to carry it against the opposition of that powerful influence, which it is one of the principal objects of the bill to moderate."[453] After the general election,

[446] This recollection became the premise of Butterfield, *George III, Lord North, and the People*, *passim*.
[447] EB, *Letter to a Noble Lord* (1796), *W & S*, IX, p. 152.
[448] Ibid.
[449] Ibid., p. 151.
[450] Ibid., p. 155.
[451] Ibid., p. 152.
[452] EB to Viscount Courtenay, 24 July 1780, *Corr.*, IV, p. 259.
[453] EB to Christopher Wyvill, 14 August 1780, ibid., p. 265. See also "The History of Europe" in *The Annual Register for 1781*, p. 141.

with Fox's success at Westminster and his own failure at Bristol, Burke was dreading his return to parliament. The divisions in his party were conspicuous. He blamed this on the activities of visionary "Schemers" whose ideas seduced the sober minded from intelligent reform, disposing them towards speculative innovation. The "*form*" of the constitution was not the problem, he explained to Harford; improvement "in point of *Substance*" was what was required.[454] Neither the Duke of Richmond nor Sir George Savile seemed to agree. By his plan to extend the vote to the mass of the male population, Richmond appeared to Burke to want to annihilate the power of freeholders. At the same time, Savile was lending his support to more frequent elections as well as additional seats for county members.[455] Neither he nor Richmond had properly considered the systematic impact these changes would have. Faced with a range of projects in the new parliament, Rockingham was keen to unite the opposition around issues that would generate consent. The election had been good for the followers of Rockingham and Shelburne, but how well this placed them was not immediately clear. Cornwallis's victory in August at the Battle of Camden gave a boost to the ministry. Nonetheless, despite a positive showing for the government in a number of divisions, the balance of forces in the new House of Commons remained uncertain throughout the autumn until after the Christmas recess.[456]

Rockingham intended to rally his troops around economical reform. According to the calculations of John Robinson, the Secretary of the Treasury, numbers in parliament were fairly evenly balanced. Full attendance might prove discomfiting for the ministry. In that atmosphere of uncertainty, Burke rose to address the House at six o'clock on 15 February 1781 to move to reintroduce his Bill from the previous year.[457] At war with the colonies, at war with the Bourbons, and divided from their allies, it was imperative that government be able to take from its overblown civil establishment "to add to their military service."[458] At the same time, a measure of retrenchment would reduce the power of influence. Burke considered his commitment to these objectives to be at one with the general attitude in the country. It had been argued by other members that the Association movement had bred commotion and upheaval. But even if this point were conceded, it was the job of administration to soothe by temperate reform the resentments that had been bred by public neglect.[459] The people had commanded "in thunder and lightening," and it now remained for parliament to execute with tranquillity.[460] Government, as a "skillful physician," should "feel the pulse of the patient" and judiciously apply the appropriate

[454] EB to Joseph Harford, 27 September 1780, *Corr.*, IV, p. 295.

[455] Ibid., p. 296.

[456] Ian R. Christie, *The End of North's Ministry, 1780–1782* (London: Macmillan, 1958), pp. 231–40.

[457] *CJ*, XXXVIII, p. 213.

[458] EB, Debate on the Bill for the Regulation of the Civil List Establishments, 15 February 1781, *Parliamentary History*, XXI, col. 1232.

[459] WWM BkP 14:8.

[460] "The History of Europe" in *The Annual Register for 1781*, p. 181.

remedy.[461] Rulers were obliged by patriotism to serve the common good, but as representatives they were bound more immediately to that duty. They were dependent on the people, "answerable for their conduct, and charged with guardianship of the constitution."[462]

North decided not to oppose the introduction of the Bill. Instead, it was defeated on the second reading by over forty votes.[463] For the remainder of the session the opposition focused its attention on the American issue, winning support from former ministerialists in June. The war in the colonies was fast approaching a moment of decision. Two days before the new session was due to meet on 27 November 1781, news of Cornwallis's surrender at Yorktown to a Franco-American force under Washington reached London. The circumstances of the surrender filled Burke with horror, producing an agitated performance in the Commons during his Speech on the Address.[464] The government survived the session, but the end was near. One problem was that the opposition remained divided, with Shelburne's supporters refusing to accept the independence of the colonies while the Rockinghams were now resigned to that outcome. Still, pressure on the ministry was not relieved. In January 1782, Lord George Germain, as Secretary of State for the Colonies, was sacrificed at the insistence of Henry Dundas in preparation for the development of a new American policy. Fox now trained his sights on the First Lord of the Admiralty, the Earl of Sandwich, moving for an inquiry into his management of the navy. In a series of votes over the course of February, the government was steadily deprived of its majority. It lost Conway's motion to reject the principle of the war on 27 February 1782. North faced a packed House to accept defeat on 20 March: "*his Majesty's ministers were no more.*"[465] For Burke, it was a victory for the independent members who best spoke the "spirit" of the people.[466] But herein lay a problem for the future: the independents held the balance in the House of Commons, yet their impartiality was often accompanied by indolence. A government had been removed, but "the most essential part of the work remained to be performed."[467] This could only be achieved with vigorous support from the independents. Passivity and lethargy would be the death of virtuous power.

In the final stages of the American conflict, the British had been fighting a war on multiple fronts. On 20 December 1780, as the Dutch were about to accede to the league of armed neutrality under Catherine II, a declaration of hostilities was announced at St. James's against what Burke described as Britain's "old and natural

[461] EB, Debate on the Bill for the Regulation of the Civil List Establishments, 15 February 1781, *Parliamentary History*, XXI, col. 1225.

[462] Ibid., col. 1232.

[463] *CJ*, XXXVIII, p. 231.

[464] EB, Speech on Address, 28 November 1781, *Parliamentary History*, XXII, col. 747.

[465] Ibid., col. 1215.

[466] EB, Debate on Change of Ministry, 20 March 1782, ibid., col. 1225.

[467] Ibid.

ally."[468] The British manifesto against the United Provinces listed an array of grievances, including a secret trade agreement between Amsterdam and the American Congress, and the ongoing commerce of the Dutch Republic with other enemy powers.[469] The first goal of the administration was therefore to launch an attack against the Antilles, beginning with a descent upon St. Vincent in early January, both as a way of bringing the United Provinces to terms, and as a means of disrupting supplies to the French and trade to the Americans. On 3 February 1781, the Dutch garrison on St. Eustatius was overwhelmed by British forces led by Admiral Rodney and General Vaughan. By 17 February, Rodney was informing the governor of Barbados that "France, Holland, and America, will most severely feel this Blow that has been given to them."[470] Two months before the incursion, the island had been devastated by a hurricane, leaving its inhabitants in a peculiarly vulnerable state.[471] As the king informed his commanders in advance of the operation, significant resistance to the onslaught was not expected.[472] The island, although a "barren rock," was a lucrative site of international trade—"the grand free port of the West-Indies and America."[473] After staging diversionary operations on the neighbouring island of Martinique, Rodney and Vaughan arrived on St. Eustatius in considerable force. Fourteen ships of the line and a number of frigates unloaded a contingent of 3,000 soldiers onto this diminutive Caribbean emporium, protected by a mere fifty troops in garrison.[474] Saba and St. Martin were also reduced. The governor, Johannes de Graaff, surrendered and appealed for clemency. Nonetheless, in the aftermath of Rodney's victory, the residents on the island—including British, Dutch, French and Jewish merchants—were treated as prisoners of war. Their properties were seized and confiscated indiscriminately. As Rodney had threatened, the "just revenge" of Britain was shown to be slow but sure.[475]

St. Eustatius possessed a tremendous magazine of supplies, providing Britain with an immediate and prodigious conquest. The value of the commodities taken

[468] *Morning Chronicle*, 26 January 1781. The motives behind the offensive are discussed in H. M. Scott, *British Foreign Policy in the Age of the American Revolution* (Oxford: Oxford University Press, 1990, 2001), pp. 305–9.

[469] *Parliamentary History*, XXI, cols. 968–72. The trade agreement had been discovered in the papers of Henry Laurens, former president to the Congress, recently arrested and committed to the tower. See "The History of Europe" in *The Annual Register for 1781*, p. 144.

[470] Sir George Brydges Rodney to General Cunningham, 17 February 1781, in *Letters from Sir George Brydges Rodney to His Majesty's Ministers Relative to the Capture of St. Eustatius* (London: n.d.), p. 17.

[471] "The History of Europe" in *The Annual Register for1781*, pp. 30ff.

[472] "His Majesty's Instructions to Sir George Brydges Rodney" in *Letters from Sir George Brydges Rodney*, p. 6.

[473] "The History of Europe" in *The Annual Register for 1781*, p. 101; Ronald Hurst, *The Golden Rock: An Episode of the American War of Independence, 1775–1783* (London: Leo Cooper, 1996).

[474] The figures are taken from EB, Debate on St. Eustatius, 14 May 1781, *Parliamentary History*, XXII, col. 221. Rodney and Vaughan would later defend themselves before the Commons: see the *Morning Chronicle*, 11 December 1781.

[475] Sir George Brydges Rodney to General Cunningham, 17 February 1781, in *Letters from Sir George Brydges Rodney*, p. 17.

was estimated at £3,000,000. Over 250 vessels were captured in the surrounding seas.[476] After being despoiled of their goods, the merchants were dispersed. Americans and Jews were banished to St. Christopher's; the Dutch, the French and the British were variously displaced. The booty was duly auctioned off at a fraction of its value. Parliament was soon petitioned to offer redress to British West Indians.[477] There were serious fears that Britain's conduct would provoke French retaliation. Burke received news of the episode by 13 March 1781: "St Eustatius taken without resistance and without capitulat[ion]," he recorded.[478] On 3 May, he drew the attention of the Commons to the severity of the proceedings, and gave notice that he would bring the matter under the consideration of the House on Monday the 14th. The affair was detrimental to the interests of the country, but also injurious to the rights of "mankind in general."[479] When Burke rose on 14 May to recount the "inhuman" severity of the British commanders, he spoke for between two and a half and three hours on the business.[480] Britain was fighting a "calamitous war" with many enemies and "no friends."[481] The situation was virtually without precedent, providing particular reasons for proceeding with moderation: civility would lessen the impulse to retaliation, attract neutrals to support the British side, and encourage antagonists to come to terms: "By such civil regards, the resentments of our enemies might be softened; their enmity might be subdued, and their minds be brought to a favourable inclination towards peace."[482]

As the report of the speech on St. Eustatius in the *Morning Herald* indicated, Burke drew support for his argument from Vattel in particular.[483] By comparison with the Swiss author, as the *Morning Chronicle* put it, Burke regarded Grotius and Pufendorf as "barbarous and savage writers."[484] Yet despite this disparagement, it is clear that his argument drew on sixteenth- and seventeenth-century sources in addition to relying heavily on Vattel.[485] After the failure of Burke's call for an inquiry into St. Eustatius, he returned to the subject at the opening of the next session, cen-

[476] "The History of Europe" in *The Annual Register for 1781*, p. 102.

[477] See P. J. Marshal, editorial headnote to EB, Speech on St. Eustatius, 14 May 1781, *W & S*, IV (forthcoming).

[478] EB to Mrs. Richard Champion, 13 March 1781, *Corr.*, IV, p. 343.

[479] *Morning Chronicle*, 4 May 1781.

[480] *London Courant*, 15 May 1781; *Public Advertiser*, 15 May 1781.

[481] EB, Debate on St. Eustatius, 14 May 1781, *Parliamentary History*, XXII, col. 218.

[482] Ibid.

[483] *Morning Herald*, 15 May 1781, appealing to "Votelle" [sic] as the "last and best writer" on the law of nations.

[484] *Morning Chronicle*, 15 May 1781.

[485] There is a general account of Burke's debt to natural law arguments in this context in Jennifer Pitts, *A Turn to Empire: The Rise of Imperial Liberalism in Britain and France* (Princeton, NJ: Princeton University Press, 2005), pp. 83–85. On the general themes, see also Peter Stanlis, *Burke and the Natural Law* (1958) (New Brunswick, NJ: Transaction Publishers, 2009), *passim*; Frederick Whelan, *Edmund Burke and India: Political Morality and Empire* (Pittsburgh, PA: University of Pittsburgh Press, 1996), pp. 275–90.

suring once more the abuse of discretion by the British commanders. This time he invoked the wisdom of Alberico Gentili, for whom discretion implied equity and virtue.[486] Yet the idea that the rights of war were circumscribed and limited had been conspicuously urged by Grotius himself. For Samuel Pufendorf, writing in 1672 in the *Law of Nature and Nations*, this was the most conspicuous feature of the Dutch jurist's position. There was all the difference in the world, Pufendorf commented, between the freedom of action to which hostile forces in a state of war could appeal and the liberty which considerations of mercy permit antagonists to take. The "*Law of Humanity*" in practice limited the rights of war. Adversaries ought therefore to moderate their conduct. "Upon this *Moderation*," Pufendorf concluded, "*Grotius* is very large."[487] As Barbeyrac interpreted Grotius in his notes to Pufendorf, while the goods of an enemy, whether sacred or profane, might fairly be destroyed, war should nonetheless not be pursued to the last extremity, but only insofar as it served the goal of peace.[488] Grotius himself illustrated the point with Cicero's claim in *De officiis* that "there are certain duties that ought to be performed even towards those who have injured us."[489] In book III, chapter 12 of *The Rights of War and Peace*, Grotius elaborated on the theme of moderation in connection with spoil. While licence in war was limited by natural justice, it was also prudently restricted by considerations of policy. Clemency, for instance, pacifies an enemy, and generosity disarms an opponent by reducing desperation.[490]

While it was clear that the tradition of modern natural law encompassing Gentili, Grotius and Pufendorf urged restraint in war and conquest, Burke's claim was that jurisprudence had nonetheless been improved by the enlightened civility of eighteenth-century practice. Above all, he argued, it was the practice of soldiers on the ground that established conventions moderating the brutality of war. Burke had in mind the security extended by modern combatants to private property on terra firma. This contrasted, he noted, with goods that were seized at sea. Yet the time was not far distant, he surmised, when even "property found afloat" would be eligible for protection.[491] This optimism was a product of a general faith in modern conventions, which had cumulatively diminished the barbarism of armed conflict. These

[486] *Morning Herald*, 5 December 1781. Burke is drawing on Alberico Gentili, *De iure belli libri tres* (1612), ed. John C. Rolfe (Oxford: Oxford University Press, 1933), 2 vols., I, p. 372, where discretion is identified with "moderatio" insofar as it is "arbitrium boni viri" (the discretion of good men). On Gentili, see Richard Tuck, *The Rights of War and Peace: Political Thought and International Order from Grotius to Kant* (Oxford: Oxford University Press, 1999, 2002), ch. 1.

[487] Samuel Pufendorf, *Of the Law of Nature and Nations*, trans. Basil Kennett (London: 1729), bk. VIII, ch. 6, § 7.

[488] Ibid.

[489] Hugo Grotius, *The Rights of War and Peace*, ed. Richard Tuck (Indianapolis, IN: Liberty Fund, 2005), 3 vols., III, p. 1420, citing Cicero, *De officiis*, I, xi: "sunt autem quaedam officia etiam adversos eos servanda a quibus inuriam acceperis."

[490] Grotius, *Rights of War and Peace*, III, pp. 1472–73.

[491] EB, Debate on St. Eustatius, 14 May 1781, *Parliamentary History*, XXII, col. 230.

conventions had benefited from the culture of enlightenment proceeding from the improved condition of manners and behaviour. They had their basis, however, in human rationality, whose provisions were established by the deity and felt by the human heart. Reason calculated in terms of "necessity" and resulted in rules that found support in sentiment.[492] That is, peaceableness and accommodation were recommended by need and utility as determined by the faculty of reason. But while the mind could see the advantage of reconciliation, the passions were inclined to embrace the same result.

In this way, Burke's argument involved the claim that the law of nations, in being founded on reason and utility, was rooted in the law of nature. At the same time, the rights of nature were endorsed by the affections, which were enhanced by the cultivation of sensibility. Therefore, under conditions of enlightenment, conventions tended to improve. Burke also claimed that the norms prescribed by reason and convention could be consulted in authoritative works of jurisprudence, and supported by precedent. While Vattel, "being a modern writer," was a valuable authority, the conquest of Grenada, as a recent example, was a valuable precedent.[493] Vattel was attractive to Burke for two reasons. First, his *Law of Nations* exempted private property from booty: "The conqueror seizes on the possessions of the state, the public property, while private individuals are permitted to retain theirs."[494] Second, Vattel descanted at length on the duties of the conqueror, which Burke took Admiral Rodney to have discounted. As soon as an enemy population submitted, Vattel contended, the rights of conquest succeeded to the duties of government: "at length every thing is to be rendered conformable to the rules of wise government, and the duties of a good prince."[495] Vattel based this conclusion on two principles. To begin with he followed Montesquieu in proposing that conquerors should acquit themselves "in the eye of humanity."[496] In addition, the norm of humanity was supported by good "policy." In other words, benign treatment was in the interest of the new ruler: "Do you wish that your conquest may prove a real addition to your strength, and be well affected to you?—treat it as a father, as a true sovereign."[497] Both arguments found their way into Burke's speech. It was in the interest of the British to secure a reputation for clemency, but such behaviour was also imposed as an obligation.

[492] Ibid.

[493] Ibid., col. 231.

[494] Emer de Vattel, *The Law of Nations, or the Principles of the Law of Nature, Applied to the Conduct and Affairs of Nations and Sovereigns*, ed. Béla Kapossy and Richard Whatmore (Indianapolis, IN: Liberty Fund, 2008), p. 598.

[495] Ibid., p. 599.

[496] Ibid., p. 600. The reference is to Charles-Louis de Secondat, Baron de Montesquieu, *De l'esprit des lois* (1748) in *Œuvres complètes,* ed. Roger Caillois (Paris: Gallimard, 1951), 2 vols., II, pt. II, bk. X, ch. 4.

[497] Vattel, *Law of Nations*, pp. 600–601.

The submission of a people to the discretion of a conqueror imposed on the new power the duties of government: "Shew me a government," Burke declared, "and I will shew you a trust."[498] Burke would later elucidate the point in his prosecution of Warren Hastings: "Name me a Magistrate, and I will name property. Name me power, and I will name protection."[499] Conquest, Burke believed, entailed a "virtual compact."[500] Failure to honour the obligations of rule dissolved the duty of obedience in the subject. Since only lawful administration commanded allegiance, force had to be succeeded by justice if it was to confer a "just title" to rule.[501] Burke judged the failure to protect the Jews of St. Eustatius to be perhaps the most culpable shortcoming of the British operation. As a "dispersed, wandering, and proscribed" people—a community without a state—the Hebrew nation depended on the offices of humanity. Their treatment by crown forces was a discredit to "this enlightened age" and still more "to the Christian character."[502] Burke held up the French conduct of the capture of Grenada in July 1779, for all its violence and crudity, as an example of superior political morality. Although the Comte D'Estaing, who had led the amphibious assault, had seized the British commander as a prisoner of war and permitted his troops to pillage the town of St. George's, nonetheless there had been "no general confiscation" and Louis XVI had restored the merchants to the quiet possession of looted goods.[503] Burke's outrage was still in evidence when he returned to the case the following winter: "my whole heart is in this business," as he put it to a correspondent.[504] He now contended that the sojourn of Rodney and Vaughan on St. Eustatius had contributed to the capture of Tobago.[505] But he was still particularly incensed by the abuse of discretion as a result of which British commanders had pursued their conquest to "destruction."[506] As Montesquieu had claimed in the *Spirit of the Laws*, such comportment was a perversion of the right of conquest, which was bound by four distinct laws: first, the law of nature, which aims at the preservation of the species; second, the law of reason ("la lumière naturelle"), which dictates that we should do unto others as we would wish done to ourselves; third, the law of political societies, which provides for the durability of civil communities; and, finally, the law of conquest itself, which, since it concerns an acquisition, urges conservation and not "destruction."[507]

[498] EB, Debate on St. Eustatius, 14 May 1781, *Parliamentary History*, XXII, col. 230.

[499] EB, Speech Opening the Hastings Impeachment, 16 February 1788, *W & S*, VI, p. 351. For discussion, see above, chapter 5, sections 5–6.

[500] EB, Debate on St. Eustatius, 14 May 1781, *Parliamentary History*, XXII, col. 229.

[501] EB, Notes for Speech on the Opening of the Hastings Impeachment, Northamptonshire MS. A. XXIX.49.

[502] EB, Debate on St. Eustatius, 14 May 1781, *Parliamentary History*, XXII, col. 223.

[503] Ibid., col. 231.

[504] EB to James Bourdieu, 5 December 1781, *Corr.*, IV, p. 387.

[505] *London Courant*, 5 December 1781.

[506] *Morning Herald*, 5 December 1781.

[507] Montesquieu, *De l'esprit des lois*, pt. II, bk. X, ch. 3.

8.7 Reverence and Utility: Reforming the Commons

Political developments soon obliged Burke to reflect on the rights of nature in the context of parliamentary reform. As the ministry of Lord North was progressively weakened, the prospect of power suddenly opened up to the Rockingham party, having been deprived of office for nearly sixteen years. On 22 March 1782, just after the fall of North, Burke impressed his patron with the need for a united ministry.[508] As it turned out, Shelburne conspired with George III to limit the Marquess's leverage.[509] On 27 March 1782, Lord Rockingham took the Treasury in the new administration, while Shelburne and Fox became Secretaries of State. Lord John Cavendish secured the position of Chancellor of the Exchequer. Nonetheless, few of Rockingham's followers succeeded to the cabinet. Burke was rewarded with paymaster general of the armed forces. Richmond, no longer a Rockinghamite, took the Ordnance. Thurlow retained the position of Lord Chancellor. Grafton became Lord Privy Seal, while Conway was appointed Commander in Chief. Divided on the American issue, the government proceeded swiftly to implement economic reform. Crewe's Bill to disenfranchise revenue officials was followed by Clerke's Bill to remove contractors from the Commons.[510] In early April, Burke was alerting Rockingham to plans to subvert the government programme by partitioning its measures into separate items.[511] The king hoped that the civil establishment might be reduced by agreement with ministers instead of being introduced as a Bill into parliament.[512] In the end, George III was won over to support for an Establishment Bill.[513] In presenting his plans to the Commons on 14 June 1782, Burke expected fewer savings than had been anticipated two years earlier.[514] The royal household was less depleted and the savings on pensions less dramatic, although major bureaucracies, like the Board of Trade and the colonial Secretary, were abolished.[515] Yet even as the new ministry pursued economic reform, agitation for parliamentary reform continued in the Commons and the country.

With Richmond and Fox in office, change in the system of national representation was a plausible proposition. Speaking before a public assembly in the last years

[508] EB to the Marquess of Rockingham, 22 March 1782, *Corr.*, IV, p. 423.

[509] John Cannon, *The Fox–North Coalition: Crisis of the Constitution 1782–4* (Cambridge: Cambridge University Press, 1969), pp. 4–5.

[510] *LJ*, XXXVI, p. 537. They passed respectively as 22 Geo. III, c. 45 and 22 Geo. III, c. 41.

[511] EB to the Marquess of Rockingham, 5 April 1782, *Corr.*, IV, p. 433.

[512] Ibid., p. 434. See also EB, Memorial on Economic Reform, WWM BkP 14:28–29.

[513] The king's message supporting the measure is printed in *CJ*, XXXVIII, p. 861. Burke's draft of the message can be found among the Rockingham Papers at the Sheffield Archives (R 81.174), reprinted in *W & S*, IV (forthcoming).

[514] For the first reading, see *CJ*, XXXVIII, p. 1057.

[515] For the details of Burke's new plan, see EB, Debate on Civil List Expenditure, 14 June 1782, *Parliamentary History*, XXIII, cols. 121–27. The legislation passed as 22 Geo. III, c. 82. A supplementary Bill to reform the Paymaster's office passed as 22 Geo. III, c. 81.

of the North administration, Fox had urged his audience to remember their "weight and consequence in the state." After all, he added, it was as a result of demonstrations concerted by the people at large that parliament had made concessions to the Irish and Americans.[516] Days later, addressing a group of supporters of the Association movement in the City of Westminster, he described the House of Commons as a mere instrument of the people: "If that delegated body fails in the execution of their trust, if they abandon the interest of their constituents, they are no more the representative of the people—they are the instruments of the crown."[517] It was at this time, French Laurence later contended, that men of talent began to gather around Fox and encourage him to favour popular causes. Speculative reforms won his support against his better judgment.[518] As it turned out, following a meeting at Richmond's house in April 1782, it was decided that a new and promising member of the Commons would revive the plan for parliamentary reform. Accordingly, on the afternoon of Tuesday 7 May 1782, the young William Pitt moved for a committee to inquire into the state of representation, coming within twenty votes of success.[519]

Two months later, Lord Rockingham died and his ministry immediately fell.[520] Shelburne now commanded a government of his own. Burke was astonished by the mendacity and opportunism of the new minister. He would later observe how all the "high-bred" republicans of the age revealed themselves to be ingratiating partisans of monarchy.[521] Shelburne was an obvious candidate for that role. In speaking of the change of ministry on 9 July 1782, Burke "abhorred that sort of accommodation, which did not leave a man possessed of a single principle he could call his own."[522] Shelburne's tenure, however, did not last long. Burke returned to office under the Fox–North Coalition in April 1783, but the ministry fell with the dramatic defeat of Fox's India Bill the following December. By the start of 1784, William Pitt was heading an administration without a majority in the House of Commons. At a meeting in Buckinghamshire on 20 March intended to raise support for the government, Burke inveighed against the hostility directed at the India Bill: "the people were not competent to decide such points: they had approved of the American war in the same useless manner they now disapproved of the India Bill."[523] A dissolution of parliament was presently announced, and a disastrous election followed for the

[516] *Gazetteer*, 1 February 1780. Fox had followed Shelburne in addressing a crowd on 29 January 1780.

[517] Charles James Fox, *The Speech of the Honourable Charles James Fox Delivered at Westminster, on Wednesday, February, 2, 1780; on the Reduction of Sinecure Places, and Unmerited Pensions* (London: 1780), p. 12.

[518] French Laurence, "Political Life of Edmund Burke: Annotated Proofs of a Contribution to the *Annual Register*" (c. 1794), OSB MS. File 8753.

[519] Ehrman, *Pitt: The Years of Acclaim*, pp. 70–1; *Parliamentary History*, XXIII, cols. 1416–38.

[520] On Fox's precipitate resignation, see EB to Charles James Fox, 3 July 1782, *Corr.*, V, pp. 5–6.

[521] EB, *Reflections*, ed. Clark, p. 222 [93].

[522] *A Complete and Accurate Account of the Very Important Debate in the House of Commons on 9 July 1782* (London: 1782), pp. 38–9.

[523] *Public Advertiser*, 20 March 1784.

opposition. Fox's energy was consumed by his contest at Westminster, where he just retained his seat having come second in the competition.[524] By the middle of April the situation was clear. The unpopularity of the coalition together with effective government influence turned the defeat of the Portland Whigs into a drubbing.[525]

With the apparent disintegration of the project of a lifetime, Burke was close to despair: "The people did not like our work; and they joined with the Court to pull it down."[526] Nine years later Burke was decisive in apportioning blame: "Mr. Pitt got into power by the mischievous intrigues of the Court," assisted by the dissenters and general corruption out of doors.[527] The new session of parliament got under way on 18 May 1784. Almost immediately Burke publicised his objections to recent proceedings, beginning with the manner in which George III had sabotaged Fox's India Bill and ending with the Address with which the new parliament had opened. He was dismayed by the king's interference in the legislative process entailed by his having signalled his opposition to the Indian measures proposed by the Foxites in December 1783. He was also alarmed that the monarch had installed Pitt at the head of the Treasury without his being in a position to command a majority in the House. The election that followed also bore the marks of incipient danger. It was preceded by a campaign of addresses in favour of the Pitt ministry and was accompanied by the deployment of considerable patronage. With the defeat of "Fox's Martyrs" Burke regarded the House of Commons "as something worse than extinguished."[528] He felt that the Rockinghams had toiled for almost twenty years to restore independence, yet their efforts had been destroyed in a matter of months: "to construct is a matter of skill; to demolish, force and fury are sufficient."[529] In response, on 14 June 1784, with the support of William Windham but without the backing of his party, Burke presented his account of the constitutional significance of recent developments to the House of Commons. This comprised a lengthy "Representation" to the king, which was printed in the *Commons Journals* and then published as a pamphlet on 5 July.[530]

Moving his Representation to the crown, Burke reprobated what he saw as the progress of new "doctrines" that would undermine the integrity of the established system of government. He pointed to two problematic claims in particular: first, the view that the constitution ought to be seen as a system of "*balances*," and second a determination to canvass popularity in ways that challenged the representa-

[524] EB to Sir Gilbert Elliot, 26 March 1784, *Corr.*, V, p. 134: "Surely a leader in a Party ought never to represent such a place; especially at a general election, when he ought to be at leisure to turn his Eye to every quarter."

[525] M. D. George, "Fox's Martyrs: The General Election of 1784," *Transactions of the Royal Historical Society*, 21 (1939), pp. 133–68; Cannon, *Fox–North Coalition*, ch. 11.

[526] EB to William Baker, 22 June 1784, *Corr.*, V, p. 154.

[527] EB, *Observations on the Conduct of the Minority* (Spring 1793), *W & S*, VIII, pp. 447–50.

[528] EB to William Baker, 22 June 1784, *Corr.*, V, p. 154.

[529] EB, *A Representation to His Majesty by the Right Honourable Edmund Burke on Monday, June 14, 1784* (London: 1784), p. ii.

[530] *CJ*, XL, pp. 198–204. For the pamphlet publication, see Todd, *Bibliography*, p. 126.

tive function of the Commons.[531] Burke targeted the commitments of Richmond and Shelburne in particular, both of whom had variously promoted these ideas.[532] He naturally recognised that the constitution should preserve its balance in the metaphorical sense of maintaining the existing system of counterweights. But the reality which the metaphor of equipoise depicted comprised a system of reciprocal checks rather than literally equal balances.[533] The branches of the British government did not "equally" share in the powers of the state. Instead, they held their privileges individually and disproportionately. A doctrine of equality was a recipe for ill-considered revision that would undermine the Glorious Revolution and destroy the Bill of Rights. Recent pretensions to the contrary, Burke protested, amounted to no more than a "dangerous fiction." The three principal components of the British system of government enjoyed their "separate powers and privileges . . . no balance or equality exists or . . . was intended between them."[534]

The representation of popular sentiment was an equally delicate issue. Burke laid out his case by first recurring to a basic, longstanding commitment: "the sense of the people, however erroneous at times, must always govern the legislature of this country."[535] Yet the "sense" of the population was often difficult to determine. Was a fleeting, furious feeling to be preferred to considered resolve? The interposition of representatives between their constituents and the executive was a means of avoiding precipitate decisions. "This House will be, as it ever ought to be, anxiously attentive to the inclinations and interests of its constituents," Burke declared.[536] Yet the quality of deliberation was essential to safeguarding those interests. For this reason, under the British constitution, representation and parliamentary deliberation were combined. "The *Tribunitian* power in this country," Burke observed, "as in ancient Rome, was wisely kept distinct and separate from the executive power."[537] Government was not transacted by securing acclamation for the monarch. For that reason, the presentation of ministerial petitions on behalf of the people to the Commons was a subversion of the relationship between the legislature and the executive. The popular sense was represented by the Commons, not the king.[538] It was to that House

[531] *Morning Herald*, 15 June 1784,

[532] EB, *Representation to His Majesty* (1784), pp. 2n, 6, 7n, where Burke takes issue with the Earl of Shelburne's claim of 8 April 1778 that the Lords were "equally the representatives of the people," *Parliamentary Register* (Almon), X, p. 392, and the Duke of Richmond's argument that the Commons had been usurping the powers the Lords and the crown in *A Letter form His Grace the Duke of Richmond to the Queries Proposed by a Committee of Correspondence in Ireland* (London: 1783). Burke also drew attention to key passages in the King's Speech of 5 December 1781, 5 December 1782 and 19 May 1784.

[533] On these idioms, see David Wootton, "Liberty, Metaphor and Mechanism: 'Checks and Balances' and the Origins of Modern Constitutionalism" in David Womersley ed., *Liberty and American Experience in the Eighteenth Century* (Indianapolis, IN: Liberty Fund, 2006).

[534] WWM BkP 25:45. Cf. EB, *Representation*, p. 6.

[535] *Morning Herald*, 15 June 1784.

[536] EB, *Representation to His Majesty* (1784), p. 2.

[537] *Morning Herald*, 15 June 1784.

[538] EB, *Representation to His Majesty* (1784), p. 3.

that the people ought to carry their complaints. If the court were to become a vehicle for popular protest or petition, it would derogate from the representative authority of the Commons. This would create a "prerogative party in the nation," an insidious court populism that would unhinge the constitution.[539] This was nothing other than patriot monarchy revived, Burke's bête noire since the *Present Discontents* of 1770. The purpose of the House of Commons was to ascertain the desires of the people, to deliberate on the basis of their inclinations, and to scrutinise the exercise of power on their behalf. This role was threatened when the monarchy made a bid for popular endorsement or when the people strove to undermine the process of deliberation.

After 1789, with the eruption of the French Revolution, the popular destruction of a due deliberative process became a constant preoccupation of Burke. But before the event he had already signalled his alarm. This was made necessary by a motion for parliamentary reform introduced by Alderman John Sawbridge on 16 June 1784. On this occasion Pitt judged the proposition "out of season," though Fox thought the moment highly opportune.[540] Burke struggled to get a hearing, though he made his position known.[541] His notes for the debate give a fuller account of his thought than the meagre surviving reports.[542] What stirred Burke to intervene was the rising chorus of support from influential figures in parliament for the idea of "personal" representation. Richmond, for instance, on 3 June 1780, had declared in favour of "the natural, inalienable and equal right of all the Commons of Great Britain . . . to vote in the election of their representatives in parliament."[543] Burke was struck by the continual barrage of criticism directed at the Commons while the constitution of the king and Lords received scarce any comment. Faced with perpetual adverse discussion of the representative component of the system of government, public confidence in the architecture of the state was being undermined. This posed a problem: where the constitution of a polity was subject to disgrace, "patriotism"—which meant allegiance—would be "destroyed in its very source."[544] Opinion on the appropriate course of action had become so divisive that it might be best simply to avoid the matter in public. But with Pitt, North, Fox and Richmond all pushing in different directions, it was now advisable to present an analysis of what was implied by their recommendations.[545]

[539] Ibid., p. 10.

[540] *Parliamentary History*, XXIV, col. 976. For Fox, see the *Public Advertiser*, 17 June 1784.

[541] The hostile reception Burke met is recorded in the *Morning Herald*, 17 June 1784. A brief outline of his intervention appears in the *Morning Chronicle*, 17 June 1784.

[542] Burke's first editors, French Laurence and Walker King, originally dated this intervention to 7 May 1782. Peter Marshall, in *W & S*, IV (forthcoming), has corrected this to 16 June 1784. I follow Marshall in the dating but have used the text of the speech included in *The Works of the Right Honourable Edmund Burke* (London: 1808–13), 12 vols., X, pp. 92–108.

[543] *Parliamentary History*, XXI, col. 686.

[544] EB, Speech on the State of the Representation of the Commons (16 May 1784), *Works* (1808–13), X, p. 93.

[545] Ibid.

There were two arguments in support of parliamentary reform that Burke was eager to challenge. One, he claimed, was "political" in form, the other "juridical" in nature. The first—the political theory—amounted to the claim that the form of government had degenerated from its original principles. Burke found this proposition difficult to credit. It implied that the facts of the British government should be determined on the basis of antecedent theory, whereas in truth the theory of the constitution could only appeal to the evident facts. The theory, or "principles," of the constitution could only be known by inferring them from the manner of its construction. Since the composition of the House of Commons—comprising knights, citizens and burgesses—had been a constant feature since its inception, there was no basis on which to argue that its original character should be restored.[546] The rights of government, in the first instance, were prescriptive in nature: one had to begin with how things now were, and how they had been before.[547] Despite appearances, this did not mean that the legitimacy of the system of government was simply grounded on its existence "time out of mind."[548] Burke's was not an argument crudely founded on tradition. He did believe that the "authority" of government was a matter of *mos maiorum*.[549] However, its legitimacy was based on both its utility as well as its authority: a constitution might remain faithful to its old customary principles and yet have every appearance of being "a bad one."[550] The question then became one of how to evaluate the constitution, and to Burke the answer was resoundingly clear: by its "expedience" or "convenience," not by its conformity with a theory of right.[551] An entitlement to individual rights—like the claims of property or conscience—could be rationally inferred from the laws of nature. But political rights, by definition, were benefits of civil society and therefore could not be derived from the rights of nature: "all *natural* rights must be the rights of individuals; as by *nature* there is no such thing as politick or corporate personality; all these ideas are mere fictions of Law, they are creatures of voluntary institution."[552]

"Voluntary" support for a prescriptive constitution was nothing but a description of popular consent: government required the backing of opinion, and trust or "presumption" operated in its favour.[553] This, however, was never an empty prejudice or blind attachment. It was based on the assurance of tried usage. This practical criterion contained two elements: a feeling of reverence for the antiquity of past customs

[546] Ibid., pp. 98–99.

[547] Ibid., pp. 96–97.

[548] The phrase appears in ibid., p. 96. For Burke's debt to the common law tradition here, see J.G.A Pocock, "Burke and the Ancient Constitution: A Problem in the History of Ideas" in idem, *Politics Language and Time: Essays on Political Thought and History* (Chicago, IL: University of Chicago Press, 1971, 1989).

[549] See below, chapter 13, section 3.

[550] EB, Speech on the State of the Representation of the Commons (16 May 1784), *Works* (1808–13), X, p. 99.

[551] Ibid., pp. 100, 105.

[552] Ibid., p. 94.

[553] Ibid., p. 96.

along with a tangible sense of positive benefit. Both elements were constitutive of the sentiment of allegiance, although their content and proportions were historically variable. Under a mixed system of government like Britain's, which included a representative component, the judgment of utility, based on a conception of public benefit, predominated over deferential acclamation. The judgment of utility could only appeal to experience, which, in the British case, delivered a clear verdict by pointing to "a growing liberty and a growing prosperity for five hundred years."[554] This, of course, had been a fitful and fortuitous acquisition that might easily be lost. Under a free government the first signs of distemper would be evident in the discontent of the people. It was the job of representatives to be sensitive to discontent, and the recent election had provided candidates with the relevant exposure. Yet no place which Burke encountered demanded parliamentary reform: "not one word, either in the towns or country, on the subject of representation."[555] The reason was not difficult to ascertain. Warwick was represented, and Birmingham was not, yet no one could claim that the latter was sacrificed to the former.[556] Virtual representation provided "equal" representation to the extent that actual representation protected local interests while serving the larger good of the whole.

Criticism of the House of Commons was based not on substantive complaints but on a theory of political justice. This brought Burke to the "juridical" theory of reform that he opposed. This doctrine was ultimately based on a moral theory, inappropriately applied to political affairs. It drew on the idea of a right to self-government, by which actual government was to be measured and judged. This idea had been gradually publicised since the advent of conflict with the colonies, and was exemplified by the writings of Richard Price. The "people," Price proposed in an attack on Burke in 1778, "are their own legislators."[557] Two years earlier he had claimed that the ideal of "self-direction," although optimally realised in small republics, could be approximated under a system of representation where the elected substituted for the electors.[558] This whole conception, Burke believed, was the wrong place to begin if one sought to understand or improve relations between rulers and ruled. On Price's assumptions, the division of political labour was no division at all, since politicians were mere deputies of the individual wills that made up the community. Yet on this basis, Burke argued, the reforms desired by the likes of Richmond, Shelburne and Price were not credible adjustments to the constitution at all, since as currently configured they would fall badly short of realising the principle on which they were

[554] Ibid., p. 100.

[555] Ibid., p. 101.

[556] Ibid., pp. 101–2.

[557] Richard Price, "Introduction," *Two Tracts on Civil Liberty* (1778) in *Price: Political Writings, ed.* D. O. Thomas (Cambridge: Cambridge University Press, 1991), where Price is responding to EB, *Letter to the Sheriffs of Bristol* (3 April 1777), *W & S*, III, pp. 317–18, where Burke charged him with subverting all authority. For further discussion, see below, chapter 13, section 2.

[558] Richard Price, *Observations on the Nature of Civil Liberty* (1776) in *Price*, ed. Thomas, pp. 22, 24.

founded. "Parliamentary reform," Burke would argue ten years later, "was the pretext for all the sedition that has been sown for many years in this country."[559]

The elimination of rotten boroughs, the addition of county seats, the shortening of parliaments and the introduction of manhood suffrage, cumulatively or individually, would not deliver any kind of "personal" representation since the Commons would still be obliged to share power with the monarchy and the peerage. Yet even with the abolition of the king and Lords, the reforms envisaged would still fall short of the ideal. For the ideal to be realised, generals would have to be put to the vote, along with admirals and bishops. Judges and justices of the peace would also have to be elected.[560] If reform was to relieve a set of justified complaints, why did the measures fail to address the full scope of abuse?[561] If political justice required that legislators should be deputies of the people, then governors should be delegates as well. However, this was scarcely a plausible conception of civil society, whose very construction had been intended as a restraint upon individual wills. Now it was being proposed that each of those wills should retain their right to self-government, albeit via the ministry of ambassadors styled "representatives." Burke was amazed by the abstruseness and unworkability of this ideology. It needed to be tackled before its tenets gained momentum. Yet astonishingly, as Burke would discover, within five years it would revolutionise the politics of Europe.

[559] EB, Speech on Suspension of Habeas Corpus, 16 May 1794, *W & S*, IV (forthcoming).

[560] EB, Speech on the State of the Representation of the Commons (16 May 1784), *Works* (1808–13), X, pp. 95–96.

[561] Ibid., p. 103.

IX

CONSENT AND CONCILIATION

AMERICA, 1774–1783

9.1 Introduction

Burke's first three years in parliament as a member for Bristol were dominated by the deteriorating situation in the colonies. The following six were devoted to retrieving them for the Empire. Relations were first soured by a group of "intolerable" Acts passed during the aftermath of the Boston Tea Party. Amongst these the Massachusetts Bay Regulating Act, which received the royal assent on 20 May 1774, overturned the province's 1691 charter.[1] Another intolerable measure was the new Bill for the government of Quebec that was debated in the Commons the same summer. The discussion centred on the obligations imposed on victors after a conquest. The principle of moderation was accepted on all sides. For some that meant retaining the settled customs of the French Canadians. Yet for Burke this should not include the institutions of despotism as advocated by aristocratic elements among the local population. He recognised that the new government would have to be based on consent, but insisted that this should not preclude introducing improvements from Britain. He believed that legislation should be devoted to public utility even if this offended the factional interests of the French *noblesse*. His arguments, however, did not prevail. The reaction to the Quebec Act in the colonies was one of suspicion.[2] In particular, the failure to provide for an elected assembly in the province encouraged Americans to view the provision as another symptom of British tyranny. By December 1774, as defiance in New England grew in strength, Congress agreed to boycott British trade if the recent spate of coercive legislation were not repealed. The government responded with stern measures. In February 1775, Massachusetts was officially declared to be in a state of rebellion. The following March, limitations were imposed on New England commerce. Then in April these restraints were extended to other provinces.

[1] 14 Geo. III, c. 45.
[2] 14 Geo. III, c. 83.

As tensions between the metropole and the provinces rose, Burke pleaded the case for appeasement. Ever since his *Speech on American Taxation* of April 1774, he had been arguing for a systematic approach to the Empire that would properly anatomise relations of cause and effect. This ought to begin with a renunciation of metropolitan pride and proceed to a restoration of the original terms of informal empire. This unwritten charter between the colonies and the mother country combined confining the right of commercial regulation to Britain with vesting control of provincial taxation in the Americans. Although it was Grenville who first put an end to this arrangement, Burke argued that Chatham and Townshend had perpetuated the new trend. He claimed that the conduct of both ministers pointed to a structural problem. Townshend played to the gallery, sacrificing prudence to acclaim; Chatham clung to a posture of remoteness from parliament, thereby failing to collaborate with his colleagues in office. Both dispositions led to incoherent fluctuations in policy and pointed to the decline of party politics in Britain. As Burke regarded the matter, only a principled "connection" committed to the common good could hope to offer resolute and consistent policies that would hold their course against the seduction of popularity or the court. From this perspective, party not only promised to repair the distempers of domestic politics; it also held the key to retrieving the Empire from the brink.

Burke elaborated on his conception of imperial relations in his classic intervention of 22 March 1775, the *Speech on Conciliation with America*. After outlining his vision of the astonishing progress of American commerce and civilisation, he proceeded to elucidate the practical limits on British policy. The pursuit of empire in the new world for the sake of revenue was now impossible: entrenched attitudes among the colonists confined British options to empire for trade. That choice excluded the possibility of a free trade, although regulations could of course be usefully relaxed. Complete commercial freedom in the absence of fiscal control would bring about an end to the project of empire altogether. That would probably entail the loss of existing benefits from trade and compromise the strategic interests of Westminster, handing considerable advantages to its European rivals. Burke therefore pushed for the reform of an imperfect system that at least functioned, even at the cost of the persistence of monopoly. America could be recovered by reverting to that system. Burke denied the claims of men like Josiah Tucker that the colonies were committed to realising their independence. He accepted that the southern provinces were haughty and that the northern ones were litigious. Together they seemed reluctant to constrain their liberty out of deference to authority. Nonetheless, Burke insisted that they were amenable to established patterns of accommodation. He also rejected the argument of Thomas Pownall that the colonies should be incorporated as provinces of an imperial union. Pownall believed that annexation generally led to representation in the history of British constitutional development, and thus that the colonies should be integrated into the parliamentary system. Yet for Burke this was a fantasy based on an ideal of equal subjection. The reality was that the Empire was less a unitary structure of subordination than a diversified collection of incomparable jurisdictions. These had to be made compatible with parliamentary authority. In the aftermath of the Glorious Revolution, it was not possible to run the Empire on the model of a composite monarchy since parliament as much as the king controlled the agenda of domestic affairs. Yet it was possible to revive the composite parliamentary Empire in which British supremacy accommodated provincial immunities and privileges. On that basis, Burke believed, the colonies could be restored to their historic allegiance.

Within a month of Burke's conciliation Speech all plans for rapprochement met with new challenges. With the first military engagements at Lexington and Concord in April 1775, a full-scale collision with the mother country loomed into focus. Burke was anxious to make concessions before all-out conflict arrived. Already he feared the entrance of the Bourbon powers into the contest. However, opinion was firmly ranged against the Rockinghams and their allies: the king was with the ministry and the country behind the king. Burke saw the merit of building even a compact coalition prepared to agitate against current government policy, but Lord Rockingham was lethargic and therefore slow to lead. In the face of inactivity on the part of Whig grandees, Burke insisted on campaigning to win new partisans. He followed the lead of Franklin in condoning the colonial position: it was, firstly, defensive in inspiration and character; and it was, secondly, fundamentally loyal to imperial sovereignty. On this reading, the principle of the Declaratory Act was still appropriate to the situation. As Burke made clear in his second conciliation Speech delivered in November 1775, American protests were directed not against traditional allegiance but against a novel application of reserve parliamentary powers. On this assumption, if parliament agreed to treat with the colonies as a body, repeal coercive laws and renounce the intention of laying taxes, harmony could be restored to trans-Atlantic relations.

News of the Prohibitory Act blockading American trade was received across the Atlantic in February 1776. Burke claimed that the measure propelled the colonies to adopt a more extreme position. Petitions in support of parliament pushed them further towards separation. That summer, the Continental Congress asserted colonial independence, driving Burke to fear for the worst from both London and America. He certainly expected a British military victory, yet he assumed that this would be accompanied by a twofold disaster: a radical reordering of the domestic constitutional balance coupled with the ongoing inability actually to govern American territory. By 1777, as Burke assessed the impact of the debts on the civil list on George III's powers of patronage, he was also registering his anxiety that developments across the Atlantic would contribute to the ruin of the mixed system of government. In his *Letter to the Sheriffs of Bristol* of that year, he hoped to avoid that outcome by reconceptualising the Empire. He traced the current difficulties to the existence of two legislative bodies competing within a single imperial frame. Relations between parliament and the assemblies should be reconfigured on the basis of a formal compact between the metropole and the provinces that would specify the terms of political trade between the two.

However, events overtook Burke's latest plan for a comprehensive settlement. Six months after the *Letter to the Sheriffs of Bristol*, General Burgoyne met with defeat at Saratoga, marking a major turning point in the war. In February 1778, the French agreed a treaty of alliance with the Americans. The following year, as the ranks of the Volunteers continued to swell in Dublin and Lord George Gordon encouraged sectarian animosity in London, the Spanish added their military weight to the French. By now Burke had relinquished his support for British supremacy, hoping to recover the colonies as partners in an imperial alliance. In 1781, as he immersed himself in the details of the Select Committee on Indian affairs, news of the British surrender at Yorktown arrived. The following April the Commons voted to terminate the war. The Treaty of Paris confirmed complete secession in 1783. The whole process had been a colossal mistake in Burke's opinion. In misconstruing the theory of imperial sovereignty, the British government had overstretched its executive competence. A system of authority had been incrementally destroyed in the misguided attempt to assert the parliamentary right to excessive powers.

9.2 *Speech on American Taxation*

Writing to the Committee of Correspondence of the New York assembly on 6 April 1774, Burke lamented the demise of political moderation on either side of the Atlantic. He was unimpressed by the combative mood that had seized the American colonies, but also dismayed by the militancy of parliamentary opinion. The counsels of "Temperate Men" had been swamped by an attitude of dogmatism on both sides. Temperate measures, Burke went on, included the defence of the rights of man—of the "real essential Rights of mankind," as he put it. But this was in no sense incompatible with imperial subjection. The true friends of America accepted "proper subordination" as an ineluctable maxim of the government of the Empire, which the self-appointed champions of liberty in the colonies were in danger of subverting.[3] This subordination, however, had to protect provincial rights, without which colonial consent would never be forthcoming. As Burke had emphasised in a statement to the Commons on 7 March 1774, government in the colonies was "popular government," which, as such, would never yield to hostile acts of power: "If such a government as that is universally discontented, no troops under heaven [can] bring them to obedience."[4] The security of popular rights, and the consent which that security promoted, were fundamental conditions without which no honest broker could

[3]EB to the Committee of Correspondence of the New York Assembly, 6 April 1774, *Corr.*, II, pp. 528–29. Subsequent commentary, in Chathamite spirit, has tended to regard Burke's combination of sovereignty and conciliation as paradoxical or contradictory. See, typically, Charles R. Ritcheson, *Edmund Burke and the American Revolution* (Leicester: Leicester University Press, 1976), *passim*.

[4]EB, Address of Thanks, 7 March 1774, PDNA, IV, p. 44.

reasonably wish "the dependence of one Country upon another."[5] However, with the declaration of its intention to close Boston port on 14 March 1774, the ministry managed to alienate colonial trust in imperial measures.

By the time that Burke next wrote to the Committee of Correspondence, on 4 May, he was able to report that in the interim colonial affairs had almost completely engaged the attention of Westminster.[6] A series of coercive or "Intolerable" measures had been introduced into the Commons in April, beginning with the Massachusetts Bay Regulating Bill on the 15th, followed by two temporary Bills, introduced on the 21st and 29th, one to facilitate the conduct of fair trials for the supporters of government measures in America, and the other to transfer the authority for billeting troops from Massachusetts magistrates to the governor.[7] Each of these Bills was approved in the Commons by early May. Burke's first stand against coercion since the passage of the Boston Port Bill, his famous *Speech on American Taxation*, came on 19 April, occasioned by a motion from Rose Fuller seeking the repeal of the duty on tea as a token of the desire for reconciliation with the colonies.[8] Burke's speech won the "highest applause," Horace Walpole recalled, amounting to a tirade against the government "in a year of fine harangues."[9] Over the course of two hours, the *London Evening Post* noted, Burke excelled himself, delivering possibly "the most excellent speech" ever to have been presented before a public assembly.[10] His intervention fell into a number of identifiable parts—a section analysing government policy relating to America; another presenting the history of previous measures; a series of depictions of prominent political characters; and an overarching statement about how to resolve the current crisis. His basic contention was that if Fuller's repeal were to pass without the ministry's coercive provisions, leniency was sure to succeed in pacifying the colonies. As things stood, however, with a succession of stern measures set to dismay American opinion, the response to a conciliatory gesture remained uncertain. But one thing was for sure: coercion mixed with "lenity" stood a "better chance of success."[11]

It is clear that Burke's speech was a means of commending a posture of magnanimity in the face of repeated acts of governmental severity. But its deeper aim was to give an account of the sources of ministerial folly, and to set out how mismanagement might be avoided in the future. Towards this end, Burke was clear that what was needed was a proper "theory" of how to proceed. This was accompanied by an injunction to avoid purely "speculative" rumination, and to steer clear of political

[5] EB to the Committee of Correspondence of the New York Assembly, 6 April 1774, *Corr.*, II, p. 529.

[6] Ibid., p. 531.

[7] P.D.G. Thomas, *Tea Party to Independence: The Third Phase of the American Revolution, 1773–1776* (Oxford: Oxford University Press, 1991), ch. 5.

[8] See PDNA, IV, pp. 180ff.

[9] Walpole, *Last Journals*, I, pp. 332–33.

[10] *London Evening Post*, 23 April 1774.

[11] EB, *Speech on American Taxation* (19 April 1774), *W & S*, II, p. 461.

doctrines founded on metaphysical pretensions. Speculation was the habit of ungrounded innovators, experience the proper basis for constructive thought, and only the latter could succeed in reconciling disagreements about the content of the "*summum ius*." As Burke would later underline in his *Reflections on the Revolution in France*, abstract disputation about ideal rights could happily be left to the "schools."[12] Yet this did not amount to a general scepticism about political theory.[13] The aim of policy, Burke was clear, was to set out a course of action that was both "consistent in theory and valuable in practice."[14] Despite the rhetoric of his later assault on revolutionary ideas in France, Burke was never a straightforward antagonist of generalising theory.[15] "I do not vilify theory and speculation," he insisted in 1784: "no, because that would be to vilify reason itself."[16] In fact, he held that the principal problem with his political opponents was that "they never had any kind of system" at all, and were constantly obliged to sustain their position by resort to ad hoc expedients—to "some miserable tale for the day," as Burke presented it.[17] What was needed, instead, was "large and liberal ideas." However, this course was rendered impossible by the approach of successive ministries: "Never have the servants of the state looked at the whole of your complicated interests in one connected view."[18] A "connected" view implied a systematic approach, which depended on a theory of how the Empire should be run.

In his notes for a speech prepared in the early 1770s, Burke was more explicit still about what he thought the crisis in America required. Each fresh disturbance in the colonies, he felt sure, was just a symptom of an underlying "distemper of the Whole . . . Empire."[19] It is apparent here that Burke saw the problem as affecting British affairs in the east and the west, since it derived from the disposition of ministries, and their role in the constitution. "It is the same folly that has lost you at once the benefit of the West and of the East," Burke asserted in 1774.[20] This folly was a matter not simply of either men or measures, but of the ideas that informed the organisation of domestic and imperial power. In the case of America, Burke had earlier

[12] Ibid., pp. 456–58. Cf. EB, *Reflections*, ed. Clark, p. 217 [86].

[13] For an example of pervasive misunderstanding on this point, see Conor Cruise O'Brien, "Edmund Burke: Prophet against the Tyranny of the Politics of Theory" in *Edmund Burke, Reflections on the Revolution in France*, ed. Frank Turner (New Haven, CT: Yale University Press, 2003).

[14] Ibid., p. 456. Cf. WWM BkP 6:202, where Burke argues that "method" (or practice) must be guided by "principle" (or theory).

[15] His later stance was perfectly compatible with his position in the 1770s. For his later denunciation of French revolutionary theory, see below, chapter 13. See also Richard Bourke, "Theory and Practice: The Revolution in Political Judgement" in Richard Bourke and Raymond Geuss eds., *Political Judgement: Essays for John Dunn* (Cambridge: Cambridge University Press, 2009).

[16] EB, Speech on the State of the Representation of the Commons (16 May 1784), *The Works of the Right Honourable Edmund Burke* (London: 1808–13), 12 vols., X, p. 99.

[17] EB, *Speech on American Taxation* (19 April 1774), *W & S*, II, p. 415.

[18] Ibid.

[19] Northamptonshire MS. A. XXVII.63.

[20] EB, *Speech on American Taxation* (19 April 1774), *W & S*, II, p. 416.

declared, it pointed to "the miserable want of any sound Theory or any consistent practice for the government of that vast critical part of the British dominions."[21] A succession of administrations had been given years "to order and arrange" the affairs of the Empire, but instead they proceeded with piecemeal tinkering, blindly reacting to circumstances without any rules of procedure.[22] Governments themselves should have the wherewithal to plot a course of action rather than haplessly wait upon events.[23] With this end in view, they might usefully follow the procedures underpinning "Lord Bacons [*sic*] idea of physic": preparation, organisation, prioritisation and generalisation.[24] Generalisation, of course, had to be distinguished from a process of pure "invention": it had to be based on experience, and experience had to draw on a fund of historical data.[25] Moreover, these data were not merely raw bundles of information from the past, but schemes for the instruction of political behaviour. Burke's approach was thus empirical and systematic at the same time—a science of politics, as Hume had recommended.[26] In managing America, this meant breaking out of the vicious circle of "occasional arguments and temporary expedients" in order to develop a comprehensive response.[27]

Such a project would have to begin by exposing accumulated folly. The errors of government had their origin in successive ministries' failure to master their own passions in the service of the domestic and the imperial interest. The offending passion was that of pride, a disproportionate preoccupation with the honour of British government, which expressed itself, as Burke had long observed, in an excessive concern for restoring national "dignity."[28] The pursuit of honour in this way had been defeated in its objective, resulting in the loss of power, a diminution of authority, and a decline in colonial reverence for the constitution.[29] Britain had sacrificed its interest in chasing a delusion—a "phantom," a mere "quiddity," as Burke described it.[30] All the while, the government had led itself to believe that it was activated by "commercial" principles, whereas in fact its motives were political from the start. This was made clear by the manner of the repeal of Townshend's legislation. The

[21] Northamptonshire MS. A. XXVII.63.

[22] Ibid.

[23] Ibid. Burke at this point cites a letter from Monsieur de Villeroy to Pierre Jeannin, intendant of finances under Henry IV, stating that "le Roi entend que vous tiriez de vous-même la principale instruction de ce que vous aurez à faire en ce voyage," reproduced in *Collections des mémoirs relatifs à l'histoire de France, depuis l'avènement de Henri IV, jusqu'à la paix de Paris*, ed. M. Petitot (Paris: 1821), XII, p. 1.

[24] Northamptonshire MS. A. XXVII.63.

[25] EB, *Speech on American Taxation* (19 April 1774), *W & S*, II, pp. 410–11.

[26] Hume, "Of the First Principles of Government" (1742) in idem, *Essays Moral, Political and Literary*, *passim*.

[27] EB, *Speech on American Taxation* (19 April 1774), *W & S*, II, p. 409.

[28] Ibid., pp. 414, 418. Cf. Marquess of Rockingham to George Dempster, 13 September 1774, *Rockingham Memoirs*, II, p. 255. On the concern with honour driving British policy, see also chapter 6, section 2 above.

[29] On the embittering effect of disappointed pride ("the haughtiness of disgrace") see further WWM BkP 6:202.

[30] EB, *Speech on American Taxation* (19 April 1774), *W & S*, II, p. 418.

charges that were withdrawn by reversing the taxation measures of 1767 were in fact the most sensible from a commercial point of view: the duties on lead and glass were unlikely to damage trade, since there was no contraband to compete with British sales. The other imports originally taxed, like paints and paper, were comparatively trivial components of the national commerce.[31] Tea, on the other hand, was a major export, whose trade was threatened by Britain's commercial rivals on account of the high price of the East India Company stock: "If commercial principles had been the true motives to the Repeal . . . Tea would have been the last article we should have left taxed for a subject of controversy."[32]

But while the conduct of the government was driven by politics rather than commerce, its political motivation was neither coherent nor consistent. Its wavering posture was best exemplified by Lord Hillsborough's circular letter to the colonies of 13 May 1769, which implicitly accepted American arguments against taxation for revenue, thus prostrating parliament before the claims of provincial assemblies, despite the fact that only four days earlier, in a speech from the throne, the government had been hurling its "thunders" against the pretensions of the colonies. In this way, the ministry had "blustered like tragic tyrants" at home before going "mumping with a fore leg in America, canting, and whining, and complaining of faction."[33] Yet their belated supplication made no practical sense, since in retaining the duty on tea they undermined the suggestion that their primary goal was the regulation of trade. "Your reasons were political, not commercial," Burke insisted.[34] The pretence to the contrary had an air of fraud, and oppressed American minds with apprehension and alarm. It did so because it unravelled a long history of colonial relations that had been based, not on political, but on commercial regulation: the management of trade was not intended to enforce subordination through taxation, but to benefit the mother country by the maintenance of commercial monopoly.[35] This arrangement certainly entailed subjection to the metropole, yet in restricting the freedom of trade it preserved the political freedom of the colonies. From the navigation acts down to the Seven Years' War, this balanced combination of liberty and authority underwrote the relationship between Westminster and its provinces. The form of management was "purely commercial," although the commerce in question was obviously "restrictive."[36] Restriction involved confining the trade of America to the import, mainly, of British manufactures and the export of colonial merchandise in exchange. This arrangement also permitted sale to foreign markets when the circle of British commerce was exhausted. The ensuing regulations led, between 1660 and

[31] For Burke's original endorsement of these duties, see EB, Speech on Townshend Duties, 15 May 1767, *W & S*, II, p. 62.

[32] EB, *Speech on American Taxation* (19 April 1774), *W & S*, II, p. 415.

[33] Ibid., p. 423. For the citation of Hillsborough's circular and the speech from the throne, see ibid., pp. 419–20.

[34] Ibid., p. 425. "Mumping" here means begging.

[35] Ibid., p. 426.

[36] Ibid.

1763, to a series of detailed "enumerations," specifying the terms of trans-Atlantic traffic—"an infinite variety of paper chains," embodied in twenty-nine Acts of parliament, that bound imperial commerce into a system.[37]

At the conclusion of the war, however, this intercontinental contract was torn up. Burke noted a change in the midst of the negotiations for peace: in the session of 1762–3, when he sat as a visitor in the gallery of the Commons, the taste of victory encouraged parliament to assert its power rather than enjoy its security. It was then that a military establishment in the colonies was publicly mooted, despite the fact that the French now posed less of a threat on the American continent.[38] With the country gentlemen constitutionally averse to an increase in taxation, Townshend dazzled parliament with the prospect of paying for defence without increasing the burden on the British public—"playing before their eyes the image of a revenue to be raised in America."[39] It was at this time that the first glimmerings of a "new Colony system" began to dawn, and it was soon to be championed by the modus operandi of Grenville.[40] The attitude of Grenville exacerbated the basic problem with the new dispensation. He brought to the political economy of the Empire a narrow "legal" perspective, by which Burke meant an entrenched bureaucratic approach. Bred into the legal profession, "the first and noblest of the human sciences," he had become a prisoner of its forms, constantly exhibiting a concern for procedure at the expense of wider judgment and thus continually sacrificing substantive concerns to the routines of administration. Individuals immersed in the habits of "office" are rarely minds of significant "enlargement," Burke remarked. They could cope well when affairs fell into a familiar groove, "but . . . when a new and troubled scene is opened, and the file affords no precedent, then it is that a greater knowledge of mankind, and a far more extensive comprehension of things, is requisite than ever office gave, or than office ever can give."[41] Grenville's manner was poorly fitted to the predicament of commercial empire. The expansion of trade was an effect of exuberant freedom, whereas Grenville placed his trust in legislation. Like so many others, he thought of national revenue in the simple terms of taxation, and was inclined to confuse commerce with regulation.[42] The way he proceeded consequently militated against enterprise and growth.

In concrete terms, in accordance with this underlying disposition, the Grenville ministry fixated on restraining the contraband trade and strangled commercial ex-

[37] Ibid., p. 427.

[38] Ibid., p. 430.

[39] Ibid., p. 431. Burke is referring to an early intervention by Townshend on the subject, most likely on 18 March 1763.

[40] Ibid. Later Israel Mauduit, in response to the published version of Burke's speech on American Taxation, which appeared on 10 January 1775, claimed that Grenville offered the colonies the opportunity to raise an adequate revenue themselves. See his handbill, *Mr. Grenville's Offer to the Colony Assemblies to Raise the Supply Themselves, instead of Having it Done by a Parliamentary Stamp Act* (London: 1775), rejected by EB in his Reply to Mauduit, *W & S*, III, pp. 91–96.

[41] EB, *Speech on American Taxation* (19 April 1774), *W & S*, II, p. 432.

[42] Ibid.

pansion in the process. To Burke this effort to regularise trade proved immediately counterproductive. Evasion of the laws of navigation did not, as many thought, imply fundamental disobedience any more than smuggling in Britain was an index of underlying dissent.[43] Besides, Grenville's attempts to manage colonial contraband led to the contraction of legitimate or "fair" trade.[44] The regulations of the early 1760s, culminating in the Sugar Act and the Stamp Act, threatened colonial commerce with baneful restrictions, and the assemblies with political annihilation. The home government, effectively, struck "terror" into the colonies, and then professed surprise at the reaction.[45] More than representing a series of unwelcome threats to established liberties, Grenville shook the obedience of the colonies to its foundations. Historically, the American provinces had implicitly consented to the terms of their subordination, accepting commercial subservience in exchange for particular privileges. Burke described this as a mixture of "commercial servitude and civil liberty."[46] Neither the servitude nor the liberty was complete in itself, but their combination, which produced tangible benefits, gave rise to a situation to which the colonists had become habituated. As Burke accordingly registered, human beings will become inured to imperfect liberty when the alternatives are less prepossessing. The colonies had acclimatised to their situation, partly because subjection to rival European empires held no attractions, but also because the compensations of British commerce were conspicuous. In due course, Adam Smith would observe the advantages of a regular system of justice, which the colonists imported into the wilderness. Under conditions of security, the abundance of land and the generous reward of labour led to rapid improvement and population growth, the main ingredients of increasing prosperity.[47] Burke, for his part, noted a further compensation: British capital had fed the development of commerce in the colonies. Without it, colonial fisheries, ship building and agriculture would have expanded at a far more languid pace: "This capital was a hot-bed to them. Nothing in the history of mankind is like their progress."[48]

The commercial advantages of imperial subordination were augmented by the political benefits. The provinces replicated the "image" of the British constitution, as well as much of its "substance": by approximating the condition of self-government, they mirrored the institutions of the mother country; by enjoying a local system of representation, they shared in its privileges.[49] The initiatives of Grenville, followed by the measures of Townshend, cast these compensations into doubt, first by contracting American trade, and then by constraining political freedom. Despite these

[43] Ibid., p. 429.

[44] Ibid., p. 433.

[45] Ibid.

[46] Ibid., p. 429.

[47] Adam Smith, *An Inquiry into the Nature and Causes of the Wealth of Nations*, ed. R. H. Campbell and A. S. Skinner (Indianapolis, IN: Liberty Fund, 1976), 2 vols., II, pp. 565–66.

[48] EB, *Speech on American Taxation* (19 April 1774), *W & S*, II, pp. 428–29.

[49] Ibid., p. 429.

obvious causes behind the disturbances in the colonies, commentators insisted on blaming resistance on repeal: concessions, it was argued, bred rebelliousness in the colonists.[50] In the same vein, the motive for the repeal was ascribed to the Rockinghams' spinelessness. For Burke, however, the measure bore the marks of circumspection. In an "enlightened" age, Montesquieu wrote, one trembles even while undertaking the greatest goods.[51] In this sense, Burke conceded, the repeal may have been timid, yet such timidity, when adopted in the service of the well-being of one's country, exemplified "heroic virtue."[52] Besides, as Burke was at pains to underline, the government had conceded the wisdom of reversing taxation policy by partially withdrawing the Townshend duties. If insubordination was triggered by conciliation, then further opposition ought to have followed as a result.[53] In fact, however, the colonies were then quiet.[54] Nonetheless, each time the British ministry managed to pacify its provinces, it squandered the goodwill it had won. This came down to the personalities of individual players, but more particularly to their role in the wider system of administration. Chatham, naturally misanthropic, failed to concert with colleagues in order to sustain a coherent policy.[55] Townshend, eager for praise, followed the moods of the House of Commons, and so could not stick to a single course of action.[56] Between them they illustrated the foibles of the deliberative process, permitting imprudent counsels to prevail.

Chatham's role was vividly depicted in Burke's speech, but the point was not that so much depended on the stature of this one man, although the extent of Pitt's imposing presence "in the eye of mankind" was acknowledged.[57] He was a great minister, Burke once acknowledged, "bold in his undertakings."[58] This above all applied during national crisis: "He inspired the people with War-like ardour when it was necessary."[59] In his Speech on American Taxation, however, Burke's focus was not on Pitt's virtues, but on the problems that followed from the departure from constitutional propriety that he had unwittingly promoted.[60] The British mixed system of government, combining parliamentary deliberation with a court administration, required concerted action by parties in parliament if the Commons was to hold its own against the designs of the executive. Chatham, however, was an unsociable

[50] This was originally a Grenvillite charge. For Burke's response, see EB, Tandem to the *Public Advertiser*, 4 August 1768, *W & S*, II, pp. 87–90, 93.

[51] Charles-Louis de Secondat, Baron de Montesquieu, *De l'esprit des lois* (1748) in *Œuvres complètes*, ed. Roger Caillois (Paris: Gallimard, 1951), 2 vols., II, "Préface" (p. 230).

[52] EB, *Speech on American Taxation* (19 April 1774), *W & S*, II, p. 441.

[53] Ibid., pp. 411–13.

[54] Ibid., p. 448.

[55] Ibid., p. 450.

[56] Ibid., p. 453.

[57] Ibid., p. 450.

[58] Notes from the Commonplace Book of Samuel Rogers, Add. MS. 47590, fol. 26.

[59] Ibid.

[60] The issue thus connects to Burke's wider theory of party. See above, chapter 5, section 2.

creature, and averse to party collaboration. Presuming that all men of honour were knaves, he was without a friend in the world.[61] Consequently the ministry he formed in 1766 was an extravagant piece of "diversified Mosaic"—an incoherent combination without any centre of action.[62] His supporters in government, who regarded him with awe, were incapable of standing their ground. As a result, when Chatham found himself betrayed by cabinet colleagues, his immediate followers were outmanoeuvred.[63] The result was a form of administration bent on a struggle over policy. Chatham's publicly declared principles were rapidly thrown overboard. This was all the more easily achieved, since these principles did not go very deep. In reality, Pitt held to a series of "popular opinions" that lacked any serious philosophical foundation.[64] When the country swung against America, he was ultimately prepared to follow, especially when those in the ascendant in his ministry were happy to lead the way. To Burke the lesson was obvious: in the absence of party organisation, governments would fumble and falter, ultimately handing the initiative to an irresponsible executive.

If Pitt's failings stemmed in part from a regard for his popularity at the expense of party connections in parliament, Townshend's derived from a longing for applause within the House of Commons. He had, Burke argued, "an immoderate passion for fame," inclining him to seek the praise of his peers.[65] This made him, Burke concluded, "truly the child of the house."[66] Since the Commons abhorred obstinacy, Townshend exhibited malleability to the point of appearing flippant. This aptitude for readjustment also assisted his ambition: observing a procession of courtiers climb the heights without firm principles, he set about tailoring his own to fit the requirements of the moment.[67] Burke's message was again clear: only the principled cohesion of political friends in parliament could protect the constitution against the volatility of the deliberative process and the advantages which this handed to the ambitions of the court. In the absence of such an arrangement, politics was reduced to a "woeful variety of schemes" unhappily succeeding one other—a sequence of "shiftings," "jumblings" and "changes," oscillating between bullying and submission, which could only end in the need for outright coercion.[68] Coercion, however, was at loggerheads with authority, which had to be distinguished from force. Force, moreover, was bound to fail since, as Burke observed in a set of notes on America around this time, troops at a distance were as disposed to disobedience as "colonies

[61] On this, see Burke's comments at WWM BkP 6:55.
[62] EB, *Speech on American Taxation* (19 April 1774), *W & S*, II, p. 450.
[63] Ibid., p. 451.
[64] WWM BkP 6:55.
[65] EB, *Speech on American Taxation* (19 April 1774), *W & S*, II, p. 453.
[66] Ibid., p. 454.
[67] Ibid., p. 455.
[68] Ibid.

at a distance."[69] Parliament, consequently, had to recover its authority by respecting colonial liberty. This meant presiding, magisterially, over the provinces of the Empire without presumptuously trespassing on any of their powers.[70]

9.3 The Quebec Act

While Burke was presenting his speech on American taxation, parliament was proceeding with its coercive measures against the colonies. Most controversial among these was the Massachusetts Bay Regulating Bill, intended to revise the popular components of the province's 1691 charter. The aim here was to reclaim control of the council, which had become a tool of the assembly on account of its members being elected by vote of the general court, comprising the outgoing council itself, together with the sitting assembly. In addition, the election of jurors and magistrates within the judicial system, as well as the political power of town meetings in the province, encouraged the ministry to subject the democratic elements of the constitution to executive control. "I propose, in this Bill," North announced to the Commons on 28 March, "to take the executive power from the hands of the democratic part of the constitution."[71] Without this measure, the system of magistracy in the province would continue to fail, and execution, impeded by the legislature, would have to fall back on naked force. Burke challenged North's proposals on Monday 2 May, in a major debate on the third reading lasting from 4 p.m. until 2 a.m.[72] John Dunning, Shelburne's follower, led the opposition to the measure, with Burke closing for the Rockinghamites early on the Tuesday morning.[73] An attempt to institute a system of magistracy without any regard to popular sentiment in Massachusetts would, Burke believed, bring into existence what North hoped to avoid: the military administration of the province.[74] Securing the submission of colonists to a force which aimed to dismantle their inherited privileges was simply "impossible," he claimed.[75] Such an endeavour might stand some chance of success among "the miserable Inhabitants of Bengal," but never among a people born to freedom.[76] Burke

[69] WWM BkP 6:101.

[70] EB, *Speech on American Taxation* (19 April 1774), *W & S*, II, pp. 459–60.

[71] *Parliamentary History*, XVII, col. 1193.

[72] PDNA, IV, pp. 397ff. There is an account of the debate in Bernard Donoghue, *British Politics and the American Revolution: The Path to War, 1773–1775* (London: Macmillan, 1964), pp. 95–99. Cf. Thomas, *Tea Party to Independence*, pp. 80–82.

[73] EB to the Committee of Correspondence of the New York Assembly, 4 May 1774, *Corr.*, II, p. 532.

[74] EB, Speech on Massachusetts Regulating Bill, 2 May 1774, *W & S*, II, p. 464. Cf. WWM BkP 6:101.

[75] WWM BkP 27:229.

[76] Ibid.

looked into the future with grave apprehension, feeling himself "shrunk to nothing" before the magnitude of the situation.[77]

In the *Account of the European Settlements in America*, the Burkes had presented the charter governments of New England as poorly fitted to the business of administering an extended empire. Great power was invested "in the whole body of the people" at the expence of steady imperial control.[78] Massachusetts, in particular, even though its governor was appointed by the crown, depended on the whims of popular government to transact business: without an established revenue to support the needs of the governor, the office was made dependent on the favour of the assembly.[79] Accustomed to this arrangement, the population, largely comprising yeoman farmers who cultivated their own freeholds, possessed a "very free, bold, republican spirit."[80] In the early 1770s, Burke still retained much the same perspective: the religion of the New Englanders was "republican" and their education "democratical," largely on account of their popular forms of government.[81] In effect, in Massachusetts, the form of the constitution was a "mere" democracy, meaning that it was *purely* democratic in character.[82] Since the executive could not hope to manage the assemblies, legislation, Smith later noted, more nearly represented the attitudes of the population at large.[83] Among a people bred to resistance, Burke insisted, popular support for these arrangements could not be circumvented. The colonists were "Englishmen," he declared; more particularly, they had their origins among the "unmanageable" portion of seventeenth-century puritan dissent.[84] Their accompanying political tastes were "rustick," founded on the primitive ideals of liberty celebrated by the canon of radical Whig polemicists.[85] Flying in the face of these cherished ideals, what was being proposed by the North ministry was the most improbable system of government imaginable to humankind—a "Republican despotism," as Burke termed it, whereby a governing power would subject a subordinate polity accustomed to the forms of freedom to a system of military servitude. The best hope was that under this set-up the colonists might grow enamoured of the figure of the king "as a sort of emanation of the divinity," providing consolation for their sorry condition, yet threatening the domestic balance of power.[86]

Two days after his performance in the Commons, Burke was still exhausted from the experience. He felt "full of trouble," and conscious that his advice would have

[77] Ibid.

[78] [Edmund and William Burke], *Account of the European Settlements in America* (London: 1757), II, p. 300.

[79] Ibid., p. 302. Cf. ibid., p. 170.

[80] Ibid., p. 167.

[81] WWM BkP 27:229.

[82] [Burkes], *Account*, II, p. 300.

[83] Smith, *Wealth of Nations*, II, p. 585.

[84] WWM BkP 27:229.

[85] Ibid. On the particular resonance of radical Whig ideology in the colonies, see Bernard Bailyn, *The Ideological Origins of the American Revolution* (Cambridge, MA: Harvard University Press, 1967, 1992).

[86] WWM BkP 27:229.

little impact.[87] What the government had proposed was nothing less than a complete forfeiture of the corporate franchise originally invested in the province of Massachusetts, which could never be legitimate in the absence of proven "delinquency."[88] It was a Bill, Burke went on, "to take away the Rights of man."[89] In all times, and in all places, including also in Britain, "Oceans of Blood" had been shed on account of constitutional interference of the kind, and there was little to encourage optimism in this instance: "This sort of unhappy Conflict may bring on Effusion of Blood."[90] This prediction became all the more credible when unrest in the colonies was further inflamed by the ministry's attempt to settle the outstanding issue of Quebec. A Bill to that end was introduced into the Lords in early May, with the topic coming before the Commons within another two weeks. On 30 May, Burke wrote to the New York assembly about the administration's dual purpose of "establishing a new Mode of Government" in Canada while also adjusting its territorial boundaries.[91] Discussion about the organisation of Quebec went back to the Proclamation of 1763, which the Rockingham ministry attempted to modify in preparation for legislation between 1765 and 1766. The Chatham ministry subsequently took up the issue in the late 1760s, before North's administration addressed it again in 1771. The problems to be resolved included the form of government to be settled on the colony, particularly whether a representative assembly should be established; the provision for the Catholic religion in the province; its territorial boundaries; and the system of judicial regulation.[92] By early 1773, the government's law officers were ready with a series of reports, which were to form the basis of the legislation that would follow.[93] When the matter came before parliament in 1774, Burke complained that it had suffered from nine years of neglect.[94]

The report from the Solicitor General, Alexander Wedderburn, established the terms on which the government would later defend its policy. Apart from a refusal to establish the Jesuits in Canada, a sect that he alleged could form no part of a regular community, Wedderburn proposed toleration for the Catholic religion, together with "a proper establishment of parochial clergymen to perform the offices of

[87] EB to the Committee of Correspondence of the New York Assembly, 4 May 1774, *Corr.*, II, p. 534.

[88] WWM BkP 27:230.

[89] Ibid.

[90] Ibid. See also EB to the Committee of Correspondence of the New York Assembly, 4 May 1774, *Corr.*, II, p. 531.

[91] EB to the Committee of Correspondence of the New York Assembly, 30 May 1774, ibid., p. 539.

[92] Reginald Coupland, *The Quebec Act: A Study in Statesmanship* (Oxford: Oxford University Press, 1925); Donoughue, *British Politics*, ch. 5; Philip Lawson, *The Imperial Challenge: Quebec and Britain in the Age of the American Revolution* (Montreal: McGill-Queen's University Press, 1989).

[93] Thomas, *Tea Party to Independence*, pp. 94–95.

[94] WWM BkP 6:5.

religion."[95] In addition, given the practical difficulties involved in conferring a system of government on a majority Canadian population sharing territory with a far smaller contingent of British settlers, he claimed that it would be best not to establish a representative assembly, but instead to form a government comprising a governor and council.[96] Finally, since Canada was not in the condition of "a new settled country," but was inhabited by a population with established customs and attachments, it would be wisest to match the system of law to existing colonial usage.[97] Given that the precise details of what had constituted Canadian practice since the Proclamation of 1763 was itself a matter of dispute, the exact form of provision for both civil and criminal jurisdiction had yet to be determined. Nonetheless, the broad principles of Wedderburn's recommendations were clear. Canada was a country of conquest, yet it would be impolitic as well as unjust for the conqueror to "impose such laws as he pleases" on those whom he has subdued. The object of conquest was not defeat but "dominion," as stipulated by the law of nations observed "in more civilized times."[98] Edward Thurlow, the Attorney General, happily concurred: "moderation" should guide the policy of civilised states, as recommended under common law and the *ius gentium* of Europe.

In advocating moderation, Thurlow was explicitly thinking in terms of the criterion of *temperamentum* invoked by Hugo Grotius as limiting the rights of war. Cicero had declared that certain duties should be observed even against those who have injured us in war.[99] In *De iure belli ac pacis*, Grotius resuscitated this argument as a prelude to stipulating the obligations of victorious powers over adversaries whom they had defeated, based at once on humanity and prudence.[100] In book III, chapter xv of *De iure*, in examining the use of *temperamentum* in the acquisition of *imperium*, Grotius cited a range of historic Roman practice whereby the laws of conquered peoples were retained after their loss of sovereignty.[101] This principle of conduct was cited by Thurlow as marking a policy of moderation whereby conquest was taken to bestow only the right of empire over subject, "but not to extend beyond that": "no change," he went on, "ought to be made to the former laws beyond what shall be fairly thought necessary to establish and secure the sovereignty of the conqueror."[102] In making this claim, Thurlow was accepting the judgment of

[95] "Report of Solicitor Alex. Wedderburn" in Adam Shortt and Arthur G. Doughty eds., *Documents Relating to the Constitutional History of Canada, 1759–91* (Ottawa: J. de L. Taché, 1918), 2 vols., I, p. 428.

[96] Ibid., pp. 425–26.

[97] Ibid., p. 430.

[98] Ibid., p 425.

[99] Cicero, *De officiis*, I, 33.

[100] Grotius, *De iure belli ac pacis*, bk. III, ch. xi, § 1, for the citation of this passage from Cicero.

[101] Ibid., bk. III, ch. xv, § 10.

[102] "Report of Attorney General, Edwd. Thurlow" in Shortt and Doughty eds., *Documents Relating to the Constitutional History of Canada*, I, p. 440, citing Grotius as the authority. Both Thurlow and Wedderburn reiterated this position in opposition to John Glynn in debate on the Quebec Bill on 26 May 1774.

previous law officers, Charles Yorke and William de Grey, published back in April 1766, invoking a maxim of the common law to the effect that a people should retain their customs until the conqueror "shall declare new laws." Any change, they went on, should be introduced "gently," all the more so since Canada was a "great and antient Colony long settled and much Cultivated, by French Subjects."[103] Here, once again, was the norm of *temperamentum*, which had become a standard principle of European policy by the middle of the eighteenth century. It was exemplified by Montesquieu's argument in the *Spirit of the Laws* that Christian morals had grafted onto the rights of war a code of moderate conduct in accordance with which the vanquished ought always to have their religion and property secured.[104]

The ideal of "gouvernement modéré" as expounded by Montesquieu was specifically invoked by Burke in his notes on the Quebec Bill.[105] The "Right of Conquest," he contended, conferred a power to act, but the "Rights of Nature" imposed a duty of political restraint.[106] The "inviolable Charter of mankind" held violence to account, and attempts to evade its injunctions had visited misery on many places—"In Ir[e]land particularly," Burke claimed, where wars of "desecration" were followed by servile forms of peace.[107] It was in this context that Burke cited the Euripidean adage, "Spartam nactus es, hanc exorna": Sparta is your inheritance, improve it.[108] This was an exhortation to build on the materials that custom had dealt you. However, by 1774, it was not entirely clear what custom in Canada comprised since sundry British practices had been superimposed on local usage in the aftermath of 1763. Burke underlined this point in the Commons on 31 May 1774, after a petition from the proprietors of Pennsylvania had been introduced concerning the colony's border with Quebec. Since Burke was charged with monitoring any change to the boundary with New York, the proposed territory of Quebec drew his immediate attention. The following August, in a letter to the New York assembly, he linked the desire to extend the boundary of Canada to a determination to limit the expansion of the

See PDNA, IV, pp. 442ff. Glynn counterposed the enforced conformity of Ireland to English norms. On the Irish versus the Minorcan "model" of assimilation in British debate in the period, see Stephen Conway, "The Consequences of the Conquest: Quebec and British Politics, 1760–1774" in P. Buckner ed., *Revisiting 1759: The Conquest of Canada in Historical Perspective* (Toronto: University of Toronto Press, 2012).

[103] "Report of Attorney and Solicitor General (Yorke and De Grey), regarding the Civil Government of Quebec," in Shortt and Doughty eds., *Documents Relating to the Constitutional History of Canada*, I, p. 255. For the use of common and natural law arguments in the debates over the Quebec Bill, see Richard Bourke, "Edmund Burke and the Politics of Conquest," *Modern Intellectual History*, 4:3 (November 2007), pp. 403–32.

[104] Montesquieu, *De L'esprit des lois*, pt. V, bk. xxiv, ch. 3.

[105] WWM BkP 6:7, where Montesquieu is cited.

[106] Ibid.

[107] WWM BkP 6:5. For reference to the "inviolable Charter," see WWM BkP 6:7.

[108] The original quotation is spoken by Agamemnon to Menelaus in Euripides' *Telephus*, and was cited in the original Greek by Cicero in *Ad Atticum*, IV, vi, 2. The translation into Latin as cited by Burke is from Erasmus.

old colonies. It was now common, he explained, to attribute the refractory spirit of North America to the "pride and presumption" of the more established provinces, arising out of their rapid expansion and growth.[109] The territorial extent of Quebec, Burke went on, was not a mere question of "Geographical Distinction" given that the border would separate constitutional polities to the south from an unaccountable system of government to the north: "this was a boundary discriminating different principles of Jurisdiction and Legislation; where on one part the subject lived under Law, and on the other under Prerogative."[110] On this basis, Burke opposed the ministry's scheme for the settlement of Canada, and was accordingly drawn into the larger question of the appropriate constitutional and juridical arrangements to be conferred upon the new colony.

Rejecting the suggestion that the Quebec Bill posed a threat to colonial freedom, Wedderburn argued that the imposition of a system of British liberty amounted to a graver "act of tyranny" than the continuation of a system of law to which the inhabitants had grown accustomed.[111] Burke responded directly to this challenge. The government was preparing to authorise the use of British criminal law together with the civil law imported by France into North America. But did the ministry in fact understand the provisions of this civil code? It had its origins in the "coutume de Paris," which had been modified by the heavy hand of monarchical power in France, but which had also developed its own peculiarities in the course of its application in the New World.[112] It was being claimed that this civil code, to be administered in the absence of juries, had proved a peculiar benefit to French Canadians. However, no evidence had been produced for this alleged fact. In the wake of the Proclamation, common law provisions had been in operation in the province, without any apparent detriment to the population. There existed no credible reason to reverse this arrangement: "Until I know the people of Canada condemn the British law, I shall not impose another, which their own enlightened judgement would have rejected."[113] Seven years later, in a speech on the Bengal Judicature Bill, Burke would argue that an enlightened apparatus of law could not reasonably be imposed without the consent of the population.[114] In the case of Quebec, he was claiming that the absence of popular compliance was a government fiction. Habituated to British forms, the enlightened preferences of the Canadians had to take precedence over their superstitious attachment to despotic arrangements inherited from France.[115]

[109] EB to the Committee of Correspondence of the New York Assembly, 2 August 1774, *Corr.*, III, p. 14.

[110] Ibid., p. 17.

[111] PDNA, IV, p. 489.

[112] Ibid., p. 490.

[113] Ibid., p. 491.

[114] EB, Speech on Bengal Judicature Bill, 27 June 1781, *W & S*, V, pp. 140–41.

[115] PDNA, IV, p. 491.

For Burke, the ultimate justification of law did not derive from either prescription or antiquity, nor from the customs of the people who supported its institution.[116] These characteristics increased the credit of legal systems, since they added the authority of usage to the utility of the law. Nonetheless, utility trumped the prescriptive authority of laws, assuming that the benefits of a legal establishment were apparent. In the absence of evidence supporting the concrete advantages of a particular system of laws, it was legitimate to resort to presumption in favour of enduring usage. "I will go on presumption," Burke declared, "when I have no other method to go upon."[117] However in general, he went on, the a posteriori method of judging institutions was the surest means for evaluating their legitimacy. This involved calculating the "beneficial advantage" derived from them, based on an assessment of whether the population was flourishing.[118] Such calculations of utility underpinned the "reason" behind particular laws, which might in addition have the support of "authority" based on precedent. Lawyers addressing parliament in connection with particular policies "seldom give their authorities without their reasons."[119] Nonetheless, in the case of Quebec, Wedderburn had cited Canadian precedent as his main authority without providing any account of the benefit of this arrangement. To Burke this way of proceeding was mischievous, and aroused suspicion. Here was a scheme to introduce into a British dominion a judicial and political set-up that amounted to "despotism" on Whig assumptions. "Am I sure [that] this despotism is not meant to lead to universal despotism?," Burke wondered.[120] This, of course, was a question of immediate interest in the old colonies.

On 2 and 3 June, a Commons committee examined witnesses in some detail, while on 6 June the boundary of Quebec with New York and Pennsylvania was debated. It was not until 7 June that Burke returned to the question of the constitution of the province. The evidence presented five days earlier had not tempted him to change his mind on the subject. In his notes on the Bill, he evidently accepted that new arrangements would have to be based on consent. He refused to countenance the idea that there existed an "abstract principle for the right government of any people": he would give them whatever system they seemed to "like." What people liked was generally what they had become accustomed to—"However," he added, "it is

[116]For Burke's use of common law ideas of immemorial custom in the defence of institutions, see J.G.A. Pocock, "Burke and the Ancient Constitution: A Problem in the History of Ideas" in idem, *Politics, Language and Time: Essays in Political Thought and History* (Chicago, IL: University of Chicago Press, 1971). For the claim that legitimacy in fact derives from prescriptive right, see Paul Lucas, "On Edmund Burke's Doctrine of Prescription; Or, an Appeal from the New to the Old Lawyers," *Historical Journal*, 11:1 (1968), pp. 35–63. For a recent discussion of the issues, see Sean Patrick Donlon, "Burke on Law and Legal Theory" in David Dwan and Christopher J. Insole eds., *The Cambridge Companion to Edmund Burke* (Cambridge: Cambridge University Press, 2012).

[117]PDNA, IV, p. 491.

[118]Ibid., p. 490.

[119]Ibid., p. 491.

[120]Ibid., p 492.

sometimes otherwise."[121] On the floor of the Commons he opposed the ministerial claim that the laws of England were "not desirable" to the Canadians.[122] The government's position, Burke pleaded, involved a breach of trust in reneging on the promises set out in the 1763 Proclamation. On the back of this argument, he proceeded to spell out his terms for an equitable settlement: "I would have English liberty carried into the French colonies," he proclaimed.[123] This preference was based not on any assumed "right of conquest," but on the duty of optimising the quality of rule.[124] "You have by the hand of Providence got these people to govern," Burke declared, "they are intitled [*sic*] to the best government you can give them."[125] This would have to extend beyond mere legal forms to encompass a popular share in the form of government.[126] On 10 June, in the midst of debating whether a jury system should be adopted for Quebec, Burke announced that he was prepared to override local prejudices regarding the issue. More specifically, he was prepared to ignore the inclinations of the *noblesse*. They were animated, he contended, by an "oligarchical spirit," which instilled in them a desire of "lording it over their brethren."[127] "Unequal liberty," he proposed, "is slavery"—it is the subjection of one portion of the population and the "dominion" of the other.[128] Trial by jury, he proposed, was "one of the greatest excellencies [*sic*] our constitution produced."[129] It was a bulwark against oppression by an aristocratic faction, and should be preserved for the protection it offered "the majority of the people" in the face of partisan arrogance and pride.[130]

As Burke foresaw, the passage of the Quebec Bill added to the fears in the colonies created by the coercive legislation against Massachusetts. In response to the sequence of Intolerable Acts from the spring of 1774, the first Continental Congress was now planned, which would be summoned at Philadelphia in September. In the interim, outrage in America grew general.[131] Opposition was apparent in county committees and provincial conventions.[132] News of unrest, which arrived in Britain through the summer, was nonetheless met by ministerial hopes that the situation might improve. The mood in government circles in any case was resolute, with

[121] WWM BkP 6:5.

[122] PDNA, V, p. 22.

[123] Ibid.

[124] Ibid., p. 132.

[125] WWM BkP 6:7.

[126] WWM BkP 6:5: "When I would extend the formal Justice of England to Canada, I do *not* mean, that the people of the Country should have no share in the constitution of it—Because this, instead of Liberty, would be the most cruel of all Servitude."

[127] PDNA, V, p. 206.

[128] WWM BkP 6:5b.

[129] EB, Speech on Quebec Bill, 10 June 1774, *W & S*, II, p. 473. Cf. WWM BkP 6:5b: "A jury too is a good institution—but it is so, because the same persons become reciprocally the Judges & the Citizens."

[130] PDNA, V, p. 206.

[131] Jerrilyn Greene Marston, *King and Congress: The Transfer of Political Legitimacy, 1774–1776* (Princeton, NJ: Princeton University Press, 1787), pp. 70–75.

[132] David Ammerman, *In the Common Cause: American Responses to the Coercive Acts of 1774* (New York: Norton, 1975), pp. 19–51.

George III expressing his determination on 11 September: "The colonies must either submit or triumph," he declared.[133] Two days later, on the other side of the Atlantic, the Suffolk County Resolves betrayed the mood of defiance in Massachusetts. In the middle of the same month, the Continental Congress endorsed the Suffolk Resolves, threatening to boycott British goods unless the Intolerable Acts were repealed. The government braced itself for confrontation, bringing forward the General Election to October 1774. The results extended ministerial control over the Commons: "The Court seems to have as great a strength in this as in the last Parliament," Burke informed the New York assembly after the new parliament had assembled.[134] At the same time, the depth of disaffection in New England became apparent as information about the challenge to British authority reached Westminster. Arms were being collected and military exercises taking place in Massachusetts, Connecticut and Rhode Island.[135]

Although resistance in North America was continually strengthening, Rockingham nonetheless thought it unlikely that the disturbances would sway the public from its current support for ministerial measures. It was the case, he predicted, that over the course of a twelve-month period from September 1774, discontent in the colonies would spread, yet the chances of the British people reversing their current attitudes, thereby saving the Empire from "perdition," seemed remote.[136] Burke was similarly discouraged by the "Stupefaction" of the public, which had fallen into line with the administration's perception that the feeling of outrage across the Atlantic was transient in nature.[137] Rockingham, for his part, noted that the "considerable people" of Philadelphia kept their distance from the "*demagogues*" of Boston. Nonetheless, he was persuaded that America acted in a "common cause" and that Congress strove to ensure the "reciprocal security" of the colonies.[138] Burke, on the other hand, doubted that the popular clamour could be kept up, since to have an effect it would have to be channelled through resistance among the British. This looked highly improbable to Rockingham and Burke alike, even if the complacency of the government appeared ill judged.[139] By November this complacency was jolted as news of American uproar spread throughout the mother country. "I am sorry to be confirmed, by your letter, that the affairs of North America are now in so dangerous a state," Rockingham wrote to Lord Mansfield at this time.[140] Yet, despite the worsening situation, when the new parliament met on 30 November the ministry was not in a position to publicise any new policy.

[133] *Correspondence of George III*, III, p. 130.

[134] EB to the Committee of Correspondence of the New York Assembly, 3 January 1775, *Corr.*, III, p. 82.

[135] Donoughue, *British Politics and the American Revolution*, ch. 9.

[136] The Marquess of Rockingham to EB, 13 September 1774, *Corr.*, III, p. 25.

[137] EB to the Marquess of Rockingham, 18 September 1774, ibid., pp. 30–31.

[138] The Marquess of Rockingham to EB, 13 September 1774, ibid., p. 25.

[139] EB to the Marquess of Rockingham, 18 September 1774, ibid., pp. 30–31.

[140] *Rockingham Memoirs*, II, p. 258.

In a debate on the Address on 5 December 1774, Lord North conceded that reconciliation would have to be sought with America, yet he argued that a first approach would have to come from the colonies.[141] Burke proceeded to itemise the negative effects of the government's stand. He had long noted that division among the provinces in America was a precondition for successful imperial rule: the colonies, he argued in 1769, had to be "kept out of conspiracy with one another."[142] The year before, in a letter to Portland, he wished that they would exhibit as much "disunion" as did the cabinet.[143] Now, in 1774, he commented on how the pursuit of coercive measures against Massachusetts had rendered American conspiracy all the more effective: "The cause of Boston is become the cause of all America."[144] He was convinced that many members of the last parliament who were now in the House of Commons would never have voted for the coercive measures of the previous session if they had realistically anticipated the consequences. It could only be hoped that wanton blindness would not repeat itself.[145] By the middle of December, the situation in America had become clearer. A trade embargo against Britain had been agreed upon by Congress, and the defiance of Massachusetts had intensified.[146] A petition to the king from Congress pleaded for redress, yet by now the authority of parliament to legislate for the colonies was openly being called into question. Burke declined in his capacity as New York agent to present the petition with his fellow agents to George III.[147] Nonetheless, he expected that the document might encourage the government to moderate its stand. Before the petition and the resolutions of Congress, the ministry looked set to "persevere in carrying into Execution the Measures of the last Session."[148] Now at least Lord North had promised to lay papers before the Commons with a view to developing some kind of assuaging plan.[149] "The season for action is drawing near," Burke commented on 5 January.[150] Rockingham's followers, in general, were despondent about future prospects,

141 PDNA, V, p. 241.

142 EB, *Observations on a Late State of the Nation* (1769), *W & S*, II, p. 194. It was a position he reversed by the time the Second Continental Congress had petitioned George III for relief: see EB, Second Speech on Conciliation, 16 November 1775, *W & S*, III, p. 196, where the desirable end of colonial unity was contrasted with factionalism.

143 EB to the Duke of Portland, 30 July 1768, *Corr.*, II, p. 11.

144 PDNA, V, p. 242.

145 WWM BkP 27:232.

146 Lord Dartmouth received news of the proceedings of Congress on 13 December 1774. See *The Diary and Letters of his Excellency Thomas Hutchinson, Esq.*, ed. P. O. Hutchinson (London: 1883–86), 2 vols., I, 323.

147 *Public Advertiser*, 22 January 1775. For Benjamin Franklin's request to Burke to collaborate in the petition, see his letter to EB, 19 December 1774, *Corr.*, III, pp. 80–1.

148 EB to the Committee of Correspondence of the New York Assembly, 3 January 1775, *Corr.*, p. 82.

149 *Parliamentary History*, XVIII, cols. 59–60.

150 The Marquess of Rockingham to EB, *Corr.*, II, p. 88.

while Chatham extolled the spirit of the colonists.[151] The session of 1775 would be dominated by American affairs, but the opposition would not manage to coalesce around a campaign.

9.4 Passivity and Resistance

The government had been actively providing for military defence and negotiating policy when parliament met after the recess on 19 January 1775. Its specific measures were revealed piecemeal over the following weeks, leading Burke to wonder whether a fixed plan had been formed at all.[152] In the Commons on 19 January, he adverted to the "critical and alarming" situation across the Atlantic, as the opposition began disparately to range against the ministry.[153] Over the preceding weeks, Burke had been preparing to rise to the seriousness of the occasion, but felt hamstrung by the obtuseness of Chatham's attitude as well as by the apparent passivity of the public. Over the previous three sessions, Burke complained to Rockingham, opinion out of doors had been pathetically acquiescent—"supine with regard to its most essential Interests."[154] This state of affairs had obliged the Rockinghams since 1773 to follow a course of inertia: dynamic opposition without popular backing wore an appearance of uncompromising zeal. Spiritedness among the people might now be rising, Burke thought, but it would be spent or even abused without proper guidance: "we know by abundant Experience that unless it [be] tempered, directed, and kept up, it never can operate to any purpose."[155] Burke's disappointment, the evidence suggests, went beyond what was strictly merited since opposition to coercion was gaining momentum in the country.[156] His objections were focused on the merchants in particular who might have averted disaster by earlier intervention.[157] Now, it seemed, they were beginning to stir, and the Rockinghams hoped to guide them. A group of some 400 merchants trading to America, having met on 4 January at the King's Arms Tavern in Cornhill, London, offered an opportunity to channel indignation, although their submissiveness towards the ministry was disconcerting: "they had nothing like the Sentiments of honest, free, and constitutional resentment," Burke reported.[158] Two days later their disposition was described in terms of "habitual deference," while

[151] The Earl of Chatham to Stephen Sayre, 24 December 1774, *Chatham Correspondence*, IV, p. 368; Thomas, *Tea Party to Independence*, pp. 172–74.

[152] EB to the Committee of Correspondence of the New York Assembly, 14 March 1775, *Corr.*, III, p. 135.

[153] EB, American Disturbances, 19 January 1775, PDNA, V, p. 267.

[154] EB to the Marquess of Rockingham, 5 January 1775, *Corr.*, III, p. 88.

[155] Ibid.

[156] James E. Bradley, *Popular Politics and the American Revolution in England: Petitions the Crown and Public Opinion* (Macon, GA: Mercer University Press, 1986), pp. 1–15.

[157] EB to Richard Champion, 10 January 1775, ibid., p. 95.

[158] Ibid.

their petition was depicted as "cold and jejune."[159] Alderman Hayley presented the London petition to the Commons on 23 January, with Burke complaining of the duration of the Christmas recess—a month of festive distraction while so "material" a "question was depending."[160] Looking back in March at the campaign against the administration since January, Burke noted the ministerial effort that had been put into convincing the merchants that forcible reduction of the colonies held out the only hope for the security of trade.[161] For this reason, a hearing for moderation had proved difficult to achieve.

Burke had thrown himself into a number of petitioning campaigns, supported but unassisted by most of his opposition colleagues. Twenty-four petitions were presented to the Commons in January 1775, with Burke collaborating through the rest of the year to draft a number from London, Bristol, Leeds, Westbury, Abingdon and Berkshire, and possibly those from Nottingham and Bridgwater.[162] Eighteen called upon parliament to seek conciliation. Richard Champion informed a correspondent that "Burke's friends in particular have forwarded this Business."[163] It became clear that both a concern with trade and opposition to coercion were significant features of opinion out of doors.[164] The government's strategy, however, was to refer successive petitions to a committee erected for the purpose—the "committee of oblivion" as Burke dubbed it on 23 January.[165] Three days later, debating a second petition submitted by London merchants, he again urged the importance of giving their grievances a hearing. On the back of this, he lamented the "national calamities" which he expected would befall the kingdom—civil war, a diminished revenue, the decline of commerce, a hike in the poor rate, an increase in taxes, bankruptcies, and the failure of credit were all anticipated.[166] In considering the American petitions from Birmingham on 31 January, he conceded that it was a mistake to believe that every addition to the power of the people was necessarily for their benefit: such a doctrine was fit for a constitution other than the British, "for ours is founded upon principles wholly repugnant to that Idea."[167] Nonetheless, the popular mood ought

[159] EB to the Marquess of Rockingham, 12 January 1775, ibid., pp. 97–98.

[160] Petition of London Merchants, 23 January 1775, PDNA, V, p. 293.

[161] EB to the Committee of Correspondence of the New York Assembly, *Corr.*, III, p. 135.

[162] Bradley, *Popular Politics and the American Revolution*, pp. 17–36, 543–44.

[163] *The American Correspondence of a Bristol Merchant, 1766–1776: Letters of Richard Champion*, ed. G. H. Guttridge (Berkeley, CA: University of California Press, 1924), p. 40.

[164] *Pace* Ian Christie and Benjamin Labaree, *Empire or Independence, 1760–1776: A British-American Dialogue on the Coming of the American Revolution* (Oxford: Phaidon, 1976), pp. 216, 232, 234, 256, 257.

[165] PDNA, V, p. 293. This meant, according to Richard Burke, that the petitions were "in Effect rejected." See *Corr.*, III, p. 106, citing Richard Burke to Richard Champion, 24 January 1775, Northamptonshire MSS.

[166] PDNA, V, pp. 312–13, 318, as reported in *Parliamentary History*, XVIII, cols. 185ff. and *London Evening Post*, 7 February 1775, respectively. The latter is reproduced in *W & S*, III, pp. 78–82.

[167] WWM BkP 6:59.

by right to be heard on the brink of this "true crisis" of British power.[168] When the bond of common liberty is dissolved, "there is no other that can hold the Empire together."[169] Any petition conveying that insight should be received as an example of wise counsel.

Burke was bound to underline the gravity of the *vox populi* since the opposition was incapable of concerting on the American issue.[170] Chatham, Burke believed, was the problem. "One cannot help feeling for the unhappy situation in which we stand from our own divisions," he wrote to Rockingham on 5 January.[171] Two days later Rockingham informed Burke of his recent discussions with Chatham, when Pitt ascribed the American crisis to the retention of the Declaratory Act.[172] The argument could only have been intended as a rebuke, and an announcement of his political independence. Burke was clear that this stance betrayed a hunger for high office: Chatham's distance from parliamentary colleagues was a product of his ambition to count alone at court: "The least peep into the Closet intoxicates him," Burke asserted, "and will to the End of his Life."[173] Divisions among the opposition became public on 20 January, the day after North had laid American papers before the Commons.[174] "This day," Burke remarked, "the Earl of Chatham made a motion . . . desiring an address to the crown." The point was that he had proceeded "without concert or communication," leaving potential allies in the lurch.[175] As it turned out the Rockinghams were happy to support his motion, but their anxiety about Chatham still persisted. On 1 February he introduced his "Provisional Act" before the Lords, a scheme for rapprochement that failed to win the support of parliament, but also one that failed to bring the Rockinghams on board, or indeed to win any backing among the colonies themselves. Chatham notified Lord Rockingham the day before his motion. Lady Rockingham, ironically styling him "the *greatest* of all *Earls*," updated Burke at nine that evening on the current state of play: "There will be a *plan offer'd*, but there are *no explanations* of the Plan."[176]

Burke had been warning of the danger of being out-manoeuvred on the American issue for some time, urging a forward campaign in the face of Rockingham's comparative indolence. "There are others in the world, who will not be inactive because we are so," he anticipated.[177] The government, as it turned out, did indeed prove active, winning support in the Commons on 2 and 6 February for an Address declaring

[168] *Morning Post*, 3 February 1775. Cf. PDNA, V, p. 351.

[169] WWM BkP 6:59.

[170] Charles R. Ritcheson, *British Politics and the American Revolution* (Norman, OK: University of Oklahoma Press, 1954), pp. 180–85.

[171] EB to the Marquess of Rockingham, 5 January 1775, *Corr.*, III, p. 89.

[172] The Marquess of Rockingham to EB, 7 January 1775, Ibid., p. 91.

[173] EB to the Marquess of Rockingham, 5 January 1775, ibid., p. 89.

[174] *CJ*, XXXV, pp. 64–66.

[175] EB to the Citizens of Bristol, 20 January 1775, *Corr.*, III, p. 101. Cf. EB to John Hely Hutchinson, 20 January 1775, ibid., pp. 104–5.

[176] Ibid., p. 109.

[177] EB to Marquess of Rockingham, 24 January 1775, ibid., p. 107.

Massachusetts in a state of rebellion, urging the king to take measures to induce obedience to the supreme legislature of the Empire.[178] This amounted to "a declaration of civil war," Cavendish contended.[179] Burke, Walpole recorded, made a "pathetic speech" against the proceedings.[180] He expressed dismay at the prospect of colonial opponents of ministerial policy being tried for treason in Smithfield under a revived statute of Henry VIII—simply for rejecting the idea of virtual representation.[181] This measure for trying Americans in Britain, "tearing a man from his family and friends the other side of the Atlantic," had been another coercive provision, the fifth of a total of seven, which amounted to acts of tyranny that justified defiance.[182] Burke was in effect accepting the legitimacy of the colonial refusal to submit to government measures since 1768: "He stated seven acts of Tyranny which justified resistance."[183] Resistance, however, had to be distinguished from rebellion. The disobedience of the colonies had been reasonable self-defence rather than an assault upon the authority of Britain. There was a widespread misconception, prevalent in parliament, contending "*that the Americans attack the Sovereignty of this country*."[184] This, Burke agreed, would indeed be unacceptable, amounting to a rebellion in the provinces against the Empire. Rebellion entailed an act of war against the sovereignty of the state, yet no aspect of American behaviour matched that description.

The ministry's definition of rebellion, Burke went on, was in fact "the oddest he had ever heard."[185] Tea parties in the provinces were being likened to an insurrection, with the population denying the right of the mother country to rule. However, Burke claimed that opposition to particular policies was not an assault on the imperial entitlement to sovereignty. Since 1773, resistance in the colonies had been widespread, Burke conceded, but actual rebellion was virtually unheard of. Fox later suggested that the confrontation illustrated the "true constitutional Whiggish principle of resistance."[186] But on top of misidentifying obstruction as rebellion, the administration was insisting that resistance was confined to Massachusetts. The truth, however, was "that from one end of the continent to the other, the like resistance had been found."[187] Its pervasiveness was a warning against the idea that it could be easily subdued. If it merited military intervention then the government

[178] Lord North concluded that Massachusetts was in a state of rebellion on 19 October 1774: see *Diary of Thomas Hutchinson*, I, 296–98. The law officers, Wedderburn and Thurlow, produced their judgment on 13 December 1774, declaring that there was "an open rebellion and war in the Province of Massachusetts Bay": see TNA, PRO, CO, 5/159, fol. 3.

[179] Report from Committee on American Papers, 6 February 1775, PDNA, V, p. 359.

[180] Ibid., p. 358.

[181] EB, Speech on American Disturbances, 6 February 1775, *W & S*, III, p. 84. Burke is referring to a ministerial scheme for reviving 34 Hen. VIII, c. 2, introduced in the 1768–69 session.

[182] Ibid., pp. 84, 83.

[183] Ibid., p. 83.

[184] Ibid.

[185] Ibid.

[186] Committee on American Papers, 2 February 1775, PDNA, V, p. 438.

[187] EB, Speech on American Disturbances, 6 February 1775, *W & S*, III, p. 83.

should prepare for all-out war instead of counting on the relatively modest increase in troop numbers actually being planned.[188] In the face of legitimate complaint, parliament was resorting to violent coercion, but without sufficient means to secure its goal. Opposition was being mistaken for insurgency, confusing Whig-style resistance with Jacobite revolt: the latter had been a subversive attempt to overturn the constitution, whereas the former was a legitimate assertion of civil rights. Burke feared that the Americans were "*now* . . . what we were" in 1745: constitutional protestors against violent innovation. Lord North was nonetheless determined to clip the colonies' wings, introducing into the Commons a motion to restrict New England trade and fishery on 10 February, still on the assumption that Massachusetts was in rebellion—the evidence for which was promptly contested by the opposition.[189] The government, it seemed to Burke, was bent upon compulsion.

Ten days later, North changed tack, moving a conciliatory resolution before a committee of the whole House. Raising revenues for civil administration and defence was now to be left to the North American assemblies, on condition that they met the requirements of the Empire as determined by parliament. Burke claimed that he had come to the House expecting to support the promised concessions, only later coming to see that North's seeming generosity was a form of duress.[190] The next day, he described the proposal as a "resolution for forcing the Colonies, by a continuance of penal Statutes, and the sending of Troops, to offer such a revenue as King and Parliament should approve, in lieu of our exercise of Taxation."[191] Under North's scheme, the colonies would determine the mode of revenue collection, yet parliament would decide on the amount since it was free to condemn what was offered as inadequate. Burke took the measure to be a product of an impractical compromise. Its object was to please the more militant ministers and pacific merchants at the same time.[192] The merchants were to be reconciled by the appearance of leniency, while government supporters, like Dundas and Ellis, were to be brought round by a show of severity. For Ellis, however, North's offer was a "degradation" of British power.[193] Its success, North responded, would only require endorsement by a single colony, since then North American unity would be broken, restoring imperial initiative by resort to *divide et impera*.[194] Burke alerted the New York assembly to this objective

[188] Cabinet meetings on 13 and 21 January agreed to put three additional forces at the disposal of General Gage, comprising three regiments of infantry and one of light dragoons, together with a reinforcement of marines: see Christie and Labaree, *Empire or Independence*, p. 229. O'Hara sent Burke news of troop movements in Ireland in preparation for their departure from Cork to America on 25 January 1775: see Hoffman, *Burke*, p. 576. For his part, Gage had sought a contingent of 20,000 troops: see *Correspondence of Gage*, I, pp. 380–81.

[189] PDNA, V, pp. 410–11.

[190] EB, Speech on North's Conciliatory Proposition, 20 February 1775, *W & S*, III, pp. 86–87.

[191] EB to John Noble, 21 February 1775, *Corr.*, III, p. 118.

[192] There seems also to have been some desire to bring the opposition on board: see Lord North to EB, 19 February 1775, *Corr.*, III, p. 115.

[193] Committee on American Papers, 20 February 1775, PDNA, V, p. 437.

[194] Ibid., p. 436.

the following month: "the chain of opposition to our Rights would be broken."[195] In truth, Burke believed, the scheme would unite rather than divide the colonies: it was a recipe for strengthening the conspiracy against the government.[196] As it turned out, by the time that the proposal reached the North American seaboard, the clashes at Lexington and Concord had occurred.

On 6 March, a motion to engross a restraining Bill limiting New England trade was put before the Commons, prompting Fox to declare that the measure would drive the colonies into manifest rebellion: "Hitherto rebellion was only asserted, and that ambiguously, of one colony."[197] Now a state of war would seize the continent as a whole. Charles Jenkinson on the other hand argued that the Americans had "aimed at a rebellious independence from the beginning."[198] This perception, Burke concluded, was a typical error of the ministry, forever rushing headlong to implement draconian measures that would ultimately fill the statute book with "a black and bloody roll of proscriptions, a frightful code of tyranny and rigour."[199] In order to preserve its authority, the government was destroying its dominions. Soon Burke was describing the prohibition of trade as "an infamous Bill for famishing the four Provinces of New England."[200] His mind revolted against such punitive acts of vengeance which struck at the very livelihood of the colonists.[201] The idea was, Burke later surmised, that the brutality of the provision carried the merciful implication that its savage effects would bring about the speediest submission.[202] On 9 March, the administration set about extending the restraints on trade to encompass New Jersey, Pennsylvania, Maryland, Virginia and South Carolina. The imposition of penalties, as Burke had predicted, seemed unrelenting. "We talk of starving hundreds of thousands of people with far greater ease and mirth than the regulations of a Turnpike," he remarked to Champion.[203] He approved of "firm government," he stated, but was horrified by the tyranny that was needed to support a weak one. Hitherto, he had been determined to advocate the supremacy of the mother country, but he was fast losing his enthusiasm as he saw what its power aimed to produce.[204]

[195] EB to Committee of Correspondence, 14 March 1775, ibid., p. 134. Cf. EB to James De Lancey, 14 March 1775, ibid., p. 137: "Ministry place their best hopes in dissolving the union of the Colonies."

[196] EB, Speech on North's Conciliatory Proposition, 20 February 1775, *W & S*, III, pp. 88–89.

[197] New England Trade and Fishery Prohibitory Bill, 6 March 1775, PDNA, V, p. 503.

[198] Ibid., p. 504.

[199] EB, Speech on Restraining Bill, 6 March 1775, *W & S*, III, p. 98.

[200] EB to Richard Champion, 9 March 1775, *Corr.*, III, p. 131.

[201] See Burke's MS notes on the restraining bill reproduced in *Correspondence* (1844), IV, p. 472: "we make our war, not on the armed hand, or the rebellious head, but on the vital principle of our own national strength."

[202] EB to the Committee of Correspondence of the New York Assembly, 14 March 1775, *Corr.*, III, p. 134.

[203] EB to Richard Champion, 9 March 1775, *Corr.*, p. 132.

[204] Ibid.

Chatham and North had presented their blueprints for settling the American crisis, and the press was by now teeming with proposals for a solution.[205] Among the Rockinghams, Burke had been in dialogue with Richmond, Cavendish and Rockingham himself in order to produce effective resolutions.[206] These had been distributed to Savile and Hartley, and even been run past Lord Camden.[207] Since December, the need for a definite opposition platform had been pressing itself upon anti-ministerial observers. At the beginning of the session, Rose Fuller had approached Burke with the idea of formulating a coherent approach. According to William Burke, Edmund had been fast acquiring a reputation for moderation by standing up to belligerence on both pragmatic and "philosophical" grounds.[208] Nonetheless, it was apparent that an endless barrage of criticism launched against each isolated measure of the administration would look like incoherent rancour: it was becoming obvious, as Burke put it, that "we must produce our hand."[209] This would involve building on his speech on American taxation in such a way as to formulate clear "principles of Colony Government."[210] O'Hara reckoned his earlier major statement on America "a prophecy" realised by its accomplishment.[211] A new statement of principles held out the best hope of pacification in the face of rising acrimony on either side of the Atlantic. Burke's original idea had been to introduce a Bill on 16 March 1775, but he was forced to postpone until the 22nd of the month. On that day, he rose at 3:30 in the afternoon, and "rivetted" the attention of the House for two and a half hours.[212] He had never spoken more brilliantly, James Harris remarked to Hardwicke.[213] His words exuded "humanity, temper, and moderation."[214] It was a watershed performance, winning universal parliamentary applause, and entrenching Burke's reputation as a formidable orator and thinker.[215]

9.5 *Speech on Conciliation*

Burke placed at the centre of his conciliation speech an apparently simple proposition: "The proposition is Peace," he declared.[216] The idea was to trade on the immediate appeal of a pacific plan, behind which lurked a political manoeuvre and a

[205] Solomon Lutnick, *The American Revolution and the British Press, 1775–1783* (Columbia, MO: University of Missouri Press, 1967), ch. 3.

[206] WWM R-1559, cited in *W & S*, III, p. 104n.

[207] *Rockingham Memoirs*, II, pp. 272–3.

[208] William Burke to Charles O'Hara, December 1774, Hoffman, *Burke*, pp. 573–74.

[209] EB, *Speech on Conciliation with America* (22 March 1775), *W & S*, III, p. 107.

[210] Ibid.

[211] Charles O'Hara to EB, 23 January 1775, Hoffman, *Burke*, p. 575.

[212] *Gentleman's Magazine*, 22 March 1775, p. 201. Cf. *St. James's Chronicle*, 23 March 1775.

[213] Add. MS. 35612, fol. 191.

[214] *London Evening Post*, 23 March 1775.

[215] Richard Burke Sr. to Richard Champion, 22 March 1775, *Corr.*, II, pp. 139–40.

[216] EB, *Speech on Conciliation with America* (22 March 1775), *W & S*, III, p. 108.

complex theoretical construction. Burke was acutely aware of the belligerent mood that predominated among sections of parliament and the ministry. That mood could find an audience among the public at large, and was confirmed in government by the attitude of the king. But it had been challenged by other voices within the administration, who had encouraged the idea that reconciliation might bear fruit. Moreover, a gesture of the kind had been made in the form of North's plan for appeasement, which had already won parliamentary approval. Burke was able to capitalise on this ministerial measure: the prospect of conciliation was officially "admissible"—"free Grace and Bounty" had been offered by the administration.[217] More than this, the government's gesture had been made before any concession from America. There had been a tacit admission that the tax on tea had been misconceived, and that therefore colonial complaints had at least some justification.[218] Burke drew from this the implication that a return to the system of colonial government that predated 1763 was natural and logical, thereby proposing an intricate vision of government under the guise of business as usual. Burke openly spurned the projector's solution to the current crisis by discounting the idea of a purely speculative approach: a new plan could not be based on unworldly abstraction, nor constructed on the basis of geometrical reasoning, but had to be grounded in evidence and fact.[219] America could be governed not in accordance with "general theories," but on the basis of a theory that was compatible with current reality. This was not, as is commonly thought, a repudiation of theory, but a rejection of any "partial, narrow, contracted, pinched, occasional system" of government.[220] While preaching prudent management, Burke was presenting a theory of imperial governance based on a view of commerce and an analysis of popular consent.

It was essential to build a picture of both colonial trade and provincial consent since these were the primary ingredients of imperial government in the new world. British America comprised subject territories within a detached and extensive empire—remote from the seat of power, yet encompassing great tracts of the globe. Their subjection was a product of commercial policy, which risked problematising the basis of popular allegiance. Burke tackled both these issues in due order. First came his analysis of the political economy of the Empire, based on a vision of enterprise lightly constrained by the hand of government. Central to this account is his panoramic sketch of the burgeoning growth of agriculture, fisheries and trade. Within the space of three generations, between 1704 and 1772, the commerce of the colonies had expanded exponentially, such that their imports from the mother country underwent a twelvefold increase in the period.[221] This meant that British commerce with the colonies during the American crisis had risen almost to equal

[217] Ibid., p. 109.

[218] Ibid., p. 110.

[219] Ibid., p. 157, where Burke cites Aristotle, *Nicomachean Ethics*, I, in support of the idea that theories should be shaped by their subject matter.

[220] Ibid., p. 111. For discussion see chapter 9, section 2 and chapter 8, section 7 above.

[221] EB, *Speech on Conciliation with America* (22 March 1775), *W & S*, III, pp. 112–13.

Britain's international trade at the start of the century.[222] This clearly represented a prodigious increase, occurring within the memory of man. As Burke had noted in *The Annual Register* back in 1766, it was this growth in imperial trade rather than revenue through regulation that proved advantageous to the economy of the mother country.[223] At the same time as British exports had multiplied, imports from America added to luxury and spurred productivity: taken together, colonial produce invigorated the "springs of national industry," while animating and extending "our foreign and domestic commerce."[224] Burke recognised the political pressures that had led to regulation, but he revelled in the consequences of liberalising trade. He took a panoptic view of the advance of commerce and civilisation, noting that waves of conquest, settlement and improvement in Britain extending over a period exceeding a millennium and a half—a succession of "civilising conquest and civilising settlement"—could not compete with the progress of opulence stimulated by the colonies over a span of merely seventy years.[225]

The problem was that the metropole had responded to these developments with uncertainty based on fear. The mother country had lost any definite sense of what overseas provinces might be for. At one moment, they were colonies for taxation, at another they were colonies for trade. Under Lord North, each of these objectives became a pretext for the other: first it was admitted that raising a revenue was practically hopeless, although the attempt was defended insofar as it symbolised the right to control imperial trade; but then it was conceded that the control of commerce was unconducive since trans-Atlantic traffic followed the irresistible laws of exchange based on reciprocal demand. On this assumption, the trade laws were maintained as a sign of the right to tax. Altogether, it came to seem that "you keep up revenue laws, which are mischievous, in order to preserve trade laws that are useless."[226] Burke's aim in his first conciliation speech was to untangle these confused objectives in order to establish the rationale for commercial empire. This was no easy task since, at bottom, empire was a political rather than a commercial enterprise although, ironically, in the case of the colonies, political arrangements were designed to service trade. Given the acclimatisation of the Americans to these conditions, it would be impossible to convert the colonies into a source of direct taxation even if in theory such a relationship could make sense. Above all, on top of imposing restrictions on their trade, revenue extraction would feel like heaping slavery upon subordination. Equally, although commercial growth would prosper best without restrictions, the politics of empire meant that duties could not simply be relinquished, just as monopolistic privileges could not be abolished by decree. Monopolies, it was true, were constricting. But a free trade in the absence of any form of fiscal subjection would amount to relinquishing the project of empire altogether. In 1775, neither British

[222] Ibid., p. 114.

[223] "The History of Europe" in *The Annual Register for the Year 1765* (London: 1766), p. 25.

[224] EB, *Speech on Conciliation with America* (22 March 1775), *W & S*, III, p. 116.

[225] Ibid., p. 115.

[226] Ibid., p. 137.

politics nor the European balance made this an attractive or even viable option, although it would later become imperative when civil war rendered the colonies ungovernable.

In his account of the reign of Elizabeth I in his *History of England*, Hume drew attention to the monopolistic practices of exclusive companies as destructive of liberty and therefore of commerce.[227] He went on to observe that many such practices were annulled under James I and VI, although the privileged status accorded trading corporations persisted. This meant that all foreign traffic, with the exception of Britain's trade with France, "was brought into the hands of a few rapacious engrossers, and all prospect of future improvement in commerce was for ever sacrificed to a little temporary advantage of the sovereign."[228] While Burke certainly knew these passages, there is no evidence indicating from where his preference for freeing up overseas commerce derived. The third edition of Hume's *Political Discourses* appeared in 1754, providing extensive justification for liberalising foreign commerce as an incentive to labour and industry.[229] Hume did not discount the benefits to be had from imposts on foreign trade, but he nonetheless championed the cause of competitive emulation in place of restrictions.[230] In this spirit, in the late 1740s, Burke's later opponent on American policy, Josiah Tucker, considered commercial monopoly as "the Bane and Destruction of a free Trade."[231] The interest of merchants, he later noted, was not in the general interest of trade, underlining how the mercantile constituency lobbied for exclusive privileges that reduced productivity.[232] The origins and development of Burke's ideas about commerce cannot be definitively identified, but he certainly took an interest in criticisms of the prevailing mercantile system developed in the 1750s. In *The Annual Register* for 1762, he published a letter from the *Journal oeconomique* which took Girolamo Belloni's 1750 *Del commercio dissertazione* to task for presuming to reduce political economy to a science of legislation.[233] The letter, which is reprinted from a selection of essays translated from the French, extolled the wisdom of regulating commerce by competition rather than excessive "police."[234] In his *Speech on Conciliation*

[227] David Hume, *The History of England* (Indianapolis, IN: Liberty Fund, 1983), 6 vols., IV, p. 145.

[228] Ibid., V, p. 20.

[229] See David Hume, "Of Commerce" in idem, *Essays Moral, Political, and Literary*, ed. Eugene F. Miller (Indianapolis, IN: Liberty Fund, 1985, 1987), pp. 263–64.

[230] Hume, "Of the Balance of Trade" in *Essays*, p. 324.

[231] Josiah Tucker, *A Brief Essay on the Advantages and Disadvantages, which Respectively Attend France and Great Britain, with Regard to Trade* (London: 1749), p. 25.

[232] Josiah Tucker, *The Case of Going to War for the Sake of Procuring, Enlarging, or Securing of Trade* (London: 1763), p. 51. Tucker's case for the "natural right" to a free commerce is more fully outlined in his *A Preliminary Discourse, Setting Forth the Natural Disposition, Or Instinctive Inclination of Mankind Towards Commerce* (London: 1755). For discussion, see George Shelton, *Dean Tucker and Eighteenth-Century Economics and Political Thought* (New York: St. Martin's Press, 1981).

[233] Belloni's work was translated into English as *A Dissertation on Commerce* (London: 1752). An excerpt appeared in the *Journal oeconomique* (March 1751), pp. 93–121.

[234] "Literary and Miscellaneous Essays," in *The Annual Register for the Year 1762* (London: 1763), p. 179. The letter was originally translated in *Select Essays in Commerce, Agriculture, Mines and Fisheries* (London: 1754), pp. 328–35. It first appeared in French as a "Lettre à l'auteur du Journal oeconomique,

with America, Burke likewise recommended leaving commerce to the determination of "nature" instead of seeking to manage its progress by artificial restraints.[235] This would involve liberalising trade without establishing a comprehensively free trade since, as shown, commercial liberty in the absence of fiscal obligations on the part of the colonies would entail the practical dissolution of empire.

The establishment of a freer trade was, in effect, what Burke was advocating in applauding what he referred to as the "salutary neglect" that obtained in the years prior to Grenville's intervention.[236] What impressed Burke was the growth of commerce in spite of the constraints imposed by "watchful and suspicious government."[237] It was the role of the metropolis to balance interests and coordinate purposes in the service of the welfare of the whole. This implied a plenitude of reserved power but not a constant exercise of interference and restraint. Under such distant and magnanimous supervision, much of the political process should be devolved to colonial governments and commercial development be left to follow its natural course. Grenville's scheme of management had entailed an opposite course: bypassing provincial legislatures and constricting colonial trade. This assumed that the consent of the colonies could largely be taken for granted, whereas the evidence suggested that it had to be cultivated. Burke's endorsement of a return to the *status quo ante* 1763 could be presented as a continuation of ancestral policy, appealing to the idea of customary practice against meretricious "modern polish," but behind it lurked an awareness of the modernity of the colonies, and the need to adapt metropolitan attitudes to their changing situation.[238] This was forward-looking politics masquerading as tradition. Its twin pillars were a vision of commerce, lightly superintended, and a view of popular consent, nurtured by the centre. What provincial opinion cherished above all was its sense of freedom, which could be sustained under conditions of economic growth and the right measure of political indulgence. It was sheer folly to rely on the passive obedience of the colonies since their cultural pedagogy had fostered an acute sense of the need for consent. An appreciation of this fact should lead to an understanding of the "*Temper* and *Character*" of the people, and it was on this basis that Burke examined their predisposition to venerate liberty: "a love of Freedom is the predominating feature, which marks and distinguishes the whole."[239]

Liberty, Burke realised, is an abstract idea, made real by its association with concrete privileges. In British constitutional history the relevant privilege resided in the right to consent to taxation, and the colonies, by cultural affinity, prized the same image of freedom: "Their love of liberty . . . [is] fixed . . . on this specific point of

---

au subject de la dissertation sur le commerce de M. le Marquis Belloni," *Journal oeconomique* (April 1751), pp. 107–17.

[235] EB, *Speech on Conciliation with America* (22 March 1775), *W & S*, III, p. 118.

[236] Ibid.

[237] Ibid.

[238] Ibid., p. 147.

[239] Ibid., p. 119.

taxing."[240] What was remarkable was the tenacity of their conviction, fed by a series of attitudes derived from society, politics and religion. Their politics was formed in the image of their constitutions, some of these being purely democratic in nature.[241] This contributed to their jealous assertion of popular rights against the presumptive authority of parliament. Their Protestantism equally contributed to the persistence of this "free spirit" since its origins lay in dissent from established earthly powers. The Church of England, like the Catholic Church, formed an alliance with regular government, whereas dissenting interests found themselves in opposition to ruling powers. Herein lay the "dissidence of dissent" and the "protestantism of the protestant religion": without the patronage of established authority, the existence of dissent depended on an assertion of natural liberty and a right of resistance against antagonistic powers.[242] The forms of enthusiasm that had been so subversive in seventeenth-century Europe proved serviceable to the Americans when populating the wilderness but now their religious sentiments encouraged a spirit of independence.[243] Burke's aim was conciliation and so his rhetoric was concessive, yet his anatomy of colonial manners pointed to a wilfulness and ferocity that had to be accommodated even if it was not to be admired. The Americans, Burke commented in 1768, were of a "high, not to say a turbulent and licentious, Spirit."[244] Accommodation involved recognising the facts on the ground, central amongst which was the fact of dissent: it would be neither dragooned nor persecuted out of existence.[245]

The same went for the social attitudes and mental habits of the Americans. The haughty attachment to liberty in the slave-owning south could not simply be wished away.[246] Similarly, legal training among the colonists had to be reckoned with: where litigiousness combined with learning is not won for the support of state, it becomes a powerful instrument of opposition. The posture of protest is then liable to pass from the legal establishment to society at large: "'*Abeunt studia in mores*.'"[247] All these factors contributed to resistance in the colonies, but no power could hope to abolish them. The distance of America was another consideration limiting the possibilities of political control. As Burke had argued in debate a year earlier, remote provinces had to be governed by a "light hand" since even the army that might ultimately be obliged to manage them would prove impossible to govern in its turn: "that very

240 Ibid., p. 121.

241 Ibid.

242 Ibid., p. 122. Recent scholarship has gone farther, and claimed that heterodoxy itself, rather than ecclesiastical defensiveness, prompted American resistance. On this, see J.C.D. Clark, *The Language of Liberty, 1660–1832: Political Discourse and Social Dynamics in the Anglo-American World* (Cambridge: Cambridge University Press, 1994).

243 For the comparison between American and European enthusiasm, see [Burkes], *Account*, II, pp. 144–5.

244 EB, Tandem to the *Public Advertiser*, 4 August 1768, *W & S*, II, p. 89.

245 EB, *Speech on Conciliation with America* (22 March 1775), *W & S*, III, p. 118.

246 Ibid., p. 122.

247 Ibid., pp. 124–25. The Latin quotation is from Ovid, *Herodias*, XV, line 53: "Enthusiasms pass over into habit."

military authority which you set up to govern ag[ains]t the genius of a people, will become the very means of putting an End to your authority."[248] In addition to this, the rapidly expanding population of the colonies made authority difficult to maintain. Imperiousness in the face of growing importance would always meet with defiance. Burke rejected the proposal from Josiah Tucker that this argued for abandoning the colonies altogether.[249] Empire was beset by problems, but it was not lightly to be sacrificed. Land settlement, Burke recognised, was yet another problem: if the Americans continued to push deeper into the back country, they could ultimately be transformed into a hostile frontier. This was not an argument for halting new settlements, or for permitting colonisation beyond the limits of the law. Instead, farmers should carry into the wilderness a reverence for the institutions of government by receiving titles to property under British jurisdiction.[250] From that point on, given the peculiarities of the American sensibility, jurisdiction could only be maintained on the basis of active consent. Consent, however, could not be secured by a contest over rights. For Josiah Tucker, the colonial attachment to inalienable rights was a primary cause of their turbulence, and was now an ineliminable feature of imperial relations. For Burke, however, it was a symptom of practical disagreements: if the grounds of dispute were removed, the zeal for rights would be tranquillised.

Disagreement between Tucker and Burke went back to 1766 when the Dean of Gloucester argued in *A Letter from a Merchant in London to His Nephew in North America* that opposition to the Stamp Act in parliament had encouraged the colonists to revolt.[251] In his Speech on American Taxation of 19 April 1774, Burke singled out this allegation for scorn: "This Dr. Tucker is already a dean, and his earnest labours in this vineyard will, I suppose, raise him to a bishoprick."[252] Tucker returned the compliment with a scathing attack on Burke soon after the publication of his conciliation speech, examining the constituent elements that for Burke composed the "fierce" spirit of liberty among the colonists. According to Tucker, these factors did not make up an attitude which policy could hope to mollify. Instead, they pointed to a theory of obedience that was incompatible with British authority, leaving separation as the only course of action.[253] American Protestantism, Tucker observed, was not hostile to all establishments, but only to church establishments that were not Presbyterian in character. In a letter to John Cruger back in 1772,

[248] EB, Notes on Massachusetts Bay Regulating Bill, 2 May 1774, WWM BkP 27:229.

[249] EB, *Speech on Conciliation with America* (22 March 1775), *W & S*, III, p. 128.

[250] Ibid., pp. 128–29.

[251] Josiah Tucker, *A Letter from a Merchant in London to His Nephew in North America* (London: 1766). For the context of Tucker's arguments, see J.G.A. Pocock, "Political Thought in the English-Speaking Atlantic, 1760–1790: (i) The Imperial Crisis, (ii) Empire, Revolution and the End of Early Modernity" in idem ed., *The Varieties of British Political Thought, 1500–1800* (Cambridge: Cambridge University Press, 1993).

[252] EB, *Speech on American Taxation* (19 April 1774), *W & S*, II, p. 446.

[253] Josiah Tucker, *A Letter to Edmund Burke, Esq., in Answer to His Printed Speech* (London: 1775), p. 20. In a letter to Richard Champion of 19 July 1775, Burke commended Tucker's wit but disregarded his arguments: see *Corr.*, III, p. 180.

Burke had made his own assessment of the "danger" of colonial dissent, expecting that toleration would advance by degrees.[254] For Tucker, however, the history of American Protestantism had its origins in the antinomian association of dominion with grace, and from there it had grown to identify legitimacy with republican institutions in church and state alike.[255] Locke was allegedly the progenitor of their political principles, which were currently supported by Priestley having been endorsed by Jean-Jacques Rousseau.[256] The tendency of this doctrine was to devolve power upon the people, perpetually threatening government with dissolution. In addition, as Tucker tended generally to observe, colonies usually struck for independence as soon as their reliance on the mother country subsided.[257] However, Burke believed that the situation could be brought back from the abyss if the government learned to reconcile imperial supremacy with colonial privilege.

Modern overseas empires, Burke contended, were best seen as composite political communities.[258] Nowhere was this more obvious than in the case of the American colonies where, at the very moment that imperial government began to fail, a system of administration sprang spontaneously from the people: as soon as the metropolitan power prorogued the local assemblies, Burke noted, the Americans managed to administer their affairs without recourse either to bloodshed or to elections.[259] This pointed to the power of tacit consent in the colonies, and the existence of incipient autonomy as a consequence. The attempt to criminalise the attendant corporate sensibility was bound to fail, leaving the British with no option but to accept American attitudes for all their apparent recalcitrance to authority. In Burke's mind, the resulting balance of forces pointed to a conception of the Empire as "an aggregate of many States" rather than a unitary edifice.[260] In arguing this, Burke was still rejecting claims originating in seventeenth-century Ireland to the effect that parliament was not entitled to bind its dominions since they lay outside the realm.[261] More

[254] EB to John Cruger, 30 June 1772, *Corr.*, II, p. 310.

[255] Josiah Tucker, *A Letter to Edmund Burke, Esq., in Answer to His Printed Speech* (London: 1775), pp. 18–19.

[256] Ibid., pp. 11–13. Tucker's arguments were developed in his *A Treatise Concerning Civil Government* (London: 1781), pt. I, where Priestley, Price and Rousseau are taken to task. On this subject, see J.G.A. Pocock, "Josiah Tucker on Burke, Locke and Price: A Study in the Varieties of Eighteenth-Century Conservatism" in idem *Virtue, Commerce, and History: Essays on Political Thought and History, Chiefly in the Eighteenth Century* (Cambridge: Cambridge University Press, 1985).

[257] See, for example, Josiah Tucker, *The True Interest of Great Britain, Set Forth in Regard to the Colonies* (Philadelphia, PA: 1776), p. 13.

[258] EB, *Speech on Conciliation with America* (22 March 1775), *W & S*, III, p. 132.

[259] Ibid., p. 126.

[260] Ibid., p. 132.

[261] For Irish Confederate claims to legislative independence for Ireland, see Robert L. Schuyler, *Parliament and the British Empire* (New York: Columbia University Press, 1929), pp. 48–49. For the influence of these arguments in America, see Charles McIlwain, *The American Revolution: A Constitutional Interpretation* (New York: Macmillan, 1924), pp. 33ff. Cf. Bailyn, *Ideological Origins*, pp. 216–29; Gordon S. Wood, *The Creation of the American Republic, 1776–1787* (Chapel Hill, NC: University of North Carolina Press, 1969), pp. 344–54; John Phillip Reid, *Constitutional History of the American Revolution IV:*

immediately, he was also taking issue with the opposite suggestion that the British Empire ought to form an incorporated union. In the face of colonial arguments for the relative autonomy of the dominions, Burke played down his commitment to the supremacy of parliament. However, he was forthright in his repudiation of the idea of an imperial union. Most explicitly, he challenged the proposal by Thomas Pownall for the establishment of an integrated "marine dominion" comprising both the provinces and the realm.[262]

Pownall first put his case in 1764 in a pamphlet on the *Administration of the Colonies*. By 1777, the work had gone through six editions, with major revisions being added in 1768, the edition that Burke first seems to have read, and the one that he annotated.[263] From the beginning, Pownall had been anxious to unite the administration of the colonies under a single effective department of government that would form a centre of information and action.[264] By the fourth edition, with the response to the Townshend duties having raised the temperature of imperial relations, Pownall was looking back on the 1754 Albany debates about a prospective American union as a watershed. He now predicted that either a British or an American union would be established, having concluded that there was no middle way.[265] Like Adam Smith, Pownall was aware of the military benefits to be derived from a marine establishment based on commercial monopoly.[266] But unlike Smith, he was also committed to the maintenance of commercial restrictions on the importation of competitive European produce to provide a spur to domestic improvement.[267] What he hoped for was therefore a liberalised trade still governed by a framework of regulation. On that basis, he was keen to propose the union of the colonies with the seat of empire. By union, however, Pownall meant a political or "incorporating" union, which would render the colonies participating members within a single British realm. This

---

The Authority of Law (Madison, WI: University of Wisconsin Press, 1993), *passim*; Eric Nelson, "Patriot Royalism: The Stuart Monarchy in American Political Thought, 1769–75," *William and Mary Quarterly*, 68:4 (October 2011), pp. 533–72.

[262] Thomas Pownall, *The Administration of the Colonies* (London: 1764), p. 6. For discussion, see John A. Schutz, *Thomas Pownall, British Defender of American Liberty: A Study of Anglo-American Relations in the Eighteenth Century* (Glendale, CA: A. H. Clark Co., 1951); Peter N. Miller, *Defining the Common Good: Empire, Religion and Philosophy in Eighteenth-Century Britain* (Cambridge: Cambridge University Press, 1994), pp. 202–32,

[263] See G. H. Guttridge, "Thomas Pownall's *The Administration of the Colonies*: The Six Editions," *William and Mary Quarterly*, 26 (1969), pp. 31–46. Burke's annotated copy of Pownall's *Administration* can be found in the British Library (c. 60. i. 9). Burke first engaged with the argument in print in EB, *Observations on a Late State of the Nation* (1769), *W & S*, II, pp. 180–81.

[264] Thomas Pownall, *The Administration of the Colonies* (London: 1764), pp. 10–14.

[265] Thomas Pownall, Dedication to Grenville in *The Administration of the Colonies* (London: 4th ed., 1768), pp. xvii–xviii.

[266] Pownall's commentary on Smith can be found in "A Letter from Governor Pownall to Adam Smith" in *The Correspondence of Adam Smith*, ed. Ernest Campbell Mossner and Ian Simpson Ross (Indianapolis, IN: Liberty Fund, 1977, 1987), Appendix A, p. 357.

[267] Ibid., p. 359.

would entail a departure from existing colonial arrangements, based on a conception of the colonies as dominions of the crown. After the restoration, and even more so after the Glorious Revolution, independent subjection to the monarchy was no longer viable since this would encroach on the authority of parliament.[268] As a consequence, the North American provinces came to be seen as annexed to the realm.[269] Annexation, however, fell short of incorporation, which depended on representation in the House of Commons. Accordingly, Pownall recommended extending the right of representation to the colonies on the grounds that their growing importance had earned them parity with British counties and boroughs.[270]

As Pownall saw it, this meant that the constitutional development of the colonies would follow the trajectory of the incorporation of Wales, or the transformation of palatinate jurisdictions like Durham and Chester into represented members of the British realm.[271] The case of Ireland was different, since it enjoyed the benefit of its own parliament, giving subjects the wherewithal to consent to their taxation.[272] Still, the thrust of the argument was clear: the extension of British power was accompanied by an extension of British benefits, tending towards political union. In his conciliation speech, Burke responded to this argument, taking Pownall's cases one by one.[273] He agreed that the standing policy of the kingdom stipulated that law and liberty follow British arms. To support his position, he drew on the famous tract by the Jacobean lawyer Sir John Davies, on the constitutional subjugation of Ireland. Davies's 1612 *Discoverie of the True Cause why Ireland was never Entirely Subdued* remained an authoritative piece of advocacy into the eighteenth century, having recently been invoked in parliamentary debates on the Quebec Act.[274] Burke would later modify his support for Davies's claims, but in 1775 he was happy to recommend a central plank of his argument to the effect that, as Burke paraphrased him, it was not "English arms, but the English constitution, that conquered Ireland."[275] A similar process was traced in the case of Wales, where marcher lordships were transformed under Henry VIII into civil communities: "A political order was established;

[268] It became viable after the demise of personal monarchy in British politics. On this, see J.G.A. Pocock, "1776: The Revolution against Parliament" in idem ed., *Three British Revolutions: 1641, 1688, 1776* (Princeton, NJ: Princeton University Press, 1980).

[269] Pownall, *Administration of the Colonies* (1768), p. 140.

[270] Ibid., p. 149.

[271] Ibid., pp. 138, 144–46.

[272] Ibid., p. 139.

[273] For Burke's objection to Pownall's use of analogy, see his marginal comments in Pownall, *Administration of the Colonies* (1768), copy at British Library (c. 60. i. 9), p. 62.

[274] See Bourke, "Edmund Burke and the Politics of Conquest," *passim*: both Wedderburn and Glynn invoked his argument. See also above, chapter 4, section 7 and below, chapter 14, section 6.

[275] EB, *Speech on Conciliation with America* (22 March 1775), *W & S*, III, p. 140. For Burke's fuller view, see the discussion of the *Letter to Sir Hercules Langrishe* (1792), below, chapter 14, section 6. There is also a further enigmatic reference to the text in WWM BkP 6:202, reproduced in, *W & S*, III, p. 204.

the military power gave way to the civil; the marches were turned into counties."[276] The cases of Chester and Durham presented a further parallel. Lawful freedom, rather than servitude, opened the path to civility.[277] In the case of palatine counties, full membership of the British polity brought with it the right of representation. Burke accepted that in principle the same treatment should be applied in America, except the practicality of the measure was not at all apparent.[278] Nonetheless, the idea of a virtual representation of the colonies seemed equally redundant.[279] Burke had made plain his scepticism in 1769: "a great people, who have their property, without any reserve, in all cases, disposed of by another people at an immense distance from them, will not think themselves in the enjoyment of freedom."[280] However, with the colonies located on the other side of the Atlantic, parliamentary procedure could not accommodate their representation.[281]

This brought Burke back to his original intuition: contrary to Pownall's simplified conception, the Empire was not to be regarded as a unitary state. It was best seen as a composition of subordinate jurisdictions, variously circumstanced and so variously constituted.[282] "I do not know what this unity means," Burke protested: "The very idea of subordination of parts, excludes this notion of simple undivided unity."[283] Nonetheless, the subordination of a liberty-loving population required political compensation if their consent to established institutions of government was to be maintained. Burke was clear that North's conciliatory propositions did not meet this requirement.[284] To hope to meet it, the ministry would have to begin by repealing the tranche of oppressive legislation passed by parliament since 1767.[285] But even this would leave the exclusion of the colonies from parliamentary representation without any form of redress. Accordingly, Burke proposed a "substitute" that he was confident would work.[286] The content of this replacement had two component parts: first, the assemblies in the colonies ought to have their "*competency*" recognised as sources of revenue for maintenance of government; and second, their freedom to grant supply, rather than their obligation to meet parliamentary demands,

[276] EB, *Speech on Conciliation with America* (22 March 1775), *W & S*, III, p. 142.

[277] Ibid., p. 143.

[278] Ibid., p. 145.

[279] On this topic in the period more generally, see J. R. Pole, *Political Representation in England and the Origins of the American Republic* (New York: Macmillan, 1966), and John Phillip Reid, *The Concept of Representation in the Age of the American Revolution* (Chicago, IL: University of Chicago Press, 1989).

[280] EB, *Observations on a Late State of the Nation* (1769), *W & S*, II, p. 196n.

[281] Ibid., pp. 178–79.

[282] This vision is explored in J.G.A. Pocock, "Empire, State and Confederation: The War of American Independence as a Crisis of Multiple Monarchy" in John Robertson ed., *A Union for Empire: Political Thought and the Union of 1707* (Cambridge: Cambridge University Press, 1995).

[283] EB, *Speech on Conciliation with America* (22 March 1775), *W & S*, III, p. 158.

[284] Ibid., pp. 158ff.

[285] Ibid., pp. 152ff.

[286] Ibid., p. 145.

should govern the process by which they managed taxation.[287] Burke's solution here was very much based on his understanding of the cause of conflict with America. As he saw it, the reasons for colonial disaffection had been consistent from the start, and so addressing these would bring about a solution even now.

There was, Burke argued, a "radical cause of trouble" in the colonies, which was identical with the origins of the dispute.[288] It was this assumption that guided Burke's proposals for conciliation. The Americans, he thought, were not questioning British authority, but merely what they saw as its inappropriate exercise. It had all begun with taxation, and by meeting complaints on this score, continuing contention would be laid to rest. The regulation of trade had not originally been a cause for concern, so any recent irritation in connection with commerce could be soothed by resolving more fundamental tensions. There had been "new disputes" fomented on the back of the basic issue, but these would fade when the underlying differences were resolved.[289] The problem with this line of argumentation was that it could give no account of colonial grievances that went beyond the subject of taxation. Burke made up for this deficiency by resorting to two intellectual moves. First, he took the most recent protests to be a product of provocation that had brought colonial aggravation to a temporary peak. Allegedly, when circumstances allowed passions to be brought down from this extreme, the historical trajectory of discontent in the colonies could be erased, leaving the disagreement where it had originally stood.[290] This was to assume that the historical development of the process of recrimination might somehow leave the people who had driven it forward unscathed: apparently, basic attitudes remained constant despite the addition of new attitudes.[291] To this assumption Burke added his second framework of understanding based on a conception of the appeal of liberty. This term, he thought, usually staked out more than was sought under its banner. Born in the crucible of protest, it laid claim to more than it could practically hope to realise. As a device of Whig political rhetoric, its avowed pretensions went beyond the arrangements for which it habitually settled. In calmer moods and at more settled moments, the desire for freedom would revert to a sort of constitutional medium produced by an inevitable spirit of compromise.[292] On this basis, Burke concluded, American antagonism was amenable to artful pacification. By comparison, fifteen years later, French insurgency would come to strike him as beyond redemption.

[287] Ibid., p. 146.

[288] Ibid., p. 138.

[289] Ibid.

[290] Ibid., p. 156.

[291] The difficulty with this position, as evidence by its failure to command parliamentary support, is examined in Robert W. Tucker and David C. Hendrickson, *The Fall of the First British Empire: Origins of the War of American Independence* (Baltimore, MD: Johns Hopkins University Press, 1982), pp. 393–95.

[292] EB, *Speech on Conciliation with America* (22 March 1775), *W & S*, III, p. 158.

9.6 Speculative Supremacy and Practical Accommodation

Burke's first bid in parliament for conciliation failed, going down by 78 to 270 votes. The mood of the government was captured by Charles Jenkinson, for whom the idea of conceding control over revenue to the Americans seemed an abdication of power and responsibility. Even the taxation of Ireland was not precluded under current arrangements.[293] But irrespective of ministerial doggedness, the situation was in any case transformed by the events of 19 April 1775. On that day, Lieutenant Colonel Francis Smith set out to seize control of the arms store at Concord, meeting with resistance as he approached Lexington in the morning. News of the ensuing tragedy reached London late in May. Burke himself was fully informed by the 27th of that month.[294] The situation appeared to be grave indeed, with Burke relaying the unfortunate turn of events to Charles O'Hara. "All our prospects of American reconciliation are, I fear, over," he predicted. Blood had now been shed, and the "sluice . . . opened."[295] According to Burke's sources, although American troops had not deliberately sought confrontation, they mobilised for action as soon as they tasted danger. Within a week, the north of the continent was under arms, particularly in the villages around Boston, with the "Massachusetts Army cantoned" about the area.[296] Officers were beginning to gain sway over angry troops. As news spread south, the people were roused in support of the stand taken in New England. The whole of the continent was "enraged," as Rockingham put it to Burke at the end of June.[297] In New York, arms stores were looted, and vessels carrying weaponry unloaded.[298] To Burke's dismay, the loyalty of that province had been ebbing since early spring. Its disaffection stood as a sign of deepening general crisis.

At the start of May, in his capacity of agent for the colony, Burke had received from New York a petition for the king, a memorial for the Lords and a remonstrance for the Commons.[299] Dartmouth approved their tone of deference, but balked at some of their content. What unsettled Dartmouth rattled Burke as well: the assembly claimed an exclusive right over internal taxation, casting doubt on the legitimacy of parliamentary sovereignty.[300] Presenting the remonstrance to the Commons on

[293] PDNA, V, p. 598. Charles O'Hara saw fit to comment ironically on this intervention: "till Jenkinson & company told us we were slaves, we never knew it": see Charles O'Hara to EB, 5 June 1775, Hoffman, *Burke*, p. 585.

[294] Paul Farr had written to him with newspaper reports from America. The Marquess of Rockingham had received further reports from Keppel at this time. See J. E. Tyler, "An Account of Lexington in the Rockingham MSS at Sheffield," *William and Mary Quarterly*, 10 (1953), pp. 99–107.

[295] EB to Charles O'Hara, c. 28 May 1775, *Corr.*, III, p. 160.

[296] The phrase is Charles O'Hara's from a letter to Burke of 5 June 1775 in Hoffman, *Burke*, p. 584.

[297] The Marquess of Rockingham to EB, 23 June 1775, *Corr.*, III, p. 172.

[298] EB to Charles O'Hara, c. 28 May 1775, ibid., pp. 160–61.

[299] EB to Lord Dartmouth, 11 May 1775, ibid., p. 155.

[300] *Parliamentary History*, XVIII, cols. 650–55.

15 May, Burke was reported to have "said little."[301] His commitment to the Declaratory Act was on the record and unchanged, yet he did not wish to reiterate his conception of British sovereignty.[302] At the end of July, he had occasion to restate his original position to Charles O'Hara, who had read Burke's conciliation speech after it had been published on 22 May and construed his design as an intention to separate taxation from legislation.[303] "No bounds ever were set to the Parliamentary power over the colonies," Burke asserted in reply. Any such limitation would have to have been established by convention, and a convention to this effect could not be found.[304] Burke recapitulated the doctrine that he propounded nine years earlier: sovereignty by its nature was theoretically unaccountable, yet in practice its exercise was always limited by circumstance.[305] Burke felt the practical restraints on imperial power all the more keenly as he despaired of moderation on the part of the ministry. The *London Gazette* for late July carried a report on Bunker Hill, which Burke immediately interpreted as a Pyrrhic victory to the British.[306] Earlier in the month, on the 19th, he had expected Gage's orders to result in some form of military engagement, insisting that any British success would be a disaster in policy terms: "we shall then be so elevated here as to throw all moderation behind us."[307] In truth, many triumphant battles would represent setbacks to the imperial power since they would defer any recognition that the need for rapprochement was paramount. Victory at Bunker Hill merely confirmed Burke's grim assessment.[308]

The second Continental Congress assembled in Philadelphia on 10 May, and sat until its adjournment on 1 August. Its putative aim was to prosecute some form of reconciliation, but as it deliberated preparations for war proceeded. Rockingham noted the plan to address "*the King, and the People of England*," omitting any reference to negotiation with parliament.[309] Burke applauded the British occupation of New York, but was generally distraught by the escalation of hostility.[310] The Duke of Richmond matched his mood of gloom: "I believe our meridian is past," he wrote

[301] James Harris to Hardwicke, Add. MS. 35612, fol. 221, reprinted in PDNA, VI, p. 34. The fullest account of what Burke said appears in *W & S*, III, pp. 171–74. Part of his reticence was owing to exhaustion and illness: see EB to the Committee of Correspondence of the New York Assembly, 7 June 1775, *Corr.*, III, p. 164.

[302] *Pace* Paul Langford, prefatory note on EB, Speech on New York Remonstrance, 15 May 1775, *W & S*, III, p. 172. During a debate on the Land Tax on 20 December 1774, Burke appears to have stated his preparedness to throw the Declaratory Act overboard if it could be shown to be an obstacle to peace: see *W & S*, III, p. 77. The point was, however, that he was certain that the Act posed no such problem.

[303] For the publication of the *Speech on Conciliation*, see Todd, *Bibliography*, p. 84. For O'Hara's letter, see Hoffman, *Burke*, pp. 584–8. He further clarified his understanding of Burke's case on 4 August in ibid., p. 590.

[304] EB to Charles O'Hara, 26 July 1775, *Corr.*, III, p. 181.

[305] Ibid., pp. 181–82.

[306] *London Gazette*, 22–25 May 1775; EB to Charles O'Hara, 26 July 1775, *Corr.*, III, p. 182.

[307] EB to Richard Champion, ibid., p. 180.

[308] EB to Charles O'Hara, 26 July 1775, ibid., p. 182.

[309] The Marquess of Rockingham to EB, ibid., p. 177.

[310] EB to Richard Champion, ibid., p. 175.

to Burke.[311] In late July, Admiral Graves and General Gage were recalled from the colonies, while a proclamation of rebellion was signed by the government in late August. Just days before, Richard Penn had presented the Olive Branch Petition from Congress to Lord Dartmouth, but the offer was rejected by the king.[312] The government accepted the drift towards deepening conflict, while the Rockinghams lamented both the war and its popular endorsement, with a majority of addresses approving a policy of coercion.[313] Burke nonetheless set about drafting a petition from the merchants of Bristol commending the pacific intentions of their comrades across the Atlantic.[314] He was almost alone among the Rockinghams in urging a programme of agitation. The colonists were now galvanised by righteous zeal. In September, the British commander-in-chief resolved to evacuate Boston, although British forces remained in position until the following March. Lord George Germain replaced Dartmouth in November 1775, and the government prepared for an intensified assault in the spring. But none of this gave any hope to the Rockinghams. Burke was appalled by the mood at home and in awe of the tenacity of the Americans.

"The spirit of America is incredible," he wrote to O'Hara on 17 August.[315] He was singularly impressed by Washington's aide-de-camp, the Quaker Thomas Mifflin, whose religious principles had been overwhelmed by a rising tide of "political Enthusiasm."[316] Burke recognised that it was in the nature of such enthusiasm to abate, but by then it would be embodied in a disciplined political movement.[317] He saw in the Americans a revival of ancient virtue, a preparedness for self-sacrifice for the sake of the common good.[318] They exhibited the kind of heroic spirit reminiscent of the characters depicted in Dutch painting: they represented human nature in its more sublime dimensions, demonstrating that the virtues of ordinary people could achieve an exceptional purity of purpose: "In New England you have turned a mean shifty peddling Nation into a people of heroes."[319] In the face of such spiritedness, the might of the British Empire could only succeed in prolonging conflict and entrenching bitterness. By comparison, the government was seized by "madness," but

[311] The Duke of Richmond to EB, 16 June 1775, ibid., p. 170. His despondency persisted through the next session: see Richmond to Rockingham, 11 December 1775, *Rockingham Memoirs*, II, p. 290.

[312] For the text of the petition, see the *Gentleman's Magazine*, 45 (1775), p. 433. Burke endorsed the ideas expressed in the petition, but declined to present the document himself. His role as New York agent made him reluctant to get involved. See EB to Charles O'Hara, 17 August 1775, ibid., p. 185; EB to Arthur Lee, 22 August 1775, ibid., pp. 188–89; EB to William Baker, 23 August 1775, ibid., pp. 196–7; *Magazine of American History*, 7 (1881), p. 359.

[313] Bradley, *Popular Politics*, pp. 137, 235–6.

[314] EB, Bristol Petition, 27 September 1775, *W & S*, III, pp. 175–77. The petition was first printed in the *Morning Chronicle* on 13 October 1775.

[315] EB to Charles O'Hara, 17 August 1775, *Corr.*, III, p. 187.

[316] Ibid.

[317] WWM BkP 6:192.

[318] Ibid., BkP 6:194.

[319] Ibid.

not by a passion to succeed.[320] All opposition, at the same time, appeared listless and without direction. In early August, Burke was already anticipating an unavailing parliament: its members, as he advised Rockingham, had been seduced into war on the basis of irrational fears and implausible promises.[321] The only chance of averting disaster was by deflecting government supporters from the course they had adopted. The king, for his part, was fully behind his ministers, and the Commons looked set to fall into line. At the same time, public opinion was for the most part behind the current policy. Therefore, the only hope of affecting change lay in converting people out of doors to a more considered programme in the future. This, in turn, was the only means of recalling parliament to its senses. Given this situation, Burke reckoned that the Rockinghams faced a singular dilemma. He recognised that popular sentiment was committed to the current path, and so there was nothing to turn the juggernaut of government around. This maddening stasis particularly afflicted public life in the 1770s: in the 1760s, Burke felt, it had been possible to mobilise opinion against an imprudent course. This had been the experience of the Rockinghams in 1766, yet within a matter of years, Burke now thought, "there has been a great Change in the National Character": the British were no longer a "jealous, fiery people."[322]

Faced with this barren prospect, Burke pushed for a campaign. The people would not quit their present enervated condition unless prompted by compelling leadership: "All direction of public humour and opinion must originate in a few."[323] Based on the experience of 1766, one might have expected action from the merchants of London and the regions. However, facts on the ground suggested otherwise: the merchant class in general looked to administration, since it naturally banked on power to facilitate its ambitions. Circumstantial causes confirmed this inclination: first, many regarded America as already lost, and saw all forms of protest as costly and forlorn.[324] Alternatively, they read the situation as likely to right itself, as seemed to have occurred at moments of crisis before.[325] Additionally, while the conflict with America adversely affected some branches of commerce, trade and manufacture had stumbled on new sources of business. Both stood to benefit, in other words, by feeding off the cadaver of a "Lucrative War."[326] The carrying trade was up, commerce with eastern Europe increased, shipping production rose, and provisions for the army were in demand.[327] All this led Burke to a dispiriting conclusion: the merchants, he

[320] EB to Charles O'Hara, 17 August 1775, *Corr.*, III, p. 185.

[321] EB to the Marquess of Rockingham, 4 August 1775, ibid., p. 183.

[322] EB to the Marquess of Rockingham, 22 August 1775, ibid., p. 190.

[323] Ibid.

[324] On the colonies as a lost cause, see ibid., p. 191; on the reluctance to protest, see EB to the Marquess of Rockingham, 14 September 1775, ibid., p. 208.

[325] Ibid., p. 209.

[326] EB to the Marquess of Rockingham, 22 August 1775, p. 191.

[327] Ibid. Some of these claims are confirmed in G. H. Guttridge ed., *The American Correspondence of a Bristol Merchant, 1766–1776: Letters of Richard Champion* (Berkeley, CA: University of California Press, 1934), p. 60; *Morning Post*, 15 July 1776.

wrote, "are gone from us, and gone from themselves."[328] However, this did not imply that public engagement should be abandoned. Burke was clear that majority sentiment could not be won for moderation, but a minority could nonetheless be secured and educated. "A Minority cannot make or carry on a War," Burke duly noted: "But a Minority well composed and acting steadily may clog a War in such a manner, as to make it not very easy to proceed."[329] The city provided a constituency from which support could be carved out, reviving a resource on which the Rockinghams had previously capitalised.[330] Lord John Cavendish supported trying out this scheme, and the decline of Chatham increased its chance of success. Portland could be encouraged and Savile pressed to act. Mercantile friends across Britain could likewise be inspired.[331] Burke was clearly desperate to rouse his colleagues from their slumbers, and above all keen to prick Rockingham into providing forward momentum.[332]

His ambition, however, was soon stymied. The best that Rockingham was prepared to offer was an early return to London to discuss drafting a memorial, which in the end was not produced. Nothing would rouse the populace in Rockingham's opinion, so he resolved to focus on parliament instead.[333] At length, he hoped, the lethargy of the public would subside.[334] But by then, Burke thought, the Empire would be undone. Rebuffed by Rockingham, he turned to Richmond, insisting that political leadership should give direction rather than wait for the climate of opinion to change automatically. The mass of the people was not born for politics; they simply wanted to promote their private affairs. For the common good they depended on the judgment and exhortation that the political class was able to provide.[335] It was not enough to rely on parliament in this extraordinary situation: out-of-doors opinion would have to be cultivated. In fact, the political system of the Empire might usefully be mobilised, not least since Irish politics might be opposed to British policy. Here, Richmond's influence in Ireland might provide leverage against the government at home. Since Britain now depended on their military assistance, the Irish held "the Balance of the Empire" in their hands.[336] If Richmond and the Cavendishes intervened to sway their relations, the Irish parliament might prove an instrument of liberty against the ministry.[337] Burke's hopes, it turned out, were ultimately dashed. In October and November the Irish parliament lent support to its British counter-

[328] EB to the Marquess of Rockingham, 22 August 1775, *Corr.*, III, p. 191. Cf. the Duke of Richmond to the Marquess of Rockingham, 11 December 1775, *Rockingham Memoirs*, II, p. 290.

[329] EB to the Marquess of Rockingham, 22 August 1775, *Corr.*, III, p. 194.

[330] Burke reported to Rockingham on 14 September 1775 that he had been politicking in the city with William Baker. See ibid., p. 211.

[331] EB to the Marquess of Rockingham, 22 August 1775, ibid., p. 194.

[332] O'Gorman, *Rise of Party in England*, pp. 341–42.

[333] The Marquess of Rockingham to EB, 24 September 1775, *Corr.*, III, p. 215.

[334] The Marquess of Rockingham to EB, 11 September 1775, ibid., p. 203.

[335] EB to the Duke of Richmond, 26 September 1775, ibid., p. 218.

[336] Ibid.

[337] Ibid., p. 219.

part, provoking Burke to complain of its irredeemable "servility."[338] In the meantime he had the opportunity to vent his anger in the Commons in response to the Address of 26 October 1775. The Americans had all along been contending for independence, a spokesman for the government now suggested.[339] Burke retorted that they were virtually independent now.[340]

Virtually, but not quite: there was a final remaining opening in which conciliation might be tried. Accordingly, on 2 November, Burke gave notice of his aim to introduce a revised plan for America, which he finally put to the House on the sixteenth.[341] Looking back on his performance the following January, he considered it to have been his most effective intervention to date: "I rather think it was my best in that way of proposition."[342] Predictably, Burke's motion was defeated, not least since neither Camden nor Shelburne could be brought to support its provisions.[343] But for the Rockinghams it served to provide an update of their position as the government's military preparations were underway, and in advance of the ministry publicising its own policy. Burke began with the observation that there were three proposals for winning back the colonies on the table. These were outright conquest, by direct assault or attrition; some form of concession following on from military coercion; or an offer of conciliation prior to the use of force.[344] Burke's preference for the latter course was well established by now. The urgency of pursuing it stemmed from the threat from the Bourbon powers, whose involvement in the imminent conflict now seemed "certain"—a conflict in which the British would be worsted.[345]

Faced with such a probable catastrophe, it was imperative that American grievances should be considered on reasonable terms. Despite the ministry's claims, and the extreme posture of some Americans, Burke was certain that independence was not the colonists' objective. The American Revolution, he later observed, had begun as a defensive war: "he thought that their cause grew daily better, because daily more defensive."[346] Burke made this remark in August 1791, contrasting American resistance with the wilful insurgency of the French. His comments were intended as an indictment of British policy, but also as an assessment of colonial ambitions. For this he had partly relied on the testimony of Franklin with whom he had been trying to

[338] EB to Charles O'Hara, 7 January 1776, ibid., p. 244.

[339] PDNA, VI, pp. 94–95. The claim was repeated by Charles Jenkinson in a debate on army estimates on 8 November: see ibid., p. 198.

[340] Ibid., p. 117.

[341] Advance notice was given in the *Public Advertiser*, 11 November 1775. The Bill was postponed first from the 10th to the 13th, and then to the 16th.

[342] EB to Charles O'Hara, 7 January 1776, *Corr.*, III, p. 246.

[343] Rockingham's attempt to win over other members of the opposition is recorded in the Marquess of Rockingham to EB, 7 November 1775, ibid., pp. 235–36.

[344] EB, Second Speech on Conciliation, 16 November 1775, *W & S*, III, pp. 185ff.

[345] Ibid., pp. 186–87.

[346] EB, *An Appeal from the New to the Old Whigs, in Consequence of some Late Discussions in Parliament, relative to the Reflections on the Revolution in France* (London: 1791), p. 39.

collaborate in the winter of 1774–75.[347] Burke now revealed that he had held "a very long conversation" with Franklin in the days before he left London for Philadelphia on 20 March 1775. In the aftermath of his high-handed treatment by Wedderburn over the Hutchinson–Oliver letters, Franklin's mind was undoubtedly "soured and exasperated" with the metropolis. Nonetheless, in common with the generality of American opinion, he sought a return to imperial relations prior to 1763 rather than a dissolution of British power.[348] The aim of American protest was manifestly not complete autonomy, not least since that outcome was so clearly contrary to the interest of the colonies.[349] Their goal was not power but relief, specifically relief from taxation. Burke reiterated his position of 22 March: "the cause of the quarrel was taxation; that being removed, the rest would not be difficult."[350] This, once again, was to speculate that the accumulated aggravations to which the colonists had been subjected had not substantially affected their underlying dispositions.[351]

Interestingly Burke was capable of entertaining the very different thought that exasperation might force an aggrieved population to relinquish its original objectives. Violence and aggression, he observed, might supply grounds against "ever submitting to a power capable of such Hostility."[352] Nonetheless, despite this observation, Burke felt confident that the colonists were still in the grip of filial affection—that they revered the imperial connection even though they felt it had been abused. Their attitudes were shaken, but not transformed, as evidenced by the manner in which they pursued the cause of war: "It is from their mode of carrying on hostility that I judge their friendship."[353] On this basis, Burke assumed that the solution to the ongoing dispute lay in satisfying the original cause of complaint. On this assumption, in order to obtain peace, it was sufficient, as Burke proposed, that parliament renounce any future intention of raising subsidies in America, that revenue from trade be put at the disposal of provincial assemblies, and that the British government be prepared to treat with these assemblies as one body. In addition, parliament should repeal offensive legislation without tampering with other necessary regulations which had not been controversial since 1763.[354] Less might have pacified the Americans in 1767, but even now they broadly accepted both the Empire and British supremacy.

[347] Burke refused to be party to a petition being organised by Franklin in December 1774, but registered his respect for his having struck out to "give Laws to new Commonwealths" in October 1775. See Benjamin Franklin to EB, 19 December 1774, *Corr.*, VI, pp. 80–81; EB to Count Patrick Darcy, 5 October 1775, ibid., p. 228.

[348] EB, *Appeal from the New to the Old Whigs*, p. 38. Burke based his assessment above all on nine indicators of the colonial disposition as well as "the reiterated solemn declarations of their assemblies." A number of the nine indicators can be found at WWM BkP 6:203.

[349] EB, Second Speech on Conciliation, 16 November 1775, *W & S*, III, p. 196.

[350] Ibid.

[351] See WWM BkP 6:200: "go to the Origin of the Quarrel—remove the original Ground."

[352] WWM BkP 6:192.

[353] WWM BkP 6:203.

[354] EB, Second Speech on Conciliation, 16 November 1775, *W & S*, III, pp. 198–201.

It might be that, with all the original discontents of the colonists redressed, a small percentage would persist in pursuing the goal of independence. This only applied, however, to a factious rump whose room for manoeuvre would be exhausted should the British conciliate: the majority accepted the principles behind the Declaratory Act, and would be won back for the Empire by a show of magnanimity.[355]

Burke regarded his Bill as embodying that very gesture. It proffered a course of moderation, not a demonstration of pusillanimity. It contained an argument for limiting the plenitude of power, not for relinquishing the reserves of national strength. However, as Burke saw it, the objective correctness of a policy of moderation was disadvantaged by its rhetorical vulnerability. Statesmanship supported the case for imperial restraint whereas demagogy preferred to flatter national pride. Populism, in other words, became an instrument of bigotry, and proceeded to cast generosity as weakness and prevarication.[356] The truth, however, was that the mere existence of sovereignty did not imply that its powers should be employed. The Declaratory Act had been a statement of the rights of supremacy that had been misinterpreted and misrepresented by a range of opinion. On the government side since the fall of the Rockinghams in 1766, it had been construed as an injunction to demonstrate political potency. On the opposing side, among many self-appointed friends of American liberty, it was represented as granting a licence to usurpation. Richard Price was a prominent example of this position. In his 1776 *Observations on the Nature of Civil Liberty*, he cited the parliamentary claim in the 1766 Act to the effect that Britain could bind the colonies "in all cases whatever" as holding out the prospect of "Dreadful power": "I defy anyone to express slavery in stronger language," he exclaimed.[357] The British Empire, he went on, was held together by a common executive head, by ties of mutual interest and affection, and by "*compacts*" among its peoples.[358] There was no absolute legislature to be found that reigned supreme over subordinate populations. A right to legislate for the colonies implied a reserve of supreme power, and supremacy meant discretion and therefore tyranny, he contended.

As far as Burke was concerned, however, the Declaratory Act had been intended as a claim of right, not a statement of policy; it ought not therefore to be confused with measures enacted in its name: British sovereignty had not been the cause of imperial taxation policy; rather, taxation had invoked sovereignty as a pretext for the abuse of power.[359] While the claim to sovereignty specified a right to supremacy, it did not imply that supreme authority should prove its will by acts of power. Equally, supremacy was perfectly compatible with a distribution and delegation of powers.

[355] Ibid., pp. 196–97.

[356] WWM BkP 6:196.

[357] Richard Price, *Observations on the Nature of Civil Liberty, the Principles of Government, and the Justice and Policy of the War with America* (London: 7th ed., 1776), p. 35.

[358] Ibid., p. 36. On Burke and Price in this context, see John Faulkner, "Burke's First Encounter with Richard Price" in Crowe ed., *An Imaginative Whig*.

[359] EB, Second Speech on Conciliation, 16 November 1775, *W & S*, III, p. 195.

The history of British sovereignty demonstrated this point: originally, supremacy in the British constitution was represented in the person of the monarch, but under Edward I's *statutum de tallagio non concedendo*, reasserted in 1628 in the Petition of Right, it was accepted that authority in matters of taxation should be invested in the community and not the king.[360] Supremacy, Burke concluded, did not imply the use of power. It might be that the right of taxation was inherent in the supreme power of a commonwealth; however, that did not prevent its exercise by subordinate parts of the body politic.[361] Writing to Richard Champion in March 1776, Burke restated the idea that sovereignty was a theoretical attribute of power.[362] Among competing jurisdictions, some claim of right had to be supreme as a means of adjudicating between rival powers. This, however, remained a speculative claim to universality: in theory, ultimate authority could determine all matters of legislation; but, in practice, sovereignty had to be accommodated to the reality of politics. Richard Price might "rail" against the claim to supremacy in the Declaratory Act, Burke commented, but in the real world speculative supremacy had to be reconciled to an imperial structure of countervailing delegated powers. It was an irony that the Chathamites, who sought to limit British supremacy, endeavoured in policy terms to increase its practical power.[363]

Burke preferred to vindicate the rights of imperial sovereignty while accommodating its exercise to existing power and opinion. The attempt to vindicate those rights by means of a declaration of supremacy may have been mistaken, Burke conceded, since it did not enhance the reputation of government or eliminate future contention.[364] But this concession on Burke's part did not derogate from the claims of parliamentary supremacy. Equally, Burke refused to identify the rights of sovereignty with an unregulated use of power. Altogether, there were two points being made here: first, Burke was drawing attention to the fact that a shadow of an imperial right was not a plenitude of power; and second, he recognised that competing powers in the Empire could not be regulated without juridical subordination, ultimately terminating in a *summum ius*, which by definition had to be legally unaccountable. Both these points had been variously canvassed in seventeenth-century natural law thinking.[365] As Grotius had argued, in analysing sovereignty it is necessary to distinguish between the right of supremacy itself, and the exercise of that right in politi-

[360] Ibid., p. 194. See J. P. Kenyon ed., *The Stuart Constitution, 1603–1688* (Cambridge: Cambridge University Press, 1986), pp. 68–71.

[361] EB, Second Speech on Conciliation, 16 November 1775, *W & S*, III, p. 193.

[362] EB to Richard Champion, 19 March 1776, *Corr.*, III, p. 254.

[363] Ibid. Part of Burke's reason for targeting Price stemmed from his association with Shelburne. See Peter Brown, *The Chathamites: A Study in the Relationship between Personalities and Ideas in the Second Half of the Eighteenth Century* (London: Macmillan, 1967), pt. 2. Price responded to Burke's rebuke in the Introduction to Richard Price, *Two Tracts on Civil Liberty* (London: 1778).

[364] EB to Richard Champion, 19 March 1776, *Corr.*, III, p. 254.

[365] For their persistence in eighteenth-century political argument in Britain, see Jack P. Greene, *Peripheries and Centre: Constitutional Development in the Extended Polities of the British Empire and the*

cal practice.[366] As regards the right, its possession varied with the form of the state, although its absolute authority remained constant: it always acted as a final resort in any jurisdictional conflict.[367] Yet in the process of exercising the right of sovereignty, further complications arise, not least where supreme authority is employed in complex systems of government.[368]

These complications were discussed by Pufendorf in terms of the problems of political union, which could take one of three forms: first, distinct political societies might come together under one common head; second, they might confederate for security whilst otherwise retaining their independence; and finally, a polity might form an "irregular" union in which the location of sovereignty was in dispute.[369] By Pufendorf's standards, the British Empire in the eighteenth century might be described as one such *respublica irregularis*, yet Burke was very clear that it was a viable product of circumstance. Grotius had observed that sovereignty must be one and indivisible, although its prerogatives might be delegated to be exercised by distinct "parts" (*partes*).[370] As Burke saw, in the case of the British Empire, these parts could be diversely exercised across a mass of distant territory, so long as the question of sovereignty was not brought into contention. Taxation might be integral to the supreme power of a commonwealth, but there was nothing to prevent its exercise by a subordinate branch of administration. Imperial policy, however, went the other way: anxiety among ministers bred a determination to concentrate power, leading the Americans to call their authority into question. The British responded by bolstering their authority with their will, resorting first to penal and then to military intervention. Even as Lord North prepared to send Peace Commissioners to examine colonial grievances, Burke saw his proposed method of negotiating with the Americans as better suited to foreign enemies than provinces in a state of rebellion.[371] It was an attempt to preserve the Empire "by destroying our Dominions."[372] At the same time, Burke was dismayed by the military methods to which the government seemed prepared to resort. British severity could be contrasted with American magnanimity. A parting of the ways had come: "I look upon that people as alienated for ever let the Event of the War be what it may."[373]

United States, 1607–1788 (New York: Norton, 1986), ch. 7. See also Jack P. Greene, *Understanding the American Revolution: Issues and Actors* (Charlottesville, VA: University of Virginia Press, 1995), pp. 5–6.

366 Grotius, *De iure belli ac pacis*, bk. I, ch. iii, § 24.

367 Ibid., bk. I, ch. iii, § 8.

368 The term "systems," *sustêma*, derives from Strabo, referring to forms of political alliance. See ibid., bk. I, ch. iii, § 7.

369 Samuel Pufendorf, *De officio hominis juxta legem naturalem libri duo* (Lund: 1673), bk. II, ch. viii, §§ 12–15.

370 Grotius, *De iure belli ac pacis*, bk. I, ch. iii, § 17.

371 WWM BkP 27:227, Notes on American Prohibitory Bill, 20 November 1775.

372 WWM BkP 6:182, Notes on American Prohibitory Bill, 1 December 1775.

373 EB to Charles O'Hara, 7 January 1776, *Corr.*, III, p. 245.

9.7 Right to Revolution

The Declaration of Independence rendered the Peace Commission redundant, but antipathy had in any case been mounting since the new year. News of North's Prohibitory Act reached the colonies in February 1776, deepening the mood of disaffection.[374] Before then, Burke later commented, the people of Massachusetts chose not "to proceed to extremities."[375] It was petitions in support of government, betraying an attitude of hostility, that first prepared the minds of Americans for disengagement.[376] Thomas Paine's *Common Sense*, appearing on 10 January, depicted the mood of the British in terms of belligerence and resentment, encouraging his readers to conclude that the "last cord" was now "broken."[377] The Prohibitory Act, Burke argued, introduced the final cleavage, implicitly treating the colonies "as a foreign nation at War."[378] On 17 March 1776, under bombardment from American cannon on Dorchester Heights, General Howe was forced to flee the town of Boston.[379] "The News from America is not very pleasing," Burke wrote to Elizabeth Montagu on 3 May.[380] The progress of British arms was so counterproductive that the ministry could be mischievously painted as seeking to emancipate the colonies.[381] Since the new session, Burke had been comparatively silent on colonial affairs. With the loss of Boston he "resumed his former Ardour," though he was largely confined to repeating his case against earlier government measures.[382] To this he added criticism of the terms on which the Peace Commissioners were charged with treating the Americans: for the colonists, everything hinged on the attitude of parliament, yet under North's scheme the attitude of parliament was the one thing that could not be known.[383] Relations with America had deteriorated since January. The British had become "a people who have just lost an Empire," Burke commented to Champion at the end of the session.[384] Government successes would stall any offer of meaningful concessions, while American victories would encourage the ministry to intensify its campaign. Either way, only disaster lay ahead.

The American advance into Boston was matched by setbacks in Canada. Colonial assaults on Quebec had been effectively resisted by the crown, until the rebels were forced to retreat with the arrival of the British navy. More of "the same bad

[374] 16 Geo. III, c. 5.

[375] EB to the Marquess of Rockingham, 3 May 1776, *Corr.*, III, p. 265.

[376] EB, *Letter to the Sheriffs of Bristol* (3 April 1777), *W & S*, III, pp. 305–6.

[377] Thomas Paine, *Common Sense*, ed. Isaac Kramnick (Harmondsworth: Penguin, 1976,), p. 99. The verdict was noted by Burke in EB, *Letter to the Sheriffs of Bristol* (3 April 1777), *W & S*, III, p. 306.

[378] EB, Notes on American Prohibitory Bill, WWM BkP 6:119.

[379] For comment, see EB to the Marquess of Rockingham, 3 May 1776, *Corr.*, III, p. 264.

[380] Ibid., p. 266.

[381] EB, Motion for Address for Copies of Dispatches from America, 6 May 1776, PDNA, VI, p. 517.

[382] EB, Speech on Loss of Boston, 6 May 1776, *W & S*, III, p. 229.

[383] EB, Speech on Conway's Motion, 22 May 1776, ibid., p. 236. Cf. PDNA, VI, pp. 293–94.

[384] EB to Richard Champion, 30 May 1776, *Corr.*, III, p. 269.

kind" could be expected in the future, which would only serve to protract the ongoing conflict.[385] The colonists would continue to suffer "heavy Blows," although even so the British could not expect to decide the contest soon.[386] In the process of continuing strife, colonial antagonism would become increasingly entrenched. Rockingham wrote to Burke on 3 July with news that the "New Englanders have instructed their delegates to declare *independency*, if the Congress should think it proper."[387] The following day, Burke openly mused over the possible fate of the colonists: "What will become of this People . . . I know not."[388] Just over a month later the *London Gazette* carried a comment from General Howe announcing that the Congress had declared for independence.[389] Fox wrote to Burke on 17 August urging some kind of response.[390] Across the Atlantic, Washington had the Declaration read to his troops stationed in New York. At the same time, General Howe was preparing to attack the American stronghold from Long Island, ultimately managing to drive the rebels across the East River. Burke regarded these events as "terrible" developments, not least since there was no tangible gain to the British imperial interest.[391] For Fox, colonial defeats told a miserable tale about modern politics: a claim to independence was purely rhetorical in nature if it could not be supported by acts of resistance. The colonial stand, it seemed, was falling before British arms, a popular rising overwhelmed by modern military discipline: "The introduction of great standing armies into Europe," he remarked to Burke, had rendered "mankind irrecoverably slaves."[392] Burke drew a similar conclusion three months later as British forces occupied the middle coast of America, and looked set to control the access points to all the rebellious colonies: "they cannot look standing Armies in the face."[393] But even as they were on the point of being overwhelmed by the British, the Americans were nowhere near being actually conquered; and if they were subdued, they could not then be governed.[394]

The King's Speech opening the new session on 31 October 1776 reported the government's successes in Canada and New York, as well as relaying the Americans' renunciation of "all allegiance" to the crown.[395] A week earlier, Rockingham had reiterated Burke's sense that British victories would feed ministerial "insolence."[396]

[385] EB to the Duke of Portland, 4 June 1776, ibid., p. 272.

[386] EB to the Marquess of Rockingham, 4 July 1776, ibid., p. 278.

[387] Ibid., p. 277.

[388] EB to the Marquess of Rockingham, 4 July 1776, ibid., p. 278.

[389] *London Gazette*, 6–10 August 1776.

[390] Charles James Fox to EB, 17 August 1776, *Corr.*, III, p. 291.

[391] EB to Richard Champion, 10 October 1776, ibid., p. 293.

[392] Charles James Fox to EB, 13 October 1776, 13 October 1776, ibid., p. 294.

[393] EB to the Marquess of Rockingham, 6 January 1776, ibid., p. 309. Cf. EB, *Letter to the Sheriffs of Bristol* (3 April 1777), *W & S*, III, p 329, where Burke reasserts the threat posed by standing armies to modern liberty.

[394] Burke was to underline the point in ibid., p. 304.

[395] *Parliamentary History*, XVIII, cols. 1366–68.

[396] The Marquess of Rockingham to EB, 13 October 1776, *Corr.*, III, p. 296.

A week before the opening of parliament, he drew attention again to the administration's "*exultation*" after New York, a mood of triumph slavishly replicated among the public.[397] Before that, support for the war had to be purchased by artifice and subterfuge. However, after the battle of Long Island, all reticence among the public was relinquished, and "the phrensy of the American war broke in upon us like a deluge."[398] Some of the Rockinghamites were now pressing for a secession from parliament, though Fox pushed for a petition calling for immediate conciliation. Towards that end, Burke drafted an amendment to the Address. As the crisis deepened, the menacing prospect of widening conflict appeared, with the Americans likely to fall back on support from the Bourbons.[399] In the face of this real threat, the ministry held out the unreal promise of a "*free*" assembly in New York convened under the influence of a victorious British army in order to express colonial support for imperial measures.[400] All the while, Burke observed, "no ground has been laid for removing the original Cause of these unhappy differences."[401] In the face of this, the Rockinghams proposed recovering the "real permanent grounds of connection" between Britain and the colonies, based at once on dependence and liberty.[402] They had not moved from their position of the previous year, hoping that the bid for independence could be undone. At the same time, the basis of that bid was openly justified: since government had reneged on its duty of protection, and offered little hope that it would be able to reassume that role, the Americans were driven to fall back on their own resources.[403] The claim to independence was a form of self-defence.

The separation of the colonies had been achieved, but Burke did not rule out some form of "reunion."[404] Franklin was en route to Paris to negotiate with Versailles, prompting Burke to flirt with the notion of following him to the French capital. He was soon disabused of the idea, though he persisted in thinking that "the Whigg party," by which he meant the Rockinghamites, "might be made Mediatours of the Peace."[405] The government, now dubbed "Tories," had become an obstacle to rapprochement, but if Franklin could press Congress to accept the Rockinghams' conciliatory scheme, then the Whigs could represent the Americans before a Tory administration, acting as both a domestic and an imperial counterweight. Nothing came of this proposal for mediation, although Burke continued to urge a programme of action on his party. Since 26 August 1776, Rockingham and his followers had been debating the wisdom of seceding from parliament, oscillating between the be-

397 The Marquess of Rockingham to EB, 22 October 1776, ibid., p. 297.

398 EB, *Speech at Bristol Previous to the Election* (6 September 1780), *W & S*, III, p. 628.

399 EB to Richard Champion, 2 November 1776, *Corr.*, p. 298.

400 Ibid., p. 299.

401 EB, Amendment to Address, 31 October 1776, *W & S*, III, p. 248.

402 Ibid., p. 250.

403 Ibid., p. 249. This interpretation is reproduced in David Ramsay, *The History of the American Revolution* (1789), ed. Lester H. Cohen (Indianapolis, IN: Liberty Fund, 1990), 2 vols., II, p. 633.

404 EB to Francis Masères, 1776, *Corr.*, III, p. 307.

405 EB to the Marquess of Rockingham, 6 January 1777, ibid., p. 310.

lief that it was their duty to oppose and the fear of complicity in a policy that would undermine the constitution.[406] It seemed clear that a British victory could shatter the domestic power balance, handing initiative and authority to George III.[407] In the face of this probable eventuality, Burke argued for secession in a letter to Rockingham on 6 January: disassociation from the government was by now a matter of honour, and fruitless sniping against the ministry made opposition seem unpatriotic. A "weak, irregular, desultory, peevish opposition" was beneath the dignity of the American cause.[408] It was difficult being a patriot out of favour with the public, as Savile complained to Rockingham.[409] The only solution, Burke felt certain, was to take a stand on principle, publicly abjuring injustice by abandoning their parliamentary role. The Commons, the Lords, the Church and the law were all against the Whigs in the scales of politics. Impeachment or a Bill of Pains and Penalties might be brought against those who seceded.[410] Nonetheless, a display of indignation against the present state of affairs offered the only hope of recalling the British public to their senses.[411] Even so, it was a slim hope, as the people grew infatuated with the spirit of military triumph. There was a current "zeal for civil war," which looked like an enduring feature of the political landscape.[412] The Rockinghams were close to desperation: France was by now colluding in the colonial rebellion, rendering any support for the cause of resistance problematic, while ministerial oppression made it impossible to back the government.[413]

The secession was doomed from the start: the Chathamites did not participate, and the Rockinghamites were divided, leading to the abandonment of the policy in April. Throughout this period, while Burke accepted the reality of American independence, he insisted on providing for the possibility of readmission on the terms outlined by his own conciliation proposals. Readmission to the Empire depended on three factors, laid out in Burke's *Address to the King* of January 1777. First, it was necessary to recognise the validity of colonial grievances, rooted in the denial of a meaningful role in governing themselves.[414] Second, acts of hostility should not be permitted to inflame American animosity further, such as the use of Indians and

[406] O'Gorman, *The Rise of Party*, pp. 349–52; G. H. Guttridge, "The Whig Opposition in England during the American Revolution," *Journal of Modern History*, 6 (1934), pp. 1–13.

[407] See the Marquess of Rockingham to the Duke of Manchester, 28 June 1775, cited in O'Gorman, *The Rise of Party*, p. 606 n18. On the constitutional threat posed, in the eyes of the Rockinghams, by the American war, see John Brewer, "The Faces of Lord Bute: A Visual Contribution to Anglo-American Political Ideology," *Perspectives in American History*, 6 (1972), pp. 95–116.

[408] EB to the Marquess of Rockingham, 6 January 1776, *Corr.*, III, p. 313.

[409] Sir George Savile to the Marquess of Rockingham, 15 January 1777, *Rockingham Memoirs*, II, pp. 304–6.

[410] EB to the Marquess of Rockingham, 6 January 1776, *Corr.*, III, pp. 312–13.

[411] The Marquess of Rockingham to EB, 6 January 1777, ibid., pp. 315–16.

[412] EB, *Letter to the Sheriffs of Bristol* (3 April 1777), *W & S*, III, pp. 302–3.

[413] EB to Richard Champion, 15 January 1777, *Corr.*, III, p. 320; EB to Richard Champion, 21 January 1777, ibid., p. 320.

[414] EB, *Address to the King* (January 1777), *W & S*, III, pp. 263–64.

emancipated slaves for the purpose of waging war.[415] And finally, a disposition to reconciliation should be made apparent by holding out an assurance of advantages to be derived from membership of an imperial community.[416] Regrettably, ministerial policy had veered the other way, threatening domestic order with constitutional derangement by asserting military government over "distant Regions."[417] Arbitrary power in the dominions, Burke was contending, would entail a reversion to arbitrary power at home. At this point Burke's rhetoric came closest to Whig doctrine exemplified by the principles of 1688: the reversion he apparently feared was a regression to Stuart dogma enshrined in the idea of passive obedience. Military government in America would become an engine of the destruction of constitutional freedom in the mother country, beginning with the executive and then corrupting the Houses of Parliament.[418] Opinion would soon follow the example of power, introducing "other maxims of government and other grounds of obedience, than those which have prevail'd since the glorious revolution."[419] The ministry ought to have deferred to Whig opinion in America; instead, Tory doctrine was being fostered by absolute government in Britain.

According to Burke, behind the vicissitudes of opinion lay a clear-cut obligation, which governments were in principle constrained to follow: they had to earn the trust of their subjects by securing them their rights. Burke would later articulate this commitment in his speeches on India, just as he had defended it in his notes for his second conciliation speech. Authority, Burke thought, imposed a sacred obligation to uphold the "*eternal*" laws that bound individuals to one another as members of the creation.[420] Political morality, he believed, was a holy trust founded on the rules of social morality. Above all, this enjoined the duty of protection. Protection meant securing the rights of liberty and property to the extent that these were compatible with the common welfare. Where these rights were violated, subjects were entitled, indeed had a duty, to resist.[421] The Glorious Revolution exemplified such resistance conducted in the name of the *salus populi*. The safety of the people was paramount to all positive institutions of law and government, and for that reason stood as *suprema lex*.[422] It was on the basis of this principle that the "people" in 1688 "reenter'd into their original rights." Similarly, between 1775 and 1776, the colonists had been driven to assert their right to self-defence in the face of an imperial abdication of authority. The Prohibitory Act, Burke claimed, implied a dissolution of government;

[415] Ibid., pp. 267–68.
[416] Ibid., p. 270.
[417] Ibid., p. 272.
[418] Ibid.
[419] Ibid., p. 273. Cf. EB, *Letter to the Sheriffs of Bristol* (3 April 1777), *W & S*, III, p. 327.
[420] EB, Notes for Second Conciliation Speech, 16 November 1775, WWM BkP 6:197(a).
[421] See below, chapter 12, section 6.
[422] EB, *Address to the King* (January 1777), *W & S*, III, p. 273.

it entailed a withdrawal of protection, and consequently a release from the duty of obedience.[423]

Two months later, in his *Letter to the Sheriffs of Bristol*, Burke was more explicit about the right to revolution that fell to the Americans after the passage of the Prohibitory Act. Since the Peace Commissioners dispatched by North did not arrive for months after the passage of a measure that effectively outlawed colonial trade, there was no means of applying for readmission into civil allegiance: "there was no man on the whole continent, or within three thousand miles of it, qualified by law to follow allegiance with protection."[424] The political attitudes leading to this situation appeared to Burke a betrayal of Christian manners underpinning the humanity of "enlightened and polished times."[425] Even so, it still seemed that the dependency of the colonies, and thus their submission to what Burke still interestingly regarded as the *de jure* sovereignty of the king-in-parliament, offered the best hope of securing the welfare of the Americans.[426] This was partly because Britain could offer security against the threat posed by the Bourbons, but also because there was a likely prospect of internal dissension among the colonies when their contest with the mother country was over. What the Americans sought, Burke suggested, was "fair equality": a system of private property under a representative regime in which individuals had equal access to protection under law.[427] Only a mixed system of government could plausibly provide this, and only Britain could realistically be expected to maintain an arrangement of the kind: "None but England can communicate to you the benefits of such a Constitution. We apprehend you are not now, nor for ages are likely to be capable of that form of Constitution in an independent State . . . [Y]our present union . . . cannot always subsist without the authority and weight of this great and long preserved Body, to equipoise, and to preserve you amongst yourselves in a just and fair equality."[428]

But even as Burke wrote, the promise of "fair equality" was being radically undermined by the ministry's handling of the war. The American Treasons Act and the Letters of Marque Act were just passing into law, enabling colonial vessels to be seized as prize and suspending habeas corpus among the colonists.[429] The latter in particular threatened equality in the Empire by discriminating against a portion of the trans-Atlantic British community: "Other laws may injure the community;

[423] Ibid., p. 269. On 1688 as instancing the dissolution of the "compact," with "all right and power" reverting "to the people," see EB, Speech on the King's Illness, 22 December 1788, *Parliamentary History*, XXVII, col. 823.

[424] EB, *Letter to the Sheriffs of Bristol* (3 April 1777), *W & S*, III, p. 312.

[425] EB, *Address to the Colonists* (January 1777), ibid., pp. 281–82.

[426] Ibid., p. 283. See EB, *Address to the King* (January 1777), ibid., p. 270, on the idea that Britain remained sovereign by right after the Declaration of Independence.

[427] EB, *Address to the Colonists* (January 1777), ibid., p. 283.

[428] Ibid.

[429] 17 Geo. III, c. 9 and 17 Geo. III, c. 7.

this tends to dissolve it. It destroys *equality*, which is the essence of community."[430] Distressed by the strategic blunder of participating in a partial secession, Burke composed his *Letter to the Sheriffs of Bristol* in April 1777 to object to recent legislation and defend his general approach.[431] The result was a major reckoning with the situation in America in the light of recent developments in Britain. By now, Burke's expertise in colonial affairs was widely acknowledged, and his industry in acquiring up to date information admitted. "I think I know America," he felt ready to assert. "If I do not, my ignorance is incurable, for I have spared no pains to understand it."[432] That understanding now brought him to a new conception of the imperial crisis in terms of the historic complication of "two legislatures"—the existence of parliament on the one hand and the assemblies on the other—within a single state.[433] In Pufendorfian terms, a "double legislature" presented an example of a *respublica irregularis*, and Burke now conceded that this arrangement could pose a problem, though equally the problem could with goodwill be resolved. Down to his first conciliation speech he had defended the informal nature of the imperial constitution. He now continued to defend its character as "a mighty and strangely diversified mass" in which unity was preserved in the midst of tremendous variations in law and administration. "I could never conceive that the natives of *Hindostan* and those of *Virginia* could be ordered in the same manner," he explained.[434] But while applauding this aptitude for accommodation to the diverse practical circumstances, Burke now recognised the wisdom of establishing a new charter, replacing the informal pact that underpinned the colonial Empire.

Imperial arrangements had "grown up" rather than been designed. With the rise to power of Britain and the increase in population and prosperity in the colonies, it appeared that the original understanding had been "outgrown."[435] Burke noted in his *Address to the Colonists* that hitherto it had been hoped that relationships within the Empire could be managed on the bases of equity and discretion, although now it seemed clear that a more formal agreement should be reached, "a ratified security for your liberties and our quiet."[436] The *Letter to the Sheriffs of Bristol* made clear that this had to involve a compact. This resolution was implicit in Burke's second conciliation speech, where he accepted that the right of taxation should be ceded to the colonies: a tacit understanding should be replaced by an explicit arrangement.[437]

[430] EB, *Letter to the Sheriffs of Bristol* (3 April 1777), *W & S*, III, p. 297.

[431] See Richard Burke Sr. to Richard Champion, 2 April 1777, *Corr.*, III, pp. 332–33 and EB to Richard Champion, 3 April 1777, ibid., pp. 333–34.

[432] EB, *Letter to the Sheriffs of Bristol* (3 April 1777), *W & S*, III, p. 304.

[433] Ibid., p. 321.

[434] Ibid., p. 316.

[435] EB, *Address to the Colonists* (January 1777), ibid., p. 285.

[436] Ibid.

[437] EB, Second Speech on Conciliation, 16 November 1775, *W & S*, III, pp. 190–95. There is some discussion of the shift in Burke's thinking about the character of the Empire at the time of the Second Conciliation Speech in Peter J. Stanlis, "Edmund Burke and British Views of the American Revolution: A Conflict over the Rights of Sovereignty" in Ian Crowe ed., *Edmund Burke: His Life and Legacy* (Dublin: Four Courts Press, 1997).

Burke now presented this as a new imperial covenant, necessitated by the kind of situation that always called for "compacts": "I mean, habits of soreness, jealousy, and distrust."[438] This was a significant modification of Burke's original position. When he first explored the issue of imperial supremacy, he assumed that parliament possessed unlimited legislative power over the colonies. This assumption was confirmed by an examination of the statute book, which pointed to a history of command and obedience. The effective possession of full powers implied in Burke's mind a title to possession, which meant the existence of sovereignty in the mother country.[439] The right of sovereignty could not be parcelled out among discrete organs of administration, even if the Chathamites pretended that it could. Burke now emphasised, however, that some of the powers of sovereignty could be contracted to a delegated authority. Formerly he had thought it best not to transfer powers by covenant, since these might, as times changed, be needed in reserve. However, prudence now dictated otherwise, since sovereignty had to stand upon opinion, and opinion was subject to historical variation, as the fate of Star Chamber and the Convocation of the Clergy under the British constitution illustrated.[440]

Burke was arguing that a right to power had to be supported by a recognition of that right if it was to be effectively wielded. That meant that authority was dependent on consent, and could only command obedience where it was endorsed by popular opinion as this happened to be historically constituted. Equally, freedom varied circumstantially with the idea of freedom, and was never an unqualified or abstract possession. Among reforming and dissenting publicists in Britain since the crisis of the American colonies broke, contention over sovereignty bred disputatiousness about the nature of liberty. Commentators like Price had debated the subject of freedom with such a degree of metaphysical distance from reality that they were driven into purely speculative conception of the nature of obligation, demarcating where liberty in theory began and where authority by comparison ended.[441] Twelve and a half years before the publication of the *Reflections on the Revolution in France*, in the midst of his defence of the American Revolution, and in the context of a bid for reconstituting the Empire on the basis of a new covenant for the distribution of its powers, Burke was trying to expose purely speculative theories of government and the abstract conception of freedom that accompanied them. That involved arguing that supreme right in the state, along with the enjoyment of liberty under it, had to be accommodated to power and opinion if it was to have any traction in the

[438] EB, *Letter to the Sheriffs of Bristol* (3 April 1777), *W & S*, III, p. 323.

[439] Ibid., p. 314. Cf. Friedrich von Gentz, *The Origins and Principles of the American Revolution Compared with the Origins and Principles of the French Revolution*, trans. John Quincy Adams (Indianapolis, IN: Liberty Fund, 2010), p, 38: "the right of a European nation over their colonies must always be a wavering, insecure, undefined, and often undefinable right."

[440] EB, *Letter to the Sheriffs of Bristol* (3 April 1777), *W & S*, III, pp. 315–16.

[441] Ibid., pp. 317–18. On dissenters like Price in connection with the American Revolution, see Colin Bonwick, *English Radicals and the American Revolution* (Chapel Hill, NC: University of North Carolina Press, 1977), esp. ch. 1.

practical world of affairs. That requirement demanded a new dispensation for America whereby the "two legislatures" on either side of the Atlantic would have to be reconciled on new terms. Simple subordination would no longer work; rapprochement required an agreement to repartition the powers of sovereignty so that its right could be rendered compatible with opinion.

9.8 A New State of a New Species

Burke continued to be disheartened through the summer and into the autumn of 1777. Winter brought no relief. At this time he began his correspondence with Philip Francis, then stationed in Bengal. But even as his renewed interest in Indian affairs was being kindled, America, he told Francis, engrossed his attention. He had laboured to avoid this war, he wrote, yet still it raged with popular support, and without causing serious discomfort to the administration: "I never approved of our engaging in it, and I am sure it might have been avoided."[442] In this melancholy state, he sensed that his predictions were being falsified by events. He never expected American resistance to endure, at least without the open intervention of France and Spain. As he commented to William Robertson at this time, every speculation that he had ventured to make had "proved fallacious."[443] Robertson's *History of America* had just appeared, and Burke noted how the current sorry situation in the Empire, while supplying copious material for future historians, provided evidence that those responsible for the current crisis had not so far profited from historical instruction.[444] The same old insensitivity to the lessons of the past continued in government circles. Howe's successes in battle would only perpetuate the damaging delusion of progress, drawing parliament ever more deeply into a patriotic frenzy of war.[445] Under these circumstances, it was crucial for the Rockinghamites to adopt a definite plan independent of the fortunes of the struggle in America. Along with Fox, Burke was disdainful of waiting on "contingencies," as he outlined in a letter sent in October.[446] It was necessary for the Whigs to storm the citadel, Fox thought, but instead his colleagues were indolently waiting on events.[447]

Burke added his own observations to this perception on Fox's part. Enterprise and activity were not characteristics of the great, and consequently they were prone to slide into torpor. They were habitually discouraged by unavoidable setbacks, as Burke wrote to William Baker at this time: "Ill success, ill health, minds too delicate for the rough and toilsome Business of our time, a want of stimulus to ambition,

[442] EB to Philip Francis, 9 June 1777, *Corr.*, III, p. 349.

[443] EB to William Robertson, 9 June 1777, ibid., p. 351.

[444] Ibid., pp. 351–52.

[445] EB to Richard Champion, 25 September 1777, ibid., p. 377.

[446] 8 October 1777, ibid., p. 381, responding to Charles James Fox to EB, 8 September 1777, *Correspondence* (1844), II, pp. 181–82.

[447] EB to Charles James Fox, 8 October 1777, *Corr.*, III, p. 381.

a degeneracy in the Nation"—these all inhibited proactive determination in politics, especially among the remnant of old Whigs.[448] The "degeneracy" of public opinion particularly troubled Burke, having developed as a concern since 1773. His senior colleagues were insufficiently disposed to "despise" its expression, while also lacking the necessary skills to "cure" it.[449] The evidence of popular abasement was everywhere to be seen, Burke confided in a lengthy letter to Fox. In Bristol opposition had all but disappeared, while in Liverpool merchants loved the war as much as they suffered from it. These attitudes had allegedly been brought about by a resurgence of "party Spirit," by which Burke meant a revival of Toryism in the country.[450] Despondency was the reaction among the Rockingham grandees, and even the dissenters were slow to take a stand against the administration.[451] "In truth, we can do nothing essential," as Rockingham put it to Burke on 26 October, unless some "great change of sentiments" should arise among the public.[452] He sensed that fatigue with the war was beginning to set in, although any acknowledgement that serious errors had been made would be slow to develop. In the meantime, Burke continued to press for consistency in the party's principles, and to underscore the importance of corresponding enterprise.[453]

Parliament was due to meet on 18 November 1777. News of Howe's victory over Washington at Brandywine in September had reached London two weeks before parliament convened, giving rise to a "wild tumult of Joy" on the streets of the capital.[454] The Earl of Abingdon had attacked the Declaratory Act in a riposte to Burke's *Letter to the Sheriffs of Bristol*, and Richmond now began to recommend the idea of its repeal.[455] The populace, Burke complained, was "ready to declare for the conqueror," with its mood growing more "vehement" and "ferocious" by the day.[456] It increased in imperiousness with every military success, and only moderated its attitude when disappointment struck. The public, it seemed, was truly a prisoner of fortune, incapable of sticking to a decided course. After three years of war, the government should set an example by promoting leniency. Instead, as Burke put it in his Speech on the Address on 20 November, they offered no alternative to "UNCONDITIONAL SUBMISSION."[457] France would soon be forced into the war, and even without this intervention the Americans could not be conquered. It

[448] EB to William Baker, 12 October 1777, ibid., p. 388.

[449] Ibid., pp. 388–9.

[450] EB to Charles James Fox, 8 October 1777, ibid., pp. 382–83.

[451] Ibid., p. 383.

[452] Ibid., p. 392.

[453] EB to the Marquess of Rockingham, 5 November 1777, ibid., p. 399.

[454] EB to Champion, 1 November 1777, ibid., p. 394; EB to the Marquess of Rockingham, 5 November 1777, ibid., p. 399.

[455] Earl of Abingdon, *Thoughts on the Letter of Edmund Burke, Esq.; to the Sheriffs of Bristol* (London: 1777). For Burke's response, see EB to the Earl of Abingdon, 26 August 1777, *Corr.*, III, pp. 368–70. For Richmond's position, see EB to the Marquess of Rockingham, 5 November 1777, ibid., pp. 398–99n.

[456] EB to William Baker, 9 November 1777, ibid., p. 401.

[457] EB, Speech on Address on King's Speech, 20 November 1777, *W & S*, III, p. 343.

was imperative to ask what conceivable interest Britain could have in vainly striving to subjugate "13 independent states."[458] Vast expense and effusion of blood had brought the ministry to this impasse in which it refused to treat with the enemy unless they prostrated themselves in advance.[459] Chatham had moved in the Lords for a recall of troops from North America on the first day of the session, and Richmond pressed for an inquiry into the state of the nation on 2 December. On the same day, Fox also moved for an inquiry in the Commons, with Burke using the occasion to reflect on the vacuity of British power. They had authority over the continent *de jure*, Burke conceded, yet the possession of territory de facto is what counted: "as they enjoy the right, *de facto*, and we alone *de jure*, we must and ought to treat with them on the terms of a foederal union."[460]

Burke's rejection of informal empire in favour of federation had been implicit in his arguments since November 1775. Now, in 1777, his assertion of British right against the united authority of the colonies was a statement of principle made in the face of the fact of American power: the mother country possessed military might but not actual authority, although it maintained its residual claim to sovereign right; the colonists had the consent of the North American population, while feeling challenged by the force of British arms. A federal union was the best that Britain could hope for under the circumstances—asserting its claim of right in the expectation of reclaiming its authority by compacting with the people of America. But as Burke formulated his conception of federation with the colonies, British arms were facing impediments across the Atlantic. Germain had approved plans for dividing the middle and southern colonies from New England by bifurcating the continent with a large army at Albany. This was to be achieved by moving General Burgoyne's forces south from Quebec to gain control of the Hudson valley while General Howe took his forces north, with the aim of supporting Burgoyne. When Howe was diverted to Philadelphia, Burgoyne met with defeat at Saratoga on 13 October 1777. The bad news reached the king late in the evening on 2 December. A heated debate in the Commons took place the following day, with angry exchanges between Burke and Wedderburn bringing them close to a duel.[461] Burgoyne's fate stung Burke with remorse—nothing but the devastation of America could be more "deplorable," he confided to Richard Champion on 7 December.[462]

[458] Notes for Speech on Address, 20 November 1777, WWM BkP 6:63.

[459] EB to Richard Champion, 1 December 1777, *Corr.*, III, p. 405.

[460] EB, Speech on Fox's Motion, 2 December 1777, *W & S*, III, p. 345. David Hartley proposed ending the war and establishing a federation on the basis of American independence on 5 December. See *Parliamentary History*, XIX, cols. 549ff.

[461] EB to Alexander Wedderburn, 3 December 1777, *Corr.*, III, pp. 406–7. See *London Chronicle*, 4–6 December 1777.

[462] EB to Richard Champion, 7 December 1777, *Corr.*, III, p. 409. See also EB on North's responsibility for the fiasco in *Parliamentary History*, XIX, cols., 537–39, and his account of Fox's indictment of military strategy in EB to the Duchess of Devonshire, 20 March 1778, *Corr.*, III, p. 422.

Nonetheless, defeat for the British portended a moment of reckoning. As Burke saw it, this was a highly "critical" moment for public opinion, as well as for the party and for Rockingham himself.[463] In the following months, Burke's colleagues began to support the idea of American independence, with the Chathamites strenuously opposing the very notion.[464] Fox urged the strategy of treating with the colonies while simultaneously broaching the question of independence, although he expected that this would find them divided in their preferences. Burke argued for securing colonial subordination to the extent that this was compatible with their "consent."[465] In practice, this meant recognising that they had an opinion of their own, and that Britain would have to negotiate on the assumption of independence. The Empire of liberty had been fractured, perhaps irreparably ruined.[466] "I conceive that America will never again assent to this country's having actual power within the continent," Rockingham revealed to Chatham early in the new year.[467] On 6 February 1778, France signed a treaty of alliance with the colonies, prompting Richmond to argue for the "independency of America" as the best means of averting impending disaster.[468] A month later, William Meredith moved for a Bill to repeal the Declaratory Act, with Burke lending his support to the measure as a possible means by which the affections of the Americans might be regained.[469] Then, on 10 April, he publicly confirmed his support for independence.[470] Burke had been sceptical about North's plan for conciliation with the colonies, introduced on 23 February. It was nothing but a doomed attempt to bypass parliament in dealing with the Americans, "extending the prerogative" in proportion as the dimensions of the Empire were inadvertently diminished.[471] At the same time, public debts had accumulated, 30 million pounds had been spent, ships had been lost, trade curtailed, and the army increased to a menacing extent.[472] For four successive years, "national honour" had been disgraced.[473]

[463] EB to the Marquess of Rockingham, 16 December 1777, *Corr.*, IX, p. 416,

[464] See, for example, the Earl of Shelburne to the Earl of Chatham, 23 December 1777, *Chatham Correspondence*, IV, p. 480.

[465] Debate on Hartley's Motion Relative to the Expence of the War, *Parliamentary History*, XIX, col. 560.

[466] On the impact of the American war on perceptions of the Empire, see Stephen Conway, *The British Isles and the War of American Independence* (Oxford: Oxford University Press, 2000), ch. 9.

[467] 26 January 1778, *Chatham Correspondence*, IV, p. 491.

[468] The Duke of Richmond to the Marquess of Rockingham, 15 March 1778, *Rockingham Memoirs*, II, pp. 347–48. A draft of his resolution had been corrected by Burke. See the Duke of Richmond to EB, 15 March 1778, *Corr.*, III, pp. 419–20. On 23 March 1778 Richmond moved for an Address requesting the withdrawal of troops, and on 7 April he demanded American independence. See *Parliamentary Register* (Almon), X, pp. 369–70.

[469] EB, Speech on Repeal of Declaratory Act, 6 April 1778, *W & S*, III, p. 374.

[470] EB, Speech on Powys's Motion on American Commission, 10 April 1778, ibid., p. 376.

[471] EB, Speech on North's Conciliatory Bill, 23 February 1778, ibid., p. 368.

[472] EB, Petition for Bristol, February 1778, ibid., p. 370.

[473] EB, Fox's Motion on State of the Troops in America, *General Evening Post*, 12 February 1778.

As Burke explained to parliament at the end of the year, it was "incumbent" on Great Britain to acknowledge independence.[474]

The intervention of France had altered the nature of the game. As Burke later expressed it, "in every American victory" he had glimpsed the germ of the rising naval power of France, and indeed of Spain.[475] Now the Empire was divided, perhaps irretrievably, and the American contingent of the British people "engrafted" on the power of France, casting a shadow of fear over the mother country.[476] But the ferocity of the war itself gave reason enough for a change of course. Burke had repeatedly denounced the use of foreign mercenaries in America, but on 6 February he descanted on the use of Indians against the colonists, the "chef-d'oeuvre" of Burke's orations at this time, as Walpole remarked.[477] Their mode of waging war was brutal in the extreme, with mutilation standing as the most popular token of glory.[478] Burke believed that the use of Indians implied an intention on the administration's part to switch from a war of conquest to one of intimidation and terror. Previous involvement with the savage tribes of the continent was an ineluctable feature of the politics of North America, whereas now alliance with the natives was both unjust and unnecessary. The Indians were a remnant rather than a "people" proper, and there was consequently little need to collaborate with them in peace or war.[479] Burke recalled that Lafitau and Charlevoix had presented extensive evidence of the savagery of the manners of the natives of North America, underscoring the immutable character of their behaviour. In Burke's mind, recourse to Indian allies was of a piece with the incitement of negro slaves such as occurred under Lord Dunmore's proclamation of 7 November 1775: it was a reckless attempt to employ a brutalised people against the Americans to cow them into unconditional submission.[480]

By the end of the session, a peace commission, headed by the Earl of Carlisle, had been dispatched. Leaving in April and returning in November, it was destined for certain failure.[481] Thirteen "democracies" would not readily bend to overtures from the administration, Burke observed. Nothing but a change of "MIND" on the government side could hope to win favour.[482] Chatham had finally gasped his last after a bitter exchange in the Lords on 7 April. North had begun to succumb to doubts about his capacity to lead, although the king was quick to stiffen his resolve. Throughout this time, the opposition turned out substantial minorities against ministerial policy, although negotiations for a new government never made serious

[474] EB, Speech on Army Estimates, 14 December 1778, *W & S*, III, p. 394.

[475] EB, *Speech at Bristol Previous to the Election* (6 September 1780), ibid., p. 629.

[476] Ibid., p. 646.

[477] Walpole, *Last Journals*, II, p. 104.

[478] EB, Speech on Use of Indians, 6 February 1778, *W & S*, III, p. 356.

[479] WWM BkP 27:244, reprinted in EB, Speech on Use of Indians, 6 February 1778, ibid., p. 365.

[480] Ibid., p. 359.

[481] See report on North's Conciliatory Bill, *General Evening Post*, 19 February 1778, for the suggestion from Fox and Burke that the measure was "too late."

[482] EB, Notes on North's Instructions to American Commission, WWM BkP 6:121.

progress.[483] Burke likened national politics to a "stagnated Pool" in which even the residue of a current flowed against the opposition.[484] War strategy now switched from a land campaign to reliance on the navy, yet a military stalemate was not to be broken until 1781. In the new session opening on 26 November 1778, the Rockinghams concentrated their energy on distinguishing the benighted American war from the necessary contest with France. With Spain in prospect of joining in the French campaign, Burke stood aghast at the improvidence of the government.[485] Even so, the Rockinghams did not launch themselves into an assault on American policy until after the Easter recess in 1779. Then, on 29 March, a committee of inquiry into the conduct of the war was established, which sat from 22 April until 30 June. A motion to question Cornwallis on "*general and particular Military matters*" succeeded in reducing the government majority to 181 against 158.[486] The administration were unsettled, and the Rockinghamites were emboldened: "There is a very great desire among almost all our friends to revive the mater," Burke enthused.[487]

But even as the opposition rallied, the government stood firm. Writing to Champion in June, ministers seemed to Burke "so much in Spirits."[488] With a body of refugees as well as loyalists in Maryland and Virginia declaring for the king, sentiment within the administration was lifted.[489] Burke was flabbergasted by this display of unshakeable complacency: a rupture with Spain was by now "absolutely certain," Burke claimed; indeed the breach was announced by North the following day in the House of Commons. It was in effect "a declaration of War," Burke noted in a postscript to Champion on the sixteenth.[490] In parliament on the same day he inveighed against the ministry: "Whenever we have talked of a Spanish war in addition to that of France and America, with what contempt have Ministry heard it?"[491] On 11 June, Burke had insisted that the British lacked "the most distant prospect of success."[492] "Was not the dependency of America already given up," he asked in the Commons on 13 May?[493] But now, with the Spanish supporting the French, the situation was altogether more desperate: the British would have to struggle for survival. The negligence of Lord North justified his impeachment, which Burke called

483 Ritcheson, *British Politics and the American Revolution*, ch. 7.

484 EB to Richard Champion, 9 October 1778, *Corr.*, IV, p. 25.

485 EB to Philip Francis, 24 December 1778, ibid., p. 33.

486 *St. James's Chronicle*, 29 April–1 May.

487 EB to the Marquess of Rockingham, 30 April 1779, *Corr.*, IV, p. 65.

488 EB to Richard Champion, 15 June 1779, ibid., p. 89.

489 On the ministerial hope that loyalism would rally and deliver a British victory, see P. J. Marshall, *The Making and Unmaking of Empires: Britain, India, and America c.1750–1783* (Oxford: Oxford University Press, 2005), pp. 357–58.

490 EB to Richard Champion, 16 June 1779, *Corr.*, IV, p. 91.

491 EB, Speech on Breach with Spain, 16 June 1779, *W & S*, III, p. 446.

492 EB, Meredith's Motion for Peace with America, *Gazetteer*, 15 June 1779.

493 EB, *Parliamentary History*, XX, col. 758.

for in his intervention on 16 June.[494] By the following autumn, it seemed salvation could be found in nothing less than a "total" failure of British policy.[495] In the King's Speech opening the session on 1 November 1780, British successes in Georgia and Carolina were highlighted against the background of the grave threat posed by the monarchies of France and Spain.[496] But, ironically, it was at this time that the crown forces came under pressure in the southern theatre of the war. After suffering severe losses in the Battle of Guilford Courthouse on 15 March 1781, Cornwallis retreated to Wilmington, North Carolina, and then to Virginia. The climax of the conflict was drawing near.[497]

On 30 May 1781, Hartley moved for peace with America, stirring Burke to belittle the government's current strategy of unleashing disaffected loyalists against triumphant rebel arms.[498] On 12 June, in possession of an admission from Cornwallis that America could not be conquered, Fox repeated Hartley's call for peace. Recalling an analogy of Benjamin Franklin's, he likened the current conflict to a bloody crusade with ministers professing the goal of liberating the colonies while actually threatening them with brutal subjugation.[499] As the American General Nathanial Greene was left free to roam the Carolinas and Georgia, Burke sensed the rebels were gaining an advantage. It looked as though the war was "in swift decay," he wrote to Portland.[500] Cornwallis, having been reinforced from the north, fortified himself with access to the coast at Yorktown in Virginia. On 5 September, the French secured a naval victory against Admiral Graves in Chesapeake Bay, cutting off both a supply route and a means of escape for Cornwallis's men. After a siege, and successive bombardments, the British surrendered on 19 October 1781. On 22 February 1782, Conway moved an Address for an end to the war, losing by a single vote but securing victory in a repeat performance five days later. Burke wrote in tones of jubilation to Benjamin Franklin the following day: "I trust it will lead to a speedy peace between the two branches of the English nation, perhaps to a general peace."[501]

Burke sketched out how he envisaged a rapprochement between the combatants in a memorandum that he composed in the middle of March 1782. Independence was a fact, but this did not rule out re-establishing formal political ties. The Americans, he thought, might be brought to recognise the king. Also, the Act of Navigation might be resuscitated and reformed.[502] As Burke pondered the possibilities for re-engagement with America, Lord North set about tendering his resignation. In

[494] EB, Speech on Breach with Spain, 16 June 1779, *W & S*, III, p. 447. He even drafted articles to that effect: see EB, Articles of Impeachment, Autumn 1779, ibid., pp. 454–63.

[495] EB to the Marquess of Rockingham, 16 October 1779, *Corr.*, IV, p. 155.

[496] *Parliamentary History*, XXI, col. 809.

[497] Piers Mackesy, *The War for America, 1775–1783* (Lincoln, NE: University of Nebraska Press, 1964, 1993), ch. 23.

[498] *Parliamentary History*, XXII, cols. 354–56.

[499] Ibid., cols. 514–15.

[500] EB to the Duke of Portland, ante 24 October 1781, *Corr.*, IV, p. 380.

[501] Ibid., p. 419.

[502] WWM BkP 27:219.

April the Commons finally voted to end the war. Between the earliest peace overtures and the achievement of an agreement, the Rockinghams entered government but then swiftly fell from power. The treaty was therefore negotiated by a ministry headed by Shelburne. Burke thought the terms on offer derisory from a British perspective, with little to offset the generous concessions to the former colonies.[503] There now existed "a *new State* of a new species in a *new* part of the Earth," and both Britain and the other European powers would have to come to terms.[504] The Treaty of Paris was concluded on 3 September 1783.[505] Criticising the peace proposals in the Commons the previous February, Burke complained about how much the government was prepared to relinquish. Huge tracts of territory had been ceded across the Atlantic, with little reciprocation from the Americans; France and Spain had been rewarded; the plight of the loyalists was galling.[506] The following month, when trade with America was being negotiated, Burke counselled against constructing a system of jealous regulation.[507] The fundamental goal of the British should be to secure an interest in the new regime and to reconnoitre their position with regard to their old enemies. "A great Revolution has happened," Burke contended.[508] Britain should stabilise its position in the new order. It was still bracing to think that the current situation had it origins in an empty dispute.

As Burke put it in a letter three years before the Peace of Paris, half an empire had been lost on account of "one idle quarrel."[509] The experience had been aggravating, but also deflating in the extreme. After Yorktown, Burke wrote to Franklin claiming that although he had always been free of personal exultation, nonetheless he used to rejoice in feelings of national power: the Empire had filled him with a sense of public pride.[510] However now, he admitted, "all the props of my pride are slipped from under me."[511] This feeling for the honour and dignity of the metropole had been founded on its role as patron of an Atlantic community of Britons. Accordingly, Burke thought, the authority of the seat of empire should be based on its disposition to act as a benefactor, disseminating justice in that capacity. What then was the "idle quarrel" that had torn the Empire asunder? It was the "rage for equality," Burke

[503] *Morning Chronicle*, 27 February 1783.

[504] WWM BkP 6:165.

[505] For the peace negotiations, see P. J. Marshall, *Remaking the British Atlantic: The United States and the British Empire after American Independence* (Oxford: Oxford University Press, 2012), pp. 34–54.

[506] EB, Debate on Preliminary Articles of Peace, 17 February 1783, *Parliamentary History*, XXIII, cols. 466ff.

[507] EB, Debate on American Intercourse Bill, 7 March 1783, ibid., cols. 611–14.

[508] WWM BkP 6:165.

[509] EB to Job Watts, 10 August 1780, *Corr.*, IV, p. 261. Cf. EB, Speech on Trade Concessions to Ireland, 6 December 1779, *W &S*, IX, p. 542: "It was our metaphysical quarrel about mere words, that had caused the American war."

[510] EB to Benjamin Franklin, post 20 December 1781, *Corr.*, IV, p. 396.

[511] Ibid.

believed, which kindled the war in America.[512] He later identified this syndrome in terms of "the unhappy phantom of a compulsory *equal taxation*."[513] This represented a violation of the "fair equality" that the colonists had been seeking. Burke's distinction had its roots in classical theories of justice: distribution could be deemed fair if it accorded with differential merit, whereas undifferentiated equality applied in every case delivered unequal justice.[514] Undifferentiated equality had to be forced on unequal circumstances, drawing on resources of rage for its implementation. A rage for equal subjection under the rubric of "*equal taxation*" had unleashed a spirit of domination.

Moreover, it was the same commitment to the "doctrine of equality" that had facilitated the government in protracting the conflict. It was a commitment born of "Knavery" and sustained by "Envy" and "Malice," preaching that since all are equal, all must be equally corrupt—both ministry and opposition alike.[515] On this basis, although the public came to despise the conduct of the government, they saw no reason to draw upon the resources of their opponents. This protected the administration from fearing the judgment of public opinion, condemning Britain to a tragic fate for lacking "moderation."[516] Interestingly, after 1774, Burke refused to ascribe a similar "rage for equality" to the Americans, although it was the "equal" rights of man that would later form the basis of his indictment of Revolutionary France.[517] Originally, he had been acutely conscious of republican zeal and democratic manners among the Americans. Insurgent ambition, it must have seemed, was a product of these attitudes. But after publicising conciliation as the cornerstone of Rockinghamite policy in March 1775, it became appropriate politically to accommodate rather than condemn existing tendencies in the colonies. In the aftermath of 1789, Burke's point was that American goals could be practically and morally accommodated.[518] The French Revolution, by comparison, was an abomination. The cases of France

[512] EB to John Bourke, November 1777, ibid., III, p. 403.

[513] EB to Samuel Span, 23 April 1778, ibid., p. 433.

[514] The *locus classicus* for the distinction can be found in Aristotle, *Nicomachean Ethics*, book V, though the distinction had been formulated earlier in Plato, *Gorgias*, 508a1–9, in terms of mathematical and geometrical proportionality.

[515] EB to Richard Champion, 9 October 1778, *Corr.*, IV, p. 25.

[516] EB to the Duke of Portland, 25 May 1782, ibid., p. 455.

[517] For a comparison of Burke on American and France, see J.C.D. Clark, "Burke's Reflections on the Revolution in America (1777): OR, How Did the American Revolution Relate to the French?" in Crowe ed., *An Imaginative Whig*. For France and America in the period generally, see Jacques Godechot, *La grande nation: l'expansion revolutionaire de la France dans le monde de 1789 à 1799* (Paris: Aubier, 1983), ch. 1; Robert R. Palmer, *The Age of Democratic Revolution* (Princeton, NJ: Princeton University Press, 1959–64), 2 vols. See also Gordon S. Wood, *The Radicalism of the American Revolution* (New York: Vintage, 1991), p. 231, concerning the "myth that the American Revolution was sober and conservative while the French Revolution was chaotic and radical."

[518] EB, *Appeal from the New to the Old Whigs*, p. 38: "He considered the Americans as standing at that time . . . in the same relation to England, as England did to king James the Second, in 1688."

and America were not "upon a Par," he insisted in 1797 when writing about French affairs.[519] In an exchange with Richard Price in January 1789, Thomas Jefferson contended that it was the American Revolution that had first prepared the ground for launching the French.[520] The following March, Price informed John Adams that it was the American war that had first released the "spirit" that was evidently "working its way thro' Europe."[521] In general, both revolutions were identified in the minds of Burke's detractors, although they remained radically separate in his own. "That an avowed friend of the American revolution should be an enemy of the French," wrote Joseph Priestley in 1791, "is to me unaccountable."[522] For Burke, however, it was essential to distinguish the two events if one was to understand the causes and consequences of each.

[519] EB to William Windham, 12 February 1797, *Corr.*, IX, p. 241. Cf. EB, Debate on Fox's Motion to Send a Minister to Paris, 15 December 1792, *Diary*, 17 December 1792: "Mr. Burke spoke of the differences between the crimes of Paine and Franklin, and said, that it was [as] wide as the difference between the insurrection of France and America."

[520] Thomas Jefferson to Richard Price, 8 January 1789, *The Papers of Thomas Jefferson*, ed. Julian F. Boyd (Princeton, NJ: Princeton University Press, 1950–), 40 vols. to date, XIV, pp. 420–24.

[521] Richard Price to John Adams, 5 March 1789, *The Correspondence of Richard Price*, ed. W. B. Peach and D. O. Thomas (Durham, NC: Duke University Press, 1994), 3 vols., III, p. 208.

[522] Joseph Priestley, *Letters to the Right Honourable Edmund Burke* (Birmingham: 1791), p. iv. Cf. Charles Pigot, *Strictures on the New Political Tenets of the Rt. Hon. Edmund Burke* (London: 1791), p. 21.

X

A DREADFUL STATE OF THINGS

MADRAS AND BENGAL, 1777–1785

10.1 Introduction

As Burke pondered the implications of a formal pact with the American colonies that might help bring to an end two years of angry warfare, the affairs of India were unexpectedly thrust onto the parliamentary agenda. It was in the aftermath of the violent deposition of Lord Pigot from his position as Governor of Madras in August 1776 that Burke's attention was newly focused on the transactions of the subcontinent. For two years from the spring of 1777 he concerned himself in particular with developments in the south. This culminated in the joint publication with William Burke of the *Policy of Making Conquests for the Mahometans* in the summer of 1779.[1] The *Policy* sought to expose the implication of East India Company servants in the depredations perpetrated by the Nawab of Arcot in the Carnatic region of southern India. The Nawab had undertaken a series of conquests with the aid of loans drawn on prominent Company officials. Since his success was a precondition for repayment of the debts, prominent servants were determined to facilitate his exploits. As the Nawab, Muhammad Ali, pushed south towards the cape in an effort to absorb competing dynasties, he set his sights on the fertile terrain of the Kingdom of Tanjore. In supporting this venture, wayward elements within the Company in effect subverted official policy. British power and resources were put at the disposal of an upstart usurper, committing the Company to the pursuit of empire by proxy. The Nawab's project of aggrandisement by the sword seemed to Burke a typical instance of despotic usurpation of a kind that had long been associated with the proclivities of "oriental" power. In the face of this ruthless bid for expropriation and oppression, Burke proposed that the might of the British should be put in the service of current possession by defending existing territorial boundaries in the Deccan. In this way, the ancient Indian constitution could be secured against the ferocity of "Mahometan" conquest.

[1] *Public Advertiser*, 22 June 1779.

Burke's understanding of the affairs of the subcontinent drew on British historical writing that began to appear in the 1760s. Commentators from Robert Orme to Alexander Dow had cast doubt on the highly schematised perspectives that survived down to Montesquieu from the Jesuit literature of the late seventeenth century. It emerged from British observers that the brutality of regional commanders like the Nawab of Arcot was a symptom of the disintegration of Mughal authority between 1707 and 1740. At the same time, it was commonly understood that this relatively recent eruption of marauding expansionism violated primordial Hindu rights that had survived the various waves of Islamic inundation since the twelfth century. What increasingly disturbed Burke after 1779 was the suggestion that the greatest threat to the established principalities and property in India was less the recidivist barbarism of opportunists like the Nawab of Arcot than the paramount power of British arms in both Madras and Bengal. With the American war consuming the energy of parliament in 1780 as the reform movement was mobilised in the counties of England and the manpower of the Volunteers in Ireland grew, Burke's focus on the subcontinent turned from the south back to the north. Controversy over the judgments produced by the Supreme Court of Judicature in Bengal prompted Burke to consider the limits of enlightened judicial procedure in the face of customary opinion in South Asia. Disputes over the remit of British laws led to the establishment of a Select Committee on Indian affairs, on which Burke played a major role between 1781 and 1783. At the same time, in response to the military campaigns of Haidar Ali in the Carnatic, a Secret Committee was set up under the chairmanship of Henry Dundas. India was now at the forefront of British parliamentary concerns. Above all others, Burke applied himself to probing the pathologies of the subcontinent.

Burke authored the most acute reports that were published by the Select Committee. By the time that the ninth and eleventh reports appeared between June and November 1783, delivering penetrating analysis of the political and commercial deformations of the Company, Burke occupied the position of paymaster of the forces under the Fox–North coalition. The government soon committed itself to introducing measures for the reform of the East India Company. Responsibility for the administration of British territories in Asia was to be invested in a commission to be staffed by members of parliament. The Company, in other words, was to be externally regulated. At the same time, patronage and oversight were to be separated from the court. When the Bill failed, and the government fell, Burke's outrage over the treatment of Indians only increased. The management of South Asia had been committed to a corporation for which the welfare of its subjects was a practical irrelevance. The objective of the Company was not good governance but corporate profit. Remarkably, the profit it sought was political rather than strictly commercial in nature. When Burke returned to consider Madras in 1785 in the aftermath of the devastation visited on the Carnatic by Haidar Ali, he remained astounded by the indifference of British officials in the region. As famine threatened and the reservoirs stood battered, the Company fixated on its debts rather than the prosperity of the population. Devoted now to exposing an entrenched system of exploitation, Burke began to train his sights on the contribution of Warren Hastings, back in Britain after a decade as Governor General of India.

10.2 Lord Pigot, the Nawab of Arcot and the Raja of Tanjore

In 1784, in the third edition of the *Wealth of Nations*, Adam Smith commented on how the Regulating Act of 1773 had failed to put an end to mismanagement in the government of India. Despite having at one time swelled the treasury at Calcutta and extended its sway over a vast accession of territory, the East India Company had gradually "wasted and destroyed" its acquisitions.[2] In fact, Smith believed, the political and financial reforms of the 1760s and 1770s had most likely caused a bad situation to deteriorate still further: if the mercantile community had been remarkable for its fundamental indifference to the plight of its subjects prior to the intervention of Westminster, government measures such as reducing the size of the Company's dividend, together with its share in its profits, were hardly calculated to induce a sense of paternal responsibility.[3] Eighteen years had passed since the Company was first subjected to a parliamentary inquiry, yet it was now facing the possibility of bankruptcy. All plans for redeeming British fortunes in the east inclined Smith towards one particular conclusion: namely, that the Company was "unfit" to govern its territorial possessions.[4] Back in 1776, in the first edition of the *Wealth of Nations*, he had already underlined the difference between the form of government under which the North American colonies had prospered and that by which Bengal had been devastated: the spirit and the letter of the laws in both jurisdictions had to be radically distinguished.[5] At this time, Burke was similarly convinced that the Regulating Act held out no hope of improving the administration of the subcontinent, although—unlike Smith—he believed that the Company could in principle be formed into a government of laws.[6] In the years that followed, Burke's confidence

[2] Adam Smith, *An Inquiry into the Nature and Causes of the Wealth of Nations*, ed. R. H. Campbell and A. S. Skinner (Indianapolis, IN: Liberty Fund, 1976), 2 vols., II, p. 753. For an examination of Smith's position, see Robert Travers, "British India as a Problem in Political Economy: Comparing James Steuart and Adam Smith" in Duncan Kelly ed., *Lineages of Empire: The Historical Roots of British Imperial Thought* (Oxford: Oxford University Press, 2009).

[3] Smith, *Wealth of Nations*, II, pp. 752–53.

[4] Ibid., p. 753. On the addition of a new "exposition of the Absurdity and hurtfulness of almost all our chartered trading companies" to the third edition of the *Wealth of Nations*, see Smith, Letter to William Strahan, 22 May 1783, *The Correspondence of Adam Smith*, ed. Ernest Campbell Mossner and Ian Simpson Ross (Indianapolis, IN: Liberty Fund, 1977, 1987), p. 266.

[5] Smith, *Wealth of Nations*, I, p. 91.

[6] *The Wealth of Nations* was reviewed in *The Annual Register for the Year 1776* (London: 1777), but it is a perfunctory review, and its authorship is uncertain. For Burke's admiration for Smith's *Wealth of Nations*, see Dugald Stewart's record of a conversation with Burke to be found in the Burke/Stewart Correspondence at the Centre for Research Collections, Edinburgh University Library, Dc. 6. 111: "Memoir Written on a Visit to Lord Lauderdale with Mr Burke and Adam Smith" (1784). For commentary on Burke's relationship to Smith, including their intellectual connections, see Bisset, *The Life of Edmund*

in this prospect sharply declined: he remained determined that East India affairs should be kept out of the clutches of the court, yet he also became convinced that the depredations of the Company were traceable to what Smith termed "irresistible moral causes" intrinsic to the way in which mercantile administration on the subcontinent was governed by the Directors in London.[7]

This did not mark, as is usually argued, a comprehensively new departure in Burke's assessment of the problems of India.[8] However, it did represent a new realisation of the depth of the Company's iniquity. The origins of this realisation can be traced to Burke's deepening concern with developments in southern India. On 9 June 1777 he dashed off a note to Lord Rockingham reminding him to prepare a letter to be delivered in person by William Burke to Lord Pigot, "the shortlived Governour of Madras."[9] William had been actively seeking an opening in India since March 1776 as a means of recovering his financial situation, ruined by the crash in East India stock in 1769.[10] Having lost his parliamentary seat in 1774, William was exposed to the demands of his creditors and therefore seized the opportunity to act as a messenger for the Court of Directors in London carrying orders to Madras.[11]

Burke (London: 2nd ed., 1800), 2 vols., II, p. 429; Jacob Viner, *Guide to John Rae's Life of Adam Smith* (New York: A. M. Kelly, 1965), pp. 23–33; James Conniff, "Burke on Political Economy: The Nature and Extent of State Authority," *Review of Politics*, 49:4 (Autumn 1987), pp. 490–514; Donald Winch, *Riches and Poverty*, part II. None of these works discusses their shared interest in the East India Company. Carl B. Cone, *Burke and the Nature of Politics: The Age of the American Revolution* (Lexington, KY: University of Kentucky Press, 1957), p. 326 and *Burke and the Nature of Politics: The Age of the French Revolution* (Lexington, KY: University of Kentucky Press, 1964), pp. 490–91, denies any significant overlap in their ideas.

[7] Smith, *Wealth of Nations*, II, p.752. Burke's detailed views on the failure of the 1773 Act are given in EB, *Ninth Report of the Select Committee* (25 June 1783), *W & S*, V, pp. 198–222. The Select Committee had been established to inquire into the conduct of the Supreme Court of Judicature in Bengal. Smith's indictment of trading corporations is outlined in A. W. Coats, "Adam Smith and the Mercantile System" in A. S. Skinner and Thomas Wilson eds., *Essays on Adam Smith* (Oxford: Oxford University Press, 1975). For a fuller treatment, see Sankar Muthu, "Adam Smith's Critique of International Trading Corporations: Theorizing 'Globalization' in the Age of Enlightenment," *Political Theory*, 36:2 (April 2008), pp. 185–212. See also Emma Rothschild, "Adam Smith in the British Empire" in Sankar Muthu ed., *Empire and Modern Political Thought* (Cambridge: Cambridge University Press, 2012).

[8] Conor Cruise O'Brien, *The Great Melody: A Thematic Biography and Commented Anthology of Edmund Burke* (London: Sinclair-Stevenson, 1992), p. 257; Frederick Whelan, *Edmund Burke and India: Political Morality and Empire* (Pittsburgh, PA: University of Pittsburgh Press, 1996), p. 44. See also F. P. Lock, *Edmund Burke: 1730–1797* (Oxford: Clarendon Press, 1998–2006), 2 vols., II, p. 35, construing EB to Lord Macartney, 15 October 1781, *Corr.*, X, p. 11, as a reversal of Burke's opposition to the Regulating Act of 1773. In fact, the grounds of Burke's criticism remain constant, and are implicit in Fox's India Bill of 1783: in his letter to Macartney, he was merely accepting the 1781 Regulating Act as effectively a renewal and amplification of the 1773 Act but by which ministerial power was at least rendered more visible.

[9] EB to the Marquess of Rockingham, 9 June 1777, *Corr.*, III, p. 347.

[10] AAC, IOR/J/1/9, fols. 232–3, a "Memorial" of William Burke to the Court of Directors from 29 November 1776, offering his services as "Secretary, or in any other Capacity where [he] may be of most Use."

[11] AAC, IOR, Court Minutes, B/93, pp. 145–46.

Rockingham hoped that he might in the process liaise with Governor Pigot.[12] Pigot had been imprisoned on the Coromandel coast by a conspiracy of Company troops together with a majority of members on the Madras Council on 26 August 1776 as a consequence of his support for the Raja of Tanjore, Tuljaji, in his ongoing dispute with the Nawab of the Carnatic, Muhammad Ali Khan Wallajah, based at Arcot.[13] Pigot had been an associate of the Rockinghams since 1766 along with his brother, Admiral Hugh Pigot. When news of the coup in the Carnatic reached London in the early spring of 1777, Lady Rockingham helped concert a campaign to secure the Governor's reinstatement by the Court of Proprietors.[14] By 2 April Burke was writing of his pleasure at Pigot's "triumphant success" in the ballot of 31 March.[15] In due course it was decided that both Pigot and his Council should be recalled to London, but by the time that William Burke reached Madras via Suez in August, Pigot had already died in captivity on St. Thomas's Mount.[16]

This outcome fanned the controversy that already surrounded Pigot's governorship. He had led, according to one critic, a "violent and despotic" administration in southern India, motivated by an "inordinate love of wealth and power."[17] But Pigot's supporters were no less committed to redeeming his reputation than his detractors were determined to expose his failings.[18] For Pigot's supporters, the abandonment of India to avidity and corruption had rendered it a "theatre of oppression, stratagems, slavery, and assassination."[19] The fate of Pigot exemplified this descent into lawlessness. In response to Lord North's decision to have a new Governor and Council appointed in Madras, George Johnstone introduced a series of resolutions in the House of Commons calling for the reinstatement of Pigot and the dismissal of his opponents as a prelude to a planned motion for a Bill aimed at "the better securing our settlements in the East Indies."[20] Burke spoke in the debate of 21 May 1777, endorsing Johnstone's resolutions in support of the Rockinghamite line: it was absurd to punish the victim of a rebellion within the Presidency on the grounds, as

[12] The Marquess of Rockingham to EB, 9 June 1777, *Corr.*, III, p. 347.

[13] For the emergence of the Carnatic out of the remnants of Mughal imperial organisation in the south, see J. F. Richards, "The Hyderabad Karnatik, 1687–1707," *Modern Asian Studies*, 9:2 (1975), pp. 241–60.

[14] EB to Lady Rockingham, 28 March 1777, *Corr.*, IX, p. 414.

[15] Ibid., p. 415

[16] AAC, IOR/E/4/867, fol. 237, for the appointment of a "Temporary Government" to replace Pigot.

[17] [Anon.] *An Inquiry into the Conduct of Lord Pigot, from his Arrival at Fort St. George, to his Expedition to Tanjore* (London: 1778), Preface.

[18] See, for example, Alexander Dalrymple, *The Very Extraordinary Revolution which Happened in the Fort St. George* (London: 1777).

[19] [Anon.], *An Impartial View of the Origin and Progress of the Present Disputes in the East India Company, Relative to Mahomed-Ally Khan, Nabob of Arcot, and Tulja-gee, Raja of Tanjore* (Edinburgh: 1777), p. 5.

[20] Debate on the Affairs of the East India Company, 21 May 1777, *Parliamentary History*, XIX, col. 276.

was being alleged, that faction was pervasive at Fort St. George. This was a recipe for promoting the Nawab of Arcot to mastery over the Company in the Deccan since "this same Prince" had grown expert in fomenting divisions to serve his interests.[21] Those within the ranks of the government who were by their own admission anxious to discountenance rebellion in America "might have been supposed an equal enemy to it in the East," Fox observed.[22] Burke shared the sentiment: "They are not satisfied with a rebellion in the West. They must have one in the East."[23] A general recall was tantamount to condoning insubordination, a move that would threaten the position of the Company in Asia. As John Lind claimed in a pamphlet attacking the enemies of Pigot, the fate of the Company depended on a resolution of the Madras imbroglio, which would ultimately determine "the stability of our public credit."[24]

In the surviving draft notes for a planned speech on Johnstone's resolutions, Burke similarly pointed to the size of the looming crisis. If due subordination was not restored in southern India, the position of the British on the subcontinent could be at risk. To concede to the wishes of Pigot's enemies in the Madras Presidency was to submit to the designs of Muhammad Ali: having employed East India troops to extend his hold over the south-east, he was indebted to Company servants for the cost of this military support. In practice, this made his creditors dependent on maintaining his position to facilitate repayment, tying them to an alliance whose terms they were not free to dictate.[25] Specifically, this meant that the Company was not at liberty to offend the Nawab, forever bending policy to fit his purposes. As far as Burke was concerned, the Council at Bengal had conceded as much in ratifying the actions of the insurgent Council at Madras: they complained, he noted, that "the Nabob had taken offence at the conduct of Lord Pigot."[26] Burke derived this information from the printed version of a letter encapsulating the response of the Bengal Council to events in Madras. Since the Madras Presidency had been subordinated to the authority of Bengal under the terms of North's Regulating Act, Warren Hastings, as Governor General, was empowered to call Lord Pigot to account for alienating, as his letter put it, "the mind of the Nabob."[27] This reprimand, however, was in contravention of Company instructions, and implied that the Nawab should determine British policy in the region. It also assumed that the role of the government in London was to ratify whatever measures might keep the Nawab sweet. Should the

[21] *Morning Post,* 26 May 1777; cf. *Parliamentary Register* (Almon), VII, p. 231.

[22] *Morning Post,* 26 May 1777.

[23] EB, Speech on Restoring Lord Pigot, 22 May 1777, *W & S*, V, p. 40.

[24] John Lind, *Defence of Lord Pigot* (London: 1777), p. 2.

[25] J. D. Gurney, "The Debts of the Nawab of Arcot, 1763–1776" (PhD thesis, University of Oxford, 1967).

[26] EB, Speech on Restoring Lord Pigot, 22 May 1777, *W & S*, V, pp. 38–39. For Hastings's approval of the measure, see his letter to George Stratton, 18 Sept. 1776, Add. MS. 29137, fol. 338.

[27] *Copy of a Letter from the Governor-General and Council, to George Lord Pigot, President &c. of the Council at Fort St. George* (London: 1776), p. 1.

ministry now resolve to punish Pigot and appoint new officials to Fort St. George, the Nawab of Arcot would have his designs confirmed by the British government, in effect placing him in possession "of Half your Empire in India."[28] This was an unnerving, indeed an alarming prospect: if Muhammad Ali switched allegiance to support the ambitions of the French, the British might be facing extinction on the subcontinent.[29]

Lord Pigot had been sent out to restore the position of the Company on the Coromandel coast to the condition it had occupied at the end of his first stint as Governor in 1763. Upon his return in December 1775, the power of Nawab Muhammad Ali had been enhanced in the region: having originally sought to consolidate a durable dynastic state for himself in the territory south of the river Kistna to Trichinopoly, the Nawab had then pushed further south towards Cape Comorin, harassing Hindu Maravar states like Ramnad and Sivaganga, and attacking tributary princes in Tinnevelly along with the Poligars of Tamilnadu.[30] Tanjore, the wealthiest and most fertile area along the coast, was the most attractive potential prize and, in 1773, the principality was duly annexed and bestowed upon the Nawab's younger son.[31] The Directors in Leadenhall Street charged Pigot with reversing this situation. As *The Annual Register* subsequently interpreted their policy, restoring the Raja would "conciliate the minds of the Gentoos," apprehensive at the extension of Muslim power at their expense. This gesture was in turn likely to placate the Hindu Marathas, a "powerful and warlike people". If the Marathas were provoked into revolting from the British interest in India, the French might seek an alliance with a confederation of Hindus against their enemies.[32] From this perspective, the defence of Tanjore had become a British reason of state. Accordingly, the supporters of the Raja were disposed to highlight the legitimacy of his rule by comparison with the instability of the Mughal interest in the region exemplified by Nawabs who were "appointed during pleasure."[33] The advocates of this thesis could draw support for their position from Orme's *History of Military Transactions in Indostan*, which described the territory of the Deccan as divided between those parts governed "by Mahommedans," whom Europeans "improperly call Moors," and those that remained under their "original princes or Rajahs."[34] As Orme saw it, with the disintegration of Mu-

[28] EB, Speech on Restoring Lord Pigot, 22 May 1777, *W & S*, V, p. 38. See the "History of Europe" in *The Annual Register for the Year 1781* (London: 1782), p. 176 for the comment that Indian Princes had become "the authors of cabals, and the leaders of parties, in the capital of Great Britain."

[29] EB, Speech on Restoring Lord Pigot, 22 May 1777, *W & S*, V, p. 39.

[30] Jim Phillips, "A Successor to the Moguls: The Nawab of the Carnatic and the East India Company, 1763–1785," *International History Review*, 7:3 (August 1985), pp. 364–89, esp. p. 368; K. Rajayyan, *The Rise and Fall of the Poligars of Tamilnadu* (Madras: University of Madras Press, 1974).

[31] K. Rajayyan, *A History of British Diplomacy in Tanjore* (Mysore: Rao and Raghavan, 1969).

[32] "The Chronicle" in *The Annual Register for the Year 1777* (London: 1778), p. 253.

[33] Ibid., p. 252.

[34] Robert Orme, *A History of the Military Transactions of the British Nation in Indostan, from the year 1745, to which is Prefixed a Dissertation on the Establishments Made by Mahomedan Conquerors in Indostan* (London: 1763–78), 2 vols., I, pp. 35–36.

ghal authority after the death of Aurangzeb, Muslim rulers in the south increasingly acquired their positions by intrigue, without the support of either the Emperor or his Subahdar: they were dissident dependants on rebellious overlords.[35] The father of Tuljaji, by comparison, had acquired his throne "by the general concurrence of the principal men in the kingdom."[36] This placed him, Lind later claimed, in much the same position as William III in England.[37]

When Pigot arrived with instructions to repair the damage inaugurated by the Nawab's "reduction of Tanjore," he found himself opposed by a majority on the Madras Council.[38] Feelings were running high, with powerful members of the British settlement facing potential ruin if Muhammad Ali were to be deprived of the revenues of Tanjore, an essential resource for servicing his debt repayments to Company officials.[39] The spirited Pigot opted for drastic action, suspending George Stratton and Henry Brooke from the Council, thereby giving himself a bare majority to carry out the instructions of the Court of Directors regarding the situation in Tanjore. Did Pigot have the authority to subvert the Council's determination? The defendants at the Coroner's inquest into the death of Pigot insisted that he did not, underlining the irregularity and arrogance of his behaviour.[40] For his part, Burke was prepared to grant that Pigot's approach had been out of the ordinary, although he noted that the actions of his antagonists had been more extreme.[41] Based on their own evidence, these antagonists had resorted to violent measures to put a stop to an irregularity committed in the service of Company policy: "They are," Burke pointed out, "as irregular as he is."[42] This, however, was rhetorical understatement: as Burke went on to make plain, he regarded what Pigot had described as the "late

[35] For more recent analysis, see Susan Bayly, *Saints, Goddesses and Kings: Muslims and Christians in South Indian Society, 1700–1900* (Cambridge: Cambridge University Press, 1989), ch. 4.

[36] Ibid., p. 112.

[37] Lind, *Defence of Lord Pigot*, p. 4.

[38] The phrase is from the instructions to Pigot contained in a Letter from the Court of Directors to Fort St. George, 12 April 1775, reproduced in *Copies of Papers Relative to the Restoration of the King of Tanjore, the Arrest of the Right Hon. George Lord Pigot, and the Removal of his Lordship from the Government of Fort St. George* (London: 1777), 2 vols., I, p. 1.

[39] The key treatments are Gurney, "Debts of the Nawab of Arcot"; Jim Phillips, "The Development of British Authority in Southern India: The Nawab of Arcot, the East India Company, and the British Government, 1775–1785" (PhD thesis, Dalhousie University, 1983).

[40] *Defences of George Stratton, Esq., and the Majority of the Council at Madras, in Answer to the Accusation of Murder Brought against them for the Supposed Murder of Lord Pigot* (London: 1778), *passim*.

[41] EB, Speech on Restoring Lord Pigot, 22 May 1777, *W & S*, V, p. 38. Pigot's defence of his actions during this episode were published as *Lord Pigot's Narrative of the Late Revolution in the Government of Madras, 11 September 1776* (London: 1777).

[42] EB, Speech on Restoring Lord Pigot, 22 May 1777, *W & S*, V, p. 38. The conduct of Pigot had been retailed by his opponents in *The Following Facts are Taken from the Consultations of the Presidency of Fort St. George, and Lord Pigot's Letters to the Court of Directors* (London: 1777).

very extraordinary revolution" in Madras as posing a threat to the very edifice of British government in the East Indies.[43]

The East India Company's management of its territories on the subcontinent was dependent in the last instance on a system of military government. Adam Smith contended that any system of mercantile administration was inevitably "military and despotic" in character.[44] A council of merchants could never generate popular support based on civilian respect for its perceived authority. Being therefore incapable of naturally inspiring a population with awe, the Presidency fell back on "force" as the final means of commanding obedience.[45] For Burke, since the establishment of the Company was based on conquest rather than popular consent, its legitimacy could only be justified in terms of the security of the subject. Under these circumstances, the obedience of its officers could alone ensure "the freedom of the people."[46] This freedom naturally fell short of a comprehensive plan of liberty: true liberty blended security with the assent of the population embodied in representative institutions. It had not "yet" been possible, Burke explained, to introduce a system of constitutional freedom underpinned by Whig principles into the government of the east. But it would be a fatal error, he went on, to sacrifice the only arrangements that could make a system of rule unaccountable to the population over which it exercised authority "*tolerable*."[47] What made unaccountable authority bearable was the protection it could still offer to the *salus populi* in the form of individual freedom.

The freedom that Burke had in mind here was clearly not public freedom exercised through popular restraint on institutionalised power, but rather freedom from arbitrary harm and the security of private property. These liberties could find protection under unaccountable government on two conditions: first, where a military government in-the-last-instance was moderated by its exercise through a civil arm; and second, where the due subordination of offices, including the routine subjection of the army to the civil administration, was rigorously observed. The revolt against Pigot, however, had subverted the subordination of offices and tipped the balance in favour of the military against civilian government. This cast doubt upon the viability of British control over its territories on the subcontinent by questioning "whether the *subordinate* was to depose the *superior*," whether the military was to "mount over" the civil power, and whether a "*foreign* prince" in the guise of the Nawab of Arcot was to impose himself on Britain's "*Domestick* Councils."[48]

As was the case with contemporary America, the situation in Madras raised the question of the legitimacy of rebellion, an issue that had engaged Burke's attention throughout the American crisis, and one that was to return to haunt him after 1789.

[43] The phrase appears in Pigot's *Letter to the Court of Directors* (London: 1777), p. 1, originally sent on 15 October 1776.

[44] Smith, *Wealth of Nations*, II, p. 638.

[45] Ibid.

[46] EB, Speech on Restoring Lord Pigot, 22 May 1777, *W & S*, V, p. 39.

[47] Ibid.

[48] Ibid.

A resort to arms for the redress of grievances, Burke now contended, "*may* be right" where a form of government of popular origin had ceased to answer to the purposes for which it was instituted.[49] This was government from the bottom up, based on the principle of consent or public utility, under which the ruled expected to call their rulers to account by a regulated yet effective process. But government from the top down, based on the principle of pure subjection, was destroyed by official insubordination: rebellion in this case subverted the rights of government altogether by attacking the very principle on which it was founded.[50] On the basis of his knowledge of the recent rebellion in Madras, it now seemed to Burke that the administration of distant provinces under the auspices of absolute government brought with it two distinct difficulties. First, as we have just seen, there was the problem of maintaining orderly subjection. The revolt against due subordination by the opponents of Pigot highlighted the precariousness of this arrangement in South Asia, raising the spectre of a new inquiry into the Company's affairs. Burke's horror at past inquiries, he now made clear, had not been based on an aversion to scrutinising the Company; instead, his disapproval had been a response to the purpose which he supposed previous inquiries were intended to serve. This, Burke reiterated, was the purpose of advancing "*Court influence*," an objective that ought not to be confused with the establishment of "*public Control*."[51] Control, Burke admitted, was desirable. However at this point there arose the second difficulty that affected the British government of India, namely the problem of how an administration bereft of popular accountability could nonetheless be brought to book by responsible checks upon its procedures.

Checks on power were a means of civilising its application. Since the administration of Britain's East Indian territories took the form of an absolute government, it was essential, in addition to maintaining an orderly structure of command, to preserve the exercise of authority from degenerating into despotism. This meant ensuring that the dictates of the Company were compatible with civil liberty—or, in Humean terms, that absolute government would be deployed in the form of civilised power: although popular control might be absent, the freedom of the subject would be guaranteed.[52] Back in 1773, Burke had wanted to organise prospective checks on Company authority in such a way that they would not subtract from the autonomy of the corporation. He assumed that these restraints could be supplied

[49] Ibid., p. 40.

[50] Ibid.

[51] Ibid., p. 36.

[52] David Hume, "Of Liberty and Despotism" in *Essays, Moral and Political* (Edinburgh: 1741), reprinted as "Of Civil Liberty" in idem, *Essays and Treatises* (London: 1758), p. 60: "It may now be affirmed of civilized monarchies, what was formerly said in praise of republics alone, *that they are a government of Laws, not of Men*. They are found susceptible of order, method, and constancy, to a surprising degree. Property is there secure; industry encouraged; the arts flourish." Cf. EB, *Reflections*, ed. Clark, p. 295 [189], for the same judgment applied to France. Nonetheless, against Hume, Burke would ultimately prize the security of liberty under mixed regimes over the freedom enjoyed under modern monarchies: see EB, *Letter to the Sheriffs of Bristol*, 3 April 1777, *W & S*, III, p. 299, and above, chapter 8, section 5.

by a code of laws devised by parliament but administered by the Company itself. Government directly invading the prerogatives of the Company could only be justified, he believed, as a response to either "necessity" or corporate "delinquency."[53] These criteria were to reappear in Burke's *Reflections* sixteen years later—the former explicitly, the latter covertly—as means of judging the legitimacy of revolution: both of them were found wanting in the case of France.[54] The situation in India was clearly different. During the debates surrounding North's Regulating Bill, the issue was not the rights of popular resistance but the propriety of government breaching its contractual obligations. As far as Burke was concerned, Lord North could not plead necessity as a justification for such a breach, since his government was not faced with a truly existential emergency. "Necessity is a thing that never can be mistaken," Burke contended: "it admits of no degrees . . . it stands upon a precipice."[55] Equally, he went on, the Company might in theory be deemed to have forfeited its rights where its delinquency could be shown to be sufficiently "great," but in practice this delinquency would have to be "ascertained."[56] Yet as Burke's exposure to the conduct of the East India Company increased through William's involvement in the Madras controversy, his suspicion that enormities had been committed began to mount.

In a letter of 9 June 1777 to Philip Francis, Burke admitted that his attention had recently been focused on the affairs of America to the detriment of his awareness of the current state of "Eastern politics."[57] He had first met Francis in England four years earlier through a common friend, John Bourke, before Francis's departure as a new member of the Bengal Council.[58] Burke was now making contact to alert him to the imminent arrival of William in Madras, just in case he should make it north to Francis's base in Bengal.[59] From the perspective of British politics at that time, Burke wrote to Francis, the case of America was not more important but it was more "distracted" than the Indian subcontinent, and it consequently absorbed the attention of the House of Commons.[60] Moreover parliament, as Burke complained five months later, "troubles itself little with such matters."[61] Only the approaching expiration of the Regulating Act would stir the government into action, and then its

[53] On this topic, see above chapter 9, section 3, and below, chapter 13, section 3.

[54] See chapter 13 below.

[55] WWM BkP 9:17.

[56] Ibid.

[57] EB to Philip Francis, 9 June 1777, *Corr.*, III, p. 349.

[58] EB to John Bourke, 12 October 1773, *Corr.*, II, p. 471. See also Francis's letter to the editors of Burke's works, n.d., copied 30 May 1812, WWM BkP 31:16, for an account of their first encounter.

[59] John Bourke had prepared the ground for Burke's letter, writing to Philip Francis on 29 April 1777 and alerting him to the arrival of William Burke in Madras: "Should any accident take him to Bengal, you will have an opportunity of gratifying your inclination to oblige E. B." by helping his "nearest and dearest friend." See Joseph Parkes and Herman Merivale eds., *Memoirs of Sir Philip Francis* (London: 1867), 2 vols., II, pp. 100–101.

[60] EB to Philip Francis, 9 June 1777, *Corr.*, III, p. 349.

[61] EB to John Bourke, November 1777, *Corr.*, III, p. 404.

aim would be to confirm "the power of the Crown over the Company."[62] For his own part, however, on William's return to England on 6 May 1778 after he accepted an appointment as agent for the Raja of Tanjore, Burke applied himself more diligently to the study of southern India, with growing alarm about the condition of its affairs.[63]

Francis followed Burke's prompting and wrote to William in Madras in October 1777, urging him not to get involved in "our damned Indian politicks." The scene was almost irretrievably corrupted, Francis implied, predicting that the current possessors of supreme power in Calcutta would "tumble" if the dimensions of their guilt should ever meet with proportionate punishment.[64] A year later, back in England, William made clear to Francis the extent of his immersion in the Tanjore business. The Raja wished not to make Britain a party to his own cause, he explained to Francis, but only that she should preserve "an equal hand" between him and his neighbours.[65] This had been the drift of William's argument in a *Memorial* that he presented to Lord North on behalf on the Raja in 1778.[66] Tuljaji had been a victim of a "ferocious and exterminatory system," crudely justified by force of arms. Dominion, William asserted, might be vindicated in terms of prescription, valid grant or legitimate convention, but never by the simple fact of power.[67] Burke had doubtless contributed to the implicit conception of political subjection: the claim that the fact of force could never justify the rights of sovereignty is a pervasive Burkean contention.

Around this time, William also put together a *Memorial of the King of Tanjore* in which he argued that, since the struggle in southern India was occurring in the midst of the dissolution of the Mughal Empire, territorial rights in the Deccan could only be underpinned by right of current possession.[68] Once again, the hand of Burke can be surmised in this formulation, which became a governing assumption in his writings on southern India over the following years.[69] Burke's outrage at developments in Madras had been prompted by William's supply of information, but the

[62] Ibid.

[63] Lucy S. Sutherland, *The East India Company in Eighteenth Century Politics* (Oxford: Oxford University Press, 1952), p. 328.

[64] WWM BkP 1:996, 1 October 1777.

[65] WWM BkP 1:1118, 14 December 1778.

[66] William Burke's *Memorial on behalf of the King of Tanjore Presented to Lord North* (London: 1778), can be found at AAC, Home Miscellaneous, 284, and is mentioned in a letter from William to Philip Francis at WWM BkP 1:1118. The *Memorial* is also mildly criticised by George Johnstone in a letter to William Burke of 4 February 1779, WWM BkP 1:1133. William Burke sent it, together with his *Memorial of the King of Tanjore* (London: 1778), to be found at AAC, MS. Eur. E. 36, pp. 817–30, to Charles Jenkinson in a letter of 1 June 1780, Add. MS. 38404, fol. 166.

[67] William Burke, *Memorial to North*, pp. 10, 14.

[68] Ibid., p. 13. For Burke's view of prescription as confirming a right from current possession, see above, chapter 5, section 4 and below chapter 12, section 3.

[69] Edmund and William Burke's close cooperation over Tanjore at this time can been seen from EB's detailed annotations to William Burke, "Reflections on the Nabob [of Arcot]'s Debts, written in 1778. By W. B.," Bodl. MS. Eng. Hist. C. 17, fols. 318–60, which includes Edmund's marginal recalculations of William's financial computations.

construction of a response in juridical terms is most likely to have derived from Edmund.[70] Burke's distress at conditions in the south comes through in a letter of 2 December 1780 to a member of the North ministry, where he confesses that he had become "strongly impressed with the Idea of the misconduct of the English Subjects in India towards the Natives, and of their disobedience to Lawful authority." He was now convinced of "the dreadful State of things in that part of the World," and searching for ways to effect some form of redress.[71] The first sign of his efforts in this direction appeared the previous year, in June 1779, with the publication of the *Policy of Making Conquests for the Mahometans*. The pamphlet was part of William's programme of action as agent for the Raja of Tanjore, but Edmund was a major contributor to its production.[72]

10.3 *The Policy of Making Conquests for the Mahometans*

The *Policy of Making Conquests for the Mahometans* was conceived in the aftermath of a petition to parliament planned in 1778 by one of the agents of the Nawab of the Carnatic, John Macpherson, for the purpose of having the kingdom of Tanjore restored to the Nawab. Together with William Waldegrave, another agent of the Raja, William Burke sought to arrange a counter-petition with Edmund's support. As it happened, both petitions were refused, but Macpherson launched a new campaign the following year, aiming once again to bend the ear of parliament: the "whole Business of Tanjore" was soon to be brought before the Commons, he informed Warren Hastings on 10 February 1779.[73] The idea was to prepare the ground with a pamphlet composed in collaboration with his cousin, James Macpherson. The *Policy* was the Burkes' joint "answer" to the intervention by the Macphersons—namely, *Considerations on the Conquest of Tanjore and the Restoration of the Rajah*. It was intended, as William later put it, as a vindication of an "oppressed" prince, traduced by misrepresentations concocted by the supporters of a predatory Nawab.[74]

The Macphersons implicitly acknowledged that the East India Company had been placed in an anomalous position by developments on the Coromandel coast

[70] EB to Lord Loughborough, 17 December 1780, Unpublished Letters, III, p. 947, where Burke identifies himself with the positions set out by William.

[71] EB to Unknown, 2 December 1780, *Corr.*, IV, p. 320; cf. EB to Lord Loughborough, 24 December 1780, Unpublished Letters, III, p. 949: "some reformation should be undertaken very speedily, by giving security to such of the Gentû governments as are still existing, & for restoring to their natural Government the miserable people who have been oppressed & plundered with so many circumstances of the grossest inhumanity."

[72] Whelan, *Burke and India*, pp. 31–32, 136–37, generally treats this work as a product of Burke's pen; however, it seems clear that William played a major role in its production. See William Burke to Charles Jenkinson, 1 June 1780, Add. MS. 38404, fol. 166. Nonetheless, various manuscript pages from the *Policy* survive in Edmund's hand among the Northamptonshire MSS. (A. XIV.9; A. XXIX.54; and A. XXXVI.3). For details, see the note by P. J. Marshall in *W & S*, V, p. 41.

[73] Add. MS. 29143, fol. 53.

[74] William Burke to Charles Jenkinson, 22 August 1780, Add. MS. 38404, fol. 172.

since the decline of French power in southern India. Having been drawn into rival alliances during their contest with the Compagnie des Indes Orientales, they continued through the 1760s to become involved in the ambitions of friendly country powers, which drew them inexorably into the politics of the region. Thus, although the Company was charged under the terms of its charter with the pursuit of trade, it was also obliged to protect its "property and commerce." This did not, as the *Considerations* put it, entitle it to pursue projects of independent conquest, but it did cast the corporation in the role of "auxiliaries to the Nabob."[75] For the Macphersons, this amounted to nothing more sinister than an assurance of creditable support for a dependable ally, but for the Burkes it succeeded in deranging the politics of southern India. Much of William's and Edmund's original perception of the situation in the Carnatic derived from the accounts supplied by William Ross, a Company servant in Madras, fluent in Marathi, and so in a position to translate the correspondence of the Raja of Tanjore.[76] For Ross, the Raja may have been prone to indulge in dissolute court pleasures, but he was still a mild and capable ruler held in affection by the Tanjoreans, and fundamentally pious in observation and outlook. The Nawab, by contrast, was a rapacious and brutal tyrant bent on personal aggrandisement, and an existential threat to the Company as a result.[77] Muhammad Ali, Ross alleged, had been borrowing from the British to bribe Company officials into participating in assorted schemes of conquest in the south, "dispossessing all the Gentoo Princes in the Country." This made the British government at Madras, along with assorted traders in the settlement, more focused on increasing their private fortunes on the subcontinent than on enhancing the general welfare of the native populations. It also undermined the political authority of the Company, contributing to the demise of its "tottering power."[78] Ross was a critic not of British imperial power, but of its corruption and misapplication in the context of Indian politics. It was a perspective he would pass on to the Burkes.

As far as Ross was concerned, conditions in the Deccan markedly deteriorated after 1770 under the influence of the principal agents of the Nawab of Arcot—first the Macphersons, then Lauchlin Macleane—who infected him with notions about his status and his rights, inflaming an established desire to increase his power in the region. His ambitions were facilitated by the pervasive "traffick in lending money," which further corrupted the venal culture of the Company.[79] Ultimately, according to Ross, the Nawab sought to supplant the position of the British in the south. In the meantime, the Company had become an instrument of oppression in the hands

[75] James Macpherson and John Macpherson, *Considerations on the Conquest of Tanjore and the Restoration of the Rajah* (London: 1779), p. 67.

[76] A substantial briefing letter to William Burke can be found as the first item in the bound notebook, "Correspondence Relative to the Kingdom of Tanjore in the Years 1777, 1778, 1779 & 1780," Add. MS. 39856.

[77] Ibid., fols. 5–6.

[78] Ibid., fol. 10.

[79] Ibid., fol. 14.

of a despot with the consequence that "the name of Englishman, once honourable, is detested."[80] The devastation that the Nawab perpetrated was presented as overwhelming: "Polygars and Rajahs, even those who are under the Company's particular protection, are dispossessed, others harassed with unjust demands, the debts of the Company unpaid, a whole Country is depopulated, and violence is practiced, with impunity, within the bounds of Madras where English laws ought to protect the subject from oppression."[81] Tanjore was a victim of the general spirit of rapacity, most conspicuously on account of two successive wars visited on the Raja by the Nawab with the assistance of the British, the first in 1771 and the second in 1773. The Burkes' general position in the *Policy* was that both these assaults were flagrant violations of those clauses in the Treaty of 1762 subsequently ratified by the Treaty of Paris that defined the relations between the Raja and the Nawab. Tuljaji successfully bought off the first attack on his territory, but he was deposed as a result of the second, with his kingdom placed at the disposal of his assailant until the Raja was restored by Pigot's intervention in 1776. The motives for these acts of aggression were allegedly masked by a series of pretexts fabricated by the agents of the Nawab. The *Policy of Making Conquests for the Mahometans* set about systematically demolishing each of these dubious defences mounted by the supporters of the ruler of Arcot.

In advancing their case, the Burkes claimed, the authors of the *Considerations* had wilfully ignored existing accounts of the controversy, principally those presented by George Rous and John Lind. Rous was a member of parliament and counsel to the East India Company who published *The Restoration of the King of Tanjore Considered* as a general defence of the Directors' position against two pamphlets that appeared in 1777, the *State of the Facts relative to Tanjore* and *Original Papers Relative to Tanjore*.[82] The *State of the Facts* had sought to publicise the debauchery of Tuljaji in an effort to delegitimise his authority to rule.[83] Rous's opposing strategy was to cast Mohammad Ali as an exemplar of the "spirit of Mahomedan conquerors."[84] On this account, the Muslim spirit of conquest was a contemporary legacy of historic waves of subjugation perpetrated over a period of eight centuries by martial adventurers pouring into the subcontinent from Persia, Arabia and northern Asia. This resulted in a ruling Islamic "nation" presiding over the more numerous native inhabitants whose religious differences preserved them from a "union with their conquerors" such that "the Hindoos at this day continue a perfectly distinct race, even in the countries under a Mahomedan Government."[85]

[80] Ibid., fol. 10.

[81] Ibid.

[82] George Rous, *The Restoration of the King of Tanjore Considered* (London: 1777); Anon., *Letter from Mohammed Ali Chan . . . to which is Annexed A State of the Facts relative to Tanjore* (London: 1777); Anon., *Original Papers relative to Tanjore* (London: 1777).

[83] Anon., *State of the Facts*, pp. 34–35.

[84] Rous, *Restoration of the King of Tanjore*, p. 26.

[85] Ibid., p. 3.

As Rous presented it, the Nawab of Arcot was a continuation of the original spirit of usurpation seeking to operate in the new geo-political context created by the arrival of European trading companies. During the controversy surrounding the introduction of North's Regulating Bill, Thomas Pownall had ascribed the corruption of the East India Company in Bengal to the contradictory role that the corporation was obliged to play in acting at once as merchant and as sovereign.[86] The south, however, was different, and the consequences arguably worse. Commerce and dominion were also "united" in the Madras Presidency, Rous pointed out, but in a way that distinguished it from arrangements in the north: in the Carnatic, the Company's power involved deploying "force" without owning responsibility.[87] Its officers were arbiters in a regional power struggle, not bearers of sovereign authority as they were in Bengal: "they have no right to invest themselves with sovereign authority," the Macphersons recognised.[88] It was under these circumstances, as the *Policy* put it, that the Madras Presidency "chose to submit an English army to the ambition of a Barbarian."[89] This surrogacy meant that the predominant power of the British in the region was put in the service of Muslim oppression: the wherewithal of "a Christian and free people" was made an instrument of oriental despotism.[90] The hallmark of this despotism was a disregard for property in the form of unremitting oppression and extortion. With the Company lending its support to a petty tyrant in this way, "Asiatic avarice was supported by European arts and discipline."[91] As the Burkes saw it, this was achieved by a process that involved undermining binding treaty obligations, that conflicted with the principles of territorial integrity in the Carnatic, and that subverted the natural order of domestic politics in the region. The method followed by the *Policy* was to subject each of these violations to forensic scrutiny with a view to exposing the political dysfunction of the Company. Its aim was to "look to the cause and forget the men"—to incriminate the system instead of particular individuals: "I endeavour . . . to confine myself to the measures themselves. . . . Collective descriptions are always chosen; and acts done in corporate capacities are alone discussed."[92]

For this indictment to succeed, the rights of the Raja had to be defended in the face of the claims of the Nawab of Arcot. The Macphersons had been anxious to depict the Raja of Tanjore as a feudal dependent of the Nawab who had failed to honour his obligations in the payment of tribute, or *Peshkash*.[93] The presentation

[86] Thomas Pownall, *The Right, Interest, and Duty of the State, as Concerned in the Affairs of the East Indies* (London: 1773), pp. 8, 42.

[87] Rous, *Restoration of the King of Tanjore*, p. 1.

[88] Macphersons, *Considerations*, p. 67.

[89] William Burke and EB, *Policy of Making Conquests for the Mahometans* (1779) in *W & S*, V, p. 102.

[90] Ibid., pp. 118–19.

[91] Ibid., p. 114.

[92] Ibid., pp. 61–62.

[93] Macphersons, *Considerations*, pp. 46, 67. Warren Hastings shared these views. See P. J. Marshall, *The Impeachment of Warren Hastings* (Oxford: Oxford University Press, 1965), p. 9.

of Tuljaji as a vassal of Muhammad Ali had been a staple strategy pursued by the Nawab's agents since the Pigot controversy broke, but it had been challenged by John Lind in 1777, insisting that "Tanjore is not a fief; it is an hereditary kingdom."[94] Lind referenced Orme in support of this historical judgment, a judgment then adopted by the Burkes.[95] The Raja was not, they protested, a "feudatory" or "vassal," but "a hereditary sovereign Prince, in undisturbed possession," whose principality had "always gone in succession."[96] In addition, harmonious relations between the prince and the population had given rise to an opulent regime, exemplified by the magnificence of the Raja's court. Colonel Lawrence's depiction of the splendours of the royal palace, reproduced in Richard Owen Cambridge's *Account* of the wars on the Coromandel coast, are cited as an indication of the flourishing state of the kingdom prior to its subjugation by the Nawab of Arcot.[97] The harmony alleged to have subsisted between the Raja and his people is explained in terms of a shared culture of "religion and manners," binding the prince's subjects in allegiance.[98] These shared habits, practices and principles inevitably bred a "reciprocal partiality," the Burkes contended—the very basis of patriarchal as opposed to constitutional government.[99] The violent intervention of a Muslim potentate shattered this "natural" scheme of subordination, introducing an oppressive and enterprising dominance among the "milder" and "more tractable" Hindu people.[100] The great casualty of this transaction was less the "rights of Princes" than the "wretched" population subject to a Muslim interloper: the "utter detestation" of the Tanjoreans for their conquerors was an underlying assumption guiding the analysis in the *Policy*.[101]

The credentials of the Raja were contrasted with those of the Nawab, the second son of the marauding "adventurer," Muhammad Anwaruddin, originally appointed as military governor, or *Faujdar*, to the Subahdar of the Deccan under the Mughal Emperor at Delhi.[102] The "genius" of the system of government that animated the

[94] Lind, *Defence of Pigot*, p. 8.

[95] See Orme, *Transactions*, I, pp. 111–13.

[96] William Burke and EB, *Policy of Making Conquests for the Mahometans* (1779) in *W & S*, V, pp. 63–64, 49.

[97] Ibid., p. 65, citing Richard Cambridge, *An Account of the War in India* (London: 1761), p. 58.

[98] William Burke and EB, *Policy of Making Conquests for the Mahometans* (1779) in *W & S*, V, p. 49.

[99] Ibid., p. 113.

[100] Ibid. The alleged mildness of the Hindus pervades the literature of the period: see, for example, Luke Scrafton, *Reflections on the government of Indostan, with a Short Sketch of the History of Bengal, from 1738 to 1756* (London: 1770), p. 16; Alexander Dow, "A Dissertation Concerning the Customs, Manners, Language, Religion and Philosophy of the Hindoos" in *The History of Hindostan from the Earliest Account of Time to the Death of Akbar, translated from the Persian of Muhummud Casim Ferishta of Delhi; together with a Dissertation Concerning the Religion and Philosophy of the Brahmins, with an Appendix, Containing the History of the Mogul Empire from its Decline in the Reign of Muhummud Shaw, to the Present Times* (London: 1768–72), 3 vols., I, p. xxxiv; Adam Smith, *Wealth of Nations*, II, p. 732.

[101] William Burke and EB, *Policy of Making Conquests for the Mahometans* (1779) in *W & S*, V, pp. 112–13.

[102] Ibid., p. 63.

Nawab's rule drove him insatiably to conquest.[103] In practice this meant pursuing an alleged policy of extermination under which he targeted and sought to extinguish "near twenty native hereditary princes," of which the Raja of Tanjore was one significant example.[104] Orme had related in his *Transactions* how, after the British had defeated the French at Pondicherry in 1761, Muhammad Ali proceeded to harass whichever "chiefs and feudatories" he had "pretensions to call to account," including the greater and lesser Maravars in the Carnatic.[105] This episode, the Burkes reckoned, was indicative of the Nawab's characteristic traits of avarice, ambition and vindictiveness.[106] The Company itself concluded that his plans for redesigning the foundations of social organisation among the Maravars required "*extremities of a shocking nature*."[107] The effects of such usurpatory expeditions included the subversion of royal houses, the uprooting of nobility and the destruction of manufacturing classes—ultimately leading to poverty and depopulation.[108] The British, as the Burkes conceded, could not match the ruthless cruelty of native despotism in India, but they did make their arms available for its support.[109] The Select Committee of the Madras Presidency established in 1769 for the purpose of monitoring the Company's acquisitions had counselled against expansion and urged respect for "*present possessions*," but the advice was never heeded and a policy of conquest was pursued.[110]

By the time that the Burkes came to write the *Policy of Making Conquests for the Mahometans*, there existed a considerable literature on the forms of government to be found on the subcontinent.[111] François Bernier had famously described the Mughal Empire as a system of rule under which the great lords of the provinces ("Omrahs," *umara*) were wholly dependent on the favours of their common superior. This meant that there existed no nobility in the European sense since property was held at the pleasure of the Emperor.[112] As a consequence, the number of civil laws could be kept to a minimum. In a volume of *Lettres édifiantes et curieuses*, a collection of travel reports compiled from the correspondence of Jesuit missionaries, Père Bouchet remarked in this vein that Indian society was administered in accordance with

[103] Ibid., p. 114.

[104] Ibid., p. 114.

[105] Orme, *Transactions*, II, p. 725.

[106] William Burke and EB, *Policy of Making Conquests for the Mahometans* (1779) in *W & S*, V, p. 66n.

[107] Ibid., p. 104.

[108] Ibid., pp. 114–16.

[109] Ibid., p. 113.

[110] Ibid., p. 58.

[111] For discussion, see Asma Ahmad, "British Enlightenment and Ideas of Empire in India," *passim*; Marshall, *Making and Unmaking of Empires*, pp. 201–3; Robert Travers, "Ideology and British Expansion in Bengal, 1757–1762," *Journal of Imperial and Commonwealth History*, 33:1 (2005), pp. 7–27; Travers, *Ideology and Empire*, esp. pp. 58–66.

[112] François Bernier, *The History of the Late Revolution of the Great Mogul . . . To which is Added, A Letter to the Lord Colbert* (London: 1671–2), 2 vols., I, pp. 30–31, 68–69. Cf. Henri de Boulainvilliers, *Histoire de l'ancien gouvernement de la France* (The Hague: 1727), 2 vols., I, p. 67: "La barbare loi de l'Orient anéantit la propriété des biens."

religious precepts in the absence of a codified set of laws.[113] Montesquieu, citing Bouchet, reproduced the observation in *The Spirit of the Laws*: "when travelers describe counties to us where despotism reigns, they rarely speak of civil laws."[114] This clearly informed his conception of frictionless power under eastern governments. Such governments comprised, as he famously contended, a system of administration lacking intermediary powers and fundamental laws.[115] Montesquieu further observed that in those parts of Asia under Muslim rule, absolute government was a consequence of the spirit of Islam: "The Mohammedan religion, which speaks only with a sword, continues to act on men with the destructive spirit that founded it."[116] This claim is also prominent in Jean Chardin's *Voyages en Perse*, which Montesquieu evidently studied.[117] But the argument was extended by the sceptic Nicolas Antoine Boulanger, a member of the d'Holbach circle who proposed in his posthumously published *Recherches sur l'origine du despotisme oriental* of 1761 that despotism was a product of the error-prone human tendency to practise idolatry—of which Islamic theocracy was an enduring example.[118] Nonetheless, despite the impact of a pre-existing polemical literature on the interpretation of Asian culture, by the early 1760s French and British accounts of Mughal authority had begun to offer a more historically nuanced analysis of political arrangements on the subcontinent.[119]

The writings of Abraham-Hyacinthe Anquetil-Duperron are, perhaps, the most notorious examples.[120] Extracts from his 1761 address to the Académie des Sciences

[113] "Lettre du Père Bouchet à M. le président Cochet de Saint-Vallier: de la religion et de l'administration de la justice," Pontichéry, 2 October 1714, *Lettres édifiantes et curieuses* (Paris: 1720), XIV, pp. 326–32.

[114] Charles-Louis de Secondat, Baron de Montesquieu, *De l'esprit des lois* (1748) in *Œuvres complètes*, ed. Roger Caillois (Paris: Gallimard, 1951), 2 vols., II, pt. I, bk. VI, ch. 1.

[115] Ibid., pp. 17–19. On this topic in Montesquieu, see Robert Shackleton, *Montesquieu: A Critical Biography* (Oxford: Oxford University Press, 1961), p. 269; Sharon Krause, "Despotism in the *Spirit of the Laws*" in D. W. Carrithers et al. eds., *Montesquieu's Science of Politics: Essays on "The Spirit of the Laws"* (Oxford: Rowman and Littlefield, 2001). On his conception of monarchy in contradistinction to despotism, see Sonenscher, *Before the Deluge*, pp. 121–49. For an account of ancient and modern usages of "despotism," see Richard Koebner, "Despot and Despotism: Vicissitudes of a Political Term," *Journal of the Warburg and Courtauld Institutes*, 14:3/4 (1951), pp. 275–302. For a continuation of the story into the eighteenth century, see Franco Venturi, "Oriental Despotism," *Journal of the History of Ideas*, 24:1 (January–March 1963), pp. 133–42; J.G.A. Pocock, *Barbarism and Religion II: Narratives of Civil Government* (Cambridge: Cambridge University Press, 1999), ch. 7.

[116] Montesquieu, *De l'esprit des lois*, II, pt. V, bk. 24, ch. 4.

[117] Jean Chardin, *Voyages du Chevalier Chardin en Perse, et Autres Lieux de l'Orient* (Paris: 1811), 10 vols., V, p. 339. See Montesquieu, *De l'esprit des lois*, II, pt. I, bk. 2, ch. 5.

[118] Nicolas Antoine Boulanger, *Recherches sur l'origine du despotisme oriental* (Paris: 1761).

[119] For the British context, see P. J. Marshall, "'A Free though Conquering People': Britain and Asia in the Eighteenth Century" in idem, *A Free though Conquering People: Eighteenth-Century Britain and the Empire* (Aldershot: Ashgate, 2003).

[120] On Anquetil-Duperron, see George Sarton, "Anquetil-Duperron (1731–1805)", *Osiris*, 3 (1937), pp. 193–223; Siep Stuurman, "Cosmopolitan Egalitarianism in the Enlightenment: Anquetil Duperron on India and America," *Journal of the History of Ideas*, 68:2 (April 2007), pp. 255–78. For his critique of Montesquieu, see Frederick G. Whelan, "Oriental Despotism: Anquetil-Duperron's Response to Montesquieu," *History of Political Thought*, 22:4 (2001), pp. 619–47. For overlap with Burke, see Jennifer Pitts,

on Zoroastrianism were reproduced in *The Annual Register* for 1762, prefaced by Burke's editorial note commending Duperron's "virtue and learning" by way of contrast with the "cravings of avarice and ambition" that usually drove European colonial enterprise.[121] Anquetil-Duperron would in due course set out a powerful challenge to earlier accounts of the putative despotism of the east in his *Législation orientale* of 1778. However, Burke's analysis of Mughal politics would largely depend on British historical sources. Prominent among these were works by former Company servants like Robert Orme and Alexander Dow, although their writings were amenable to a variety of interpretations depending on the aspect of their analyses that one chose to emphasise. One pivotal facet of the accounts of Orme and Dow involved the fate of the Mughal emperors after the death of Aurangzeb in 1707: since then, they contended, authority and initiative had been wrested from the centre by powerful deputies in the provinces such as the Nawabs of Bengal and the Nizams of Hyderabad.[122] But before the rise of these provincial deputies, there survived throughout the subcontinent, along with the Hindu religion, what Richard Cambridge described as "the old form of government" under native Rajas as well as a number of smaller tributary rulers, like the Poligars of Tamilnadu.[123] However, the significance of both the Mughal and the pre-conquest components of India's ancient constitution could be variously anatomised, carrying diverse implications for contemporary conceptions of political legitimacy in the post-Mughal era.[124] In 1779, Burke was happy to present southern Muslim adventurers like Muhammad Ali as brutal exemplars of the spirit of Islamic conquest; but later he would champion the idea of regulated government in South Asia that respected the rights of the subject and accommodated Hindu culture. "In short," Burke later declared at the end of the Hastings trial, "every word that Montesquieu has taken from idle and inconsiderate Travellers is absolutely false."[125] From this angle, Muslim rapacity was not endemic, but an aberration which stood in need of an explanation.

"Empire and Legal Universalisms in the Eighteenth Century," *American Historical Review*, 117:1 (February 2012), pp. 92–121.

[121] "Antiquities" in *The Annual Register for the Year 1762* (London: 1763), p. 103.

[122] This process has been widely examined in recent historiography. C. A. Bayly, "Introduction" to idem, *Rulers, Townsmen and Bazaars: North Indian Society in the Age of British Expansion* (Oxford: Oxford University Press, 1983, 2000), provides an overview. For the dynamic struggle between the centre and the provinces under the later Mughals, see Muzaffar Allam, *The Crisis of Empire in Mughal North India: Awadh and Punjab, 1707–1748* (Oxford: Oxford University Press, 1986, 2001). For the shifting balance of power in Indian society at large, see C. A. Bayly, *Indian Society and The Making of the British Empire* (Cambridge: Cambridge University Press, 1988, 1993). For Bengal, see Philip B. Calkins, "The Formation of a Regionally Oriented Ruling Group in Bengal, 1700–1740," *Journal of Asian Studies*, 99:4 (1970), pp. 799–806. For Awadh, see Richard B. Barnett, *North India between Empires: Awadh, the Mughals, and the British, 1720–1801* (Berkeley, CA: University of California Press, 1980). For the Deccan, see Karen Leonard, "The Hyderabad Political System and its Participants," *Journal of Asian Studies*, 30:3 (1971), pp. 569–82.

[123] Cambridge, *Account*, p. xxiv.

[124] Travers, *Ideology and Empire*, *passim*.

[125] EB, Speech in Reply, 28 May 1794, *W & S*, VII, p. 265.

Robert Orme, who won the admiration of William Robertson as well as Joshua Reynolds and James Boswell, acknowledged the enduring integrity of Hindu political culture while also adverting to the capriciousness of Muslim rule.[126] His writings could therefore be scanned for evidence of eastern despotism as well as for indications of moderation. According to Orme's reckoning, the native population of Rajas, petty princes and their subjects outnumbered a total of 10 million Muslim settlers by ten to one, making it necessary for the colonial latecomers to respect the original sovereignties that preceded waves of Muslim usurpation, on condition that Hindu princes paid the appropriate tribute.[127] Yet despite this de facto observance of established custom, Orme went on, laws in the Empire were reducible to a few maxims. A decade later, Alexander Dow, in a historical study of successive Islamic empires on the subcontinent that was to remain a standard work for sixty years, reiterated the same point: "The Mahommedans of Hindostan have no written laws," except for religious precepts and immemorial usages, very occasionally written down.[128] On Orme's account, the political dependants of the Great Mughal were granted property for life in the form of revenue assignments which reverted to the Emperor on the death of the imperial deputy.[129] However, by way of contrast with the terms of tenure among the *umara*, the "estates of all those who are not feudatories descend to the natural heirs."[130] For Dow, however, insecurity of property affected the whole of society: "The lives and properties of the greatest Omrahs are as much at [the Emperor's] disposal, as those of the meanest subjects."[131] Between them, Orme and Dow presented a complex picture of Indian politics as a moderated despotism. Nonetheless, for both, in the declining state of the Empire, absolute authority was devolving to viceroys in the provinces, without any plausible check upon their power.[132]

[126] See, for example, James Boswell, *Boswell's Life of Johnson, Together with Journal of a Tour to the Hebrides and Johnson's Diary of a Journey into North Wales*, ed. G. B. Hill, rev. L. F. Powell (Oxford: Oxford University Press, 1934–50, 1971), 6 vols., III, p. 284.

[127] Orme, *Transactions*, I, pp. 24–25. This can be contrasted with the picture set out in Orme's 1753 *General Idea of the Government and People of Indostan* which appeared in Robert Orme, *Historical Fragments of the Mogul Empire, of the Morattoes, and of the English Concerns in Indostan* (London: 1805).

[128] Dow, *History of Hindostan,* I, p. xvi. For an account of Dow's *History* and its impact, see J. S. Grewal, *Muslim Rule in India: The Assessments of British Historians* (Oxford: Oxford University Press, 1927), ch. 2; Ranajit Guha, *A Rule of Property: An Essay on the Idea of Permanent Settlement* (1963; Durham, NC: Duke University Press, 1996), pp. 12–36.

[129] For the difference between the theoretical and practical claims of Mughal nobles on their *jagirs*, see John F. Richards, *The Mughal Empire* (Cambridge: Cambridge University Press, 1993, 2008), p. 66.

[130] Orme, *Transactions*, I, p. 27. Cf. Nathaniel Halhed, *A Letter to Governor Johnstone on Indian Affairs* (London: 1783), p. 29, on "the feodal maxims of the Mogul Government."

[131] Dow, *History of Hindostan*, p. xiv. Cf. William Watts, *Memoirs of the Revolution in Bengal Anno Dom. 1757* (London: 1764), p. 5: "The Mogul . . . is . . . the sole Possessor of Property, the single Fountain of Honour, and the supreme Oracle of Justice. The whole country belongs to him; all Honours are Personal."

[132] Dow, *History of Hindostan*, p. xvii. As a result of his identification of Asia with inveterate despotism, Burke later described the "history of Dow" as having "no authority in the world." See EB, Speech in Reply, 5 June 1794, *W & S*, VII, p. 385.

The Burkes' argument in the *Policy* was indebted to this picture of a declining empire in which unaccountable authority, having been located at the centre, was being appropriated by unscrupulous military governors in the provinces. In the process, they implied, the Mughal practice of leaving the authority of Hindu rulers undisturbed was breaking down under pressure from a resurgence of the spirit of conquest among rapacious upstart adventurers like Muhammad Ali. Britain's duty in the region coincided with her interest, which was to seek to improve the condition of her dependants on the subcontinent by extending the benefits of enlightened practices and principles.[133] However, instead of what they clearly ought to have done, the British supported the cause of "intolerable despotism" inspired by "the spirit of Mahometan domination."[134] In practice, this involved bolstering the aggressive expansionism of the Nawab of Arcot at the expense of an effective balance of power in the Carnatic.[135] The British were foreign interlopers in South Asia whose military and commercial superiority brought with it the inescapable obligations of authority—to serve justice in proportion to the effectiveness of one's power. Burke was acutely aware that the British position on the subcontinent rested on force. The East India Company itself, he knew, had long been a military operation that added to the might of the Empire: as he reminded his audience during the debate on the Judicature Bill back in 1772, "they have given you an army of thirty thousand men . . . they have given you a Fleet of ninety sail."[136] Despite its foundation in blood and conquest, Burke was consistent in defending the rights of British imperial sovereignty in Asia, albeit on condition that these were exercised judiciously.

In Bengal, the rights of empire had been derived from a revolution in government whose outcome was decided by the preponderance of British arms. During this process of revolutionary change Indian politics had been plunged into what Burke recognised as sheer "tumult."[137] He had articulated this perception in 1773 when reflecting on British fortunes in the period 1757–65: Clive and his associates had been driven to act from necessity—in the midst of hostile forces, guided by "the eye of the assassin."[138] The reference here to assassins underlines Burke's appreciation of the decisiveness of violence in the acquisition of dominion. The followers of the Persian founder of Syrian assassination squads, Hassan-i Sabbāh, still famous in the eighteenth century as "the Old Man of the Mountain," was invoked by Vattel in 1758 as an exemplar of callous brutality.[139] *The Annual Register* for 1760 carried an essay that recounted his ruthlessly "sanguinary" measures.[140] For Burke to claim

[133]William Burke and EB, *Policy of Making Conquests for the Mahometans* (1779) in *W & S*, V, p. 114.

[134]Ibid., pp. 114–15.

[135]Ibid., p. 115.

[136]EB, Speech on Judicature Bill, 30 March 1772, Eg. MS. 239, fol. 265.

[137]EB, Proceedings against Clive, 21 May 1773, Eg. MS. 248, fol. 360.

[138]Ibid.

[139]Emer de Vatttel, *The Law of Nations*, ed. Béla Kapossy and Richard Whatmore (Indianapolis, IN: Liberty Fund), p. 559.

[140]"An Account of the Origin, Customs, Manners, &c., of the Assassins of Syria" in *The Annual Register for 1760* (London: 1761), p. 57.

that British dominion had been secured under the eye of the assassin was very much a refusal to shroud subjugation in mystique. It was inappropriate, he was arguing, to expect the savage business of conquest to be held back by the civility of laws.[141] Nonetheless, he further contended, the obligations of justice immediately followed upon success in the military contest.

In southern India the balance of forces was somewhat different: British paramountcy did not take the form of territorial sovereignty as it did in Bengal. Instead, the Company was established as a hegemon in the region surrounded by jealous rival powers. But along with its position of superiority, the Company also inherited binding political duties. As the Burkes presented the matter in the *Policy*, the duty of geo-political justice in the Carnatic was coterminous with maintaining a proportionate balance among the principalities of the region. This obligation had to begin with an enforcement of legitimate political boundaries. In the context of the dissolution of a great empire such as had been in progress on the subcontinent since the 1720s, this had to mean policing territories in accordance with actual "*possession*."[142] It was not in Britain's interest that any "antiquated claims should be revived," not least since her own title was based on the fact of current possession.[143] On the basis of this title, the British also enjoyed supremacy, which made them in reality the final arbiters of the Carnatic, acting through subordinate dependants. Native governments, identical in heritage and culture to their subjects, were interposed between the Company and the indigenous populations, obliging the British to serve their purposes by acting through local surrogates—"as in wisdom perhaps they ought to do."[144] This was the only acceptable scheme of conquest under the circumstances: holding out a prospect of civilisation and improvement without recourse to the expedient of direct subordination, which was liable to provoke a counter-reaction. But instead of pursuing a course of civilising conquest, the Company had become mired in expropriating usurpation, acting as the instrument of Muslim domination and thus compromising national honour along with domestic reason of state.

10.4 The Secret Committee, the Select Committee and the Bengal Court of Judicature

It was the events surrounding the deposition of Lord Pigot that had driven the Rockinghamite faction in parliament into an engagement with Indian politics in the late 1770s. Nonetheless, as Burke immersed himself in the affairs of the Carnatic, developments in Bengal were proving equally controversial. General John Clavering, Col-

[141] Proceedings against Clive, 21 May 1773, Eg. MS. 248, fol. 360.
[142] William Burke and EB, *Policy of Making Conquests for the Mahometans* (1779), *W & S*, V, p. 113.
[143] Ibid.
[144] Ibid.

onel George Monson and Philip Francis had arrived in Calcutta in October 1774 as newly appointed members of the Supreme Council, joining Richard Barwell and Warren Hastings. Hastings had been appointed as Governor of Bengal in the spring of 1771, arriving to replace John Cartier on 13 April 1772. Under instructions from the Company Directors, he set about abolishing Clive's dual system of government by which the Nawab's deputy or *naib*, in the person of Muhammad Reza Khan, administered the *Diwani*.[145] This reform entailed bringing the territorial revenues of Bengal and adjacent provinces under the direct management of East India Company servants. Along with this transfer of responsibility, legal administration was recast, bringing about a degree of centralisation by the setting up of courts of appeal in Calcutta, with clearer lines demarcating civil and criminal jurisdictions. In the process, the judicial functions of the Zamindars were curtailed, while a codification of Hindu and Muslim law was undertaken.[146] But as Hastings proceeded with his policy of retrenchment and reorganisation, the government of the Company was reconfigured under the terms of North's Regulating Act. Together with the appointment of members to the newly constituted Supreme Council, this involved the creation of a Supreme Court of Judicature, headed by Elijah Impey as Chief Justice, assisted by three appointed judges.[147]

These reforms were soon beset by disabling complications. In addition, immediately after Monson, Clavering and Francis had arrived in Calcutta, conflict between them and Hastings began to surface as the new majority on the Council busily searched for indices of corruption on Hastings's part.[148] Francis later revealed how he originally understood his mission: "I conceived that we were to be armed with extraordinary Powers to correct enormous Abuses," as he put it in his *Autobiography* around 1776.[149] Within a month and a half of assuming his new role, he was confiding to John Bourke that he had been sent to "save and govern" a "Glorious" empire in the east, now "tottering on the verge of Ruin." His correspondent was urged to "Talk to Ned Burke" and alert him to the "putrefied" condition of affairs in Bengal.[150] Along with his fellow opponents of the Hastings regime, Francis began to deluge

[145] Keith Feiling, *Warren Hastings* (London: Macmillan, 1966), ch. 8.

[146] M. E. Monckton-Jones, *Warren Hastings in Bengal, 1772–74* (Oxford: Oxford University Press, 1918), p. 4; Neil Sen, "Warren Hastings and British Sovereign Authority in Bengal, 1774–80," *Journal of Imperial and Commonwealth History*, 25:1 (1997), pp. 59–81.

[147] Misra, *Central Administration of the East India Company*, pp. 19–20.

[148] A reassessment of Francis's career and ambitions is provided by T. H. Bowyer, "Philip Francis and the Government of Bengal: Parliament and Personality in the Frustration of an Ambition," *Parliamentary History*, 18:1 (1999), pp. 1–21.

[149] Parkes and Merivale eds., *Memoirs of Philip Francis*, I, p. 367.

[150] AAC, MS. Eur. E. 13/A, fols. 37–44, corrected from Parkes and Merivale, *Memoirs of Philip Francis*, II, p. 18. A copy of the letter can also be found at WWM BkP 9:114. For Francis's cultivation of Burke, see also Philip Francis to John Bourke, ibid., II, p. 64, and Philip Francis to John Bourke, 23 September 1776, AAC, MS. Eur. E. 13/C, fol. 790.

the Court of Directors with damning dispatches about the Governor's conduct.[151] This hostility, leading to moves for the recall of the Governor General, mobilised Hastings's supporters in the Court of Proprietors in London, with Richard Becher insisting before a General Court in May 1776 that Hastings had in effect single-handedly purged the Company of "venality and peculation" in the north-east.[152] In the meantime, Francis was accumulating evidence against the equity of the new system of farming out the collection of revenues instituted by Hastings. Equally, Hastings's treatment of the Rohillas arising out of the Company's alliance with the Wazir of Awadh was coming under intense scrutiny. At the same time, friction between the Supreme Council and the Bengal Court of Judicature became manifest, challenging the viability of the Regulating Act itself. The Act was due to expire in 1779, with the Company Charter coming up for renewal within another year. With these deadlines in view, John Robinson began work at the Treasury on a new settlement in the summer of 1778.[153] In January 1780, Burke was championing the merits on an inquiry into Company affairs as a prelude to removing the "*Causes* of extortion & usury."[154] With the American war dominating parliamentary business, a "French War" then "added to the American," and the government in mounting disarray, measures were not brought forward until 1781.[155] These resulted in the passage of an Amending Bill in the Commons on 3 July, which was accepted in the Lords without alteration.[156]

The months preceding the enactment of North's Amending Bill were crowded by an upsurge in South Asian politics. "The affairs of India now began to require and to attract the most serious attention of the House of Commons," as *The Annual Register* commented in 1782 on the previous year's proceedings.[157] The regulations introduced in 1773 were widely held to have perpetuated, or even introduced, "disorder" and "confusion" into the affairs of the subcontinent.[158] The sense of alarm intensified when news reached London in April of Haidar Ali's victory over British troops near Madras as a sizeable French fleet operated off the Coromandel coast.[159] This prompted Lord North to appoint a Secret Committee under the Lord Advocate,

[151] The relations between the majority members of the Council and their dispatches to the Court of Directors are discussed in T. H. Bowyer, "Philip Francis and the Government of Bengal: Parliament and Personality in the Frustration of an Ambition," *Parliamentary History*, 18:1 (1999), pp. 1–21.

[152] *Morning Chronicle*, 17 May 1776.

[153] His plans can be found among the Liverpool Papers at Add. MSS. 38398, fols. 107ff. and 38403, fols. 2ff. These are discussed in Sutherland, *East India Company Politics*, pp. 337–39.

[154] EB to Lord Loughborough, 8 January 1781, Unpublished Letters, III, p. 952.

[155] The phrase appears in EB to Philip Francis, 24 December 1778, *Corr.*, IV, p. 33.

[156] 21 Geo. III, c. 65. Burke's response to the Act is given in his letter to Lord Macartney, 15 October 1781, *Corr.*, X, p. 11.

[157] "The History of Europe" in *The Annual Register for the Year 1781*, pp. 175–76.

[158] Ibid., p. 176.

[159] B. Sheikh Ali, *British Relations with Haidar Ali* (Mysore: Rao and Raghavan, 1963), ch. 7.

Henry Dundas, to inquire into the affairs of the Carnatic.[160] Discontent in Bengal likewise impacted on the government. Two months earlier, a petition had been received regarding the Court of Judicature from the Governor General and Council, with further complaints being issued by both the Company and British residents in Bengal.[161] These petitions were debated in the Commons on a motion proposed by Richard Smith on 12 February 1781. Smith protested that the Court presided arbitrarily over British subjects, while having also in practice extended its jurisdiction over the native population, exercising its powers oppressively over assorted Muslim and Hindu notables. It was sheer "madness," Smith exclaimed, to establish legal practices among the inhabitants of Bengal that were antipathetic at once to their "religion and customs," and that might plausibly drive the local inhabitants to "phrensy and desperation."[162] The outrageousness of the Court's actions had been so obvious to the Supreme Council that it had been reduced to the "indispensable necessity" of resorting to force to restrain it.[163]

Controversy over the Court of Judicature led to the establishment of a Select Committee of fifteen under Richard Smith to inquire into judicial arrangements in Bengal.[164] Burke was to play a decisive role in composing its Reports, and in directing many of its conclusions.[165] The proceedings of the Select Committee ran alongside the activities of the Secret Committee over the course of the next two and a half years, being disbanded with the defeat of the Fox–North Coalition in December 1783. During that time, the administration of Lord North disintegrated, the American colonies were finally lost, and India moved to the centre of British political debate. "The State of India is the greatest Object that ever can come before the Nation," Burke insisted to a returning British naval officer in March 1781.[166] Throughout the spring of that year, he had been engaging with the wider issue of the government of the Company in addition to collecting evidence for the Select Committee. The essential elements of his original hostility to ministerial interference in a corporate concern resurfaced at this time. Once again he defended the proposition that "the Company's territorial acquisitions belonged entirely to themselves,"

[160] Its proceedings are discussed in Jim Phillips, "Parliament and Southern India, 1781–1783: The Secret Committee of Inquiry and the Prosecution of Sir Thomas Rumbold," *Parliamentary History*, 7:1 (1988), pp. 81–97.

[161] *CJ*, XXXVIII, pp. 97–99, 159–62, 278–80.

[162] *Morning Herald*, 12 February 1781.

[163] Richard Smith in *Parliamentary History*, XXI, col. 1190.

[164] *CJ*, XXXVIII, p. 202.

[165] The Select Committee originally reported in the spring of 1781, only to be reconvened on 4 December and run for a further two years, issuing eleven Reports. On the authorship of these Reports, see P. J. Marshall, "Appendix B," *W & S*, V, pp. 626–28. The "Observations" of the *First Report* can be attributed to Burke, as can the *Ninth* and *Eleventh Report*. He may also have had a hand in the *Third Report*. He had little share, however, in the *Fourth*, *Seventh* or *Tenth Report*, while the *Fifth* and *Eighth Report* are mainly composed of citation.

[166] EB to John Blankett, 2 March 1781, *Corr.*, IV, p. 340.

challenging what he saw as the improvident ambition of Dundas and Lord North to plunder the corporation for the supply of revenue.[167] Resuming his rhetoric of the late 1760s, he urged the government to desist from managing East Indian affairs by "violence" lest it compromise the credit of the Company and the nation.[168] Just as he had emphasised in the early 1770s, Burke complained once more that North's ministry had been determined from the beginning to "obtain money under a pretence of establishing a political reform," in addition seeking in 1781 to interfere with its monopoly and reallocate its trade.[169] However, unlike his earlier reaction to the allegations of Indian misgovernment levelled by Burgoyne's Select Committee, his suspicion of North's intentions in the 1780s took place against the background of a general concern shared across the opposition benches that the Company had betrayed its trust and stood in need of supervision.[170]

In a debate on 30 April on Haidar Ali's military adventures in the Carnatic, Fox declared that "our settlements in the East Indies were reduced from a most glorious style of prosperity, almost to ruin."[171] The reference seems to have been to Bengal rather than Madras, but the impression made was that South Asia in general was declining under British management. It was by this time widely believed that the Supreme Court in Calcutta had contributed significantly to the emerging crisis. Richard Smith restated his case on 23 May 1781: government by English laws, he claimed, was "completely inconsistent with the customs, manners, and religious principles of the Indians." Among the victims of the imposition of a foreign jurisdiction, he went on, were "the Zemindars or feudatory princes of India."[172] *The Annual Register* elucidated the significance of this complaint. The Zamindars, it was explained, were "the present great landholders of India," who operated in practice as "hereditary princes."[173] They formed a crucial intermediary role between the peas-

[167] 23 May 1781, *Parliamentary History*, XXII, col. 321. Cf. 8 May 1781, ibid., col. 139.

[168] 9 April 1781, ibid., col. 113.

[169] 23 May 1781, ibid., col. 316.

[170] Burke's reaction to Burgoyne's speech of 13 April 1772 can be found at WWM BkP 9:14. In notes on the debate, Burke reports Burgoyne as having "displayed great & pathetick powers of Eloquence" with a view to representing "in the strongest colours the miseries of the natives of Bengal."

[171] Ibid., col. 132.

[172] Ibid., col. 303.

[173] "The History of Europe" in *The Annual Register for the Year 1781*, p. 177. See the definition provided by the Glossary in Harry Verelst, *A View of the Rise, Progress, and Present State of the English Government in Bengal: Including a Reply to the Misrepresentations of Mr. Bolts, and Other Writers* (London: 1772), "*Zeméen-dár*, literally a land-holder, accountable to government for the revenue." Cf. the definition in Henry Vansittart, *A Narrative of the Transactions in Bengal from the Year 1760 to the Year 1764* (London: 1766), 3 vols., I, Glossary: "Zemindar, A person who holds a certain tract of land immediately of the government, on condition of paying the rent of it." Cf. also Robert Orme, *General Idea of the Government and People of Indostan* (1753) in idem, *Historical Fragments of the Mogul Empire* (London: 1805), p. 403: "Zemindar . . . is the proprietor of a tract of land given in inheritance by the King or the Nabob, and who stipulates the revenue which he is to pay for the peaceable possession of it." For a recent account, see Ratna Ray and Rajat Ray, "Zamindars and Jotedars: A Study of Rural Politics in Bengal," *Modern Asian Studies*, 9:1 (1975), pp. 81–102.

ant population and the governing class of Nawabs, retaining their social ascendancy in the aftermath of the conquest of the country. In the wake of successive waves of Muslim subjugation, they subsisted as feudatories in territories which "their ancestors possessed in sovereignty," while "the people" continued to regard them "with the highest degree of attachment and reverence."[174] Prior to Hastings's reforms, along with their pivotal role in the assessment and collection of revenue, the Zamindars had taken charge of the civil courts in the localities in accordance with the "established laws and constitution" of the country, "which had till now been acknowledged by all conquerors."[175] Even if barbarous military invaders into the subcontinent had not entirely respected, they had at least acknowledged, the antiquity and popularity of the "Gentoo civilization." By comparison, the Supreme Court at Calcutta, dispatching English bailiffs deep into the countryside, amounted to a "total revolution" in the affairs of the region, appearing to the population as an absolute despotism supervening upon the older structure of a relatively benign authority.

The perspective advanced in *The Annual Register* is identical to the position that Burke was developing at this time. In the notes for his speech on the Judicature Bill of 19 June 1781, he drew attention to the fundamental problem of governing the subcontinent. The native population had long been subjected to "great oppressions" since it had always had the misfortune to be governed "by a foreign people."[176] While the subjugation of "native" by "foreign" populations similarly characterised the history of Europe after the fall of Rome, the invading hordes of Europe had gradually blended with their conquered subjects. In India, on the other hand, political subordination polarised the natives in relation to the newcomers, although subjection was still sustained without the application of violence: Hindu practices and customs were consistently preserved. As a result, South Asia could be characterised as a moderated despotism, but never as a specimen of tyranny. Under Hastings's government, however, moderation came to an end. The replacement of the old Mayor's Court in Calcutta with the new Supreme Court of Judicature headed by Elijah Impey had brought an end to the earlier forms of constitutional restraint. The imposition of British laws onto an Indian social order amounted simply to "folly joined to Tyranny," Burke declared.[177] In the language of the Bill that he himself drafted in the spring of 1781 with a view to alleviating the system of perceived legal oppression in Bengal, the current arrangement of political power in north-east India had not only succeeded in pitting the Governor General and Council against the Supreme Court, it had also afflicted the inhabitants with "Fears and Apprehensions."[178]

[174] "The History of Europe" in *The Annual Register for the Year 1781*, p. 177.

[175] Ibid.

[176] WWM BkP 9:4.

[177] Ibid.

[178] "A Bill to Explain and Amend so much of an Act [13 Geo. III, c. 630] as Relates to the Administration of Justice in Bengal," *House of Commons Sessional Papers of the Eighteenth Century*, ed. Sheila Lambert (Wilmington, DE: Scholarly Resources, 1975–76), 147 vols., XXXIII, p. 264. Richard Smith, in a speech of 20 November 1783, reported in the *Morning Herald* the following day, confirmed that

The evidence collected by the Select Committee, whose first Report was submitted before parliament on 8 June 1781, recapitulated these fears and apprehensions in some detail.[179] British subjects had charged the Supreme Court with executing rough justice, but the native population had also suffered by its actions. This outcome stemmed from a fundamental misconception of the relationship between enlightenment and empire: an enlightened system of government could not simply be foisted on a people inured to absolute subjection. The British Empire could hope to offer protection to the native inhabitants of the subcontinent, ultimately improving the constitution of India as the manners of the people were freed from habits of subordination through the experience of durable security. But the passage towards enlightenment would be arduous and fraught with difficulty, requiring both vigilance and circumspection. To begin with, the British settlements in the East Indies resembled the barrier towns fortified by the Dutch in the Austrian Netherlands: civil conditions simply did not apply under these circumstances, so administration could not be subjected to judicial regulation. To this extent, the powers of the Governor and Council would have to be regarded as "arbitrary."[180] Moreover, a system of "equal freedom," exemplified by the enlightened constitutional arrangement of Great Britain, certainly could not be established in Bengal contrary to the dispositions of the Indians themselves. As Burke emphasised during his speech on the Bengal Judicature Bill of 27 June 1781, the denizens of South Asia were "familiarized to a system of rule more despotic, and familiarity had rendered it congenial."[181] This was indeed the meaning of government by consent: the "enlightened" were obliged to conform their administration to the expectations even of those who "resist the lights of philosophy," however much this conformity betrayed the forms of British freedom.[182]

The previous month, in a speech urging publicity on the secret proceedings of Dundas's proposed Committee on the condition of affairs in the Carnatic, Burke underlined Britain's obligation to win the affection of the natives in competition with the Country powers as well as European rivals. This could only be achieved by the open administration of "equal justice."[183] But equality here meant impartiality, not the subversion of established hierarchies and distinctions. In the process of drafting his Bill on the Bengal Judicature, Burke consulted William Jones in an ef-

---

the Bill had been substantially drawn up by Burke. The Bill was revised by Lord Thurlow in the Lords, later passing as 21 Geo. III, c. 70. Burke's adverse comments on Thurlow's reduction of the Bill to a mere "triffle" can be found in EB to Henry Dundas, 1 June 1787, *Corr.*, V, p. 334.

[179] *Report from the Committee to Whom the Petition of John Touchet and John Irving . . . were Severally Referred* (1781) in *Commons Sessional Papers*, ed. Lambert, LXXXVIII, *passim.*

[180] 22 June 1781, *Parliamentary History*, XXII, col. 550. The powers of the Council were arbitrary because military in character. Burke went on to argue that "the idea of establishing civil liberty in India was absurd." In due course he would modify these claims.

[181] EB, Speech on Bengal Judicature Bill, 27 June 1781, *W & S*, V, p. 141. On Burke's developing views of the constitution of politics in South Asia, see Whelan, *Edmund Burke and India*, pp. 242–60.

[182] EB, Speech on Bengal Judicature Bill, 27 June 1781, *W & S*, V, p. 141.

[183] EB, Speech on Secret Committee, 30 April 1781, ibid., pp. 136–37.

fort to comprehend what these hierarchies and distinctions entailed.[184] For Jones, they could be ascertained from the terms of "the old Mogul constitution," which should be retained as the basis for any future judicial reforms.[185] Like many others, Burke accepted that British policy should be founded on the provisions of the ancient Mughal constitution—the question was what this constitution had actually comprised, and which of its constituent elements could practically be revived.[186] The answer to the question turned on the status of the Zamindars, which formed a central plank of inquiry for Burke and his colleagues on the Select Committee. In a letter to John Bourke from November 1777, written soon after reading Philip Francis's *Plan for a Settlement of the Revenues of Bengal*, Burke confessed that he had come round to Francis's perspective: he had hitherto considered the Zamindars to be less secure in their position than English copyholders, although he had now been brought to recognise that "the occupier of the Soil, and not the Government, is the true proprietor of the land of Bengal."[187]

The issue that Burke was addressing concerned whether the Zamindars were to be regarded as subordinates under the viceroys of the Mughal Emperor, as officials subject to the whims of their political superiors, or as landed proprietors who enjoyed hereditary rights within their districts. Philip Francis, who returned from India in October 1781 in time to supply Burke with evidence to be used in later Reports of the Select Committee, had made his position clear in a letter sent from Calcutta to Charles Boughton Rouse back in June 1776. As with the establishment of feudal government in Europe, the Mughal constitution was based on a "System of Conquest". However, in India, the Muslim invaders did not distribute conquered territory among their followers, but instead installed them in subordinate political offices whilst retaining the original proprietors—the Zamindars—in possession of their lands on condition that they paid tribute to the Emperor.[188] As Francis put it in his *Plan* of 1776, it appeared, according to the terms of their grants (*sanads*) from the Emperor, that they held of the sovereign "*in capite*." But this appearance was nothing less than a "feodal fiction," Francis claimed, since in reality territorial lords held their property securely provided they paid a moderate tribute.[189]As a result,

[184]William Jones to Viscount Althorp, 29 June 1781, *The Letters of Sir William Jones*, ed. Garland Cannon (Oxford: Oxford University Press, 1970), 2 vols., II, pp. 478–79. See also EB to William Jones, post 13 June 1781, *Corr.*, IV, p. 352.

[185]William Jones, "Thoughts on a System of Judicature," WWM BkP 9:137.

[186]For the idea of an "ancient Mughal constitution" in British thought down to 1780, see, again, Travers, *Ideology and Empire*, *passim*. There is also some discussion in Sudipta Sen, *Distant Sovereignty: National Imperialism and the Origins of British India* (London: Routledge, 2002), pp. xx–xxi.

[187]EB to John Bourke, November 1777, *Corr.*, III, pp. 403–4, discussing Philip Francis, *Plan for a Settlement of the Revenues of Bengal, Baha and Orixa* (22 January 1776), reproduced in idem, *Original Minutes of the Governor-General and Council of Fort William on the Settlement and Collection of the Revenues of Bengal, with a Plan of Settlement* (London: 1782). For treatment of Francis's *Plan*, see Guha, *Rule of Property*, ch. 4.

[188]Weitzman, *Hastings and Francis*, Appendix II, no. 2, p. 305.

[189]Francis, *Plan for a Settlement*, p. 72.

while the "form of their government was despotic," in truth it was not oppressive to "the mass of the conquered people."[190] Citing the first volume of Hume's *History of England* on the moderate nature of the Roman conquest of Europe, Francis took the Mughal Empire to be similarly "civilised" in form.[191] Armed with these insights, he presented the Zamindars as hereditary landed princes who performed official duties as administrators and magistrates with an independent stake in the country. Francis looked upon Rouse as a loyal ally against Hastings, especially since, as a collector in Bengal down to 1778, he had shared his views on the management of the revenue. Rouse also became important to Burke as a source of information in connection with the Bengal Judicature.[192] His evidence to the Select Committee is recorded in the first *Report*: ever since the "Subjection of Bengal to Mogul Government," he asserted, the Zamindars had enjoyed the status of hereditary proprietors, in that capacity exercising local jurisdictions and attracting the "Devotion" of their people.[193]

The evidence of George Vansittart and Harry Verelst to the Select Committee confirmed the perspective advanced by Boughton Rouse. The Zamindars were in effect "tributary Princes," Vansittart contended, enjoying substantial freedom in the management of their districts.[194] Verelst explained the historical foundations on which this autonomy rested. The "Gentoos," he insisted, were profoundly committed to their native customs and traditions, with the result that their Islamic conquerors, who had generally subjugated their victims "by the Edge of the Sword," had been obliged to "sheath the Sword" in the face of this dogged attachment. The only alternative to tolerating an independent Hindu culture, and thus maintaining its mode of social organisation intact, was to "deluge the country in Blood" as a prelude to conversion.[195] A decade earlier, Verelst had already arrived at this conclusion, but he supported it with a different explanation: despotism was milder or more "tolerable" in India than "it ever before appeared in the history of mankind." This, however, was seemingly a result of the submissiveness rather than the tenacity of the subject population: secure in the face of their placid conquered subjects, the Mughals could afford to indulge this "timid race."[196] Oppression was not therefore endemic to the Mughal constitution, but had instead gradually crept in with the onset of its dilapidation when provincial Nawabs began to extend their power as central authority at Delhi receded: "during this progress to independence, burthens multiplied on the people."[197] However, this kind of oppression was belatedly superimposed upon a sys-

[190] Ibid., p. 30.

[191] Ibid., p. 79.

[192] EB, Bill to Amend 1784 India Act, 22 March 1786, *W & S*, VI, p. 67. See also EB to Lord Macartney, 16 October 1781, *Corr.*, X, p. 12.

[193] *Report form the Committee* (1781) in *Commons Sessional Papers*, ed. Lambert, LXXXVIII, p. 30.

[194] Ibid.

[195] Ibid., p. 37.

[196] Verelst, *A View of the Rise*, p. 65.

[197] Ibid., p. 66. Cf. ibid., p. 145n. The same point is made in Henry Vansittart, *A Narrative of the Transactions in Bengal*, I, pp. v–vi.

tem of absolute authority that was fundamentally concessive in nature, founded on an acceptance of native manners and opinions.

In challenging the authority of Montesquieu on the nature of despotic government, Voltaire had made it his business to dispel the notion that absolute authority was coterminous with violent expropriation. In the process, he redefined feudal subordination in contradistinction to political enslavement. Not only was the organisation of the German Empire presented as a feudal edifice compatible with liberty, but the Mughal Empire was likened to its European counterpart: "The Grand Mughal is the same as the Emperor of Germany. The Subahdars are princes of the Empire, each having become a sovereign in his province."[198] This verdict was the culmination of a longstanding determination to take issue with what Voltaire saw as contradictory characterisations of eastern despotism, depicted, on the one hand, as lacking in all restraint and, on the other, as exhibiting the symptoms of moderation.[199] In his *Essai sur les mœurs*, he chided Bernier, Tavernier and Catrou for their incoherence, since the forms of despotism which they confidently associated with Asia would in fact be incapable of maintaining any authority whatever: such "pretended" despotisms were a chimera, he insisted.[200] The apparently simplified models of eastern governments publicised by the Jesuit literature on India had been gradually revised in British historical representations since the 1760s. In 1770, Luke Scrafton claimed that the Tartar institutions of India protected the ancient Hindu laws, the most immutable of which was "the hereditary right to all lands, which even extends to the tenants."[201] Even Dow, for whom the principles of passive obedience were "carried through every vein of the state," argued that Muslim government on the subcontinent was not "so terrible in its nature, as men born in free countries are apt to imagine."[202] Moreover, the administration of the Rajas, while also despotic, seemed "milder than the most limited monarchy in Europe."[203]

For Robert Orme, while the relationship between the Emperor and his viceroys was purely despotic, and while the circulation of property and offices was designed to prevent a great concentration of estates in particular families, the "body of the people" was comparatively secure in its liberties: the right of sale and bequest inhered in the cultivators of the soil, and the estates of territorial princes "descended

[198] Voltaire, *Fragments sur l'Inde, sur le General Lalli, et sur le comte de Morangiés* (Paris: 1773), p. 11.

[199] For discussion, see Pocock, *Barbarism and Religion II: Narratives of Civil Government*, pp. 83–159.

[200] Voltaire, *Essai sur les mœurs et l'esprit des nations*, ed. René Pomeau (Paris: Garnier, 1963), 2 vols., II, p. 404, taking issue with François Bernier, *Suite des mémoires de l'empire du grand Mogol* (Paris: 1671); Jean-Baptiste Tavernier, *Six voyages en Turquie, en Perse et aux Indes* (Paris: 1679); and Père Catrou, *Histoire générale de l'empire du Mogol* (Paris: 1705). Voltaire's discussion is cited by Francis, *Plan for a Settlement*, p. 80.

[201] Luke Scrafton, *Reflections on the Government of Indostan, with a Short Sketch of the History of Bengal, from 1738 to 1756* (London: 1770), pp. 24–25.

[202] Dow, "A Dissertation Concerning the Origins and Nature of Despotism in Hindustan" in idem, *History of Hindustan*, III, p. xxiii.

[203] Ibid., p. xxxiv.

to the natural heirs."[204] Even so, for Verelst, none of this detracted from the "impossibility of introducing English laws" among eastern governments, however moderated they might be in their despotism.[205] Burke accepted Verelst's contention that British legal forms had no place in the judicial administration of India, insisting in his speech on the Bengal Judicature Bill of 27 June 1781 that laws had to be adapted to the "genius of the people."[206] Back in May 1774, Burke had described the population in general as "submissive," formed to obedience by "nature, religion & inveterate custom."[207] On this assumption, he expressed the view in 1781 that British constitutional arrangements and legal provisions were superior to their Asian counterparts, yet he still contended that the government of a territory depended on the preferences of the population over which it ruled.[208] In the case of India, the subject population had grown accustomed to a form of rule that was "more despotic" than British norms, and so enlightened power had little option but to accommodate illiberal attitudes and practices. Enlightenment could not be brought about by tyrannical imposition: "even a free and equal plan of government, would be considered despotic by those who desired to have their old laws and their ancient system."[209] Back in 1772, Verelst had given some sense of what this "ancient system" involved. It was based, he believed, on personal rather than civil subordination, on account of which the experience of subjection to immediate authority seemed to offer more security than the remote promise of public utility.[210] Ties of personal authority underpinned all social arrangements, defining relations between masters and servants, merchants and manufacturers, and husbands and wives. As a consequence, while there might be considerable overlap between the laws of contract in Britain and India, public and domestic law diverged sharply between both jurisdictions.[211] Native laws and legal officers ought therefore to be retained. To prevent Bengal ultimately achieving independence on account of this effective autonomy, the Supreme Council should be invested with the power to issue edicts, while British judges should be charged with regulating the conduct of *pandits* and *qazis*. In practice, therefore, "some enlightened minds" would watch with parental care over a subordinate yet improving system of despotism.[212]

Burke was similarly concerned about the prospect of Bengali independence in the event of a failure to secure Indian "consent" to British rule: "must we abandon

[204] Orme, "A Dissertation on the Establishments Made by the Mahomedan Conquerors in Indostan" (1763) in idem, *A History of Military Transactions*, I, p. 27.

[205] Verelst, *A View of the Rise*, p. 131.

[206] EB, Speech on Bengal Judicature Act, 27 June 1781, *W & S*, V, p. 140.

[207] Notes for Speech on Massachusetts Bay Regulating Bill, WWM BkP 27:229.

[208] EB, Speech on the Bengal Judicature Bill, 27 June 1781, *W & S*, V, p. 141. Cf. EB, "Observations" to the *First Report* of the Select Committee, 5 February 1782, ibid., p. 184.

[209] EB, Speech on the Bengal Judicature Bill, 27 June 1781, ibid., p. 141.

[210] Verelst, *A View of the Rise*, p. 135.

[211] Ibid., pp. 135–38.

[212] Ibid., pp. 145–48.

the government of the country rather than agree to rule over them by laws inimical to ourselves?" The answer to the rhetorical question was clear: "surely not."[213] The recent behaviour of the Supreme Court in violating the "dearest rights" of Indians, including systematic disrespect for both their "ladies" and their "religious ceremonies," risked contributing to the destruction of the government of a few thousand Britons presiding over 30 million natives.[214] Burke had no difficulty in endorsing the wisdom of the "laws of England," but he considered any attempt to force them onto another civilisation as tantamount to exhibiting a "savage & tyrannical contempt for the rights of mankind at large."[215] After all, to impose civil institutions and judicial arrangements by violence was to trespass against the "first principle" of freedom, which is liberty in the choice of one's own laws.[216] This choice could not take the form of resolutions by the people—"Civil Liberty," Burke contended, was "out of the Question" in India—but would instead have to be understood in terms of tacitly expressed opinion made manifest through the customs of India's "little platoons & clusters." These customs had formed a bulwark against domination in the past, so it would be a singular piece of folly to disregard them now. "Manners stand in the place of Laws in Asia," Burke observed: "it is by them that the ferocity of despotism has been corrected."[217] Directly transplanting the "heterogeneous mixture called the law of England" into the subcontinent could never succeed in meliorating the condition of the natives.[218] Instead of introducing the forms of liberty, it was more likely to add weight to the "chains of their servitude."[219] Even the idea of providing a jury system was misconceived since, under the circumstances, juries could not operate as popular tribunals aimed at guarding the "inferior people against the violence of power."[220] To subject the inhabitants of Bengal to the judgment of British juries was to place the vulnerable many in the hands of the empowered few. Moreover, given that the few in question were often of "low" standing, this arrangement would amount to the "worst sort of oligarchy" under which a tiny demotic minority would determine the fate of the mass of the population.[221]

[213] EB, Speech on Bengal Judicature Bill, 27 June 1781, *W & S*, V, p. 141.

[214] Ibid. Burke is referring, inter alia, to the recent Patna case, discussed in detail in Travers, *Ideology and Empire*, pp. 191–205.

[215] Draft notes on the Bengal Judicature Bill, Northamptonshire MS. A. XXVIII.6.

[216] Ibid.

[217] Ibid.

[218] See EB, *Letter to the Sheriffs of Bristol* (2 April 1777), *W & S*, III, pp. 304–5: "I could never conceive . . . that the *Cutchery* Court and the grand Jury of *Salem* could be regulated on a similar plan."

[219] Ibid. On the wider context for this analysis, see Robert Travers, "Contested Despotism: Problems of Liberty in British India" in Jack P. Greene ed., *Exclusionary Empire: English Liberty Overseas, 1600–1900* (Cambridge: Cambridge University Press, 2009).

[220] Northamptonshire MS. A. XIV.66.

[221] Draft notes on the Bengal Judicature Bill, Northamptonshire MS. A. XXVIII.6. A jury comprising native inhabitants was another matter. This was an arrangement that Burke came to support in 1783: see Burke, *Ninth Report*, p. 205.

10.5 The *First* and *Ninth Report* of the Select Committee

With the fall of Lord North in March 1782, British high politics entered a period of rapid change. Over the following two years, the question of the relationship between the East India Company and the British state moved to the centre of parliamentary concerns. The decision of that question was partly determined by the machinations of the political establishment, but its urgency was pressed upon successive ministries by the pace of external events. The increasingly beleaguered financial condition of the Company, partly stemming from the drain of war against the Marathas and Haidar Ali, made the impact of Company affairs on the House of Commons unavoidable. In addition, as the ongoing struggle with France, originally framed by the contest with the colonies, threatened to spill over onto the subcontinent, the weariness of the mother country called for a solution to outstanding East Indian problems.[222] Burke's work on the Select Committee along with Dundas's on the Secret Committee did much to drive and shape the inevitable reforms that would follow.[223] The centrality of both politicians to the terms of the India debate was guaranteed by the extension of the remit of the Secret Committee on 30 November 1781 and of the Select Committee at the start of December, since the Reports of each would continue to inform discussion over a period of two years.[224] Principle, as well as party, would now dominate the political agenda, and Burke would play a pivotal role in formulating its content.[225] The relative importance of both committees shifted after the demise of North, depending on the composition of the ministries under which they sat: Burke's prevailed under the second Rockingham administration, while Dundas's came to the fore after he accepted office under Lord Shelburne. Between them, they pushed for Sir Thomas Rumbold to be disciplined for his conduct of affairs in the Carnatic, for the recall of Elijah Impey for judicial mismanagement in his capacity as Chief Justice, and for the repudiation of Warren Hastings for dishonouring the policy of the British nation. In addition, they drafted major Bills aimed at reforming the Company. Each of these developments was flanked by the publication of at least one of the Committees' reports.

The first *Report* of the reconstituted Select Committee appeared on 5 February 1782, having occupied Burke throughout the previous month.[226] During that time, he was completing the "Observations" included in the *Report*, expanding its range of reference from a specific concern with Elijah Impey's contradictory role as judge presiding over the higher civil court in Calcutta, the Sadr Diwani Adalat, as well

[222] Sutherland, *East India Company Politics*, pp. 365–67.

[223] Phillips, "Parliament and Southern India," pp. 84–87.

[224] *CJ*, XXXVIII, pp. 598, 599–600.

[225] Sutherland, *East India Company Politics*, pp. 368–69.

[226] It was published as *First Report from the Select Committee, Appointed to take into Consideration the State of the Administration of Justice in the Provinces of Bengal, Bahar, and Orissa* (London: 1782).

as acting as Chief Justice of the Supreme Court of Judicature.[227] Hastings had appointed Impey to his position on the civil court in October 1780 as a gesture of conciliation during their disputes over the jurisdiction of the Supreme Court, but in practice it meant that the head of the main court of appeal from the provincial courts in Bengal was also the head of the Supreme Court to which plaintiffs might want to appeal should they seek redress against the decisions of the civil court.[228] The conflict here was tangible, since the Chief Justice of the Supreme Court had been appointed as a check on the Company, although he was now acting as a judge in one of its courts. "One and the same Man," Burke commented, "possesses, and in Effect blocks up, all the Avenues to Justice."[229] Since the organisation of the courts of a subordinate jurisdiction was a matter of grave legislative concern, Burke's attention was drawn from the judicial administration of Bengal to the wider issue of the general constitution of the powers of the Company. It was important, Burke thought, that the limitations of these powers ought in principle to be recognised, not least since they were commonly interpreted as enjoying an unbounded extent.

The reason for this was to be found in a pervasive yet erroneous perception of the basis of the Company's authority on the subcontinent. It was commonly assumed that the corporation had inherited the rights enjoyed in practice by the Nawabs of Bengal in the aftermath of the decline of central Mughal authority: since Nawabi power in this period seemed bent on securing its independence from the Emperor while also appearing to exercise its prerogatives oppressively, the Company was often assumed to have inherited the despotic authority improperly appropriated by Mughal deputies in the provinces as a matter of right. But for Burke this claim was patently absurd. In the first place, it made no sense to assume an entitlement to illegitimate authority: such an assumption was an intrinsic juridical nonsense, amounting to "a rule to have no rule" in the conduct of affairs.[230] It was, moreover, preposterous to pretend that parliament could ever have intended such an arrangement. But not only was the idea of a *right* to arbitrary power intrinsically confused, it was also based on a false picture of the history of government in South Asia. The Mughal polity had never been literally arbitrary, Burke insisted—the "Mahomedans were subject to Mahommedan Law," based on the Koran and its judicial interpretation, giving rise to the customary usages of the Empire.[231] The Hindu population was likewise bound by its legal customs: as Hastings's protégé Nathaniel Halhed had recently demonstrated in translating *A Code of the Gentoo Laws*, the provisions of the pandits were as extensive as they were respected.[232]

227 This matter was taken up again in Burke, *Ninth Report*, p. 206.

228 For an account of this arrangement see M. P. Jain, *Outlines of Indian Legal and Constitutional History* (Nagpur, New Delhi: Wadhwa and Co., 2006).

229 EB, *"Observations" on the First Report of the Select Committee* (5 February 1782), *W & S*, V, p. 163.

230 Ibid., p. 170.

231 Ibid., p. 171.

232 Nathaniel Halhed, *A Code of Gentoo Laws, or Ordinances of the Pundits* (London: 1776), cited in Burke, *"Observations"*, *W & S*, V, p. 171. The review of Halhed in *The Annual Register for the Year 1777*,

While Company servants were in the habit of claiming arbitrary power as a bequest from their predecessors, their conduct was also commonly justified in terms of the rights of conquest. Here, Burke confessed, matters grew "dark and arduous."[233] As a matter of historical record, Burke well knew, power was frequently established by the rights of war. Yet it was equally clear that civil authority rarely if ever claimed those rights as a guide to political conduct: as Hume had argued in 1742, even the most severely despotic government depended on the support of the population that it ruled.[234] In any case, however extreme the rights of sovereignty based on conquest might be assumed to be, it was inconceivable that parliament would transfer such awesome authority to a subordinate agency of government.[235] Burke believed that sovereign power was unimpeachable by its nature, yet its rights could never be delegated to a representative agency. In a set of notes drafted for a speech on India in the 1780s, Burke emphasised the fact that "the supreme power in any constitution of Government must be absolute."[236] Absolute power of the kind might be rendered increasingly arbitrary by a process of corruption, although, in any decent system of government, procedural mechanisms could be relied upon to correct such deviation, preventing power from descending into a pure "Government of Will."[237] Yet however absolute the theoretical rights of sovereignty might be, by definition such authority could never be invested in a subordinate jurisdiction. Consequently, the idea of "*an intermediate arbitrary power*" amounted to a contradiction in terms.[238] Besides, since the Company habitually acted as if it derived its title from a grant conferred by treaty with the Emperor, it followed that it had assumed responsibilities of office that could not plausibly be equated with the rights of war.[239]

Nonetheless, it seemed obvious that the Company had in practice acted without restraint. By this stage Burke had long surrendered all residual doubt about the gravity of East India Company abuses, explicitly recognising that its servants had acted with devastating impunity as they imposed their will on the natives while disregarding "ancient Establishments."[240] All the while the Direction had failed to curb their

---

p. 246, argues that the record of Hindu law might profitably be used to soften British laws by paying due regard to "the peculiar and national prejudices of the Hindoo." In 1794, Burke recommended Halhed's book as demonstrating the "enlightened" state of jurisprudence on the subcontinent. See EB, Speech in Reply, 28 May 1794, *W & S*, VII, p. 267.

[233] Ibid., p. 172.

[234] David Hume, "Of the First Principles of Government" (1742) in idem, *Essays Moral, Political and Literary*, pp. 32–33: "The Soldan of EGYPT, or the emperor of ROME, might drive his harmless subjects, like brute beasts, against their sentiments and inclination: But he must, at least, have led his *mamalukes*, or *praetorian bands*, like men, by their opinion." For Burke's general debt to this line of argument, see Richard Bourke, "Sovereignty, Opinion and Revolution in Edmund Burke," *History of European Ideas*, 25:3 (1999), pp. 99–120.

[235] Burke, *"Observations"*, *W & S*, V, p. 172.

[236] Northamptonshire MS. A. XIV.5.

[237] Ibid.

[238] Ibid. Cf. EB, *"Observations"*, *W & S*, V, p. 172.

[239] Ibid.

[240] Ibid., p. 175.

servants' behaviour. As Burke saw it, the interposition of Leadenhall Street was only very "occasional"; attempts to reform the Directors had failed to improve their performance; and, in any case, the Direction was powerless to control those whom it scrutinised.[241] The introduction of the Supreme Court under Impey was intended to provide relief. In the absence of popular control or established privileges among the people, the only resort against oppression lay in the effectiveness of the judiciary. Yet in India this resource occasioned alarm rather than redress as a consequence of its corruption under the influence of Warren Hastings.[242] Given the customs and manners of the native population, the corruption of due process would prove singularly destructive. Long habituated to existence under an unaccountable regime, the people of South Asia were concessive and "dissembling," and so only roused with difficulty to complaint.[243] These traits were commonly associated with banyans and gomasthas who operated as brokers and agents for Europeans. Their condition, Burke was proposing, had socialised them into the "miserable Arts and Subterfuges of Servitude," which made them ready candidates for complicity in oppression. As a result, Europeans would bring to perfection the despotic manners of the east instead of delivering on the promise of enlightenment. Indeed, they would ultimately become victims of the culture they were helping to entrench: "the Europeans, by being brought themselves into the same Condition, which produced those habits in others, instead of improving the natives by the Boldness and Openness of European Manners, will themselves be led gradually into the Refinement, Mystery, Dissimulation, and Prevarication of Indian Banians and Gomastahs."[244]

The second Rockingham administration came into office a month after the publication of the first *Report* of the Select Committee. The *Report* was referred to a committee of the whole House, giving rise to a series of resolutions highly critical of Impey and Hastings, which were carried on 24 April 1782. At this time, however, the initiative in Indian affairs was passing to Dundas since the ministry was divided on how to proceed in the business.[245] Shelburne, now in the Cabinet, supported Sulivan and Hastings, a situation that prompted Burke to urge Rockingham to attach Dundas to his interest before Shelburne gained the upper hand in shaping South Asian politics. Adam Smith, who had access to the Lord Advocate's sentiments via the Duke of Buccleuch, had informed Burke that Dundas might be seduced, yet Rockingham could not be moved to act. Shelburne had already taken up Thomas Orde, a favourite of the Advocate and an important presence on his Secret Committee. A cabal, Burke feared, was in the process of forming that could dislodge the Rockinghams' position in the Commons. He made an explicit appeal on 27 April: "I am sorry, that your Lordship thinks slightly of India in the Scale of our

241 Ibid., pp. 145, 151–52.

242 Ibid., p. 179.

243 Ibid., p. 184.

244 Ibid.

245 Dundas's Secret Committee had turned to investigate the "rise, progress, [and] conduct" of the Maratha War the previous December. See *CJ*, XXXVIII, p. 600.

politicks."[246] Burke envisaged the remnants of the Bedfords joining forces with Dundas and his friends in support of Shelburne, consolidating their coalition "upon this Indian Ground." Since Shelburne was irretrievably ignorant about the subject, and bent on serving Sulivan, Impey and Hastings, there was a danger that this alliance would make a "Jobb" of East Indian reform, "to the utter ruin of that Country and of this."[247]

Dundas, as it happened, stood aloof from every blandishment, advancing his case from a position of independence. On 9 April, with the publication of the sixth *Report* of the Secret Committee before the House, he had spoken at length of the disastrous consequences that had accompanied the shift to "offensive military operations" on the subcontinent, inflaming the powers of the region against the British.[248] The servants of the Company had "broken through the policy laid down by Lord Clive" of operating defensively in India, fancying themselves as latter-day reproductions of Alexander the Great.[249] Burke echoed these sentiments in his contribution to the same debate, but he remained nervous that Dundas's planned reforms would increase the powers of the crown: he was, he made clear, averse to the idea that the ministry should take "any part in the direction of India."[250] Parliament, and not the government, was the "Cure" for India's ills.[251] But by July, when the ministry collapsed on the death of Lord Rockingham, Dundas was recruited by Shelburne to serve in his short-lived government. With the opening of parliament on Tuesday 5 December, the India issue was prominent in the King's Speech, with details of a new Bill drafted by Dundas leaking out at the end of January.[252] Shelburne, however, fell on 24 February 1783, and attempts to form a new government descended into disarray. In the midst of the ensuing confusion, on 1 March, Burke wrote to Dundas with information relevant to provisions for the security of the Raja of Tanjore to be included in the new India Bill.[253] Interference by the former Governor of Madras, Thomas Rumbold, in the management of one of the districts of Tanjore had had a blighting effect on the revenue stream. The deposition of Chait Singh, the Raja of Benares, had had a similar effect on the Company coffers. Burke drew a general conclusion intended to guide Dundas's conduct: "Native government can alone combine

[246] EB to the Marquess of Rockingham, 27 April 1782, *Corr.*, IV, p. 449.

[247] Ibid.

[248] *Parliamentary History*, XXII, col. 1276.

[249] Ibid., col. 1279.

[250] Ibid., col. 1303; EB, Speech on Secret Committee Resolutions, 15 April 1782, *W & S*, V, p. 190.

[251] Northamptonshire MS. A. XXVIII.5. Cf. *Morning Post*, 16 April 1782; *Gazetteer*, 16 April 1762; *London Courant*, 16 April 1782. The form of the administration in Bengal, on the other hand, seemed appropriate to Burke. See Major John Scott to Warren Hastings, 24 April 1783, Add. MS. 29159, fol. 47: "The present constitution [Burke] said was a good one, & all that was wanted was a Change of Men," meaning the substitution of Philip Francis for Warren Hastings.

[252] *Parliamentary Register* (Debrett), XI, p. 7, where the government looks forward to framing "some fundamental laws" regarding India; on details of the new Bill appearing in January, see Sutherland, *East India Company Politics*, pp. 391–2.

[253] EB to Henry Dundas, 1 March 1783, *Corr.*, V, pp. 67–69.

the prosperity of the Country with the regularity of payments—and this is not only true of Tanjour, and Benares; but of every other mediate or immediate dependency in India."[254] As Burke cast about for the best means of remedying the situation in the east, he began to consider the responsibility of individuals. "I have but a poor opinion of regulations, that are not supported either by punishment or reward," he wrote to Loughborough in 1781.[255] Two years later Laurence Sulivan was presented as "the principal Cause of the distress & ruin of our affairs in the East," being "closely connected with the delinquents at home & abroad."[256] The general character of Burke's ideas was now clear: no amount of regulation internal to the Company itself was sufficient to hold its servants to account; external scrutiny, unlike in Dundas's Bill, was to be enforced by parliamentary committees rather than the arm of government; and the administration of Indian territories was to be conducted through local rulers. Ultimately, it was only on the basis of accommodation to Asian practices and sensibilities that society and politics in the region would be enlightened by means of the long-term, indirect influence of British principles of government.

With the formation of the Fox–North Coalition in April 1783, Dundas's Bill was quietly allowed to perish.[257] By this time, a draft of the *Ninth Report* of the Select Committee was more or less complete, having been written almost exclusively by Burke.[258] The *Report* represents Burke's most sustained analysis of the constitution of the East India Company, presenting an exhaustive indictment of both its commercial and political organisation, encompassing all its internal and external relations. It begins by outlining the inadequacy of North's Regulating Act of 1773, contending that, although that Act had been passed in the aftermath of five detailed reports compiled by Burgoyne's Select Committee, and another five by the government's Secret Committee, it had failed to capitalise on the extensive information made available to the Commons. North's reforms, comprehending the constitution of the Court of Proprietors and the Court of Directors, as well as the judicial, administrative and supervisory systems of government placed over the subcontinent, had consequently failed. The reform of the Court of Proprietors exemplified the government's simplistic understanding of the problem. Under North's Act, voting in the General Court had been confined to the holders of larger shares of stock on the assumption that this reduction in the democratic character of the Court of Proprietors would both diminish faction and increase responsibility.[259] But this was on the assumption that

[254] Ibid., pp. 68–69.

[255] EB to Lord Loughborough, 2 February 1781, Unpublished Letters, III, p. 953.

[256] EB to Lord North, 28 March 1783, Unpublished Letters, I, p. 12.

[257] Dundas had moved for "leave to bring in a Bill for the better regulation of the government of India" on 14 April 1783, which was duly granted. See *Parliamentary Register* (Debrett), IX, pp. 608–13.

[258] On the authorship of the *Report*, see Phillip Francis to French Laurence and Walker King, copied 30 May 1812, WWM BkP 31:16; on the date of composition, see Charles Boughton Rouse to Burke, 19 March 1783, WWM BkP 1:1776.

[259] The populism of the General Court continued to be a target under North: see the comments of his Secretary to the Treasury, John Robinson, in the summer of 1778 in Add. MS. 38398, fols. 114–15: "nothing can be more preposterous than the present System: The Concernment of several Asiatic

Company abuses would depreciate the value of shares, and that the motives for holding stock were purely commercial in nature. The fact was, however, that Company shareholders viewed their votes as a passport to political patronage rather than as an immediate source of emolument: "The India Proprietor . . . will always be in the first instance a Politician; and the bolder his Enterprize, and the more corrupt his Views, the less will be his Consideration of the Price to be paid for compassing them."[260]

The reform of the Direction proved no more successful. The idea was to increase the independence of the directors by extending their tenure of office, subjecting them to rotation, and extending their authority. However, their authority was, if anything, reduced. By balloting the Proprietors for the composition of the Court of Directors, the General Court continued to hold sway over their superiors. Besides, the Directors were not compelled to prosecute delinquency among Company servants, nor disposed to reward their most qualified employees. Their orders, consequently, were "habitually despised" at all levels among the operatives on the ground.[261] Rules for promotion through the ranks had not been established, with the result that potentially honourable merchants were left to despair of ascending to higher offices on the basis of decent efficiency, obliging them "to make up in Lucre what they can never hope to acquire in Station."[262] Lacking a culture of meritorious reward and the instruments of punitive correction, the Directors steadily dwindled in respect.

As Burke had been at pains to emphasise since 1781, the introduction of the Court of Judicature had also been counterproductive, ultimately proving "terrible to the Natives."[263] The new Bengal Council, headed by a Governor General, was similarly poorly designed: its authority over the other Presidencies in matters of war and peace was indeterminate, while its estimate of its own administrative powers was excessive in the extreme.[264] In theory, this framework of rule could be reined in by the British government: through control over appointments and powers of inspection the Supreme Council could be disciplined by ministerial intervention. However, national government proved no more sensitive to meritorious appointment than the Directors were in monitoring promotion. The gradations of rank on which seniority in the Company had originally been based were disregarded in key appointments to the Council.[265] Equally, the government's powers of inspection were no match for East Indian corruption: incoming, but not outgoing, correspondence could be

---

Provinces at six thousand miles distance is ultimately in the hands of the Court of Proprietors, the most Democratick Body of this Country."

[260] EB, *Ninth Report of the Select Committee* (25 June 1783), *W & S*, V, p. 201.

[261] Ibid., pp. 203–4. This was the subject of the *Second Report from the Select Committee, Appointed to Take into Consideration the state of the Administration of Justice in the Provinces of Bengal, Bahar, and Orissa* (London: 1782).

[262] EB, *Ninth Report of the Select Committee* (25 June 1783), *W & S*, V, p. 212.

[263] Ibid, p. 205.

[264] Ibid., p. 207.

[265] Ibid., p. 216. Burke focuses on the example of Stephen Sulivan, the son of Laurence Sulivan, who, having been appointed to the posts of secretary and then Persian translator, was ultimately nominated to the Council without any obvious qualification.

scrutinised, although actual orders could never be modified.[266] In the absence of any effective system of regulation guiding the activities of the Company, disorders and abuses had multiplied in the aftermath of North's reforms: judicial and executive arrangements proved dysfunctional; aggressive wars were undertaken; the Country powers were oppressed; and orders were ignored. Underlying all this was not merely a failure to correct delinquency, but a fundamental error of policy: the pursuit of profit was given precedence over the welfare of the Indians. This, of course, amounted to a complete perversion of the contract of government. Any scheme of reformation would have to begin by an inversion of priorities, restoring Indian affairs to their "natural Order": "The prosperity of the Natives must be previously secured, before any Profit from them whatsoever is attempted."[267]

Burke's criticism here went beyond the contention that the obligations of government had been corrupted under the influence of commercial greed. The principles of commerce had themselves been distorted by diverting fiscal revenue into the Company's trade. With the assumption of the *Diwani* in 1765, a "great Revolution" in the organisation of the Company's business had suddenly occurred.[268] Having hitherto paid for its "investment" by the import of European bullion, the corporation from now on employed its territorial revenues to procure its merchandise for export.[269] The alternative, as the Company saw it, would have been to remit silver bullion to Europe, where it commanded a lower price, leaving nothing to be done but to export it back to Bengal. It was therefore employed as an article of trade, with a negative effect on domestic manufacture, starving the country of the product of its industry and depriving other European traders of their customary volume of commerce. As James Steuart had observed of the new arrangement, "the industry of the workman was paid for with the money of his own country."[270] A percentage of the revenue was also absorbed by the British Treasury and the Company's dividend, increasing the drain on specie in India and reducing the means of investment, which began to be replenished by credit. Power and influence, instead of commercial utility, governed the Company's trade.[271] As early as December 1780 Burke had been

[266] Ibid., p. 220. Burke had complained about this arrangement two and a half years earlier. See "Minutes taken on Ideas on East India Affairs, suggested by Mr. Burke for Consideration, 12 January 1781," Add. MS. 38405, fol. 10r–v.

[267] EB, *Ninth Report of the Select Committee* (25 June 1783), *W & S*, V, p. 221.

[268] Ibid., p. 223.

[269] In fact the export of bullion ceased after 1757. From 1760, the revenues of Burdwan, Midnapore and Chittagong were used for investment. The income form the Zamindari of Twenty-Four Parganas was also available to the Company. See N. R. Sinha, *The Economic History of Bengal: From Plassey to the Permanent Settlement* (Calcutta: Firma K. L. Mukhopadhyay, 1965), 2 vols., I, pp. 11–12; Bayly, *Indian Society and the Making of the British Empire*, p. 53.

[270] James Steuart, *The Principles of Money Applied to the Present State of the Coin of Bengal* (London: 1772). On Steuart's general account, see William J. Barber, *British Economic Thought and India, 1600–1858: A Study in the History of Development Economics* (Oxford: Oxford University Press, 1975), ch. 4.

[271] EB, *Ninth Report of the Select Committee* (25 June 1783), *W & S*, V, pp. 224–27. Burke's analysis here became a staple of Indian historiography in the early twentieth century. See the extensive citation of

enumerating the results: Company servants, he believed, were guilty of "tyranny to the natives" as a consequence of their hunger for "dominion."[272] The substitution of political ambition in the place of mercantile interests had deranged the commerce of Britain and India: it had directly ruinous effects on the prosperity of the subcontinent; it created a mirage of commercial buoyancy that inflated the price of Company stock, resulting in the crash of 1769; and, although individual fortunes were made, Britain's commercial profit steadily declined.

The drain on native wealth was further increased by the charges on the revenue incurred by British civil and military establishments, of which the Company, but not India, was made a beneficiary. This immediately impacted on the Muslim population, which depended on remuneration through its monopoly on government posts, having left "the antient Gentû Proprietors" in possession of their lands.[273] While a stipend had been stipulated by treaty to the Nawab in 1765, this was steadily reduced over the succeeding years. Opportunities in the army likewise declined: although Indians made up nine-tenths of the fighting force, none occupied its higher ranks, and all lucrative contracts for supplies were tendered to the British.[274] At the same time, overland trade had been suffered to decline. Although the northern provinces of the Mughal Empire had never much depended on maritime commerce, the trade with the western coast of the subcontinent, along with that to Persia and to Tartary, had long been extensive. But with the fall of Nadir Shah, the Persian trade was destroyed, as was a substantial proportion of domestic commerce with the decline of Mughal power. At the same time, the campaigns of Haidar Ali had devastated the Carnatic, while British arms had devastated Awadh and Rohilkhand.[275] All the while, Britain's position as territorial ruler enabled its servants to extend their private monopolies on articles of trade, beggaring local traders and corrupting commercial logic.[276] Saltpetre, opium and salt were gradually monopolised by the Company, leading to the distortions in the pattern of supply and demand that so astonished Adam Smith.[277]

With the depletion of South Asia's resources, it was only a matter of time before the impact on the Company was felt. Since neither the commerce, manufacture nor agriculture of the subcontinent was improved while land rents were being raised to

the *Ninth Report* in Romesh Chunder Dutt, *The Economic History of British India* (London: Kegan Paul, Trench, Tübner & Co., 1902), pp. 48–50.

[272] Speech to the General Court of the East India Company, December 1780, reported in John Barrow, *Some Account of the Public Life of the Earl of Macartney* (London: 1807), 2 vols., I, pp. 73–74; EB, Speech on Secret Committee, 30 April 1781, *W & S*, V, p. 137. It was at this point that Burke first raised the prospect of impeachment: see ibid., p. 138.

[273] EB, *Ninth Report of the Select Committee* (25 June 1783), *W & S*, V, pp. 228.

[274] Ibid., pp. 229.

[275] Ibid., pp. 229–30.

[276] Ibid., pp. 244–46.

[277] An account of these monopolies takes up a substantial portion of the argument of the *Ninth Report* in ibid., pp. 247–306. Much of this was apparently drawn up by Philip Francis. See Francis to the editors of Burke's works, n.d., copied 30 May 1812, WWM BkP 31:16. For Smith's criticism of the monopoly on the opium trade, see *Wealth of Nations*, II, p. 636.

supply the demand for revenue, the Company had come to depend on a sinking supply of funds. This drove it, on Burke's analysis, to desperate lengths: "they plunged deeper . . . and were drawn from Expedient to Expedient for the Supply of the Investment, into that endless Chain of Wars, which this House and its Resolutions, has so justly condemned."[278] An imperial pathology had evolved: the politicisation of commerce had promoted the spirit of conquest. This was facilitated by the discretion afforded to Company officials, based on their own interpretation of the latitude they enjoyed for action. The obedience of officials was a *sine qua non* of imperial justice. Where servants operated in the face of major temptations to abuse and were invested with considerable powers over a timid population, a culture of disobedience could be devastating. Under Hastings, it became "uniform" and "systematic," ultimately being embraced as a matter of principle on the basis of an arrogant interpretation of the Governor's prerogatives.[279] The presumptuousness of the Company increased with the diminution of the role in government played by Mohammad Reza Khan: where a portion of the Nawab's authority was preserved in the hands of the *naib*, who retained, under Clive's provisions, responsibility for criminal justice, the natives were screened from the reality of a change of power. This, as Burke saw it, prevented Bengal "from wearing the dangerous Appearance, and still more, from sinking into the terrible state, of a Country of Conquest."[280] With the removal of Reza Khan from office, Burke contended, Hastings and Richard Barwell came to see themselves as the heirs to an absolute conquest with direct access to positive power over the natives. This power, Burke observed, was tangibly "real" while authority in Britain was "purely formal." When, under the circumstances of remote empire, these two jurisdictions clash, "their opposition serves only to degrade the Authority that ought to predominate, and to exalt the Power that ought to be dependent."[281] Free governments, Hume had warned, are liable to be as oppressive to their subject provinces as they are jealous of their hard-won liberty.[282] In India, Burke complained, this syndrome had grown rampant: despotism had become endemic within a provincial administration that flouted the authority of the mother republic.

10.6 Fox's India Bills

Nine months of acute political attention was focused on the affairs of the East India Company after the formation of the Fox–North Coalition in April 1783. By 20 August, Burke was at work on material that would be incorporated into Fox's

[278] EB, *Ninth Report of the Select Committee* (25 June 1783), *W & S*, V, p. 232.
[279] Ibid., pp. 307, 311, 318.
[280] Ibid, p. 321.
[281] Ibid., p. 333.
[282] David Hume, "That Politics May Be Reduced to a Science" (1742) in idem, *Essays Moral, Political and Literary*, pp. 18–19.

India Bills, presented to a packed House the following November.[283] On the day on which the first and more controversial of the two Bills was first introduced, by which time Burke's views on the treatment that should be meted out to Hastings diverged from the more conciliatory posture being adopted by Fox, the *Eleventh Report* of the Select Committee appeared, seeking to expose the Governor General's personal corruption, exemplified by his "taking of *Gifts* and *Presents*."[284] One aspect of this charge was that of simple peculation, but a more serious element was that of extracting donations from native rulers as a means of direct oppression and exploitation. Many of Burke's examples were to figure prominently in his case against Hastings presented during the impeachment trial, but a central component of his argument in the *Eleventh Report* was that the presents Hastings received were not products of princely munificence but examples of high-handed extortion whereby Hastings had preyed on the indigent on the basis of their need for protection.[285] Burke would spend a considerable amount of effort from the mid 1780s to the mid 1790s excoriating the character of Hastings for such behaviour, but his deeper purpose in 1783 was to point to underlying causes that invited abusive conduct. Burke cast doubt upon the virtues ascribed to Hastings by his defenders, taking his cue from the suffering "millions" of Bengal.[286] In the language of Fox's Bill for restructuring the government of the Company, these victims had been subjected to "disorders of an alarming nature and magnitude."[287] Yet the key objective of Burke's great speech on the Bill was to demonstrate that these disorders had been at once "habitual" and "incorrigible."[288]

The purpose of Fox's Bill was to vest control of the Company in a board of seven Commissioners, to be drawn from and appointed by the Houses of Parliament in the first instance, and subsequently to be appointed by the crown. A body of assistant Commissioners was to supervise commercial activity, and the tenure of the Commissioners was to be for a period of four years.[289] The Commission was to act in a quasi-judicial capacity, subjecting administration to expert scrutiny. Its principles were modelled on those of "a Court of Judicature," Burke revealed.[290] At the same time, the board was to be an arm of government, with extensive patronage at its disposal—a fact that deeply alarmed its parliamentary opponents. Yet it was not to be

[283] The first of Fox's Bills concerned the government of the Company, the second the code of administration in India. On the authorship of the Bills, see Vincent T. Harlow, *The Founding of the Second British Empire, 1763–93* (London: Longmans, Green and Co., 1952–64), 2 vols., II, pp. 124–26. On the timing of Burke's involvement, see Marshall, *Impeachment*, p. 20; Cannon, *Fox–North Coalition*, p. 107.

[284] EB, *Eleventh Report of the Select Committee* (18 November 1783), *W & S*, V, p. 334. For Burke's authorship of the Report, see Philip Francis to the editors of Burke's works, n.d., copied 30 May 1812, WWM BkP 31:16.

[285] EB, *Eleventh Report of the Select Committee* (18 November 1783), *W & S*, V, pp. 350–1.

[286] See, for example, the debate on the Reports of the Select Committee, 18 April 1782, *Gazetteer*, 19 April 1782.

[287] The Bill is reprinted in *Parliamentary History*, XXIV, cols. 62ff.

[288] EB, *Speech on Fox's India Bill* (1 December 1783), *W & S*, V, p. 433.

[289] Cannon, *Fox–North Coalition*, p. 108.

[290] EB, *Speech on Fox's India Bill* (1 December 1783), *W & S*, V, p. 444.

a newfangled instrument of the court, and its period in office could readily diverge from the tenure of a given ministry. This, of course, was deliberate: the Commissioners did not hold office at the pleasure of the king, preserving them from the forms of corruption standardly associated with court "influence."[291] "Let it once get into the ordinary course of administration," Burke wrote, "and to me all hopes of reformation are gone."[292] The idea was to found the Commission as a "parliamentary establishment," rooted in the "uncorrupt public virtue of the representatives of England."[293] In its constitution it was to be inoculated against secret machinations: its watchword was publicity and impartiality of conduct supported by its dependence on the confidence of the Commons.[294] The intention behind these arrangements was to institute a scheme of inspection integrated into the political system yet insulated from what Burke and Fox regarded as its pitfalls: the Bill inculcated "the wisdom of a jealousy of power," Fox believed. Every clause exuded suspicion, supposing that "men were but men" and thus prone to various degrees of malversation.[295]

Burke's great contribution to the debate was delivered on a motion to go into committee on the Bill, enabling him to respond to the objections aired during the first and second readings. Nathaniel Wraxall considered the result the "finest composition" he had witnessed in the House between 1780 and 1794.[296] It was certainly a powerful and authoritative intervention. The opposition had variously styled the Bill a "monstrous" and abhorrent measure, threatening to monopolise vast opportunities for patronage while violating the chartered rights of the Company.[297] Archibald Macdonald went so far as to challenge the Bill as doing violence to the very "rights of men."[298] John Wilkes continued in the same vein even after Burke had delivered his oration: anxious to deprecate the "heterogeneous traffic of war and trade" in India, Wilkes nonetheless saw fit to criticise the Bill's provisions as destabilising every charter, contract and corporation in the kingdom.[299] Burke opened his speech with a rebuke to this kind of misconceived polemic: his own aim, he insisted, was to defend the rights of men, but these had to be distinguished from the privileges of a corporation. A charter of rights, such as Magna Carta, might be instituted to restrain power in the name of natural duties that obliged governments to their subjects; but

[291] It is on these grounds that modern historians have sometimes viewed the Bill as somehow impractical, which of course it was from the perspective of the court. See Sutherland, *East India Company Politics*, pp. 265ff.; John Ehrman, *Pitt the Younger: The Years of Acclaim* (London: Constable, 1969), pp. 120ff.

[292] EB, *Speech on Fox's India Bill* (1 December 1783), *W & S*, V, p. 442.

[293] Ibid.

[294] Ibid, pp. 444–46.

[295] *Parliamentary Register* (Debrett), XII, p. 291.

[296] *The Historical and Posthumous Memoirs of Sir Nathaniel Wraxall, 1772–84*, ed. Henry B. Wheatley (London: 1884), 5 vols., III, p. 173.

[297] *Parliamentary History*, XXIV, e.g. cols. 10, 11, 15. The point was sometimes conceded by ministerial supporters, like William Eden: see *John Courtenay, incidental Anecdotes and a Biographical Sketch* (London: 1809), pp. 135–38.

[298] *Parliamentary History*, XXIII, col. 1299.

[299] *Parliamentary History*, XXIV, col. 20.

the East India Company charter created powers rather than circumscribing authority, and as such it should be accountable for its exercise of those powers.[300]

The charter of the East India Company originally conferred a monopoly on commerce, and by happenstance had become a charter of dominion. This outcome was a decree of providence and yet, since providence was inscrutable, British power in the east had to be viewed in political terms as a justifiable product of contingent circumstances. "Whatever might be the design in the inscrutable ways of Providence," Burke remarked, "was not for him or any other to determine."[301] A "great empire," he elaborated, had been "thrown" into "our hands."[302] He "trembled" to reflect on the justice with which conquest had originally been accomplished, but it was now an established fact, and one that could be justified in terms of policy and humanity. Of course, British usurpation had been preceded by earlier waves of conquest perpetrated by a sequence of Arab, Tartar and Persian invasions, each irruption into the territory having been "ferocious, bloody, and wasteful in the extreme."[303] The British entry, by comparison, was less dramatic in its violence, yet still it did not make for a pretty picture, having been carried out by subterfuge and opportunism.[304] However, these methods did not delegitimise the achievement. The justification of British authority had two bases. First, it was now "impractical" to surrender what had been acquired: withdrawal would leave the natives in a more miserable situation, prey to spoliation by competing local powers and exposed to intervention by the French.[305] There was no claimant to power on the subcontinent in a better position to provide for the welfare of the population, not least since the Country powers were mutually afflicted by "incurable, blind and senseless animosity."[306] Second, there was nothing in the nature of things that made a trading company essentially unfit for territorial power. Here Burke openly dissented from the conclusions of Adam Smith: "I have known merchants with the sentiments and the abilities of great statesmen; and I have seen persons in the rank of statesmen, with the conceptions and character of pedlars."[307] It was clear that the British system of government in South Asia had grown systematically abusive in nature, but it also seemed clear that these abuses could be remedied by transferring the powers of the Directors to a parliamentary Commission whose inspections and deliberations would be independent of the crown and guided by an impartial regard for the prosperity of Indians.

[300] EB, *Speech on Fox's India Bill* (1 December 1783), *W & S*, V, pp. 381–82.

[301] EB, Speech on Secret Committee Resolutions, 15 April 1782, *London Courant*, 16 April 1782.

[302] EB, Speech on Secret Committee Resolutions, 15 April 1782, *Gazetteer*, 16 April 1782.

[303] EB, *Speech on Fox's India Bill* (1 December 1783), *W & S*, V, p. 401.

[304] Ibid. Cf. Burke's more indulgent verdict in Proceedings against Clive, 21 May 1773, Cavendish Diary, Eg. MS., 248, fol. 261.

[305] EB, Speech on Secret Committee Resolutions, 15 April 1782, *Gazetteer*, 16 April 1782.

[306] EB, *Speech on Fox's India Bill* (1 December 1783), *W & S*, V, p. 401.

[307] Ibid., p. 387. See Smith, *Wealth of Nations*, II, p. 638, on the "essentially and perhaps incurably faulty" nature of mercantile administration.

The British had erected in the east what Burke described as "an oppressive, irregular, capricious, unsteady, rapacious, and peculating despotism."[308] Under the current dispensation of power, such depraved management was beyond redemption. However, overhauling the structure of authority offered a route to reformation short of dismantling the administrative edifice of the Company on the subcontinent. Reform was enjoined by the obligations under which all governments operated: the duty to deliver on the trust invested in them.[309] These obligations were derived from the moral ties that bound human beings to one another more generally—derived, that is, from what Burke termed "the faith, the covenant, the solemn, original, indispensable oath, in which I am bound, by the eternal frame and constitution of things, to the whole human race."[310] As a result of this primordial covenant, all power is ultimately answerable for its conduct, obliged to serve the purpose for which it was instituted—namely, the benefit of those over whom it was established, as judged by men acting as moral dependants of the deity.[311] The contract of government, in this sense, was undeniable, and liable to be rescinded, as Burke had argued in 1773, when its terms were violated by a degree of delinquency that deprived the ruling power of all trust.[312] As Burke was to make plain in relation to French politics in the 1790s, the question of the basis on which a breach of sovereign trust could be said to have taken place, and of who had the right to act where such a breach was deemed to have occurred, were matters of considerable delicacy. A breach of trust on the part of a subordinate jurisdiction, however, was far easier to determine, and more readily acted upon: it could be called to account, not by anything so indeterminate as the multitudinous "people," but by a sovereign parliament "which is alone capable of comprehending the magnitude of its object, and its abuse; and alone capable of an effectual legislative remedy."[313]

Burke's speech on Fox's India Bill is among his most carefully constructed performances. Since one of its primary purposes is to call into question the legitimacy of an established regime of government, it is largely taken up with elucidating the criteria for dismantling one structure of authority and substituting another in its place. As the title to government is compromised by a violation of trust, the bulk of Burke's attention is devoted to anatomising the criteria for delinquency, in terms of which any alleged breach of trust must be tested. Delinquency most conspicuously

[308] EB, *Speech on Fox's India Bill* (1 December 1783), *W & S*, V, p. 430.

[309] On this theme in Burke, see James Conniff, "Burke and India: The Failure of the Theory of Trusteeship," *Political Research Quarterly*, 46:2 (June 1993), pp. 291–309. See also Richard Bourke, "Liberty, Authority and Trust in Burke's Idea of Empire," *Journal of the History of Ideas*, 61:3 (Summer 2000), pp. 453–71; David Bromwich, "Introduction" to idem ed., *On Empire, Liberty and Reform: Speeches and Letters. Edmund Burke* (New Haven, CT: Yale University Press, 2000), p. 16.

[310] EB, *Speech on Fox's India Bill* (1 December 1783), *W & S*, V, p. 425. For relevant discussion, see P. J. Marshall, "Review of *On Empire, Liberty and Reform: Speeches and Letters. Edmund Burke*," *Reviews in History*, 154 (31 August 2000): http://www.history.ac.uk/reviews/review/154.

[311] On this theme in Burke, see below, chapter 12, section 6, and chapter 13, section 6.

[312] WWM BkP 9:17.

[313] EB, *Speech on Fox's India Bill* (1 December 1783), *W & S*, V, p. 385.

delegitimises government, Burke proposed, where four characteristics are combined: first, where the magnitude of the object of abuse is substantial; second, where the extent of the delinquency is significant; third, where the mismanagement is systematic; and finally, where it cannot be removed without constitutional reorganisation. The printed version of Burke's speech proceeds, more or less in order, to apply each of these tests to both the internal and external governance of the Company, and to its internal and external commerce. He begins, captivatingly, with an outline of the dimensions of the territory, illustrating the breadth of British responsibility: "Through all that vast extent of country there is not a man who eats a mouthful of rice but by permission of the East India Company."[314] But the importance of these territories is further underlined by contrasting the advanced civilisation which they host with the "gangs of savages . . . who wander on the waste borders of the river of the Amazons, or the Plate."[315] Even so, Burke observes, the abstract dignity and distinction of this polished and pious culture has not been sufficient to evoke sympathy for its plight in the imaginations of European statesmen.[316] To achieve this, Burke reckons, the subject must somehow be brought nearer by rendering its relative strangeness familiar.[317] Failing that, he is left appealing to conscience within the framework of Christian natural law through a presentation of the scale of abuse for which Europeans have been responsible.

The catalogue of abuses that Burke itemises is rolled out in cataclysmic tones. Who would have thought, just fifty years back, that the mighty dominion of the Mughal Emperor could, within the space of a generation, have been treated with insult and reduced to indigence? "Awful lessons" are taught by the spectacle of such vicissitudes.[318] Burke examines the fallout of this revolution in affairs: the violation of obligations to the Mughal in favour of the Wazir of Awadh; the "*extirpation*" of the Rohillas; the deposition of successive Nawabs; the breaking of countless treaties; the ruin of the Zamindars of Bengal; and the repeated betrayal of dependent powers from Benares to the Carnatic.[319] In all this, Burke thought, Hastings had much to answer for; but the problem went deeper. Previous conquests on the subcontinent had begun in ferocity and ended in durable establishments: "Fathers there deposited the hopes of their posterity; and children there beheld the monuments of their fathers."[320] The British, on the other hand, began with an establishment, and allowed it to degenerate into a means of oppression and extortion. The opportunity for

[314] Ibid., p. 389.

[315] Ibid.

[316] On this strategy, together with the significance of sympathy in Burke's thought, see Uday Singh Mehta, *Liberalism and Empire: A Study in Nineteenth-Century British Liberal Thought* (Chicago, IL: Chicago University Press, 1999), ch. 5; Jennifer Pitts, *A Turn to Empire: The Rise of Imperial Liberalism in Britain and France* (Princeton, NJ: Princeton University Press, 2005), pp. 72–73, dissenting from Sara Suleri, *The Rhetoric of English India* (Chicago, IL: University of Chicago Press, 1992), ch. 2.

[317] EB, *Speech on Fox's India Bill* (1 December 1783), *W & S*, V, p. 390.

[318] Ibid., p. 392.

[319] Ibid., pp. 392–430. By extirpation, Burke meant political destruction, not mass extermination.

[320] Ibid., p. 401.

commerce gave way to an appetite for conquest, channelling the avidity of youthful Company adventurers into a heady enjoyment of power. No enduring settlements resulted, no roots were cast, no monuments were erected. Waves of petty interlopers descended, and soon departed with their spoil, leaving little to the native population but "the hopeless prospect of new flights of birds of prey and passage."[321]

In Burke's analysis, there is a precise reason why these birds of prey come and go with such impunity: forming no attachments or bonds of sympathy in India, they are not subject to any supervision from outside either. This is because, in political terms, the responsible agencies had no incentive to correct their errant behaviour and, in commercial terms, the motives of profit and loss had been suspended. While in theory the servants were answerable to the Directors and the Directors regulated by the Proprietors, both the Direction and the terms of subordination between these offices had been perverted and inverted at the same time. The roles of Company Director and Proprietor of stock were no longer coveted simply on the basis of their capital value or on the expected return on the dividend. These benefits were as nothing compared to the spoils of patronage, rendering the Company a political rather than a commercial enterprise: fluctuations in the dividend or the price of stock were of marginal concern to their beneficiaries by comparison with the opportunities for acquiring lucrative contracts or allocating positions of power to family members in India.[322] Under these circumstances, a vote in the General Court was hardly to be used to control wastage or peculation; its use was to acquire influence and carve out opportunities, leading to rewards. This perversion of commercial practice came with an inversion of relations of authority. The Directors no longer controlled the servants on the ground: instead, the servants ultimately gained the wherewithal to appoint Directors who would serve their interests.[323]

The creation of a parliamentary Commission was intended as a means of establishing a supervisory body freed from the avid interests that now governed Company behaviour. Central importance was attached to ensuring that this new arrangement did not imperil the constitutional integrity of the metropole: while the population of India was to be relieved of its oppression, the British constitution was to be preserved "from its worst corruption."[324] The prospect of corruption was focused on the tenure of the members of the Commission. If the Commissioners were to be appointed and removed "at pleasure" by the crown, they would be absorbed into the processes of clandestine influence which, as Burke and Fox saw the matter, had adversely affected Britain's constitutional balance. If, on the other hand, they were appointed on the basis of their Foxite party principles and were to enjoy their position for a fixed term of years, they would be immune to the means of corruption as these operated at the time. The objection to this solution as one that had been

321 Ibid., p. 402.
322 Ibid., p. 437.
323 Ibid.
324 Ibid., p. 383.

determined by party preference was in reality nothing other than a "party objection" itself, loaded to serve the interests of the court.[325] Burke had long argued that party was ineliminable from a free constitution, meaning that partisanship was an intrinsic feature of a mixed system of government. Either the court party or their opponents were bound to benefit from specific measures.[326] In the case of the Indian reforms comprehended in this Bill, any benefit to the Foxites was of an incidental nature: the key thing was to appoint partisans of Indian reform openly, selected on the basis of their standing and expertise. Should the ministry appoint to the Commission on any other basis, it would lose the confidence of the Commons and, with that, the basis of its power.[327]

After the debate on Fox's India Bill had ended, the House voted to go into committee on its provisions, which were submitted to the upper House when they passed on the third reading. It was in the Lords that it met with defeat under the direct influence of George III, leading to the fall of the Coalition and the installation of a ministry headed by Pitt.[328] Earl Temple wrote to Burke on 19 December 1783 informing him that the king had "no further occasion" for his service as paymaster general.[329] At the start of the new year, the younger Pitt was ready with his first India Bill, adapted from Dundas's earlier Bill of 1783.[330] The day before its second reading in the Commons, Burke wrote to William Richardson, Professor of Humanity at the University of Glasgow, indicating that the plight of the Hindus was engrossing his "whole heart," and causing him "in truth . . . some sleepless nights."[331] As it turned out, the Bill was defeated on 23 January by 222 votes to 214.[332] Coincidentally, a week later, Lord Macartney wrote to Burke from Fort St. George warning that without some fundamental reform in the organisation of the Company "you might bid adieu to your Empire in Asia."[333] However, effective reorganisation looked improbable to erstwhile Coalition supporters as concern increased that the public was largely indifferent to the India business. Only the prospect of bankruptcy, William Eden complained, would engage "the Feelings of the People" about the situation in Asia.[334] "I totally despair of anything which can be done in the future," Burke replied. The "havock" and "destruction" of their brethren in the east did not seem to touch the humanity of the British.[335]Against this backdrop, with his position con-

[325] Ibid., p. 445.

[326] Ibid., p. 447.

[327] Ibid., p. 445. This, Burke thought, was a particularly potent argument since the introduction of economical reform.

[328] Cannon, *Fox–North Coalition,* ch. 7.

[329] Earl Temple to EB, 19 December 1783, *Corr.*, V, p. 119.

[330] Sutherland, *East India Company Politics*, p. 408.

[331] EB to William Richardson, 22 January 1783, *Corr.*, V, p. 124.

[332] Burke spoke in opposition on 16 January, objecting that the Bill "put the whole East-India Company into the hands of the Crown." See *W & S*, V, p. 452.

[333] Lord Macartney to EB, 31 January 1784, *Corr.*, V, p. 125.

[334] 13 May 1784, ibid., pp. 146–47.

[335] 17 May 1784, ibid., p. 151.

siderably strengthened by the addition of about seventy supporters in the general election of 1784, Pitt introduced a second India Bill on 6 July.[336] Francis wrote on the 27th that he delivered his "Soul" in his speech on the second reading of amendments to the Bill, leaving Burke to make his stand on the veracity of the Select Committee's reports the following day.[337] It was a final desperate plea, as he informed Sir Gilbert Elliot on 3 August. Pitt's measures, he lamented, represented pure iniquity, having been enabled by a corrupted House of Commons.[338]

10.7 The Avenging Prophet

As Burke saw it, the corruption of the Commons began with a parliamentary faction that had conspired with George III to instal the ministry of Pitt. It was then consolidated by the general election of March–April 1784. Burke regarded the independence of the House as all but lost.[339] The labours of the previous parliament in reforming the constitution had been undone at a single stroke. As Burke argued in a pamphlet written about these developments, *A Representation to His Majesty* of 1784, protracted skill in construction could be dismantled in one moment of fury.[340] The work of demolition was in the process of reducing the standing of the Commons to a "mere Appendage" of administration under the pretence of endeavouring to save the constitution from an improper attempt upon the crown by the ambitions of a party in parliament.[341] In their work of destruction, Burke noted, the Pitt ministry was abetted by the servitude of the people who had allegedly sunk to a level of depravity that outdid the "worst times of the Roman Republick."[342] "I fear everything is gone," Burke later remarked, citing Lucan's *Pharsalia* on the state of the Roman Republic after Pompey: "nec *color* imperii, nec *frons* erit ulla Senatus."[343] The government, the monarch, and the people out of doors, had conspired in their indifference to the condition of India. In ancient Rome, by comparison, as aristocratic factions contributed to the ruin of the imperial provinces, "such men as Verres,

[336] C. H. Philips, *The East India Company, 1784–1834* (Manchester: Manchester University Press, 1940), p. 32.

[337] Philip Francis to EB, ibid., p. 161; EB, Speech on Pitt's Second India Bill, 28 July 1784, *W & S*, V, p. 455.

[338] EB to Sir Gilbert Elliot, post 5 August 1784, *Corr.*, V, p. 166.

[339] 22 June 1784, ibid., p. 154. Burke was responding to Baker's letter of 20 June, in which he had extolled Burke's motion of 14 June defending the conduct of the Coalition, printed in ibid., pp. 153–4. Burke's motion, seconded by Windham, appears in *CJ*, pp. 198–204.

[340] EB, *A Representation to His Majesty by the Right Honourable Edmund Burke on Monday, June 14, 1784* (London: 1784), p. ii.

[341] Ibid., pp. 16, 12.

[342] EB to William Baker, 22 June 1784, *Corr.*, p. 155.

[343] EB to Sir Gilbert Elliot, 3 August 1784, ibid., p. 166, Burke's emphasis, citing Lucan, *Pharsalia*, bk. IX, line 207: "There will be neither the outward show of authority nor the facade of the senate."

and such practices as his, were always odious to the people at Large."[344] In the face of the degenerate politics of 1784, Burke opted to play the role of Cicero in his condemnation of the delinquent Verres, albeit confronted with a less amenable audience: he stood as the grand accuser of imperial malpractice embodied in the figure of Warren Hastings. The "power of representation only is on my side," as Burke put it to Thurlow at the end of the year.[345] Others were in a position to act, whereas he could at best personify what he took to be the pleas of disenfranchised millions stationed on a remote continent.

Impeachment would be Burke's instrument of representation. He had long pledged to bring to justice "the greatest delinquent that India ever saw."[346] He now realised that an act of justice could double as an act of representation, reversing what he presented in his speech on the fate of Almas Ali Khan as a protracted design to "keep the poor natives wholly out of sight."[347] Accordingly, five months after Hastings had resigned his governorship, Burke greeted his return to Britain with a comment on the utility—the "propriety and advantage"—of staging some form of inquiry into his conduct in Asia.[348] If no one else stood forward to undertake the business, Burke himself would assume the role of advocate, bearing in his person the cause of a broken people. Between 1784 and 1785, while being subjected to mocking jibes from youthful supporters of Pitt's government, and sensing that all hope of redress through the offices of power was receding, Burke increasingly, and consciously, assumed the persona of an avenging prophet, threatening his colleagues with the only authority that was paramount to their own. Pleading the case of an abused revenue collector from the frontier territories of Awadh, he declared himself compelled to "preach a sermon" on the subject.[349] In the course of his speech, he laid his hands on what he termed the "sacred volumes" of the Committee reports and, calling upon "*great God*," repeatedly adverted to the mounting vengeance of a "dreadful Providence" whose negative judgment on the British for their conduct of empire in the east was evident in the misfortunes of the nation.[350]

While Burke continued to fulminate against the audacity of Hastings, the issue of the debts of the Nawab of the Carnatic came before the Commons again, having lain comparatively dormant since the late 1770s. With an inquiry into the financial affairs of the Carnatic being resisted by Pitt's Board of Control and the terms for the settlement of the Nawab's debts in dispute, Burke prepared to attack the new dispensation in India, together with its chief manager, Henry Dundas, in a major speech in the Commons on 28 February 1785. He launched his case after Fox's call

[344] Ibid. For Burke's recourse to Cicero's *Verrine Orations* in his prosecution of Hastings, see below, chapter 12, section 2.

[345] EB to Lord Thurlow, 14 December 1784, *Corr.*, V, p. 203.

[346] 28 April 1783, *Parliamentary History*, XXIII, col. 800.

[347] EB, Speech on Almas Ali Khan, 30 July 1784, *W & S*, V, p. 461.

[348] EB, Notice of Motion on Hastings, 20 June 1785, ibid., p. 617.

[349] *Morning Herald*, 31 October 1784.

[350] Ibid., and EB, Speech on Almas Ali Khan, *W & S*, V, pp. 468, 472, 475, 477.

for papers had been refused, using the occasion to anatomise the system of empire in southern India. Central here was the contrast with arrangements in the north-east: while the military and political conquest of Bengal had whetted the acquisitive appetites of traders, exciting "an emulation" in all parts of the service, the Directors in London had grown alarmed by the new pressures on Company finances, repeatedly urging modesty and retrenchment as a result.[351] However, "vehement passion is ingenious in its resources," Burke observed. Faced with calls for restraint being issued from Leadenhall Street, servants in Madras sought to advance their position indirectly. Whereas presents had corrupted officials in Bengal, servants made their killing by issuing loans in Madras; while wars were openly pursued in the north-east, aggrandisement occurred under cover in the Carnatic. As Burke had been emphasising since the 1770s, all this was compassed through the pivotal figure of the Nawab of Arcot, whose mind had allegedly been inspired by the British with the most grandiose ambition to establish an empire in the Deccan. As he proceeded to overturn established sovereignties of the region, his debts to the Company proportionately "grew and flourished."[352]

The Nawab's project encountered major resistance in the figure of Haidar Ali, who was striving to expand through the south-west from his base in Mysore as the Company indirectly advanced from the south-east through Muhammad Ali. Faced with provocation, and the bad faith of the Company, Haidar Ali's rapacious ambition was unleashed upon the Carnatic: "He resolved," as Burke phrased it, "in the gloomy recesses of a mind capacious of such things, to leave the whole Carnatic an everlasting monument of vengeance."[353] This "menacing meteor," as Burke styled him, poured a torrent of ruthless aggression upon his enemies, wasting whole territories with fire and steel, driving the dispossessed into the hands of their assailants, leaving a devouring famine in its wake. Its victims perished in scores every day in the streets of Madras. For a year and a half the terror of Haidar Ali and his son, Tipu Sultan, battered what Burke reminded the Commons were their beleaguered "fellow citizens" until a "dead uniform silence reigned over the whole region."[354] This wasteland comprised, in Burke's simile, an extent of territory comparable in size to England—extending "from Thames and Trent" along a north–south axis and "from the Irish to the German sea" moving from east to west.[355] Yet the East India Company, instead of proceeding to employ all available resources to reanimate its subject territories in the wake of their military devastation, opted to press its usual revenue claims based on calculations made in the years of peace and plenty. To call this policy "tyranny, sublimed into madness" would be to understate the turpitude of the undertaking, Burke declared.[356] The situation was one that called for public provision

[351] EB, *Speech on the Nabob of Arcot's Debts* (28 February 1785), *W & S*, V, p. 516.
[352] Ibid., pp. 517–18.
[353] Ibid., p. 518.
[354] Ibid., pp. 519–20.
[355] Ibid., p. 520.
[356] Ibid., p. 521.

on a massive scale: government would have to maintain the population before the population could support the government again, and here "the road to oeconomy lies not through receipt, but through expence."[357] Propagation of the species, and the rudimentary sustenance on which that propagation depends, would have to precede the resumption of the original levels of revenue extraction: population and cultivation were prerequisites of taxation.

Burke's aim here was to show the extent to which the British government along the Coromandel coast conducted itself without any awareness of its primary responsibility to its Indian subjects: the government sought to maximise its advantage over a population towards which it was obliged by a duty of care. As he spoke, Burke laid out before the House his own copy of Thomas Barnard's map of the territories along the coast ceded to the Company in 1763. Here it could be seen how dependent the agriculture of the region was on human providence and public provision: the irrigation of the lands required a supply of innumerable reservoirs, which Barnard's map shows scattered throughout the country.[358] Art was required to compensate for the deficiencies of nature, and a succession of native governments had committed themselves to the construction and maintenance of this shared public resource: "these are the grand sepulchers built by ambition; but by the ambition of an unsatiable benevolence."[359] Yet as things now stood, public munificence in the Carnatic had disappeared as a consequence of the Company's "avarice run mad."[360] Burke referred to Dundas' *Fourth Report* for the Committee of Secrecy to demonstrate beyond controversy the level of culpable negligence: "the great reservoirs, by which the lands are supplied with water, were going to decay," the *Report* had stated.[361] Further decay, it must have seemed obvious, would mean crop failure and famine. Burke noted that agricultural and commercial enterprise required the "previous provision of habitation, seed, stock, capital."[362] India's reservoirs in the south represented capital on a grand scale. Where this provision had been drastically depleted, government was needed to supply what the calamity of war had reduced to a level that threatened the survival of the community. However, under the Company, the public treasury was employed as a means of extracting tribute rather than as an instrument of the common welfare. At the same time, all attempts to restore the infrastructure necessary for economic growth were being sacrificed to the demands of Company creditors for the immediate repayment of debts that Burke held to be basically fictitious in na-

[357] Ibid.

[358] See *A Map of the East India Company's Lands on the Coast of Coromandel by Thomas Barnard* (1778). This map was published by Alexander Dalrymple on a reduced scale from Barnard's original map of 1774. Dalrymple also published an *Explanation of the Map of the East India Company's Lands on the Coast of Coromandel by Thomas Barnard* (London: 1778).

[359] EB, *Speech on the Nawab of Arcot's Debts* (28 February 1785), p. 522.

[360] Ibid., p. 521.

[361] *Fourth Report of the Committee of Secrecy* (6 February 1782) in *Commons Sessional Papers*, ed. Lambert, CXLIII, p. 670.

[362] EB, *Speech on the Nawab of Arcot's Debts* (28 February 1785), *W & S*, V, p. 522.

ture. The health of the system of credit was essential to sustainable recovery, yet the fact remained that, under exigent circumstances, "the first creditor is the plow," and under conditions of dire want the claims of creditors "must hold off their profane unhallowed paws from the holy work" of cultivation, propagation and nutrition.[363]

Burke's speech on the debts of the Nawab of Arcot was delivered after eight years of intense engagement with the politics of South Asia. It is a sustained examination of the systematic deformation of government responsibility in the Carnatic, which matches in depth his analysis of the Indian predicament as presented in his reports for the Select Committee and his speech on Fox's India Bill. However, while the *Eleventh* and *Ninth* reports were intended to influence policy, and Fox's Bill was designed to reconfigure the government of India, the Arcot speech was an attack on what Burke took to be a corrupt ministry aided by a degenerate House of Commons. Throughout 1784 and 1785, he felt exposed to political ridicule by Pitt's supporters in the Commons, cut off from his own allies after the demise of the Coalition, and in despair about the prospect of making an immediate political impact. He would now proceed, as he admitted to Francis, on the basis of "the single Vote, to which I am reduced."[364] When it came to the question of India, there was no mileage, he felt, in strategic alliances with the followers of North: he would act in the name of justice against his enemies and opponents, hoping that Fox and Francis would be prepared to follow. Solitary campaigning would be given precedence over party politics as well: Fox might crave a following, but Burke did not.[365] The situation obliged him to focus on the delinquency of an individual, rather than on the defects of the system of administration in India, which was supported by the government of William Pitt. Under the circumstances, Burke resolved to concentrate on the career of Warren Hastings, deciding to expose his guilt by embarking on his impeachment.[366] Burke was frank that this was an approach by which he could "justify" himself, but it was also one by which the Commons would have to record a moral stand: in the absence of wielding power, there was nothing else to be done.[367]

[363] Ibid., p. 523.

[364] EB to Philip Francis, 23 November 1785, *Corr.*, V, p. 240.

[365] EB to Philip Francis, 10 December 1785, ibid., p. 243.

[366] The idea that Burke's animus against Hastings was motivated by the latter's having slighted William Burke was first peddled by Charles McCormick, *Memoirs of the Right Honourable Edmund Burke* (London: 1798), but has been generally rejected by commentators since, beginning with Robert Bisset, *The Life of Edmund Burke* (London: 1798), p. 413.

[367] EB to Philip Francis, 10 December 1785, *Corr.*, V, p. 243.

PART V

Whiggism, Jacobinism, Indianism and Ascendancy, 1785–1797

OVERVIEW

The period covered by the final part of this book is usually taken to mark a significant shift in Burke's career. The reforming Whig is commonly seen as succumbing to reaction, pitting him against progress, enlightenment and revolution. However, Burke's final phase can more accurately be seen in terms of a commitment to positive change: in the Empire at large—in India and Ireland in particular—he remained wedded to the project of ongoing renovation. The battle for subjecting the East India Company to parliamentary control had been lost with the failure of Fox's India Bills in 1783. Nonetheless, in launching the impeachment of Warren Hastings in 1786, Burke hoped to establish cosmopolitan norms by which the government of India could be judged. The venture proved exhausting and exacting in equal measure. By the middle of February 1788, Burke had concluded the opening of the trial proceedings and was celebrating the prospect of a common front against Hastings. Yet the prosecution dragged on for over half a decade, draining its chief manager and ending in defeat. As Burke saw it, reform had been embarrassed by the forces of reaction. Throughout the same period, Burke campaigned energetically for ameliorating the plight of Irish Catholics. In 1792 we find him pleading for them to be granted the parliamentary franchise. Then in 1795 under the Lord Lieutenancy of Earl Fitzwilliam he further urged admitting them to seats in the Irish parliament. However, as Burke viewed the events that followed, prudent reform was sacrificed to petty jobbery in Irish politics, and by 1797 much of the country had been "Jacobinised."

Burke's attempts to improve conditions in Ireland and South Asia came on the back of a lifelong effort to secure domestic reform. Since the 1760s he had pressed for changes to the regulation of metropolitan trade; through the 1770s he was urging a constitutional role for party; most recently he had been pushing for economical reform. Measures of the kind were intended to presage renewal: reform was intended to restore arrangements under which progress could continue, not trigger crises that would arrest improvement and encourage the advent of destruction.[1] What Burke opposed was the emergence of a new idiom of reform couched in the language of the rights of man. His antipathy was not directed against the principle of natural rights or the contention that civil entitlements had a basis in the laws of nature. Burke's defence of property, his promotion of toleration, and his championship of values that ought to guide the government of India were all conducted on the assumption of fundamental rights. What disturbed Burke was the appropriation of the rhetoric of rights to serve the advancement of what he saw as two calamitous political programmes. The first was the goal of resorting to the natural right of self-government as a means of determining the shape of existing civil societies. This agenda received encouragement during the course of the American Revolution, and its ideals began to infect the project of parliamentary reform in Britain. The second programme turned on the idea that the original rights of nature could challenge the distribution of wealth in established societies. As Burke saw it, both these sets of pretensions to primordial "rights" in man compelled the French Revolution along its avid course, progressively diminishing the chances of securing any civil entitlements.

From this perspective, French rights supplied an armoury against the principles of natural law. Of course, those principles had been variously interpreted from the scholastics to Grotius, Pufendorf and Locke. Burke followed modern jurisprudence in interpreting the laws of nature as means of promoting the progress of society through the pursuit of personal utility. That pursuit was tamed by restraints imposed on behaviour by the operation of manners and morals, yet Burke still thought that individuals were swayed by the motive of self-interest. Self-interest served the objective of social and civil improvement. Indeed, government had been created to promote that very objective. Yet for Burke, following Locke, although authority was the servant of a higher purpose it was not the bearer of any privileged supernatural sanction. Consequently it was permissible—indeed obligatory—to resist its power where it endeavoured to subject the rights of man to the dictates of arbitrary command. Arbitrary power was an essential feature of the spirit of conquest. In Burke's eyes, resistance or revolution was a legitimate response. Yet the French Revolution had begun not as a rebellion against an oppressive monarch but as a wilful campaign on the part of a faction to usurp the constitution of the state.

In this sense, the Revolution had its origins in a bid for domestic conquest. Before long it turned its energy against the powers of Europe. Through the 1790s, Burke interpreted the invasions and annexations engineered by the French as an expression of an implacable crusade. Originally inspired by demagoguery and a rage for

[1] For consideration of these processes in a general eighteenth-century context, see Franco Venturi, *The End of the Old Regime in Europe*, trans. R. Burr Litchfield (Princeton, NJ: Princeton University Press, 1989–91), 3 vols.; Reinhart Koselleck, *Kritik und Krise: Eine Studie zur pathogenese der bürgerlichen Welt* (1959) (Frankfurt am Main: Suhrkamp, 1973).

equality, the Revolution steadily increased its military power. With the execution of Louis XVI at the start of 1793 and the subsequent establishment of an unaccountable regime, Burke came to view the French polity as a military state—governed by force within and bent on subjugation abroad. The formation of the Directory in 1795 merely perpetuated this appetite for republican expansionism. By the autumn of that year, Burke believed that significant numbers of dissenters in Britain were devoting their energies to dismantling the established Church. Conditions in the metropolis and the provinces were likewise unnerving: as alarm about food shortages spread across the country, artisanal radicalism was reviving in London. At the same time, Foxite Whigs were irreparably divided over France, with the Duke of Portland assuming office in a coalition under Pitt. Having retired from the House of Commons in 1794, Burke was cheered that many of his old friends were now cooperating with the ministry, but he was soon dismayed by the approach of the administration towards the war. Balance-of-power politics was now over in Europe, he believed. France had no conception of agreed limits to its sphere of interest as it persisted in overwhelming long-established sovereignties on the continent. Burke ended his days railing against plans to accommodate this lawless power. He saw himself not as a prophet against the progressive principles of the age, but as a champion of liberties under assault from a system of tyranny. Property, religion and government were under attack from a godless creed. Its maxims were gaining converts under the influence of French arms. Burke concluded that its onward march could only be reversed by opposing it with military force.

XI

THE ADVENT OF CRISIS

INDIA, BRITAIN AND FRANCE, 1785–1790

11.1 Introduction

By the mid 1780s, the glory days of collaboration among the Rockingham Whigs had given way to simmering fractiousness among Fox's followers. Burke, above all others, was dismayed by this turn of events, though he was rapidly absorbed by new developments. With Hastings's return to Britain in 1785, he saw an opportunity to advance the cause of good government by prosecuting the Governor General for misconduct in the east. He had little hope at this point that the enterprise would succeed. Nonetheless, having focused on the iniquities of the system of government under the East India Company, Burke seized the chance to concentrate on the culpability of a single man. By rousing the Commons against Hastings, standards of justice would be asserted in British public life. At the same time, the incrimination of the Governor General would affirm the existence of imperial norms based on the universality of fundamental rights. The commitment to such values guided Burke's support for a range of causes that won an audience in the Commons from the middle of the decade: principally, opposition to the transportation of convicts in 1785 and moves to abolish the slave trade in 1789. Yet in the same period Burke felt compelled to defend the authority of prescription. In opposing Pitt's Bill for parliamentary reform in 1785 and his attempt to impose restraints on the conduct of the regent in 1788–9, Burke supported existing arrangements in terms of established convention. Pragmatic conventions and original rights then collided with the French Revolution. From the beginning, Burke argued for an intelligent combination of both principles. Prescription could not override inalienable rights, yet rights would have to be reconciled with social utility. By the early autumn of 1789, Burke was adamant that the rage in France against established usage would prove destructive of the principles of society and government. Britain had a vested interest in countering the storm: the proximity of France, and the appeal of its demotic slogans, posed a threat to social distinctions along with the British constitution. European developments were now an acute domestic concern.

11.2 The Return of Hastings

The years between 1785 and the advent of the French Revolution imposed new strains on the opposition Whigs. After the defeat of Fox's martyrs in 1784, the party was in need of a sense of purpose and direction.[1] Voting cohesion among the Foxites gave an impression of unity, which was supported by the development of party institutions. At this time, under the supervision of William Adam, funds were created for the purpose of contesting elections, agents were charged with coordinating campaigning and propaganda, and the Whig Club was established in May 1784.[2] Even so, with the decline in the party's popularity since Pitt's accession to power, members were divided on how best to concert their plans.[3] In due course, the Hastings impeachment and the regency crisis would deepen these divisions; French developments from 1789 drove them to breaking point. Looking back on the period from the vantage of 1793, Burke commented in his *Observations on the Conduct of the Minority* that his final breach with Fox on 6 May 1791 had been preceded by a long period of "distance, coolness, and want of confidence."[4] According to French Laurence, writing three years later, the seeds of the breach were planted during Fox's election for Westminster in 1780. It was then that he felt his triumph over the power of the crown with the aid of the people. With the death of Rockingham two years later he fell under the influence of men of letters naturally disposed to favour "popular courses." This tendency was confirmed in 1783 when the Foxites fell from power: "Their second dismissal within a year and a half from the service of the crown, fixed their conviction of a determined proscription, and threw them still more upon the people."[5] Yet it was in the middle of the decade that the division between Fox and Burke became conspicuous over questions of opposition tactics. Their dispute soon grew critical over the issue of parliamentary reform. However, at the outset, the pursuit of Hastings promised to focus opposition Whiggism, lending purpose to Fox's followers after the experience of defeat.

Conditions in the mid 1780s would lead to what Burke later termed his "total alienation" from Fox.[6] It was a remarkable development since they started from

[1] Frank O'Gorman, *The Whig Party and the French Revolution* (London: Macmillan, 1967), p. 5.

[2] L. G. Mitchell, *Charles James Fox and the Disintegration of the Whig Party, 1782–94* (Oxford: Oxford University Press, 1971), pp. 102–3; Donald E. Ginter, "The Financing of the Whig Party Organization, 1783–1793," *American Historical Review*, 71:2 (January 1766), pp. 421–40; Archibald S. Foord, *His Majesty's Opposition, 1714–1830* (Oxford: Oxford University Press, 1964), pp. 406–7; Eugene Charlton Black, *The Association: British Extraparliamentary Political Organisation, 1769–1793* (Cambridge, MA: Harvard University Press, 1963), p. 217.

[3] B. W. Hill, "Fox and Burke: The Whig Party and the Question of Principles, 1784–1789," *English Historical Review*, 89:350 (January 1974), pp. 1–24.

[4] EB, *Observations on the Conduct of the Minority* (Spring 1793), *W & S*, VIII, p. 407.

[5] French Laurence, "Political Life of Edmund Burke: Annotated Proofs of a Contribution to the *Annual Register*" (c. 1794), OSB MS. File 8753.

[6] Ibid.

the common position of being aggrieved at the conduct of William Pitt and George III. Years later, the Duke of Portland would reveal that his loyalty to Fox stemmed from the commitments he contracted at this time.[7] These were based on perceptions that he shared with Burke: sabotaging Fox's India Bill had been an outrage; the creation of an administration without the support of the Commons a disgrace; the use of executive power to secure the election for Pitt an affront. No one felt more strongly than Burke that all this had both weakened and discredited the House of Commons, and augmented the power of George III. Pitt's own behaviour was culpable in the extreme.[8] Nonetheless, Burke came to believe that it was friends of Fox who were open to a coalition with the new government.[9] Certainly Foxites had failed to capitalise on the principles that had been betrayed. Instead, as Burke saw things, Fox himself withdrew from the scene of combat, holed up for almost a year at St. Anne's Hill in Surrey, and refused to rebuild the party on the basis of shared ideas. This brought home to Burke the fact that the days of the Rockinghams were at an end: the collaboration of friends around shared constitutional ideals had given meaning and cohesion to the party. By comparison, Fox merely sought to harry Pitt with piecemeal attacks on individual issues: "All opposition, from that period to this very Session," Burke reflected in 1793, "has proceeded upon separate measures."[10] The party was struggling, and needed to be rallied; that required a concerted and deliberate plan of action, supported by vigorous campaigning. In seeking to deliver such a result, Burke felt that Fox was fitful in providing backing. There was no trace of a "plan of Conduct" among the leaders of the opposition, Burke complained to Windham in 1784. Fox was pleased to trust in what "accidents" might throw up.[11] He was also disinclined to turn to Burke for counsel. His adherents tended to follow suit: Burke could scarcely conceal his delight in the autumn of 1786 when reporting to a correspondent that some of "our army" had accepted his advice on the Hastings trial.[12] Issues were important, but they had to be systematically pursued. That required establishing a reputation for consistency based on a commitment to core goals. All this was very foreign to the modus operandi of Fox, whose eloquence and force of personality were extraordinary assets, but whose behaviour could seem lax and fluctuating.[13]

Fox, Burke thought, was excessively concerned with immediate advantage. This made him crave a retinue, and therefore veer towards popular causes. It was a strategy that disturbed Burke already in 1785, and one that appalled him as the 1790s dawned. He first noted it in connection with the conduct of the Hastings business.

[7] The Duke of Portland to EB, 10 October 1793, *Corr.*, VII, p. 448.

[8] EB, *Observations on the Conduct of the Minority* (Spring 1793), *W & S*, VIII, pp. 447–48.

[9] Ibid., p. 448.

[10] Ibid.

[11] EB to William Windham, 14 October 1784, *Corr.*, V, p. 177.

[12] EB to Thomas Lewis O'Beirne, 29 September 1786, ibid., p. 281.

[13] Nathaniel Wraxall, *A Short Review of the Political State of Great Britain at the Commencement of the Year 1787* (London: 1787), pp. 28–9.

From the start, the quest for the Governor General was merely a party matter for Fox. According to the musings of Nathaniel Wraxall, although Burke's push against Hastings became mingled with enmities and resentments, he was originally actuated by "benign and enlarged principles."[14] The case of Fox was different: the impeachment was merely one opportunity among others, to be discarded when it no longer served his ambitions at Westminster.[15] He had involved himself, Burke later commented, in matters of great significance with which he had no genuine "sympathy."[16] Certainly Fox's attitude was more detached than Burke's: on 7 February 1787, the day on which Richard Brinsley Sheridan brought forward the fourth article of charge in his notoriously rousing speech on the abuse of the Begams of Awadh, Fox was absent at Newmarket. By comparison, in 1785–6, when the indictment of Hastings seemed liable to discomfit Pitt, Fox had embraced it with enthusiasm. Pitt himself realised that the issue presented an opportunity to the opposition to increase its appeal, and decided to back as well as neutralise the impeachment. When immediate political capital started to drain from the proceedings, Fox began to distance himself from the trial, and was seeking its discontinuance by 1789. On the other hand, Burke, who had originally expected the business to last no more than a year, pressed on for another five at great personal and political cost.[17] It had to be pursued, Burke came to think, irrespective of opposition fortunes. Equally, it should not be seen as a passport to popularity: the Commons, and the people, were by now corrupted; true Whigs would have to stand on higher ground.[18] Unlike Fox, as he explained to Francis, Burke grew less inclined to base his politics on the pressure of drawing numbers.[19]

In his darker moods, Burke could sense that misconduct in India was actually popular with the electorate.[20] Therefore, almost by definition, the indictment of malfeasance would have to be made a matter of principle. The process of bringing Hastings to trial was underway by early 1786, although the roots of the prosecution went back to the beginning of the decade. It was after the debate on the King's Speech opening parliament on 24 January 1786 that Hastings's agent, Major John Scott, rose to ask Burke when he planned to launch an investigation into the conduct of the Governor General, recently arrived in Britain from Calcutta.[21] Burke responded with a tale from Pierre de L'Estoile's *Journal du règne de Henri IV*, relat-

[14] *The Historical and Posthumous Memoirs of Nathaniel Wraxall*, ed. Henry B. Wheatley (London: 1884), 5 vols., VI, p. 301.

[15] Ibid., p. 302. On Fox's opportunism, see Ian R. Christie, "Charles James Fox" in idem, *Myth and Reality in Late-Eighteenth-Century British Politics and Other Papers* (Berkeley, CA: University of California Press, 1970), p. 139.

[16] WWM BkP 25:90.

[17] EB to Adam Smith, 7 December 1786, *Corr.*, V, p. 296.

[18] EB to William Baker, 22 June 1784, ibid., pp. 154–55.

[19] EB to Philip Francis, 10 December 1785, ibid., p. 243.

[20] EB to William Baker, 22 June 1784, ibid., p. 155.

[21] *Parliamentary Register* (Debrett), XIV, p. 32; G. R. Gleig ed., *Memoirs of the Life of the Right Honourable Warren Hastings* (London: 1841), 3 vols., III, p. 276.

ing how in 1590 the Duke of Parma advised the French king that he would meet his enemy in battle on terms of his own choosing.[22] However the fact was, as Scott baited him, Burke had already drafted what would become his first article of charge against Hastings.[23] Unaware of this advance preparation, Hastings grew optimistic when the issue of a public inquiry came before parliament in the new year since it seemed that he would be accused of political error rather than criminal misconduct.[24] Yet, whatever the Governor General thought, Burke would soon describe his proposed inquiry as "the greatest and most important" that had ever before been presented to "*a human Tribunal*."[25] He was obviously keen to emphasise the gravity of these proceedings, the enormity of the crimes that had allegedly been committed, and the burden of judgment that would fall on the House of Commons. The matter to be adjudicated went beyond narrow legal reasoning, requiring investigation in terms of "the liberal principles of truth and justice."[26] Part of Burke's motive in pressing for an inquiry into Hastings's behaviour was to justify his past efforts in vilifying Company politics. But he also had a domestic patriotic purpose in wanting to vindicate the honour of both parliament and nation.[27] However, the plan to launch an inquiry included yet another ambition: to undermine the resort to moral scepticism in public life. It was this aim that would link Burke's dogged pursuit of Hastings with his campaign against the Revolution in France.

Burke had been observing Hastings closely since the early 1780s. During the process of compiling the *First Report* of the Select Committee in January and February 1782, he had evidently come to the conclusion that Hastings had betrayed the trust of his office. In the "Observations" to the *First Report*, Burke noted the widespread tendency to misconstrue the administrative prerogatives of the Governor General and Council as equivalent to legislative authority, and then to interpret that authority as having been conferred without limitation.[28] This resulted in the paradoxical assumption that the management of affairs in Bengal had been invested in a

[22] Speech on Address from the Throne, *W & S*, VI, p. 45; cf. EB, *Heads Written for Consideration &c* (November 1792), *W & S*, VIII, p. 396, on the Duke of Parma. See Pierre de L'Estoile's *Journal du règne de Henri IV* (The Hague: 1741), 4 vols., I, p. 84: "le Duc de Parme avoit sagement répondu . . . qu'il fera ce qui lui conviendra le mieux." Burke's interest in the career of Henri IV was evident as early as 1770. It was an interest that was to last into the 1790s. See EB to Pierre-Gaëton Dupont, 28 October 1790, *Corr.*, VI, pp. 145–48.

[23] EB to Philip Francis, 23 December 1785, *Corr.*, V, p. 245.

[24] Gleig, *Memoirs*, III, pp. 278–79.

[25] EB, Speech on Notice of Motion on Hastings, 13 February 1786, *W & S*, VI, p. 46; cf. EB, Speech on Method of Proceeding against Hastings, ibid., p.75.

[26] EB, Speech on Notice of Motion on Hastings, 13 February 1786, ibid., p. 46;

[27] EB, Motion for Papers on Hastings, 17 February 1786, ibid., p. 47. Cf. EB, Speech in Reply, 28 May 1794, *W & S*, VII, pp. 231–32: "It is the British Nation that is upon its trial before all other Nations, before the present time and before a long, long posterity."

[28] EB, "Observations" to the *First Report* of the Select Committee, 5 February 1782, *W & S*, V, p. 170.

subordinate yet absolute government whose powers could be exercised to the utmost extent of caprice. This was, Burke seems to have concluded, a shocking assumption: it undermined the authority and legality of the legislative process, and it absolved executive power on the subcontinent of responsibility. This not only freed provincial administration from any practical restraint, it also implied the absence of any standard of moral conduct. In the "Observations," Burke took these characteristics of imperial rule in India to have been exemplified by the behaviour of Hastings as manifested by his treatment of Maharaja Nandakumar.

The case of Nandakumar had been examined at length in the original 1781 *Report* on judicial proceedings in Bengal. The Maharaja had been charged with forgery by the Supreme Court of Judicature under Elijah Impey after having accused the Governor General of accepting bribes or "entertainment."[29] Nandakumar was duly executed on 5 August 1775, immediately spreading "terror" and "alarm" in Calcutta and beyond, ultimately arousing suspicion that a judicial murder had been ordered.[30] The Select Committee examined a succession of witnesses stationed across Bengal and adjacent territories at the time, each one reporting the mixture of horror and resentment that the fate of Nandakumar had inspired amongst the native population, dismayed by the brutality of British legal practice. The following February, the *First Report* added to these concerns: not only did the punishment of forgery as a capital offence appear severe in the extreme to all Bengalis, but the verdict itself was seen as a "political Measure."[31] Hastings was being accused of tampering with the judicial process as a means of doing away with an opponent. By March 1782, rumours were circulating that Burke would seek the recall of the Governor, and within a month resolutions against Hastings were carried in the House of Commons.[32] On 16 December, Burke declared that he was prepared to pledge his own character against Hastings's, accusing him of outright criminality.[33]

[29] Differing interpretations of these events can be found in N. K. Sinha, "The Trial of Maharaja Nandakumar," *Bengal Past and Present*, 78 (1959), pp. 135–45 and D. M. Derrett, "Nandakumar's Forgery," *English Historical Review*, 75 (1960), pp. 223–38. The controversy was discussed extensively in the nineteenth century. See Thomas Babington Macaulay, "Warren Hastings" (October 1841) in idem, *Critical and Historical Essays, Contributed to the Edinburgh Review* (Leipzig: 1850), 5 vols., IV, pp. 213–349; John Morley, *Edmund Burke: A Historical Study* (London: 1867), pp. 202–3. A revisionist account was first offered by James Fitzjames Stephen, *The Story of Nuncomar and the Impeachment of Sir Elijah Impey* (London: 1885), 2 vols., esp. I, pp. 139, 186 and II, p. 37. The most useful modern discussions appear in Marshall, *Impeachment of Hastings*, pp. 135–42; Whelan, *Burke and India*, pp. 146–8; Lock, *Burke II*, pp. 224–29.

[30] *Report from the Committee to Whom the Petition of John Touchet and John Irving . . . were Severally Referred* (London: 1781), pp. 59–63.

[31] EB, "Observations" to the *First Report* of the Select Committee, 5 February 1782, *W & S*, V, p. 183.

[32] Major John Scott to Warren Hastings, 28 March 1782, Add. MS. 29153, fol. 494.

[33] *Morning Herald*, 17 December 1782; Major John Scott to Warren Hastings, 21 December 1782, Add. MS. 29157, fol. 232.

Despite all this, in a letter to Lord Thurlow written in December 1784, Burke was keen to insist that he was "no Enemy of that man": if anything, he had originally been prejudiced in his favour as a figure of dependable character and great ability.[34] But the facts spoke for themselves: the country had been pillaged and reduced under his care.[35] In the spring of 1783, Burke had been complaining that Hastings's disregard for Company orders had become flagrant and habitual—conduct that he appeared to justify on "principle."[36] In the *Eleventh Report*, Burke further charged that Hastings presumed to "legalize" in retrospect activities that had been expressly forbidden by the Company.[37] It was being rumoured in the early months of 1783 that Burke was weighing up the merits of a Bill of Pains and Penalties, though the matter was left to lie during the Fox–North Coalition.[38] By the time that he gave notice of his intention to begin parliamentary proceedings against Hastings on 20 June 1785, the Governor General's management of affairs in India challenged in Burke's mind the legitimacy of the British political process, and indeed raised the question of the justice of government altogether. Since Hastings had, as Burke saw it, reduced administration on the subcontinent to an arbitrary exercise of personal whim, he was taken to have snubbed parliamentary control and degraded public morality.

Hastings was Burke's junior by two years, and had joined the East India Company at the age of eighteen. By 1758, after the Plassey revolution and the overthrow of Siraj-ud-Daula, he had risen to the rank of resident at the court of Mir Jafar in Murshidabad. Having returned to London following the fall of Mir Kasim in 1764, he accepted a new posting as second in Council at Fort St. George in 1768. Three years later, he was appointed Governor of the Bengal settlement, where he would remain in command for a total of thirteen years.[39] Charged with reconstructing the government of Bengal, he resolved to rule the population "according to their own ideas, manners, and prejudices."[40] This approach was based on a commitment to tolerant administration, at least as this was understood by Hastings. Nathaniel Halhed, whom Hastings undertook to sponsor at this time, set out the relevant principle in the Preface to his 1776 translation of *A Code of Gentoo Laws*. As the Romans had governed their provinces, wrote Halhed, so the British should conduct themselves in India—adjusting their administration to local circumstances, practising toleration in religion, and preserving such "institutes" of the country as were compatible with

[34] *Corr.*, V, p. 204. For confirmation and restatement of this position, see EB to Sir Thomas Rumbold, 23 March 1781, *Corr.*, IV, p. 345; EB, Speech on Pitt's Second India Bill, 28 July 1784, *W & S*, V, p. 459; EB, Speech on Almas Ali Khan, 30 July 1784, ibid, pp. 475–76.

[35] *Corr.*, V, p. 204.

[36] EB, *Ninth Report*, *W & S*, V, p. 311.

[37] EB, *Eleventh Report*, ibid., pp. 354–56.

[38] James Macpherson to Warren Hastings, 28 February 1783, Add. MS. 29158, fol. 322.

[39] Keith Feiling, *Warren Hastings* (London: Macmillan, 1966), chs. 1–7.

[40] Gleig, *Memoirs*, I, p. 404.

imperial sovereignty.[41] Hastings's application of these tenets of enlightened administration impacted in the first place on revenue collection and secondly on civil and criminal jurisdiction. In each case, the pursuit of tolerant reform appeared to Hastings's opponents as an exercise in rapacious usurpation.

With his appointment as Governor General under the terms of North's Regulating Act of 1773, Hastings's direct and indirect involvement in diplomacy ramified and deepened. This included adopting measures relative to developments in Awadh while engaging with the moving frontier of Maratha interests across the subcontinent. It also involved staving off the advances of the rulers of Mysore, and managing the ambitions of the Nizam of Hyderabad. [42] With the entry of France into the American war in 1778, Hastings expected the emerging coalition of country powers ranged against the British to receive support from Britain's main European enemy. As it turned out, the British survived the arrival of a French expeditionary force in 1781. Pressurising the Maratha states into a peace in 1783, just before the Treaty of Paris confirmed the independence of the American colonies, Hastings began to present himself as a saviour of the British Empire. To Burke, however, these escapades were provocative and imperious. In practice, Hastings's interventions meant extending the defence of British interests beyond the maintenance of a legitimate sphere of influence through the formation of alliances into a policy of active expansion, subordination and extortion achieved by means of treachery and bad faith. This policy of apparently deliberate conquest began in 1774 with the expulsion of the Rohillas from the region abutting the territory of the Wazir of Awadh and, as Burke came to represent things in the early 1780s, proceeded as an unrelenting imperial pathology until Hastings's return to Britain in 1785.

During his speech on 10 June 1773 on the East India Regulating Bill, Burke had connected misgovernment in India with the person of the Governor: if it was true, as the Select and Secret Committees had recently insinuated, and as speakers in the chamber had reiterated, that the affairs of India were being systematically mismanaged, why was Hastings, who had occupied senior roles in the Company throughout the period of alleged malpractice, most recently as Governor of Bengal, being appointed to the new position of Governor General under North's Act? Hastings, surely, was guilty of everything charged against the Company.[43] Later, when Burke became properly convinced that corruption was endemic to the Company and that

[41] Nathaniel Halhed, *A Code of Gentoo Laws, or Ordinances of the Pundits* (London: 1776), pp. ix–x. On Hastings's promotion of "Oriental" learning, see P. J. Marshall, "Warren Hastings as Patron and Scholar" in Anne Whiteman et al. eds., *Statesmen, Scholars and Merchants: Essays in Eighteenth-Century History Presented to Dame Lucy Sutherland* (Oxford: Oxford University Press, 1973). On Halhed and British scholarship in India, see P. J. Marshall, "Introduction" to idem ed., *The British Discovery of Hinduism in the Eighteenth Century* (Cambridge: Cambridge University Press, 1970).

[42] Hastings's original method for extending British influence is recorded in a letter to Alexander Elliott of 12 January 1777 in Gleig, *Memoirs*, II, pp. 131–50. For discussion, see Weitzman, *Hastings and Francis*, pp. 87–88.

[43] Eg. MS. 250, fol. 208.

Hastings had led the way in perpetrating outrages, his response oscillated between diagnosing fundamental failures in the system of government and indicting the culpability of the Governor General. This variation in approach was partly due to circumstances: given the opportunity to overhaul the Company, Burke focused on anatomising its constitutional inadequacies. But, with the fall of the Coalition, succeeded by the triumph of Pitt in the general election of 1784, Burke was forced to concentrate on exemplary punishment in the absence of any prospect of remedying the underlying dysfunction. The ministry, he feared, had been bought, and the Commons corrupted. In this situation, the only available resort was to incriminate the "scourge of India," to expose the "dreadful colossus" in the name of "humanity."[44]

Writing to William Baker on 22 June 1784, Burke judged the situation in Britain to be more depraved than even "the worst times of the Roman Republick."[45] As he would later observe, while provincial magistrates in the Roman Empire were known to have "abused their trust," this had prompted the institution of "several wholesome Laws to check their arrogance."[46] After 1784, however, effective supervision of the kind had become impossible in the British Empire: the ministry was abetting a system of iniquity in India and gaining popularity in the process. In drafting Fox's India Bill, Burke had placed his faith in the supreme authority of parliament. After the failure of the Bill, he conceded that the "idea of an absolute power" such as was enjoyed by the sovereign parliament of Britain had "its terrors."[47] Yet it was the only appropriate tribunal for examining the abuses of the Company. Parliament comprised a vast array of what were in effect diverse "judges and jurors," mutually correcting one another's prejudices through a process of free and public discussion.[48] It therefore offered the only viable means of imperial supervision. But with Fox's following having been routed in the general election and a "wretched Gang of a Parliament" lending its support to Pitt, Burke could only hope to record his dismay at imperial abuses that for the moment could not be materially redeemed.[49] "I am utterly without resource," he confided to Walker King in late July 1785.[50] Nearly twenty years had passed since he first set out to "cure the disorders" of India, yet now the miscreants responsible for the mayhem were in a position to wreak revenge on their accusers.[51]

[44] EB, Speech on Almas Ali Khan, *W & S*, p. 476.

[45] *Corr.*, V, p. 155. On the brighter outlook that Burke actually faced, see Marshall, *Impeachment of Hastings*, ch. 2.

[46] EB, Notes for Rohilla War Speech, WWM BkP 9:65.

[47] EB, *A Representation to His Majesty, Moved in the House of Commons . . . June 14, 1784* (London: 1784), p. 24n.

[48] Ibid.

[49] EB to Sir Gilbert Elliot, 3 August 1784, *Corr.*, V, p. 166.

[50] *Corr.*, V, p. 214. On Burke's solitary determination in this context, see Thomas Macknight, *History of the Life and Times of Edmund Burke* (London: 1858–60), 3 vols., III, p.140.

[51] *Corr.*, V, p. 215. Burke is particularly concerned here about what he took to be a malicious scheme on the part of the new ministry to remove William Burke from his post of Deputy Paymaster in India. It is interesting that he views his conduct in regard to India since 1766 as having been wholly consistent.

It was under these circumstances that Burke resolved to concentrate his efforts on prosecuting Hastings. In the debate on the Address of Thanks to the Throne on 25 January 1785, he went out of his way to stress his view that the situation in India comprised a subject of "the greatest magnitude"—beside it, the question of parliamentary reform and the problems of Ireland paled into insignificance.[52] There existed in India as great a political disaster "as ever the world had produced," yet the prime culprit responsible for this catastrophe "was at this moment commanding our armies, and directing the expenditure of our revenues in Bengal."[53] A month earlier, Thurlow had insisted to Burke that Hastings was bereft of friends in the ministry, on the Board of Control, and among the Directors, but Burke still expected the worst from his campaign against the Governor General.[54] The actual conviction of Hastings, he thought, was "a thing we all know to be impossible."[55] He would be presenting material before a tribunal that had "conceived a favourable opinion" of Hastings's character.[56] Criminality, which resided in intention, would therefore be almost impossible to prove under circumstances where the judges had been effectively "bribed."[57] As Burke presented the situation in early 1786, he would proceed in his campaign as a solitary missionary—"without power, without access to records, without support."[58] All that he could hope for was a select minority following his lead. Fox, and even Francis, might seek to draw a retinue in train, and for that purpose compromise on the gravity of the charges against the accused. But Burke's aim was to vindicate his own political judgment together with his theory of political justice in the eyes of posterity, for which evidence of misdeeds on a substantial scale was required.[59]

The government of India under Warren Hastings raised three resounding issues. First, there was the question of Hastings's character as an administrator. Burke complained of the endless chorus of "panegyrics" circulated by Hastings's backers in celebration of their master.[60] In debate on the Select Committee Reports he relayed how he had often heard it said that the Governor of Bengal "was a very worthy man, of great abilities, and unquestionable integrity."[61] In his Speech on Almas Ali Khan, Burke distinguished between the private virtue and public conduct of officials: the question was not, he insisted, "whether he was a good father, a good husband, a good friend."[62] In outlining his position on Pitt's second India Bill, Burke was more em-

[52] *Parliamentary History*, XXIV, col. 1400.
[53] Ibid.
[54] Lord Thurlow to EB, 14 December 1784, *Corr.*, V, p. 202.
[55] EB to Philip Francis, 10 December 1785, ibid., p. 243.
[56] Ibid., p. 241.
[57] Ibid.
[58] EB, Motion for Papers on Hastings, 17 February 1786, *W & S*, VI, p. 48.
[59] EB to Philip Francis, 10 December 1785, *Corr.*, V, pp. 242–43.
[60] EB to Lord Thurlow, 14 December 1784, *Corr.*, V, p. 204.
[61] *Gazetteer*, 18 April 1782.
[62] 30 July 1784, *W & S*, V, p. 477.

phatic still. The purely "private virtues" of a "public man" were not fit subjects for examination. The issue was whether he counted as a "good governor," and his alleged domestic qualities as an individual ought not be permitted to screen the abundant evidence pointing to his malevolence as an administrator.[63] The fundamental question for the government of the subcontinent was how a public official of such palpable inadequacy had prospered inside the ranks of the East India Company. Burke had spent much of the early 1780s addressing this very topic: what in the constitution of the Company had facilitated the rise of such domineering characters, and how might these dangerous arrangements be set to rights? But now, in 1786, he switched tack, focusing on the man rather than the system of administration, hoping that by pillorying the former he might at least indict the latter, even if systematic reform could not be expected. It might have been hoped that this would rally the troops, but only as part of a long-term campaign to build the reputation of the opposition Whigs in parliament and the country. Fox, however, was impatient for more immediate results, and his relations with Burke began to deteriorate.

11.3 Rights and Reform: Representation, Regency, Slavery

On 16 March 1785, Burke rose to address the issue of the treatment of British convicts since it was rumoured that plans were in progress to transport them to Africa. This might affect up to 100,000 individuals thus condemned. Given the perils of the journey, and the inhospitable conditions on arrival, this seemed an excessively punitive measure—amounting, in some cases, to the enforcement of a death penalty without regard to the magnitude of the crime.[64] In a country justly proud of the leniency of its criminal laws, it might be expected that the aim of punishment should be to improve delinquents "by provisions dictated by clemency."[65] Yet pestilence, plague and famine awaited those transported. As Burke underlined when he returned to the subject on 11 April, such treatment was an affront to the humanity of the House of Commons.[66] Burke, of course, had his doubts about the calibre of parliamentary members admitted to the Commons in 1784, yet in the end he was keen to defend the principles determining their selection. The grounds of that defence were submitted to the House in the middle of April. The articulation of those grounds indicated

[63] 28 July 1784, ibid., p. 456.

[64] For context, see Alan Frost *Botany Bay: The Real Story* (Melbourne: Black, 2011). I am grateful to Peter Marshall for drawing my attention to Burke's intervention.

[65] EB, Convicts Sentenced to Transportation, *Parliamentary History*, XXV, col. 391. At the end of the decade, Burke would call for a drastic revision of Britain's criminal law in the context of objecting to the proliferation of penal statutes. See *Public Advertiser*, 29 May 1789. For discussion, see Leon Radzinowicz, *A History of the Criminal Law and its Administration* (London: Stevens and Sons, 1948–60), 5 vols., I, pp. 484–86.

[66] *Morning Chronicle*, 12 April 1785.

Burke's mounting alarm about new doctrines related to the right of representation that he believed posed a threat to the security of the British constitution. The organisation of public power was a delicate contrivance based on historically accumulated compromises.[67] Impulsive revision might trigger a collision of forces whose current configuration guaranteed freedom and the common good. As Burke had learnt from Montesquieu, the enlightened reformer should detect not only abuses but also corruption arising from reform itself.[68]

Burke's intervention was prompted by Pitt's attempt on 18 April 1785 to introduce a Bill to secure "a Reform in the Representation of the People."[69] Since the start of the new session, Pitt had been looking for an opportunity to redeem the failure of his previous attempts to reconfigure the composition of the Commons.[70] When the chance came, Pitt spoke to a packed chamber for about two and a half hours, finally meeting with opposition from the followers of Lord North together with a variety of ministerial supporters and opponents.[71] Each new attempt by Pitt at parliamentary reform, Burke remarked, was conspicuously different from the last, and was therefore poorly calculated to inspire confidence in the plan.[72] This time around, the idea was to increase the county membership by reallocating seats from thirty-six "decayed" boroughs.[73] This would provide for seventy-two new members, an outcome to be achieved with the consent of the electors in the old boroughs. In addition to county members, Pitt hinted at an increase in representation for London.[74] He also indicated that he favoured the admission of copyholders to the franchise.[75] A fund was to be established for buying out the borough patrons amounting, in the first instance, to one million pounds.[76] Fox voted for the Bill, though he expressed misgivings.[77] Burke, on the other hand, was completely opposed. This points to an interesting early divergence from Fox, and indicates some of the grounds on which Burke would later judge ill-conceived reform to be a harbinger of revolutionary change.

[67] EB, *Thoughts on the Cause of the Present Discontents* (1770), *W & S*, II, p. 311.

[68] Charles-Louis de Secondat, Baron de Montesquieu, *De l'esprit des lois* (1748) in *Œuvres complètes*, ed. Roger Caillois (Paris: Gallimard, 1951), 2 vols., I, Préface: "On voit encore les abus de la correction même."

[69] *Parliamentary History*, XXV, col. 432.

[70] William Pitt to the Duke of Rutland, 12 January 1785, *Correspondence between the Rt. Hon. William Pitt and Charles, Duke of Rutland, Lord Lieutenant of Ireland* (London: 1890), p. 84.

[71] I. R. Christie, *Wilkes, Wyvill and Reform: The Parliamentary Reform Movement in British Politics, 1760–1785* (London: Macmillan, 1962), p. 217.

[72] *Morning Chronicle*, 19 April 1785.

[73] Grafton, *Autobiography*, p. 379.

[74] *Parliamentary History*, XXV, col. 448.

[75] Ibid., col. 447.

[76] Christopher Wyvill, *Political Papers, Chiefly Respecting . . . a Reformation of the Parliament of Great Britain* (York: 1794–1802), 6 vols., IV, pp. 62–65.

[77] *London Chronicle*, 16–19 April 1785.

Pitt's plan had two main features: first, his aim was to reform anomalous representation; second, he wanted to lay down a rule for likely changes in the future. In both cases, he presented his scheme as a historical necessity: as circumstances changed, with demography and wealth subject to alteration over time, representation should keep pace with new developments. This in fact was in keeping with the spirit of the constitution: it was an ancient provision of the law of the land that "the state of representation was to be changed with the change of circumstances."[78] This was not innovation, but reform—or at least innovation within the framework of constitutional precedent.[79] Opposition to such enlightened and principled adaptation was nothing less than a superstitious reverence for the past that fretted over every increment of historical improvement.[80] In changing the proportion between borough and county seats, a larger proportion of MPs would represent populous districts instead of "places that had neither property nor people."[81] Pitt was clear about the principles on which representation should generally operate: the Commons should share an "interest" with the population at large, who ought in turn to be bound to it by ties of "sympathy and union."[82] This was a far cry, Pitt insisted, from competitor schemes based on "individual representation." Any new arrangement founded on this principle was delusive, and liable to launch the public upon "unbounded" seas.[83] However, Burke suspected that it was precisely into these uncharted territories that Pitt's proposals would ultimately lead.

Burke objected to Pitt's proposals on three principal grounds. He accepted the general argument that the Commons represented an amalgam of interests, and that it secured this status by a process of deliberation among its members who identified with the diversity of the people out of doors.[84] This identification or "sympathy" with the electorate was achieved on account of the dispositions of the various constituencies in the lower House. One key constituency was made up of the country seats, whose members' independence helped make them a voice of the landed interest. Pitt's plan would involve adding more weight to this particular constituency, at the expense of the fund of talent that gained access through "rotten" boroughs—like Pitt himself, who sat for Appleby, or Burke, who sat for Malton. "The influence of the country Gentlemen in Parliament," Burke pointed out, "was always known to preponderate, when they were united in opinion."[85] Burke's first complaint was therefore that Pitt's scheme would merely increase this bias: "Where then was the prudence of throwing into that scale, in whose power the balance already was, that

[78] *Parliamentary History*, XXV, col. 435.

[79] Ibid., col. 438.

[80] Ibid., cols. 432–33.

[81] Ibid., col. 441.

[82] Ibid., col. 435.

[83] Ibid.

[84] Hanna Fenichel Pitkin, *The Concept of Representation* (Berkeley, CA: University of California Press, 1967), ch. 8.

[85] *Morning Herald*, 19 April 1785.

share of power which was pretended to be the means of keeping all parts of the House on the same level."[86] Reform should have a purpose, yet Pitt's stated objective made little political sense. This brought Burke to his second complaint. Pitt claimed that his scheme would offer finality, yet how could "he truly say this"?[87] The Duke of Richmond was in the ministry, and hankered after a more comprehensive rearrangement. What was the guarantee that, once Pitt's plan had been accepted, Richmond would not reappear in his publicly respectable role with the aim of bringing into being "his scheme also"?[88] This brought Burke to his third point, which was really an insinuation: Pitt's measure was merely an element of a more capacious and menacing programme to subvert the prescriptive basis of the existing constitution. This was to suggest not that Pitt was part of a conspiracy, but that he was a tool of others' designs. Burke singled out Richmond and Wyvill as the agents of this more sinister purpose.

Burke's speech of 18 April was reputed to be "one of his best," yet its content was not extensively reported.[89] Nevertheless, in three separate reports his alarm can be discerned. In one, he is presented as focusing attention on a recent plan which, "of all others he had read or heard of, paid the most respect to the original rights of men."[90] This was a reference to the Duke of Richmond's programme that had been circulated just two years earlier.[91] In another report Burke is presented as having referred to a "doctrine" which had recently gained ground, founded on the principle of "universal representation."[92] In addition to Richmond, Burke singled out the ideas of Christopher Wyvill for comment, noting above all his correspondence that had been published.[93] Wyvill, according to the account of Burke's speech in the *Morning Chronicle*, had been busy "disseminating notions, tending to disturb the minds of poor industrious men, who were quiet and easy before they were told the Constitution was ruined."[94] Since Pitt's avowed intention of making a "final" addition to the preponderance of the country members in the House made no practical sense, Burke concluded that, at best, it opened the way for more devious aims or, at worst, Pitt's current plan was a preparation for a more ambitious scheme. Insofar as that scheme was likely to assist the highly subversive idea of basing representation on the natural rights of man, it would have to be vehemently opposed. In introducing his plan, Pitt had been explicit: "Those who went further—those who went to ideas of individual

[86] Ibid.

[87] *General Evening Post*, 16–19 April 1785.

[88] Ibid.

[89] *Morning Herald*, 19 April 1785.

[90] *General Evening Post*, 16–19 April 1785.

[91] Charles Lennox, third Duke of Richmond, *An Authentic Copy of the Duke of Richmond's Bill for a Parliamentary Reform* (London: 1783). This reproduced a proposal originally introduced by Richmond into the House of Lords in 1780.

[92] *Morning Herald*, 19 April 1785.

[93] *Ibid.*; *General Evening Post*, 16–19 April 1785.

[94] *Morning Chronicle*, 19 April 1785.

representation, deluded themselves with impossibilities."[95] However, Burke's sense was that Pitt's ideas were insufficiently differentiated from what he regarded as the quixotic enterprises of Wyvill and Richmond.

We have already noted that, during the American war, Richmond had come under the influence of Cartwright's pamphlet, *Take Your Choice!* Four years later, he joined the Society for Constitutional Information to agitate for a more equal representation. By 1783, he had adopted Cartwright's proposals for annual parliaments and universal manhood suffrage, and was publicising proposals for comprehensive reformation.[96] That same year, Henry Joy wrote on behalf of the committee of correspondence of the Irish Volunteers in Ulster seeking Richmond's support for a plan of parliamentary reform to be proposed at the third Dungannon Convention of 8 September 1783. In response, Richmond set out his commitment to the "full, clear, and indispensable Rights of Universal Representation." In the wake of the failure of more moderate plans in the British parliament, this could only be achieved by direct action by "the People at large."[97] Richmond expected that this fundamental change would be compatible with the existing mixed system of government, avoiding its transformation into a democratic republic, and a consequent resurgence of levelling principles in Britain.[98] What counted for him, however, was less the convenience of the measure than the opportunity to assert the "unalienable" right. Constitutional precedent could not impede an "eternal Principle of Justice and Wisdom."[99] For Burke, however, Richmond's ideas were "the most impractical that could be imagined."[100]

Wyvill had campaigned in favour of Pitt in the election of 1784. The coalition, above all its India Bill, had led to his radical estrangement from the Foxites.[101] The following year, during the debate on reform, he attracted a large proportion of Burke's vituperation. Burke noted, in particular, the range of his correspondence, which had included a published record of his exchanges with the Volunteers. "It is a right of mankind to be governed by their own consent, or by Representation," Wyvill had written.[102] It was the duty of government to serve the "people," rather than an exclusive aristocratic interest, and this indeed had been the original aim of the Saxon constitution.[103] This obligation was commonly abandoned under circumstances where wealth was concentrated in fewer hands, enabling the consolidation

[95] *Parliamentary History*, XXV, col. 834.

[96] Alison Gilbert Olson, *The Radical Duke: Career and Correspondence of Charles Lennox, Third Duke of Richmond* (Oxford: Oxford University Press, 1961).

[97] *A Letter of His Grace the Duke of Richmond, in Answer to Queries Proposed by A Committee of Correspondence in Ireland* (London: 1783), p. 32.

[98] Ibid., pp. 40–41.

[99] Ibid., p. 35.

[100] *General Evening Post*, 16–19 April 1785.

[101] Christie, *Wilkes, Wyvill and Reform*, p. 192.

[102] *Letters Addressed to the Committee of Belfast, on the Proposed Reformation of the Parliament of Ireland* (York: 1783), p. 12.

[103] Ibid., p. 13.

of aristocratic privilege. Institutional mechanisms had to be developed to counteract this tendency since the rights of property should remain inviolate. The best means of providing for redress lay in the purification of representation, although this, for Wyvill, should stop far short of universal enfranchisement. The right to consent by representation was fundamental, but it was necessarily overridden by the principles of reason of state. In practical terms, national preservation required the restriction of the suffrage to responsible elements within the community, meaning public-spirited citizens of property.[104] As Burke noticed, this prudential restriction was nonetheless added to an underlying commitment to a natural right that conferred the privilege of suffrage universally. On that basis Wyvill's ideas were rejected by Burke. Pitt's proposals were judged to be "in conformity" with the same doctrine.[105] Fundamental rights secured the individual from expropriation and oppression, but they could not dictate the form of government as such. This proved to be a fundamental commitment of Burke's, which would shape his response to the Revolution in France.

Burke had occasion to defend his prescriptive conception of the British constitution in the context of the regency crisis. This began with the first signs of George III's illness in June 1788. The symptoms were at first physical, but indications of mental debility began to appear in October.[106] Rumour was soon rampant that the situation was irretrievable, and the expectation rose that George Augustus Frederick, the dissolute Prince of Wales, would promptly replace the incapacitated king. On 24 November, Fox returned exhausted from his travels in Italy, only to find his colleagues in disarray. Sheridan was pursuing negotiations with the Lord Chancellor, Edward Thurlow, to prepare for the installation of a new ministry. In the process he was winning the support of Carlton House, raising Burke's suspicions, and unsettling Fox himself. Meanwhile Alexander Wedderburn, created Baron Loughborough in 1780, had his sights set on the seals in any new administration, and was advising the prince on constitutional procedure. Burke, who wanted Thurlow replaced on the woolsack, agreed with this approach: the constitution made no provision for an interregnum, and so the regent should succeed as a matter of right.[107] This would best be achieved on the initiative of the prince, who might then consult both Houses for their advice.[108] The situation appeared more ambiguous after the examination of the royal doctors before the Privy Council on 3 December, with Pitt expecting the king's return to normality before long. His strategy from now on was to play for extra time, with Fox growing ever more restless as the prospect of power drew steadily closer. By 10 December, during the debate on the report from the Commons committee on the state of the king's health, Fox had resolved to argue for the prince's right to the regency without the imposition of restrictions of the kind that Sheridan had been prepared to endorse. To that extent he had accepted the analysis propounded by

[104] Ibid., p. 14.

[105] *Morning Herald*, 19 April 1785.

[106] Ida Macalpine and Richard Hunter, *George III and the Mad Business* (London: Penguin, 1969).

[107] Mitchell, *Charles James Fox*, pp. 124–26.

[108] EB to Charles James Fox, post 24 November 1788, *Corr.*, V, pp. 428–9.

Burke, delivered despite his awareness of his declining influence in the party. Fox was most likely guided by a determination to sideline Sheridan.

Fox was anxious to dissuade the House from searching into precedents as a means of establishing a correct mode of procedure. Above all, he wanted to emphasise the fact that the judgment of the Commons could not resolve the exigency it currently faced: "The circumstance to be provided for did not depend on their deliberations as a house of parliament; it rested elsewhere."[109] It was naturally in the power of parliament as a whole to alter the terms of succession to the throne, yet this was not a right possessed by the Lords and Commons alone.[110] Pitt professed himself astounded at the assumptions of his adversary. His aim was now to portray Fox's intervention as a defence of the rights of the executive against the authority of parliament. Burke, in turn, marvelled at the opportunism of Pitt's manoeuvre. From the start, Burke had been anxious to remove himself from the heat of the present contentions. He had little to expect from the formation of a new government, and viewed developments as creating a constitutional precedent.[111] The issues were thus in need of cool and penetrating analysis.[112] Over the following days and weeks, as Burke urged a course of moderation on his colleagues in the Commons, his performances became ever more vituperative and desperate. Allegations of insanity steadily rained down upon him.[113] His outbursts were the product of overwhelming frustration, the causes of which had been accumulating over the previous four years. One element was the beleaguered position of the opposition, operating in a parliament that had grown meek to the point of docility.[114] This, as the Foxites saw it, was the legacy of 1784. Burke's rage against Pitt for his role in that calamity surged during the debates on the regency. The calculating ambition cloaked by the punctiliousness of the first minister was endlessly upbraided. Yet the role of the opposition also drove Burke to exasperation, not least for the way in which his colleagues had marginalised him in the party.

On 22 December 1788, Burke spoke at length on an amendment to Pitt's resolution that the House should define the terms of the regency. He spoke, we are told, "with more than usual solemnity."[115] To Burke, Pitt's proposal ranked as the most

[109] *Parliamentary History*, XXVII, col. 706.

[110] Ibid., col. 711. However, see EB, Speech on the Civil Establishment Bill, 8 March 1780, *W & S*, III, p. 555: "the present Royal family were called to the Throne by the free voice of the people . . . his Majesty was the *creature of public institution*, and could not hold his throne a moment, if the other orders of the state chose to put a negative on his being any longer King."

[111] In the *World*, 23 December 1788, Burke is reported to have said: "A probability of a change in the Administration had been suggested; for his part, he knew nothing of it: power might shift hands, but he neither wished nor expected it to fall into his." Burke was right: according to opposition plans, he was likely to rank no higher than paymaster general in any new administration.

[112] EB, Debate on the Committee Report on the State of the King's Health, 10 December 1788, *Parliamentary History*, col. 713.

[113] John W. Derry, *The Regency Crisis and the Whigs, 1788–1789* (Cambridge: Cambridge University Press, 1963), ch. 4.

[114] EB, Speech on the King's Illness, 19 December 1788, *Parliamentary History*, XXVII, col. 817.

[115] *World*, 23 December 1788.

abject demagoguery, flattering the people "at their own expense."[116] By comparison, Burke assured his audience that he had never made a speech either "to please the court" or to "captivate the people."[117] What concerned him was the integrity of the constitution in the face of an unanticipated exigency. This exigency was certainly pressing but it was not, in the technical sense, an overriding necessity: no absolute political emergency existed since the constitution adequately catered to the situation at hand.[118] A vacancy on the throne might create an emergency, for which a convention parliament would be required to provide for the defect. This predicament had obtained in 1688: necessity, which in practice meant the threat of constitutional implosion, leading inexorably to civil war, had dictated that a deviation from the royal line was inescapable. As Burke would underline nearly two years later in the *Reflections*, this dire emergency was remedied by appeal to the rights of war.[119] An alteration in the succession occurred in order to secure the hereditary principle. However, Pitt's approach to the current incapacity of George III threatened to create a form of elective monarchy.[120] This might be licensed by a false analogy with the Glorious Revolution, but the speciousness of the comparison foretold the death of British liberty.[121] In 1688, the government was not merely "convulsed and disjointed, but annihilated and reduced to atoms."[122] Under these circumstances, extra-constitutional conspiracy became legitimate.[123] However, 1788 presented a very different scene. A prospective regency had to be distinguished from a revolution in the state. Nonetheless, on the Pittite model, given the incapacity of George III, Britain ought first to resolve itself into a popular regime before it could reconstruct itself as a monarchical republic. This was to imagine that Britain in 1788 was in the position of the Americans in 1787.[124]

What in America would count as an act of construction could only figure in Britain as a project of deconstruction. On this basis, Burke likened the plan of the ministry to the designs of "fifth Monarchy-men," disassembling the pillars of the constitution.[125] By early February 1789, Burke's animus against attempts to impose restrictions on the regency had become focused on the ambitions of William Pitt. The "heaven-born" minister, as Burke now styled him, was bent upon the revival of

[116] EB, Speech on the King's Illness, 22 December 1788, *Parliamentary History*, XXVII, col. 819.

[117] WWM BkP 15:35.

[118] WWM BkP 15:6, 7, 25, 36.

[119] EB, *Reflections on the Revolution in France*, ed. J.C.D. Clark (Stanford, CA: Stanford University Press, 2001), p. 177 [39]. See below, chapter 13, section 3.

[120] Burke later connected the principles canvassed during the regency crisis to the democratic ideas purveyed by sections of dissenting opinion. See EB to William Weddell, 31 January 1792, *Corr.*, VII, p. 56.

[121] *Morning Chronicle*, 23 December 1788.

[122] *World*, 23 December 1788.

[123] *Times*, 23 December 1788.

[124] EB, Speech on the King's Illness, 22 December 1788, *Parliamentary History*, XXVII, col. 821. The *Morning Herald*, 23 December 1788, misreported America as "Africa."

[125] *World*, 23 December 1788.

divine-right despotism, promoted under cover of democratic zeal.[126] However, at the same time, Burke's open contempt for Pitt disguised his mounting disdain for his colleagues. "I sincerely wish to withdraw myself from this scene for good and all," he confided to Windham.[127] The desire to surrender was largely based on his sense of powerlessness in the party. Despite the strength and cogency of his opinions from the start of the crisis, his arguments were largely disregarded by his colleagues. However, the issue for Burke was not merely the personal feeling of being slighted, but the petty hankering for office evident in the conduct of Fox and Sheridan. This was a very tangible break with the posture of the Rockinghams, and it was not a world in which Burke was keen to continue. The madness of George III raised a basic issue of constitutional propriety: Fox and Sheridan should have been prepared to forgo their place in government in order to prevent "further outrages on the Constitution."[128] The question of the succession involved a fundamental principle. As Burke was to make plain to Lord Fitzwilliam in 1791, it touched on the very idea of prescriptive right. To compromise that idea would prove perilous to government as well as to its propertied supporters: "I was convinced to a certainty," he recollected, "that whatever tended to unsettle the succession, and to disturb the recognised ranks and orders, and the fixed properties in the nation would be of all men the most fatal to your friends . . . and the chiefs of your party."[129]

Because prescription was intended for the preservation of justice, only the overriding claims of humanity could be permitted to challenge it. In the spring of 1789, Burke publicised his commitment to one such claim. "We are greatly delighted at the prospect of slavery being abolished," Mary Leadbeater wrote to her father Richard Shackleton at this time. She was particularly pleased to find that in "such a discussion our honoured friend Burke could not be silent."[130] Since the end of the American war, the movement for the abolition of the slave trade had been gaining ground in Britain. It emerged against the background of buoyant and lucrative commerce involving Bristol, Liverpool and London: through the eighteenth century down to 1807, a total of about 2¾ million African slaves were delivered in English ships to the American market.[131] International rivalry was fierce, with Spanish, Portuguese, French, Danish, Dutch and American traders competing.[132] In the Commons on 9 May 1788, Pitt summarised the current state of the debate in Britain. Everyone agreed, he stated, that something would have to give: either the African trade would

[126] EB, Debate on the Regency Bill, *Parliamentary History*, XXVII, col. 1170.

[127] EB to William Windham, c. 24 January 1789, *Corr.*, V, p. 437.

[128] Ibid., p. 439.

[129] WB to Earl Fitzwilliam, 5 June 1791, *Corr.*, VI, p. 272.

[130] Mary Leadbeater to Richard Shackleton, 30 May 1789, OSB MSS. 50, Box 2.

[131] David Richardson, "The Eighteenth-Century British Slave Trade: Estimates of its Volume and Coastal Distribution in Africa," *Research in Economic History*, 12 (1989), pp. 151–95; Kenneth Morgan, *Bristol and the Atlantic Trade in the Eighteenth Century* (Cambridge: Cambridge University Press, 1993) p. 129.

[132] James A. Rawley, *The Transatlantic Slave Trade* (New York: W. W. Norton, 1981); Philip D. Curtin, *The Atlantic Slave Trade: A Census* (Madison, WI: University of Wisconsin Press, 1969).

have to be abolished, or some system of regulation would have to be introduced.[133] Contributing to the debate, Burke declared that "he was one of those who wished for the abolition of the Slave Trade. He thought it ought to be abolished on the principles of humanity and justice."[134] He had always espoused the view that if political circumstances rendered abolition impossible, then a system of regulation ought to be introduced.[135] In 1780, he had drafted a "Code" with a view to humanising the trade, yet even then he expressed the general view that the tenets of morality and religion demanded an end "to all traffic in the persons of men, and to the detention of their said persons in a State of Slavery."[136] Two years earlier, he was reported as having condemned the practice as being "of the most inhuman nature, a traffic for human bodies."[137] Back in 1757, the *Account of the European Settlements in America* had described the British trade as more ferocious than any of its rivals. Indeed, nothing could excuse such a base form of commerce except the consideration that British slaves had been African slaves already.[138] By 1789, opinion in the Commons in favour of abolition was backed by what Burke later called "a popular spirit" in the form of over a hundred petitions directed against the trade.[139] On 12 May in that year, William Wilberforce moved for a committee to examine these petitions, leading him to recommend "total abolition."[140] Wilberforce's performance, culminating in twelve specific resolutions on the subject, seemed to Burke to have been presented on principles "so admirable" as to "equal anything he had heard in modern oratory."[141] He then proceeded to outline his fundamental point: the trade was so despicable in all its circumstances that neither prudence nor dire necessity could be pleaded in its defence.[142] Since abolition was clearly right, the question was how this outcome should be achieved.

When Burke returned to this subject in 1792, after it had been agreed that this branch of commerce should be gradually terminated, he adverted to some of the serious complications involved. In the end, from a cosmopolitan point of view, it was slavery rather than the slave trade that was the fundamental problem. "I am very

[133] *Parliamentary History*, XXVII, cols. 495–96.

[134] EB, Speech on the Slave Trade, 9 May 1788, ibid., col. 502.

[135] A review of George Wallace, *A System of the Principles of the Law of Scotland* (Edinburgh: 1760) in *The Annual Register for the Year 1760* (London: 1761), pp. 263–65, argues strenuously against modern slavery and its trade, though the authorship of the piece cannot be established with certainty.

[136] EB, "Sketch of a Negro Code," *W & S*, III, p. 563. The "Code" had been circulated among colleagues. It was commended by Charles Rose Ellis to the House of Commons on 6 April 1797: see *Parliamentary History*, XXXIII, col. 253.

[137] *Public Advertiser*, 14 May 1778. Cf. EB, Speeches on African Slave Trade, 5 June 1777, *W & S*, III, pp. 340–41.

[138] [Edmund and William Burke], *An Account of the European Settlements in America. In Six Parts.* (1757) (London: 6th ed., 1777), 2 vols., II, pp. 128–29. A form of gradual and regulated manumission was also considered. See ibid., pp. 130–31.

[139] EB to Henry Dundas, 9 April 1792, *Corr.*, VII, p. 122.

[140] *Parliamentary History*, XXVII, cols. 41, 62.

[141] EB, Speech on Wilberforce's Resolutions, 12 May 1789, *ibid.*, col. 68.

[142] Ibid., col. 69.

apprehensive," Burke wrote to Dundas, "that so long as the slavery continues some means for its supply will be found."[143] The best course of action was therefore to render demand redundant. When this occurred, those inured to slavery would be delivered up to freedom, yet it was advisable that this be preceded by careful preparation. Slavery was degrading and dehumanising at once. Its victims were unfit to exercise responsible liberty.[144] As a result, the route to abolition would have to be regulated in detail, directed by the guiding hand of power. In 1789, however, Burke emphasised the urgent need to achieve eradication. The slave trade was a system of "absolute robbery" for which nothing could be pleaded in mitigation.[145] Nine days earlier, on 12 May, Burke had been more emphatic still. There was nothing about the slave trade that could be reasonably justified: it violated people's property in themselves, thereby subverting their human status as bearers of natural rights. Intriguingly, therefore, within days of the Estates General having met at Versailles, propelling the French state towards revolutionary crisis, Burke was protesting the rights of man against despotic subjection. As he knew, Locke had argued in the second of the *Two Treatises of Government* that servitude involved such a radical denial of the duty of self-possession that it was incompatible with the obligation of self-preservation.[146] Burke shared this view that the original right of self-mastery was inalienable; one did not possess the liberty to dispose of oneself as one wished, and so one could not sell one's freedom to another.[147] Yet Burke also insisted that the practical exercise of natural freedom was constrained by the requirements of civil society. The confusion, as he saw it, between natural and civil rights was fundamental to the ruling ideas of Revolutionary France.[148] Under the influence of those ideas, social rights were dismantled in the name of primordial rights. The consequences of that confusion would absorb Burke's attention for the remainder of his career.

[143] EB to Henry Dundas, 9 April 1792, *Corr.*, VII, pp. 123–24.

[144] EB, Debate respecting the Slave Trade, 12 May 1789, *Parliamentary History*, XXVIII, col. 71.

[145] EB, Debate on Wilberforce's Resolutions, 21 May 1789, *ibid.*, col. 96.

[146] John Locke, *Two Treatises of Government*, ed. Peter Laslett (Cambridge: Cambridge University Press, 1960, 1990), II, iv, § 23. Locke was taking up a position against Suárez, Grotius and Pufendorf. On this, see Richard Tuck, *Natural Rights Theories: Their Origin and Development* (Cambridge: Cambridge University Press, 1979), pp. 49–57; Stephen Buckle, *Natural Law and the Theory of Property: Grotius to Hume* (Oxford: Oxford University Press, 1991, 2002), pp. 48–52, 118–22, 175–79. On the wider complexities of Locke's theory of slavery, see John Dunn, *The Political Thought of John Locke: An Historical Account of the Argument of the "Two Treatises of Government"* (Cambridge: Cambridge University Press, 1969), pp. 108–10, 174–77; Jeremy Waldron, *God, Locke, and Equality: Christian Foundations in Locke's Political Thought* (Cambridge: Cambridge University Press, 2002), pp. 197–206; James Farr, "Locke, Natural Law, and New World Slavery," *Political Theory*, 36:4 (August 2008), pp. 495–522; David Armitage, *Foundations of Modern International Thought* (Cambridge: Cambridge University Press, 2013), pp. 111–12.

[147] Northamptonshire MS. A. XXIX.49. For discussion, see below, chapter 12, section 6. Cf. John Locke, "Of Ethic in General" (c. 1686–88?) in *Political Essays*, ed. Mark Goldie (Cambridge: Cambridge University Press, 1997), p. 302: natural law "is not made by us, but for us."

[148] EB, *Reflections*, ed. Clark, pp. 217–18 [87–8].

11.4 The Franco-British Contest

"England is a moon shone upon by France," Burke is reported to have once said. Britain's great European and imperial rival, he went on, "has all things within herself; and she possesses the power of recovering from the severest of blows. England is an artificial country: take away her commerce, and what has she?"[149] Throughout Burke's career in the House of Commons, France loomed as a potential threat to the security of Europe, and consequently to the power and prestige of the British state. From 1789, relations between both countries grew more complicated. At that point, the French Revolution was poised to reconfigure the balance of power in Europe. France was distracted, and depleted of resources, but for all that posed a range of new and insidious challenges to the British. As Burke saw it, this development represented a sudden change of fortune. Back in 1769, reflecting on French political economy in the aftermath of the Seven Years' War, he had expected "some extraordinary convulsion" in that country, with effects on Europe that were difficult to predict.[150] However, in the midst of the American war, the situation began to look different. First, with Turgot occupying the position of controller-general of French finances, Burke sensed a spirit of amity pervading the court at Versailles. Philosophy, along with "a certain System d'oeconomie politique," had passed from among the learned into the counsels of the king, and from there it had started to humanise "the minds of the people" at large.[151] As a result, a decline in national chauvinism seemed reasonable to expect, even though any show of goodwill was likely to prove temporary. More significantly, in the space of just a few generations, France had passed from occupying the dominant position in Europe to "fourth in the Scale" of power on the continent.[152] None of this, however, meant that France was a spent force. Some great minister, recalling the days of glory, might press for a return to the goal of universal empire.[153] By the middle of the 1790s, Burke came to the conclusion that revolutionary turbulence was a by-product of the ambition to resuscitate this objective. From its sorry condition in the autumn of 1789, French power was evidently on the rise again.

[149] Notes from the Commonplace Book of Samuel Rogers, Add. MS. 45790, fol. 27.

[150] EB, *Observations on a Late State of the Nation* (1769), *W & S*, II, p. 151.

[151] WWM BkP 6:200, reproduced in *W & S*, III, p. 212. On the impact of Turgot, see Colin Jones, *The Great Nation: France from Louis XV to Napoleon* (London: Penguin, 2002), pp. 292–301.

[152] WWM BkP 6:200, reproduced in *W & S*, III, p. 212. Burke placed France behind Russia, Austria and Prussia, but also Britain, putting her in fifth position overall: cf. EB, Second Speech on Conciliation, 16 November 1775, *W & S*, III, p. 187. For a study of Britain's relations with France in the period, see Derek Jarrett, *The Begetters of Revolution: England's Involvement with France, 1759–1789* (London: Longman, 1973).

[153] WWM BkP 6:200, reproduced in *W & S*, III, p. 212.

This recovery could be placed within a longer train of development. After the appointment of Jacques Necker as director of the treasury under Louis XVI in October 1776, Burke began to comment on the rehabilitation of French finances.[154] Writing to the Duke of Portland in 1779, he noted Necker's success in managing the national debt without the introduction of new taxes.[155] This was a recovery on which Burke had already dwelt during his speech on the army estimates the previous year. As Britain drained its resources to service the American war, largely by increasing its land forces across the Atlantic, France had been reinvesting in the capacity of its navy. Months after France had joined forces with the colonies, its credit and prosperity, as well as its military might, easily put Britain in the shade.[156] By the following year, Burke's anxiety was still greater. A "*war of oeconomy*" now existed between the two powers, and Britain looked certain to be worsted. Under Lord North, the administration had increased "dissipation and profusion"—the prerogative of monarchies rather than republics.[157] In his *Speech on Economical Reform* in February 1780, Burke further developed his thesis: by means of Necker's skill and Louis XVI's virtue, a truly "patriot" scheme was restoring France to greatness.[158] This was largely a consequence of redeeming public credit by reining in the excesses of a notoriously prodigal court. Sound finances depended upon confidence and trust: confidence in public economy and trust in the constitution. Britain enjoyed the latter by comparison with the French monarchy, yet Necker had secured the former by retrenchment and public accounting. It was in this context that Burke was moved to comment: "I am far from being sure, that a monarchy, when once it is properly regulated, may not for a long time, furnish a foundation for credit upon the solidity of its maxims, though it affords no ground of trust in its institutions."[159]

By 1787, it was clear to British observers that Necker's enterprise had failed. *The Annual Register* for that year, still under Burke's editorship, with close allies like Thomas English and French Laurence contributing copy, argued that the colossal expense of the American war had added to the unmanageable burdens facing

[154]Later generations were to be far more critical, but for a more sympathetic account see Robert D. Harris, "Necker's Compte Rendu of 1781: A Reconsideration," *Journal of Modern History*, 42:2 (June 1970), pp. 161–83. See also J. F. Bosher, *French Finances, 1770–1795: From Business to Bureaucracy* (Cambridge: Cambridge University Press, 1970), ch. 8.

[155]EB to the Duke of Portland, 16 October 1779, *Corr.*, IV, p. 154.

[156]EB, Speech on Army Estimates, 14 December 1778, *W & S*, III, p. 396.

[157]EB, Speech on Public Expenses, 15 December 1779, ibid., pp. 468–69.

[158]EB, *Speech on Economical Reform*, 11 February 1780, *ibid.*, p. 488. For Necker's appreciation of Burke's comments, see EB to Jacques Necker, 5 May 1780, *Corr.*, IV, p. 233. Burke returned to the subject in EB, Debate on the Bill for the Regulation of the Civil List Establishments, 15 February 1781, *Parliamentary History*, XXI, cols. 1235–36.

[159]EB, *Speech on Economical Reform*, 11 February 1780, *W & S*, III, p. 489. For the theme of public debt in eighteenth-century political thought, also in relation to Burke, see Sonenscher, *Before the Deluge*, ch. 1. For the wider British context, see Hont, *Jealousy of Trade*, ch. 4.

France.[160] "From this war," the *Register* commented, "an immense new debt being laid upon the back of the old, already too great, the accumulation became so vast, that it seemed to swell beyond the common bounds of examination and enquiry."[161] Nonetheless, there were grounds for optimism despite the depth of the crisis. The monarchy, partly under the influence of the controller-general, Charles-Alexandre Calonne, sought to win the public over to its measures.[162] It was generally true that, since the beginning of the king's reign, compulsory loans and arbitrary exactions had consistently been avoided. Now, in addition, the regime sought endorsement of its measures from public opinion. This took the concrete form of summoning the assembly of notables for 22 February 1787.

As the analyst in *The Annual Register* saw it, this decision represented the latest instalment of a general tendency since the days of Necker to seek the establishment of an ever freer constitution in France whereby the acclamation of the public was actively sought by the government.[163] This development, Burke thought, had deeper roots in the eighteenth century. Even under Louis XV, the Parisian and provincial *parlements* had steadily arrogated authority to themselves, emerging as a bulwark between the people and their oppression.[164] Commenting on this development in the historical essay opening *The Annual Register* for 1764, Burke depicted this growth in freedom as a "capital revolution," the consequences of which remained to be discerned.[165] The effects of the spirit of liberty were more obvious in 1787. As the year progressed, *The Annual Register* noted, it became increasingly clear that the assembly of notables was unequal to the task of resolving the kingdom's problems: "nothing less than an assemblage of the general states of the kingdom . . . could effectually remove the present grievances."[166] With the convocation of the Estates General

[160] Thomas W. Copeland, "Burke and Dodsley's *Annual Register*," *Publication of the Modern Language Association*, 54:1 (March 1939), pp. 223–45; idem, "A Career in Journalism" in idem, *Burke*.

[161] "History of Europe" in *The Annual Register for 1787* (London: 1788), pp. 177–78. Borrowing had boomed particularly after 1781. See Jones, *The Great Nation*, p. 318. For the impact of the war on the French financial situation, see Robert D. Harris, "French Finances and the American War, 1777–1783," *Journal of Modern History*, 48:2 (June 1976), pp. 233–58; Derek McKay and H. M. Scott, *The Rise of the Great Powers, 1648–1815* (London: Longman, 1983), p. 265.

[162] On Calonne's methods, and his failure, see Albert Goodwin, "Calonne, the Assembly of French Notables of 1787 and the Origins of the 'Révolte Nobiliaire'," *English Historical Review*, 61:240 and 241 (May and September 1946), pp. 329–77 and 202–34.

[163] "History of Europe" in *The Annual Register for 1787*, pp. 179–80.

[164] This view was largely dismissed by post-Revolutionary histories, though more recently it has found comparative favour: see William Doyle, "The Parlements of France and the Breakdown of the Old Regime 1771–1788," *French Historical Studies*, 6:4 (Autumn 1970), pp. 415–58; Bailey Stone, *The Parlement of Paris, 1774–1789* (Chapel Hill, NC: University of North Carolina Press, 1981); Julian Swann, *Politics and the Parlement of Paris under Louis XV, 1754–1774* (Cambridge: Cambridge University Press, 1995).

[165] "History of Europe" in *Annual Register for the Year 1764* (London: 1765), p. 10.

[166] "History of Europe" in *Annual Register for the Year 1787* (London: 1788), p. 184.

now in prospect, it suddenly seemed that the "ancient Gallic constitution" was being revived.[167]

As the assembly of notables convened at the end of February 1787, a new commercial and navigation treaty, negotiated the previous year between William Eden and Conrad Alexandre Gérard de Rayneval, was being debated in the British Houses of Parliament.[168] The treaty was negotiated against the background of recent French successes in European diplomacy, notably the treaty of Fontainebleau, masterminded by Vergennes, which promoted an alliance with the Dutch and provided access to the Scheldt estuary.[169] In the first year of Pitt's administration, there were fears for the fate of Britain under the domination of France. Consequently, there was a degree of suspicion when the government encouraged negotiations aimed at liberalising trade with a historic rival. The talks were the outcome of a clause proposed by Shelburne in the 1783 Treaty of Versailles designed to open up commerce between Britain and France, but they gained momentum when William Eden was appointed by Pitt to lead the discussions.[170] Under the Eden treaty, signed on 26 September 1786, Britain continued its prohibition on the importation of silks, while both countries restricted the export of machinery. Nonetheless, more importantly, provision was made for a radical departure from the system of regulation in operation between the two states since the Treaty of Utrecht. In effect, that meant providing for ease of entry into both territories, arranging a significant reduction in duties on produce and manufactures, and granting reciprocal rights of commerce.[171] All this came with substantial advantages to the British, yet, when the measures were debated in the House of Commons, the Foxites had resolved to oppose the government. On 2 February 1787, when Pitt gave notice of his intention to seek ratification of the treaty ten days later, Burke argued for a postponement. On 5 February, he went on the offensive, focusing on the political defects of the Treaty. Originally, he informed the House, he was happy to believe that the French had been duped into making concessions, since it was not clear that they stood to gain by the agreement.[172] He then detected a deeper plot, and sounded the alarm: "We [are] about

[167] Ibid., p. 185.

[168] For Calonne's involvement in the negotiations along with Rayneval, see Marie Donaghay, "Calonne and the Anglo-French Treaty of 1786," *Journal of Modern History*, 50:3 (September 1978), pp. D1157–D1184; for the Maréchal de Castries, see idem, "The Maréchal de Castries and the Anglo-French Commercial Negotiations of 1786–87," *Historical Journal*, 22:2 (June 1979), pp. 295–312.

[169] J. Holland Rose, "The Franco-British Commercial Treaty of 1786," *English Historical Review*, 23:92 (October 1908), pp. 709–24; Orville T. Murphy, "DuPont de Nemours and the Anglo-French Commercial Treaty of 1786," *Economic History Review*, 19:3 (1966), pp. 569–80.

[170] Donald C. Wellington, "The Anglo-French Commercial Treaty of 1786," *Journal of European Economic History*, 21:2 (1992), pp. 325–37.

[171] W. O. Henderson, "The Anglo-French Commercial Treaty of 1786," *Economic History Review*, 10:1 (1957), pp. 104–12; Jeremy Black, *British Foreign Policy in an Age of Revolutions, 1783–1793* (Cambridge: Cambridge University Press, 1994), p. 111.

[172] Northamptonshire MS. A. XXVII. 50.

to truckle," he argued, "and to join ourselves with that power against which nature designed us as a balance."[173]

Pitt took issue with this perception on 12 February. It "supposed the existence of diabolical malice in the original frame of man."[174] However, Burke remained suspicious of the intentions of the French. Previously, France had not tended to regard its commerce as an overriding concern. "Her great Object is Power," Burke observed.[175] On 21 February he aired his suspicions in detail. His alarm, he insisted, was not based on a simple view of commercial rivalry. On this score, he was anxious to demonstrate that he entertained no fears that British manufactures would be sacrificed to France: "he was ready to declare that he had no jealousy."[176] In fact jealousy, he claimed, was "a tempter ill suited to acknowledged strength, and decided superiority."[177] Petitions from Manchester and Gloucester had welcomed the treaty, yet for Burke the grasping short-sightedness of merchants ought not to be regarded.[178] Commerce could not be distinguished from the wider national interest: "I have never known in the intercourse of Nations any Case in which the Commerce was not influenced by the policy of the contracting Countries," he remarked.[179] If nothing was to be considered but the trade of the two countries, then there was little that could be objected to in the treaty. However, the fact was that the French were cunningly seeking to promote their political interest by packaging state ambition as commercial liberality. While Burke was happy to welcome a genuinely cosmopolitan spirit, he was not prepared to attribute benign motives to the French: "she had no design of amity towards this country."[180] The proposed concessions to British manufactures were part of a deeper plan to gain access to the benefits of the British financial market. France, he surmised, was prepared to sacrifice its short-term trading interest in order to service a long-term commercial advantage. In pursuit of this long-term goal, France was keen to secure access to British capital markets. To illustrate his argument, Burke presented a picture of cooperative harmony in British society comprising the commercial, financial and landed interests: "in this country the Landed Interest, the

[173] *Parliamentary History*, XXVI, cols. 358–59. Cf. Adam Smith, *An Inquiry into the Nature and Causes of the Wealth of Nations*, ed. R. H. Campbell and A. S. Skinner (Indianapolis, IN: Liberty Fund, 1976), 2 vols., I, p. 496: "Being neighbours, they [France and Britain] are enemies, and the wealth and power of each becomes, upon that account, more formidable to the other; and what would increase the advantage of national friendship, serves only to inflame the violence of national animosity."

[174] *Parliamentary History*, XXVI, col. 392. Pitt's attitude on this core is discussed in John Ehrman, *The Younger Pitt: The Years of Acclaim* (London: Constable, 1969, 1984), p. 493.

[175] Northamptonshire MS. A. XXVII.50.

[176] *Parliamentary History*, XXVI, col. 487.

[177] Northamptonshire MS. A. XXVII.50.

[178] *Parliamentary History*, XXVI, col. 487.

[179] Northamptonshire MS. A. XXVII.50. For contemporary debate on the relations between trade and policy, see John E. Crowley, "Neo-Mercantilism and *The Wealth of Nations*: British Commercial Policy after the American Revolution," *Historical Journal*, 33:2 (June 1990), pp. 339–60.

[180] *Gazetteer*, 22 February 1787.

Monied Interest, and the Commercial Interest formed one grand partnership," he contended.[181] This was an exceptional achievement on whose basis the strength of British banking had arisen. The cheapness of credit and the robustness of the insurance industry were both products of this social partnership. In gaining access to Britain's commerce, the French stood to gain from its financial and insurance markets: "we shall enable her to support her trade with English capitals."[182]

Burke's claim was that the strength of British commerce had substantially been built on the solidity of its credit and insurance facilities, which provided for both the ease and the security of British trade. The "powers of capital were irresistible to trade," Burke observed: "it domineered, it ruled, it even tyrannized in the market."[183] Under the Eden treaty, France would be permitted to share in this facility, enabling her to rival British commerce around the globe, thereby increasing her navigation and consequently her political power. Therefore, in 1787, as political developments across the Channel prepared the ground for revolution, Burke looked to France as posing an ongoing threat to Britain. He noted the massive fortifications at Cherbourg along with the programme of extending political alliances in Europe and took these as an index of French ambition. Britain was being deceived by a siren voice on the continental mainland while gleefully "singing ballads to our manufacturers."[184] The old determination to achieve universal empire remained the animating purpose behind Britain's political rival. Yet, within a year, Burke's perspective would undergo fundamental change. Domestic political crisis would challenge the potency of French government, and diminish the standing of the country in the international arena. French ambition might remain constant, but the country's fortunes were about to plummet, forcing a reappraisal of the politics of Europe. The stability of the continent required the continuance of French power, since otherwise the security of Germany would be threatened. At the same time, it was necessary to monitor the belligerence of France since any change might tip the balance against the British interest. As the dazzling spectacle of 1789 progressed, it became apparent that France could avail of new methods of sabotage to be achieved through an alliance with subversive elements in Britain. In the late winter of 1787, Burke warned the Commons of the peril lurking in the pacific pronouncements of the French, recalling the Achaean gift that overwhelmed the Trojans.[185] Within two and a half years, the nature of the danger would be transformed, though the persistence of a threat could not be doubted. Over time, the French Revolution would remodel the power politics of Europe.

[181] *Morning Chronicle*, 22 February 1787. Cf. EB, *Third Letter on a Regicide Peace* (1797), *W & S*, IX, p. 374: "while the landed interest, instead of forming a separate body, as in other countries, has, at all times, been in close connexion and union with the other great interests of the country, it has been spontaneously allowed to lead and direct, and moderate all the rest."

[182] *Public Advertiser*, 22 February 1787.

[183] *Parliamentary History*, XXVI, col. 488.

[184] *Public Advertiser*, 22 February 1787.

[185] *Parliamentary History*, XXVI, col. 489.

11.5 The Revolution in France

After the dismissal of the assembly of notables on 25 May 1787 and the exile, and then recall, of the Paris *parlement* in the same year, the Estates General was finally summoned in the summer of 1788, scheduled to meet on 1 May 1789.[186] By that stage, extreme weather had caused drastic damage to the 1788 harvest, confidence in government solvency had plummeted to an all time low, and both Loménie de Brienne and Malesherbes-Lamoignon had fallen from the ministry. The whole process, Thomas Jefferson observed, was being driven by an "illumination of the public mind" regarding "the rights of the nation."[187] For his part, Burke sensed that he was witnessing the "Total" eclipse of France as a major power—corrupted "in the very glow of her meridian Splendour."[188] Necker had been recalled in November 1788, and Burke stood aghast at the machinations of the court. As the American constitution was being successfully ratified, and Burke was enjoying the company of Thomas Paine at Beaconsfield, the standing of the French monarchy seemed in a sorry state of decline.[189] But even as the country appeared to be floundering in the early autumn of 1788, it was another year before the affairs of France drew further comment from Burke. The Hastings impeachment and the regency crisis dominated the intervening period.[190] Both episodes brought frustration and disappointment to Burke. Yet he battled on, against the current, without much hope of success. When, on 10 June 1789, the Abbé Sieyès moved that the third estate unilaterally verify its powers, Burke was immersed in presenting the sixth article of impeachment against Hastings. The whole session of the trial proved a setback for the prosecution, leaving Burke with a feeling of perpetual disappointment. Endless misfortune, even in the service of the best causes, detracts from "the opinion of a man's Judgment," Burke wrote to Lord Charlemont in July.[191] But just one month later, again in a letter to Charlemont, Burke was risking his judgment in an assessment of the Revolution that would ultimately restore his reputation in Britain, and indeed Europe, yet divide him from former friends in his own party.[192]

"Party" was a key concern of Burke's around this time. He was explicit in commending its utility to Charlemont.[193] In the face of ongoing challenges to the integrity of Whig politics, principled public actors should unite to defend the com-

[186] In the end, it actually convened on 5 May 1789. For the events preceding its being summoned, see Jean Egret, *The French Pre-Revolution, 1787–1788* (Chicago, IL: University of Chicago Press, 1977). See also, Michel Vovelle, *The Fall of the French Monarchy, 1787–1792* (Cambridge: Cambridge University Press, 1984), ch. 3.

[187] Thomas Jefferson to Richard Price, 8 January 1789, *Papers of Jefferson*, ed. Boyd, XIV, pp. 420–24.

[188] EB to Gilbert Elliot, 3 September 1788, *Corr.*, V, p. 414.

[189] Ibid., p. 415.

[190] Mitchell, *Charles James Fox*, chs. 3 and 4.

[191] EB to Lord Charlemont, 10 July 1789, *Corr.*, VI, pp. 1–2.

[192] EB to idem, 9 August 1789, ibid., p. 10

[193] Ibid., pp. 9–10.

monwealth. The problem for Burke was that the basis for unity was eroding among the Foxite connection. "How much the greatest event . . . that ever happened in the World!" Fox had exclaimed to Richard Fitzpatrick just ten days earlier.[194] As his friend the Marquis de Lafayette later expressed it, he shared with aristocratic reformers in France a "Sympathie de Liberté" that encouraged him to welcome the developments in France.[195] Burke was more circumspect: current events presented a "wonderful Spectacle," he remarked, but without its final significance being apparent to view. By 13 June 1789, clerics from the first estate had broken ranks with their own order, and over the next days there were further defections to the commons. "They are disposed to reduce the state to one order as much as possible," Jefferson observed to Richard Price.[196] On 17 June, Sieyès felt ready to propose that this new body should constitute itself under the title of a National Assembly. "They have at one stroke converted themselves into the long parliament of Charles I," Arthur Young recorded.[197] At the same time, it was proposed that existing taxation be annulled, retaining only provisional validity until new arrangements could be devised. As Young noted in general, a "great crisis of the fate of four-and-twenty millions of people" was now in process.[198]

When the deputies to the Assembly arrived at the Salle des États in Versailles, they found their chamber locked and surrounded by soldiers with bayonets. Defying authority by decamping to the Jeu de Paume, and later resisting attempts to have the Assembly disbanded, the commons won the backing of the Paris streets, and, on 27 June, the king duly ordered the second estate to join the National Assembly.[199] Richard Price expressed his astonishment to Count Mirabeau on 4 July that so much could be achieved "without violence or bloodshed."[200] Nonetheless, by degrees, *The Annual Register* commented, the third estate had been encroaching upon the sovereignty of the whole: "one branch of the legislature" had endeavoured to "swallow up all the other powers of the state."[201] Concurrently, journalism disseminated disaffected opinion, and the bookshops brimmed with publications on current affairs.[202] "Nineteen-twentieths" of these, according to Young's calculations, came out

[194] Charles James Fox to Richard Fitzpatrick, 20 July 1789, *Memorials and Correspondence of Charles James Fox*, ed. Lord John Russell (London: 1853–7), 4 vols., II, p. 361.

[195] Marquis de Lafayette to Charles James Fox, 6 Nivôse 1800, Add. MS. 51468, fol. 49.

[196] Thomas Jefferson to Richard Price, 19 May 1789, *Papers of Thomas Jefferson*, ed. Boyd, XV, pp. 137–9.

[197] Arthur Young, *Travels during the Years 1787, 1788 and 1789 [in] the Kingdom of France* (Bury St. Edmonds: 1792), p. 115.

[198] Ibid., p. 102.

[199] See the *London Chronicle*, 31 June–2 July 1789.

[200] Richard Price to Comte de Mirabeau, 2–4 July 1789, *The Correspondence of Richard Price*, ed. W. B. Peach and D. O. Thomas (Durham, NC: Duke University Press, 1983–94), 3 vols., III, p. 230.

[201] "History of Europe," *Annual Register for the Year 1789* (London: 1792), p. 227.

[202] See *The Diary and Letters of Gouverneur Morris*, ed. Anne Cary Morris (London: 1888), 2 vols., I, p. 262: "Already Marat, Camille Desmoulins, Loustalot, and the principal journalists of the Revolution, had forced themselves before the public."

"in favour of liberty," and were "commonly violent against the clergy and nobility."[203] At the same time, the coffee houses in the Palais Royal teemed with orators, haranguing crowds with various schemes for sedition and revolt.[204] Political opinion seemed set against a separation of powers, promoting the possibility of popular despotism growing "wild."[205] With Louis XVI's capitulation on the 27th, "tyranny," the *Diary* commented, "is no more in France."[206] To Young, the "whole business" now seemed over—the "revolution complete," as he put it.[207] In actual fact the struggle was just beginning.

In early July the *World* observed that Paris was consumed in "*general exultation*."[208] Only the military was in a position to oppose the insurgency of the people, although the army now appeared to have allied with the third estate. Consequently, it was imperative that Britain should consider whether French republicanism posed a danger to its own strategic interests.[209] After all, the flame of liberty might spread "by contact and approximation" to the other nations of Europe, the *World* speculated.[210] On the other hand, as the *London Chronicle* predicted, this might in turn give rise to a spirit of peace emanating from the French capital.[211] Nonetheless, domestically, popular fury stalked the streets of Paris. "The spirit it is impossible not to admire," Burke confessed in August, yet he further noted that the "old Parisian ferocity" was on the prowl.[212] A citizens' militia had been established in Paris in mid-July, while the population in general scrambled to arm itself.[213] The archbishop of Paris had been humiliated, yet troops had refused to intervene "against their *fellow citizens*."[214] On the fourteenth, the Bastille was stormed for armaments with the assistance of the French Guards. According to the *World*, the ensuing tumult resembled the Gordon Riots of 1780.[215] The mood lightened momentarily on

[203] Young, *Travels in France*, p. 104. Cf. the *World*, 18 July 1789 on the profusion of pamphlets. See also "History of Europe," *Annual Register for the Year 1789*, p. 228.

[204] *Diary or Woodfall's Register*, 3 July 1789; Young, *Travels in France*, p. 122.

[205] Ibid., p. 107.

[206] *Diary or Woodfall's Register*, 3 July 1789.

[207] Young, *Travels in France*, p. 123. Cf. the *London Chronicle*, 31 June–2 July 1789: "liberty is established, property assured, and the constitution fixed." The same conclusion was drawn by an acquaintance of Burke's in a letter to Richard Burke Jr., sent on 29 June 1789. See *Corr.*, VI, pp. 10–11n.

[208] *World*, 4 July 1789. For a cursory account of the British press at the time of the French Revolution, see Jeremy Black, "The Challenge of the Revolution and the British Press," *Studies on Voltaire and the Eighteenth Century*, 287 (1991), pp. 131–41. See also William Palmer, "Edmund Burke and the French Revolution: Notes on the Genesis of the Reflections," *Colby Quarterly*, 20:4 (December 1984), pp. 181–90.

[209] *World*, 4 July 1789. Cf. *World*, 17 July 1789, for military defections from the king: "Deserted by his own . . . thus miserable, at this period, is the condition of the King of this extensive Empire."

[210] *World*, 22 July 1789.

[211] *London Chronicle*, 25–28 July 1789.

[212] EB to Lord Charlemont, 9 August 1789, *Corr.*, VI, p. 10.

[213] *Diary or Woodfall's Register*, 22 July 1789.

[214] "History of Europe," *Annual Register for 1789*, p. 230.

[215] *World*, 20 July 1789.

17 July: amid scenes of jubilation at the Hotel de Ville, the king promised to relocate from Versailles to Paris, accepting a tricolour cockade from the hands of the city's mayor, Sylvain Bailly, as a symbol of national rapprochement.[216] However, the wider context remained ominous. Reports of scenes of decapitation at the Place de Grève reached London at the end of July.[217] Bertier and Foulon were mutilated on the 22nd.[218] Applauding the determination of the National Assembly, the *London Chronicle* still grimly forecast that "France will be deluged in blood."[219] It was predicting "civil war" by the end of the month.[220] The *World* was soon citing the prognostications of Lord Mansfield: "the reigning *confusion* is such, that out of it, it is *impossible* that any *order* can ever arise."[221] The spread of violence through the provinces was noted in the *Diary*.[222] Burke pondered the significance of the popular violence when writing to Charlemont: it might be that some of the recent scenes of vengeance represented nothing more than a "sudden explosion" of animosity, incidental rather than essential to the character of affairs.[223] However, equally, the displays of violence might exemplify a general frenzy, proving that the people were as yet unfit for liberty. Renovating a constitution required "Wisdom" as well as "spirit," and it remained to be seen if the French were in possession of what was needed.[224]

In September, Burke's son was updated on the impact of the Great Fear on the region of Auxerre in central France, where he had stayed with the Parisot family in 1773 and 1774.[225] In response to the agrarian unrest radiating through the countryside, the National Constituent Assembly had voted on 4 August to abolish the seigniorial rights of the nobility and the tithes of the clergy, urged on by the Duke d'Aguillon and Viscount de Noailles. Legislation detailing the overthrow of "feudalism" followed between the fifth and eleventh, culminating in the ringing

[216] *L'Ancien moniteur* in *Réimpression de l'Ancien moniteur* (Paris: 1858–63), 31 vols., I, p. 173.

[217] *Diary or Woodfall's Register*, 22 July 1789; *World*, 28 July 1789.

[218] It was discussed by deputies in the National Assembly soon after: *Archives parlementaires*, VIII, pp. 863–67. See Burke on this episode in EB to Adrien-Jean-François Duport, post 29 March 1790, *Corr.*, VI, p. 107. Cf. EB, *Reflections*, ed. Clark, p. 230 [103], including comment on Barnave's alleged reaction: "ce sang était-il donc si pur?" Barnave later regretted the remark. See *Œuvres de Barnave*, ed. M. Bérenger (Paris: 1843), 4 vols., I, pp. 107–9. Burke returns to the incident in EB to William Windham, 18 December 1796, *Corr.*, IX, p. 186: "God save me from falling into the merciful hands of those who think the Business of Foulon and Bertier—no act of cruelty." The event was still troubling Hippolyte Taine one hundred years later. See Hippolyte Taine, *The French Revolution* (Indianapolis, IN: Liberty Fund, 2002), 4 vols., I, pp. 54–55. Cf. François Furet, *Interpreting the French Revolution* (Cambridge: Cambridge University Press, 1981), p. 63, linking such violence proleptically to 1792.

[219] *London Chronicle*, 14–16 July 1789.

[220] Ibid., 18–21 July 1789.

[221] *World*, 1 August 1789.

[222] *Diary or Woodfall's Register*, 4 August 1789.

[223] EB to Lord Charlemont, 9 August 1789, *Corr.*, VI, p. 10.

[224] Ibid.

[225] Madame Parisot to Richard Burke Jr., 14 September 1789, ibid., pp. 16–20.

declaration: "The National Assembly entirely destroys the feudal regime."[226] These were frenzied, knee-jerk measures, embraced under the pressure of events.[227] Over the past months, the outbidding of opponents in terms of the extremity of one's proposals had been a tendency among orators in the Assembly. The exposure of the chamber to intervention by the public had been noted by the British press since early July.[228] Meetings lacked procedure, and were swamped by hectoring crowds. The applause of the spectators appealed to the vanity of the speakers. Lists of the "unpatriotic" were dispatched to the centre of Paris.[229] The friends of privilege were advertised as *ennemis du peuple*. The security of the people, on the other hand, would be guaranteed by a national constitution, currently under construction in the Assembly. A prefatory statement of principles, the Declaration of the Rights of Man and the Citizen, was agreed on 26 August, although versions of the prospective manifesto had been trailed in the *Diary* throughout the preceding weeks.[230] An admirer of Burke's in the Commons, William Windham, had visited France in the period between the "elimination" of feudalism and the negotiation of the Declaration of Rights. Returning to England on 6 September 1789, he sent Burke a range of accounts of events since the beginning of the troubles.[231] The "new Constitution will be settled without a struggle," he expected.[232] Burke, responding two weeks later, did not agree.[233]

By now, in addition to the subversion of taxes, dues and tithes, designs on the property of the Church had been reported.[234] Such comprehensive programmes of disestablishment seemed unconnected to any concrete plan for reform. The monarchy, now openly dependent on the decrees of the Assembly, had effectively been transformed in appearance into a democracy, since the commons gave the law to both the king and the other orders. This appearance, however, was misleading, Burke thought. It would be some time before any durable constitutional form could be settled on the population of France. The source of sovereignty, the third article of the Declaration declared, resided "essentiellement dans la Nation."[235] It was more likely,

[226] Cited in William Doyle, *The Oxford History of the French Revolution* (Oxford: Oxford University Press, 2nd ed., 2002), p. 117.

[227] For the pivotal nature of the reforms, see Michael P. Fitzsimmons, *The Remaking of France: The National Assembly and the Constitution of 1791* (Cambridge: Cambridge University Press, 1991), pp. 52–61; for their extent and "swingeing" nature, see P. M. Jones, *Reform and Revolution in France: The Politics of Transition, 1774–1791* (Cambridge: Cambridge University Press, 1995), pp. 178–85.

[228] *Diary or Woodfall's Register*, 8 and 10 July 1789.

[229] "History of Europe," *Annual Register for 1789*, pp. 224, 229. For recent discussion, see Barry M. Shapiro, *Revolutionary Justice: Paris, 1789–90* (Cambridge: Cambridge University Press, 1993), pp. 42–3.

[230] See, for example, the text of Target's proposals in the *Diary or Woodfall's Register*, 12 August 1789.

[231] William Windham to EB, 15 September 1789, *Corr.*, VI, p. 21.

[232] Ibid.

[233] EB to William Windham, 27 September 1789, ibid., pp. 24–26.

[234] *Diary or Woodfall's Register*, 24 August 1789.

[235] Stéphane Rials, *La déclaration des droits de l'homme et du citoyen* (Paris: Hachette, 1988), p. 22. The final text of article three is a modification of drafts originally composed by Lafayette: see ibid., p. 591. For discussion, see Keith Michael Baker, *Inventing the French Revolution* (Cambridge: Cambridge

Burke argued, that the location of sovereignty would continue to be a matter of contention. The Assembly might in theory ascribe sovereignty to itself, but in practice it lacked the authority to get its provisions heeded: "it does not appear to me," he wrote to Windham, "that the National Assembly have one Jot more power than the King." Now they lead, but next they follow, the demands of the popular voice in promoting schemes to undermine "all orders, distinctions, privileges[,] impositions, Tythes, and rents."[236]

It was evident to Burke that French arrangements were more "truly democratical" than those of North America. So far, the French had retained the hereditary succession to the crown, but in every other respect they outdid the Americans in popular spirit.[237] Two years after the conclusion of the American war, Burke was happy to articulate his disparagement of the former colonists, at least in private conversation. During a visit to Gilbert Elliot in 1785, he had freely aired his disapproval of the "democratic party." The federalists, by comparison, were wise and patriotic.[238] Accordingly, Burke happily approved of the federal constitution after its agreement in 1787. "From the part Mr Burke took in the American Revolution," Paine commented in 1791, "it was natural that I should consider him a friend to mankind."[239] The expectation was based on a simplified analysis. In debate on the second Quebec Bill on 6 May 1791, despite the rancour underlying his comments in 1785, Burke conceded that the Americans had formed a constitution well adapted to their situation.[240] Based on their education and the colonial experience of provincial government, they had originally been disposed to popular excesses. Nonetheless, they had been acclimatised to obedience by the experience of war. On the basis of that experience, they were primed to construct a constitutional order, under which one branch of power was checked by another in the service of the common good. Given the composition of American society, its political organisation did not reflect a society of orders, and so the regulation of the polity depended on purely constitutional restraints. Still, it was a mixed republican system, at least comparable to the British, and thus remote from the French "absurdity" of governing the "nation" through the "nation," implying that a people could literally govern itself.[241] In the French case,

University Press, 1990), ch. 11. Cf. idem, "The Idea of a Declaration of Rights" in Dale Van Kley ed., *The French Idea of Freedom: The Old Regime and the Declaration of Rights of 1789* (Stanford, CA: Stanford University Press, 1994). For the language of rights in the Declaration, see also Jeremy Jennings, *Revolution and the Republic: A History of Political Thought in France since the Eighteenth Century* (Oxford: Oxford University Press, 2010), pp. 32–37.

[236] EB to William Windham, 27 September 1789, ibid., p. 25.

[237] Ibid.

[238] Conversation recorded in Thomas Somerville, *My Own Life and Times, 1741–1814* (Edinburgh: 1861), p. 222.

[239] Thomas Paine, *Rights of Man, Common Sense and Other Political Writings*, ed. Mark Philp (Oxford: Oxford University Press, 1995, 2008), p. 86.

[240] *Parliamentary History*, XXIX, col. 365.

[241] Ibid., col. 366.

the spirit of democracy was subject to the reality of anarchy. As Burke remarked to Windham in the autumn of 1789, when representatives sought to deliberate over a course of action, there commonly appeared "a Mob of their constituents ready to Hang them if They should deviate into Moderation."[242] In form, the French had resolved to erect a constitutional democracy; but the edifice was exposed to anarchic dictation from the populace.

By the time Burke made these observations, plans for a second chamber supported by the *monarchiens* on the constitutional committee of the National Assembly had been defeated.[243] Five days later, on 15 September 1789, the king was reduced to possessing merely a suspensive veto over legislation: complete authority had effectively been ceded to the National Assembly.[244] Writing to his son after the march on Versailles of 5–6 October, Burke took Mirabeau to be the prime mover in devising a constitution in the Assembly: "Mirabeau presides as the Grand Anarch," he complained.[245] The king himself seemed a pitiable cypher.[246] Having arranged what *L'Ami du peuple* would soon represent as an offensive banquet to welcome the Flanders Regiment to Versailles, both Louis XVI and Marie Antoinette were assailed in the royal palace by a troop of baying women who had travelled from Paris to register their protest.[247] The episode later inspired the famous passage in the *Reflections*: "the age of chivalry has gone.—That of sophisters, oeconomists, and calculators, has succeeded."[248] Writing privately a year earlier, without needing to portray the event to full rhetorical effect, the monarch appeared more "ridiculous" than tragic.[249] To date, Louis XVI's tergiversations had betrayed his lack of spine and resolution. Striking a comic note, Burke entertained the possibility that he might swap the palace guard for this Amazonian delegation from the Paris markets. Faced with the radical transmogrifications of the Revolution, Burke was never sure whether to laugh or cry.[250] He was certain, nonetheless, that an era was over: the king, now removed to the Tuileries, was effectively a prisoner in his own palace.

[242] EB to William Windham, 27 September 1789, *Corr.*, VI, p. 25. Cf. EB, *Reflections*, ed. Clark, pp. 227–9 [100–102].

[243] The vote was lost by 89 to 849, with 122 abstentions. On the *monarchiens*, see Ran Halévi, "Monarchiens" in *Critical Dictionary of the French Revolution*, ed. François Furet and Mona Ozouf (Cambridge, MA: Harvard University Press, 1989). See also James L. Osen, *Royalist Political Thought during the French Revolution* (Westport, CT: Greenwood Press, 1995).

[244] The suspensive veto passed by 673 to 325, with 11 abstentions. For the debates leading to this verdict, see R. K. Gooch, *Parliamentary Government in France: Revolutionary Origins, 1789–1791* (Ithaca, NY: Cornell University Press, 1960), pp. 90–96.

[245] EB to Richard Burke Jr., c. 10 October 1789, ibid., p. 30.

[246] See the account in the *London Chronicle*, 10–13 October 1789.

[247] *L'Ami du peuple, ou le publiciste Parisien*, 27, 7 October 1789, in Jean-Paul Marat, *Œuvres politiques, 1789–1793* (Brussels: Pôle Nord, 1989–95), 10 vols., I, p. 248; *Diary or Woodfall's Register*, 10 and 13 October 1789; *The Times*, 10 October 1789.

[248] Burke, *Reflections*, ed., Clark, p. 238 [113].

[249] EB to Richard Burke Jr., c. 10 October 1789, *Corr.*, VI, p. 30.

[250] Burke, *Reflections*, ed. Clark, pp. 154–55 [11–12].

At this point Burke began to believe that the decline of France would be difficult to reverse. Popular hostility in Paris seemed uniform, leaving opponents of the insurgency without recourse.[251] After the October Days, Lally-Tollendal left France, while Mounier withdrew to Dauphiné.[252] "All that are firm against the Parisians are obliged to fly," Burke grumbled.[253] On 2 November 1789, with the encouragement of Talleyrand and Mirabeau, the property of the Church was placed "at the disposal" of the Assembly.[254] In due course it would be employed as security for the issuing of *assignats*.[255] Writing ten days later to Fitzwilliam, Burke now regarded the Revolution as a concerted process, and the country as irretrievably "undone."[256] The "pillage" of the Church was only the latest in a procession of ruinous decrees. It was part of a more general "convulsion of property" that threatened civil society with dissolution.[257] The crown, in capitulating early to the third estate, had eased the way to its own demise. Bankruptcy seemed the only means of recovering from financial disaster, and a civil war the only hope of devising a constitution. Neither option, however, was realistically in prospect. Public deliberation lacked determination and insight, and coherent opposition to the ongoing destruction was not available. Plans for a national bank devised in the aftermath of the seizure of *biens nationaux* in the form of Church property seemed as deluded as every other scheme to date.[258] The emergence of a popular dictator prepared to restore the constitution was the only hope for France: "One man may change all."[259] But such deliverance was not credibly in evidence. The Assembly was now the servant of the will of the people—or, more specifically, "the Will of the Burghers of Paris."[260] Government, in other words, was effectively extinct.[261]

[251] On this, see EB to Unknown, January 1790, ibid., p. 79: "I see no way, by which a second revolution can be accomplished."

[252] Jean Egret, *La Révolution de notables: Mounier et les monarchiens* (Paris: Armand Colin, 1950), pp. 195, 211.

[253] EB to Richard Burke Jr., 11 November 1789, *Corr.*, VI, p. 33.

[254] The debate in the National Assembly was covered in the *Gazetteer*, 6 November 1789. For discussion of this episode, see Georges Lefebvre, "La vente des biens nationaux" in idem, *Études sur la Révolution française* (Paris: PUF, 1954, 1963), pp. 307–37.

[255] This occurred on 19 and 21 December 1789. See Florin Aftalion, *The French Revolution: An Economic Interpretation* (Cambridge: Cambridge University Press, 1990), pp. 65–6.

[256] EB to Earl Fitzwilliam, 12 November 1789, *Corr.*, VI, p. 36. According to François Furet, Burke was the earliest observer to view the Revolution as "an undivided whole, *comme un bloc*." See his "The French Revolution, or Pure Democracy" in Colin Lucas ed., *Rewriting the Revolution* (Oxford: Oxford University Press, 1991), p. 42.

[257] EB to Earl Fitzwilliam, 12 November 1789, *Corr.*, VI, pp. 36–37. Cf. EB to Philip Francis, 15 November 1789, ibid., p. 39.

[258] Various plans were presented to the Assembly between 21 and 27 November 1789: *Archives parlementaires*, X, pp. 158–295. The scheme examined by Burke was published in Pierre-Nicolas Haraneder, *Plan de M. le Vicomte de Macaye, pour l'établissement d'une banque nationale* (Paris: 1789). Burke discusses the plan in EB to Philip Francis, 11 December 1789, *Corr.*, VI, pp. 50–55.

[259] EB to Earl Fitzwilliam, 12 November 1789, ibid., p. 37.

[260] Ibid., p. 36.

[261] EB to Philip Francis, 15 November 1789, ibid., p. 39.

The relationship between an apparently democratic constitution and popular protest was a central concern of Burke's between the summer and winter of 1789–90. Two issues absorbed him above all. First, having resolved itself into a sovereign representative of the people, the Constituent Assembly was an undivided power: a pure democracy, and thus unimpeded by any legitimately opposing force. Secondly, democratic legislation lacked integrity and cohesion, being constantly exposed to the "voice of Multitudes."[262] In other words, although France had been reconfigured as an unmixed popular state, its constitutional processes were subjected to unmanageable popular pressure.[263] This Burke termed "democratic fury," and its destructive impulses were evident in the practice of executing enemies by hanging them from lamp irons.[264] This constant derangement, whereby constitutional deliberation was driven by the anarchic forces of popular resentment, could not long persist. "A total anarchy is a self-destructing thing," Burke recognised.[265] Now that violence had been adopted as an instrument of political change, it would be impossible to resist its potency in future. This made it impossible to predict the constitutional future of French democracy: "The French may be yet to go through more transmigrations," as Burke put it.[266] In the end, however, violence would be welcomed as the arbiter of violence: anarchy would be governed by military force.

It might be that France was henceforth trapped in a cycle of anarchy and despotism. At either extreme of this dialectic, property would be prey to avarice and resentment. Its vulnerability had already been made conspicuous by the actions of France's anarcho-democracy. As Burke commented in early 1790, its legislators had struck at "prescriptive Right, long undisturbed possession."[267] This implicitly involved overturning "an uninterrupted stream of Regular judicial determinations"—an unbridled indulgence of arbitrary power. Under such a regime, no possession would seem secure, as the very notion of private property was abolished.[268] Comparison with the American Revolution appeared facile in the context of this diagnosis. It was an established principle of natural law that government was created for the security of property.[269] By any eighteenth-century reckoning, an attack upon its institution was a radical subversion of the enabling conditions of civil society. Richard Price's enthusiasm for the Revolution was viewed by Burke in this context. So too was the reforming zeal of all divisions of the French Estates. Equally, the attitudes of Fox and Sheridan appeared remarkable to Burke: uncomprehending and affected at the

[262] EB to Charles-Jean-François Depont, November 1789, ibid., p. 49.

[263] Later, in a letter to Adrien-Jean-François Duport, post 29 March 1790, ibid., p. 106, Burke argued on this basis that the National Assembly, like the French king, was in a "captivated" condition.

[264] EB to Unknown, January 1790, ibid., p. 80.

[265] Ibid., p. 79.

[266] EB to Charles-Jean-François Depont, November 1789, ibid., p. 46.

[267] Ibid., p. 44.

[268] Ibid.

[269] Locke, *Two Treatises*, II, § 140. On the legitimacy of unequal appropriation in Locke, see Jeremy Waldron, *God, Locke, and Equality: Christian Foundations in Locke's Political Thought* (Cambridge: Cambridge University Press, 2002), ch. 6.

same time.[270] In October 1789, Fox was recorded as having toasted the majesty of the French people.[271] Such gestures, it seemed to Burke, carried an onus of responsibility. The following January, he commented darkly to a correspondent that flirtation with French democracy in British political circles was exceeding the bounds of judiciousness: "it is high time for those who wish to preserve the *morem maiorum*, to look about them."[272] The posture of political dissent had been troubling Burke for some years. Now, the disposition of opposition Whigs added cause for concern.[273] It was time to make a public stand on the issue of the Revolution.

11.6 *Speech on the Army Estimates*

News of the feud among leading Foxites had reached Paris by early February 1790. It was reported there that, at a meeting at Burlington House aimed at patching up differences, Sheridan had done everything he could to appease Burke's anger. His efforts, however, were in vain.[274] Mounting hostility, intensified by disagreements over the regency crisis and the Hastings trial, was soon to be aired in parliament.[275] By now, Burke had immersed himself in the details of French affairs over a period of several months, having familiarised himself with selections from the *cahiers de doléances* and reports of debates in the National Assembly.[276] He had also embarked on the composition of the *Reflections*, having stolen time, as he would later comment, from the prosecution of Hastings to deliver himself over to a consideration of French affairs.[277] Back in the autumn of 1789, Windham had sent him books to help him inform himself about recent developments.[278] Since then, he had made it his business to consult the official documentation on the Revolution, as well as

[270] See the account in Bisset, *Life of Burke*, pp. 461ff.

[271] Mitchell, *Charles James Fox*, p. 155.

[272] EB to Unknown, January 1790, *Corr.*, VI, p. 81.

[273] This was later explained by Burke's Foxite critics in bemused terms as an "ill humour" that "broke out" at the time of the Revolution. See Henry Richard Vassall Fox, third Baron Holland, *Memoirs of the Whig Party during my Time* (London, 1852–54), 2 vols., I, pp. 9–11.

[274] Journal of Lady Elisabeth Foster, 4 February 1790, cited in Mitchell, *Charles James Fox*, p. 155. Divisions in the opposition had been a matter of press speculation for some months: see *Morning Post*, 3 November 1789; *Public Advertiser*, 2 February 1790.

[275] Burke's mounting disaffection is retrospectively recorded in Sylvester Douglas, *The Diaries of Sylvester Douglas*, ed. Francis Bickley (London: Constable, 1928), 2 vols., I, p. 154.

[276] *Pace* Copeland, "Burke, Paine, and Jefferson" in idem, *Burke*, p. 165; Alfred Cobban, *The Debate on the French Revolution, 1789–1800* (London: 2nd ed., Adam and Charles Black, 1960), p. 5; Alfred Cobban and Robert A. Smith, "Introduction" to *Corr.*, VI, pp. xv, xx; L. G. Mitchell, "Introduction" to idem ed., *W & S*, VIII, pp. 1–3. For Burke's prodigious determination to be informed about the subjects he addressed, see Lock, *Burke*, II, pp. 248–49. James Mackintosh, recalling his conversations with Burke at the end of 1795, confirmed his minute grasp of developments in France: see Thomas Green, *Extracts from the Diary of a Lover of Literature* (Ipswich: 1812), p. 139.

[277] EB, *Reflections*, ed. Clark, p. 415 [356].

[278] William Windham to EB, 15 September 1789, *Corr.*, VI, p. 21.

following the press in Britain and France.[279] He certainly felt his grasp surpassed the reports in the newspapers: in France, these were prey to the wider national confusion, and in Britain they tended to follow dominant opinion in the country.[280] Long before his first intervention in public on the issue, he had examined the *Procès-verbal* of the Constituent Assembly as well as the writings of the Comte de Mirabeau.[281] Since then, as he informed Adrien Duport, a former *conseiller* in the Paris *parlement*, he had plunged deeper into mastering the transactions of the neighbouring power.[282] The proximity of France drove the urgency of engagement: the fate of Britain was bound up with French fortunes. It was this fact that pushed Burke into declaring his position in public, responding to Fox in the debate on the Army Estimates in February 1790.

In the King's Speech opening parliament on 21 January 1790, European war, together with the "internal situation of different parts of Europe," drew passing comment.[283] In the debate on the Address, Viscount Valletort, MP for Fowey, pointed more explicitly to the situation in France, drawing attention to the "internal tumults of an ungovernable populace."[284] He also noted the situation in the Netherlands, along with wider discontent among European states. However, none of this, he suggested, threatened the tranquillity of Britain.[285] On 5 February, on the first day of the debate on the Army Estimates, Fox returned to the subject of the current peace. Back in July, he had declared that he would be happy to jettison his inveterate anxiety about France "if this Revolution has the consequences I expect."[286] By February 1790 this expectation seemed to have been fulfilled: the Revolution appeared to be converting France to a pacific disposition.[287] One aspect of Fox's perception was more generally shared: since the summer of 1789, French turmoil had boosted the British sense of security. For example, in the autumn of that year, William Grenville saw the shambles across the Channel as guaranteeing an "invaluable peace" to Britain.[288] However, there was a considerable difference between ascribing British safety to French mayhem, as Grenville had done, and attributing existing harmony

[279] Including, it seems the *Courier de Provence*, an organ of the Comte de Mirabeau. See EB to Unknown, January 1790, *Corr.*, VI, p. 79n

[280] Ibid., p. 79.

[281] See Burke's citations from the *Procès-verbal*, for example in EB, *Reflections*, ed. Clark, p. 348 [259]. The *Procès-verbal* was authorised as an official publication on the day that the Third Estate assumed the title of National Assembly, on 17 June 1789.

[282] EB to Adrien-Jean-François Duport, post 29 March 1790, ibid., p. 105.

[283] *Parliamentary History*, XXVIII, col. 300.

[284] Ibid., col. 304.

[285] Ibid., cols. 305–6.

[286] Charles James Fox to Richard Fitzpatrick, 30 July 1789, *Memorials*, II, p. 361.

[287] See Frank O'Gorman, *The Whig Party and the French Revolution* (London: Macmillan, 1967), pp. 45–6, and John W. Derry, *Charles James Fox* (London: B. T. Batsford, 1972), p. 296, on Fox's predetermined response to French events.

[288] William Wyndham Grenville to the Marquis of Buckingham, 14 September 1789, *Memoirs of the Court and Cabinet of George III*, ed. Duke of Buckingham and Chandos (London: 2nd ed., 1853–55), 2 vols., II, p. 165

to shared values between both states, as Fox was now proposing. It was "universally known throughout all Europe," Fox argued, "that a man, by becoming a soldier, did not cease to be a citizen."[289] This was an explicit commendation of the recent conduct of the French military.[290] It was an interjection that struck Burke as remarkable. Fox was applauding the commitment of the Royal Army to democracy, which included belated support for its dereliction of duty, distressingly in evidence between 14 July and the October *journées*.

Burke was absent from the Commons on 5 February, but evidently read the reports of Fox's speech. An opportunity to respond arrived on Tuesday, 9 February, when the report of the committee of supply was made available to the parliament. Before it was presented, Burke rose immediately after Henry Flood, recently transferred to the British House of Commons, and gave notice of his intention to introduce the question of parliamentary reform later in the session.[291] Flood was at this time a member of the Society for Constitutional Information, founded in 1780 and increasingly dominated by the practical intelligence of Horne Tooke as John Jebb and Major John Cartwright passed from the scene after 1786.[292] Burke thanked Flood for providing the Commons with due time for reflection, since the topic was a particularly serious one at the current juncture—during a period that could be regarded as "the most eventful that ever occurred in the history of Europe."[293] With a "wild storm" gathering over the continent, members of parliament would best be advised to dedicate their vigilance to preserving the benefits of the constitution. When the debate on the Army Estimates resumed, Fox returned to his original thesis. The situation of France meant that she posed no current threat beyond her borders. On the contrary, the cast of affairs was such as to encourage nothing less than exultation. While the condition of this once mighty empire could not plausibly imbue onlookers with feelings of alarm, neither should its predicament "excite us to indignation." The current "anarchy and confusion" of the country, Fox concluded, was "incidental" to the true nature of the Revolution, whose long-term consequences would render its interests more congruent with British policy.[294] It was this congruence that Burke

[289] *Parliamentary Register* (Debrett), XXVII, p. 55; *Parliamentary History*, XXVIII, col. 330. Cf. *London Chronicle*, 4–6 February 1790: "recent events warranted an universal congratulation, that men becoming soldiers lost not the sentiments, the feelings, the patriotic actions of citizens." The same report is reproduced in the *Public Advertiser*, 6 February 1790. For similar wording, see also the *World*, 6 February 1790.

[290] Fox's sentiments were reprobated by Colonel Phipps in the House of Commons. See Prior, *Life of Burke* (1854), p. 300.

[291] *CJ*, XLV, p. 226. There is an account of Flood's proposal in George Stead Veitch, *The Genesis of Parliamentary Reform* (1913) (London: Constable, 1965), pp. 113–14. Burke recalled Flood's proposal in EB, *Letter to Sir Hercules Langrishe* (1792), *W & S*, IX, p. 627.

[292] Albert Goodwin, *The Friends of Liberty: The English Democratic Movement in the Age of the French Revolution* (London: Hutchinson, 1979), pp. 114–17.

[293] *Parliamentary Register* (Debrett), XXVII, p. 65. Cf. *Public Advertiser*, 10 February 1790; *World*, 10 February 1790.

[294] *Parliamentary Register* (Debrett), XXVII, pp. 75–77.

angrily disputed. It was clear that France no longer posed a conventional threat to British power, but that did not diminish the significance of subtler dangers.

Burke had been pondering the implications of the French ordeal for the European balance since November 1789. At that stage, he wrote to Fitzwilliam expressing his sorrow at the diminished state of a former hegemon. There was no doubt that he wished to see France "circumscribed within moderate bounds" rather than in a position "despotically to give the Law to Europe." Nonetheless, there were serious ramifying consequences that accompanied the extinction of a major player within "our Western system."[295] The following January, Paine delivered his own perspective on some of these consequences in a long letter to Burke, analysing the significance of the Revolution. As Paine explained in the Preface to the *Rights of Man*, in 1787 he had appealed to the philosophic statesman André Morellet to promote a pacific scheme to improve relations between Britain and France.[296] The following year, Paine made the fruits of their discussions available to Burke.[297] After the summer of 1789, some of Paine's fondest hopes had already been realised, and in January 1790 he outlined to Burke how European politics would be affected. "The Revolution in France is certainly a forerunner to other Revolutions in Europe," he predicted.[298] As his speech on the Army Estimates on 9 February would make clear, this was exactly what Burke dreaded. Paine provided his own picture of what the deluge might involve. The National Assembly, which had hitherto shown its preparedness to "set fire to the four Corners of the Kingdom," now controlled events, in unison with the "Mass of the Nation" and supported by the army. The exhilarating reception of Louis XVI by Parisian crowds on 17 July 1789 fuelled Paine's enthusiasm: "everyone [was] armed with something.—Those who had no Muskets or Swords, got what they could."[299] It was this alliance between popular force and the military that promised so much and, as Paine saw it, offered an example for other monarchies to follow.

On the international front, what the Revolution made available was a "new mode of forming Alliances" among European powers.[300] Paine envisaged a subversive pact operating transnationally. This would be based on the emergence of patriotic confederacies across the continent that would polarise the politics of all countries. Fraternal citizens, he expected, would array themselves against courts. These cosmopolitan conspiracies would agitate against foreign despots in sympathy with their allies across the borders of Europe. Apparently based on his reading of the French press,

[295] EB to Earl Fitzwilliam, 12 November 1789, *Corr.*, VI, p. 36.

[296] Paine, *Rights of Man*, ed. Philp, p. 87. The episode is relayed in John Keane, *Tom Paine: A Political Life* (London: Bloomsbury, 1995), pp. 267–75.

[297] Paine's letter, sent on 7 August 1788, can be found at the American Philosophical Society Library, Philadelphia, B/P165. Morellet's position is set out in a letter to Paine of 18 August 1787, forwarded to Burke. See WWM BkP 1:2080.

[298] Thomas Paine to EB, 17 January 1790, *Corr.*, VI, p. 71. Cf. Paine, *Rights of Man*, pp. 196–97.

[299] Thomas Paine to EB, 17 January 1790, *Corr.*, VI, p. 70. Cf. Paine, *Rights of Man*, pp. 104–5, on the armament of the citizens of Paris in mid-July 1789.

[300] Thomas Paine to EB, 17 January 1790, *Corr.*, VI, p. 71.

Paine pointed to conditions in Poland, Brabant, Rome and Bohemia as favouring this progressive insurgency.[301] The potency of its doctrines was already evident in Spain where the Declaration of Rights had been publicly condemned. Prussia was alleged to be contemplating direct action against France on the grounds that its own army was exposed to the "Contagion."[302] With the appearance of the *Reflections* in the autumn of 1790, Burke likewise observed the spread of Revolutionary ideals. Prior to 1789, literary talent in France had devoted much energy to pursuing foreign alliances and correspondence.[303] The pace of exchange quickened after the creation of the National Assembly. Fanaticism was disseminated like a plague in the states of Europe, with Berne, Germany and Spain seeing a rise in proselytism. The revolt against Christianity was a virtual epidemic, with hostility to establishments being diffused in its wake.[304] For Paine, the principal benefit of this zealotry would be the corruption of the armed forces. His optimism about the military derived from the example of France—beginning with the failure of the Duc de Broglie, one-time commander-in-chief of the French armed forces, to ensure the loyalty of his troops. Jefferson had informed Paine about popular sympathies in the royal army, while Paine himself applauded the discipline of the National Guard that had just formed under Lafayette.[305] "I suppose France will on some occasions be introduced into the debates of your Parliament this Meeting," Paine speculated.[306] With its introduction into the new session during the debate on Army Estimates in February 1790, Burke was ready to meet Paine's ardour with his own assessment of the current peril.

Burke's purpose in his speech was to lay down a marker, and to admonish his colleagues about the extent of that peril. Fox was the most immediate object of his attention, largely on account of his celebration of the French military four days earlier. It is clear from Burke's comments that uppermost in his mind was the crisis in the armed forces that had become steadily apparent since the previous spring.[307] A riot in the faubourg Saint-Antoine had been put down in April 1789, and over

[301] Ibid., pp. 71–72. Foreign developments of the kind were reported in *L'Ancien moniteur*, 12 and January 1790, in *Réimpression de l'Ancien moniteur* (Paris: 1858–63), 31 vols., III, pp. 93, 125–26.

[302] Thomas Paine to EB, 17 January 1790, *Corr.*, VI, p. 71.

[303] Burke noted the example of French publicists insinuating themselves into the court of Frederick the Great, whose posthumous works had just been published by Thomas Holcroft: EB, *Reflections*, ed. Clark, p. 277 [167].

[304] Ibid., pp. 325, 327 [226–27, 229]

[305] Thomas Jefferson to Thomas Paine, 11 July 1789, *Papers of Jefferson*, ed. Boyd, XV, pp. 266–9; Thomas Paine to EB, 17 January 1790, *Corr.*, VI, p. 73. For these developments, see Jules Leverrier [Albert Soboul], *La naissance de l'armée nationale, 1789–1794* (Paris: Éditions Sociales Internationales, 1939), pp. 34–39.

[306] Thomas Paine to EB, 17 January 1790, *Corr.*, VI, p. 74.

[307] More recent accounts trace the origins of insubordination to the officer class, and date its open manifestation to the summer of 1788. See Samuel F. Scott, *The Response of the Royal Army to the French Revolution* (Oxford: Oxford University Press, 1978), pp. 47–50. See also Rafe Blaufarb, *The French Army, 1750–1820: Careers, Talent, Merit* (Manchester: Manchester University Press, 2002), ch. 2; Michael Sonenscher, *Sans-Culottes: An Eighteenth-Century Emblem in the French Revolution* (Princeton, NJ: Princeton University Press, 2008), p. 287ff.

succeeding months major troop reinforcements were stationed in the Île-de-France. Since then, propaganda encouraging insubordination had been distributed among the soldiers: "We are citizens before being soldiers," one pamphlet declared.[308] Another extolled the courage to disobey.[309] The crescendo came in mid-July with the rebellion of the *Gardes françaises*, the subsequent desertion of 760 soldiers from their number, and their incorporation into the militia. Desertions continued into the autumn. The comportment of the Flanders regiment on 5–6 October was equally discouraging: officers could not bank on controlling their troops, who openly fraternised with the crowds. [310] In the reported version of what Burke said in response to Fox on 9 February, he was emphatic that the French were now saddled with an army that "acknowledged no head."[311] He also noted that the Assembly "dared not venture to discuss their conduct," despite the failure of the military to rally to the royal standard and the defections among the French Guards in mid-July.[312] Burke further noted the existence of the recently formed militia, charged, as he put it, with watching over "the national army."[313] Under such an arrangement, despite Fox's paean, it was not clear how any soldier might truly be a citizen, nor a citizen pledge allegiance to the army. The difficulty of reconciling the military with constitutional government had been a concern of Burke's since the 1750s.[314] More recently, he had joined Fox in highlighting the dangers that standing armies posed to liberty in the midst of the American war.[315] Yet now insubordination within European armies revealed how military subversion might facilitate popular rebellion. Republican sentiment had long been expected to prosper in militias; as it turned out, a standing army became a vehicle for demotic zeal.

In the published version of his speech, which appeared on 20 February, Burke elaborated on his original remarks.[316] The most disconcerting result of the Revolutionaries' many misguided actions was the state of the military, he asserted.[317] Reflecting on the performance of the royal troops of the line, he insisted that these "soldiers

[308] Anon., *Avis aux grenadiers et soldats*, Bibliothèque nationale, 8° Lb39 1867, cited in Scott, *Response of the Royal Army*, p. 56.

[309] Anon., *Adresse aux soldats françois et allies* (Paris: 1789), p. 1.

[310] Jean-Paul Bertaud, *The Army of the French Revolution: From Citizen-Soldiers to Instrument of Power* (Princeton, NJ: Princeton University Press, 1988), pp. 25–26; Scott, *Response of the Royal Army*, pp. 75–76.

[311] *Parliamentary Register* (Debrett), XXVII, p. 91.

[312] Ibid.

[313] Ibid.

[314] EB, "Considerations on a Militia" (1757) in Richard Bourke, "Party, Parliament and Conquest in Newly Ascribed Burke Manuscripts," *Historical Journal*, 55:3 (September 2012), pp. 619–52, at pp. 647–52.

[315] Charles James Fox to EB, 13 October 1776, *Corr.*, III, p. 294; EB to Marquess of Rockingham, 6 January 1776, ibid., p. 309.

[316] According to Gilbert Elliot, in a letter to William Elliott, it did not actually appear until the 23rd. See Todd, *Burke Bibliography*, p. 140.

[317] EB, *Substance of the Speech of the Right Honourable Edmund Burke in the Debate on the Army Estimates* (London: 1790), p. 13.

were not citizens, but base hireling mutineers, and mercenary sordid deserters, wholly destitute of any honourable principle."[318] Burke did not underestimate the difficulty of rendering a military force compatible with constitutional freedom: "An armed, disciplined body is, in its essence, dangerous to liberty; undisciplined, it is ruinous to society."[319] Yet, at the same time, he could not imagine a less provident arrangement than had been settled on by the French. The existence of Lafayette's forces alongside a mutinous national army pointed, at best, to a divided command. "They have set up, to balance the Crown army, another army . . . a balance of armies, not of orders." Burke pleaded: "Are any of these armies? Are any of these citizens?"[320] Such divisions heralded civil war, not peace and harmony. Burke would return to the theme of the army in the later sections of the *Reflections*, recalling how the soldier "is told he is a citizen," which in practice meant he was becoming averse to subordination. He reiterated the peril of two distinct armies, one popular and the other monarchical, without either possessing a functioning chain of civil and military command.[321]

The condition of the French armies highlighted a crisis of insubordination that lay at the root of the Revolutionary meltdown. Sheridan might later present this pervasive rebelliousness as directed against, and indeed caused by, a moribund feudal despotism.[322] But the truth was, Burke contended, it was aimed at the entirety of a social order, which in practice meant waging war upon established obligations and distinctions: on taxes, dues and classes, and, by extension, on revenues and possessions.[323] Only the most wildly antinomian political project could seriously advocate such devastation. Certainly, in their right minds, neither Sheridan nor Fox could credit such convulsive proceedings, unless they were duped into admiring a mirage of liberty while discounting, in the process, the reality of despoliation. In addition to an assault on every form of social distinction, the Church had been attacked as an exemplar of the old regime, its treatment openly illustrating the objective of the Revolution: the disestablishment of property and religion.[324] In promoting an adherence to "enlightened" atheism, toleration was effectively annihilated; in pillaging large concentrations of private property, social security was substantially abolished.[325] Burke had a vivid sense of what the disintegration of civil society entailed, dissolving everything from the contract of government to the institution of the family.[326] These

[318] Ibid., p. 21.

[319] Ibid., p. 24.

[320] Ibid., pp. 24–26.

[321] EB, *Reflections*, ed. Clark, pp. 388 [318], 395 [327–28].

[322] *Parliamentary Register* (Debrett), XXVII, p. 98. The same perspective was adopted by Burke's first, hostile biographer, who therefore opted to explain his response to the Revolution in terms of apostasy. See Charles McCormick, *Memoirs of the Right Honourable Edmund Burke: Or, an Impartial Review of his . . . Life* (London: 1798), pp. 314, 319–20.

[323] EB, *Speech on the Army Estimates*, p. 22.

[324] Ibid., p. 12.

[325] *Parliamentary Register* (Debrett), XXVII, p. 91.

[326] Ibid., p. 92.

would all be under threat if the war on society were to succeed. The object of this war, Burke proposed, was to destroy all order and level all distinctions: "to raise soldiers against their officers; servants against their masters; tradesmen against their customers; artificers against their employers; tenants against their landlords; curates against their bishops; and children against their parents."[327]

How could such a programme begin to succeed? Burke turned to Tacitus to formulate his answer. Revolutionary agitation was driven by malevolence while putting on a show of public virtue—exhibiting a "*falsa* species *libertatis*."[328] Speciousness was at the heart of its proceedings: actions were legitimised in the name of justice, yet self-advancement was their underlying object; equality was advertised as their ultimate goal, yet their real aim was to level all distinctions.[329] However, even levelling did not mean parity, but additional increments of advantage. The revolution in privilege was justified as self-evidently meritorious, although aspirants to equality were to be arbiters of their own merit.[330] Herein lay the intrinsic appeal of republican insurgency: whereas it was difficult to induce a people to embrace its servitude, popular rhetoric captivated the ambitions of mankind. It "flattered," as Burke put it, our "natural inclinations"—namely, the feeling of desert, underlying claims of merit, driven by the passion for self-regard.[331] Seen in this way, the revolutionary animus of 1789 did not arise from a species of "democratic sociability" that was transposed, as Cochin argued, from the "clubs" to the arena of politics.[332] It was driven, instead, by a peculiar sensibility, rooted in the passion for primitive justice. The desire for primitive justice entailed extinguishing privilege, or at least those privileges that adversely affected one's own standing.[333] This process was fanned by accumulated resentments, stimulated over the course of a struggle for power.

The political vehicle best suited to popular ambition of the kind might seem to be democratic government, but here again appearance had to be distinguished from reality. In practice, in France as it was now circumstanced, democratic government meant the subversion of constitutional procedure under the influence of popular agitation. As a result, political decision-making was devolved from the National Assembly to the "nation," which, in practice, was disaggregated into competing popular

[327] EB, *Speech on the Army Estimates*, p. 22.

[328] EB, *Speech on the Army Estimates*, p. 11. Emphasis in the original. Burke is citing Tacitus, *Histories*, I, i.

[329] On the distinction between levelling and equalising, see chapter 13, section 4 below.

[330] On these themes in eighteenth-century political thought more generally, see Sonenscher, *Sans-Culottes*, *passim*.

[331] EB, *Speech on the Army Estimates*, p. 11.

[332] Augustin Cochin, *Les sociétés de pensée et la démocratie moderne* (Paris: Plon-Nourrit, 1921). For an attempt to rehabilitate Cochin, see Furet, *Interpreting the French Revolution*, pt. II, ch. 3. For criticism, see Michael Sonenscher, "The Cheese and the Rats: Augustin Cochin and the Bicentenary of the French Revolution," *Economy and Society*, 19:2 (1990), pp. 266–74.

[333] It was a "desperate democracy, formed of desperate men" according to the report of Burke's speech in the *London Chronicle*, 9–11 February 1790.

sects. France was thus administered, as Burke saw it, by a "mob of democracies."[334] Yet since, in the end, such a mob of competing popular forces would have to submit to direction if it was not to self-destruct, the provinces would be subjected to the republic of Paris, and the people of Paris to the prevailing agents of the popular will. In this situation, popular representation would be illiberal and coercive: nothing less than a popular tyranny. Compared to every other form of despotism, Burke observed, "a democratic despotism was the most abominable."[335] What this meant in France had by now become clear: a "cruel, blind, and ferocious democracy" had taken the place of regulated government.[336]

Burke was anxious to point out that his condemnation of the Revolution did not entail a retrospective endorsement of the French monarchy. This had, under Louis XIV, been no better than a "gilded tyranny."[337] Its learning, its gallantry and its magnificence merely occluded political and religious oppression. As a dominant military power in the period, French taste and manners permeated other European courts, disseminating a partiality for absolute monarchy in the process, as Voltaire had long ago observed.[338] The contagion of France was thus an established problem, although now it stood as a more potent danger than ever. The vicinity of France made it a permanent source of influence, yet in addition it held out the seductions of democratic rebellion for emulation. In rejecting inherited privileges and distinctions, this rebellion also extinguished every constitutional restraint—those "balances and counterpoises which serve to fix the state."[339] From Burke's perspective, these counterweights had been available in the spring of 1789. He claimed that the French were in possession of a viable constitution "the day the States met in their separate orders."[340] At that point, unlike in Britain in 1688, the executive was angling to facilitate reforms. Deviating from that agenda, the Assembly opted to revolutionise French politics and society, destroying the possibility of productive renovation. Comparisons with the Glorious Revolution had grown common but were redundant, Burke protested.[341] In the first place, militarily, English resistance had been coordinated by peers and commoners, "the flower of the English Aristocracy."[342] It was also prosecuted with discipline in the ranks. Thereafter, while the monarchy was limited by parliament, the "order of the state" was not transformed: a mixed system of government remained, its component parts intact, representing a society whose gradations were preserved: "The nation kept the same ranks, the same orders, the

[334] EB, *Speech on the Army Estimates*, p. 20.

[335] *Parliamentary Register* (Debrett), XXVII, p. 91.

[336] Ibid., p. 90.

[337] EB, *Speech on the Army Estimates*, p. 9.

[338] Ibid., p. 10. For Voltaire's point of view, see *Le siècle de Louis XIV* (Berlin: 1751), 2 vols., I, p. 5 and II, p. 138.

[339] EB, *Speech on the Army Estimates*, p. 18.

[340] Ibid., p. 17.

[341] The published version adds detail to Burke's original statement of position in light of Fox's comments on 1688 to be found at *Parliamentary Register* (Debrett), XXVII, p. 96.

[342] EB, *Speech on the Army Estimates*, p. 27.

same privileges, the same franchises, the same rules for property, the same subordinations, the same order in law, in the revenue, and in the magistracy; the same lords, the same commons, the same corporations, the same electors."[343] It was, in truth, "a revolution, not made, but prevented."[344]

Sheridan, Burke now believed, was a lost cause. On 9 February he declared that he was "*separated*" from him in politics.[345] Fox was another matter: Burke's intervention was partly a bid to reclaim him for constitutional Whiggism in the face of his toleration of Revolutionary principles. Factions were forming in the kingdom for the subversion of Whig doctrine, masquerading as an attempt to promote its precepts. Men of "political weight" should not be suffered to lend their support.[346] Fox insisted in response that he would "never lend himself to any cabal," while Burke reiterated his suspicion of "clubs and associations."[347] Immediately after the publication of Burke's speech on the Army Estimates, Earl Stanhope objected to this apparent aspersion as a calumny against the Revolution Society.[348] The Society, founded in 1700, was dedicated to the principles of 1688, and on that basis saluted the ideas of 1789.[349] It was incomprehensible to Stanhope that Burke should denigrate the import of those ideas merely as a consequence of the unruly manner in which their implementation was being forwarded in France. Revolutionary violence was an unfortunate concomitant of legitimate reform, determined by the excesses of the preceding regime.[350] This was an analysis that was shared by Sheridan and Fox, but also by Thomas Mercer, a merchant from the north of Ireland who had recently befriended Burke, having stood as a witness at the Hastings trial. The Revolution, Mercer thought, was a kind of restitution, an adjustment of affairs in favour of the disadvantaged. Having encountered Burke's reaction to French developments in the British press, Mercer focused on his outrage at the invasion of Church property: was depriving "pampered and luxurious prelates" of a portion of their livings accumulated in an age of "ignorance and superstition" truly to be castigated as an act of injustice? Surely this was a legitimate means of reparation

[343] Ibid., p. 29.

[344] Ibid., p. 28.

[345] *Parliamentary Register* (Debrett), XXVII, p. 100.

[346] *World*, 10 February 1790.

[347] *Parliamentary Register* (Debrett), XXVII, pp. 96–7. Cf. *World*, 10 February 1790, for Burke's remarks on Sheridan's political clubability: he meant factiousness. For an account of attempts to repair the breach, see Cone, *Burke*, II, pp. 304–5.

[348] Charles Stanhope, *A Letter from Earl Stanhope to the Right Honourable Edmund Burke, Containing a Short Answer to his Late Speech on the French Revolution* (London: 1790), p. 20.

[349] The foundation is thus dated in "Rules of the Revolution Society," n. d., Dr. Williams Library, MS. 24.90(1). On 4 November 1789, Richard Price moved an address to the Revolution Society applauding the "glorious example given in France" of an assertion of the rights of man. See "Minute Book of the Revolution Society, 16 June 1788–4 November 1791, Add. MS. 64814, fols. 22–23.

[350] Ibid., pp. 7–12.

enacted in the spirit of Christian charity.[351] Mercer's query went to the bottom of Burke's convictions, and elicited a response that explained his purpose in the Army Estimates speech, as well as the reason for his vehemence against the Revolution.

Speaking on 9 February, Burke had charged the Revolution with aiming at the destruction of "all" order, subverting every mechanism of social compliance, extending from the army and the professions to the family.[352] This verdict seemed excessive to members of Burke's audience, both then and later: a shock to society had occurred, but all-out war had not ensued, deranging every relationship on which society was founded. However, it was in fact perfectly evident to Burke that commercial exchange and family piety continued to exist in France. His point was that the enabling condition of these ties had been seriously undermined. What was being shattered was established opinion at large, puncturing the beliefs that supported social and political arrangements. On account of its constitutional reforms, exemplified by the Declaration of the Rights of Man, the National Assembly had, as the third edition of the Army Estimates *Speech* phrased it, "destroyed every hold of authority by opinion."[353] Existing loyalties had been replaced with a doctrine of allegiance lacking any purchase on the minds of the people. At the same time, with the expropriation of the Church, combined with attacks on the principle of aristocracy, a fundamental "breach of faith" had occurred—namely, trust in the security of property.[354] It was on this outcome that Burke dwelt in his response to Mercer, pointing out that the exponents of the rights of man had damaged confidence in the idea of any durable right at all. Every authority in jurisprudence was agreed that civil society had been invented for the security of property. The right to property, Burke went on, was guaranteed in the minds of men by the experience of possession over time: title was conferred by authority and confirmed by prescription.[355] Where government confiscated and settled opinion was undermined, the sense of justice would be extinguished from society altogether.[356]

As Burke understood it, the Revolution was promoting the pretensions of natural right against the provisions of established justice. In practice, this meant that the institution of property was being sacrificed in the name of pre-civil rights of individual entitlement. On this basis, the provisions of civil justice could not stand. As Burke saw things, security of property over time inevitably gave rise to inequalities in distribution. Since the primitive sense of justice was disposed to find this natural process

[351] Captain Thomas Mercer to EB, 19 February 1789, *Monthly Magazine*, XIII (1802), part I, pp. 317–18.

[352] *Parliamentary Register* (Debrett), XXVII, p. 92.

[353] EB, *Substance of the Speech of the Right Honourable Edmund Burke in the Debate on the Army Estimates* (London: 3rd ed., 1790), p. 19.

[354] Ibid.

[355] See Lucas, "Burke's Doctrine of Prescription" (1968) pp. 56ff., contra Pocock, "Burke and the Ancient Constitution" (1960), on the centrality of prescription based on associationist psychology, rather than on common law custom, to Burke's characteristic way of arguing about hereditary rights.

[356] EB to Captain Thomas Mercer, 26 February 1790, *Corr.*, VI, pp. 94–95.

of allocation unfair, it was essential for unequal property to find support in popular opinion as well as being underwritten by the state. Belief in Providence, and an appreciation of general social utility, were prerequisites for submission to a regime of inequality. The promise of a scheme of ultimate restitution that compensated for secular misfortune offered one source of protection against antisocial avidity. This explains Burke's exclamation in his letter to Mercer that "God is the distributor of his own blessings."[357] It was, therefore, the height of presumption to disturb "impiously" the established order of property. Rapacious redistribution, even in the name of the "purity of religion and Christian charity," would compromise those attitudes that lent support to inequality, without which both landed property and commercial society would dissolve.[358] Even with the sanction of Providence, the accumulation of property was potentially exposed to the charge of privilege, and so could conceivably be beset by envy. Ordinarily, although envy is pervasive in any complex association, it does not operate as a radically destabilising sentiment since it is restrained by a shared countervailing interest in preserving property relations. In addition, as Hume and Smith had observed, envy is offset by social admiration, sustained by sympathy and by the aesthetic appreciation of social beauty.[359] In Burke's eyes, 1789 had shown how resentment could undermine the belief in rank, especially when public authority combined with popular ideology to sap the attitudes that bolstered social distinctions. What was endangered by this process was not just privilege, but property. Those who cheered the process while enjoying the benefits of wealth were hypocrites in the pose of well-meaning Samaritans.[360]

Burke underlines this charge in the published version of his Army Estimates speech: "He wished the House of Commons to consider, how the members would like to have their mansions pulled down and pillaged."[361] The justification of the threat to property in the minds of the propertied stemmed from a failure to appreciate that the stability of possession depended on a general agreement of interests. This would be undermined by opinions that were adverse to that agreement. Interests, in the end, were governed by prejudice, and corroborated by custom over time.[362]

[357] Ibid., p. 95.

[358] Ibid., p. 94. Cf. Henry Home, Lord Kames, *Sketches of the History of Man*, ed. James A. Harris (Indianapolis, IN: Liberty Fund, 2007), 3 vols., I, p. 71, building on Henry Home, Lord Kames, *Historical Law-Tracts* (London: 1758), Tract III, "History of Property."

[359] See Hume, "Of Our Esteem for the Rich and Powerful," in *Treatise of Human Nature*, II, ii, 5; Smith, "Of the Origin of Ambition, and of the Distinction of Ranks," in *Theory of Moral Sentiments*, I, iii, 2. On the support which the feeling of beauty provides to that of sympathy in the disposition to admire the contrivances that accompany great wealth, see Smith, "Of the Beauty which the Appearance of Utility Bestows upon the Production of Art," ibid., IV, i.

[360] In November 1789, Richard Price had invoked the parable of the good Samaritan as a means of advertising the possibilities of revolutionary cosmopolitanism: see Richard Price, *A Discourse on the Love of Our Country, Delivered on Nov. 4, 1789* (London: 3rd ed., 1790), p. 3.

[361] EB, *Speech on the Army Estimates* (1st ed.), pp. 22–23.

[362] For an early statement of this position, which Burke must have known, see Berkeley, *Discourse Addressed to the Magistrates* (1736), pp. 484–6.

The opinion that historic concentrations of property were detrimental to justice was a powerfully destabilising presumption. What encouraged that presumption, as Mercer himself had shown, was the idea that property amassed in "times of ignorance and superstition" bore the marks of the illegitimacy of the age in which it was acquired. For Burke, this involved confusing the historical origins of European societies with the subsequent process of their improvement: by condemning the former under the banner of "feudalism," the latter was simultaneously denied. As Paley had argued in 1785, hereditary honours, the descent of property, tithes, tolls, rents and services, the privileges of the nobility and the immunities of the clergy, were all founded in the popular mind "upon prescription."[363] Exploding attachments confirmed by time exposed society to a resurgence of the spirit of conquest.

There was no one who ought to appreciate that fact more keenly than a product of County Down in Ireland, such as Mercer was. "It is possible," Burke wrote ironically, "that many estates about you were originally obtained by arms, that is, by violence." Burke was happy to clinch his point by referring Mercer to their joint awareness of the waves of plunder and confiscation by which the Irish polity had been settled in the seventeenth century. Here was a process of usurpation more brutal than any feudal yoke. Nonetheless, Burke accepted, this was "*old violence*," albeit not as old as the Frankish and Norman conquests. The passage of years had conferred legitimacy on the new regime of property by the silent operation of prescription.[364] Establishments of the kind could be improved by judicious reform, but they could not be overhauled by revolution. It might seem that the negative consequences of a process of revolution could be mitigated by the good intentions of its perpetrators. To Burke, however, this judgment involved reducing political theory to the vagaries of personality. The King of Prussia and the Czarina of Russia, much like the King of France, were most probably highly imperfect characters. Nonetheless, to the extent that they presided over a system of government their personal defects were mitigated.[365] By contrast, if the future of France were to be placed in the hands of 24 million well-intentioned reformers, the results would be disastrous. Politics could not thrive under a reign of virtue exercised directly by the community at large: violent factions would soon subvert the fellowship of the fraternal republic.[366] The administration of civil society required an effective division of labour by which rulers represented the ruled. Political wisdom strove to reconcile that separation of function with the responsibility of governors and the security of the governed.

363 William Paley, *The Principles of Moral and Political Philosophy* (Indianapolis, IN: Liberty Fund, 2002), p. 287. The observation did not lead Paley to accept Burke's argument in the *Reflections*: see William Paley to Edmund Law, 28 November 1790, TNA PRO 30/12/17/4, fol. 33: "The French revolution I think he has traduced grossly." I am grateful to Niall O'Flaherty for this reference.

364 EB to Captain Thomas Mercer, 26 February 1790, *Corr.*, VI, p. 95.

365 Ibid., p. 96.

366 Ibid., p. 97.

A translation of Burke's speech on the Army Estimates soon appeared in Paris.[367] Anacharsis Cloots responded on 12 May 1790, extolling both the procedures and the objectives of the Revolution.[368] More immediately, Adrien Duport objected to Burke's stance in a speech to the National Assembly on the reform of the French judiciary delivered on 29 March.[369] On receiving a copy of the speech, Burke opted to respond. It was all very well setting about renovating the French judiciary, he argued, but this may prove counterproductive under circumstances where "the foundations of property are destroyed."[370] Constitutional and judicial forms were crucial but ineffective where the will to operate them dispassionately had atrophied or did not exist.[371] On Burke's reckoning, the sense of justice in France had been radically compromised by replacing due process of law with demotic vengeance. At the beginning of his literary career, in the *Vindication of Natural Society*, Burke had associated such vengeance with the condition of "natural" society: artifice, dismissed by Bolingbroke, was in truth the foundation of civilisation.[372] In 1739, Hume had championed the artifice of a common social pact against the natural partiality of humankind.[373] Such artifice, Burke later contended, was natural to man, based on an in-built instinct for company and emulation.[374] Faced with the accumulated effects of this natural process of socialisation, the desire for justice could be represented as "natural" and "rude," as Burke suggested in his letter to Duport.[375] Next to this native acceptance of social distinctions and differences in wealth, the determination to level accumulated privilege appeared unnatural as well as destructive. It looked like a species of "artificial ignorance" grafted on to pre-existing social impulses, rooted in human nature and refined by the wisdom of ages.[376] This newfangled yet barbarous and antisocial artifice was the product of aberrant modern philosophies, and Burke's *Reflections* set about exposing both their principles and their implications.

[367] EB, *Discours de M. Burke sur la situation actuelle de la France* (Paris: 1790). It was reviewed in *Révolutions de Paris*, April 1790, pp. 126–31, and in the *Journal historique et littéraire*, 15 June 1790, p. 266. The earliest report of the speech appeared in *L'Ancien moniteur*, 24 February 1790, III, p. 442.

[368] Baron Jean-Baptiste Cloots to EB, 12 May 1790, *Corr.*, VI, pp. 109–15, later printed as a pamphlet entitled *Adresse d'un Prussien à un Anglais* (Paris: 1790). Burke retorted briefly in August 1790: see ibid., pp. 135–36.

[369] Adrien-Jean-François Duport, *Principes et plan sur l'établissement de l'ordre judiciare*, 29 March 1790, printed in *Procès-verbal de l'assemblée nationale*, vol. XVI, no. 244, with a footnote taking issue with Burke at pp. 105–6.

[370] EB to Adrien-Jean-François Duport, post 29 March 1790, *Corr.*, VI, p. 107.

[371] Ibid., p. 108.

[372] EB, *Vindication of Natural Society* (1756), *W & S*, I, *passim*. For discussion, see above chapter 2, section 3.

[373] Hume, *Treatise of Human Nature*, III, ii, 2.

[374] See EB, *Appeal from the New to the Old Whigs* (London: 1791), p. 130: "Art is man's nature." For the naturalness of sociability, see *Philosophical Enquiry*, p. 224. For discussion, see above chapter 3, section 2.

[375] EB to Adrien-Jean-François Duport, post 29 March 1790, *Corr.*, VI, p. 108.

[376] Ibid.

XII

THE OPENING OF THE HASTINGS IMPEACHMENT, 1786–1788

Figure 5. Burke early in the Hastings impeachment is cast as Cicero in his prosecution against Verres. In the background on the floor, Britannia lends support to a personified India. Fox stands in the background watching on as Lord North turns his back on the proceedings. John Boyne, *Cicero against Verres* (1787). Private collection. BM 7138 (in Robinson, p. 92).

12.1 Introduction

As France awaited the results of the elections to the Estates General in the spring of 1789, Burke was immersed in the process of prosecuting Hastings. That April he was hard at work on the details of the sixth article of impeachment. But it had taken years of labour to reach this stage in the proceedings. The preliminaries for mounting a compelling case against the accused had been underway since February 1786. This chapter takes the story from the beginning of that process to the great speech that opened the impeachment two years later. Between 4 April and 5 May 1786, Burke's twenty-two articles of charge outlining allegations of high crimes and misdemeanours against the Governor General were delivered to the House of Commons. It was on the basis of these articles that the Commons was to decide either to impeach Hastings before the House of Lords or to abandon all accusations against him. Burke presented the first article of charge, implicating Hastings in the Rohilla war, on 1 June 1786. Fox presented the Benares charge thirteen days later. But with the session about to end, grounds for a prosecution had still to be fully proved. Burke and his allies resumed their case in 1787. That February, Sheridan triumphed with a rousing oration on the Begams charge, received as one of the pre-eminent performances of the age.[1] In the months after the debate on the French commercial treaty in February 1787, further crimes were being alleged by opposition members. Soon it was clear that Hastings would have a case to answer. A committee under Burke's chairmanship now drafted articles of impeachment. On 10 May 1787, the Commons voted that Hastings should face trial, clearing the way for Burke to hold the alleged miscreant to account. The proceedings finally opened on 15 February 1788.

Burke believed that the Rohilla war charge, which sought to implicate Hastings in a project of foreign conquest on the subcontinent, encapsulated the depravity of the former Governor, ultimately stemming from his avarice. This cupidity brought a cascade of wrongdoing in its train. Acquisitiveness, it was alleged, encouraged corruption and rapacity, culminating in attempts to advance Company power in the region. Hastings thus embodied the spirit of conquest in South Asia. His imperiousness was equally evident in his attitude to the Raja of Benares whose government he treated with contempt. To indict Hastings, Burke drew on a conception of sympathy to which he had committed himself in the 1750s after being steeped in Anglican moral theory. He accepted with John Tillotson that benevolence was an instinct, a natural appetite with which the deity had equipped individuals to advance the purposes of humanity as a whole. From this perspective, stoic apathy, which remained an eighteenth-century ideal, seemed a species of unnatural rationalism. Cosmopolitan benevolence was based on principle not passion, and could not hope to sustain the sentiment of genuine fellow-feeling. Under the Roman Empire, malfeasance

[1] *The Life and Letters of Sir Gilbert Elliot, First Earl of Minto*, ed. Countess of Minto (London: 1874), 3 vols., I, p. 124.

could be brought to justice by means of established judicial procedures, but in Britain the Houses of Parliament offered the only means of redress. To mobilise this resource, Burke was obliged to prick the consciences of fellow members by appealing to the native impulse to sympathise with affliction. Sympathy, however, was partial and parochial in nature. Identification with remote suffering was therefore hard to elicit. Burke would have to capture the imagination of his auditors by making Company victims seem somehow familiar while depicting their predicament as extreme. Accordingly, his harrowing representation of the Rangpur atrocities was designed to stir the depths of human outrage. As the 1790s were about to dawn, Burke saw himself as appealing to a sense of moral injury, not as an opponent of mainstream "enlightened" values but as a critic of the failure to have them implemented in India.

The dramatic speech with which Burke launched the impeachment was extended over four days in the middle of February 1788. It constituted a major statement of his position on India, presenting an analysis of the history and politics of the subcontinent. It covered the structure of Company government and its corruption under Hastings; the disposition of the directors, proprietors and servants; the fraught relationship between power and trade; the character of the population over which the Company presided, above all the Hindu majority; the decline of Mughal authority, and the rise of British power; and the natural and civil obligations under which the Company stood.

The administration in Bengal was subordinate to the British state, but it was also bound by overriding normative constraints. According to Burke, government was a repository of trust as well as the subject of duties. He acknowledged with seventeenth-century lawyers like Grotius and Pufendorf that it was created as an instrument of human convenience founded on consent or "contractual" agreement. In this sense it was an artificial construction intended to serve social utility. At the same time, as both Grotius and Pufendorf recognised, it was providentially ordained as a means of furthering the satisfaction of needs. For Burke, however, the authority of government, whatever its expediency, should be subject to definite limits. In this context, he agreed with Locke that the title to command depended on the protection of fundamental rights. The violation of these rights imposed upon its victims the obligation of resistance. Strikingly, just under two years before the appearance of the *Reflections* in print, Burke was underlining the duty of resistance in the name of the rights of man.

12.2 A More Extended Virtue: Britain and Rome

On 17 February 1786 Burke moved for papers connected with Hastings's period as Governor General to be laid before a committee of the whole House. This material was to be considered on 3 April, although Burke had yet to produce his actual articles of charge. The idea was that witnesses might be examined in committee along with the papers supplied by the government. In the end, Burke gave way in the face of objections from the law officers, and proceeded to present his case, beginning the next day and lasting throughout April. Preparations for the impeachment of Warren Hastings had now begun. The twenty-two charges against Hastings covered the whole period of his career.[2] Burke's aim was clear: to put on record a readily comprehensible account of a protracted history of corruption, identifying criminality in its various manifestations and setting out what its consequences had been.[3] The purpose here was to amass evidence of nefarious conduct that would morally indict even if it failed legally to convict under the adverse circumstance of partiality towards Hastings among members of the House of Commons. To achieve this ambition, Burke needed to awaken greater sympathy for his cause, which meant stirring feelings of humanity among his audience. The need to evoke sympathy in connection with India was not new. Explaining his motion for papers on Elijah Impey on 9 February 1785, Burke had professed himself astounded by the idea that parliament might prove deaf to the "pleadings of humanity" represented by the sufferings of the people of Bengal. The situation to which Impey had subjected the natives, he went on, would inevitably trigger those "impulses of conscience" to which "every feeling mind" ought to be disposed.[4] The previous year, at his most despairing, Burke had presented his stand for India as "the battle of humanity" conducted in the face of "insensibility" and indifference.[5] Facing a parliament in early 1786 that had not been schooled in the history of Indian abuses, Burke would have to reacquaint his audience with the facts, gathering these into a meaningful narrative capable of stirring the sentiment of compassion and loading Hastings in the process with an appearance of guilt. This was the best that could be done for the inhabitants of the Indian Empire. Impugning, even if not convicting, a former Governor General offered a means of establishing standards for the future government of the subcontinent.

On 17 February 1786 Burke walked the new members of the Commons through the history of recent parliamentary proceedings in connection with South Asia, from the establishment of Burgoyne's Committee in 1772, through the passage of North's Regulating Act of 1773, to the setting up of the Select and Secret Committees in 1781.[6] Running in parallel with this narrative, Burke also sketched developments on the subcontinent after 1764: the dispatch of Clive by the East India Company to restrain the "rage of Conquest" that had seemingly taken root among servants after 1757, and to correct the manifold "corruptions" that had come to infect the organs of government.[7] When reform was undertaken by parliament in 1773, it was approached under mistaken assumptions: namely, that the Court of Directors was

[2] P. J. Marshall, *The Impeachment of Warren Hastings* (Oxford: Oxford University Press, 1965), pp. 39–40. The articles are summarised in F. P. Lock, *Edmund Burke: 1730–1797* (Oxford: Clarendon Press, 1998–2006), 2 vols., II, pp. 81–90.

[3] EB to Philip Francis, 23 December 1785, *Corr.*, V, p. 245.

[4] *Gazetteer*, 10 February 1785.

[5] EB, Speech on Almas Ali Khan (30 July 1784), *W & S*, V, pp. 476, 474; cf. ibid., pp. 473, 471.

[6] EB, Speech on Notice of Motion for Papers on Hastings, 13 February 1786, *W & S*, VI, pp. 48–50.

[7] Ibid., p. 49.

capable of reining in Company servants so long as it was invested with sufficient authority to perform the task.[8] The implications of Burke's rendition here are clear. The problems of the British Empire in India derived not simply from the activities of runaway servants in Bengal and the Carnatic, but from the very constitution of the Company itself: both the Court of Directors and the Court of Proprietors had been captured in the east by politics on the ground instead of acting as means of regulation and supervision.[9] "From this aera," Burke observed, "wealth did what it generally does, it opened the door to corruption."[10] This remark was intended to suggest not that commerce corrupts morals, but that politics corrupted commerce in the circumstances of South Asia, where avidity took the place of habitual mercantile prudence: "Abuse crept in upon abuse, till all India became one continued scene of peculation, rapine, fraud, injustice, and disgrace."[11]

Burke's determination to bring the perpetrators of these misdeeds to book was informed, as he explained to the Commons on 20 February 1786, by the "awful" sense of duty that he owed to "the interests of humanity."[12] Despite this, unlike Cicero in his campaign against Verres, he was being hampered in his access to relevant documents before proceeding.[13] Burke's repeated recourse to Cicero's prosecution of Verres during the course of his stand against Hastings served a number of related purposes.[14] Most obviously, it conferred a kind of classical dignity and solemnity upon the undertaking. Second, it enabled Burke to cloak himself in the mantle of pure patriotism: as with Cicero in his "impeachment" of the malevolent Sicilian administrator, so Burke's pursuit of the Governor General could be presented as an attempt to salvage the national reputation.[15] Beyond these advantages, however, there was an additional significance which Cicero's conduct held for Burke: the trial against Verres was an intervention into a Roman constitutional crisis, and Burke was keen to imply that British politics had become similarly unhinged. As Cicero saw the matter, popular suspicion of senatorial domination of the courts dealing with provincial extortion was mounting after the election of Pompey and Crassus in 70 BC and, by the time that Verres was being tried in the late summer of the

[8] Ibid.

[9] Burke had already presented this analysis in EB, *Ninth Report of the Select Committee* (25 June 1783), *W & S*, V, pp. 201–4.

[10] EB, Speech on Motion for Papers on Hastings, 17 February 1786, *W & S*, VI, p. 54.

[11] Ibid.

[12] Ibid., p. 62.

[13] *Morning Chronicle*, 21 February 1786.

[14] There is a general discussion of Burke's use of Cicero in this context in H. V. Canter, "The Impeachments of Verres and Hastings, Cicero and Burke," *Classical Journal*, 9 (February 1914), pp. 199–211. See also Geoffrey Carnall, "Burke as Modern Cicero" in Geoffrey Carnall and Colin Nicholson eds., *The Impeachment of Warren Hastings* (Edinburgh: Edinburgh University Press, 1989).

[15] The reports of Burke's speech regularly referred to Cicero's prosecution as an "impeachment": see, for example, ibid. In fact it was an action launched before the question *de pecuniis repetundis* based on charges of extortion. See Frank Hewitt Cowles, *Gaius Verres: An Historical Study* (Ithaca, NY: Cornell University Press, 1917).

same year, this had already led to calls for a restoration of the powers of the tribunes, posing a threat to Cicero's model of a balanced constitutional order.[16] Burke noted how the vitals of the Roman Empire had been poisoned on account of a reluctance to punish provincial malversation.[17] This failure of nerve, he believed, contributed to the derangement of the organs of public power. As he addressed himself to the British public in 1786, he had likewise come to the conclusion that the corruption of popular opinion required a reassertion of senatorial wisdom, even if the intervention was likely to fail.

Burke defended his stand against the corruption of public morals by appeal to an overriding sense of duty. This he identified with the Christian obligation to charity understood as more than a merely "partial charity which contracted its views to the situation of an individual." The charity that Burke had in mind was not a matter of compassion directed towards particular persons, but a species of moral generosity derived from what he described as "a more extended virtue" that aimed at nothing less than doing "justice to millions."[18] In resorting to this capacious virtue, Burke's intention was not to recharge the stoic idea of universal kinship, which he had done so much to disparage earlier in his career, and would again debunk as he examined French affairs in the 1790s.[19] In the Verrine orations, Cicero himself had spoken of forms of human suffering that were liable to stir up indignation, even among the insentient.[20] This universal capacity for fellow-feeling is given ethical force in Cicero within a stoic framework of moral thought.[21] *Against Verres* invokes this framework by pointing to the existence of a community of justice among peoples.[22] In *De officiis* this community is described as constituting the "law of nations" (*ius gentium*), the violation of which offends against human society.[23] In *De finibus* this sense of humanity is presented as a comprehensive affection that ultimately extends to the human race (*gens humanae*).[24] Yet although Cicero identifies this feeling by the term *caritas*, Burke's charity was anti-stoic rather than neo-stoic in character.

[16] Cicero, *The Verrine Orations*, ed. L.H.G. Greenwood (Cambridge, MA: Harvard University Press, 1928), 2 vols., I, xv, 44.

[17] EB, Speech on Motion for Papers on Hastings, 17 February 1786, *W & S*, VI, p. 63. See also WWM BkP 9:76, citing Asconius' commentary on Cicero, in *Q. Caecilium oratio quae divinatio dicitur*.

[18] *Public Advertiser*, 21 February 1786. To confirm Burke's specific use of the virtue of "charity" in this debate, cf. *Morning Herald*, 21 February 1786.

[19] See below, chapter 14, section 3.

[20] Cicero, *Verrine Orations*, V, cxvi, 172–72.

[21] Stoic elements in Cicero's thought occur within a wider framework of scepticism, constituting a notoriously eclectic mix. On Cicero's moral thought in connection with previous Hellenistic traditions, see the essays in J.G.F. Powell ed., *Cicero the Philosopher* (Oxford: Oxford University Press, 1995) and Andre Laks and Malcolm Schofield eds., *Justice and Generosity: Studies in Hellenistic Social and Political Philosophy* (Cambridge: Cambridge University Press, 1995).

[22] Cicero, *Verrine Orations*, I, iv, 13.

[23] Cicero, *De officiis*, III, 21, 23.

[24] Cicero, *De finibus*, V, 65, discussing the moral theory of Antiochus of Ascalon. For the stoic background, see Malcolm Schofield, *The Stoic Idea of the City* (Cambridge: Cambridge University Press, 1991); Gisela Striker, "Origins of the Concept of Natural Law" in idem., *Essays on Hellenistic Epistemology and Ethics* (Cambridge: Cambridge University Press, 1996). For Cicero's departure from stoic doc-

The true foundation of charity was an important consideration for Burke, constituting the means by which human beings might act in accordance with the laws of nature. Throughout the impeachment of Hastings, he appealed to universal morality founded on the sentiment of humanity. But this is not to be confused with the doctrine of "universal benevolence" that he later came to associate with the philosophy of Rousseau. Cosmopolitan generosity on the Genevan's part seemed to Burke a notional commitment without any basis in genuine emotion: although a theoretical "lover of his kind," Rousseau in fact comported himself as a "hater of his kindred."[25] This outcome was determined by a rational commitment to humanity that was devoid of any tangible affection for the species. According to Tillotson, it was the Christian religion's peculiar devotion to charity that surpassed all heathen sects of morality.[26] Tillotson discussed this virtue in terms of what he took to be an Aristotelian conception of sociability with a view to undermining the moral doctrines of Thomas Hobbes.[27] But its distinguishing feature, he thought, was its status as a "natural instinct" that preceded the decrees of abstract reason: in the sphere of moral conduct, he contended, "mankind hardly need to consult any other oracle, than the mere propensions and inclinations of their nature."[28] Burke accepted, as he would later reveal during the course of the war against Revolutionary France, that the "Scheme of Charity ought certainly to take in mankind," but it had to do so on the basis of a "graduated Scale."[29] Enlarged benevolence was spurious where it supplanted more immediate attachments.

Since Burke's case against Hastings depended on setting out the principles of legitimate government, the terms on which he sought to elucidate the foundations of political morality became particularly important for his involvement in Indian affairs in the late 1780s and early 1790s. Anglicans like Tillotson provided Burke with the intellectual equipment to vindicate fundamental norms within a framework of natural law while rejecting both stoic universalism and deist rationalism along with the cosmopolitanism he came to associate with Rousseau. The motivation behind moral action was based on sentiment, not reason—on "propensions and inclinations," as Tillotson put it. As Burke had made plain in the 1750s, reason was required to evaluate our duties but was insufficient by itself to inspire their adoption

---

trine under the influence of Antiochus, see Richard A. Horsley, "The Law of Nature in Cicero and Philo," *Harvard Theological Review*, 71 (January–April 1978), pp. 35–59. See also Elizabeth Asmis, "Cicero on Natural Law and the Laws of the State," *Classical Antiquity*, 27:1 (April 2008), pp. 1–33. On Antiochus of Ascalon, see Jonathan Barnes, "Antiochus of Ascalon" in Jonathan Barnes and Miriam Griffin eds., *Philosophia Togata: Essays on Philosophy and Roman Society* (Oxford: Oxford University Press, 1989).

[25] EB, *Letter to a Member of the National Assembly* (1791), *W & S*, VIII, pp. 314–15. For discussion, see below, chapter 14, section 3.

[26] *The Works of the Most Reverend Dr. John Tillotson* (London: 1728), 3 vols., I, pp. 169–73. On Burke's debt to Anglican moral thought, see above, chapter 2, section 3.

[27] Tillotson, *Works*, I, p. 305.

[28] Ibid., II, pp. 298–99.

[29] WWM BkP 10:36.

by human beings.[30] For that purpose, providence in its wisdom had equipped us with animating passions that concerned us with the welfare of our fellows.[31] Burke was happy, in other words, to acknowledge the effectiveness of our "moral passions," although he insisted that sensibility was inadequate to determine duty or to oblige us to its actual performance. Reason was required to establish a proper "science of our duties," with the performance of those duties depending in the last instance on the awesome prospect of reward or punishment.[32] But the plain fact was that we were constituted with affective instincts that moved us to compassion for the plight of suffering humanity. Sympathy of the kind depended on stimulating the imagination, through which we could identify with the condition of our fellow creatures. For that reason, it was vital for Burke's purposes that circumstances in India could be compassed by the minds of his British auditors in the House of Commons. For this he had to ensure that they invested in the affairs of India, which could only be achieved by a process of imaginative identification. Early in the proceedings against Hastings, Burke sensed that this design was proving successful. "Hitherto all goes reasonably well," he reported to Gilbert Elliot around 20 February 1786: "now I think we shall go on powerfully."[33]

Both in parliament and out of doors, opinion had been busily running against Burke since the election of 1784. By the beginning of the new session in 1786, he feared that he was in danger of losing his reputation altogether. However, by the spring there was a palpable sense of progress in Burke's correspondence, and by the autumn he was celebrating his successes: "India is no longer new to the Ears or understandings of the nation," he wrote to a political ally, Thomas Lewis O'Beirne.[34] Burke had long been concerned that British opinion was determined to care little about the subcontinent, obliging him to prick MPs' consciences by filling their minds with lurid accounts of the afflictions of multitudes. The veracity of concrete details had become so important to Burke that he challenged Thurlow's dismissal of the Select and Secret Committee Reports as amounting to "*idle fables*" during his first motion for papers against Hastings.[35] The next day, the king was complaining to Pitt of Burke's "fertile imagination."[36] Nonetheless, it was precisely imagination that was required to evoke in his audience the feeling of charity, and so it was this resource that Burke drew upon in crafting his case against Hastings. As he bluntly stated at the start of June 1786, to secure the conviction of Hastings for acts of al-

[30] EB, *A Philosophical Enquiry into the Origin of our Ideas of the Sublime and Beautiful* (1757, rev. ed. 1759), *W & S*, I, p. 272.

[31] For discussion, see the account of Burke's parliamentary intervention on St. Eustatius above, chapter 8, section 6.

[32] The phrase cited appears in EB, *Philosophical Enquiry* (1757, rev. ed. 1759), *W & S*, I, p. 272.

[33] EB to Sir Gilbert Elliot, c. 20 February 1786, *Corr.*, V, pp. 259–60.

[34] EB to Thomas Lewis O'Beirne, 29 September 1786, ibid., p. 281.

[35] EB, Speech on Motion for Papers on Hastings, 17 February 1786, *W & S*, VI, p. 55. Thurlow had compared the Reports in the House of Lords on 9 December 1783 to "the history of Robinson Crusoe." See *Parliamentary Register* (Debrett), XIV, p. 21.

[36] Historical Manuscripts Commission, *Twelfth Report*, Appendix, Part IX (Smith MSS.), p. 350.

leged turpitude, he was obliged to appeal to the "hearts and consciences of gentlemen," and ultimately to their sense that their innermost dispositions were available for divine inspection.[37]

The bulk of Burke's charges were presented to the Commons in April 1786, with the last being delivered on 5 May.[38] By then, Hastings himself had already appeared before the House, but his defence against Burke's allegations had been unconvincing.[39] The examination of witnesses followed between 2 and 24 May, with the Commons voting on Burke's first articles in June. The first charge, on the Rohilla war, was defeated by 67 to 119 votes.[40] However, with Pitt's support the second charge, concerning Chait Singh of Benares, was approved by 119 to 79, with further consideration of the remaining charges being deferred from 21 June till the new session.[41] This approval was an important victory for Burke, and explains his upbeat tone the following September. He now felt that he had begun to surmount the assumption that India was somehow beyond British comprehension.[42] Adam Smith, he thought, would approve of his conduct thus far.[43] Both men shared the view that the acquisition of territorial sovereignty had politicised the commercial enterprise of the East India Company, leading to the perverse arrangement whereby the corporation administered a polity with a view to exploiting it for profit while it sought commercial advantage via a system of political patronage. As a result, the Company played two roles, both incompatible with its interest, and therefore detrimental to the welfare at once of Britain and the East Indies: "If the trading spirit of the East India Company renders them very bad sovereigns; the spirit of sovereignty seems to have rendered them equally bad traders."[44] This was exactly the conclusion that Burke had arrived at in his *Ninth Report* of 1783. What interested both Smith and Burke was how a project of commerce had descended into a project of conquest in the east, giving rise to what Smith believed was perhaps the worst system of government that could conceivably be devised for "any country whatever."[45] Clearly Burke shared this devastating verdict, which he had been publicising himself since 1781. Five years later, in debate on the Rohilla war, he confessed that he had never lost the

[37] EB, Speech on Rohilla War Charge, 1 June 1786, *W & S*, VI, p. 111.

[38] *CJ*, XLI, pp. 483–536, 568–95, 612–23, 627–29, 648–54, 750–61.

[39] Ibid., pp. 668–733.

[40] *Parliamentary History*, XXVI, cols. 51–91; *General Evening Post*, 3 June 1786.

[41] *Parliamentary History*, XXVI, cols. 91–115; Marshall, *Impeachment of Hastings*, pp. 39–51; Lock, *Burke II*, pp. 76–96.

[42] EB to Sir Gilbert Elliot, 20 February 1786, *Corr.*, V, pp. 259–60.

[43] EB to Adam Smith, 7 December 1786, ibid., p. 296.

[44] Adam Smith, *An Inquiry into the Nature and Causes of the Wealth of Nations*, ed. R. H. Campbell and A. S. Skinner (Indianapolis, IN: Liberty Fund, 1976), 2 vols., II, p. 819. For discussion of Smith's thesis, see Gary M. Anderson and Robert D. Tollison, "Adam Smith's Analysis of Joint-Stock Companies," *Journal of Political Economy*, 90:6 (December 1982), pp. 1237–56.

[45] Smith, *Wealth of Nations*, II, p. 570. The original European transformation of a project of commerce into a programme of conquest was associated by Smith with the Spanish in the new world. See ibid., p. 564.

feeling of anger that the situation in India originally inspired—"an uniform, steady, public anger," as he characterised it, "but not a private anger."[46] He had no personal animosity against Hastings, he was saying, but he did condemn the system over which he presided, making his campaign against the Governor General quite the opposite of a "personal contest": it was instead "a national and imperial question."[47]

When Smith passed judgment on the administration of Bengal in 1776, he was adamant that it was the "system of government" that he wished to censure—"not the character of those who have acted in it."[48] Servants and governors merely acted the parts that their situation dictated. In the period 1781–3, Burke's emphasis likewise fell on the culpability of the system of political organisation rather than on Company personnel, although he did nonetheless obviously believe that individual cases of malpractice had exacerbated misgovernment. Now, with the impeachment of Hastings, he had opted to concentrate his energy on exposing personal malfeasance, although he remained aware that corporate corruption formed the context in which misconduct operated. In fact, that was still largely the point: as he advised the Commons during his Rohilla war speech on 1 June 1786, "Mr. Hastings was out of the question." With Lord Cornwallis about to depart for the east to assume the role of Governor General, proceedings against Hastings went beyond simply disciplining a former Company chief. What was being established was "a set of maxims and principles to be the guide and rule of future Governors in India."[49] Burke continued to abhor the terms under which the new Governor General would operate. He was going out, as Burke put it to Smith, with "powers totally unlimited," including the authority to overrule his council and to act as commander-in-chief.[50] Burke interpreted this as confirmation that the British government was extending its control over the Empire in the east. It was a means, as Burke had declared the previous March, of introducing "arbitrary and despotic Government in India" under the pretence of establishing a vigorous administration.[51] But while a people might eagerly submit to authority, they would never willingly subject themselves to arbitrary authority, which would always inspire resistance while at the same time lacking vigour.[52] Given the reality of Pitt's India Act, Burke's case against Hastings could never by itself refashion the government of India into a form that he could approve. All he could hope for was to improve the general standard of political conduct, recognising that administration would still be forced to operate in the absence of credible mechanisms of accountability. The Commons could lay down "principles" for the

[46] EB, Speech on Rohilla War Charge, 1 June 1786, *W & S*, VI, p. 104.

[47] Ibid.

[48] Smith, *Wealth of Nations*, II, p. 641.

[49] EB, Speech on Rohilla War Charge, 1 June 1786, *W & S*, VI, p. 105.

[50] EB to Adam Smith, 7 December 1786, *The Correspondence of Adam Smith*, ed. Ernest Campbell Mossner and Ian Simpson Ross (Indianapolis, IN: Liberty Fund, 1977, 1987), p. 297. Cornwallis's powers were conferred under 26 Geo. III, c. 16, sec. 7.

[51] EB, Speech on Bill to Amend 1784 India Act, 22 March 1786, *W & S*, VI, p. 66.

[52] Ibid., p. 67.

government of distant provinces even in circumstances where the ministry refused to introduce the arrangements most likely to protect those principles in practice.[53]

In Burke's mind, an independent committee of the House of Commons still offered the best means of scrutinising and disciplining wayward political behaviour. In its absence, misconduct could best be tried by alternative judicial means. Launching an impeachment offered the sole remaining method of publicising a code of practice by exposing political corruption to shame and disgrace.[54] It facilitated the kind of "Vigilance" that "Large Empire" fundamentally required.[55] Nonetheless, by comparison with the means available to Roman prosecutors of imperial misconduct, impeachment was a judicial instrument that was poorly adapted to Burke's purpose. The corruption of provincial administrators in the Roman Empire was altogether more amenable to judicial inquiry and prosecution.[56] Burke noted a range of circumstantial reasons why this was inevitably the case. In the first place, the Roman Empire was a geographically continuous body, while the British was widely separated by great stretches of sea and land.[57] Equally, all denizens of Roman provinces could communicate through the Greek language, enabling "Praetors and Governors to converse intelligibly with the natives."[58] Indian subjects, on the other hand, were reduced to effective silence.[59] This disenfranchisement was reinforced by the fact that would-be Indian complainants were bereft of any effective corporate personality, whereas Roman provinces could submit their grievances collectively to the capital.[60] Because the subcontinent also lacked a substantial colonial population, the British Empire, unlike the Roman, had no political roots in its acquired provinces, depriving the native population of potential patronage and protection, and so leaving them without representation in the colonists' mother country.[61] For the same reason, the seat of Empire saw no influx from the subcontinent, leaving both populations socially and politically separated.[62]

The British had no existing body of law that addressed the problem of imperial extortion and oppression, whereas Rome, given its situation, had succeeded in developing a series of provisions under the title of *lex pecuniae repetundae* intended to bring spoliation to justice.[63] Burke had commented on these provisions as early as his *Abridgement of English History*, which pointed to an account of Tacitus in the

[53] EB, Speech on Rohilla War Charge, 1 June 1786, *W & S*, VI, p. 105.

[54] Burke had rejected the only two other possibilities, prosecution by the Attorney General before the King's Bench and a Bill of Pains as Penalties such as Dundas had introduced against Rumbold, as inappropriate under the circumstances. See EB, Motion for Papers on Hastings, 17 February 1786, ibid., p. 51.

[55] EB, Notes on Rohilla War Speech, WWM BkP 9:65.

[56] EB, Speech on Rohilla War Charge, 1 June 1786, *W & S*, VI, p. 105.

[57] Ibid.

[58] *Morning Herald*, 2 June 1786.

[59] EB, Speech on Rohilla War Charge, 1 June 1786, *W & S*, VI, pp. 105–6.

[60] Ibid., p. 106.

[61] Ibid., p. 94.

[62] Ibid., p. 106.

[63] Burke notes these various provisions in WWM BkP 9:65.

Annals of various laws introduced against exploitation in the provinces.[64] The availability of impeachment proceedings did not wholly compensate for the lack of such an arrangement in Britain since earlier trials appeared to have been explicitly partisan, thus failing to establish an acceptable precedent for prosecuting political offences.[65] Extending to the accused the rights of regular due process undermined the interest of justice from the opposite direction. As Burke subtly noted, the legal security due to a population against exploitation by magistrates could never be provided by a judicial process that entitled the perpetrator of public abuses to the protection due to a defendant in a criminal trial. If Hastings in his public capacity was deemed to enjoy the full range of civilian protections, then misdemeanours could never be plausibly proved against him, thus depriving the governed of appropriate protection against their governors.[66] The issue here turned on the rules of evidence that should be appropriately used, a topic that would exercise Burke when the impeachment proper got under way. In the interim he recognised that British arrangements did offer redress. "I will not condemn the frame of our Government," he remarked in this context.[67] The constitution, through the House of Commons, enabled representation, and as such it could take the part of the Indian people.

The great problem here, Burke was aware, was that the Indians "had never transmitted any complaint to this country."[68] Burke was never an unconditional admirer of the forms of government in South Asia. To the extent that they won the allegiance and promoted the welfare of their populations they were certainly to be respected and maintained. Nonetheless, neither the paternalism of Tanjore nor that of the various Nawabs in the north had ever exemplified a system of responsible government. Indeed, the original Mughal edifice had been some kind of despotic arrangement, although clearly this was not arbitrary in nature: despite Hastings's preconceptions, even the *Institutes* of Timur "were dictated by the spirit of justice," as Burke noted.[69] Burke later made similar claims for the provisions of Genghis Khan, above all his preservation of a system of ranks.[70] Nonetheless, the historical exercise of authority in India had rendered the population both passive and concessive.[71] Burke believed that Hastings had capitalised on this passivity, and awed his many victims into silence and submission—a fact which "redoubled the horror" of

[64] EB, *An Essay towards an Abridgement of English History* (1757–c. 1763), *W & S*, I, p. 373; Tacitus, *Annals*, XV, 22.

[65] On earlier impeachments, see Lock, *Burke, II*, pp. 65–71.

[66] EB, Speech on Rohilla War Charge, 1 June 1786, *W & S*, VI, p. 94.

[67] WWM BkP 9:65.

[68] *Morning Herald*, 2 June 1786.

[69] *Public Advertiser*, 2 June 1786. Hastings had invoked Timur or "Tamerlane" as having been a fit guide for his behaviour.

[70] EB, Speech in Reply, 28 May 1794, *W & S*, VII, pp. 268–9, drawing on Pétis de la Croix, *The History of Genghizcan the Great, First Emperor of the Ancient Moguls and Tartars* (London: 1722), pp. 49–50.

[71] See EB, Speech on Bengal Judicature Bill, 27 June 1781, *W & S*, V, pp. 140–41. Cf. EB, "Observations" to the *First Report* of the Select Committee, 5 February 1782, ibid., p. 184.

their oppression.[72] The only means of redress which the victims of oppression could hope for under the circumstances resided in the representative role enjoyed by the House of Commons—a body of citizens who stood for those subjected to its authority. The Commons could represent the voices of the exploited to the extent that its members could sympathise with their plight.[73] They ought to be "full of warm and animated Sympathy, for those who suffer under the abuses of *power*."[74] In a passage deleted from his notes for his speech on the Rohilla war charge, Burke amplified this thought: as prosecutors taking the part of a "suffering people" on the subcontinent, members of parliament "virtually" represented the aggrieved.[75] Although Indians had not voted for them, members of the Commons could personify their complaints to the extent that they experienced "fellow feeling" for their predicament.[76] "These unfortunate people," Burke insisted, "had undoubtedly the common feelings of mankind."[77] Their humanity meant that, even in the absence of articulated discontent, their representatives could voice the misery that they must feel through the "sympathy pervading human nature."[78]

12.3 The Rohilla War Charge

Burke believed that by reporting Hastings's involvement in the sorry fate of the Rohillas, the basic principles of his Bengal administration would be revealed. Hastings himself also believed that the war would prove the weak link in his defence, sensing—as was later confirmed—that it "would be decisive of all the business."[79] Rohilkhand was a fertile stretch of territory situated along the north-west frontier of Awadh.[80] Early in the eighteenth century, the country had been settled by the Rohillas, a group of Pathan military chiefs who had descended from Afghanistan to establish their supremacy in the urban centres of the region over a majority Hindu population.[81] They administered the territory through a loose confederacy headed by Hafiz Rahmat Khan, establishing what Burke described as "the most orderly and

[72] *Public Advertiser*, 2 June 1786.

[73] EB, Speech on Rohilla War Charge, 1 June 1786, *W & S*, VI, p. 94.

[74] WWM BkP 9:65.

[75] Ibid.

[76] Ibid.

[77] *Morning Herald*, 2 June 1786.

[78] Ibid.

[79] "Minutes of the Proceedings of the Trial of Warren Hastings," Add. MS. 24225, fol. 39.

[80] There is a very positive account of the prosperity of the country in *The Origin and Authentic Narrative of the recent Maratta War; and also, the Late Rohilla War, in 1773 and 1774* (London: 1781), which correspondingly casts the intervention of Hastings in a poor light.

[81] C. A. Bayly, *Rulers, Townsmen and Bazaars: North Indian Society in the Age of British Expansion* (Oxford: Oxford University Press, 1983, 2000), pp. 23–5, 120–22.

regulated Government that had hitherto been seen in India."[82] With the surge of the Marathas from the south to occupy Delhi in 1771, Rohilkhand became a significant buffer zone separating Maratha power from Awadh, which at this time was established as a crucial British ally securing East India Company provinces against invasion from the Maratha enemy. The Wazir of Awadh, Shuja-ud-Daula, had his own designs on Rohilkhand, first agreeing with the British in 1772 to protect the Rohillas against Maratha attacks and then, when their leaders refused to pay for the privilege, marching against their territory in April 1774 with the support of British forces under Colonel Alexander Champion, driving some 20,000 individuals from the country across the Ganges, thereby extirpating politically a whole people from the region.[83] Champion later complained that the Nawab had pursued his prey with ruthless inhumanity, drawing the British into aiding and abetting a savage conquest.[84] The enterprise was motivated, Hastings later conceded, by the need to relieve the Company's financial distress and deliver it from political vulnerability.[85]

Dundas had introduced a resolution against Hastings on the back of the *Fifth Report* of the Secret Committee on 28 May 1782, censuring the "iniquitous" management of the Bengal administration.[86] Over the following five years, the conduct of the Rohilla war had acquired such notoriety that Charles Hamilton, in his 1787 historical account of the "rise, progress and final dissolution" of the Rohilla Afghans, singled out the campaign of 1774 as having done more than any other event to foster a reputation for depravity among Company servants.[87] Nonetheless, when Dundas rose to debate the issue on 2 June 1786, he was adamant that "policy" trumped "morality" in judging the rights of war, further insisting that his earlier resolution

[82] EB, Speech on Rohilla War Charge, 1 June 1786, *W & S*, VI, p. 100. For a summary of other contemporary responses, see H. H. Dodwell ed., *The Cambridge History of India V: British India, 1497–1858* (Delhi: S. Chand & Co., 2nd ed., 1963), p. 222.

[83] For debate on the meaning of "extirpation," see John Strachey, *Hastings and the Rohilla War* (Oxford: Oxford University Press, 1892), pp. 179–82. The term, commonly used to describe the fate of the Pathan chiefs, was according to Strachey a mistranslation of the Persian for "expulsion." It seems, however, that the confusion properly developed in the nineteenth century. In his evidence to a Committee of the Whole House on the articles of charge against Hastings, reprinted in *Minutes of the Evidence Taken before a Committee of the House of Commons, Appointed to Consider the Several Articles of Charge of High Crimes and Misdemeanours, Presented to the House against Warren Hastings* (London: 1786), Sir Robert Baker was clear that "it was never intended to remove the cultivators of the soil but to remove the governors of it" (p. 11). Whether this amounted to extirpation was nonetheless debated in the House of Commons on 1 June 1786. See in particular the contribution by Powys in *The Debate on the Rohilla War in the House of Commons on the 1st and 2nd June 1786* (London: 1786), p. 17. For Burke's use of the same term as a synonym for "removal" in connection with the Caribs of St. Vincent, see EB to James De Lancey, 20 August 1772, *Corr.*, II, p. 328.

[84] Champion's evidence is reprinted in ibid., pp. 12–28.

[85] For harsh verdicts on the policy of Hastings, see James Mill, *The History of British India* (London: 5th ed., 1858), 10 vols., III, p. 397; John Morley, *Edmund Burke: A Historical Study* (London: 1867), pp. 204–5.

[86] *CJ*, XXXVIII, p. 1029.

[87] Charles Hamilton, *An Historical Relation of the Origin, Progress, and Final Dissolution of the Government of the Rohilla Afghans* (London: 1787), pp. xii–xiv.

against Hastings had not charged him with criminal behaviour in his conduct of foreign relations.[88] In the process, he downgraded the significance of the removal of the Rohillas to be resettled beyond the Ganges since they were, as was generally recognised, recent colonists of Rohilkhand, and to that extent could be considered mere strangers and intruders. Dundas was implicitly accepting Hastings's description of the Rohilla settlers as a band of "foreign adventurers" rather than a "nation" proper.[89] Burke retorted with an example from the seventeenth-century conquest of Ireland: would Dundas consider it so unobjectionable if the Scottish planters of the previous century were to be forcibly relocated and stationed beyond the Tweed? The place "where a man's ancestors had settled and fixed their residence, became, he said, to all intents and purposes, his home, and it was as great an act of injustice to remove him from thence, as if it had been his by the most remote and ancient possession."[90]

Burke's judgment here is significant: recent prescription rather than antiquity gave title to property and government, although this was in turn dependent on observing the obligations of rule.[91] While the Rohillas did have a prescriptive right to their territories, this was not based on remote antiquity, since they had colonised northern India as recently as the 1720s. In addition, their prescriptive claims to exercising power had to be supplemented by their performance of the duties of governors. Ultimately, neither the origins nor the longevity of a system of rule was sufficient to establish its legitimacy. "All the Mahomedans in India are strangers," Burke noted, with the implication that prior occupancy carried with it no entitlements.[92] Muslim government on the subcontinent over the course of previous centuries had been established by military adventurers from Tartary and Persia, yet "every distinguished person" that the country could claim as its own had settled as an invader from the north or south, frequently exploited by the throne at Delhi as a means of subduing more established populations who proved refractory in their dealings with the Mughal Emperor.[93] This applied equally to Rohilla mercenaries as well as to the Wazir of Awadh, although the East India Company chose to legitimise and support the rapacity of the latter in his campaign to annihilate the government of the former, exactly the type of conduct that a claim to previous occupancy could never hope to justify. On Burke's telling, the campaign against the Rohillas was at bottom Hastings's design, a malicious scheme in which the perfidious Nawab became an instrument of British conquest. Even the *Fifth Report* of the Secret

[88] *Debate on the Rohilla War*, p. 76.

[89] *The Defence of Warren Hastings at the Bar of the House of Commons . . . in the Year 1786* (London: 1786), p. 23.

[90] Ibid., p. 80.

[91] On prescription, see above, chapter 5, section 4 and chapter 8, section 7. For the prescriptive basis of Burke's theory of government, see also Paul Lucas, "On Burke's Doctrine of Prescription; Or, An Appeal from the New to the Old Lawyers," *Historical Journal*, 11:1 (1968), pp. 35–63, criticised in Francis Canavan, "Burke on Prescription of Government," *Review of Politics*, 35:4 (October 1973), pp. 454–74.

[92] EB, Speech on Rohilla War Charge, 1 June 1786, *W & S*, VI, p. 99.

[93] Ibid., pp. 99–100.

Committee recognised the advantages that Hastings expected to flow from the Nawab's assault upon his neighbours.[94] Burke underlined a passage in a letter from Hastings included in one of the appendices to Dundas's *Report* confirming that, in the event of the Rohilla chiefs refusing to abide by their agreements with Shuja-ud-Daula, "we will thoroughly exterminate them."[95] Burke's dismay at Hastings's behaviour towards the Rohillas resulted not simply from abhorrence at a perceived violation of the rights of war, but more particularly from what looked like the Governor General's determination to destroy politically a flourishing polity.

Burke went so far as to contrast conquest with extirpation: "The motives, the object, and the ends of them were materially different."[96] Conquest might in fact prove glorious if its origins and outcomes could themselves be justified—presumably, as in Clive's case, where the enterprise conformed to the rights of war, and where victory was succeeded by a project of civilising empire: "acquiring the government of a worthy race of men . . . improving them in science or morals . . . making them more happy or rich."[97] The prospect of such an outcome had been held out to the British after 1757, but instead of instituting an empire of laws, the achievements of Clive were followed by a scheme of usurpation, employing the rights of conquest as a pretext for expropriation when military ascendancy could only justify an equitable settlement, and thus the beginning of an end to conquest proper. Burke was a critic not of either empire or colonial settlement but of the exercise of forms of power that disregarded the welfare of subjects. Colonial plantation had its uses, above all after the fact, while empire as such was unavoidable in human affairs: certainly neither could be dispensed with a priori or on principle. However, wilful extirpation was another matter altogether. It represented an assault on property achieved by routing the leadership of a community—and so, effectively, the destruction of the community itself.[98] It was not every single member of a nation that was likely to be affected by the elimination of its political and propertied classes: "It was the chief land-holders, the principal manufacturers, the nobles, the superior clergy, and the men of property of all ranks" who were commonly the victims of extirpating conquest.[99] Nonetheless, such targeted destruction ought properly to be regarded as amounting, in Dundas's phrase, to a political "Extermination."[100]

[94] *Fifth Report of he Committee of Secrecy, Appointed to Enquire into the Causes of the War in the Carnatic* (London: 1782), p. 21.

[95] Ibid., Appendix 21: Letter to Shuja-ud-Daula, 22 April 1773. Burke's annotated copy of the *Fifth Report* can be found at the British Library, 749.d.1.

[96] EB, Speech on Rohilla War Charge, 1 June 1786, *W & S*, VI, p. 111.

[97] Ibid.

[98] Burke estimated the number of expelled Rohillas at 60,000—the bulk of the population itself—whereas in his evidence to the Commons Colonel Champion estimated the number at 20,000. See *Minutes of the Evidence Taken before a Committee of the House of Commons, Appointed to Consider the Several Articles of Charge of High Crimes and Misdemeanours*, p. 22.

[99] EB, Speech on Rohilla War Charge, 1 June 1786, *W & S*, VI, p. 111.

[100] For Dundas's description, forming part of his resolutions against Hastings in 1782, see *CJ*, XXXVIII, p. 1029. For Hastings's own gloss on "extirpation" as having "consisted in nothing more than

As Burke saw it, Hastings's treatment of the Rohillas was of a piece with his general comportment on the subcontinent, which he allegedly approached as a country of conquest. In the process, he rendered the duties of government coterminous with the needs of administration, identifying the obligations of rule with limitless rights of war: on this assumption, self-interested expediency and necessity alone set the limits to legitimate behaviour. When it came to dealing with Indian rulers outside the provinces immediately subject to British authority, this conduct acquired an especially wilful and oppressive aspect since these territories were in fact "not subject to us by conquest": it was their trust in East India Company policy, their "easy faith," that had "given the sword of Indian jurisdiction into the hands of British honour."[101] Nonetheless, Hastings assumed that India was inured to conquest, and that consequently its people were disposed to rebellion. They could only therefore be governed by constant "strictness."[102] In a letter to Nathaniel Smith included as a preface to Charles Wilkins's 1785 translation of the *Bhagvat-geeta,* Hastings had underlined the cultural distance separating Europe from the east. European standards of propriety were, he argued, inapplicable to the taste, morality and religion of Indian civilisation.[103] Nonetheless, as Hastings went on to argue, an awareness of Asian beliefs and practices, for all their remoteness from British norms, could help to conciliate differences, and thereby "lessen the weight of the chain by which the natives are held in subjection." Knowledge humanised by inducing familiarity; it could imprint the obligations of benevolence "on the hearts of our own countrymen." This, Hastings claimed, would alleviate the severity of dominion founded on "the right of conquest."[104] For Burke, however, it was the presumptuous exercise of that right that made "*despotism*" such an outstanding feature of "Mr. Hastings's government in India."[105] This, however, was not to be confused with the "civilised" despotism of the Mughals: it represented instead the arbitrary caprice of the Governor's absolute authority.[106]

In a memoir that Hastings composed during his return trip from Bengal to England, the former Governor openly complained of the inadequacy of "delegated and fettered power" to command Asian territories that exceeded the dimensions of the parent state.[107] Hastings completed *The Present State of the East Indies* in January 1786, and John Stockdale published an unauthorised version in March. Official publication followed in October of the same year, publicising still more widely

in removing from their offices the Rohellas who had the official management of the country, and from the country the soldiers who had opposed us in the conquest of it," see *Defence of Hastings*, p. 24

[101] *Public Advertiser*, 2 June 1786.

[102] Ibid.

[103] *Bhagvat-geeta, or Dialogues of Kreeshna and Arjoon*, trans. Charles Wilkins (London: 1785), p. 7.

[104] Ibid., p. 13.

[105] Ibid.

[106] Cf. EB, *Reflections*, ed. Clark, p. 295 [189] on the comparative despotisms of Turkey, Persia and France. See also Burke on the Ottoman Empire during his contribution to the debate on the Ochakov affair, 29 Mary 1791, *Parliamentary History*, XXIX, cols. 76–77.

[107] Warren Hastings, *The Present State of the East Indies* (London: 1786), p. 98.

Hastings's sense that, notwithstanding the fact that his powers had been confined by the constitution of the Company, the "first executive member" of the Bengal government ought to possess "a power absolute within himself, and independent of control."[108] Given this requirement of the office, he admitted that during his tenure he had been obliged to defend what he perceived to be the "public safety" in violation of express orders from the Court of Directors that might, in his view, have compromised the security of the Empire.[109] In his Speech on the Rohilla war charge on 1 June, Burke traced this felt need for unconstrained authority to a fundamental motivating or "ruling" impulse in Hastings—namely, "avarice," the shameless pursuit of profit at all costs, which Grotius had depicted by the Greek term "aischrokerdeia" when defending the commercial and political rights of the United Dutch East India Company in the early seventeenth century—a "vile disease of spirit," as he put it, "characterized by complete disrespect for law and morality."[110] According to Burke, it was excessive covetousness of the kind that drove the Governor General to embrace a range of subsidiary principles. These included the tendency to disregard orders, to dominate his colleagues, to oppress the natives, to bribe reluctant collaborators, and to pursue a policy of war as an instrument of financial increase.[111] Each of these tendencies had been represented in the articles of charge brought before the House of Commons in April and May, and they would form the basis of the impeachment the following year.

The domineering spirit of the Hastings government was particularly manifest in his management of the Company's external relations, which Burke took to consist of a policy of plunder of a kind that he had anatomised in the *Ninth Report* of the Select Committee.[112] The pursuit of conquest as a means of supply subverted every prudent rule of political economy and betrayed the principles of common justice. These principles were not founded on positive institutions but were traceable to obligations under natural law. Burke conceded that the protocols of the British constitution, for example the provisions of Magna Carta, might not be expected to gain any traction in India, but nonetheless the "law of nature and nations" ought to be applicable in every jurisdiction of the globe.[113] This law ought properly to regulate international relations as well as the terms on which civil magistrates were obliged to their subjects. They comprised, Burke insisted, the "great and fundamental axioms" on whose basis all societies were constructed.[114] They diverged in point of detail from the positive institutions of individual states, but they nonetheless provided

[108] Ibid., p. 100.

[109] Ibid.

[110] Hugo Grotius, *Commentary on the Law of Prize and Booty* (c. 1604), ed. Martine Julia van Ittersum (Indianapolis, IN: Liberty Fund, 2006), p. 11. For an original use of the Greek term, see Sophocles, *Antigone*, line 1056. Grotius' manuscript was not published until the nineteenth century.

[111] EB, Speech on Rohilla War Charge, 1 June 1786, *W & S*, VI, pp. 95–96.

[112] See EB, *Ninth Report of the Select Committee* (25 June 1783), *W & S*, V, p. 232.

[113] EB, Speech on Rohilla War Charge, 1 June 1786, *W & S*, VI, p. 109.

[114] Ibid.

a bedrock of public morals against which existing arrangements could be judged. Together with the guidance supplied by judiciously selected experience, the *ius naturae* directed statesmen in their adherence to the principles of justice, disqualifying the resort to arbitrary caprice as a criterion of political conduct.

The same laws of nature that restrained the domestic behaviour of governments formed the basis of legal relations in the international arena. Grotius had begun *The Rights of War and Peace* with the claim that few in the history of philosophical inquiry into the nature of law had examined the foundations of the law of nations—that is, the law that determines relations between states. Moreover, no one had studied it "comprehensively and methodically." [115] In seeking to do so for the first time, Grotius set about undermining the common sceptical insistence on reducing natural justice to self-interest.[116] Burke did not cite Grotius but he shared his purpose and adopted some of his fundamental principles: for both, justice was not reducible to the arbitrary whims of power but was based on the disposition to form orderly social relations.[117] The appetite for society, along with the impulse to self-preservation, was a fundamental part of human nature, intended to comply with the divine purpose: God "willed that there should be such principles in us," as Grotius claimed.[118] Mutual regard underlay relations based on justice, outlawing individual caprice as a viable foundation for human society. Reciprocation of the kind could be generated on the basis of a calculation of interest by anticipating the balance of pleasure and pain in the pursuit of agreement as against conflict.[119] The same utilitarian calculus could yield rules for relations between states, although these were more extensively evident in the common practice of civil societies, frequently exemplified in the literature of the ancients.[120] As Burke put it, while the law of nature was accessible to the reasoning intellect, the law of nations could be ascertained by the "collected experience

[115] Hugo Grotius, "Prolegomena to the First Edition" (1625), *The Rights of War and Peace*, ed. Richard Tuck (Indianapolis, IN: Liberty Fund, 2005), 3 vols., III, p. 1745. For the earlier distinction between the law of nations and a universal civil law in Francisco Suarez, see Annabel Brett, *Changes of State: Nations and the Limits of the City in Early Modern Natural Law* (Princeton, NJ: Princeton University Press, 2011), p. 85.

[116] Thucydides and Carneades are the named targets in Grotius, "Prolegomena to the First Edition" (1625), *Rights of War and Peace*, III, pp. 1745–46. On Grotius' purposes in refuting ancient and modern scepticism, see Richard Tuck, "Grotius, Carneades and Hobbes," *Grotiana*, 4 (1983), pp. 43–62, For Grotius' debt to classical and medieval jurisprudence, see Brian Tierney, *The Idea of Natural Rights: Studies on Natural Rights, Natural Law, and Church Law, 1150–1625* (Michigan, MI: William B. Eerdmans, 1997), ch. 13.

[117] Grotius, "Prolegomena" (1625), *Rights of War and Peace*, III, p. 1747; idem, "Preliminary Discourse" (1631–2), *Rights of War and Peace*, I, pp. 84–85.

[118] Grotius, "Prolegomena" (1625), *Rights of War and Peace*, III, p. 1749. Cf. EB, *Philosophical Enquiry*, pp. 218–20.

[119] Grotius, "Prolegomena" (1625), ibid., III, p. 1748; idem, "Preliminary Discourse," *Rights of War and Peace*, I, p. 87.

[120] *Rights of War and Peace* , III, pp. 1756, 1758.

of ages, the wisdom of antiquity, and the practice of the purest times."[121] Yet there was nothing in this archive that could be found to legitimise the conduct of Warren Hastings.

Burke's ultimate contention was that Hastings's management of affairs in the East Indies contravened the norms of justice that bound governors to their subjects, their allies, and foreign potentates. He claimed that Hastings had flouted these norms as a matter of preferred principle, most conspicuously in his extirpation of the Rohillas. Burke drew attention to what he took to be the basic tendency of Hastings's conduct by citing the published record of his response to the articles of charge. In his defence against the third article of charge, on the treatment of the Raja of Benares, Hastings had referred to the "many *despotic principles* in the Mogul system of government." Where these existed, "the *powers* of the prince" were everything, the "*rights* of the subject nothing."[122] Burke fastened on to declarations of this kind, most usually penned by Hastings's trusted associates, as indicative of the Governor's basic principles of government.[123] They pointed, Burke contended, to an avowed "system of . . . arbitrary power" more repugnant than any other with which he was acquainted.[124] Therefore, not only did this system contravene the laws of nature but, more than this, there did not exist a single example of a comparable code of practice in the annals of the law of nations. Thus, for Burke, the Rohilla war exemplified the spirit of conquest in operation, perpetuating military aggrandisement and political subjugation, thereby resuscitating the goal of usurpation in an age of "doux commerce."[125] For this reason, it enjoyed an important status in the campaign against Hastings, highlighting the former Governor's political attitudes together with their underlying causes that Burke would explore at length when he came to open the impeachment.

[121] EB, Speech on Rohilla War Charge, 1 June 1786, *W & S*, VI, p. 109. For the foundation of natural law in "our rational nature," see EB, *Tracts Relating to Popery Laws* (1756), *W & S*, IX, p. 456.

[122] *Defence of Hastings*, p. 91n. The footnote was added, most likely by one of Hastings's assistants, to the published version of the defence. Burke returned to these claims in EB, Speech in Reply, 28 May 1794, *W & S*, VII, pp. 258–60.

[123] Nine associates contributed to the composition of Hastings's defence, delivered on 1–2 May 1787. On this, see Rosane Rocher, *Orientalism, Poetry and the Millennium: The Checkered Life of Nathaniel Brassy Halhed* (Delhi: Motilal Banarsidass, 1989), pp. 132–35.

[124] EB, Speech on Rohilla War Charge, 1 June 1786, *W & S*, VI, p. 107. Examining John Benn at the Hastings trial in the spring of 1788, Burke concluded that both trade and revenue were exploited at Benares "for the private advantage of Dependants of Mr. Hastings." See Add. MS. 24224, fol. 168.

[125] The phrase is adapted from Charles-Louis de Secondat, Baron de Montesquieu, *De l'esprit des lois* (1748) in *Œuvres complètes*, ed. Roger Caillois (Paris: Gallimard, 1951), 2 vols., II, pt. IV, bk. xx, ch. 1, and is commonly associated with the doctrine that commerce promotes social bargaining, and therewith a disposition to peace. See Albert O. Hirschman, *The Passions and the Interests: Political Arguments for Capitalism before its Triumph* (Princeton, NJ: Princeton University Press, 1977), *passim*, for an overview. On its pathological manifestations after the Seven Years' War, see Muthu, "Adam Smith's Critique of International Trading Companies," pp. 199, 206.

12.4 The Trial Begins: The Government of the Company

In book XX, chapter 2 of the *Spirit of the Laws*, Montesquieu cites Caesar's remark in the *Gallic Wars* to the effect that the commerce of Marseilles had corrupted the mores of the Gauls with the result that, having been formerly the vanquishers of the Germans, they now became their victims.[126] In modern societies such corruption had identifiably positive effects. Trade opened up international commerce, spreading knowledge ("connoisssance") of foreign customs. Knowledge awakened less the will to power than the impulse to compare. That impulse facilitated reciprocation, arising out of mutual dependence, rooted in the spirit of compromise. Market morality, while it reduces individual humanity to a trade in utilities, draws diverse nations towards the arts of peace, replacing the spirit of conquest with "l'esprit de commerce."[127] Modern overseas trade, however, began in conquest rather than mutual dependence: the Portuguese, having rounded the Cape, traded with the East Indies "as conquerors," and the Dutch in due course followed suit. The Spanish meanwhile subjugated great tracts of territory in the west, treating their newly discovered lands as "objets de conquête" where other more refined peoples, like the British and the French, would later discover their potential as "objets de commerce."[128] Burke's clear vision was that in the period after the publication of *The Spirit of the Laws*, and even more intensely after the Treaty of Paris in 1763, the spirit of British commercial enterprise yielded to the spirit of conquest.[129] Clive's successes between the Battle of Plassey and the Treaty of Allahabad in 1765 represented legitimate conquests secured under the rights of war, providing the British with an extended territorial base from which to expand their commerce. However what followed, instead, was a corruption of commerce in the service of political ambition. Hastings, for Burke, was the perfect vehicle for the pathologies that ensued, and the Rohilla war encapsulated his method of procedure.

Burke led his charges against Hastings with the fate of the Rohillas because the Governor's conduct in this connection displayed a range of his tactics, and pointed to the greed that formed their underlying motive. The charges as a whole compose a picture of how this motive was put to work. They covered much of the thirteen years of Hasting's Governorship in Bengal, and related to his management of justice and revenue in the province, his treatment of dependants and allies in the region, and his conduct of external affairs. According to Burke, the pursuit of war and rapacity along with the use of bribes were evident in his handling of foreign relations, while his management of internal affairs was characterised by general corruption: the

[126] Montesquieu, *De l'esprit des lois*, pt. IV, bk. xx, ch. 1n, citing Caesar, *De bello Gallico*, VI, 24.

[127] Montesquieu, *De l'esprit des lois*, pt. IV, bk. xx, chs. 1–2.

[128] Ibid., pt. IV, bk. xxi, ch. 21.

[129] See EB to Lord Loughborough, 24 December 1780, Unpublished Letters, III, p. 950. Adam Smith traces the change to the exact publication date of Montesquieu's work, dating the shift in British conduct to the Treaty of Aix-la-Chapelle. See Smith, *Wealth of Nations*, II, p. 749.

spurious allocation of contracts, the inappropriate award of appointments. Covetousness, disobedience and oppression were conspicuous throughout. The "eyes of Europe" were consequently fixed on the proceedings, as Ernst Brandes assured Burke after his success with the Benares charge in the spring of 1786.[130] By May 1787, a number of further charges had succeeded: the Begams charge, led by Sheridan, passed on 7 February; the Farrukhabad and Faizullah Khan charges were carried in March; the Presents and Revenue charges were accepted in April; and the "Misdemeanours in Oude" charge passed in May.[131] The articles of impeachment, as these were drafted by Burke, his assistants and their legal advisors, comprised just under half of the original articles of charge, rearranged and subdivided in the interest of legal clarity and precision.[132] These included allegations of taking bribes, mishandling the revenues and the abuse of contracts, but they focused above all on Hastings's activities outside the borders of Bengal and Bihar, where he was accused of abusing his power in connection with Indian rulers.[133] After the Commons had approved the impeachment on 10 May, Burke presented his twenty articles to the Lords between the 14th and the 28th of the same month.

By the close of the parliamentary session Burke was relieved: "The House of Commons has cleared itself of the stain which its Eastern Government has fixed upon the nation."[134] The first stage of what Burke termed his "long Indian Journey" was now complete. In the interval before the next leg, which would last until the early summer of 1794, the legal "Caravan" had a chance to pause, "and our Camels may unload and rest."[135] It remained to be seen how the Lords would respond to the allegations brought by the lower House. The new parliamentary session opened in late November, with the impeachment beginning in February 1788. A committee of managers was selected to prosecute the trial, with Philip Francis dramatically excluded from their number—a "blow," as Burke admitted, to his management of an affair that was nearest to his heart of any issue "in the World."[136] The previous July, he was already conscious of difficulties that lay ahead. A number of bishops were known to be sympathetic to Hastings's cause, leaving the task of defending Christian principles to members other than the Lords Spiritual.[137] Burke was equally doubtful about the intentions of a number of Law Lords whom he expected would tie the managers to technical forms of pleading, confining them to the strictest rules of evidence.[138] The jurisprudence of the upper House had grown self-consciously

[130] Ernst Brandes to EB, 12 January 1787, *Corr.*, V, p. 306.

[131] Marshall, *Impeachment of Hastings*, pp. 52–58.

[132] EB, Articles of Impeachment, 14–28 May 1787, *W & S*, VI, pp. 125–258.

[133] See the summary presented by Marshall in ibid., pp. 127–33.

[134] EB to Thomas Burgh, 1 July 1787, *Corr.*, V, pp. 340–41.

[135] Ibid., p. 340.

[136] EB to Henry Dundas, 7 December 1787, ibid., p. 360. Burke was terribly anxious to secure Francis's local knowledge for the prosecution: see EB to Dundas, ibid., p. 361; EB to Philip Francis, 18 December 1787, ibid., p. 370.

[137] EB to Thomas Burgh, 1 July 1787, ibid., p. 341.

[138] Ibid.

specialised, rendering its procedures increasingly "unparliamentarily," as Burke saw it: the professionalism of the judicial process made the lawyers suspicious of grand causes.[139] It was therefore essential to secure Westminster Hall as the venue for the proceedings, exposing the Lords to the scrutiny of the public, imposing some kind of check upon their collective judgment by making them sensitive to the sentiments of humanity.[140]

"The Trial, so long impending, of Mr. Hastings opened today," as Fanny Burney signalled the event in her diary entry for 13 February 1788.[141] The business began around twelve in the afternoon, as the managers for the prosecution arrived with Burke at their head, his brow knit with "deep labouring thought."[142] Two days later, after the preliminaries, Burke began in earnest to address the assembled peers and commoners.[143] His great speech would last from Friday 15 to Tuesday 19 February, taking up between three and four hours of the afternoon on each of the first two days, a further three hours the day after and two hours on the final day. Burney described her reaction to the second day of Burke's speech, recording the mixture of fluent narrative and thunderous declamation that characterised the performance. His style, she claimed, was brilliant and absorbing, even to suspicious auditors such as she was. Copious stores of information, quotation and allusion dazzled those present, with sudden bursts of vivid depiction captivating even the sceptics in the audience.[144] Against all expectation, Robert Stewart, later Viscount Castlereagh, informed his mother, "Burke's wild imagination travel'd within the bounds of reason."[145] This was a trial of the quality of British justice, and Burke rose to the solemnity of the occasion. The fundamentals of "State morality" were at stake, and with them the legitimacy of the British constitution itself.[146]

In the months before the impeachment got under way, Burke became acutely aware of the "load upon my Shoulders," as he felt a weight of responsibility which few, he thought, would be able to "conceive."[147] The enormous burden of the preparatory work was almost complete, and Burke set by a period in which to recover. Nonetheless, after years of anticipation, the proximity of the trial filled him with "moments of nausea."[148] Then illness struck in the days before the event, straining

[139] Ibid. See Marshall, *Impeachment of Hastings*, pp. 64, 68; William Holdsworth, *A History of the English Law* (London: Methuen, 1903–52), X, pp. 609–11. Professionalisation among the Law Lords steadily progressed into the nineteenth century: see Arthur Turberville, *The House of Lords in the Age of Reform, 1784–1837* (Fair Lawn, NJ: Essential Books, 1958).

[140] EB to Thomas Burgh, 1 July 1787, *Corr.*, V, p. 341; EB to General Burgoyne, 7 November 1787, ibid., p. 358.

[141] Fanny Burney, *Diary and Letters of Madame D'Arblay* (Philadelphia, PA: Carey and Hart, 1842), 2 vols., II, p. 28.

[142] Ibid., p. 29.

[143] *LJ*, XXXVIII, p. 80.

[144] Burney, *Diary*, II, pp. 48–49.

[145] Robert Stewart to Lady Frances Stewart, post 19 February 1788, OSB MS. File 9225.

[146] EB, Speech on the Opening of Impeachment, 15 February 1788, *W & S*, VI, pp. 271–72.

[147] EB to Henry Dundas, 7 December 1787, *Corr.*, V, p. 362.

[148] EB to Philip Francis, c. 3 January 1788, ibid, p. 372.

his voice and sapping his general spirits.[149] However, when the moment arrived, with ticket-holders flocking into the court from around 9:30 in the morning, Burke grew energised. A faint hoarseness in his voice could still be detected, but as soon as he had launched himself into the case he became animated, inspired by the sheer "magnitude of the surrounding multitude," stirred by the "awfulness" of the occasion.[150] On one side of the Hall the representatives of the Commons and of the crowned heads of Europe were seated; on the other, the peeresses and the general public were assembled.[151] As he began to present his arguments against Hastings, Burke was aware that he was wielding a vital constitutional resource that distinguished the constitution of Great Britain. Impeachment, he declared, "is the individuating principle that makes England what England is."[152] It offered a means of subjecting magistracy to inspection and control. Just over a year before the advent of the French Revolution, Burke found the politics of Europe in a state of agitation, with many established securities to liberty being discarded.[153] In that context, the deployment of such an inveterate legal instrument as impeachment in order to restrain the abuse of public power stood as a lesson to the wanton innovations of the Continent.[154]

The aim of Burke's opening speech was to establish that Hastings's conduct during his period as Governor General represented a connected system of criminality, informed throughout by a set of malign maxims. Hastings's behaviour, he insisted, was not the product of error; nor was it explicable in terms of ordinary human frailty.[155] Burke could perfectly appreciate how the pressure of circumstances in a demanding and unfamiliar situation might adversely affect a statesman's adherence to the rules of propriety. However, the activities of the Governor General amounted to a series of drastic offences against what Burke described as the "eternal laws of justice."[156] Ordinary municipal regulations were inadequate to the task of trying such violations against basic norms. For this purpose, a wider "Imperial justice" appeared requisite, since the impeachment concerned the oppression of a remote and diverse population, culminating in the denial of their fundamental rights. In notes for a speech on India drafted two years earlier, Burke had outlined the content of these basic entitlements. The "great End of all Government," he proposed, was the protection of the life, liberty and property of the subject, and the specific forms into which government might be cast could only be justified in terms of their ability to serve that purpose.[157] At a minimum, imperial justice, vindicating the "cause of Asia in the presence of Europe," ought to guarantee the security of these entitlements,

[149] EB to Edmond Malone, 12 February 1788, ibid., p. 379.
[150] *Morning Herald*, 16 February 1788; *World*, 16 February 1788.
[151] *Gazetteer*, 16 February 1788.
[152] EB, Speech on the Opening of Impeachment, 15 February 1788, *W & S*, VI, p. 272.
[153] WWM BkP 9:67.
[154] EB, Speech on the Opening of Impeachment, 15 February 1788, *W & S*, VI, p. 272.
[155] Ibid., pp. 271–74.
[156] Ibid., p. 275.
[157] Northamptonshire MS. A. XXVIII.7.

conferred on civil societies by natural law. It was in terms of these universal obligations that a Christian power could be held accountable in the exercise of its authority over distinct religious communities rooted in ancient civilisations.[158]

While Burke held Hastings to be accountable under comprehensive laws of nature, he also recognised that he was responsible to a more tangible tribunal. The Governor's authority had been delegated by the East India Company, which was itself answerable for the exercise of its powers. In the first place it was answerable to the terms of its charter, granted by act of parliament since 1698.[159] From hence it derived its existence as a corporate entity, responsible to the "supreme power of this kingdom," which confided power without ceding sovereignty.[160] Secondly, the Company received its powers under the authority of the Mughal Emperor, above all by its grant of *Diwani* over Bengal, Bihar and Orissa in 1765. With this grant of civil jurisdiction, the Company was obliged to serve the welfare of the natives, an obligation annexed to the office of *Diwan* in perpetuity, irrespective of what might befall the Emperor himself. In accepting responsibility for the powers thus bestowed on the Company, the British government implicitly contracted with the Mughal Empire to promote the interest of the population for which they shared responsibility. This established, Burke contended, a "virtual union" between both polities, whereby they were jointly obliged to preserve the rights and liberties of their subjects.[161]

The Company's exercise of jurisdiction on these terms had itself been a complex development, starting with the corporation's original commercial purpose and culminating in its recent status as a territorial power. As a trading company operating in a remote theatre, exposed to competition and armed rivalry from the start, any absolute distinction between the politics and commerce of the corporation had always been more notional than real. Since "its intercourse was with many great, some barbarous, and all of them armed nations, where not only the Sovereign but the Subjects were also armed in all places," it was found necessary to enlarge the powers of the Company early on.[162] The most dramatic increase in its prerogatives occurred during the reign of Charles II. First rights of naval discipline, then martial law, and then criminal jurisdiction—over factories, settlements and servants—were conferred upon what was in theory a commercial enterprise. With the transfer of the powers of war and peace, it seemed that in practice "the whole power and sovereignty" of the British government had been "sent into the East."[163] This created a novel political and juridical arrangement, whereby a subordinate sovereign power operated under the authority of a remote superior, thus making it practically sovereign from the

[158] EB, Speech on the Opening of Impeachment, 15 February 1788, *W & S*, VI, pp. 278–79, 307.

[159] Originating as a royal charter in 1600, the grant was authorised by parliament from the end of the seventeenth century. See W. R. Scott, *The Constitution and Finance of English, Scottish and Irish Joint Stock Companies to 1720* (Cambridge: Cambridge University Press, 1910–12), 3 vols., II, pp. 89–179.

[160] EB, Speech on the Opening of Impeachment, 15 February 1788, *W & S*, VI, pp. 280–81.

[161] Ibid., pp. 281–82.

[162] Ibid., p. 282.

[163] Ibid., p. 283.

point of view of its subjects, yet dependent upon parliament as the original source of this high trust. It wore the appearance, therefore, of a company-state: an international actor exercising an array of civil functions, answerable to a European power.[164]

This novel combination of features had come about, Burke noted, by an inversion of the known development of political societies. In the ordinary course of events, commonwealths were first founded before trade could be pursued, since commerce required the protection of a political establishment to proceed. With the pursuit of overseas enterprise on the part of the East India Company, however, that order was reversed so that the commercial concerns pursued by a trading organisation became subordinated to the political ambitions that accompanied its expanding territorial rights. This expansion took place against the background of the rise of European power and the comparative decrease in the military competitiveness of its Asian rivals, forming the Company by degrees into a "great Empire, carrying on subordinately . . . a great commerce."[165] This combination of attributes became conspicuous in the eighteenth century, especially as the century progressed. It created conditions under which the deployment of British power took place in the context of a confusion of roles: the role of *dominus* on the one hand, and that of *mercator* on the other.[166] Potentially this confusion was highly consequential, since the duty of a ruler was to promote the interest of his subjects while the duty of a trader was to promote his own advantage.[167] A reversal of roles, Burke saw, would convert the East India Company into a territorial power bent on the pursuit of its advantage at the expense of natives subject to its jurisdiction. It was this unpropitious mixture of characteristics that had so manifestly disturbed Adam Smith. A "company of merchants," he remarked, "are, it seems, incapable of considering themselves as sovereigns, even after they have become such."[168] By this he did not mean that they had no interest in power: like Burke he came to see how much this was a commodity after which they hankered. The problem was that they strove for power for the purpose of securing their private interest—that is, with a view to commercial rather than public utility.

There were two problems associated with this prioritisation. First, in seeking its private over the public advantage, in line with what a trading corporation was expected to do, the Company put itself in conflict with the welfare of the population it ruled. But, at the same time, in assuming substantial political responsibilities, the Company began to misconstrue its original commercial vocation. On the one hand, it transformed itself from a profit-seeking into a rent-demanding organisation, as

[164] This mixture of characteristics forms the basis of the historical analysis provided by Philip J. Stern, *The Company-State: Corporate Sovereignty and the Early Modern Foundations of the British Empire in India* (Oxford: Oxford University Press, 2011).

[165] EB, Speech on the Opening of Impeachment, 15 February 1788, *W & S*, VI, p. 283.

[166] Burke mentions the distinction in Roman law between the power appropriate to "a Trader" and that which should be wielded by "a Lord" in ibid., p. 283.

[167] Unless, of course, the relationship comprised that between *dominus* and *servus*, in which case the rule was in the interest of the master and therefore, by Aristotelian definition, despotic in nature.

[168] Smith, *Wealth of Nations*, II, p. 637. For discussion, see Muthu, "Adam Smith's Critique of International Trading Companies," pp. 200–201.

Burke had emphasised at length in his *Ninth Report*, and as Smith observed in the third edition of the *Wealth of Nations*: revenue, rather than trade, came to dominate its agenda.[169] On the other hand, with the growth of territorial power came an expansion of opportunities for place and patronage, the quest for which began to absorb Company servants on the ground and to animate the Directors and Proprietors in London. As Smith noted, the government of the Company in this way received a share in the appointment of the "plunderers" of the country, and therefore lacked the incentive to curtail their thirst for booty.[170] A forced trade in booty should not be confused with commercial traffic, and the government of such an enterprise is not driven by business acumen. Neither commercial nor political in nature, the Company became an instrument of avaricious extraction—strictly, a bureaucracy bent upon exploitation.[171] In perversely marrying politics and trade, it corrupted the character of both, transforming itself into an engine of economic oppression at the expense of any provincial or imperial benefit.

From Burke's perspective, this overriding pathology did not derive from the methods of East Indian administration so much as from the fundamental character of the government. The Company's means of administering its territories provided ample occasions for enforcing responsibility. The problem was that, although accountability ascended upwards, there was no point at which the welfare of the natives became an official concern. As a "State in the disguise of a Merchant," the corporation had preserved the forms and structures appropriate to a mercantile venture, albeit infusing these with the ambitions of the politician.[172] As a bureaucracy, the organisation retained the system of subordination together with the mechanisms of scrutiny characteristic of a corporate business enterprise. As instruments of administration, these provided effective means for affecting accountability—in this sense, national government might usefully learn from the procedures of the "Counting-house."[173] Company servants and counsellors were obliged to record and report their activities to their superiors, thus creating a paper trail amounting to a "government of writing": "it was in the power of a man siting in London to form an accurate

[169] EB, *Ninth Report of the Select Committee* (25 June 1783), *W & S*, V, pp. 222–3; Smith, *Wealth of Nations*, II, pp. 750–51. The extant literature comparing the economic ideas of Burke and Smith tends to ignore their shared views about the political economy of India. See Donal Barrington, "Edmund Burke as Economist," *Economica*, 21:83 (August 1954), pp. 252–8; W. L. Dunnes, "Adam Smith and Burke: Complementary Contemporaries," *Southern Economic Journal*, 71 (1941), pp. 330–46; Rod Preece, "The Political Economy of Edmund Burke," *Modern Age*, 24:3 (Summer 1980), pp. 266–73; Francis Canavan, *The Political Economy of Edmund Burke: The Role of Property in His Thought* (New York: Fordham University Press, 1995), ch. 6. The fullest comparison is in Donald Winch, *Riches and Poverty: An Intellectual History of Political Economy in Britain, 1750–1834* (Cambridge: Cambridge University Press, 1996), chs. 7 and 8.

[170] Smith, *Wealth of Nations*, II, p. 752. Burke presented the same argument in EB, *Ninth Report of the Select Committee* (25 June 1783), *W & S*, V, p. 201.

[171] EB, ibid., *passim*; Smith, *Wealth of Nations*, II, pp. 752–54.

[172] EB, Speech on the Opening of Impeachment, 15 February 1786, *W & S*, VI, pp. 283–84.

[173] Ibid., p. 296.

judgment of every thing that happened upon the Ganges."[174] This enabled the Directors to track the activities of servants, and to appraise their executive integrity and capacity. Effective monitoring presupposed a delineated system of subordination, and this was provided by the constitution of the Company, which organised its members into stratified gradations, spanning writers, factors, junior merchants, senior merchants, counsellors, presidencies and the governorship. Promotion was determined by probation over time. Each level was thus intended as an apprenticeship to the next rung, generating a hierarchy of competence and authority.[175] If these regulatory structures had ever been configured with a view to serving the interest of Indians, magisterial control could have been easily implemented. However, nothing of the kind was ever attempted. Indeed, as Burke maintained, the whole edifice was unceremoniously dismantled by Hastings, the better to promote the advantage of the Company to the detriment of its subject multitudes.[176] This made Hastings more than a mere a cog in the machine: he was, in fact, perfectly adapted to a system of endemic mismanagement, which he went beyond the bounds of duty in endeavouring to perfect. Herein lay his peculiar culpability.

A striking example of Hastings's subversion of established gradations came with his establishment of the Committee of Revenue in 1781, designed to put the temporary and avowedly inadequate system of tax collection established in 1773 on a durable and coherent basis. Hastings embarked upon the scheme after the departure of Philip Francis for Europe, leaving him in charge of the Calcutta Council now that his opponents had all "sickened, died, and fled."[177] The aim of the reform was to centralise the administration of the revenue with a view to reducing the costs of collection. This was to be achieved by the establishment of a four-member Committee of Revenue, assisted by Ganga Govind Singh as *Diwan*.[178] Burke would in due course inveigh against the calibre of this *Diwan*, but for the moment he noted how the new appointments fell to Hastings—awarded, as it seemed, on the basis of personal patronage. This potentially bestowed on Committee members an authority unconnected with ability or experience, disrupting the order of seniority in the Company. Just as Hastings broke in upon the established hierarchy of offices, he also undermined the accountability of officers by relaxing the duty to record correspondence and by employing agents on Company business whose primary loyalty was to the Governor himself.[179] It seemed clear that Hastings's actions were woven into a systematic scheme of abuse. "He ought to be forced to produce his Letter

[174] Ibid., pp. 296–97.

[175] Ibid., p. 284.

[176] Ibid., p. 285.

[177] G. R. Gleig ed., *Memoirs of the Life of the Right Honourable Warren Hastings* (London: 1841), 3 vols., II, p. 330.

[178] Dodwell ed., *Cambridge History*, p. 427.

[179] EB, Speech on the Opening of Impeachment, 15 February 1788, *W & S*, VI, p. 298.

Books," Burke insisted to Dundas in March of the previous year.[180] Earlier that same month, he had written to John Michie, a senior official at Leadenhall Street, urging him to fill the outstanding gaps in Company correspondence caused by Hastings's disregard for the standing orders of the Court of Directors.[181] Hastings flouted the rules, Burke felt, as a means of covering his tracks. The Court had requested him to complete his files, yet he claimed that there was nothing he had withheld.[182] Burke took him to be indulging in prevarication and dissimulation as a means of escaping the scrutiny of his seniors, and with that any regulation of his behaviour.[183]

On 5 April 1787 Burke had written to Dundas complaining of Hastings's refusal to deliver up the papers of William Palmer and William Davy, his military secretary and Persian translator respectively, both of whom had been sent to Awadh in 1782 to negotiate a loan with the Wazir, Asaf-ud-Daula, and to transfer a "present" to Hastings.[184] These proceedings, Burke reckoned, were typical of the Governor, involving at once manipulation and peculation. Palmer remained in Awadh as Hasting's representative, thus supplanting the official Awadh resident, while neither his nor Davy's correspondence was publicly recorded.[185] Typically, as Burke saw it, Hastings had bypassed the official structures, and then evaded the possibility of scrutiny. Burke was not optimistic about recovering the evidence from Hastings: "He will have time enough to have fresh Copies made . . . leaving out and falsifying as he pleases."[186] This is what had become of the ethos of service and the government by correspondence which might have facilitated an equitable administration of the territories: they were replaced by personal rule carried on through clandestine machinations. Three circumstances favoured these irregular proceedings, as Burke saw things. First, the youth of Company servants counted against their circumspection, as they eagerly indulged their expectations of gain without education into a code of honour or restraint. Such men were even appointed to preside in the lower courts, exercising jurisdiction without any commitment to impartial justice.[187] Second, the system of emoluments was ineffective: great offices were rewarded with pay rather than reputation while the occupants of the lower positions were left to prey on the population.[188] Finally, the service was animated by a tight *esprit de corps* which rendered its members averse to outside accountability. Servants appeared in Asia as

[180] EB to Henry Dundas, 29 March 1787, *Corr.*, V, p. 317.

[181] EB to John Michie, 14 March 1787, ibid., pp. 309–10.

[182] The Court of Directors approached Hastings on 21 March 1787: Add. MS. 29170. Hastings responded within two days: *Papers Relative to Hastings' Impeachment* (London: 1786–7), 3 vols., II, p. 988.

[183] These arguments were later to figure prominently in the trial itself. See Add. MS. 24226, fols. 271–72, for typical comments by Burke on Hastings's attempts to destroy all proof of his guilt.

[184] EB to Henry Dundas, 5 April 1787, *Corr.*, V, p. 321.

[185] Hastings defended his actions in a letter to the Court of Directors on 23 March 1787. See *Papers Relative to Hastings' Impeachment*, II, p. 988.

[186] EB to Henry Dundas, 5 April 1787, *Corr.*, V, p. 321.

[187] EB, Speech on the Opening of Impeachment, 15 February 1788, *W & S*, VI, p. 288.

[188] Ibid., pp. 286–87.

merchant-visitors rather than colonial settlers, keeping them out of sympathy with the natives. They were closed in upon themselves, a mini republic in isolation, wielding public power without any connection to the population—amounting to "a Nation of placement," a "Kingdom of Magistrates."[189]

A further, external resource promoted parasitism on the subcontinent. Indian commercial agents, or banians, in European service mediated between senior Company servants and the native population—playing the role, in Burke's reconstruction, of eunuchs in an unhappy seraglio. Banians were for the most part descended from the merchant or Vaishya caste. While they were therefore disrespected in their original station, they were elevated into a relatively commanding position by their association with European traders.[190] Among the British their reputation for dissimulation was well publicised. A letter sent in 1767 from William Bolts to the then President of the Calcutta Council, Harry Verelst, included as an appendix to his *Considerations on Indian Affairs*, highlights the "political wiles and customs of the Banyans."[191] They tended, Bolts had earlier explained, to act at once as "interpreter, head book-keeper, head secretary, head broker, the supplier of cash and cash-keeper, and in general also secret-keeper" to the British.[192] Burke regarded them as depraved intermediaries, bred to baseness and the arts of subterfuge by an "apprenticeship in servility."[193] Their breeding at the same time made them skilful oppressors, trained in "all the artifices and contrivances, by which abject slavery secures itself against the violence of oppression."[194] Coming into the power of these conniving hirelings, British masters were being captured by their own native agents and inured to a culture of treachery and oppression.[195] This completed Burke's outline of the constitution of the Company: the pursuit of trade had given way to the pursuit of power; power was sought as a privilege instead of a public benefit; the Directors and Proprietors had no investment in the welfare of the natives; the servants operated at a distance from the local population, with senior traders transacting business through an intriguing class of brokers.

[189] Ibid., pp. 285–86.

[190] C. A. Bayly, *Indian Society and The Making of the British Empire* (Cambridge: Cambridge University Press, 1988, 1993), pp. 55, 72. Some banians had been Brahmins, but for the most part they rose from humble origins. For a general treatment, see P. J. Marshall, "Masters and Banians in Eighteenth-Century Calcutta" in Blair B. Kling and M. N. Pearson eds., *The Age of Partnership: Europeans in Asia before Dominion* (Honolulu: University of Hawaii Press, 1979).

[191] William Bolts, *Considerations on India Affairs, Particularly Respecting the Present State of Bengal and its Dependencies* (London: 1772), p. 473.

[192] Ibid., I, pp. 83–84.

[193] Northamptonshire MS. A. XIV.10.

[194] EB, Speech on the Opening of Impeachment, 15 February 1788, *W & S*, VI, pp. 292–3.

[195] Ibid., pp. 293–94; cf. EB, "Observations" to the *First Report* of the Select Committee (5 February 1782), *W & S*, V, p. 184.

12.5 The Trial Continues: Native Rule and European Conquest

Burke was now three quarters of the way through the first instalment of his speech, and at this point turned from his treatment of the banians to characterise the population as a whole, dealing first with the original Hindu inhabitants and then examining the impact of successive Muslim invasions on the society and politics of South Asia. Burke faced the task of having to depict the customs of peoples of considerable antiquity who had been the subjects of complex processes of historical development. His aim throughout was to contrast the relations between the Hindu and Muslim inhabitants with the later arrangements introduced under the British. He began with an account of India's oldest civilisation. While the Hindu culture of the country exhibited a peculiar stability, rooted in the continuity of its socio-religious institutions, its adherents were also singularly sensitive to being subject to disgrace, and vulnerable to exploitation on that account.[196] The Hindu faithful seemed to Burke to be expressly uncosmopolitan in manners while nonetheless being well disposed to the rich diversity of creation. They were bound fast to the integrity of their own traditions, just as they were fixed to the locality of their own soil.[197] Correspondingly, they avoided conspicuous hospitality, yet still operated within a framework of general benevolence. On account of their unalterable commitment to their inherited ways of life, they remained deeply resistant to cultural penetration, and would therefore have to be governed in accordance with their own persuasions. The manners, social order and religious precepts that constituted the empire of opinion among Hindus amounted to a uniform set of attitudes and practices distinguished from the diverse streams from which European culture had been composed—the "mixed system of opinion and sentiment," as Burke presented it in in the *Reflections on the Revolution in France*, that had "given its character to modern Europe."[198] By comparison, piety and honour within Hindu civilisation comprised a single coherent code of behaviour and belief. It would take considerable violence to disassemble this consolidated ethic, and it would be sacrilege ever to attempt to do so.[199]

Caste was the central fact of Hindu civilisation, giving rise to a form of life that was turned in upon itself, while still being well disposed towards outsiders: outward benevolence, Burke surmised, had grown all the more affordable as a consequence of communal confidence.[200] Separation between the orders themselves was likewise categorical, virtually compartmentalising each of the four castes into distinct commonwealths, defined by their own duties, occupations and ceremonies. Any violation of the precepts of one's own caste carried with it the penalty of permanent

[196] EB, Speech on the Opening of Impeachment, *W & S*, 15 February 1788, VI, pp. 301, 305.

[197] Ibid., p. 301.

[198] EB, *Reflections*, ed. Clark, pp. 238–39 [113].

[199] EB, Speech on the Opening of Impeachment, 15 February 1788, *W & S*, VI, pp. 302–3.

[200] Ibid., p. 302.

exclusion, and exclusion meant excommunication from society at large: "speak to an Indian of his caste, and you speak to him of his all."[201] Being shamed was not only a temporal affliction; it also carried pollution into the hereafter. And since disgrace might be incurred involuntarily, or even imposed on unwilling victims from outside, the Hindus were left exposed to the threat of external defilement. Moreover, they were vulnerable to oppression on the strength of that external threat—a situation which, in Burke's eyes, Hastings was happy to exploit.[202] There was nothing that a would-be conqueror might not achieve if he resorted to this instrument of tyranny. In resorting to it, Hastings was able to reduce the Hindus in a way previous marauders never could to the sorry status of a "conquered people."[203]

Burke admitted that, prima facie, Hastings's precursors were more likely to subjugate the Hindu population than the enlightened empire that British power supposedly represented. Yet, remarkably, the opposite proved to be the case: the "era of the Prophet Mahomet" had opened the way to three waves of invasion, all of which proved more conducive to pacific accommodation than the European era that succeeded them. The first wave comprised an Arab incursion into central Asia under the Umayyad Caliphate in the seventh and eighth centuries. This was followed, in Burke's narrative, by the second main incidence of central Asian conquest, this time perpetrated in the fourteenth century by the Tartar chief Timur, largely with a view to ousting his Muslim predecessors.[204] The final instalment of Muslim penetration took place in the sixteenth century under Emperor Akbar, who brought Bengal under Mughal rule in 1576. Akbar, like Timur, supplanted a dynasty without, strictly speaking, conquering the country. In both cases, native princes and landholders were preserved in possession of their property and authority, forming the country into a republic of rulers under a common head.[205] This depiction differed considerably from the picture of a uniform despotism grafted onto a nation of inveterate slaves such as had dominated European representations down to 1748. Burke directly challenged Montesquieu's presentation: Muslim conquerors, Burke conceded, had indeed been ardent enthusiasts, disposed to spread the despotism to which their religion was inclined.[206] Yet in practice Islamic usurpation accommodated what it could not subdue, transcending the "destructive spirit" which Montesquieu claimed as its foundation.[207] It was this earlier, Montesquieuian account to which Hastings appealed when painting himself as the inheritor of the mantle

[201] Ibid., p. 303.

[202] Ibid., p. 304. Hastings's willingness to place his own banian, Krishna Kanta Nandy ("Cantoo Baboo"), in judgment over Brahmins was one of Burke's favourite examples of his preparedness to violate the rules of caste. See ibid., pp. 294–95.

[203] Ibid., p. 309.

[204] These events are covered in James Fraser, "A Short History of the Hindostan Emperors, Beginning with Temur" in idem, *The History of Nadir Shah, Formerly Called Thamas Kuli Khan, the Present Emperor of Persia* (London: 1742).

[205] EB, Speech on the Opening of Impeachment, *W & S*, VI, 15 February 1788, pp. 307–10.

[206] Ibid., p. 307.

[207] Montesquieu, *De l'esprit des lois,* pt. V, bk. xxiv, ch. 4.

of Genghis Khan, as he had done in his defence against the Benares charge in 1787: ultimately, he hoped, the arbitrary maxims of his Asian precursors might give way to the "liberal spirit of the British legislature," but for the present the inhabitants of India were habituated to the remnants of the "Mogul system."[208]

The next stage of Burke's narrative was crucial to his argument. It covered the decline of central Mughal authority, the emergence of imperial viceroys into relative independence, competition among European powers during the War of the Austrian Succession, and the establishment of British paramountcy after the Seven Years' War. It was during what Burke termed this "era of the independent Soubahs" that European power advanced on the subcontinent, and Burke's aim was to analyse the legitimacy of its progress.[209] In *The Annual Register* for 1761, Burke had included an excerpt from Richard Cambridge's *Account of the War in India* which charted the progress of war between the British and the French on the Coromandel coast after 1750, and which opened with a general overview of the recent history of the subcontinent, focusing on the military capacity of the home-grown population.[210] At the outset, Cambridge explained how the peninsula never was completely subordinated to Mughal authority until the reign of Aurangzeb. But almost immediately, with the death of Aurangzeb in 1707, and above all after the capture of the Mughal Emperor by Nadir Shah in February 1739, the power of Delhi precipitously declined, with authority and initiative shifting to the Nawabs in the provinces.[211] What struck Cambridge was how a mere "handful of Europeans" could influence so dramatically the politics of these provinces.[212] The answer lay in the tactics adopted by Indian armies. While the Emperor's cavalry was impressive, his infantry was under-resourced, and discipline in general was insufficiently imposed. At the same time, mounted soldiers feared for the safety of their horses before British canon, while supporting troops were inexpert in the use of artillery.[213] It was against this background, Burke noted, and in the context of the British military struggle against the French, that the "power, force and efficacy of European discipline" began to be felt in open contests with provincial governors.[214]

The most famous of these contests came in 1756 with Siraj-ud-Daula's attempt on the British settlement in Calcutta, avenged by Robert Clive a year later at the Battle of Plassey. It was from that point that Burke dated the British "patronage" of Bengal, whereby the East India Company usurped the provincial power of the

[208] *Defence of Hastings*, pp. 101–2n.

[209] EB, Speech on the Opening of Impeachment, 15 February 1788, *W & S*, VI, p. 311.

[210] "Characters" in *The Annual Register for the Year 1761* (London: 1762), pp. 6–10, amounting to lightly edited excerpts from Cambridge, *An Account of the War in India*, pp. xxiii–xxxviii.

[211] Cambridge, *An Account of the War in India*, pp. xxiii–xxiv.

[212] Ibid., p. xxvi.

[213] Ibid., pp. xxxi–xxxii.

[214] EB, Speech on the Opening of Impeachment, 16 February 1788, *W & S*, VI, p. 316.

Nawabs.[215] In doing so they were succeeding to an unstable political system presided over in the recent past by habituated tyrants.[216] Reflecting on the fate of the Nawabs during the "era" of the Subahdars, Burke commented that it was their independence that brought about their ruin. When Alivardi Khan became Nawab in 1740, he did so by destroying the incumbent, Sarfaraz Khan, in the process demonstrating how the resort to arms paved the way to an acquisition of power.[217] Alivardi's reign was plagued by successive Maratta raids, leaving the province depleted upon the accession of Siraj-ud-Daula.[218] It was with this history behind them that the British secured Bengal, succeeding by force of arms to the responsibilities of government. "There is a secret veil to be drawn over the beginnings of all governments," Burke observed in this context.[219] Power most usually has its roots in the brutal fact of violence, which may be justified by the rights of war or the demands of necessity.[220] But war only gives way to peace by pronouncing an amnesty on the past, and then employing moderation to consolidate the new regime: conciliating the vanquished by conforming to their opinions and instituting a regular system of justice. The transfer of power in Bengal was achieved by force and usurpation, on the back of timely initiative and military virtue. While the business could be justified, it could not be wholly admired; prudence and discretion dictated burying it in obscurity on the understanding that a new era marked an opportunity for reconstruction.[221] Reconstruction would be necessary since the status quo was not an option: the British were coming in the footsteps of a succession of brutal rulers lacking any prescriptive claim to authority in the country.[222]

Like all conquests, the conquest over Bengal had been achieved through revolution. As an event, the revolution could be justified as an act of necessity, but it could only win legitimacy by establishing regular government, and thus by bringing the process of revolution to an end.[223] Burke was clear that the British revolution should put a stop to revolutions of the kind that had been initiated by Alivardi Khan. Instead, it became a trigger for still more.[224] This outcome required an explanation

[215] Ibid. The phrase "patronage" echoes Cicero's definition of the Roman Empire as a *patrocinium* of the world: see *De officiis*, II, 27.

[216] Burke emphasises the usurpations and cruelty of the Nawabs in oppressing Zamindars and Rajas in his notes on John Zephaniah Holwell, *Interesting Historical Events Relative to the Provinces of Bengal and the Empire of Indostan* (London: 1766–77), 2 vols., at Northamptonshire MS. A. XIV.6A.

[217] Burke's narrative here depends on Holwell, *Interesting Historical Events*, I, pp. 70ff. For his use of this material, see EB to Philip Francis, 13 April 1788, *Corr.*, V, p. 387.

[218] EB, Speech on the Opening of Impeachment, 15 February 1788, *W & S*, VI, p. 311.

[219] Ibid., pp. 316–17. On this theme, cf. EB, *Reflections*, ed. Clark, p. 166 [25].

[220] This bloody origin of regimes is likewise emphasised in Holwell, *Interesting Historical Events*, I, pp. 17–19.

[221] EB, Speech on the Opening of Impeachment, 16 February 1788, *W & S*, VI, p. 317.

[222] Ibid., p. 315.

[223] This was the only way to "justifye" the "mysterious ways of almighty providence" by which British dominion had been acquired over a country with which "Nature almost forbad intercourse." See Northamptonshire MS. A. XIV.6A.

[224] EB, Speech on the Opening of Impeachment, 16 February 1788, *W & S*, VI, p. 317.

since it thwarted expectations of the disposition of British power. As an enlightened European state, it was reasonable to hope it would establish a regular administration, putting an end to capricious personal rule. Indeed, as the "most enlightened" regime coming from the enlightened portion of the European continent, an impartial administration based on popular consent might in addition have been expected.[225] Impartiality would entail securing property by the rule of law, and consent would amount to governing in accordance with native opinion. Burke's thought seems to have been that enlightened British power comprised a system of regulated justice under a tolerant and representative regime. The practice of toleration was an enlightened product of the "reformed religion," making the world safe for liberal politics and civil justice.[226] What distinguished the British constitution in Europe was precisely this combination of features. The security of property had been made compatible with a popularly instituted political regime. Popular consent was embodied in a parliamentary system without prejudice to the impartiality of the laws. When power fell to this species of government via a corporate delegate in the east, it was to be expected that British principles would guide the construction of a constitution in Bengal: while it was impractical to expect that a properly representative regime could be established, nonetheless native opinion could be rigorously respected, a jury system could be instituted, and impartial laws attuned to local customs could be administered.[227]

In broad outline, this arrangement would involve fidelity to British principles while amounting to a restoration of the ancient Mughal constitution, established on the subcontinent before the tyranny of the independent Nawabs.[228] Guided by the example of enlightened British practice, this restoration might then have been improved by consensual reforms implemented gradually over time. Burke's approval of the possible introduction of a jury system provides an example of a possible agenda for reform.[229] Toleration, civil liberty, improved accountability and government by consent could have recovered "native government" from the strife and confusion

[225] Ibid., pp. 314–15.

[226] Ibid., p. 315.

[227] Ibid. The interpretation of Burke's argument at this point implied by French Laurence and Walker King's editorial reconstruction in *The Speeches of the Right Honourable Edmund Burke on the Impeachment of Warren Hastings* (London: 1857), 2 vols., I, p. 58, correctly emphasises the prospective "advantage" that the "spirit" of British principles promised to South Asia, as well as noting the absence of British constitutional "forms" in India; but they go beyond Burke's text in concluding that these "forms" were not "communicable" abroad: practically, of course, and especially in the short term, a parliamentary system could not be transplanted. However, Burke was clear that much of the East India Company's "government of writing" as well as the British jury system had much to recommend themselves on the subcontinent. British "forms," nonetheless, could not be imposed since in that case they would be introduced in the spirit of despotism. On this point, see EB, Speech on the Opening of Impeachment, 16 February 1788, *W & S*, VI, p. 345.

[228] On this, see above, chapter 10, section 3 and Travers, *Ideology and Empire, passim.*

[229] On this, see EB, *Ninth Report of the Select Committee* (25 June 1783), *W & S*, V, p. 205. Earlier, and consistent with this, he had objected to the idea of British-only juries sitting in judgment on Indians: see Northamptonshire MS. A. XIV.66.

inaugurated by the ambition of India's provincial "grandees."[230] A year and a half later, in the *Reflections on the Revolution in France*, Burke would claim that the values of charity and honour, derived respectively from Christianity and a system of graduated ranks, facilitated the moderation of power in European politics, conferring on the constitutions of its more enlightened regimes an "advantage" over Asian modes of government.[231] India under the Mughals had not been an unmitigated despotism, but it had not been a fully civilised monarchy either since it lacked the essential characteristic of "noble equality" that underlay both politics and law in Europe, distinguishing it from ancient factionalism and eastern subordination.[232] What India lacked in the "forms" of a properly constitutional monarchy, Britain might supply by means of liberal "spirit," introducing the will to improvement and a genius for accountability into what was already a government of laws in Asia.[233] In return for its beneficence, Britain would acquire an ally, which might prove a significant asset in a future geo-political contest. As Burke had declared three months earlier at an anniversary celebration of Fox's election at the Shakespeare Tavern in Westminster, "To secure India justice, and to extend to her the humanity of Britain, would be the means of making her a great and useful ally, and the time might come when in the hour of distress or danger she might repay the obligation."[234]

The fact was, however, it "happened otherwise."[235] Enlightened government in Europe would soon be represented by unexampled despotism in Asia, beginning with a rise in conspiracy and exploitation among Company servants in Bengal immediately after the death of Siraj-ud-Daula. With the departure of Clive for Europe after 1757, the example of previous depositions of rulers fostered an inclination to engineer yet more, making way for "new wars and disturbances, and for that train of peculation which ever since has vexed and oppressed that Country."[236] A princely coup had proved enormously profitable, encouraging venality among the servants who had conspired to bring it about. With the removal of Siraj-ud-Daula fresh in their memories, a number of Clive's successors conspired in 1760 to topple Mir Jafar, inaugurating an era of mercenary behaviour which Clive, and then Hastings, were later charged with correcting—unhappily, without success.[237] Burke relates the dark dealings among rival factions through the 1760s, first to oust Mir Jafar and replace him with Mir Kasim, then to abandon Mir Kasim and restore his predecessor. In due course, the office of *naib* was settled on Mahomed Reza Khan, allegedly

[230] EB, Speech on the Opening of Impeachment, 16 February 1788, *W & S*, VI, p. 314.
[231] EB, *Reflections*, ed. Clarke, p. 239 [113].
[232] Ibid.
[233] EB, Speech on the Opening of Impeachment, 16 February 1788, *W & S*, VI, p. 315.
[234] *Gazetteer*, 11 October 1787. I am grateful to P. J. Marshall for this reference.
[235] EB, Speech on the Opening of Impeachment, 16 February 1788, *W & S*, VI, p. 317.
[236] Ibid.
[237] Ibid., p. 318.

at a cost of £20,000, and the succession to Mir Jafar bestowed on Munni Begam.[238] The Company actors were motivated throughout by the usual mercenary aims: the acquisition of territory, and with it a revenue stream; personal remuneration by the receipt of presents; and the chance to expand their private trade at the expense of the native population.[239] When this sequence of revolutions began, Hastings was a "young gentleman" of about "27 years of age": this was the nursery in which he learned to advance his goals by subterfuge, disobedience, perfidy and oppression.[240]

There is an interlude in Burke's presentation between this sequence of revolutions and the instalment of Hastings as President and then Governor General in Bengal. This intermission is taken up with the exploits of Clive, who was returned by the Company to settle its affairs in the wake of the monstrous upheavals of the previous years. In Burke's eyes, the system implemented by Clive stood as an isolated moment of "Glory" in the annals of the Company: he outlawed the practice of bribing, or accepting presents, among Company servants; he settled British relations with Awadh and Benares; he retained the Emperor in his dignity while increasing the power of the Company; he placed the civil power in British hands, and law and order in the hands of the natives. In short, he established the foundations for a constitutional settlement of the country.[241] But these reforms were not to last: with the promotion of Hastings to the highest offices of authority in India, the native infrastructure of government was systematically dismantled, while the Governor himself proceeded to act on arbitrary principles, which he then defended as embodying the customary practice of Asia.[242] Burke's attack on what he saw as Hastings's convenient reliance on "Geographical morality," using what he chose to interpret as local norms as a cover for nefarious behaviour, forms the centrepiece of the second day of Burke's speech.[243] Hastings's treatment of Benares is taken to exemplify this attitude, where the alleged "anarchy" of the country is invoked to justify its oppression. In particular,

[238] Ibid., pp. 338–39.

[239] Ibid., pp. 319–37. The course of events is more clearly relayed in *Speeches on the Impeachment of Warren Hastings* (London: 1857), I, pp. 62–84. For a contemporary account of the proceedings which Burke recollected, see Henry Vansittart, *A Narrative of the Transactions in Bengal from the Year 1760 to the Year 1764* (London: 1766), 3 vols., who justified the deposition of Mir Jafar with reference to the financial exigencies of the Company, satisfied by the cession of Burdwan, Midnapore and Chittagong (I, p. 45). Vansittart's perspective was vigorously challenged in Luke Scrafton, *Observations on Mr. Vansittart's Narrative* (London: 1766).

[240] Northamptonshire MS. A. XXXVI.4.

[241] EB, Speech on the Opening of Impeachment, 16 February 1788, *W & S*, VI, pp. 340–42; Northamptonshire MS. A. V.40.

[242] Burke reconstructs what he takes to have been the guiding principles of Hastings's conduct based on an examination of his Company correspondence, the maxims to which he averted in his defence in the House of Commons, and his code of conduct as he presented this to the Lords. For the last two, see *Defence of Hastings*, pp. 98, 101–2 and 105–7, where he is presented as having comported himself as any Nawab would in the face of the confused jumble of Indian law and politics, and *LJ*, XXXVIII, p. 56, where he defends his rule in terms of Asian precedent.

[243] EB, Speech on the Opening of Impeachment, *W & S*, VI, p. 346.

Hastings took Benares to be a dependent territory whose Raja, or chief Zemindar, was at once a tributary and a rebel: his inferior station, in an Asian context, was held to inspire resentment and encourage rebellion. Under these circumstances, as Hastings saw it, the Raja required strict discipline if he was to be controlled by his British superiors.[244]

12.6 Rights of Nature: The Benares Revolution

The exact sequence of events in Benares between its period as an autonomous but tributary state to Awadh after 1756 and its falling under the supremacy of the East India Company during the leadership of Chait Singh beginning in 1775 forms an important part of Burke's basic case against Hastings.[245] According to Burke, this period covered an epoch in which the obligations of Benares as an independent tributary were respected in much the same way as, under the feudal law of Europe, nominally restricted tenure under a "Lord Paramount" was in practice enjoyed as a hereditary fiefdom.[246] Burke contrasted this arrangement with Hastings's treatment of the Raja from 1778 onwards. From that point on, Chait Singh was made subject to rigorous exactions at the behest of Hastings, leading three years later to a punitive fine for his failure to pay, in turn provoking a rebellion culminating in the Raja's exile.[247] The "necessary tendency" of Hastings's actions, Burke believed, was "to produce revolt & War."[248] On 16 August 1781, with turbulence mounting in the city, two separate detachments of East India Company sepoys came under attack from

[244] Hastings's position here was drafted by Nathaniel Halhed and is presented in *Defence of Hastings*, p. 106. On Halhed's contribution, along with that of Major Scott, William Markham and Nathaniel Middleton, to Hastings's defence before the Commons on 1–2 May 1786, see Rocher, *Orientalism*, pp. 132ff. Halhed's authorship is confirmed by Scott in *Minutes of the Evidence Taken at the Trial of Warren Hastings, Esquire, Late Governor General of Bengal, at the Bar of the House of Lords* (London: 1788–95), 6 vols., I, pp. 368–69.

[245] Burke's original charge on this score is presented in *CJ*, XLI, pp. 494–503, 694–97. The Benares charge is examined in Marshall, *Impeachment of Hastings*, ch. 5. Relevant context is supplied by Bernard S. Cohn, "The Initial British Impact on India: A Case Study of the Benares Region," *Journal of Asian Studies*, 19:4 (August 1960), pp. 418–31, and idem, "Political Systems in Eighteenth Century India: The Banaras Region," *Journal of the American Oriental Society*, 82:3 (July–September 1962), pp. 312–20.

[246] Northamptonshire MS. A. XXII.60. Burke considers Shuja-ud-Daula has having held of the great Mughal on the same terms: see ibid. In Northamptonshire MS. A. XXXVI.13 he compares the arrangement with Germany.

[247] Burke dwelt on the particular indignities to which Chait Singh was subjected during the trial itself, recorded at Add. MS. 24224, fols. 281–89. Burke's verdict on the propriety of Hastings's conduct is contained in Northamptonshire MS. A. XXII.60: he "Calls Robbery a fine."

[248] Northamptonshire MS. A. XXII.60. In Northamptonshire MS. A. XXIX.36 Burke claims that Hastings "precipitated the Rebellion" through a process of humiliation. During the trial, on 22 February 1788, Fox claimed that the term "rebellion" was a misnomer, meaning that the insurrection had been a justified revolt. At this point Fox and Burke were at one on the rights of revolution. See *Speeches of the Managers and Counsel in the Trial of Warren Hastings*, ed. E.A. (London: 1859–61), 4 vols., I, p. 252.

Chait Singh's retainers.[249] Within a month, the Raja's troops had been dispersed and Chait Singh himself had escaped to Ramnagar.[250] Burke's famous invocation of the obligations of rulers under the laws of nature in his speech of 16 February 1788, which subsequent commentary has held up as an essential ingredient of his opposition to the rights of revolution, was in fact deployed in the context of his justification of rebellion in response to Hastings's abuses in 1781.[251]

Burke later accepted that it was not possible to specify a priori the occasions on which a people "may or may not resist". Nonetheless, the treatment of Benares offered a clear example of when oppression permitted a country to "take up arms."[252] In seeking to vindicate his conduct against the Raja of Benares, Hastings appeared to Burke to have embraced despotism on principle, justifying its maxims as necessary responses to disobedience.[253] However, insurrection on Chait Singh's part, Burke argued, was the last resort of conscience in the face of insupportable oppression. Magistracy enjoined the duty of protection, Burke insisted. Therefore, the abrogation of that duty on the part of a sovereign licensed an appeal to natural right on the part of the subject: power at that point could be limited by "downright revolt" without the morality of insurrection being tainted by any "criminal" characteristics.[254] The right of revolution, in other words, was based on the rights of man. A close examination of Burke's writings after 1790 shows that he did not suddenly abandon this commitment with the advent of Revolution in France, but instead specified the conditions on which an appeal to such rights could be made, and elucidated the civil entitlements which the rights of nature in fact prescribed. "Far am I from denying," Burke declared in the *Reflections*, the "*real* rights of men."[255] As his response to the Benares episode two years earlier showed, he certainly meant what he said.

Hastings's account of the rights of the subject was altogether different. In the case of Benares, he observed, the subject was himself a ruler in a dependent jurisdiction.

[249] An account was later provided by William Markham under examination as a witness on 17 March 1792. See *Minutes of the Evidence Taken at the Trial of Warren Hastings*, III, pp. 1689–98.

[250] Marshall, *Impeachment of Hastings*, pp. 104–5. There is a description of the bloody struggle at the Palace given by David Birrell under examination as a witness at the trial on 6 June 1792 in *Minutes of the Evidence Taken at the Trial of Warren Hastings*, III, pp. 1772–76.

[251] For the programmatically conservative appropriation of Burkean natural law principles, see Russell Kirk, "Burke and Natural Rights," *Review of Politics*, 13:4 (October 1951), pp. 441–56; Peter J. Stanlis, *Edmund Burke and the Natural Law* (1958) (New Brunswick, NJ: Transaction Publishers, 2003); idem, "The Basis of Burke's Political Conservatism," *Modern Age* 5:3 (Summer 1961), pp. 263–74. Stanlis's argument draws on the problematic distinction between "natural law" and "natural rights" traditions of thought set out in Jacques Maritain, *The Rights of Man and Natural Law*, trans. Doris C. Anson (New York: Charles Scribner's Sons, 1943) and Leo Strauss, *Natural Right and History* (Chicago, IL: University of Chicago Press, 1953).

[252] EB, Speech in Reply, 30 May 1794, *W & S*, VII, p. 323.

[253] EB, Speech on the Opening of Impeachment, 16 February 1788, *W & S*, VI, pp. 347–49, citing and discussing *Defence of Hastings*, pp. 106–7.

[254] Northamptonshire MS. A. XXII.56, reproduced in EB, Speech on the Opening of Impeachment, *W & S*, VI, Appendix, p. 470.

[255] EB, *Reflections*, ed. Clarke, p. 217 [86].

In setting out his rights in a memorandum on the status of the Zamindar composed for Pitt two days before the presentation of the Benares charge in June 1786, Hastings elucidated a "fundamental principle of Despotism" in terms of the illegitimacy of resisting or disputing superior authority "under any pretence."[256] At the same time, since on Hastings's analysis the Zamindar was only the proprietor of the soil while his superior was the owner of its produce, the supreme magistrate was entitled to alienate or assume direct control of a Zamindarry in cases where the Zamindar was deemed to have rebelled, including where he failed to pay his dues.[257] In a published letter to the Court of Directors from 1785, Hastings described the Raja's position as one of "absolute obedience."[258] He had previously elucidated the meaning of that condition: it bestowed upon the Company "absolute authority," entitling it to punish any appearance of "contumacy."[259]

Presenting his case before the Lords in 1788, Burke took the behaviour that corresponded to this defence to exemplify Hastings's wantonly capricious conduct on the subcontinent. As Burke set out his case, Hastings accepted that his authority derived from the mother country as entrusted to the East India Company. Nonetheless, as Hastings argued, the power thus transmitted was obliged to operate in the context of the systematic disloyalty characteristic of Asian political culture, encouraging the Governor to act the part of arbitrary despot, as Burke complained. In Burke's eyes, Hastings was claiming the right of degrading the depraved.[260] In addressing this situation, Burke's argument was not simply that no such authority had been delegated by the British parliament; nor was it simply that Hastings had wilfully misdescribed conditions in South Asia. His further point was that civil power was at bottom a sacred trust that could never be whimsically exercised by its possessor. No one had a right to govern, in Locke's potent phrase, by the "boundless extravagancy of his own will."[261] Moreover, Burke further contended, again in a Lockean vein, individuals did not have the right to govern even themselves in whatever way they might happen to wish: "My Lords, the East India Company have not arbitrary power to give. . . . No

[256] Warren Hastings, "A Definition of the Nature of the Office of a Zemindar . . . for the Use of Mr. Pitt," Add. MS. 29202, fols. 33–37. The point was generalised by Major John Scott in a debate on the repeal of the India Judicature Bill on 27 February 1787, drawing a sharp rebuke from Burke. See *Parliamentary History*, XXVI, cols. 638–39.

[257] Ibid. An alternative understanding of the status of Chait Singh is presented by Fox in *The Debate on the Charges relating to Mr. Hastings' Conduct to Cheyt Sing, at Benares* (London: 1786), p. 1. Cf. EB, Speech in Reply, 5 June 1794, *W & S*, VII, p. 384, citing Harry Verelst, *A View of the Rise*, Appendix, p. 163.

[258] *Copy of a Letter from Warren Hastings, Esq. to the Court of Directors, Relative to their Censure on his Conduct at Benares* (London: 1786), p. 7.

[259] Warren Hastings, *A Narrative of the Late Transactions at Benares* (London: 1782), pp. 11–19.

[260] Northamptonshire MS. A. XXIX.17. Burke later commented on deleterious effects on a subject people of this attitude on the part of a ruler. See EB, Speech in Reply, 28 May 1794, *W & S*, VII, p. 264: "according to the ordinary course of human nature . . . those whom you despise you never will treat well."

[261] John Locke, *Two Treatises of Government*, ed. Peter Laslett (Cambridge: Cambridge University Press, 1960, 1990), bk. II, ch. ii, § 8. On Burke's debt to Locke's political thought, see below, chapter 13, section 2.

man can govern himself by his own will, much less can he be governed by the will of others."[262] Since human beings were subject to the norms of nature, they could not determine the extent of their obligations themselves.

In *De iure praedae*, Grotius had presented lawlessness as essentially inhuman.[263] In this vein, Burke contended that "man is born to be governed by law."[264] Since the manuscript of *De iure praedae* was not published until the nineteenth century, it is clear that Burke was not aware of its contents. However, he was certainly familiar with *The Rights of War and Peace*, which evidently reproduced some essential features of the earlier argument. In the 1605 work, Grotius had baldly stated, "What God has shown to be His Will, that is law."[265] In *The Rights of War and Peace*, Grotius takes the divine will to be evident from the ends and aptitudes of human nature.[266] Those ends comprised the desire for an orderly social existence as well as the instinct for self-preservation. For Grotius, these objectives were compatible with the individual right to govern their own behaviour, including, as Rousseau later observed, the right to alienate one's liberty altogether to another.[267] But whereas Burke accepted that both self-preservation and sociability were fundamental parts of divinely orchestrated human nature, he insisted that the right to preserve oneself did not extend to the right to pursue that aim however one saw fit.[268]

All "power," Burke contended, "is of God."[269] For this reason, the exercise of power cannot be finally justified in terms of a "contract" by which it is bestowed on an individual or group.[270] Power might be acquired by natural means, as with a father over his children, or by force, as in the case of military conquest. But conquest could only be legitimised by winning popular consent to an arrangement that was first instituted by resort to violence. In this sense, consent was needed to confer legitimacy upon authority—or, in the terms in which this point was generally made, lawful government was founded on a "contract." However, as Burke was at pains to emphasise, while "contractual" agreement might be a necessary element in the foundations of legitimate government, it was certainly not sufficient to ground that legitimacy. In this spirit, Burke claimed that law did not arise from merely human "institutions," from contingent "conventions" based on circumstantial needs.[271] Such conventions

[262] EB, Speech on the Opening of Impeachment, 16 February 1788, *W & S*, VI, p. 350.

[263] Grotius, *Commentary*, p. 36.

[264] EB, Speech on the Opening of Impeachment, 16 February 1788, *W & S*, VI, p. 351.

[265] Ibid., p. 19.

[266] Grotius, *Rights of War and Peace*, I, pp. 82–3, 93–4.

[267] Ibid., II, p. 557; see Jean-Jacques Rousseau, *Du contrat social* (1762) in *Œuvres complètes*, III, pp. 352–33.

[268] Cf. Locke, *Two Treatises*, bk. II, ch. iv, § 23: "For a Man, not having the Power of his own Life, *cannot*, by Compact, or his own Consent, *enslave himself*, to any one, nor put himself under the Absolute, Arbitrary Power of another, to take away his Life, when he pleases."

[269] EB, Speech on the Opening of Impeachment, 16 February 1788, *W & S*, VI, p. 350.

[270] Ibid.

[271] Ibid. Cf. Samuel Pufendorf, *De iure naturae et gentium libri octo* (Lund: 1672), bk. III, ch. iv, sect. 4.

did indeed develop in order to satisfy human needs, but they nonetheless remained answerable to "one great, immutable, pre-existent law, prior to all our devices, and prior to all our conventions, paramount to our very being itself, by which we are knit and connected in the eternal frame of the universe, out of which we cannot stir."[272]

It was a commonplace of modern natural law that, as Pufendorf himself put it, "CIVIL GOVERNMENT" is "from GOD."[273] This did not mean, as assorted neo-Aristotelian traditions had proposed, that human beings were naturally disposed to political cooperation, even though they evidently possessed social aptitudes and appetites.[274] Rather, cooperation was brought about by political subjection, which was itself secured by agreement based on the calculation of its utility among creatures whose passions would otherwise lead them to conflict. The divine will commanded the goal of civil existence, yet this was achieved by means of general consent based on calculation, not by a pre-given appetite for "community."[275] For Pufendorf, this civil condition was accompanied by a "peculiar *Veneration*" (*peculiare sanctimonium*) owed to the sovereign on the part of the subject, such that the subject ought to endure whatever "Severities" (*asperitas*) might be imposed in addition to the usual duty of obedience to reasonable commands. Under conditions of extreme oppression, citizens should attempt to flee rather than "draw their Swords" against the fatherland.[276] For all Burke's recognition of the force of natural law arguments specifying the indirect divine sanction that underlay the civil contract, his conclusions ran counter to Pufendorf's injunction in favour of the passivity of the oppressed. A marginal note in his manuscript makes his position perfectly clear:

[272] EB, Speech on the Opening of Impeachment, 16 February 1788, *W & S*, VI, p. 350. Cf. Northamptonshire MS. A. XXIX.49: "great, primary, preexisting, Law." See also EB, Speech in Reply, 28 May 1794, *W & S*, VII, p. 280. Jurisprudential opinion varied on the source of this immutability. On the two dominant positions, see Pufendorf, *De iure naturae et gentium*, bk. II, ch. iii, sect. 5.

[273] Samuel Pufendorf, *The Whole Duty of Man, according to the Law of Nature*, ed. Ian Hunter and David Saunders (Indianapolis, IN: Liberty Fund, 2003), p. 198. Cf. Samuel Pufendorf, *De iure naturae et gentium*, bk. VII, ch. iii. For the divergence of Protestant natural law from earlier traditions on this score, see Knud Haakonssen, "Protestant Natural Law Theory: A General Interpretation" in Natalie Brender and Larry Krasnoff eds., *New Essays on the History of Autonomy* (Cambridge: Cambridge University Press, 2004), p. 96. For another overview with a different emphasis, see Richard Tuck, "The 'Modern' Theory of Natural Law" in Anthony Pagden ed., *The Languages of Political Theory in Early-Modern Europe* (Cambridge: Cambridge University Press, 1987). For Burke in relation to modern natural law, see David Armitage, "Edmund Burke and Reason of State," *Journal of the History of Ideas*, 61:4 (October 2000), pp. 617–34.

[274] Failure to draw this distinction has encouraged commentators to classify Burke as some kind of unreconstructed Aristotelian or Thomist, beginning with Ernest Barker, *Essays on Government* (Oxford: Oxford University Press, 1945, 1951), p. 218: "Burke was always an Aristotelian, perhaps because he was also, even if unconsciously, a Thomist." See also Ross J. Hoffman and Paul Levack, Preface to *Burke's Politics: Selected Writings and Speeches on Reform, Revolution and War* (New York: Alfred A. Knopf, 1949); Stanlis, *Burke and the Natural Law*, pp. xxxiiiff.; Canavan, *Political Reason of Edmund Burke*, *passim*.

[275] Samuel Pufendorf, *The Whole Duty of Man*, pp. 187–89, where Pufendorf takes issue with Aristotelian natural law.

[276] Ibid., p. 209.

neither "conquest," "succession" nor "compact" could justify civil injustice.[277] It was simply impermissible to wield power in order "to extinguish the rights of the people." Indeed, "to bear" despotism was itself a "crime" where its yoke could be "rationally shaken off."[278] We are forced to surmise what Burke meant by "rational" here: presumably a reasonable calculation of success, such as Chait Singh made, although he actually failed in the attempt—saving himself but losing his territory. On Burke's scheme, not only was the use of arbitrary power a criminal enterprise, but enduring it was equally nefarious. Power of the kind had to be resisted, and only "absolute impotence" could justify the failure to rise against it.[279]

Burke's defence of the divine sanction underpinning the civil obligations of rulers was explicitly conceived in opposition to moral scepticism. The "great, immutable, pre-existent law" that imposed upon political authorities the duty to serve the benefit and justice of the people was, he insisted, "paramount to all our Ideas and all our sensations."[280] Modern Epicurean doctrine, embraced by Hobbes and taken by many in the late seventeenth century to have been entailed by Locke's "way of ideas," was interpreted by Burke to undermine the natural rights of justice. However, as Montesquieu had argued in *The Spirit of the Laws*, the possibility of relations of justice must pre-exist the institution of terrestrial laws.[281] Burke had striven in the 1750s and early 1760s to render his own commitment to the authority of natural justice compatible with his opposition to rational dogmatism in a way that inclined him to a kind of "academic" scepticism.[282] We must "learn to doubt," Burke had argued in the early 1750s. This required that we "humble the understanding" in its overweening pretensions to have access to the fundamental reason of things.[283] As far as Burke was concerned, this pretension lay at the heart of early to mid eighteenth-century deist attempts to expose the mysteries of religion, which in turn entailed compromising the foundations of moral duty.[284] Burke abandoned his philosophical ambitions some time after 1759, and so never succeeded in reconciling his commitment to the transcendent authority of duty with his acute awareness of the limitations that bounded human knowledge. Nonetheless, as his political career down to Hastings's impeachment shows, he never lost his original commitment, which was deployed with strenuous vigour in the opening speech of 1788.

This commitment to popular rights enjoined two duties in particular: to uphold the institution of property and to preserve the population from oppression and

[277] Northamptonshire MS. A. XXIX.49.

[278] Ibid.

[279] EB, Speech on the Opening of Impeachment, 16 February 1788, *W & S*, VI, p. 351.

[280] Northamptonshire MS. A. XXIX.49.

[281] Montesquieu, *De l'esprit des lois*, pt. I, bk. I, ch. 1.

[282] See above, chapter 2, section 3. For Burke's interest in academic scepticism, see EB, *A Philosophical Enquiry into the Origin of our Ideas of the Sublime and Beautiful* (1757, rev. ed. 1759) in *W & S*, I, p. 191, where he cites Cicero, *Academica*, II, 127.

[283] EB, "Philosophy and Learning" in *A Notebook of Edmund Burke, ed.* H.V.F. Somerset (Cambridge: Cambridge University Press, 1957), pp. 88–89.

[284] EB, "Religion" in ibid., p. 70: "*Moral Duties are included in Religion, and enforced by it.*"

violence: "Name me a Magistrate, and I will name property. Name me power, and I will name protection."[285] Justice and security were imposed as inescapable obligations on government by virtue of the sacredness of its trust. Optimally, that trust could be enforced by a well-regulated constitution under which restraints would be imposed on the ruling power, either by the action of countervailing magistracies or by the impact of influential "orders" in the state.[286] Even in a constitutional regime, however, supreme power was by definition legally unaccountable. Nonetheless, supremacy did not divest sovereignty of moral responsibility even though it guaranteed it juridical autonomy. According to Burke, it was this conflation of the legal unaccountability of sovereignty with its moral irresponsibility that encouraged Hastings to believe that the possession of authority gave licence to exercise its prerogatives at will. Burke had been perturbed by the pervasiveness of what he now termed this "gross confusion and perversion of ideas" since his first engagement with the American crisis in 1766.[287] By the nature of things, supreme jurisdiction could not be subjected to "penal prosecution" for its actions, since that would imply a superior jurisdiction to which supremacy could be held to account.[288] To render sovereignty accountable would be to dissolve the final authority of the state.[289] Short of such a dramatic course, power could be regulated without prejudice to the principle of supremacy by dividing the public offices through which sovereignty was exercised. The principle of such a division underlay every constitutional limitation on the exercise of power. But under a truly absolute monarchy, which for Burke represented the only serviceable meaning of "despotism," neither magistracies nor laws controlled the will of the government, leaving justice to depend on the moderation of the ruler. In the absence of all moderation, where the government put itself in a state of hostility with the governed, the people would be forced to rebel against established authority.[290] By November 1790, Burke was at pains to argue that nothing remotely resembling a violation of the rights of man, let alone a state of war between the prince and his people, captured conditions during pre-Revolutionary France. However, with equal confidence he assured his audience in February 1788 that these conditions did apply in Benares seven years earlier.

From Burke's perspective, therefore, having subverted the very purpose for which government had been invented, namely the security of property in civil society,

[285] EB, Speech on the Opening of Impeachment, 16 February 1788, *W & S*, VI, p. 351.

[286] Northamptonshire MS. A. XXII.56.

[287] EB, Speech on the Opening of Impeachment, 16 February 1788, *W & S*, VI, p. 351; EB, Speech on Declaratory Resolution, 3 February 1766, *W & S*, II, p. 47. For Burke's views on sovereignty, see above, chapter 6, section 4 and chapter 9, section 6.

[288] EB, Speech on the Opening of Impeachment, 16 February 1788, *W & S*, VI, p. 351. See Bourke, "Sovereignty, Opinion and Revolution in Edmund Burke," *History of European Ideas*, 25:3 (1999), pp. 99–120.

[289] EB, Speech on the Opening of Impeachment, 16 February 1788, *W & S*, VI, p. 352.

[290] Ibid., p. 470, reproducing Northamptonshire MS. A. XII.56.

Hastings proceeded to justify his conduct by presenting Asian governments as unconstitutional despotisms to whose practices he was obliged to adhere.[291] It was a position which Hastings's counsel was later to reiterate in a speech for the defence in 1792, embellishing the argument with the tales of travellers and the opinion of Montesquieu.[292] Two years later, in his speech in reply closing the prosecution's case, Burke returned again to question these assumptions.[293] This scepticism went back to the beginning of the impeachment. Accordingly, the remainder of Burke's speech on 16 February 1788 was taken up with an attempt to demonstrate that Hastings's notions about eastern governments simply could not be sustained. In order to clinch the point, Burke set about illustrating how the monarchies of the east were manifestly regimes of law, subject to the Koran along with experts in its provisions: "every Mahomedan Government . . . is by its principles a Government of law."[294] The fact that Muslim governments were governments by law was further underlined by the fact not only that judicial power was separated from the executive, but that the executive was itself divided into distinct compartments whenever power was delegated: "they have subdelegated their power by parcels," as Burke put it.[295] This applied in particular to the complex division of responsibility among legal officers, but it also applied to the separation of civil from criminal jurisdiction in the offices of *Nazim* and *Diwan*. "In India there is a partition of the powers of Government," Burke emphasised, challenging accounts of the constitution of the subcontinent made popular by Tavernier, Montesquieu and their disciples.[296] In addition to Muslim institutions, there was also Hindu law.[297] Altogether, Burke concluded, when it came to consciousness of what constituted violations of basic norms, Asia was "in that respect" fully as enlightened as Europe.[298] In other respects, it must have seemed, it was not. In the end, Burke maintained his partiality for the British constitutional system: "we have better institutions for the preservation of the rights of men than

[291] See EB, Speech on the Opening of Impeachment, 19 February 1788, *W & S*, VI, p. 454, on Hastings's project "to defeat the ends which all Governments ought in common to have in view."

[292] Speech of Edward Law, 14 February 1792, *Speeches of the Managers in the Trial of Warren Hastings*, II, pp. 532–46. See Montesquieu, *De l'esprit des lois*, pt. II, bk. xi, ch. 6: "Chez les Turcs, où ces trois pouvoirs [du gouvernement] sont réunis sur la tête du sultan, il règne un affreux despotisme."

[293] EB, Speech in Reply, 28 May 1794, *W & S*, VII, pp. 262–3.

[294] EB, Speech on the Opening of Impeachment, 16 February 1788, *W & S*, VI, p. 363.

[295] Ibid., p. 364.

[296] Ibid., p. 464, reproducing sections from Northamptonshire MS. A. XXIX.49. Burke specifically cites *The Six Voyages of John Baptista Tavernier, Baron of Aubonne through Turky, into Persia and the East-Indies* (London: 1677) against the author's overall thesis in his Speech on the Opening of Impeachment, *W & S*, VI, p. 362. The same strategy is deployed in Voltaire, *Essai sur les mœurs et l'esprit des nations*, ed. René Pomeau (Paris: Garnier, 1963), 2 vols., II, p. 404. For Burke's rejection of the applicability of "oriental despotism" to the east, see chapter 10 above.

[297] EB, Speech on the Opening of Impeachment, 16 February 1788, *W & S*, VI, p. 364.

[298] Ibid., p. 367.

any other Country in the World."[299] No state, however, could renege on its responsibility to maintain those rights, and India under the Mughals had been particularly dedicated to ensuring their inviolability.

12.7 The Rangpur Atrocities

According to Burke's analysis, the dedication to civil rights had sharply declined in the era of the independent Nawabs, and Hastings modelled his behaviour on these immediate predecessors, from Alivardi Khan to Kasim Ali.[300] On 18 February 1788, on the fifth day of the trial, Burke set about dramatising the consequences of Hastings's approach by dwelling on the atrocities committed by the revenue collectors of Rangpur in northern Bengal under the administration of Raja Devi Singh. The charge against Hastings was that he had been bribed into awarding revenue farms to Singh, thus implicating him remotely in the abuse of cultivators or *raiyats* by collectors during Singh's tenure.[301] In essence, Burke's claim was that Hastings's avarice got the better of his concern for the welfare of the people. The British government of India had its origins in the need for "safety," Burke reflected, but was soon diverted by desperate ambition into the wilful pursuit of self-interest. Next, "as generally happens in conquest," ambition was channelled into pecuniary greed, which Hastings's "sale" of responsibility to Devi Singh apparently exemplified.[302] Hastings's defence insisted that he could not be plausibly connected to events in Rangpur, but Burke was determined to damn him by association. "Oh! what an affair," Burke declared to Francis six weeks before his speech, "I must dilate upon that."[303] The affair seemed to Burke to go to the heart of the "Presents" charge, but it also had the additional advantage of enabling his prosecutors to "work upon the popular Sense."[304] This was of course essential to Burke's purpose: his best hope was to affect popular sentiment through the impeachment, thereby putting pressure on the Lords to condemn the accused. To that end, all the art of rhetoric was required to evoke the extremity of Hastings's abuse of East India Company authority.

Burke appreciated that such an enterprise ultimately had to be an exercise in well-judged oratory, leading the feelings of the public to a sense of perfect outrage by identifying events at Rangpur with epic cruelty and associating Hastings with those

[299] Ibid., p. 352. On the other hand, the jurisprudence of the east was as enlightened "as perhaps any Nation ever possessed." See EB, Speech in Reply, 28 May 1794, *W & S*, VII, p. 267.

[300] EB, Speech on the Opening of Impeachment, 16 February 1788, *W & S*, VI, p. 367.

[301] The claim was that Devi Singh had acquired the farms by the corrupt payment of *peshkash* through Ganga Govind Singh, though the charge turned out to be false. See Hastings's notes, Add. MS. 29193, fols. 92ff. For a general treatment of Indian officials in the period, see P. J. Marshall, "Indian Officials under the East India Company in Eighteenth-Century Bengal," *Bengal Past and Present*, 84 (1965), pp. 95–120; on Ganga Govind Singh in particular, see ibid., pp. 111–20.

[302] Ibid., p. 377.

[303] EB to Philip Francis, c. 3 January 1788, *Corr.*, V, p. 372.

[304] Ibid.

events. The previous year, in December 1787, Gilbert Elliot had opened proceedings against Elijah Impey with a panegyric celebrating the virtues of Burke as a statesmen. The day after the performance, Burke conveyed his thanks via Lady Elliot, extolling the merits of Elliot's speech as a whole—"the Method, the arguments, the Sentiments, the Language, the manner, the action, the Tone and modulation of Voice were all exactly of a piece."[305] This was a master indicating what mastery required, providing a glimpse of what Burke thought would be needed for his speech on Rangpur. Elliot, Burke commented, "drew Tears from some of his auditory."[306] He did so by stirring their sentiments to correspond with his own, which had themselves been roused to pity extreme distress. "In Truth the whole came from the heart, and went to the heart," he went on: sincerity was a prerequisite for evoking proper sympathy.[307] This was a view that Burke shared with Elliot himself: "what a powerful ingredient in eloquence a *sincere feeling* in the speaker is."[308] The business of the orator was to identify emotionally with his subject and to inspire his audience to share in these emotions. However, this required a thorough command of ornament and artifice, without ever showing the art by which it was achieved. When Elliot later came to comment on Sheridan's fourteen-hour speech of mid-June 1788 on the Begams charge, he remarked upon the self-consciously ornate character of the performance. His rhetorical "*bouquets*" served as a distraction, diminishing the importance of the cause.[309] For Burke, however, the whole of Elliot's earlier performance had shown the "finishing hand" of a maestro, conveying moral urgency without exhibiting its methods. It recalled, he thought, the "flame of zeale severe" ignited by Abdiel in rebuking Satan in Book V of *Paradise Lost*.[310] Elliot, as Burke saw it, had like himself set out to expose the awful presumptuousness of gross impiety. What was needed for the purpose, Burke indicated, was "Taste": the ability to fabricate a community of sentiment without advertising the means of fabrication. In this way, "humanity" could be drawn to "pass a stern Sentence upon Cruelty and oppression."[311] This was the task that Burke set himself on 18 February 1788.

Burke's account of the atrocities that were supposed to have accompanied attempts to enforce a revenue settlement on Rangpur was largely drawn from three reports drafted by John Patterson after the outbreak of rebellion in January 1783. Burke acquired a Company copy of Patterson's work some time after 1786, which he annotated extensively along with correspondence and enclosures bound with the reports.[312] The unreliability of these documents was later indicated by a commission

[305] EB to Lady Elliot, 13 December 1787, ibid., p. 369.

[306] Ibid.

[307] Ibid.

[308] Sir Gilbert Elliot to Lady Elliot, 13 December 1787, *Life and Letters of Sir Gilbert Elliot, First Earl of Minto, from 1751–1806* (London: *Longmans, Green and Co.,* 1874), 3 vols., I, p. 177.

[309] Ibid., pp. 206–15.

[310] Milton, *Paradise Lost*, V, line 807.

[311] EB to Lady Elliot, 13 December 1787, *Corr.*, V, p. 369.

[312] Add. MS. 24268, with summaries and commentary on nearly every page in Burke's hand.

that exonerated the worst of the "horrid Cruelties" allegedly perpetrated by Devi Singh's agents, accepting nonetheless that oppression had occurred.[313] In Burke's version of events, after the farm of Rangpur had been entrusted to Devi Singh, innumerable small Zamindars in the district were incarcerated with a view to enforcing the extraction of excess rents. This was followed by the imposition of new taxes, leading to the sequestration of estates on account of the inability to pay.[314] The situation of the *raiyats* was accordingly imperilled: in a year of low grain prices, they could not meet the cost of the new burdens being imposed. Facing desolation, they sold their effects and then fell prey to usury.[315] Next came their resort to the most dreadful expedients available: they sold their wives and children.[316] Having reduced them to penury, "stripped of every thing," their tormentors sought still more, hoping to extort any hidden means of subsistence by the application of torture. Burke proceeded to treat his audience to a rendition of the methods applied, expatiating on refinements in physical abuse to which the victims were allegedly subjected. Every possible means was used to afflict the body and offend the mind.[317]

The oppressors were then confronted by the inevitable result as the *raiyats* rose in rebellion against "delegated Tyranny."[318] Patterson had noted that the "voice of the whole people" called out against their persecutors. "The minds of everyone great and small were ripened for revolt by Despair," he later remarked.[319] A "veil," Burke commented, had been lifted: those pleasing illusions by which subordination is made bearable were no longer effective under conditions where brutal subjection was without mitigation and beyond disguise.[320] In the margins of one of Patterson's reports he copied this summary judgment: "The wonder would have been if the people had not risen."[321] In India of all places, only complete repression could drive the people to

[313] "Report of Enquiry into the Causes of the Insurrection at Rungpore," AAC, IOR, P/51/6, fols. 1–302, quotation on fol. 5. See *Maharaja Deby Sinha* (Calcutta: Kuntaline Press, 1914), pp. 470–522.

[314] EB, Speech on the Opening of Impeachment, 18 February 1788, *W & S*, VI, pp. 413–14.

[315] Ibid., pp. 416–18.

[316] This is reported by John Patterson in Add. MS. 24268, fol. 102, and underlined by Burke.

[317] EB, Speech on the Opening of Impeachment, 18 February 1788, *W & S*, VI , pp. 419–21.

[318] EB to George Patterson, 7 April 1788, *Corr.*, VI, p. 381. For accounts of the insurgency, see S. B. Chaudhuri, *Civil Disobedience during the British Rule in India, 1765–1857* (Calcutta: World Press, 1955), pp. 58–76, and Narahari Kaviraj, *A Peasant Uprising in Bengal, 1783: The First Formidable Peasant Uprising against the Rule of the East India Company* (New Delhi: People's Publishing House, 1972); for a recent revision of subaltern assumptions about the uprising, see Jon Wilson, "A Thousand Countries to Go to: Peasants and Rulers in Late Eighteenth-Century Bengal," *Past and Present*, 189:1 (2005), pp. 81–109.

[319] Add. MS. 24268, fols. 105, 159. The European district collector Richard Goodlad, on the other hand, could detect no compelling reason for the revolt. See his letter to David Anderson, 27 January 1783, reprinted in *Maharaja Deby Sinha*, p. 323.

[320] EB, Speech on the Opening of Impeachment, 18 February 1788, *W & S*, VI, pp. 422–23. The phrase "pleasing illusions" occurs, of course, in *Reflections*, p. 239 [114].

[321] Add. MS. 24268, fol. 242.

revolt: the Indians, Burke accepted, were "patience itself."[322] Nonetheless, as he read in Patterson, "let the mind of Man be ever so much inured to servitude, still there is a point where oppression will rouse it to resistance."[323] In the early 1780s Burke had traced this passive obedience to a history of subjection to illiberal government; in 1788 he still considered the posture "criminal."[324] Obedience to rule that betrayed the public good was both slavish and immoral, and so the fact of the peasants of Rangpur having, as Burke put it, "burst at once into a wild universal uproar" was bound to produce sympathy in Britain.[325] At least, therein lay Burke's only hope for the future. On the following day, summing up his case before the Lords, he lighted upon the principle of charity as the highest of moral vocations. Closing his opening speech, Burke realised that a guilty verdict depended on the sentiments of humanity rather than the processes of municipal legal judgment. "I impeach him in the name of human nature itself," he declared.[326] However, while Burke believed that the sentiment of humanity had been a great achievement of Christian culture, it was weaker than the nearer affections supporting family, friendship and national allegiance. The challenge was to inspire cosmopolitan charity with an effective charge.

At the end of his speech, Burke recalled that the undertaking to impeach Hastings had represented a watershed for the House of Commons. There had not been a more valuable tribute to human nature, nor a more glorious justification of British politics, than the achievement of a sense of "moral community" binding the lower House to the plight of her Indian subjects, bringing them to resent "as their own" the indignities of a people separated from Britain by considerable geographical and cultural barriers.[327] Now the task was to rekindle that resentment in the hearts of British peers. To that end, Burke flattered the august stature of his audience, both anciently and newly ennobled, distributed into their various gradations of rank between the crown and the people, as a fitting body to pass judgment on an issue of imperial significance.[328] Above all, he exalted the Bishops in the Hall, a "true image of the primitive Church," purified of accretions of Roman superstition, standing for a religion of love. But in raising them high, his aim was to remind them of their true vocation as originally represented by the mission of Christ: to renounce the pathos of distance, to walk among the people, to cultivate "sympathy with the lowest."[329] Burke closed with a vision of a Christian empire comprising multiple faiths, at once tolerant and charitable. The question was how to make this vision effective.

[322] Ibid., p. 422.

[323] Ibid., fol. 242. The passage was underlined by Burke.

[324] *"Observations" on the First Report of the Select Committee* (5 February 1782), *W & S*, V, p. 184; EB, Speech on the Opening of Impeachment, 18 February 1788, *W & S*, VI, p. 422.

[325] Ibid.

[326] Ibid., p. 459.

[327] Ibid., pp. 457–58.

[328] Ibid., p. 458.

[329] Ibid., p. 459.

XIII

THE GREAT PRIMAEVAL CONTRACT

REFLECTIONS ON THE REVOLUTION IN FRANCE, 1790

Figure 6. John Jones after George Romney, *Edmund Burke* (1790) National Gallery of Art, Washington, D.C.

13.1 Introduction

Burke's *Reflections on the Revolution in France* occupies a non-standard position within the canon of past political thought. Its production was determined by immediate circumstance rather than philosophical reflection. Cicero's *Republic* was written in retirement and Machiavelli's *The Prince* after the author's fall from office. In terms of the conditions of its composition, the *Reflections* is roughly comparable to Locke's *Two Treatises of Government* insofar as both were prompted by compelling practicalities. But even here, Locke was a scholar and tutor turned counsellor and polemicist whereas Burke was a responsible politician. Many classic texts, from Aristotle to Tocqueville, were partly framed as responses to existing conditions in public life, and are therefore rightly seen as interventions into local debates.[1] However, Burke's intervention was directly shaped by the pressure of events. This hardly makes it exceptional in the history of political writing, but it does help account for aspects of its style and structure. As an occasional work it has often seemed diffuse in its subject matter. Despite the intensity of its engagement, it appears to circle around a series of disparate concerns. But in reality these preoccupations are tightly interconnected.

The *Reflections* is a defence of the British constitutional setup, including existing relations between church and state. As such it is an attack on figures hostile to the Anglican establishment as well as to the principle of parliamentary monarchy. Its immediate target was the nonconformist preacher Richard Price, who sought with various fellow travellers to undermine ecclesiastical and political arrangements in Britain. Noble patrons of dissent, like the Earl of Shelburne, and aristocratic critics of the national Church, like the Duke of Grafton, are treated with particular disdain. For Burke, their public support for the values of Revolutionary France exposed them to justifiable derision. They were driven, he supposed, by a kind of demagogic enthusiasm which hid their goal of self-serving ambition. In the process they helped publicise an attitude to politics and religion that would ultimately be destructive of both. Burke was desperate to consolidate Whig antipathy to such principles and recover Charles James Fox from the temptations of populism by counterposing the enlightened values of British domestic politics with the chaos of ideas that was serving to dismantle contemporary France.

It seemed to Burke that French ideas might lend force to British doctrines that were subversive of the domestic constitution in church and state. He therefore targeted both, roughly in sequence rather than together, beginning with a critique of assaults on the 1688 settlement. The principal target here was Price's idea of freedom as self-government, which extended civil liberty to include a right to public power. It was on this basis, Burke believed, that Price had mistaken the Whig

[1] On this, see the contributions to James Tully ed., *Meaning and Context: Quentin Skinner and His Critics* (Princeton, NJ: Princeton University Press, 1988).

conception of legitimate resistance for a licence to resort to revolution as a matter of convenience. With this approach, it was suggested, neither parliament nor monarchy could stand. Burke accepted that, fundamentally, government was indeed an instrument of convenience. However, he also thought that constitutional government should provide a way of deliberating over the character of that convenience. This required the provision of means for scrutiny, debate and execution under conditions of stability and allegiance. For this reason, Burke dwells at some length on the emotions that support continuity in national counsels and attachment to the welfare of the community. These included moral and aesthetic sentiments that encourage respect, as well as feelings of veneration for enduring customs and the national past. None of this was intended to affirm an empty reverence for "tradition." Instead, support for authority was interpreted as a means of advancing the common good. As Burke was at pains to emphasise in his speech opening the Hastings trial, the failure to protect the good of the community provided grounds for legitimate resistance. More expansively, the *Reflections* dwells on the duty of obedience as well as protection. He claimed that both should be comprehended under the "great primaeval contract" that defines the moral relations between rulers and ruled.[2] Burke recognised the right to revolution against the state but he also appreciated the gravity of recourse to insurrection. The situation in France, he thought, could scarcely justify resort to violence, still less an attempt upon the pillars of established government.

Burke claimed that civil society was a mechanism for survival as well as a vehicle for human progress towards perfection. It was consequently an object of both reverence and piety as well as a beneficiary of trust. In France it had fulfilled its trust only to be treated with contempt. Full-scale resistance had begun not with popular insurgency but with the treachery of disaffected courtiers and nobles. These were soon abetted by disgruntled men of letters who found themselves in league with aspiring agents of the monied interest. Between them they launched an offensive against the property of the Church, condemned as a bastion of corporate privilege. On Burke's analysis the Revolution was fuelled by resentments about inequality rooted in the ambitions of rising talent along with competitiveness over standing among the divisions of the aristocracy. The diverse appeal of equality focused hostility against the monarchy, giving rise to a reckless spirit of innovation. That mood was eagerly heightened by the deputies in the Assembly, who were in Burke's opinion bereft of practical wisdom and the inclination to pursue sustainable reform. Superstitious fear of timeworn institutions conflated historic abuses with current political practice. Luxury was widely taken to be the cause of misery. The determination to overturn the consolations of providence made the spectacle of unmerited prosperity seem unbearable. As corporate bodies and social divisions were progressively undermined, the military looked poised to extend its powers without resistance. The spirit of conquest was reborn under the cloak of liberty.

[2] EB, *Reflections*, ed. Clark, p. 261 (144].

13.2 Liberty and Dissent

Burke's response to the American crisis, together with his writings on party government, sustained his reputation down to the 1880s as an exemplar of liberal reform. His *Reflections on the Revolution in France*, on the other hand, was to become a conservative classic. Both these outcomes are indicative of processes of transmission that distorted the original significance of his career. As the most recent editor of the *Reflections* has emphasised, neither "liberalism" nor "conservatism" had any meaning for Burke.[3] "Liberal" was a pervasive epithet in the political language of the eighteenth century, yet its espousal as an ideal by parliamentarians like Burke is not to be confused with the doctrines of nineteenth-century liberalism. Similarly, Burke certainly believed that the essential ingredients of beneficent stability should be conserved. Ultimately, this was little more than a common-sense position. However, he was very far from believing that traditional arrangements should be maintained at the expense of progressive change. In writing the *Reflections*, he was presenting a defence of a particular political order, as anyone might do when confronted with a fundamental challenge to what seemed to them necessary to preserve. The interesting question has to be about what Burke was defending, and the methods he adopted in seeking to do so.

The political order that Burke set about vindicating was conceptualised in two dimensions: first, in terms of Britain's religious and political establishment; and second, in terms of the principles underlying European politics. These two concerns were related to one another, since the situation in Europe, it seemed to Burke, was adversely affecting the interests of Britain. In practical terms, Europe here meant the monarchy of France, although Burke associated the Revolutionary attack on property and religion with a general assault on the heritage of post-feudal Christendom. Writing to Calonne as the *Reflections* was about to appear, Burke claimed that his true object "was not France, in the first instance, but this Country."[4] In political terms, this was of course correct. The *Reflections* was occasioned by Burke's alarm about the determination of sections of the dissenting community in Britain to publicise their allegiance to the principles of Revolutionary France. To the extent that support for these principles could be expected to spread among the political class, the British constitution would be imperilled. Having said this, the success of French

[3]EB, *Reflections*, ed. Clark, "Introduction," pp. 109–11. The point is effectively conceded in Harvey C. Mansfield, "Burke's Conservatism" in Ian Crowe ed., *An Imaginative Whig: Reassessing the Life and Thought of Edmund Burke* (Columbia, MO: University of Missouri Press, 2005), p. 60. More usually, Burke is seen as combining conservatism with liberalism. See, typically, Yves Chiron, *Edmund Burke et la Révolution française* (Paris: Téqui, 1987), p. 149; Jean-Clément Martin, *Contre-révolution, révolution et nation en France, 1789–1799* (Paris: Éditions du Seuil, 1998), pp. 99–103. For a more intricate picture, see Michael A. Mosher, "The Skeptic's Burke: *Reflections on the Revolution in France*, 1790–1990," *Political Theory*, 19:3 (August 1991), pp. 391–418.

[4]EB to Charles-Alexandre de Calonne, 25 October 1790, *Corr.*, VI, p. 141.

ideas would depend on the fate of France. It was therefore essential for Burke's purposes to evaluate the probable fortunes of the neighbouring power. That required an analysis of its animating maxims, and an assessment of how these were likely to play out.

Burke's preoccupation with these matters determined his choice of genre. The *Reflections* takes the form of a letter "intended to have been sent to a gentleman in Paris."[5] The gentleman in question was Charles-Jean-François Depont, with whom Burke had been acquainted since 1785.[6] Depont was twenty-two in 1789, and had by then been elevated to *conseiller* of the *parlement* of Paris.[7] On 4 November 1789, he made contact with Burke again, seeking his advice on whether the Revolution was likely to succeed in its stated aims.[8] That same month, Burke drafted a lengthy reply, amounting to his most considered engagement with France to date, though he decided to hold the letter back.[9] Depont pressed him for an answer on 29 December, at which point Burke embarked upon a lengthier response. It was this reply that was destined to grow into the *Reflections*. Burke originally intended it to comprise an analysis of the principles underlying the various institutions which the French had revolutionised since the summer of 1789, above all the organisation of constitutional powers, together with the restructuring of the army, and of course the Church. His aim, as he indicated in the *Reflections* itself, was "to compare the whole of what you have substituted in the place of what you have destroyed, with the several members of our British constitution."[10] But soon the project swelled to unmanageable proportions, obliging Burke to abandon his detailed account of the British system of government, leaving him to concentrate on the main facets of the French. He thus held in reserve what he had wanted to say about "the spirit of our British monarchy, aristocracy, and democracy, as practically they exist."[11] Some discussion of this topic made its way into the *Reflections*, but Burke never published his full account.

Before long, the original plan for what was to become the *Reflections* became complicated by domestic developments relating to the publication of *A Discourse on the Love of Our Country*, a sermon by Richard Price celebrating the Glorious Revolution, which concluded with a panegyric on developments in France.[12] Al-

[5] EB, *Reflections*, ed. Clark, p. 141: facsimile reprint of the title page of the first edition. The importance of the epistolary form is considered by Christopher Reid, *Burke and the Practice of Writing* (Dublin: Gill and Macmillan, 1985), p. 8.

[6] Richard Burke Sr. to EB, 10 November 1785, *Corr.*, V, p. 235.

[7] H.V.F. Somerset, "A Burke Discovery," *English*, 8:46 (1951), pp. 171–78.

[8] Charles-Jean-François Depont, 4 November 1789, *Corr.*, VI, pp. 31–32.

[9] Though the letter was subsequently sent: see EB, *Reflections*, ed. Clark, p. 143 [iii]: Preface. A copy can be found in *Corr.*, VI, pp. 39–50.

[10] EB, *Reflections*, ed. Clark, p. 335 [241].

[11] Ibid., p. 335 [242].

[12] Price's sermon provoked a considerable number of hostile responses: twenty-seven pamphlets in all, twenty-one before the appearance of the *Reflections*. See Gayle Trusdel Pendleton, "Towards a Bibliography of the *Reflections* and the *Rights of Man* Controversy," *Bulletin of Research in the Humanities*, 85 (1982), pp. 65–103.

ready by the early spring, a substantial draft of Burke's response to Price's sermon was complete. At that point, it bore the title "Reflections on certain Proceedings of the Revolution Society of the 4th of November 1789, concerning the Affairs of France," indicating the work's principal subject matter.[13] The title identified Burke's underlying purpose. It may be that he had not yet decided to amalgamate this material with his reply to Depont, but at some point the two projects were combined into the *Reflections*, which would begin with a response to Price's sermon to the Revolution Society, followed by a more detailed examination of France.

The Revolution Society had been reanimated in the summer of 1788 to prepare for the centenary of the Glorious Revolution. Toward that end, it brought together members of the Society for Constitutional Information, politically minded elements from among the dissenting clergy, and supporters of parliamentary and religious reform.[14] By 6 October 1788, the Society had produced a draft version of agreed principles.[15] The following year, on 4 November, its chairman, Earl Stanhope, saluted the spirit of liberty in France, with Richard Price moving an Address to the National Assembly, applauding "the glorious example given in France to encourage other Nations to assert the unalienable rights of Mankind and thereby to introduce a general reformation in the Government of Europe."[16] By 26 March 1790, the Revolution Society was collaborating with the Society for Constitutional Information to submit reform proposals before parliament.[17] With an election looming in the summer of 1790, the Foxites were keen to repair their damaged relations with the dissenters who had deserted Rockingham for Pitt in 1784.[18] Under these

[13] *London Chronicle*, 13–16 February 1790: Advertisement.

[14] Eugene Charlton Black, *The Association: British Extraparliamentary Political Organisation, 1769–1793* (Cambridge, MA: Harvard University Press, 1963), pp. 214–15; Albert Goodwin, *The Friends of Liberty: The English Democratic Movement in the Age of the French Revolution* (London: Hutchinson, 1979), ch. 4.

[15] Minute Book of the Revolution Society, 16 June 1788–4 November 1791, Add. MS. 64814, fol. 5. A final draft was proposed on 4 December: see Revolution Society, *An Abstract of the History and Proceedings of the Revolution Society, in London* (London: 1790), pp. 14–15.

[16] Minute Book of the Revolution Society, 16 June 1788–4 November 1791, Add. MS. 64814, fols. 22–3. The Address was presented to the Assembly by the Duke de la Rochefoucauld. The Archbishop of Aix offered a response. See *Procès-verbal*, 25 November 1789. The correspondence between members of the Assembly and the Revolution Society was published in the *London Chronicle*, 29–31 December 1789, and in the *Diary or Woodfall's Register*, 31 December 1789. There is an account of the exchange in George Stead Veitch, *The Genesis of Parliamentary Reform* (1913) (London: Constable, 1965), pp. 121–25. See also E. Pariset, "La société de la révolution de Londres dans ses rapports avec Burke et l'Assemblée Constituante," *La Révolution française*, 29 (1985), pp. 297–325. Relevant materials were collected in the Appendices to Richard Price, *A Discourse on the Love of Our Country* (1789) (London: 3rd ed., 1790). Burke used the third edition of Price's work.

[17] "Papers Relating to the London Corresponding Society and Society for Constitutional Information: Meetings Held 14 Mar 1783–7 Oct 1791," TNA TS 11/961/3507, fols. 212ff.

[18] The attempt to establish a rapprochement is evident in Burke's and Fox's dealings with Priestley in the autumn of 1789: see EB to Charles James Fox, 9 September 1789, *Corr.*, VI, p. 15: "Dr P. is a very considerable Leader among a Set of Men powerful enough in many things, but most of all in Elections."

circumstances, Burke was determined that any engagement between the parliamentary opposition and the nonconformists should be conducted in terms of the principles espoused by the Rockingham Whigs.[19] This required the production of a manifesto that would target the ingredients of antagonistic constitutional ideas. Price's sermon on the love of country, delivered at the Old Jewry on 4 November 1789 immediately prior to the presentation of his Address to the National Assembly, provided Burke with the materials for his attack. Already by the end of December the *Diary* could comment on how Price's sermon was "in the hands of so many people."[20]

In castigating Price, who had long been seen by Burke as a dangerous associate of Shelburne's, Burke was disparaging a presumptively Whig ideology that he believed was actually subversive of the basic tenets of Whig doctrine. Shelburne he ranked as "a disappointed statesman," a "fallen politician" who still wanted to make an impact by cultivating a band of flattering agitators.[21] Faced with this accretion to the main body of Whiggism, Burke wished his book, he later wrote, "to be, in the first instance, of service to the public, in the second, to the party."[22] The two were intimately intertwined in Burke's assessment of current politics. After all, the tenets of the party were essential to the commonweal. Price's pronouncements before the Old Jewry were anathema to those principles, which made it essential to expose their divergence from Whig fundamentals. A common cause had brought dissenting ideas about liberty into apparent harmony with the Rockinghams during the campaign against the ministry's prosecution of the American war. But the differences in shared vocabularies were now plain to see, and every form of alliance had to be scrutinised and possibly terminated. Even in 1777, Burke had insisted on the disparity between Price's precepts and the Rockingham position. But by 1790 incommensurability had become a yawning gap. This mounting antagonism was not being caused by a shift in doctrine so much as by the expansion of Price's audience. In 1791, Burke would complain of the positive reception accorded the credenda of "Paine, Priestley, Price, Rouse, Mackintosh, Christie, &ca." at Brooks's.[23] What stunned Burke even prior to this was the encouragement given to Price and his colleagues by the National Assembly in 1789: "The National Assembly of France has given importance to these gentlemen by adopting them."[24] The progress of subversive principles had to be curtailed.

Burke first took issue with Price in public in his *Letter to the Sheriffs of Bristol*: "There are people, who have split and anatomized the doctrine of free Government, as if it were an abstract question concerning metaphysical liberty and necessity; and

[19] Albert Goodwin, "The Political Genesis of Burke's Reflections on the Revolution in France," *Bulletin of the John Rylands Library*, 50:2 (1968), pp. 336–64.

[20] *Diary or Woodfall's Register*, 30 December 1789.

[21] WWM BkP 10:4.

[22] EB to Earl Fitzwilliam, 5 June 1791, *Corr.*, VI, p. 272.

[23] Ibid., p. 273.

[24] EB, *Reflections*, ed. Clark, p. 147 [4]. The Revolution Society's Address was printed in French in *L'Ancien moniteur*, 10 November 1789, in *Réimpression de l'Ancien moniteur* (Paris: 1858–63), 31 vols., II, pp. 171–72.

not a matter of moral prudence and natural feeling."[25] The reference was to Price's *Observations on the Nature of Civil Liberty*, published under Shelburne's patronage in February 1776.[26] Burke's purpose was to damn the pamphlet's conception of freedom by association with Price's Platonising *Review of the Principal Questions in Morals* of 1758.[27] In the Preface to the fifth edition of the *Observations*, which appeared in March 1776, Price advertised his indebtedness to Locke's second *Treatise*.[28] This meant little more than tracing the origins of civil society to the consent of the people, on whose trust the legitimacy of government depended. Boswell claimed that Burke once commented that Locke, "who shewed such extraordinary powers in analyzing human understanding, shewed he had very little use of it himself, when he attempted to apply it practically to the subject of government."[29] This cannot be taken to stand as Burke's considered view of Locke, although it may be that he was keen to dissociate himself from the contemporary reception of the great philosopher, which had been anatomised by Josiah Tucker in the early 1780s.[30] Nearly four years later, in the midst of the war against Revolutionary France, Burke was reported as describing the *Two Treatises of Government* as "one of the worst" books ever written.[31] It seems Burke's relation to Locke was a mixture of indebtedness and disavowal: he distanced himself from aspects of the moral psychology that

[25] EB, *Letter to the Sheriffs of Bristol,* 3 April 1777, *W & S*, III, p. 317. For the history of Burke's engagement with Price, see John Faulkner, "Burke's First Encounter with Richard Price" in Crowe ed., *An Imaginative Whig*. See also, Frederick Dreyer, "The Genesis of Burke's *Reflections*," *Journal of Modern History*, 50:3 (September 1978), pp. 462–79.

[26] For Price's relationship with Shelburne, see Lord Fitzmaurice, *Life of William, Earl of Shelburne* (London: 1912), 2 vols., I, p. 432. See also Peter Brown, *The Chathamites: A Study in the Relationship between Personalities and Ideas in the Second Half of the Eighteenth Century* (London: Macmillan, 1967), part II.

[27] Price's work set about undermining the sensationalism of Locke's *Essay* and Hutcheson's moral sense thesis by way of recourse to Plato and Cudworth. See Richard Price, *A Review of the Principal Questions and Difficulties in Morals* (London: 1758), pp. 4, 18, 24n, 26. For discussion, see Martha K. Zebrowski, "Richard Price: British Platonist of the Eighteenth Century," *Journal of the History of Ideas*, 55:1 (January 1994), pp. 17–35. For the relationship between Price's moral and political thought, see Susan Rae Peterson, "The Compatibility of Richard Price's Politics and Ethics," *Journal of the History of Ideas*, 45:4 (October 1984), pp. 537–47; Gregory I. Molivas, "Richard Price, the Debate on Free Will, and Natural Rights," *Journal of the History of Ideas*, 58:1 (January 1997), pp. 105–23.

[28] Price, *Observations* (7th ed.), Preface. Cf. ibid., pp. 16, 93, 100. See also his rejoinder to Burke in Price, *Two Tracts*, pp. ii–viii.

[29] James Boswell, *The Hypochondriak, Being the Seventy Essays by the Celebrated Biographer*, ed. Margery Bailey (Palo Alto, CA: Stanford University Press, 1928), II, pp. 270 and 270n9.

[30] For his attack on the putative Lockeanism of dissenters, see Josiah Tucker, *A Treatise Concerning Civil Government* (London: 1781). For discussion, see J.G.A. Pocock, "Josiah Tucker on Burke, Locke and Price: A Study in the Varieties of Eighteenth-Century Conservatism" in idem, *Virtue, Commerce, and History: Essays on Political Thought and History, Chiefly in the Eighteenth Century* (Cambridge: Cambridge University Press, 1985), ch. 9.

[31] *Morning Chronicle*, 18 April 1794. This was a report of Burke's speech on the debate about accepting French dissidents into the British armed forces of 17 April 1794. The phraseology in the *Oracle* for 24 April 1794 reporting the same speech is milder. Both versions are presented by P. J. Marshall in *W & S*, IV (forthcoming).

came to be associated with the *Essay*, yet he accepted Locke's denial that individuals had a right voluntarily to submit to the arbitrary authority of rulers.[32] At the same time he believed, with the author of the *Two Treatises*, that legitimate government required popular consent.

However, the meaning of this condition was complicated in the thought of Locke, accounting for Burke's wary reception of his ideas.[33] Locke famously emphasised the role of consent in the establishment of political obligation on a basis of reasonable subjection. For the most part, according to this view, quotidian government operated without directly addressing the psychological preferences of the governed.[34] It was Burke, and not Price, who accepted the restriction of consent to the formation of a reasonable political order. Short of militant resistance, there was no mechanism for appeal from rulers to the ruled, except insofar as the constitution provided for representation. For Price, on the other hand, magistracy is deputed to do the people's bidding: legitimate government depended on tangible consent, not merely on an underlying framework of agreement.[35] Price believed that Locke had been a patron of this view. As Burke saw it, Price's approach to obligation involved conferring absolute liberty on the subject at the expense of civil freedom. As be put it in his *Letter to the Sheriffs of Bristol*, natural liberty represented the "extreme" of freedom, which "obtains no where" in established political societies.[36] The idea that a population could appeal against its government in the name of natural freedom was ultimately "destructive to all authority," and so was incapable of contributing to progressive reform.[37]

[32] See John Locke, *Two Treatises of Government*, ed. Peter Laslett (Cambridge: Cambridge University Press, 1960, 1990), II, iv, § 23. For Burke's use of the argument in connection with the Hastings trial, see above chapter 13. Burke's affinity with Locke is the subject of Frederick A. Dreyer, *Burke's Politics: A Study in Whig Oligarchy* (Waterloo, Ontario: Wilfrid Laurier University Press, 1979). Cf. Ofir Haivry, "The 'Politick Personality': Edmund Burke's Political Ideas and the Lockean Inheritance" (PhD thesis, University College London, 2005).

[33] A manuscript transcription of a speech by Burke in French Laurence's hand on the American crisis from around 1770 refers to the "many sober & good citizens, who are swayed by the authority of Locke & other constitutional politicians" into discrediting the rights of the House of Commons. See OSB MS. File 2237.

[34] Locke, *Two Treatises,* II, xiii, § 149. On the role of consent in Locke's thought, see John Dunn, "Consent in the Political Theory of John Locke" in idem, *Political Obligation in Historical Context* (Cambridge: Cambridge University Press, 1980). See also John Dunn, " 'Trust' in the Politics of John Locke" in idem, *Rethinking Modern Political Theory* (Cambridge: Cambridge University Press, 1985); John Dunn, "From Applied Theology to Social Analysis: The Break between John Locke and the Scottish Enlightenment" in Istvan Hont and Michael Ignatieff eds., *Wealth and Virtue: The Shaping of Political Economy in the Scottish Enlightenment* (Cambridge: Cambridge University Press, 1986).

[35] Price, *Observations* (7th ed.), p. 7. According to D. O. Thomas, *The Honest Mind: The Thought and Work of Richard Price* (Oxford: Oxford University Press, 1977), p. 191, the argument is closer to Milton's *Tenure of Kings and Magistrates* (1650) than to Locke.

[36] EB, *Letter to the Sheriffs of Bristol*, 3 April 1777, *W & S*, III, p. 318.

[37] Ibid.

Burke took up this argument again in the *Reflections*, as he had done in his first letter to Depont. Freedom, he believed, is the birthright of the species. More than this, no one has the "right" to forfeit it.[38] Nonetheless, true freedom has to be distinguished from pre-social freedom, which acts without any reference to civil justice. As with all political values, the meaning of liberty can only be derived from its context. It has no content when presented "in all the nakedness and solitude of metaphysical abstraction."[39] Freedom in society is a form of power, and so its justification depends on how that power is used.[40] In the *Reflections*, Burke noted how it had been invoked to the detriment of private property, the armed forces and the collection of revenue.[41] He well knew, he commented, how rousing the rhetoric of liberty could be, but freedom, to be useful, had to be fitted to government, without which it was at best a kind of folly.[42] Despite this, the spirit of untamed freedom was applauded by members of parliament—by Shelburne, now the Marquis of Lansdowne, and Stanhope in particular—as well as by dissenting divines like Price.[43] Between them, they amalgamated politics and religion into an insidiously corrupting combination. The results were evident in what Burke regarded as Price's mongrel sermon, the *Discourse on the Love of Our Country*. It was a work, he thought, that reeked of fanaticism: infusing political passions with the unworldliness of religion, it fed reforming zeal with visionary expectations and infected religious sentiment with the ambitions of power. Its tone and ideas recalled the days of the Catholic League in France and the Solemn League and Covenant in Scotland.[44] Price's true exemplar was Hugh Peter, the Independent chaplain who had fortified the army before it marched on London for Pride's purge in 1648.[45] Like Price, in preaching love to mankind, Peter is alleged to have spread hatred among fellow citizens.

It was no accident that Burke chose to juxtapose Price's sermon with the exhortations of a seventeenth-century regicide preacher. It was part of his argument that British defenders of 1789, in interpreting the French Revolution as a reprise of 1688, had confused the glorious deliverance accomplished by William III with the tragedy of the 1640s. Peter had played a notorious role in the climax of that decade, conspiring with Ireton and Cromwell to secure the execution of the king. On the eve of Charles I's death, he delivered a gruesome sermon based on Isaiah 14:19–20: "thou art cast out of thy grave like an abominable branch."[46] An address at St. James's

[38] EB to Charles-Jean-François Depont, November 1789, *Corr.*, VI, p. 41.

[39] EB, *Reflections*, ed. Clark, p. 151 [7].

[40] Ibid., p. 153 [9].

[41] Ibid., p. 152 [9].

[42] Ibid., p. 412 [352–53].

[43] Stanhope, along with Henry Beaufoy and Benjamin Vaughan launched their parliamentary careers on Shelburne's interest. See Goodwin, *Friends of Liberty*, pp. 10–13.

[44] EB, *Reflections*, ed. Clark, p. 157 [13].

[45] Ibid., pp. 156–57 [13]. See R. P. Stearns, *The Strenuous Puritan: Hugh Peter, 1598–1660* (Urbana, IL: University of Illinois Press, 1954).

[46] Ian Gentles, *The New Model Army in England, Ireland, and Scotland, 1645–1653* (Oxford: Blackwell, 1992), p. 309.

Chapel on 28 January 1648 beseeching the saintly to "bind their *kings* with chains, and their *nobles* with fetters of iron" enjoyed notoriety even after the restoration.[47] In the fifth volume of his *History of England*, Hume cited Peter's tirade as a favourite "among the enthusiasts of that age."[48] It was most probably Hume's account that put Burke in mind of a zealous chaplain whose activities during the civil war exemplified the perils of politicised religion. "No sound ought to be heard in the church but the healing voice of Christian charity," Burke asserted: "politics and the pulpit are terms that have little agreement."[49] Religion was in the habit of polluting politics, Hume had argued. Politics was inclined to corrupt religion, Burke responded. Despite this subtle divergence, both shared a common perspective on the course of events after 1642: the pretensions of popular politics and egalitarian ideology were pushed to extremes by their confederation with religion. In Burke's mind, Price's posture recalled the excesses of 1648 insofar as he opened religion to the passions of politics. Pride and ambition drowned out the voice of humility. At the same time, expectations of political change were divorced from practical life. As a result, "theological politicians" like Price, comprehensively ignorant of the ordinary course of affairs, were captivated by passions which political experience usually moderated: "they have nothing of politics but the passions they excite."[50]

In delivering his sermon on the anniversary of the Glorious Revolution, Price admitted that he had been led to dwell more extensively on political subjects than "would at any other time be proper in the pulpit."[51] Since his subject was the impact of Christianity on the progress of society, the combined theme of religion and politics was unavoidable. In addressing this theme, Price's aim was to commend the principle of universal benevolence embodied in the Christian sentiment of charity: this, he argued, should restrain patriotic feeling and limit national prejudice by fostering cosmopolitan fellowship.[52] True patriotism, he contended, rose above the clannish instincts of nationality in embracing virtue, liberty and knowledge. As the *Public Advertiser* summarised Price's thesis, "by cultivating truth, virtue, and universal liberty, we shall be enabled also to combine general philanthropy to all mankind, which will tend so essentially to produce public peace among men."[53] Moreover, the principles of liberty, virtue and knowledge constructively reinforced one another. Political and religious liberty facilitated the refinement of virtue, but it also created conditions in which knowledge could advance. Knowledge, in turn, contributed to the enlightenment of political and religious precepts, giving rise to "those revolutions

[47] Psalm CXLIX, cited in EB, *Reflections*, ed. Clark, pp. 156–57 [13].

[48] David Hume, *The History of England* (Indianapolis, IN: Liberty Fund, 1983), 6 vols., V, p. 515n.

[49] EB, *Reflections*, ed. Clark, p. 157 [14].

[50] Ibid.

[51] Richard Price, *A Discourse on the Love of Our Country, Delivered on Nov. 4, 1789* (London: 3rd ed., 1790), p. 2.

[52] Ibid., pp. 4–9.

[53] *Public Advertiser*, 25 December 1789.

in which every friend to mankind is now exulting."[54] The advancement of learning, however, had to be tempered by virtue if its impact on society was to be beneficial. At the same time, the pursuit of virtue without knowledge was liable to promote enthusiasm, and so prudence dictated that both should be cultivated together.

The practice of virtue, Price went on, included the public duties of religion. In Britain, however, the forms of worship and the tenets of faith were constrained by the decrees of public authority. Such an arrangement, Price contended, constricted the avenues to truth by closing down the freedom of inquiry. In this connection, Price urged "men of weight," like the Duke of Grafton, to campaign against the "application of civil power to the support of particular modes of faith which obstructs human improvement and perpetuates error."[55] Burke mocked Price's notion that religious congregations should be permitted to proliferate without limit. "It is somewhat remarkable," he commented, "that this reverend divine should be so earnest for setting up new churches, and so perfectly indifferent concerning the doctrine which may be taught in them."[56] The truth was, however, that Price was unconcerned about the multiplication of beliefs because he assumed that in the long run error would succumb to truth. Moreover, as he saw things, the process of dissent had always been blameless in the past. In his *Observations on the Importance of the American Revolution* of 1785, Price conceded that public criticism had often been followed by strife, but responsibility for civil breakdown lay with the dogmatism of the authorities.[57] This insistence on the unimpeachable innocence of dissent was rooted in Price's brand of millennialist Christianity.[58] Although the process of enlightenment might be interrupted by a period of darkness, the progress of knowledge would inevitably resume. Price offered a concrete example to support his case: although the illumination of classical antiquity was followed by the barbarism of scholastic thought, philosophy and Christianity had flourished anew with the revival of learning and the advent of experimental science.[59] Given the evident pattern of improvement through the ages, criticism should be subject to neither civil nor ecclesiastical restraints. In fact, even speculative atheism was preferable to enforced conformity.[60]

[54] Price, *Discourse on the Love of Our Country*, p. 14.

[55] Ibid., p. 18. Grafton was a Unitarian member of the House of Lords. His *Hints Submitted to the Serious Attention of the Clergy, Nobility and Gentry, by a Layman* (London: 1789), to which Burke alluded, argued for a reform of the Anglican liturgy.

[56] EB, *Reflections*, ed. Clark, p. 158 [15].

[57] Richard Price, *Observations on the Importance of the American Revolution* (London: 1785), p. 27.

[58] Jack Fruchtman, *The Apocalyptic Politics of Richard Price and Joseph Priestley: A Study in Late Eighteenth-Century English Millennialism* (Philadelphia, PA: American Philosophical Society, 1983), esp. ch. 3.

[59] Price, *Importance of the American Revolution*, p. 4. Cf. Richard Price, *The Evidence for a Future Period of Improvement in the State of Mankind* (London: 1787), pp. 13–14.

[60] Price, *Importance of the American Revolution*, p. 38.

The millennium was "hastening," Price felt certain.[61] Yet before the commencement of the kingdom of the Messiah, the Antichrist would undoubtedly fall.[62] This would take the form of the liberation of religion from civil control, which in Britain would mean the disestablishment of the Anglican Church. Everything, as Price read the signs, was pointing in this direction. By the autumn of 1789, he was reported to have "great hopes" that the struggle in France was the harbinger of the progressive expansion of liberty.[63] Freedom to philosophise was the surest means of expediting these forecasts. In practical terms, this freedom entailed the liberty to criticise public authority, and the right to publish any species of theoretical doctrine. By 1790, Burke himself had devoted a quarter of a century in public life to defending the principle of publicity and calling executive power to account. He had also consistently committed himself to the principle of toleration, albeit in the context of a defence of the established Church. Yet enlightened ideals, he also believed, had to preserve their own enabling conditions. It made no sense to permit the freedom of religious speculation to destroy the very foundations of religion. Similarly, it was counterproductive to allow liberty of discussion and publication to destroy the conditions of political freedom. In the *Reflections*, Burke was happy to tolerate Price's ideas about the desirability of dissent, even though he thought they posed a threat to national tranquillity. However, he regarded some of his political principles as more directly subversive: "His doctrines affect our constitution in its vital parts."[64] However much Price propounded his adherence to enlightened principles, his commitments in fact subverted what he expected them to deliver. From this perspective, it can be seen that the *Reflections* is largely an enlightened assault on the pretensions of self-appointed representatives of enlightenment whose doctrines promised to overthrow what they hoped to realise. Its rhetoric was deployed against a brand of *faux* "enlightenment," not against the spirit of criticism leading to social and intellectual improvement.[65]

13.3 To Frame a Government for Ourselves

The doctrines advanced by Price that Burke found peculiarly subversive were presented towards the end of the *Discourse on the Love of Our Country*. The principal offending dogma was Price's claim that "civil authority is a delegation from the

[61] Price, *Future Period of Improvement,* p. 25.

[62] Ibid., p. 19.

[63] James Wodrow to Samuel Kenrick, 25 October 1789, Dr. Williams Library, Wodrow–Kenrick Correspondence, 24.157 (141).

[64] EB, *Reflections*, ed. Clark, p. 159 [16].

[65] For discussion of the relationship between criticism and enlightenment, see Reinhart Koselleck, *Kritik und Krise: Eine Studie zur pathogenese der bürgerlichen Welt* (1959) (Frankfurt: Suhrkamp, 1973). For the relationship of criticism and "opinion" to the French Revolution, see Roger Chartier, *The Cultural Origins of the French Revolution* (Durham, NC: Duke University Press, 1991), pp. 16ff.

people."[66] The meaning of Price's sentence depended on the verb "delegation." Burke himself accepted that government was held in trust on behalf of the people, but that did not make the populace direct arbiters of public decisions: such an arrangement negated any effective division of labour between rulers and ruled. Nonetheless, *delegation* could be construed in these terms, implying not that public power was answerable to the common good but that it should in practice be controlled by the competing whims of the population. To Burke's mind, the anarchic subjection of French representatives in the National Assembly to menacing intervention by the crowd encapsulated the idea of delegation. Ultimately, it undermined all constitutional government whilst pretending to further the cause of the public interest. It was a conception that first gained ground in England in the 1640s, and was revivified during the conflict with the colonies. In 1776, the Reformed Baptist publicist Caleb Evans reinvigorated this idea of popular political control. In his *Political Sophistry Detected*, he commented that a violation of the public trust entitled a population to resist established authority and recover political power "into [its] own hands."[67] The Glorious Revolution, he continued, and thus the monarchy of George III, was founded upon this very ideology.[68] In 1777 Burke argued that radical precepts of the kind, conjoined with antinomian ideas, corrupted "our understandings" and tore up "the foundations of human society."[69] In 1790 these axioms appeared all the more alarming as men like Sheridan and Lansdowne connived in their dissemination.

It was not the criticism of particular establishments that bothered Burke, but what seemed an attack on any form of establishment at all. Price's notion that civil authority was a delegation from the people had been widely promulgated by various publicists throughout the course of the American crisis. Immediately after the war, it continued to be broadcast. In the *Discourse on the Love of Our Country*, Price himself associated the argument with the events surrounding 1688. It was at that moment, he wrote, that "the rights of the people were asserted": a monarch was expelled, "and a sovereign of our own choice appointed in his room."[70] Three principles were established in connection with these developments: first, the right to liberty of conscience; second, the right to resist abusive government; and, finally, "the right to chuse our own governors, to cashier them for misconduct, and to frame

[66] Price, *Discourse on the Love of Our Country*, p. 34. For discussion, see D. O. Thomas, "Richard Price and Edmund Burke: The Duty to Participate in Government," *Philosophy*, 34:131 (October 1959), pp. 308–22.

[67] Caleb Evans, *Political Sophistry Detected, Or, Brief Remarks on the Rev. Mr. Fletcher's "American Patriotism"* (Bristol: 1776), p. 17. These doctrines, along with those of Price and John Shebbeare, were systematically attacked in John Wesley, *Some Observations on Liberty: On a Late Tract* (Edinburgh: 1776).

[68] Evans, *Political Sophistry Detected*, pp. 17–18. Evans was replying to John Fletcher's attack on both himself and Richard Price in *American Patriotism Further Confronted with Reason, Scripture, and the Constitution* (Shrewsbury: 1776).

[69] EB, *Letter to the Sheriffs of Bristol*, 3 April 1777, *W & S*, III, p. 318.

[70] Price, *Discourse on the Love of Our Country*, p. 32.

a government for ourselves."[71] It was this last set of clauses that caused Burke to take alarm.[72] The same claim had been made by the dissenting minister, Robert Robinson, in 1784: constituents, as the term implied, "constitute or appoint" delegates to administer their rights, and thus in Britain a mixed monarchy had been ordained by popular choice.[73] Robinson further believed that religious institutions ought also to be the product of choice: political and religious societies alike derived from a right of inquiry and election "in the people."[74] During the debate on Fox's motion for the repeal of the Test and Corporation Acts on 2 March 1790, Burke cited the work of Robinson as liable to form a rising generation of dissenters into "determined enemies" of the Church.[75] The indoctrination that they practised as leaders of congregations had long been found objectionable by Burke, but in the aftermath of November 1789 in France, when animosity towards the Gallican Church gave rise to deliberate spoliation, hostility to religious establishments had to be treated with particular caution.

Fox had himself addressed the condition of the French Church in moving his motion for toleration on 2 March.[76] However much he might rejoice in the "emancipation" of the neighbouring people, he condemned the "summary and indiscriminate forfeiture of the property of the church."[77] Nonetheless, he went on, actions and opinions had to be distinguished: it was one thing to advocate the reform of institutions, but another to seek to dismantle them by violence. Priestley was widely cited at this time as a committed opponent of the constitution, yet Fox thought that his opinions did not pose any tangible threat.[78] However, for Burke, such a perspective failed to distinguish between ideas that might harmlessly be debated by the public and an agenda that openly incited subversive agitation. Marking the difference involved attending at once to "acts," "declarations" and the "avowed intentions" of propagandists.[79] In Robinson's case, Burke could see only a trail of "misanthropy,"

[71] Price, *Discourse on the Love of Our Country*, p. 34.

[72] Charles James Fox defended Price's view, and his formulation, in the Debate on the King's Message, 1 February 1793, *Parliamentary History*, XXX, col. 310. Burke responded caustically in EB, *Observations on the Conduct of the Minority* (Spring 1793), *W & S*, VIII, p. 439.

[73] Robert Robinson, *A Political Catechism, Intended to Convey Just Ideas of Good Civil Government and the British Constitution* (London: 3rd ed., 1784), pp. 33–35. A powerful precedent for the argument can be found in the polemics of the country Whig John Tutchin, whose *Observator* argued in June 1702 that the throne was founded on "consent, approbation and the election of the people" (cited in J. P. Kenyon, *Revolution Principles: The Politics of Party, 1689–1720* [Cambridge: Cambridge University Press, 1977, 1990], p. 107).

[74] Robert Robinson, *A Plan of Lectures on the Principles of Nonconformity for the Instruction of Catechumens* (Cambridge: 1778), p. 58.

[75] *Parliamentary History*, XXVIII, col. 436. He is also reported as having referred to a work by Samuel Palmer, an Independent minister based in Hackney.

[76] For an account of the debate, see G. M. Ditchfield, "The Parliamentary Struggle over the Repeal of the Test and Corporation Acts, 1787–1790," *English Historical Review*, 89:352 (July 1974), pp. 551–77.

[77] *Parliamentary History*, XXVIII, col. 397.

[78] Ibid., col. 401. Cf. his still more comprehensive defence in the Debate on the King's Measure for the Augmentation of Forces, 1 February 1793, *Parliamentary History*, XXX, col. 310.

[79] *Parliamentary History*, XXVIII, col. 436.

"anarchy" and "confusion." In the case of Priestley, the prospect was no less disturbing. Burke cited the Preface to his recent *Letters to the Rev. Edward Burn* as evidence of wilful animosity against Anglicanism.[80] This was by no means a trivial concern: the ecclesiastical configuration of the British polity was a facet of national political cohesion. Priestley admitted that he was happy to contribute to the explosive mixture that would detonate under the edifice of the Church of England.[81] A key ingredient in that mixture was the doctrine of the rights of man, which, as Burke saw things, was a recipe for undermining the harmony of the British church–state coalition. More fundamentally, "it broke asunder," as he claimed, "all those ties which had formed the happiness of mankind for ages."[82]

Despite its incendiary content, Fox publicly approved the "general principles" of Price's sermon.[83] Yet this was to condone Price's stated conviction that the achievements of the Glorious Revolution were imperfect, and awaiting completion through a reform of parliamentary representation: the "INEQUALITY OF OUR REPRESENTATION," as Price put it, was the gravest defect of the constitution.[84] However, in Burke's mind, a reform of the system of representation in the name of the rights of man would capsize the constitution altogether. Price's attempt to describe the events of 1688 in the language of natural right could serve no other purpose than that of unpicking the Revolution settlement, and with that the peace and prosperity of the three kingdoms. For that reason, the first fifty pages of the first edition of the *Reflections* were taken up with a presentation of the meaning of 1688 from the perspective of what Burke saw as the principles publicised by the Junto Whigs and the managers at the trial of Henry Sacheverell. This involved taking each of Price's propositions in turn, refuting, first, the claim that the Revolution established an elective monarchy in Britain; second, that it created a precedent whereby the monarch could be punished and deprived of office for "misconduct"; and, finally, that it bequeathed a right to recompose the polity at will.[85] In all this, Burke was not denying

[80] Ibid., col. 438.

[81] Joseph Priestley, *Letters to the Rev. Edward Burn of St. Mary's Chapel, Birmingham* (Birmingham: 1790), pp. ix–x.

[82] *Parliamentary History*, XXVIII, col. 435.

[83] Ibid., p. 401.

[84] Price, *Discourse on the Love of Our Country*, p. 39. On interpretations of the Glorious Revolution in the eighteenth century, see H. T. Dickinson, "The Eighteenth-Century Debate on the 'Glorious Revolution'," *History*, 62:201 (February 1976), pp. 28–45. See also idem, *Liberty and Property: Political Ideology in Eighteenth-Century Britain* (London: Methuen, 1977). For "true Whig" scepticism about the achievements of the Revolution, see Mark Goldie, "The Roots of True Whiggism, 1688–1694," *History of Political Thought*, 1:2 (Summer 1980), pp. 195–236. For developments under George III, see Kathleen Wilson, "Inventing Revolution: 1688 and Eighteenth-Century Popular Politics," *Journal of British Studies*, 28:4 (October 1989), pp. 349–86. For Burke's response, see Ben James Taylor, "Political Argument in Edmund Burke's *Reflections*: A Contextual Study" (PhD thesis, University of Birmingham, 2010), ch. 3.

[85] On this last point, the Whig publicist William Atwood had taken John Locke to task in *The Fundamental Constitution of the English Government* (London: 1790), p. 101: there was no dissolution between December 1688 and February 1789, since, in the absence of a presiding monarch, the government, being mixed, could effectively continue, and deliberate over the succession.

the right of resistance to unjust rule: "The punishment of real tyrants is a noble and awful act of justice."[86] Still less was he disputing the limited nature of the British monarchy. Instead, he was challenging what he took to be the extraordinary claim that the constitution was controlled by extra-constitutional powers.[87]

Much of Burke's argument hinged on the limited nature of the action taken in 1688–9, together with the character of the principles informing that action. One month after the appearance of the *Reflections*, arguing for the continuance of the impeachment against Hastings, Burke recalled the events of the Popish plot between 1678 and 1681, when Titus Oates spread rumours of a Catholic conspiracy to assassinate Charles II. Burke assured his audience that he did not mean in any way to palliate the displays of bigotry stirred up at the time, yet he did condone the reasonableness of precaution under the circumstances: "Were not the circumstances of the King, having sold himself to a foreign power, and the Heir of the Crown having declared himself a Roman Catholic, sufficient grounds of apprehension?"[88] This apprehension gave rise to the exclusion policy of the first Earl of Shaftesbury, forming the context for the composition of Locke's *Two Treatises of Government*, and the first appearance of Whig ideas of resistance.[89] After 1685, the prospect of a Catholic dynasty succeeding to the throne grew yet more real, and Whiggism united with influential Tory leaders to secure the "abdication" of James II.[90] For Burke, the replacement of a sitting monarch with the Dutch Stadholder, William III, Prince of Orange-Nassau, had been obtained "by a just war."[91] The armies of William and James never came within one hundred miles of one another, yet the threat of force was implicit in the campaign. James II had withdrawn himself in the face of im-

[86] EB, *Reflections*, ed. Clark, p. 245 [122]. Cf. EB to Charles-Jean-François Depont, November 1789, *Corr.*, VI, p. 48: "A positively Vicious and abusive Government ought to be chang'd, and if necessary, by Violence, if it cannot be, (as sometimes it is the case) Reformed."

[87] For the emergence of rival interpretations of 1688–89 as affirming either popular or parliamentary sovereignty, see Steve Pincus, *1688: The First Modern Revolution* (New Haven, CT: Yale University Press, 2009), ch. 2.

[88] EB, Speech on Continuation of the Impeachment, 23 December 1790, *W & S*, VII, p. 92.

[89] J. R. Jones, *The First Whigs: The Politics of the Exclusion Crisis, 1678–1683* (Oxford: Oxford University Press, 1961). On Locke in this context, see still Peter Laslett, "Introduction" to idem ed., *Two Treatises, passim*. See also Richard Ashcraft, *Revolutionary Politics and Locke's Two Treatises of Government* (Princeton, NJ: Princeton University Press, 1986).

[90] J. R. Jones, *The Revolution of 1688 in England* (London: Weidenfeld and Nicolson, 1972); J. R. Western, *Monarchy and Revolution: The English State in the 1680s* (London: Blandford, 1972). For the divisiveness underlying this common front, see Pincus, *1688*, ch. 10. On the charge of abdication, see the original phrasing in the parliamentary resolution alleging that James II had violated the terms of his contract in *Debates of the House of Commons: From the Year 1667 to the Year 1694*, ed. Anchitell Grey (London: 1763), 10 vols., IX, p. 25: "King *James* the Second . . . having withdrawn himself out of this Kingdom, has abdicated the Government." For the persistence of claims of abdication, see Gerald M. Straka, *Anglican Reaction to the Revolution of 1688* (Madison, WI: State Historical Society of Wisconsin, 1962).

[91] EB, *Reflections*, ed. Clark, p. 180 [43].

pending confrontation; resistance had certainly occurred.[92] Burke followed Whig argumentation in seeing the resistance as justified.[93]

However, what interested Burke in 1790 was less the fact of resistance than the process of reconstruction that followed. This occurred, he was adamant, not by recourse to natural rights but by an appeal to history: the deliberations and resolutions of the convention parliament in 1689 had been conducted with a view to rendering the caesura of 1688 compatible with constitutional precedent. Burke's overwhelming emphasis on this aspect of the Revolution is liable to obscure the criteria he invoked to justify the event. Burke accepted that popular consent, in the sense of general utility, was a necessary ingredient in any legitimate regime. For that reason governors, including hereditary monarchs, were bound by considerations of the common interest. "Kings," as Burke put it, ". . . are undoubtedly the servants of the people."[94] It was inconceivable that obligation could have any other basis, since the goal of magistracy was to serve the "general advantage" of society.[95] But how were governments' attempts to fulfil this function to be judged? By regular constitutional procedure, Burke supposed. Dissenting from this conclusion, Price intimated that an apparatus of power should be held to account by stepping outside established constitutional restraints and appealing directly to the population at large. According to this view, popular accountability was not simply a matter of representatives being answerable to the public, or of governments being morally constrained to cater to opinion. Instead, it was assumed that the actual system of rule ought to be permanently on trial, subject to arbitration by the people. For Burke, on the other hand, not only was such an arrangement likely to prove unpopular, as he thought it certainly would be in the case of Britain, but on that basis no system of government could be expected to endure: it was a recipe for perpetual dissolution.

In endeavouring to show just how repugnant to popular sentiment such a method of procedure had previously been, Burke wanted to demonstrate how strenuously the British establishment strove to avoid a dissolution of government in 1689.[96] Government was based on consent, Burke recognised, and consent was partly formed out of the sense of public convenience. But the idea of permanently subjecting the constitution of a country to ongoing revision at the behest of transient preferences

[92] On this, see J.G.A. Pocock, "The Fourth English Civil War: Dissolution, Desertion, and Alternative Histories in the Glorious Revolution" in Lois G. Schwoerer ed., *The Revolution of 1688–1689: Changing Perspectives* (Cambridge: Cambridge University Press, 1992).

[93] For the context of such justifications down to the advent of Whig ascendancy, see Kenyon, *Revolution Principles*.

[94] EB, *Reflections*, ed. Clark, p. 179 [41].

[95] Ibid. For discussion of the utilitarian basis of political argument in Burke, see David Dwan, "Burke and Utility" in David Dwan and Christopher Insole eds., *The Cambridge Companion to Edmund Burke* (Cambridge: Cambridge University Press, 2012).

[96] EB, *Reflections*, ed. Clark, p. 170 [35]. Hume, *History of England*, VI, p. 517, refers to a "temporary dissolution of government" between the flight of James II and the determinations of the convention parliament.

among its people was a recipe for perpetual civil war. Stable government required more than the "present sense of convenience, or the bent of a present inclination."[97] A project of ongoing fundamental revision would inevitably involve a programme of serial dissolution, decomposing "the whole civil and political mass, for the purpose of originating a new civil order out of the first elements of society."[98] For that reason, all systems of government, in fostering consent, relied on respect for enduring procedures as well as the variable sense of public convenience.[99] This attitude of respect was fed by various elements in human psychology: first, by admiration, and the deference that it inspired; second, by a veneration for the antiquity of past practice; and, finally, by an aesthetic sense of reverence for power. The first two components in particular are mutually related since veneration for the past grows out of admiration for elders. The efficacy of this combination of admiration and veneration in constituting respect for authority dominates Burke's censure of Price's ideas, and consequently his account of 1688–9. Since the Revolution was focused on the fate of the monarchy, the mode of succession was the issue under discussion. British monarchical succession was determined by heredity. Accordingly, it was this principle, and not election, which guided deliberation when the succession to James II became an issue.[100] Moreover, it was this principle which had underpinned the British monarchy through the ages, however it might have originally been based on some version of popular choice: "the inheritable principle survived through all transmigrations."[101]

The principle of hereditary office, like that of hereditary honours, carried with it two assets that benefited the constitution: first, it explicitly advertised the fact of continuity; and second, it associated continuity with family tradition.[102] Both

[97] EB, *Reflections*, ed. Clark, p. 175 [30]: "They acted by the ancient organized states [i.e. the Commons and Lords], in the shape of their old organization [i.e. parliament], and not by the organic *moleculae* of a disbanded people [i.e. as if in the state of nature]."

[98] Ibid., p. 170 [29].

[99] The French, however, had rejected every "principle of attachment, except a sense of present convenience." See ibid., p. 252 [131–32].

[100] Charles James Fox was to contest this claim three years later. See Fox, Debate on the Address of Thanks, 13 December 1792, *Parliamentary History*, XXX, col. 22.

[101] Ibid., p. 171 [30]. The elective nature of the original European ("German") monarchies was emphasised by Charles-Louis de Secondat, Baron de Montesquieu, *De l'esprit des lois* (1748) in *Œuvres complètes*, ed. Roger Caillois (Paris: Gallimard, 1951), 2 vols., II, pt. VI, bk. 31, ch. 4, following Tacitus, *Germania*, I, 7: "reges . . . sumunt (they select their kings)." For discussion, see Michael Sonenscher, *Before the Deluge: Public Debt, Inequality, and the Intellectual Origins of the French Revolution* (Princeton, NJ: Princeton University Press, 2007), pp. 137ff. Burke follows Montesquieu at *Reflections*, ed. Clark, p. 161 [19]. He had long accepted the point: see EB, Speech on the Civil Establishment Bill, 8 March 1780, *W & S*, III, p. 555: "Property and subjects existed before Kings were elected." Cf. EB, Speech on the Duration of Parliaments, 8 May 1780, ibid., p. 590: "there are few Nations whose Monarch was not originally elective." For Hume, *History*, I, pp. 161–62, the Saxon monarchies combined election with heredity. Burke followed him in EB, *An Essay towards an Abridgement of English History* (1757–c. 1763), *W & S*, I, pp. 434–35. William Robertson, *The History of Scotland* (London: 1759), 2 vols., I, p. 14, follows Montesquieu.

[102] Cf. EB, *Letter to a Noble Lord* (1796), *W & S*, IX, p. 183.

involved the idea of entailment, as with an estate. Burke cited the terms of the Declaration of Right and the Act of Settlement to drive home the point, the one being an Act for "*settling*" the "*succession*" of the crown, the other an Act which bound "us and our *heirs*, and our *posterity*, to them, their *heirs*, and their *posterity*."[103] Unlike the elective arrangements that periodically shook the Polish commonwealth and the Holy Roman Empire, the principle of heredity added the prescriptive authority of historical transmission to the certainty of succession.[104] Antiquity and continuity were integral to allegiance, adding the support of ancestral attachment to the feeling of consent based on an appreciation of the common interest. Burke cited Virgil's *Georgics* on the lifecycle of the beehive to explain the ancestral appeal: "the race remains immortal (*genus immortale manet*) . . . and the grandfathers of grandfathers (*avi . . . avorum*) are enumerated."[105] Burke's acute sense of the legitimating effect of historical precedent is usually ascribed to his exposure to the common law.[106] It would be truer to say that the common law, like the oracles of the Glorious Revolution, illustrated for Burke a disposition of the human mind to venerate the idea of pedigree.

Pure pedigree can be distinguished from a reasonable tradition transmitted by a process of accredited deliberation exemplified by the common law. Antiquity as such was capable of conferring authority on the body of past usages exclusively on the basis of the idea of heritage. Long-established practices commonly embodied wisdom, deriving from the accumulated verdict of artificial reason.[107] In this way, prejudice found support in the fund of refined judgment handed down from enlightened predecessors: "We are afraid to put men to live and trade each on his own private stock of reason; because we suspect that this stock in each man is small, and that the individuals would do better to avail themselves of the general bank and

[103] The Declaration of Right of March 1689 was given statutory form in the Bill of Rights of 16 December 1689. Burke cites it, with his own italics, in *Reflections*, ed. Clark, p. 163 [22]. For discussion, see Lois G. Schwoerer, *The Declaration of Rights, 1689* (Baltimore, MD: Johns Hopkins University Press, 1981). Burke also adds his own emphasis to the citation above from the Act of Settlement (1701), Clause I, in *Reflections*, ed. Clark, p. 173 [33].

[104] Burke commented in his "History of Europe" in *The Annual Register for the Year 1763* (London: 1764), p. 44, that the experience of elective monarchies in modern Europe proved "beyond all speculation, the infinite superiority, in every respect, of hereditary monarchy." Earlier, in "That Politics May Be Reduced to a Science," *Essays*, p. 18, Hume argued that the superiority of hereditary over elective monarchy was a universally defensible maxim of politics.

[105] EB, *Reflections*, ed. Clark, p. 171 [30–31], citing Virgil, *Georgics*, IV, lines 208–9.

[106] See J.G.A. Pocock, *The Ancient Constitution and the Feudal Law: A Study of English Historical Thought in the Seventeenth Century* (Cambridge: Cambridge University Press, 1957, 1987), pp. 242–43. Cf. J.G.A Pocock, "Burke and the Ancient Constitution: A Problem in the History of Ideas" in idem, *Politics, Language and Time: Essays on Political Thought and History* (Chicago, IL: University of Chicago Press, 1971, 1989). For criticism, see Paul Lucas, "On Edmund Burke's Doctrine of Prescription; Or, an Appeal from the New to the Old Lawyers," *Historical Journal*, 11:1 (1968), pp. 35–63.

[107] See EB, *Reflections*, ed. Clark, p. 259 [141] on jurisprudence as "the collected reason of ages." See above, chapter 2, section 2 for Burke's early admiration for the reliance of common lawyers on the cumulative refinements of artificial reason.

capital of nations, and of ages."[108] Yet prejudice could equally draw credit from its purely venerable status. There was a "powerful prepossession towards antiquity" in British culture, and it expressed itself when justifying rights and franchises "as an *inheritance*."[109] Imagining the polity in terms of its historical continuity was to view it on the analogy of change in nature: as with natural and human reproduction, continuity is evident amidst change.[110] The naturalness of "preserving the method of nature in the conduct of the state" meant that the authority of prescription was itself a law of nature.[111]

Viewing national politics as an inheritance stamped it in the image of "a relative in blood."[112] Here Burke drew on the idea of the *mos maiorum*, which blended the authority of the past into the authority of elders.[113] Tradition was thus imagined as preserving kinship along with custom. On this basis, the state in classical theory was commonly personified in the form of a progenitor. The laws of the city, as Plato argued in a famous passage in the *Crito*, should be regarded as the "parents" of the citizen.[114] The same familial emblem pervades the literature of Rome.[115] For this reason, devotion to *familia* and *patria* could be brought together under the common duty of *pietas*: "piety admonishes us to sustain our duty towards our country, our parents, and our kin."[116] Reinvigorating these attitudes, Burke invoked what he called a "pious predilection" for the past.[117] This predilection illustrated powerful human instincts that moved the mind to revere precedent and tradition. This gave

[108] EB, *Reflections*, ed. Clark, p. 251 [130].

[109] Ibid., p. 182 [45].

[110] Ibid., p. 184 [48].

[111] Ibid., pp. 184–85 (48–49]. Burke later cites Jean Domat, *The Civil Law in its Natural Order, together with the Public Law*, trans. William Strahan (London: 1722), 2 vols., I, pp. 483–97, to this effect. See EB, *Reflections*, ed. Clark, p. 322 [233]. Cf. EB, *Letter to Richard Burke* (post February 1792), *W & S*, IX, p. 657.

[112] EB, *Reflections*, ed. Clark, p. 185 [49]. On this theme in Burke, see Ali ʿAl'Amin Mazrui, "Edmund Burke and Reflections on the Revolution in the Congo," *Comparative Studies in Society and History*, 5:2 (January 1963), pp. 121–33, which substantially influenced Conor Cruise O'Brien, "Introduction" to Edmund Burke, *Reflections on the Revolution in France* (Harmondsworth: Penguin, 1970). For O'Brien's notes and comments on this article, see Conor Cruise O'Brien, "Burke," New York University Archives, the Albert Schweitzer Chair in the Humanities, Conor Cruise O'Brien Files, box 5, folder 8. Cf. idem, *The Great Melody: A Thematic Biography of Edmund Burke* (London: Sinclair-Stevenson, 1992).

[113] See Suetonius, *De grammaticis et rhetoribus*, XXV, i, 15: "All innovation contrary to the usage and customs of our ancestors does not seem right." Cf. EB, *An Appeal from the New to the Old Whigs, in Consequence of some Late Discussions in Parliament, relative to the Reflections on the Revolution in France* (London: 1791), p. 70.

[114] Plato, *Crito*, 51e. This section of the dialogue is cited in David Hume, "Of the Original Contract," *Essays*, p. 487; Smith, *Theory of Moral Sentiments*, p. 233.

[115] See, for example, Cicero, *De re publica*, fragments of the Preface preserved in Nonius Marcellus, 428.8, repr. in Cicero, *On the Commonwealth and On the Laws*, ed. James E. G. Zetzel (Cambridge: Cambridge University Press, 1999), p. 1: "our country . . . is a parent prior to our biological parents."

[116] Cicero, *De inventione*, II, 66. On this topic, see Gertrude Emilie, "Cicero and the Roman *Pietas*," *Classical Journal*, 39:9 (June 1944), pp. 536–42.

[117] EB, *Reflections*, ed. Clark, p. 187 [51].

to the feeling of allegiance the weight of authority, based on deference to seniority and standing: "We procure reverence to our civil institutions on the principle upon which nature teaches us to revere individual men; on account of their age; and on account of those from whom they are descended."[118] This was nothing other than the mental disposition supporting the "right to POWER," which Hume had examined in 1742. Its operation can be observed, he wrote, in "the attachment which all nations have to their ancient government, and even to those names, which have the sanction of antiquity."[119] Building on Adam Smith, the Foxite Scottish theorist John Millar studied the effects of authority through a diversity of settings, from primitive peoples to modern commercial states.[120] For Burke, authority added dignity to the evanescent assent that underwrote national allegiance. It consolidated attachment through the idea of descent. It lent patriotism "an imposing and majestic aspect."[121] As a consequence, it restrained the spirit of freedom under the influence of habit: "By this means our liberty becomes a noble freedom."[122]

But if the binding force of inherited custom stabilised allegiance, it did not determine its content altogether. Speaking on the continuation of proceedings against Hastings on 21 December 1790, Burke had occasion to address the role of precedent in legal argument. Its authority, he then recognised, was entirely circumscribed. Legal rules had to be "agreeable to the general tenor of legal principles which overrule precedents."[123] They had to be agreeable, in other words, to the overriding principle of the good of the community. In general terms, therefore, citizens acquiesced in their obligations to government on the basis of the common interest as well as past authority. It followed that acquiescence did not make allegiance unconditional.

[118] Ibid., p. 185 [50]. Cf. Cicero, *De inventione*, II, 66: "reverence [*observantia*], by which we respect and cultivate those who are superior in age, wisdom, honour or standing."

[119] David Hume, "Of the First Principles of Government," *Essays*, p. 33. On this theme in Hume and Smith, see Istvan Hont, "Commercial Society and Political Theory in the Eighteenth Century: The Problem of Authority in David Hume and Adam Smith" in Willem Melching and Wyger Velema eds., *Main Trends in Cultural History: Ten Essays* (Amsterdam: Editions Rodopi B.V., 1994). See also Donald Winch, *Riches and Poverty: An Intellectual History of Political Economy in Britain, 1750–1834* (Cambridge: Cambridge University Press, 1996), ch. 7; cf. idem, "The Burke–Smith Problem in Late Eighteenth-Century Political and Economic Thought," *Historical Journal*, 28:1 (1985), pp. 231–47. Hume's argument was indebted to William Temple, for which see Bourke, "Sovereignty and Opinion in Burke," pp. 100, 115–16.

[120] John Millar, *The Origins of the Distinction of Ranks* (1771), ed. Aaron Garrett (Indianapolis, IN: Liberty Fund, 2006), ch. 3; John Millar, *An Historical View of the English Government* (1787, 1803), ed. Mark Salber Phillips and Dale R. Smith (Indianapolis, IN: Liberty Fund, 2006), pp. 795ff. The first edition of the work was dedicated to Charles James Fox. For criticism of Burke as having deserted "his former tenets" in 1790, see p. 806n. For Millar's debt to Smith, see Smith, *Lectures on Jurisprudence*, p. 318: "everyone naturally has a disposition to respect an established authority, and superiority in others." Cf. Smith, *Theory of Moral Sentiments*, p. 231.

[121] EB, *Reflections*, ed. Clark, p. 185 [49].

[122] Ibid. Cf. Hume, *History of England*, VI, p. 533: "a regard for liberty, though a laudable passion, ought commonly to be subordinate to a reverence for established government."

[123] EB, Speech on Continuation of the Impeachment, 23 December 1790, *W & S*, VII, p. 83.

It was surely right that no government "could stand a moment, if it could be blown down with any thing so loose and indefinite as an opinion of 'misconduct.'"[124] Nonetheless, Burke standardly regarded the obligation to obedience as susceptible of being relinquished on two grounds: on the basis of "necessity" on the one hand, and on account of "delinquency" on the other.[125] In dismissing the idea that a British monarch might be deposed on the grounds of "misconduct," Burke appears to have abandoned the criterion of delinquency in the *Reflections*. On closer inspection, however, its ongoing role is clear. Delinquency implies rather more than incidental misconduct: it points to persistent abuse in the exercise of power. At that stage, resistance becomes legitimate. "The speculative line of demarcation, where obedience ought to end, and resistance must begin, is faint, obscure, and not easily definable," Burke commented. Government must be "deranged indeed" before it can be resorted to.[126] But where the ends of government were themselves subverted by the misapplication of power, the duty of allegiance was brought to an end. As Hume had similarly argued, it was impossible to prescribe rules in advance of a rebellion that would ring-fence the inviolable rights of the people.[127] The betrayal of trust was a matter of practical judgment and a question of popular sentiment. Nonetheless, there were circumstances under which the justice of resistance would be evident to judgment, and rebellion would ensue.

Burke felt able to endorse rebellion a number of times during the course of his career. The resistance of America in 1776 was the most momentous of those occasions. The passage of the Prohibitory Act in 1775, together with the delay in sending commissioners to the colonies as a means of providing redress, exposed the Americans to hostility without any means of peaceful submission.[128] As Burke pointed out in October 1776, this dissolved the duty of obedience based on the provision of protection.[129] For this reason, in the notes he prepared for his speech on the Prohibitory Bill, he described the measure as "a solemn publick act made for separating the Colonies from the British Empire, a complete abdication of your authority."[130] What Burke's response shows is that he understood delinquency as creating a *need* for resistance. Accordingly, he took the Revolution of 1776 as having been a matter

[124] EB, *Reflections*, ed. Clark, p. 177 [38].

[125] Burke first invoked these criteria in a discussion about the culpability of the East India Company in 1773. See WWM BkP 9:17. Cf. EB, *Fox's India Bill*, p. 387. For discussion, see above, chapter 10, sections 5–6.

[126] EB, *Reflections*, ed. Clark, p. 181 [43].

[127] Hume, *History of England*, VI, pp. 293–94.

[128] See above, chapter 9, sections 6–7.

[129] EB, Amendment to Address, 31 October 1776, *W & S*, III, p. 249. David Hartley had already expatiated on the right of resistance in the debate on the expense of the American war on 5 December 1775 in *Parliamentary History*, XIX, esp. col. 554. However, unlike Burke, he took the right to have been adumbrated in the Bill of Rights.

[130] WWM BkP 6:119.

of "*necessity*" rather than "*choice*."[131] Later, in 1777, he contended that it was the "hostile mind" of the administration towards the American people that fully justified "a change of government" by force.[132] Burke was prone to arguing that, in general, rebellion was provoked by misrule, rather than being fomented by the ideology of malcontents.[133] Certainly this was the defence he offered for the insurgency of Chait Singh, the Raja of Benares, in 1781. As Burke argued at the Hastings trial in 1788, a resort to arms in this case was enjoined by the rights of man.[134] Their violation put the East India Company into a state of war with a portion of its subjects, triggering the necessity of recourse to revolution. Necessity was likewise the justification for 1688, with Burke resorting to Livy for the legitimating adage: "iustum est bellum . . . quibus necessarium."[135] The Revolution in France was different: no necessity existed here. Insurrection had been fostered rather than compelled. In December 1781 Burke had described the conditions of incarceration at the Bastille as "ridiculously grand" even though it was regarded as "the horridest jail of a despotic and arbitrary government."[136] The truth was, he now suggested, that long before the storming of the prison on 14 July 1789, "all arbitrary imprisonments, with all other effects of Arbitrary power[,] were at an End."[137] The jail may have been symbolic, but Burke's point was substantive. The French had rebelled against "a mild and lawful monarch"; bizarrely, they had revolted against their protection under a moderate regime.[138]

Necessity in 1688 was determined by the absence of an alternative: either a temporary deviation in the strict order of succession to the crown had to be undertaken, or the peace of the kingdom would be definitely squandered.[139] This was a "grave and over-ruling necessity," Burke wrote: a necessity "in the strictest moral sense in which necessity can be taken."[140] That is, it was an act of war undertaken in an "extreme emergency" as a means of avoiding protracted civil war.[141] *Necessitas non habet legem*, Burke was aware. Dire exigency did not provide a rule for future action. Resistance should be an act of extra-legal desperation, not a constitutional procedure that could be scripted in advance. Burke excoriated the allegedly antinomian doctrines

[131] EB, Speech on Cavendish's Motion on America, 6 November 1776, *W & S*, III, p. 253. Cf. EB, Address to the King, 1777, ibid., p. 269.

[132] EB, *Letter to the Sheriffs of Bristol*, 3 April 1777, *W & S*, III, p. 306. Cf. ibid., pp. 292, 307, 312.

[133] Ibid., p. 310.

[134] Northamptonshire MS. A. XXII.60. For discussion, see above chapter 12, section 6.

[135] Livy, *Ab urbe condita*, IX, i, 10–11, cited in EB, *Reflections*, ed. Clark, p. 180 [43]: "*iusta bella quibus necessaria*."

[136] EB, Debate on the Case of Henry Laurens, 17 December 1781, *Parliamentary History*, XXII, col. 858.

[137] WWM BkP 10:16.

[138] EB, *Reflections*, ed. Clark, pp. 190–91 [56]. Cf. EB, *Appeal from the New to the Old Whigs*, p. 18.

[139] Burke considered the matter in detail during the regency crisis. See WWM BkP 15:6, and WWM BkP 15:25.

[140] EB, *Reflections*, ed. Clark, pp. 177 [39], 165 [24]. See also ibid., p. 261 [144]. Cf. EB, *Appeal from the New to the Old Whigs*, pp. 58ff.

[141] EB, *Reflections*, ed. Clark, p. 169 [29].

of dissenters in 1777, but he did not expect domestic subversion to proceed from their commitment to the rights of popular resistance. By 1790, however, things had changed. In the aftermath of the Revolution in France, ideologically driven assaults on the British constitutional *pax* posed a threat to the security of the domestic political order. Events across the Channel recalled 1648, not the glorious deliverance of forty years later. The problem with Paine, Priestley and Price was that they could not offer an account of the 1640s, which could hardly be presented as an unproblematic success. Weighing up the consequences of the execution of Charles I in the penultimate volume of his *History of England*, Hume pointed to prudent restrictions that ought perhaps to limit public reasoning on political subjects. The doctrine of resistance, he argued, was capable of such devastation that its tenets ought at the very least to be officially opposed: "it is dangerous to weaken, by . . . speculations, the reverence, which the multitude owe to authority."[142] True enlightenment involved combatting false prophets of enlightenment. The *Reflections*, faced with a resurgence of the attitudes of the 1640s, was Burke's response to what he saw as the specious illumination of fanatics.

13.4 The True Moral Equality of Mankind

By comparison with previous "great" rebellions, the French Revolution had been unprovoked and had nothing noble in view. Thinking even of England in the late 1670s, Burke could understand the inevitability of "great heats and tempestuous passions" awoken by fears of oppression.[143] Such fear could spark the ambition to secure a regime of liberty. However, freedom in France meant nothing but contending for the rights of man. It was, in truth, an expression of petty resentments rather than outrage at abuse. Motivated as this was by grasping passion rather than moral rectitude, Burke thought of it as brought about by an "unforced choice" instead of on account of imposing reasons of state.[144] It had begun with the treachery of the nobility, and was sustained by the petty discontents of an aspiring commons.[145] This contrasted markedly with the stand adopted by the protagonists in the French wars of religion, and likewise by the leaders of the Fronde. Even more conspicuously, the character of the modern partisans of rebellion could be distinguished from that of Cromwell, "one of the great bad men of the old stamp."[146] As Burke painted him, Cromwell was austere, but not degraded: he shone by his own talents, appearing less as an upstart than as aiming to assert his "natural place in society."[147] As he rose, he

142 Hume, *History of England*, V, p. 544. The phrasing is identical in the 1754 edition.

143 EB, Speech on Continuation of the Impeachment, 23 December 1790, *W & S*, VII, p. 92.

144 EB, *Reflections*, ed. Clark, p. 193 [58].

145 On this motif, see EB, *Letter to a Noble Lord* (1796), *W & S*, IX, p. 171, reprimanding "a misguided populace, set on by proud great men, themselves blinded and intoxicated by a frantick ambition."

146 EB, *Reflections*, ed. Clark, p. 204 [70].

147 Ibid., p. 204 [70–71].

exalted those who followed in his wake, and sought to preserve the dignity of the state. Similarly the French in the sixteenth century, even in the midst of civil war, retained the idea of distinction and the practice of emulation: "All the prizes of honour and virtue, all the rewards, all the distinctions, remained."[148]

For Hume, the early period of the Stuart reign had encouraged the spread of knowledge resulting in a fermentation of ideas. Views were enlarged, and expectations of liberty increased.[149] The gothic components of the constitution soon collided as the power of the Commons rose. Yet in the 1630s and, above all, in the 1640s, this rise was overtaken by attitudes of resistance that at first espoused the rights of parliament and later championed democratic ideas. These ideas had originally been promoted in the city, and were later disseminated through the army.[150] As Hume presents it, the ideology became prevalent among the Independents.[151] In the late 1640s, it prospered among the soldiers campaigning against the monarchy, captivating pious militants by the appeal of equality: "An entire parity had place among the elect: And, by the same rule, that the apostles were exalted from the most ignoble professions, the meanest sentinel, if enlightened by the spirit, was entitled to equal regard with the greatest commander."[152] It is notable that Burke, who paid such attention to Hume's *History*, was insistent that, even in the midst of these currents, rebellion never degenerated into rapacity. In England at least, there was no assault on property, and Leveller ideas proved marginal to Cromwell's plans. Even as the conquest of the country advanced by the hand of a "destroying angel," there was dignity in contention, and a long-term purpose in the resort to war.[153] With France, by comparison, there was a levity in its proceedings, mysteriously galvanised by popular fury. What drove this was the promise of popular equality, displacing the "true" equality of differentiated orders.

The distinction here is subtle but important. In the *Reflections*, Burke was anxious to extol the "true moral equality of mankind," which he contrasted with the "monstrous fiction" of parity among ranks.[154] Distinctions in society might take many forms, based on differences between power, wealth, rank and merit. True equality reconciled these differences with justice. To this extent, Burke's position was identical with Rousseau's. Civil equality, Rousseau commented, could never be equated with the equality of the state of nature. Every political society was obliged to implement

[148] Ibid., p. 205 [71].

[149] Hume, *History of England*, V, pp. 18–19.

[150] Ibid., pp. 293, 387.

[151] Ibid., pp. 442–43.

[152] Ibid., 513. Cf. ibid., VI, pp. 3–4.

[153] EB, *Reflections*, ed. Clark, p. 204 [71].

[154] Ibid., p. 189 [53]. On Burke's commitment to what might be termed the "unequal equality" of civil society, see Ian Harris, "Paine and Burke: God, Nature and Politics" in Michael Bentley ed., *Public and Private Doctrine: Essays in British History Presented to Maurice Cowling* (Cambridge: Cambridge University Press, 1993). See also idem, "Introduction" to *Burke: Pre-Revolutionary Writings* (Cambridge: Cambridge University Press, 1993); idem, "Burke and Religion" in David Dwan and Chris Insole eds., *The Cambridge Companion to Edmund Burke* (Cambridge: Cambridge University Press, 2012).

a system of distributive justice whereby distinctions were reconciled with the prevailing sense of justice. In the final note to his *Discours sur l'origine de l'inégalité*, Rousseau justified his commitment to reasonable inequality: the citizens of a state should be "distingués" and "favorisés" on the basis of their services to the public.[155] Strict or "mathematical" equality, what Rousseau termed "egalité rigoureuse," in failing to make proportionate distinctions among members of society, was equivalent to what Burke described as fictional equality. It was based on a "pretence" of identity between citizens, which even its exponents failed to honour.[156]

Rousseau sought to clinch the point by citing Isocrates on the "two sorts of equality" that were carefully distinguished among the Athenians: one sort, which provided for advantages to be distributed indifferently among the populace; and another, which required that they be allocated differentially according to merit.[157] Only the latter was compatible with civil society, Rousseau thought, and Burke agreed: "those who attempt to level, never equalize."[158] Where Burke departed from the Genevan was in his attachment to forms of distinction rooted in what he described as "the old common law of Europe."[159] What he had in mind here was an idea of equality based on accommodation rather than autonomy. Dependence was a fact of social and political life, based on various gradations of authority and prestige. Equalisation across these differences meant moderating their severity by substituting mutual reliance in the place of illiberal subjection. From this perspective, the opposite of dependence was subjugation, not autonomy, since radical independence was not compatible with a society of ranks. It appeared remarkable to Burke that the French saw fit to receive their theology from Helvétius and Voltaire and their politics from the writings of Rousseau: "We are not the converts of Rousseau; we are not the disciples of Voltaire; Helvétius has made no progress amongst us."[160] The *Contrat social* in particular, he wrote, was a "performance of little or no merit."[161] The price of self-government under the form of popular sovereignty envisaged by Rousseau pre-

[155] Rousseau, *Discours sur l'origine de l'inégalité* in *Œuvres complètes*, III, p. 222.

[156] See EB, *Reflections*, ed. Clark, p. 210 [77], where Burke refers to Price's goal as a "pretence" of equality.

[157] Isocrates, *Areopagitica*, 21–22. Distribution according to merit was dubbed "geometrical" proportionality in Aristotle, *Nicomachean Ethics*, 1130b30–1131b24. Heinrich Meier traces Rousseau's thought to a footnote by Barbeyrac to his edition of Pufendorf, *Droit de la nature*, I, 7, § 11, n. 2: see Jean-Jacques Rousseau, *Diskurs über die ungleicchheit*, ed. Heinrich Meier (Munich: Schöningh, 1984), pp.380–81n. For Rousseau on equality, see Michael Sonenscher, *Sans-Culottes: An Eighteenth-Century Emblem in the French Revolution* (Princeton, NJ: Princeton University Press, 2008), ch. 3. For the political context, see Richard Whatmore, *Against War and Empire: Geneva, Britain, and France in the Eighteenth Century* (New Haven, CT: Yale University Press, 2012), ch. 3. For Burke and Rousseau, see below, chapter 14, section 3.

[158] EB, *Reflections*, ed. Clark, p. 205 [72].

[159] Ibid., p. 188 [53].

[160] Ibid., pp. 249–50 [127].

[161] EB to Unknown, January 1790, *Corr.*, VI, p. 81.

supposed a level of national cohesion that could not be achieved in modern societies based on a diversity of roles and significant differences in standing.

This vision of heterogeneity was fundamental to Burke's social and political thought, and underpinned the argument of the *Reflections*. Inequality, he thought, could never be removed; consequently, enlightened politics should aim to make it compatible with reciprocity. Distinctions of power and wealth existed in civil life "as much for the benefit of those whom it must leave in an humble state, as those whom it is able to exalt to a condition more splendid, but not more happy."[162] General commercial prosperity was the most obvious advantage, based on an unequal command of resources and a complex division of labour. In the face of this benign yet potentially aggravating arrangement, delusive claims to equality, stoking "vain expectations," would merely embitter social relations that supported accommodation irrespective of differences in power and wealth.[163] The progress of European civilisation had mitigated differential antagonism, liberalised interaction, and facilitated emulation and improvement. At the same time, inequality was assuaged by the path to happiness available to the virtuous of all conditions. To subvert this achievement by overturning the whole edifice of artificial society was to undo every viable relationship in the name of natural equality. Much like a "palsy," egalitarian ideologues were in the process of attacking "the fountain of life itself."[164] Since society in its progress generated distinctions, a war against that process was sure to be as devastating as it was bound to be counterproductive: "some description must be uppermost," Burke asserted; the Revolutionaries could only hope to invert established distinctions, never to secure their abolition.[165] Even Price himself, as Burke observed, disregarded what he termed the "*dregs*" of the people.[166]

The singular success of modern European civilisation had resulted from grafting a market society onto a society of orders. The combination of these two modes of interaction formed the basis of domestic peace and prosperity across the continent. Market society, driven by exchange, founded on reciprocal need, promoted equality of standing in the midst of inequality of resources. Commercial sociability of the kind in Europe was superimposed upon a society of ranks. European rank-ordered society, Burke claimed, was ultimately indebted to the "spirit of a gentleman."[167] It was allegedly the pre-existence of this "spirit" that facilitated the emergence of a peaceful commercial order.[168] Governed by the principle of "*Fealty*," the culture of

[162] EB, *Reflections*, ed. Clark, p. 189 [54].

[163] Ibid.

[164] Ibid., p. 205 [71–72].

[165] Ibid., p. 205 [72].

[166] Ibid., p. 214 [83].

[167] Ibid., p. 241 [117]. On this, see J.G.A. Pocock, "The Political Economy of Burke's Analysis of the French Revolution" in idem, *Virtue, Commerce, and History*.

[168] Northamptonshire MS. A. XXVII.75: "The refined state of Europe in a great measure due to it."

gentility was based on the idea of moral equality underlying a hierarchy of status.[169] The constitutional organisation of mainstream European politics was underpinned by this mechanism of social accommodation, distinguishing it to its advantage from the regimes of the east and the republican polities of the ancient world.[170] Fealty was not based on need, and so could not be reduced to commercial utility. The mutual allegiance between vassal and lord was a reciprocal tie of loyalty based, as Burke presented it, on disinterested attachment. Pledged to fidelity, the medieval knight was at the same time typically animated by chivalry and piety. His code of honour thus bound him to God, women, the vulnerable and his superiors.[171] The love of women was idealising rather than sensual; the love of God promoted an ethic of devotion; and loyalty to one's benefactor inspired an attitude of service that rejected the temptations of spoil.[172] According to William Robertson, it was this mentality that softened the manners of medieval Europe, conspicuously diminishing the ferocity of war.[173] As Adam Ferguson observed in a similar vein, feudal heroism, unlike the republican heroism of the ancient city-states, appeared admirable to the extent that it was compatible with commiseration.[174] In Burke's hands, this matrix of values became the "mixed system" of sentiments that underlay modern social and sexual attitudes, extending from the battlefield to the salon.[175] Its crucial feature, in the context of the *Reflections*, was that it reconciled the disparity of conditions by means of sympathetic goodwill.

As a result of the successful dissemination of these dispositions, loyalty to rank and sex was made "generous."[176] This point was essential to Burke's argument. Commerce, as Robertson had argued in passages of his *History of the Reign of Charles V* that Burke still recalled, "unites" by ties of interest.[177] Yet for Burke the bonds of utility would prove insufficient to hold the divisions of a complex society together,

[169] See Richard Bourke, "Edmund Burke and Enlightenment Sociability: Justice, Honour and the Principles of Government," *History of Political Thought*, 21:4 (2000), pp. 632–55.

[170] EB, *Reflections*, ed. Clark, p. 239 [113].

[171] William Robertson, *The History of the Reign of the Emperor Charles V* (Dublin: 1762–71), 2 vols., I, pp. 61ff. Cf. Adam Ferguson, *An Essay on the History of Civil Society*, ed. Fania Oz-Salzberger (Cambridge: Cambridge University Press, 1995, 2003), pp. 191ff. This work was given an enthusiastic review, possibly by Burke, in *The Annual Register for the Year 1767* (London: 1768), pp. 307–13. The review is attributed to Burke in Thomas Copeland, "Edmund Burke and the Book Reviews in Dodsley's *Annual Register*," *Publications of the Modern Language Association*, 57:2 (June 1942), pp. 446–68, though the attribution cannot be certain.

[172] See Millar, *Distinction of Ranks*, pp. 137–39.

[173] Robertson, *Reign of Charles V*, I, p. 62: "War was carried on with less ferocity, when humanity came to be deemed the ornament of knighthood no less than courage."

[174] Ferguson, *History of Civil Society*, p 191.

[175] EB, *Reflections*, ed. Clark, p. 238 [113]. For discussion, see R. J. Smith, *The Gothic Bequest: Medieval Institutions in British Thought, 1688–1863* (Cambridge: Cambridge University Press, 1987), pp. 119–20.

[176] EB, *Reflections*, ed. Clark, p. 238 [113].

[177] Robertson, *Reign of Charles V*, I, p. 71.

above all where property and status were unequally distributed: "in destroying the original principle of modern manners—arts & commerce may suffer also."[178] Liberality of manners was needed to support the pursuit of interest if social harmony was to be preserved.[179] Historically, this had been bequeathed by the nexus of chivalry and fealty. By the operation of these principles, divisions were supplanted by mutual accommodation: in the midst of social distinctions, a "noble equality" was diffused through "all the gradations of social life."[180] The pride of the great bowed down before the esteem of their admirers; the resentment of the aspiring succumbed to the elegance of the powerful. Authority was made gentle; submission was freely given. Burke sometimes described this rapprochement in the language of friendship: *amicitia* involved loyalty based on deferential benevolence.[181] More commonly, however, Burke thought of the harmony of orders as a peculiarly European achievement, indebted to the dynamics of admiration. As Burke saw it, the key feature of admiration was appreciation, not profit. In this sense, it was founded on an aesthetic sensibility, or the pleasures of a "moral imagination."[182] In being captivated by the beauty and sublimity of manners, social distinction could be relished rather than resented.

In arguing that deference was inspired by taste, Burke wanted to show two things at once: first, that moral sensibility was refined by elegance: "vice," he wrote, "lost half its evil, by losing all its grossness."[183] Second, he wanted to show that the assimilation of ranks was not based on considerations of interest alone. One could appreciate refinement in a disinterested fashion: one did not have to "possess" it.[184] For this reason, all the artifice of elegant life, what Burke termed its "pleasing illusions,"

[178] Northamptonshire MS. A. XXVII.75.

[179] Cf. EB, Speech on Traitorous Correspondence Bill, 9 April 1793, *Parliamentary History*, XXX, col. 645: "commerce was a subservient instrument to her greater interests, her security, her honour and her religion."

[180] EB, *Reflections*, ed. Clark, p. 239 [113].

[181] See Cicero, *De amicitia*, IX, 31. For discussion, see chapter 5, section 6 above. Cf. Richard Bourke, "Liberty, Authority and Trust in Burke's Idea of Empire," *Journal of the History of Ideas*, 61:3 (Summer 2000), pp. 453–71, p. 469.

[182] EB, *Reflections*, ed. Clark, p. 239 [114]. On this, see Richard Bourke, "Pity and Fear: Providential Sociability in Burke's *Philosophical Enquiry*" in Michael Funk Deckard and Koen Vermeir eds., *The Science of Sensibility: Reading Edmund Burke's Philosophical Enquiry* (Dordrecht: Springer, 2012). For a different reading of this passage in Burke, see David Bromwich, "Moral Imagination," *Raritan*, 27:4 (Spring 2008), pp. 4–33.

[183] EB, *Reflections*, ed. Clark, p. 238 [113].

[184] The same principle applied to the appreciation of female beauty as determined by the culture of chivalry: see Robertson, *Reign of Charles V*, I, pp. 62–3. For the intellectual origins of the idea that beauty could be relished without profit, see Francis Hutcheson, *Inquiry into the Original of Our Ideas of Beauty and Virtue*, ed. Wolfgang Leidhold (Indianapolis, IN: Liberty Fund, 2004), p. 26: "there must be a Sense of Beauty, antecedent to Prospects even of . . . advantage." For discussion, see Paul Guyer, "Beauty and Utility in Eighteenth-Century Aesthetics" in idem, *Values of Beauty: Historical Essays in Aesthetics* (Cambridge: Cambridge University Press, 2005).

inspired assent and approbation without the prospect of advantage.[185] On that basis, human life was progressively clothed in "decent drapery," conferring dignity and estimation on "unaccommodated" man.[186] To "uncover our nakedness" was to strip away the accretions of civilisation.[187] To want to do so was a cynical exercise in conflating humanity with its animal functions.[188] Under the influence of aesthetic sensibility, the temptations of bestial appetite were kept at bay by their repulsiveness. With the assault on the queen in her quarters at Versailles on the morning of 6 October 1789, however, taste was degraded, respect for rank and sex exploded, and human relations stripped to the naked impulse of rapacity. This amounted to a revolution in the inclination to "politeness," a reduction to natural equality as satirised by Burke in his *Vindication of Natural Society* thirty-four years before.[189] Equality of the kind, he then saw, was no more than a rudimentary animality.[190] By way of contrast, the artifice of civilisation, based on the refinement of manners, supported the impulse to humanity and the affection to rank. It ensured that the various "shades of life" were harmoniously allied to one another.[191] Building on these instincts, public life in general was made decorous and delightful: high office appeared sublime, and the *patria* beautiful: "love, veneration, admiration, [and] attachment" bound citizens to their polity.[192]

Burke dwelt at great length on the events of 5–6 October 1789 in the *Reflections* because they so perfectly captured the revolt against humanity that governed the Revolution. It was, he proposed, "the most horrid, atrocious, and affecting spectacle, that perhaps ever was exhibited to the pity and indignation of mankind."[193] The descent of the *poissardes* upon Versailles, the assault on the queen's bedchamber, the

[185] EB, *Reflections*, ed. Clark, p. 239 [114].

[186] Ibid. The reference to "unaccommodated man" here is to William Shakespeare, *King Lear*, Act III, Scene iv. For the resonance of the play in the depiction of Marie Antoinette, see Seamus Deane, *Strange Country: Modernity and Nationhood in Irish Writing since 1790* (Oxford: Oxford University Press, 1997), pp. 10–11.

[187] EB, *Reflections*, ed. Clark, p. 255 [135].

[188] Cf. EB, "Several Scattered Hints Concerning Philosophy and Learning Collected Here from My Papers" (c. 1755) in *A Notebook of Edmund Burke: Poems, Characters, Essays and Other Sketches in the Hands of Edmund and William Burke*, ed. H.V.F. Somerset (Cambridge: Cambridge University Press, 1957), p. 91: "What shall we say to that philosophy, that would strip it naked?" For discussion, see above, chapter 2, section 3. See further George Berkeley, *Alciphron; or the Minute Philosopher* in *The Works of George Berkeley*, ed. Alexander Campbell Fraser (Oxford: Oxford University Press, 1901), 4 vols., II, p. 119: "one would think the intention of these philosophers was, when they had pruned and weeded the notions of their fellow-subjects, and divested them of their prejudices, to strip them of their clothes, and fill the country with naked followers of nature, enjoying all the privileges of brutality."

[189] EB, *Reflections*, ed. Clark, p. 231 [104].

[190] EB, *Vindication of Natural Society* (1756), *W & S*, I, p. 138: "The original Children of the Earth lived with their Brethren of the other Kinds in much Equality."

[191] EB, *Reflections*, ed. Clark, p. 239 [114].

[192] Ibid., pp. 240–41 [115–16]; cf. ibid., p. 366 [286]. On "delight," see above, chapter 3, section 2. On "national love" or patriotism, cf. Hutcheson, *Inquiry into the Original of Our Ideas of Beauty and Virtue*, pp. 114–15.

[193] EB, *Reflections*, ed. Clark, p. 226 [99].

forced address to the crowd from the royal balcony, the procession to Paris with the heads of decapitated guards on pikes, and the triumphal return of the captive royals to the Tuileries palace, together depicted a world turned upside down.[194] Such events could not fail to shock "the moral taste of every well-born mind."[195] To Philip Francis, however, the meditation on the queen's suffering was "mere foppery," as indeed it has often appeared to subsequent readers.[196] But to Burke a detailed narration of the ordeal of Marie Antoinette served a definite and defensible purpose. His aim in the *Reflections*, he confided to Francis, was to expose Price, and through him Lansdowne, to "hatred, ridicule, and contempt."[197] As Burke read Price's *Discourse*, he appeared to be revelling in the vengeful humiliation of persons of distinction. Price later pointed out, in the Preface to the fourth edition of his sermon, that his exultation had in fact been focused on events of mid-July, not the "riot and slaughter" perpetrated after the women's march on Versailles.[198] Nonetheless, from Burke's perspective, an evocation of the vicious spirit of denigration exhibited on 6 October could best be achieved by conjuring with the spectacle of tragedy, arousing great emotions in the face of a fall from greatness.[199] Are not "high Rank, great Splendour of descent, great personal Elegance, and outward accomplishments ingredients of moment in forming the interest we take in the Misfortunes of Men?" he asked.[200] Burke was to repeat the observation four years later, commenting on how it was "wisely established in the constitution of our heart that mankind interests itself most in the fall and fate of great personages."[201] In the face of such catastrophe, only the most unfeeling could fail to be moved to pity and fear.

Behind Burke's rousing hymn to fealty and chivalry, there was an intention to recover the historical foundations of civilised behaviour. This had to be based on the disinterested appreciation of human qualities, not merely on the usefulness of

[194] After Burke, Carlyle made much of these developments. See Thomas Carlyle, *The French Revolution: A History* (Boston: 1838), 2 vols., I, pp. 244ff. On the same episode, see, more recently, Simon Schama, *Citizens: A Chronicle of the French Revolution* (London: Penguin, 1989), pp. 386–99; Barry Schapiro, *Revolutionary Justice in Paris, 1789–1790* (Cambridge: Cambridge University Press, 1993), ch. 4.

[195] EB, *Reflections*, ed. Clark, p. 226 [99].

[196] Philip Francis to EB, 19 February 1790, *Corr.*, VI, p. 86.

[197] EB to Philip Francis, 20 February 1790, ibid., p. 92.

[198] Richard Price, Preface to the Fourth Edition, *A Discourse on the Love of Our Country* in D. O. Thomas ed., *Price: Political Writings* (Cambridge: Cambridge University Press, 1991), p. 177. For discussion, see Richard Bourke "Theory and Practice: The Revolution in Political Judgement" in *Political Judgement,* ed. Richard Bourke and Raymond Geuss (Cambridge: Cambridge University Press, 2009), pp. 90–99.

[199] Paley argued that the *Reflections* should be regarded as a tragedy, though not in dramatic form: see William Paley to Edmund Law, 28 November 1790, TNA, PRO 30/12/17/4/ 33–35.

[200] EB to Philip Francis, 20 February 1790, ibid., p. 90. Burke returned to the theme in EB to the Bishop of Salisbury, 31 July 1791, *Corr.*, VI, p. 309.

[201] EB, Speech in Reply at Hastings Impeachment, 3 June 1794, *W & S*, VII, p. 340.

our fellows.[202] The chivalric veneration of the "fair sex" dramatised this capacity, since it pointed to the possibility of admiring women "without any consideration whatsoever of enjoying them."[203] Similarly, the obligations of trust and loyalty that characterised fealty were based on generosity, not market worth. Burke advertised these capacities to explain the prerequisites of cohesion, not to recommend the habit of self-abasement. After the appearance of the *Reflections*, he pleaded with Francis: "When did you find me totally unmoved at the distress of hundreds and thousands of my equals, and only touched with the sufferings of guilty greatness?"[204] His aim in the *Reflections* was not to extol cringing compliance, but to elucidate the preconditions of mutual concession. Without concession, there would be conflict, and "natural equality" was essentially a recipe for this conflict. Fawning was repugnant to Burke's Whiggish proclivities: "I am naturally inclined to those who do not command," he affirmed in this period.[205] In other words, he was not a partisan of submissive servitude. There was no virtue in either abject genuflection or short-sighted hostility to property. Creeping "sycophants" who idolised power were as abhorrent as the adversaries of established rank.[206] Between these extremes, Burke styled himself an advocate of personal freedom.[207] Freedom, however, had to be civil freedom. It was, Burke thought, "another name" for justice: "It is not solitary, unconnected, individual, selfish Liberty."[208] It implied the enjoyment of rights secured against the powerful, but it was not to be identified with egalitarian self-assertion. An equality of natural right entailed the subversion of *meum et teum*. The promotion of such values embittered attitudes to social distinctions, and was bound to unleash the furies of the mob.

13.5 Privilege and Merit

A central aim of the *Reflections* was to show how these values had gained momentum by being embodied in a tenacious political force. This involved accounting for the origins of the Revolution, and then explaining how its direction was sustained. Burke largely skated over the early stages of the conflict, beginning with the convo-

[202] On this theme, see the review of Adam Ferguson's *Essay on the History of Civil Society* in *The Annual Register for the Year 1767*, which praises Ferguson's argument for challenging the doctrine of the animality of the human species (associated with Rousseau's *Second Discourse*), and vindicating the idea of amicable or benevolent moral sentiments. For this aspect of Ferguson's thought, see Iain McDaniel, *Adam Ferguson and the Scottish Enlightenment: The Roman Past and Europe's Future* (Cambridge, MA: Harvard University Press, 2013), ch. 3.

[203] EB to Philip Francis, 20 February 1790, *Corr.*, VI, p. 91.

[204] EB to Philip Francis, 19 November 1790, ibid., p. 171.

[205] EB to John Noble, 14 March 1790, ibid., p. 103.

[206] EB, *Reflections*, ed. Clark, p. 208 [76].

[207] On this, see EB, "Observations" to the *First Report* of the Select Committee, 5 February 1782, *W & S*, V, p. 184.

[208] EB to Charles-Jean-François Depont, November 1789, *Corr.*, VI, p. 42.

cation of the Assembly of Notables on 22 February 1787. Soon after gathering at Versailles, members of the Assembly found themselves on a collision course with Calonne that exploded into acrimony in mid-March.[209] By 8 April, the Comptroller-General had been dismissed, with Brienne appointed minister by the end of the month. Yet Brienne's attempts to control the Notables proved as unavailing as his predecessor's, and the Assembly was dissolved at the end of May. Burke explained the deteriorating situation as an effect of the designs of misleading counsellors.[210] Here he had in mind less the machinations of the court than the posture of the provincial and Parisian *parlements*. In June and July, the *parlements* had been expected to register new taxes being proposed by the ministry. It was at this stage that the magistrates of the *parlements* called openly for the summoning of the Estates General, but the gesture appeared to Burke to be grounded in perfidy. In calling for the Estates, "bold and faithless" men, under pretence of honest counsel, planned to use this organ as a weapon against the monarchy.[211] To illustrate his point, Burke emphasised how the convocation was pursued without precaution. This amounted to saying that an opportunity had emerged in 1787–8 to reconstruct a mixed system of government in France, loosely based on the "ancient" constitution of the kingdom.[212] But the chance was squandered by the treachery of the "leaders" of France, not least those in the *parlements* who clamoured for the Estates without adequately preparing for their impact on affairs.[213]

In advancing this narrative of subterfuge by the elite, Burke was partly trading on the suspicion that the Duc d'Orléans had set about subverting the regime.[214] The events of 1788 exposed the mounting distrust between the monarchy and the organs it consulted.[215] This standoff culminated in the attempted evisceration of the *parlements* in July 1788, followed by the threat of imminent bankruptcy in August. That threat undid the royal coup against the *parlements*: the monarchy now capitulated, the Estates General was called, and Necker returned to office. Burke represented the

[209] For an interpretation of the significance of these events, see Albert Goodwin, "Calonne, the Assembly of French Notables of 1787 and the Origins of the 'Révolte Nobiliaire'," *English Historical Review*, 61:240 (May 1946), pp. 202–34, and idem, "Calonne, the Assembly of French Notables of 1787 and the Origins of the 'Révolte Nobiliaire' (Continued)," *English Historical Review*, 61:241 (September 1946), pp. 329–77.

[210] Recent scholarship emphasises the incoherence of the monarchy. See François Furet, *Revolutionary France, 1770–1880* (Oxford: Blackwells, 1992) p. 42.

[211] EB, *Reflections*, ed. Clark, p. 190 [55].

[212] Ibid., p. 186 [50].

[213] Ibid., p. 190 [55]. Burke developed this argument in EB, *Letter to a Member of the National Assembly* (1791), *W & S*, VIII, pp. 327ff. For discussion, see below, chapter 14, section 3.

[214] For the role of the Duc d'Orléans, and his connection with publicists like Sieyès conspiring against the regime, see George Armstrong Kelly, "The Machine of the Duc D'Orléans and the New Politics," *Journal of Modern History*, 51:4 (December 1979), pp. 667–84.

[215] William Doyle, "The Parlements of France and the Breakdown of the Old Regime 1771–1788," *French Historical Studies*, 6:4 (Autumn 1970), pp. 415–58; Jean Egret, *The French Pre-Revolution, 1787–1788* (Chicago, IL: University of Chicago Press, 1977); William Doyle, *Origins of the French Revolution* (Oxford: Oxford University Press, 1980, 1999), ch. 8.

decision to summon the Estates as a product of the perfidy of *parlementaire* counsel. The magistrates of the *parlements* "should bear their part in the ruin which their counsel had brought on the sovereign and their country."[216] What he detected was a move on the part of treacherous *parlementaires* against the re-establishment of a balanced constitution. A conspiracy against privilege by the beneficiaries of privilege ensued, with Emmanuel-Joseph Sieyès deputed to spearhead the attack through his *Essai sur les privilèges* of November 1788. It was at this point that the French might have productively addressed themselves to consolidating their monarchy, reforming their clergy, disciplining their army, and establishing reciprocal ties between the nobility and commons.[217] This process of renovation would have supplied the elements of a mixed constitution, founded on a combination and opposition of forces essential to the preservation of liberty.[218] But, instead, there emerged a series of attacks on the idea of privileged orders—liable to resolve itself into a war of all against all as esteem became detached from established marks of social distinction.[219]

After the Estates had assembled, this assault on aristocracy was fomented by noble renegades in league with the general tendency of the *tiers état*. Writing to Philip Francis the month the *Reflections* appeared, Burke insisted that he did not blame the populace for the French calamity. Instead, he wrote, "I charge these disorders . . . on the Duke of Orleans, and Mirabeau, and Barnave, and Bailly, and Lameth, and Lafayette, and the rest of that faction."[220] Ambitious nobles and enterprising commoners had been prepared to flatter democratic sentiment in order to seize control of the political machine. The creation of an unmixed sovereignty in the form of the National Assembly was part of that design, although it transpired that the political process spiralled out of control. Burke was determined to obstruct any equivalent development before it gained any momentum in British public life. The problem was a general one: "Turbulent, discontented men of quality, in proportion as they are

[216] EB, *Reflections*, ed. Clark, p. 190 [55].

[217] Ibid., p. 189 [53].

[218] Ibid., p. 187 [50–51].

[219] See Emmanuel-Joseph Sieyès, *Essai sur les privilèges* in Roberto Zapperi ed., *Écrits politiques* (Brussels: Éditions des Archives Contemporaines, 1994), where the *esprit de corp* of exclusive hereditary privileges bestowed by princely favour is contrasted with the natural respect arising from worthy emolument and spontaneous national honour. Sieyès himself, of course, recognised distinctions, so long as they were based on a general appreciation of merit. For the juxtaposition of Burke and Sieyès on this subject, see the running commentary in *An Essay on Privileges, and particularly on hereditary nobility . . . Translated into English* (London: 1791), esp. pp. v, 16–17, 27–29.

[220] EB to Philip Francis, 17 November 1790, *Corr.*, VI, p. 172. Later, Burke charged Lafayette with being the "origin and the author of all the calamities of France": EB, Debate on the Detention of Lafayette, 17 March 1794, *Parliamentary History*, XXXI, col. 48. For the conspiratorial activities of the Duc d'Orléans, see also Thomas Jefferson to Richard Price, 13 September 1789, *Price Correspondence*, III, p. 258; Thomas Paine to EB, 17 January 1790, *Corr.*, VI, p. 73. Cf. EB, *Letter to a Noble Lord* (1796), *W & S*, IX, pp. 183–4 on "the Orleans, the Rochefoucaults, and the Fayettes, and the Viscomtes de Noailles, and the false Perigords, and the long et caetera of perfidious Sans Culottes of the Court, who like demoniacks, possessed with a spirit of fallen pride, and inverted ambition, abdicated their dignities."

puffed up with personal pride and arrogance, generally despise their own order."[221] In Britain, the Marquis of Lansdowne exemplified the type. He encapsulated the "profligate disregard for . . . dignity" common among highborn traitors to their class.[222] Driven by ambition, they consorted with "low instruments" and conspired in demagogic projects.[223] Lansdowne in particular was a calculating calumniator, happy to sew sedition for his own purposes.[224] Since his efforts were motivated by the prospect of power, his dedication to liberty was mere hypocrisy.

Duplicity of the kind was a temptation among men of rank: "Almost all the high-bred republicans of my time have, after a short space, become the most decided, thorough-paced courtiers."[225] The slow, tedious and practical conduct of resistance was left to others, capable of campaigning without the seductions of grand ideas or the spectacle of magnificent effects. As Burke understood it, party spirit—the virtue of aristocratic connection—actively conspired against this brand of fawning ambition. For this reason, attempts to capture the soul of the Whigs by Sheridan, possibly followed by Fox, had to be closed down. As Burke's son, following in the footsteps of his father, saw the matter, Sheridan had been departing from the principles of honest connection, putting himself "at the head of innovation in this country."[226] At the same time Fox, wearied by the laboriousness of protracted opposition, with little beyond a reversionary hope for conducting a future government, was exposed to the seductions of popular rhetoric.[227] Both men represented a danger hovering over the Commons of a kind that Lansdowne and Stanhope were indulging in the Lords. They were in the process of destroying the Rockinghamite approach of using the party as a bulwark between monarchy and the people. Since this was the only dependable way in which a mixed monarchy could be made to work, a new departure was a threat to the constitution.

Events in France vividly illustrated the problem. In the summer of 1789, treacherous nobles sought leverage by aligning with the third estate, although they were soon consumed by the commotion of the popular chamber. Before long, the National Assembly itself was captured by the Paris mob.[228] With its establishment, orators tendered their talents to the public, becoming "instruments, not guides of the people."[229] In this way, would-be politicians, fraternising in clubs, dictated to their putative representatives.[230] For its part, the Parisian crowd became captivated by rumours of plots and conspiracies.[231] Gatherings at Versailles, the Palais Royal and the

[221] EB, *Reflections*, ed. Clark, p. 201 [68].
[222] Ibid. On the French equivalents, see ibid., pp. 364–65 [284].
[223] Ibid., p. 203 [70].
[224] EB to Philip Francis, 20 February 1790, *Corr.*, VI, p. 92.
[225] EB, *Reflections*, ed. Clark, p. 222 [93].
[226] Richard Burke Jr. to Earl Fitzwilliam, 29 July 1790, *Corr.*, VI, p. 126.
[227] Ibid., p. 129.
[228] EB, *Reflections*, ed. Clark, pp. 227–29 [100–2].
[229] Ibid., p. 413 [353].
[230] Ibid., p. 302–3 [198].
[231] Ibid., p. 303 [198].

Hôtel de Ville weighed upon the deliberations of the deputies.[232] In the Assembly, some of the popular leaders were "men of considerable parts," but they were constitutionally averse to negotiating the complexities of practical judgment.[233] They perpetually strove to cheat the obdurate facts of the social world, replacing calculation with airy hope and imagination. Hating vice too much, they respected "men too little."[234] Burke claimed that as soon as he read the list of deputies returned to the Estates General, he knew the game was up. Having noted the descriptions and professional affiliations of the deputies to the third estate, there was nothing they might do that would surprise the seasoned observer.[235] Burke believed it was important to consider qualification for rule when evaluating the competence of a deliberative body. In the case of the third estate, the picture was not encouraging. Among the 600 members of that body, the legal profession was heavily represented.[236] This mostly comprised "obscure provincial advocates"—the "inferior, unlearned, mechanical, merely instrumental" end of the profession.[237] Not being held in great esteem, they did not respect themselves. They lacked both gravity and deliberation, not least since they had little at stake in their reputations. They were consequently prone to regard their narrow interest rather than the wider national situation. They were at once jobbing, petty and litigious. "Was it to be expected," Burke therefore asked, "that they would attend to the stability of property?"[238]

In addition to the lawyers, there were the traders. Since these were lacking in substance, they would be overborne by the lawyers. Equally, the medics did not constitute a significant counterweight to the dominant interest, while the financiers saw in the security of landed property an opportunity for converting their ephemeral assets into solid gains.[239] All this meant that there was scarcely any representation of the landed acreage of the country, not least since the members of the clergy were drawn from the menial ranks. Occupying the first estate, a preponderance of *curés*

[232] On public and crowd behaviour, see Colin Lucas, "The Crowd and Politics between 'Ancien Regime' and Revolution in France," *Journal of Modern History*, 60:3 (September 1988), pp. 421–57.

[233] EB, *Reflections*, ed. Clark, p. 338 [245].

[234] Ibid., p. 341 [250–51].

[235] Ibid., p. 193 [59]. See *Liste, par ordre alphabétique, de bailliages et sénéchaussées, de MM. les députés aux États Généraux, convoqués à Versailles le 27 Avril 1789* (Paris: 1789). For analysis, see François Furet and Ran Halévi, "Introduction," *Orateurs de la Révolution française: les constituants* (Paris: Gallimard, 1989); Timothy Tackett, *Becoming a Revolutionary: The Deputies to the French National Assembly and the Emergence of a Revolutionary Culture, 1789–1790* (Philadelphia, PA: Pennsylvania State University Press, 1996, 2006).

[236] They constituted about 43 per cent of the whole. For an analytical breakdown, see Harriet Applewhite, *Political Alignment in the French National Assembly, 1789–1791* (Baton Rouge, LA: Louisiana State University Press, 1993), pp. 39–46.

[237] EB, *Reflections*, ed. Clark, p. 196 [61]. Cobban identifies 166 deputies as *avocats* or *notaires*, with the remainder holding venal legal-administrative offices in the provinces or municipal centres: Alfred Cobban, *Aspects of the French Revolution* (London: Jonathan Cape, 1968), pp. 100–102. For modification, see Applewhite, *Political Alignment*, pp. 40–41.

[238] EB, *Reflections*, ed. Clark, p. 197 [62–63].

[239] Ibid., p. 198 [64]. See Tackett, *Becoming a Revolutionary*, pp. 35–47.

was to be found among the clergy.[240] Thus, altogether, between the first and third estates, the deputies apparently had limited horizons, and were easily swayed and corrupted. Most importantly, Burke noted, they were primed to look on extensive wealth with envy. As a body, they combined "ignorance, rashness, presumption, and lust of plunder."[241] It was not encouraging that they were guided by a cohort of "Renegadoes"—"a dozen persons of quality" who had "betrayed their trust in order to obtain . . . power."[242] Epitomised by the seditious scheming of Mirabeau, they had forsaken their allegiance to their aristocratic platoons in the hope of cutting a figure in the state.[243]

It was a grim outlook. Even the more talented orators in the assembly, largely comprising experimental "men of theory," were obliged to conform their opinions to attitudes that predominated in the mass.[244] The results, Burke predicted, would be inevitably disastrous: the rapacious and incompetent would wield authority over the propertied. From this position, they would be disposed to wage war against existing stratifications that permeated politics and society. Sieyès had himself conceded in his *Essai sur les privilèges* that some form of stratification was unavoidable since rulers had to preside over the ruled.[245] This was based on the division of mankind into two classes, with the distinction founded on the superiority of employments.[246] Controversy only arose with the question of who was best qualified to exercise the ruling function. In contrast to Burke's "spirit of a gentleman" and "spirit of religion," Sieyès traced the foundations of European politics to the attitudes inspired by militarism and monasticism, and the exclusive orders in which each of them was embodied. The administration of a polity on the basis of estates was a perpetuation of that "false" hierarchy.[247] Under it, a mere 200,000 privileged individuals would

[240] They made up 231 (70 per cent) of a total of 330. For their attitudes, see Timothy Tackett, *Religion, Revolution and Regional Culture in Eighteenth-Century France: The Ecclesiastical Oath of 1791* (Princeton, NJ: Princeton University Press, 1986), pp. 141–46.

[241] EB, *Reflections*, ed. Clark, p. 201 [67].

[242] Ibid., p. 209 [77]. The appellation "Renegadoes" appears in EB to the Duchesse de Biron, 20 March 1791, *Corr.*, VI, p. 235.

[243] For Mirabeau's pre-revolutionary thought down to 1789, see François Quastana, *La pensée politique de Mirabeau, 1771–1789: "Républicanisme classique" et régénération de la monarchie* (Aix-en-Provence: PUAM, 2007). For his intellectual milieu, and connection with Shelburne (later Lansdowne), see Jean Bénétruy, *L'atelier de Mirabeau: quatre proscrits genevois dans la tourmente révolutionnaire* (Geneva: Alex Julien 1962), pp. 148, 178ff. See also Whatmore, *Against War and Empire*, pp. 12–14.

[244] EB, *Reflections*, ed. Clark, p. 194 [59].

[245] On Sieyès's conception of the political division of labour, see Keith Michael Baker, *Inventing the French Revolution* (Cambridge: Cambridge University Press, 1990), pp. 244–51.

[246] Sieyès, *Essai sur les privilèges*, p. 103. For discussion, see Murray Forsyth, *Reason and Revolution: The Political Thought of the Abbé Sieyès* (Leicester: Leicester University Press, 1987), ch. 4.

[247] On this basis, government by estates represented a continuation of the spirit of conquest. See Emmanuel-Joseph Sieyès, *What Is the Third Estate?* (1789) in Michael Sonenscher ed., *Sieyès: Political Writings* (Indianapolis, IN: Hacking, 2003), p. 99. For Sieyès's constitutional ideas in opposition to the "*anglophiles*" doctrines of the monarchiens, see Pasquale Pasquino, *Sieyès et l'invention de la constitution en France* (Paris: Éditions Odile Jacob, 1998), ch. 1.

illegitimately dominate 24 million souls.[248] To Burke this complaint looked suspiciously close to being a purely arithmetic objection, directed against the unexceptional fact that the few ruled over the many. It was, he wrote, "ridiculous" to think of the problem in mathematical terms.[249] Standards of rule were not reducible to the number of those who held sway: rather, the criteria should be grounded on the aptitude of governors.

A system of government did not represent the individuals over whom it presided; instead, it was obliged to represent the common interest.[250] However, as Burke saw it, the fact was that a government of "five hundred country attornies and obscure curates" could not be trusted to administer 24 million citizens.[251] Everyone could agree that a system of rule required pre-eminence insofar as the rulers pursued decisions on behalf of the ruled. In practical terms, this meant that the good of the whole had to be provided for by a minority. For that to happen, the minority would have to govern in the interest of the whole. It could not simply achieve this by embodying the desires of the many since, as Burke put it, the "will of the many, and their interest, must very often differ."[252] The common interest resided in the preservation of liberty and property. These, in turn, were best safeguarded by a constitutional system that blended popular consent with the impartial administration of justice. Under British arrangements, consent was provided by means of the electoral component of the constitution, while justice was guaranteed by the stability of property underwritten by the hereditary elements of the regime. Configured in this way, a government still had to preserve itself as it confronted variable circumstances, for which it would have to be able to adapt to change. This flexibility demanded skill on the part of rulers. A successful regime, therefore, had to combine ability and stability by drawing its representatives from the ranks of the talented as well as the propertied. From this perspective, the fact that the "property of France" did not "govern it" was a recipe for serious injustice.[253]

Any assembly was a potentially destabilising forum, whose management was a precondition of effective government. Its composition was a vital element in its character, determining how deliberation would be conducted and controlled.[254] The temper of the deputies was therefore a major consideration. It was to be hoped that they would be worthy of the tasks that confronted them, and so be estimable "in point of condition of life, of permanent property, of education, and of such habits as enlarge and liberalise the understanding."[255] This was intended not as a catalogue of exclusions, but as an inventory of qualifications: the exigent, the dependent, the

[248] Sieyès, *Essai sur les privilèges*, p. 95.

[249] EB, *Reflections*, ed. Clark, p. 209 [76].

[250] On this, see Michael Sonenscher, "Introduction" to *Sieyès: Political Writings*, p. xix.

[251] EB, *Reflections*, ed. Clark, p. 209 [76].

[252] Ibid.

[253] Ibid., p. 209 [77].

[254] Philippe Raynaud, "Préface" to EB, *Réflexions sur la Révolution de France*, ed. Alfred Fierro and Georges Liébert (Paris: Hachette, 1989), p. xlvi.

[255] EB, *Reflections*, ed. Clark, p. 194 [60].

ignorant and the bigoted were poorly equipped to rule. Burke contrasted the National Assembly with the British House of Commons as a forum in which merit had an opportunity to rise, but in which social standing and professional achievement were also recognised.[256] "Everything ought to be open," Burke accepted, "but not indifferently to every man."[257] Election implied discrimination, and discrimination in favour of practical virtue seemed wise. Prudent statesmanship of the kind required independence and judgment. The first was unavoidably linked to the means to independence, and the second required both leisure and freedom from constricted modes of thought. Constriction, Burke thought, was imposed by "faculty habits" of mind, such as he associated with bureaucratic or purely procedural intelligence.[258] The room for reflection that came with leisure was its antidote. Leisure was of course a relative concept, but it implied at least the chance to survey the great political subjects that fell under the purview of the politician. The process of deliberation required penetration and solidity, and so it was best conducted by including both the talented and the responsible.

For that purpose, the House of Commons accommodated ability as well as property. Indeed, the British constitution as a whole embraced both principles, the one dynamic in nature—"vigorous and active"—and the other circumspect—"sluggish, inert and timid."[259] Burke insisted that he did not wish to restrict power to the unmeritorious, simply confining authority to blood and titles. Anyone might possess the attributes of outstanding leadership, for which there was no qualification but virtue and wisdom.[260] Burke had underlined this commitment in dissenting from Adam Smith who had disparaged the capacity of the mercantile class to rule.[261] There were, nonetheless, preferable attributes among rulers, and there were conditions under which these qualities were likely to prosper. The immediate aim of government ought to be the protection of property, and so the determination to protect it had to be safeguarded. This was best achieved by placing its defence in the hands of the propertied since they were most committed to ensuring its conservation. For this reason, property "must be represented . . . in great masses of accumulation, or it is not rightly protected."[262] Without property, there could be no society; without its accumulation, there could be no prosperity. The advance of the under-privileged depended on its accumulation, which was best preserved from danger by placing it

[256] Ibid., p. 198 [65].

[257] Ibid., p. 206 [74].

[258] Burke invoked these shortcomings to criticise the abilities of Grenville in the 1760s and Hastings in the 1780s. See his indictment of Grenville's narrow legalism in EB, Speech on American Taxation, 19 April 1774, *W & S*, II, p. 432, and of Hastings's bureaucratic mind-set in EB, Speech in Reply, 14 June 1794, *W & S*, VII, p. 620.

[259] EB, *Reflections*, ed. Clark, p. 207 [75].

[260] Ibid., p. 206 [73–74].

[261] Adam Smith, *An Inquiry into the Nature and Causes of the Wealth of Nations*, ed. R. H. Campbell and A. S. Skinner (Indianapolis, IN: Liberty Fund, 1976), 2 vols., II, p. 638. Cf. Edmund Burke, *Speech on Fox's India Bill*, 1 December 1783, *W & S*, V, p. 387.

[262] EB, *Reflections*, ed. Clark, p. 208 [75].

under the superintendence of the wealthy. The inviolability of heritable estates thus formed a rampart against the invasion of the assets of the vulnerable. It was the role of the House of Lords under the British constitution to guarantee this distribution, which might otherwise be held out as a temptation to the disadvantaged, as it had been, delusively, in France.

It was for this reason that some preference should be given to birth, without of course this preference constituting an absolutely privileged order. Hereditary honours and a hereditary chamber constituted a partial privilege in the midst of legal equality. Yet its purpose was to ensure the general advantage. The government of a civil society always involved this kind of trade-off, which created distinctions in order to serve the goals of justice and the common welfare. As circumstances changed, the nature of the trade-off might need adjustment, calling for political reform. However, reform without due wisdom risked sacrificing what it wished to secure, and therefore had to be based on deliberation. This required experience, historical judgment and general ability, and should not be made a matter of mere chance: rulers should govern on the basis of their ability rather than the pretence of their equality. Government by equality meant determining the future of the polity by lot. Yet it was not plausible that "rotation" or "appointment by lot" could positively serve a government obliged to tackle important affairs.[263] The selection of a political class, a task performed by the constitution, ought to be conducted so as to fit the appropriate ruler to each task. A systematic misfit would spell disaster, bringing the apparatus to its knees. Every state demanded of its system of rule a capacity for adaptation and conservation. The new French government could manage neither, lacking the political skills for the one and the requisite inclination towards the other. France had been placed under popular rule, but it failed to regard the welfare of its people. It was a specimen of "unnatural inverted domination."[264] The worst, rather than the best, had been appointed to rule, and the arts of flattery replaced the duty of leadership.

There is a dark, Tacitean undercurrent in the *Reflections*. Burke was keen to show that the language of liberty masked a process of enslavement. Aspects of the Augustan revolution resonated with the Revolution of 1789. After the accession of Octavian, Tacitus commented, there was a complete absence of opposition: the people were bought off, as was the army, while Augustus strove to "protect the plebs" by "tribunician right."[265] Burke saw that the abjection of court minions and the slavishness of demagogues forced them to trade in the same currency.[266] They capitalised on a rising tide of flattery, and helped destroy the republic. However, Burke believed that French populism was more baleful than Roman autocracy. Under the absolute government of a prince, the public, however cowed, limited its scope for action. But under a pure or "perfect" democracy, this restriction was lost. The most despotic

[263] Ibid., p. 206 [74].

[264] Ibid., p. 258 [139].

[265] Tacitus, *Annals*, I, i, 1–5: "ad tuendam plebem tribunicio iure."

[266] See EB, *Reflections*, ed. Clark, p. 258 [140]: the French populace was "prey to the servile ambition of popular sycophants or courtly flatterers."

monarch stood in need of assistants, and each assistant was a potential break on the untrammelled will of the prince. Ultimately, if he was not curtailed by rebellion, he could be murdered by his own janissaries.[267] However, with the exercise of unadulterated popular power, the absence of resistance was immediately felt. The abuse of power was not concentrated, and was therefore exempt from disgrace. "A perfect democracy," as Burke famously put it, "is the most shameless thing in the world."[268] On this understanding, a regime of equality, based on the rights of man, was distinguished as a despotism beyond constraint.

13.6 The Consecration of the Commonwealth

Burke had begun the *Reflections* early in 1790, combining the substance of two pamphlets: one, a response to Depont on the state of France; and the other, a response to Price, whose sermon he first read before the opening of parliament on 21 January.[269] By April, Gilbert Elliot was referring to the work as just about to appear.[270] He later clarified that what he had then read was only a fraction of what was finally published.[271] Between May and August Burke settled down to expand the compass of his argument, leaving us with a long epistolary pamphlet, serving at least two purposes, and composed in at least two distinguishable periods.[272] Despite this, there are no divisions in the work, and the composition is deliberately loose. But while it is ruminative, and prone to digression, it is not without structure.[273] Having treated the significance of the Glorious Revolution in comparison with the French, and then the competence of the National Assembly as an organ of deliberation, interspersed with an examination of the principles underlying the civilisation of modern Europe, Burke turned to the role of religion in relation to public life. Here he is above all concerned to justify the principle of an established Church against what he saw as a joint assault advanced by freethinkers and dissenters. Burke was of course aware that heterodox Christians like Priestley and Price were not in league with deists or atheists in England and France. English deism, for one thing, had been largely consigned to the past. Its impact had peaked by the 1750s, and thereafter it had radically declined. Having attacked the sect in his *Vindication of Natural Society* of 1756, Burke had scarcely given them any consideration since.[274] Who, he asked, born in the last

[267] Ibid., p. 257 [138].

[268] Ibid., p. 258 [139].

[269] EB to William Weddell, 31 January 1792, *Corr.*, VII, p. 56.

[270] Sir Gilbert Elliot to Lady Minto, 22 April 1790, *The Life and Letters of Sir Gilbert Elliot* (London: 1874), 3 vols., I, pp. 357–8.

[271] WWM BkP 1:22–64.

[272] On the probable stages of composition, see F. P. Lock, *Burke's Reflections on the Revolution in France* (London: George Allen & Unwin, 1985), pp. 58–59.

[273] A surviving manuscript sketch for a section of the *Reflections* gives some sense of Burke's concern with structure. See Northamptonshire MS. A. XXVII.75.

[274] EB, *Vindication of Natural Society* (1756), *W & S*, I, *passim*.

forty years, had actually read the British luminaries of anti-Christian polemic, whom Burke now painted as "Atheists and Infidels"?[275] John Toland, Matthew Tindal, Anthony Collins, Viscount Bolingbroke, Thomas Chubb and Thomas Morgan had always been relatively marginal to the mainstream of British society.[276] For the most part they were unconnected, lacking influence in the state.[277] However, it now transpired that their enemies, heterodox Christian dissenters, might bring about what the deists had failed to achieve: the debasement of the authority of the Christian religion wrought by an offensive against the established Church.[278]

Unlike the class of freethinkers in the first half of the eighteenth century, dissenters in Britain in the 1780s and 1790s were aided by an alliance with the political mainstream. They shared this advantage with atheists in France, who had found a vehicle among deputies in the third estate hostile to the clerical establishment.[279] Despite the outright animosity of rational dissenters towards irreligion, Burke regarded the two groups as constituting a common peril. First of all, he ascribed to both a similar intellectual approach; and second, he noted their shared antagonism to established religion. Burke accounted for both these features in terms of a shared attitude of "enthusiasm." [280] Ascribing an enthusiastic spirit to English dissent and French heterodoxy was of course an affront to both, since they separately prided themselves on supplanting credulity by means of rigorous, rational procedure. Two forms of excessive credulity came under attack in the seventeenth and eighteenth centuries: superstition on the one hand, and enthusiasm on the other. Both presumed to sustain belief on the basis of insufficient evidence, driven, it was often claimed, by excessive fear in the case of superstition, and by disproportionate hope in the case of enthusiasm.[281] Burke took many of the heterodox, congratulating themselves on their success in overcoming superstition, to have slipped into enthusiasm, pretending in the process to have achieved enlightenment. He sought to turn the

[275] EB, *Reflections*, ed. Clark, p. 253 [133].

[276] For their resuscitation in France, see, for example, Voltaire, *Lettres à S. A. Mgr. l prince de *** sur Rabelais et sur d'autres auteurs accusés d'avoir mal parlé de la religion* in idem, *Mélanges*, ed. Jacques van den Heuvel (Paris: Gallimard: 1961), pp. 1228ff., for whom the advocates of irreligion in England were "prodigieux."

[277] EB, *Reflections*, ed. Clark, p. 254 [133].

[278] For an account of the uneasy alliance between freethinkers and dissenters in the early 1650s see Hume, *History of England*, VI, p. 59.

[279] On pre-Revolutionary anticlericalism, see Dale Van Kley, "Church, State, and the Ideological Origins of the French Revolution," *Journal of Modern History*, 51:4 (December 1979), pp. 630–64; Tackett, *Religion, Revolution and Regional Culture*, ch. 10. For the anticlericalism of the third estate, see Tackett, *Becoming a Revolutionary*, pp. 65–74.

[280] EB, *Reflections*, ed. Clark, pp. 217 [85], 319 [218]. On the significance of enthusiasm in the *Reflections*, see J. G A. Pocock, "Introduction" to Edmund Burke, *Reflections on the Revolution in France*, ed. idem (Indianapolis, IN: Hackett, 1987); J.G.A. Pocock, "Edmund Burke and the Redefinition of Enthusiasm: The Context as Counter-Revolution" in François Furet and Mona Ozouf eds., *The French Revolution and the Creation of Modern Political Culture: The Transformation of Political Culture, 1789–1848* (Oxford: Pergamon, 1989), 3 vols., III.

[281] See above, chapter 2, section 4.

tables on what he saw as intellectual complacency, implying that for Priestley, Price and Helvétius, reason operated less as a means of genuine enlightenment than as a kind of spiritual "illumination."[282] In seeking to purge belief of all superstition, *faux*-enlighteners confused reasonable assent with the foundationless "Fancies of a Man's Own Brain," as Locke had put it.[283] Reason among deists and rational dissenters was merely a presumptuous mental persuasion, Burke thought: the feeling of certainty that it communicated was a kind of intellectual conceit.

The term "conceit" has two senses here: it refers, first, to a whimsical notion; and second, to the presumptuousness of treating personal fancies as tokens of divine revelation. The belief that reason reveals to the mind the truths of nature by introspection combines both meanings into a comprehensive conceit amounting to a self-regarding confidence in one's opinions without reference to probable evidence. In this vein, Locke described enthusiasm as arising from the "Conceits of a warmed or over-weening Brain," groundlessly seduced by its own conviction.[284] Burke was particularly concerned to expose the pretensions of ethical enthusiasm. Revolutionary agitators in France shared with rational nonconformity in England a determination to impose moral truths of reason on the actions and opinions of individuals already existing under the discipline of civil society. This bespoke an extraordinary arrogance: to begin with, it equated personal preferences with rational norms of conduct; next, it strove to impose these values irrespective of circumstances. The procedure was both sophistic and pedantic at the same time, and therefore dubbed by Burke a regressive "political metaphysics."[285] All judgments of experience, and consequently all existing arrangements, could only be validated by the abstract ideals of doubtful speculation. Given the remoteness of these ideals from the existing order of things, the criticism of concrete abuses gave way to exposing the foundations of legitimacy.[286] The most reasonable prejudice was restlessly discarded.[287] Since actual political attitudes and institutions would never "quadrate" with the amplitude of pre-civil rights, their illegitimacy was a foregone conclusion of the theory.[288] This mode of dissection masqueraded as enlightened critique by public opinion, but in truth it was a recipe for antinomian destruction. Every civil restraint was branded an illicit "privilege," all government deemed a form of "usurpation."[289] Improvement was predicated on what Priestley projected as "the fall of the civil powers," and the means to reform was supplanted by permanent insurrection.[290]

282 EB, *Reflections*, ed. Clark, p. 225 [98].

283 John Locke, *An Essay Concerning Human Understanding* (1689), ed. Peter H. Nidditch (Oxford: Oxford University Press, 1975, 1979), IV, xix, § 3.

284 Ibid., bk. IV, ch. xix, § 7.

285 EB, *Reflections*, ed. Clark, p. 217 [86].

286 Ibid., pp. 214–15 [82–84].

287 Ibid., p. 256 [136].

288 Ibid., p. 217 [86].

289 Ibid., p. 215 [84].

290 Joseph Priestley, *An History of the Corruptions of Christianity* (Birmingham: 1782), 2 vols., II, p. 484. The phrase is cited, in italics, in EB, *Reflections*, ed. Clark, p. 216 [85]. This, and many other

The fervour of Priestley was replicated by the impetuousness of Jean-Paul Rabaut Saint-Étienne, a deputy to the third estate for Nîmes, who was elected president of the Constituent Assembly in March 1790. For Burke, Rabaut Saint-Étienne typified the recklessness of the National Assembly in perpetually discounting recalcitrance to change. This fed a fantasy of absolute purgation, requiring the elimination of every obstacle to progress. As Burke cites Rabaut Saint-Étienne, this would involve a revolution in laws, manners and ideas—"tout détruire; puisque tout est à recréer."[291] What particularly disturbed Burke was his sense that this taste for calamity was generally focused on the eradication of ecclesiastical establishments. Rabaut Saint-Étienne, a Calvinist pastor, had made his mark before the Revolution by campaigning for the extension of toleration to French Protestants.[292] The problem for Burke was less his project than his rhetoric of extirpation, which resonated with a wider discourse of anti-Christian polemic. Since the 1750s, Burke had been on his guard against the rise of irreligion, regarding the belief in "particular" providence as a precondition for social life. He was recorded in 1784 as considering Dowdeswell's flirtation with atheism as his sole weakness, though even this was "mere folly and I trust that his soul is now with God."[293] French unbelief, by comparison, was a more serious affair. Reynolds had written to Burke from Paris in 1768 criticising the "bigotry" of the enemies of the Christian religion.[294] On his own visit to Paris in 1773, Burke had been dismayed by the public profession of scepticism. Writing to the Abbé Barruel in the final months of his life, he confirmed his correspondent's account of a conspiracy against Christianity, which he believed he had witnessed first hand twenty-four years before.[295]

What astounded Burke was the association of the dogmatic claims of deism with the achievements of philosophical learning. He was likewise perplexed by the identification of enlightened ideals with hostility towards Christian establishments. The truth was, he countered, the origins of enlightenment lay in the rebirth of modern letters, cultivated by the clergy and patronised by the nobility.[296] The progress of

---

quotations from the writings of dissenters used by Burke, can be found in Anon., *A Look to the Last Century: Or, the Dissenters Weighed in their Own Scales* (London: 1790). The passage cited here appears on p. 113, with the author commenting: "The language of Price is not much behind."

[291] EB, *Reflections*, ed. Clark, p. 339n [247]. Burke added the quotation as a note in the third edition.

[292] Allying himself with Malesherbes, he contributed to the promulgation of Louis XVI's Édit de Tolérance of 7 November 1787.

[293] Dugald Stewart, "Memoir Written on a Visit to Lord Lauderdale with Mr Burke and Adam Smith" (1784), Burke/Stewart Correspondence, Centre for Research Collections, Edinburgh University Library, Dc. 6. 111.

[294] Joshua Reynolds to EB, September 1768, *Corr.*, II, pp. 17–18.

[295] EB to the Abbé Barruel, 1 May 1797, *Corr.*, IX, p. 320. Barruel, who had taken refuge in England in 1792, had just published the first volume of his *Mémoires pour servir à l'histoire du Jacobinisme* (London: 1797–98), 4 vols., and set out "les principaux auteurs de la conspiration" in ch. 1 (I, pp. 1ff.). On the significance of Burke's letter to Barruel, see Darrin M. McMahon, "Edmund Burke and the Literary Cabal: A Tale of Two Enlightenments" in EB, *Reflections on the Revolution in France*, ed. Frank M. Turner (New Haven, CT: Yale University Press, 2003), p. 245.

[296] EB, *Reflections*, ed. Clark, p. 242 [117].

modern knowledge did not begin in the eighteenth century, but was a process that had its origin in the renaissance. It was advanced by the reformation, and confirmed by modern science. Humanism, theology and the experimental method were mutually supporting pillars of philosophy, each building on the accretions of past wisdom. For this reason, the improvement of knowledge was best secured without obliterating its foundations in the gothic structure of European civilisation. Enlightenment, from this perspective, meant "meliorating, and above all preserving the accessions of science and literature."[297] It did not imply a revolt of reason against the tenets of faith.[298] It recognised, instead, that its beginnings were "monkish," and continued its intimate entanglement with religion.[299] Reason was not the enemy but rather the support of belief. Both prospered by an alliance with ecclesiastical establishments, as illustrated by the history of the Anglican Church. A "radical" assault upon the foundations of this alliance risked destroying both its achievements and its enabling conditions. Burke's attack upon this assault was neither "conservative" nor "counter-enlightenment."[300] On its own terms, it was a defence of the advance of liberality in conjunction with the progress of society and learning.

As Burke saw it, spurious emissaries of enlightenment in France promised nothing more edifying than an anti-Christian establishment founded on persecution. They proffered liberation from the authority of the past, but would in practice deliver a ruthless tyranny; they held out the prospect of toleration, but would end by heightening religious oppression. Christian charity should be taken as the "measure of tolerance," Burke later argued, not apathy or hatred towards religion.[301] The self-appointed representatives of "light" in Britain would similarly squander toleration by capsizing the Church under which it was provided. In the absence of that ecclesiastical structure, sectarianism would proliferate, and animosity deepen. At the same time, public life would lose its connection to the sanctity of religion. Religion was essential to the progress of culture: containing the germ of the moral life, it laid the foundations for humane behaviour. Without it, regression to brutishness was assured. The endeavour to destroy organised belief would vitiate morals, and manners

[297] Ibid., p. 264 [149].

[298] Modern scholarship has been largely based on the opposite assumption. See Peter Gay, *The Enlightenment: An Interpretation. The Rise of Modern Paganism* (New York: Alfred Knopf, 1966); Jonathan Israel, *Enlightenment Contested: Philosophy, Modernity, and the Emancipation of Man, 1670–1752* (Oxford: Oxford University Press, 2006). For John Robertson, *The Case for the Enlightenment: Scotland and Naples* (Cambridge: Cambridge University Press, 2005), the enlightenment was a project focused on secular improvement.

[299] EB, *Reflections*, ed. Clark, p. 265 [149].

[300] For the existence of an English, "conservative" Enlightenment, see J.G.A. Pocock, "Clergy and Commerce: The Conservative Enlightenment in England" in R. Ajello et al. eds., *L'età dei lumi: studi storici sul settecento europeo in onore di Franco Venturi* (Naples: Jovene, 1985); on "counter-enlightenment," see Isaiah Berlin, "The Counter-Enlightenment" in Henry Hardy ed., *Against the Current: Essays in the History of Ideas* (Princeton, NJ: Princeton University Press, 2013), and for Burke's alleged role see Isaiah Berlin to Conor Cruise O'Brien, 10 April 1992, reprinted in O'Brien, *The Great Melody*, pp. 612–15.

[301] EB to the Rev. Thomas Hussey, *Corr.*, VIII, pp. 245–46.

accordingly would become depraved. The enterprise, however, was bound to fail. Man, Burke claimed, was "by his constitution a religious animal."[302] Any attempt to eviscerate the influence of religion from the human mind could only succeed in creating yet more mysterious forms of persuasion, at once "uncouth, pernicious, and degrading."[303]

While religion was the basis of moral edification, it was also a pillar of the state: in the first place, God prescribed the formation of civil society; and in the second, the sanction of religion operated as a check upon its rulers.[304] Both these natural law precepts can be traced to diverse sources in the history of jurisprudence, and they found expression in one of the pivotal paragraphs of the *Reflections*. "Society is indeed a contract," the paragraph begins.[305] By "Society" Burke meant civil society, and he was signalling his belief that the state was founded on reciprocal obligations.[306] These were neither as arbitrary nor as perishable as the contingent interests that were served by ordinary agreements in business or trade. The national interest was rather an enduring interest that bound one generation to the next. The personality of the state was a product of human artifice and could not be reduced to its transitory parts.[307] Equally, its objectives were not exhausted by the mere "animal existence" of the individuals who composed it. Since civil society was enjoined by the divinity as a mechanism for realising human ends, it was a means of advancing towards the perfection of science, art and virtue.[308] This did not mean, in neo-Aristotelian fashion, that it was the state's purpose to realise the perfection of human nature, but that, in protecting society, and thus religion too, it facilitated the objective of mental and moral improvement.[309] In combining their aptitudes for that

[302] EB, *Reflections*, ed. Clark, p. 255 [135].

[303] Ibid.

[304] On the first point, cf. Samuel Pufendorf, *The Whole Duty of Man, according to the Law of Nature*, ed. Ian Hunter and David Saunders (Indianapolis, IN: Liberty Fund, 2003), p. 198. For Burke's natural law sources, see chapter 12, sections 3, 4 and 6 above.

[305] EB, *Reflections*, ed. Clark, p. 260 [143]. The paragraph has been variously misinterpreted as an Aristotelian or Thomistic dissertation. See, originally, Ernest Barker, *Essays on Government* (Oxford: Oxford University Press, 1945, 1951), p. 218.

[306] Thus Friedrich Gentz, in his 1793 translation of the *Reflections*, correctly translates the opening line of the paragraph: "Die bürgerliche Gesellschaft ist . . . ein Kontrakt." See EB, *Über die Französische Revolution*, trans Friedrich Gentz, ed. Hermann Klenner (Berlin: Akademie Verlag, 1991), p. 193.

[307] On the wider theme, see Quentin Skinner, "The State" in Terence Ball, Russell L. Hanson and James Farr eds., *Political Innovation and Conceptual Change* (Cambridge: Cambridge University Press, 1989); for a longer trajectory, cf. idem, "A Genealogy of the Modern State," *Proceedings of the British Academy*, 162 (2009), pp. 325–70.

[308] EB, *Reflections*, ed. Clark, p. 261 [143]. Cf. Northamptonshire MS. A. XXVII.75, final para. See also Edmund Law, *Considerations on the State of the World, with regard to the Theory of Religion* (Cambridge: 1745), on the human vocation for perfection via the gradual improvement of our faculties. See further William Warburton, *The Alliance between Church and State; Or, the Necessity and Equity of an Established Religion and a Test-Law* (London: 1736), pp. 18–19.

[309] Improvement involved the pursuit of happiness, not conformity with the *telos* of the species. Cf. John Locke, *An Essay Concerning Human Understanding* (1689), ed. Peter H. Nidditch (Oxford: Oxford University Press, 1975, 1979), II, 21, § 51: "the highest perfection of intellectual nature lies in careful and constant pursuit of true and solid happiness."

purpose, citizens were subject to the duty of obedience while sovereigns were bound by the obligation to protect. Accountability, in both directions, was fixed by a law of nature. Burke dubbed this the "great primaeval contract of eternal society."[310] It implied the subjection of nature to divine will. It was on the basis of this subjection that the responsibility of human conscience to a higher law was commanded.

In response to the French onslaught against the state, Burke prescribed the importance of reverencing its institutions. As Hobbes had done before him, he cited Ovid's fable about the daughters of Pelias who, deceived by Medea, dismembered their father as a means to his rejuvenation.[311] To forestall such violence against the body politic, Burke claimed that "we have consecrated the state." Its faults should be approached like "the wounds of a father, with pious hands."[312] However, as we have already seen, this did not proscribe resort to the most radical of remedies when the security of the citizens was in peril. Despite appearances, the *Reflections* contains a developed defence on the rights of man and the citizen against despotic oppression by the state. Since they were rights of nature, these popular entitlements did not exist as a positive charter. As Burke's treatment of the rebellion of Benares two years earlier suggested, they were an urgent last resort.[313] Similarly, in commenting on the brutal treatment of the people of Rangpur, Burke recognised that there was a point at which oppression provoked resistance.[314] Nonetheless, unlike his ideological opponents in Britain and France, he also recognised that this appeal to force was in practice a "resort to anarchy," which could not be blithely authorised in the hope of speculative improvements.[315] Violent resistance could only be adopted as a "dreadful" exigency, Burke believed. Yet when it became necessary it was enjoined by the law of nature: the ordinary protocols of morality were suspended in favour of a higher principle of preservation.[316]

The association of the polity with the sacredness of the Church was not an attempt to confer divine authority on the form of government. Nonetheless, in the heated atmosphere of 1790–1, this section of the *Reflections* was read by many

[310] EB, *Reflections*, ed. Clark, p. 261 [144].

[311] Ibid., p. 260 [143]. Cf. EB, Speech on the State of the Representation of the Commons (16 May 1784), *The Works of the Right Honourable Edmund Burke* (London: 1808–13), 12 vols., X, p. 108: "I look with filial reverence on the Constitution of my Country, and never will cut it in pieces, and put it into the kettle of any magician, in order to boil it, with the puddle of their compounds, into youth and vigour." For Ovid's narration, see *Metamorphoses*, VII, lines 297ff. For Hobbes's appropriation of the fable, see Thomas Hobbes, *Elements of Law, Natural and Politic*, ed. Ferdinand Tönnies (London: Frank Cass & Co., 1969), p. 178; Thomas Hobbes, *Leviathan*, ed. Noel Malcolm (Oxford: Oxford University Press, 2012), 3 vols., II, pp. 526–27.

[312] EB, *Reflections*, ed. Clark, p. 260 [143].

[313] See Burke's notes on the opening of the Hastings impeachment at Northamptonshire MS. A. XXII.60. For discussion, see above, chapter 12, section 6.

[314] Report by John Patterson on Rangpur atrocities, annotated by Burke, at Add. MS. 24268, fol. 242. See above, chapter 12, section 6.

[315] EB, *Reflections*, ed. Clark, p. 261 [144].

[316] Ibid., p. 304 [199].

contemporaries as bordering on a defence of government by divine right, not to say preaching the doctrine of passive obedience. Within a year of the work's appearance, Burke took Fox to be accusing him of apostasy, while Priestley directly condemned him for reviving Toryism.[317] The fact was, however, that Burke's Whiggism was perfectly compatible with the idea that the deity approved the creation of the state. His argument did not imply any mystical sanction for a particular polity; instead, it meant that the general utility of the formation of civil society should be recognised as a decree of providence.[318] From this perspective, the establishment of a civil existence among human beings was at once useful and ordained by natural law.[319] Its utility was acclaimed by the individuals who composed it, and so the system of government, if it was to be legitimate, had to be based on their consent. Allegiance ended when the civil condition ceased to be useful in its current form, specifically where it posed a threat to the life and liberty of the subject. At that point there occurred a violation of juridical consent. It was this violation that provoked the "necessity" of resistance. Nonetheless, short of that extremity, obedience was obligatory. Under the British constitution, the feeling of allegiance was presented as a duty on

[317] EB to Earl Fitzwilliam, 5 June 1791, *Corr.*, VI, p. 274; Priestley, *Letters to the Right Honourable Edmund Burke, Occasioned by his Reflections on the Revolution in France* (Birmingham: 1791), p. viii. Recent commentary has been subtler but still assumes that a major "reordering" of Burke's priorities occurred in 1790, if not soon before. See Nigel Aston, "A 'Lay Divine': Burke, Christianity, and the Preservation of the British State, 1790–1797" in idem ed., *Religious Change in Europe, 1650–1914: Essays for John McManners* (Oxford: Oxford University Press, 1997), p. 186. For high Church orthodoxy, see Richard A. Soloway, "Reform or Ruin: English Moral Thought during the First French Republic," *Review of Politics*, 25:1 (January 1963), pp. 110–28; Nigel Aston, "Horne and Heterodoxy: The Defence of Anglican Beliefs in the Late Enlightenment," *English Historical Review*, 108:429 (October 1993), pp. 895–919; F. C. Mather, *High Church Prophet: Bishop Samuel Horsley (1733–1806) and the Caroline Tradition in the Later Georgian Church* (Oxford: Oxford University Press, 1992), pp. 228–30. According to J.C.D. Clark, "Religious Affiliation and Dynastic Allegiance in Eighteenth-Century England: Edmund Burke, Thomas Paine and Samuel Johnson," *English Literary History*, 64:4 (Winter 1997), pp. 1029–67, there is evidence for the late influence on Burke of the high Church Anglicanism, indicated by the presence of Horsley's tracts against Priestley in the sale catalogue of his library.

[318] This was a standard proposition of Protestant natural law. See, for example, the argument to this effect set out by the Cambridge latitudinarian and Grotius scholar Thomas Rutherforth, in his *Institutes of Natural Law, Being the Substance of a Course of Lectures on Grotius's De Iure Belli ac Pacis* (Cambridge: 2nd ed., 1779), p. 10. Cf. Warburton, *Alliance between Church and State*, pp. 7–8.

[319] For this reason, utility-based and natural law arguments in Burke are perfectly compatible with one another. As Samuel Pufendorf, *De iure naturae et gentium* (Amsterdam: 1688), 2 vols., I, p. 134, argued, that which provided for long-term *utilitas* also catered to *honestum*. For utilitarian strands of argument in Burke, see John Dinwiddy, "Utility and Natural Law in Burke's Thought: A Reconsideration," *Studies in Burke and His Time*, 16:2 (1974–5), pp. 105–28. For a recent discussion of Burke in relation to natural law traditions, see Chris Insole, "Burke and the Natural Law" in Dwan and Insole eds., *Cambridge Companion to Burke*. For further analysis, see above, chapter 12, section 6. The utilitarian foundations of natural law were evident to David Hume: see his *An Enquiry Concerning the Principles of Morals*, ed. Tom Beauchamp (Oxford: Oxford University Press, 1998, 2007), p. 92: "Examine the writers on the laws of nature; and you will always find . . . they are sure to assign . . . as the ultimate reason for every rule they establish, the convenience and necessities of mankind."

account of the union of church and state. William Warburton had argued that this union was an "alliance" based on a federal agreement under which salvation and civil protection could be separately secured under a common "league" of defence.[320] For Burke the British church-state constituted a unity rather than an alliance, although crucially this union did not imply an identity of function.[321] The existence of such a united body, based on a politico-ecclesiastical compact, operated as a reminder that obedience was a virtue sanctioned by religion as well as interest.[322]

The consecration of the commonwealth did not merely serve to inculcate obedience to the national will, it also reminded rulers of the sacredness of their trust. Governors should be practically accountable to the governed, but they were morally accountable to God. To fulfil their office, they ought to act with appropriately "high and worthy notions" of civic responsibility.[323] In the English context, the union of church and state helped to fix their sights on the gravity of their duty. Human beings, as creatures substantially of their own making, for whom liberty was therefore an opportunity as well as a burden, were best kept in awe by the feeling of sublimity before an omnipotent God.[324] This principle applied a fortiori to the population of a free state since they played the roles of sovereign and citizen at the same time. Their freedom gave them a share in public power which, to be lawful, had to be purged of purely selfish will. Without religion, it was impossible that such purification could ever succeed.[325] A purely civil constitution, in other words, was insufficient to manage the appetites of those over whom it presided. For that reason, every state required the support of ecclesiastical institutions whose aim was to promote the perfection of human nature.[326] The association of holy institutions with the civil order consolidated the virtual "oblation" of the state to the deity.[327] As Cicero had written in his account of the dream of Scipio that survived into the eighteenth century as a fragment of *De re publica*, nothing was more pleasing to God than the creation of a community in justice.[328]

[320] Warburton, *Alliance between Church and State*, p. 53. For the terms of this federal union, Warburton refers to Grotius, *De iure belli ac pacis*, I, iii, § 21.

[321] See EB, Debate on Fox's Motion for Unitarian Relief, 11 May 1792, *Parliamentary History*, XXIX, col. 1383: "By a Christian commonwealth there was established no alliance, as had often been erroneously stated, between church and state. Church and state were one and the same." Cf. Northamptonshire MS. A. XXXVIII.11(c): "In a Christian Commonwealth, the Church and the State are one and the same thing."

[322] Burke parts company here with Hume and Smith, for whom allegiance was founded on purely secular principles. Cf. Adam Smith, *Lectures on Jurisprudence*, ed. R. L. Meek, D. D. Raphael and P. G. Stein (Indianapolis, IN: Liberty Fund, 1982), pp. 318–21.

[323] EB, *Reflections*, ed. Clark, p. 256 [137].

[324] Cf. EB, *A Philosophical Enquiry into the Origin of our Ideas of the Sublime and Beautiful* (1757, rev. ed. 1759), *W & S*, I, pp. 236, 239ff.

[325] EB, *Reflections*, ed. Clark, p. 258 [140]. Cf. Warburton, *Alliance between Church and State*, p. 8.

[326] EB, *Reflections*, ed. Clark, p. 262 [146].

[327] Ibid., p. 263 [146]: "I had almost said oblation of the state itself."

[328] Cicero, *De re publica*, VI, xiii, cited in EB, *Reflections*, ed. Clark, p. 262 [145].

A federal union of church and state implied an alliance without subordination. As the French dismantled the autonomy of their own ecclesiastical establishment, Burke was anxious to underline how the Anglican Church retained its independence by controlling its property and revenues. A clergy dependent on the crown would increase the power of the court, while a church controlled by parliament would foster factionalism within its ranks.[329] However, ecclesiastical independence did not mean the isolation of the Church from powerful elements in society. By placing education in the hands of the clergy, gentlemen were integrated into the establishment.[330] Their Protestantism, Burke insisted, was a Protestantism of "zeal."[331] Their faith was genuine, not instrumental, which alone could ensure the use of religion in consolidating authority.[332] Devotion among the great provided a balm for their own lassitude, but it also gave them conviction in justifying providence to the poor, without which the condition of social inequality would prove unbearable. Devotion required respect for the institution through which it was channelled. That meant maintaining the dignity of the Church and its ceremonies. The provision of dignity was an antidote to enthusiasm and superstition, since worship in the absence of tangible objects promoted self-adulation, while excessively pompous observances tended to enslave the mind. For that reason, the rituals of the Church should be conducted with "modest splendour, with unassuming state, with mild majesty and sober pomp."[333] None of this amounted to a defence of superstition: the argument was that religious excesses had to be reformed with due solicitude, and that they were in any case preferable to impiety.[334] To a fanatic, this might look like fawning idolatry, but to a statesman it was prudent moderation.

For Burke, such prudence ought to be carried over into a defence of the Church's endowment. Those who pleaded for disestablishment, like Price and Priestley, advanced their case by way of appeal to the unaffected simplicity of the primitive church, arguing for the poverty and austerity of the Christian mission. For Burke, however, the wealth of the Church secured its independence, and guaranteed its

[329] EB, *Reflections*, ed. Clark, p. 265 [150].

[330] Ibid., p. 264 [148].

[331] Ibid., p. 255 [135].

[332] Ibid., p. 266 [151]. Cf. EB, "Religion of No Efficacy Considered as a State Engine" (c. 1755) in *Notebook*, ed. Somerset.

[333] EB, *Reflections*, ed. Clark, p. 263 [146].

[334] On this, see Edward Gibbon to Lord Sheffield, 5 February 1791, *The Letters of Edward Gibbon*, ed. J. E. Norton (London: Cassell, 1956), 3 vols., III, p. 216, commenting on Burke's *Reflections:* "I approve his politics, I adore his chivalry, and I can even forgive his superstition." Burke's argument is confused with support for superstition in G. W. Chapman, *Edmund Burke: The Practical Imagination* (Cambridge, MA: Harvard University Press, 1967), pp. 188–90; Ernest Barker, "Burke on the French Revolution" in *Essays on Government*. For Derek Beales, "Edmund Burke and the Monasteries of France," *Historical Journal*, 48:2 (June 2005), pp. 415–36, Burke's defence of the Gallican Church merged into a defence of superstition, directed against Hume. However, for a comparable justification of ceremonial pomp which deliberately falls short of superstition, see *The Folger Library Edition of the Works of Richard Hooker IV: Of the Laws of Ecclesiastical Polity*, ed. John E. Booty (Cambridge, MA: Harvard University Press, 1982), pp. 33–34.

standing in society at large, eliciting respect as a consequence of its equal standing with leading persons of rank within the nation.[335] Wealth was a form of insurance for the professors of religion against contempt from their lay peers: their position, with its material support, was a passport to estimation in the eyes of their flock. Those who slighted the virtue of the Church by criticising its wealth might gain credibility by extending their own charity to the point where it seriously diminished their personal property. Short of that, their complaints appeared fraudulent.[336] In France, the attempt to reduce the standing of the Church by an attack upon its property had been animated by selfishness masquerading as virtue. Demoting the clergy into pensioners of the state, they were degraded from enjoying corporate rights within the kingdom to living off the alms doled out by an atheistic republic. The process of humiliation began in hypocrisy and deceit, and ended in outright plunder. Burke cautioned: "At home we behold similar beginnings. We are on our guard against similar conclusions."[337]

13.7 The Fatal Junction

Having examined the impact of Revolutionary ideology on the French Church, and restated the principles of ecclesiastical polity in England as a prophylactic against developments across the Channel, Burke next turned to consider the causes behind the progress of the Revolution in France. He had already drawn attention to the opportunistic betrayal of their order by prominent members of the French nobility. That was intended to explain the disintegration of the Estates General. Burke was now obliged to account for the trajectory of policy in the National Assembly. His analysis is commonly characterised as a kind of conspiracy theory, as if conspiracy were not essential to the prosecution of revolution, the pursuit of which depends on concerted action. Nonetheless, in important respects, Burke's was not a conspiratorial narrative. His purpose, he claimed, was not to explain the machinations of the Assembly, detailing the origin of every policy, but to account for the orientation of legislation in general. He sought a "*cause*" for "the general fury" which drove the attack upon ecclesiastical privilege.[338] He discovered this in the social and political impact of two groups, the monied interest and the republic of letters. What he noted was their "junction," not their *coniuratio*.[339] These distinct though sometimes overlapping camps came to share an independently generated, yet still common interest.

[335] EB, *Reflections*, ed. Clark, pp. 267–68 [153–54]. Cf. EB, Speech on Church *Nullum Tempus* Bill, 17 February 1772, Northamptonshire MS. A. XXXI.27A: "I very well know the propriety of maintaining the sacred Order with decency, with a sober dignity. [A] poor Clergy in an opulent Nation are a disgrace to its religious Sentiments."

[336] EB, *Reflections*, ed. Clark, p. 269 [155–56].

[337] Ibid., p. 270 [157].

[338] Ibid., p. 278 [168].

[339] Ibid.

Under the circumstance of the Revolution, it became a shared purpose. The purpose was to dismantle the power of the Church, although that objective served what had started as distinguishable ambitions.

For their part, the leading lights of literature in France had formed "a regular plan for the destruction of the Christian religion."[340] To achieve this they targeted the doctrines and governance of the Gallican Church. Since senior appointments to bishoprics and abbeys were part of the patronage of the crown, providing the incumbents with admission to the ranks of nobility, an assault on the property of the Church was an attack on both aristocracy and monarchy.[341] It was the goal of the monied interest to pursue such a project of aggression. To this extent, its members shared an objective with the literary cabal in seeking to undermine the authority of religion. An attempt on the Church was a *coup de main* against the aristocracy. The motives behind the animus among the monied men against the nobility had deep roots in the social and political structure of the French monarchy, pointing to a fundamental instability in the regime, and uncovering the socio-political causes of the Revolution. The junction between money and letters showed how these socio-political causes coincided with hostility against religion. It was these overlapping purposes that explained the centrepiece of the Revolution, the confiscation of church property as a means of securing national credit.

Burke required a motive for the invasion of ecclesiastical property since the professed reasons of the Revolutionaries did not stack up. It was claimed that the confiscation was activated by a concern for "national faith"—meaning, a determination to secure the credit of the body politic.[342] With the advent of European deficit financing, public borrowing had originally offered security to states in the context of international rivalry: credit helped to fund a military establishment. Yet in its excess, debt became a means of government "subversion."[343] As the French case illustrated, financial interests burgeoned to become a power in the state, finally dictating policy to their political representatives.[344] As Burke pointed out, to honour creditors was nothing other than to confirm a claim to property. Therefore, to mortgage

[340] Ibid., p. 276 [165]. On this theme in Burke, see Seamus Deane, *The French Revolution and Enlightenment in England, 1789–1832* (Cambridge, MA: Harvard University Press, 1988), ch. 1. For general reviews of historiography on the subject, see Thomas E. Kaiser, "This Strange Offspring of Philosophie: Recent Historiographical Problems in Relating the Enlightenment to the French Revolution," *French Historical Studies*, 15:3 (Spring 1988), pp. 549–62; Michael Sonenscher, "Enlightenment and Revolution," *Journal of Modern History*, 70:2 (June 1998), pp. 371–83.

[341] EB, *Reflections*, ed. Clark, p. 275 [164].

[342] Ibid., p. 272 [160].

[343] Ibid., p. 326 [228]. On this theme in eighteenth-century British thought, see Istvan Hont, "The Rhapsody of Public Debt: David Hume and Voluntary State Bankruptcy" in idem, *Jealousy of Trade: International Competition and the Nation-State in Historical Perspective* (Cambridge, MA: Harvard University Press, 2005).

[344] On the rise of the financial interest in France to a position of power in the state, see Jacques Necker, *De l'administration des finances de la France* (Lausanne: 1784), 3 vols., III, ch. 12. Burke used the French edition in writing the *Reflections*.

church lands in order to underwrite the title of financiers was to privilege one form of property over another. In fact, it was to violate landed property for the security of paper, an inversion of the priority of actual wealth over the speculative claims of *propriété financière*.[345] Under ordinary conditions, public credit had a claim upon the resources of the state, not upon the fortunes of its individual members. The truth was, Burke concluded, the National Assembly kept the pledges that it suited it to keep, abandoning those interest groups which it considered expendable.[346] The preferential treatment accorded rentier or capitalist interests over those of immoveable property involved a radical shift in policy towards an established cleavage in French society between the claims of the old aristocracy of titles and the new aristocracy of wealth. The political Revolution was at the same time a social Revolution involving a vast transfer of wealth.[347] This transfer was conducted under cover of a campaign against privilege, whereas in fact it confirmed the conquest of monied privilege over its main rival.[348]

This conquest was an act of vengeance, Burke contended. Since the days of Louis XIV, the French aristocracy had been riven by antipathy between the established nobility and the new wealth of the mercantile and financial classes.[349] But if there was a struggle for equality among the divisions of the elite, the conduct of the nobility towards the lower classes was humane. In comparison with the disdain that characterised the medieval nobility of Germany and Italy, the higher ranks in France were relatively concessive and accommodating.[350] There were of course problems, for instance with old French tenures, but there was no systematic oppression of the masses: apart from anything else, although the aristocracy enjoyed distinction, it lacked concrete institutional power.[351] Hostility towards privilege was a demagogic strategy rather than an expression of uninstructed popular feeling.[352] The desire to foment discord derived from within the upper ranks as a consequence of a fault-line between the "two" aristocracies—the aristocracy of titles and the aristocracy of

345 Cf. P. M. Jones, *Reform and Revolution in France: The Politics of Transition, 1774–1791* (Cambridge: Cambridge University Press, 1995), p. 203, on the number of *constituantes* who were rentiers and stockholders.

346 EB, *Reflections*, ed. Clark, pp. 272–73 [160–62].

347 On the historiographical tension between the "political" and "social" interpretations of the Revolution, see Alfred Cobban, "Political versus Social Interpretations of the French Revolution" in idem, *Aspects of the French Revolution*. For analysis, see Michael Sonenscher, "The Cheese and the Rats: Augustin Cochin and the Bicentenary of the French Revolution," *Economy and Society*, 19:2 (1990), pp. 266–74.

348 EB, *Reflections*, ed. Clark, p. 278 [168].

349 EB, *Reflections*, ed. Clark, p. 274 [163]. Cf. Alexis de Tocqueville, *The Old Regime and the Revolution*, ed. François Furet and Françoise Mélonio (Chicago, IL: University of Chicago Press, 1998–2001), 2 vols., I, pp. 157–58, where Tocqueville takes issue with Burke before, not untypically, reproducing his argument.

350 EB, *Reflections*, ed. Clark, p. 304 [199].

351 Ibid., p. 307 [203]. Burke was seeking further evidence to support these claims in a letter to the Vicomte de Cicé, 24 January 1791, *Corr.*, VI, pp. 207–8.

352 EB, *Reflections*, ed. Clark, p. 308 [205].

wealth.[353] The aristocracy of wealth, much of it recently ennobled, and sometimes intermarried with the old order, incurred the envy and hostility of sections of the old nobility, especially the bearers of "unendowed pedigrees," left brandishing mere titles before the splendour of *arrivistes*.[354]

In this way, on the eve of the Revolution, the exclusive pride of the titled *noblesse* confronted the ambitious pride of the monied interest.[355] Political upheaval offered the opportunity to financial interests to leverage themselves at the expense of their antagonists. Moreover, by now, the historic antipathy in French society to monied wealth, deriving from the reaction against the financial experiments of John Law, had been at least partially redressed in the public mind by a literary campaign headed by allies of Turgot.[356] The Church offered a soft target to the adversaries of landed property: it exemplified the privilege of hereditary wealth, and it had long been traduced by its literary opponents. The scene was set for overturning long-standing prescriptive titles that had been ratified down the generations by successive legal decisions. When Mirabeau proposed that Church estates be put "at the disposal of the nation," it passed on 2 November 1789 by 568 votes to 346.[357] The king's chaplain, the Abbé Maury, battled in vain in the Assembly against Talleyrand and Thouret.[358] Burke concluded: the "service of the state was made a pretext to destroy the church."[359] The following December, under pressure to pay off the short-term debt of the Caisse d'Escompte, but unwilling to establish a national bank for the purpose, the Assembly opted to employ the funds anticipated from the sale of estates as security for the issuance of paper notes, styled "assignats."[360] The auction of property began on 14 May 1790.

[353] Ibid.

[354] Ibid., pp. 274–75 [163–64]. For recent comment on the struggles within a complicatedly divided elite, see Daniel Roche, *France in the Enlightenment* (Cambridge, MA: Harvard University Press, 2000), ch. 12. On intermarriage, see William Doyle, *Aristocracy and its Enemies in the Age of Revolution* (Oxford: Oxford University Press, 2009), p. 21.

[355] Cf. Guy Chaussinand-Nogaret, *The French Nobility in the Eighteenth Century: From Feudalism to Enlightenment* (Cambridge: Cambridge University Press, 1985), p. 115, on an open elite in terms of access that was closed in terms of ideology.

[356] The identification of Turgot and his literary associates as friends of financial speculation occurs in a footnote added to the 1803 edition of the *Reflections*. See EB, *Reflections*, ed. Clark, p. 278n. EB, *Réflexions sur la Révolution de France*, ed. Fierro and Liébert, p. 673n singles out Helvétius and d'Holbach as allies. On John Law, see EB, *Reflections*, ed. Clark, p. 408 [346]. For discussion, see Antoin E. Murphy, *John Law: Economic Theorist and Policy-Maker* (Oxford: Oxford University Press, 1997). For the significance of his system for subsequent financial thought, see Sonenscher, *Before the Deluge*, pp. 108–20. For discussion in relation to Burke, see above, chapter 7, section 3.

[357] Marcel Marion, *La vente des biens nationaux pendant la Révolution* (Paris: Honoré Champion, 1908).

[358] Louis Bergson, "National Properties" in François Furet and Mona Ozouf eds., *A Critical Dictionary of the French Revolution* (Cambridge, MA: Harvard University Press, 1989), pp. 211–12.

[359] EB, *Reflections*, ed. Clark, p. 287 [179].

[360] Ibid., p. 288 [180]: "instead of paying the old debt, they contracted a new debt, at 3 per cent, creating a new paper currency, founded on an eventual sale of the church lands." Cf. ibid., pp. 323 [224–25], 359–60 [276]. The currency comprised "billets assignés sur les biens du clergé," bearing interest at 5 per

It was the extent of the subversion of the corporate rights of the Church that staggered Burke. He compared it to the offensive of Henry VIII against the English monasteries, and found the actions of this committed tyrant relatively tame.[361] "We have lost the republic completely," Cicero declared in *De officiis*[362] He was thinking of the corruption of justice after the descent into civil war, followed by proscription and the expropriation of enemies. Sulla and Marius were the principal culprits he had in mind, subjecting the estates of opponents to forced sale.[363] Yet here again, the scale of Roman violence in Burke's mind was dwarfed by the French.[364] Moreover, while the depredations at Rome occurred on the back of political strife, in France they were a product of calculated hostility premeditated under conditions of of civil peace. More than peace, it was a period of relative happiness and prosperity. The regime supported justice and the population flourished. Burke compared its condition to the state of the Ottoman Empire, languishing without cultural or agricultural improvement.[365] In effect, he accepted Hume's judgment that France was a civilised monarchy, "a despotism rather in appearance than in reality."[366] In terms of demographic expansion and the extent of its national wealth, the French Kingdom had been prospering through the 1780s. Much of Burke's evidence came from Necker's *De l'administration des finances*, which had appeared in 1784. The quantity of specie in the country was indicative: its sheer volume, as recorded by Necker, pointed to a bustling economy—to buoyant industry and healthy trade, founded on the security of property. Compared to the devastation of the Deccan, first under the Nawab of the Carnatic and then by Haidar Ali, which Burke had cause to complain of before the House of Commons, France before the Revolution was the embodiment of abundance: construction, navigation, manufacture and cultivation were all thriving.[367]

None of this amounted to an endorsement of the French regime. The regime was, as Burke put it, only the best of the absolute monarchies of Europe, not a model of constitutional perfection.[368] It was, in fact, studded with abuses, many of these elucidated by Necker himself: the administration exacerbated civil inequalities; it

---

cent. See Florin Aftalion, *The French Revolution: An Economic Interpretation* (Cambridge: Cambridge University Press, 2002), ch. 4.

[361] EB, *Reflections*, ed. Clark, pp. 281–2 [172–73].

[362] Cicero, *De officiis*, II, 29.

[363] Ibid., II, 27. For indictment of these same figures, see EB to the Duchesse de Biron, 20 March 1791, *Corr.*, VI, p. 235.

[364] EB, *Reflections*, ed. Clark, pp. 280–1 [171–72].

[365] Ibid., p. 295 [189]. His information was based on Demetrius Cantimer, *History of the Growth and Decay of the Othoman Empire* (London: 1756), cited in EB, Evidence on Begams of Oudh, 22 April 1788, *W & S*, VI, p. 476.

[366] EB, *Reflections*, ed. Clark, p. 295 [189]. Cf. EB, *Letter to a Member of the National Assembly* (1791), *W & S*, VIII, p. 332 for the depiction of France as "a mild paternal monarchy." See David Hume, "Of Civil Liberty" in idem, *Essays Moral, Political, and Literary*, ed. Eugene F. Miller (Indianapolis, IN: Liberty Fund: 1985, 1987), p. 94.

[367] EB, *Reflections*, ed. Clark, pp. 298–9 [193–95]. For the waste of South Asia, see EB, *Speech on the Nawab of Arcot's Debts* (28 February 1785), *W & S*, V, p. 522.

[368] EB, *Reflections*, ed. Clark, p. 294 [187–88].

was overly dependent upon the financial interest; and the sale of offices multiplied exemptions from taxation while corrupting the manners of the nobility.[369] Nonetheless, the nobility and the monarchy sought improvement, as evidenced by the performance of the latter since the 1770s and by the former in their *cahiers des doléances*.[370] Fiscal exemptions rankled, but this could have been addressed by means of reform. In the meantime, both the clergy and the nobility contributed meaningfully to the exchequer.[371] But instead of seeking national renovation, the Revolutionaries sought remedies in the form of abolition irrespective of the obstacles they might encounter, or the institutions and habits they might destroy. The reconstruction of a polity required a different approach, under which the theory of government would harmonise with forces on the ground. In arguing his case, Burke proved himself a subtle constitutional theorist, averse at once to the vacuity of aprioristic moralism and the blindness of impressionistic empiricism.

13.8 Luxury and Superstition

In practice, this meant that Burke aimed to marry practical reform with constitutional theory. His approach to reform was guided by fitting available means to ends, which meant achieving goals by using existing attitudes and arrangements. This, however, was not a purely mechanical exercise since policy was guided by a conception of the constitution. This conception, in turn, was derived from classical constitutional thought, modified by subsequent historical experience, and further refined with reference to current circumstances. This approach to theory and practice is strongly contrasted by Burke with the attitude to legislation manifested by the deputies in the National Assembly. Their attitude was underpinned by impoverished constitutional ideas and an inadequate conception of how government should do business. In relation to the constitution, they were dogmatically attached to a single site of sovereignty, wielded by the democratic forces in the state. "Have these gentlemen never heard, in the whole circle of theory and practice, of any thing between the despotism of the monarch and the despotism of the multitude?" Burke wondered.[372] But while the outward shape and rhetoric of the state was democratic, it would soon be controlled by an oligarchy of financial interests.[373] In each of its incarnations, the form of government would be exercised without restraint, uncontrolled by any countervailing force and unresponsive to the desires of the public. All the while, usurpation would be justified in the language of the rights of man, encouraged by the spirit of innovation. This spirit was animated by a form of intellectual presump-

[369] Necker, *De l'administration des finances*, III, chs. 12, 14.
[370] EB, *Reflections*, ed. Clark, pp. 294 [188], 299 [195], 304–5 [200].
[371] Ibid., p. 286 [178].
[372] Ibid., p. 291 [184].
[373] Ibid., p. 291 [185].

tion that promoted a vision of the future based on a disregard for the limitations of prevailing circumstances.

Hitherto, the success of the Revolution could be accounted for in terms of the affected popularity of its prominent leaders. Mirabeau, Barnave, Sieyès, Lameth, Duport, Lafayette and Thouret secured their ambitions under the banner of equality. But it was hostility to religion that accounted for the animus that drove Revolutionary zeal. Atheistic bigotry, Burke thought, had suffused much of the intellectual culture of the late monarchy of France, directing opinion against the Church which would then be pillaged by the monied interest. This amounted to a malignant disavowal of Christian belief, forwarded by proselytising and conspiring men of letters.[374] Having lost the support of court patronage bestowed under Louis XIV, they determined to survive by their own wits, congregating in academies, and collaborating on projects.[375] Their fanaticism ultimately betrayed them. Assuming the mantle of enlightenment, they soon became ambassadors of persecution. The cause of religious bigotry spread like an epidemic, reminiscent of the spiritual contagion of sixteenth-century Germany.[376] Underneath the show of speculative benevolence, a fund of animosity had festered, fostering antinomian beliefs among the population at large. Publicists became preachers of intolerance under the guise of enlightened civilisation. Philosophers had grown monkish in their manners. The abettors of light and learning bred a resurgence of superstition.[377]

Superstition expressed itself as an antithetical prejudice, contemptuous not merely towards individuals but to whole descriptions of men. Burke characterised this antagonism as a form of collective disdain whereby the behaviour of current members of the Church government of France was conflated with the corporate existence of the whole body. The incorporation of individuals was a means to their preservation, but here it was being exploited as an excuse for persecution.[378] This procedure was typically a prelude to a programme of extirpation. Individuals were tarnished with collective characteristics. Then, their corporate identity was defined

[374] EB, *Reflections*, ed. Clark, pp. 276–7 [165–67]. For the measures directed against the French Church by the Constituent Assembly, see Norman Hampson, *Prelude to Terror: The Constituent Assembly and the Failure of Consensus, 1789–1791* (Oxford: Basil Blackwell, 1988), ch. 9.

[375] EB, *Reflections*, ed. Clark, pp. 275–26 [165]. The *Encyclopédie* was a key example of the kind of collaboration Burke had in mind. For a recent (though indeterminate) treatment of its impact, see Robert Darnton, *The Business of Enlightenment: A Publishing History of the Encyclopédie, 1775–1800* (Cambridge, MA: Harvard University Press, 1979). See also Daniel Roche, "Encyclopedias and the Diffusion of Knowledge" in Mark Goldie and Robert Wokler eds., *The Cambridge History of Eighteenth-Century Political Thought* (Cambridge: Cambridge University Press, 2006).

[376] EB, *Reflections*, ed. Clark, p. 324 [225–26].

[377] Ibid., p. 321 [235]. The paradox has been ignored in much of the intellectual history of the enlightenment and the Revolution, which variously aligns the anti-Christian enlightenment with Revolutionary radicalism. See, for example, Robert Darnton, *The Literary Underground of the Old Regime* (Cambridge, MA: Harvard University Press, 1982), pp. 36ff. For criticism of Darnton's archival methods, see Mark Curran, "Beyond the Hidden Best-Sellers of Pre-Revolutionary France," *Historical Journal*, 56:1 (March 2013), pp. 89–112.

[378] EB, *Reflections*, ed. Clark, p. 310 [207].

in trans-historical terms so that their current dispositions were convicted by past actions in which they had played no part. This led to two absurd results. First, instead of correcting particular forms of behaviour, the institutions through which aberrant passions expressed themselves were abolished: instead of restraining pride, arrogance, avarice and rapacity, governments, churches and legal establishments were attacked. Second, since contemporary establishments were entirely blended with their history, the present was subverted out of hostility to the past. The Constituent Assembly was "gibbeting the carcass" of past abuses instead of attending to remediable faults: "You are terrifying yourself with ghosts and apparitions," he advised Depont, "whilst your house is the haunt of robbers."[379] The clergy were guilty of excesses typical of their profession, but these had been treated as monumental crimes. Accordingly, the Church was punished with the destruction of its independence in preparation for the abolition of the Christian religion. Under the Constitution of the Clergy, which was voted by the Assembly on 12 July 1790, the Church hierarchy were to be elected by the citizens of France.[380]

The treatment of the monastic orders captured for Burke how the legislators of France approached their task. Eight months after the publication of the *Reflections* he noted in a letter to the Comte de Rivarol how the attempt to purge religious culture was liable to provoke unmanageable fury in its turn.[381] Founded on abstemiousness and devotion to good works, monasteries offered a ready "*purchase*" for advancing the public welfare, a potent means of promoting the common good.[382] But the superstitious bias of the apostles of irreligion condemned this corporate lever of public beneficence by branding it an exemplification of irrational devotion. In truth, as Burke saw it, superstition and enthusiasm were "rival follies," both of which could still be used in combatting disbelief.[383] Monkish superstition in France had the added bonus of employing its stocks as a stimulus to improvement. Here Burke was taking a stand against the common assumption that monastic orders were condemned by their idleness. This allegation merged with Sieyès's case against the nobility as parasitical upon the labour of the peasants and manufacturers. As Sieyès saw it, while agriculture, industry, trade, the professions and public service all contributed to the welfare of society, the profits of landed wealth were squandered unproductively.[384] For Burke, however, the charity supported by this "feudal" relic

[379] Ibid., p. 311 [208–9].

[380] Ibid., p. 318 [217–18].

[381] EB to Claude-François de Rivarol, 1 June 1791, *Corr.*, VI, p. 266. He was responding to a copy of Rivarol's *Les Chartreux: poëme et autres pièces fugitives* (Paris: 4th ed. 1789), sent to him by the author.

[382] EB, *Reflections*, ed. Clark, p. 329 [232]. The emphasis in Beales, "Burke and the Monasteries of France," is different, presenting Burke as an apologist for superstition. For the notion of leverage or a "purchase" in politics, cf. EB, *Letter to a Member of the National Assembly* (1791), *W & S*, VIII, p. 330, on Archimedes' δόσ μοι ποῦ στῶ (give me a place to stand).

[383] EB, *Reflections*, ed. Clark, p. 331 [235].

[384] Sieyès, *What Is the Third Estate?* (1789) in Sonenscher ed., *Political Writings*, pp. 94–5. On this idiom in the context of French political economy, see John Shovlin, "Political Economy and the French

ought to be seen as a social benefit.[385] Moreover, from the perspective of political economy, religious orders surviving on their revenues from rent assisted in the circulation of goods and services in society. As leisured rentiers, monks performed the same function as all landlords, enabling agricultural labour and to that extent spurring industry.[386] Their use to society was no different from that of the landed nobility, or any other group that profited from rent: their surplus revenues remunerated the wages of labour by purchasing manufactures or maintaining domestic servants. Couched in these terms, an attack on religious assets was an attack on commercial society masquerading as an assault on feudal barbarism.

In their economic aspect, therefore, the monasteries were a part of "the great wheel of circulation."[387] What stung Burke's conscience was not the idleness of their inhabitants, but the condition of labouring wretches in the cities, condemned to work from "dawn to dark" in an assortment of servile roles: "I should be infinitely more inclined forcibly to rescue them from their miserable industry, than violently to disturb the tranquil repose of monastic quietude."[388] In *De l'administration des finances*, Necker had reacted against the common claim that luxury was the cause of poverty. The truth, he argued, was that any attempt to abolish hardship by diminishing wealth was a recipe for social and economic regression.[389] As Adam Smith had argued in the *Wealth of Nations*, public efforts to balance the distribution of wealth were usually productive of still greater inequalities.[390] Burke termed the coexistence of poverty and plenty the inescapable "yoke of luxury."[391] That yoke could not be broken without detriment to the whole. "In a civilized country," as Smith once commented, "the poor provide both for themselves and for the enormous luxury of their superiors."[392] Consequently, the suspicion of luxury had become a pervasive

---

Nobility, 1750–1789" in Jay M. Smith ed., *The French Nobility in the Eighteenth Century* (Philadelphia, PA: Pennsylvania State University Press, 2006).

[385] On the "myth" of feudalism in the French Revolution, see Alfred Cobban, "The Myth of the French Revolution" in idem, *Aspects of the French Revolution*, pp. 95–99. Cf. idem, *The Social Interpretation of the French Revolution* (Cambridge: Cambridge University Press, 1964), ch. 4. On landed "capitalism" in eighteenth-century France, see George V. Taylor, "Types of Capitalism in Eighteenth-Century France," *English Historical Review*, 79:312 (July 1964), pp. 478–97.

[386] EB, *Reflections*, ed. Clark, p. 331 [236]. For discussion, and comparison with Adam Smith in this context, see Winch, *Riches and Poverty*, pp. 215–16.

[387] EB, *Reflections*, ed. Clark, p. 332 [237].

[388] Ibid.

[389] Necker, *De l'administration des finances*, III, ch. 11. For this topic in eighteenth-century thought, see Istvan Hont, "The Early Enlightenment Debate on Commerce and Luxury" in Mark Goldie and Robert Wokler eds., *The Cambridge History of Eighteenth-Century Political Thought* (Cambridge: Cambridge University Press, 2006).

[390] Adam Smith, *An Inquiry into the Nature and Causes of the Wealth of Nations*, ed. R. H. Campbell and A. S. Skinner (Indianapolis, IN: Liberty Fund, 1981), 2 vols., I, p. 135.

[391] EB, *Reflections*, ed. Clark, p. 332 [237].

[392] On this, see Adam Smith, "'Early Draft' of Part of the *Wealth of Nations*" in idem, *Lectures on Jurisprudence*, ed. R. L. Meek, D. D. Raphael and P. G. Stein (Indianapolis, IN: Liberty Fund, 1982), pp. 562–63.

attitude, particularly attractive to the labouring masses. Yet their acceptance of inequality was a condition of social existence: without it, the institution of property, and thus the acquisitions of labour, would dissolve.[393] In the midst of the disappointments which must inevitably intervene between human effort and the expectations of reward, only providence could offer compensation: human effort must be taught its consolation "in the final proportions of eternal justice."[394]

For many modern readers of Burke, this form of recompense may look like sorry comfort. Yet the only alternative was the hope that secular satisfactions would be sufficient to bear the weight of social discouragement. Unlike Burke, Bolingbroke and Hume were happy to gamble social stability on the prospect of psychological submission to the effects of luxury. However, Burke believed that this gamble would not pay off. From his vantage, the sceptical critique of providence compromised the order of society: depriving the masses of the consolations of religion would "deaden their industry" and therefore strike "at the very root of acquisition and conservation."[395] The unequal accumulation of property required the promise of future rewards. Alongside the rejection of deism implicit in this formulation lay a common perspective shared by Hume and Smith as well as Burke.[396] They believed that human industry was the engine of improvement, but this depended on the security of acquisition. In modern Turkey and India, and even in England under feudalism, fear of expropriation led to the concealment of riches, and thus a reduction in capital wealth and commercial prosperity.[397] Since property was ultimately rooted in the opinions that lent it support, it was an inherently fragile institution. It was liable to be destroyed if undermined by redistribution. Short of its destruction, it might be subject to violent competition, as exemplified by the current struggle between forms of property in France.

Statesmanship implied an ability to balance the freedom to accumulate with the state's claims on private wealth through public borrowing and fiscal extraction. This ability to balance presupposed an opportunity to acquire, conserve and augment property. Easing the freedom of acquisition pointed towards a stratified distribution of wealth, and a corresponding division into ranks. In modern commercial societies built on a feudal past, this division into orders was founded in part on the inequality of wealth but also on the kinds of deferential respect into which individuals had become socialised. As Burke saw it, this did not involve servile submission so much as an acceptance of a concentration of riches in select hands from which the many

[393] Northamptonshire MS. A. XXVII.75.

[394] EB, *Reflections*, ed. Clark, p. 411 [351]. On this, see above, chapter 2, section 5.

[395] EB, *Reflections*, ed. Clark, p. 411 [351].

[396] On the strict obligations of justice in eighteenth-century jurisprudence, see Istvan Hont and Michael Ignatieff, "Needs and Justice in the *Wealth of Nations*: An Introductory Essay" in idem, *Wealth and Virtue: The Shaping of Political Economy in the Scottish Enlightenment* (Cambridge: Cambridge University Press, 1983).

[397] Smith, *Wealth of Nations*, I, pp. 285, 277, for these points respectively.

could expect no tangible advantage.[398] The constitution of any republic should reflect these social divisions, as lawgivers among the ancients testified.[399] Different aptitudes and powers among the members of society should be proportionately represented by competing branches within the system of rule. Montesquieu remarked that in any state there will exist distinctions, and that in Europe these tend to be based on a mixture of birth, riches and honours. Where the privileged orders were mixed promiscuously with the mass, the freedom of all would soon be reduced to the slavery of all.[400] By implication, as Burke noted, where the population of a European state was abstracted and equalised into a common mass, the disparate interests that underlay this fabricated equality would lose all corporate means to protect themselves. The government of such a people would become, as Burke observed, echoing Montesquieu, "the most arbitrary power that has ever appeared on earth."[401] Since the French had destroyed the integrity of their orders, they had little prospect of resisting this fate: every barrier against despotism had been progressively extinguished.

The organisation of the executive, legislative and judicial power of France reflected this outcome: the clergy, as we have seen, had been reduced to dependence on the public; an absolute veto to be exercised by the monarch was denied on 11 September 1789; the *parlements* were abolished the following November.[402] Equally, there were no plans to offset the popular chamber by the creation of the equivalent of a senate.[403] With executive power in the hands of an impotent and degraded king, its effectiveness was hamstrung and its dignity destroyed.[404] Judicial authority had been deputed to dependent, elective officials.[405] Everything therefore depended on the legislative assembly and the process of election that would select its future members. The plans for this were laid out on 29 September 1789, presented by Thouret, based on Sieyès's ideas.[406] Burke predicted that this would create an unaccountable oligarchy, disconnected from the voters in the primary constituencies. It would also serve to carve up the territory of France into fissiparous and competing

398 EB, *Reflections*, ed. Clark, p. 411 [351].

399 Ibid., p. 357 [272–73].

400 Charles-Louis de Secondat, Baron de Montesquieu, *De l'esprit des lois* (1748) in *Œuvres complètes*, ed. Roger Caillois (Paris: Gallimard, 1951), 2 vols., II, pt. 2, bk 12, ch. 6.

401 EB, *Reflections*, ed. Clark, p. 359 [275].

402 These were discussed by Burke in ibid., pp. 377 [301] and 289 [182] respectively.

403 Ibid., p. 367 [287].

404 Ibid., pp. 368–72 [288–94].

405 Ibid., pp. 375–76 [299].

406 *Archives parlementaires*, IX, pp. 202ff. Cf. Emmanuel-Joseph Sieyès, *Observations sur le rapport du Comité de constitution sur la nouvelle organisation de la France* in Zapperi ed., *Écrits*, p. 262. For the electoral scheme and its subsequent revision, see Malcolm Crook, *Elections in the French Revolution* (Cambridge: Cambridge University Press, 1996, 2002), ch. 2. For context, see Michael P. Fitzsimmons, "The Committee of the Constitution and the Remaking of France, 1789–1791," *French History*, 4:1 (1990), pp. 23–47. For Burke's verdict on Sieyès's constitutional experimentation, see EB, *Letter to a Noble Lord* (1796), *W & S*, IX, pp. 177–78.

jurisdictions.[407] The only principle of unity was to be found in false displays of harmony exemplified by the festival of the Revolution staged on 14 July 1790.[408] Under the circumstances, the only means of coherence was violent enforcement of the public will. Two methods of achieving this were already apparent: a programme of confiscation and the dominance of Paris. The final arm of coercion would be the military. "Everything depends on the army in such a government as yours," Burke concluded: "you have industriously destroyed all the opinions, and prejudices, and, as far as in you lay, all the instincts which support government."[409]

Burke's alarm about developments in the defence forces had been apparent since his Speech on the Army Estimates in February 1790. Now he focused his attention on a speech by the Comte de la Tour du Pin, minister of war since August 1789, delivered before the Assembly on 4 June 1790. Here the minister dwelt on the collapse of military discipline occurring along with the spread of popular ideology. Turbulent committees of soldiers recalled the Roman *comitia*.[410] Effectively, a military democracy was being established, which would ultimately determine the form of the state.[411] The Assembly's remedy for this revolt was to infuse the soldiers with civic spirit by means of fraternisation in the municipalities. They were trying to cure the distemper by the distemper itself, Burke complained.[412] The mingling of civilian conspirators with military reprobates would blend mutiny with sedition, with results that would prove fatal to the republic. "There must be blood," Burke anticipated.[413] Popularity would replace discipline as the principle of command, obliging officers to fall back on the wiles of the Roman tribunes. At the same time, the constitution of the executive was such that the senior posts in the army could take their cue from either the king or the Assembly. This was a recipe for faction, since officers would become pleaders in two courts, that of the acting monarch and that of the representatives of the people. As the examples of Marius and Cromwell had shown, it was only a matter of time before "some popular general" would take advantage of the crisis of authority: "Armies will obey him on his personal account."[414] Lafayette's militia was already leading the way. Modern policy since the sixteenth century had

[407] In 1791, Burke described the state as comprising no less than 48,000 republics: see EB, *Appeal from the New to the Old Whigs*, p. 20. He was thinking of the 40,000-odd municipalities (or communes) created under the administrative reforms of 1789–90. I am grateful to Malcolm Crook for guidance on this.

[408] EB, *Reflections*, ed. Clark, p. 359 [275–76]. Cf. EB, *Letter to a Member of the National Assembly* (1791), *W & S*, VIII, pp. 310–11. On this, see Mona Ozouf, *Festivals of the French Revolution* (Cambridge, MA: Harvard University Press, 1988), ch. 2.

[409] EB, *Reflections*, ed. Clark, p. 390 [320].

[410] *Archives parlementaires*, XVI, pp. 95–96.

[411] EB, *Reflections*, ed. Clark, p. 381 [308].

[412] Ibid., p. 386 [314].

[413] Ibid.

[414] Ibid., p. 388 [318]. Cf. Smith, *Lectures on Jurisprudence*, pp. 233–34, 240 on Dionysius, the Roman *imperatores* and Cromwell as exemplars of "military monarchy." The spectacle of a republican seizure of power culminating in the "arbitrary and despotic government of a single person" had been analysed by Hume, *History of England*, VI, p. 54.

been dedicated to supplanting the spirit of usurpation which had dominated European politics back in the age of military fiefdoms. However, events in France since the summer of 1789 had been cumulatively reversing that trend.

Back in 1757, Burke had shown his restiveness about allowing arms to fall into the wrong hands. Even the ancient republics refused to allow armed troops within the walls of the city.[415] Back then, Burke feared disturbances from artisans concentrated in cities should they have access to the weaponry of a patriotic militia. As it turned out, the danger came from subversion within the ranks of a standing army, abetted by the example of an urban militia. The combination of relative deprivation with dense interaction in populous cities provided the materials for tumult and sedition. This had been the experience of both Paris and Ghent in the high middle ages, and it was a permanent threat in commercial states in the eighteenth century. Britain was an obvious example: "By the distribution of trade, it may be all considered as one great manufacturing City, where the People being close together, the fire of Sedition may easily catch from one to another until it spreads over the kingdom."[416] It transpired that popular insurgency occurred in France, beginning with a process of reform at the top affecting the allegiance of the crown's forces. From July 1789, the dynamics of agitation in the streets of the capital contributed to the transfer of power to demagogic leaders. An extraordinary spectacle ensued, embracing the collapse of a civilised monarchy and an assault on the Gallican Church. A new and malign force had emerged within the heart of a polite trading empire, and it threatened to undermine the guiding principles of European politics.

[415] EB, "Considerations of the Militia" (1757) in Richard Bourke, "Party, Parliament and Conquest in Newly Ascribed Burke Manuscripts," *Historical Journal*, 55:3 (September 2012), pp. 619–52, p. 651.

[416] Ibid., p. 652.

XIV

WHIG PRINCIPLES AND JACOBIN DOGMA, 1791–1793

Figure 7. Burke bombards a tearful Fox with accusations. Pitt reclines unperturbed by the mayhem in the background.
Anon., Sketch for *The Wrangling of Friends or Opposition in Disorder* (1791) Collection House of Commons (Robinson, p. 151)

14.1 Introduction

After 1790, Burke's career was substantially shaped by the reaction to the *Reflections*. The work was a sophisticated polemical assault on attempts to reduce the rights and responsibilities of citizenship to a perilous ideal of self-government. However, it was widely construed as an attack on the equality of human beings and the accountability of governments to the people whom they ruled. In fact it was a critique of the resort to primitive equality as a justification for destroying equitable relations in civil society. At the same time, its aim was to distinguish responsible government from popular tyranny. From Burke's vantage, the doctrine of the rights of man represented a crusade against the values of cohesion and responsibility and was therefore liable to shatter society and government altogether. The force of his argument has been drowned out by subsequent political rhetoric. This has been based on the assumption that liberalism and democracy form a natural union of values that set European society on the path to progress after 1789. Of course for Americans the route to improvement begins in 1776. Accounts of linear development since the end of the eighteenth century are therefore prone to identify the French with the American Revolution. From this angle, the "Age of Revolutions" was the parent of liberal democracy. This conclusion is a product of a politicised reading of history. To sustain it, it has become necessary to disregard Burke's view of the French Revolution and thus to condemn him as a leading opponent of modernity. In the face of this simplified picture of the past, it is important to try to reconstruct Burke's positions impartially. This has to begin by piecing together the content of his thought. That involves recovering the perspective from which the Revolution posed a threat to the steady growth of civilisation. Given that threat, it seemed urgent that its principles should be challenged and disabled. By early 1791, Burke was certain that the Revolutionary dynamic could not be stopped in the absence of interference by outside powers. In January of that year, as part of his plea for intervention, he sought to demonstrate that the culture of the Revolution was beyond reprieve. Towards that end, in *A Letter to a Member of the National Assembly*, he scrutinised the character of prevailing attitudes in France in order to explain how the values of 1789 could gain such purchase on the legislators in the National Assembly.

In accounting for the transformation of opinion among the French, Burke presented the work of Rousseau as a decisive influence on the Revolution. This was not because the Assembly tried to implement his proposals but on account of the code of conduct he promoted: on Burke's telling, Rousseauian "virtue" became the fashion after 1789. But how could his ideals have such a devastating effect? Burke focused on the impact of the *Confessions* and the *Nouvelle Héloïse*. They both contributed significantly to a revolution in taste. The new code of manners dispensed with morality altogether by attacking its twin foundations: common human sentiment, based on mutual affection; and the sense of duty, grounded in respect for the Almighty. Rousseau replaced these values with a "school" of vanity. Self-regard supplanted the fear of God and man. Common attachments were destroyed by the lure of paradox, and obligations were ousted by a cult of "humanity." Burke took this ideal of humanity to be a thinly disguised expression of self-love. It was *amour propre* masquerading as universal benevolence. According to Burke, it was this duplicity, or hypocrisy, that impelled the Revolution. Angry self-assertion took the place of accommodation and justified its behaviour in the name of cosmopolitan justice.

Only a change in the ethical outlook of society could explain the sudden effectiveness of Revolutionary ideology. Burke claimed that the collapse of the old regime was triggered by the weakness of the king allied to the treachery of his advisors. In accepting the recommendation to reform the mode of selection to the first estate and revise the proportions between the second and the third, Louis XVI transformed the foundations of the ancient government of France. Burke observed that this resulted in the creation of *démocratie royale*—a popular regime under a parade of royalty—at the very moment that strong leadership was needed for reform. As a consequence, reform was overwhelmed by the drive towards innovation supported by the self-regarding taste for *humanité*. The results in 1790 and 1791 were staggering. The effect on British domestic politics was no less remarkable, emboldening critics of the constitution of church and state, and straining relations among the Foxite Whigs. By the spring of 1791, Burke's relationship with Fox was close to breaking point. The final rupture came on 6 May during a debate on the Canada Bill: Fox described the American and Glorious Revolutions as inspired by adherence to the rights of man while Burke associated the same tenets with permanent anarchy. In the *Appeal from the New to the Old Whigs*, which appeared on 3 August 1791, Burke proceeded to distinguish the Whiggism of the Rockinghams from the Francophile Whig doctrine promoted by Fox and inadequately differentiated from the republicanism of Thomas Paine.

As the Revolution troubled the atmosphere at Westminster it also upset the balance of political forces in Ireland. By the autumn of 1791, the Society of United Irishmen had been formed to pursue fundamental constitutional reform. Rumours began to circulate that Catholics and Dissenters planned to combine to promote their interests on a common front. At the same time, a newly configured Catholic Committee was actively campaigning for the repeal of all remaining anti-popery legislation. Faced with reluctance on the part of the Dublin administration to enfranchise Catholics and resistance from the Irish parliament to further relief from the penal laws, Burke began to agitate for political rights for the majority. By January 1792, in his *Letter to Sir Hercules Langrishe*, he was urging the wisdom of admitting Catholics to the vote as the best means of preserving them from the temptations of Jacobin zeal. Burke believed that Protestant domination in Ireland was at bottom a betrayal of Reformation principles: it was not an attempt to protect conscience from the abuse of power but rather an effort to preserve a political monopoly under the pretence of religious piety.

As pressure for reform intensified in Ireland, the Brissotins appeared to be gaining leverage in France. Militancy began to win an audience in the Legislative Assembly. At the same time, on the home front, Burke believed that rational dissent was assuming the form of a civil faction rather than a spiritually motivated sect. He also feared that general subversion in Britain was continuing to build momentum. Even so, the Foxites persisted in publicising their sympathy for France. Then, on 20 April 1792, the French Assembly voted for war against the Habsburg monarchy. The following autumn the Revolutionary forces won their first major victories against Austria. By the time that the French king was executed at the start of 1793, Britain was in the process of preparing to join the war. Burke hoped that the conflict would be pursued as a campaign of doctrinal annihilation rather than as a strategic struggle for geo-political advantage. He insisted that there was no problem justifying interference with the French regime: the population could scarcely be depicted as a "people", the country was divided into antagonistic factions, and the Revolution was incompatible with the balance of power in Europe. As early as his *Thoughts on French Affairs* of late 1791, Burke claimed that European politics was riven by mutually hostile parties that would divide established sovereignties into opposing ideological camps. He now claimed that the Revolutionary contingent in that division was motivated by a relentless will to conquer. Burke concluded that French republicanism had revived the spirit of domination and would seek enlargement by a mixture of proselytism and the sword.

14.2 Aftermath of the *Reflections*

By the time that the *Reflections* appeared on 1 November 1790, it had gone through multiple revisions since the previous February.[1] At one point Burke was rumoured to have given up on the book.[2] The memorialist, Charles McCormick, recorded how all Burke's powers of mind and body had been employed in producing the work over a period of ten months.[3] One of McCormick's sources was the Burkes' secretary, William Thomas Smith, whom Edmund had been urging to forward publication since late October.[4] McCormick described how Burke had been drawn into a process of endless revision: he "wrote, blotted, re-wrote, printed, cancelled, [and] re-printed it so often."[5] James Prior later confirmed this cycle, relaying Dodsley's account of how a dozen new drafts had been printed and destroyed.[6] This diligence

[1] EB confirmed to Philip Francis, 27 October 1790, *Corr.*, VI, p. 142, that he had taken the book "in hand" early in that year.

[2] The information was relayed in a letter from Thomas Paine to Thomas Christie, reporting news from John Debrett, as recorded in William E. Woodward, *Tom Paine: America's Godfather, 1739–1809* (New York: E. P. Dutton and Company, 1945), pp. 186–87.

[3] Charles McCormick, *Memoirs of the Right Honourable Edmund Burke* (London: 1798), p. 339.

[4] EB to William Thomas Smith, c. 25 October 1790, *Corr.*, VI, pp. 141–42. Smith had sold a tranche of Burke Papers to McCormick. See TNA, C12/2186/2: Burke v. Swift, 1797.

[5] McCormick, *Memoirs of Burke*, p. 339.

[6] James Prior, *Life of the Right Honourable Edmund Burke* (1824) (London: 5th ed., 1854), p. 310.

was rewarded with extraordinary success. At five shillings, the *Reflections* was not cheap, yet within a week it was reputed to have sold 7,000 copies.[7] By December, the *St. James's Chronicle* reported that around 13,000 had been sold.[8] After the publication of the eighth impression of the third edition in May 1791, that number had risen to about 19,000.[9] Having read his copy of the work, William Windham testified to its impact, noting its capacity to redirect "the stream of opinion throughout Europe."[10] Burke at this time stood decried and disregarded, yet his position was about to be transformed. "One would think, that the author of such a work, would be called to the government of his country," Windham reflected.[11] Many enemies, as well as friends, became enthusiastic admirers.[12] William Markham was reported to be "in raptures" over its content.[13] Robert Hall, the Baptist minister, was astounded by the performance: "The excursions of his genius are immense."[14] The coverage in the press was instantaneous and extensive.[15] The *Reflections* promptly became a major point of political reference, beginning its career as a controversial classic.[16]

If the work was widely applauded, it was also derided, and even excoriated. The Presbyterian minister James Wodrow, writing to Samuel Kenrick in March 1791, portrayed it as a "furious puff" whose only merit was its power to provoke.[17] More specific derision came from Ewan Law: he informed his brother, Edward Law, chief counsel in the defence of Warren Hastings, that its argument was largely derived from William Paley's *Principles of Moral and Political Philosophy*.[18] However, Paley

[7] Horace Walpole to Mary Berry, *The Yale Edition of the Correspondence of Horace Walpole* (New Haven, CT: Yale University Press, 1937–83), 48 vols., XI, p. 132. Cf. Richard Burke Sr. to Richard Shackleton, 8 November 1790, OSB MSS. File 2423. The price of the *Reflections* can be put in perspective: a common labourer might earn between six and eight shillings a week.

[8] *St. James's Chronicle*, 2–4 December 1790. Cf. EB to Gilbert Elliot, 29 November 1790, *Corr.*, VI, p. 177. The *Public Advertiser*, 10 January 1791, reported that 14,000 had been sold, and that a new impression was printing.

[9] William B. Todd, *A Bibliography of Edmund Burke* (Godalming: St. Paul's Bibliographies, 1982), p. 150. By Burke's death, this had risen to 30,000: see Prior, *Life of Burke*, p. 311.

[10] *The Diary of the Right Hon. William Windham, 1784–1810*, ed. Mrs. Henry Baring (London: Longmans, Green and Co., 1866), p. 213.

[11] Ibid.

[12] Many of Burke's oldest friends expressed their support, including Richard Brocklesby, John Burgoyne and Michael Kearney. See WWM BkP 1:2256, 2258 and 2261. Gilbert Elliot was effusive: see his letter to EB, 6 November 1790, *Corr.*, VI, pp. 155–56. See also John Douglas to EB, 9 November 1790, ibid., p. 157; Lord John Cavendish to EB, 14 November 1790, ibid., pp. 160–61.

[13] Edward Law to John Law, 23 November 1790, TNA, PRO 30/12/17/3/255–7.

[14] Robert Hall, "On Theories and the Rights of Man" in *The Miscellaneous Works and Remains of the Rev. Robert Hall* (London: 1849), p. 196.

[15] See F. P. Lock, *Edmund Burke: 1730–1797* (Oxford: Oxford University Press, 1998–2006), 2 vols., II, pp. 333–36.

[16] Thomas Macknight, *History of the Life and Times of Edmund Burke* (London: 1858–60), 3 vols., III, pp. 329–30.

[17] James Wodrow to Samuel Kenrick, 28 March 1791, Dr. Williams Library Wodrow–Kenrick Correspondence, 24.157 (159).

[18] TNA, PRO 30/12/17/2/ 98.

himself was not so sure: he credited Burke's scepticism about the "rights of man," and endorsed his refutation of Price's conception of the contract of government. Yet he went on to comment that Burke had "traduced" the Revolution: the disorder was incidental rather than intrinsic to the process, falling short of the public violence unleashed against Charles I.[19] This mixture of agreement and dissent on the part of a single respondent indicates the complexity of the impact of the work. The debate sparked by Burke along with Price, and subsequently Paine, generated a literature comprising more than 300 titles.[20] The larger Revolution controversy, which overlaps with that debate, inspired something in the region of 600 pamphlets.[21] In both cases, debate is usually cast in terms of polar ideologies, denominated by morally charged categories. In standard accounts, "conservatism" did battle with "radicalism" and "reformism," with Burke deputed to represent the forces of reaction.[22] By extension, he is commonly seen as a partisan of *ancien régime* Europe, opposed at once to progress and to constitutional reform.[23]

This is both a value-laden and a Manichean perspective. Describing the British constitution in *The Spirit of the Laws*, Montesquieu presented it as a system of "liberté politique extrême," not obviously preferable to an arrangement more "modérée."[24] From a European vantage, there was nothing typical about British politics in the eighteenth century, and so it hardly embodied the principles of a generic "old

[19] William Paley to Edmund Law, 28 November 1790, TNA, PRO 30/12/17/4/ 33–5. I am grateful to Niall O'Flaherty for this reference.

[20] Gayle Trusdel Pendleton, "Towards a Bibliography of the *Reflections* and the *Rights of Man* Controversy," *Bulletin of Research in the Humanities*, 85 (1982), pp. 65–103, identifies 340 titles at p. 65.

[21] Gregory Claeys, "The French Revolution Debate and British Political Thought," *History of Political Thought*, 11:1 (Spring 1990), pp. 59–80, at p. 60.

[22] Alfred Cobban, "Introduction" to idem ed., *The Debate on the French Revolution, 1789–1800* (London: Nicholas Kaye, 1950); Marilyn Butler, "Introduction" to idem ed., *Burke, Paine, Godwin and the Revolution Controversy* (Cambridge: Cambridge University Press, 1984); Ian R. Christie, *Stress and Stability in Late Eighteenth-Century Britain: Reflections on the British Avoidance of Revolution* (Oxford: Oxford University Press, 1984, 1986), pp. 164ff., 170–71; J.G.A. Pocock, "The Varieties of Whiggism from Exclusion to Reform: A History of Ideology and Discourse" in idem, *Virtue, Commerce, and History: Essays on Political Thought and History, Chiefly in the Eighteenth Century* (Cambridge: Cambridge University Press, 1985, 1995), p. 276; Thomas Philip Schofield, "Conservative Political Thought in Britain in Response to the French Revolution," *Historical Journal*, 29:3 (September 1986), pp. 601–22; Harry T. Dickinson, "Popular Loyalism in Britain in the 1790s" in Eckhart Hellmuth ed., *The Transformation of Political Culture: England and Germany in the Late Eighteenth Century* (Oxford: Oxford University Press, 1990), p. 504; Mark Philp, "Introduction" to idem ed., *The French Revolution and British Popular Politics* (Cambridge: Cambridge University Press, 1991). Emma Vincent MacLeod, "La question du citoyen actif: les conservateurs britanniques face à la Revolution française," *Annales historiques de la Révolution française*, 4 (2005), pp. 47–72. Recent contributions to the discussion are summarised in idem, "British Attitudes to the French Revolution," *Historical Journal*, 50:3 (September 2007), pp. 689–709.

[23] For the "ancien régime" as a generic category, see J.C. D.Clark, *English Society, 1688–1832* (Cambridge: Cambridge University Press, 1985).

[24] Charles-Louis de Secondat, Baron de Montesquieu, *De l'esprit des lois* (1748) in *Œuvres complètes*, ed. Roger Caillois (Paris: Gallimard, 1951), 2 vols., II, pt. 2, bk. 12, ch. 6. Cf. Montesquieu, *Mes pensées*, in ibid., I, p. 1429: "gouvernement modéré, c'est-à-dire où une puissance est limitée par une autre puissance."

regime." Since Burke in 1790 was defending party government based on popular consent as the best means of securing the system of liberty analysed by Montesquieu, it makes no sense to describe his position as a retreat to a conservative norm. Equally, as a proponent of reform throughout the 1790s, Burke is scarcely reducible to a hidebound ideologue, cleaving to the integrity of existing establishments: in relation to Ireland, India and the slave trade, he continued to press the case for reform. Even in connection with France, at the start of 1791, Burke was advocating the wisdom of "real reform," to be distinguished from the specious improvements being peddled by the National Assembly.[25] It is true that the *Reflections* proved a divisive text, yet it divided Burke from opponents in a variety of ways, not simply along a single axis. The reaction of Philip Francis is instructive in this regard. Francis read an early draft and later studied the finished product.[26] "All that you say of the Revolution in England is excellent," he remarked.[27] Clearly this was not a point of contention between the two. Moreover, Francis was averse to revolutionary expedients, much like Burke: "you dread and detest commotion of every kind. And so do I."[28] Nonetheless, *in extremis*, as the American Revolution and the revolt of Chait Singh showed, both were prepared to justify resistance against authority. What separated them was the question of whether such action was reasonable in France. Has not "God himself commanded or permitted the Storm to purify the elements?" demanded Francis.[29] Burke was confident that the answer had to be "no."

It seems strange to divide the political orientation of a whole epoch on the basis of rival interpretations of a single event about which, evidently, some were more right than others, but without anyone being absolutely correct in their predictions. Gibbon was avowedly delighted with the *Reflections* as offering "an admirable medicine against the French disease."[30] Horace Walpole, equally, could not suppress his appreciation. As with other adherents of the Whig cause, his loyalty to Fox was paramount, yet the power of Burke's arguments could not be denied. As Walpole saw it, revolution across the Channel was on the rampage: it would, "like Ceres with blazing torches . . . set fire to, and destroy all the harvests upon earth, because her daughter's liberty had been ravished."[31] By contrast, Fox, Sheridan, Francis, Mackintosh, Price, Priestley, Wollstonecraft and Paine all disputed Burke's account of developments in

[25] EB, *Letter to a Member of the National Assembly* (1791), *W & S*, VIII, p. 305.

[26] Francis's annotated copy can be found at the Houghton Library, Harvard University, *EC75. B9177.790r.

[27] Philip Francis to EB, 3 November 1790, *Corr.*, VI, p. 151.

[28] Ibid., p. 154.

[29] Ibid.

[30] Edward Gibbon to Lord Sheffield, 1791, *The Private Letters of Edward Gibbon*, ed. Rowland E. Prothero (London: 1896), 2 vols., II, pp. 236–37. Cf. Horace Walpole to Mary Berry, 26 February 1791, *Yale Edition of the Correspondence of Horace Walpole*, ed. W. S. Lewis (New Haven, CT: Yale University Press, 1937–83), 48 vols., XI, p. 209: "Gibbon admires Burke to the skies, and even the religious parts, he says."

[31] Horace Walpole to Lady Ossory, 9 December 1790, *Correspondence of Horace Walpole*, ed. Lewis, XXXIV, p. 101.

France, yet this is hardly sufficient to characterise their politics, let alone to help us distinguish progress from reaction. Both these categories, plainly, beg the question: from what vantage does a position constitute "progress"? Francis, like Price and Priestley, objected to Burke's defence of ecclesiastical establishments. To Francis, the government of congregations by "priests, bishops, and by cardinals" seemed tantamount to spiritual usurpation.[32] Territories had been laid waste to found monasteries, he believed. Yet Burke feared that the revival of superstition in Europe would be generated by this hostility to priestcraft. It was for history to decide which position was correct: in the eighteenth century the future was opaque.[33] Subsequent commentators, anxious to locate themselves on the right side of history, have habitually endeavoured to pre-empt its verdict. Since, from the perspective of the present, all eighteenth-century publicists were prisoners of their own circumstances, the conduciveness of their politics is best left out of account. Burke's contemporaries were variously divided on Revolutionary France, on the utility of church establishments, and on the scope for political reform. Much of this diversity was instigated by Burke's text. Yet it was frequently based on extravagant misinterpretations of his intentions.

In the aftermath of the *Reflections*, Burke was standardly taken to be championing sentiment over reason, to be subordinating utility to tradition, and to be prioritising prescription over natural right.[34] Each of these reconstructions involves a degree of misrepresentation, based on exaggerated accounts of Burke's original emphasis. Like most of the protagonists in the debate on the Revolution, he set about vindicating the "liberty, safety, and happiness" of the people, yet how this was to be achieved proved controversial.[35] Like Burke, most of his antagonists sought to reconcile merit with privilege. It was an undertaking that has failed to produce consensus even

[32] Ibid., p. 152. But cf. Capel Loft, *Remarks on the Letter of the Right Hon. Edmund Burke Concerning the Revolution in France* (London: 1790), p. 48, on the impropriety of despoiling the monastic orders.

[33] As Joseph Priestley himself put it in his *Letters to the Right Honourable Edmund Burke, Occasioned by his Reflections on the Revolution in France* (Birmingham: 1791), p. vii: "After all, mankind in general will judge the event. If they succeed in establishing a free government, they will be applauded for their *judgment* . . . and if they fail, they will be condemned for their precipitancy and folly."

[34] Mary Wollstonecraft, *A Vindication of the Rights of Men, in a Letter to the Right Hon. Edmund Burke* (1790) in idem, *A Vindication of the Rights of Men and A Vindication of the Rights of Woman,* ed. Sylvana Tomaselli (Cambridge: Cambridge University Press, 1995, 2009), pp. 8, 13, 54; [David Williams], *Lessons to a Young Prince on the Present Disposition in Europe to a General Revolution* (London: 5th ed., 1790), pp. 120–21; Joseph Towers, *Thoughts on the Commencement of a New Parliament* (London: 1790), p. 124; Thomas Christie, *Letters on the Revolution in France, and on the New Constitution Established by the National Assembly* (Dublin: 1791), p. 15; [Catherine Macaulay], *Observations on the Reflections of the Right Hon. Edmund Burke, in a Letter to the Right Hon. Stanhope* (London: 1790), p. 16; Brooke Boothby, *A Letter to the Right Honourable Edmund Burke* (London: 1791), p. 20. Burke acknowledged receiving a number of responses to the *Reflections,* but claimed that he had "not read any of them": see EB to Unknown, 26 January 1791, *Corr.*, VI, p. 214.

[35] EB to Philip Francis, 19 November 1790, ibid., p. 172. Cf. [David Williams], *Lessons to a Young Prince on the Present Disposition in Europe to a General Revolution* (London: 1st ed., 1790), p. 68, on the positive improvements made by the American Revolution: "security, liberty, and happiness are more diffused."

down to our own time. Burke insisted that the proposed means of reconciliation sketched in the *Reflections* was intended to secure property in the interest of commerce while also underwriting a system of responsible government.[36] In the midst of revolution, this involved articulating hitherto unstated principles: it was their elucidation that prompted erstwhile collaborators to object, stirring Fox into disapproval and inciting Sheridan to compose a reply.[37] The usual charge against Burke was the inconsistency of his principles. He was conscious of this allegation from the start, believing that it arose from a failure on the part of his critics to grasp the implications of their own. Writing to Gilbert Elliot on 29 November 1790, he recalled that he had declared his enduring credentials on the hustings back in 1774: advertising his candidacy to the Bristol electorate, he had stood, as he put it to Elliot, "on a Whigg Interest and on that only."[38] He was confident that he had not subsequently deviated from that commitment. Describing his position back in 1774, he proclaimed his allegiance to two fundamental values: the dignity of a system of regulated authority, represented by the constitution, and the prospect of sustainable economic prosperity, guaranteed by the progress of commerce.[39] Now, in 1790, he was clear that both these depended on the "spirit of a gentleman." As he claimed to Gilbert Elliot on 29 November, he would have protested then, as he was loudly protesting now, against the "destruction" of the system of ranks in any European country.[40]

Most of Burke's Whig detractors were similarly disposed to retain the government of crown and parliament in the interest of land and commerce, with a view to supporting property and prosperity. Their departure from Burke resulted from their denial that conditions in France threatened these fundamental principles. The trenchancy of Burke's judgments increased the likelihood of their divergence. Faced with massive upheaval, it proved difficult to project confidently the probable course of events, yet Burke was ready with an unwavering assessment. Exposed to his emphatic pronouncements, many of them subversive of vulgar Whig pieties, it was more comfortable to fall back on established modes of evaluation, many of these enjoying the status of national shibboleths directed against a rival power. In France itself, with politics subdividing into acrimonious factions, the *Reflections* met with

[36] For [Williams], *Lessons to a Young Prince* (1st ed.), p. 68, on the other hand, social hierarchy blighted industry.

[37] For Fox's response, see Joseph Farington, *The Farington Diary* (London: Hutchinson, 1923), 8 vols., IV, p. 22. Cf. his claim that it was written in "very bad taste" in Add. MS. 47590, fol. 24. Sheridan was rumoured to be composing a response to Burke's *Reflections* at this time, but his pamphlet never appeared: see L. G. Mitchell, *Charles James Fox and the Disintegration of the Whig Party, 1782–94* (Oxford: Oxford University Press, 1971), p. 158, citing Lady Elizabeth Foster's account given in the Chatsworth MSS. Richard Burke Jr. confirmed as much in a letter to Fitzwilliam on 23 November 1790: see EB to Gilbert Elliot, 29 November 1790, *Corr.*, VI, p. 179n.

[38] EB to Gilbert Elliot, 29 November 1790, ibid., p. 178.

[39] EB, Speech on Arrival at Bristol, 13 October 1774, *W & S*, III, p. 59.

[40] EB to Gilbert Elliot, 29 November 1790, *Corr.*, VI, p. 179.

a variable reception.[41] A list compiled after November 1790 detailing the "noms de ceux qui ont ecrit [*sic*]" to Burke from France itemises approximately forty persons.[42] Opponents of the Revolution often disputed his analysis, but usually acknowledged the inspiration his work afforded: the Abbé Maury, the Comte de Montlossier, Jean-Jacques Duval d'Eprémesnil, Jean Joseph Mounier, Charles Alexandre de Calonne and Jacques Antoine Marie de Cazalès were quick to acknowledge it.[43] If nothing else, the *Reflections* came to enjoy a symbolic significance as a clear-sighted rejection of the recent course of French affairs. Mirabeau implicitly recognised as much on 28 January 1791 in representing the work to the National Assembly as a superstitious assault on "la raison humaine."[44]

There was no doubting that the book had created a stir. But even among those favourably disposed to Burke's animus against the Revolution, his message was unlikely to be greeted by a uniform response. François-Louis-Thibault de Menonville, elected deputy to the Estates General from Mirecourt in Lorraine, wrote soon after the appearance of the first edition of the *Reflections* with a sympathetic critique of some of its judgments. To begin with, he noted that minor errors in Burke's text gave fuel to his determined adversaries.[45] More generally, he observed how many of Burke's negative characterisations could be appropriated as endorsements by Jacobin ideologues.[46] But above all, Menonville challenged Burke's indictment of opponents of French policy who continued to participate in the business of the Assembly. He protested: "There are some Gentleman . . . who have thought, it was their bounden Duty, to stand to the last, in the Post they have been trusted into, by their constituents."[47] This raised the complex issue of complicity with the new regime. Burke urged compliant opponents of the Revolutionary juggernaut to consider the means available of resorting to resistance.

This advice came in the form of an open reply to Menonville, published as *A Letter to a Member of the National Assembly*. Burke had finished his response by

[41] There is a tendentious sketch in L. G. Mitchell, "Introduction" to idem ed., *W & S*, VIII, pp. 14–15. A brief critical reaction is recorded in *L'Ancien moniteur* in *Réimpression de l'Ancien moniteur* (Paris: 1858–63), 31 vols., VI, pp. 78–79. More detailed responses appeared in the *Journal historiques et littéraire*, 1 June 1791; *Révolutions de Paris*, April 1790 (reviewing the Army Estimates speech); *Le Spectateur national*, 5 December 1790; *Journal de Paris*, 23 December 1790; and *Chronique de Paris*, 3 December 1790.

[42] WWM BkP 10:18.

[43] Their correspondence with Burke can be found among the Fitzwilliam Papers at the Northamptonshire Record Office. See Colin Lucas, "Edmund Burke and the Émigrés" in François Furet and Mona Ozouf eds., *The French Revolution and the Creation of Modern Political Culture: The Transformation of Political Culture, 1789–1848* (Oxford: Pergamon, 1989), 3 vols., III, pp. 103–4.

[44] *Archives parlementaires*, XXII, p. 536. The words were in fact written by Étienne Dumont: see idem, *Souvenirs sur Mirabeau, et sur les deux premières assemblées legislatives*, ed. J. Bénétruy (Paris: Presses Universitaires de France, 1951), p. 147.

[45] François-Louis-Thibault de Menonville to EB, 17 November 1790, *Corr.*, VI, p. 163.

[46] Ibid., pp. 164–65.

[47] Ibid., p. 166.

19 January 1791, dispatching it to his correspondent nine days later.[48] The *Letter* appeared in Paris at the end of April, having been circulated in Britain during its progress through the press.[49] Alexander Haliday, the Belfast Whig politician, expected the work to raise more "clubs of citizens" against it than inspire "companies of adventurous knights" to support its message.[50] The main purpose of the letter was to publicise Burke's sense that the situation in France was irremediable. In the *Reflections*, he had written caustically of the remnants of the Constituent Assembly remaining after the October *journées* as "dregs and refuse".[51] It was at that point that Lally-Tollendal and Mounier had withdrawn, sensing that the tide of politics had shifted against them.[52] Burke's endorsement of their retirement stung Menonville: these two prominent *monarchiens* had, in truth, betrayed their cause, having already created conditions that would lead to its subversion. Lally-Tollendal had contributed to the *Declaration of the Rights of Man and the Citizen*, while both he and Mounier had facilitated the union of the Estates. Then, alarmed by the course of events to which their actions had contributed, they deserted the ranks of their followers.[53] However, for Burke, they had abandoned a hopeless situation. If one traced the views of those directing the vanguard of the Revolution, he proposed, it was evident that their designs predated May 1789. The agenda of men like Sieyès and Mirabeau had been formulated long before the first meeting of the Estates, and their principles were now being institutionalised as they purged the commonwealth of the influence of its landed property.[54] Burke concluded that there was no chance that their programme of action could be halted in its tracks: its proponents controlled events, and their supporters could not be turned. This meant that there were no domestic means of overturning the new regime.

From Burke's perspective, the forlorn state of the French polity was a result of the fatal collusion between the legislators and the multitude. The deputies in the Assembly seemed chained to the vagaries of the crowd as a consequence of their resort to direct popular legitimation, while the crowd had been inflamed by the promise of public power. In effect, the dynamics of popular politicisation sabotaged constitutional procedure. Insurgency replaced orderly representation. As Burke saw it, the initiative had been seized by knaves in the Assembly, abetted by dupes among the population at large. With the tangible success of the Revolution, the knaves could not be deflected and the populace would not be reformed. Desperation precluded

[48] For the delay, see EB to the Comtesse de Montrond, 25 January 1791, ibid., p. 212.

[49] James Bland Burges informed Burke on 6 May 1791, ibid., pp. 252–3, that George III had "perused it with much attention."

[50] Alexander Haliday to the Earl of Charlemont, *The Manuscripts and Correspondence of James, First Earl of Charlemont* (London: 1894), 2 vols., II, p. 140.

[51] EB, *Reflections*, ed. Clark, p. 238 [101].

[52] For his defence of this move, see Trophime Gérard de Lally-Tollendal, *Lettre de Monsieur de Lally-Tollendal à Madame la Comtesse de **** (N.P.: 1789).

[53] François-Louis-Thibault de Menonville to EB, 17 November 1790, *Corr.*, VI, p. 167.

[54] EB, *Letter to a Member of the National Assembly* (1791), *W & S*, VIII, p. 298.

moderation in a world turned upside down. Politicians were consumed by their own fraud while the mob grew intoxicated by the thrill of upheaval. Routine political process seemed dreary on account of its humdrum procedures:

> The shifting tides of fear and hope, the flight and pursuit, the peril and escape, the alternate famine and feast . . . after a time, render all course of slow, steady, progressive, unvaried occupation, and the prospect only of a limited mediocrity at the end of long labour, to the last degree tame, languid, and insipid.[55]

Above all, ferment was beguiling because it flattered the illusion of empowerment: the people of Paris, just yesterday immured in undistinguished normality, were now captivated by the impression that they had become "a people of princes."[56] Activists in clubs and orators in coffee-houses supported themselves with "the imagination" that they were "generals of armies, prophets, kings and emperors."[57] For such an illusion of liberation there was no cure.

There appeared to exist no domestic means of reversing the tide of affairs. Since leading politicians were bewitched by their own sophistries, nothing would induce them to reason consequentially.[58] At the same time, their minions were dazzled by the fantasy of their own efficacy.[59] Burke felt that nothing could turn back this flood of mutual corruption, leaving the residual "sound part of the community" as the only resource against further destruction. This section of the population might be large, but it was nonetheless evidently in the minority.[60] Besides, it was completely bereft of the means of effective action. The reason for this lay in the previous history of the kingdom. As Voltaire and Montesquieu had powerfully attested, the French monarchy had reduced its independent nobility in the course of the seventeenth century: while they rose in splendour, they declined in power.[61] As Tocqueville later emphasised, administrative centralisation was an achievement of the old regime.[62] When the authority of Louis XVI was eroded, this left a power vacuum. Once this was filled by the democratic forces of the Assembly, the new incumbents could act without resistance. Burke presented his own assessment of the legacy of centralisation after the French wars of religion in a letter to the Chevalier de la Bintinaye, nephew of Jean-Baptiste-Marie, Champion de Cicé, the Bishop of Auxerre in Burgundy, with

[55] Ibid., p. 301.

[56] Ibid.

[57] Ibid., p. 305. For the specific reference to clubs and coffee-houses dictating to the Assembly, see EB to the Comtesse de Montrond, 25 January 1791, *Corr.*, VI, p. 213.

[58] EB, *Letter to a Member of the National Assembly* (1791), *W & S*, VIII, p. 298.

[59] Ibid., p. 305.

[60] Ibid.

[61] Voltaire, *Le siècle de Louis XIV* (Berlin: 1751), 2 vols., II, pp. 138–41; Montesquieu, *De l'esprit des lois*, pt. I, bk. viii, ch. 6.

[62] Alexis de Tocqueville, *The Old Regime and the Revolution,* ed. François Furet and Françoise Mélonio (Chicago, IL: University of Chicago Press, 1998–2001), 2 vols., I, p. 118.

whom Burke was acquainted since his son's visit to France in 1773.[63] "To strengthen itself the Monarchy had weakened every other force," Burke wrote. "To unite the Nation to itself," he continued, "it had dissolved all other ties." Therefore, when the king fell into the rank of a minor officer of state, the commonwealth reverted to a condition of "disconnection."[64] Behind this description lay a comparison with Britain, whose politics was organised around the principle of "connection," by which the nobility and gentry could unite against the crown. Party, or principled connection, illustrated this system at its best.

In the absence of any obstacle of the kind, the conquest of France could be secured without any show of domestic resistance. In 1742, Hume had famously contrasted eastern states with the organisation of monarchy in Europe. In the latter, unlike the former, an independent system of honour and rank served to curb the untrammelled will of executive power. Yet this same political significance accorded to the nobility meant that the conquest of a monarchy graced with intermediate powers was both more difficult to achieve and harder to retain if its government should ever be overturned.[65] Burke's point was that, with the exception of their role in the *parlements* before 1789, the gentlemen of France had no means of combination and therefore little effective clout. Certainly their judicial authority was not matched by a network of independent organisation such as characterised the governing class in Britain. There was no "force or union" below the level of the monarch that could sustain the kingdom's corporations.[66] Consequently, when the king was discredited, there was no means of supporting either the clergy or the nobility, or of mobilising the people against the new regime. This left Lally-Tollendal appealing to the memory of Quintus "Capitolinus" Catulus, consul at Rome in 78 BC, whose stand against Marcus Lepidus' march on Rome seemed to embody patriotic virtue in opposition to militant populism.[67] Burke had been sent a copy of Lally-Tollendal's pamphlet in December 1790, but he admired its spirited eloquence more than its strategic sense.[68] Lally was appealing to the civic devotion of the French, yet his audience, in Burke's mind, were already beyond recovery: "He speaks, as if he applied himself to the high-minded military Republicans, or to an antient spirited French Nobility, wholly devoted to political and martial Glory."[69] In fact he was speaking to renegades and their habitués.

[63] The Burkes knew both men through the Parisot family, with whom Richard Burke Jr. had stayed. See Madame Parisot to Richard Burke Jr., 14 September 1789, *Corr.*, VI, pp. 17–18.

[64] EB to the Chevalier de la Bintinaye, March 1791, ibid., p. 242.

[65] David Hume, "That Politics May Be Reduced to a Science" in idem, *Essays Moral, Political and Literary*, ed. Eugene F. Miller (Indianapolis, IN: Liberty Fund, 1985, 1987), pp. 22–23.

[66] EB to the Chevalier de la Bintinaye, March 1791, *Corr.*, VI, p. 242.

[67] Trophime Gérard Lally-Tollendal, *Quintus Capitolinus aux Romains* (Paris: 1790).

[68] EB to John Trevor, January 1790, *Corr.*, VI, p. 217.

[69] EB to the Comtesse de Montrond, 25 January 1791, ibid., p. 212.

Burke drew what seemed the obvious conclusion: in the absence of any viable internal remedy, assistance would have to come "from *without*."[70] "Your sole hope seems to me to rest in the disposition of the Neighbouring powers and in their ability to yield you assistance," as he put it to Bintinaye.[71] Burke had by now committed himself to counter-revolution, and assumed that its success would depend on external assistance. The monarchy, being a virtual prisoner, had no autonomous means of acting, and no figure of weight and ability had surfaced in a leading role.[72] This predicament threw France at the mercy of outside forces that might sympathise with its misfortune or realise that their interests were opposed. Reason of state was more likely to determine the policy of European powers, but they would have to be brought to see that the Revolution posed a threat. At present, with France in a parlous state, the danger was less immediately apparent. Nonetheless, "times and occasions make dangers," Burke observed. Above all, it was possible that the French would inspire sympathetic rebellion in another country.[73] In the meantime, Burke was anxious to vindicate the legitimacy of intervention. He tentatively canvassed three grounds for interference: the policy interest among rival powers in maintaining a monarchical constitution in France; the obligation to restore a system of justice to an oppressed neighbour; and the duty to defend a Christian culture under assault. To bolster his case, he set about further anatomising the moving "principle" of the French regime.

14.3 The Paradoxes of Rousseau

In pursuing this course, Burke built up a drastic picture of the "*disposition*" governing France.[74] This, he claimed, had been formed from materials supplied by Jean-Jacques Rousseau.[75] Burke was capitalising on the recognition accorded Rousseau after the National Assembly voted for a statue in his honour on 21 December 1790.[76] Between 1790 and 1791, a street was also named after him, and a section after the *Contrat social*. A copy of that work, along with a bust of its author, had already been given pride of place in the Assembly. Burke thought that the literature of an era was a window on its taste, and that consequently the official endorsement of a particular

[70] EB, *Letter to a Member of the National Assembly* (1791), *W & S*, VIII, p. 305. Cf. EB to John Trevor, January 1790, *Corr.*, VI, p. 217.

[71] EB to the Chevalier de la Bintinaye, March 1791, *Corr.*, VI, p. 242.

[72] Ibid., pp. 241–42.

[73] EB, *Letter to a Member of the National Assembly* (1791), *W & S*, VIII, p. 306.

[74] Ibid., p. 311.

[75] For Burke's treatment of Rousseau in the context of the Revolution, see the discussion in Iain Hampsher-Monk, "Rousseau, Burke's *Vindication of Natural Society*, and Revolutionary Ideology," *European Journal of Political Theory*, 9:3 (2010), pp. 245–66. For an older literature on Burke and Rousseau, see above, chapter 2, section 3, as well as David Cameron, *The Social Thought of Rousseau and Burke: A Comparative Study* (Toronto: University of Toronto Press, 1973).

[76] *Archives parlementaires*, XXI, p. 619.

figure was a powerful index of the public will. It was one thing to tolerate the free use of public discussion, which Burke, like Kant, encouraged.[77] It was quite another for the state to canonise an author of "mixed or ambiguous morality."[78] Clearly Burke's intention was not to condemn Rousseau as a reprobate, but to draw attention to his ambivalent status as a moralist.[79] He had been familiar with Rousseau's writings since the 1750s, attracted by his originality and soaring eloquence.[80] The rhetorical passion to be found in Rousseau's writings was a vehicle for a philanthropic ethic that distinguished him as a conscientious icon of the age. But to Burke's mind his bearing was ultimately equivocal.[81] Overriding the posture of indignation in his prose was the persistent impulse to scandalise his audience, to astound by offending customary beliefs about morality. It might be, of course, as Rousseau would claim, that customs could act as covers for injustice. But equally customs might operate as conductors for moral truths. Rousseau's method, however, was paradoxical: it aimed to subvert the common sense or δόχα (*doxa*) of the age.

As Burke well knew, this reproduced a rhetorical strategy fostered by the stoics. Contrary to standard accounts, Burke's point was not so much that the leading orators in the National Assembly adopted doctrines wholesale from their Swiss master, but rather that they mimicked an aspect of his style and values: "I less consider the author, than the system of the Assembly in perverting morality, through his means."[82] The "means" at issue referred to Rousseau's resort to a stoic mode of moral reasoning, overturning the *sensus communis* with outlandish moral claims.[83] In book IV of *De finibus*, Cicero referred to the verbal deceptions (*praestigiae*) of the stoics as the means by which they supported outrageous moral positions.[84] In

[77] Immanuel Kant, *Was ist Aufklärung*, ed. Horst D. Brandt (Hamburg: Felix Meiner Verlag, 1999). See, however, EB to Richard Burke Sr., 24 July 1791, *Corr.*, VI, p. 307, on the need to deal severely with treasonable publications.

[78] EB, *Letter to a Member of the National Assembly* (1791), *W & S*, VIII, p. 312.

[79] Burke was sent an anonymous pamphlet by its author comparing his thought to the Rousseau who had written the *Considérations sur le gouvernement de Pologne*, but in his response Burke ignored the comparison: see EB to Unknown, 26 January 1791, *Corr.*, VI, pp. 214–15. The work sent was Anon., *A Comparison of the Opinions of Mr Burke and Monsr Rousseau* (London: 1791).

[80] Even in 1791, he was prepared to concede that his style was "glowing, animated, enthusiastic": see EB, *Letter to a Member of the National Assembly* (1791), *W & S*, VIII, p. 318.

[81] There is a sketch of Burke's response to Rousseau in Henry Mackenzie, "The Political Character of Burke" (n.d.), Beinecke Library, Yale University, Osborn fd1.

[82] EB, *Letter to a Member of the National Assembly* (1791), *W & S*, VIII, p. 318. For discussion of Rousseau's impact, or otherwise, on French Revolutionary politics and society, see Gordon H. McNeil, "The Cult of Rousseau and the French Revolution," *Journal of the History of Ideas*, 6:2 (April 1945), pp. 197–212; Joan McDonald, *Rousseau and the French Revolution, 1762–1791* (London: Athlone Press, 1965); Norman N. Hampson, *Will and Circumstance: Montesquieu, Rousseau and the French Revolution* (Norman, OK: University of Oklahoma Press, 1983).

[83] The British, by comparison, were more widely exposed to "the authors of sound antiquity": see EB, *Letter to a Member of the National Assembly* (1791), *W & S*, VIII, p. 318.

[84] Cicero, *De finibus bonorum et malorum*, IV, 74.

Pro Murena, he attacked Cato as a leading patron of these counter-intuitive norms.[85] The resulting paradoxes were born of a revolt against vice which risked contempt for human beings as the progenitors of foul deeds. "By hating vices too much, they come to love men too little," Burke wrote of Revolutionaries in the *Reflections*.[86] The idea is derived from his suspicion of stoic moralism, exposed by Cicero but perpetuated by Rousseau. Burke claimed to have discovered Rousseau's method of composition from Hume, which allegedly consisted in striking the imaginations of his readers by fastening on to "marvelous" episodes in ordinary life. On this basis, he would fabricate "new and unlooked for strokes in politics and morals."[87] It was a method, Burke reminds us, exemplified by Cato: "Cicero ludicrously describes Cato as endeavouring to act in the commonwealth upon the school of paradoxes which exercised the wits of the junior students in stoic philosophy."[88] In his *Paradoxa stoicorum*, Cicero elucidated this procedure, presenting Cato as opposed to the common opinions of mankind, expressing his unworldly views in a rudimentary style.[89]

The crude rhetorical method of the stoics mirrored their coarse lifestyles: "they become increasingly uncouth, severe and harsh, in both their speeches and their morals."[90] Burke himself invoked the rough morality of the stoics by citing Horace on the poorly clad, bare-footed Cato, who had inspired a cult of austerity in his own day.[91] In promoting independence from worldly fortune, strands of stoicism became averse to the refinements of civilised existence, cultivating a cynic antipathy to artificial desires.[92] This resulted in opposition to common sensibility as recorded in the annals of the *ius gentium*. According to Cicero, Socrates was the source of this predilection for "παράδοχα" (*paradoxa*).[93] By common consent the attitude was popularised by Diogenes of Sinope who became a byword for contempt for the world of mere "opinion."[94] Diogenes, in turn, as Plato is alleged to have remarked,

85 Cicero, *Pro Murena*, 60–66.

86 EB, *Reflections*, ed. Clark, p. 341 [251].

87 Ibid., p. 342 [252].

88 Ibid., p. 342 [251].

89 Cicero, *Paradoxa stoicorum*, 2.

90 Cicero, *De finibus bonorum et malorum*, IV, 78.

91 EB, *Reflections*, ed. Clark, p. 342 [251], quoting Horace, *Epistles*, I, xix, line 12.

92 For early modern depictions of members of the cynic school as sponsors of a rude antipathy to civility, see Johann Jacob Brucker, *Historia critica Philosophiae* (Leipzig: 1742–44), 5 vols.; Ephraim Chambers, *Cyclopaedia: Or, an Universal Dictionary of Arts and Sciences* (London: 1751), 2 vols.

93 Cicero, *Paradoxa stoicorum*, 4. Cf. Cicero, *Academica*, II, 136. See also Diogenes Laertius, *Vitae philosophorum*, I, 15. For the Socratic pedigree of the stoics and the cynics, see Eric Brown, "Socrates in the Stoa" in Sara Ahbel-Rappe and Rachana Kamtekar eds., *A Companion to Socrates* (Oxford: Blackwells, 2009)

94 Burke commented adversely on Diogenes' contempt for common practices (like burial) in EB, "Several Scattered Hints Concerning Philosophy and Learning Collected Here from My Papers" (c. 1755) in *A Notebook of Edmund Burke: Poems, Characters, Essays and Other Sketches in the Hands of Edmund and William Burke*, ed. H.V.F. Somerset (Cambridge: Cambridge University Press, 1957), p. 91. On Diogenes, along with Rousseau's perceived debt to cynic moral philosophy, see Michael Sonenscher,

appeared to be a "Socrates gone mad."[95] In reviewing Rousseau's *Lettre à d'Alembert sur les spectacles* in 1760, *The Annual Register* associated its argument with the misanthropic rigidities of stoic and cynic philosophy.[96] Its assessment of Rousseau's message substantially overlapped with the estimate subsequently presented in the *Reflections*, where the Genevan is associated with the paradoxes of Cato.[97] *The Annual Register* had been particularly explicit: the "tendency to paradox" compromised the character of the work. This was expressed in terms of a "satire upon civilized society" born of underlying "splenetic" habits of mind. In the *Letter to a Member of the National Assembly*, the philosophy of Rousseau is equated with Diogenes: the famous author of the *Confessions* and the *Nouvelle Héloïse* was now dubbed "the insane *Socrates* of the National Assembly."[98]

Burke's longstanding interest in Rousseau was based on a fascination with his peculiar combination of characteristics. The reviewer of the *Lettre à d'Alembert* in *The Annual Register*, most probably Burke, declared that no other contemporary writer had "a greater share of talent or learning than Rousseau."[99] This admiration was matched by the fact that the *Register* regularly featured material associated with Rousseau. This included, in 1762, an extract from a *Prophétie Par M. de V*****, published in 1761 and purporting to be by Voltaire, which charged Rousseau with launching a cynical attack on civilisation through a combination of hypocrisy and enthusiasm.[100] The following year, *The Annual Register* carried a review of *Émile*, as well as two lengthy extracts from the work, the first on the utility of instruction through the medium of fable, the second comprising the Savoyard Vicar's comparison between Socrates and Christ.[101] The review describes Rousseau, once again, as "a paradoxical genius." We are told that the doctrines canvassed by *Émile* are, predictably, set against the "received notions" of the age, resulting in a high-sounding moral crusade that was in fact "dangerous to piety and to morals."[102] For Burke, the most

Sans-Culottes: An Eighteenth-Century Emblem in the French Revolution (Princeton, NJ: Princeton University Press, 2008), pp. 138ff.

[95] Diogenes Laertius, *Vitae philosophorum*, VI, 54.

[96] *The Annual Register for the Year 1759* (London: 1760), p. 479. For the reception of Rousseau in Britain in the 1750s, see Edward Duffy, *Rousseau in England: The Context for Shelley's Critique of the Enlightenment* (Berkeley, CA: University of California Press, 1979), ch. 1.

[97] EB, *Reflections*, ed. Clark, p. 342 [251].

[98] EB, *Letter to a Member of the National Assembly* (1791), *W & S*, VIII, p. 314. The comparison was more widespread: see Gabriel Brizard, "Socrate et Jean-Jacques, ou parallèle de Jean-Jacques Rousseau avec Socrate," Bibliothèque de l'Arsenal, Paris, MS. 6099.

[99] *The Annual Register for 1759*, p. 479. The attribution of reviews in *The Annual Register* is a notoriously perilous activity. In this case, the coincidence between its judgments and Burke's later views is striking.

[100] "A Prophecy by Monsieur Voltaire" in "Miscellaneous Essays" in *The Annual Register for the Year 1761* (London: 1762), reproducing portions of [Anon.], *Prophétie Par M. de V***** (Geneva: 1761).

[101] *The Annual Register for the Year 1765* (London: 1766) also carried a refutation of Rousseau's ideas for inculcating the idea of God in children, pp. 215–16, and the appropriate method for reasoning with children according to Locke and Rousseau's *Émile*, pp. 217–19.

[102] "Account of the Books for 1762" in *The Annual Register for the Year 1762* (London: 1763), p. 227.

significant danger posed to morals by the arguments presented in *Émile* derived from the challenge to revealed religion mounted by the Savoyard Vicar's "Profession de Foi" in book IV of the work, a portion of which was excerpted in *The Annual Register* for 1762. In preaching a religion of nature, based on the intimations of the heart, the Savoyard Vicar dispenses with the centrality of the Bible to religious faith. Nonetheless, in the midst of delivering his argument, the "sceptical" Vicar articulates such a compelling account of the veracity of Christ's sacrifice that even the most dogmatic deist could not fail to be moved by the performance.[103] Rousseau inspires, yet he undermines; he enjoins piety and justice, yet he destroys their foundation. All this was done, Burke suspected, to undermine habitual beliefs, less from the spirit of genuine inquiry than from motives of self-promotion. He was driven into sophistry out of a desire for applause.

For this reason, Burke characterised Rousseau in the *Letter to a Member of the National Assembly* as "the great professor and founder of the *philosophy of vanity*."[104] Vanity, he went on, was "omnivorous."[105] As he later observed, it was capable of deranging the common habits of morality by promoting an excessive "sensibility for ourselves."[106] It had long been the besetting sin of self-deluding stoics.[107] Yet in Rousseau its operation was still more insidious. He did not merely contradict in practice the virtues that he advocated in theory: he further made a virtue of the contradiction, raising hypocrisy to a new level of knowingness. What drove this process was an insatiable self-regard, sacrificing sincerity on account of a need for approval. He extolled independence while slavishly craving attention. Disingenuousness was transformed into a habit of existence. The *Confessions* constructed a model for acolytes to follow: "in his life," as Burke emphasised, by which he meant his autobiography, Rousseau offered a standard of behaviour.[108] There he exposed his own failings on a pretext of candour while in fact exonerating his shortcomings as he made a parade of himself: he advertised his vices to "excite surprize and draw attention" with a show of openness, perverting even duplicity into systematic falsity.[109] Those who aped this behaviour became mere painted creatures—"spurious, fictitious"—affecting attitudes and discounting the social cost.[110] What counted was the outlandish appeal of sophistic argument beside which actual consequences were of little concern. In Rousseau this conceitedness gave rise to a code of manners, depicted in noble language with ignoble effects: "universal benevolence" was championed while betrayal became a norm; education was recommended yet its precepts were depraved; love

[103] "Literary and Miscellaneous Essays," ibid., pp. 160–62.

[104] EB, *Letter to a Member of the National Assembly* (1791), *W & S*, VIII, p. 313.

[105] Ibid., p. 314.

[106] EB to Claude-François de Rivarol, 1 June 1791, *Corr.*, VI, p. 269.

[107] For this anti-stoic indictment, see Christopher Brooke, *Philosophic Pride: Stoicism and Political Thought from Lipsius to Rousseau* (Princeton, NJ: Princeton University Press, 2012).

[108] EB, *Letter to a Member of the National Assembly* (1791), *W & S*, VIII, p. 312.

[109] Ibid., p. 314.

[110] Ibid., p. 315.

was celebrated yet its content was debauched. In a letter to the Comte de Rivarol from June 1791, Burke meditated on the combination of moral enthusiasm and vice that had come to characterise French manners in Rousseau's wake. Humanity was made to substitute all other virtues, extinguishing norms of behaviour that limited the passions.[111] Obligations born of restraint gave way to self-congratulatory benevolence: a self-regarding commitment to cosmopolitan fellow-feeling masked the eradication of fidelity to duties.[112]

Burke associated this mode of dissimulation with the principles adumbrated in Rousseau's *Nouvelle Héloïse*. In the *Confessions*, Rousseau pointed to the ambivalent reception of that work—uniformly cherished by society at large, unevenly appreciated by "the literary people."[113] This diversity, he claimed, could be accounted for in terms of the sentiments that the work expressed—its "subtleties of heart," as Rousseau put it.[114] In a continent like Europe, where virtue was entirely corrupted, the kinds of decency, purity and tenderness displayed in the *Nouvelle Héloïse* were still hankered after.[115] Yet to Burke this apparent purity was simply the work of *amour propre*, disposed to seduce the mind from its proper duty. As he wrote to Rivarol: "I have observed that the Philosophers in order to insinuate their polluted Atheism into young minds, systematically flatter all their passions natural and unnatural."[116] The erotic transports of Julie's tutor, Saint-Preux, were examples of lust exalted into a pretence of virtue. He was a charmer in the guise of a teacher, a despoiler masquerading as a lover. Between Rousseau's renunciation of fatherhood through his abandonment of his children, and his degradation of the passion of love in the *Nouvelle Héloïse*, he attacked the taste and morals of the age.[117] He targeted the nursery of fidelity and honour: namely, the family. "Ever since all the sentiments of nature have been stifled by extreme inequality," Rousseau wrote in the second Preface to the work, "it is from the iniquitous despotism of fathers that the vices and misfortunes of children arise." It was therefore necessary to initiate reform by redeeming the source of corruption: one had to begin "with domestic morals."[118] Domestic morals,

[111] EB to Claude François de Rivarol, 1 June 1791, *Corr.*, VI, p. 270.

[112] Including the duty of patriotic allegiance. For its subversion by specious French fraternity, see EB, *Observations on the Conduct of the Minority* (Spring 1793), *W & S*, VIII, pp. 434–35.

[113] Jean-Jacques Rousseau, *The Confessions, and Correspondence, including the Letters to Malesherbes*, ed. Christopher Kelly, Roger D. Masters and Peter G. Stillman (Hanover, NE: University Press of New England, 1995), p. 456. For the reception in England, see James H. Warner, "Eighteenth-Century English Reactions to the Nouvelle Héloïse," *Publications of the Modern Language Association*, 52:3 (September 1937), pp. 803–19.

[114] Rousseau, *Confessions*, p. 457.

[115] Rousseau originally claimed that purity of sentiment appeared "unnatural" to the debased feelings of civilised observers: see Jean-Jacques Rousseau, *Julie, or the New Heloise: Letters of Two Lovers Who Live in a Small Town at the Foot of the Alps*, ed. Philip Stewart and Jean Vaché (Hanover, NE: University Press of New England: 1997), p. 3. In the *Confessions* the argument was that their remoteness made them desirable.

[116] EB to Claude François de Rivarol, 1 June 1791, *Corr.*, VI, p. 270.

[117] EB, *Letter to a Member of the National Assembly* (1791), *W & S*, VIII, pp. 315–16.

[118] Rousseau, *Nouvelle Heloise*, pp. 17–18.

Burke agreed, were a pivot of society. For him, marriage was a mainstay of European civilisation. Without it the social freedom enjoyed by women would be impeded, since their movements would be patrolled by jealous men.[119] In fact, the advantages of Europe over non-European societies were derived from the combination of liberty of movement with a rigorous marriage bond, without which the culture of gallantry could never have endured.[120]

As Burke perceived it, Rousseau's renovation of family sentiment would bring about its destruction. To begin with, its binding sentiment, love, was vitiated in the novel, perverted into a form of "philosophical" crudity. It combined lewdness with gloomy rumination into a single brew.[121] Rousseau's portrayal of a family instructor in the guise of a passionate gallant seemed indicative to Burke. It showed how the mind might be tempted in imagination to dismantle socially necessary prejudices: "When the fence from the gallantry of preceptors is broken down, and your families are no longer protected by decent pride, and salutary domestic prejudice, there is but one step to a frightful corruption."[122] Saint-Preux, in Voltaire's blunt description, was merely "une espèce de valet Suisse."[123] The difference in rank between Julie and Saint-Preux encapsulated the risk of promiscuous liaisons between the sexes, enacting the fantasy of an egalitarian breach of social barriers. In this way, Rousseau prefigured in fiction what the Constituent Assembly would enforce by law. By copying the sentiments promoted by his writings, French legislators unleashed an angry struggle between the orders.[124] Works like the *Nouvelle Héloïse* provided food for the levelling impulse. Inadvertently, they were vehicles of social resentment.

Burke was at pains to emphasise how Rousseau combined base desires with sublime morals in a peculiarly seductive vein. It was this that made his example such a perilous one. It was not so much particular values as the "*general spirit and tendency*" of his *oeuvre* that had proved mischievous.[125] This served as a canker to every possible civil existence, poisoning the roots of domestic tranquillity, religious duty and social trust. It was in this very spirit of vain sophistry that the judicial system of France had been destroyed. "Nothing seems to me to render your internal situation more desperate than this one circumstance of the state of your judicature," Burke

[119] The theme had been central to Montesquieu's *Lettres persanes* (1721), dramatised in the relationship between the characters of Usbek and Roxanne. On gallantry as key to European social life, see Charles-Louis de Secondat, Baron de Montesquieu, *De l'esprit des lois* (1748) in *Œuvres complètes,* ed. Roger Caillois (Paris: Gallimard, 1951), 2 vols., II, pt. VI, bk. XXVIII, ch. 22. For discussion of Montesquieu's ideas about freedom and subordination in the context of Asian and European gender relations, see Michael A. Mosher, "The Judgmental Gaze of European Women: Gender, Sexuality, and the Critique of Republican Rule," *Political Theory*, 22:1 (February 1994), pp. 25–44.

[120] EB, Speech on the Divorce Bill, 29 April 1772, *W & S*, II, p. 357.

[121] EB, *Letter to a Member of the National Assembly* (1791), *W & S*, VIII, p. 317.

[122] Ibid.

[123] Voltaire, *Lettres à M. de Voltaire sur La Nouvelle Héloïse (ou Aloïsa) de Jean-Jacques Rousseau, citoyen de Genève* in idem, *Mélanges,* ed. Jacques van den Heuvel (Paris: Gallimard, 1961) p. 399.

[124] Ibid.

[125] Ibid., p. 318.

commented to Menonville.[126] Work on the reform of the judiciary had begun with Nicolas Bergasse's report to the National Assembly of 17 August 1789, but consideration of the matter was deferred until after the passage of the Declaration of the Rights of Man and the Citizen.[127] It was then postponed again while administrative and electoral arrangements were debated. The issue was revived at the end of the year, beginning with a report by Thouret presented on 22 December.[128] A proper investigation only got under way on 24 March 1790, with heated exchanges between Roederer and Cazalès leading to a determination to reconstruct the whole system.[129] This was largely done on the basis of the agenda set on 31 March by Bertrand Barère, which was debated over the course of the spring and summer. The overhaul of the judiciary included the introduction of justices of the peace, the abolition of the order of barristers, the establishment of juries, the right to defend oneself or to appoint a *défenseur officieux* for the purpose, and the popular election of judges.[130] By comparison, Burke observed, even during the Cromwellian revolution in government, the judicial apparatus of the commonwealth retained its essential structure, as well as its leading personnel.[131] The French goal of comprehensive reconstruction illustrated the powerful "spirit of system" that had seized the deputies.[132] According to Burke, as we have seen, this was motivated by the attraction to intellectual sophistry, animated by voracious vanity. By this means, French legislators were infected with the "contagion of project and system."[133] They had been tainted by the vacuous "chatter" of philosophy, epitomised by the *Encyclopédie* and sustained by individuals like Condorcet and Raynal.[134]

The inducement of the spirit of system had drawn the members of the National Assembly into revising every existing social arrangement, destroying in the process subordination and respect. This accounted for the resort among the population to assassination and terror tactics.[135] It released "the fury of rash speculation" at large.[136]

[126] Ibid., p. 302. Burke had briefly treated this in a later edition of the *Reflections*: see EB, *Reflections*, ed. Clark, Appendix I, p. 421.

[127] *Archives parlementaires*, VIII, pp. 440–50.

[128] *Archives parlementaires*, X, p. 718.

[129] *Archives parlementaires*, XII, pp. 348–99.

[130] See Michael P. Fitzsimmons, *The Remaking of France: The National Assembly and the Constitution of 1791* (Cambridge: Cambridge University Press, 1994, 2002), pp. 97ff.

[131] EB, *Letter to a Member of the National Assembly* (1791), *W & S*, VIII, pp. 302–3; cf. EB, *Remarks on the Policy of the Allies* (Spring 1793), *W & S*, VIII, pp. 497–98.

[132] Cf. Adam Smith, *The Theory of Moral Sentiments*, ed. D. D. Raphael and A. L. Macfie (Indianapolis, IN: Liberty Fund, 1982), p. 232.

[133] EB, *Letter to a Member of the National Assembly* (1791), *W & S*, VIII, p. 324.

[134] EB to Claude-François de Rivarol, 1 June 1791, *Corr.*, VI, pp. 267–68.

[135] EB, *Letter to a Member of the National Assembly* (1791), *W & S*, VIII, p. 319. Cf. EB, *An Appeal from the New to the Old Whigs, in Consequence of some Late Discussions in Parliament, relative to the Reflections on the Revolution in France* (London: 1791), p. 10. For Burke's longstanding interest in assassination, see "An Account of the Origin, Customs, Manners, &c., of the Assassins of Syria" in *The Annual Register for 1760* (London: 1761), p. 57.

[136] EB, *Letter to a Member of the National Assembly* (1791), *W & S*, VIII, p. 325.

The effects of the ensuing violence were potentially devastating since the people were generally armed.[137] Consequently, not only would the reconquest of the country have to be led from outside, but the process would be gruesome and protracted.[138] On the far side of this bloody struggle, it was impossible to anticipate what system of government might be imposed. Burke chided Calonne for having specified terms of peace with the Revolutionaries in his *De l'état de la France*.[139] Any political reform had to begin with the balance of forces as these were pitted against one another in society. This would require taking the measure of "the conjunctions and oppositions of men and things."[140] That had to be the objective of any political science, yet it was an approach that the Revolutionaries had steadfastly rejected. Even a straightforward attempt to foist the provisions of the British constitution on France would lead to counterproductive results. A wise plan still had to adapt to shifting circumstances. In previously arguing for the substitution of a "British" model into the place of the French monarchical system, Burke had never favoured a literal transplantation. Lally, Mounier, Menonville, Cazalès and Maury had variously extolled the virtues of the British scheme of government, but they had scarcely grasped its abundant complexities, and they misunderstood its applicability to France.[141]

The French Revolution had begun with an offer of reform, Burke recalled. In the spring of 1788, Louis XVI had held out the prospect of a new Magna Carta for France when he offered to convene the Estates General. This would have represented the established orders of the French monarchy, not reproduced the divisions of the British state: in the strict sense, neither a House of Lords nor a House of Commons was envisaged, and the monarchy would have continued to play the predominant role in legislation and administration.[142] Moreover, the clergy were to occupy a major part in the constitution. All this, however, was undermined by an act of treachery. For Burke the Revolution had occurred in 1788. The terms on with the Estates were to be convoked were the central issue. Since this body was to act as a major organ of deliberation, it was vital that it should reflect the different orders in the state. It was the job of the Paris *parlement* to advise on its constitution, yet it was here that it betrayed its crucial trust.[143] In acting, in effect, as counsel to the king, the *parlement* had failed to secure his welfare by recommending measures that would compromise the monarchy: "Under the pretence of resuscitating the antient constitution, the Parliament [*sic*] saw one of the strongest acts of innovation, and

[137] Ibid., p. 301.

[138] Ibid., p. 320.

[139] EB to John Trevor, January 1791, *Corr*. VI, pp. 218–19. Calonne's recommendations, which were in fact identical with the measures proposed by Louis XVI at the *séance royale* of 23 June 1789, were set out in his *De l'état de la France, présent et à venir* (London: 3rd ed., 1790), pp. 392ff.

[140] EB, *Letter to a Member of the National Assembly* (1791), *W & S*, VIII, p. 327.

[141] EB to John Trevor, January 1791, *Corr*., VI, p. 219.

[142] EB, *Letter to a Member of the National Assembly* (1791), *W & S*, VIII, pp. 330–32.

[143] Ibid., p. 327.

the most leading in its consequences, carried into effect before their eyes."[144] It had been the *parlement*'s customary task to maintain the integrity of constitution, yet here it had ensured its subtle perversion. In tampering with the mode of selection to the first and third estates, and destroying the old proportions between the commons and the rest, the historic representation of the state had been demolished with hazardous consequences for the future. At one point Burke went further, blaming the monarchy itself: "These changes, unquestionably the King had no right to make."[145] Almost a year later, he was even more explicit in accusing Louis XVI: "With his own hand . . . [he] pulled down the pillars which upheld the throne."[146]

From Burke's perspective, the monarchy in the spring of 1789 would have had to act as the pivot of any prospective reconfiguration of the French state. Its powers would need to be greater than the considerable prerogatives of George III since it offered the only means of consolidating the divergent interests of the Estates. How its commanding influence might thereafter be reduced would be a matter for modification over time. In the interim, it was essential that its authority be maintained. Instead, by the summer of 1789, the French had established what Calonne termed a "démocratie royale."[147] Already in November 1790, Burke had begun to incorporate some of the arguments of Calonne into later editions of the *Reflections*.[148] Calonne's aim had been to commend the wisdom of basing reform on the recommendations of the *cahiers de doléances*.[149] Burke left his positive proposals to one side, accepting instead his diagnosis. The establishment of a *démocratie royale* meant creating a form of popular power under which the mere shadow of monarchical authority was retained.[150] In other words, it was, in practical terms, a pure democracy over which a pageant of royalty presided. We have seen how Burke claimed in the *Reflections* that this ambitious popular leviathan would resolve itself into a persecuting oligarchy, still appealing to the legitimating principle of equality, and goaded into action by the vanity of its governors. Such a beast could not be tolerated for long at the heart of European politics: "no Monarchy limited or unlimited, nor any Republics, can possibly be safe as long as this strange, nameless, wild, enthusiastic thing is established in the Centre of Europe," Burke wrote at this time.[151] The design of the *Letter to a Member of the National Assembly* was to provoke discussion about its removal. It

[144] Ibid., p. 328.

[145] Ibid.

[146] EB, *Thoughts of French Affairs* (December 1791), *W & S*, VIII, p. 374.

[147] Calonne, *De l'état de la France*, p. 374. He took the phrase from the Abbé Maury, whom he cited, at p. 194, as claiming that the Revolutionary conspirators had sought to establish "une démocratie royale, avoient evahi tous les pouvoirs du Roi." Burke adverts to the idea in EB to Claude-François de Rivarol, 1 June 1791, *Corr.*, VI, p. 262, in EB to William Weddell, 31 January 1792, *Corr.*, VII, p. 60, and again in EB, *Remarks on the Policy of the Allies* (Autumn 1793), *W & S*, VIII, p. 458.

[148] EB, *Reflections*, ed. Clark, Appendix I, pp. 420, 422.

[149] Calonne, *De l'état de la France*, pp. 3, 367ff.

[150] Ibid., p. 373.

[151] EB to John Trevor, January 1791, *Corr.*, VI, p. 218.

suggested that intervention into the affairs of a state of this kind could be justified in terms of policy and justice. Now it remained to be examined how such an outcome might be procured.

14.4 Division amongst the Whigs

Burke's emphasis on the moral depravity of France in the *Letter to a Member of the National Assembly* had been designed to establish the impossibility of any serious internal resistance to the new regime. As he put it to the British minister at Turin, John Trevor: "Nothing else but foreign force can or will do."[152] Burke felt that an initiative was urgently called for, since every day the Revolutionary regime increased its grip on the public mind. However, for any kind of expedition to succeed, a minimum precondition was that Britain and Prussia would at least have to "acquiesce" in the measure.[153] Burke claimed to be in the dark about how affairs on the continent were developing. Even so, he was confident that the transformation bequeathed by the Revolution to European politics had not yet fully dawned on the leading figures in the states affected: "I am astonished at the blindness of the States of Europe, who are contending with each other about points of trivial importance . . . on old, worn out Topics of Policy."[154] In any case, Burke scarcely had much concrete political influence abroad. He was feted among opponents of the Revolution as a philosopher-statesman, "un véritable homme d'état," as Montlosier put it in the summer of 1791.[155] But this did not award him any tangible political power. On the home front, he was equally impotent. Writing to the royalist émigrée, the Comtesse de Montrond, in January 1791, he declared himself "a very private man." He was, moreover, "totally destitute of authority and importance in the State," and arguably out of favour "with those who possess its powers."[156] Just as crucial, he was by this time out of favour with important men in his own party. He was desperately fighting to keep the prosecution against Hastings alive whilst countering his marginalisation by Fox and his supporters. The divisiveness of events in France continued to widen the breach. Contributing to the debate on Horne Tooke's petition regarding the Westminster election on 7 February 1791, Burke alluded to the present as a time of "dangerous innovation."[157]As soon as the French crisis reappeared on the public stage, a deterioration in relations among the Foxite Whigs was bound to ensue.

[152] Ibid., p. 217. Cf. EB to the Abbé Foullon, 1 June 1791, ibid., p. 263; Richard Burke Jr. to the King of France, 6 August 1791, ibid., p. 319.

[153] EB to John Trevor, January 1791, ibid., p. 218.

[154] EB to the Chevalier de la Bintinaye, March 1791, ibid., p. 242.

[155] Comte de Montlosier to EB, 31 August 1791, Northamptonshire MS. A. IX.72.

[156] Comtesse de Montrond, 25 January 1791, *Corr.*, VI, p. 211.

[157] *Parliamentary History*, XXVIII, col. 1271.

The moment of reckoning came on 6 May 1791 when Fox and Burke openly quarrelled on the floor of the Commons. On that same day, before the advent of contention, Burke's son wrote from a committee room in the British parliament to Thomas Lewis O'Beirne in Longford alerting him to the impending crisis among the Whigs. The party now headed by Fox was perhaps "the Greatest" that had ever existed in the kingdom yet its future hung very much in the balance.[158] As Richard saw it, Fox himself was the cause of the current political impasse. In this he was clearly ventriloquising his father's views. He found it impossible, he admitted, to divine what was impelling Fox to embrace ideas whose tendency was subversive of Whig doctrine, yet there was no doubting that he had positioned himself as a critic of the *Reflections* and a friend to the ideal of liberty proclaimed from Revolutionary France.[159] His most recent declaration of principles had been delivered in the midst of a debate on the Oczakov affair on 15 April 1791. In March, parliament had been notified of the ministry's determination to back the Ottomans against Catherine II of Russia in her refusal to cede the fortress of Oczakov on the Black Sea.[160] With Pitt in an exposed position at the time, government policy presented Fox with an opportunity.[161] Burke's intervention came on 29 March when he objected to the prospect of alliance with an unfriendly and unchristian power that had not previously been admitted into the European balance. "What had these worse than savages to do with the powers of Europe, but to spread war, destruction, and pestilence amongst them?" he implored. When Fox opposed the measure on 15 April 1791, he likewise turned to the issue of the balance of forces within Europe, but he focused on how this had been affected by the Revolution in France.

Fox reiterated his position of February 1790, underlining the absence of any threat from across the Channel. But he went further in celebrating the virtues of the new government: altogether, he considered France to be "the most glorious edifice of liberty, which had been erected on the foundation of human integrity in any time or country."[162] It was a bold manifesto that brought Burke to his feet, already stung by his allies' attempts to silence him on France. Again he was stymied: loud cries went up in the chamber for the question to be put, with Burke deferring to the prevalent mood of the Commons. He was now in search of an occasion on which to make his opinion known. That came during the debate on the committee stage of the Quebec Bill, whose introduction into the Commons had been first signalled by

[158] Richard Burke Jr. to Thomas Lewis O'Beirne, *Corr.*, VI, p. 254.

[159] Ibid., p. 255.

[160] King's Message respecting War between Russia and the Porte, 28 March 179, *Parliamentary History*, XXIX, cols. 31–33. For the wider context, see Jeremy Black, *British Foreign Policy in an Age of Revolutions, 1783–1793* (Cambridge: Cambridge University Press, 1994), pp. 257–328.

[161] John Holland Rose, *William Pitt and the National Revival* (London: George Bell and Sons, 1911), ch. 27; John Ehrman, *Pitt the Younger II: The Reluctant Transition* (London: Constable, 1983), pp. 6–32.

[162] *Parliamentary History*, XXIII, col. 1271. It was this line that Burke was to cite in the *Appeal from the New to the Old Whigs* as indicative of Fox's confused political principles: see EB, *Appeal from the New to the Old Whigs*, p. 16.

the King's Message of 25 February 1791 calling for the division of the province into Upper and Lower Canada.[163] As Pitt presented the proposal on 4 March, its aim was to compose the "differences of opinion" between the original French colonists and newer inhabitants settled from Britain and America, particularly since the Quebec Act of 1774.[164] In addition to the division of territory, this would involve establishing new constitutional arrangements for each of the two jurisdictions. Burke rose to address the issue on 6 May, with conflict between himself and Fox anticipated by the Pittite press since late April.[165] In any case it was long expected from his own side, with Portland warning Fitzwilliam on 21 April that "something disagreeable is likely to happen, & such a Political Schism & Division as may end in the dissolution of the Party."[166] In a set of instructions which Burke composed for a conversation to be staged between Fox and Portland at this time, he made plain that the point to be explained was not whether Fox meant to "introduce the Fr[ench] revol[ution] here—But why—if he does not—he extolls & magnifies it in the language & sentiments of those who do."[167] Burke began his speech of 6 May by observing that if the doctrine of the rights of man were to be admitted, the Commons would be surrendering its competence to legislate for "a distant people" like the Canadians.[168] The truth was, however, that Canada had been acquired by right of conquest under the law of nations. By that right, together with the fact of the cession of Quebec by France, and the prescriptive right of thirty years' possession, Britain was entitled to frame a government for her colonists.[169] This right should be exercised with due regard being paid to justice and circumstance, not on the model of French Revolutionary doctrine, whose drastic impact in Saint-Domingue was already apparent.[170]

Soon Burke felt the pressure of opposition from his own side. "It was unfortunate," he confessed, "sometimes to be hunted by one party, and sometimes by another."[171] Fox declared that he would prefer to absent himself from the House than to listen to a dissertation on the demerits of the French Revolution in the midst of a debate on Quebec. He then proceeded to deliver his own sentiments on the rights of man, insisting that these had justified the English and American revolutions. He recalled how this had been shared ground between himself and Burke: "During the American war they had together rejoiced at the successes of a Washington, and sympathized almost in tears for the fall of a Montgomery."[172] Burke now felt personally

[163] Frank O'Gorman, *The Whig Party and the French Revolution* (London: Macmillan, 1967), pp. 63–69.

[164] *Parliamentary History*, XXIII, col. 1377.

[165] Mitchell, *Charles James Fox*, p. 161.

[166] Duke of Portland to Earl Fitzwilliam, 21 April 1791, WWM, Fitzwilliam MS. F115–54.

[167] "Instructions by EB Intended for the Use of the Duke of Portland in a Conversation Expected to Take Place between Him and Fox. May 1791," OSB MS. File 2231.

[168] *Parliamentary History*, XXIX, col. 364.

[169] Ibid.

[170] Ibid., cols. 366–67.

[171] Ibid., col. 374.

[172] Ibid., col. 379.

assailed, and embarked on a refutation of Fox that would sacrifice a political friendship of twenty-two years' standing to what seemed to him the overriding national interest. He felt compelled to alert the public to the threat from subversive ideas. While harmony reigned in British society and the government operated effectively, there existed an opportunity to oppose obnoxious doctrines without triggering a catastrophic reaction. The shocking scenes of the Gordon Riots were only eleven years in the past. Three hundred thousand men were under arms in France. Now was the time to extinguish the rhetoric of resistance in Britain.[173]

In choosing to adopt this idiom as his own, Fox had embarked on a course that put an end to his friendship with Burke. He was now in tears as Burke thundered his disagreement. Having composed himself, he reiterated his mantra: "the original rights of men were . . . the foundation of all governments and all constitutions."[174] By this stage Burke was weary. The previous February he had alluded to his retirement from the Commons. He now described himself, at sixty-one, as being "an old man," determined to serve a righteous cause without support from party friends.[175] He would withdraw, as he told Fitzwilliam, into his own circle.[176] Separation from the remnants of the Rockingham party would mark the period of his "declining hours."[177] Nonetheless, this would enable him to maintain the integrity of his principles—conferring, as he soon admitted, "an inward peace."[178] He was confident of the consistency that had characterised his behaviour as a defender of a mixed system of government: during the Gordon Riots he had happily inclined towards prerogative as a specific against demotic subversion while in general he had campaigned against the expansion of court influence. As a report of a speech by Burke in the *Dublin Evening Post* put it at this time, there was currently "no occasion to cry out in favour of Democracy."[179]

Pitt had naturally been happy to sow suspicion between Burke and Fox.[180] Fox had accused Burke of serving the designs of the ministry at a meeting in April.[181] The truth was, however, that senior opposition Whigs were also alarmed by Fox's behaviour. According to Burke's recollection, Fox had privately asserted that, in declaring his partisanship towards the new regime in France, he was faithfully representing the bulk of the Whig opposition.[182] If this was Fox's belief, it did not chime with the assumptions of friendly Whig grandees. To them his recent statements smacked of

[173] Ibid., col. 386.

[174] Ibid., col. 392.

[175] Ibid., col. 396. This now became a regular refrain: see EB, Debate on Mr. Grey's Notice of a Motion Relative to Parliamentary Reform, 30 April 1792, ibid., col. 1317.

[176] EB to Earl Fitzwilliam, 5 June 1791, *Corr.*, VI, p. 275.

[177] Ibid.

[178] EB to the Marquis de Bouillé, 13 July 1791, ibid., p. 291.

[179] *Dublin Evening Post*, 17 May 1791. An extract is preserved at OSB MS. File 2230.

[180] He and Lord Grenville had arranged to meet to discuss Burke's statement on the Revolution on the morning of 21 April 1791: see Lord Grenville to EB, 20 April 1791, *Corr.*, VI, p. 248.

[181] Duke of Portland to Earl Fitzwilliam, 21 April 1791, WWM, Fitzwilliam MS. F115–54.

[182] Ibid.

waywardness. To others they seemed to be founded on presumption and ignorance. In the weeks before his final bruising encounter with Burke in the Commons, he spent his time recuperating at the races in Newmarket. He had yet to read Paine's *Rights of Man*, which had appeared on 16 March. Even so, he was happy to conjure with the language of revolution. By the end of May, he had still to read Burke's *Letter to a Member of the National Assembly*, although he was content to support the idea that its argument was "mere madness."[183] Fox's commitment to France was personal. From early on he had been an admirer of French society and manners. Burke saw him as being saddled with an outmoded set of perceptions. As he later commented, Fox's attachment to the country was as blind as it was interminable, "and like a Cat, he has continued faithful to the house after the family has left it."[184] Under these circumstances, it was not easy for Fox to induce the opposition in the Lords to follow him. Concern for party cohesion was his major asset.

On Burke's reckoning, however, the Duke of Portland, Earl Fitzwilliam, the Duke of Devonshire, Lord John Cavendish, Frederick Montagu "and a long et cetera of the old stamina of the Whiggs" approved of the position first set out in the *Reflections*.[185] After 6 May, certainly Portland and Fitzwilliam remained sympathetic to Burke, yet they maintained their loyalty to Fox for the sake of party unity.[186] They were utterly opposed to the tenor of French affairs, although they could not grasp the magnitude of the events. Even after the slave revolt on Saint-Domingue the following August, their attitudes were unmoved: "one of them does not even read the Newspaper—and the Business is not suffered to occupy their reflections."[187] Nonetheless, they were inclined to accept the values underpinning Burke's message. Many others, he felt confident, were following suit.[188] Therefore, over the summer of 1791, the situation within the ranks of the party was finely poised. Morally, Burke had backing; but politically, at least for the present, he was in the wilderness. Writing to Fitzwilliam in early June, he reflected on his unenviable position on 6 May. Despite his provocative avowal of "French Whiggism" during the Quebec debate, Fox's following in the Commons applauded him "as to a man."[189] Burke's isolation was virtually complete: "It was an exhibition absolutely new, to see a man who had sat twenty six years in Parliament, not to have one friend in the House."[190] As a lone eminence, Burke now embarked on his *Appeal from the New to the Old Whigs* both to vindicate his conduct and to define the creed of his party.

[183] Charles James Fox to Lord Holland, 26 May 1791, *Memorials and Correspondence of Charles James Fox*, ed. Lord John Russell (London: 1853), 4 vols., II, p. 363.

[184] Notes from the Commonplace Book of Samuel Rogers, Add. MS. 47590, fol. 26.

[185] EB to Gilbert Elliot, 29 November 1790, *Corr.*, VI, p. 178.

[186] Richard Burke Jr. to Thomas Lewis O'Beirne, 6 May 1791, ibid., p. 255.

[187] EB to Richard Burke Jr., 28 October 1791, ibid., p. 439.

[188] EB to the Marquis de Bouillé, 13 July 1791, p. 291: deference to Fox ensured that they did not "speak out so clearly."

[189] EB to Earl Fitzwilliam, 5 June 1791, ibid., pp. 273–74.

[190] Ibid., p. 275.

14.5 *Appeal from the New to the Old Whigs*

The *Appeal* ultimately appeared on 3 August 1791, with Burke having steadily revised it through the summer at Margate.[191] He began it soon after his public rift with Fox, spurred on by a provocative notice in the *Morning Chronicle*. On 12 May 1791, the *Chronicle* passed its verdict on the contest between Burke and Fox: the latter was declared to have maintained the "pure doctrines" of opposition Whiggism. "The consequence is," the paper concluded, "that Mr. Burke retires from parliament."[192] It was not surprising that the *Chronicle* would swing behind Fox. The following September, after the *Appeal* had appeared, the paper was still pursuing its agenda against Burke, publishing the "true" principles animating Fox's conduct over the course of the previous decade.[193] His opponent's words and actions were simply "contradictory," Fox maintained.[194] For his part, Burke found the implicit effort to silence him reprehensible. The *Reflections* never pretended to stand as a party credo, so the determination to disavow it seemed out of proportion.[195] A further design to disparage Burke's refutation of this disavowal might reasonably be depicted as excessive. Burke opened the *Appeal* with a frontal assault on his deprecation. If his opponents wanted to exclude him like a latter-day Diogenes from the objects of his political affection, in response he would condemn them to their blind allegiance.[196] Fox and his adherents were profuse in declaring for liberty, and no one could reasonably fault this rhetorical ploy in a popular assembly. But an avowed preference for a particular example of freedom demanded some supporting illustration.[197] Burke would show that Fox's enthusiasm, like Sheridan's, was for a system of methodical social and political anarchy. At issue was not the opposing merits of monarchies and republics, but the choice between a system of moderate government and disorganised popular tyranny.[198] This being demonstrated, Burke claimed provocatively, the stubborn stalwarts of the French Revolution ought not to be classed as "mistaken politicians," but more drastically as "bad men."[199]

In July 1791, in the midst of composing the *Appeal*, Burke wrote to the Marquis de Bouillé, a commander in the French Army with known sympathies for the

[191] The forthcoming appearance of the work was announced in the *St. James's Chronicle* on 18 June 1791. Burke made revisions to subsequent impressions of the first edition, with the help of French Laurence in the third impression. A change in the order of presentation was announced in the second but carried out in the third impression. See Todd, *Bibliography*, pp. 172–5.

[192] *Morning Chronicle*, 12 May 1791.

[193] *Morning Chronicle*, 28 September 1791.

[194] Notes from the Commonplace Book of Samuel Rogers, Add. MS. 47590, fol. 14.

[195] EB, *Appeal from the New to the Old Whigs*, p. 6.

[196] Ibid., pp. 1–2.

[197] Ibid., p. 16.

[198] Ibid., p. 10.

[199] Ibid., p. 14.

French king, insisting that he had not lost his "Spirit" or his "principles."[200] One reason for his buoyancy was confidence in his national support. "I have spoken the sense of infinitely the majority of my Countrymen, and that also of most of my late party."[201] Burke was now particularly sure of himself since news of the capture of the royal family after the abortive flight to Varennes had reached London.[202] Before his flight, the king had declared in favour of the new French constitution; after his escape, he published a document disavowing it completely.[203] The sympathy of the British masses clearly lay with the French sovereign. The cause of the king, Burke wrote, "is that of all the Sovereigns of Europe."[204] Within days it was clear that the royals had definitely been recaptured, and Burke predicted hideous results: "I believe we must prepare ourselves for very great and awful events both abroad and at home."[205] The *Public Advertiser* carried a report from the *Journal de Paris*: "The King has been stopped at Varennes."[206] Troop movements in Spain, Austria and Prussia were reported, as sympathy for counter-revolution rose.[207] Before the capture, the London crowds were jubilant at the prospect of the escape. "The joy was almost universal," Burke reported.[208] The public sorrow following his arrest was no less real.[209] Burke knew that the current of opinion was running with him, even if fury among French democrats had increased.[210] Fox tried to dissuade Sheridan from attending the celebrations of Bastille Day; the Whig Club declined to attend the dinner after the event.[211] An arson attack against Priestley's home during the Birmingham riots in mid-July further darkened the mood in government circles.[212] Under the circumstances, Burke was only too happy to step forward as a representative of the national sensibility. He now stressed how, all along, he had been supported "by the nation whose sentiments he had undertaken to describe."[213] He believed he had succeeded in capturing British feeling.

By extension, it was being claimed that Fox represented a fraction of public opinion. Nonetheless, he was a powerful figure with substantial influence within opposition Whiggism. His arguments would therefore have to be contested. Fox did not, of course, approve every Revolutionary episode. He simply justified what he took to be the objective of the Revolution, interpreting disorder and violence as regrettable

[200] EB to the Marquis de Bouillé, 13 July 1791, *Corr.*, VI, p. 291.
[201] Ibid.
[202] *London Gazette*, 25 June 1791.
[203] EB, *Thoughts of French Affairs* (December 1791), *W & S*, VIII, pp. 338–39.
[204] EB to James Bland Burges, 26 June 1791, *Corr.*, VI, p. 278.
[205] EB to James Bland Burges, 29 June 1791, ibid., p. 279.
[206] *Public Advertiser*, 27 June 1791.
[207] Ibid.
[208] EB to the Marquis de Bouillé, 13 July 1791, *Corr.*, VI, p. 291.
[209] Ibid.
[210] See Pierre-Gaëton Dupont to EB, 7 July 1790, ibid., p. 283, on "le dédain du peuple pour le Roy."
[211] Charles James Fox to Lord Holland, 26 May 1791, *Memorials*, II, pp. 263–64.
[212] R. B. Rose, "The Priestley Riots of 1791," *Past and Present*, 18 (November 1960), pp. 68–88.
[213] EB, *Appeal from the New to the Old Whigs*, p. 4.

distractions along the road to liberty. He resorted to what became a common refrain of pro-French Whigs: "These Calamities must attend on all great Changes however proper in their principle or however well conducted."[214] However, to Burke this was to confuse declarations of intent with actual outcomes: advocates of the Revolution promised peace and concord within and between nations, yet they forwarded only persecution and violent struggle.[215] The justification of revolution was a matter for political judgment, not aprioristic moral reasoning. It was therefore never amenable to purely abstract analysis. An account of projected benefits was required, and this demanded more than airy "prattling about the Bastille."[216] The right of resistance was a precious resource, but prone to casuistical wrangling.[217] In reality, it could "never be defined": its permissibility could not be specified in advance of the relevant facts.[218] The legitimacy of the act depended on circumstances and consequences. Resort to it therefore presupposed a calculating prudence that would compute the costs of flying to arms to dismantle a regime. This had to involve two assessments at once. First, the oppressiveness of the government to be deposed would have to be weighed in the balance: the domination of a Nero, for instance, should never be conflated with the admittedly absolute rule of a Trajan or a Galba.[219] Monarchs might well be fairly cashiered, but their culpable delinquency would have to be great.[220] At the same time, the cost of dissolving the frame of government would have to be estimated. In such cases, the "burthen of proof lies heavily on those who tear to pieces tho whole frame and contexture of their country."[221] The new Whigs were following their French masters: they wilfully exaggerated conditions under Louis XVI, and subscribed to a process of revolution without reckoning on its results.

A particular charge against Burke was that he chose to pass judgment on developments in France at an inappropriate juncture in the parliamentary calendar.[222] This was partly a result of his having opted to publicise his views during the committee stage of the Quebec Bill. But it also stemmed from the sense that he aimed to identify Fox with a republican agenda—to ascribe to him "a predilection for Republican

[214]EB to Richard Burke Jr., 28 October 1790, *Corr.*, VI, p. 439. This is Burke's synopsis of new Whig sentiment, not the reported speech of Fox.

[215]EB, *Appeal from the New to the Old Whigs*, pp. 11–12.

[216]Ibid., p. 20. Paine had devoted considerable attention to the storming of the Bastille in *Rights of Man*: see Thomas Paine, *Rights of Man, Common Sense and Other Political Writings*, ed. Mark Philp (Oxford: Oxford University Press, 1995, 2008), pp. 104–10. For Burke's views on the Bastille, see WWM BkP 10:16.

[217]EB, *Appeal from the New to the Old Whigs*, pp. 123–24.

[218]Ibid., p. 20.

[219]Ibid., p. 18.

[220]See above, chapter 8, section 7 and chapter 11, section 5. For this criterion, cf. EB, *Fox's India Bill*, 1 December 1783, *W & S*, V, p. 387.

[221]EB, *Appeal from the New to the Old Whigs*, p. 19.

[222]Thomas Grenville to Earl Fitzwilliam, 22 April 1791, WWM, Fitzwilliam MS. F115–55: "how notorious it was that we were giving to government by such a discussion at this moment every advantage."

Principles & a Republican Form of Government."[223] This seemed peculiarly treacherous on Burke's part, since an association of the kind would inevitably damage Fox's chances of forming a government. Burke, in any case, denied the allegation. He then came to the main business of the *Appeal*. This was to defend himself against charges of inconsistency, above all in his profession of Whig principles.[224] After a brief survey of his conduct in relation to parliamentary reform, the subscription controversy, the prerogatives of the monarchy, and the American war, he proceeded to defend his representation of the Glorious Revolution by comparing this with canonical statements within the Whig tradition. For this purpose, he turned to the prosecution of the high Church divine Henry Sacheverell, which had absorbed the efforts of Whig grandees in the spring of 1710.[225] "The impeachment of Dr. Sacheverell was undertaken by a Whig Ministry and a Whig House of Commons, and carried on before a prevalent and steady majority of Whig peers," Burke recalled.[226] Its proceedings could therefore be trusted to represent Whig views. Moreover, since a major reason for Sacheverell's prosecution lay in his denial that the fate of James II confirmed the right of resistance, a reprise of the Whig response offered an opportunity to compare Burke's precepts with the ideas presented at the trial.[227]

Burke's method was to collect representative statements from leading figures associated with the Whig Junto, including Nicholas Lechmere, John Hawles, Earl Stanhope, Robert Walpole, Joseph Jekyl, Robert Eyre and John Holland in order to establish two fundamental commitments. The first of these was a point that he had laboured in the *Reflections*, where the Glorious Revolution was justified as an act of "necessity"—an emergency measure designed to ward off a more cataclysmic conflict.[228] The second pivotal doctrine that Burke examined in the *Appeal* was the idea of popular sovereignty. Since this involved specifying the nature of supreme authority within a polity, Burke's discussion included an investigation of the character of the British government, and the juridical status of the "people" to whom it was answerable. Given that the government in question was a "mixed" arrangement, with monarchical, aristocratic and popular components, this proved a complicated undertaking. For one thing, while these components acting together represented the "people" as a whole, one element, namely the Commons, was often identified as the "people." In addition, while the constituent parts of the government were bound to one another, the government as a whole was obliged to serve the people. Both

[223] Duke of Portland to Earl Fitzwilliam, 21 April 1791, WWM, Fitzwilliam MS. F115–54. The issue is raised in EB, *Appeal from the New to the Old Whigs*, p. 23. For Burke's earlier denial during debate on the Quebec Bill on 11 May 1791 of involvement in a "*Dark Plot*," see the *Oracle*, 12 May 1792. For Fox's rejection of the charge, see *The Annual Register for the Year 1791* (London: 1795), p. 118.

[224] EB to William Cusac Smith, 22 July 1791, *Corr.*, VI, p. 303.

[225] For general treatment, see Geoffrey Holmes, *The Trial of Dr. Sacheverell* (London: Methuen, 1973).

[226] EB, *Appeal from the New to the Old Whigs*, p. 55.

[227] Henry Sacheverell, *The Perils of False Brethren, both in Church, and State* (London: 1710).

[228] EB, *Appeal from the New to the Old Whigs*, pp. 57–82.

relations implied the existence of a covenant or "contract." This taxonomic ambiguity gave scope to controversy within Whiggism. The existence of two meanings of "contract" along with two senses of the term "people" contributed to conditions in which antagonistic visions of British politics could emerge.

One powerfully dissident conception of the British constitutional order had been publicised by Thomas Paine in the pages of his *Rights of Man*.[229] Burke had been brooding an attack on that work since April 1791.[230] What distinguished Paine's argument was his explicit disdain for mixed government based on hereditary privilege. Commitment to a purely republican constitution of the kind distinguished Paine from contemporary critics of post-Walpolean politics, from Catherine Macaulay and James Burgh to Thomas Hollis and Richard Price.[231] In the absence of legitimate distinctions in social "degree," civil society became incompatible with a division into corporations represented by means of a mixed constitutional order.[232] Paine's position became more explicit in his *Rights of Man*, part II, as the predicament of the king of France shifted the terms of the debate.[233] Still, the foundation for his more fully developed argument had been laid in the earlier work, where "the people" were presented as having mutually contracted to establish a form of government. In this, Paine was not referring to a historic moment in British history. Quite the reverse: British history had been "disfigured" by the legacy of the Norman conquest and therefore stood in need of comprehensive regeneration.[234] Monarchy and aristocracy were the tangible marks of a usurpation that could only be purged by "a general revolution in Europe."[235] For this transformation to be brought about, it was

[229] Modern scholarship has followed Burke in ascribing to Paine a pivotal role in the Revolution debate. See R. R. Fennessy, *Burke, Paine and the Rights of Man: A Difference of Political Opinion* (The Hague: M. Nijhoff, 1963); H. T. Dickinson, *British Radicalism and the French Revolution, 1789–1815* (Oxford: Blackwells, 1985); Claeys, "Revolution Debate," pp. 62–7.

[230] Thomas Grenville to Earl Fitzwilliam, 22 April 1791, WWM, Fitzwilliam MS. F115–55: "it was not the Quebec Bill, but Mr. Payne's pamphlet, & some notes of the Unitarian Society upon it, that had determined him to speak at large upon these matters." A toast to Paine at a meeting of the Unitarian Society on 14 April 1791 is recorded in the *Morning Chronicle*, 15 April 1791. Burke was informed of the proceedings in Henry Wisemore to EB, 16 April 1791, *Corr.*, VI, p. 247. Wisemore commented that "*aristocracy, Church Power* and national prejudices" would fall all the sooner for Burke's "Romantic attempt to support them."

[231] Richard Whatmore, "'A Gigantic Manliness': Paine's Republicanism in the 1790s" in Stefan Collini, Richard Whatmore and Brian Young eds., *Economy, Polity, and Society: British Intellectual History, 1750–1950* (Cambridge: Cambridge University Press, 2000).

[232] Paine, *Rights of Man*, pp. 117–19.

[233] For the relevant context, see Gary Kates, *The Cercle Social, the Girondins, and the French Revolution* (Princeton, NJ: Princeton University Press, 1985); William Doyle, "Thomas Paine and the Girondins" in idem, *Officers, Nobles and Revolutionaries: Essays on Eighteenth-Century France* (London: Hambledon Press, 1995).

[234] Paine, *Rights of Man*, pp. 123, 127. For discussion, see Gregory Claeys, *Thomas Paine: Social and Political Thought* (Boston: Unwin Hyman, 1989), chs. 3 and 4.

[235] Paine, *Rights of Man*, p. 193.

necessary to refer any programme of reform to an ideal situation against which actual conditions could be judged. Originally, as Paine put it, "*individuals themselves*, each in his own personal and sovereign right, *entered into a compact with each other* to produce a government."[236] As a consequence, Paine went on, the civil community was charged with securing the rights of its members. This conclusion, however, could be variously interpreted, with widely divergent consequences stemming from alternative interpretations. The strategy pursued by Burke in the *Appeal* was first to insinuate complicity between pro-French Revolutionary Whiggism and the *Rights of Man*, and then to discredit each one of Paine's assumptions.

Paine directed considerable effort in the earlier portion of the *Rights of Man* towards undermining Burke's insistence that the existence of a state implied an intergenerational commitment that could not blithely be sacrificed to passing convenience. This claim has been widely misinterpreted to mean that all future legislation must be confined by the decree of the past. On the basis of this misunderstanding, Burke is assumed to have believed that it is the job of politics to conserve tradition. As Paine ascribed this idea to him, he is accused of promoting government from "beyond the grave."[237] Paine proceeded to identify this alleged commitment with the outlandish doctrines of Papal infallibility and divine right monarchy, doubly condemning Burke as a crypto-Catholic and a Tory.[238] This provocative representation is then extended by Paine to include the charge that Burke was averse to all legislative reform: "he tells the world to come, that a certain body of men, who existed a hundred years ago, made a law; and that there does not now exist in the nation, nor ever will, nor ever can, a power to alter it."[239] Burke's parliamentary career, before and after 1789, offers ample testimony to his belief in the right of the state to "alter" its legislation. What preoccupied him in the *Reflections* and the *Appeal*, however, was the putative right of the nation to dismantle its constitution at will. In the end, it seems, Paine accepted this point in his analysis of France: future legislative assemblies were free to make whatever laws they saw fit, but they would be bound in their mode of procedure by the terms set by the constitution previously agreed in the Constituent Assembly. Only a national "convention," assembled for the purpose, had the right to revise the constitution of the state.[240]

Throughout the *Appeal* Burke emphasised that the British system of government comprised "three members." These members each had different "natures," with the result that the monarchical component could not be justified in terms of the principles that supported the democratic element.[241] To imagine that the monarchy might be subject to popular election was precisely to seek to blend distinct principles of

[236] Ibid., p. 122.
[237] Ibid., p. 92.
[238] Ibid., pp. 93, 101–2, 121.
[239] Ibid., p. 93.
[240] Paine, *Rights of Man*, p. 124.
[241] EB, *Appeal from the New to the Old Whigs*, p. 31.

legitimation. To place the choice of monarch in the hands of the "people" was in practice to subject the crown to the power of the Commons. Burke's aim was not to deny the supreme right of sovereignty in the state, which he had been defending since the start of the American crisis. The legislative will of the community was indeed the final arbiter of the fate of the polity, as Paine implied. "Such a power," Burke affirmed, "must reside in the complete sovereignty of every kingdom."[242] In the case of Britain, an Elizabethan statute confirmed this juridical conclusion. Burke therefore conceded that the sovereign will in any state had supreme authority over acts of legislation. It clearly followed that past legislation could not bind future acts of sovereignty. However, what past consensus should determine, as if forever, was the terms on which this sovereignty was exercised. The expectation of permanence was a bulwark against fundamental innovation that might threaten the very survival of the state. To confer upon the people the right to revise the constitution of sovereignty entailed ceding control of the polity to the popular element in the state. That, of course, was a recipe for civil dissension since all the competing powers of government would be subordinated to the rule of one. In response, Burke declared his intention to show that the Commons, "taken separately from the legislature which includes the crown," had no right to alter the monarchical succession "at . . . pleasure." Still less, he went on, was the popular chamber entitled, purely of its own accord, "to set up a new form of government."[243] The same rule, of course, applied to the king and Lords themselves: they could not simply abolish rival components of the national compact.

If the supreme competence of sovereign legislation was not in doubt, the wisdom of wielding its powers with "*sound discretion*" was equally evident.[244] As Burke had endlessly argued in connection with the Declaratory Act, while sovereignty was absolute, its use should be practically constrained. It was constrained by the need to win consent for its effective application. Consent was rooted in opinion, and opinion was shaped by history. Supreme authority should therefore operate with reference to past custom. For this reason, Burke adopted the *mos maiorum* as "not indeed his sole, but certainly his principal rule of policy."[245] Properly understood, therefore, the past did not bind legislative authority in the present: it simply guided it. It indicated how government could operate in conformity with the forces prevailing in society and state. The alternative was to act in conflict with them, replacing political negotiation with militant acts of will. The need to proceed by violence was made inevitable by explicitly contending with the configuration of the state's powers. Cooperation between these powers sustained the commonwealth as a "body corporate," which, from a juridical point of view, was a permanent entity: it survives

[242] Ibid., p. 69.
[243] Ibid., p. 68.
[244] Ibid., p. 69.
[245] Ibid., p. 70.

the lives of its individual members, and "never dies."[246] The achievement of cooperation between the constituent parts of government is the labour of history: it is "the result of the thoughts of many minds, in many ages."[247] It is brought about by either habitual collaboration or official contractual engagement. The British constitution was a product of both procedures—customary practice, and legislative compact. Together they formed the "contract of government," the "*original contract* of the British state," which was "fundamentally and inviolably fixed in King, Lords, and Commons."[248] It could only be unilaterally relinquished by a radical breach of faith.

An attempt on the constitution would begin with such a breach, whereby one component would seek to engross the powers of the rest. The historic struggle between prerogative and privilege in seventeenth-century England illustrated this dynamic, with the monarch and then the people vying in contention. As the 1640s proved, this kind of dissension was bound to "lacerate the commonwealth."[249] Attempts upon the state, by either the king or the Commons, proceeded by appeal to prevalent opinions: to the idea of passive obedience or the idea of popular consent. Of course, the public might register its approval by actively embracing either precept, as the parties of Great Britain demonstrated. Equally, the people might be tyrannised in the name of either doctrine. Flattery might promise freedom yet deliver slavery, as occurred in France through an "equal usurpation on the prince and people."[250] To Burke, this was in fact the lesson taught by the history of the English commonwealth.[251]

New Whiggism held out the same blandishments in the 1790s by preaching that all power was the property of the people: "These new Whigs hold, that the sovereignty, whether exercised by one or many, did not only originate from the people . . . but that, in the people the same sovereignty constantly and unalienably resides."[252] On this construction, the sovereignty of the people might reclaim government as its immediate national property. Burke quoted Paine's *Rights of Man* to this effect:

[246] Ibid., p. 69. Cf. EB, Speech on the State of the Representation of the Commons (16 May 1784), *The Works of the Right Honourable Edmund Burke* (London: 1808–13), 12 vols., X, p. 94. Underlying Burke's discussion is the idea of the state as a *persona ficta*. On this, and particularly its resuscitation by Hobbes, see Quentin Skinner, "Hobbes and the Purely Artificial Person of the State" in idem, *Visions of Politics III: Hobbes and Civil Science* (Cambridge: Cambridge University Press, 2002); Istvan Hont, "The Permanent Crisis of a Divided Mankind: 'Nation-State' and 'Nationalism' in Historical Perspective" in idem, *Jealousy: International Competition and the Nation-State in Historical Perspective* (Cambridge, MA: Harvard University Press, 2005); David Runciman, *Pluralism and the Personality of the State* (Cambridge: Cambridge University Press, 1997), ch. 1.

[247] EB, *Appeal from the New to the Old Whigs*, p. 113.

[248] Ibid., p. 57.

[249] Ibid., p. 119.

[250] Ibid., p. 138.

[251] See above, chapter 13, section 4.

[252] EB, *Appeal from the New to the Old Whigs*, p. 56.

"Sovereignty, as a matter of right, appertains to the Nation only."[253] This proposition was modelled on Article III of the Declaration of the Rights of Man and the Citizen, originally drafted by Lafayette.[254] It was designed as a challenge to the conjoint sovereignty of the monarch and Estates of France, but it succeeded in generally blurring relations between sovereignty and government. Burke accepted that the people were the legitimate source of all power, but he rejected the claim that its exercise might continue in their hands. Popular sovereignty had to be distinguished from democratic government under which power was devolved from the representative organs of the state to the multitude in whose name it had been instituted. A purely democratic administration of the kind was a notional construct which ordained that the levers of power were to be operated directly by the people. In practice this could only amount to a system of popular anarchy under which factions would compete for the control of the state. Government would continually be dissolved into the people, in whom sovereignty "constantly" resided. This was, in effect, a government without government, which therefore approached the condition of the state of nature. Rousseau, and later Kant, balked at such an arrangement.[255] To express the authority of the people by devolving power into their hands was a recipe for dissolving the commonwealth into its constituent elements. For Burke, the people would optimally control their government, but they could not both exercise and control its powers at the same time: "to exercise and to control together is contradictory and impossible."[256] One department of government might usefully control another, but undivided power was impossible to restrain. Pure popular power was boundless in precisely this way. Consequently, "no legislator, at any period of the world, has willingly placed the seat of active power in the hands of the multitude."[257] In Rome, and even Athens, government was distinct from sovereignty.

Burke recognised that the new Whiggism was a composite dogma based on a vague and generalised commitment to popular enfranchisement. At its most benign, it amounted to little more than a rhetorical endorsement of the original rights of the people. At this point the new Whiggism merged with old Whig pieties of a kind

[253] Paine, *Rights of Man*, p. 193. Cited in EB, *Appeal from the New to the Old Whigs*, p. 89.

[254] Stéphane Rials, *La Déclaration des droits de l'homme et du citoyen* (Paris: Hachette, 1988), p. 22. See above, chapter 11, section 5. Lafayette's assertion of the rights of the nation was extolled by Paine in *Rights of Man*, pp. 95–96, 166. Paine singles out Article III of the Declaration for comment in ibid., p. 141, 165. For Paine's debt to Lafayette, see Gary Kates, "From Liberalism to Radicalism: Tom Paine's Rights of Man," *Journal of the History of Ideas*, 50:4 (October–December 1989), pp. 569–87. For Lafayette's role in the drafting of the Declaration, see L. Gottschalk and M. Maddox, *Lafayette in the French Revolution: Through the October Days* (Chicago, IL: University of Chicago Press, 1969).

[255] Jean-Jacques Rousseau, *Du contrat social* in *Œuvres complètes III: Du contrat social, écrits politiques*, ed. Bernard Gagnebin and Marcel Raymond (Paris: Gallimard, 1946), pp. 404–5; Immanuel Kant, *Über den Gemeinspruch: Das mag in der Theorie richtig sein, taugt aber nicht für die Praxis* in *Über den Gemeinspruch: Das mag in der Theorie richtig sein, taugt aber nicht für die Praxis und Zum ewigen Frieden*, ed. Heiner F. Klemme (Hamburg: Felix Meiner Verlag, 1992), p. 62.

[256] EB, *Appeal from the New to the Old Whigs*, p. 120.

[257] Ibid.

that Burke himself paraded during the American war.[258] What distinguished the two was the preparedness of the new Whigs to condone the brand of popular rights being exercised in France: this gave precision to equivocal assumptions, and demanded a statement of principle. It was true that no section of opposition Whiggism had openly embraced the anti-constitutional ideas bandied about in London clubs and societies. It was also the case that the support for pure democracy in British politics comprised an infinitesimally small constituency. Their statements, however, were countenanced, and therefore in practice indulged. In the absence of outright opposition, Burke feared an insidious corruption of British constitutional ideals. False ideas had gained a footing; they were encouraged by party "go-betweens"; soon the staunchest Whigs in parliament would be drawn into the degenerate mix.[259] Burke therefore saw a "new, republican, frenchified Whiggism" in prospect.[260] What drove this process was passive assent, encouraged by moral inertia. Innovators like Fox and Sheridan gained acquiescence from grandees like Portland who were supported by the unassuming apathy of their followers in the Commons—men like William Weddell, the "equestrian order" of the party, whom Burke was hoping to turn.[261] For that purpose, he was keen to appeal to their provident fear that Britain might not be definitively proof against ideological and political subversion. There was therefore a battle to be won in the struggle to gain opinions. To define his cause, Burke targeted Paine, not because his position attracted substantial support among Foxites, but because he exemplified the incendiary doctrines that inattention would allow to prosper. Modern factions fed on zeal rather than tangible hardship.[262] They appealed by means of speculative schemes instead of discontent. Burke needed to diminish Paine's imaginative allure by exposing his empty promise.

Burke wrote to French Laurence just as the *Appeal* was about to appear confirming that the Foxites harboured a contingent "who like the Principles of Payne," albeit rendered palatable by disguise.[263] It was Paine's success in proselytism that made him a worthy opponent, not his intellectual penetration. He was, Burke thought, "utterly incapable of comprehending" his subject. He gave an impression of "art and skill," although he was completely lacking in learning. What sustained him was his "audacity," and his disregard for consequences.[264] Burke's goal was to point to the consequences that would follow from a consistent application of his ideas. That aim was facilitated by a common point of departure: both Burke and Paine began with the

[258] See, for instance, EB to the Committee of Correspondence of the General Assembly of New York, 6 April 1774, *Corr.*, II, p. 529; EB, *Address to the King*, January 1777, *W & S*, III, p. 269; WWM BkP 27:230.

[259] EB, *Appeal from the New to the Old Whigs*, pp. 96–97.

[260] EB to William Weddell, 31 January 1791, *Corr.*, VII, p. 52.

[261] EB, *Appeal from the New to the Old Whigs*, p. 97. Burke succeeded with Weddell: see EB to William Weddell, 31 January 1792, *Corr.*, VII, pp. 50ff.

[262] Ibid., p. 99

[263] EB to French Laurence, 2 August 1791, *Corr.*, VI, p. 312.

[264] EB to William Cusac Smith, 22 July 1791, ibid., pp. 303–4.

arguments of Hobbes. In the *Rights of Man*, Paine had explicitly stated that governments had originally risen "out of the people."[265] Their origin identified the legitimate source of their power. This popular reserve of power could never be alienated to a ruling order since the original contract preceded the establishment of government: "there could originally exist no governors to form such a compact with." Civil society was therefore founded on an antecedent agreement among each individual to establish a sovereign power.[266] This had famously been Hobbes's position, from the *Elements of Law* to *Leviathan*: "A *Common-wealth* is said to be *Instituted*, when a *Multitude* of men do Agree, and *Covenant, every one, with every one*," to confer authority upon a common representative of their wills.[267] In the *Elements of Law*, Hobbes was even more explicit on this point: in the creation of a commonwealth, "there passeth no covenant, between the sovereign and any subject." This was because, as Paine would later confirm, prior to the formation of political society, "there is no sovereign with whom to contract."[268]

Although Paine was prepared to recognise the binding character of the constitutional provisions of the Constituent Assembly over future legislative procedures, nonetheless he was adamant that "a Nation has at all times an inherent indefeasible right to abolish any form of Government it finds inconvenient."[269] This meant that any system of representation that embodied popular sovereignty was perpetually revocable by the people. Since election and popular representation were the only principles of political legitimation recognised by Paine, this meant that the constitution of the state was permanently up for revision by a bare majority of the electorate. Burke singled out this suggestion for attack in the *Appeal*: "We hear much from men, who have not acquired their hardiness of assertion from the profundity of their thinking, about the omnipotence of a *majority*." As Paine had drawn on Hobbes for his conception of an original covenant, Burke had recourse to the same author to contradict Paine's conclusions about the capacity of the people to reclaim their original sovereignty. He did this, in Hobbesian fashion, by indicating that there had been no original "sovereignty" at all. A multitude, in a state of nature, have power but not sovereignty. Since each individual covenants with each to create a sovereign to harmonise their wills, popular sovereignty cannot pre-exist the formation of a sovereign will.

As Burke read him, Paine's idea seemed to be that a simple majority from among the electorate might reclaim the sovereignty that they had previously conferred, thus reserving the right to reconfigure the constitution of the state. Hobbes had dwelt on this possibility in particular detail in section 20 of chapter 4 of *De Cive*: "Someone

[265] Paine, *Rights of Man*, p. 122.

[266] Ibid., pp. 121–2.

[267] Thomas Hobbes, *Leviathan*, ed. Noel Malcolm (Oxford: Oxford University Press, 2012), 3 vols., II, p. 264.

[268] Thomas Hobbes, *Elements of Law, Natural and Politic*, ed. Ferdinand Tönnies (London: Frank Cass & Co., 1969), p. 119.

[269] Paine, *Rights of Man*, p. 193.

will perhaps infer that the *summum imperium* can be abolished by the simultaneous consent of all the subjects."[270] To refute this inference, Hobbes referred to the terms of the original contract as comprising a comprehensive agreement of each with each. The contract of sovereignty, in other words, was founded on unanimity. An attempt to undo this covenant on the basis of a bare majority was therefore a violation of the terms of the compact. The appeal to a majority entailed recourse to an artificial expedient. The principle of majority rule required antecedent agreement, and so could not be a provision of the state of nature: "it is not by nature that the consent of the greater number should be regarded as the consent of all."[271] Burke followed Hobbes's logic closely. The right to act on the basis of agreement by a majority, Burke contended, depended on two preconditions: first, the existence of a corporate will brought about by unanimous decision; and second, a further unanimous agreement that an outright majority might count as standing in for the consent of the whole. "We are so little affected by things which are habitual," Burke commented, "that we consider this idea of the decision of a majority as if it were a law of our original nature."[272] A majority decision procedure, however, was an artificial construct. It was one possible means among many of ascertaining the general will. Moreover, people would only become inured to it by protracted civil discipline. Under many circumstances, they might prefer to be represented by one individual or by a few.

For their part, the French had dissolved all civil discipline, and with it the terms of their incorporation. They were, as a consequence, scarcely a "people" at all, but a disbanded populace or "multitude." Burke now advanced his own conception of the "character" of a genuine people, which applied where the ruling order acted with justice and authority. "When the multitude are not under this discipline, they can scarcely be said to be in a civil society."[273] On the basis of his account of a proper scheme of civil discipline, Burke aimed to support two different claims at once. First, in denying to France a properly civil condition, he was laying down a criterion that would justify going to war: "They may lawfully be fought with, and brought under, whenever an advantage offers."[274] Defending this position would preoccupy Burke for the following six years. But he was also using the occasion to defend his preferred constitutional system. On 31 January 1792, six months after the *Appeal* had appeared, he elaborated on this topic in response to a letter that he had received from William Weddell. The Rockinghamites and their descendants, he told

[270] Thomas Hobbes, *De Cive (The Latin Version)*, ed. Howard Warrender (Oxford: Oxford University Press, 1983), p. 148: "inferet forte aliquis *summum imperium* consensu omnium subditorum posse tolli." I have slightly modified the translation in Thomas Hobbes, *On the Citizen*, ed. Richard Tuck and Michael Silverthorne (Cambridge: Cambridge University Press, 1998), p. 89.

[271] Hobbes, *De Cive*, p. 149: "non enim a natura est quod consensus maioris partis habeatur pro consensu omnium."

[272] EB, *Appeal from the New to the Old Whigs*, pp. 125–26.

[273] Ibid., p. 129.

[274] Ibid., p. 131.

Weddell, were an "aristocratic" party.[275] This did not mean that they were wedded to arbitrary privilege. Burke's argument was social, political and constitutional at the same time. Its implications were social, since every system of government had to support a regime of property. At the same time, his case was inevitably political, since the class of legislators invested with power ought to show willingness and capacity in pursuing that goal. Finally, Burke's case was inescapably constitutional, since the powers of the state would have to collaborate in reproducing a class of rulers that would not prejudice the integrity of the system of rule.

As Burke saw it, in the British context, an aristocratic party best answered these objectives. This did not mean that he was a fawning admirer of social privilege, or a partisan of aristocratic government. Actors on the public stage were obliged to serve the people: despite their appearance in physical form, human beings were bound by moral duties imposed by a superintending intelligence.[276] Nonetheless, public security could only be guaranteed by constitutional restraints, never by purely normative commitments. That meant that the components of public power had to be regulated, balanced and disposed to the common good. This objective was best served, not by an aristocratic form of government, under which the few dictated without liability or constraint, but by a system of government that was aristocratic in spirit in the etymological sense of the term: what was required was a system of government under which the best—οἱ ἄριστοι (*hoi aristoi*)—were permitted to rule. This was an ideal conception on Burke's part, which he signalled by denominating the best form of rule as based on a "*natural* aristocracy."[277] From the perspective of conjectural history, political aristocracy was a product of social aristocracy. Beyond the most rudimentary conditions of existence, social differentiation inescapably emerged, giving rise over time to "a variety of conditions and circumstances in a state." This variety was artificial, insofar as it implied development from an original state of simplicity, yet it was natural to the extent that such development proceeded from human aptitudes and desires. "Art," Burke remarked in this context, "is man's nature."[278] The natural political corollary to this development, was the hegemony of those best equipped to rule. Since government was an artifice intended to serve the interest of the many, it was necessary to discover how the welfare of the populace—those who were *numero plures*—could best be served by those who were *virtute et honore majores*: predominant in their ability and sense of duty.[279]

The question for the legislator was how this ideal arrangement could best be approximated in practical terms. To achieve this, a system of rule would have to be devised in which public virtue would combine with political prudence. The combination of these characteristics would provide for the cultivation of popular consent, the security of private property, and the protection of personal liberty. This could

[275] EB to William Weddell, 31 January 1792, *Corr.*, VII, p. 52.

[276] EB, *Appeal from the New to the Old Whigs*, pp. 120–22.

[277] Ibid., p. 130.

[278] Ibid. See below, chapter 15, section 2.

[279] EB, *Appeal from the New to the Old Whigs*, p. 129.

never be achieved under the naked domination of an aristocracy—"the worst imaginable government," in Burke's eyes.[280] Instead, it would have to be accomplished under a mixed system of government in which the spirit of aristocracy prevailed. In any mixed polity, constituting a "republic" in its true sense, there would be partisans inclined to the competing elements of the legislature.[281] As Burke represented them, the Rockinghamites and their descendants were partisans of "aristocracy." That meant that they supported an alliance between the Lords and the Commons oriented towards preserving the constitutional balance against the ambitions of the crown and popular leaders in the lower House. As he put it to Weddell, they were a party "equally removed from servile court compliances, and from popular levity, presumption, and precipitation."[282] He had underlined the point the previous November to Fitzwilliam: an aristocratic party stood between popular whim and monarchical usurpation.[283] It could achieve this position because the core of the party was both "independent" and "embodied": they were secure in their own power, and represented in the state.[284] Their independence did not make them a separate force in society, but an integral part of the national compact. The strength of the old Whigs lay in their property, above all in their landed wealth, which bound them to the idea of inheritance, and thus to established constitutional practices: they were a party whose "Temper" derived from landed independence, attaching them "to the antient tried usages of the Kingdom."[285] They were committed, therefore, to the compact of government between king, Lords and Commons, and the distribution of wealth which that compact was designed to secure.

It is important to grasp the thought behind this commitment. For Burke, the preservation of an unequal distribution of wealth was in the long-term interest of social justice. The old couplet associated with the medieval Lollard preacher John Ball encapsulated the principles of British revolutionaries: "When Adam delved and Eve span, / Who was then the gentleman."[286] Burke's point was that this simple egalitarian precept conflicted with its probable results. As he explained to William Cusac Smith in July 1791, a rigorous process of reasoning would show that what passed for poverty in the popular imagination would count as wealth compared to the deprivation

[280] EB, *An Essay towards an Abridgement of the English History* (1757–?), *W & S*, I, p. 547.

[281] As Fox intimated on 11 May 1791, a "*res publica*" could take a variety of forms (*Diary*, 12 May 1791). Cicero's term translates Plato's πολιτεία (*politeia*), meaning a composite polity. As Fox well knew, "republic" could also designate a "pure" republic in which the constitution was governed by its democratic component. For his part, he would defend his own brand of "Republicanism" against the innuendo of Pitt (*Oracle*, 12 May 1791). In "The History of Europe" in *The Annual Register for 1791*, p. 111, Burke was presented as disdaining to use the word "*republicanism*" in "an obnoxious sense."

[282] EB to William Weddell, 31 January 1792, *Corr.*, VII, p. 53.

[283] EB to Earl Fitzwilliam, 21 November 1791, *Corr.*, VI, p. 450.

[284] EB to William Weddell, 31 January 1792, *Corr.*, VII, p. 56.

[285] Ibid., p. 52.

[286] EB, *Appeal from the New to the Old Whigs*, p. 133. Burke's account of Ball's programme was based on Thomas Walsingham, *Historia Anglicana*, ed. William Camden (Frankfurt: 1603).

that enforced equality would engineer.[287] An aristocratic party, in preserving that knowledge, reconciled order with prosperity. That reconciliation was based on a benign prejudice. As Burke articulated it in the *Reflections*, in the words of Cicero, *Omnes boni nobilitati semper favemus*: "all good citizens always favour nobility."[288] On 11 May 1791, Fox had indicated his support for such well-disposed partiality. Nobility was founded on the unity of property and rank, and it helped to maintain the delicate balance of the constitution. In Britain, the role of the aristocracy was to be applauded: "that prejudice for ancient family, and that sort of pride that belonged to Nobility, was right to be encouraged in a country like this, or one great incentive to virtue would be abolished."[289] However, in the same speech, thinking of conditions in Canada, he also "recommended an imitation of the Government of the United States of America" as the best model "now existing" for the peoples of the new world.[290] In the *Appeal*, Burke avoided explicit comparisons, and presented instead a general defence of the principle of aristocracy.

This involved itemising the positive contribution which distinguished members of society were likely to make to its government. He included more than nobility within this aristocracy, extending its bounds to encompass outstanding members of the professions, officers in the military, the upper reaches of trade, professors of science and the humanities, and of course the highborn themselves, freed from sordid interests and blessed with leisure. Together, these made up "what I should call a *natural* aristocracy, without which there is no nation."[291] This last clause was a reference to the situation in France: its "people" no longer existed since the conditions of government had been subverted. The British constitution, by comparison, strove to approximate the ideal of a natural aristocracy. Burke was happy to indict the actual nobility of the country for their inertia, indolence and incapacity. However, the combination of property, experience and talent which the British system of government promoted offered the best opportunity among constitutions currently available to cultivate the public virtues. It encouraged the aspiration to excellence, fostered accountability and nurtured prudence. It might of course fail, as it had done in its management of India and America. But government founded on the subversion of aristocracy was guaranteed to fail, as the course of the French Revolution served to demonstrate.

On 8 August 1791, immediately after the appearance of the *Appeal*, Burke wrote to his old friend the Earl of Charlemont, explaining his current position on France

[287] EB to William Cusac Smith, 23 July 1791, *Corr.*, VI, p. 304.

[288] EB, *Reflections*, ed. Clark, pp. 308–9 [205], citing Cicero, *Pro Sestio*, IX, 21.

[289] *Diary*, 12 May 1791.

[290] *Oracle*, 12 May 1791; cf. *Morning Post*, 12 May 1791: "that Government was, for its inhabitants, and its circumstances . . . the best that he knew of in the whole world." See also Fox on the Address of Thanks, 14 December 1792, in the *Morning Chronicle*, 15 December 1792: "for them most certainly the best form of Government upon earth." Burke had compared America with France on 6 May 1791: see *Parliamentary History*, XXIX, col. 365.

[291] EB, *Appeal from the New to the Old Whigs*, p. 130.

while confirming his friendship after more than a year's silence. He expected the French Revolution would have driven them apart, yet still he wished to assert his affection and respect. He had thought of Europe as generally improving, although this progress would now be reversed by precipitate violence in France. As a result of his published views, many opposition Whigs chose to maintain their distance, although the truth was that he had been disowned more in appearance than in reality—"privately I know there are eminent exceptions."[292] These included Portland and Fitzwilliam. Burke hoped that Charlemont would lend at least his moral support as well. Within a week he received his answer: while there were indeed differences between them on the Revolution in France, Charlemont's admiration for Burke remained undiminished. Writing to Alexander Haliday at the end of July, Charlemont reaffirmed the inspiration he drew from Paine, though he rejected his subversive conception of the constitution.[293] Now, with Burke, he professed to "despise" French philosophy, to "disapprove" of many of the measures adopted by the National Assembly, and to "abominate" the excesses of the people. He was also alarmed by the probable "contagion" of French ideas, especially "in a country circumstanced like ours."[294] Ireland, he felt, was particularly prone to revolutionary upheaval. His apprehension, as would soon become clear, was already felt by Burke.

14.6 Revolution and Ascendancy in Ireland

The Dublin barrister and politician Theobald Wolfe Tone famously described the controversy between Burke and Paine as having helped—"in an instant"—to transform the politics of Ireland."[295] Writing to Burke's son on 11 April 1791, Thomas Lewis O'Beirne noted the ongoing impact of the *Reflections* on public debate in Ireland, "notwithstanding the unremitting Efforts of almost all the Presbyterians and Atheists of the Country to give circulation to Payne's answer."[296] In fact, despite the success of Burke's argument among sympathetic publicists, enthusiasm for Paine

[292] EB to the Earl of Charlemont, 8 August 1791, *Corr.*, VI, pp. 330–31.

[293] The Earl of Charlemont to Alexander Haliday, 30 July 1791, *Correspondence and Manuscripts of Charlemont*, II, p. 142.

[294] The Earl of Charlemont to EB, 13 August 1791, ibid., p. 144.

[295] Theobald Wolfe Tone, *Life of Theobald Wolfe Tone: Compiled and Arranged by William Theobald Wolfe Tone* (Dublin: 1998), p. 39. For the ramifications of the controversy, see Paul Bew, *Ireland: The Politics of Enmity, 1789–2006* (Oxford: Oxford University Press, 2007), pp. 7–13; Ultán Gillen, "Monarchy, Republic and Empire: Irish Public Opinion and France, c.1787–1804" (DPhil thesis, University of Oxford, 2006), chs. 2 and 3.

[296] Northamptonshire MS. A. VII.2. Irish pamphlets supporting Burke against Paine included [William Cusac Smith], *Rights of Citizens* (London: 1791); Thomas Goold, *A Vindication of the Right Hon. Edmund Burke's Reflections on the Revolution in France* (Dublin: 1791). For comment, see Tadhg O'Sullivan, "Burke, Ireland and Counter-Revolution, 1791–1801" in Donlan ed., *Burke's Irish Identities.*

was spreading even to the Irish Whigs.[297] In due course, Christopher Wyvill would note how it had spread "to an alarming degree" through both islands.[298] O'Beirne, who had been born a Roman Catholic, became associated with the Rockingham Whigs in the early 1780s and succeeded to a living in Longford after the death of the incumbent, John Ryder.[299] He had considerable connections in Irish political circles, not least since he had helped to organise opposition to Pitt's plans for a commercial union with Ireland in 1785.[300] He was therefore in a position to monitor the cast of Irish attitudes in 1791. The young Richard Burke was of course pleased to learn that his father's work was still making converts on the neighbouring island. An Irish edition of the *Reflections* appeared in November 1790, and numerous editions were to follow.[301] Nonetheless, its fortunes had to progress "despite the adverse Exertions of the many."[302] In Richard's lexicon, the "many" did not signify a majority in the country but the partisans of democratic ideas. As his tone of disdain indicated, he was becoming increasingly involved in his father's campaign against France. After an approach from Calonne in July 1791, Burke encouraged the participation of his son in an unofficial diplomatic mission to Coblenz.[303] This resulted in the appointment of the chevalier de La Bintinaye as emissary to the British government for the émigré princes at Worms. Richard's involvement at Coblenz was followed by another commission: his appointment as London agent for the Irish Catholic Committee.[304] He now had a definite interest in what the "many" thought in Ireland. More immediately he had to concern himself with the views of its political establishment.

The Catholic Committee had staked out its claim to act as the "medium" through which the voice of Irish Catholics should be conveyed to government at a general

[297] For divergent reactions among the Whigs, compare the responses of Richard Sheridan and Alexander Haliday in *Correspondence and Manuscripts of Charlemont*, II, pp. 137, 139–40, 142. On Paine in Ireland, see David Dickson, "Paine and Ireland" in David Dickson, Dáire Keogh and Kevin Whelan eds., *The United Irishmen: Republicanism, Radicalism and Rebellion* (Dublin: Lilliput, 1993).

[298] Christopher Wyvill to William Burgh, 16 May 1792, in Christopher Wyvill, *Political Papers, Chiefly Respecting . . . a Reformation of the Parliament of Great Britain* (York: 1794–1802), 6 vols., V, p. 67.

[299] O'Beirne owed his accession to Portland: see Thomas Lewis O'Beirne to EB, *Corr.*, V, p. 29. For an overview of his career, see Caroline Gallagher, "Bishop Thomas Lewis O'Beirne of Meath (c.1747–1823): Politician and Churchman," *Ríocht na Mídhe*, 20 (2009), pp. 189–208.

[300] See Thomas Lewis O'Beirne, *A Reply to the Late Treasury Pamphlet Entitled "The Proposed System of Trade with Ireland Explained"* (London: 1785).

[301] R. B. McDowell, *Ireland in the Age of Imperialism and Revolution* (Oxford: Oxford University Press, 1979, 1991), p. 353. See also R. B. McDowell, *Irish Public Opinion, 1750–1800* (London: Faber and Faber, 1944), p. 164, for the serialisation of the *Reflections* in the Irish press.

[302] Richard Burke Jr. to Thomas Lewis O'Beirne, 6 May 1791, *Corr.*, VI, p. 353.

[303] Charles-Alexandre de Calonne to EB, c. 20 July 1791, ibid., pp. 300–301; EB to Charles-Alexandre de Calonne, c. 20 July 1791, ibid., p. 302; EB to Charles-Alexandre de Calonne, December 1791, ibid., pp. 473ff. For an account of Richard Burke Jr.'s mission, see F. P. Lock, *Edmund Burke* (Oxford: Oxford University Press, 1998–2006), 2 vols., II, pp. 391–93.

[304] Edward Byrne to Richard Burke Jr., 15 September 1791, *Corr.*, VI, pp. 396–97.

meeting convened on 15 November 1783.[305] For the next seven years, however, its outward campaigning went into abeyance.[306] But then, against a backdrop of international crisis, English Catholics began to seek relief from penal restrictions in Britain. Correspondingly, in the summer of 1790, the situation began to shift in Ireland. A meeting of the electorate of the Catholic Committee from all the towns and parishes in the country instructed their representatives on 3 June 1790 to press for further relief from anti-popery legislation. To that end, it was resolved in the first instance to compose "An Appeal to the Nation" as a means of preparing opinion to support the measure. The services of Richard Burke Jr. were to be sought out for the purpose. Accordingly, the Chair of the Committee requested that Thomas Hussey, a leading Catholic cleric, should intercede with Richard on their behalf.[307] Hussey had known the Burkes since 1779, and had recently been approached to further the cause of English Catholics.[308] Having failed to locate Richard at Lincoln's Inn in mid-August, Hussey appealed directly to Edmund Burke, recognising his interest in the "oppressed State of the R: Catholicks" of Ireland.[309] He then wrote to his son at the end of the month, apprising him of the probable course of events in Ireland. As a consequence of the controversy over Nootka Sound, war with Spain now threatened.[310] Since toleration in Ireland had previously been driven by a context of foreign conflict, future concessions might be expected from a similar conjunction of events. Yet it was "absurd," Hussey argued, to allow policy to be dictated by the advent of a national emergency.[311] It was more prudent to concede from motives of justice in the present what necessity would in any case later compel.

Developments in France made a prompt decision mandatory. Hussey was already concerned by the spread of the "*french disease*."[312] Hitherto, he noted, Catholic attitudes had been cowed, seeking redress in a spirit of submission. Burke traced this passivity to the impact of the penal laws: the Catholic landed gentry of the late seventeenth century who remained in Ireland after the Treaty of Limerick had maintained "something of the Spirit of Struggle" on account of their indignation at their

[305] R. Dudley Edwards ed., "Minute Book of the Catholic Committee, 1773–1792," *Archivium Hibernicum*, 9 (1942), pp. 2–172, p. 88.

[306] Eamon O'Flaherty, "The Catholic Convention and Anglo-Irish Politics, 1791–93," *Archivium Hibernicum*, 40 (1985), pp. 14–34.

[307] Baron Hussey of Galtrim to Thomas Hussey, 6 August 1790, *Correspondence* (1844), III, pp. 152–55.

[308] See Dáire Keogh, "Thomas Hussey, Bishop of Waterford and Lismore, 1797–1803, and the Rebellion of 1798" in W. Nolan ed., *Waterford: History and Society* (Dublin: Geography Publications, 1992); idem, "Thomas Hussey, Edmund Burke and the Irish Directory" in Seán Patrick Donlan ed., *Edmund Burke's Irish Identities* (Dublin: Irish Academic Press, 2006).

[309] Thomas Hussey to EB, 13 August 1791, *Corr.*, VI, p. 133.

[310] EB to the Earl of Charlemont, 25 May 1790, ibid., p. 118. Burke, unlike Hussey, thought war in the end unlikely.

[311] Thomas Hussey to Richard Burke Jr., 28 August 1790, ibid., p. 134.

[312] Ibid.

reduced conditions.[313] However, this generation had all passed away by the time that Burke reached manhood, leaving their progeny, the "second Growth" after the latest revolution in Ireland, in a comparatively defeated state: whether Catholics or converts, they were psychologically beaten, and accordingly they were abject in attitude. Advancement required reconciliation with existing circumstances. For converts, like the father of the current Lord Chancellor of Ireland, that requirement bred a fear of raising any "disturbance" that might conflict with personal ambition or family fortune.[314] For those who retained their Catholic faith, it meant maximising opportunities for increasing commercial wealth. By 1790, the industry of this class had raised them to ample wealth: "a new race of Catholics have risen . . . to considerable opulence," Burke observed to his son.[315] The great landowners who had fled Ireland after the Williamite wars sought distinction in Germany and France, but their achievements never matched their pedigree. The few remaining grandees, like Lord Kenmare, were hostile rather than sympathetic to successful merchants and large farmers, and so the Catholic interest was bound to fragment, as indeed it did with a split in the Catholic Committee at the end of 1791.[316]

As Hussey saw matters, it was events in France that encouraged an attitude of insurgency among Catholics. They would no longer "bear the lash of Tiranny and oppression." The change of mind was evidenced by new attitudes on the Catholic Committee supportive of French Revolutionary ideals. Hussey argued that the minds of men had been "sublimated" by what had passed since 1789, by which he meant that their enthusiasm had been fired.[317] During the mid 1780s, elements within the Irish Volunteers, particularly among its new light Presbyterian contingent in the north, had begun to propose the gradual enfranchisement of Catholics in the context of a general bid for parliamentary reform.[318] In 1783, Henry Joy, the editor of the *Belfast News-Letter*, endorsed the idea of a comprehensive Christian "right of election."[319] Richard Price, acknowledging the particular circumstances of Ireland, nonetheless commended the proposal.[320] Against this background, the

[313] EB to Richard Burke Jr., 20 March 1792, *Corr.*, VII, p. 101.

[314] Ibid.

[315] EB to Richard Burke Jr., post 3 January 1792, ibid., p. 9. For the social context that Burke is addressing, see Maureen Wall, "The Rise of a Catholic Middle Class in Eighteenth-Century Ireland," *Irish Historical Studies*, 11:42 (September 1958), pp. 91–115; Louis Cullen, "Catholics under the Penal Laws," *Eighteenth-Century Ireland*, 1 (1986), pp. 23–36; Ian McBride, *Eighteenth-Century Ireland: Isle of Slaves* (Dublin: Gill and Macmillan, 2009), ch. 6.

[316] The "country gentlemen" consequently presented a separate address to the Lord Lieutenant on 27 December 1791: see Francis Plowden, *An Historical Review of the State of Ireland* (Philadelphia, PA: 1806), 5 vols., IV, Appendix I, pp. 1–3.

[317] Thomas Hussey to Richard Burke Jr., 28 August 1790, *Corr.*, VI, p. 134.

[318] Ian McBride, *Scripture Politics: Ulster Presbyterians and Irish Radicalism in the Late Eighteenth Century* (Oxford: Oxford University Press, 1998), pp. 134–44.

[319] *A Collection of Letters which have been Addressed to the Volunteers of Ireland, on the Subject of Parliamentary Reform* (London: 1783), p. 23.

[320] Ibid., p. 83.

Catholic Committee began to acquire new weight and independence, and to press for a fresh campaign.[321] On 18 February 1791 a sub-committee of eight reported the determination of the General Committee to secure the relief of the Catholic community from their "degraded" condition by mitigating existing penal laws.[322] Early in March, criticising the penal statutes then in force in England, Burke recognised the wisdom of regulating religion as a necessary part of sound statecraft. However, Catholicism posed no genuine threat to the British constitution since the deposing power of the Pope was disregarded. He added, ironically, that the current pontiff did not seem to have been active in fomenting insurrection.[323] Nonetheless, restiveness about Catholic allegiance to the constitution continued in the Whig clubs of Belfast and Dublin.[324]

In this context, it was resolved by the Irish Catholic Committee on 3 December 1791 that Burke's son be approached to serve as "*agent in London*" to present its applications to the British ministry.[325] He was being sent to stir up in Ireland the kind of confusion that his father was struggling to prevent in England, Edmond Malone wryly commented to Charlemont.[326] In the middle of December, Richard was still undecided about travelling to Ireland. However, by the end of the month, he had set out from Beaconsfield for Dublin.[327] The Chair of the Catholic Committee, Edward Byrne, assured Richard of the ground shared between his colleagues and Burke's son. Before any significant progress could be made, the "Prejudices" of the opponents of Catholic relief would have to be dissipated.[328] The key question was how this objective might be achieved. Young Burke was intervening in the midst of a delicate balance of forces. Already on 12 March 1791 the Lord Lieutenant, the Earl of Westmorland, was alerting the British government to opposition in the Irish parliament to any advance on the Relief Acts of 1771, 1774, 1778 and 1782.[329] However, rumours of collaboration between Catholics and dissenters, especially in the north-eastern counties of Ireland, were now passing between London and Dublin. In August, Wolfe Tone's advocacy of Catholic emancipation as a precondition for

[321] Jim Smyth, *The Men of No Property: Irish Radicals and Popular Politics in the Late Eighteenth Century* (Dublin: Gill and Macmillan, 1992), pp. 94–59.

[322] Edwards ed., "Minute Book of the Catholic Committee, 1773–1792," pp. 23, 33–35.

[323] EB, Catholic Dissenters Relief Bill, 1 March 1791, *Parliamentary History*, XXVIII, cols. 1369–72, based on the report in the *Diary*, 2 March 1791. A shorter version appears in the *Morning Chronicle*, 2 March 1791. For the relevant issues and principles at stake as viewed from Dublin, see *Original Papers Relevant to the Current Application to the British Parliament for Relief of the Roman Catholics in England* (Dublin: 1791).

[324] *Correspondence and Manuscripts of Charlemont,* II, pp. 114–16, 120.

[325] Ibid., pp. 136–37.

[326] 3 December 1792, ibid., p. 204.

[327] EB to Richard Burke Jr., 13 December 1791, *Corr.*, VI, p. 456n; Richard Burke Jr. to Henry Dundas, 27 December 1791, ibid., p. 471. Richard departed with John Keogh two days later.

[328] Edward Byrne to Richard Burke Jr., 15 September 1791, ibid., p. 397.

[329] Thomas Bartlett, *The Fall and Rise of the Irish Nation: The Catholic Question, 1690–1830* (Dublin: Gill and Macmillan, 1992), p. 125.

the achievement of liberty in Ireland appeared in print.[330] The following October, the Society of United Irishmen was formed in Belfast. In November, another branch was set up in Dublin.[331] Activists on the Catholic Committee, like John Keogh and Richard McCormick, were to be found among its members.[332] At the same time, a distinct Catholic Society, with some of its membership overlapping with the Catholic Committee, was established under the leadership of Theobald McKenna. The prospect of a complex pattern of polarisation within and between dissent, the Anglican establishment and distinct sections of Catholic opinion began to appear.

Richard Burke's first move as London agent for the Catholic Committee was to sound out Henry Dundas, the Home Secretary, on the position of the British government.[333] However, Dundas and his colleagues were determined not to be drawn.[334] Burke wrote to Richard on 15 December 1791 reprobating what appeared to be the current ministerial position.[335] On his last trip to Dublin, in the autumn of 1786, he had wanted to introduce his son to "the Country from whence he originated and, to make him a little known there."[336] Just over a month before the journey, he had written to O'Beirne lamenting the poorly constructed constitution of the country.[337] Clearly, in Burke's mind, the Relief Acts passed in the preceding years had not adequately addressed the role of Catholics in the state. Now, writing to his son at the end of 1791, he was anxious to repair what seemed an anomalous situation in which the majority population was excluded from participation in the political life of the country on the grounds of religion. More immediately, he pointed to the folly of seeking to drive a wedge between Catholics and dissenters without first establishing civil equality between them.[338] Collaboration between these two poles of Irish society had been mooted after the Bastille celebrations in Belfast in July 1791.[339] In the same month, the Earl of Westmorland wrote to Dundas to communicate his

[330] [Theobald Wolfe Tone], *An Argument on Behalf of the Catholics of Ireland* (Dublin: 1791).

[331] Marianne Elliott, *Partners in Revolution: The United Irishmen and France* (New Haven, CT: Yale University Press, 1982, 1989), pp. 22–33.

[332] Eamon O'Flaherty, "Irish Catholics and the French Revolution" in David Dickinson and Hugh Gough eds., *Ireland and the French Revolution* (Dublin: Irish Academic Press, 1990).

[333] Thomas H. D. Mahoney, *Edmund Burke and Ireland* (Cambridge, MA: Harvard University Press, 1960), p. 163.

[334] Henry Dundas to Richard Burke Jr., 6 October 1791, *Corr.*, VI, pp. 429–30. For a report of Dundas's meeting with Burke Jr. on 9 October, see the *Morning Chronicle*, 10 October 1791. Richard sent a summary of the meeting to Pitt, who had already discussed the issues with Edmund Burke. See Northamptonshire MS. A. XII.8. For Pitt's acknowledgement, see William Pitt to Richard Burke Jr., 13 October 1791, *Corr.*, VI, p. 436.

[335] EB to Richard Burke Jr., 15 December 1791, ibid., pp. 461–63.

[336] EB to John Hely Hutchinson, 11 November 1786, *Corr.*, V, p. 289.

[337] EB to Thomas Lewis O'Beirne, 29 September 1786, ibid., p. 282.

[338] EB to Richard Burke Jr., 15 December 1791, ibid., pp. 461–63.

[339] Simon Butler, "Introduction to the Digest of the Popery Laws" in William James MacNeven ed., *Irish History Illustrative of the Condition of the Catholics of Ireland* (New York: 1807), pp. 14–15.

alarm.[340] William Grenville, as Foreign Secretary, was presented with evidence of early conspiracy by Burke's son.[341] By the end of December, Dundas was outlining the government's ambition to deter any Catholic resort to a seditious alliance with dissent by supporting their plea for an end to some of their civil disabilities.[342] The Burkes and the British government seemed to be moving in the same direction. After a meeting with the Chief Secretary to the Lord Lieutenant, Major Robert Hobart, Richard informed his father that the Irish executive, still effectively controlled from London, was "convinced of the necessity of conciliating and gaining the R[oman] C[atholics] to the interests of Government."[343] The question was whether they would support a measure for full political enfranchisement, and pressurise the Irish parliament into adopting it.

Writing to the Earl of Charlemont on 29 December, Burke reiterated his determination in the aftermath of the *Appeal* that the British constitution "should be thoroughly understood." He was also keen that its benefits should be "widely extended."[344] Here he was thinking of the need for reform in Ireland. By now, Dundas had apprised Dublin Castle of the ministry's support for a range of concessions to Catholics. Faced with stern resistance from Westmorland and Hobart, confirmed by the dismay of established Protestant opinion, the British agreed to reduce the number of privileges to be granted.[345] Sir Hercules Langrishe, a pro-administration member of the Irish Commons, was to introduce a new Bill before the House on 25 January 1792. The previous December, Langrishe had set out for Burke his own thinking on emancipation. Burke composed a lengthy reply at speed, dispatching it to Ireland on 3 January.[346] Burke's *Letter to Sir Hercules Langrishe* was then published in Dublin on 18 February 1792.[347] According to Hobart, it had been eagerly, indeed anxiously, awaited in Dublin as a near representation of the views of Henry Dundas.[348] It has been described as "an appeal to the Irish Parliament itself."[349] More specifically, it was an appeal over the heads of the administration at Dublin Castle. It was already clear to the Irish government that a considerable proportion of the

[340] The Earl of Westmorland to Henry Dundas, 26 July 1791, cited in W.E.H. Lecky, *History of Ireland in the Eighteenth Century* (London: Longmans, Green and Co., 1913), 4 vols., III, p. 10.

[341] Lord Grenville to Henry Dundas, 29 October 1791, *The Manuscripts of J. B. Fortescue Preserved at Dropmore* (London: 1894), 2 vols., II, p. 221.

[342] Lecky, *History of Ireland*, III, pp. 37–39.

[343] Richard Burke Jr. to EB, 15 December 1791, *Corr.*, VI, p. 463. Hobart had been a school fellow of Richard's at Westminster.

[344] Ibid., p. 472.

[345] Lecky, *History of Ireland*, III, pp. 49ff.; Bartlett, *Fall and Rise of the Irish Nation*, pp. 137–42.

[346] Burke had started it in December, and had finished by 1 January. See EB to Richard Burke Jr., 1 January 1792, *Corr.*, VII, p. 4.

[347] *Morning Post*, 18 February 1792. See EB to Richard Burke Jr., c. 8 March 1792, *Corr.*, VII, pp. 94–95.

[348] Robert Hobart to Henry Dundas, 17 January 1792, TNA, HO 100/36/ fol. 60.

[349] Conor Cruise O'Brien, *The Great Melody: A Thematic Biography and Commented Anthology of Edmund Burke* (London: Sinclair-Stevenson, 1992), p. 476.

MPs on College Green were profoundly opposed to admitting Catholics to a share in the franchise. "To them I have nothing to say," Burke declared in his *Letter* to Langrishe.[350] His hope was that Pitt and Dundas would be able to induce the Irish parliament to accept major change.[351] His pamphlet was an attempt to broaden the constituency to which they might appeal. Langrishe, he thought, presented an example of a member of parliament who was currently prepared to follow the lead of the administration in perpetuating residual penal legislation against his better judgment.[352] If he could be brought to accept the logic of his endorsement of Catholic toleration, others similarly disposed might follow suit.

It was part of Burke's purpose to argue that men like Langrishe who had previously embraced measures of Catholic relief but who now opposed attempts to introduce complete emancipation were struggling against the inevitable tide of history. Towards the end of January 1792, he insisted that the battle for Catholic enfranchisement would be won: "They *will* have it; because the nature of things *will* do it."[353] The previous month, Dundas had laid out the measures which Irish Catholics might be led to expect: all laws which restricted membership of trades or professions should be repealed; interdenominational marriage should be permitted; regulations which inhibited access to education should be lifted; the ban on carrying arms should be revoked; participation in grand and petty juries should be allowed; and provisions for participation in elections might be considered.[354] During the course of a probing correspondence conducted with Westmorland and Hobart over the following weeks, these concessions were radically qualified. Admission to the suffrage, even on the limited basis proposed, was to be denied.[355] Membership of grand juries and the right to bear arms was also to be withheld.[356] The remaining measures passed after a series of spirited debates held at the end of January.[357] Pitt and Dundas had been brought to agree that, as things now stood, Britain could not govern through a parliamentary administration in Ireland without the compliance of mainstream Protestant opinion.[358] Nonetheless, Burke correctly sensed that the British government was in principle opposed to a system of proscription that condemned an

[350] EB, *Letter to Sir Hercules Langrishe* (1792), *W & S*, IX, p. 598.

[351] EB to Richard Burke Jr., post 3 January 1792, p. 9, shows that Burke had banked on Westminster as the means of supplying forward momentum.

[352] EB, *Letter to Sir Hercules Langrishe* (1792), *W & S*, IX, p. 595.

[353] EB to Richard Burke Jr., 26 January 1792, *Corr.*, VII, p. 40.

[354] Henry Dundas to the Earl of Westmorland, 26 December 1791, TNA, HO 100/33, fols. 205ff.

[355] The franchise sought was for admission of 40 shilling freeholders in the counties who in addition rented or owned land worth £20 per annum. See Richard Burke Jr. to Henry Dundas, post 16 December 1791, *Corr.*, VI, p. 469.

[356] Bartlett, *Fall and Rise of the Irish Nation*, p. 141.

[357] These were duly published in pamphlet form: see *A Report of the Debates in Both Houses of Parliament, on the Roman Catholic Bill* (Dublin: 1792). Langrishe defended the government's proposals in terms of civil rather than natural rights, criticising ideas publicised by Paine. See ibid., p. 6.

[358] Lecky, *History of Ireland*, III, p. 54.

entire Christian denomination to a state of civil inequality. "Our constitution is not made for great, general, proscriptive exclusions; sooner or later, it will destroy them, or they will destroy the constitution."[359] The aim of the *Letter to Sir Hercules Langrishe* was to build up a constituency for bringing an end to the relevant exclusions.

Burke's main leverage lay in the fears of establishment Protestants. These resulted, he surmised, less from genuine alarm about the spread of rival theological tenets, or even from the threat posed by an international Catholic alliance.[360] Such grounds for apprehension were in fact perennial pretexts, and they hid the true source of anxiety.[361] Accordingly, zeal for the fate of Protestantism was a dissimulating pretence.[362] The current impasse, Burke proposed, was not so much a product of the Reformation as a consequence of a complex colonial history. This inheritance would shape the resolution of the ongoing conflict. Religion, of course, played a crucial role, but it was important to grasp the nature of its past significance as well as its contemporary purchase on men's minds. The current age was one in which "men are infinitely more likely to heat themselves with political than religious controversies."[363] This statement carried three important implications. First, it acted as a reminder that hostilities in Ireland originated in a struggle over power, not religion. The Statutes of Kilkenny, passed by the Irish legislature in 1366, enshrined a code of antipathy between settler and native, and established a pattern of future animosity and proscription.[364] Religious conflict, which emerged under the reign of Elizabeth I, merely inflamed a struggle that had already become entrenched. Secondly, Burke's point was that the Protestant establishment could no longer bank on the unconditional support of Britain on account of shared religious loyalty. The common enmity of 1691 had abated among the British since at least the 1760s.[365] Finally, as the French Revolution had shown, a population might be seduced from its religious commitments on the basis of a newfound political allegiance. But if, as a result of a failure to address their grievances, Roman Catholics were driven to consider an alternative creed, the Church of Ireland would certainly not be their choice.[366] Burke was intimating that, however one configured the future balance of forces, the current constitution of the Irish church-state was bound to lose if it did not opt for conciliation.

Confronting Anglican opinion in Ireland with the range of possible options, Burke's intention was to appeal to rational suspicions over imaginary fears. It was

[359] EB, *Letter to Sir Hercules Langrishe* (1792), *W & S*, IX, p. 601.

[360] Ibid., p. 620.

[361] On this, see also EB, *Letter to Richard Burke* (post February 1792), *W & S*, IX, p. 646: "I speak here of their pretexts, and not the true spirit of the transaction, in which religious bigotry I apprehend has little share."

[362] Ibid., p. 641.

[363] EB, *Letter to Sir Hercules Langrishe* (1792), *W & S*, IX, p. 633.

[364] Ibid., p. 615.

[365] Ibid., p. 616.

[366] Ibid., p. 633.

certain that the current arrangement would not endure since the elements supporting it were in flux: new alignments were emerging, and new constitutional arrangements projected. No matter in what direction the current stalemate might shift, self-preservation dictated that the Protestant establishment should court Catholic opinion by revising the terms of its own ascendancy. Despite the rhetoric of Burke's proclamations in his writings on France, he was adamant that change was a staple of politics: "We must all obey the great law of change."[367] To direct its progress intelligently, thus avoiding an inadvertent subversion of one's intentions, it was necessary to proceed with circumspection. The ambitions of those who were set to gain would have to be managed, lest the intoxication of acceding to new powers should get the better of their reasonable expectations. At the same time, the attachments of those in the ascendant would have to be protected so as to avoid inducing despair at the prospect of decline. In any event, a static equilibrium was not a future option. Under the current dispensation, Catholicism might collaborate with reform-oriented dissent to undermine the connection between property and representation, in which case established Protestants would become politically marginal: in this scenario, two thirds of the population would combine with half of the remainder to monopolise political power for themselves. Alternatively, if the British government should pursue a policy of parliamentary union, the enfranchisement of Catholics was bound to accompany the measure. In that case, representatives of the Protestant ascendancy might find themselves canvassing for the electoral favour of currently excluded Catholic voters. Burke concluded: "Take what course you please—union or no union; whether the people remain Catholics, or become Protestant Dissenters, sure it is, that the present state of monopoly, *cannot* continue."[368]

The Church party cherished the Irish constitution of 1782, yet it clung to the possibility of an incorporating union as a reserve insurance policy. The achievement of any such outcome, Burke predicted, would be fraught with difficulty: "Great divisions and vehement passions would precede this union."[369] It was unlikely that the result would benefit the welfare of either kingdom. More pertinently still, it would not advance the dominance of established Protestantism in Ireland. It was crucial for Churchmen to grasp that an epochal shift in imperial policy was observable in the aftermath of the Seven Years' War. Britain was loath to risk "another American war in Ireland," intervening in support of insupportable monopoly.[370] Above all, its government was unwilling to defend a religious minority against the wishes of the preponderating population. The Quebec Act and the recent Canada Act exhibited the disposition of the official mind.[371] The same attitude was in evidence in the management of the Indian Empire: sectarian differences were never invoked in justification of civil disabilities. "We did not fly from our undertaking," Burke observed, "because

[367] Ibid., p. 634.
[368] Ibid., p. 633.
[369] Ibid., p. 632.
[370] Ibid., p. 633.
[371] Ibid., p. 636.

the people were Mahometans or Pagans."[372] There no longer existed a strictly Protestant interest binding the members of the religious establishment in Britain and Ireland no matter what. Gradually, during the aftermath of the Treaty of Limerick, a distinct patriot programme had emerged in the smaller island, asserting "an *independent Irish interest*."[373] Ultimately, this consciousness of an interest distinguishable from metropolitan policy found political expression in the Volunteer movement, and the bid for a properly authoritative parliament in 1782. With this shift in constitutional priorities came a change in domestic politics: "With their views, the *Anglo-Irish* changed their maxims."[374] They were impelled toward a rapprochement with 2 million of their Catholic brethren. The need to recognise a common welfare shared between the denominations of the island accompanied the reorganisation of relations between metropole and province.

On the basis of these developments, Burke defined the advent of Grattan's parliament, granted together with an extension of religious toleration, as the moment when the principles of 1688 finally obtained in Ireland.[375] Two weeks after Burke had signed off on his *Letter to Sir Hercules Langrishe*, Westmorland wrote to Pitt outlining Britain's dependence on the goodwill of the Church party in Ireland. The frame of the government there, he observed, was that of "a Protestant garrison."[376] He indicated that he had taken the image of a garrison from Burke, but in actual fact he seems to have mistaken Burke's usage. For the best part of the eighteenth century, Burke contended, the property, power and magistracy of Ireland had been in the possession of Church of Ireland descendants of colonial settlers. However, in the 1770s, their radically exclusive tenure started to come to an end as Catholics and Presbyterians began to be relieved of their disabilities. The British government, which drove Catholic reform, recognised that the majority population in the country would no longer endure the government of Ireland acting "the part of a *garrison*."[377] After the failure of his son's attempt to petition the Irish Parliament on behalf of the Catholic Committee in late January, Burke wrote to him in February about the pretensions of the administration. The Protestant interest in Ireland had long pretended to advocate a patriot agenda, whereas in fact it was currently playing

[372] Ibid., p. 637. On Muslim, Pagan and Jewish toleration from the late seventeenth century, see John Marshall, *John Locke, Toleration and Early Enlightenment Culture: Religious Intolerance and Arguments for Religious Toleration in Early Modern and "Early Enlightenment" Europe* (Cambridge: Cambridge University Press, 2006), ch. 19.

[373] EB, *Letter to Sir Hercules Langrishe* (1792), *W & S*, IX, p. 617.

[374] Ibid. For discussion, see Eamon O'Flaherty, "Burke and the Irish Constitution" in Seán Patrick Donlan ed., *Edmund Burke's Irish Identities* (Dublin: Irish Academic Press, 2006), esp. pp. 114–15.

[375] Admission to the franchise would therefore constitute a complete "restoration" of the Glorious Revolution by extending its provisions to Ireland. See EB, Debate on the Address of Thanks, 14 December 1792, *Parliamentary History*, XXX, col. 74.

[376] Lecky, *History of Ireland*, III, p. 48.

[377] EB, *Letter to Sir Hercules Langrishe* (1792), *W & S*, IX, p. 618.

the role of a tyrannising faction.[378] This, Burke thought, was to proceed with business as usual, except now dominion was asserted with a fraudulently enhanced claim to legitimacy.

That move was facilitated by a new coinage: Protestant domination was qualified by the term "*ascendancy*."[379] According to Burke, the term had recently been minted in Dublin Castle, only to be adopted by the corporation and then parliament.[380] It certainly played a role in the special pleading of Robert Hobart: the British connection, he explained to Dundas, could only be maintained on the basis of "Protestant ascendancy," since the management of the country relied on the executive control of parliament, which depended in turn on Protestant predominance in the constitution.[381] The phrase can be traced to the paper war of 1786–8, but it now gained particular traction in parliamentary debate over Langrishe's Bill.[382] For Burke, however, it was merely a piece of subterfuge, dignifying oppression with an appearance of acclaim: "New *ascendancy* is the old mastership. It is neither more nor less than the resolution of one set of people in Ireland, to consider themselves as the sole citizens in the commonwealth."[383] It was of this reality that Burke sought to persuade Langrishe in January. "You hated the old system as early as I did," Burke reminded him.[384] For his part, Burke had arrived at his current view as early as 1760.[385] With Langrishe, he shared a belief in the futility of excluding the greater part of a country from its constitutional benefits. On 24 January 1792, Langrishe would himself castigate the attempt to "build a code of religious laws on the ruins of almost every moral virtue and obligation."[386] But while he was prepared to grant full toleration to the exercise of religion, he was not prepared to modify the organisation of political power. As Langrishe informed Burke on 10 December 1791, "the Catholics should

[378] EB, *Letter to Richard Burke* (post February 1792), *W & S*, IX, pp. 641–42, 650. On this theme in Burke, see Seamus Deane, "Factions and Fictions: Burke, Colonialism and Revolution" in idem, *Foreign Affections: Essays on Edmund Burke* (Cork: Cork University Press, 2005).

[379] EB, *Letter to Richard Burke* (post February 1792), *W & S*, IX, pp. 642–43.

[380] For discussion, see Eamon O'Flaherty, "Burke and the Catholic Question," *Eighteenth-Century Ireland*, 12 (1997), pp. 7–27.

[381] Lecky, *History of Ireland*, III, p. 51, based on Robert Hobart to Henry Dundas, 17 January 1792, TNA, HO 100/36/ fols. 58ff.

[382] James Kelly, "The Genesis of 'Protestant Ascendancy': The Rightboy Disturbances of the 1780s and their Impact upon Protestant Opinion" in Gerard O'Brien ed., *Parliament Politics and People: Essays in Eighteenth-Century Irish History* (Dublin: Irish Academic Press, 1989); Jacqueline Hill, "The Meaning and Significance of 'Protestant Ascendancy', 1787–1840" in Lord Blake ed., *Ireland after the Union: Proceedings of the Second Joint Meeting of the Royal Irish Academy and the British Academy* (Oxford: Oxford University Press, 1989); James Kelly, "Eighteenth-Century Ascendancy: A Commentary," *Eighteenth-Century Ireland*, 5 (1990), pp. 173–87; W. J. McCormick, *The Dublin Paper War of 1786–8* (Dublin: Irish Academic Press, 1993).

[383] EB, *Letter to Richard Burke* (post February 1792), *W & S*, IX, p. 644.

[384] EB, *Letter to Sir Hercules Langrishe* (1792), *W & S*, IX, p. 637.

[385] Ibid., p. 635.

[386] Hercules Langrishe, *Sir Hercules Langrishe's Speech in the House of Commons, 24 January 1792* (Dublin: 1792), p. 4.

enjoy every thing *under* the state, but should not be *the state itself*."[387] Langrishe described this arrangement as determined by the status of Ireland as a Protestant state, as laid down at the Glorious Revolution and confirmed by the Act of Settlement. However, his whole conception, as Burke tried to show, was based on fundamental misapprehension.

Burke's response addressed three issues: the nature of a popular state, the meaning of a Protestant establishment, and the legacy of the Glorious Revolution. The term "state," of course, had two meanings: the commonwealth itself and its government or administration.[388] It was clear that each and every member of a commonwealth could not equally participate in its government.[389] Nonetheless, under a mixed popular constitution, such as Burke thought to be characteristic of Britain and Ireland alike, it was not practicable to exclude a considerable proportion of the population, let alone the preponderant segment, from the basic franchises definitive of citizenship. To do so, in fact, was to condemn the bulk of the people to civil servitude, negating the very notion of a commonwealth itself. A state that was based on aristocratic sovereignty might well confine political privilege to a particular order of citizens. The republic of Venice best exemplified this arrangement, under which the people were indemnified for their exclusion from the Maggior Consiglio by having a monopoly on trade bestowed upon them: this served, in some sense, to "balance" distinct orders.[390] However, the constitution of Ireland offered no such compensation. Moreover, as an oligarchy, it was in conflict with its own animating principle. While citizenship and government were confined to the few, this restriction was founded on a popular conception of government: in theory, the system of parliamentary representation was intended as a vehicle for popular sovereignty. The sovereignty was distributed among three components: the crown, the Irish Lords and the Irish Commons. However, this last, "plebeian" element comprised only a fraction of the population since the majority had been deprived of their electoral franchise in 1728.[391] This meant that the disenfranchised were obliged to defer to their social equals in their capacity of being political masters. This was, Burke concluded, a constitutional "monster": a "plebeian oligarchy" to which the mass of the country was crudely subordinated.[392] Power commanded without authority, and so obedience was founded on submission, not acquiescence.

[387] Cited by Burke in EB, *Letter to Sir Hercules Langrishe* (1792), *W & S*, IX, p. 596. The existence of the letter is confirmed in *Corr.*, IX, p. 467.

[388] EB, *Letter to Sir Hercules Langrishe* (1792), *W & S*, IX, p. 598.

[389] A "*universal unmodified capacity*" for executive power was little more than a pretence of "fanatics": ibid., p. 600.

[390] Ibid., p. 599.

[391] Northamptonshire MS. A. XXVII.83: "I had always before been of opinion that the multitude of those who suffer any Grievance is a great argument in favour of its redress." On the loss of the franchise, see J. G. Simms, "Irish Catholics and the Parliamentary Franchise, 1692–1728," *Irish Historical Studies*, 12 (March 1960), pp. 28–37.

[392] EB, *Letter to Sir Hercules Langrishe* (1792), *W & S*, IX, p. 600.

In his *Letter to Richard Burke*, which followed over a month after the *Letter to Sir Hercules Langrishe*, Burke spelt out just how little would be sacrificed by including Catholics in the franchise.[393] It was a dangerous mistake to perpetuate the idea that any concession would act as a harbinger of social revolution by overturning the confiscations of the seventeenth century.[394] Burke balked at the suggestion that the beneficiaries of past conquest might be "turned out of their Houses, if Catholicks obtain any security in theirs."[395] It was the procurement of consent that would secure the balance of property. Likewise it was allegiance that would secure constitutional stability. Admission to the suffrage could not materially alter the balance of power in the state, whereas continued debarment threatened pernicious consequences. Not the least of these was the ease with which criminal behaviour among disaffected Catholics was liable to be misrepresented as treasonous in intention without the voices of the accused ever being heard. Burke's first-hand experience of the Whiteboy disturbances of the 1760s had confirmed his worst fears: Catholics "have no hold on the gentlemen who aspire to be popular representatives."[396] Not only were Catholics refused literal representation under the constitution, they were denied virtual representation as well.[397] As a consequence, in addition to religious persecution under the popery laws, they continued to be subject to civil persecution by their exclusion from the privileges of citizenship. The reasons for this predicament were historical in nature, extending back through the events of the sixteenth and seventeenth centuries.

According to Burke's analysis, the constitution of Ireland had been formed by a process encompassing the Norman Conquest and extending to Catholic defeat in the Williamite wars. In pre-Tudor Ireland, the failure to amalgamate the Pale, the marches and the native population prevented the incorporation of Irish society into the system of English property and law. This failure determined English policy from the middle of the sixteenth century: on the testimony of Patrick Finglas, Edmund Spenser and John Davies, the aim was to secure a "perfect" conquest.[398] The attempt to extend the jurisdiction of the Pale in the wake of the military contests of

[393] EB, *Letter to Richard Burke* (post February 1792), ibid., p. 652.

[394] Northamptonshire MS. A. XXVII.78.

[395] Northamptonshire MS. A. XXVII.80.

[396] EB, *Letter to Sir Hercules Langrishe* (1792), *W & S*, IX, p. 603. The Rightboy disturbances of the mid 1780s produced a similar response, about which Burke was again critical in 1792: see EB, *Letter to Richard Burke* (post February 1792), *W & S*, IX, p. 648. For the context, see J. S. Donnelly, "The Rightboy Movement, 1785–1788," *Studia Hibernica*, 17/18 (1977–78), pp. 120–202.

[397] EB, *Letter to Sir Hercules Langrishe* (1792), *W & S*, IX, pp. 601–2, 629. See, however, Cullen, "Catholics under the Penal Laws," p. 27 on the indirect political influence of intermediate Catholic landlords.

[398] EB, *Letter to Sir Hercules Langrishe* (1792), *W & S*, IX, p. 615. Burke is referring in this context to Patrick Finglas, *Breviat of the Getting of Ireland and of the Decaie of the Same* in Walter Harris, *Hibernica: Or, Some Antient Pieces Relating to Ireland* (Dublin: 1747); Edmund Spenser, *A View of the Present State of Ireland* (1598), ed. W. L. Renwick (Oxford: Oxford University Press, 1934, 1970); and John Davies, *Discoverie of the True Cause why Ireland was never Entirely Subdued nor Brought under Obedience of the Crowne of England, untill the Beginning of His Majesties Happie Raigne* (London, 1612).

the Elizabethan period was accompanied by colonial settlement in the north. This set the pattern for future conflict: military subjugation was followed by plantation. The strategy was pursued with particular vigour during the upheavals of the seventeenth century: the Cromwellian settlement after 1641 and the final reduction of the Irish in 1691 involved extensive expropriation.[399] Burke's objection was not to the facts of war and conquest, but to the policy that attended the achievement of peace. The spirit of conquest persisted after the victory of arms in defiance of all principles of jurisprudence. Only pacification could justify a process of usurpation. The blending of previously hostile populations indicated the passage from belligerence to a civil condition.[400] With the introduction of penal statutes against Catholics in the wake of the Williamite victory of 1688–91, successful military extirpation was consolidated by political means. The popery laws were instruments of subjugation masquerading as tokens of rehabilitation. They were "the effects of national hatred and scorn towards a conquered people."[401]

The resistance to franchise reform on the part of the Protestant establishment was the final instalment of this policy of acrimony. It pitted the "Protestant" interest against its imagined assailants without bothering to define the content of the dominant creed.[402] This pointed, in effect, to an epochal reversal whereby the interests of religion were confused with those of power. Such a project inverted the priorities of enlightenment. These had been to gain for religion the protection of civil society without confusing the dictates of conscience with the ambitions of political power. On Burke's understanding, under the circumstances that prevailed in the British and Irish kingdoms, this delicate balance could only be preserved under a regime in which a religious establishment was combined with toleration in matters of faith together with the civil freedom of all denominations. In the face of this requirement, on which the constitutional harmony of Britain and Ireland depended, the apologists for "Protestant Ascendancy" represented a double anachronism. The achievement of an enlightened political culture relied on a practical reconciliation between opinions and interests.[403] In the seventeenth century, opinion had been dominated by theological commitments that sought to prevail over the management of interests in the political sphere. The result was religious and political commotion leading to civil war. The proscriptions enforced by the Irish constitution were a relic of that era. However, viewed sceptically, this residue of theology was in reality a charade: the Protestant ascendancy prized its "interests" over its "opinions," meaning its object was political mastery rather than the security of its doctrines.[404] To maintain the charade, it was necessary to present the Church as falling into danger, thus pretending

[399] EB, *Letter to Sir Hercules Langrishe* (1792), *W & S*, IX, p. 616.

[400] Ibid., p. 614.

[401] Ibid., p. 616.

[402] Ibid., pp. 604–13.

[403] Ibid., p. 647.

[404] Ibid.

that Protestant theology was under assault from hostile forces.[405] The truth was, however, that any crusade that might be launched by antagonistic theological tenets was firmly a phenomenon of the past. The abiding danger to civil society stemmed not from the ambitions of an adverse religion, but from the claims of inimical political ideas.

This was the constant refrain of Burke's commentary on Ireland in the 1790s: the Revolution in France had changed the game of politics, inaugurating a new menace. This spelled peril not to some particular establishment alone, but to religious and political establishments altogether. The Revolution had transformed the world of opinion, spreading like a religion but in opposition to religion: "It is this new fanatical Religion, now in the heat of its first ferment, of the Rights of Man, which rejects all Establishments, all discipline, all Ecclesiastical, and in truth all Civil order, which will triumph, and which will lay prostrate your Church."[406] The prospect of sedition in Ireland was real, but its source was not the pronouncements issuing from the Papal See. Instead, the risk was that if Catholic grievances were not relieved, the population would be driven into a subversive confederation.[407] The United Irishmen represented the most immediate threat, with key members having defected from the Whig clubs.[408] The best way to disarm them was to seduce the Catholic masses from all support for their enterprise. So far, the coalition between Catholics and dissenters was rudimentary and marginal: "the greater, as well as the sounder part of our excluded countrymen, have not adopted the wild ideas, and wilder engagements, which have been held out to them."[409] The Catholic Committee was advancing its cause by means of deferential petitions rather than associating in a show of strength.[410]

[405] Alarm about the fate of the Church of Ireland, as Burke may have known, had been publicised above all by Richard Woodward, bishop of Cloyne, from 1787, in response to the current campaign against tithes. See Jacqueline R. Hill, "Popery and Protestantism, Civil and Religious Liberty: The Disputed Lessons of Irish History1690–1812," *Past and Present*, 118 (February 1988), pp. 96–129, at pp. 123–24.

[406] EB, *Letter to Sir Hercules Langrishe* (1792), *W & S*, IX, p. 647.

[407] EB, *Letter to Sir Hercules Langrishe* (1792), ibid., p. 603.

[408] Ibid., p. 625. Burke mentioned James Napper Tandy and Simon Butler in particular. On relations between Whiggism and the United Irish creed, see S. J. Connolly, *Divided Kingdom: Ireland, 1630–1800* (Oxford: Oxford University Press, 2008), pp. 434–49.

[409] EB, *Letter to Sir Hercules Langrishe* (1792), *W & S*, IX, p. 625. John Keogh, however, was already a member of the United Irishmen.

[410] Ibid.: the intention here was to contrast the Catholic Committee with the activities of Theobald McKenna's Catholic Society of Dublin, established in the summer of 1791. The Society published an appeal in the form of Anon., *Declaration of the Catholic Society of Dublin* (Dublin: 1791). Westmorland blamed this "mischievous" Declaration for arousing Protestant opposition to concessions: see Westmorland to Dundas, 28 November 1791, National Library of Ireland, MS. 394, fol. 57. For context, see Stephen Small, *Political Thought in Ireland, 1776–1798* (Oxford: Oxford University Press, 2002); Tadhg O'Sullivan, "Between Toleration and Preservation: The Popery Laws and Irish Anglicanism, 1782–1808," *Eighteenth-Century Ireland*, special issue no. 1, ed. John Bergin et al., (2011), pp. 249–74.

The real danger to constitutional progress lay, as Richard Burke advised Dundas on 12 January 1792, in "a junction between the Catholics and the Dissenters."[411]

Dundas responded to Burke's son eight days later. He did not appreciate the persistent tone of menace in Richard's letters, intimating an inevitable resort to militancy among Catholics if the appropriate concessions were not granted. Dundas made plain that if "the Catholicks should chuse to have recourse to violence of any kind they do it at their own Peril."[412] Burke himself had earlier clarified the position. There was no question of endorsing unconstitutional methods: "To warn, is not to menace."[413] Richard returned to London in early April 1792. Langrishe's Bill appeared to Burke to be both "mischievous and insolent."[414] Its content, together with the ungracious treatment of the Catholic petition, had only served to aggravate opinion on the Committee.[415] In the face of disappointment, Burke counselled moderation and patience: the Catholics "should consider themselves but in the *beginning* of a great work."[416] They should try to make sense of the attitudes of their opponents and begin the work of neutralising "the acid of old sour prejudices."[417] Even so, while promoting the wisdom of such *politique* sentiments, Burke also admitted to his share of frustration: "I can never persuade myself, that any thing in our thirty nine articles, which differs from their articles, is worth making three millions of people Slaves."[418] Burke considered the doctrine of Protestant ascendancy to be a subversion of the Christian principle of toleration. It was, indeed, a species of "Mahometanism," prone to persecution on account of erecting power into the secular tribunal of conscience.[419]

The day after Langrishe had presented his Bill before the Irish Commons, Burke observed how much the policy of Dublin Castle diverged from the cast of British affairs since the accession of George III.[420] In Ireland, by comparison with Britain, a mock zeal pervaded fidelity to the established Church. For Burke, there was something suspicious about baring one's conscience as a token of pride. Nonetheless, he estimated his commitment to the security of Anglicanism above that of the stalwarts of Protestant ascendancy in Ireland. The Anglican Communion was a pillar of the British constitution. It bound the state to religion as a source of moral duty, establishing a national creed without coercing freedom of conscience. At the same time, it was a great solvent in fixing the relationship between Britain and Ireland: it

[411] *Corr.*, VII, p. 25.

[412] Ibid., p. 33.

[413] EB, *Letter to Sir Hercules Langrishe* (1792), *W & S*, IX, p. 630.

[414] EB to Richard Burke Jr., 29 February 1792, *Corr.*, VII, p. 83.

[415] Richard Burke Jr. to EB, c. 1 March 1792, ibid., p. 88.

[416] EB to Richard Burke Jr., 19 February 1792, ibid., pp. 65–66.

[417] Ibid.

[418] EB to Richard Burke Jr., 23 March 1792, ibid., p. 118.

[419] Ibid.

[420] EB to Richard Burke Jr., 26 January 1792, ibid., p. 40. He was thinking above all of the attitudes of the Lord Chancellor, John Fitzgibbon, the head of the Revenue department, John Beresford, and the Speaker, John Foster.

kept "these two Islands, in their present critical independence of Constitution, in a close connexion of *opinion and affection*."[421] The irony was that the Protestant establishment in Ireland was a prime beneficiary of that connection. Its members were dependent on British power for their survival. Given that dependence, they would ultimately bend to the will of the metropolis. What disturbed Burke was that by then concessions would have been extorted rather than bestowed. In the current state of Europe, with Jacobinism maintaining its dominance in France, such niggardliness from government would prove a strategic error: "it is of infinite Moment, that matters of Grace should emanate from the old sovereign authority."[422] The opportunity for munificence had now passed, but France was still in disarray, and Ireland had not been placated.

14.7 France and Europe

"I have, from the very first," Burke commented to Dundas in the autumn of 1791, "attended with more care than is common [to] the effects of this French malady on the minds of men in England and Ireland."[423] Burke's preoccupation with the dissemination of Revolutionary ideas in Britain and Ireland developed in the context of a deepening concern with the likely impact of affairs in France on the balance of power in Europe. He was by now utterly convinced of the need to challenge the new regime militarily, and he cast about for means to justify a resort to intervention. Over the past year, he had despaired of France supplying material for counter-revolution itself. In fact, little could be securely predicted about the probable course of domestic events: "The people of that Country are ill of so anomalous, and in every respect, so new a distemper, that no one can possibly prognosticate any thing concerning the Crisis or its indications of cure."[424] Under these circumstances, crude and desperate enterprises, such as the abortive *journée des poignards* of 8 February 1791, were to be discouraged.[425] Any engagement needed a plausible chance of success. Burke was adamant that this presupposed the involvement of European sovereigns, preferably allied with a determined British power.[426] The legitimacy of such an expedient could be defended on at least three grounds. First, as Burke emphasised in the *Appeal from the New to the Old Whigs*, France no longer existed as a genuinely corporate "people."

[421] EB, *Letter to Richard Burke* (post February 1792), *W & S*, IX, p. 649.

[422] EB to Richard Burke Jr., 26 January 1792, ibid., p. 40.

[423] EB to Henry Dundas, 30 September 1791, *Corr.*, VI, p. 419.

[424] EB to John Trevor, January 1791, ibid., p. 217.

[425] EB to the Abbé Honoré-Charles-Ignace Foullon, 1 June 1791, ibid., pp. 263–4.

[426] For discussion of Burke on intervention, see Jennifer M. Welsh, *Edmund Burke and International Relations* (Basingstoke: Palgrave: 1995); Iain Hampsher-Monk, "Edmund Burke's Changing Justification for Intervention," *Historical Journal*, 48:1 (March 2005), pp. 65–100; Brendan Simms, "'A False Principle in the Law of Nations': Burke, State, Sovereignty, [German] Liberty, and Intervention in the Age of Westphalia" in Brendan Simms and D.J.B. Trim eds., *Humanitarian Intervention: A History* (Cambridge: Cambridge University Press, 2011).

Second, despite its condition of virtual anarchy, the country could still be said to be "divided" against itself. As Burke underlined as early as August 1791, even the "very republican Writer Vattell" endorsed the right of neighbouring powers to take sides in a civil war under the "Law of Nations."[427] In a policy document composed in December 1791 and intended for circulation in government circles, the *Thoughts on French Affairs*, Burke returned to the right of intervention "in the case of a divided kingdom."[428] He also added a final ground on which recourse to war could be justified: the manifest incompetence of an imprisoned king.[429]

Burke's rising alarm about the disposition and influence of France took place against the backdrop of a British commitment to neutrality. In late August 1789, William Eden, then ambassador in Paris, informed Pitt that the "anarchy" of France was virtually "complete."[430] Nonetheless, the British ministry avoided taking an explicit stand on the progress of the Revolution. There had been anxiety about the possibility of France intervening to assist the Dutch patriot party in 1787, and British wariness about French intentions emerged again after the revolt in the Austrian Netherlands against Emperor Joseph II in July 1789. Even so, in his public statements, Pitt emphasised the absence of any immediate threat from France.[431] When, in December 1789, the Comte d'Artois sought British support for restoring the French monarchy to its full powers, Pitt was inclined to support existing arrangements across the Channel.[432] He continued to stand aloof for the next two years. Throughout the summer of 1791, the courts of Europe constantly sought a British statement of principle. However, developments on the continent were allowed to proceed without any commitment from the ministry. The Vienna Convention of 25 July laid the foundations for a new Austro-Prussian alliance. The Declaration of Pillnitz followed on 27 August, establishing a pact against the doctrines of the Revolution. Yet Britain's refusal either to intervene or to lend assistance to a European campaign persisted until 1792. In February of that year, Pitt proposed a reduction in the subsidy to the armed forces and looked forward to a period of enduring peace.[433]

By comparison, Burke had continued to urge outside interference through the summer of 1791. Optimistically, even before the Declaration of Pillnitz, Richard

[427] EB to Richard Burke Jr., 5 August 1791, *Corr.*, VI, p. 317. Hampsher-Monk, "Burke's Changing Justification for Intervention," claims that Burke abandoned Vattel as an authority after the advent of war against France. On this, see also Iain Hampsher-Monk, "Burke's Counter-Revolutionary Writings" in David Dwan and Christopher J. Insole eds., *The Cambridge Companion to Edmund Burke* (Cambridge: Cambridge University Press, 2012), pp. 216–17. However, Burke was still invoking Vattel in the summer of 1793: see EB, Speech on Fox's Motion for Peace with France, 17 June 1793, *Parliamentary History*, XXX, col. 1012.

[428] EB, *Thoughts of French Affairs* (December 1791), *W & S*, VIII, p. 340.

[429] Ibid.

[430] Black, *British Foreign Policy*, p. 343.

[431] Ehrman, *Pitt the Younger*, II, p. 47.

[432] Jennifer Mori, *William Pitt and the French Revolution, 1785–1795* (Edinburgh: Keele University Press, 1997), p. 69.

[433] *Parliamentary History*, XXIX, col. 826.

Burke Jr. wrote to assure the king of France that external assistance "*is coming*."[434] Meanwhile, Lally-Tollendal was despairing in an open letter to Burke about the prospect of "l'intervention des princes étrangers pout dévaster et asservir la France."[435] That prospect receded with Louis XVI's acceptance of the new French constitution on 13 September 1791.[436] The Austrians now retreated from the idea of action against France even if the Prussians, with whom they remained allied, were more disposed to intervene. In general terms, the Declaration of Pillnitz was more a gesture than a statement of purpose: without British support, Leopold II was opposed to counter-revolutionary measures.[437] For its part, as Burke observed, Britain continued to preserve a state of "ambiguous neutrality," attending to the machinations of Russia and the Prussians instead of what ought to be the priority of all states: the restoration of the monarchy of France.[438] At this time, it seemed clear that Frederick William II of Prussia, eager to make his mark in European affairs, favoured a forward policy in regard to France, but he would have to concert with the Habsburg crown if he was to be able to act at all. Sympathy for the French royal family together with appeals from the émigré princes were not without an effect on European sovereigns, but only a concrete change of circumstances would trigger an armed response.

At this time, Burke was enjoying cordial relations with leading members of the ministry. He dined with Dundas at Wimbledon on 19 August, and with Charles Jenkinson, now Lord Hawkesbury, four days later.[439] Dundas even chose to compliment the argument of the *Appeal*.[440] At a dinner with Pitt, Grenville and Addington in September, it became clear to Burke that the government remained wedded to the "Idea of neutrality."[441] Pitt nonetheless tried to reassure Burke: "we shall go on as we are, until the day of judgement."[442] Burke, however, was unconvinced. The "old order of Europe" was currently on trial: the delicate reconciliation between monarchies and republics which secured the equilibrium of the continent was being exploded in France, and, sooner or later, Britain would have to act if the whole edifice was not to be erased.[443] The Treaty of Sistova had just brought the Habsburg–Ottoman conflict to an end, Poland was momentarily pacified, the Dutch revolt had subsided,

[434] Richard Burke Jr. to the King of France, 6 August 1791, *Corr.*, VI, p. 319.

[435] Thomas Arthur Comte de Lally-Tollendal, *Post-scriptum d'une lettre de M. le Comte de Lally-Tollendal à M. Burcke* (N.P.: 1791).

[436] Michel Vovelle, *The Fall of the French Monarchy, 1787–1792* (Cambridge: Cambridge University Press, 1984), p. 143.

[437] T.W.C. Blanning, *The Origins of the French Revolutionary Wars* (London: Longman, 1986), pp. 87–89.

[438] EB to Richard Burke Jr., 18 August 1791, *Corr.*, VI, p. 357.

[439] EB to Richard Burke Jr., 25 August 1791, ibid., p. 367; EB to Richard Burke Jr., 1 September 1791, ibid., pp. 376–77.

[440] Henry Dundas to EB, 12 August 1791, WWM BkP 1:2468.

[441] EB to Richard Burke Jr., 26 September 1791, *Corr.*, VI, p. 410.

[442] *The Life and Correspondence of the Right Hon. Henry Addington, First Viscount Sidmouth* (London: 1847), 2 vols., I, p. 72.

[443] EB to Lord Grenville, 21 September 1791, *Corr.*, VI, p. 407.

and the Austrian Netherlands were independent. Above all, the Prussians and the Emperor were beginning to concert. Such a favourable moment for building an alliance against France was unlikely ever to emerge again.[444] Did the British government believe that the character of the Revolution was likely to change? If not, they would have to consider its medium-term significance for Britain's interest. Burke believed that the ministry was naïvely trusting in the immunity of its own affairs from the contagion of French ideas.[445] He now determined to try to disabuse them. "Every now and then I seemed to make an impression on them," Burke reported of a meeting in September.[446] He now embarked upon his *Thoughts on French Affairs*, hoping to capitalise on his access to ministerial favour.[447]

The *Thoughts* endeavoured to set out the gravity of the problem facing contemporary international affairs. Hitherto, European politics had been a child of the Reformation. That comprehensive revolution in doctrine had determined the relationship between domestic and foreign affairs among all the states of Europe since the sixteenth century. National interests were not simply a function of religious affiliations, but they were nonetheless permanently qualified by them. The crucial point was that sectarian denominations enjoyed a cosmopolitan significance: loyalty to particular rituals and tenets extended beyond the bounds of purely domestic allegiance. As a result, zealots in each state "were more affectionately attached to those of their own doctrinal interest in some other country than to their fellow citizens."[448] This was the predicament of modern party. Hume had argued that it was the emergence of "parties from principle" that served to distinguish the character of modern politics: "Parties from principle, especially abstract speculative principle, are known only to modern times."[449] Their emergence, he went on, was among the most extraordinary occurrences in the history of politics. Burke was concerned with two developments that followed on from their emergence: first, the extent to which they influenced the course of international politics; and, second, the way in which the same speculative zeal had been transferred from religious doctrines to systems of politics. In other words, after 1789, political allegiance became a doctrinal issue that would divide the affairs of Europe into rival factions. The divisiveness of political principles was not unprecedented: the competition between democratic and aristocratic ideologies, animated by the ancient struggle between Athens and Sparta, indicated that the problem had its source in "human nature."[450] It was not religious zeal that proved contentious, but zeal itself. And now, for the first time in modern history, a "spirit

[444] EB to Henry Dundas, 30 September 1791, ibid., p. 422.

[445] EB to Richard Burke Jr., 26 September 1791, ibid., p. 411.

[446] Ibid., p. 412.

[447] He seems to have been planning it from late September: see EB to Lord Grenville, 21 September 1791, ibid., p. 408.

[448] EB, *Thoughts on French Affairs* (1791), *W & S*, VIII, p. 342.

[449] David Hume, "Of Parties in General" (1741) in idem, *Essays Moral, Political, and Literary*, ed. Eugene F. Miller (Indianapolis, IN: Liberty Fund, 1985, 1987), p. 60.

[450] EB, *Thoughts on French Affairs* (1791), *W & S*, VIII, p. 342.

of general political faction" had surfaced that was distinct from religious sectarianism but that nonetheless formed partisans within rival jurisdictions.[451] This was an epochal shift in the nature of reason of state that would require a drastic reassessment of international policy.

From now on, it could be expected that European wars would be contests between principles as much as they would be driven by the struggle of interests.[452] Principles formed opinions that shaped the perception of interests. The stability of interests would thus be shaken by the vagaries of opinions that, *in extremis*, would determine the very content of interests.[453] French Revolutionary principles were reducible to the idea of the sovereignty of a mathematical majority, entitled not merely to make decisions but to overturn every settlement at will. It was a doctrine, in short, of permanent revolution that militated against lasting forms of government and an effective division of political labour. It uprooted establishments by attacking the solidity of landed interests, enfranchising money against territory in the name of natural equality. Although France stood at the head of this ideological faction, the system of old Europe "has no head."[454] This left the passive partisans of the old order in a peculiarly exposed position since the French had inspired foreign acolytes in other countries of Europe. Britain, Burke insisted, was conspicuous amongst them: discontent was apparent among the habitually disaffected, but also among infidels, deists and socinians. Burke's attention was above all focused on dissenters, the "Phalanx of a Party," as he put it to Dundas, nine tenths of whom were allegedly disposed to conspire against the constitution.[455] Together with resurgent republicans, whose antiquated politics had been dormant since the civil war, they were gaining ground by dissimulation and fraud.[456] They would be abetted, Burke now anticipated, by a cabal of British nabobs, resentful of their status on the basis of their wealth.[457]

Pitt attributed domestic security to two facets of the current situation: first, to British internal tranquillity, and second to the prospect of a French bankruptcy. Burke took both parts of this assessment to be based on complacency. The impression of enduring tranquillity was an illusion. It was based on the assumption that

[451] Ibid.

[452] These two governing maxims were subsequently artificially distinguished by the historiography of the French Revolution, characterising the wars that emerged in its wake as, on the one side, *Prinzipienkriege* (wars of principle) and, on the other, wars of policy. For discussion, see Blanning, *Origins of the Revolutionary Wars*, pp. 70ff.; Philip Schofield, "British Politics and French Arms: The Ideological War of 1793–1795," *History*, 77:250 (June 1992), pp. 183–201. See also J. Holland Rose, "The Struggle with Revolutionary France, 1792–1802" in A. W. Ward and G. P. Gooch eds., *The Cambridge History of British Foreign Policy, 1783–1919* (Cambridge: Cambridge University Press, 1922), 3 vols., I, pp. 216–308; M. Duffy, "British Policy in the War against Revolutionary France" in Colin Jones ed., *Britain and Revolutionary France: Conflict, Subversion and Propaganda* (Exeter: University of Exeter Publications, 1993).

[453] EB, *Thoughts on French Affairs* (1791), *W & S*, VIII, p. 342.

[454] Ibid., p. 345.

[455] EB to Henry Dundas, 30 September 1791, *Corr.*, VI., p. 419.

[456] Ibid., p. 420.

[457] EB, *Thoughts on French Affairs* (1791), *W & S*, VIII, p. 345.

British society promised mobility whereas exclusivism in France upset the ambition of rising classes. It was true, Burke still felt, that the spirit of exclusion among the French nobility proved aggravating to the aspiring, but it was also true that money, merchants and men of letters were conspicuously honoured in France.[458] It was an aspect of British society, just as it had been of French, that the envy of striving wealth and talent might rebel against a system of honours adapted to a monarchy and a landed gentry under the law of primogeniture. Under this circumstance, durable wealth in property was held in greater respect than fugitive and seemingly precarious achievements. In this, policy simply followed manners. It was in no sense preordained that rising ambition would not revolt, as it had done in France, against settled opinions governing public esteem.[459] The danger in Britain was therefore also that a grasping drive towards equalisation would undermine the conditions of political society. The Habsburg Emperor's secret regard for the campaign against aristocracy and clericalism in France was of a piece with the British indulgence of its indefinite continuance.[460] What observers missed, Burke believed, was that the attack on nobility entailed an attack on monarchy, and that both facilitated a deeper assault on property, religion and government.[461] Incipient fury against privilege in Britain would add to the moving cascade.

Burke's judgment about the prospects for European security was based on this fundamental sense that an epochal shift in the framework of politics had irreversibly occurred. A new, imperious dogma was on the move that would sweep all opposition before it unless it was openly resisted by force of arms. Even bankruptcy was powerless to halt its progress, as Burke underlined to Pitt the previous autumn.[462] He emphasised the point once more in *Thoughts on French Affairs*: in reality, the French state was already bankrupt, having forced a paper currency on its creditors, but this had not disabled it from pursuing its course energetically.[463] In the face of this resilience, Burke's aim was to demonstrate the profoundly adverse effects that were certain to proceed from France's effective departure from the Westphalian system of politics signalled by its renunciation of the "feudal" past. The precondition for European harmony was the tranquillity of Germany, dominated by two mutually checking powers. Should Prussia and Austria shift from the current policy of impeding the aggrandisement of its rival, the consequences for peace would be catastrophic:

[458] Ibid., pp. 346–47.

[459] Ibid., p. 347.

[460] For Leopold II's views, see Adam Wandruszka, *Leopold II: Erzherzog von Österreich, Großherzog von Toskana, König von Ungarn und Böhmen, Römishcer Kaiser* (Vienna and Munich: Herold, 1963–65), 2 vols., II, pp. 353–5. Burke recognised the problem, blaming his ministers in equal measure: see EB, *Thoughts on French Affairs* (1791), *W & S*, VIII, pp. 375–77. On Kaunitz and Cobenzl as supporters of the "french system," see EB to Henry Dundas, 23 September 1791, *Corr.*, VI, p. 409.

[461] EB to Richard Burke Jr., 26 September 1791, *Corr.*, VI, p. 413.

[462] Ibid., pp. 411–12.

[463] EB, *Thoughts on French Affairs* (1791), *W & S*, VIII, pp. 362–3.

"A great revolution is preparing in Germany; and a revolution, in my opinion, likely to be more decisive upon the general fate of nations than that of France itself."[464]

Burke was anticipating a revival of the destruction of the Thirty Years' War, fuelled by Revolutionary ideology. The key to this revolution was the dissemination of the principle of the *droits de l'homme* throughout the German territories together with France's abandonment of its traditional role of guarantor of restraint on the part of the leading princes of the Empire. Under the Treaty of Westphalia, the French were to insure the balance and independence of Germany, yet this compact had in effect become "an antiquated fable."[465] The Revolutionary principles of war and peace would in the long term involve a commitment either to the amicable communication of the rights of man or to their violent imposition on reluctant sovereigns. Either way, the role of France was no longer to safeguard the liberties of Europe, which were now construed as relics of the old tyranny: new rights were set to replace old wrongs. The acquisition of Alsace as well as Avignon and Comtat Venaissin exemplified the new dispensation: both were hailed by the National Assembly on the basis of plebiscitary right rather than under the terms of inter-state agreements or antecedent treaties.[466] For good measure, as Burke noted, the French also excavated an old *arrêt*, legitimising the accession of Avignon.[467] "It is known that they hold out from time to time the idea of uniting all other provinces of which Gaul was antiently composed," Burke remarked.[468] Yet the recourse to precedent merely illustrated Revolutionary hypocrisy. In the end, a new *esprit de conquête* would seize the initiative, licensed by plebiscitarian ideology.[469]

Armed with this insight, Burke proceeded to survey the general condition of Europe, noting the insurgent threat posed to established powers in Italy, Spain, Sweden, Russia, Poland and Holland.[470] Sedition could hope to prosper in each of these territories, but Switzerland, after Germany, presented the most pressing problem, partly because its cohesion was fundamentally precarious, but also because it was divided into aristocratic and democratic republics, each of them differently affected by developments in France.[471] However, the crisis was likely to begin along the western German frontier, in the Bishopric of Münster and the Ecclesiastical Electorates of Mainz, Trier and Cologne. It was in relation to these vulnerable principalities that Austria and Prussia were first likely to exercise their ambitions. Britain, depen-

[464] Ibid., p. 349.

[465] Ibid., p. 352.

[466] *Archives parlementaires*, XX, pp. 83–84 (28 October 1790); *Archives parlementaires*, XXX, pp. 631–32 (14 September 1791).

[467] Blanning, *Origins of the Revolutionary Wars*, p. 78.

[468] EB, *Thoughts on French Affairs* (1791), *W & S*, VIII, p. 353.

[469] A policy of conquest had been denounced in the National Assembly on 22 May 1790. See *Archives parlementaires*, XV, p. 662: "la nation française renonce à entreprendre aucune guerre dans la vue de faire des conquêtes." From Burke's perspective, all this could mean in practice was a rejection of "Feudal" conquest in favour of democratic usurpation.

[470] EB, *Thoughts on French Affairs* (1791), *W & S*, VIII, pp. 354–62.

[471] Ibid., p. 353.

dent on its marine, was of course powerless to stop them. However, internal dissent within the Ecclesiastical territories could be expected to be swift: attachment to the rights of man among sections of the newly subject populations would "preclude the two Sovereigns from the possibility of holding what they acquire."[472] This would be the beginning of the end of the Empire, and the start of a general conflagration in Europe. There was nothing in the culture or infrastructure of diplomacy to retard this progress, and the process would be abetted by the government of France. The Legislative Assembly succeeded the Constituent on 1 October 1791. The triumvirate of the Feuillants—Barnave, Duport and Lameth—were losing the Revolutionary initiative while seeking to ingratiate themselves into the counsels of the king.[473] With many of their number ineligible for the new Assembly, they intrigued to advance their cause with the ministry.[474] Burke disregarded their anxiety to distinguish themselves from their opponents, lumping them with the Fayettistes together with the Jacobins as the "Chiefs of the Regicide Faction."[475] The Feuillants were now keen to rally to the monarchy to stabilise what their members had originally disturbed, but they would only, on Burke's reckoning, "preserve as much of order as is necessary for the support of their own usurpations."[476]

While Burke understood the ministry to be in the hands of the Feuillants, he saw the Assembly as increasingly in the power of Brissot. In reality, only about 38 from among the 745 deputies in the Legislative Assembly were clearly associated with Brissot in the autumn of 1791.[477] Nonetheless, Burke took his rhetoric to exemplify the character of the new chamber. France, he later observed, "was distracted by a violent party."[478] He calculated that the Assembly was populated by around 400 lawyers, 60 peasants, 60 priests and 120 military men.[479] "The assembly has not fifty men in it," he believed, "who are possessed of an hundred pounds a year in any description of property whatsoever."[480] Deputies of substance were often in thrall to republican politics. Condorcet, he thought, had assumed the role of Brissot's chief supporter.[481] Both men had swung openly behind an explicitly republican agenda

[472] Ibid., p. 352.

[473] Georges Michon, *Essai sur l'histoire du parti Feuillant: Adrien Duport* (Paris: Payot, 1924), pp. 345–69; Ran Halévi, "Feuillants" in François Furet and Mona Ozouf eds., *A Critical Dictionary of the French Revolution* (Cambridge, MA: Harvard University Press, 1989). In the early days of the assembly, they still retained a significant following: around 250 deputies against the Jacobins' 136. See Vovelle, *Fall of the French Monarchy*, pp. 211–12.

[474] Without, as it happens, genuine success: see Max Lenz, "Marie Antoinette im Kampf mit der Revolution," *Preußischer Jahrbücher*, 78 (1894), p. 2, cited in Blanning, *Origins of the Revolutionary Wars*, p. 125 n.17.

[475] EB, *Thoughts on French Affairs* (1791), *W & S*, VIII, p. 378.

[476] Ibid., p. 379.

[477] M. J. Sydenham, *The Girondins* (London: Athlone Press, 1961), p. 99.

[478] *Star*, 1 May 1792.

[479] WWM BkP 10:23–24.

[480] EB to William Weddell, 31 January 1792, *Corr.*, VII, p. 61. The number was still lower in EB, Debate on Parliamentary Reform (20 April 1792), *Star*, 1 May 1792.

[481] EB, *Thoughts on French Affairs* (1791), *W & S*, VIII, p. 382.

after the failed flight to Varennes, and they now led a contingent of deputies seeking to extend the Revolution abroad.[482] Between October and December, Vergniaud, Isnard, Gaudet, Lasource and others, along with Brissot and Condorcet, agitated for war in the Assembly and the Jacobin club.[483] Conspiring with Clavière at Madame de Staël's salon, they strove to muster support for a revolutionary crusade.[484] On 20 October 1791, on a motion regarding the émigrés introduced by Condorcet, Brissot mounted the tribune "au milieu des applaudissements d'une partie de l'Assemblée."[485] He reminded his audience of France's renunciation of conquest, but then asserted that this was conditional upon reciprocal respect. In the absence of respect for a free constitution, a free people would display its vengeance: "la vengeance d'un peuple libre est lente, mais elle frappe sûrement."[486] Delacroix called for Brissot's speech to be printed and distributed to all members of the Assembly, and the proposal was virtually unanimously decreed.[487] Brissot's oration, Burke declared, was "full of unexampled insolence towards all the Sovereign States of Germany, if not of Europe."[488] As long as the rest of Europe remained on a defensive footing, Burke expected its message to percolate through the continent, spreading "by an internal corruption (a sort of dry rot)" that would wither established principles of allegiance.[489]

Burke's fear was that Brissot's principles would find an internationally receptive audience: European monarchs along with their ministries were increasingly disposed to French ideas, just as the diplomatic corp was generally partial to the rights of man.[490] All things considered, Burke believed that the power of France was now more "formidable" than at any previous period of its existence.[491] To impress the urgency of the situation on British ministers, he tried to spark their fear and apprehension. The effort, however, did not succeed, and the following February he was complaining of their distance and coldness.[492] All along, he realised, the risk had been that alarm might drive them deeper into neutrality out of anxiety that excessive precaution would exacerbate the problem. The most he could therefore hope for was to prevail upon their "enlightened foresight."[493] Beyond that, he had to resign his

[482] Leopold von Ranke, *Ursprung und Beginn der Revolutionskriege, 1791 und 1792* (Leipzig: 1875), pp. 177ff.; Heinrich von Sybel, *Geschichte der Revolutionszeit von 1789 bis 1795* (Dusseldorf: 1853–70), 4 vols., I, pp. 289ff.; H.-A. Goetz-Bernstein, *La diplomatie de la Gironde* (Paris: Hachette, 1912), pp. 29–35; Georges Michon, *Robespierre et la guerre révolutionnaire* (Paris: Marcel Rivière, 1937), ch. 2; Keith Michael Baker, "Condorcet" in Furet and Ozouf eds., *Critical Dictionary of the French Revolution*, p. 206.

[483] See, for example, Jacques-Pierre Brissot de Warville, *Discours sur la nécessité de déclarer la guerre aux princes allemands qui protègent les émigrés, prononcé, le 16 décembre, à la Société* (Paris: 1791).

[484] Sydenham, *Girondins*, pp. 101–3.

[485] *Archives parlementaire,* XXXIV, p. 309.

[486] Ibid., p. 316.

[487] Ibid., p. 317.

[488] EB, *Thoughts on French Affairs* (1791), *W & S*, VIII, pp. 381–82.

[489] Ibid., pp. 368–9.

[490] Ibid., pp. 371–72, 373–75.

[491] Ibid., p. 384.

[492] EB to Richard Burke Jr., 29 February 1792, *Corr.*, VII, p. 81.

[493] EB, *Thoughts on French Affairs* (1791), *W & S*, VIII, p. 385.

feelings to an unstoppable political fate. The *Thoughts on French Affairs* was intended by Burke to be his final intervention into policy debate on France.[494] It was written in a mood of cosmic surrender: "we must wait the good pleasure of a higher hand than ours," he confided to Fitzwilliam.[495] This was a lesson in resignation which Burke had learned late, he informed his son: "Non mihi res."[496] He accepted that true wisdom and the dictates of religion counselled resignation before the tide of events. Faced with the scale of the upheaval caused by France, Burke struggled to submit to his own teaching. He informed Fitzwilliam that his aim was to stand aloof from parliament, unless the constitution was threatened or the question of France was forced.[497] However, circumstances prevented him from lowering his sights. In February 1792, Paine published part II of the *Rights of Man*, explicitly advocating democratic revolution. Almost immediately it was denounced by Burke as an "infamous libel" on the constitution.[498]

14.8 The Progress of Dissent and Revolution

The occasion for this verdict was the notice brought forward in parliament by Charles Grey on 30 April 1792 of a motion to be introduced on the theme of parliamentary reform. Grey's plans were unspecific, yet the move was significant insofar as it constituted the first attempt at Commons reform since Flood's motion of 4 March 1790, which had been withdrawn in the face of a discouraging reception.[499] By now, the Sheffield Constitutional Society was circulating a cheap edition of Paine's new work; soon, a Manchester branch was commending it "to every Nation under Heaven," and corresponding with the Jacobin Club in Paris.[500] In January 1792, Thomas Hardy formed the London Corresponding Society, with a membership drawn largely from the artisanal classes.[501] On 20 March, Philip Francis was publicly endorsing the need for constitutional change.[502] Within a month, a group of Foxite supporters, including Sheridan, Grey, Francis, Thomas Erskine and Lord

[494] Ibid., p. 386.

[495] EB to Earl Fitzwilliam, 21 November 1791, *Corr.*, VI, p. 453.

[496] EB to Richard Burke Jr., 1 September 1791, ibid., p. 378: "it is not my fortune" (Lucan, *Pharsalia*, VII, line 264).

[497] EB to Earl Fitzwilliam, 21 November 1791, *Corr.*, VI, p. 452.

[498] EB, Speech on Parliamentary Reform (30 April 1792), *Gazetteer*, 1 May 1792.

[499] *Parliamentary History*, XXVIII, cols. 452–79.

[500] John Cannon, *Parliamentary Reform, 1640–1832* (Cambridge: Cambridge University Press, 1972), p. 121; G. S. Veitch, *The Genesis of Parliamentary Reform* (1913) (London: Constable, 1965), p. 201; Albert Goodwin, *The Friends of Liberty: The English Democratic Movement in the Age of the French Revolution* (London: Hutchinson, 1979), pp. 198ff.

[501] Thomas Hardy, "Letter to a Friend, Written in 1799" in idem, *Memoir of Thomas Hardy, Founder of, and Secretary to, the London Corresponding Society* (London: 1832), Appendix, pp. 98ff.; E. P. Thompson, *The Making of the English Working Class* (1963) (London: Victor Gollancz, 1968), ch. 5.

[502] Add. MS. 27814, fol. 32.

Lauderdale, had formed the Association of the Friends of the People to promote the cause of "moderate" reform.[503] Many of the Friends of the People would later repent of their folly.[504] Through March, April and May of 1792, the evidence was mounting that republican principles and levelling schemes were spreading through the manufacturing towns and cities under the influence of Paine. In the spring of 1791, the Society for Constitutional Information was reviving due to the success of part I of Paine's pamphlet, and commending the work in a public Declaration.[505] However, even before the Declaration appeared in print, Jeremiah Batley, who had drafted it, was disowning the ideas expressed in the *Rights of Man*.[506] Later Batley explained to Burke how soon afterwards he had quit the Society, being an admirer of the existing "mixed Government" of Britain.[507] By the spring of 1792, Burke's worry was that plans for temperate reform would be used to advance more extreme positions. It was by now clear that Paine's doctrines were finding eager audiences beyond Sheffield and Manchester in Wakefield and Leeds.[508] Christopher Wyvill was disturbed by the sheer speed of dissemination, which he had not reckoned on when writing his *Defence of Dr. Price* as a means of promoting judicious reform by constitutional means.[509] Nonetheless, he soon realised that "we are drawing near to a more serious crisis than we before experienced."[510]

To Burke, while there seemed to exist a "halcyon calm" on the surface of affairs, confusion was brimming underneath.[511] Division among opposition Whigs now began to emerge, although both sides were held together through the summer and into autumn. Fox admitted to being alarmed by the present state of France; on 7 March, he openly praised the British monarch in a debate in the Commons.[512] Burke construed the mood of restraint as an index of retreat.[513] In truth, however, Fox's aim was to placate Sheridan and Grey without repelling Portland and his supporters.[514] Fox was unhappy about the strategic impact of Grey's motion, although he voted in support of its introduction. However, Pitt was determined to criticise

[503] *Some Account of the Life and Opinions of Charles, Second Earl Grey* (London: 1861), p. 10. For aspects of the ideological development of the Society, see Iain Hampsher-Monk, "Civic Humanism and Parliamentary Reform: The Case of the Society of the Friends of the People," *Journal of British Studies*, 18:2 (Spring 1979), pp. 70–89.

[504] Herbert Butterfield, "Charles James Fox and the Whig Opposition in 1792," *Cambridge Historical Journal*, 9:3 (1949), pp. 203–330, at p. 304.

[505] Declaration Proposed to the Constitutional Society, 28 May 1791, in Wyvill, *Political Papers*, V, pp. iv–v.

[506] Jeremiah Batley to Christopher Wyvill, 14 April 1791, in ibid., pp. 3–7.

[507] Jeremiah Batley to EB, 8 April 1793, WWM BkP 1:2816.

[508] Christopher Wyvill to William Burgh, 16 May 1792, in Wyvill, *Political Papers*, V, p. 67.

[509] Christopher Wyvill, *A Defence of Dr. Price and the Reformers of England* (London: 1792); Christopher Wyvill to James Martin, 28 April 1792, Wyvill, *Political Papers*, V, p. 23.

[510] Christopher Wyvill to William Mason, 10 May 1792, ibid., p. 32.

[511] EB to the Rev. Robert Dodge, 29 February 1792, *Corr.*, VII, p. 86.

[512] O'Gorman, *Whig Party*, p. 80.

[513] EB to the Rev. Robert Dodge, 29 February 1792, *Corr.*, VII, p. 85.

[514] Mitchell, *Charles James Fox*, p. 173.

the timing of the proposal, and the notice was easily defeated. In the midst of his contribution, Fox raised the subject of Paine's new pamphlet, describing it as a pitch for "an entire[ly] new constitution."[515] In fact he had not read Paine's new production, though from what he had heard he could not approve its contents. He went on to add that Burke's *Reflections* did not give him any more pleasure, though both works had at least contributed to debate.[516] In replying, Burke concentrated on the dynamics of reform. He presented himself as accepting that Grey's intentions were benign; so too, he claimed, were the aims of the Friends of the People. However, the same could not be said of the societies and clubs publicly extolling the virtues of Paine's new book.[517] Which cause would Grey be serving in tampering with the constitution, that of British Jacobins or that of the Friends of the People? Reformers had to consider the character of fellow travellers, lest the enthusiasm of subversives destroy the prospects for moderation. In this context, Burke recalled the fate of John Hampden after 1642: "Hamden, who took up arms against the abuses of Government, would never have been impelled to an exterminatory war against the constitution."[518] As this case showed, Whig resistance was easily hijacked by wanton incendiaries. For this reason, as all "history and experience" demonstrated, those who initiated revolutions were rarely if ever in a position to bring them to a conclusion.

It was as a subversive political combination that Burke treated the 2,000 signatories of a Unitarian petition presented to parliament that spring.[519] On 11 May 1792, Fox moved for a committee of the whole House to consider a motion for repealing legislation introduced under the 1698 Blasphemy Act and clause 17 of the 1689 Toleration Act as it specifically affected arian and socinian heresy.[520] Given the current atmosphere in the Commons, Fox's presentation of the case for toleration in terms of "the fundamental, unalienable rights of man" may have seemed a provocation to its opponents.[521] By the late eighteenth century, socinianism had risen to a powerful position within the Unitarian community. At the same time, with the decline of deism after the 1750s, the rejection of the doctrine of the trinity, particularly the denial of the pre-existence and atonement of Christ, represented the extreme of theological dissent.[522] Above all, Priestley's materialist and necessitarian philosophy seemed to many barely compatible with Christian doctrine. Nonetheless, Burke followed Fox in setting to one side the Christological significance of Unitarian dissent,

515 *Gazetteer*, 1 May 1792.

516 *Diary*, 2 May 1792. On 11 May 1792 he added that the *Reflections* was "a libel on every free constitution in the world": see *Parliamentary History*, XXIX, col. 1402.

517 *Star*, 1 May 1792.

518 *Gazetteer*, 1 May 1792.

519 *Morning Chronicle*, 9 March 1792; G. M. Ditchfield, "Public and Parliamentary Support for the Unitarian Petition of 1792," *Enlightenment and Dissent*, 12 (1993), pp. 24–48.

520 *CJ*, XLVII, pp. 787–9.

521 *Parliamentary History*, XXIX, col. 1371.

522 G. M. Ditchfield, "Anti-Trinitarianism and Toleration in Late Eighteenth-Century British Politics: The Unitarian Petition of 1792," *Journal of Ecclesiastical History*, 42:1 (January 1991), pp. 39–67, at p. 62.

focusing instead on its political intentions. Burke had been collecting the public correspondence of the Revolution Society since 1789, including a message from Stanhope in 1792 expressing satisfaction with the French ambition to "introduce a general reformation in the governments of Europe."[523] At the same time, he had been following the sermons and pronouncements of Priestley, by now a leader of the Unitarian movement.[524] In a *Discourse* delivered in April 1791, Priestley had inveighed against the "unnatural" authority of the Church of England, and proceeded to detect in the "*signs of the times*" confirmation of supposed scriptural prophecies of "great revolutions" to come.[525] Burke annotated his copy of Priestley's sermon extensively, noting its reference to the "*idolatrous worship of Christ*."[526] He also noted its interest in "abolishing" distinctions that were the "offspring of a barbarous age."[527] Against this background, when he rose to speak on the Unitarian petition on 11 May 1792, he was happy to strip the question of its "theological vestment" and proceed to investigate the issue in terms of "policy and prudence."[528]

Being in a position to enumerate examples of Priestley's habit of blending politics and religion, Burke must have been surprised to hear that Fox could find "nothing of politics" in his religious writings, and to hear that his "political works seemed free from religion."[529] Throughout his notes for his speech on the Unitarian petition, Burke returned to the doctrines of Priestley and Price as extreme yet typical expressions of the views of advanced dissent.[530] At one point, in fact, he singled out Priestley's 1787 *Letter to William Pitt* as an exemplary attack on the idea of a Christian establishment.[531] In the *Letter*, Priestley construed toleration as coterminous with disestablishment, seeking to found all churches on voluntary allegiance.[532] From Priestley's perspective, this would enable dissenters to "impugn" the doctrine of the trinity, and more generally to found religion on freedom of discussion.[533] "What we are aiming at," he wrote, "is to enlighten the minds of the people."[534] The process of enlightenment, he went on, would in time produce "a rational and permanent uniformity."[535] Burke similarly embraced the goal of enlightenment, yet he

[523] Northamptonshire MS. A. VII.21.

[524] Burke refers to him as its "patriarch" in *Parliamentary History*, XXIX, col. 1384.

[525] Joseph Priestley, *The Proper Objects of Education in the Present State of the World, Represented in a Discourse, Delivered on . . . 27th of April 1791 . . . in the Old Jewry* (London: 1791), pp. 9, 14.

[526] Northamptonshire MS. A. XIV.64.

[527] Ibid.

[528] *Parliamentary History*, XXIX, col. 1382.

[529] Ibid., col. 1402.

[530] See, for example, Northamptonshire MS. A. XXVII.98. Burke does not distinguish Price's arianism from Priestley's socinian doctrines.

[531] Northamptonshire MS. A. XXVII.96.

[532] Joseph Priestley, *A Letter to the Right Honourable William Pitt . . . on the Subject of Toleration and Church Establishments* (London: 2nd ed., 1787), pp. 2, 17.

[533] Ibid., pp. 24, 25.

[534] Ibid., p. 22.

[535] Ibid. p. 30.

wondered how it could be best achieved. The history of Europe suggested that the expectation of purely rational agreement on doctrinal and ceremonial matters was deluded. Disputes in religion were more likely to beget fury and fanaticism, leading to the derangement of both church and state.[536] Violent diversity could only be composed by acts of authority, above all where authority could command the most general assent. This implied the establishment of an authority to teach, based around a minimum of shared beliefs. In the case of the Church of England, the framework of ecclesiastical authority was well fitted to the form of state. It also acted as a "barrier" against fanaticism and infidelity.[537] An establishment of the kind was perfectly compatible with free inquiry, and indeed with complete liberty of conscience. The only issue was the question of the "quantum of Liberty" to be conceded to corporate bodies actively dissenting from the constitution in church and state.[538]

As Burke saw matters, the freedom of corporate religious bodies should be regulated in the same way that the liberty of the subject should be restrained: liberty was conditional on the absence of an intention to harm. The profession of belief might be assumed to be generally harmless, except where it sought to trespass on the beliefs and institutions of others. "I know they say, that Religion is the Empire of God," Burke observed.[539] This was true, he conceded, where only conscientious relations between man and God were at issue. In the case of Unitarianism in the 1790s, it could not be said that it presented a purely "passive . . . dissent on account of an overscrupulous habit of mind."[540] On the basis of their own statements, and the actions proceeding from these statements, it was clear that the Unitarian petitioners were not merely a theological sect: "they do not aim at the quiet enjoyment of their own Liberty", but were instead associated "for the express purpose of *Proselytism*."[541] Proselytism, in this case, meant collecting a sufficient following to overturn the established Church "by *force & violence*."[542] This design was concurrent with the aim of subverting the state by the dissemination of French principles of government. Religion had to be viewed as a spiritual project, but it operated in a social and political environment. Founded on opinion, it was animated by passion, and it assembled in congregations. When a congregation sought to dismantle religious or political establishments, it became by that very fact a faction in the state, giving rise to a competition between rival powers.[543] The danger posed by this competition was a matter for prudential judgment, yet where the object under assault was of surpassing value,

[536] Northamptonshire MS. A. XXVII.98.

[537] Northamptonshire MS. A. XXVII.100; Northamptonshire MS. A. XXVII.103a.

[538] Northamptonshire MS. A. XXVII.94.

[539] Northamptonshire MS. A. XXVII.102; Northamptonshire MS. A. XXXVIII.11(b). Cf. Northamptonshire MS. A. XXXVIII.11(f).

[540] Northamptonshire MS. A. XXVII.98.

[541] Northamptonshire MS. A. XXVII.96; Northamptonshire MS. A. XXXVIII.11(a).

[542] Northamptonshire MS. A. XXVII.96.

[543] Northamptonshire MS. A. XXVII.100.

responsible apprehension was the duty of the statesman. Fear, under these circumstances, was the best guarantee of safety.[544]

Burke's sense of alarm deepened his suspicion of Fox through the summer and into the winter. Reynolds had died on 23 February, and then Richard Shackleton passed away on 28 August, but public affairs still bore down on Burke throughout 1792. France declared war on the Habsburg monarchy on 20 April 1792. Soon after, negotiations over a coalition between the Pitt administration and the Portland Whigs got under way. These highlighted the tensions among Burke's old friends. On 29 May he wrote to Loughborough indicating the extent of Portland's distaste for proceedings in France, even if the "minds of his friends" seemed otherwise disposed.[545] Those with a favourable attitude to collaboration with Pitt judged Fox to be open to some form of conciliation, yet Burke saw him as a potential addition to ministerial inactivity. Above all, he represented a misguided willingness to indulge "the French and dissenting scheme of things."[546] The Jacobin ministry had fallen in the middle of June, with Dumouriez dispatched to command on the northern front. In protest, the Cordeliers club organised a large demonstration at the Tuileries to intimidate the king. "The proceedings at Paris are frantick," Burke exclaimed at the start of August.[547] A week earlier, the Duke of Brunswick, heading the allied forces, issued a Declaration announcing his determination to secure the French royal family. In response, the Assembly ordered the arming of the citizenry of Paris. Brissot now, belatedly, rallied to the cause of the king, but, on 10 August, the Paris sections moved against the Tuileries Palace and established a Revolutionary commune.[548] "I looked for some such Event for a long time," Burke claimed seven days later.[549] The monarchy was now suspended while its fate was decided. On 13 August the royal family was transferred to the Temple prison. Burke was personally horrified, but also on the point of political despair. He wrote to Fitzwilliam: "Surely all this will be enough to satiate even Mr Fox, and Mr Sheridan, or Dr Priestley."[550] The sluggish pace of allied arms offered little comfort.

The Duke of Brunswick did not cross the French border until 19 August. The day before, Burke was complaining to Lord Grenville of what he described as the English Jacobin denial of a right to interfere in the internal affairs of the new republic. The menace of subversion was simmering in Britain, compromising security as it celebrated the French example. A second round of negotiations between govern-

[544] Northamptonshire MS. A. XXVII.98.

[545] EB to Lord Loughborough, 27 May 1792, *Corr.*, VII, p. 144.

[546] Loughborough to EB, 13 June 1792, ibid., p. 149; EB to Lord Loughborough, 13 June 1792, ibid., p. 151.

[547] EB to the Abbé de la Bintinaye, 3 August 1792, ibid., p. 167.

[548] On the hypocrisy of Brissot and his faction at this time, see the retrospective comment in EB, Speech on Sheridan's Motion relative to Seditious Practices, *Parliamentary History*, XXX, col. 553; cf. EB, *Preface to Brissot's Address to his Constituents* (1794), *W & S*, VIII, p. 514.

[549] EB to James Bland Burges, 17 August 1792, *Corr.*, VII, p. 169.

[550] EB to Earl Fitzwilliam, 17 August 1792, ibid., p. 172.

ment and the opposition ended in failure at the end of August. The sticking point, from Burke's perspective, was the disposition of Fox. He continued to cultivate the enterprising spirits in his own party, but fell short of causing a rupture with the Duke of Portland. Portland, meanwhile, cleaved to Fox, and refused to push the issue of their divergence regarding France. Burke, on the other hand, was determined to test his opponent, urging "a total Hostility" to French republican practice as a condition of future collaboration with Fox.[551] In September, as the Convention Assembly formed, Burke devoted himself to the fate of the French clergy in exile against the background of the massacres in Paris. After the Prussian capture of Verdun on 2 September, the populace in the capital butchered the city's prisoners.[552] Despite the descent into disorder in France, the British ministry persisted with neutrality. The Bristol MP John Baker Holroyd, now Lord Sheffield, exclaimed to William Eden that the ministry would deserve "the execration of all the world" if they did not swiftly move to crush the "barbarous spirit" of the French.[553] Burke was now convinced that, without action against France, the fabric of the British constitution would be overturned. The government was completely opposed to the tenets of the Revolution, yet it persisted in believing that the country was immune from the effects of those very principles: no matter what the condition of Europe, the administration treated the peril unleashed by France as advancing without any destructive consequences "to this Kingdom."[554] As two hundred members of the Legislative Assembly and eighty-three from the Constituent were returned to the Convention Assembly—including Brissot, Robespierre, Marat and Pétion—Burke considered this assumption to be unhinged.

As if to underline the problem, Thomas Paine and Joseph Priestley were elected to the new Assembly.[555] Burke wrote to a French correspondent in October that "La France en ce moment est hors d'elle. Toutes ses vertus se sont évaporés."[556] By now, the Convention had abolished the monarchy, and Louis XVI had been put on trial.[557] Saint-Just and the Montagnards pressed for an execution. On 15 January 1793, the guilt of the king was almost unanimously declared; six days later, he went to the scaffold. "It was the necessary result of all the preceding parts of that monstrous Drama," Burke wrote to Loughborough.[558] As the fate of the French monarch was being determined, Burke's distress about the balance of European forces reached new lows. On 20 September 1792, the Duke of Brunswick, at the head of the Prussian

[551] EB to William Burke, 3 September 1792, ibid., pp. 192–94.

[552] For the early course of the war, see T.W.C. Blanning, *The French Revolutionary Wars, 1787–1802* (London: Arnold, 1996), ch. 3; for the Foxite dismay at the September massacres, see the *Morning Chronicle*, 12 September 1790.

[553] The Earl of Sheffield to Lord Auckland, 21 October 1792, OBS MS. File 13483.

[554] EB to Lord Grenville, 19 September 1792, *Corr.*, VII, p. 218.

[555] Priestley declined the honour. See the *Morning Chronicle*, 4 October 1792.

[556] EB to Monsieur de Sandouville, post 13 October 1792, *Corr.*, VII, p. 359.

[557] For Burke's public response, see EB, Debate on the Royal Family, 20 December 1792, *Parliamentary History*, XXX, col. 139.

[558] EB to Lord Loughborough, 27 January 1793, *Corr.*, VII, p. 344.

army, met with defeat at the Battle of Valmy. Burke was unsparing in his vitriol: "The United military glory of Europe has suffered a Stain never to be effaced."[559] Dumouriez now set his sights on the Austrian Netherlands, and the occupation of the Rhineland could begin. Decisiveness and vigour had triumphed on the French side, while sloth and hesitation characterised the allies.

Procrastination was a function of puzzled Austrian politics supported by Prussian irresolution. Burke traced the problem to the underlying policy deficiency. In a memorandum circulated among the ministry and opposition in November 1792, he observed that in the space of a mere three weeks the wheel had turned: France had been permitted to conquer Savoy; it was on the verge of victory at Jemappes; and it was in a position to overwhelm the Swiss.[560] France's domestic vices drove her military success. On the other side, the Austro-Prussian alliance was defeated by insufficient ambition: focusing exclusively on the fate of the royals and disregarding the internal condition of France, the German courts proceeded without a concern for the French nation.[561] Their venture, consequently, smacked of conquest rather than constitutional restoration. They ignored the émigrés and the prospective framework of the state while hoping to reinstate the original power of the country. The assumption was that "the person of the Monarch of France was every thing; and the Monarchy, and the intermediate orders of the State, by which the Monarchy was upheld, were nothing."[562] The limited nature of their political aims compromised the allies' military strategy by disposing the Duke of Brunswick to negotiate rather than subdue.[563] It was a shame virtually without precedent in military history.[564] The only hope lay in the prospect of a British resolution to form a defensive alliance with the old European order.[565]

Burke believed that the government's ongoing inertia was partly owing to the want of public support from leaders of opinion in the country at large, including from the grandees among the opposition Whigs.[566] By this point, Burke was in harness with Windham and Loughborough, once more pressing the case for a coalition. "Dangerous is the situation of England," commented the diarist Robert Johnson, an admirer of Burke on tour from America at this time: "every step taken by the

[559] EB to Richard Burke Jr., 17 October 1792, ibid., p. 271.

[560] EB, *Heads Written for Consideration &c* (November 1792), *W & S*, VIII, p. 387. For its circulation, see William Windham to EB, 14 November 1792, *Corr.*, VII, pp. 288–89; EB to Earl Fitzwilliam, 29 November 1792, ibid., pp. 309, 310. On the situation in Europe, see also EB to the Abbé de la Bintinaye, 23 November 1792, ibid., p. 302.

[561] This was the position articulated in the Brunswick Manifesto of 25 July 1792. See Antoine-Henri, baron de Jomini, *Histoire critique et militaire des guerres de la Révolution* (Brussels: 1837–39), 15 vols., II, pp. 286–90.

[562] EB, *Heads Written for Consideration &c* (November 1792), *W & S*, VIII, p. 393.

[563] EB to Earl Fitzwilliam, 29 November 1792, *Corr.*, VII, p. 309.

[564] See EB to Earl Fitzwilliam, 23 October 1792, ibid., pp. 276–77; EB to Richard Burke Jr., 6 November 1792, ibid., p. 284.

[565] EB, *Heads Written for Consideration &c* (November 1792), *W & S*, VIII, p. 401.

[566] EB to Earl Fitzwilliam, 29 November 1792, *Corr.*, VII, p. 301.

Minister is important Indeed."[567] Three things now seemed essential to Burke on the domestic front: national harmony on the legitimacy of the British monarchy, unity among the erstwhile parties of the country, and concessions to relieve dissension in Ireland.[568] Every step towards these goals proved arduous and protracted. In late November, Loughborough was offered the great seal, but he declined it.[569] The following January, with war between Britain and France imminent, he finally accepted.[570] The decision represented the first major defection from the Portland Whigs. It was an outcome that had been determined by rising tensions over the previous months. As Loughborough himself informed Burke on 30 November, Portland and Devonshire were convinced of the case against France, yet both men inexplicably clung to the hope of a united opposition.[571] This prospect dwindled as the French government insisted upon its right to navigate the Scheldt estuary, threatening the freedom of the United Provinces. Within days the French were extending fraternal support to all peoples seeking to recover their liberty.[572] Next, to Burke's dismay, came the decree of 15 December 1792 promulgated by Joseph Cambon: "guerre aux châteaux, paix aux chaumières."[573] Early that same winter, the British ministry, along with prominent figures in the opposition, began to settle on a policy of war. By early December, the die was cast.[574] Through the preceding month, alarm had been mounting about the advent of insurrection in Britain, and plans were afoot to embody the militia. After a bad harvest, discontent and riots over food prices and wages spread through the country.[575] The London Corresponding Society,

[567] Robert C. Johnson, "Diary of Travels in England, France and Italy, October 1792–March 1793," Gen. MSS. File 3, Beinecke Library, Yale University.

[568] EB to Richard Burke Jr., 18 November 1792, *Corr.*, VII, p. 292; cf. EB to Richard Burke Jr., post 21 November 1792, ibid., p. 298; EB to Earl Fitzwilliam, 29 November 1792, ibid., p. 312. The plan included reconciling George III with the Prince of Wales.

[569] Lord Loughborough to EB, 27 November 1792, ibid., p. 303.

[570] *Later Correspondence of George III*, ed. A. Aspinall (Cambridge: Cambridge University Press, 1962), 5 vols., I, p. 647.

[571] Lord Loughborough to EB, 30 November 1792, *Corr.*, VII, p. 319.

[572] This was the Decree in the Convention of 19 November 1792 extending support to all peoples who strove to recover their liberty: see J. M. Roberts, J. Hardman and R. C. Cobb eds., *French Revolution Documents* (Oxford: Blackwell, 1966–73), 2 vols., II, p. 389. For comment, see Black, *British Foreign Policy*, p. 416. For Burke's response, see EB, Speech on Aliens Bill, 28 December 1792, *Diary*, 29 December 1792: "By the famous Decree of the 19th of November . . . the Republic of France had resolved to pull down the Constitution, and all public institutions in every country possessed by her armies." See also, EB, *Observations on the Conduct of the Minority* (Spring 1793), *W & S*, VIII, p. 424, where it is stated that the decree was explicitly aimed at Britain. Cf. John Bowles, *The Real Grounds of the Present War with France* (London: 1793; 6th ed., 1794), pp. 11–13.

[573] *Archives parlementaires*, LV, p. 70: "Ils se sont demandé d'abord quel est l'objet de la guerre que vous avez entreprise. C'est sans doute l'annéantissement de tous les privilèges. Guerre aux châteaux, paix aux chaumières." For Burke's alarm, EB, *Observations on the Conduct of the Minority* (Spring 1793), *W & S*, VIII, pp. 424–25.

[574] *Diaries and Correspondence of James Harris, First Earl of Malmesbury* (London: 1844), 4 vols., II, pp. 501–2.

[575] Ehrman, *Pitt the Younger*, II, pp. 214–16.

together with assorted urban associations across Britain, was transmitting addresses of support to the Convention Assembly. In December, these developments came to a climax in a series of confrontations among the parliamentary class.

Burke reiterated his views in the controversy that followed, beginning with the debate on the address of thanks on 13 December 1792. Fox opened with a denial of the existence of an insurrection, the fear of which had caused the government to call out the militia.[576] He then ranged widely over conditions on the continent and in Britain—applauding the triumph over allied arms in the recent struggles, and inveighing against the resurgence of "exploded" Tory doctrines.[577] The speech risked an open breach with Portland and Fitzwilliam in shifting the common ground of opposition Whiggism.[578] Fox taunted Burke more openly the next day.[579] Burke responded with an anatomy of European republics, presenting contemporary France as a singular aberration that strove for a confraternity of international sedition.[580] Its example brought to mind the policy of Mohammed, seducing populations to a new faith "with the Koran in this hand, and a sword in the other."[581] The following day, Fox proposed dispatching an ambassador to Paris.[582] Burke took the opportunity to oppose French policy, above all its temerity in flouting the law of nations. He then resolved to vindicate his conduct hitherto: he was nothing now if not an independent member of the Commons, for which he was commonly persecuted and reviled. He became indignant: "I have made no provision for myself or family. We are not in possession of any office; neither cajoled by the reversion of place, nor by the promise of pension."[583] Allegations of self-interest from Fox and his allies rankled. Suspicion of the Foxites continued in the weeks that followed. On 28 December, rising to speak on Dundas's Bill for the registration of aliens, Burke reminded the Commons of his treatment at the hands of his former colleagues, now styled the "phalanx": "What endeavours had been used to make him odious to the public, and to his private friends, all the world knew."[584] The truth was, he had stood by his prin-

[576] On the idea of "*Insurrection*," see Charles James Fox to the Duke of Portland, 1 December 1792, *Memorials*, IV, p. 291.

[577] *Parliamentary History*, XXX, cols. 12–34; *Morning Chronicle*, 14 December 1792. Fox's intervention on 13 December was, as Edmond Malone commented to Burke three days later, the "most dangerous speech that was ever uttered in parliament": *Corr.*, VII, p. 323. Cf. Edmond Malone to Lord Charlemont, 22 December 1792, *Correspondence and Manuscripts of Charlemont*, II, p. 209.

[578] Fox's motives were later defended in a couple of pamphlets by Robert Adair: *A Whig's Apology for His Consistency* (London: 1795); *The Letter of the Rt. Hon. C. J. Fox to the Electors of Westminster, with an Application of its Principles to Subsequent Events* (London: 1802).

[579] *Parliamentary History*, XXX, cols. 61–62. See also *Morning Chronicle*, 15 December 1792.

[580] *Parliamentary History*, XXX, cols. 69–70. The French republic was in fact "*sui generis*": *Diary*, 15 December 1792.

[581] *Parliamentary History*, XXX, col. 72.

[582] Ibid., cols. 80–81. It was this speech that led many Whig stalwarts to separate from Fox. See Mitchell, *Charles James Fox*, p. 205.

[583] *Parliamentary History*, XXX, col. 110; cf. *Morning Chronicle*, 17 December 1792.

[584] *Parliamentary History*, XXX, col. 180; *Morning Chronicle*, 29 December 1792. Pitt sent Burke a copy of the Aliens Bill as it was first introduced in the Lords. See William Pitt to EB, 22 December 1792,

ciples, which had now led him to support the ministry systematically—not with "a layer of support and a layer of opposition," but with the level of backing necessary to a government at war.[585]

The debate on the Aliens Bill concluded with histrionics. It was in this context that, famously, Burke threw a concealed dagger onto the floor of the House of Commons to symbolise the intentions of the French: "When they smile, I see blood trickling down their faces."[586] He abominated their hypocritical fraternising zeal: their true aim was to "cram" fraternity down the throats of lesser powers.[587] Yet, astonishingly, it was a programme that won the approval of Fox, who had celebrated the French victory at Jemappes. The previous November, Burke relayed to Fitzwilliam what he understood to be the position of his old associate: Fox apprehended no threat to the internal state of Britain, and believed that the French republic should be recognised. He could not see what Burke obviously feared: that France now aimed at "universal Empire."[588] At that time, Burke was not without hope that his old friend might still be brought round—that the second Revolution of August 1792, followed by the spectacle of the September massacres, offered him an honourable retreat. Yet it seemed that Fox's mind was still fixated on "the growth of Tory principles."

As far as Burke was concerned, the Whigs had always "supposed & asserted Monarchy even when they would most limit it."[589] In the 1770s and again after 1784, it was vital that its prerogatives should be brought within bounds. In 1789, however, the world changed, with democracy, rather than monarchy, posing a danger to the constitution. Fox remained imprisoned within an anachronism. On 27 January 1793, Burke summed up his feelings. Loughborough had just joined the administration, and Burke expressed his sympathy for his detestation of Francophile Whiggism.[590] Everything should be done to defend the liberties of Europe as well as the constitution of Great Britain. Burke called for resolution: vigorous exertion and a comprehensive policy were needed to crush the ambition of Revolutionary power. However, it soon transpired that the government's determination fell short of what Burke believed was now required. On 12 February 1793, Fox declared that if France were really the monster that some of its enemies had claimed, then nothing less than a war of extermination was called for.[591] It was a policy that Burke would duly advocate.

Corr., VII, p. 324. According to EB, *Observations on the Conduct of the Minority* (Spring 1793), *W & S*, VIII, p. 445, the "phalanx" was originally a self-description.

585 *Parliamentary History*, XXX, col. 181.

586 Ibid., col. 189. Burke acquired the dagger from James Bland Burges, and had presented a copy to Dundas the day before, on 27 December. See EB to Henry Dundas, 27 December 1792, *Corr.*, VII, p. 328.

587 *Parliamentary History*, XXX, col. 184.

588 EB to Earl Fitzwilliam, 29 November 1792, *Corr.*, VII, p. 316.

589 Northamptonshire MS. A. XXVII.99.

590 EB to Lord Loughborough, 27 January 1793, *Corr.*, VII. p. 344. Loughborough joined the administration on 18 January 1793.

591 Debate in the Commons on the King's Message respecting War, 12 February 1793, *Parliamentary History*, XXX, col. 364: "*bellum internecinum*."

XV

THE PURSUIT OF HASTINGS, 1788–1796

Figure 8. Burke sinks on the acquittal of Hastings as the accused receives an Horation endorsement: *Virtus repulsae nescia sordidae incontaminatis fulget honoribus* (virtue which knows nothing of sordid rejection beams with uncontaminated honours).
James Sayers, *The Last Scene of the Managers Farce* (1795). BM 8647, Private Collection (Robinson p. 172).

15.1 Introduction

Writing for the *Edinburgh Review* in 1841, Macaulay presented Warren Hastings's tenure in office as following in the footsteps of the darkest period of British rule in India. In the decade after the conquest of Bengal, the more powerful civilisation, as Macaulay viewed the British, began to flaunt its might and then break loose "from all restraint."[1] Against this background of disorder and ruthlessness, Hastings had managed to bring efficiency and vigour to administration. He was nonetheless deemed guilty of considerable offences: morality could not justify his wilful expediency.[2] It was Burke who had sought to bring this abuse of justice before the public. In applauding his conduct, Macaulay also recognised that his zeal had been ferocious while nonetheless insisting that his principles were pure.[3] To a subsequent generation Burke's motives seemed less disinterested. Writing on the fate of Nandakumar in the 1880s, James Stephen chided the later Burke by resorting to his own language, condemning him as "contumacious, arrogant, confident, and assuming."[4] However for Burke the conduct of Hastings could not be justified by circumstance. There was consequently no limit to legitimate vituperation. Having followed Burke's polemic against Revolutionary France to the threshold of international crisis, this chapter turns back to take up the thread of the Hastings impeachment in order to trace Burke's Indian crusade to its final conclusion. While championing the cause of custom and precedent in connection with France, the Hastings trial would show Burke to be an advocate of forward-looking reform. Tradition should never overwhelm improvement, he insisted. Law, like policy, was a creature of rational deliberation intended to serve humanity and justice. It ought not to be a prisoner of common law regulations in thrall to the judgments of the past.

The final years of Burke's protracted stand against wrongdoing in India brought setbacks followed by radical disenchantment. He delivered the Presents and Contracts charges with stamina and gusto, but the prolongation of the trial soon began to count against him. He started to reflect again about the sentiment of humanity: it was fortified by custom among people who shared a culture, yet it required the support of rhetoric if it was to gain traction among strangers. The force of persuasion could not sustain the cause through the dreariness of judicial proceedings. In pressing his case, Burke tried to leave his audience with an acute awareness of the toxic nature of bribery; he also treated them to penetrating insights on the "economics"

[1] Thomas Babington Macaulay, "Warren Hastings" (1841) in idem, *Critical and Miscellaneous Essays* (Philadelphia: 1843–44), 5 vols., IV, p. 90.

[2] Ibid., p. 175.

[3] Ibid., p. 183.

[4] James Fitzjames Stephen, *The Story of Nuncomar and the Impeachment of Sir Elijah Impey* (London: 1885), 2 vols., II, p. 87. On key shifts in the Victorian ideology of empire, see Karuna Mantena, *Alibis of Empire: Henry Maine and the Ends of Liberal Imperialism* (Princeton, NJ: Princeton University Press, 2010).

of empire. But technicalities would inevitably prove wearying and thus inhibit the expression of compassion for native Indians. For this reason, Burke was dismayed by the legalism of Hastings's barristers as they deflected the trial into humdrum points of order. The defence counsel expected the petty provisions of the lower courts to determine procedure in what to Burke was a truly grand affair of state. The meanness of their approach befitted the bent of the accused: the scandal of the former Governor was the banality of his delinquency. He appeared sordid, unscrupulous and contemptible in his vices. Schooled in the habits of low and unaccountable administration, he had the audacity to disguise his iniquity as virtue. He was a "Jacobin" in morals though not in ideology: conducting himself without a flicker of fear for his maker, he played the role of tyrant by presuming to rebel against all principles. After the acquittal of his adversary in April 1795 Burke was disheartened; with the award of an annuity to Hastings the following year he felt beaten. Campaigning through his final illness against the search for peace with France while striving to save Ireland from the prospect of dreadful strife, Burke would look back on the India business as a draining undertaking. At first the trial publicised noble principles of government but it ended by traducing the cause of justice it strove to promote.

15.2 The Sentiment of Humanity

With the completion of Burke's opening speech of the impeachment in February 1788, 139 days of the trial still remained. The next six years over which that process stretched plunged Burke into the controversies of the French Revolution, and forced a realignment in British affairs. In connection with India, the same period proved a disappointment for Burke as he battled to save the impeachment from defeat, only to face the acquittal of Hastings in the end. In the sessions of 1788–91, the prosecution delivered its case on only four of its original articles of charge, leaving 1792 and 1793 for the defence to present its response. The obstacles to Burke's success began immediately after he completed his opening speech. On 19 February 1788, Fox gave notice on behalf of the managers that it was their intention to proceed to a conclusion of the trial by presenting evidence on each charge separately, with the defence presenting their case at each stage.[5] But the proposal was contested by the chief counsel for the defence, Edward Law, insisting that the prosecution should offer an overarching demonstration of Hastings's putatively malign purpose, as it had originally proposed to do. When the issue came to be debated in the Lords on 21 February, Edward Thurlow began with a eulogy of Burke, accepting that his charges pointed to "crimes of so deep a dye" that even the severest outcome for Hastings would be insufficient punishment. This, however, assumed that guilt could actually be demonstrated.[6] The following day proved inauspicious for the Com-

[5] *LJ*, XXXVIII, pp. 83ff.; *Parliamentary History*, XXVII, col. 54.
[6] Ibid., col. 55.

mons managers, with the Lord Chancellor declaring that the prosecution should present its entire case first. This increased the likelihood that the trial would last for years, during which the tide of popular interest was sure to recede.[7] By the end of the session, in June 1788, with only the Benares and Begams charges having been presented, proceedings had become repeatedly embroiled in wrangling over technicalities. At the same time, Hastings's supporters were busy stirring up resentment over costs. There was no expense that would be "too great for the obtainment of justice," Burke retorted.[8] In a fit of blind passion he advised James Bland Burges, one of Hastings's keenest supporters, that he would regard any attempt to press the issue as a personal attack, and despised it accordingly.[9] Nonetheless, by 4 May, he was remarking in a letter to John Burgoyne that one of his fellow managers, Charles Grey, believed that the public would tire of the length and expense of the trial.[10] Even Sheridan's outstanding performance in summing up the Begams charge in June did not lift the gloom that threatened to settle over the trial.[11] Within less than a year, the Duchess of Devonshire was reporting how Sheridan hoped that "Hastings would run away and Burke after him."[12] Partisans of the enemy were "disseminated everywhere," Burke had earlier announced to Burgoyne. The judges, he was certain, were entirely "partial," the records were "mangled," the witnesses "unwilling," the Commons "reluctant" and the public "indifferent."[13]

As the prospect of success receded, and Burke's mood darkened, his feeling of embattlement grew more intense. On 7 March, he rose to lambast the East India Declaratory Bill during a debate on its amendment. Having generally sought to extend the powers of the Board of Control since its establishment under Pitt's India Act of 1784, Dundas was now specifically aiming to subject the British armed forces in India to ministerial control, and to charge the expense on the Company itself.[14] Defending that intention, Pitt belatedly explained the purpose behind the 1784 Act on 5 March: the principal object in framing it had been "to take from the Company

[7]Burke later insisted that he had anticipated a lengthy trial from the start: see EB, Speech on Limitation of the Impeachment, 14 February 1791, *W & S*, VII, p. 98.

[8]EB, Speeches on Impeachment Costs and on Charge against Impey, 9 May 1788, *W & S*, VI, p. 480. Cf. EB to the Lords of the Commissioners of the Treasury, 15 April 1788, *Corr.*, V, pp. 388–91; EB to Charles Wolfran Cornwall, 1 May 1788, ibid., pp. 393–94; EB, Debate in the Commons Respecting the Expenses of Hastings's Trial, 6 June 1788, *Parliamentary History*, XXVII, cols. 543–47.

[9]Reported by James Bland Burges to his wife on 10 May 1788. See *Selections form the Letters and Correspondence of Sir James Bland Burges, Bart.*, ed. James Hutton (London: 1885), pp. 99–102.

[10]EB to General John Burgoyne, 4 May 1788, *Corr.*, V, p. 395. The five barristers acting as counsel to the managers soon offered their services free of charge. See Add. MS. 24266, fols. 360–61, and Burke's praise of their "true public national Charity" given in a letter in response on 26 May 1788, *Corr.*, V, p. 399.

[11]On the "wonder" inspired by that speech, see Sir Gilbert Elliot to Lady Elliot, 3 June 1788, *Life and Letters of Sir Gilbert Elliot, First Earl of Minto, from 1751–1806 (London: 1874)*, I, p. 211.

[12]Diary entry of 20 November 1788, reprinted in Walter Sichel, *The Life of Richard Brinsley Sheridan* (London: Constable, 1909), 2 vols., II, p. 404.

[13]EB to General John Burgoyne, 4 May 1788, *Corr.*, V, pp. 395–96.

[14]C. H. Philips, *The East India Company, 1784–1834* (Manchester: Manchester University Press, 1940), pp. 54–60.

the entire management of the territorial possessions, and the political government of the country."[15] This revelation inevitably stung both Fox and Burke, since clearly such an invasive degree of "management" would entail transferring the patronage of India from the Court of Directors to the ministers of George III. The government was endeavouring, Burke reflected on 7 March, to acquire no less than the Company's "military power, the management of their politics, the management of their revenue, and as much as could be taken of their Commerce."[16] Instead of allocating the patronage of the corporation, as proposed under Fox's Bill, to a commission of "seven of the most respectable men in the kingdom," the Declaratory Bill was making a job of the administration of India.[17] The situation stirred painful memories in Burke about the treachery of the Commons in 1784, its reduction to a demotic mob in search of imperial tribute, and its abandonment of the cause of imperial justice.[18] The impeachment of Hastings had offered some kind of redemption, although the Lords now threatened to undo its effect.

Burke's appreciation of the task ahead is illustrated by his intervention into a debate on the Begams charge on 22 April 1788. By then, Fox, Sheridan, Anstruther, Grey and the other managers, together with their five counsel, had been applying themselves to their particular areas of responsibility, with Burke contributing to the prosecution on an ad hoc basis.[19] Sheridan's original speech on the "Begums of Oudh" in February 1787 had made the alleged misappropriation by the Wazir of his mother's and grandmother's property under pressure from Hastings a notorious act of pillage. Burke's intervention on the use of evidence in support of the managers' case in April 1788 was designed to show how the tenets of the "Mahometan religion" uniformly prevailed throughout every jurisdiction that subscribed to the faith, producing regularity in the manners, customs and institutional arrangements of the "several Countries" in which Islam was adhered to.[20] Conspicuous among these salient customs was a general reverence for the sanctity of motherhood, placing women of rank in particular in positions of independent authority and wealth. Hastings's pressure on the Wazir had led to a violation of the usual homage, thus offending against basic attitudes rooted in Islamic culture. An attack upon customs of the kind was an attack upon the order of things, Burke contended, since habits were deeply embedded in human nature itself.[21] Humanity was "in the habit" of acquiring

[15] *Parliamentary History*, XXVII, col. 93.

[16] EB, Speech on East India Declaratory Bill, *W & S*, VI, p. 473.

[17] Ibid. Cf. WWM BK. 9:53.

[18] EB, Speech on East India Declaratory Bill, *W & S*, VI, p. 474.

[19] The managers engaged the following barristers as counsel: Arthur Leary Pigott, William Scott, French Laurence, Sylvester Douglas and Richard Burke Sr.

[20] EB, Evidence on Begams of Oudh, 22 April 1788, *W & S*, VI, p. 476. Burke sought to underline his point by invoking the authority of Demetrius Cantimer's *History of the Growth and Decay of the Othoman Empire* (London: 1756).

[21] EB, Evidence on Begams of Oudh, 22 April 1788, *W & S*, VI, p. 478.

habits, so much so that the tendency to form and adhere to them was a fundamental component of the human frame.[22]

This observation pointed to the problem that Burke faced in the trial as a whole. Sympathy for humanity was part of our nature, and it had been awakened in the Commons during the campaign to launch the impeachment. Nonetheless, this was clearly a faint and under-motivated proclivity, which needed additional impetus for its concrete mobilisation. In the ordinary course of life, this extra stimulus was supplied by shared customs. In their absence, "it is the most difficult thing in the world to bring ourselves to a proper degree of sympathy when we are describing those circumstances which are not ingrafted in our nature by custom."[23] Laughter, much like sorrow, spreads infectiously among mankind, Burke noted. The observation had been a common one in the moral and aesthetic psychology of the ancients, famously invoked by Horace in his *Ars poetica*: "As people's faces smile on those who smile, so they respond to those that weep."[24] Such natural, instinctive responses, however, were greatly enforced by local culture: by custom, habit, religion and institutional setting. The common reactions of humanity, in fact, were easily drowned out and replaced by habitual responses. The reverse situation was equally the case: humanity felt especially outraged when its acquired prejudices were offended. Custom could thus intensify the reactions of natural sensibility. Six years later, during his speech in reply to the defence, Burke underlined the point by distinguishing between the "physical" and "moral" elements of man.[25] The "inborn sentiments of people," such as the feelings of shame and disgrace, were particularly liable to being provoked where natural responses were fortified by manners and usages. Such cultural accretion made up a people's "second nature", determining their sensitivities and therefore their reactions, playing an essential role in eliciting their consent.[26]

Burke's conclusion in 1788 was that the key to managing moral psychology was to graft the habits of our second nature onto primary human aptitudes, thus infusing them with motivating zeal. To be most effective, abstract moral values like humanity

[22] For "habits," see above, chapter 2, section 4. According to EB, *Philosophical Enquiry*, *W & S*, I, p. 265, while habit, being indifferent, is not a cause of pleasure, nonetheless a departure from custom, our "second nature," is liable to cause discomfort. On this, see John Tillotson, "Of the Education of Children" in *The Works of the Most Reverent Dr. John Tillotson* (London: 1728), 3 vols., I, p. 508; "It is an acquired and a sort of *Second* Nature, and next to Nature it self a principle of greatest power. Custom bears a huge sway in all Human Actions." Cf. EB, *Reflections*, p. 357. For discussion, see James Chandler, *Wordsworth's Second Nature: A Study of Poetry and Politics* (Chicago, IL: University of Chicago Press, 1984), ch. 4.

[23] EB, Evidence on Begams of Oudh, 22 April 1788, *W & S*, VI, p. 478.

[24] Horace, *Ars poetica*, lines 101–2: "ut ridentibus arrident, ita flentibus adsunt/humani voltus." Burke cites the preceding lines of the passage in *Reflections*, p. 241. On this, see Richard Bourke, "Pity and Fear: Providential Sociability in Burke's *Philosophical Enquiry*" in Michael Funk Deckard and Koen Vermeir eds., *The Science of Sensibility: Reading Edmund Burke's Philosophical Enquiry* (Dordrecht: Springer, 2012), pp. 151–75, and above, chapter 3, section 2.

[25] EB, Speech in Reply, 12 June 1794, *W & S*, VII, p. 540.

[26] Ibid. On this, see Burke's statement during debate on the Quebec Bill reported in the *Oracle*, 12 May 1791: "to that Second Nature of Man founded in his Habits . . . all Political Science should be referred." Cf. EB, *Appeal from the New to the Old Whigs*, p. 130.

and honour, the dearest possessions of human life, required additional impetus supplied by cultural prejudice. Where honour is fused with custom, it acts as one of the "strongest influences" governing the mind.[27] In transactions relating to a remote and alien culture, however, that fusion must be brought about by imaginative identification. Burke's rhetoric was commonly deployed with that objective in mind. Addressing the Commons in 1790, he reminded his audience of the "magic" power of eloquence: by means of it, he insisted, remote suffering could be "brought home to our bosoms"—"time and place disappear to the sympathy" as the art of persuasion succeeds in uniting "all mankind in all countries, and the sphere and empire of benevolence is extended every way, and upon every side."[28] But while the impact of eloquence could be momentarily decisive, it was nonetheless limited in its effect, dissipating soon after its immediate application. It would soon become clear that nothing acted so drastically to dissipate the sentiment of humanity as the dulling effect upon the imagination of a drawn-out judicial process that became enmeshed in tedious detail, ambiguous evidence and the technicalities of legal procedure. Ambivalence and distraction then appeared, squandering the original moral charge.

Burke's colleagues were themselves early in succumbing to distraction: attendance by the managers at preparatory meetings before the reopening of the trial on 21 April 1789 was patchy, with Fox and Sheridan absenting themselves altogether.[29] Over the preceding months, the drama of the regency crisis had absorbed the attention of the opposition, as Burke recalled at the start of his four-day speech opening the Presents charge.[30] On 30 March, Sheridan was already appearing noncommittal in his responses to Burke's pleas for assistance.[31] Through the following month, Burke continued to rouse his fellows with appeals to the "terrors" of duty, prompting William Windham to consent on 7 April to be "harnessed" to the impeachment train, which Burke led like a "dragon."[32] When Major Scott petitioned the Commons to protect Hastings from allegations that made no appearance in the official charges after Burke had openly accused the former Governor of murdering Nandakumar "by the hands of Sir Elijah Impey," Burke grew eager to articulate the depth of his determination: "Neither hope, nor fear, nor anger, nor weariness, nor discouragement of any kind, shall move me from this trust," he declared to Frederick Montagu, one of the managers in the trial.[33] Burke's doggedness, however, was the

[27] EB, Evidence on Begams of Oudh, 22 April 1788, *W & S*, VI, p. 478.

[28] EB, Speech on Continuation of the Impeachment, 23 December 1790, *W & S*, VII, p. 91.

[29] L. G. Mitchell, *Charles James Fox and the Disintegration of the Whig Party, 1782–94* (Oxford: Oxford University Press, 1971), ch. 3.

[30] "Minutes of Proceedings of the Trial of Warren Hastings," Tuesday 21 April 1788, Add. MS. 24229, fols. 1–2.

[31] Richard Brinsley Sheridan to EB and EB to Richard Brinsley Sheridan, 30 March 1789, *Corr.*, V, pp. 457–58.

[32] William Windham to EB, 7 April 1789, ibid., p. 463.

[33] EB to Frederick Montague, 1 May 1789, ibid., p. 468. For the allegation in relation to Nandakumar, see "Minutes of Proceedings," Add. MS. 24229, fol. 55. For Burke's eulogy of Montagu, see EB, Speech on Limitation of the Impeachment, *W & S*, VII, p. 100.

exception, obliging him to discount any insinuation that he was driven by malice, or indeed activated by any party views.[34] He was conscious of the sacrifices that both he and his associates had made, prizing his honesty in a noble cause. "My friends have suffered; I have not gained," he confided to his old friend Joseph Emïn in late March.[35] Frustration drew him to meditate on the frailty of human things: "Who could have thought . . . that this kingdom would rule the greater part of India? But kingdoms rise and pass away . . . Pedlars become Emperors."[36] Burke had come to feel powerless as a spectator in the midst of events. Having adopted a principled stand, the ability to shape things slipped away.

The Presents charge was central to the import of Burke's stand. "Presents," he emphasised, was a misnomer, to cover what was in truth a system of bribes. Hastings's method was to justify peculation by means of a simple "perversion" of names, presenting a scheme of extortion as a native practice of exchanging gifts.[37] It had been part of Hastings's brief to eradicate the resort to presents, whereas in fact he had entrenched and extended its usage. This pointed to "a general systematic plan of corruption" on Hastings's part, which he pursued in the interest of greed and at the expense of all integrity, revolutionising the government of India for the purpose.[38] It was with this in mind that Burke had previously pointed to avarice as the driving force that guided Hastings's actions.[39] It was not a case of the vices of the time and place infecting the character of the man, but a case of "vitium hominis" spreading outwards, on account of which corruption was made more profound.[40] Bribery, Burke thought, was the original, fundamental, "endemical & ruinous distemper" that had afflicted the affairs of the Company since the acquisition of territorial power.[41] It lay at the root of the confusion between its commercial and political purpose, contributing to the derangement of either goal: it its wake, commerce degenerated into a species of strategic placement, and politics into a system of exploitation. On these terms, it made no sense to seek the "economic" roots of domination and expansion in India: commerce was conducted for the sake of patronage and politics in the interest of private advantage, so neither trade nor empire as ordinarily understood existed under the auspices of the Company.[42] Presents were the life-blood

[34] EB to Frederick Montagu, 1 May 1789, *Corr.*, V, p. 468.

[35] EB to Joseph Emïn, 29 March 1789, ibid., p. 456.

[36] Ibid.

[37] "Minutes of Proceedings," Add. MS. 24229, fol. 17.

[38] Ibid., fol. 12.

[39] EB, Speech on Rohilla War Charge, 1 June 1786, *W & S*, VI, pp. 95–96.

[40] "Minutes of Proceedings," Add. MS. 24229, fol. 16.

[41] Ibid., fol. 15.

[42] On the theme of economic imperialism in seventeenth- and eighteenth-century political and economic thought, see Jacob Viner, "Power versus Plenty as Objectives of Foreign Policy in the Seventeenth and Eighteenth Centuries" (1948) in idem, *Essays on the Intellectual History of Economics*, ed. Douglas A. Irwin (Princeton, NJ: Princeton University Press, 1991); Pocock, *Machiavellian Moment*, ch. 13; Istvan Hont, "Free Trade and the Economic Limits to National Politics: Neo-Machiavellian Political Economy Reconsidered" (1990) in idem, *Jealousy of Trade: International Competition and the Nation-State in*

of this malformed monster, and Hastings perfected the means of their circulation. Having first consolidated their role in the political economy of India, he then justified the outcome as an integral part of native society.

Burke was very clear about what the Governor's priorities ought to be: he ought to have introduced British standards of probity into the east. Corruption in India, he believed, could not be justified by an appeal to the venerable customs of the natives. At one point on 25 April 1789, on the second day of his Presents speech, Burke recalled a passage from Coke's *Institutes* in which the so-called Brehon "law" was described as a mere "lewd custome."[43] Coke's point was clear: primitive Irish practices were not legally grounded, and should therefore not enjoy either force or authority. Burke was similarly unsentimental about Indian practices where these conflicted with the provision of basic justice, which the British constitutional order was capable of delivering. He had announced on the opening day of the Presents charge that the Commons appeared at Westminster as the "representatives of the inhabitants of Bengal" charged with defending the rights of their remote subjects.[44] It was this capacity to deliver substantive, "representative" justice that connected human activity to the first cause in the chain of existence.[45] Provincial customs could never be pleaded against the provisions of imperial justice. "A governor is to conform himself to the law of his Country," to which local arrangements ought to be made subordinate.[46] It is easy to mistake Burke's reverence for established custom for a commitment to the primacy of tradition. When it came to administering political life in Bengal, no authoritative practice in the east could palliate a breach of laws "enacted in the west."[47] It was of course true, as Burke saw the matter, that provincial sentiment had to be respected, but never at the expense of basic principles of justice. Throughout his career, Burke adhered to the idea that among European and Asian powers, the British polity was best constituted to protect individual rights and the general welfare. This did not entail reconstructing subject provinces in the image of the metropolis, but it did mean that the British constitution was peculiarly well adapted to winning the consent of the people while upholding the liberties of the subject.

Historical Perspective (Cambridge, MA: Harvard University Press, 2005). For an application of the theme in the Indian context, see P. J. Marshall, "Economic and Political Expansion: The Case of Oudh," *Modern Asian Studies*, 9 (1975), pp. 465–82.

[43] "Minutes of Proceedings," Add. MS. 24229, fol. 107. The reference is to Edward Coke, *The Fourth Part of the Institutes of the Laws of England* (London: 1644), p. 358.

[44] "Minutes of Proceedings," Add. MS. 24229, fol. 7. Cf. EB, Speech in Reply, 7 June 1794, *W & S*, VII, p. 458: "The Commons, who represent Lucknow."

[45] "Minutes of Proceedings," Add. MS. 24229, fol. 3.

[46] Ibid., fol. 107.

[47] Ibid., fol. 17. Burke went on to point out that in the case of the local arrangements he was discussing, there was in fact no conflict between east and west.

The irony was that bribery was in any case alien to Indian practice: any temptation to believe otherwise was a "perfect mistake."[48] It had been introduced into South Asia with the corruption of Mughal power and accelerated by the activities of the East India Company. Above all, the practice had increased under the governorship of Hastings—like a stream of "insect vices" flowing form a "reptile mind."[49] Burke was fascinated by the inglorious character of Hastings's calamitous rule. His sins were those of a "low, sordid and illiberal" character; their effects were never spectacular or astounding.[50] Yet herein lay their progressively destructive effect. The very magnitude of great crimes proved a hindrance to their virulence. Petty, knavish behaviour, on the other hand, could be endlessly corrupting, degrading public morals by infectious emulation. For this reason, bribery in public office proved a devastating virus, permeating an administration by a process of imitation as officials took their lead from a degenerate head. The mischief stemmed more from the example than the act itself since the standard set by authority determined behaviour down the chain of command, polluting the code of conduct through all subordinate positions. Indian experience thus refuted the Mandevillian dogma that personal vices could result in public benefits: on the contrary, Burke argued, private immorality perverted the ethics of public power.[51] Therefore bribery was not a purely personal failing: it had ramifying political consequences, radiating from the top as a signal to follow suit. It laid waste the two inhibiting passions that regulated the use of power—shame or disgrace on the one hand, and fear of detection on the other.[52] How could one fear detection when one's superior endorsed the practice? How can one feel disgrace when the general culture is debauched? The degradation of authority represented the greatest threat to politics of all: whereas tyranny could never extend its tentacles to the utmost reaches, the ugly vices of debased authority spread like a contagion.

In the face of such insidious and catastrophic corruption, the ardour of Burke's pursuit would not be dampened. However, Fox was not so convinced of the merit of continuing the impeachment. After the Commons' censure of Burke's accusation of murder against Hastings on 4 May 1789, attitudes among the managers were divided.[53] Burke later revealed that "Mr. Fox strongly urged me to relinquish the prosecution at this time."[54] At a meeting of most of the managers on 5 May, Burke learned that Fox intended to move for an adjournment, opening the way to resignation. The trial might have terminated there, but Fox failed to arrive at the House of Commons on time. As a result, Burke's view prevailed, and the managers headed to Westminster Hall for the thirty-eighth day of the trial. "I had not the least Idea

[48] Ibid.

[49] EB, Speech on Sixth Article: Presents, 21 April 1789, *W & S*, VII, p. 33.

[50] Ibid., p. 35

[51] Ibid., p. 33.

[52] Ibid., pp. 33–34, 36.

[53] Mitchell, *Charles James Fox*, pp. 107–17.

[54] Prior, *Life of Burke*, p. 286.

that you wished me to move the house for a Message to the Lords to adjourn the Trial," Burke insisted in disingenuous tones to Fox.[55] His defiant determination to continue stood out as "the most brilliant day of my life," he later confided.[56] He had a powerful conviction in his mission at this time, intensifying his feeling of isolation, and reminding him of the sacrifices he had made. He had settled on a particular course in deciding to pursue the impeachment no matter what, and with this came inevitable setbacks. "By cultivating Interests nearer home," he wrote to Richard Bright, he might have provided "Service" to his friends and family.[57] But he had dedicated himself to a higher cause, and was prepared to pay the price. Since the "Massacre" of Fox's martyrs in the general election of 1784, Burke had felt the loss of the old Rockinghamite corps. "My strength was always in those admirable Men . . . with whom I had been connected," he now confessed: "Stripped of them I am nothing."[58] He had increasingly been subject to humiliation and insults, but it had fortified him in the determination to assist the "cause of humanity."[59] With or without Fox, he would continue to the end.

15.3 Precedent and Convenience

The sittings for the Hastings trial in 1790 extended over thirteen days between 16 February and 9 June. Repeated disputes over evidence dominated the proceedings. The previous December, Burke had revealed to Francis that he "totally" despaired for the future, longing for an "honourable retreat" from the prosecution. He suspected that the voice of the public was against him.[60] A week later he was complaining of the "depravity of England," which he was as powerless to remedy as he was the folly of France. He felt betrayed by his friends and supporters, disowned by the attitude of the Commons, and alarmed by the mounting weariness among the public about the trial.[61] He was aware that Hastings's supporters planned to have the impeachment scuppered but, despite Fox's reticence, he was keen to pursue the Contracts charge after the completion of the article on Presents.[62] Early in March he drafted a paper in relation to planned resolutions aimed at renewing the Commons'

[55] EB to Charles James Fox, 11 May 1789, *Corr.*, V, p. 473. Even Hastings had heard of a plan among the managers to resign by 11 a.m. on 4 May. See Hastings's Diary, 4 May 1789, Add. MS. 39881, fols. 192–93.

[56] Prior, *Life of Burke*, p. 285.

[57] EB to Richard Bright, 8 May 1789, *Corr.*, V, p. 470.

[58] Ibid., p. 471.

[59] Ibid.

[60] 11 December 1789, *Corr.*, VI, p. 55. His mood was partly determined by the acquittal of the publisher John Stockdale on 9 December 1789 in relation to an alleged libel against the Commons in connection with the impeachment, and then by the Commons support for the prosecution of the printers of libels against Elijah Impey.

[61] EB to Philip Francis, 17 December 1789, *Corr.*, VI, pp. 55–56.

[62] Ibid., p. 57.

commitment to the impeachment. He immediately sought ministerial support for the undertaking, writing to the Secretary of State, William Grenville, for the purpose. Grenville replied indirectly in mid-April, via John King, contending that the prosecution had failed to act with sufficient dispatch either to serve the interest of justice or to sustain support for their cause.[63] Burke's resolutions passed on 11 May, although the trial was interrupted by the dissolution of parliament in June.[64] Would the impeachment continue as usual after a new parliament had assembled? The question was raised in the Commons the following November.[65]

On 23 December 1790, Burke addressed a committee of the whole House on the same subject.[66] If the crown was permitted to bring an impeachment to a close by dissolving parliament, "the Constitution would be destroyed," he asserted.[67] Such an arrangement would potentially hand the initiative to the accused, and in any case transfer the prerogatives of the Commons and the independence of the judicial process to the reigning ministry. This amounted, Burke concluded, to an "abominable" doctrine.[68] The rights of the popular element in the constitution were the principal foundation of its authority: in contending for them "we fight *pro aris et focis*," Burke declared.[69] Supported by Fox and Pitt, Burke's view prevailed, despite the contrary position shared by most of the lawyers.[70] On 17 December, Burke had announced that he and his colleagues had resolved to present only one more charge, that concerning contracts. During the trial of John Stockdale, Thomas Erskine had famously claimed that British dominion in the east was founded on nothing other than "violence and terror," implicitly endorsing Hastings's rule as somehow adapted to circumstance.[71] The defence against the Presents charge had adopted this position, contending that the Governor General was merely conforming to local precedent. This fitted in with the general thesis of Hastings's supporters to the effect that his behaviour had been a product of necessity. For Burke, the article on contracts served to show how the pretence of exigency was a screen behind which lurked deliberate oppression. According to the prosecution, Hastings had squandered vast sums in awarding contracts, thus his violence in raising funds cannot have been a result of

[63] William Wyndham Grenville to John King, 14 April 1790, Unpublished Letters, I, p. 126.

[64] See EB, Speech on Resolutions on Future of the Impeachment, 11 May 1790, *W & S*, VII, pp. 74ff., and *CJ*, XLV, p. 459.

[65] For Burke's speech on 30 November, see *Parliamentary History*, XXVIII, cols. 900–901.

[66] This was the final day of a series of debates that began on 17 December. See *Parliamentary History*, XXVIII, cols. 1018–74, 1074–1127. For his preparation for the debate, see EB to Philip Francis, 4 December 1790, *Corr.*, VI, p. 188.

[67] EB, Speech on Continuation of the Impeachment, 23 December 1790, *W & S*, VII, p, 83.

[68] WWM Bk 9:71.

[69] EB, Speech on Continuation of the Impeachment, 23 December 1790, *W & S*, VII, p. 86.

[70] *CJ*, XLVI, p. 136. The Lords set up a committee to examine precedents. See EB to Philip Francis, 4 December 1790, *Corr.*, VI, p. 188.

[71] *A Complete Collection of State Trials*, ed. T. B. Howell and T. J. Howell (London: 1816–26), 34 vols., XXII, p. 278. See EB to Henry Dundas, 22 March 1792, *Corr.*, VII, p. 112.

genuine urgency.[72] On 14 February 1791, Burke introduced a motion limiting the scope of the impeachment so as to include this final charge.[73] However, the issue was not debated until the end of May, when it failed to attract the attention of the public.

More striking was the rift between Fox and Burke that had erupted in the Commons on 6 May 1791. Burke's speech on the army estimates in February 1790 followed by the publication of the *Reflections* in November had put pressure on his dealings with the opposition Whigs. These tensions burdened his collaboration with some of the trial managers, affecting his relations with his oldest ally in the pursuit of Hastings. Philip Francis had written to Burke from Newmarket in early November, detailing his criticisms of his friend's views on the French Revolution. Burke replied on the 19th with a polite repudiation. Their common position on India helped to shape his response: "When did you find me totally unmoved at the distress of hundreds and thousands of my equals, and only touched with the sufferings of guilty greatness?" Burke implored.[74] The real question was whether the grievances of the French were at all comparable to the distresses of the undone millions of South Asia, and whether the revolutionaries who acted in the name of the citizens of France could plausibly pretend to be redressing the complaints of their own subjects. Burke, along with Francis, was prepared to argue for his "equals"; at issue was the character and content of that equality. Civil equality, Burke believed, had been destroyed by the French experiment, which could never be justified by the imperfections of the previous regime. A similar appeal to a precursor political order underlay the defence of Hastings's actions: his advocates had sought to palliate his criminal activities "by an attempt to prove, that the Moorish dominion was productive of many more and worse instances of inhumanity and perfidy than the English."[75] Burke could not accept that the wickedness of a prior establishment could vindicate the excesses of its successor: "I feel myself much more disposed to sentiments of resentment and indignation against the tyranny of Mr Hastings and Monsr Barnave, than against that of Aurangzeb, and Lewis the 14th." Anything that Francis might say about the "despotism" of pure monarchies had been heard "a thousand times before."[76] Burke was also a defender of the British mixed system of government, but that would not excuse him in supporting perfect tyranny in opposition to imperfect monarchical rule.

Burke had raised the possibility of resigning from the House with William Windham in early 1789, yet the "India business" bound him in point of honour to remain.[77] In the spring of 1791, the same desire was tempting him again. In February he announced to the Commons that, after three years, his "resolution to persevere"

[72] EB to William Adam, 4 January 1791, *Corr.*, VI, p. 198.

[73] *Parliamentary History*, XXVIII, cols. 1225–37.

[74] EB to Philip Francis, 19 November 1790, *Corr.*, VI, p. 171, discussed above, p. 708.

[75] Ibid.

[76] Ibid.

[77] EB to William Windham, c. 24 January 1789, *Corr.*, V, p. 437.

in seeing the trial to an end was unabated.[78] Yet nonetheless in March he was "hinting at retiring." It was the impeachment, once more, that kept him going: "dropped by him it never will be, nor can be."[79] In the event, the managers for the prosecution concluded their evidence on 30 May, with Burke writing to Francis the following day asking him for a conference on how they were to handle the defence.[80] On 2 June 1791, Hastings's counsel began to present their case. Looking back a year later on how the defence team had proceeded, Burke conveyed his conviction that they were playing for time, hoping to exhaust the patience of the public: "It is plain that it is Hastings's plan to continue the Trial until Peers, commoners, and spectators run away from it."[81] The day before, Major Scott had moved for an account of the expenses incurred by the impeachment since 1788. Two weeks later Burke wrote to Dundas seeking his support, believing that the intention of Hastings and his agents was to ensure that the proceedings "should never come to Judgement."[82] However Burke had too much invested to withdraw. He had spent twelve years enmeshed in "this one India pursuit." Nothing but an "irresistible Sense of Duty" could have sustained him in such an unprofitable enterprise. "I am now an old man," he reflected. He had been rewarded with neither wealth, rank, power nor official commendation. The least he could do under the circumstances was to serve his reputation insofar as that would also serve the reputation of his country. As "an old worn out soldier" left in an exposed position, he could not afford to be subject to disgrace by being associated with the excessive costs of the impeachment.[83] Neither would he accept being hung out to dry: this was not a contest between Burke and Hastings, it was a prosecution brought in the name of the Commons.[84]

Burke suspected that Hastings's supporters wanted to explain away his campaign as a product of merely personal rancour to detract from the plausibility of the charges themselves. He also believed that they aimed to smother the case in a mass of detail—"a confused miscellaneous heap," as Burke phrased it.[85] To these tactics they further tried to add an intellectual defence by describing British rule in terms of acclimatisation rather than usurpation: since the Indians had no privileges, property or rights, there was nothing that could ever have been usurped.[86] When this thesis was advanced by Halhed to general consternation, Hastings had affected to disown it; but after Erskine made use of the doctrine in the trial of John Stockton, Hastings's counsel decided to rejuvenate these claims.[87] They returned, as Burke put

[78] EB, Speech on Limitation of the Impeachment, 14 February 1791, *W & S*, VII, p. 98.

[79] Jane Burke to William Burke, 21 March 1791, *Corr.*, VI, p. 238.

[80] Ibid., p. 262.

[81] EB to Richard Burke Jr. c. 8 March 1792, *Corr.*, VII, p. 93.

[82] EB to Henry Dundas, 22 March 1792, ibid., p. 111.

[83] Ibid., p. 116.

[84] Ibid., p. 114.

[85] Ibid., p. 113.

[86] Ibid., p. 112.

[87] Speech of Edward Law, 14 February 1792, *Speeches of the Managers in the Trial of Warren Hastings*, II, pp. 524ff.

it, to their own "Vomit."[88] Yet nothing would cause Burke to relent: "I will pursue him," he insisted—"Mr Hastings shall not escape Judgment." This was, Burke proclaimed, "the great Object for which I live," and he would not leave it short of satisfaction that he had done his utmost to prove the substance of his charges.[89] However, the obstacles in his way still multiplied. His fellow managers, he felt, were deserting him, while the ministry was undermining his criticisms of Company servants. Rumours that John Shore, a former member of Hastings's Committee of Revenue, was to succeed Cornwallis as Governor General reached Burke in the autumn. It was almost the final straw, Burke told Fitzwilliam: "This, I confess, has almost beaten me to the Ground."[90]

The appointment of Shore was perplexing and insulting since it compromised the purpose of the impeachment. The threat of it made Burke fear for "the breaking of my heart," bringing to mind his enemies who were determined to ruin him and his family—in "the present Age and to all posterity." He was, he protested, drifting "on the last Planck of his wreck."[91] In his eyes Shore had been implicated in the scandals of the Hastings years, and was adept as a Company bureaucrat at subterfuge and evasion.[92] Burke felt the burden of opposing the measure as he was cut loose from Fox's supporters—lying, as he complained to Dundas, under the "unprovoked" and "implacable" hostility of his former peers.[93] This feeling of isolation continued until Hastings's counsel had completed delivering their evidence. As they finished their submissions in the spring of 1793, Burke spent his time at Westminster Hall and in its environs. The court was now sitting from the morning into the evening, with Burke present on 25 May from 9 a.m. until 6 p.m. On that day, he was subject to an animated attack by Archbishop Markham, reported two days later in the *World*.[94] "The manner exceeded the matter," as Burke's brother informed his son: such "furious agitation, and bodily convulsion" was wonderful to behold.[95] The day after this outburst, Burke wrote to Arthur Murphy, underscoring the commitment that had sustained his career: he had sought to defend two "sacred" principles, each fundamentally dependent on the other: liberty on the one hand, and authority on the other.[96] Recently, in connection with France and India, he had been driven to challenge two malign excrescences nurtured by the perversion of those principles—the "Tyranny of Freedom," paraded in France, and the "Licentiousness of Power," let

[88] EB to Henry Dundas, 22 March 1792, *Corr.*, VII, p. 112.

[89] EB to Captain John Grey, post 7 June 1792, ibid., p. 148.

[90] 5 October 1792, ibid., p. 233.

[91] Ibid.

[92] Dundas had been impressed by Shore during his work with Cornwallis on the Permanent Settlement in the summer of 1792. See Phillips, *East India Company*, pp. 69–70.

[93] EB to Henry Dundas, 8 October 1792, *Corr.*, VII, p. 247.

[94] *World*, 27 May 1793.

[95] Richard Burke Sr. to Richard Burke Jr., 29 May 1793, *Corr.*, VII, pp. 369–70.

[96] Ibid., p. 367. On the centrality of these values to Burke's career, see Richard Bourke, "Liberty, Authority and Trust in Burke's Idea of Empire," *Journal of the History of Ideas*, 61:3 (Summer 2000), pp. 453–71.

loose in India.[97] Each effort, however, spluttered into the void, leaving Burke only his conscience as consolation.

Counsel for the defence closed on 28 May 1793, concluding with a degree of swiftness that threw the managers off balance. Their speeches in reply were now scheduled for 5 June, cutting them little slack with which to prepare their material. Hastings himself was in dire straits, expecting the prosecution to spin out the trial for another year.[98] The managers were indeed planning to have the affair extended, though Burke feared they might be thwarted by the "Indian Interest" inside parliament.[99] He began raising the alarm about a conspiracy among the bishops, and the ongoing hostile designs of Stanhope and Thurlow.[100] On 7 June postponement was finally granted, with the trial set to resume in February 1794. This last session of the impeachment was the longest, forcing a deferral of judgment until 1795. It also began with tragedy for Burke: his brother, Richard, died suddenly a week before its commencement. Burke was devastated, and contemplated giving up his Westminster seat, thus abandoning the conduct of the trial to others.[101] But by the beginning of March 1794 ongoing wrangles over the admissibility of evidence prompted him to plan a protest against the conduct of the trial. Towards that end, he began work with the managers' solicitor to produce a report on the legal attitudes that had guided the judges in the impeachment, based on a comparative study of past judgments in the Lords' *Journals*. The *Report* was finally presented to the Commons on 30 April.[102] The interpretation of the rules of evidence and pleading over the course of the impeachment, Burke believed, set a damaging precedent for future prosecutions of the kind. This would sap the power of the House of Commons in its capacity as accuser, and so undermine parliamentary responsibility.[103]

The arguments of Burke's *Report* grew out of his experience of the previous three years, supplemented by a lifetime of reflection on the historical nature of British law. Over the recent period, he had repeatedly been accused of pursuing his quarry out of personal venom, and so of employing delaying tactics to satisfy the same motive.[104] However, from Burke's angle, the length of the trial had been determined by the volume of challenges to the managers' evidence and to the manner in which they prosecuted their case. These challenges were facilitated by an insistence on applying the rules of proceeding in the lower courts to the conduct of the impeachment. Appeal to such rules was a piece of opportunism on the part of the defence, but Burke thought that these appeals were made effective by a mixture of attitudes

[97] EB to Arthur Murphy, 26 May 1793, *Corr.*, VII, p. 368.

[98] *Speeches of the Managers in the Trial of Warren Hastings*, III, pp. xxviii–xxxii.

[99] EB to Henry Dundas, 7 June 1793, *Corr.*, VII, p. 371.

[100] Ibid., p. 372.

[101] William Windham to Richard Burke Jr., 11 February 1794, ibid., p. 531, editorial note.

[102] Burke had worked himself "almost blind" on the proofs close to publication. See EB to John Ley, 22 April 1794, ibid., p. 539.

[103] EB to Henry Addington, 14 March 1794, ibid., p. 534.

[104] On this theme, see EB to Lord Loughborough, c. 17 March 1796, *Corr.*, VIII, p. 426.

on the part of the Lords: first, by the narrow professional ethos that had come to predominate among its robed members, but also by the corruption that had captured many peers. Burke had earlier drawn attention to the fact that even Hastings had recognised the extent to which "the sons of great families" in Britain had come to India to acquire "immense premature fortunes."[105] This situation made the Lords a tainted tribunal before which the case of the natives of India would not be impartially heard. Burke had scoured the Governor's minutes where Hastings complained of the pressure he was under from "Persons of high Rank and Station" in Britain to offer their friends and relations preferment and protection in India, including those sons of the great who were "aspiring to the rapid Acquisition" of wealth before returning to settle in the mother country.[106] This gave rise to what Burke termed a species of "false patriotism," whereby the extraction of wealth through patronage in India was mistakenly seen as a commercial boon to the Company and to Britain. These attitudes pervaded the House of Commons as well, leaving some of the representatives of the eastern empire in the hands of what Burke thought of as the "antichrist of representation": namely, members who served the interest of their fortunes instead of India's.[107] Since all this militated against an effective prosecution of malefactors for high crimes and misdemeanours, Burke felt that the disadvantageous interpretation of impeachment procedures by the legal profession in the Lords imposed an additional slant on the partiality of the tribunal. It therefore required examination and criticism.

Burke had first mounted his criticisms in a systematic way in mid-February 1791. The law, he made clear, was a profession that he greatly admired, although it was peculiarly inclined to foster an *esprit de corps* amongst its members. From thence derived their hostility to impeachments, since these were a means of holding even the legal body to account.[108] Accordingly, they employed forms of procedure as obstacles to justice by foisting the technicalities of the common law upon parliament acting in its judicial capacity. The law comprised persons who were subject to the infirmities of their species, above all the disposition to extend their powers—in the case of lawyers, this impulse was geared towards extending the jurisdiction of their profession, and hence to weakening any "Power by which they may be limited and controlled." They shunned accountability before another body, and so it was "the Business of the House of Commons to counteract this Tendency."[109] In securing that objective, parliament was entitled to conduct itself in accordance with its own distinct precedents and usages, free of the judicial principles of either the common

[105] EB, Speech on Limitation of the Impeachment, 14 February 1791, *W & S*, VII, p. 102.

[106] This material is cited in EB, Speech in Reply, 14 June 1794, ibid., pp. 629–31.

[107] EB, Speech on Limitation of the Impeachment, 14 February 1791, ibid., pp. 102–3. Cf. Burke's worry that "the breakers of law in India" might become "the makers of law for England" in EB, *Reflections*, ed. Clark, p. 199 [66].

[108] EB, Speech on Limitation of the Impeachment, 14 February 1791, *W & S*, VII, p. 103.

[109] EB, *Report from the Committee of the House of Commons Appointed to Inspect the Lords Journals*, 30 April 1794, *W & S*, VII, p. 151.

or the civil law, based on its superior dignity and wisdom.[110] Burke's *Report* of 1794 was intended to demonstrate that a thorough examination of the Lords' *Journals* confirmed that these assumptions underpinned previous parliamentary trials. This was crucial ground for Burke to establish since the preservation of what he saw as the "Law of Parliament" was a precondition for defending "the Rights and Liberties of the Subject."[111] If judicial and executive power could not be subjected to parliamentary scrutiny, the constitutional provision of a separation of powers would be undermined. Such scrutiny, however, depended on inquiries being conducted on terms set by parliament, since otherwise the judiciary would be its own judge and jury. As Coke put it, in a passage from the *Fourth Part of the Institutes* that Burke cited, "As every Court of Justice hath Laws and Customs for its direction . . . So the High Court of Parliament, *suis propriis legibus & consuetudinibus subsistit*."[112] In practice, this meant adopting the principle of publicity, as respected by the courts at large; proceeding on the basis of common understanding rather than the technicalities of the law; adopting a flexible position on the use of evidence, including, where appropriate, the admissibility of circumstantial proof; and a refusal to model the high court of parliament on the practices of the courts below.

Burke concluded his *Report* with this final recommendation, observing that the constitution of a parliamentary court had to be distinguished from the composition of judicial bodies lower down. In trials below, a judge interposed himself between the evidence and the jury in order to save such a body "taken promiscuously from the Mass of the People" form error based on unavoidable ignorance.[113] However, the situation concerning the Lords in the high court of parliament was entirely different, since the peers had to be considered equal to the assessment of evidence without the intercession of any legal power. These were people of "high Rank, generally of the best Education, and of sufficient Knowledge of the World; and they are a permanent, settled, a corporate, and not an occasional and transitory Judicature." They ought, in that capacity, to deliberate and adjudicate as equals. Should they consider themselves reliant on expert advise, and so dependent, much like a jury, on guidance from the legal profession, the jurisdiction of the Lords would be threatened with bifurcation, separating the bishops and lay members from the lawyers.[114] This would have the additional adverse consequence of sacrificing a more capacious political prudence to the narrow, specialised judgments of a professional body of men. The *Report* was intended to highlight the negative results that might follow from this, based on the experience of the Hastings impeachment. One positive principle cherished by the common law which professionalisation among the Law Lords threatened to undo was the principle publicly employed in recording the reasons for specific judgments. This, in fact, was the rationale behind law reports: unlike the

[110] EB, Speech on Limitation of the Impeachment, 14 February 1791, *W & S*, VII, pp. 104–5.

[111] EB, *Report from the Committee*, p. 116.

[112] Coke, *Fourth Part of the Institutes*, pp. 15–16, cited by EB, *Report from the Committee*, p. 120.

[113] Ibid., p. 192.

[114] Ibid., pp. 192–93.

digests, institutes and codes of the Roman law, common law records rested not on the authority of supreme power, but on the authority of legal reasoning. Without this procedure, the judgment against John Hampden in the Ship Money case would never have been subject to public suspicion.[115] Thus public reasoning in legal judgments was a means of conforming the laws of the country to common opinion rather than to the demands of power.[116]

The principle of publicity appeared to Burke to be a staple part of "the Character and Spirit of our Judicial Proceeding, continued from Time immemorial."[117] Its justification rested not exclusively on its antiquity, however, but on its ongoing utility as judged by practical experience and theoretical reflection. A public record of reasoned argumentation served the dual purpose of preserving continuity within the body of the law while also marking appropriate departures from established precedent. This facilitated a process of orderly change rather than chaotic innovation; it was the basis of progressive political improvement secured against whimsical departures from sound practice. It enabled the provision of justice to keep pace with developing affairs, above all with improvements in principles and policy that accompanied the expansion of commercial empire.[118] Where judgments were to be rendered affecting the comportment of state power, the verdict ought not to be shrouded in the mysteries of legal jargon, but ought to be presented in language accessible to the population at large based on common understanding. Burke cited the legal authority, Michael Foster, to make his point: it was appropriate for the conduct of parliamentary trials "*loquendum ut vulgus*."[119] The resort to professional vocabularies was an assault not just on common speech, but on common sense as well, representing a throwback to the barbarisms of pre-enlightened civil science. Burke criticised the jurisprudence of classical civil law in these terms, and chastised its modern followers for substituting "subtle Disquisitions" in the place of a workable system of legal practice.[120] The law was concerned with human affairs rather than metaphysical entities, and could not be completely reduced to rules without remainder. Its application required judgment depending on circumstances instead of inflexible maxims. Flex-

[115] Ibid., p. 141.

[116] For the seventeenth-century history of this idiom of thought, see Alan Cromartie, *The Constitutionalist Revolution: An Essay on the History of England, 1450–1642* (Cambridge: Cambridge University Press, 2006); J.G.A. Pocock, *The Ancient Constitution and the Feudal Law: A Study of English Historical Thought in the Seventeenth Century* (Cambridge: Cambridge University Press, 1957, 1987).

[117] EB, *Report from the Committee*, p. 142.

[118] Ibid. See also EB, *Letter to the Sheriffs of Bristol*, 3 April 1777, *W & S*, III, p. 295. Cf. William Blackstone, *Commentaries on the Laws of England* (London: 1765–9), 4 vols., I, pp. 69–70.

[119] EB, *Report from the Committee*, p. 131, citing Michael Foster, *A Report of Some Proceedings on the Commission of Oyer and Terminer and Gaol Delivery for the Trial of the Rebels in the Year 1746* (Oxford: 1762), pp. 389–90.

[120] EB, *Report from the Committee*, p. 158. For his understanding of Roman imperial jurisprudence, including its adoption of stoic precepts, Burke relies on Giovanni Vicenzo Gravina, *Origines iuris civilis* (Leipzig: 1708), pp. 84–85. Bartolus of Sassoferrato and Petrus Baldus of Ubaldis are identified by Burke as scholastic inheritors of stoic casuistry.

ibility, in fact, was an index of liberality which arrived with a more enlightened legal science, after the extension of Roman ideas of equity and advances in modern jurisprudence alike.[121] In modern Europe, with the extension of empire and commerce, in tandem with the development of the law of nature and nations, the technical severities of an earlier age gave way to a more civilised and humane approach to legal judgment: "as new Views and new Combinations of Things were opened, this antique Rigour and over-done Severity gave Way to the Accommodation of Human Concerns, for which Rules were made, and not Human Concerns to bend to them."[122]

Burke drew on Hardwicke's famous judgment of 1744 in *Omychund v. Barker* to reinforce his argument.[123] The case turned on the admissibility of witnesses' evidence—specifically, those connected to the Indian merchant, "Omychund," who was seeking to make good his claim in the English Court of Chancery for the recovery of debt against the estate of Hugh Barker. Disregarding the protestations of Barker's counsel, Hardwicke ruled that evidence taken from Hindu witnesses was admissible in English courts, despite the impossibility of their swearing the Christian oath.[124] This involved setting to one side authoritative legal opinion in Bracton, Fortescue and Coke regarding infidels. The Solicitor General, William Murray, later Lord Chief Justice Mansfield, acting as one of the counsel for Omychund, cited Christopher St. Germain's 1528 *Dialogus de fundamentis legum Angliae* to the effect that "reason" was the ground for all laws, and that consequently legal judgment should serve justice and convenience rather than slavishly adhering to inapplicable precedents.[125] Burke proceeded to cite the Attorney General, Dudley Ryder, as well as the Chief Justice, John Wills, in support of Murray's claim that the legal rules should fit the case, as modified by human reason to suit the circumstance in the interest of justice.[126] Next Burke drew attention to the opinion of Thomas Parker expressed in *Wells v. Williams* that "the necessity of trade has mollified the too rigorous rules of the old laws in their . . . discouragement of aliens." Previously a Jew, regarded as an enemy alien, was not permitted to sue for justice in the English courts. "But now commerce has taught the world more humanity," Parker declared.[127] This example, like Murray's, enjoined liberality in the face of cosmopolitan experience as

[121] According to Gravina, *Origines iuris civilis*, p. 86, which Burke cites again, Roman law was mired in crudely superstitious forms before its liberalisation around the age of Cicero.

[122] EB, *Report from the Committee*, p. 163.

[123] Ibid., p. 164.

[124] John Tracy Atkins, *Reports of Cases Argued and Determined in the High Court of Chancery* (1765–8), ed. Francis William Sanders (London: 3rd ed., 1794), 3 vols., I, pp. 21ff.

[125] Ibid., p. 32.

[126] EB, *Report from the Committee*, pp. 164–65, citing Atkins, *Reports*, I, pp. 31–50. For discussion of the case, see David Lieberman, *The Province of Legislation Determined: Legal Theory in Eighteenth-Century Britain* (Cambridge: Cambridge University Press, 1989), ch. 4. For Mansfield in general, see James Oldham, *The Mansfield Manuscripts and the Growth of English Law in the Eighteenth Century* (Chapel Hill, NC: University of North Carolina Press, 1992), 2 vols.

[127] Robert Raymond, *Reports of Cases Argued and Adjudged in the Courts of the King's Bench and Common Pleas* (London: 1765), 3 vols., I, pp. 282–83.

international developments opened new avenues to justice, each of which was embraced in accordance with the "*Genius*" of the law of England but without what Burke termed "artificial circumscriptions."[128] By this means, British jurisprudence would be able to conform "to the Growth of our Commerce and our Empire."[129] In this way, Burke could argue that although *doux commerce* had descended into conquest and belligerence in Asia, it had facilitated enlightenment and liberality in Britain.

15.4 Counterfeit Virtue

On 7 May 1794 Burke wrote to the Speaker, Henry Addington, sketching how the prosecution might structure its response to Hastings's defence.[130] Between 8 and 27 May, Grey, Sheridan, Fox and Taylor presented their final statements. Then, on 28 May, Burke began his speech in reply. This epic speech extended over nine days, beginning with a restatement of the principal grounds of the prosecution's case, and proceeding to reiterate the main elements of the Benares and Begams articles before considering the outlines of the Presents and Contracts charges. While Burke retraced many of the arguments laid out at the opening of the impeachment, he also used the opportunity to break new ground. This involved offering an analysis of Hastings's character, deflating any suggestion that this was a heroic, if brutal, conqueror—"We never said he was a tiger and a lion," Burke reminded the judges. "No. We said he was a weasel and a Rat."[131] Here Burke was returning to a thesis about Hastings that he had begun to develop when opening the Presents charge in 1789. His purpose was not merely to diminish Hastings by comparing him to some of the more degraded creatures to be found in the animal kingdom. He further likened him to "a despicable insect" among a "swarm of locusts" capable of more devastation than the most powerful beast in the field.[132] But the point was precise: an insidiously corrupting creature could be more catastrophically destructive than the depredations committed by heroic violence. Hastings had held the bullock contract in Bengal in 1760–1, and Burke repeatedly drew attention to this base employment. But he did not intend this to be interpreted as a piece of social disparagement. It was, instead, an exercise in political discrimination. Hastings, Burke believed, was unfit to rule; he had been "exalted to great unmerited power."[133] He was a sordid, aspiring business contractor, disposed to serve his immediate interest, and thus ill-

[128] EB, *Report from the Committee*, pp. 167–68.

[129] Ibid., p. 168. In the same spirit, Burke drew upon the arguments of Francis Buller and John Fonblanque. Burke identified Buller with the cause of Hastings: see EB to William Windham, 8 January 1795, *Corr.*, VIII, p. 113.

[130] *Corr.*, VII, pp. 540–41.

[131] EB, Speech in Reply, 28 May 1794, *W & S*, VII, p. 277.

[132] Ibid.

[133] Ibid.

adapted to responsibility for great affairs of state. "We have not accused him of the vices of conquerors": these might over time be transformed into the virtues of the statesman. For Burke, unlike Smith, there was nothing that barred a merchant or contractor from exercising authority—although, equally, there was nothing about these roles that fitted their occupants for statesmanship. A corrupt contractor, however, posed a particular problem: a great official, like a great trader, might rise above his immediate preoccupations to enjoy a position of public responsibility, but a crooked dealer was irredeemably concerned with swindling his way into profit.

Hastings, Burke noted, was a "creature of the bureau."[134] His vices were mean rather than great in stature, but they carried horrendous consequences all the same. Bureaucratic corruption spread like a pestilence, extending the culture of bribery and extortion without restraint. What the experience of British involvement in South Asia demonstrated was that a man is not less obnoxious on account of his insignificance, but potentially more so. Base and mercenary habits could blight a whole civilisation: "such minds placed in an unsuitable power, mind and power unsuitable, can do more mischief to a country . . . than the proudest high and mighty conquerors."[135] The motto of imperial subjection could best be borrowed from Virgil—*parcere subiectis et debellare superbos*.[136] Such an exercise of force promised benign reconstruction in the wake of carnage and destruction. Corrupted power, however, pretended to aim at upright conduct whilst actually operating by chicane. It thus produced a range of "counterfeit, hypocritical virtues" more pernicious than cruelty itself.[137] Acts of naked, violent passion were susceptible to moderation whereas principled exploitation was unrelenting in its thoroughness. For this reason, "it is better to have no principles than false principles of Government."[138]Driven by low, crafty self-interest while faking public virtue, Hastings was compelled to rob his subjects of their rights, property, distinctions, usages, laws and sense of honour.[139] Against this despotic impulse, founded on a fantasy of eastern slavery, Burke counterposed Luke Scrafton's account of society in Asia structured around rank, equity, privilege and respect.[140] In effect, Burke believed, Hastings perfected the British assault upon this structure. On the penultimate day of his speech, on 14 June 1794, he recalled how Hastings had been dispatched to reform a degenerate system of administration. At that point, "Mr. Hastings ought to have laid aside all the habits of a Bullock Contractor" since his instructions required him to play the part of "a great

[134] Ibid.

[135] Ibid., 5 June 1794, p. 383.

[136] Virgil, *Aeneid*, VI, line 853, cited in EB, Speech in Reply, 5 June 1794, *W & S*, VII, p. 286.

[137] Ibid., 28 May 1794, p. 232.

[138] Ibid., 30 May 1794, p. 289.

[139] Ibid., p. 284.

[140] Ibid., 28 May 1794, p. 279, citing Luke Scrafton, *Reflections on the Government of Indostan* (London: 1770). For the context of this debate, see above, chapter 12, section 5.

Minister for the reformation of a great service full of abuses."[141] But instead he spread these abuses like a poison through all that he touched.

This was an attack not upon Hastings's birth but on his character. His perpetual defence was that he had inherited a malignant system. Burke's claim was that he further deformed a dysfunctional administration by exercising his evidently "abominable talents" in the service of his "more abominable dispositions."[142] His inclination was fundamentally that of a rebel against restraint; it was this that made him tyrannise over populations. "He that is a Tyrant will be a Rebel," Burke concluded. Both roles derived from an underlying attitude, depending only on opportunity for their expression: "according as the relation varies, the man is a Tyrant if superior, a Rebel if inferior."[143] Hastings needed appropriate instruments for his purpose, as he made out that he was governing whilst actually engaging in oppression. For this he had to administer by means of masquerade, "where no one thing appears to you as it is": slavish exploiters were made to appear in the guise of respectable rulers, established princes as if they were longstanding slaves.[144] But in the end it was the Governor General pulling the levers behind the scene, conducting "the great Opera of India, an Opera of fraud, deceptions, tricks and Harlequin proceedings."[145] The astonishing fact was how few levers were needed to have so dramatic an effect. The British Empire in India was composed of "three systems of people": the Muslim minority who comprised the old regime, the Hindu majority who made up both the landed and monied interest, and the governing interest now vested in the British. This last component was "infinitely small"—"scarcely," in fact, "to be mentioned."[146] Nonetheless, they wielded enormous power through their control of revenue and arms. Burke thought Hastings adept at finding suitable natives to collaborate in his enterprise, but he could also draw on the cadre of Company servants who were fit for purpose. With the extinction of the old Muslim administrative class, and the impoverishment of the landed interest of the country, these servants had a crucial role to play. They came into Hastings's hands as ready material for exploitation: desperate to succeed yet without education or worthy exemplars, they were offered either oblivion or conspiracy in corruption.[147]

Burke had already expended great effort in setting before parliament the damage inflicted by servants on the government of Bengal, on the external relations of the Company in the Carnatic, on the situation in Benares and the affairs of Rohilkhand. He once more summed up his main conclusions over the course of his speech in reply, but he now lavished particular attention on the affairs of Awadh, the

[141] EB, Speech in Reply, 14 June 1794, *W & S*, VII, pp. 619–20.
[142] Ibid., 5 June 1794, p. 386.
[143] Ibid., 3 June 1794, p. 339. Cf. ibid., 5 June 1794, p. 400.
[144] Ibid., p. 388. Cf. p. 414.
[145] Ibid., p. 409.
[146] Ibid., 12 June 1794, pp. 568–69.
[147] Ibid., 14 June 1794, pp. 616–17.

treatment of which had been the subject of fourteen of the twenty original articles of impeachment.[148] Since 1724 Awadh, "in extent about the size of England," had enjoyed effective autonomy as a quasi-independent province within the Mughal Empire.[149] It came to terms with the British after the Battle of Buxar in 1764, finally signing up to the Treaty of Benares in 1773. This imposed on the Wazir of Awadh, Shuja-ud-Daula, the obligation to accept troops stationed in his territory while paying a subsidy to the British for the privilege. The Wazir's successor, Asaf-ud-Daula, agreed to increase this subsidy under the Treaty of Faizabad in 1775, at the same time ceding Benares to the Company. East India Company involvement in the affairs of Awadh steadily deepened, with the Wazir's dependence increasing in tandem with his debts.[150] To guarantee their subsidy, the Company moved to control the revenue of the country; it also set about raiding some of its treasures. Much of this activity was conducted by the Company's resident in the Wazir's court at Lucknow—for the most part Nathaniel Middleton in alternation with John Bristow. Together with their accompanying officials and a staff of military personnel, they descended, as Burke put it, like a "swarm of locusts" on the country.[151] Exploitation intensified after the Treaty of Chunar, concluded in 1781.[152] The collection of revenues farmed out to military officers continued despite promises that this burden would be lifted, leading to allegations of direct extortion and oppression.

All of this was an affront to the law of nations, Burke insisted. On the second day of his speech he had turned to consider the duties of a reigning power as these ought to be observed towards its dependents. Such duties entailed obligations that were not merely a matter of convention but were stipulated by the law of nature itself. For this conclusion Burke drew on the work of Vattel rather than the authority of Grotius.[153] In *Le droit des gens*, translated into English in 1760 and 1793, Vattel opened with a history of the emergence of the idea of a "law of nations," showing how in the modern era the inadequate conception of Hugo Grotius, who tended to reduce its content to "the common consent of mankind," gave way to the "true idea of the law of nations," notably in Barbeyrac's revision of Grotius' argument given in a note to

[148] EB, Articles of Impeachment, 14–28 May 1787, *W & S*, VI, pp. 147–56, 201–58: namely, Article Two and Articles Twelve through Twenty.

[149] The quotation appears in *W & S*, VII, 5 June 1794, p. 383.

[150] Cuthbert C. Davies, *Warren Hastings and Oudh* (Oxford: Oxford University Press, 1939).

[151] EB, Speech in Reply, 3 June 1794, *W & S*, VII, p. 381.

[152] The impact of the treaty is discussed in Barnett, *North India between Empires*.

[153] EB, Speech in Reply, 3 June 1794, *W & S*, VII, 30 May 1794, p. 291. Cf. ibid., p. 282, on a state's being "bound in all transactions with foreign Powers to act according to the known, recognized rules of the Law of Nations, with regard to all powers that are Sovereign, or appear to be Sovereign, whether dependent or independent." For Burke's criticisms of Vattel, see EB, *Remarks on the Policy of the Allies* (1793), *W & S*, VIII, p. 474, as well as chapter 8, section 6, and chapter 14, section 7 above, and chapter 16, section 2 below. F. P. Lock, *Edmund Burke: 1730–1797* (Oxford: Clarendon Press, 1998–2006), 2 vols., II, p. 454, n. 66, suggests that Burke's reticence about Vattel was partly rhetorical.

the text of *De iure belli ac pacis*.[154] There Barbeyrac took issue with the Grotian claim that the authority of the "*Right of Nations*" derived from common practice among states, citing Dio Chrisostom's notion that law was founded on custom.[155] Vattel, in opposition, refers his reader to Pufendorf, elucidating his position with the claim that the principles of the law of nations are consistent with the fundamental laws of nature.[156] Vattel goes on to claim that a proper understanding of how the law of nations, while based on natural law, nonetheless involved a modification of its principles in practice, was the particular achievement of Christian Wolff, on whose results he himself intended to build.[157] In his speech in reply, Burke draws attention to one particular practical principle as set out by Vattel in chapter 16 of book I.[158] This concerns the protection due to a weaker state reliant on the offices of a more powerful hegemon to whom it is tied by treaty arrangements. Vattel had been thinking about the responsibilities of the Dukes of Austria towards the city of Lucerne. However Burke, despite Vattel's allegedly "Republican" cast of mind, applied his ideas to relations between Benares and Bengal.[159] Nonetheless, the same principle was applicable to the Company's relationship to Awadh. Where a powerful neighbour fails to ensure the protection it is obliged to provide, its dependent is released from all its corresponding duties.[160]

Hastings met Asaf-ud-Daula on 19 September 1781 after the revolt of Chait Singh in Benares and agreed to relieve the Wazir of some of his burdens incurred by British pensioners, as well as some of the troops stationed in his territory. At the same time, a decision was made to continue the use of military personnel in managing short-term revenue farms. As it turned out, all promises of relief were not delivered and the measures to improve efficiency proved oppressive. As with Benares, the Company reneged upon its obligation to protect and rebellion was the justifiable result. On Vattel's terms, "a compact" had been "dissolved," and so the weaker party was entitled to resume its rights.[161] Accepting this judgment in the case of Awadh,

[154] Emer de Vattel, *The Law of Nations, or the Principles of the Law of Nature, Applied to the Conduct and Affairs of Nations and Sovereigns*, ed. Béla Kapossy and Richard Whatmore (Indianapolis, IN: Liberty Fund, 2008), pp. 8–9.

[155] Hugo Grotius, *The Rights of War and Peace*, ed. Richard Tuck (Indianapolis, IN: Liberty Fund, 2005), 3 vols., I, pp. 162–63. See Dio Chrysostom, *Orationes*, De consuetudine, LXXVI, 1.

[156] Grotius, *Rights of War and Peace*, I, p. 163, Barbeyrac's note 3, referencing Pufendorf, *De iure naturae*, II, iii, 23. Burke follows suit: see EB, Speech in Reply, 30 May 1794, *W & S*, VII, p. 291: "the Law of Nations . . . is the Law of reason and the Law of nature, drawn from the pure sources of morality."

[157] Vattel, *Law of Nations*, p. 10. On Vattel's relationship to Wolff, see Simone Zurbuchen, "Vattel's Law of Nations and Just War Theory," *History of European Ideas*, 35 (2009), pp. 408–17, revised in Isaac Nakhimovsky, "Carl Schmitt's Vattel and the 'Law of Nations' between Enlightenment and Revolution," *Grotiana*, 31 (2010), pp. 141–64.

[158] EB, Speech in Reply, 30 May 1794, *W & S*, VII, p. 291.

[159] Vattel, *Law of Nations*, p. 209. For Burke's criticism of Vattel's apparent indulgence of the "Right of the People" to claim the sovereignty of their state, see EB, *Remarks on the Policy of the Allies* (1793), *W & S*, VIII, p. 474.

[160] Vattel, *Law of Nations*, p. 208.

[161] Ibid., p. 209.

Burke had earlier noted, in the thirteenth article of impeachment, that the country fell under the protection of the East India Company, and that consequently the Governor General was bound to attend to its prosperity and "religiously abstain from any Act which had a Tendency to the Prejudice thereof."[162] When Hastings failed to deliver, the country apparently rose up "as if it were by common consent."[163] Burke's understanding of developments at the time is substantially derived from the evidence of Robert Holt, assistant to the resident at the Wazir's court from 1779, who had witnessed conditions in the districts of Bahraich and Gorakhpur under the administration of Colonel Alexander Hannay.[164] Holt testified to the use of corporal punishment, the confinement of "refractory Zemindars" bound in irons in mud forts and bamboo structures, the emigration of immiserated population, and the sale of children in times of distress.[165] This led, Burke contended, to a "general Insurrection" in response to the violation of natural rights.[166]

Two rights in particular were violated, Burke argued. First, the alleged forced sale of children offended against the order of nature: "The love that God has placed in the Parents to their own children, the first fruit of that second conjunction which has been made among mankind, is the first bond and first formation of society. It is stronger than all laws, for it is the law of nature."[167] Second, the displacement of persons fleeing in distress was an affront to the natural attachment of individuals to their "natal soil," and so is only likely to be induced by direct oppression.[168] Accordingly, Burke charged that the native subjects under Hannay's sway "rose in a just rebellion" in response to a de facto ruler who had acted in defiance "of the laws and rights of the people."[169] Since, as Burke saw it, Hastings "had the whole Government of Oude in him" from 1776 to 1784, responsibility for abuses rested upon his shoulders.[170] In any case, his self-declared efforts to improve the situation, notably by the Treaty of Chunar in 1781, seemed to Burke almost calculated to fail. Hastings's refusal to honour his own commitments in the case of Awadh was taken to exemplify a wider pattern of perfidy. Since the business of government had been invested in the Governor General, it fell to him to assume responsibility for its three great offices: the regular administration of revenue, maintaining the magistracy in respect, and securing the people in their moveable and immoveable property.[171] Not only did Hastings fail to honour these obligations, he also violated explicit undertakings to do so.

[162] EB, Thirteenth Article of Impeachment, *W & S*, VI, p. 216.

[163] EB, Speech in Reply, 5 June 1794, *W & S*, VII, p. 417.

[164] *Minutes of the Evidence Taken at the Trial of Warren Hastings*, I, pp. 381–82.

[165] Ibid., pp. 283–85.

[166] EB, Thirteenth Article of Impeachment, *W & S*, VI, p. 220; EB, Speech in Reply, 5 June 1794, *W & S*, VII, p. 417. Against Burke it was claimed that the rising was fomented by the Begams at Faizabad.

[167] Ibid., p. 416.

[168] Ibid.

[169] Ibid., p. 417.

[170] Ibid., p. 394.

[171] Ibid., p. 412.

This went towards illustrating the extent to which the Governor General had undermined imperial trust. Good faith, Burke contended, might have secured India as a legitimate conquest—the "most glorious" that had ever been seen in the world. This opportunity, however, had been sacrificed to the "perpetual tissue of perfidy and breach of faith" that characterised Hastings's *modus operandi*.[172] If the British Empire were to fall, it would fall through violence and breach of trust; it could only be maintained through public faith.[173] Yet under Hastings it had proceeded by violent conquest and confiscation, as though mimicking the pathologies of Jacobinism. Burke concluded his speech on 16 June 1794 by invoking events in France since 1789 as amounting to the most astonishing "moral earthquake" that had ever convulsed terrestrial existence.[174] Caught in the storm of the great shifts in moral and political sensibility that had engulfed the affairs of France and Europe over the previous five years, the Lords could offer nothing but justice to offset the cataclysmic character of the times. Should the Houses of the British parliament ever suffer the fate of the *parlement* of Paris, their only consolation would be the virtue of their past decisions. Justice in the trial of Hastings would be a blow against "Indianism" since it represented a stand in favour of morality in public life. But it would also, Burke was implying, amount to a stand against Jacobinism since Indian corruption shared the same tendency to expropriation and oppression. Where a tide of iniquity threatened to overwhelm the civilised conduct of affairs, the defence of justice operated as a mode of defiance. Whatever lay in store for Warren Hastings, the principles of right would still persist even when the globe was "burned to ashes."[175]

On 20 June 1794, the Commons voted its thanks to the managers of the trial. Burke responded by reminding the House that he had cast no aspersions on individual servants, but had endeavoured to blame the contagion of rapacity in India by exposing the captain general at the helm.[176] "My engagement with the publick is fulfilled," Burke wrote to Fitzwilliam the following day.[177] That evening, he applied for the stewardship of the Chiltern Hundreds, an office of emolument under the crown—the traditional way of surrendering a House of Commons seat. He was happy now to escape the daily bustle of Westminster, conscious of having given himself to combatting what he presented as "the two great Evils of our time, Indianism and Jacobinism."[178] It had been a long and, as he put it to Pitt, "possibly a fruitless Struggle."[179] With the death of Burke's son in August, the news of Hastings's acquittal in April 1795 only added despair to grief. Whether he would take on any new work in his retirement would depend on Richard's recovery, he informed French

[172] Ibid., p. 390.
[173] Ibid., pp. 392–93.
[174] Ibid., p. 693.
[175] Ibid.
[176] EB, Speech on Vote of Thanks to the Managers, ibid., p. 695.
[177] EB to Earl Fitzwilliam, 21 June 1794, *Corr.*, VII, p. 552.
[178] Ibid., p. 553.
[179] EB to William Pitt, 25 June 1794, ibid., p. 554.

Laurence in late July, at a point when his son's condition was badly worsening.[180] When he died on 2 August, Burke was overwhelmed by remorse: "I have not husbanded the Treasure that was in my hands," as he expressed himself to Fitzwilliam.[181] Receiving the news from Pitt that he was to be granted a pension from the civil list on 30 August 1794, he was pleased at the prospect of security but aggrieved that his son could not now benefit.[182] It was "but watering old withered stumps," he confided to Laurence.[183] Yet the depth of Burke's sorrow did not curb his outrage when the fate of Hastings finally became public. The Lords had "dishonourd [*sic*] themselves forever," as he wrote to Dundas the following May.[184]

The verdict on Hastings was delivered on 23 April 1795. He was acquitted on every charge by a majority of the twenty-nine peers voting.[185] On 13 May a group of proprietors of East India stock gave notice of their intention to call a General Court with a view to finding a way to recompense Hastings for his services to the Company and to indemnify him against losses resulting from the impeachment. Burke was appalled: this amounted, he complained, to a tax on Indian suffering.[186] The following day, Dundas assured him that his fears were without foundation since the Board of Control would have to consent to any payment to Hastings.[187] In early June the Court of Proprietors resolved to compensate Hastings. "They will not be satisfied with an escape," Burke commented to Dundas: "They must have a Triumph."[188] To Burke's relief the crown law officers ruled that the Company could not award an annuity to its former Governor General without the consent of the government. Nonetheless, the Chairman and Deputy Chairman of the Company were charged by the Court of Proprietors with taking up the issue with the ministry in October. Agreement was reached over the course of the winter months, with news reaching Burke of a rapprochement in February. There are things which "cannot be compromised," he protested to Dundas.[189] He was ready to sacrifice his relations with the minister to secure this point of honour: he would prefer exile, prison or beggary to a retrospective concession that the prosecution had been malicious: "I cannot go down to the Grave leaving such a charge as a Monument to my Memory."[190]

On 1 March 1796 the Board of Control under Dundas formally approved a pension for Hastings. Burke's ensuing breach with the minister stung him severely,

[180] EB to French Laurence, 31 July 1794, ibid., p. 562.

[181] EB to Earl Fitzwilliam, post 4 August 1794, ibid., p. 568.

[182] Ibid., pp. 574–5. A brief political autobiography written by Burke in this context justifying his conduct since 1782 can be found at OSB MS. File 2235.

[183] Extract from MS. letter cited in *Corr.*, VII, p. 575.

[184] EB to Henry Dundas, 13 May 1795, *Corr.*, VIII, p. 240.

[185] The debate and final vote can be found in *Debates of the House of Lords, on the Evidence Delivered in the Trial of Warren Hastings* (London: 1797).

[186] EB to Henry Dundas, 13 May 1795, *Corr.*, VIII, p. 240.

[187] Ibid., p. 241.

[188] 5 June 1795, ibid., p. 260.

[189] EB to Henry Dundas, post 3 February 1796, ibid., p. 385.

[190] Ibid., p. 386.

giving rise to what he described as "pain inexpressible."[191] The reward of an annuity to Hastings's accuser followed by the reward of an annuity to the accused was too much for Burke to bear. "It is flagitious," Burke announced to Fitzwilliam, and he planned a petition to parliament as his "dying act."[192] On the same day, he post-scripted a letter to the Speaker with the ominous phrase, "Fiat justitia et ruat cœlum."[193] As he made clear to William Windham the day before, he in fact expected the heavens to fall.[194] Aged, weak and dispirited, Burke never petitioned the Commons against the government's reward of Hastings. Arranging his speeches on the impeachment with an introductory history would constitute his best protest against what had happened, Laurence advised him.[195] Loughborough had already written to Burke, explaining that compensation for loss was not a reward, and that in any case the acquittal had gone some way towards excusing Hastings in the minds of conscientious members of the public. Burke's pursuit of an acquitted patriot would appear vindictive to a public for whom a rebellion in Benares was a barely memorable event. However, Burke would not be appeased. Seething with anger, he composed a response, re-casting his dismay in the form of a personal defence through three successive drafts.[196] For men like Loughborough, debate about India was a lever in British politics; for Burke it encompassed issues of profound and enduring significance. For fourteen years he had persevered in the cause of imperial justice, and he would not capitulate now to the belated consensus that the accusations against Hastings had been groundless.

It might be tempting to see Burke's doggedness as a form of righteous dogmatism, but that is to miss the nature of his conviction. Apart from his rancorous dissent from the government over the Nawab of Arcot's debts in 1785, Burke had for the most part endeavoured to work with successive administrations, largely because there had been common ground between them. There was a shared sense that the British management of the subcontinent had been productive of great injustices, that the East India Company was complicit in the perpetuation of these violations, and that Hastings bore the brunt of responsibility for corruption. These were not the conclusions of personal malevolence on Burke's part, but common perceptions of ministries and oppositions in the 1770s and 1780s. If North, Robinson, Dundas and Pitt had all meant what they said, a gross betrayal of the duties of government had been permitted to occur in India. It made no sense to pretend that these assumptions had never been espoused, and Burke for one would not be party to a hypocritical revision. During their conferences in the spring of 1780, North had been clear that he regarded Hastings as "highly culpable." It was the intervention of Gilbert

191 EB to Dundas, 6 March 1796, ibid., p. 401.

192 EB to Earl Fitzwilliam, 6 March 1796, ibid., p. 403; EB to the Duke of Portland, 6 March 1796, ibid., p. 404.

193 Ibid., p. 405: "Let justice be done, though the heavens fall."

194 Ibid., p. 404: "Gods [*sic*] ways are unreachable. But I think the Bolt will fall."

195 French Laurence to EB, 15 March 1796, ibid., p. 418.

196 EB to Lord Loughborough, c. 17 March 1796, ibid., pp. 422–23, 423–25, 425–35.

Elliot, Lord Mansfield and others that saved him.[197] The Select and Secret Committees had grown out of this unease, leading Dundas to conclude, along with Burke, that the Governor General was the "True Cause" of the evils that the Committees uncovered. When Adam Ferguson moved for Hastings's recall, it was at Dundas's instigation.[198] It was again Dundas who had moved forty-five resolutions in the Commons as a means of establishing an effective "Code of Laws" for the government of the subcontinent.[199] Equally telling was the fact that both Fox and Pitt's India Bills shared the common objective of taking the government of India out the hands of the East India Company. The Board of Control, like Fox's Commissioners, was intended to end the collusion between Leadenhall Street and the Governor General: however deeply Hastings led the Company into nefarious practices, their reprobation ended by indulging his projects and schemes. Hastings was never their servant, but always secretly their "Master"—a servant permanently in rebellion against the Direction, but one whose rebellion managed to conscript the authorities he opposed.[200] The Lords' verdict had inadvertently complied with this collusion, and the Commons was now effectively condoning this complicity. This way of proceeding threatened the integrity of the British constitution, and violated the principles of fundamental justice.

It is easy in retrospect to represent alarm about the potential subversion of the Revolution settlement as betraying excessive caution, but the fact is that the settlement was regarded as a deliverance that was exposed to the possibility of fatal corruption. Fear of this eventuality haunted much of Burke's career. It was hardly a concern without foundation: a constitution is a pact that might subtly be undone. Since that pact involved rival players, the aggrandisement of one at the expense of the others posed a serious threat to the harmony of the whole. The crown's empowerment through its empire was one possible source of imbalance; the control of the ministry from the imperial provinces presented an alternative means of corruption. Burke reminded Loughborough that the Declaration of Right had been intended to curb the dispensing powers of the crown, yet this appeared as little more than a "contemptible" provision beside the indulgence of a corporation that was permitted to stand outside the law while commanding the resources of a vast empire. Next to the power of the East India Company, the dominion of James II had been but a "paltry Frame," yet the Company was dictating to parliament in a way that should outrage any Whig.[201] The disregard for due process was a gathering "distemper" that would undermine the framework that preserved British politics against anarchy. For this reason, Indianism joined Jacobinism as posing a threat to the British government. Indianism, Burke concluded, was "the worst by far," since it sapped the means

[197] Ibid., p. 429.
[198] Ibid.
[199] Ibid., p. 430.
[200] Ibid., p. 431.
[201] Ibid.

of dealing with a revolt against property and religion.[202] Constitutional propriety offered protection to due process, while due process secured society and politics against implosion. A disregard for law and government along with the procedures that regulated them was an invitation to explode the bonds of society: "it furnishes Jacobinism with its strongest arms against all *formal* Government."[203]

Burke drafted his last surviving letter to Dundas in the period when he was composing his response to Loughborough.[204] He wanted the evidence presented in the Hastings trial digested with an accompanying commentary to leave a record of the case that had been pursued and failed.[205] The ordeal should form a part of British history. This was in fact the only trial that the Commons had ever lost, and it was the only impeachment whose proceedings had not been published.[206] He confessed himself "sore" and "hurt" by what had transpired; it had pierced him "to the quick."[207] Burke saw himself as having endured years of persecution, with loss of wealth, standing and opportunity, for having hunted down systematic criminality that degraded human nature.[208] A blow was now being struck at his reputation for all posterity, threatening to bury his crusade in obloquy and contempt. With both himself and Hastings rewarded for their services to the British interest, the ruined multitudes of India might remember the impeachment as a sham. That prospect was terrible, but it was a possibility that Burke was forced to entertain for his final year and a half.

[202] Ibid., p. 432.
[203] Ibid.
[204] Three drafts survive in ibid., pp. 435–33, 436–37, 437–42.
[205] Ibid., p. 439.
[206] EB to Henry Addington, 7 March 1796, ibid., p. 405.
[207] EB to Henry Dundas, c. 17 March 1796, ibid., p. 436.
[208] Ibid., pp. 437–38.

XVI

REVOLUTIONARY CRESCENDO

BRITAIN, IRELAND AND FRANCE, 1793–1797

Figure 9. Burke in retirement (otium cum dignitate: leisure with dignity) broods over the horrible consequences of a prospective peace with regicide France. James Sayers, *Thoughts on a Regicide Peace* (1796). BM 8826, private collection (Robinson, p. 182).

16.1 Introduction

On 1 February 1793, as Hastings's defence was delivering its response to the prosecution in the impeachment trial, France declared war on Britain. Nine days later, Pitt's government reciprocated with its own declaration of hostilities. Burke now regarded French territory as occupied by an austere republic that had substituted enthusiasm for the military virtues for a culture of sociability and politeness. Given the exigent circumstances afflicting the British Empire, Burke considered Fox's position as excessively indulgent towards France. For this reason, in his *Observations on the Conduct of the Minority*, composed between February and June 1793, he strove to detach Portland and his followers from the clutches of the Foxite Whigs. Yet memories of Pitt's subterfuge in 1784 bound Burke's one-time party associates in opposition to the government. It was not until January 1794 that the Duke of Portland lent his authority to the administration. The following summer he entered a formal coalition with the government, leaving the Foxites in the wilderness as a derisory minority.

Through the summer of 1793, the revolt in the Vendée region of western France was in progress. Equally encouraging for Burke at this time, the allies recaptured most of the Austrian Netherlands. Then on 23 July a coalition of German forces finally re-took Mainz. However, Burke soon despaired that the allies had not capitalised on their victories. In December 1793, Napoleon seized Toulon. Even more disappointingly, over the following months Prussia and Russia were distracted by the second partition of Poland; then in June 1794 the coalition army succumbed in Flanders. Burke lamented that the allies had not attempted to march on Paris. He was also distraught at any suggestion that the enemy might be brought to terms. He was not blind to the distinctions among the political factions in France, yet he was persuaded that the various partisans of the Revolution shared a vision that excluded them from European norms. A sequence of conspirators from Lafayette to Barère had pledged themselves against any system of government that reflected the society of orders. To Burke this signalled their opposition to forming a genuinely mixed regime under which hereditary property would be secure. To Burke's mind, an effective constitution ought to reflect existing social forces so that its system of checks and balances was supported by the underlying division of ranks. It followed that an unmixed regime catering to an undifferentiated "nation" was a recipe for unremitting tyranny. In Burke's eyes, the French tyranny took the form of a military republic devoted to the spread of its doctrines by means of cultural and territorial aggrandisement.

This process of enlargement was still evident in Ireland despite the passage of major reforms in 1793. Burke hoped that the appointment of Earl Fitzwilliam to the Lord Lieutenancy under the coalition government would lead to Catholic relief from the last of the popery laws, giving the majority population the right to sit in parliament. However, by the spring of 1795 Fitzwilliam's viceroyalty had ended in failure. Through his last two years, Burke inveighed against the myopia of the Castle administration for indulging the mood of apprehension over the future of Protestant ascendancy. "Ascendancy," for Burke, meant the aspiration to supremacy in defiance of all sound Reformation principles. Faced with the zeal of Anglican persecution in Ireland and the persistence of atheistic bigotry in France, he longed for irenic cooperation among the Christian denominations of Europe. The Roman Catholics of Ireland in his estimation offered a model of reformed piety reminiscent of the primitive church: charitable, conscientious and without pomp. Yet its adherents were being driven into the hands of the United Irishmen as the Dublin government resorted to coercive measures against Catholic Defenderism. The goal of separation was gaining ground among all the main religious sects. Yet for Burke the only credible choice for the inhabitants of the island was between dependence on the benign authority of the British and subjection to the popular despotism of France. Catastrophically, in attempting to manage a population facing these alternatives, the Irish government drove the Catholic masses towards support for revolution.

The fortunes of the coalition powers in the war by now looked grim. At the start of January 1795, the Batavian Republic was declared. Three months later, Frederick William II's Prussia made peace with France. That summer, émigré forces were defeated at Quiberon Bay on the Brittany coast. The continent now looked vulnerable to being overwhelmed by Jacobinism. Two months before this, Burke had reflected on the conditions that had prepared Europe for revolution: extensive luxury bred an attitude of self-satisfaction among the privileged orders while rising talent was faced with exclusion from important offices at court.[1] Economic depression and an increase in the price of wheat boosted the appeal of the "rights of man." In the autumn of 1795, scarcity of corn following an unsatisfactory harvest in Britain encouraged calls for market regulation along with a rhetoric of hostility between rich and poor. In response, as the government was signalling its preparedness to come to terms with France, Burke launched a vigorous apology for the rights of property. In his *Thoughts and Details on Scarcity*, he defended accumulated capital as a benefit to labour, a free market in grain as the best precaution against famine, and improving conditions for labour as advantageous to productivity. In his late invective against the idle opulence of the great, the *Letter to a Noble Lord* of 1796, he married this commitment to the benefits of industry to his awareness of the advantages of heritable wealth. Burke could understand the sentiment of class antagonism that had prospered since the Revolution, but he remained determined to broadcast his assessment of its counterproductive consequences.

As Burke persisted with his opposition to British overtures for peace between the autumn of 1796 and the spring of 1797, he made clear what he thought the costs of the Revolution had been, and how he expected its system of values to affect the future of Europe. By a mixture of philosophical sermonising and military engagement, it had uprooted the attachment to prescription in France and was threatening neighbouring countries with contagion. This had undermined the institution of property

[1] EB, *Letter to William Elliot* (26 May 1795), *W & S*, IX, p. 39.

in general, posing a danger to the prosperity of all members of society. It also compromised belief in the authority of government, without which liberty, he believed, would ultimately disappear. Finally, since the Revolution had campaigned for the destruction of religion, Burke feared that it was eroding the foundation of morals based on the principle of self-denial. In this he was returning to some of his earliest concerns, holding that the sense of honour alone was not enough to sustain the obligations of duty. Without the binding tribunal of conscience, moral value would be dissolved into the vagaries of taste. As we have seen, Burke assumed that this would usher in an age of false "humanity" under the impact of the ideas of Rousseau. Under his influence, ordinary feelings would be suppressed out of deference to abstract norms, the metaphysical love of man would encourage contempt for individual men, and the idlest fantasy of social improvement would be sufficient to justify limitless suffering.

16.2 Revolutionary War in Europe

The political tensions that had mounted over the winter session between Fox and the opposition Lords subsided during the Christmas recess, which had been delayed until 4 January 1793. Portland fled from Burlington House in London to his seat at Bulstrode. For the present, a fatal rupture was delayed. Yet still the pressure continued, and the Portland Whigs began to unravel as members defected individually from Fox.[2] The news that Louis XVI was to be executed reached London on 21 January. The death itself was announced in the British press just three days later.[3] In the Commons on 1 February, Fox declared his horror at what had befallen the French king.[4] Nonetheless, he went on, the crimes perpetrated in one state were not the concern of another.[5] Moreover, it seemed clear that Austria and Prussia were the current aggressors of Europe, with France merely responding defensively.[6] Fox proceeded to vindicate the theory of equal rights and the doctrine of the sovereignty of the people, signalling the depth of division overwhelming the opposition.[7] Later in the year, Burke suggested that these ideas derived from the writings of Rousseau, and associated them with France's 1791 constitution.[8] From the perspective of Burkean

[2] L. G. Mitchell, *Charles James Fox and the Disintegration of the Whig Party, 1782–94* (Oxford: Oxford University Press, 1971), pp. 212–13.

[3] Frank O'Gorman, *The Whig Party and the French Revolution* (London: Macmillan: 1967), p. 117.

[4] *Parliamentary History*, XXX, col. 302.

[5] Ibid., col. 303.

[6] Ibid., cols. 304–7.

[7] Ibid., cols. 309–10. The ground for this new commitment had been prepared in his speech to the Whig Club on 4 December 1792: see Charles James Fox, *Speech Containing the Declaration of His Principles, respecting the Present Crisis of Public Affairs* (London: 1792), p. 2.

[8] EB, *Observations on the Conduct of the Minority* (Spring 1793), *W & S*, VIII, p. 438. Burke had in mind Rousseau's *Contrat social*, and connected this to Titre III, Article 1 of the Constitution de 1791: "La Souveraineté est une, indivisible, inaliénable et imprescriptible. Elle appartient à la Nation; aucune section du peuple, ni aucun individu, ne peut s'en attribuer l'exercice."

orthodoxy, their endorsement by Fox was a singular aberration: popular sovereignty as conceived in the aftermath of 1789 undermined the society of orders, posed a challenge to the conjoint sovereignty of the estates of the kingdom, and confused the exercise of government with its popular legitimation. As such ideas began to circulate in the Whig Club and among the Friends of the People, Malmesbury, Windham and Elliot became alienated from Fox; it was only a matter of time before Portland would decide to split.

Britain declared war against France on 9 February 1793. Burke greeted the advent of conflict with relief. For the previous four years, he told the Commons, his inability to convince the government of the imminence of catastrophe had almost killed him.[9] Throughout that time he had stood "almost alone in his sentiments."[10] At last the illusion of security had been exposed.[11] But while the confrontation had to be welcomed, there could be no denying that the impending struggle would be "terrible." France was now a military republic, driven by an *esprit de conquête*. Having destroyed religion and social distinctions, and sacrificed arts and commerce, there was nothing left for her citizens but to become soldiers.[12] It was this development that determined the country along a path of conquest, extending territorial empire under cover of brotherly peace.[13] It represented a new form of public "enthusiasm" under whose influence trade would be "bartered" for the sword.[14] The military virtues would be cultivated in tandem with Revolutionary doctrine: "War to the palace, and peace to the cottage."[15] This policy was accompanied by the idea that modern wars were an expression of aristocratic pride, so a war against rank would be a war to end all wars.[16] Since the ideology was destructive of property, and therefore of commercial society, the pillage that it recommended was the only means by which it could be sustained. Plunder would become the necessary means of military aggrandisement, and war would be undertaken for the purpose of supply.[17] Perpetual peace would be sought through permanent war: this, Burke commented that autumn, had been the "drift" of Jacobin doctrine since 1789.[18]

Introducing his own resolutions against the war on 18 February, Fox set about drawing attention to the extremity of Burke's position by emphasising the difference of opinion between him and Pitt. For the government, war against France was justified by the enemy's actions on the continent, above all its interference with the

[9] EB, Debate on the King's Message respecting War, *Parliamentary History*, XXX, col. 383.

[10] *Star*, 13 February 1703.

[11] EB, Debate on the King's Message respecting War, 12 February 1793, *Parliamentary History*, XXX, col. 383.

[12] Ibid.

[13] Ibid., col. 384.

[14] Ibid., col. 386.

[15] Ibid., col 385. Burke is referring to Joseph Cambon's adoption on 15 December 1792 of the motto of Nicolas de Chamfort: *Archives parlementaires*, LV, p. 70.

[16] EB, *Observations on the Conduct of the Minority* (Spring 1793), *W & S*, VIII, p. 434.

[17] *Parliamentary History*, XXX, col. 387.

[18] EB, *Observations on the Conduct of the Minority* (Spring 1793), *W & S*, VIII, p. 434.

navigation of the Scheldt. However for Burke the issue was rather the "*malus animus*" of the French, which rendered her an implacable opponent.[19] The problem, in other words, was the malevolent spirit of militant republicanism, proceeding from the domestic constitution of the state. Burke clarified his argument in response to Fox's charge. His "principal objection" to France was indeed its internal organisation. It was as a consequence of this that the Revolution was compelled to spread towards new frontiers. There was no material difference between him and Pitt, but a shared purpose under distinct pretexts.[20] Had the French confined the effects of their Revolution to themselves, the right of interference might be questioned.[21] The fact was, however, that France was bent on general European subversion. Revolution abroad had been adopted as a domestic reason of state.[22]

Fox's argument was entirely pertinent: Burke's terms for peace were far removed from those of the administration, even if for the moment they shared a common agenda. A Pittite pamphlet from early 1793 drew attention to the anarchy of France.[23] In February, this situation could be shown to have consequences for policy. For Burke, it meant that the enemy was not in a position to negotiate since no one could be held responsible for the conduct of the state, and indeed its commitments could not be credited as binding into the future.[24] The point illustrated Burke's divergence from the ministry. Not only was France implacable, it was incapable of negotiation. As a consequence, unlike Pitt, Burke was not content with a strategy of containment; he was committed to the extermination of a regime. He proceeded to vilify the personnel of the new French empire, condemning both the ministry and the Convention alike: Roland, Le Brun, Condorcet, Brissot, Chauvelin, Santerre, Robespierre and the Duc d'Orléans were equally denounced.[25]

Between February and June, as Burke and Fox progressively clarified their positions, bitterness between the old allies continued to fester. Ructions were soon felt in the Whig Club: on 19 February, Portland offered his support to a declaration to be made the next day in favour of Fox, prompting the resignation of over forty members.[26] By the end of the month, Burke was charging Fox with leading his followers into the wilderness. He seemed to be heading a party, but he was in fact in charge

[19] Ibid., col. 424. For further discussion, see Richard Bourke, "Edmund Burke and International Conflict" in Ian Hall and Lisa Hill eds., *British International Thinkers from Hobbes to Namier* (Basingstoke: Palgrave Macmillan, 2009).

[20] *Parliamentary History*, XXX, cols. 435–36.

[21] *Star*, 13 February 1793.

[22] *Morning Chronicle*, 19 February 1793; *Star*, 19 February 1793.

[23] [Anon.], *The Letter of the Rt. Hon. C. J. Fox . . . Anatomized* (London: 1793).

[24] EB, Speech on Fox's Resolutions against War, 18 February 1793, *Parliamentary History*, XXX, col. 438. Cf. EB, *Observations on the Conduct of the Minority* (Spring 1793), *W & S*, VIII, pp. 430–31.

[25] Ibid., cols. 438–9. Cf. EB, Speech on Fox's Motion for Peace with France, 17 June 1793, *Parliamentary History*, XXX, cols. 1010–11.

[26] *Oracle*, 23 February 1793; *Morning Chronicle*, 6 March 1793.

of a faction.[27] The suggestion here was coded, but still clear: Fox's rhetoric was subversive of the British constitution, servicing the ambitions of the French state. On 12 and 18 February, Burke had drawn attention to the remarkable coincidence between Fox's advocacy and the policy of the Brissotins. Fox's arguments, he alleged, were derived from the French newspapers.[28] Every part of what he had said in opposition to the war offered succour to the militants in France. Its substance could be gleaned from "the speeches of Brissot in the National Convention."[29] Earlier in the century, in dealing with the menace of Jacobitism, the British government had stood firm against the faction at home as much as it resisted their allies abroad. However, now, both Sheridan and Fox were proposing to strengthen the hand of internal enemies while ignoring the magnitude of the threat from an external foe.[30] The determination of the Foxites to press for parliamentary reform raised suspicions about the purpose of their agitation. They had yet to reveal the content of their plans for the constitution. Fox himself was a source of serious anxiety: while he distanced himself from every concrete plan of reform, he goaded his eager acolytes in the Commons.[31]

Burke returned to these allegations during his speech on the Traitorous Correspondence Bill on 22 March: "We have now a foreign enemy who have attempted to form a domestic faction in favour of their views, and have in part succeeded."[32] The charge of faction against Foxites was again stated with a defence of the principle of party: whereas the former was directed against the constitution, the latter was a combination to support the common good. Both Whig and Tory partisans promoted the public interest; however, the "opposition phalanx" aimed at sabotage.[33] Burke even threatened to name the members of a treasonous cabal, the implication being that they were members of the Commons.[34] They were nothing but the tools of cosmopolitan conquest—a "*Douce Fraternité*," as Burke termed it, as duplicitous as France's earlier policy of *doux commerce*.[35] Spain and Portugal had joined the coalition against France in January 1793, yet Dumouriez, who mobilised his forces against the United Provinces, remained undaunted. The allies therefore

[27] EB, Speech on Sheridan's Motion relative to Seditious Practices, 28 February 1793, *Parliamentary History*, XXX, col. 556.

[28] EB, Speech on Fox's Resolutions against War, 18 February 1793, ibid., col. 433.

[29] EB, Speech on the King's Message respecting War, 12 February 1793, ibid., col. 380. Burke returned to the point in EB, *Observations on the Conduct of the Minority* (Spring 1793), *W & S*, VIII, pp. 431, 437.

[30] EB, Speech on Sheridan's Motion relative to Seditious Practices, 28 February 1793, *Parliamentary History*, XXX, col. 550.

[31] Ibid., col. 551.

[32] *London Chronicle*, 23 March 1793.

[33] *Star*, 23 March 1793.

[34] *Diary*, 23 March 1793. The issue was raised by Sheridan again on 26 March, but Burke declined to name specific traitors: *Morning Chronicle*, 27 March 1793.

[35] EB, Speech on Traitorous Correspondence Bill, 22 March 1793, *Parliamentary History*, XXX, col. 614. Cf. EB, Speech on Traitorous Correspondence Bill, 9 April 1793, *ibid.*, col. 645: "France had endeavoured under the specious pretext of an enlarged benevolence to sow the seeds of enmity among nations, and destroy all local attachments."

concentrated their efforts in northern Europe. The Austrians made early progress in Flanders, securing a victory against the French at Neerwinden in mid-March. By then, the National Convention was conscripting soldiers by the hundreds of thousands, with the levy provoking resistance in the provinces. The first pitched battle between the Revolutionary army and the insurrection in the Vendée was under way by 19 March. By early summer, as far as Fox was concerned, all the aims of the British had been secured, and on 17 June he moved for a negotiated peace.[36]

As Fox saw things, the real threat to British interests came from the Austro-Prussian alliance. The second partition of Poland gave rise to a disadvantageous balance of power, tilted in favour of Russia and the Germans. However, to Burke this amounted to a hollow complaint, unless Fox was proposing a campaign against every power in Europe.[37] The goal of the war, he reiterated, should be the establishment of a government in France that would offer security to peace.[38] This did not mean imposing a regime of the allies choosing on its people: "no country could force a particular form of Government upon another."[39] The following April Burke insisted that any system of government would beat the current anarcho-despotic republic.[40] In its absence there was a need to interpose on the French. Burke once again cited Vattel to confirm the right of intervention: "If, by the subversion of all law and religion, a nation adopts a malignant spirit to produce anarchy and mischief in other countries, it is the right of nations to go to war with them."[41] Circumstances should determine the form of government that should be installed, and for Burke this pointed to the restitution of the old Bourbon power.[42] Burke's opposition to Fox was by now profound and irrevocable. The Revolution had separated them, but the war

[36] Burke excoriated the politics of this gesture in EB, *Observations on the Conduct of the Minority* (Spring 1793), *W & S*, VIII, pp. 428–36.

[37] EB, Speech on Fox's Motion for Peace with France, 17 June 1793, *Parliamentary History*, XXX, col. 1009; *Morning Chronicle*, 18 June 1793. Cf. EB, *Observations on the Conduct of the Minority* (Spring 1793), *W & S*, VIII, pp. 422–23, where Burke argues that Fox, along with the *Morning Chronicle*, was effectively promoting an alliance with Jacobin France.

[38] The goal was founded on what Burke later itemised as at least ten different grounds for war: EB, *Observations on the Conduct of the Minority* (Spring 1793), *W & S*, VIII, pp. 428–29.

[39] *Star*, 18 June 1793.

[40] EB, Debate on Bill to Enable Subjects of France to Enlist as Soldiers, 11 April 1794, *Parliamentary History*, XXXI, col. 380.

[41] EB, Speech on Fox's Motion for Peace with France, 17 June 1793, *Parliamentary History*, XXX, col. 1012. In the *Diary*, 18 June 1793, Burke is reported as having read an extract from Vattel. Cf. EB, *Observations on the Conduct of the Minority* (Spring 1793), *W & S*, VIII, p. 421; EB, *Remarks on the Policy of the Allies* (Autumn 1793), ibid., p. 474. An appendix to the 1797 edition of the *Remarks* contained annotated extracts from Vattel supporting, as Burke thought, a policy of partisan intervention: see EB, *Three Memorials on French Affairs, Written in the Years 1791, 1792 and 1793* (London: 1797), pp. 200ff. Burke based his argument on Emer de Vattel, *The Law of Nations, or the Principles of the Law of Nature* (London: 1787), bk. II, ch. iv, §§ 53, 56; bk. II, ch. v, § 70; bk. IV, ch. ii, § 14; bk. II, ch. xii, § 196; bk. III, ch. iii, §§ 45, 47, 49; bk. III, ch. ix, § 165; bk. I, ch. xix, §§ 232, 230; bk. IV, ch. v, § 66. The bearing of Vattel on the issue of intervention was discussed between Windham and Fox on 21 January 1794 during the Debate on the Address of Thanks. See *Parliamentary History*, XXX, cols. 1246, 1254–55.

[42] EB, Speech on Fox's Motion for Peace with France, 17 June 1793, ibid., col. 1012.

proved still more divisive. Back in September 1792, the Earl of Upper Ossory had affirmed to Burke that Fox was "as good an aristocrate [*sic*] as any of us."[43] Burke was disposed to believe him, yet something remained awry. As late as November, Burke informed Fitzwilliam that he did not despair of recovering Fox, even if, as he recently complained to Loughborough, his adherence to French doctrines appeared almost total.[44] The second Revolution offered Fox the chance to reorientate his attitude. Instead, he continued to deny the threat of domestic conspiracy and to associate with Orléans, Talleyrand and Chauvelin.[45] The polarity that would become public in 1793 was almost complete.

Burke dated the advent of extreme aversion to the final month of 1792. From Fox's amendment to the Address of 13 December through to his ostentatious yet disingenuous endorsement of a loyalist association on the 19th, it became increasingly obvious to Burke that his old friend was caballing against the British constitution.[46] Nonetheless, both Portland and Fitzwilliam were determined to stand by him. Since their views were in fact closer to Burke's than to Fox's, they had placed themselves in an extraordinary position. In practical terms, it meant that both of them refused to relinquish their deep-seated suspicion of Pitt and wholeheartedly support the administration. In more personal terms, it carried the consequence that Fitzwilliam refused to offer Burke's son the Commons seat of Higham Ferrers in August 1793. Fitzwilliam explained his decision in response to Richard's dismay: "He [Burke] and I materially differ in politics."[47] The patronage of his son would imply support for Burke, and thus amount to a declaration of hostility to Fox. This Fitzwilliam could not do, not least since he was systematically opposed to the Pitt ministry, albeit supporting the justice of the war against France. Complete support for the government would entail a breach with Portland, and the dissolution of the remnants of the Rockingham Whig party. "I make the decision not between your father and Fox," he disclosed, "but between the true, the only parties in question, between your father and the D[uke] of P[ortland]."[48] A month later, Burke presented Portland with a lengthy memorandum, posthumously published as *Observations on the Conduct of the Minority*.[49] The *Observations* had been written between February

[43] EB to Richard Burke Jr., c. 4 September 1792, *Corr.*, VII, p. 197.

[44] EB to Earl Fitzwilliam, 29 November 1792, ibid., p. 312; EB to Lord Loughborough, 28 November 1792, ibid., p. 305.

[45] EB to Earl Fitzwilliam, 29 November 1792, ibid., p. 315.

[46] EB, *Observations on the Conduct of the Minority* (Spring 1793), *W & S*, VIII, pp. 413–18.

[47] Earl Fitzwilliam to Richard Burke Jr., 27 August 1793, ibid., p. 417. Fitzwilliam had first informed Richard of his decision on 8 August, with Richard then expressing his bewilderment at length on the 16th. See ibid., pp. 394–95, 396–410.

[48] Earl Fitzwilliam to Richard Burke Jr., 27 August 1793, ibid., p. 418.

[49] EB to the Duke of Portland, 29 September 1793, ibid., pp. 436–38. A pirated version of the *Observations* was published by J. Owen on 13 February 1797; an authorised edition appeared eight months later. See William B. Todd, *A Bibliography of Edmund Burke* (1964) (Godalming: St. Paul's Bibliographies, 1982), pp. 207–10.

and June 1793, and was intended as a vindication of Burke's conduct in that period.[50] It also aimed to elucidate the character of Fox's behaviour, and to capture the contradictions that this had forced on the opposition Whigs. If Fox had been acting in a ministerial capacity in the first six months of 1793, there was little doubt "that he would have been considered as the most criminal Statesman that ever lived in this Country."[51]

In submitting the *Observations* for Portland's consideration, Burke was responding to a situation in which a government at war was being actively opposed by an influential cohort within Whiggism: Stanhope, Lansdowne, Lauderdale, Coke, Grey, Sheridan, Erskine, Whitbread, Francis, Courtney, Lambton, Taylor and Fox had been agitating against the justice of a national campaign in alliance with more avowedly subversive organisations.[52] Subversion was being perpetrated by various means—publication, domestic conspiracy and foreign correspondence—none of which was vigorously discountenanced by the Foxites.[53] What they did disclaim, on the other hand, was the acceptability of Britain's allies, the legitimacy of the war, and the threat from internal dissension. As a powerful and effective opposition politician, Fox was perforce the leading member of the faction. He was a man, Burke wrote, "of an aspiring and commanding mind, made rather to controul, than to be controulled."[54] Those who gave succour to Fox were indirectly bolstering his faction, placing them in a position of antagonism towards their professed objectives. "It is truly alarming," as Burke put it to Portland, "to see so large a part of the Aristocratick Interest engaged in the Cause of the new species of democracy, which is openly attacking or secretly undermining the System of property, by which mankind has hitherto been governed."[55]

It was an astonishing situation from Burke's perspective. The Rockinghamites and their successors were nothing if not a party of property. This commitment, Burke thought, was based on the fundamental principles of justice. Property was a precondition of civil and social existence; on its security the progress of society depended.[56] In all ages, the first duty of government had been to provide for its defence,

[50] It seems to have been conceived after Portland backed the Whig Club's declaration of support for Fox on 20 February 1793: see EB, *Observations on the Conduct of the Minority* (Spring 1793), *W & S*, VIII, p. 408.

[51] Ibid., p. 436.

[52] Most of the names of members on this list from the lower House appear in this connection in EB, *Observations on the Conduct of the Minority* (Spring 1793), *W & S*, VIII, pp. 445.

[53] The Association for Preserving the Liberty of the Press, formed on 22 December 1792, was the latest addition, and included Horne Tooke as a member. For Burke's strictures against it, see ibid., p. 418; for its activities, see Albert Goodwin, *The Friends of Liberty: The English Democratic Movement in the Age of the French Revolution* (London: Hutchinson, 1979), pp. 273–74.

[54] EB, *Observations on the Conduct of the Minority* (Spring 1793), *W & S*, VIII, p. 447.

[55] EB to the Duke of Portland, 29 September 1793, *Corr.*, VII, p. 437.

[56] Cf. EB, Debate on Volunteer French Corps, 11 April 1794, *Parliamentary History*, XXXI, cols. 380–81: "After all, if it were asked, did he prefer property to virtue? His answer would be no. To

until the French undermined the idea of secure and enduring possession by engineering a colossal transfer of accumulated corporate wealth. Back in August 1791, Burke relayed Lord Stormont's view that Fox could not conceivably countenance such spoliation, nor consequently the philosophy that justified it: his was an entirely "unexceptional creed."[57] Within a year Burke came to doubt this assessment of Fox's position. Already in October 1791 his conduct during the Oczakov crisis raised suspicion.[58] The following spring, his reaction to Pitt's Proclamation against Seditious Practices was still more disturbing.[59] By 1793, Burke was certain that his former ally had been lost to Jacobin ideas, yet many old friends, now his ideological opponents, inexplicably lent him their backing. Writing to Windham in November 1793, Burke summed up his opinion in exasperated tones: "The conduct of our late party is so absurd, contradictory, and self destructive, that I cannot easily express it."[60] Burke felt this all the more particularly since he had by then read Portland's defence. He was a duller man than Burke, Portland remarked of himself disarmingly; he lacked Burke's imagination, and could not fully share his alarm, even if Burke's foresight had been vindicated thus far.[61] He abhorred Jacobin ideas, and could not share in Fox's sympathies, yet still he credited the man, whereas he could never trust William Pitt. The source of his conviction stemmed from 1784, when Pitt had colluded with the king to destroy the coalition and undermine the Commons. In the aftermath of the deluge of 1789, perhaps Pitt had better politics, but Fox was the better man.[62]

Portland's response grieved Burke since the whole purpose of the *Observations* had been to challenge this contradictory commitment. The critical events of 1784 had certainly represented a grave constitutional threat. Jacobinism, however, was "the most dreadful, and the most shameful evil, which ever afflicted mankind."[63] Besides, 1784 was nine years past whereas 1793 posed an immediate challenge. Whatever Fox's motives might be in supporting a version of the Jacobin peril, his decision promised only political catastrophe. Under its auspices, Foxites were agitating for a species of parliamentary reform that would ruin the current British constitution. At that point, Burke concluded, "all goes to pieces."[64] Having associated himself consistently with the proponents of such a course of action, Fox had become unacceptable to long-term adherents of the Whig cause. Burke underlined the

---

honour?—No. To morals?—No. To arts and literature?—No. But he respected property in as much as it was the basis upon which they were all erected."

[57] EB to Richard Burke Jr., 10 August 1791, *Corr.*, VI, p. 335.

[58] EB, *Observations on the Conduct of the Minority* (Spring 1793), *W & S*, VIII, pp. 409–10.

[59] The Proclamation was aimed at the Friends of the People. For Fox's reaction to it, see Debate on the King's Proclamation against Seditious Practices, 25 May 1792, *Parliamentary History*, XXIX, cols. 1509–12.

[60] EB to William Windham, c. 10 November 1793, *Corr.*, VII, pp. 481–82.

[61] The Duke of Portland to EB, 10 October 1793, ibid., p. 447.

[62] Ibid., p. 448.

[63] EB, *Observations on the Conduct of the Minority* (Spring 1793), *W & S*, VIII, p. 451.

[64] Ibid., p. 441.

extent to which discontent with him had deepened: even if the present king were to support Fox as chief minister, the response of weighty elements within the political nation would "shake this kingdom to its foundations."[65] To persist in the face of these unprecedented challenges with a superannuated system of personal loyalty seemed to Burke to be perfectly baffling: it was "a species of modern politicks" that was not only incomprehensible; it was one that "must end in the ruin of the country."[66]

As Burke pondered the unhappy state of the domestic scene, prospects in Europe brightened, if only momentarily. By the spring of 1793, Russia, Portugal and Naples had been drawn into the war, and the king of Sardinia was supported with subsidies. That summer, after a month-long campaign, the allies recaptured almost the whole of the Austrian Netherlands and began laying siege to a fortress town in the south of the Low Countries as a prelude to the invasion of France. In June, a succession of departments from Bordeaux to the Jura rose against the authority of Paris, threatening to employ federal power against the dominance of the capital. Soon, important towns like Marseilles and Lyons were in a state of rebellion.[67] The Austrians took the fortress of the Condé on 12 July; the French garrison at Mainz capitulated on the 27th. Portland, whose second son was serving on the continent, wrote to Burke on 31 July with news of a French surrender to the Duke of York at Valenciennes. Burke was ecstatic, yet in responding to Portland he paused to emphasise that this was not a war of ambition but "a War of Principle."[68] The French republic had no conception of legitimate territorial limits since the ideals to which it adhered had no regard for geographical bounds.[69] This fact had to affect the design of strategy. The war against France could not be fought with a view to a settling of accounts with a manageable enemy. Its aim, as Burke informed an officer in the imperial army, was to "Rescue the Remains of the civilised World from impiety and barbarism."[70] This could not be secured by reparations and indemnities. The Revolution was driven by an ideological commitment, bolstered by the example of success. The example would have to be punished, and the ideology accordingly damaged. This could only be achieved by a coherent plan of war. "We are at War with that principle and that Example and not with an ordinary power."[71] Spurious doctrines might be expected gradually to perish,

[65] Ibid., p. 450.

[66] Ibid., p. 452. Cf. EB to Mrs. John Crewe, c. 22 November 1794, *Corr.*, VIII, p. 82: to persist in a political connection on the grounds of loyalty despite the prevalence of contradictory principles "is surely irrational and immoral in the highest degree."

[67] Alan Forrest, *Society and Politics in Revolutionary Bordeaux* (Oxford: Oxford University Press 1975); Richard Cobb, *Paris and its Provinces, 1792–1802* (Oxford: Oxford University Press, 1975); Stephen Auerbach, "Politics, Protest and Violence in Revolutionary Bordeaux, 1789–1794," *Proceedings of the Western Society for French History*, 37 (2009), pp. 149–61; William Scott, *Terror and Repression in Revolutionary Marseilles* (London: Macmillan, 1973).

[68] James Prior, *Life of the Right Honourable Edmund Burke* (1824) (London: 5th ed., 1854), p. 380; EB to the Duke of Portland, 1 August 1793, *Corr.*, VII, p. 381.

[69] EB to Lieutenant General Edward, Count Dalton, 6 August 1793, ibid., p. 384.

[70] Ibid., p. 382.

[71] Ibid., p. 383.

but a successful case of implementation stood as a permanent temptation.[72] An allied victory was conditional on taking the war to Paris.

The Anglo-Austrian campaign soon disappointed Burke. After Valenciennes, both the Duke of York and Saxe-Coburg opted to engage in the reduction of fortified border towns instead of pressing on to the capital of the Revolution. It was a "ruinous" method of procedure in Burke's opinion.[73] He counted himself an "*alarmist*" on the domestic and foreign fronts, determined to reveal the gravity of the crisis facing Europe.[74] His opponents were cast in the roles of the self-satisfied and the duped: "These squirrels are charmed by the rattle-snake," but they risked their all in the process.[75] In September, the allies were forced back from Dunkirk, yet the real issue was how to make their campaign a success: this was not a strategic war to diminish the power of a rival but a project "to drive Jacobinism out of the World."[76] With this end in view, it was developments within France that thrilled Burke. News of the declaration of Toulon in favour of Louis XVI's son, which included the admission of a British naval squadron into its harbour, reached London on 14 September 1793.[77] Cazalès, Burke reported, was "electrified."[78] Burke was equally cheered by the response in Britain and France. Here was an internal revolt in the name of a constitutional objective, which precluded a blanket condemnation of the French enemy. Developments in the Vendée were even more inspiring. By June 1793, in the west of France in the area south of the Loire, around Poitou, a self-proclaimed Royal and Catholic Army was embodied under a military council.[79] The following September, its progress had cheered Burke, although plans launched at the end of July by the Committee of Public Safety for the savage suppression of insurrection were already afoot.[80] The tribulations of Flanders paled into insignificance by comparison with the strategic importance of supporting rebellion in the French provinces.[81]

In late September, Lord Grenville drafted a Declaration against France in which the British pledged their support to insurgents against the republic.[82] Dundas showed Burke a copy on 25 October, just over a week after the execution of Marie

[72] EB to Florimond-Claude, Comte de Mercy-Argenteau, c. 16 August 1793, ibid., p. 388.

[73] EB to William Windham, 18 August 1793, ibid., p. 413.

[74] EB, *Observations on the Conduct of the Minority* (Spring 1793), *W & S*, VIII, pp. 412–13, 416; EB to William Windham, 23 August 1793, *Corr.*, VII, p. 415.

[75] Ibid., pp. 415–16. Cf. EB to Captain Woodford, 13 January 1794, ibid., p. 522.

[76] EB to Dr. Charles Burney, 14 September 1793, ibid., p. 422.

[77] M. H. Crook, "Federalism and the French Revolution: The Revolt of Toulon in 1793," *History*, 65:215 (October 1980), pp. 383–97.

[78] EB to Gilbert Elliot, 16 September 1793, *Corr.*, VII, p. 429.

[79] Charles Tilly, *The Vendée: A Sociological Analysis of the Counter-Revolution of 1793* (Cambridge, MA: MIT Press, 1964).

[80] EB to Henry Dundas, 8 October 1793, *Corr.*, VII, p. 445.

[81] EB to Gilbert Elliot, 22 September 1793, ibid., pp. 432–33.

[82] *The Manuscripts of J. B. Fortescue Preserved at Dropmore* (London: Eyre and Spottiswoode, 1894), 2 vols., II, p. 428; *London Gazette*, 26–29 October 1793.

Antoinette.[83] Within two days, Burke was alerting the minister for war to his "very serious doubts" about the propriety of publishing such a document at this time, and pleading for an opportunity to deliver a full response.[84] On 13 October 1793, the Austrian army had been victorious at Wissembourg, although the siege of Dunkirk had been raised in early September. In the middle of October, the French drove back the Austrians at Wattignies, and in early November the rebels in the Vendée came under pressure.[85] Yet it was not each passing vicissitude that unsettled Burke, but the lack of determination on the part of the allies. It was in this mood that he composed his *Remarks on the Policy of the Allies*, intended as a memorandum for government.[86] A major declaration of intent, just as the allies were being put on the defensive, seemed ill judged. Even military victories posed a problem for the allies since they encouraged an attitude of complacency. Despite the declaration's promise to assist the victims of French oppression, "Not a man, not a Ship[,] not an article of Stores" had been sent to insurgents in the Vendée.[87] British neglect was far more revealing than any number of declarations. It seemed obvious that the government was happy to use royalists as their instruments, but they disregarded the nobility and clergy, and thus left the émigrés out of account. This implied that republicans were to be accepted, *faute de mieux*, as the de facto government of France.[88]

For Burke, the republicanism introduced under the Convention was of a piece with royal democracy established in 1791.[89] In both cases, the state was formed under an unmixed system of government—in the first instance, under a pageant of monarchy; in the second, under a republican administration. The fundamental problem with each was the absence of organised constitutional resistance and the animus against hereditary property. Both these principles, in turn, flowed naturally from the Revolution of 1789. Allied to an assault on religion, despotic government and the subversion of property proceeded without any impediment. Burke designated this conspiracy under the capacious term of Jacobinism, considering each of its subdivisions as party to a common project, quarrelling only over the distribution of power.[90] Lafayette was succeeded by Brissot, and Brissot by Barère and Robespierre, "like wave succeeding wave."[91] But the original agitators were as malign as their progeny: Lafayette, Dumouriez, De Noailles, Necker, Talleyrand and Lally-Tollendal

[83] It was published on 29 October 1793. See *Parliamentary History*, XXX, cols. 1057–60.

[84] EB to Henry Dundas, 27 October 1793, *Corr.*, VII, p. 465; Dundas sought to mollify Burke two days later: Henry Dundas to EB, 29 October 1793, ibid., p. 468.

[85] EB to William Windham, 4 November 1793, ibid., p. 472.

[86] EB to Lord Grenville, 29 October 1794, Unpublished Letters, I, pp. 132–33. Burke discusses the conditions of anxiety and isolation under which he revised the *Remarks* in EB to Lord Loughborough, 12 January 1794, ibid., p. 517.

[87] EB to William Windham, c. 10 November 1793, ibid., p. 481.

[88] EB, *Remarks on the Policy of the Allies* (Autumn 1793), *W & S*, VIII, p. 456.

[89] Ibid., pp. 458, 460–61. On *démocratie royale*, see above, chapter 14, section 3.

[90] On this, see also EB, *Preface to Brissot's Address to his Constituents* (1794), *W & S*, VIII, pp. 501, 518.

[91] EB, *Remarks on the Policy of the Allies* (Autumn 1793), *W & S*, VIII, p. 476.

seemed as culpable as any among the current "Sectaries" in the Convention.[92] Consequently, the prospect of negotiation with any faction in France filled Burke with horror. The allies ought to act through what he viewed as the expatriate substance of the country, which was to be found scattered through the territories of Europe. The restoration of royalty required a guarantee of heredity, which demanded the re-establishment of hereditary property. However, the great mass of the landed and corporate property of France by right belonged to émigrés in Flanders, Switzerland, Spain, Italy and Britain. The current campaign must, therefore, be geared towards facilitating the restoration of the intermediary bodies of France currently strewn across Europe, as a precondition for a successful reconstruction of the monarchy.[93]

Burke's proposals for France thus excluded a programme of conquest: the country was to be reconstituted by a process of "civilization."[94] Only the national representatives of property and religion, whom Burke was pleased to categorise as the true "*people*" of France, could act as instruments of this civilising mission.[95] "Frenchmen are best for French affairs," Burke insisted to Windham on the eve of his final session in parliament.[96] The advice would not be heeded, and Burke would spend his last year in the Commons continuing his fight against France as he brought the trial of Hastings to a conclusion. In December 1793, Napoleon Bonaparte recaptured Toulon from the British.[97] In the spring of 1794, the eastern allies concentrated their efforts on the second partition of Poland. As a result, by the end of June, fortune smiled on the soldiers of the Revolution when the Austrians succumbed in Flanders to the republican army under Jourdan. Two months before this climactic encounter, Burke was railing in the Commons against the "humanity" of the French—"affected humanity, devoid of justice," had been the driving force of the Revolution.[98] It was the disenfranchisement of property that had enabled this force to prosper. This was by now a familiar theme, but it was one with which Burke persisted. As he argued on 11 April 1794, "The original fault in the proceedings of the French revolution was, that property was not permitted to have a vote."[99] This set one description of citizens against another, and fed the notion that one species of property could be invalidated without catastrophic effects on the institution altogether.[100]

The new year belatedly vindicated Burke's single-mindedness: on 17 January 1794, Portland convened a meeting at Burlington House to announce his resolution to lend his full support to the war.[101] The split in the Whigs, which Fox was to

[92] Ibid., p. 477. On Lafayette in particular, see EB, Debate on La Fayette, *Parliamentary History*, XXXI, cols. 47–51.

[93] Ibid., pp. 464–67.

[94] Ibid., pp. 468–69.

[95] Ibid., p. 457.

[96] EB to William Windham, 8 January 1794, *Corr.*, VII, p. 514.

[97] For Burke's disappointed response, see 1794, ibid.

[98] EB, Debate on Seditious Practices, 17 April 1794, *Parliamentary History*, XXXI, col. 423.

[99] EB, Debate on Seditious Practices, 11 April 1794, ibid., col. 381.

[100] EB to Florimond-Claude, Comte de Mercy-Argenteau, c. 16 August 1793, *Corr.*, VII, p. 389.

[101] William Windham to EB, 18 January 1794, ibid., pp. 525–26. As late as 10 January, Burke seems not to have ruled out a coalition including Fox: see EB to Richard Burke Jr., 10 January 1794, ibid., p. 515.

describe as nothing less than a "dissolution" of the party, was complete, though Portland would still refuse to serve under Pitt.[102] However, the following July an alliance between the two men was concluded. By then, Burke had at last retired from the House of Commons, hoping to step down to a condition of "otium cum dignitate."[103] Negotiations were underway to reward him with a peerage, but the enterprise ended in failure.[104] Nonetheless, Burke now proceeded to campaign against Jacobinism out of doors. Fox, he was sure, would not return to the fold: he had relinquished his commitment to Whig principles altogether.[105] "Whig" and "Tory" were effectively at an end.[106] The "extinction" of the republican regime remained Burke's chief objective.[107] There was no hope of negotiating with such a subversive and malevolent force.[108] The struggle, Burke suggested to Portland, might be "the last struggle."[109] "We are playing for no light stakes," he later confirmed.[110] Dundas would commend the prescience of the author of the *Reflections* on 17 April 1794, though by now Burke was insisting that French politics had no equivalent in the past.[111] The power of prediction could not rely on comparison with the earlier examples: the French marvel was altogether without precedent.[112] Political judgment could not depend on a repertoire of cases, but would have to sift its materials reflectively rather than mechanically. Nothing had prepared the mind for the wonder that was the Revolution.[113] By terror alone it sustained the edifice of what trust had hitherto supplied: subordination, cooperation, and a market in money and commodities.

16.3 Not Freedom, but Dominion: The Fitzwilliam Episode

Burke retired from parliament on 21 June 1794. It was soon agreed that his son would succeed to his seat at Malton. The days of the borough's "greatest lustre" were now over, Fitzwilliam wrote.[114] Burke was touched by the compliment, and relieved

[102] Charles James Fox to Lord Holland, 9 March 1794, *Memorials and Correspondence of Charles James Fox*, ed. Lord John Russell (London: 1853), 4 vols., III, p. 65.

[103] Richard Burke Jr. to William Windham, 19 June 1794, *Corr.*, VII, p. 551: "leisure with dignity." This referred to the possibility of being awarded a peerage.

[104] Due largely to his "want of fortune." See William Windham to William Pitt, TNA, PRO 30/8/190, fol. 240.

[105] EB to Mrs. John Crewe, c. 24 November 1794, *Corr.*, VIII, p. 83.

[106] *Morning Chronicle*, 27 June 1794, cited in Mitchell, *Charles James Fox*, p. 237.

[107] EB to Lord Loughborough, 12 January 1794, *Corr.*, VII, p. 518.

[108] EB to Captain Woodford, 13 January 1794, ibid., p. 521.

[109] EB to the Duke of Portland, 20 January 1794, ibid., pp. 527–28.

[110] EB to Mrs. John Crewe, c. 22 November 1794, *Corr.*, VIII, p. 83.

[111] *Parliamentary History*, XXXI, col. 412.

[112] EB, *Remarks on the Policy of the Allies* (Autumn 1793), *W & S*, VIII, p. 498.

[113] Ibid., p. 499.

[114] Earl Fitzwilliam to EB, 26 June 1794, *Corr.*, VII, p. 555.

that his son would be catered for.[115] Richard was duly elected on 18 July.[116] The triumph made his sudden death all the more devastating to Burke. Richard Brocklesby, writing to Thomas Young two months after the tragedy, could only hope that Burke's "impetuous torrent of Grief" would be moderated by the "lenient hand of time."[117] In a state of affliction, it was the affairs of Ireland that drew Burke back into the ambit of public life. He was returning to the issue that had first sparked his interest in politics, but he was also taking up the thread of his son's last official duties. As he informed Grattan in the autumn of 1794: "I have now no Objects which can employ my Mind, but to spin out, with second hand and worn out materials, the broken Staple of his Life."[118] The toll of Richard's death almost defeated Burke through his final years. Even appearing in public was a painful experience, he informed Windham.[119] His despair was absolute, he confided some weeks later.[120] His grief also oppressed him with premonitions of his own death. "I am almost literally, a dying man," he proclaimed.[121] He later confessed that he lacked "strength and energy of mind and body, with an heart sunk and dejected, and a body tottering on the Edge of the grave."[122] There was something unseemly, he began to feel, about having survived the successor generation.[123] Trapped "in the silent gloom" of a beleaguered situation, his remaining years could be justified only as a form of repentance.[124] His involvement in Irish affairs was intended as a kind of reckoning, but also as a final penitence.[125]

Now without his seat in the Commons, Burke still had his friends in parliament, and the inclination when necessary to resort to his pen. On 10 August 1794, Earl Fitzwilliam accepted the Lord Lieutenancy of Ireland.[126] With the establishment of the coalition the previous month, Windham had accepted the post of Secretary at War and the Duke of Portland had become Secretary of State with responsibility for Home Affairs. Since the Lord Lieutenant was answerable to the Home Secretary, Burke's friends had been entrusted with a decisive role in Irish affairs. "My dearest Lord—you have undertaken Ireland," Burke enthused to Fitzwilliam. He promptly offered to make himself available for advice: "my best Ideas on that Subject are at your Service."[127] At the end of August, Burke was awarded a pension to be drawn on

[115] EB to Earl Fitzwilliam, 29 June 1794, ibid., p. 558.

[116] Richard Burke Jr. to Mrs. Thomas Haviland, c. 18 July 1794, ibid., p. 560.

[117] Richard Brocklesby to Thomas Young, 8 October 1794, OSB MS. File 1850.

[118] EB to Henry Grattan, 3 September 1794, *Corr.*, VIII, p. 4.

[119] EB to William Windham, 7 October 1794, ibid., p. 30.

[120] EB to William Windham, 16 October 1794, ibid., p. 35.

[121] Ibid., p. 42.

[122] EB to Unknown, 1794, ibid., p. 108.

[123] EB to Henry Grattan, 20 March 1795, ibid., p. 206. Cf. EB, *Letter to a Noble Lord* (1796), *W & S*, IX, p. 171: "I live in an inverted order. Those who ought to have succeeded me are gone before me."

[124] EB to Earl Fitzwilliam, 10 February 1795, *Corr.*, VIII, p. 147.

[125] EB to Henry Grattan, 20 March 1795, ibid., p. 207.

[126] E. A. Smith, *Whig Principles and Party Politics: Earl Fitzwilliam and the Whig Party, 1748–1833* (Manchester: Manchester University Press, 1975), p. 179.

[127] EB to Earl Fitzwilliam, 31 August 1794, *Corr.* VII, pp. 578–79.

the civil list, striking a pang of grief for the recent loss of his son, but nonetheless providing the security that would enable him to campaign.[128] Developments in Dublin soon absorbed him. John Hely Hutchinson, Secretary of State and Provost of Trinity College Dublin, died on 4 September 1794. Burke soon became involved in finding replacements for both positions, having been approached himself to assume the role of Provost at Trinity.[129] At the same time, there were plans afoot to endow a Catholic seminary in Ireland.[130] One of Burke's last conversations with his son had been devoted to the idea.[131] A Bill was already in prospect in February 1795.[132] An Act providing for the education of the Catholic clergy in Ireland finally passed on 5 June 1795.[133] A College was duly established in Maynooth in County Kildare, and Burke donated a selection of his son's books to the library.[134] There was also a scheme to fund clerical salaries from Dublin Castle, which might also be charged with controlling the appointment of bishops. By January 1795, proposals were under consideration among the Catholic hierarchy.[135] Burke was anxious that selection be confined to the Catholic Church.[136] He was also opposed to appointments on the basis of popular election: "The Christian religion did not in France survive this arrangement for a year."[137] But it was the fate of Fitzwilliam in the position of Lord Lieutenant that dominated Burke's thinking from the autumn of 1794 until the return of the Earl to London on 25 March 1795.

Burke assumed that Fitzwilliam would find little by way of "enlargement or manly policy" waiting in Ireland. Support for what remained of Protestant ascendancy still predominated, and with it a petty attitude of "narrow subtilty" seemed to prosper.[138] Burke was hoping for the completion of Catholic emancipation, and

[128] EB to Walker King, 31 August 1794, ibid., p. 579. The sum was later supplemented with annuities drawn on West Indian customs duties: see Walker King to Earl Fitzwilliam, 3 August 1795, *Corr.*, VIII, p. 292.

[129] EB to Lord Loughborough, 19 October 1795, ibid., p. 46; EB to Earl Fitzwilliam, 21 October 1794, ibid., pp. 53, 56.

[130] Henry Grattan to EB, 1 October 1794, ibid., p. 28.

[131] EB to Henry Grattan, 3 September 1794, ibid., p. 5.

[132] The Rev. Thomas Hussey to EB, 27 February 1795, ibid., p. 162.

[133] 35 Geo. III, c. 21. The Duke of Portland requested Thomas Hussey to establish the new institution: see the Rev. Thomas Hussey to EB., c. 14 March 1795, ibid., p. 198.

[134] The Archbishop of Dublin to EB, 13 July 1795, ibid., p. 288.

[135] The Rev. Thomas Hussey to EB, 29 January 1795, ibid., p. 125. It was also being debated more generally, along with the idea of founding a Presbyterian institution. See William Drennan, *A Letter to His Excellency Earl Fitzwilliam, Lord Lieutenant of Ireland* (Dublin: 3rd ed., 1795), p. 9.

[136] EB to the Rev. Thomas Hussey, ante 10 February 1795, *Corr.*, VIII, p. 143.

[137] EB to the Rev. Thomas Hussey, 17 March 1795, ibid., p. 204.

[138] EB to Earl Fitzwilliam, 31 August 1794, ibid., p. 579. For the persistent defence of ascendancy, see, for example, the speech before the Irish parliament of Patrick Duigenan during the Catholic relief debates of early 1793 in *A Full and Accurate Report of the Debates in the Parliament of Ireland, in the Session of 1793 on the Bill for the Relief of His Majesty's Catholic Subjects* (Dublin: 1793), pp. 127ff. Henry Grattan sent a copy of this *Report* to Burke on 15 April 1795: see *Corr.*, VIII, p. 232.

expected to encounter resistance in Dublin Castle and the Irish parliament. The previous year, major concessions to Catholics had made their way onto the statute book. They passed with ease but not without displays of peevishness.[139] Their reception was determined by the European crisis. In the months before the outbreak of war with France, Burke's son proclaimed to Dundas that "to go to War for the national existence, while there is a shadow of a doubt about Ireland, is perfect madness."[140] On Wednesday 2 January 1793, delegates from a nationwide Catholic Convention presented a petition to George III complaining of their "manifold incapacities."[141] The document enumerated a series of grievances, highlighting the disqualification of Catholics from offices of trust; the prohibition on their founding universities, colleges or schools; the denial of their right to bear arms; their exclusion on various terms from petty and grand juries; and, most ignominious of all, their continuing to be deprived of the electoral franchise.[142] As war with France grew imminent, Pitt and Dundas were anxious to meet what seemed to them reasonable demands.

Wolfe Tone, who had replaced Richard Burke as secretary to the Catholic Committee the previous July, famously declared that the proximity of the contest with France drove the government to advocate concessions: "Dumouriez was in Brabant, Holland lay prostrate before him; even London, to the impetuous ardour of the French, did not appear at an immeasurable distance."[143] On 10 January 1793, the king's speech recommending reform was read before both Houses of the Irish parliament. The franchise on equal terms with Protestants was to be granted; numerous civil and military offices were to be opened to Catholic dissenters; selection to juries was to be conceded; and the right to bear arms was to be admitted.[144] A torrent of rhetorical opposition was unleashed against the proposals, although in the end the Irish parliament capitulated under pressure from the government, with the Bill becoming law on 9 April 1793.[145] In due course, the Catholic Committee presented its thanks to the crown for bestowing "substantial benefits."[146] Yet during the debates on the Bill objections had been vigorously delivered. At the committee stage the speaker, John Foster, challenged the idea of an inherent "right" of election.[147] The

139 See Henry Grattan to Richard Burke Jr., 20 March 1793, *Corr.*, VII, p. 362, on the "peevish littleness" of the Irish Lord Chancellor during the debates.

140 Richard Burke Jr. to Henry Dundas, 27 December 1792, ibid., p. 326.

141 *The Petition of the Catholics of Ireland to the King's Most Excellent Majesty* (Dublin: 1793), p. 3.

142 Ibid., pp. 4–7.

143 Theobald Wolfe Tone, *Life of Theobald Wolfe Tone: Compiled and Arranged by William Theobald Wolfe Tone* (Dublin: 1998), p. 78.

144 Thomas Bartlett, *The Fall and Rise of the Irish Nation: The Catholic Question, 1690–1830* (Dublin: Gill and Macmillan, 1992), p. 165.

145 *An Act for the Relief of His Majesty's Popish or Roman Catholick Subjects of Ireland* (Dublin: 1793).

146 *Proceedings of the General Committee of the Catholics of Ireland, which Met on Tuesday April 16, and Finally Dissolved on Thursday April 25, 1793* (Dublin: 1793), p. 1.

147 *An Accurate Report of the Speech Delivered by the Right Hon. John Foster, Feb 27th 1793, on the Bill for Allowing Roman Catholics to Vote at the Elections of Members of Parliament* (London: 1793), p. 12. For

Lord Chancellor, John Fitzgibbon, stated his objections as the Bill passed through the Lords: "so long as the preposterous claims of the Court of Rome to universal spiritual dominion over the Christian world shall be maintained, it is utterly impossible that any man who admits them, can exercise the legislative powers of a Protestant State with temper and justice."[148]

Sentiments of the kind drew acid commentary from Burke. He was naturally in favour of healing measures aimed at Irish Catholics, as he informed the Earl of Upper Ossory in January 1793, though he could not approve of the pressure which the Catholic convention had brought to bear: "I would have the door opend [*sic*], not broken open."[149] Since the convention had been constituted by elected delegates, it performed a potentially ominous role as an organ of extra-constitutional representation for Catholic dissenters. Aspects of the Relief Bill troubled Burke more, not least the ongoing suspicion of Roman Catholics which it manifested. The extension of the allowance to keep arms was to be conditional on taking an oath denying the temporal authority of the Pope.[150] It was impossible to see in the current state of European affairs how the Bishop of Rome could threaten the security of the Irish. "I am glad," Burke commented ironically to an unknown correspondent, "that your minds are in every other respect so much at Ease in Ireland, that you can entertain yourselves with this Species of apprehension."[151] One hundred and fifty years ago, Burke later conceded, he would have seen the wisdom of an oath of abjuration. Yet now, in an age of enlightenment, an inquisition into prejudices that had already disappeared could only serve to agitate and inflame.[152]

There were, however, more tangible reasons for anxiety about Irish developments. First, there was the proposal to pursue parliamentary reform on top of measures to alleviate the condition of Catholics. Hercules Langrishe and Theobald McKenna were alike suspicious of the provisions. They were merely a means of fomenting aims that could not be satisfied.[153] To Burke they added to the arsenal of grievances fabricated by projectors.[154] His only purpose, he declared, was the "pacification" of Ire-

---

Foster in general, see A.P.W. Malcomson, *John Foster: The Politics of the Anglo-Irish Ascendancy* (Oxford: Oxford University Press, 1978).

[148] *The Speech of the Right Honourable John Lord Baron Fitzgibbon, Lord High Chancellor of Ireland, on the Second Reading of the Bill for the Relief of His Majesty's Catholic Subjects, March 13, 1793* (Dublin: 1793), p. 3. For Burke's attitude to Fitzgibbon, see above, chapter 1, section 2.

[149] EB to the Earl of Upper Ossory, 22 January 1793, *Corr.*, VII, p. 342.

[150] As set out under 13 and 14 Geo. III, c. 35, sec. I.

[151] EB to Unknown, post 18 February 1793, *Corr.*, VII, pp. 350–51.

[152] EB, *Letter to William Smith* (29 January 1795), *W & S*, IX, p. 661.

[153] Hercules Langrishe, *The Speech of the Right Honourable Sir Hercules Langrishe on the Bill to Improve the State of the Representation* (London: 1793), p. 8; Theobald McKenna, *An Essay on Parliamentary Reform, and on the Evils Likely to Ensue from a Republican Constitution in Ireland* (Dublin: 1793), p. 2.

[154] EB to the Earl of Upper Ossory, 22 January 1793, *Corr.*, VII, p. 342.

land, and the extension of the franchise had brought that outcome a step closer.[155] The "great Object" of equality had substantially been gained, he wrote to Grattan.[156] The aim now was to generate support for the new arrangements. A month before Burke wrote, the United Irishmen had mobilised a reanimated Volunteer movement to press for more extensive reforms. The previous autumn, a national battalion had been launched in sympathy with French principles, and sectarian tensions mounted in the borderlands between Munster and Leinster.[157] There were confrontations between Volunteers and the armed forces in the north-east of Ireland in March 1793. Burke complained to Grattan of a "mutinous Spirit which is in the very constitution of the lower part of our compatriots of every description." It was being leavened with an admixture of noisy republicanism that would require both "firm" and "prudent" management to defuse.[158] As it happened, the administration was in the process of restricting the importation of gunpowder and banning Volunteer parades in Ulster. That summer subversive conventions were summarily outlawed.[159] Yet as the government bore down on United Irish agitation and associated military displays, sectarian antagonism spread south from parts of Armagh into adjoining counties in Leinster, extending as far as Meath. Rioting against the new Militia Act followed through spring and summer.

The Militia Act was introduced during the passage of Catholic relief and in the aftermath of the suppression of volunteering. It was intended to provide for domestic defence during the contest with France, raising recruits by ballot, which meant that men would be chosen by lot from among the tenantry of the landlords. This introduced compulsion into the process of recruitment, igniting widespread hostility across large tracts of the country.[160] The death toll by August 1793 was five times greater than the sum of fatalities connected with insurgent or agrarian violence over the previous thirty years.[161] This led to reports that Catholics were in a general state of revolt. Burke set about contradicting this diagnosis: "The simple Truth is, that whatever their extent or violence might have been, These Tumults had no connexion

[155] EB to Unknown, post 18 February 1793, ibid., p. 350.

[156] EB to Henry Grattan, 8 March 1793, ibid., p. 360.

[157] See John Baker Holroyd to Lord Auckland, 21 October 1792, OSB MS. File 13483: "The sober people in Ireland feel no slight alarm in regard to the Roman Catholicks, & the natives have returned to their old tricks of murdering Christians and houghing [i.e. maiming] Protestant Cattle." Holroyd had land in County Meath.

[158] EB to Henry Grattan, 8 March 1793, *Corr.*, VII, p. 361.

[159] S. J. Connolly, *Divided Kingdom: Ireland, 1630–1800* (Oxford: Oxford University Press, 2008), p. 447.

[160] Thomas Bartlett, "An End to Moral Economy: The Irish Militia Disturbances of 1793," *Past and Present*, 99 (May 1983), pp. 41–64.

[161] Ivan F. Nelson, "'The First Chapter of 1798'? Restoring a Military Perspective to the Irish Militia Riots of 1793," *Irish Historical Studies*, 33:132 (November 2003), pp. 369–86.

with Religion or Politics."[162] His main aim was to deny that the violence had been encouraged by men of influence among the clergy. This was not sectarian but "*popular*" protest, and its causes should be traced to a proscriptive constitution.[163] Burke had described this as a form of "exclusive Liberty," which properly understood "was not freedom but dominion."[164] If hitherto this system had not produced Catholic insurgency, it was nonetheless promoting alienation from the establishment. This was powerfully in evidence over the course of the past year as violence perpetrated by Catholic Defenders rose.[165] Much of this had taken the form of disarming Protestants. Soon declarations were infused with Jacobin prescriptions.[166] "They talked of the famous system of liberty and equality in the most extravagant manner," one pamphleteer recorded.[167] By the beginning of 1794, Burke was advising the new Chief Secretary to the Lord Lieutenant that "Ireland is in danger of being Jacobinised."[168] He was clear that this was being inadvertently stoked by the administration in Dublin, whom he now described as an unashamedly oligarchical clique, or "click": "They have a way of forcing people into disaffection, by acting towards them as if they were in Rebellion."[169] It was into this atmosphere that Fitzwilliam was to step as the new viceroy.

As the war against Revolutionary France escalated, and the British Empire faced a struggle for its existence, Burke believed that Ireland had grown too important to be left to a coterie.[170] He underlined his sense of urgency throughout the following year. In the context of the "dreadful" contest against Jacobin revolution, the greatest interests "ever staked" were apparently at issue.[171] A great "Master-calamity" was bearing down on Britain, and Ireland played a pivotal role in its system of defence.[172]

[162] EB to John Coxe Hippisley, 3 October 1793, *Corr.*, VII, p. 442.

[163] Ibid., p. 443. Cf. EB to John Coxe Hippisley, 8 January 1794, ibid., p. 513: "Jacobins, in reality, though they happen to remain outwardly in their Communions in which they are bred, are not Christians of any description."

[164] EB to Henry Grattan, 8 March 1793, ibid., p. 360.

[165] For the aims and character of Defenderism, see Tom Garvin, "Defenders, Ribbonmen and Others: Underground Political Networks in Pre-Famine Ireland," *Past and Present*, 96 (August 1982), pp. 133–55; Thomas Bartlett, "Select Documents XXXVIII: Defenders and Defenderism in 1795," *Irish Historical Studies*, 24:95 (May 1985), pp. 373–94. See also, relatedly, Martyn J. Powell, "Popular Disturbances in Late Eighteenth-Century Ireland: The Origins of the 'Peep of Day' Boys," *Irish Historical Studies*, 34:135 (May 2005), pp. 249–65; Ian McBride, *Eighteenth-Century Ireland: Isle of Slaves* (Dublin: Gill and Macmillan, 2009), pp. 413–25.

[166] Marianne Elliott, *Partners in Revolution: The United Irishmen and France* (New Haven, CT: Yale University Press, 1982, 1989), pp. 40ff.; Jim Smyth, *The Men of No Property: Irish Radicals and Popular Politics in the Late Eighteenth Century* (Dublin: Gill and Macmillan, 1992), p. 67.

[167] [Anon.], *A Candid and Impartial Account of the Disturbances in the County Meath* (Dublin: 1794), p. 8.

[168] EB to Sylvester Douglas, post 30 December 1793, *Corr.*, VII, p. 510.

[169] Ibid., pp. 509–10.

[170] Ibid., p. 510.

[171] EB to William Fitzwilliam, 16 October 1794, *Corr.*, VIII, p. 34.

[172] EB to Lord Loughborough, 19 October 1794, ibid., p. 44. Cf. EB to Earl Fitzwilliam, c. 24 September 1794, ibid., p. 23.

If the country was not intelligently secured, he later reflected, it would be abandoned either to the French government or to "a revolutionary system" of its own making.[173] The geo-politics of Europe had transformed the significance of the sister kingdom: it was no longer "an obscure dependency" but a vital link in the old order.[174] Thirty years earlier an error in international prudence could be expected to be rectified in the medium term, yet now it threatened to imperil the remaining edifice of civilisation.[175] Ireland was a dyke against disastrous inundation.[176] The basic problem was that Irish government was in the hands of a jobbing cabal. With the coming of Fitzwilliam, the expectation was that the regime could be purified. Fitzgibbon would be removed from the position of Lord Chancellor, with John Beresford, Edward Cooke and Sackville Hamilton also being sacrificed. Writing to Grattan from London on 23 August 1794, this is exactly what Fitzwilliam promised to deliver, hoping to model his conduct on the Lord Lieutenancy of Portland. He would look to Whigs like the Ponsonbys to help him forge that result.[177] However, tensions soon emerged within the coalition government over the remit of Fitzwilliam's new position. First, there were delays in relieving Westmorland, for whom a new post had to be found. Next, Pitt was anxious about Fitzwilliam's scheme to purge the Irish government, above all his plan to dispose of Fitzgibbon's services. And finally, while the first minister urged that the Catholic question be left aside for the time being, the Lord Lieutenant assumed that the issue might be forwarded in Dublin even if the Westminster government was to stand aloof from the cause.[178]

"You certainly go to a Farm terribly havocked by the last Tenants," Burke commented after Fitzwilliam had accepted the role.[179] Yet as the Earl laid plans to overhaul the composition of the Castle administration, strains within the coalition intensified. By the middle of October the new ministry was on the verge of disintegration.[180] Burke began to fret in the face of the difficulties that arose. He was

[173] EB to the Rev. Thomas Hussey, 19 February 1795, ibid., p. 152.

[174] EB to William Windham, 16 October 1794, ibid., pp. 42–43.

[175] EB to Lord Loughborough, 19 October 1794, ibid., p. 45.

[176] The image appears in EB, *Second Letter to Sir Hercules Langrishe* (26 May 1795), *W & S*, p. 668.

[177] Earl Fitzwilliam to Henry Grattan in Henry Grattan, *Memoirs of the Life and Times of the Rt. Hon. Henry Grattan* (London: 1839–42), 4 vols., IV, p. 173. The Ponsonbys were cousins of Portland, while Lady Charlotte Ponsonby was Fitzwilliam's wife. Portland's brief tenure as Lord Lieutenant under the Rockingham administration in 1782 had involved in effect a change of personnel in the Dublin government. See R. B. McDowell, "The Fitzwilliam Episode," *Irish Historical Studies*, 15:58 (September 1966), pp. 115–30, p. 116.

[178] McDowell, *Ireland in the Age of Imperialism*, ch. 13; John Ehrman, *Pitt the Younger II: The Reluctant Transition* (London: Constable, 1983), pp. 421–27, 430–39; Bartlett, *Fall and Rise of the Irish Nation*, pp. 193–98; Deirdre Lindsay, "The Fitzwilliam Episode Revisited" in David Dickson et al. eds., *The United Irishmen: Republicanism, Radicalism and Rebellion* (Dublin: Lilliput Press, 1993); David Wilkinson, "The Fitzwilliam Episode, 1795: A Reinterpretation of the Role of the Duke of Portland," *Irish Historical Studies*, 29:115 (May 1995), pp. 315–39; Paul Bew, *Ireland: The Politics of Enmity, 1789–2006* (Oxford: Oxford University Press, 2007), pp. 27–31.

[179] EB to Earl Fitzwilliam, 9 September 1794, *Corr.*, VIII, p. 9.

[180] EB to William Windham, 16 October 1794, ibid., p. 34.

profoundly committed to the ongoing campaign against France, and consequently to the government of Pitt: "I thought that the Reputation, and the permanence of Mr. Pitts [*sic*] administration was the very corner stone of the salvation of Europe."[181] After the failure of Fitzwilliam's mission in 1795, and the consequent collapse of the policy of Catholic emancipation, Burke returned again to emphasise his devotion to Pitt: "I thought, and do still think, Mr Pitts [*sic*] power necessary to the Existence of the antient order of Europe."[182] Yet he had also been committed to the Portland contingent in the coalition.[183] Now that this was in danger, he would have to choose between the government and his friends.[184]However, happily for Burke, disagreements within the ministry were resolved in the short term. Fitzwilliam landed in Balbriggan on 4 January 1795, ready to take up his controversial brief. A raft of dismissals from the Irish administration followed, and the Catholic Committee expected emancipation to proceed, bringing their concerns up for "*immediate* consideration."[185] Burke noted the "respect and attachment of the whole body of the Catholics for the Lord Lieutenant."[186] Yet by the middle of February the cabinet in London had determined to halt the viceroy's progress. On the 23rd, Portland urged that Fitzwilliam withdraw from his post. Burke, on the other hand, insisted that the Lord Lieutenant should remain: "for Gods [*sic*] sake . . . stay where you are."[187] "Ireland is now on the brink of civil war," Thomas Hussey predicted.[188] Even after Fitzwilliam's dismissal, Burke argued for his return.[189] Both Burke and Fitzwilliam explained the recall in terms of the Lord Lieutenant's handling of Beresford, confirming their settled evaluation of the corruptions of Irish government.[190] Just as the House of Lords was getting ready to acquit Hastings, the Lord Lieutenant made preparations for his return to London. "We have an Eastern, and a Western Chief Governour before the Publick," Burke observed. Their treatment reflected ominously on the integrity of the constitution.[191]

[181] EB to Lord Loughborough, 10 October 1794, ibid., p. 45.

[182] EB to Earl Fitzwilliam, 13 March 1795, ibid., p. 190. Cf. EB to Henry Grattan, 20 March 1795, ibid., p. 207.

[183] EB to William Windham, 16 October 1794, ibid., p. 36.

[184] EB to William Windham, 20 October 1794, ibid., p. 51; EB to Earl Fitzwilliam, 21 October 1794, ibid., p. 53.

[185] Earl Fitzwilliam, *Second Letter from Earl Fitzwilliam to the Earl of Carlisle* (Dublin: 2nd ed., 1795), p. 6.

[186] EB to the Rev. Thomas Hussey, 29 January 1795, *Corr.*, VIII, p. 125. Cf. EB to the Rev. Thomas Hussey, 4 February 1795, ibid., p. 136; the Rev. Thomas Hussey to EB, 19 February 1795, ibid., p. 152.

[187] EB to Earl Fitzwilliam, c. 26 February 1795, ibid., p. 161.

[188] The Rev. Thomas Hussey to EB, 27 February 1795, ibid., p. 162.

[189] EB to the Duke of Devonshire, 11 March 1795, ibid., p. 184.

[190] The claim was refuted in [Anon.], *A Fair Statement of the Administration of Earl Fitzwilliam in Ireland* (London: 1795).

[191] EB to Henry Grattan, 20 March 1795, *Corr.*, VIII, p. 206.

16.4 Union or Separation: Fitzwilliam and After

The Bill to admit Roman Catholics to seats in the Irish parliament was introduced on 12 February 1795 and defeated on its second reading by seventy-one votes on 4 May. Under its provisions, all offices, excepting royal and ecclesiastical positions, would have been opened to every religious description. After eighty years of general enforcement, followed by twenty years of relaxation, it was time to remove the "final remnant" of penal legislation, Langrishe had argued.[192] Form the perspective of the Catholics, Burke believed, it would mean that a "stigma" had been belatedly removed, resulting in about three of their number sitting in the Commons, and possibly a peer in the House of Lords.[193] "The fear that if they had capacities to sit in Parliament they might become the Majority and persecute in their turn is a most impudent and flagitious pretence," Burke later contended. Even on the basis of the most extreme projections, including a reform of the borough franchise in Ireland, the Catholics could never amount to more than a tenth of the members on College Green.[194] A week after the Bill had been introduced, Grattan informed Burke that the Commons appeared ready to grant relief. On the back of this, the defence of the realm would be boosted by the establishment of a yeoman force.[195] For Fitzwilliam, this would have been a major benefit of the Bill, offering security against the growing threat from France. Yet it seemed to Burke, instead, as the Bill looked set to fail, that the administration would rather risk "a thousand Civil Wars" than sacrifice one single place of power or profit.[196] In claiming this he was impugning the principles of the Castle "Junto" whose politics he had been indicting since the beginning of the 1790s. Three months before Fitzwilliam first arrived in Dublin, Burke had rounded on this particular "set of men in Ireland" who were immersed in "innumerable corruptions, frauds, oppressions, and follies."[197] Foster, Fitzgibbon, Beresford and company, craving the spoils of office while resisting emancipation, had long established themselves as a "Cabal" in the administration opposed to the original principles of Whig tolerance and upright government.[198] Their whole system was built on jobbery and proscription.[199]

[192] *A Report of the Debate in the House of Commons on the Bill for the Further Relief of His Majesty's Popish or Roman Catholic Subjects* (Dublin: 1795), p. 17.

[193] EB to Earl Fitzwilliam, c. 26 September 1794, *Corr.*, VIII, p. 22.

[194] EB to French Laurence, 23 November 1796, *Corr.*, IX, p. 125.

[195] Henry Grattan to EB, 19 February 1795, *Corr.*, VIII, p. 150.

[196] EB to *Earl* Fitzwilliam, 13 March 1795, ibid., p. 192.

[197] EB to William Windham, 16 October 1794, ibid., p. 34.

[198] Ibid., p. 41.

[199] EB to Earl Fitzwilliam, 21 October 1794, ibid., pp. 53, 54. Cf. EB to the Rev. Thomas Hussey, 5 March 1795, ibid., p. 175; EB to the Rev. Thomas Hussey, 17 March 1795, ibid., p. 199; EB to Henry Grattan, 20 March 1795, ibid., p. 207; EB to Earl Fitzwilliam, 5 July 1795, ibid., p. 286.

The situation in France should stand as a warning against such corruption. The lifelong tenure that was attached to the position of Secretary of State exemplified the exclusive methods of administration in the country. "Many many causes . . . had prepared the Fall of the French Monarchy," Burke proposed to Loughborough, but extended tenures in public office and reversionary interests in positions in government had been conspicuously damaging, depriving Louis XVI of the power of patronage while at the same time fomenting resentments among aspiring talent. When a trial of strength came, the king had "nothing to manage that infinite body of discontent, which arose from the frustrated and hopeless pretentions of so many individuals."[200] The problem in Ireland was that jobbish power was married to political proscription. Despite appearances, it was not religious principles that animated this spirit, but the feeling of supremacy over a people.[201] The Protestant cause was merely a pretext for secular ambition. For this reason the ideal of "ascendancy" seemed "Deistical" to Burke, exploiting the pretence of piety as an engine of persecution whose objective was terrestrial advantage over the oppressed.[202] Under these conditions, the association of the establishment with sectarian proscription was peculiarly dangerous since it would serve to undermine the Church of Ireland itself. As a minority Church, comprising just over a tenth of the population of the country, it was vital "to keep off the idea of its being a Jobb."[203]

The fate of the Christian churches bound them increasingly together. Indifference was therefore the enemy of Protestant faith in Ireland, especially when combined with "contempt" for other denominations.[204] In the face of political prejudices infecting established religion, Burke longed to encounter before his death, as he confessed to Thomas Hussey, "an image of a primitive Christian Church."[205] Given the relative simplicity and the spirit of toleration that had been forced by violence and rapine upon Irish Catholicism, with some improvement it might approximate that condition of untrammelled piety.[206] This was a remarkable conclusion for a member of the established Church, but it pointed to the irenecism that had long underwritten Burke's religious sentiments. The Dutch Remonstrant Geeraert Brandt, whose *History of the Reformation* had been translated into English in the 1720s, had sought to promote the unity of Christian denominations by adopting the irenic

[200] EB to Lord Loughborough, 19 October 1794, ibid., p. 49

[201] EB to the Rev. Thomas Hussey, 9 June 1795, ibid., p. 264.

[202] EB to the Rev. Thomas Hussey, 21 June 1795, ibid., p. 270.

[203] EB to Earl Fitzwilliam, 21 October 1794, ibid., p. 55.

[204] EB to Earl Fitzwilliam, 10 February 1795, ibid., p. 146.

[205] EB to the Rev. Thomas Hussey, ante 10 February 1795, ibid., p. 143. James Ussher, Archbishop of Armagh from 1625 to 1676, had argued in *A Discourse of the Religion Anciently Professed by the Irish and British* (London: 1631) that Irish Christianity before the Norman Conquest had more in common with the Reformation Church than with Irish Catholicism after it had come more directly under the influence of the papacy.

[206] EB to the Rev. Thomas Hussey, ante 10 February 1795, *Corr.*, VIII, p. 143.

maxim: "*I condemn no man in whom I can find anything of Christian* [*sic*]."[207] Brandt looked to Erasmus as the patron of accommodation, renouncing inquisition as a subversion of the Christian ethic.[208] This came with an admiration for the Christianity of the "first ages," devoted to moral precepts rather than the persecution of heresy.[209] For Burke the spirit of charity could now be found among Irish Catholics, having consigned the Popish attitude of religious bigotry to history. Under the circumstances, as he explained in his *Letter to William Smith* in early 1795, "a league" between the principal denominations became plausible. In fact, some species of union had become necessary on account of the Jacobin creed, bent on destroying religion altogether: "the first, the last, and middle Object of their Hostility, is Religion."[210]

Burke's *Letter* was a response to an inquiry received from William Cusac Smith about the political ramifications of the emancipation of Catholics. Smith, who had entered the Irish Commons the previous year, had written two days before the opening of parliament in 1795, announcing his commitment to full "Civil Rights" for Catholics but questioning the extent to which they should enjoy political power.[211] He was already in print as an advocate of closer "bonds" with the majority faith, yet he now wondered at what point Protestant security might be undermined by the arrival of Roman Catholics in College Green.[212] Burke responded that the question was misconceived, since a right of admission to parliament was not equivalent to the enjoyment of power.[213] Moreover exclusion, under the circumstances, could not add to Protestant safety, whereas it would appear as an index of "jealousy and suspicion."[214] Catholics, in this situation, were liable to be tempted by Jacobinism, and if by this means their religion were to be "destroyed by infidels, it is a most contemptible and absurd Idea, that, this, or any Protestant Church, can survive that Event."[215] Before atheism acquired power through the organs of the French state, divisions among Christians had never posed an existential threat. In fact the differences of opinion bred by "overdone" piety inadvertently served to eradicate the corruptions of excessive zeal. "But now," Burke concluded, "nothing but inevitable

[207] Geeraert Brandt, *The History of the Reformation and other Ecclesiastical Transactions in and about the Low Countries* (London: 1720–23), 4 vols., I, p. vi. On Brandt's impact, see Peter Burke, "The Politics of Reformation History" in A. C. Duke and C. A. Tamse eds., *Clio's Mirror: Historiography in Britain and the Netherlands* (Zutphen: Walburg Pers, 1985).

[208] Ibid., "The Author's Preface," n.p.

[209] Ibid., "Introduction," n.p.

[210] EB, *Letter to William Smith* (29 January 1795), *W & S*, IX, p. 661.

[211] William Smith to EB, 20 January 1795, *Corr.*, VIII, p. 120. He refined his arguments [William Smith], *A Letter to His Excellency Earl Fitzwilliam by a Member of Parliament* (Dublin: 1795).

[212] William Smith, *The Patriot, or Political Essays* (Dublin: 1793), p. 7; William Smith to EB, 20 January 1795, *Corr.*, VIII, p. 120.

[213] EB, *Letter to William Smith* (29 January 1795), *W & S*, IX, p. 664.

[214] Ibid., p. 665.

[215] Ibid., p. 662.

ruin will be the consequence of our Quarrels."[216] Yet despite the possibility of impending doom, the Irish government was driven by *faux*-sectarian rancour. Even in Britain the image of the papacy persisted as a shibboleth. When Napoleon in 1796 was successfully leading republican troops against Pope Pius VI in Italy, the British government was forswearing any support for the papacy, while the Castle administration in Dublin was declaring war on his religion: "we are cutting our own throats in order to be revenged of this . . . old Pope."[217] A self-defeating mantra served outmoded bigotry: "All is well, provided Popery is crushed."[218]

Burke followed the debate of 4 May 1795 on the second reading of the Catholic Relief Bill with attention.[219] The "ability" of the House, he reported to Lord Fitzwilliam, came down on the right side of the question.[220] Nonetheless, in his *Letter to Hercules Langrishe* sent eleven days later, he complained of some of the content of the speeches.[221] Patrick Duigenan had refuted claims about the loyalty of Catholics, proposing that their admission to full political rights would confer half the power of the kingdom on its Popish inhabitants—a "crime, according to Locke . . . to be punished by deposition."[222] Duigenan based his arguments on a published account of a meeting hosted by the Catholic Committee of an estimated 4,000 aggrieved civilians at the Francis Street Chapel in Dublin on 9 April 1795. Opening the meeting, John Keogh had saluted the militant stand of America against the Empire and the progress of revolution in Holland and Brabant.[223] This had been followed by a harangue by one of the delegates, Dr. James Ryan, against a suspected design on the part of Pitt to introduce an incorporating union between the two kingdoms by capitalising on popular dissensions. This would mean "the annihilation of the Irish Parliament," ensuring the eternal superiority of one nation and the perpetual subordination of the other. As Ryan put it: "Superiority to the country to which the seat of legislative authority was transferred, and inferiority to that from which it was removed."[224] After the meeting, the Catholic Committee peremptorily disbanded, leaving the mass of the population without any credible representation.

[216] Ibid.

[217] EB to French Laurence, 25 November 1796, *Corr.*, IX, p. 133.

[218] EB to the Rev. Thomas Hussey, post 9 December 1796, ibid., p. 163. Cf. EB to Unknown, February 1797, ibid., pp. 259–60.

[219] The debate was reported in successive issues of the *Morning Chronicle* on 12, 13 and 14 May 1795, yet Burke seems to have had available to him more information than appeared in these reports, not least the content of Philpot Curran's speech.

[220] EB to Earl Fitzwilliam, 15 May 1795, *Corr.*, VIII, p. 242.

[221] EB, *Second Letter to Sir Hercules Langrishe* (26 May 1795), *W & S*, IX, p. 668.

[222] *Report on the Bill for the Further Relief of Roman Catholic Subjects*, p. 115. The other half, he expected, would be in the hands of the crown.

[223] *Orations Delivered at a Meeting of the Roman Catholics at Francis-Street Chapel on Thursday the Ninth of April 1795 on the Question of Catholic Emancipation* (Cork: 1795), pp. 6–7.

[224] Ibid., p. 18. The same suspicion was articulated in Arthur O'Connor, *Speech of Arthur O'Connor Esq. in the House of Commons of Ireland, Monday, May 4th, 1795, on the Catholic Bill* (Dublin: 1795), p. 31

"I agree with you in your dislike of the discourses in Francis-Street," Burke admitted to Langrishe.[225] The language of the speakers tended to welcome separation, which to Burke could only end in unimaginable catastrophe. He was eloquent in his opposition through the following year: "Ireland cannot be separated one moment from England without losing every source of her present prosperity."[226] In the final months of his life, he returned to this uncomfortable theme: "By such a separation Ireland would be the most completely undone Country in the world; the most wretched, the most distracted, and, in the end, the most desolate part of the habitable Globe."[227] Back in March 1795, Hussey had anticipated this shift in opinion among disaffected Catholics: "They will wish for a separation from G: Britain, and the contemptible light in which they will view their own Parliament will induce them to lay it in the dust, and to erect a convention, on the french scale, in its' [*sic*] place."[228] Burke was dismayed to see the prediction confirmed so soon. It was a foolish and vainglorious posture learned from the United Irishmen, based on the idea that Irish grievances "originate from England."[229] Britain, the idea went, sought to divide and rule.[230] The direct contrary, in fact, held true: it was the ascendancy of an oligarchical faction in Ireland that had oppressed the Catholic interest, whose only resource was the comparatively concessive instincts of the Westminster parliament.[231] As Burke later asserted: "There is a great cry against English influence. I am quite sure that [it] is Irish influence that dreads the English Cabinet."[232]

Ireland's choice was political dependence on Britain or subordination to France. If the country defected to the Jacobins, it would pay dearly for the momentary satisfaction of its pride. As things now stood, dependence on Britain would mean either the continuance of the existing autonomous legislature or the introduction of a comprehensive union between both polities. Burke had been meditating this subject since 1761. He was reported then as considering a union "*a matter of deep and difficult enquiry*."[233] After Fitzwilliam had been appointed Lord Lieutenant, the question was being agitated again. Its merit, Burke believed, would depend on the

[225] EB, *Second Letter to Sir Hercules Langrishe* (26 May 1795), *W & S*, IX, p. 668.

[226] EB to John Keogh, 17 November 1796, *Corr.*, IX, p. 113.

[227] EB to Unknown, February 1797, ibid., p. 257.

[228] The Rev. Thomas Hussey to EB, 3 March 1795, *Corr.*, VIII, p. 168.

[229] EB to the Rev. Thomas Hussey, 18 May 1795, ibid., p. 246. Cf. EB to Earl Fitzwilliam, 20 December 1796, *Corr.*, IX, p. 189; EB to French Laurence, 20 December 1796, ibid., p. 190.

[230] The claim was by now pervasive: see, for example, John Philpot Curran, *A Letter to the Right Honourable Edmund Burke on the Present State of Ireland* (Dublin: 1795), p. 6: the Irish Protestant is too "warm" to recognise that he has since the 1690s been made "the blind instrument of a scheme, equally cruel and impolitic, of dividing Ireland into two parties, who should waste and destroy each other."

[231] On this, see EB to the Rev. Thomas Hussey, post 9 December 1796, *Corr.*, IX, p. 166: constitutional independence meant that "along with the weight and authority, [the Irish] have totally lost all Benefit from the superintendancy of the British Parliament."

[232] EB to Unknown, February 1797, *Corr.*, IX, p. 259.

[233] EB to William Dennis, 1761, reported by French Laurence, *Corr.*, I, pp. 143–4.

details of the plan, although as the situation currently stood the scheme was not practical politics.[234] There was nothing left but to hope for the allegiance of Catholic opinion as a partner in the campaign against Jacobin irreligion. "I am charmed with what you tell me of the alienation of Catholics from the grand Evil of our time," Burke wrote to Hussey.[235] Yet rumours of a French invasion were already in circulation, and Fitzwilliam saw that Catholic opinion was ready for indoctrination: "they are ripe for mischief . . . they want but a cause and a leader."[236] By the middle of May Burke feared that men of talent would contract the French disease and appeal to the unpropertied with promises of fraternal justice: "Part of the property will be debauched, a part frightened; and the rest subdued."[237] Since Jacobinism aimed at the destruction of accumulated habits of mind, it began with an assault on religion as the root of all prejudice.[238] Christianity appealed to reason but was at base a prescriptive religion supported by acculturation and family attachment.[239] All the main denominations of the Christian faith in Europe could draw on that support, and for that reason they shared a common resource in perpetuating sober prejudice as a weapon in the defence of property and religion.[240] As Burke put it to Langrishe at the end of May 1795, the British Empire was at war with the enemies of that resource—first Jacobinism, which threatened to dissolve the bonds of society; but also "Ascendancy," which alienated the Catholic multitude under a pretence of commitment to religion; and finally "Indianism," which was destroying large tracts of Asia in defiance of every Christian code of conduct.[241] Together they fomented discontent and undermined the idea of providence.

Burke's worst fears continued to be realised in Ireland. There was a massacre of eleven revenue officers in Leitrim in April 1795.[242] Militant Defenderism was on the rise, and Protestant associations met it with violence. During his period as Lord Lieutenant, Fitzwilliam informed Burke, this "war of Religion between the lower orders had no existence."[243] In fact it had been stirring since the 1780s; certainly it was coming to fruition now. An organised confrontation at the Diamond crossroads

[234] EB to Earl Fitzwilliam, c. 26 September 1794, *Corr.*, VIII, p. 20.

[235] EB to Thomas Hussey, 4 February 1795, ibid., p. 136.

[236] Earl Fitzwilliam to EB, 4 March 1795, ibid., p. 171.

[237] EB to Earl Fitzwilliam, 15 May 1795, ibid., p. 243.

[238] Cf. EB, *Letter to William Elliot* (26 May 1795), *W & S*, IX, p. 39: "Religion . . . All other opinions, under the name of prejudices, must fall along with it."

[239] EB, *Letter to William Smith* (29 January 1795), *W & S*, IX, p. 662.

[240] Ibid., p. 661.

[241] EB, *Second Letter to Sir Hercules Langrishe* (26 May 1795), *W & S*, IX, p. 667 (mistranscribed). Cf. EB to Sir Hercules Langrishe, 26 May 1796, *Corr.*, X, p. 32. See also EB to Earl Fitzwilliam, 21 June 1794, *Corr.*, VII, p. 553 on "the two great Evils of our time, Indianism and Jacobinism."

[242] Edward Hay to EB, 21 June 1795, *Corr.*, VIII, p. 271; *Hibernian Journal*, 6 May 1795; Bartlett, "Defenders and Defenderism," p. 380.

[243] Earl Fitzwilliam to EB, 18 February 1796, *Corr.*, VIII, p. 386.

near Loughall in Armagh on 21 September 1795 resulted in dozens of Catholic fatalities.[244] Attacks on Catholic homes and a series of expulsions from the marshlands around Lough Neagh followed through the winter months.[245] Burke counselled against the Defenders' decision to disarm: "If the disarmament had been common to all descriptions of disorderly persons the Measure would have been excellent."[246] Deprived of their role as arbiters of communal welfare in the country, the gentry began to connive at disaffected Protestant militants.[247] It was now plain, Burke wrote to Hussey, that "Catholick *Defenderism* is the only restraint upon Protestant *Ascendency*."[248] John Keogh described the situation as the Irish equivalent of the Vendée.[249] In November 1796, Burke noted that the attacks perpetrated by Protestants had proceeded without punishment, "and hardly any discountenance from the Government."[250] He took this to be indicative of the disposition of the new regime. The second Earl of Camden had arrived to replace Fitzwilliam immediately after his departure in March 1795. Burke respected Camden's "values" but condemned the system which he chose to operate.[251] Thomas Pelham was appointed as Chief Secretary to the Lord Lieutenant. Beresford was restored to his old position in the administration. Fitzgibbon and Archbishop Agar were promoted in the Lords.[252] Keogh complained that appointments ignored the need to "Unite and Conciliate," and in fact tended to "terrify and Silence the great Body of the People."[253] Burke was similarly "afflicted" by the character of the administration.[254] To the end of his days he would excoriate their obnoxious habits of rule, driving the mass of the population from obedience to insurrection.[255] Their animosity could do more damage than the open hostility of the law.[256]

This drove to the very heart of the mismanagement of Ireland. Given the dependence of the British government on the Irish executive, policy was at the mercy of

[244] Patrick Tohall, "The Diamond Fight of 1795 and the Subsequent Expulsions," *Journal of the Armagh Diocesan History Society*, 3:1 (1958), pp. 17–50.

[245] McBride, *Eighteenth-Century Ireland*, p. 414. The expulsions are mentioned in EB to Earl Fitzwilliam, 17 January 1796, *Corr.*, VIII, p. 374.

[246] EB to the Rev. Thomas Hussey, 27 November 1795, ibid., p. 351.

[247] D. W. Miller, "The Armagh Troubles, 1784–1795" in Samuel Clark and James S. Donnelly Jr. eds., *Irish Peasants: Violence and Political Unrest, 1780–1914* (Manchester: Manchester University Press, 1983).

[248] EB to the Rev. Thomas Hussey, 18 January 1796, *Corr.*, VIII, p. 378.

[249] John Keogh to EB, 20 July 1796, *Corr.*, IX, p. 59.

[250] EB to French Laurence, 23 November 1796, ibid., p. 126.

[251] EB to Sir Hercules Langrishe, 8 April 1796, *Corr.*, X, p. 38.

[252] Bartlett, *Rise and Fall of the Irish Nation*, p. 207.

[253] John Keogh to EB, 20 July 1796, *Corr.*, IX, p. 59.

[254] EB to John Keogh, 17 November 1796, ibid., p. 113.

[255] EB to Earl Fitzwilliam, 20 November 1796, ibid., p. 121.

[256] EB to French Laurence, 23 November 1796, ibid., p. 126.

a clique of monopolists.[257] The only hope for the future lay in the dismissal of this cabal, and the reconstruction of government on a more conducive basis.[258] In the meantime, their conduct stoked the antipathy of the bulk of the population, unwittingly lending support to seditious conspiracies. This made them inadvertent patrons of the current regime in France—a "Lilliputian Directory" in league with the Gallic foe.[259] In the "petulance and riot of their drunken power," they insulted and provoked the nominal subjects of their care.[260] As the forces hostile to the establishment began to threaten and menace the country, the government began to place itself on an explicitly military footing. "In Ireland it is plain they have thrown off all sort of Political management and even the decorous appearance of it," Burke commented.[261] Official desperation was evident in the appointment of a new Commander-in-Chief of the Irish forces: on 10 October 1796 Henry Lawes Luttrell, now Earl of Carhampton, took over from Robert Cunninghame. The choice, Burke thought, was indicative of a determination to provoke conflict.[262] The previous autumn, when Carhampton had been charged with the pacification of Connaught, suspected Defenders were consigned to service in the king's fleet abroad without so much as a show of legal procedure. This seemed to be of a piece with the government's handling of strife in Armagh, where they had ultimately played a hand in fomenting discord. The Irish parliament, encouraged by Pelham, refused an inquiry into the episode.[263] By this time the United Irishman had revived, first in Ulster, as a secret society, and were coalescing with Defenders to produce a substantial fighting force. In October 1796 the movement numbered 38,000 members in the north-east of Ireland alone. By the following February that figure had risen to 69,000. "The Catholics," Burke predicted, "unprotected, disowned and persecuted by their Government will take refuge in an Alliance with the protestant republicans."[264] The Irish parliament at this point adjourned its proceedings, having passed an Indemnity Act in effect condoning Carhampton's excesses.[265] An Insurrection Act outlawed the administration of conspiratorial oaths.[266] A partial suspension of habeas corpus followed in October.

[257] EB to the Rev. Thomas Hussey, post 9 December 1796, ibid., p. 166; EB to Unknown, February 1797, ibid., p. 255.

[258] EB to Earl Fitzwilliam, post 9 December 1796, ibid., p. 158; EB to French Laurence, 29 March 1797, ibid., p. 297.

[259] EB to French Laurence, 8 December 1796, ibid., p. 151.

[260] EB to the Rev. Thomas Hussey, post 9 December 1796, ibid., p. 162; EB to William Windham, 30 March 1797, ibid., p. 301.

[261] EB to French Laurence, 18 November 1796, ibid., p. 116.

[262] Ibid., p. 117. Cf. Earl Fitzwilliam to EB, 27 November 1796, ibid., p. 136; EB to Earl Fitzwilliam, 30 November 1796, ibid., p. 139.

[263] EB to French Laurence, 18 November 1796, ibid., p. 117; Grattan, *Memoirs*, IV, p. 258.

[264] EB to Earl Fitzwilliam, 20 November 1796, ibid., p. 121. Cf. EB to John Keogh, 17 November 1796, ibid., p. 114.

[265] 36 Geo. III, c. 6.

[266] 36 Geo. III, c. 20. Introduced on 22 February 1796, it received the royal assent on 24 March 1796.

The standoff between the executive and diverse sections of the population lurched closer to militant confrontation.

Accordingly, the government introduced a yeomanry to tackle rising unrest. At the same time, tensions within the militia rose as Hussey charged that Catholics were being compelled to attend Protestant services.[267] The practice seemed to be indicative of an impulse to scourge the populace.[268] The narrow failure of a French fleet to converge on Bantry Bay in December illustrated the imminence of crisis. "I confess I tremble at the danger whilst I am rejoicing in the escape," Burke exclaimed to Windham.[269] Yet even as catastrophe loomed on the horizon, the opposition Whigs in Dublin plumped for parliamentary reform. Burke continued to believe that their plans were based on a fundamental misapprehension. The current configuration of the Irish Commons was largely a product of the incorporation of new boroughs under James I, intended as "perpetual seminaries of protestant burgesses."[270] Reform should aim at acquiring virtual representation for all members of the community, not the subversion of all hope for an adequate system of government in Ireland: "If Men have the real Benefit of a *Sympathetic* Representation, none but those who are heated and intoxicated with Theory will look for any other." Under current circumstances, the generation of sympathy would require a system of actual representation for Catholics, not a revolution in the form of the legislature such that the influence of property would be destroyed.[271] But as the opposition in parliament risked revolution by accident, militant forces out of doors deliberately threatened subversion by violence.

That prospect activated Burke's most agonised thoughts about the relationship between conscience and power. As matters stood at the close of 1796, the Catholics were descending into disorderly behaviour, for which they would have to be disciplined with the full force of the law. However, the law was in the process of being progressively suspended in order to deal with the rising defiance that the government had provoked. It was a tortuous situation that beset Burke with the deepest dilemmas. Having directed all his energy over the previous seven years against the presumptuous rights of revolutionary insurgency, he was acutely aware of the obligation to preserve the life of the state: "The first duty of a State is to provide for its own

[267] The Rev. Thomas Hussey to EB, 30 November 1796, *Corr.*, IX, p. 141. The allegations stretched back to encompass the particular case of James Hyland stationed on Carrick-on-Suir. See the Rev. Thomas Hussey to EB, 29 January 1795, *Corr.*, VIII, p. 124; EB to Earl Fitzwilliam, 10 February 1795, ibid., p. 145.

[268] EB to the Rev. Thomas Hussey, post 9 December 1796, *Corr.*, IX, p. 162.

[269] EB to William Windham, 5 January 1797, ibid., p. 2223.

[270] This description was penned by Sir John Davies, quoted in T. W. Moody, "The Irish Parliament under Elizabeth and James I: A General Survey," *Proceedings of the Royal Irish Academy*, 45 (1939–40), pp. 41–81, p. 54.

[271] EB to Unknown, February 1794, *Corr.*, IX, pp. 255–56. Cf. EB to French Laurence, 23 November 1796, ibid., p. 125; Earl Fitzwilliam to EB, 5 December 1796, ibid., p. 144; EB to Earl Fitzwilliam, 7 December 1796, ibid., p. 149; EB to French Laurence, 1 June 1797, ibid., p. 364.

conservation," he insisted to Hussey.[272] Looking back at the end of the fifth volume of his *History of England* at the revolutions in government that had led to execution of Charles I, David Hume remarked that if it became necessary to "*inculcate*" generic teaching on the duties of allegiance, then "the doctrine of obedience" ought exclusively to be taught.[273] Forty years later, reflecting on the rights of the subject in the context of incipient revolution in Ireland, Burke argued that the "Doctrine of Passive obedience, as a Doctrine, it is unquestionably right to teach."[274] Burke's point was ultimately equivalent to Hume's: while a revolution against the state can never be justified doctrinally, in practice it can be legitimate to employ violence against established authority. Hume returned to the issue in the sixth volume of his *History* when he came to treat the Test Bill intended to exclude all cases of resistance introduced into the Lords in April 1675.[275] Here Hume noted that attempts to deny resistance on principle were as obtuse as its encouragement on the basis of theoretical precepts.[276] In a similar vein, in 1796, Burke also denied that rebellion could be proscribed in every case since it made no sense to proclaim that the people possessed no right of self-defence. This, Burke claimed, should be seen as "a sort of deceit."[277] Power could only be legitimately deployed in accordance with the dictates of the law: "For if the people see, that the Law is violated to crush them they will certainly despise the Law."[278] The abandonment of due process was thus a declaration of anarchy. Burke was explicit: where violations were systematic rather than lapses from a judicious course, they had to be seen as "an encouragement . . . to riot, sedition, and a rebellious Spirit which sooner or later will turn upon those that encourage it."[279] Revolution could not be theoretically justified in advance, but in extreme circumstances it could be condoned as an appropriate course of action.

Burke was responding to the series of extra-judicial procedures made available to Irish magistrates through the course of 1796. But it was Hussey's claim that Catholics in the militia were being coerced into participating in Protestant services that distressed him most. Without any prompting from the clergy or publicists at large, such acts offended conscience and sparked defiance from "the God *within*."[280] By the end of December 1796, Burke recognised that civil relations were breaking

[272] EB to the Rev. Thomas Hussey, post 9 December 1796, ibid., p. 168.

[273] David Hume, *The History of England* (Indianapolis, IN: Liberty Fund, 1983), 6 vols., V, p. 544. On Hume on revolution, see Andrew Sabl, "When Bad Things Happen from Good People (and Vice-Versa): Hume's Political Ethics of Revolution," *Polity*, 35:1 (Autumn 2002), pp. 73–92; Andrew Sabl, *Hume's Politics: Coordination and Crisis in the "History of England"* (Princeton, NJ: Princeton University Press, 2012), pp. 103–7.

[274] EB to the Rev. Thomas Hussey, post 9 December 1796, *Corr.*, IX, p. 168. Cf. EB to Dr. William Markham, post 9 November 1771, *Corr.*, II, p. 283.

[275] For an account, see the Earl of Shaftesbury, *Letter from a Person of Quality* (London: 1675).

[276] Hume, *History*, VI, pp. 293–94.

[277] EB to the Rev. Thomas Hussey, post 9 December 1796, *Corr.*, IX, p. 171.

[278] Ibid., pp. 168–9.

[279] Ibid., p. 170.

[280] Ibid.

down. Conditions pointed to a virtual war between "property and no property."[281] The government had a substantial responsibility to bear. By February 1797, large sections of the Protestant population of the kingdom were being represented by the administration as in a state of "open Rebellion." Abandoned by public authority, the Catholic masses were being induced to join them.[282] A percentage was defecting to the ranks of the United Irishmen, though luckily the numbers in early 1797 were still low.[283] In March Burke remained assured that the bulk of the majority was "yet sound."[284] However, in the period before his death, that hope was fast receding: "Two months ago, a concession, or even a civil temporary refusal to the Catholicks, would have fixed that description."[285] With the rejection of a memorial to the king on the state of Ireland from French Laurence and Earl Fitzwilliam in March 1797, the situation seemed finally forlorn.[286] It was the ideological stance of the Junto that Burke found inexcusable, amounting to "a determined hostility to those who compose the infinitely larger part of the people."[287] Burke expected now to be finished with the Irish business "for ever."[288] In actual fact he returned to the topic for the last time on 6 June. By now he was sure that the shades were finally closing in. The Catholics were treated as a species of public enemy.[289] The administration proceeded to institute military government, a "Luttrellade" as Burke caustically described it to French Laurence, recalling the work of the Commander-in-Chief Henry Luttrell, the Earl of Carhampton.[290] Within a year of his death the dreaded rebellion finally arrived, issuing in carnage and clearing the way to union.

Burke lamented that discrimination had been conducted in the name of religion without specific moral commitments or doctrinal precepts. "Protestantism" under the circumstances was rather a negation than a religion, a principle of exclusion instead of an aid to piety.[291] Burke learned of what he took to be the results of this perversion in a sequence of letters sent from Cork in early May 1797. There was "a very great & genuine change in the minds of the people here brought about within a short period of time."[292] Expressions of loyalty such as had been roused by the French landing at Bantry Bay were now distant memories. The minds of men

[281] EB to Earl Fitzwilliam, 20 December 1796, ibid., p. 188.

[282] EB to Unknown, February 1797, ibid., p. 259.

[283] Ibid., p. 262.

[284] EB to William Windham, 30 March 1797, ibid., p. 301.

[285] EB to Earl Fitzwilliam, 7 May 1797, ibid., p. 330. Cf. EB to French Laurence, 12 May 1797, ibid., pp. 333–35.

[286] The Memorial in French Laurence to EB, c. 18 March 1797 in *The Epistolary Correspondence of the Right Hon. Edmund Burke and Dr. French Laurence* (London: 1827), pp. 157–62.

[287] EB to William Windham, 30 March 1797, ibid., p. 301. Cf. EB to the Bishop of Waterford, 22 May 1797, ibid., p. 357.

[288] EB to William Windham, 30 March 1797, *Corr.*, IX, p. 301.

[289] EB to Unknown Bishop, 6 June 1797, ibid., p. 369.

[290] EB to French Laurence, 5 June 1797, ibid., p. 368.

[291] EB to Unknown, February 1797, ibid., pp. 260–62.

[292] Extract of Letter from Cork, 3 May 1797, OSB MS. File 8750.

were so heated, one correspondent wrote, "that nothing but the horrors of Revolution can cool them."[293] When the explosion came a year later, the village of Ballitore was occupied by the yeomanry. Soldiers were quartered there in the months that followed; accusations of brutality against the inhabitants mounted. Mary Leadbeater, Richard Shackleton's daughter, directly witnessed the events. Burke's final letter to her recollected his tender memories of Ballitore.[294] Twelve months later Leadbeater would witness the troubles that besieged the village during the 1798 Rebellion.[295] Subsequently she revealed how Burke's letters to her were stolen among "the dreadful scenes of tumult and dismay which our little village for a time afforded," although a set of copies were fortuitously preserved.[296] Despite Burke's protracted hostility to anarchy and despotism, within a year of his death his childhood haunts would be overrun by a struggle between the forces he had been determined to oppose.

16.5 Scarcity and Plenty: *Thoughts and Details* and the *Letter to a Noble Lord*

After the failure of Fitzwilliam's Lord Lieutenancy in Ireland, events drew Burke to consider the situation in Britain. This was driven by a preoccupation with the rising cost of provisions that reached a peak in the summer of 1795. In the autumn of that year, the contest with France was coming to a significant turning point. In that context, pressure on the public coffers was likely to continue to rise even though trade and manufacture appeared to be in a flourishing state. Exports had regained the levels seen at the start of the 1790s; production—in textiles, paper and glass—was generally up; the number of bankruptcies had noticeably fallen.[297] And yet, as the King's Speech opening the new session of parliament on 29 October 1795 indicated, alongside the signs of prosperity, grain prices were exorbitant.[298] The cost of wheat, a staple in the subsistence diet, had conspicuously risen.[299] The winter months of 1794 had been peculiarly unfavourable to corn and grass, resulting in a low yield, even though the quality of the produce remained high. This situation affected the nourishment of cattle and therefore the cost of meat. The following year, when successive

[293] Extract from Letter from Cork, 4 May 1797, OSB MS. File 8750.

[294] EB to Mrs. William Leadbeater, 23 May 1797, *Corr.*, IX, p. 359.

[295] Mary Leadbeater, *The Annals of Ballitore* in *The Leadbeater Papers: Selections from the MSS. and Correspondence of Mary Leadbeater* (London: 1862), 2 vols., I, pp. 221–78.

[296] Mary Shackleton [Leadbeater] to Thomas O'Beirne, 11 February 1802, OSB MSS. 50, Box 2.

[297] A. D. Gayer, W. W. Rostow and A. J. Schwartz, *The Growth and Fluctuation of the British Economy, 1790–1850* (Oxford: Oxford University Press, 1953), 2 vols.; T. S. Ashton, *Economic Fluctuations in England, 1700–1800* (Oxford: Oxford University Press, 1959); Ralph Davis, *The Industrial Revolution and British Overseas Trade* (Leicester: Leicester University Press, 1979).

[298] *Parliamentary History*, XXXII, col. 142.

[299] Walter M. Stern, "The Bread Crisis in Britain, 1795–1796," *Economica*, 31:122 (May 1964), pp. 168–87; E. P. Thompson, "The Moral Economy of the English Crowd in the Eighteenth Century," *Past and Present*, 50 (February 1971), pp. 76–136.

frosts were followed by a series of heavy rains, even severer shortages obtained.[300] Amid allegations of price-fixing on the back of the disappointing harvest, the tide of popular discontent gave immediate cause for alarm. It was therefore announced that "regulations" might be recommended to parliament.[301] The previous spring and into the summer, there had been riots and demonstrations in response to bread shortages.[302] The Privy Council was deluged with appeals to increase supplies.[303] The king's coach was attacked as it made its way to the opening of parliament.[304] Pitt had been surrounded on his way to the debate.[305] In general terms, political agitation, which had been in abeyance, reappeared. In the aftermath of the treason trials of 1794, organised political protest had momentarily receded: Thomas Hardy, Horne Tooke, Thomas Holcroft and Major John Cartwright withdrew, at least for a time, from the lines of battle. Yet by the summer of 1795 demonstrations were revived. This turn of events coincided with distress over scarcity. The activities of the London Corresponding Society were rekindled; John Thelwall inaugurated a programme of educational lectures; mass meetings were convened across the capital—at St. George's Fields on 29 June and in Copenhagen Fields on 26 October.[306] At the same time, a paper war against the price of provisions got under way. Accusations against "Rogues of Grain" were issued by poetasters; farmers and middlemen were alleged to have designed an artificial dearth.[307] In this context, a debate was held on the price of corn in the House of Commons on 3 November 1795. A few days later, Burke "scribbled" his thoughts on how to respond to the distress in a memorial sent directly to Pitt.[308]

This memorial would subsequently form the main plank of Burke's *Thoughts and Details on Scarcity*, published after his death in 1800. Fragments from a surviving manuscript from late 1795 that Burke intended to be published as a series of letters to Arthur Young were interleaved with the larger manuscript by the editors of the

[300] EB, *Thoughts and Details on Scarcity* (1795), *W & S*, IX, p. 137.

[301] *Parliamentary History*, XXXII, col. 142.

[302] J. Stephenson, "Food Riots in England, 1792–1818" in R. Quinalt and J. Stephenson eds., *Popular Protest and Public Order* (London: George Allen & Unwin, 1974).

[303] Stern, "Bread Crisis," p. 171.

[304] *Parliamentary History*, XXXII, cols. 143–55; Francis Place, *The Autobiography of Francis Place*, ed. Mary Thale (Cambridge: Cambridge University Press, 1972), pp. 145–47; EB to William Pitt, 7 November1795, *Corr.*, VIII, p. 338.

[305] Ehrman, *Pitt: The Reluctant Transition*, p. 455.

[306] Albert Goodwin, *The Friends of Liberty: The English Democratic Movement in the Age of the French Revolution* (London: Hutchinson, 1979), ch. 10. For the mass meeting of 1795, see Mark Harrison, *Crowds and History: Mass Phenomena in English Towns, 1790–1835* (Cambridge: Cambridge University Press, 1988), p. 4. Burke mentions Thelwall's campaign of lectures in EB, *Letter to a Noble Lord* (1796), *W & S*, IX, p. 163.

[307] [Anon.], *The Devil the Master; or Rogues in Grain* (London: 1795); [Anon.], *A Dialogue between a Gentleman and a Farmer on the Present High Price of Provisions* (London: 1795); Thomas Wright, *A Short Address to the Public on the Monopoly of Small Farms: A Great Cause of the Present Scarcity and Dearness of Provisions* (London: 1795). For the emergence of this genre in the 1750s, see A. W. Coats, "Changing Attitudes to Labour in the Mid-Eighteenth Century," *Economic History Review*, 11:1 (1958), pp. 35–51.

[308] EB to William Pitt, 7 November 1795, *Corr.*, VIII, p. 337.

work.[309] Writing to Pitt on 7 November 1795, Burke described the original memorial as a series of "Reflections," containing in addition "a good many small details."[310] Much of this material was a reaction to proceedings in parliament on 3 November when it was proposed to establish a committee to inquire into the high price of corn. As an indication of the direction in which he thought policy might be taken, Pitt had raised the possibility of amending the law on the Assize of Bread, incentivising farmers to bring their finest wheat to market, and introducing into general consumption a greater variety of grains.[311] Some respondents blamed the current dearth on farming monopolies.[312] Others accused the government of buying up available corn.[313] John Curwen, the member for Carlisle since 1786, recommended increasing the rewards of labour so that exigencies could be met.[314] It was apparently these contributions to the debate that led Burke to go "further" than he had originally intended when he raised his voice against tampering with the provisions trade.[315] Intervention of the kind, he argued, was the "most dangerous" kind of interference into which governments could be tempted.[316]

The British press had reported economic controls introduced by the French assembly from the middle of September 1793.[317] Rising prices, hoarding and calls for an agrarian law had conspired to mobilise the Parisian sans-culottes in favour of fixed grain prices in the autumn of 1792. Supported by leading *enragés*, most conspicuously Jacques Roux, the calls for regulation spread in the early months of 1793. As tensions increased between the Montagnards and their opponents in the spring, the Convention swung behind a scheme that would lead to the regulation of the grain supply. On 4 May 1793, with pressure heaped on deputies from the galleries in the assembly, proposals for imposing a "maximum" on the price of bread passed into

[309] A work by Burke on the cost of wages was promised "Speedily" in the *London Chronicle*, the *Star* and the *Courier and Evening Gazette* on 17 December 1795. This was to take the form of a series of letters to Arthur Young. Burke's executors, French Laurence and Walker King, amalgamated what survived of this manuscript with the remains of Burke's memorial to Pitt, forming *Thoughts and Details on Scarcity*, published on 25 November 1800. The material addressed to Young is distinguished from the original memorial by Laurence and King in the Preface to EB, *Thoughts and Details on Scarcity, Originally Presented to the Right Hon. William Pitt in the Month of November, 1795* (London: 1800), p. ix, and can now be found in EB, *Thoughts and Details on Scarcity* (1795), *W & S*, IX, pp. 123–29, 130–32, 143–45.

[310] EB to William Pitt, 7 November 1795, *Corr.*, VIII, p. 337.

[311] *Parliamentary History*, XXXII, col. 235. For comment on the counterproductive character of the Assize of Bread, intended to regulate supply, see Adam Smith, *Lectures on Jurisprudence*, ed. R. L. Meek, D. D. Raphael and P. G. Stein (Indianapolis, IN: Liberty Fund, 1982), p. 364; Adam Smith, *An Inquiry into the Nature and Causes of the Wealth of Nations*, ed. R. H. Campbell and A. S. Skinner (Indianapolis, IN: Liberty Fund, 1976), 2 vols., I, p. 158.

[312] *Parliamentary History*, XXXII, col. 237; *St. James's Chronicle*, 4 November 1795.

[313] *Lloyd's Evening Post*, 2–5 November 1795.

[314] Ibid.

[315] EB to William Pitt, 7 November 1795, *Corr.*, VIII, p. 337.

[316] EB, *Thoughts and Details on Scarcity* (1795), *W & S*, IX, p. 120.

[317] *Morning Post*, 16 September 1793; *Evening Mail*, 21–23 October 1793; *True Briton*, 26 October 1793.

law. This was succeeded by the provisions of the *maximum général* of 11 and 29 September, designed to regulate the cost of all essential supplies.[318] The administration of this measure was committed to the *commission des subsistences*, placed under the supervision of the Committee of Public Safety.[319] Stockpiling and increased shortages were the result. Political competition among the factions in the Convention had fed a demagogic scheme for redistributing provisions. As the demand for a "fair" price for necessities rose in London in the autumn of 1795, Burke was acutely conscious of the disturbing precedents in Paris.

In the face of British dearth, Thomas Pownall launched a general attack on the system of regulation known as the Corn Laws, including the bounty on exportation, which came in for increasing criticism from the 1770s.[320] Only a "FREE MART" governing relations between supply and demand could deliver the optimal allocation of the resource.[321] By the time that Pownall wrote, debate about regulating the grain supply had an extensive and controversial history behind it.[322] In a lengthy digression on the corn trade added to book IV of the *Wealth of Nations*, Adam Smith had contrasted the catastrophic Bengal Famine of 1770 with bread shortages in Europe over the previous generation.[323] In general terms, countries with a naturally rich corn supply, like France and Britain, had little to fear from years of comparative dearth: "In an extensive corn country, between all the different parts of which there is a free commerce and communication, the scarcity occasioned by the most unfavourable seasons can never be so great as to produce a famine."[324] Under these circumstances, only misguided actions by government could convert scarcity into famine. It was this that explained why the drought in Bengal had ended in such catastrophe: "Some improper regulations, some injudicious restraints imposed by the servants of the East India Company upon the rice trade, contributed, perhaps, to turn that dearth into a

[318] Albert Mathiez, *La vie chère et le mouvement social sous la Terreur* (Paris: Payot, 1927); François Furet, "Maximum" in François Furet and Mona Ozouf eds., *A Critical Dictionary of the French Revolution* (Cambridge, MA: Harvard University Press, 1989).

[319] Marc Bouloiseau, *The Jacobin Republic, 1792–1794* (Cambridge: Cambridge University Press, 1983, 1987), pp. 100–106.

[320] Donald Grove Barnes, *A History of the English Corn Laws: From 1660–1846* (1930) (Oxford: Routledge, 2010), pp. 23ff.

[321] Thomas Pownall, *Considerations on the Scarcity and High Prices of Bread-Corn and Bread at the Market* (Cambridge: 1795), p. 57.

[322] Istvan Hont and Michael Ignatieff, "Needs and Justice in the Wealth of Nations: An Introductory Essay" in idem eds., *Wealth and Virtue: The Shaping of Political Economy in the Scottish Enlightenment* (Cambridge: Cambridge University Press, 1983, 1985), pp. 13–26.

[323] For discussion of the relationship between the economic thought of Burke and Smith, see Laurence and King, Preface to EB, *Thoughts and Details on Scarcity* (1800), p. vi; William C. Dunn, "Edmund Burke and Adam Smith: Complementary Contemporaries," *Southern Economic Journal*, 7 (January 1941), pp. 330–46; Donal Barrington, "Edmund Burke as Economist," *Economica*, 21:83 (August 1954), pp. 252–58; Donald Winch, *Riches and Poverty: An Intellectual History of Political Economy in Britain, 1750–1834* (Cambridge: Cambridge University Press, 1996), chs. 7 and 8.

[324] Smith, *Wealth of Nations*, I, p. 526.

famine."[325] With regard to Britain, Smith was particularly keen to refute suggestions that the price of bread was adversely affected by the avarice of inland corn traders. In fact, he claimed, the interest of the consumer was in harmony with that of the merchant even as they pursued their separate agendas. As sellers raised their prices under conditions of insufficiency, buyers were protected from the worst consequences of a scarce supply.[326]

Smith's argument amounted to saying that the trade in corn should be determined by the operations of the market. This was to contend that commercial relations should be governed by "commutative" rather than "distributive" justice: prices ought to be determined by the rights of property and the laws of trade rather than considerations of merit or desert.[327] Burke accepted this distinction, citing Pufendorf in its defence, noting in addition that describing distribution based on merit as an "imperfect" obligation of justice was to degrade what was a duty of charity: "Without all doubt, charity to the poor is a direct and obligatory duty upon all Christians."[328] The obligation, in other words, was to be taken seriously, but it did not extend to subverting market relations by public authority.[329] It was the bargain struck between consumption and production that should determine price, not an externally enforced idea of relative fairness. On 28 October 1795, Portland, in his capacity as Home Secretary, had issued instructions requesting magistrates to inquire into the state of the corn produce.[330] Burke wondered what a public official could have to do with the availability of grain, since only the market could appropriately fix the ratio between supply and demand: free bargaining settled, and could alone settle, the price of commodities by discovering the balance between the needs of producers and consumers. Any artificial distortion of that natural balance was liable to "do mischiefs incalculable."[331]

Restraints upon pricing, the establishment of public granaries, and the regulation of the export and import of grains by the imposition of duties and bounties, were common methods of interfering with the free commerce between farmers, middlemen and consumers. A further method of managing the trade in provisions was to adapt the purchasing power of the consumer. For the labourer, this could be

[325] Ibid., p. 527.

[326] Ibid., pp. 524–25.

[327] The distinction was classically formulated in Aristotle, *Nicomachean Ethics*, V, and became central to early modern natural law doctrine. See, for example, Hugo Grotius, *The Rights of War and Peace*, ed. Richard Tuck (Indianapolis, IN: Liberty Fund, 2005), 3 vols., I, pp. 142–7. Cf. Adam Smith, *The Theory of Moral Sentiments*, ed. D. D. Raphael and A. L. Macfie (Indianapolis, IN: Liberty Fund, 1982), p. 79.

[328] EB, *Thoughts and Details on Scarcity* (1795), *W & S*, IX, p. 129. For Pufendorf's terminology, see Samuel Pufendorf, *De iure naturae et gentium libri octo* (Lund: 1672), bk. I, ch. vii, sects. 7–9. Cf. Samuel Pufendorf, *The Whole Duty of Man, according to the Law of Nature*, ed. Ian Hunter and David Saunders (Indianapolis, IN: Liberty Fund, 2003), p. 110.

[329] Richard Whatmore, "Burke on Political Economy" in David Dwan and Christopher J. Insole eds., *The Cambridge Companion to Edmund Burke* (Cambridge: Cambridge University Press, 2012), p. 81.

[330] *CJ*, li, p. 85.

[331] EB, *Thoughts and Details on Scarcity* (1795), *W & S*, IX, p. 133.

affected by regulating wages, thus relieving, as the new idiom had it, the exigencies of the "labouring poor."[332] Burke had noticed the changing rhetoric pervading debate about poverty since early October 1795. It was at that time that an article in the *St. James's Chronicle* had argued for "Strictures on Wheat and Flour" to improve the lot of "the labouring poor especially."[333] The new coinage struck Burke as menacing: the "poor" had generally referred to the indigent who were incapable of labour, yet now the "labouring poor" were commonly invoked as part of an argument for a more democratic distribution of resources. Burke returned to the theme in 1797: plans for the relief of the "*Labouring Poor*" were not as "innocent" as they were "foolish."[334] Burke's target was not the poor laws, or the new Speenhamland system of outdoor relief, as has commonly been assumed: "I say nothing to the policy of the provision for the poor, in all variety of faces under which it presents itself. This is the matter of another enquiry."[335]

What concerned Burke was the ammunition that egalitarian rhetoric provided to Jacobin ideology. Late in October 1795, the *Whitehall Evening Post* carried the statement that the "price of provisions is so far advanced that the labouring poor man can scarcely provide bread for his family."[336] Soon, action was being taken in Newcastle to sell provisions at reduced prices to "the poor and the labouring poor."[337] In the House of Commons on 25 November Sir John Rous called for price regulations that might "afford real relief to the labouring poor."[338] But from the start, the conditions of labour had been linked to the affairs of France. In late October, the mayor, sheriffs and aldermen of Norwich, in Norfolk, had petitioned their representatives, William Windham and Henry Hobart, for a "restoration of peace" with the French government. It was probably Windham who drew Burke's attention to this "Memorial for Peace," which added a plea for a reduction in the cost of necessaries: "The dearness and scarcity of all kinds of provisions . . . cannot but excite alarming apprehensions for the future happiness of the labouring poor of every description."[339] Before long the plight of the labouring poor was being deployed for party advantage in the House of Commons. In the debate on seditious meetings on 17 November 1795, Sheridan

[332] For Burke's strictures on the term, see ibid., p. 121. On the malleability of the concept, see Gertrude Himmelfarb, *The Idea of Poverty: England in the Early Industrial Age* (London: Faber and Faber, 1984). Cf. Gareth Stedman Jones, *An End to Poverty: A Historical Debate* (London: Profile, 2004).

[333] *St. James's Chronicle*, 1–3 October 1795.

[334] EB, *Third Letter on a Regicide Peace* (1797), *W & S*, IX, p. 355.

[335] Ibid., p. 352. On Speenhamland, see Karl Polanyi, *The Great Transformation* (New York: Farrar and Reinhart, 1944). On the political economy of the poor laws, see A. W. Coats, "Economic Thought and Poor Law Policy in the Eighteenth Century," *Economic History Review*, 13:1 (1960), pp. 39–51.

[336] *Whitehall Evening Post*, 27–29 October 1795; cf. *Whitehall Evening Post*, 14–17 November 1795.

[337] *London Packet*, 16–18 November 1795.

[338] *Morning Post*, 26 November 1795.

[339] *Lloyd's Evening Post*, 23–26 October 1795. Cf. *St. James's Chronicle*, 24–27 October 1795; *Morning Post*, 26 October 1795. Burke refers directly to this "Memorial for Peace" in his criticism of the "squires of Norfolk" in EB, *Thoughts and Details on Scarcity* (1795), *W & S*, IX, pp. 122–23. He is mistaken by the editor to be referring to a similar measure at Suffolk: ibid., p. 123n.

celebrated the historic loyalty of working men: "he put it to the gentlemen of estates, to the merchants and manufacturers, who heard him, whether they had ever seen a poor labouring man, unthankful in his return for their bounty."[340]

Public oversight of the rewards of agricultural labour became an issue in parliament after the debates on the state of the corn supply, as signalled by Curwen's remarks on 3 November 1795. On 9 December Samuel Whitbread brought a Bill before the Commons to amend an Elizabethan Act governing the remuneration of husbandry.[341] Whitbread's aim was to complement this provision by setting a minimum level of wage. Fox intervened decisively in support of the motion: "It was not fitting in a free country that the great body of the people should depend on the charity of the rich."[342] On the second reading of the Bill, on 12 February 1796, Whitbread drew on the evidence of Richard Price to the effect that the wages of labour had lagged behind the cost of provisions over the course of the previous two centuries.[343] "Tread cautiously in the affair of Provisions," Burke had admonished Windham the previous November.[344] Debate was tending to inflame the poor against the privileges of the rich. Much of this was fanned by resentment against the "monopoly" of capital. By this Burke meant the accumulation of wealth in the hands of farmers. This, he believed, was entirely in the interest of the consumer since the farmer could only afford to drop the percentage of his profit as the size of his stock increased.[345] This was part of a larger argument about the shared interest between capital and labour, in harmony with the claims of the *Wealth of Nations*.[346] Smith saw that the "contract" of labour was founded on an opposition of interests since both parties sought to maximise their advantage.[347] Nonetheless, in general terms, the profit of the master was to the benefit of the worker: "The demand of those who live by wages . . . necessarily increases with the increase of the revenue and stock of

[340] *Morning Chronicle*, 18 November 1795.

[341] The Statute of Artificers of 1562 (5 Eliz. I, c. 4) gave magistrates responsibility for regulating agricultural wages, while guilds assumed responsibility for urban trades.

[342] *Parliamentary History*, XXXII, col. 702; *True Briton*, 10 December 1795.

[343] *St. James's Chronicle*, 13–15 February 1796. Burke refuted this in EB, *Third Letter on a Regicide Peace* (1797), *W & S*, IX, pp. 353–54.

[344] EB to William Windham, 17 November 1795, *Corr.*, VIII, p. 344.

[345] EB, *Thoughts and Details on Scarcity* (1795), *W & S*, IX, pp. 132–33. Cf. EB, *Third Letter on a Regicide Peace* (1797), *W & S*, IX, p. 347.

[346] However, see Winch, *Riches and Poverty*, pp. 203–4, which sets Burke's views in opposition to Smith's. Cf. James Conniff, "Burke on Political Economy: The Nature and Extent of State Authority," *Review of Politics*, 49:4 (Autumn 1987), pp. 490–514; C. B. Macpherson, *Burke* (Oxford: Oxford University Press, 1980), pp. 52ff. For a Manichaean version of the antithesis, see Emma Rothschild, "Adam Smith and Conservative Economics," *Economic History Review*, 45:1 (February 1992), pp. 74–96. For Burke's evident pleasure in having been consulted by Smith in connection with the *Wealth of Nations*, see EB, *Letter to a Noble Lord* (1796), *W & S*, p. 160.

[347] Smith, *Wealth of Nations*, I, p. 83.

every country, and cannot possibly increase without it."[348] In the absence of force and fraud, the objectives of the capitalist and the wage earner coincided.[349] This meant that, excepting combinations against the bargaining power of individuals, the absolute welfare of the poor improved with the prosperity of the rich.

In advancing this perspective, Burke, like Smith, was challenging earlier claims to the effect that wealth was increased by the indigence of labour. They were rejecting the idea that industry was encouraged by necessity. The argument had been powerfully challenged in 1766 by Louis Messance, secretary to the intendant of Auvergne, in a work celebrated by Smith for the clarity of its insight.[350] As Smith himself suggested: "The liberal reward of labour, as it encourages the propagation, so it increases the industry of the common people."[351] In this vein, Burke claimed that farmers benefited from the prosperity of their workers. Indeed the former were described by Burke as the "pensioners of the poor," necessarily "maintained by their superfluity."[352] The rich prospered by the maximal productivity of labour, which was boosted where wages were high and provisions cheap.[353] It was the job of government not to regulate that relation, but to disseminate information on the common benefits that attended the concentrated accumulation of wealth. Faction, greed and misguided benevolence taught that industry would benefit from public favours. The truth was that the people maintained government which could not for that reason maintain the people. Envy was the enemy of this great truth of political economy, disposing the labouring multitudes to despoil the capital of the rich. But if resentment should drive the workers to cut the throats of the wealthy, accumulated stock would be radically dispersed, barely benefiting its recipients and depriving society of its bank of capital.[354] Equalisation could only realistically level down.[355]

As Burke composed his strictures on the idea of equalising capital and labour, the Duke of Bedford attacked his merit as a pensioner of the state. Reprimanding the government for its lavishness and corruption during a debate on the Treasonable Practices Bill, he complained in the Lords on 13 November 1795 about the

[348] Ibid., pp. 86–87. For the tendency of urban "masters" to combine against "workmen," see ibid., pp. 83ff. Burke, however, was addressing himself to farmers: here, he seems to have thought, combination was less feasible.

[349] EB, *Thoughts and Details on Scarcity* (1795), *W & S*, IX, pp. 124–25. Cf. EB to Arthur Young, 23 May 1797, *Corr.*, IX, p. 361: "My constant opinion was, and is, that all matters relative to labour, ought to be left to the conventions of the parties."

[350] Louis Messance, *Recherches sur la population des généralités d'Auvergne* (Paris: 1766), cited by Smith, *Wealth of Nations*, p. 102.

[351] Ibid., p. 99.

[352] EB, *Thoughts and Details on Scarcity* (1795), *W & S*, IX, pp. 120–21.

[353] Ibid., p. 125.

[354] Ibid., pp. 120–21.

[355] Ibid., p. 127.

"extravagant" pension granted to "the preacher of economy (Mr. Burke!)."[356] The Earl of Lauderdale further branded Burke as "the author of the war" with France, leaving Lord Grenville, the Foreign Secretary, to defend his integrity along with the government's.[357] Not to be outdone, Lord Abingdon further denounced him as "a Tory and a Catholic."[358] On 14 November, a letter from "The People" thanking Bedford appeared in the *Courier*, and Curwen renewed the attack two days later in the Commons: "the manner in which the Honourable Gentleman, and some others, had deserted their old friends, took from them all credit that might otherwise have attached to them."[359] Windham was left to rally to the defence of his friend and ally. On 19 November, Lauderdale moved for an address requesting a statement of all grants awarded to Burke.[360] By then Burke had resolved to take a public stand against Bedford. He wrote to Grenville on the 15th to thank him for his intervention, and then to Windham the following day about the conduct of Curwen.[361] The latter was dismissed as a lazy prattler, scarcely capable of dinting Burke's pride. In fact, "the invectives of even the most powerful declaimers of the Age can very little hurt me."[362] Burke failed to complete his letter to William Windham, yet his letter to Grenville soon grew to a "shameful . . . Bulk," and was published on 24 February 1796 as *A Letter from the Right Honourable Edmund Burke to a Noble Lord*.[363]

The *Letter to a Noble Lord* is a powerful satire on the presumption of Bedford, depicted as a callow and posturing aristocrat. Its energy is pent-up and controlled, its rhetoric pared and concentrated. The resulting invective is restrained yet barbed, constituting one of Burke's most annihilating performances. The argument turns on the opposition between industry and indolence: the ceaseless public labours of Burke on the one hand, and the pampered lethargy of Bedford on the other. "I have

[356] *St. James's Chronicle*, 12–14 November 1795. Cf. the *London Packet*, 13–16 November 1795; *Morning Post*, 14 November 1795.

[357] *St. James's Chronicle*, 12–14 November 1795; *Star*, 14 November 1795. Burke ascribed the remark to Bedford in EB, *Letter to a Noble Lord* (1796), *W & S*, IX, p. 186. See also the *Morning Chronicle*, 14 November 1795, where Lauderdale is reported to have accused Burke of inculcating doctrines "that tended to extinguish the principles of freedom."

[358] *Oracle*, 14 November 1795.

[359] *Courier and Evening Gazette*, 14 November 1795; *English Chronicle*, 14–17 November 1795. The *Whitehall Evening Post*, 14–15 November 1795, noted that Curwen commended his character while condemning the manner in which the pension had been awarded. A further letter criticising the pension appeared in the *Morning Chronicle*, 16 November 1795.

[360] *St. James's Chronicle*, 19–21 November 1795. Also reported in: *Whitehall Evening Post*, 19–21 November 1791; *Lloyd's Evening Post*, 20–23 November 1795; *Morning Post*, 20 November 1795; *Oracle*, 20 November 1795; *True Briton*, 20 November 1795; *Star*, 20 November 1795; *Johnson's British Gazette*, 22 November 1795. Lauderdale returned to the fray at the start of December: see *St. James's Chronicle*, 1–3 December 1795.

[361] EB to Lord Grenville, 15 November 1795, Unpublished Letters, I, pp. 135–36; EB to William Windham, 16 November 1795, *Corr.*, VIII, pp. 338ff.

[362] Ibid., p. 339.

[363] EB to William Windham, 17 November 1795, ibid., pp. 341–44; EB to Lord Grenville, 16 November 1795, Unpublished Letters, I, p. 137; Todd, *Bibliography*, p. 186.

labored . . . far more," Burke wrote to Windham after Bedford's intervention, ". . . than any Member, that ever sat in the House."[364] Accordingly, in the *Letter to a Noble Lord*, unflagging toil was pitted against unproductive capital.[365] Burke even invoked the ongoing scarcity of corn to set the context in which he was resisting his unmerited disgrace: "in this hard season" he would not trade a quarter of a bushel of wheat "for all that is called fame and honour in the world."[366] Reputation was a "luxury," a "privilege" of the rich, he commented wryly: "it is an indulgence for those who are at their ease."[367] Yet while he could forgo renown, he would not endure contempt. The effect of his ironic ascription of glory to the great is to prize the humble industry of the dedicated man of business. "I was not, like his Grace of Bedford, swaddled, and rocked, and dandled into a Legislator," he remarked.[368] Unlike his opponent, it could not be said that Burke "had nothing to attend to but the lazy enjoyment of undisturbed possessions."[369] The core of the *Letter* proceeded to enumerate Burke's main achievements, and to compare his career as a statesman with the contributions of the Bedford family.

This was a dangerous strategy to pursue since it traded on a set of attitudes that encouraged revolution. In the *Letter to William Elliot* that Burke had undertaken six months earlier as a riposte to a slight from the Duke of Norfolk, he argued that European politics at the pinnacle of its good fortune had germinated the seeds of its destruction. This derived from the degeneracy of the ruling orders that dominated the courts and assemblies of the continent as a whole. Burke had in mind the hereditary nobility on the one hand, and aspiring men of ability on the other. "General wealth loosened morals, relaxed vigilance, and increased presumption," he reckoned. Under these circumstances, the dissemination of knowledge based on spurious premises perverted and dislodged established principles of political prudence. The upper ranks were corrupted while men of business grew disaffected. Laxness and incapacity spread on one side, while "dark designs" were developed on the other. Reigning ideas of distributive justice were generally called into question. Burke anatomised the result: "Men of talent began to compare, in the partition of the common stock of public prosperity, the proportions of the dividends, with the merits of the claimants."[370] Unsurprisingly they found their share disproportionate to their deserts. The spectacle of one successful challenge to the allocation of privilege was sufficient to unsettle the distribution of property in all states. Authority, in the process, lost its credit. A struggle between establishment and rapacity began.

[364] EB to William Windham, ante 17 November 1795, *Corr.*, VIII, p. 340.

[365] See, for example, EB, *Letter to a Noble Lord* (1796), *W & S*, IX, pp. 148–49, where "the total body of my services, on account of the industry which was shewn in them" is compared to the Duke of Bedford's "few and idle years."

[366] Ibid., p. 171.

[367] Ibid.

[368] Ibid., p. 160.

[369] Ibid., p. 175.

[370] EB, *Letter to William Elliot* (26 May 1795), *W & S*, IX, p. 39.

What is remarkable about the *Letter to a Noble Lord* is that Burke was prepared to highlight the injustice of a situation in which idleness could prosper while talent was rebuffed. However, although attitudes among all ranks would have to be reformed, it still seemed madness to Burke to encourage a collision between social orders.

"I had earned my pension before I set my foot in St. Stephen's Chapel," Burke pleaded in the *Letter to a Noble Lord*.[371] He had in mind his application as a student and man of letters before embarking on a career in parliament. Bedford was thirty-one in 1796, having been born in the month that the Rockinghams first formed a ministry. He succeeded to his grandfather's title in 1771, and would preside over vast estates scattered over eleven counties. As an adult he was satirised for avoiding the payment of taxes.[372] Burke lampooned this "Poor rich man" as incapable of comprehending the benefits to be derived from diligence and effort: "He can hardly know any thing of publick industry in it's [*sic*] exertions, or can estimate it's [*sic*] compensations."[373] Although Bedford attended Westminster and Cambridge, and completed the Grand Tour, he was reputed not to have read a book before the age of twenty-four.[374] Burke's passport, by comparison, was his resolution and endeavour. Knowledge, and the urge to acquire it, had determined his station in life—"Otherwise no rank, no toleration even, for me."[375] The Duke's charge against Burke was hypocrisy in receiving a gift from the crown, having subjected the royal household, and public administration more generally, to sharp reductions during the second Rockingham administration. Burke began by defending his reforms of 1782, including his revision of the civil list. He made clear that the aim had not been to deprive the state of funds to reward merit, of which he hoped his pension could stand as an example.[376] The goal was instead to tackle the excesses of influence by proceeding in a "healing and mediatorial" spirit.[377]

Since influence usually operated by royal favour, criticism of Burke's pension could strike a public nerve.[378] In the *Morning Post* he was condemned as a beneficiary of charity, reaping a harvest in the dearth of his old age.[379] However, as Burke saw it, economical reform was intended not to diminish the state's largesse, but to

371 EB, *Letter to a Noble Lord* (1796), ibid., p. 159.

372 Baron Macdonald, "The Duke and the Taxing-Man" in *Poetry of the Anti-Jacobin*, ed. Charles Edmonds (London: 1890), pp. 52–53.

373 EB, *Letter to a Noble Lord* (1796), *W & S*, IX, p. 150.

374 E. A. Smith, "Francis Russell, Fifth Duke of Bedford" in *The Oxford Dictionary of National Biography* (Oxford: Oxford University Press, 2004), 60 vols.

375 EB, *Letter to a Noble Lord* (1796), *W & S*, IX, p. 160.

376 Ibid., p. 158.

377 Ibid., p. 157.

378 The response to Burke began after the appearance of the *Letter*, which was variously summarised in the newspapers almost immediately: see *General Evening Post*, 23–25 February 1796; *St. James's Chronicle*, 23–25 February 1795; *St. James's Chronicle*, 27 February–1 March 1796; *Whitehall Evening Post*, 23–25 February 1796; *Lloyd's Evening Post*, 24–26 February 1796; *London Packet*, 24–26 February 1796; *Gazetteer*, 26 February 1796; *Public Ledger*, 26 February 1796.

379 *Morning Post*, 25 February 1796.

curb the power of the crown over parliament: "I looked on the consideration of public service, or publick ornament, to be real and very justice."[380] Since Burke was not a member when he became a pensioner, the allegations of duplicity could not stick. Ability, Burke insisted, had to be rewarded: the award of pensions to Dunning and Barré in 1782 had been a reasonable recompense for the use of their talents in public life.[381] What struck Burke as preposterous was an accusation of jobbery from an inert magnate whose personal affluence derived from the bounty of Henry VIII, bestowed upon his ancestors thanks to "the recent confiscation of the nobility of the land."[382] John Russell, the first Earl of Bedford, had been a courtier of the Tudor monarch, compensated with the estates of the Duke of Buckingham. He was subsequently granted property plundered from the Church. The Russells had been remunerated by the hand of rapacity; Burke had been paid for services by a mild and moderate king. "I was not made for a minion or tool," Burke protested.[383] The Duke of Bedford, by comparison, was. He was the "Leviathan among all the creatures of the Crown. He tumbles about his unwieldy bulk; he plays and frolicks in the ocean of Royal bounty."[384] To date he had contributed nothing to the needs of the state, whereas Burke, among other employments, had defended the nobility.

Burke's position is only difficult to access from a contemporary perspective by a wilful failure of historical imagination. To begin with, he had not launched his defence out of native obsequiousness. He fully recognised that men like Bedford held "large portions of wealth without any apparent merit of their own."[385] The Duke also enjoyed a ponderous hereditary title without having had to exert himself to acquire it. Burke was moved to support this unearned distribution on the basis of his pledge to property in general, not out of partiality to privilege as such. Family wealth, passing from generation to generation, solidified the commitment to ownership across society. At the same time, massed wealth was a shield that protected the rights of smaller assets. All degrees of prosperity would stand or fall together: "If a great storm blow on our coast, it will cast the whales on the strand as well as the periwinkles."[386] Extensive property was also a benefit to the circulation of wealth: a hoard of capital was required for commerce and industry to function since labour had to be funded from accumulated stocks. In addition to its role in promoting economic growth, landed property ineluctably attracted power. It was true that privilege should not confer a title to exercise rule. Only virtue could hope to perform that role. However, virtuous government was profoundly difficult to compose out of such treacherous materials as human beings. Virtuous rule involved servicing the common good by a mixture of conservation and reform: without conservation, Burke thought, there

[380] EB, *Letter to a Noble Lord* (1796), *W & S*, IX, p. 160.
[381] Ibid., p. 161.
[382] Ibid., p. 166.
[383] Ibid., p. 160.
[384] Ibid., p. 164.
[385] Ibid., p. 162.
[386] Ibid., p. 173.

could be no reform, but only a giddy and explosive transformation. Property and nobility were disposed to conserve; optimally, they would also militate against "selfishness and a narrow mind."[387] A defence of "inglorious sloth" was no part of Burke's agenda.[388] Nonetheless, he thought that social standing could impose a sense of responsibility. An awareness of one's position between ancestry and posterity induced a consciousness of accountability. More generally it could act as an "incitement to virtuous activity," not least on the part of industrious men of business in the Commons.[389] Having promoted the means of defending the state through the first half of the 1790s, the *Letter to a Noble Lord* offered a tribute to its reform. This was secured by the disinterested devotion of men of ability whose merit ought to obtain for them an appropriate distribution of honour.

Burke itemised his own desert without a hint of brazenness by modestly recapitulating his attainments as endeavours. He had striven to understand political economy long before the day he entered parliament, and he then put his learning to use in support of the Rockingham party.[390] He applied himself to mastering American affairs from the first months of 1766, and disseminated his findings down to 1783. Fourteen years he devoted to the business of India: "They are those on which I value myself most; most for the importance; most for the labour; most for the judgment; most for constancy and perseverance in the pursuit."[391] Throughout he had applied himself with calculating prudence. His stance regarding administrative reform could represent his attitude towards the rest: "I conceived nothing arbitrarily; nor proposed anything to be done by the will and pleasure of others, or my own; but by reason, and by reason only."[392] Proposals were pursued by planning, and planning by systematic appraisal with a view to matching causes with probable effects. This was underpinned by the objective of the statesman, which was to administer on the basis of "oeconomy." Burke contrasted this noble function with the goal of "parsimony."[393] Properly understood, it operated by careful selection and due proportion in allocation. It was nothing less than the distributive justice that attended good government; it aimed to bolster virtue by recompensing merit. In contrast to the record of the Bedford family, it was this principle that had guided Burke in public life.[394] It was also what distinguished his parliamentary conduct from the ardour of revolutionaries in France. Revolution "harpies" had inverted the science of politics. The *Let-*

[387] Ibid., p. 183.

[388] Ibid.

[389] Ibid.

[390] Burke's early application to the political economy of empire is recorded by William Markham. See William Markham to the Duchess of Queensbury, 25 September 1759, *Chatham Correspondence*, I, p. 432.

[391] EB, *Letter to a Noble Lord* (1796), *W & S*, IX, p, 159.

[392] Ibid., p. 157.

[393] Ibid., p. 162.

[394] Ibid., pp. 166–69.

ter provided one of Burke's final chances to expose their inspiration and mode of procedure.[395]

Since the Revolution had extended even "to the mind of man," Burke was keen to analyse its motivation and results.[396] Its chief outcome had been to subvert the supports of civil society—prejudice, prescription and religion. What staggered Burke was that this had been achieved by "a set of literary men."[397] Still more remarkable were the impulses that drove them. Their original inspiration was humanity, not cruelty: "They had nothing but *douce humanité* in their mouth."[398] This pose was first paraded as delicacy of feeling: "The slightest severity of justice made their flesh creep. The very idea that war existed in the world disturbed their repose."[399] Yet ultimately these were attitudes rather than tangible commitments. They were ideals instead of concrete human affections and, in the end, abstract prescription smothered moral sentiment. Such ideals had been the begetters of a new kind of fanaticism—the product less of passion than the denial of passion. The "revolutionists" suffered from the common maladies of excessive speculation, and then further exacerbated the results: they threw off the fear of God, and then the fear of man. They steeled themselves against the appeals of immediate suffering in the name of long-term expectations of progress. This was the icy calculus of the "thorough-bred metaphysician."[400] A general conception destroyed any palpable sensitivity. Millennia might be needed to realise the theoretical benefits they pursued; the human race might even be sacrificed if the goal was attractive enough. Burke's conclusion looked to the current posture of affairs: peace with such a prodigy could not sensibly be contemplated.

16.6 The Prospect of Compromise: *Letters on a Regicide Peace*

The impossibility of peace meant unremitting war. In Burke's final years he sensed that the will to prosecute it was failing. At the end of December 1794, after the exoneration of Hardy, Tooke and Thelwall on charges of treason, Burke wrote to Windham about the contest with the Jacobin foe: "There is no medium,—there is no temperament,—there is no compromise with Jacobinism."[401] Nonetheless, as he was completing his *Letter to a Noble Lord*, the government was contemplating peace with France. The turning point in the war had come on 26 June 1794. On that date, the coalition forces were defeated at the Battle of Fleurus, deciding the fate of the Austrian Netherlands. Now the Revolutionary armies went on the offensive. In the

[395] Ibid., p. 156.
[396] Ibid., p. 147.
[397] Ibid., p. 174.
[398] Ibid., p. 175.
[399] Ibid.
[400] Ibid., p. 176.
[401] EB to William Windham, 30 December 1794, *Corr.*, VIII, p. 104.

late summer of 1793, the Convention had instituted the *levée en masse*, transforming the military fortunes of the French. A citizen army of around 800,000 troops supplanted the combined forces of the old line army, the national guard and the volunteers that had hitherto occupied the field.[402] The sheer volume of fighting men available to the French could overwhelm the professional and mercenary strength of the allies.[403] After Fleurus, republican soldiers pushed northwards into the Netherlands, threatening the strategic barrier between Britain and France, and looking forward to requisitioning the naval strength of the Dutch. The determination of the allies began to slacken.

A year before Fleurus, William Eden, recently ennobled as Baron Auckland, had denounced the enemy as a "nation of unchained devils."[404] Prices were rising incrementally across the Channel, the national currency continued to fall, and flour shortages were spreading panic through the countryside and the capital. Sans-culottes stormed the Assembly demanding redress. Dragoons were dispatched to quell the rebellious countryside, and mobilisation against the coalition began in earnest. The ferocity of the French assault called for concerted opposition, Auckland thought. On 14 April 1794, Dundas emphasised the government's aim of overthrowing the French regime. In the same breath, he claimed that Burke alone had foreseen the Jacobin determination to sweep established kingdoms from the map of Europe.[405] He was supported by the implacable rhetoric of John Bowles, calling for the "extermination" of the current system in France.[406] Yet by the autumn of the same year the resolution of the government seemed to buckle. Auckland was reconsidering the position of all-out war in a detailed letter reviewing policy sent to Pitt. The French, he noted, had brought an overwhelming concentration of manpower to bear on the dispersed efforts of the members of the first coalition. Victory in Flanders showed them reaping the reward. It might soon be necessary to consider treating with the enemy without any expectation of restoring the old regime.[407] At the end of the year, Wilberforce added an amendment to the vote of thanks urging peace. Grey intro-

[402] For debate about the figures, see T.W.C. Blanning, *The French Revolutionary Wars, 1787–1802* (London: Arnold, 1996), pp. 120–21.

[403] It seemed to contemporaries, and to historians since, that dedication played a role in effectiveness too. See John A. Lynn, *The Bayonets of the Republic: Motivation and Tactics in the Army if 1791–1794* (Urbana, IL: University of Illinois Press, 1984), pp. 19–21.

[404] Lord Auckland to Lord Henry Spencer, 19 November 1793, *The Journal and Correspondence of William, Lord Auckland* (London: 1860–2), 4 vols., III, pp. 147–48.

[405] *Parliamentary History*, XXXI, cols. 412–13. Cf. William Playfair, *Peace with the Jacobins Impossible* (London: 1794), p. 17: "There was but one man in Europe, who . . . foresaw and foretold the misfortunes of Europe."

[406] John Bowles, *Reflections Submitted to the Consideration of the Combined Powers* (London: 1794), p 1. Cf. idem, *Farther Reflections Submitted to the Consideration of the Combined Powers* (London: 1794).

[407] Lord Auckland to William Pitt, 28 November 1794, *Correspondence of Auckland*, p. 274.

duced a motion to the same effect in the new year.[408] By this stage it was clear that the Dutch would capitulate to the French: the Batavian Republic was declared on 19 January 1795. Then, on 5 April, came the devastating news that Prussia had signed the Peace of Basel.[409] The Rhineland was now horribly exposed to French ambition, yet the cohesion of the first coalition continued to decline. Spain withdrew from the war on 10 July. Eleven days later, at Quiberon Bay on the Brittany coast, the French defeated the forces of the émigrés backed by Britain. The King's Speech of 29 October 1795 set the tone for the new session: the crown professed to regard the French as on the point of collapse, and was prepared to come to terms with a government that promised stability.[410] The plan of restoring the Bourbons no longer figured in ministerial rhetoric.

The shift in position was elaborated in a pamphlet by Baron Auckland, *Some Remarks on the Apparent Circumstances of the War*, published to coincide with the new parliamentary session. Auckland sent a copy directly to Burke. The effect was predictable: "I confess your address to the public, together with other accompanying circumstances, has filled me with a degree of grief and dismay which I cannot find words to express."[411] Auckland surveyed the position in the British army and navy, regarding the former as under pressure although the latter still seemed predominant.[412] He also examined the recent history of France, and was appalled: "the requisitions against farmers and shopkeepers, the law of the maximum, the forced loans, the compulsory enrollments, the domiciliary visits, the judicial massacres."[413] The events of 1793–4 had shocked all Europe: the postponement of the constitution in the name of revolutionary government; the concentration of power in a provisional executive; the accelerated progress of dechristianisation; and the bloody wave of judicial killings beginning with Marie Antoinette. Summary executions outpaced the guillotine. Together they left a death toll of over 40,000 citizens.[414] Initiative passed to the committees of safety and security and the tribunal of Revolutionary justice.[415] Immiseration followed as credit and commerce declined: "The IRON AGE of barbarism [had] returned," Arthur Young remarked.[416] Auckland was writing in the

[408] Jennifer Mori, *William Pitt and the French Revolution, 1785–1795* (Edinburgh: Keele University Press, 1997), pp. 214–15.

[409] The Peace of Basel was signed on 5 April 1795. Burke charged Frederick William IV with apostasy over the treaty in EB, *Letter to William Elliot* (26 May 1795), *W & S*, IX, p. 35.

[410] *Parliamentary History*, XXXII, col. 142.

[411] EB to Lord Auckland, 30 October 1795, *Corr.*, VIII, pp. 334–35.

[412] [Lord Auckland], *Some Remarks on the Apparent Circumstances of the War in the Fourth Week of October 1795* (London: 3rd ed., 1795), pp. 5–13.

[413] Ibid., p. 19.

[414] Donald Greer, *The Incidence of the Terror during the French Revolution: A Statistical Interpretation* (Cambridge, MA: Harvard University Press, 1935).

[415] François Furet, *Revolutionary France, 1770–1880* (Oxford: Blackwell, 1992), pp. 134–42.

[416] Arthur Young, *An Idea of the Present State of France and the Consequences of the Events Passing in that Kingdom* (London: 2nd ed., 1795), p. 11.

aftermath of 9 Thermidor Year II (27 July 1794), and the purgatorial terror of the reaction that followed. It seemed that within a year the French had become exhausted, as evidenced by their acceptance on 22 August 1795 of the constitution of Year III.[417] Auckland had little doubt about the flawed character of the new arrangements, although they seemed preferable to the military democracy that had preceded it: "Democracy is not suitable even to the government of a village," Dumouriez declared.[418] France now wore the appearance of a "mixed oligarchy" in Auckland's eyes.[419] On 25 October 1795 the Convention had declared itself dissolved and was to be replaced by the Directory on 2 November. Auckland imagined the form of the state would be modified still further, but one thing was certain: relative stability had returned to France, and Britain should reflect upon the conditions under which it would be expedient to negotiate a peace. The issue was no longer the form of government in France but the viability of a durable settlement.[420]

Auckland indicated to Burke that his sentiments had the support of senior figures in government.[421] On 8 December Pitt relayed the king's message to the Commons that a negotiated settlement was under consideration.[422] George III was in fact sceptical about Pitt's manoeuvre, and the cabinet was divided.[423] However, there was little opposition voiced in parliament, although Fitzwilliam stated his dissent in the House of Lords on the fourteenth.[424] Burke now resolved to publicise his commitment to the war. He was "confounded and dismayed" by the implications of the King's Message, and embarked on a comprehensive letter to Fitzwilliam over the Christmas period.[425] This formed the basic matter of his first letter on a regicide peace, which launched an attack on Auckland's October pamphlet. The letter, however, lay unfinished, and was published posthumously in 1812 as the *Fourth Letter on a Regicide Peace*. Burke ridiculed the idea that French policy had been tamed. The Directory showed every sign of continuing business as usual and could not reasonably be represented as incubating a pacific intent. Auckland's casual references to "France" were a sleight of hand, a mere "hocus-pocus": this was the same usurpa-

[417] Cf. [Anon.], *Considerations on the Principal Objections against Overtures for Peace* (London: 1795), p. 29. The *St. James's Chronicle*, 22–25 August 1795, reported that this was "nearly the *twentieth*" new constitution proposed.

[418] Charles-François Du Périer Dumouriez, *A Political View of the Future Situation of France* (London: 1795), p. 81.

[419] [Auckland], *Some Remarks*, p. 31.

[420] Ibid., p. 33.

[421] Lord Auckland to EB, 28 October 1795, *Corr.*, VIII, p. 333.

[422] *Parliamentary History*, XXXII, cols. 569–70.

[423] J. Holland Rose, *Pitt and Napoleon: Essays and Letters* (London: G. Bell and Sons, 1912), pp. 238–9.

[424] *Parliamentary History*, XXXII, cols. 604–7; EB to Earl Fitzwilliam, 16 December 1795, *Corr.*, VIII, p. 358–9.

[425] EB to Earl Fitzwilliam, 9 December 1795, ibid., p. 357; EB to Earl Fitzwilliam, 7 January 1796, ibid., pp. 367–68.

tory regime that had been in existence since 1789.[426] Any attempt to distinguish the newly established Directory from antecedent Revolutionary administrations could not be sustained, or indeed disguised by dubious personification under the corporate name of "France."[427] Burke would return to this topic later in 1796: a state should not be seen as a mere geographical entity comprising territory and resources: "It is not France extending a foreign empire over other nations: it is a sect aiming at universal empire."[428] The corporate legitimacy of a country rested on the security of its property.[429] The representatives of property were now in exile, however, leaving the former France in the hands of an unconstitutional faction.[430] Everything suggested that the new order would continue the old: the ambition of the Directory lay in conquest, with little sign that the polity was under serious strain.[431]

Burke's final writings on France down to 1797 were taken up with British overtures for peace. As he laid his *Fourth Letter on a Regicide Peace* to one side at the beginning of 1796, he turned to writing his *Thoughts on the Prospect of a Regicide Peace*. A pirated version of the text appeared on 19 October 1796. A revised and authorised version was published by Rivington the following day as *Two Letters on the Proposals for Peace with the Directory*, commonly referred to as the *First* and *Second* letters on a regicide peace.[432] Burke's final composition in the series, the *Third Letter on a Regicide Peace*, was never completely finished, though work on it had begun by November 1796. Taken together, these last writings represent Burke's final thoughts on the peril posed by Jacobin France, resuscitated in the guise of the Directory. In the *Reflections*, the domestic form of the state was depicted as still unsettled and its external prospects seemed to be unfavourable. It posed a greater threat in terms of propaganda than power. That threat had not diminished as the 1790s progressed, but in his final years Burke came to see the Revolution as a mammoth force—a prodigy that defied all expectations of the ordinary life cycle of states. It was, he now concluded, the "mother of monsters."[433] The description was intended to do more than terrify: the new French behemoth subverted the laws of political economy, and for that reason posed a tangible though unprecedented danger. What had been poison to the historic countries of Europe was nourishment to this colossus. The French revenues had been decimated, manufactures were depleted, commerce interrupted, the soil inadequately cultivated, and the countryside depopulated.[434] Yet despite the radical austerity, the country's military still battled on. As in Britain, the harvest of 1795 had been deficient, adding to the famine conditions experienced the previous

[426] EB, *Fourth Letter on a Regicide Peace* (1795), *W & S*, IX, p. 50.
[427] Ibid., p. 51.
[428] EB, *Second Letter on a Regicide Peace* (1796), ibid., p. 267.
[429] EB, *First Letter on a Regicide Peace* (1796), ibid., pp. 252–55.
[430] EB, *Second Letter on a Regicide Peace* (1796), ibid., p. 264.
[431] EB, *Fourth Letter on a Regicide Peace* (1795), ibid., pp. 57–58.
[432] Todd, *Bibliography*, pp. 193–98.
[433] EB, *First Letter on a Regicide Peace* (1796), *W & S*, IX, p. 223.
[434] EB, *Second Letter on a Regicide Peace* (1796), ibid., p. 288.

spring. Naval blockades rendered provisions even scarcer. In addition, produce was being requisitioned for hard-pressed troops. Burke marvelled at the fact that in the face of these exigencies the French armies could manage to conquer "the finest parts of Europe."[435] The ruthless determination of this new power was without precedent: "to burn a city, or to lay waste a province of their own, does not cost them a moment's anxiety."[436]

Shortages were exacerbated by the collapse of the currency. Within four months of the Directory assuming office, the *assignat* had finally disappeared. Early on in the new regime, the government released more paper into the economy, yet confidence in the notes could not be sustained. "We go about asking when the assignats will expire, and we laugh at the last price of them," Burke remarked.[437] Yet the government persisted in its sheer indomitability. Traders preferred to deal in silver as the value of the currency crumbled. Landowners were forced to accept half their rents in kind. The state was obliged to inflate the pay of its employees.[438] A solution to the crisis was sought in a new forced loan, imposed on 19 Frimaire Year IV (10 December 1795). Six hundred million *livres* were supposed to have been raised by February 1796, but by the summer only half of the expected sum had been collected.[439] A new currency, the *mandat*, collapsed at the same time, and was demonetised early in 1797.[440] Amid furious speculation and national bankruptcy, the polity continued to prosper as a military conqueror: "That bankruptcy, the very apprehension of which is one of the causes of the fall of the Monarchy, was the capital on which she opened her traffic with the world."[441] The French republic had exchanged the laws of commerce for the laws of war. Its finances were sustained by force of will, backed up by arms; its security was maintained by constant aggrandisement. On 30 January 1795, Boissy d'Anglais, a one-time Girondin who resurfaced as a Montagnard before reappearing on the Council of Five Hundred under the Directory, proclaimed the limits of France to be co-extensive with its natural borders.[442] The announcement outdid the audacity of Louis XIV: "Whatever his inward intentions may have been, did Lewis the 14th ever make a declaration, that the true bounds of France were the Ocean,

[435] EB, *First Letter on a Regicide Peace* (1796), ibid., p. 191.

[436] EB, *Second Letter on a Regicide Peace* (1796), ibid., p. 288.

[437] Ibid.

[438] Denis Woronoff, *The Thermidorean Regime and the Directory, 1796–1799* (Cambridge: Cambridge University Press, 1984, 1987), pp. 92–93.

[439] Marie Joseph L. Adolphe Thiers, *The History of the French Revolution* (London: 1838), 5 vols., IV, pp. 314–15; Howard G. Brown, *Ending the French Revolution: Violence, Justice and Repression from the Terror to Napoleon* (Charlottesville, VA: Virginia University Press, 2006, 2008), pp. 33–34.

[440] William Doyle, *The Oxford History of the French Revolution* (Oxford: Oxford University Press, 2nd ed., 2002), p. 324.

[441] EB, *First Letter on a Regicide Peace* (1796), *W & S*, IX, p. 191.

[442] *L'Ancien moniteur* in *Réimpression de l'Ancien moniteur* (Paris: 1858–63), 31 vols., XXIII, p. 343: "nous obligent à étendre nos frontières, à nous donner de grands fleuves, des montagnes et l'Océan pour limites."

the Mediterranean and the Rhine?"[443] British predictions that the hubris of the republic would be humbled seemed recklessly optimistic to Burke. The unwieldy bulk of the Holy Roman Empire had felt the strain under Charles V, yet here the politics of extent had found a solution: the current domination of subject territories by the French had produced an irrefragable mass.[444] The power of the republic was of an altogether "new species," Burke insisted.[445] It was animated by an undeflected purpose, and driven by unimpeded force. Everything was subordinate to public design: "The state is all in all."[446] Property was sacrificed to the goal of conquest. The force of the state was concentrated in the army alone as national territory was "barbarized and impoverished."[447] On the one hand the spectacle was reminiscent of Genghis Khan, or the prophet Mohammad, as national policy was reduced to proselytism and arms.[448] On the other hand it resembled what would later be termed "imperialism," rekindling the spirit of early Rome: France was "not a commercial but a martial republick."[449] It stood for expansive, unrelenting, Machiavellian power: "the whole is a body of ways and means for the supply of dominion, without one heterogeneous particle in it."[450]

Auckland had drawn much hope from the demise of the Jacobin terror. The end of the Convention and the agreement of a new constitution appeared more promising again. Under its provisions, the universal manhood suffrage envisaged in 1793 was repealed: only males over the age of twenty-one paying direct taxes qualified for citizenship. Political society was thus defined in terms of property.[451] Political influence was still more narrowly restricted. Higher qualifications in terms of income and age limited the electorate to the legislative assemblies to 30,000, half the number stipulated in 1791. Legislation was to be processed by two bodies conjointly, a Council of Elders, comprising 250 deputies over forty years of age, and a Council of Five Hundred, whose members had to be at least thirty. The Council proposed new laws and the Elders scrutinised. The executive, consisting of a Directory of five,

[443] EB, *Fourth Letter on a Regicide Peace* (1795), *W & S*, IX, p. 81. On the history of the idea of France's "natural" borders, see Gaston Zeller, "La monarchie d'ancien régime et les frontières naturelles," *Revue d'histoire moderne*, 8 (1933), pp. 305–33; Peter Sahlins "Natural Frontiers Revisited: France's Boundaries since the Seventeenth Century," *American Historical Review*, 95:5 (December 1990), pp. 1423–51.

[444] EB, *Fourth Letter on a Regicide Peace* (1795), *W & S*, IX, pp. 57–58. Cf. EB, *First Letter on a Regicide Peace* (1796), ibid., p. 203.

[445] EB, *Second Letter on a Regicide Peace* (1796), ibid., p. 277.

[446] Ibid., p. 288.

[447] EB to Unknown, 1795, *Corr.*, VIII, p. 363.

[448] EB, *Second Letter on a Regicide Peace* (1796), *W & S*, IX, p. 289. Cf. EB, *First Letter on a Regicide Peace* (1796), ibid., p. 199: "It is with an *armed doctrine*, that we are at war."

[449] EB, *Second Letter on a Regicide Peace* (1796), ibid., p. 292. On the late eighteenth-century language of "empire," see still Richard Koebner, *Empire* (Cambridge: Cambridge University Press, 1961); for later developments, see Richard Koebner and Helmut D. Schmidt, *Imperialism: The Story and Significance of a Political Word, 1840–1960* (Cambridge: Cambridge University Press, 1964).

[450] EB, *Second Letter on a Regicide Peace* (1796), *W & S*, IX, p. 293.

[451] *Gazette de France*, 24 September 1795.

was selected by the Elders from a list supplied by the Council. The constitution was proclaimed on 23 September 1795, and was promptly summarised in the British press.[452] Auckland supposed the politicians staffing the new Directory to be "in a course of amelioration."[453] Burke found this diagnosis depressingly naïve. The new regime was little more than a reprise of the old usurpation costumed in a fresh disguise.[454] The executive was elected on 31 October, and was taken to manifest a new dispensation—abandoning an unqualified commitment to the rights of man and renouncing radical equality as at best a "Chimera."[455] A Declaration of Rights and Duties accompanied the new regime, defending, in its fifth article, established property. Yet to Burke this paper safeguard was a testimony to insecurity: "What Government of Europe, either in its origin or its continuance, has thought it necessary to declare itself in favour of property."[456]

The anticipation of a new dawn was mocked by the requirement that the legislature be composed of two-thirds of the outgoing Convention. Equally, the executive had to be staffed by regicides: Rewbell, Barras, La Révellière-Lépeaux, Carnot and Le Tourneur were chosen.[457] The constitution was accepted by referendum on 23 September 1795, but its popularity was in question from the beginning. The turnout for the poll was conspicuously low; a large proportion of opposition votes were discounted. The government moved swiftly against the rising tide of dissent, with Bonaparte suppressing Paris insurgents on 5 October. Burke absolutely denied that the new arrangements had won support: they admitted themselves that their country was "against them."[458] Previous instalments of the Revolutionary apparatus had garnered at least outward endorsement; however, the constitution of 1795 had to be imposed: in its "very formation" it had been "generally resisted by a great and powerful party in many parts of the Kingdom, and particularly in the Capital. It never had a popular choice even in shew."[459] Twenty thousand regular troops now garrisoned the capital. A state of martial law was reported in the British press on 9 October.[460] Former terrorists were released from prison to add their weight to the military oppression. A "complete Military Government is formed," Burke observed.[461] The economy, the constitution and the administration were all creatures of force, "and nothing but force."[462]

Britain's only realistic chance against the regicide regime was external war in defence of its internal balance of power. Managing the domestic threat of political sub-

[452] *Whitehall Evening Post*, 22–24 September 1795; *Oracle*, 24 September 1795.
[453] EB, *Fourth Letter on a Regicide Peace* (1795), *W & S*, IX, p. 70.
[454] Ibid., pp. 72–73.
[455] Ibid., p. 101.
[456] Ibid.
[457] Woronoff, *Thermidorean Regime and Directory*, pp. 36–37.
[458] EB to Earl Fitzwilliam, 9 December 1795, *Corr.*, VIII, pp. 357–58.
[459] EB, *Fourth Letter on a Regicide Peace* (1795), *W & S*, IX, p. 89.
[460] *Lloyd's Evening Post*, 9–12 October 1795.
[461] EB, *Fourth Letter on a Regicide Peace* (1795), *W & S*, IX, p. 89.
[462] Ibid., p. 90.

version by resort to emergency measures would destroy the constitution: "Our constitution is not made for this kind of warfare."[463] A war of opinion was being fought against an example of its success: if the example were dismantled the maxims would retreat.[464] On the other hand, the avoidance of military engagement would increase the power of domestic faction. Under these circumstances, Hume's vision of a peaceful euthanasia of the constitution would be shattered: the British state would die a violent death.[465] Burke anatomised the opposing forces in this prospective contest in his *First Letter on a Regicide Peace*. He looked beyond the electorate to the "natural representative of the people," the constituency on which political representatives depended.[466] This comprised the literate public who had "tolerable leisure" for political debate and possessed the requisite understanding.[467] Burke calculated this at 400,000 citizens, a fifth of the 2 million adult males comprising a total population of 8 million.[468] A similar percentage was eligible to vote in elections to the Convention, amounting to about 6 million Frenchmen.[469] The majority of the British political nation was opposed by a "formidable minority" numbering in the region of 80,000 Jacobin sympathisers. Although these made up only a fifth of the politically active citizens, "they were capable of mimicking the general voice."[470] To manage such a substantial and vocal cohort by purely constitutional means risked corrupting the national organs of government as a prelude to civil war.

Only robust war against the armies of the republic offered appropriate means of weakening domestic subversion. Moreover, the contest would have to take the form of a war of annihilation: the opposing regime would have to be taken down. It was clear that the current struggle was a battle between systems of opinion, yet opinion drew its strength from the support supplied by force. The wars of religion had shown the folly of persecuting conscience, yet the current war of ideas did not take its rise from "indifferent things" (*adiaphora*) such as were characteristic of theological dispute. Combat concerned the rights of man, and consequently the basic security of *meum* and *teum*. An ideological assault on these fundamental civil precepts could only be subdued by military might.[471] Furthermore, the assault would have to be

[463] Ibid., p. 110.

[464] Ibid., p. 70; EB, *First Letter on a Regicide Peace* (1796), ibid., p. 257.

[465] EB, *Fourth Letter on a Regicide Peace* (1795), ibid., p. 119, referring to David Hume, "Of Public Credit" in idem, *Essays Moral, Political, and Literary*, ed. Eugene F. Miller (Indianapolis, IN: Liberty Fund, 1985, 1987), pp. 263–65.

[466] EB, *First Letter on a Regicide Peace* (1796), *W & S*, IX, p. 224. The electorate has been calculated at about 280,000, including the borough and country franchise: see John A. Phillips, "Popular Politics in Unreformed England," *Journal of Modern History*, 52:4 (December 1980), pp. 599–625.

[467] Ibid.

[468] F. P. Lock, *Edmund Burke: 1730–1797* (Oxford: Clarendon Press, 1998–2006), 2 vols., II, p. 539.

[469] Malcolm Crook, *Elections in the French Revolution* (Cambridge: Cambridge University Press, 1996, 2002), p. 83.

[470] EB, *First Letter on a Regicide Peace* (1796), *W & S*, IX, p. 224.

[471] EB, *Second Letter on a Regicide Peace* (1796), ibid., pp. 294–95.

total: "I never thought we could make peace with the system."[472] French animosity was determined by the ethos of the regime, bent upon "ambition and systematick hostility."[473] The antagonism of any other power could be separated from its existence, yet Jacobinism, "by it's [*sic*] very essential constitution, is in a state of hostility with us, and with all civilized people."[474] Burke had been pressing this perspective since the advent of the war, yet by 1795 it had become a constant refrain. Enmity was rooted in the very "stamina" of the new regime.[475] It was commonly assumed that French belligerence was an accidental product of domestic mayhem, whereas in fact the Revolution had its origins in ambition.[476] The *First* and *Second* letters on a regicide peace were devoted to uncovering the essential nature of that ambition, while the *Third* addressed the consequences that followed from its ongoing existence.

16.7 Philosophers and Politicians: *Letters on a Regicide Peace*

A general election was held in Britain in the summer of 1796, from which the ministry emerged in a strengthened position. Nonetheless, opinion at large was still disenchanted with the fortunes of the war, and Pitt continued to feel the strain of financial austerity. In this context, on 2 September 1796, the government began to consider negotiating a peace. Francis Jackson was charged with opening initial talks about talks.[477] Meanwhile, the Directory focused its strategy on thwarting the Austrians, assailing them by a pincer movement that was to converge on Vienna, advancing with the armies of Moreau and Jourdan in Germany while Bonaparte descended into Italy. Spain joined forces with France against what remained of the coalition. In October, the British ministry decided to apply itself more deliberately to negotiation. The Earl of Malmesbury was appointed to lead the discussions, arriving in Paris on 22 October. Within a month, the French were overcoming resistance in the Rhineland, and Bonaparte began to prevail in Italy. By 18 December the peace talks had come to an end, and Malmesbury, having been rebuffed, returned to London two days later.[478] Hoche's fleet left Brest for Bantry Bay that same month: the war against Britain would continue with a vengeance. Yet the response would not be conducted with the resolution that Burke expected. On 14 December 1796, Fitzwilliam made his case against suing for peace in the House of Lords.[479] On the 27th, the govern-

[472] EB, *First Letter on a Regicide Peace* (1796), ibid., p. 265.

[473] Ibid., p. 249.

[474] Ibid., p. 239.

[475] EB, *Fourth Letter on a Regicide Peace* (1795), ibid., p. 104.

[476] Ibid., p. 86.

[477] Ehrman, *Pitt: The Reluctant Transition*, pp. 627–28.

[478] The denouement is recorded in *Diaries and Correspondence of James Harris, First Earl of Malmesbury* (London: 1844), 4 vols., III, pp. 349–65.

[479] *Parliamentary History*, XXXII, cols. 607–8.

ment published a Declaration revealing the course of the recent talks.[480] These had been premised on entirely fallacious assumptions, Burke believed. Malmesbury had sought to re-establish a balance of power in Europe with an enemy devoted to universal empire. Previous treaties, for example those of Aix-la-Chapelle, Paris and Versailles, comprehending the period 1748–83, had all been based on obstructing the dominion of France by counterposing a coalition of antagonistic forces.[481] Insofar as Louis XV and Louis XVI had accepted these terms, they had submitted to the idea of reciprocal restraints in Europe. The partition of Poland in 1772 represented an early threat to this vision of a balanced European "commonwealth," but then France in 1792 had abandoned the principle altogether.[482] It was soon clear that French republicans strove "to erect themselves into a new description of Empire, which is not founded on any balance, but forms a sort of impious hierarchy, of which France is to be the head and the guardian."[483]

In response to the growing menace of France in 1797, it had become common to argue that Britain should come to terms on account of "necessity"—given what seemed like the precarious state of the public revenues, and the alleged decline in national prosperity more generally.[484] Yet these constraints were largely fabricated in Burke's view. In order to counteract the harbingers of distress, he offered a more sober account of the "state of the nation" in 1797, recalling his earliest review of national strength in 1769. His first political pamphlet in the guise of a Rockinghamite, the *Observations on a Late State of the Nation*, had set out to challenge William Knox's dire prognostications with a more plausible analysis of the relative strengths of Britain and France.[485] Knox, Burke recollected, was a bird of "evil presage" who had been motivated by "the common spleen of disappointed ambition."[486] He had managed to convert "the signs of national prosperity into symptoms of decay and

[480] *CJ*, LII, pp. 238–40.

[481] EB, *Third Letter on a Regicide Peace* (1797), *W & S*, IX, pp. 337–38.

[482] The detailed discussion of the first Polish partition in *The Annual Register for the Year 1772* (London: 1773), pp. 1–8, was ascribed to Burke by Sir James Mackintosh in the *Edinburgh Review*, LXXXVIII (September 1796), p. 380. The attribution is purely speculative, although certainly the author shared many of Burke's views. The ascription was accepted in Thomas Macknight, *History of the Life and Times of Edmund Burke* (London: 1858–60), 3 vols., II, p. 2 and, with due reserve, in G. L. Vincitorio, "Edmund Burke and the First Partition of Poland" in idem ed., *Crisis in the Great Republic: Essays Presented to Ross J. S. Hoffman* (New York: Fordham University Press, 1969), p. 38. Brendan Simms, "'A False Principle in the Law of Nations': Burke, State Sovereignty, [German] Liberty, and Intervention in the Age of Westphalia" in Brendan Simms and D.J.B. Trim eds., *Humanitarian Intervention: A History* (Cambridge: Cambridge University Press, 2011), follows Vincitorio.

[483] EB, *Third Letter on a Regicide Peace* (1797), *W & S*, IX, p. 339.

[484] Ibid., p. 361.

[485] The *Observations* endeavoured to take stock of the fallout from the Seven Years' War. For Burke's preoccupation with the situation in Britain then by comparison with its position in 1797, see EB to William Windham, 26 April 1797, *Corr.*, IX, p. 316.

[486] EB, *Third Letter on a Regicide Peace* (1797), *W & S*, IX, p. 371. The editor mistakes Burke's reference to his 1769 *Observations* for a reference to the 1756 *Vindication of Natural Society*.

ruin."[487] The prophets of doom oraculating in 1797 resembled the Cassandras of 1769, except the unhappy forecasts of today were more profoundly counterproductive. Those who now sought to capitalise on the apparent vicissitudes of the economy hoped, "by depressing our minds with a despair of our means and resources, to drive us, trembling and unresisting, into the toils of our enemies."[488] In truth the nation was "gamboling in an ocean of superfluity" while its detractors characterised its welfare in terms of penury and want.[489]

The events of 1797 appeared critical to many observers. In February there was a run on the Bank of England, and in the summer there were mutinies at Spithead and the Nore.[490] The British navy had been inactive in the Mediterranean since January; Russia became increasingly remote as an ally; and Austria signed a peace at Leoben in April. Despite these setbacks, Burke spent his final months assailing government passivity: offence was the only effective means of securing a practical defence.[491] The lack of ministerial resolve looked like a prelude to capitulation: "it must terminate in a peace which, like Scylla, has a thousand barking monsters of a thousand wars in its womb."[492] He applauded attempts to argue against the disposition of France, but in the end the enemy would have to be confronted with naked force.[493] In the face of this requirement, the government appeared pusillanimous and the opposition deluded. Erskine set the tone for the minority, bewailing the decline of commerce and the condition of "the laborious poor."[494] Fox explained the resort to war in terms of corruption in public life, arguing that Burke's reforms of 1782 had been deficient.[495] His allegations, Burke retorted, were nothing short of mendacious.[496] Relations with his old ally would never recover. The "French party in our parliament," Burke fulmi-

[487] EB, *Observations on a Late State of the Nation* (1769), *W & S*, II, p. 147.

[488] EB, *Third Letter on a Regicide Peace* (1797), *W & S*, IX, p. 371.

[489] Ibid., p. 384. The charge is directed against the opposition in particular in EB to William Windham, 30 March 1797, *Corr.*, IX, p. 299.

[490] For the mutinies, see EB to French Laurence, 5 June 1797, ibid., p. 368; EB to Earl Fitzwilliam, 18 June 1797, ibid., p. 370. For the general mood in 1797, see John Ehrman, *The Younger Pitt: The Consuming Struggle* (London: Constable: 1996), pp. 3ff.

[491] EB to Sir Lawrence Parsons, 8 March 1797, *Corr.*, IX p. 279; EB to William Windham, 30 March 1797, ibid., p. 300; EB to Earl Fitzwilliam, 26 April 1797, ibid., p. 317; EB to Lord Loughborough, 1 May 1797, ibid., p. 322.

[492] EB to French Laurence, 11 April 1797, ibid., p. 307.

[493] EB to John Gifford, 1 May 1797, ibid., p. 321.

[494] Thomas Erskine, *A View of the Causes and Consequences of the Present War with France, in Answer to Mr. Burke's Regicide Peace* (Philadelphia, PA: 9th ed., 1797), p. 6. Erskine triggered a series of responses, see John Gifford, *A Letter to the Hon. Thomas Erskine, Containing some Strictures on His View of the Causes and Consequences of the Present War with France* (London: 9th ed., 1797); idem, *A Second Letter to the Hon. Thomas Erskine, Containing Farther Strictures* (London: 3rd ed., 1797); John Bowles, *French Aggression Proved from Mr. Erskine's "View of the Causes of the War"* (London: 1797); [Anon.], *Reasons against National Dependency, in Refutation of Mr. Erskine's View of the Causes and Consequences of the Present War* (London: 1797). Burke commended this anonymous work in EB to William Windham, 26 April 1797, *Corr.*, IX, p. 315.

[495] French Laurence to EB, 14 March 1797, ibid., pp. 281–82.

[496] EB to French Laurence, 16 March 1797, ibid., p. 285.

nated in April, should "be treated as public Enemies."[497] Fox tried to make some kind of personal amends in the days before Burke's death, yet personal tragedy was insufficient even for private reconciliation. The breach of 1791 had caused inestimable pain. Burke had originally followed the "stern voice of his duty" and he would not now be charged with insincerity in his motives by a show of friendship that would compromise the integrity of his principles.[498] To the end, he would remain implacable in his hostility to Jacobinism, and equally to any attempt to appease it. During his final decline, he rejected once more the very idea of a regicide peace. He drew on the stock of arguments that he had been accumulating since the beginning. As early as February 1790, he had alerted the House of Commons to the danger posed by France's proximity, or "vicinity."[499] In the *Reflections* he accused her departure from "the old common law of Europe."[500] In his last years he refined his account of the commonalities among European states and the nature of the malady that set France apart.[501]

In the *Fourth Letter on a Regicide Peace*, Burke had invoked the common basis upon which the governments of Europe had "virtually" constituted an integrated "Republic."[502] The point, as he would emphasise in the *First* letter the following year, was that France had abandoned the ancient "politick communion" of Europe, supported by means of religious and legal affinities.[503] According to Vattel, diplomacy, negotiation, ties of interest and treaty obligations made Europe "a kind of republic."[504] Yet in no sense did Burke regard this European "Commonwealth" as a juridical unity: it was a "community" that existed in a state of concord in the absence of a common sovereign.[505] The ties of concord could diminish the intensity of conflict, and

[497] EB to William Windham, 26 April 1797, ibid., p. 315.

[498] Jane Burke to Charles James Fox, ante 9 July 1797, ibid., p. 373.

[499] EB, *Substance of the Speech of the Right Honourable Edmund Burke in the Debate on the Army Estimates* (London: 1790), p. 18. See above, chapter 11, section 6.

[500] EB, *Reflections on the Revolution in France*, ed. J.C.D. Clark (Stanford, CA: Stanford University Press, 2001), p. 188 [53].

[501] On Burke's late preoccupation with the commonwealth of Europe, see R. J. Vincent, "Edmund Burke and the Theory of International Relations," *Review of International Studies*, 10:3 (July 1984), pp. 205–18; David Boucher, "The Character of the History of the Philosophy of International Relations and the Case of Edmund Burke," *Review of International Studies*, 17:2 (April 1991), pp. 127–48; Jennifer Welsh, *Edmund Burke and International Relations* (Basingstoke: Macmillan, 1995), pp. 70–88; Iain Hampsher-Monk, "Introduction" to EB, *Revolutionary Writings*, ed. Iain Hampsher-Monk (Cambridge: Cambridge University Press, 2014), pp. xxxiv–xxxvi.

[502] EB, *Fourth Letter on a Regicide Peace* (1795), *W & S*, IX, p. 83. For "virtually," see EB, *First Letter on a Regicide Peace* (1796), ibid., p. 248. For the idiom, cf. Voltaire, *Le siècle de Louis XIV* (London: 1752), 2 vols., I, p. 11; Edward Gibbon, *The History of the Decline and Fall of the Roman Empire* (Dublin: 1776), 8 vols., VI, p. 368; Robert Plumer Ward, *An Enquiry into the Foundation and History of the Law of Nations in Europe* (London: 1795), 2 vols., II, p. 73; Richard Bentley, *Considerations upon the State of Public Affairs* (London: 1796), p. 67.

[503] Ibid., p. 240.

[504] Vattel, *Law of Nations*, p. 496.

[505] The distinction here is based on Thomas Hobbes, *De Cive*, ed. Howard Warrender (Oxford: Oxford University Press, 1983), 2 cols., I, ch. V, sects. v–vi. Hobbes's "anarchy" of independent states is

build consensus thanks to "resemblances," "conformities" and "sympathies."[506] They facilitated relations of amity among nations still existing in a state of war.[507] Burke refused to credit schemes designed to establish an everlasting peace. In the end, war was the only means of effecting "justice among states."[508] Nonetheless, the ferocity of war could be mitigated by a culture of agreement. A system of "correspondences" could help regulate antagonism and reduce at once the duration, the intensity and the extent of conflict. Burke's account of this underlying means of correspondence served two purposes: first, to identify the fundamental hostility between "Europe" and "France"; and second, to emphasise the total war threatened by the French republic. A "similitude" in laws, manners and beliefs enabled the states of Europe to concur in their behaviours. This was never sufficient completely to coordinate their objectives, but it saved them from perpetual wars of annihilation. Burke ascribed the existing consensus to a shared European past, which he had first explored in his *Essay towards an Abridgement of the English History*. As the *Abridgement* had shown, Britain, like France, had been constructed out of a coalescence between gothic and feudal laws. This combination, as Montesquieu had argued, informed the *ésprit* of modern European societies. By "spirit" Montesquieu basically meant "opinion." Power was never effective unless it conformed to the "ésprit général."[509] "Even liberty," he noted, "has seemed unbearable to peoples who were not used to enjoying it."[510] Burke claimed that the system of opinion in Europe lay at the root of those cultural correspondences that assuaged international antipathy and supported the balance of power.

Prevailing "opinion" had three sources in European history: first, the original gothic customs of the Germanic peoples; second, the feudal law engrafted on German mores by a process of conquest; and third, the improvement of customary laws by the digests of Roman law. This combined edifice of laws, customs and manners gave rise to the European system of estates that served to moderate the use of power in modern polities.[511] This system had not been the product of deliberate design, yet it was certainly the enabling condition of modern liberty. "That liberty," Burke wrote,

---

sometimes contrasted with Burke's "commonwealth" of European nations. This is not a strict antithesis, however. The independent constituents of the "republic" of Europe existed in a state of mutual war, as Burke saw it. Nonetheless, political and commercial cooperation existed in the midst of underlying conflict.

[506] EB, *First Letter on a Regicide Peace* (1796), *W & S*, IX, p. 247.

[507] Burke's point was that this condition of war had been refined or alleviated by the progress of artifice, giving rise to forms of cooperation that were absent in "original" nature. Cf. *The Annual Register for 1772*, Preface.

[508] EB, *First Letter on a Regicide Peace* (1796), *W & S*, IX, p. 248. Cf. the "History of Europe" in *The Annual Register for 1772*, p. 3: "Wars, however it may be lamented, are inevitable in every state of human nature; they may be deferred, but they cannot be wholly avoided."

[509] Charles-Louis de Secondat, Baron de Montesquieu, *De l'esprit des lois* (1748) in *Œuvres complètes*, ed. Roger Caillois (Paris: Gallimard, 1951), 2 vols., II, pt. III, bk. 19, ch. 4.

[510] Ibid., pt. III, bk. 19, ch. 2.

[511] EB, *First Letter on a Regicide Peace* (1796), *W & S*, IX, p. 248.

"was found, under monarchies stiled absolute, in a degree unknown to the ancient commonwealths."[512] The security of freedom lay in the principle of "obstruction": the estates were formed politically so as to block any concentration of power.[513] The equilibrium of power in the European concert mirrored this domestic arrangement of checking rising ambition. As a result, while competitors sought advantage they could not exterminate their opponents. Republican France had brought an end to this system of restraint. Yet, despite that fact, British policy continued to proceed as if the original European concert still existed. The ministry had approached the current contest as a struggle for advantage, failing to comprehend that this was a war of extirpation: "It is a war between partizans of the ancient, civil, moral and political order of Europe against a sect of fanatical and ambitious atheists which means to change them all."[514] Burke insisted that the coalition as a whole had failed to perceive this basic reality. On the continent, this could be explained in terms of the calibre of rulers: princes, and their ministers, were ill equipped for partisan warfare. "Virtue," Burke wrote, "is not their habit."[515] They were rarely stirred by conscience, or raised to embrace a higher cause: "A large, liberal and prospective view of the interests of States passes with them for romance."[516] In seeking to advance their immediate advantage in the usual way, the members of the coalition steered clear of the strategy that they should have adopted—an attack on the very vitals of the French foe that would take the war to the capital of subversion.[517] Optimally this would have been conducted as a counter-revolutionary operation that at one point could have mobilised 80,000 supporters in France galvanised by "vengeance" and "enthusiasm."[518] However, as things turned out, cooperation between Russia, Prussia, Austria and Britain proved no better than a nominal alliance in which great powers continued to act for their individual gain.[519] In the process, France was left free to defend her borders and to crush the rising tide of domestic opposition.

In advocating the proactive policy of a war of destruction against the regicide republic, Burke elucidated the "*Law of Neighbourhood*," or the rights of self-defence proceeding from "*vicinage*," in terms of which he had first justified Britain's alarm about France.[520] The French republic, like Algeria, was an outlaw from civilisation, but only the former imposed directly on the fundamental interests of Britain and

[512] EB, *Second Letter on a Regicide Peace* (1796), ibid., p. 287. Cf. EB, *Reflections*, ed. Clark, p. 239 [113].

[513] EB, *Second Letter on a Regicide Peace* (1796), *W & S*, IX, p. 287.

[514] Ibid, p. 267.

[515] Ibid.

[516] Ibid.

[517] Ibid., pp. 268, 272.

[518] Ibid., p. 273.

[519] Ibid., p. 269.

[520] EB, *First Letter on a Regicide Peace* (1796), *W & S*, IX, pp. 250–51. Cf. EB, *Substance of the Speech of the Right Honourable Edmund Burke in the Debate on the Army Estimates* (London: 1790), p. 18.

Europe.[521] Determined hostility, combined with proximity, posed a tangible and immediate threat. The danger was all the more critical given the nature of the enmity. Burke analysed its content as well as its origins. Its content was more easily observed since it comprised three basic elements which the revolutionaries openly espoused: regicide, Jacobinism and atheism.[522] The principle of regicide dictated that any government ordered on the basis of estates could legitimately be dismantled as an instance of "usurpation."[523] Jacobinism reinforced the regicide rage for conquest since it stiffened popular antipathy to prescriptive government while also inflaming sentiment against accumulated property. Jacobins could be divided into fomenters and constituents. The former headed a rebellion of talent against privilege, while the latter were inspired by indigence, irritation and spurned allegiance.[524] Both Jacobins and regicides were impelled towards devastation by the animating and malevolent energy of atheism. The French republic, Burke argued, was atheistic "*by Establishment*."[525] It rooted out core doctrines that supported morality and institutions that housed religious worship. In their place it substituted theatrical rites and vitiated principles. The depravity that accompanied deliberate impiety had concerned Burke since he embarked upon the *Vindication of Natural Society*. In the absence of the idea of a particular providence, ethical conduct lost its bearings and its motivation. In effect, morality was deprived of its basis in self-denial.[526]

The idea that impiety was at war with human morals had deep roots in European culture by the time Burke wrote.[527] Locke had famously argued that while Muslims, Pagans and Jews should be protected in their civil rights under a Christian commonwealth, atheists were simply intolerable.[528] Without the assumption of a relationship to God, there could be no faith among men: "Promises, Covenants, and Oaths . . . can have no hold upon an Atheist." Yet these were the very "Bonds" of social existence.[529] In their absence, no society could stand. Human communities could tolerate a great diversity of speculative opinions, yet this did not extend to

[521] EB, *First Letter on a Regicide Peace* (1796), *W & S*, IX, pp. 257–59.

[522] Ibid., pp. 240–41.

[523] Ibid., p. 240.

[524] EB to the Rev. Thomas Hussey, post 9 December 1796, *Corr.*, IX, p. 162. Burke is thinking of the contrast between French speculative Jacobins and practical Jacobins in Ireland.

[525] EB, *First Letter on a Regicide Peace* (1796), *W & S*, IX, p. 241.

[526] Ibid.

[527] For aspects of the idiom, see Michael Hunter, "The Problem of 'Atheism' in Early Modern England," *Transactions of the Royal Historical Society*, 35 (1985), pp. 135–57. See also Michael Hunter and David Wootton eds., *Atheism from the Reformation to the Enlightenment* (Oxford: Oxford University Press, 1992).

[528] John Locke, *A Letter Concerning Toleration* (1689) in *A Letter Concerning Toleration and Other Writings*, ed. Mark Goldie (Indianapolis, IN: Liberty Fund, 2010), pp. 58–59.

[529] Ibid., pp. 52–53. John Marshall, *John Locke, Toleration and Early Enlightenment Culture* (Cambridge: Cambridge University Press, 2006), p. 702, notes that in the amendments to the fourth edition of the *Essay Concerning Human Understanding* Locke did ultimately credit the reality of societies of atheists.

speculation about the divinity. This, Locke claimed, was a practical, not a theoretical precept since it constituted "the foundation of all morality."[530] Neither the desire for reputation nor the feeling of disgrace was sufficient to encourage moral behaviour: at best such purely secular inducements could sustain the customs and fashions of the day. True morality implied an overriding obligation dependent on a superior law that prescribed standards for action based on more than merely "ideas of our own making."[531] In his *Various Thoughts on the Occasion of a Comet*, Bayle had argued that a general faith in a providential deity was not sufficient for the mortification of sin. For that it was necessary for the heart to be "sanctified by the grace of the Holy Spirit."[532] Notoriously, this did not prevent Bayle from contending that the regulations of magistrates and the general opinions of mankind might be sufficient to bind atheists to their compacts. Nonetheless, in his *Philosophical Commentary*, he supported the idea that governors were entitled to restrain those who preached against "the Belief of a Providence, and the fear of divine Justice" since such doctrines were commonly taken to destroy the fabric of civil society.[533] As with Locke, for Burke the problem went deeper: atheists subverted the tribunal of conscience in denying the binding force of moral norms. As Henry More had argued in the 1650s, atheism is a pernicious form of enthusiasm since it leaves the satisfaction of fancy as the only measure of justice.[534]

Natural historians of religion, like Hume, had taught that religion was the cause of fanatical zeal. Burke took this claim to be little more than the product of "superficial" analysis.[535] Enthusiasm was an effect of human passion rather than a specifically religious attitude. In fact, nothing was more capable of inflaming the imagination and provoking the impulse to proselytise than the hatred of piety and worship.[536]

[530] John Locke, "An Essay on Toleration" (1667) in John Locke, *Political Essays*, ed. Mark Goldie (Cambridge: Cambridge University Press, 1997, 2006), p. 137.

[531] John Locke, "Of Ethic in General" (1686–88?) in ibid., p. 302. Cf. John Locke, *An Essay Concerning Human Understanding* (1689), ed. Peter H. Nidditch (Oxford: Oxford University Press, 1975, 1979), I, iii, § 13. On this theme in Locke, see John Dunn, *The Political Thought of John Locke: An Historical Account of the Argument of the "Two Treatises of Government"* (Cambridge: Cambridge University Press, 1969), *passim*; idem, "From Applied Theology to Social Analysis: The Break between John Locke and the Scottish Enlightenment" in idem, *Rethinking Modern Political Theory: Essays 1979–1983* (Cambridge: Cambridge University Press, 1985).

[532] Pierre Bayle, *Various Thoughts on the Occasion of a Comet*, trans. Robert C. Bartlett (Albany, NY: State University of New York Press, 2000), pp. 161–62.

[533] Pierre Bayle, *A Philosophical Commentary on these Words of the Gospel, Luke 14:23, "Compel them to Come in, that My House May be Full* (Indianapolis, IN: Liberty Fund: 2005), pp. 242–43. It has been pointed out that this formulation did not have to imply that atheists might form durable societies: see Gianluca Mori, *Bayle Philosophe* (Paris: Champion 1999).

[534] Henry More, *An Antidote against Atheism* (London: 1655), ch. 1.

[535] EB, *Second Letter on a Regicide Peace* (1796), *W & S*, IX, p. 278.

[536] Cf. Joseph Addison, *The Evidences of the Christian Religion* (London: 1733), p. 223, on the "unaccountable Zeal which appears in Atheists and Infidels . . . in a most peculiar manner possessed with the spirit of bigotry."

Atheism, in the end, was at war with God. Yet since its patrons could not strike out omnipotent divinity, they opted to deface the image of holiness in man. Men like Pierre-Victurnien Vergniaud and Maximin Isnard "worked themselves into a perfect phrensy against religion and all it's [*sic*] professors."[537] This disposed them to indulge every impulse of vainglory and to persecute the representatives of Christian morals. In alliance with politicians, these philosophers drove the Revolution. Whereas the philosophers were bent upon rebellion against God, the politicians were more immediately driven by ambition. Their goals were originally set by the court politics of the old regime: they "had the exterior aggrandizement of France as their ultimate end."[538] The means of achieving this had been controversial since the reign of Louis XV. On the one hand, the persistence of anti-Habsburg sentiment after the *renversement des alliances* of 1756 gave a focus to opposition forces conspiring at Versailles to increase the power of the monarchy by the clandestine means of the *secret du roi*; on the other hand, as first mooted by Louis XIV but finally instituted under Choiseul, the court pursued an open policy of collaboration with Austria to narrow Britain's options for continental alliances.[539] Burke marvelled at the duplicity of these two simultaneous programmes: "What is truly astonishing, the partizans of those two opposite systems were at once prevalent . . . during the latter part of the reign of Louis XV."[540] As Burke portrayed the rival factions operating in the French court, one side aimed to diminish Britain by challenging her at sea, while the other sought to overwhelm her by dominating the continent.[541] Although the adherents of the continental policy became predominant in numbers they continued to act covertly against the Habsburg alliance, latterly associated with Marie Antoinette.[542]

According to Burke, this "double diplomacy" ultimately served to unhinge the monarchy.[543] The greedy intrigues of discontented courtiers multiplied. A pivotal figure among the schemers was Jean-Louis Favier, a creature of the Duc de Broglie who composed a set of reflections on foreign affairs in the final months of Louis XV's reign.[544] His attention was fixed on the "dégradation rapide" of French power since

[537] EB, *Second Letter on a Regicide Peace* (1796), *W & S*, IX, p. 279.

[538] Ibid., p. 280.

[539] On the *secret du roi*, see the Duc de Broglie, *Le secret du roi: correspondance secrète de Louis XV avec ses agentes diplomatiques, 1752–1774* (Paris: 1978), 2 vols. On its ramifying consequences under Louis XVI, see Munro Price, *Preserving the Monarchy: The Comte de Vergennes, 1774–1787* (Cambridge: Cambridge University Press, 1995, 2004), pp. 12–13. See also John Hardman and Munro Price, "Introduction" to *Louis XVI and the Comte de Vergennes: Correspondence, 1774–1787*, ed. John Hardman and Munro Price (Oxford: Voltaire Foundation, 1998), pp. 9–10. For the inauguration of the *renversement* at the end of Louis XIV's reign, see Derek McKay and H. M. Scott, *The Rise of the Great Powers, 1648–1815* (London: Longman, 1983), p. 105.

[540] EB, *Second Letter on a Regicide Peace* (1796), *W & S*, IX, p. 279.

[541] The maritime strategy is recapitulated in Jonathan R. Dull, *The French Navy and the Seven Years' War* (Lincoln, NE: University of Nebraska Press, 2005).

[542] Price, *Preserving the Monarchy*, pp. 27–28.

[543] EB, *Second Letter on a Regicide Peace* (1796), *W & S*, IX, p. 282, including Burke's footnote.

[544] For the full context, see Gary Savage, "Favier's Heirs: The French Revolution and the *Secret du Roi*," *Historical Journal*, 41:1 (March 1998), pp. 225–58.

the losses and humiliations suffered in the Seven Years' War.[545] The rise of Russia and the partition of Poland were indices of a corresponding shift in the balance of power in Europe. The subordination of the French court to the machinations of Vienna was the fundamental cause behind the change of fortune.[546] As Burke represented it, the situation disheartened Favier and his colleagues with monarchical government altogether, and attracted a rising generation of politicians in France to republicanism as an instrument of international power politics.[547] Montesquieu and Machiavelli on the travails of the Roman commonwealth became manuals of instruction for ambitious diplomats.[548] The inadequacy of the monarchy as devised by Louis XIV became a subject of analysis and complaint. Montalembert's declamations against the ostentatious imperiousness of the regime captured the mood of rising antagonism.[549] Ambition combined with anti-monarchical sentiment laid the groundwork for an alliance with American republicanism and with popular rebellion in the Low Countries: "These sentiments were not produced, as some think, by their American alliance. The American alliance was produced by their republican principles and republican policy."[550] It now only remained for the devotees of popular government to collaborate with the antagonists of the Christian religion to dismantle the components of a polite, reforming monarchy.

Their collaboration was enabled by a "silent revolution" that accompanied the rise of the "middle classes."[551] The power of the established nobility had declined since the period of the Fronde, and with it their ability to foment and defuse popular discontent. Rising talent and new wealth became "the seat of all active politicks."[552] Mercantile and monied property supplied the route to ascendancy, while the academies, the salons and the press provided the means of influence and propaganda.[553] Before long, speculation conspired with ambition; philosophers supported embittered politicians. The alliance gave rise to a militant power the likes of which had never before been seen. An implacable lust for conquest assailed the European order.

[545] Jean-Louis Favier, *Conjectures raisonnées sur la situation actuelle de la France dans la système politique de l'Europe* (April 1773) in Louis-Philippe de Ségur ed., *Politique de tous les cabinets de l'Europe, pendant les règnes de Louis XV et Louis XVI* (Paris: 1794), 3 vols., I, p. 96.

[546] Ibid., p. 100.

[547] EB, *Second Letter on a Regicide Peace* (1796), *W & S*, IX, pp. 282–83. For discussion, see Michael Sonenscher, "Republicanism, State Finances and the Emergence of Commercial Society in Eighteenth-Century France—or, from Royal to Ancient Republicanism and Back" in Martin van Gelderen and Quentin Skinner eds., *Republicanism: A Shared European Heritage* (Cambridge: Cambridge University Press, 2002), 2 vols., II, pp. 277–78.

[548] EB, *Second Letter on a Regicide Peace* (1796), *W & S*, IX, pp. 282–83.

[549] Marc-René Montalembert, *Abrégé historique du règne de Louis XIV* in idem, *La fortification perpendiculaire* (Paris: 1776–84), 5 vols., IV, pp. 66ff. Burke singles out Montalembert in EB, *Second Letter on a Regicide Peace* (1796), *W & S*, IX, p. 283.

[550] Ibid., p. 286. For the significance of the Dutch affair, see Munro Price, "The Dutch Affair and the Fall of the Ancien Régime, 1784–1787," *Historical Journal*, 38:4 (December 1995), pp. 875–905.

[551] EB, *Second Letter on a Regicide Peace* (1796), *W & S*, IX, p. 291.

[552] Ibid.

[553] Ibid., p. 292.

Its avidity and determination knew no bounds. Its hostility to religion, property and established government pitted it against every principle of civilisation. The breach was now beyond repair: a power that would not be reduced could only be destroyed.

16.8 Shaken to Their Very Centres

Burke knew that 1797 would be his final year. "I apprehend my Stomach is irrecoverably ruind [*sic*]," he wrote to Thomas Hussey in July 1796.[554] His health continued to deteriorate, interspersed with bouts of remission, over the following twelve months. His move to Bath in the summer of 1796 was his only chance "of preserving a Life" which seemed on the point of expiring.[555] He wrote again to Hussey at the end of the year: "in all probability, I am not long for this world."[556] He was now weak, and forced to dictate his correspondence, though he continued to work on the *Third Letter on a Regicide Peace*. On 30 January 1797, he left Beaconsfield with Jane for Bath again. He remained there until 24 May, when he made his final return to Gregories to prepare to die. "I have lain a long time in a state of utter inability for any exertion of mind or body, having been reduced to the last extremity," he informed a correspondent in March.[557] From that state his condition would only worsen. In May he confirmed to Fitzwilliam that "any real recovery is a thing now out of the Question."[558] His decline was rapid: he died just after midnight on 9 July 1797. A month before the end, he was still lamenting "the dreadful evils of every kind which are impending over us."[559] French Laurence left a portentous depiction of the final moment: "When he fell, these kingdoms, Europe, the whole civilized world, lost the principal prop that remained, and were shaken to their very centres."[560]

Burke was buried next to his son and brother at Beaconsfield church. In his last days, he had requested that he be placed in an unmarked grave lest his body be exhumed and mauled by "*the French Revolutionists*."[561] At this stage he was delirious, and the direction was disregarded. His last will and testament was signed in August 1794, two days after his son's death, and updated on 22 January 1797.[562] The instructions for his funeral were carried out by his executors. William Windham, Sir Gilbert Elliot, Lord Inchiquin, Henry Addington, Earl Fitzwilliam and the Duke of Portland acted as pallbearers. The cortège left Butler's Court at 7 p.m. on 15 July.

554 EB to the Rev. Thomas Hussey, 26 July 1796, *Corr.*, IX, p. 61.

555 EB to John Keogh, 17 November 1796, ibid., p. 112.

556 EB to the Rev. Thomas Hussey, post 9 December 1796, ibid., p. 161.

557 EB to Sir Lawrence Parsons, 8 March 1797, ibid., p. 277.

558 EB to Earl Fitzwilliam, 21 May 1797, ibid., p. 355.

559 EB to French Laurence, 1 June 1797, ibid., p. 366.

560 French Laurence to Earl Fitzwilliam, 9 July 1797, ibid., p. 374.

561 Edmund Nagle to Earl Fitzwilliam, 4–5 July 1797, Northamptonshire MS., Fitzwilliam Correspondence.

562 Appendix, *Corr.*, IX, pp. 375–9.

Burke's empty coach followed the procession to the church. A simple, unassuming ceremony was held, attended by close friends and intimates of the family. Burke was happy for the mourners to arrange the proceedings to their satisfaction, so long as the service was kept within the bounds of decent modesty. For himself, he informed French Laurence, "it can be nothing. I wish no more of vain-glory: of that I have already had enough."[563]

[563] French Laurence, "Account of Edmund Burke's Funeral," OSB MS. File 8748.

CONCLUSION

Just over two months before his death Burke wrote to his protégé Lord Fitzwilliam, lamenting that all was "over" with the world as he had known it.[1] It is worth reflecting on the nature of the society into which Burke was born in comparison with the one he was about to depart.

The last of the popery laws, depriving Roman Catholics in Ireland of the vote, received the royal assent two years before Burke's birth.[2] He then spent the 1730s between Dublin and the Blackwater. In the middle of that decade, Bishop Berkeley had asked whether there existed any civilised people on earth "so beggarly, wretched, and destitute as the common Irish."[3] Between 1778 and 1782, in response to patriotic complaints about the sorry state of the country, Irish trade had been liberalised and legislative independence had been granted. By 1793, all popery laws excepting the right to sit in parliament had been repealed. Nonetheless, despite this sequence of major legislative changes, Ireland was on the brink of insurrection. Burke believed that the refusal of emancipation was breeding resentment. At the start of 1797, he claimed that he had first diagnosed the Irish problem in early manhood and that he would be advancing the same analysis while gasping for his last breath.[4] Fifteen months later, between May and September, the country was in a state of open rebellion. Soon afterwards, preparations for the Union of 1801 were underway, defining relations between both territories for another 120 years. Ireland had certainly been transformed over the course of Burke's lifetime. As he lay dying, he expected the progress he had welcomed in his native country to be overwhelmed by Jacobinism and systematically undone.

The Ireland into which Burke was born was a subordinate kingdom, subject to the sovereignty of the British crown-in-parliament. George II acceded to the throne in 1727, and through the 1730s the affairs of parliament were dominated by the figure of Walpole. Throughout Burke's boyhood, literary culture was saturated with criticism of Walpolean rule. Swift, Bolingbroke, Gay, Pope and Fielding variously

[1] EB to Earl Fitzwilliam, 26 April 1797, *Corr.*, IX, p. 317.

[2] 1 Geo. II, c. 9.

[3] George Berkeley, *The Querist* (1735–7) in *The Works of George Berkeley*, ed. Alexander Campbell Fraser (Oxford: Oxford University Press, 1901), 4 vols., IV, p. 434.

[4] EB to Unknown, February 1797, *Corr.*, IX, p. 263.

lampooned the decline in morals while lambasting the incidence of corruption.[5] In 1791, Burke dismissed these charges as the cant of treasonable Jacobites abetted by the hypocrisy of discontented Whigs. Walpole was "far from governing by corruption. He governed by party attachments."[6] Yet in his final year Burke signalled that the old parties were "nearly extinct."[7] The distinction between Whig and Tory seemed to be passing into history as Burke's erstwhile associates within the Foxite connection increasingly came to resemble a dissident faction in the state. Pitt's government was pursuing a policy of peace with the French enemy while the minority had so far refused to oppose the substance of Jacobin "maxims." Even worse, many of them seemed openly to champion these principles, obstinately insisting that the tragedies of the Revolution were incidental to the long-term benefits they still expected to be realised. The kind of destruction that Burke viewed as a conspicuous "evil" was presented by his opponents as "a matter of accident . . . wholly collateral to the system."[8] In the face of the French deluge, as Burke returned from Bath to prepare for death at Beaconsfield, he expected to finish his "long career with that of the civil and Moral World."[9] Having successfully deranged longstanding party affiliations, Jacobinism was undermining the principles of British politics.

British affairs were increasingly shaped by the Empire during Burke's lifetime. In his childhood the North American and West Indian colonies were key elements of imperial trade and power. Over the course of the eighteenth century, the volume of trans-Atlantic commerce increased by more than a factor of twelve, constituting about a third of Britain's overall trade by 1772.[10] Already in February 1766, Burke was referring to these provinces collectively as "a great[,] a growing people spread over a vast quarter of the Globe," extending from the equator as far as the polar circle.[11] Yet as soon as the importance of these settlements was appreciated, British policy began to drive thirteen of the colonies into rebellion. Then, between 25 May and 17 September 1787, the terms for a federal government were finally agreed for an independent United States of America. On 29 May 1790, Rhode Island became the thirteenth state to ratify the constitution. On 10 January 1791, a convention at Bennington authorised by the Vermont assembly voted to apply for admission to the Union. The following May, Burke publicised his admiration for the newly

[5] H. T. Dickinson, *Walpole and the Whig Supremacy* (London: English Universities Press, 1973); Bertrand A. Goldgar, *Walpole and the Wits: The Relation of Politics to Literature, 1722–1742* (Lincoln, NE: University of Nebraska Press, 1976); Isaac Kramnick, *Bolingbroke and His Circle: The Politics of Nostalgia in the Age of Walpole* (Ithaca, NY: Cornell University Press, 1992).

[6] EB, *An Appeal from the New to the Old Whigs, in Consequence of some Late Discussions in Parliament, relative to the Reflections on the Revolution in France* (London: 1791), p. 63.

[7] EB, *Third Letter on a Regicide Peace* (1797), *W & S*, IX, p. 326.

[8] Ibid., p. 304.

[9] EB to Earl Fitzwilliam, 21 May 1797, *Corr.*, IX, p. 356.

[10] EB, *Speech on Conciliation with America* (22 March 1775), *W & S*, III, pp. 113–14.

[11] EB, Speech on Declaratory Resolution, 2 February 1766, WWM Bk 6:127, reprinted in *W & S*, II, p. 49.

constructed nation.[12] He was satisfied that the current configuration of America meant the continuation of the kind of regulated government that he associated with old Europe. In the new world, at least, a system of civilised politics could survive.

In general terms, Burke was happy to commend republican arrangements: he had never "abused" either "Athens, or Rome, or Sparta," he insisted.[13] In particular he was pleased to extol the federal structure of American government. The former colonists, he claimed, "were certainly well adapted for the reception of a Democratic form of government."[14] This was not, however, a furious "agrarian" democracy: it was cast in constitutional—and, in that sense, "republican"—form.[15] There was no pretence that the "nation" was governed by the "nation," or that the people as a whole were ruled by the commonalty.[16] Like so much over the course of Burke's political career, America had been radically reconstituted. In a sense, however, the Revolution had been a restoration. From Burke's vantage, the Americans had been nursed in the school of "English" liberty: their constitution was in most respects a "copy" of the British.[17] They lacked the materials for instituting a nobility and hereditary monarchy, "but they have brought their government as near as possible to the British constitution." This was evidenced by their determination to ensure that power was restrained by the operation of "reciprocal checks."[18] In his final year Burke considered the fate of America for the last time: despite the confused perceptions of Thomas Erskine and his allies, the Revolutions in France and America were not comparable in their aims.[19]

While America dominated Burke's agenda in the 1760s and 1770s, India commanded his attention in the 1780s and 1790s. Here the course of affairs was altogether less encouraging. In his youth the Mughal Empire had been an imposing presence in the world, although beneath the show of splendour great shifts in power

[12] EB, Debate on the Quebec Government Bill, 6 May 1791, *Parliamentary History*, XXIX, cols. 365–66.

[13] EB, Debate on the Quebec Government Bill, 11 May 1791, *Parliamentary History*, XXIX, col. 418. Cf. *Public Advertiser*, 12 May 1791: "he defied any man to say that he had attacked ancient or modern Republics."

[14] *Oracle*, 7 May 1791.

[15] For Burke on the "*agrarian whims*" of France, by which he meant a project to level the distribution of property, see *Whitehall Evening Post*, 5–7 May 1791. For the claim that France, by comparison with America, was no republic at all, see EB, Debate on the Quebec Government Bill, 1 May 1791, *Parliamentary History*, XXIX, col. 418.

[16] *St. James's Chronicle*, 7 May 1791. Burke expressed this thought with reference to the character of Prettyman, a foundling son of a fisherman living as a prince in George Villier's *The Rehearsal*. As reported, Burke stated that in France, "Prince Prettyman" is set "to govern Prince Prettyman." Cf. *Evening Mail*, 6–9 May 1791; *World*, 7 May 1791.

[17] *Whitehall Evening Post*, 5–7 May 1791. Cf. Fox as reported in the *General Evening Post*, 10–12 May 1791: "Mr. Fox referred to some proceedings in the early part of the constitution of America, in which the principles of Monarchy, of Aristocracy, and of Democracy, were now so happily blended."

[18] *Oracle*, 7 May 1791; *World*, 7 May 1791.

[19] EB to William Windham, 12 February 1797, *Corr.*, IX, pp. 240–41. Burke is taking issue with Thomas Erskine, *A View of the Causes and Consequences of the Present War with France* (London: 1797).

were in train. Between the accession of Murshid Quli Khan to the position of Nawab of Bengal in 1717 and the invasion of India by Nadir Shah in 1739, the subcontinent underwent a series of "concussions."[20] Burke was no admirer of the "tyranny" of Aurangzeb, nor of the independent Subahdars who rose to power during the decline of the Mughals.[21] Nonetheless, throughout the eighteenth century down to 1757, India was governed by a "Hindoo policy" which secured the property and authority of the native inhabitants of the country.[22] For Burke, pure despotism was only established after the arrival of the British. Warren Hastings then justified East India Company oppression as a matter of fundamental principle. It was this that made Burke argue that Indianism was worse than Jacobinism.[23] The vindication of exploitation as a duty of government was a subversion of every principle of civilised subjection and a denial of the subordination of man to God. In 1796, Burke looked back on his toil in the service of India since the opening of the Hastings impeachment: "I have spent the last fourteen years of my existence in a Labour hardly credible, in hopes of obtaining Justice for an oppressed people," he wrote to Loughborough.[24] The effort, he once commented, had called forth exertion beyond his "strength," feelings beyond his "command," and application beyond his "powers."[25] His endeavours, however, were completely unavailing. Hastings was rewarded with a pension for his services. The unholy claim that servitude could be imposed on a people by right of prescription was not only unpunished but had in effect been rewarded by the British government. In the 1750s Burke had grown to expect enlightened justice from the Empire, yet he lived to see it endorse the application of the spirit of conquest in the most brutal and unmitigated fashion.

When Burke was born the British Empire thrived under the shadow of France. The War of the Spanish Succession had arrested the hegemony of Louis XIV. A struggle to balance the states of Europe in support of rival powers then dominated diplomacy for the rest of the century. Britain, France, the Dutch Republic, Prussia, Austria and Russia jostled to promote opposing schemes of paramountcy. Burke believed that this system of competition had suddenly ended in April 1792. The search for advantage among antagonists was replaced by a scheme of conquest. He claimed that France had launched a campaign of implacable aggression directed against the idea of any balance of power at all. Accordingly, he thought that Europe was confronted by inexpiable war. The image of a country beyond expiation, fundamentally incapable of atonement, was deliberately provocative on Burke's part. It pointed to both an irreparable breach and an interminable moral rupture. The French polity, from this perspective, was beyond accommodation. Its bid for conquest could only

[20] EB, Opening of Hastings Impeachment (15 February 1788), *W & S*, VI, p. 311.

[21] EB to Philip Francis, 19 November 1790, *Corr.*, VI, p. 171; EB, Opening of Hastings Impeachment (15 February 1788), *W & S*, VI, pp. 311–12.

[22] Ibid., p. 312.

[23] EB to Lord Loughborough, c. 17 March 1796, *Corr.*, VIII, p. 432.

[24] Ibid., p. 425.

[25] WWM BkP 25:90.

be met by a push for counter-conquest. The militancy of France was a product of its doctrinal ambitions: it sought to spread dominion in order to promote new principles of politics.

As Burke saw it, French Revolutionary doctrine was directed against the main elements that had constituted the history of civilisation. It was pitted against three components in particular: religion, property and prescription. It was above all in response to the Revolutionary onslaught against these elements that Burke had bemoaned to Fitzwilliam the dissipation of the world as he had known it. He articulated the same sentiment during this period to French Laurence, pointing to the demise "of the system of Europe, taking its laws, manners, religion and politics, in which I delighted so much."[26] Burke believed that this combination of ingredients had enabled the states of Europe to flourish since the downfall of feudal government, enabling them to advance towards progressive improvement, the limits of which "it would not have been easy for the imagination to fix."[27] The Revolution had rudely interrupted this steady progress by inaugurating a war "between Wealth and want."[28] At the same time, religion had been undermined, enfeebling moral habits. In the process, the idea of a just providence had been overturned, inflaming dissatisfaction with the distribution of worldly goods. Attacks on prescription then eroded the title to property while simultaneously sapping the roots of every established form of government. The "chain of human Tradition," Burke feared, would soon be broken.[29] This did not mean that he valued past custom over justice; it meant that justice was best supported with the aid of prescription.

Burke sympathised with the myriad discontents for which Jacobinism had become a vehicle, but he was contemptuous of the leading patrons of the ideology. It had begun, he believed, as a "Vice of men of parts."[30] It offered a means to aspiring talent to further its ambition. Given the circumstances of France in 1789, not least the burgeoning hostility to the privileges of the Gallican Church, an opportunity arose to requisition ecclesiastical property as a means of securing the interest of public creditors. The enemies of corporate property seized their chance. Speaking in the National Assembly in October 1789, the Abbé Maury was openly dismayed. Property, he insisted, had to be respected in its entirety: "En effet, la propriété est une, et sacrée pour nous comme pour vous."[31] The accumulated property of the Church, he went on, guaranteed the possessions of each deputy. Today's assailants might readily prove to be tomorrow's victims. For his part, Burke's commitment to the integrity of individual and corporate wealth was not based on some devotion to settled advantage. It was the duty of government, he believed, to secure justice against the

[26] EB to French Laurence, 11 April 1797, *Corr.*, IX, p. 307.

[27] EB to Florimond-Claude, Comte de Mercy-Argenteau, c. 6 August 1793, *Corr.*, VII, p. 387.

[28] EB to Earl Fitzwilliam, 20 December 1796, *Corr.*, IX, p. 189.

[29] EB to Henry Addington, post 2 March 1795, *Corr.*, VIII, p. 168.

[30] EB to Earl Fitzwilliam, 15 May 1795, ibid., pp. 242–43.

[31] *Archives parlementaires*, IX, p. 428 (13 October 1789).

rapacity of "the Multitude," but also to protect the people "from the insolence of the Rich and powerful."[32] Burke once declared that he had set himself a basic rule as a politician: "To act as representative of the people who had no power."[33] The protection of property was categorically not a defence of privilege. As Adam Smith had proclaimed, the right that each individual had to the ownership of their labour was the most "sacred and inviolable" of entitlements.[34] According to Burke, it was the job of statecraft to devise a system that could best guarantee practical security for such claims.

From Burke's perspective, this could not be achieved under an aristocratic regime. Nonetheless, the security of property meant endorsing a differential distribution of wealth. That entailed protecting social distinctions under government. It therefore seemed right to include an aristocratic component in any complex constitution. In a general sense Fox was committed to the same principle. He was certainly "no lover of pure aristocracy."[35] Nonetheless, he was also sure that "there could be no good or complete system of government without a proper mixture of monarchy, aristocracy, and democracy."[36] Fox articulated these views in the aftermath of his break with Burke during the Commons debate on the provision of a legislative council for Quebec in the spring of 1791. Aristocracy, he argued, was founded on rank or property, or alternatively on both together. In Britain it was formed on the basis of hereditary titles, which created pride in the distinction of ancient families, and thereby acted as a spur to public virtue by encouraging service to the state. Fox thought that this encouragement ought to exist under every government; it was usually even found in popular republics.[37] Burke agreed that a division of ranks thrived in all regulated regimes, but he went on to note that there existed two types of aristocracy: there was the kind that flourished in modern European monarchies and the kind that prospered in constitutional democracies. Where there was no hereditary monarchy, as in the case of the United States, aristocracy "necessarily sprang out of the democracy."[38] While such a popular aristocracy looked set to thrive in the new world, distinctions derived from monarchy were under pressure in the old.

[32] EB to the Rev. Thomas Hussey, 4 February 1795, *Corr.*, VIII, p. 139.

[33] WWM BkP 25:90.

[34] Adam Smith, *An Inquiry into the Nature and Causes of the Wealth of Nations*, ed. R. H. Campbell and A. S. Skinner (Indianapolis, IN: Liberty Fund, 1976), 2 vols., I, p. 138.

[35] *World*, 12 May 1791; cf. *Parliamentary History*, XXIX, col. 409.

[36] *Star*, 12 May 1791.

[37] *Parliamentary History*, XXIX, col. 410; cf. *Morning Post*, 12 May 1791.

[38] EB, Debate on the Quebec Government Bill, 11 May 1791, *Parliamentary History*, XXIX, col. 419. Burke was approving the creation of the Senate. On the inclusion of such a "select and stable member" in the American system of government, see James Madison, *Federalist* no. 63 in Alexander Hamilton, John Jay and James Madison, *The Federalist*, ed. George W. Carey and James McClellan (Indianapolis, IN: Liberty Fund, 2001), p. 325.

In Britain dignities were usually conferred for "Valour in the Field, Gallantry on the Ocean, or wisdom in the Cabinet."[39] This had given rise to an "open aristocracy" to the extent that honours were bestowed on the basis of personal merit. Burke contrasted this arrangement with the existence of a "closed" elite that he expected "would prove a dead weight on any government, counteracting and ultimately clogging its action."[40] It would inhibit movement to the extent that it failed to cooperate with the second chamber in the legislature. Alexis de Tocqueville, whose indebtedness to Burke was greater than he cared to admit, regarded the *noblesse* of eighteenth-century France as in effect an exclusive stratum.[41] It did not obstruct administration since it was a social rather than a political order: "The more the nobility ceased to be an aristocracy, the more it seemed to become a caste."[42] Tocqueville reprimanded Burke for failing to notice this complexity. Yet he was in fact repeating the substance of his precursor's thesis: as the French nobility withdrew from playing a responsible role in politics the system of privileges became increasingly circumscribed and restrictive.[43]

In Burke's late, great work, the *Letter to a Noble Lord*, he revealed how he had been devastated by the recent course of events on both a personal and a political level. He was bereft, degraded and disorientated at the same time. Prostrated by disappointment, only the promise of divine justice could console him. To some degree at least, he could submit to the decrees of providence. Yet still he felt he had been "torn up by the roots."[44] This was partly owing to the impact of the Revolution. Its relentless drive for renewal threatened Burke's values with extinction. He was sure that religion, property and prescription were in a state of peril. However, with the defeat of Napoleon by the sixth coalition in the Battle of Leipzig in 1813, the Revolution was forced to retreat. Paris was captured by allied forces in March 1814. The following year a series of punishing treaties were imposed on the defeated French. A Revolution had occurred, yet continuities remained. In lamenting Europe's upheavals since 1789, Burke's anatomy of the crisis taught posterity to recognise the

[39] *Oracle*, 12 May 1791.

[40] EB, Debate on the Quebec Government Bill, 11 May 1791, *Parliamentary History*, XXIX, col. 421.

[41] Tocqueville's detailed notes on Burke can be found in Alexis de Tocqueville, "Dossier M. Révolution française, jugement d'intellectuels étrangères" (1858), Archives nationales, 177/Mi/432. For a discussion of Tocqueville's study of Burke, see Robert T. Gannett Jr., *Tocqueville Unveiled: The Historian and His Source for "The Old Regime and the Revolution"* (Chicago, IL: University of Chicago Press, 2003), pp. 57–65.

[42] Alexis de Tocqueville, *The Old Regime and the Revolution*, ed. François Furet and Françoise Mélonio (Chicago, IL: University of Chicago Press, 1988), 2 vols., I, p. 156.

[43] Ibid., p. 157, presumably referring to EB, *Reflections on the Revolution in France*, ed. J.C.D. Clark (Stanford, CA: Stanford University Press, 2001), p. 304 [199]. Burke's complete view, however, was more complex: see, for example, ibid., p. 274 [163]; EB, *Letter to William Elliot* (26 May 1795), *W & S*, IX, p. 39. In his manuscript notes, Tocqueville recorded Burke's statement that "I found your nobility . . . men of high spirit" in Alexis de Tocqueville, "Dossier M. Révolution française, jugement d'intellectuels étrangères" (1858), Archives nationales, 177/Mi/432, AT 2820.

[44] EB, *Letter to a Noble Lord* (1796), *W & S*, IX, p. 171.

attitudes and structures that survived. Constitutional regulation, mixed government and the rule of law had long and complex futures ahead of them. Commerce, hierarchies of wealth and social privilege persisted. The principle of nobility endured for generations, while popular aristocracy is still with us. Burke's rhetoric speaks of an epoch suddenly submerged; his analysis allows us to see durability amidst change.

INDEX